D1712407

INTERNATIONAL
LAW REPORTS

VOLUME 115

Volumes published under the title:

ANNUAL DIGEST AND REPORTS
OF PUBLIC INTERNATIONAL LAW CASES

Vol. 1 (1919-22) } Edited by Sir John Fischer Williams, K.C.,
                     and H. Lauterpacht, LL.D.
Vol. 2 (1923-24) }
Vol. 3 (1925-26) } Edited by Arnold D. McNair, C.B.E., LL.D.,
                     and H. Lauterpacht, LL.D.
Vol. 4 (1927-28) }
Vol. 5 (1929-30)
Vol. 6 (1931-32)
Vol. 7 (1933-34)
Vol. 8 (1935-37)
Vol. 9 (1938-40)
Vol. 10 (1941-42)
Vol. 11 (1919-42) } Edited by H. Lauterpacht, Q.C., LL.D., F.B.A.
Vol. 12 (1943-45)
Vol. 13 (1946)
Vol. 14 (1947)
Vol. 15 (1948)
Vol. 16 (1949)

Volumes published under the title:

INTERNATIONAL LAW REPORTS

Vol. 17 (1950)
Vol. 18 (1951)
Vol. 19 (1952)
Vol. 20 (1953)   } Edited by Sir Hersch Lauterpacht, Q.C., LL.D.,
                    F.B.A.
Vol. 21 (1954)
Vol. 22 (1955)
Vol. 23 (1956)
Vol. 24 (1957)   Edited by Sir Hersch Lauterpacht, Q.C., LL.D.,
                    F.B.A., and E. Lauterpacht
Vol. 25 (1958-I) }
                    Edited by E. Lauterpacht, Q.C.
Vol. 26 (1958-II) }
Vols. 27—68 *and* Consolidated Tables and Index to Vols. 1—35 *and* 36—45
                    Edited by E. Lauterpacht, Q.C.
Vols. 69—115 *and* Consolidated Index and Consolidated Tables of Cases and
                    Treaties to Vols. 1—80 *and* Vols. 81—100
                    Edited by Sir Elihu Lauterpacht, C.B.E., Q.C.,
                    and C. J. Greenwood, Q.C.

Lauterpacht Research Centre for International Law
University of Cambridge

INTERNATIONAL LAW REPORTS

VOLUME
115

Edited by

SIR ELIHU LAUTERPACHT, CBE QC
Honorary Professor of International Law, University of Cambridge
Bencher of Gray's Inn

C. J. GREENWOOD, QC
Professor of International Law
London School of Economics and Political Science

and

A. G. OPPENHEIMER
Associate Editor: Civil Law Jurisdictions
Fellow of the Lauterpacht Research Centre for International Law, University of Cambridge

GROTIUS PUBLICATIONS

CAMBRIDGE
UNIVERSITY PRESS

International Standard Book Number: 0 521 64245 0

Printed in Great Britain on acid-free paper by
Gomer Press, Llandysul, Dyfed

Published by the Press Syndicate of the University of Cambridge
The Pitt Building, Trumpington Street, Cambridge CB2 1RP
40 West 20th Street, New York, NY 10011-4211, USA
10 Stamford Road, Oakleigh, Melbourne, 3166, Australia

First published 1999

A catalogue record for this book is available from the British Library

CONTENTS

Page

PREFACE   vii

EDITORIAL NOTE   ix

TABLE OF CASES (alphabetical)   xiii

TABLE OF CASES (according to courts and countries)   xv

DIGEST (main headings)   xvii

DIGEST OF CASES REPORTED IN VOLUME 115   xix

TABLE OF TREATIES   xxxiii

REPORTS OF CASES   1

INDEX   673

CONSOLIDATED TABLES OF CASES, VOLUMES 101-115   703

PREFACE

Like its predecessors, the present volume contains a wide variety of national and international decisions and is the work of many hands. Mr Andrew Oppenheimer, Associate Editor for Civil Law Jurisdictions, translated, summarized and edited the Belgian decisions, which were contributed by Joe Verhoeven, Professor of International Law at the Catholic University of Louvain. Dr Michael Byers, Associate Professor of Law of Duke University, translated the decision of the Federal Constitutional Court in Germany, which was edited and summarized by Mr Oppenheimer. Dr Jenny Kuper, London School of Economics, prepared the summaries of six United Nations Human Rights Committee cases. The other United Nations Human Rights Committee cases and the summary of the *Tangiora* case were the work of Ms Fiona Mucklow, LL M. Ms Karen Lee, MA, prepared the summaries of the *Project Blue Sky* and *Delgamuukw* cases, as well as the two decisions from Lithuania. Ms Lee also prepared the Tables of Cases and the Digest and performed invaluable work in seeing the volume through the press. The Index and Table of Treaties were again prepared by HE Miss Maureen MacGlashan, CMG, who, together with Ms Lee, also compiled the Consolidated Tables of Cases for volumes 101-115. Mrs Diane Ilott was responsible for copy-editing and Mr Adrian Lee for correcting the proofs. To all of them we extend our grateful thanks.

We are also indebted to the following publishers for their kindness in allowing us to reproduce decisions from the reports which they publish: the Registrar of the International Court of Justice (*International Court of Justice Reports*), Butterworths (Australia) Limited (*Australian Law Reports*), the Canada Law Book Company (*Dominion Law Reports*) and the New Zealand Incorporated Council of Law Reporting and Butterworths of New Zealand Limited (*New Zealand Law Reports*).

Finally, we are grateful to our publishers, Cambridge University Press, and, in particular, to Ms Finola O'Sullivan, Ms Jayne Matthews and Dr Caroline Murray, and to our printers, the Gomer Press, for the trouble which they have taken with this volume.

E. LAUTERPACHT

Lauterpacht Research Centre
  for International Law,
University of Cambridge

C. J. GREENWOOD

Law Department,
London School of Economics
  and Political Science

July 1999

EDITORIAL NOTE

The *International Law Reports* endeavour to provide within a single series of volumes comprehensive access in English to judicial materials bearing on public international law. On certain topics it is not always easy to draw a clear line between cases which are essentially ones of public international law interest and those which are primarily applications of special domestic rules. For example, in relation to extradition, the *Reports* will include cases which bear on the exception of "political offences" or the rule of double criminality, but will restrict the number of cases dealing with purely procedural aspects of extradition. Similarly, while the general rules relating to the admission and exclusion of aliens, especially of refugees, are of international legal interest, cases on the procedure of admission usually are not. In such borderline areas, and sometimes also where there is a series of domestic decisions all dealing with a single point in essentially the same manner, only one illustrative decision will be printed and references to the remainder will be given in an accompanying note.

DECISIONS OF INTERNATIONAL TRIBUNALS
The *Reports* seek to include so far as possible the available decisions of every international tribunal, e.g. the International Court of Justice, or *ad hoc* arbitrations between States. There are, however, some jurisdictions to which full coverage cannot be given, either because of the large number of decisions (e.g. the Administrative Tribunal of the United Nations) or because not all the decisions bear on questions of public international law (e.g. the Court of the European Communities). In these instances, those decisions are selected which appear to have the greatest long-term value.

Human rights cases. The number of decisions on questions of international protection of human rights has increased considerably in recent years and it is now impossible for the *Reports* to cover them all. As far as decisions of international jurisdictions are concerned, the *Reports* will continue to publish decisions of the European Court of Human Rights and of the Inter-American Court of Human Rights, as well as "views" of the United Nations Committee on Human Rights. Selected decisions of the European Commission of Human Rights will be printed, chosen by reference to the importance of the points at issue and their interest to public international lawyers generally. (All reports of decisions of the European Commission of Human Rights are published in an official series, the *Official Collection of Decisions of the European Commission of Human Rights,* as well as in the *European Human Rights Reports*). Decisions of national courts on the application of conventions on human rights will not be published unless they deal with a major point of substantive human rights law or a matter of wider interest to public international lawyers such as the relationship of international law and national law, the extent of the right of derogation or the principles of the interpretation of treaties.

International arbitrations. The *Reports* of course include arbitral awards rendered in cases between States which involve an application of public international law. Beyond this, however, the selection of arbitral decisions is more open to debate. As these *Reports* are principally concerned with matters of public international law, they will not include purely private law commercial arbitrations even if they are international in the sense that they arise between parties of different nationality and even if one of them is a State. (For reports of a number of such awards, see *Yearbook Commercial Arbitration* (ed. Pieter Sanders, under the auspices of the International Council for Commercial Arbitration)). But where there is a sufficient point of contact with public international law then the relevant parts of the award will be reported. Examples of such points of contact are cases in which the character of a State as a party has some relevance (e.g. State immunity, stabilization clauses, *force majeure*) or where there is a choice of law problem involving discussion of international law or general principles of law as possible applicable laws. The same criteria will determine the selection of decisions of national courts regarding the enforcement of arbitral awards.

DECISIONS OF NATIONAL TRIBUNALS
A systematic effort is made to collect from all national jurisdictions those judicial decisions which have some bearing on international law.

EDITORIAL TREATMENT OF MATERIALS
The basic policy of the Editors is, so far as possible, to present the material in its original form. It is no part of the editorial function to impose on the decisions printed in these volumes a uniformity of approach or style which they do not possess. Editorial intervention is limited to the introduction of the summary and of the bold-letter rubric at the head of each case. This is followed by the full text of the original decision or of its translation. Normally, the only passages which will be omitted are those which contain either statements of fact having no bearing on the points of international law involved in the case or discussion of matters of domestic law unrelated to the points of international legal interest. The omission of material is usually indicated either by a series of dots or by the insertion of a sentence in square brackets noting the passages which have been left out.

Presentation of Materials

The material in this volume is of two kinds, material reproduced photographically and material which has been freshly set for this volume.

Material photographically reproduced. This consists exclusively of reports originally printed in the English language. The material can usually be recognized by the differences between its type-style and the Baskerville type otherwise used in these *Reports*. The source of the material is identified by the reference to the "Report" in square brackets at the end of the case. Where more than one citation is given, the report used is the one first listed. The bold type figures in square brackets in the inner margin of each page refer to the pagination of the original report. The smaller figures in square brackets in the margins of these cases are the indicators of footnotes which have been editorially introduced.

Other material. The remaining material in the volume has been typeset for this volume. This includes all material specially translated into English for these *Reports* as well as some material in English which in its original form was not suitable for photo-reproduction. The source of all such material is indicated by the reference to the "Report" in square brackets at the end of the case. The language of the original decision is also mentioned there. The bold figures in square brackets in the body of the text indicate the pagination of the original report. Small figures in square brackets within the text are indicators of footnotes which have been editorially introduced.

Notes

Footnotes. Footnotes enclosed in square brackets are editorial insertions. All other footnotes are part of the original report.

Other notes. References to cases deemed not to be sufficiently substantial to warrant reporting will occasionally be found in editorial notes either at the end of a report of a case on a similar point or under an independent heading.

Digest of Cases

With effect from Volume 75 the decisions contained in the *Reports* are no longer arranged according to the traditional classification scheme. Instead a Digest of Cases is published at the beginning of each volume. The main headings of the Digest are arranged alphabetically. Under each heading brief details are given of those cases reported in that volume which contain points covered by that heading. Each entry in the Digest gives the name of the case concerned and the page reference, the name of the tribunal which gave the decision and an indication of the main points raised in the case which relate to that particular heading of the Digest. Where a case raises points which concern several different areas of international law, entries relating to that case will appear under each of the relevant headings in the Digest. A list of the main headings used in the Digest is set out at page xvii.

CONSOLIDATED INDEX AND TABLES

A Consolidated Index and Consolidated Tables of Cases and Treaties for volumes 1-80 was published in two volumes in 1990 and 1991. A further volume containing the Consolidated Index and Consolidated Tables of Cases and Treaties for volumes 81-100 was published in 1996. The present volume contains Consolidated Tables of Cases for volumes 101-115.

TABLE OF CASES REPORTED

ALPHABETICAL

(Cases which are reported only in a note are distinguished from cases which are reported in full by the insertion of the word "note" in parentheses after the page number of the report.)

Adams v. Jamaica (Communication No 607/1994) 286

Biocare (SA) v. Gécamines (Zaire) and Republic of Zaire 415
Bordes and Temeharo v. France (Communication No 645/1995) 254
Bosnia and Herzegovina v. Yugoslavia. See Case concerning Application of the Convention on the Prevention and Punishment of the Crime of Genocide (Bosnia and Herzegovina v. Yugoslavia) (Preliminary Objections) (Order on Counter-claims)

Case concerning Application of the Convention on the Prevention and Punishment of the Crime of Genocide (Bosnia and Herzegovina v. Yugoslavia) (Order on Counter-claims) 1, 206
Case concerning Application of the Convention on the Prevention and Punishment of the Crime of Genocide (Bosnia and Herzegovina v. Yugoslavia) (Preliminary Objections) 1, 10
Centre for Industrial Development v. Naidu 424
Collée v. Gécamines Commerciale 435 (note)

De Queiroz v. State of Portugal 430
Delgamuukw and Others v. The Queen in Right of British Columbia and Others; First Nations Summit and Others, Interveners 446

Faurisson v. France (Communication No 550/1993) 355
Former Syrian Ambassador to the German Democratic Republic (Case No 2 BvR 1516/96) 595
François v. State of Canada 418

Genocide, Application of the Convention on the Prevention and Punishment of

the Crime of. See Case concerning Application of the Convention on the Prevention and Punishment of the Crime of Genocide (Bosnia and Herzegovina v. Yugoslavia) (Preliminary Objections) (Order on Counter-claims)

Holland v. Ireland (Communication No 593/1994) 277
Human Rights Convention Case (Case No 22/94) 637

Länsman (J.) et al. v. Finland (Communication No 671/1995) 300

Morocco (Kingdom of) v. DR 421

Price v. Jamaica (Communication No 572/1994) 350
Project Blue Sky Inc. and Others v. Australian Broadcasting Authority 384
Property Restitution Case (Case No 12/93) 619

Re Reference by the Governor in Council concerning Certain Questions relating to the Secession of Quebec from Canada 536

Somers v. Hungary (Communication No 566/1993) 263
Stewart v. Canada (Communication No 538/1993) 318

T v. Belgium 442

Vaessen v. American Battle Monuments Commission 435

Wellington District Legal Services Committee v. Tangiora 655

TABLE OF CASES REPORTED

ARRANGED ACCORDING TO COURTS
AND TRIBUNALS (INTERNATIONAL CASES)
AND COUNTRIES (MUNICIPAL CASES)

(Cases which are reported only in a note are distinguished from cases which are reported in full by the insertion of the word "note" in parentheses after the page number of the report.)

I. DECISIONS OF INTERNATIONAL TRIBUNALS

International Court of Justice

1996
Case concerning Application of the Convention on the Prevention and Punishment of the Crime of Genocide (Bosnia and Herzegovina v. Yugoslavia) (Preliminary Objections) 1, 10

1997
Case concerning Application of the Convention on the Prevention and Punishment of the Crime of Genocide (Bosnia and Herzegovina v. Yugoslavia) (Order on Counter-claims) 1, 206

United Nations Human Rights Committee

1996
Adams v. Jamaica (Communication No 607/1994) 286

Bordes and Temeharo v. France (Communication No 645/1995) 254
Faurisson v. France (Communication No 550/1993) 355
Holland v. Ireland (Communication No 593/1994) 277
J. Länsman et al. v. Finland (Communication No 671/1995) 300
Price v. Jamaica (Communication No 572/1994) 350
Somers v. Hungary (Communication No 566/1993) 263
Stewart v. Canada (Communication No 538/1993) 318

II. DECISIONS OF MUNICIPAL COURTS

Australia

1998
Project Blue Sky Inc. and Others v. Australian Broadcasting Authority 384

Belgium

1989
François v. State of Canada 418
Kingdom of Morocco v. DR 421
SA Biocare v. Gécamines (Zaire) and Republic of Zaire 415

1990
Collée v. Gécamines Commerciale 435 (note)

1991
Centre for Industrial Development v. Naidu 424

1992
De Queiroz v. State of Portugal 430

1997
Vaessen v. American Battle Monuments Commission 435

1998
T v. Belgium 442

Canada

1997
Delgamuukw and Others v. The Queen in Right of British Columbia and Others; First Nations Summit and Others, Interveners 446

1998
Re Reference by the Governor in Council concerning Certain Questions relating to the Secession of Quebec from Canada 536

Federal Republic of Germany

1997
Former Syrian Ambassador to the German Democratic Republic (Case No 2 BvR 1516/96) 595

Lithuania

1994
Property Restitution Case (Case No 12/93) 619

1995
Human Rights Convention Case (Case No 22/94) 637

New Zealand

1997
Wellington District Legal Services Committee v. Tangiora 655

DIGEST OF CASES

List of Main Headings

(Those headings for which there are entries in the present volume are printed in italics. For a guide to the Digest, see the Editorial Note at p. xi.)

Air

Aliens

Arbitration

Canals

Claims

Comity

Conciliation

Consular Relations

Damages

Diplomatic Relations

Economics, Trade and Finance

Environment

Expropriation

Extradition

Governments

Human Rights

International Court of Justice

International Criminal Law

International Organizations

International Tribunals

Jurisdiction

Lakes and Landlocked Seas

Nationality

Recognition

Relationship of International Law and Municipal Law

Reprisals and Countermeasures

Rivers

Sea

Sources of International Law

Space

State Immunity

State Responsibility

State Succession

States

Territory

Treaties

War and Armed Conflict

DIGEST OF CASES REPORTED IN VOLUME 115

Page

Diplomatic Relations

Diplomatic agent—Notification by receiving State that diplomat is *persona non grata*—Vienna Convention on Diplomatic Relations, 1961, Article 9(1)—Whether such notification justiciable in municipal courts—Scope of obligation of sending State to recall diplomat in such circumstances—Belgium, Conseil d'Etat

    T v. Belgium   442

Immunity—Former head of mission—Acts performed in the exercise of diplomatic functions—Whether immunity subsists after functions have terminated—Vienna Convention on Diplomatic Relations, 1961, Article 39(2)—Immunity from criminal jurisdiction—Whether commission of particularly serious crime may preclude reliance on diplomatic immunity—Whether State may take preventative measures against abuses of diplomatic immunity—Whether criminal prosecution constitutes preventative measure—Federal Republic of Germany, Federal Constitutional Court (*BVerfG*) (Second Senate)

    Former Syrian Ambassador to the German Democratic Republic (Case No 2 BvR 1516/96)   595

Immunity—Territorial scope—Whether immunity has *erga omnes* effect in third States or is only applicable in receiving State—Whether this question is regulated by treaty or customary international law—*Agrément* (consent) as basis of immunity — Vienna Convention on Diplomatic Relations, 1961, Article 4—Exception for diplomats in transit—Article 40 of Convention—Federal Republic of Germany, Federal Constitutional Court (*BVerfG*) (Second Senate)

    Former Syrian Ambassador to the German Democratic Republic (Case No 2 BvR 1516/96)   595

Economics, Trade and Finance

Trade in services—Broadcasting—Australia–New Zealand Closer Economic Relations Trade Agreement in force 1 January 1983—Trade in Services Protocol in force 1 January 1989—Articles 4 and 5(1) of Protocol — Equal access and treatment for New Zealand film and television industry in Australian market — Australia's treaty obligations—Australia, High Court

    Project Blue Sky Inc. and Others v. Australian Broadcasting Authority   384

Page

Human Rights

Freedom of expression—Restrictions on freedom of expression—
Conditions—Requirement that any restriction be provided by
law, address a legitimate aim and be necessary for the achievement of that aim—French legislation prohibiting the denial of
certain offences connected with the Holocaust — Whether a
violation of International Covenant on Civil and Political Rights,
1966, Article 19—United Nations Human Rights Committee

Faurisson v. France (Communication No 550/1993)   355

Jus cogens character of certain human rights norms—Prohibition
of genocide—Genocide Convention, 1948—Status—Nature of
rights and obligations under Genocide Convention—Character
as obligations *erga omnes*—International Court of Justice

*Case concerning Application of the Convention on the Prevention and
Punishment of the Crime of Genocide (Bosnia and Herzegovina v.
Yugoslavia) (Preliminary Objections) (Order on Counter-claims)*   1

Minorities—International Covenant on Civil and Political Rights,
1966, Article 27—Sami reindeer herdsmen in Finland—Whether
rights violated by legislation on logging and by road-building
programmes—Consultation of Sami herdsmen by Government
of Finland—Limited impact of Government plans for logging and
road-building on culture of the Sami—United Nations Human
Rights Committee

J. Länsman et al. v. Finland (Communication No 671/1995)   300

Procedure—United Nations Human Rights Committee—Nature
of Committee—Whether a "judicial authority"—International
Covenant on Civil and Political Rights, 1966—Whether State
Party under an obligation to provide legal aid for petitioner to
Human Rights Committee—New Zealand, Court of Appeal

Wellington District Legal Services Committee v. Tangiora   655

Property rights—Confiscation of property in Hungary during
Communist period—Confiscation based on racial factors—Post-
Communist legislation providing for compensation but not for
restitution of property — Whether violation of owner's rights
under International Covenant on Civil and Political Rights, 1966
—United Nations Human Rights Committee

Somers v. Hungary (Communication No 566/1993)   263

Property rights—Recognition of indigenous land rights—Legal
rights of the Gitksan and Wet'suwet'en aboriginal peoples over

territory in British Columbia—Whether aboriginal peoples possessing aboriginal title—Whether aboriginal peoples having right to self-government—Relationship between aboriginal rights and aboriginal title—Aboriginal rights encompassing aboriginal title—Nature and content of aboriginal title—*Sui generis* character of aboriginal title—Proof of aboriginal title—Relevance of oral history evidence of use and occupation of territory—Relevance of aboriginal perspectives—Common law aboriginal title—Effect of Section 35(1) of Constitution Act 1982 recognizing and affirming existing aboriginal rights—Nature and scope of constitutional protection afforded by Section 35(1) of Constitution Act 1982— Whether any limitation to aboriginal rights—Whether aboriginal rights absolute — Whether infringement of aboriginal rights by government permissible—Test of justification—Canada, Supreme Court

Delgamuukw and Others v. The Queen in Right of British Columbia and Others; First Nations Summit and Others, Interveners   446

Property rights—Right to private ownership of property—Right not to be arbitrarily deprived of property—Right enshrined in international legal instruments—Nationalization of property in Lithuania upon its annexation by Soviet Union in 1940— Restoration of independence in Lithuania in 1990 — Right of private ownership reinstated — Whether property in Lithuania belonging to State or former landowners—Law of 18 June 1991 on the Procedure and Conditions of the Restoration of the Rights of Ownership to the Existing Real Property ("restoration law")— Amended on 15 July 1993 ("law in dispute")—Whether provisions complying with Constitution of Lithuania—Whether parts of item 3 of law in dispute amending Parts 5 and 6 of restoration law contradicting Constitution of Lithuania—Whether items 14, 15, 16, 17, 18 and 19 of law in dispute by which Article 12 of restoration law has been appended by items 10, 11, 12, 13, 14 and 15 complying with Constitution of Lithuania—Lithuania, Constitutional Court

Property Restitution Case (Case No 12/93)   619

Right to a fair trial—International Covenant on Civil and Political Rights, 1966, Article 14—Capital case—Appeal—Conduct of defence counsel on appeal—Duty of Court to take exceptional care in capital case—Commutation of death sentence—Sufficient remedy for violation of Article 6 but not for violation of Article 14—United Nations Human Rights Committee

Price v. Jamaica (Communication No 572/1994)   350

Right to a fair trial—Non-disclosure of prosecution evidence to the defence—Effects—Circumstances in which it is appropriate

Page

Human Rights *(cont.)*

for international human rights tribunal to question conduct of
trial—Actions of defence counsel—International Covenant on
Civil and Political Rights, 1966, Article 14—United Nations
Human Rights Committee

    Adams v. Jamaica (Communication No 607/1994)   286

Right to a fair trial — Trial of terrorist suspect before special
criminal court — Ireland — Whether court possessing sufficient
independence—Procedures followed—Whether communication
inadmissible—Inadmissibility *ratione temporis*—Trial occurring before
entry into force of human rights instruments for respondent State
—Concept of continuing violation — Requirement of exhaustion
of domestic remedies—United Nations Human Rights Committee

    Holland v. Ireland (Communication No 593/1994)   277

Right to life—Nuclear weapons—Testing of nuclear weapons—
Whether French nuclear tests in the South Pacific constituting a
threat to life—Whether residents of islands near test area victims
of violations of the International Covenant on Civil and Political
Rights, 1966—United Nations Human Rights Committee

    Bordes and Temeharo v. France (Communication No 645/1995)   254

Right to respect for family and private life—Right of entry to
'own country'—Alien long-term resident in State threatened with
deportation on account of criminal convictions—Family resident
in State — Whether State could be regarded as alien's 'own
country' for purposes of Covenant—Whether violation of rights
under International Covenant on Civil and Political Rights, 1966,
Articles 7, 9, 12, 13, 17 and 23—United Nations Human Rights
Committee

    Stewart v. Canada (Communication No 538/1993)   318

Self-determination—Scope and extent—Right to self-determination
in the context of an existing State — Whether part of the
population of an existing State capable of constituting a "people"
for the purpose of the right of self-determination—Internal and
external self-determination—Whether international law recognizes
a right of unilateral secession for part of the population of an
existing State—Quebec—Whether population of Quebec or part
thereof a "people"—Whether population of Quebec enjoying
internal self-determination—Declaration of Principles of Friendly
Relations between States 1970—Canada, Supreme Court

    *Re Reference by the Governor in Council concerning Certain Questions
relating to the Secession of Quebec from Canada*   536

Torture, inhuman and degrading treatment—Prison conditions
—'Death row' phenomenon—Whether length of time convicted
person held on death row amounts to inhuman treatment—
Failure of State to investigate conditions in prison—International
Covenant on Civil and Political Rights, 1966, Articles 7 and 10—
United Nations Human Rights Committee

Adams v. Jamaica (Communication No 607/1994)   286

International Court of Justice

Counter-claims—Rules of Court, Article 80—Definition of counter-
claim—Requirement of direct connection between counter-claim
and original claim—Meaning—Connection in fact and in law—
Discretion of Court—Procedure—Whether Court obliged to hold
oral proceedings on admissibility of counter-claim—International
Court of Justice

*Case concerning Application of the Convention on the Prevention and
Punishment of the Crime of Genocide (Bosnia and Herzegovina v.
Yugoslavia) (Preliminary Objections) (Order on Counter-claims)*   1

Jurisdiction—Principles on which jurisdiction based—Whether
Court should adopt strict approach to jurisdiction—Disputes
clause in multilateral treaty—Genocide Convention, 1948,
Article IX—Jurisdiction *ratione personae*—Whether Convention
in force between claimant and respondent — Date at which
Convention must be in force—Jurisdiction *ratione materiae*—Scope
of Convention—Nature of disputes covered by Article IX—
Jurisdiction *ratione temporis*—Admissibility—International Court of
Justice

*Case concerning Application of the Convention on the Prevention and
Punishment of the Crime of Genocide (Bosnia and Herzegovina v.
Yugoslavia) (Preliminary Objections) (Order on Counter-claims)*   1

International Criminal Law

Genocide—Genocide Convention, 1948—Definition—Nature of
obligations under Genocide Convention—Whether conferring
rights and imposing responsibility upon States—International
Court of Justice

*Case concerning Application of the Convention on the Prevention and
Punishment of the Crime of Genocide (Bosnia and Herzegovina v.
Yugoslavia) (Preliminary Objections) (Order on Counter-claims)*   1

Page

International Organizations

Immunity—Attachment and execution—Arbitration—Award in favour of former employee of international organization—Enforceability of award—Rejection by arbitral body of plea of jurisdictional immunity by international organization—Whether automatically implying no immunity from execution of award—Bank account of international organization—Whether immune from execution—Whether any presumption that funds in such an account are allocated for the mission of the organization—Waiver of immunity—Conditions—Headquarters Agreement between Belgium and the Centre for Industrial Development, 1978, Articles 1, 3 and 5—Whether court order of *exequatur* for award necessarily excluding immunity from execution—Belgium, Civil Court of Brussels (Jurisdiction for Attachments)

Centre for Industrial Development v. Naidu   424

United Nations — Admission of new member — Significance — Admission of Bosnia and Herzegovina as member—Whether establishing Statehood of Bosnia and Herzegovina—Recognition of President of Bosnia and Herzegovina—International Court of Justice

Case concerning Application of the Convention on the Prevention and Punishment of the Crime of Genocide (Bosnia and Herzegovina v. Yugoslavia) (Preliminary Objections) (Order on Counter-claims)   1

International Tribunals

United Nations Human Rights Committee — Competence — Admissibility of communication—Requirement that author of communication be a victim of a violation—Matter simultaneously brought before two human rights tribunals — United Nations Human Rights Committee

Bordes and Temeharo v. France (Communication No 645/1995)   254

United Nations Human Rights Committee — Competence — Domestic remedies rule—Committee not empowered to question in the abstract the compatibility of national law with the Covenant — Committee confined to investigating the communications submitted to it—United Nations Human Rights Committee

Faurisson v. France (Communication No 550/1993)   355

United Nations Human Rights Committee—Competence—Domestic remedies rule—Failure to exhaust domestic remedies—Whether communication inadmissible *ratione temporis*—Date of entry into force of International Covenant on Civil and Political Rights, 1966, and Optional Protocol for respondent State—United Nations Human Rights Committee

Holland v. Ireland (Communication No 593/1994)   277

United Nations Human Rights Committee—Competence—Procedure—Request for indication of interim measures—United Nations Human Rights Committee

J. Länsman et al. v. Finland (Communication No 671/1995)   300

United Nations Human Rights Committee—Procedure—Admissibility of communication—Failure of State to challenge admissibility—Time allowed to State to provide information on steps taken to give effect to views of Committee—United Nations Human Rights Committee

Adams v. Jamaica (Communication No 607/1994)   286

United Nations Human Rights Committee — Procedure — Interim measures — Request for stay of deportation — United Nations Human Rights Committee

Stewart v. Canada (Communication No 538/1993)   318

Jurisdiction

Territorial—Criminal jurisdiction—Offences committed in West Berlin prior to German reunification in 1990—Whether committed within the territory of the Federal Republic of Germany—Federal Republic of Germany, Federal Constitutional Court (*BVerfG*) (Second Senate)

Former Syrian Ambassador to the German Democratic Republic (Case No 2 BvR 1516/96)   595

Recognition

Of States—Of right of people to self-determination—Recognition as condonation of unlawful act—Whether likelihood of recognition of breakaway State means that there is a right to create such a State—Canada, Supreme Court

Re Reference by the Governor in Council concerning Certain Questions relating to the Secession of Quebec from Canada   536

Of States and governments—Significance—Whether establishing that entity is a State—Whether signifying acceptance of claim to succession—Recognition of particular individual as Head of State—Significance of non-recognition—Whether treaty in force

Page

Recognition *(cont.)*
between States which do not recognize one another—Subsequent
act of mutual recognition — Dayton–Paris Agreement between
Bosnia and Herzegovina, Croatia and Federal Republic of
Yugoslavia—International Court of Justice

    *Case concerning Application of the Convention on the Prevention and
    Punishment of the Crime of Genocide (Bosnia and Herzegovina v.
    Yugoslavia) (Preliminary Objections) (Order on Counter-claims)*   1

Relationship of International Law and Municipal Law

In general — Whether Supreme Court of Canada entitled to
answer question regarding application of international law —
International law as part of the law of Canada—Right of self-
determination under Canadian law and international law —
Canada, Supreme Court

    *Re Reference by the Governor in Council concerning Certain Questions
    relating to the Secession of Quebec from Canada*   536

Treaties—Effect in municipal law—Broadcasting Services Act
1992 (Cth)—Section 122 of Act empowering Australian Broadcasting Authority to determine Australian Content Standard—
Section 160(d) of Act requiring Australian Broadcasting Authority
to perform its obligations in manner consistent with Australia's
treaty obligations—Clause 9 of Standard favouring Australian
television programmes—Whether Clause 9 of Standard conflicting
with Articles 4 and 5 of Protocol—Interpretation and compatibility
of Sections 122 and 160 of Act—Whether Clause 9 of Standard
made in breach of Act—Validity of Standard—Australia, High
Court

    Project Blue Sky Inc. and Others v. Australian Broadcasting Authority   384

Treaties — Human rights — European Convention for the
Protection of Human Rights and Fundamental Freedoms, 1950
— Protocols Nos 1, 4 and 7 — Republic of Lithuania ratifying
Convention and Protocols—International obligations of Republic
of Lithuania—Requirement effectively to implement Convention
—Constitution of Republic of Lithuania—Defining rights and
freedoms to be guaranteed for individuals within jurisdiction of
the Republic of Lithuania—Article 7 of Constitution rendering
any law or legal act contradicting Constitution invalid—Whether
Articles 4, 5, 9 and 14 of Convention contradicting Articles 48,
20, 26 and 29 of the Constitution—Whether Article 2 of Protocol
No 4, 1963 contradicting Article 32 of Constitution—Lithuania,
Constitutional Court

    Human Rights Convention Case (Case No 22/94)   637

Treaties—International Covenant on Civil and Political Rights, 1966—Effect in the law of New Zealand—Whether New Zealand authorities required to grant legal aid for petition to United Nations Human Rights Committee—New Zealand, Court of Appeal

Wellington District Legal Services Committee v. Tangiora   655

State Immunity

Jurisdiction—Whether war crimes, crimes against humanity or other crimes against international law may preclude State official from relying on State immunity—Significance of Article 7 of Charter of International Military Tribunal, 1945—Whether violation of *jus cogens* might preclude reliance on immunity — Whether any distinction between diplomatic and State immunity in this regard — Federal Republic of Germany, Federal Constitutional Court (*BVerfG*) (Second Senate)

Former Syrian Ambassador to the German Democratic Republic (Case No 2 BvR 1516/96)   595

Jurisdictional immunity—Chauffeur employed by embassy of foreign State—Contract of employment—Dismissal—Claim for damages for unjustifiable dismissal—Whether foreign State entitled to jurisdictional immunity—Whether fact that employee is a foreign national is material—Relevance of European Convention on State Immunity, 1972, Article 5(1)—Whether applicable as codification of customary international law even though defendant State not a party—Belgium, Labour Court of Brussels (Sixth Chamber)

Kingdom of Morocco v. DR   421

Jurisdictional immunity—Employee of cultural and information centre of foreign State—Contract of employment—Dismissal—Claim for damages in lieu of notice—Whether foreign State entitled to jurisdictional immunity—Whether contract of employment concluded *jure imperii* or *jure gestionis*—Proper method of service of writ on a foreign State—Belgium, Labour Court of Brussels (First Chamber)

François v. State of Canada   418

Jurisdictional immunity — Expropriation — Foreign company— Claim against foreign State for damages—Policy of "Zairianization" operated by State of Zaire—Claim in Belgian courts to recover compensation payable under the law of Zaire—Whether State of Zaire entitled to invoke immunity from jurisdiction—Whether "Zairianization" of foreign-owned companies constituting an act of sovereignty—Whether recourse to procedure established by

Page

State Immunity *(cont.)*

Zairian Government for recovery of compensation constituting
an ordinary commercial act—Belgium, Civil Court of Brussels
(Second Chamber)

SA Biocare v. Gécamines (Zaire) and Republic of Zaire   415

Jurisdictional immunity—Language teacher employed in consular
section of embassy of foreign State—National of employing
State—Contract of employment—Dismissal—Claim for damages
for breach of contract — Whether foreign State entitled to
jurisdictional immunity—Whether fact that employee a national
of the employing State is relevant—Relevance of European
Convention on State Immunity, 1972, Article 5(2)—Whether
applicable as codification of customary international law even
though defendant State not a party—Belgium, Labour Court of
Brussels (Fourth Chamber)

De Queiroz v. State of Portugal   430

State entity—Whether endowed with independent legal personality
—Whether entitled to invoke jurisdictional immunity—American
Battle Monuments Commission—Locally recruited employee—
Dispute concerning contract of employment — Whether
Commission entitled to invoke jurisdictional immunity from
proceedings before municipal courts — United States of
America–Belgium Agreement of 27 November 1958 concerning
American Military Cemeteries—Provision for immunity from
civil jurisdiction—Whether Agreement may be relied upon
against individuals in the absence of its publication—Belgium,
Labour Court of Verviers

Vaessen v. American Battle Monuments Commission   435

State Responsibility

Acts of State organs—Relationship between State responsibility
and individual criminal responsibility — Genocide — Genocide
Convention, 1948—Whether State can be responsible for genocide
contrary to the Convention—Whether dispute regarding alleged
responsibility of State for genocide falling within Article IX of the
Convention—Prohibition of genocide as obligation owed *erga
omnes*—Significance—International Court of Justice

*Case concerning Application of the Convention on the Prevention and
Punishment of the Crime of Genocide (Bosnia and Herzegovina v.
Yugoslavia) (Preliminary Objections) (Order on Counter-claims)*   1

State Succession

Continuity of States—Re-emergence of State—Lithuania—End
of annexation by Soviet Union—Lithuania regaining independence
—Supreme Council of Lithuania adopting Act of 11 March 1990
on the Restoration of the Independent State of Lithuania—
Territory of Lithuania integral and indivisible—Act of 11 March
1990 on the Reinstatement of 12 May 1938 Constitution —
Annulment of all laws introduced by Soviet Union—No re-
establishment of laws in effect prior to 15 June 1940—Validity of
Chapter 8 of 1938 Constitution "National Economy" remaining
— Provisional Basic Law of the Republic of Lithuania —
Restitution of right to private ownership—Whether private or
State ownership of property—Whether property to be restored to
former owners according to prescribed laws—Whether any public
interest—Whether fair compensation appropriate—Lithuania,
Constitutional Court

Property Restitution Case (Case No 12/93)   619

Dissolution of State—Socialist Federal Republic of Yugoslavia—
Emergence of Bosnia and Herzegovina as State — Treaty
obligations of former Yugoslav State—Genocide Convention,
1948 — Whether Bosnia and Herzegovina succeeding to
obligations of former Yugoslavia — Concept of automatic
succession to certain treaties — Whether part of customary
international law—Date on which Bosnia and Herzegovina
became party to Genocide Convention—International Court of
Justice

*Case concerning Application of the Convention on the Prevention and
Punishment of the Crime of Genocide (Bosnia and Herzegovina v.
Yugoslavia) (Preliminary Objections) (Order on Counter-claims)*   1

Union of States—German reunification—Demise of German
Democratic Republic with accession of its *Länder* to Federal
Republic of Germany—Effect on treaties of German Democratic
Republic with third States—Unification Treaty, 1990, Article 12
—Effect of reunification on diplomatic relations of German
Democratic Republic with third States—Whether accreditations
expiring or taken over by Federal Republic—Continuity of the
law—Criminal law—Prosecution of former head of foreign
mission in German Democratic Republic for acts committed
against Federal Republic—Whether permissible following
absorption of German Democratic Republic into Federal
Republic—Whether any rule of customary international law
governing the position—Federal Republic of Germany, Federal
Constitutional Court (*BVerfG*) (Second Senate)

*Former Syrian Ambassador to the German Democratic Republic (Case No
2 BvR 1516/96)*   595

Page

States

Conduct of foreign relations—Diplomatic relations—Decision by
receiving State that foreign diplomat is *persona non grata* —
Notification of such decision to sending State pursuant to Vienna
Convention on Diplomatic Relations, 1961, Article 9(1) —
Whether justiciable in courts of receiving State — Whether
constituting an *acte de gouvernement*—Belgium, Conseil d'Etat

T v. Belgium　　442

Creation and dissolution—Self-determination of groups within
State—Whether conferring a right of unilateral secession—
Relationship between right of self-determination and respect for
territorial integrity of State—Canada, Supreme Court

*Re Reference by the Governor in Council concerning Certain Questions
relating to the Secession of Quebec from Canada*　　536

Existence — Admission to United Nations — Circumstances in
which State created — Significance of recognition and non-
recognition—International Court of Justice

*Case concerning Application of the Convention on the Prevention and
Punishment of the Crime of Genocide (Bosnia and Herzegovina v.
Yugoslavia) (Preliminary Objections) (Order on Counter-claims)*　　1

Territory

Conquest—Non-recognition—Annexation of Lithuania to Soviet
Union—Soviet Union introducing new laws and Constitution in
Lithuania—Subsequent nationalization of property, banks and
large-scale industry—Lithuania, Constitutional Court

Property Restitution Case (Case No 12/93)　　619

Title—Occupation of Canada by aboriginal peoples before
assertion of British sovereignty—Source of aboriginal title—
Relevance of Royal Proclamation of 1763—Requirements for
proof of aboriginal title—Relevance of physical fact of occupation
—Common law principle that occupation proving possession of
land in law—Whether claimants occupying land prior to British
sovereignty — Whether continuity between present and pre-
sovereignty occupation — Whether occupation was exclusive—
Whether aboriginal title surviving colonization — Fiduciary
obligation of Crown to aboriginal peoples—Reconciling aboriginal
interests with sovereignty of the Crown — Section 91(24) of
Constitution Act 1867 — Whether federal government having
exclusive jurisdiction over aboriginal rights—British Columbia

joining Confederation in 1871—Whether British Columbia having power to extinguish aboriginal rights after 1871—Canada, Supreme Court

Delgamuukw and Others v. The Queen in Right of British Columbia and Others; First Nations Summit and Others, Interveners 446

Treaties

Application—Genocide Convention, 1948—Nature of rights and obligations—Interpretation—Succession of new States—International Court of Justice

Case concerning Application of the Convention on the Prevention and Punishment of the Crime of Genocide (Bosnia and Herzegovina v. Yugoslavia) (Preliminary Objections) (Order on Counter-claims) 1

Effect on third parties—Requirement of publication—Treaty affecting rights and obligations of third parties—Whether treaty can be invoked against third parties in the absence of publication—Belgium, Labour Court of Verviers

Vaessen v. American Battle Monuments Commission 435

War and Armed Conflict

Character of conflict—Conflict in Bosnia and Herzegovina—Whether internal or international—Allegations of genocide—Whether affected by character of conflict—International Court of Justice

Case concerning Application of the Convention on the Prevention and Punishment of the Crime of Genocide (Bosnia and Herzegovina v. Yugoslavia) (Preliminary Objections) (Order on Counter-claims) 1

TABLE OF TREATIES

This table contains a list, in chronological order according to the date of signature, of the treaties referred to in the decisions printed in the present volume. It has not been possible to draw a helpful distinction between treaties judicially considered and treaties which are merely cited.

In the case of bilateral treaties, the names of the parties are given in alphabetical order. Multilateral treaties are referred to by the name by which they are believed commonly to be known. References to the texts of treaties have been supplied, including wherever possible at least one reference to a text in the English language. The full titles of the abbreviated references will be found in the list of Abbreviations printed in the volume containing the Consolidated Tables to Vols 1–80.

1919

Sept. 10 Allied and Associated Powers-Yugoslavia (Kingdom of Serbs, Croats and Slovenes), Treaty for the Protection of Minorities (Treaty of Saint-Germain) (1 Hudson 312; UKTS 17 (1919); 112 BFSP 514; 13 Martens NRG, 3rd ser. 521; 226 CTS 182) 32-3
      Chapter I
        Art. 11 32-3
      Chapter II
        Art. 16 32

1929

Feb. 11 Holy See-Italy, Lateran Treaty (Conciliation Treaty) (130 BFSP 791; 21 Martens NRG, 3rd ser. 18; AJIL (1929) Supp. 187; GU 5 June 1929 (extraordinary number); Acta Apostolica Sedis, 7 June 1929; Documents, 1929, 216)
        Art. 12(2) 612

1945

June 26 Charter of the United Nations (9 Hudson 327; UKTS 67 (1946), Cmd 7015; 145 BFSP 805; USTS 993; 1 Peaslee 1288; 59 Stat 1031; 1 UNTS 16; 39 AJIL (1945) Supp. 190; JOF 13 January 1946; 3 Bevans 1153)
        Preamble 657
      Chapter I
        Art. 1(3) 59-60, 657-8
      Chapter IV
        Art. 13(1)(b) 657-8
      Chapter IX
        Art. 55 656-7
        Art. 56 658
      Chapter XIV
        Art. 93(1) 173

June 26 Statute of the International Court of Justice (9 Hudson 510; UKTS 67 (1946), Cmd 7015; USTS 993; 145 BFSP 832; 1 Peaslee 1322; 3 Bevans 1179; CanTS 7 (1945); 39 AJIL (1945) Supp. 215n; JOF 13 January 1946; 59 Stat 1031)
        Art. 34(3) 11
        Art. 36(6) 35, 166

          Art. 37 32
          Art. 38(1)(b) 610
          Art. 38(1)(c) 164
          Art. 38(1)(d) 603
          Art. 40(2) 11
          Art. 63(1) 11

Aug. 8   France, UK, USA, USSR, Agreement for the Prosecution and
          Punishment of Major War Criminals (London Agreement), and
          Charter of the International Military Tribunal (Nuremberg
          Charter) (82 UNTS 279; 145 BFSP 872; UKTS 27 (1946); EAS
          472; 39 AJIL (1945) Supp. 257)
          Art. 7(1) 608-9

1948
Dec. 9   Convention on the Prevention and Punishment of the Crime of
          Genocide (78 UNTS 277; 15 BFSP 682; UKTS 58 (1970); 6 Vert
          A 49; 45 AJIL (1951) Supp. 7; Roberts 157; JOF 26 November
          1950; ATS 2 (1951); Schindler 699) 46-9, 52-3, 56-66
          Art. I 28, 39
          Art II(a)-(d) 28
          Art. III 28, 179
          Art. IV 29, 39, 44, 177-9
          Art. V 29, 39, 44, 181
          Art. VI 28-9, 39, 43, 44, 181
          Art. VII 29
          Art. VIII 39, 43, 194
          Art. IX 10-205
          Art. XI 24-7
          Art. XIII 25
          Art. XIV 193, 194
          Art. XV 194
          Art. XVI 194

1950
Nov. 4   European Convention for the Protection of Human Rights and
          Fundamental Freedoms (213 UNTS 221; UKTS 71 (1953), Cmd
          8969; 156 BFSP 915; ETS 5; 45 AJIL (1951) Supp. 24; 1 Peaslee
          354; 2 Vert A 20; 1 HRR 65; JOF 4 May 1974; 1 EYB 316; 1974
          RTAF 28)
          Art. 1 641
          Art. 2 643
          Art. 3 643
          Art. 4 646-8
          Art. 5 . . . . 643, 647-50
          Art. 5(1)(c) 366-7
          Art. 5(4) 648
          Art. 9 650-1
          Art. 10 369
          Art. 13 642
          Art. 14 651-3
          Art. 66 641
          First Protocol (20 March 1952) (213 UNTS 262; 159 BFSP 355;
          UKTS 46 (1954), Cmd 9221; ETS 9) 641

Fourth Protocol (16 December 1963) (213 UNTS 328; ETS 46) 641
    Art. 2 653-5
Seventh Protocol (22 November 1984) (ETS 117; 7 EHRR 1; 24 ILM
    (1985) 435) 641

1958
Nov. 27 Belgium-United States of America, Agreement concerning Military
    Cemeteries (115 ILR 438-9 (Articles 5(2), 7(1)(a) and 7(2))) 438-9

1961
Apr. 18 Vienna Convention on Diplomatic Relations (500 UNTS 95; UKTS
    19 (1965), Cmnd 2565; 55 AJIL (1961) 1064; 98 JDI 711; 23 UST
    3227; 1971 RTAF 32; TIAS 7502; JOF 17 April 1971)
        Preamble 607, 617
        Art. 3 607
        Art. 4 . . . . 610, 611
        Art. 9 . . . . 443, 611
        Art. 9(1) 445
        Art. 31 603
        Art. 31(1) 605
        Arts. 34ff. 614
        Art. 39(2) 603, 605, 606, 609-18
        Art. 40 . . . . 602, 603, 611

1965
Mar. 18 Convention on Settlement of Investment Disputes between States and
    Nationals of other States (575 UNTS 159; UKTS 25 (1967),
    Cmnd 3255; 17 UST 1270; TIAS 6090; 1966 UNJYB 196; 60
    AJIL (1966) 892; 4 ILM (1965) 532)
        Art. 53(1) 662

Nov. 15 Hague Convention on the Service Abroad of Judicial and
    Extrajudicial Documents in Civil and Commercial Matters (658
    UNTS 163; UKTS 50 (1969), Cmnd 3986; 20 UST 361; TIAS
    6638; 100 JDI 260)
        Art. 10(6) 440

Dec. 21 International Convention on the Elimination of All Forms of Racial
    Discrimination (60 UNTS 195; UKTS 77 (1969), Cmnd 4108; 5
    ILM (1966) 352)
        Art. 4 368

1966
Dec. 16 International Covenant on Civil and Political Rights (UN Doc.
    A/Res. 2200 (XXI); UKTS 6 (1977), Cmnd 6702; JOF 30 June
    1981; 50 Vert A 683; 6 ILM (1967) 368; 1966 UNJYB 178; 1966
    YBHR 442; 30 ZaöRV 365; Brownlie I, 270; 999 UNTS 171)
        Preamble 658-9
        Art. 2 299
        Art. 2(3) 659
        Art. 2(3)(a) 355
        Art. 4(3) 285
        Art. 5 . . . . 367, 645
        Art. 5(1) 366

Art. 6 . . . . 255-62, 354
Art. 6(2) 354
Art. 7 . . . . 288, 292, 295, 297-8, 299, 321, 323, 324, 326, 330
Art. 9 . . . . 321, 323, 324, 326, 330
Art. 10(1) 288, 292-3, 295, 297-8, 299
Art. 12 . . . . 321, 323, 324
Art. 12(3) 324
Art. 12(4) 324, 330-1, 333, 334-49
Art. 13 . . . . 321, 323, 326-7, 329, 330, 340-1, 344, 346
Art. 14 . . . . 268, 285, 326
Art. 14(1) 279, 285-6, 288, 291, 296, 298, 664
Art. 14(2) 288, 291, 296, 298
Art. 14(3)(b) 288, 291, 296, 298, 354
Art. 14(3)(c) 351, 352-3
Art. 14(3)(d) 351, 352-3, 354, 663-4, 666
Art. 14(3)(e) 288, 291-2, 296-7, 298
Art. 14(5) 352-3
Art. 14(7) 363, 364
Art. 17 . . . . . 255-62, 323, 324, 327, 329, 331-3, 334-5, 337, 338-40,
343, 349
Art. 18 268
Art. 19 . . . . 268, 368
Art. 19(2) 380-3
Art. 19(3) 368, 372-3, 374-83
Art. 20(2) 367-8, 375, 378-80
Art. 21 268
Art. 22 268
Art. 23 . . . . . . 321, 323, 324, 327, 331, 334-5, 337, 338-40, 343, 349
Art. 23(1) 331-3
Art. 24 268
Art. 26 . . . . 269, 270-6, 329, 367
Art. 27 . . . . 303-4, 306-18
Optional Protocol (First) (UKTS 6 (1977), Cmnd 6702; 6 ILM (1967)
383; 1966 UNJYB 193; Annex to UNGA Res. 2200 (XXI), Supp.
16, p. 49; 1966 YBHR 450; 8 Jo. ICJ 78; 30 ZaöRV 394;
Brownlie I, 292) 268-9
Art. 1 . . . . 259, 262, 660
Art. 2 . . . . 306, 330
Art. 3 . . . . 283, 306, 330, 660
Art. 4(2) 269, 366
Art. 5 661
Art. 5(1) 274, 316, 353, 372
Art. 5(2)(a) 258, 260, 261, 306, 352
Art. 5(2)(b) 285-6, 306, 330, 352, 365
Art. 5(4) 276, 288, 299, 301, 318, 321, 338, 351, 354, 373
Art. 6 661

1968
Sept. 27 Brussels Convention on Jurisdiction and Enforcement of Judgments
in Civil and Commercial Matters (EEC) (JO (CEE) 1978, L304/77;
Encyclopaedia of European Community Law B 11 235; 8 ILM
(1969) 229; EC 46 (1978), Cmnd 7395; 42 Vert A 579; 100 JDI 555)
Protocol
Art. IV 440

1969

May 23 Vienna Convention on the Law of Treaties (UKTS 58 (1980), Cmnd
7964; 1969 UNJYB 140; 63 AJIL (1969) 875; 8 ILM (1969) 679; 9
IndJIL 288; 29 ZaöRV 711)
Art. 2 100
Art. 2(a) 93
Art. 2(9) 93
Art. 6 100
Art. 7(2)(a) 35
Art. 8 115
Art. 11 195-8
Art. 24(3) 204-5
Art. 26 661-2
Art. 46 .... 103, 122
Art. 53 192
Art. 60(5) 67

1972

May 16 European Convention on State Immunity (Basle) (UKTS 74 (1979),
Cmnd 7742; 11 ILM (1972) 470; 66 AJIL (1972) 923; ETS 74; 20
EYB (1972) 299)
Art. 5 422
Art. 5(1) 432-4
Art. 5(2) 431-4

1978

Aug. 23 Vienna Convention on Succession of States in Respect of Treaties
(1978 UNJYB 106; 17 ILM (1978) 1488; 72 AJIL (1978) 971; 18
IndJIL 393; 39 ZaöRV 279)
Art. 2 158-9
Art. 2(4)(b) 158
Art. 6 158-61
Art. 34(1) 62, 185-91
Art. 46 191

Nov. 29 Belgium-Centre for Industrial Development, Headquarters Agreement
Art. 1 428
Art. 3 428
Art. 5 428

1982

Dec. 10 Convention on the Law of the Sea (21 ILM (1982) 1261; Misc 11
(1983), Cmnd 8941; Brownlie I, 129)
Art. 207(1) 122

1983

Jan. 1 Australia-New Zealand Closer Economic Relations Trade Agree-
ment
Trade in Services Protocol of 1 January 1989 (115 ILR 387 (Articles
4 and 5(1))) 407-10
Art. 4 .... 387, 395-6, 403
Art. 5(1) 387, 395-6, 403

1984
Dec. 8   ACP-EEC Convention (Lomé III) (EC 19 (1985), Cmnd 9511;
          UKTS 15 (1988), Cm 321) 427

1990
Aug. 31   FRG-GDR, Treaty on the Establishment of German Unity (Unification
          Treaty) (30 ILM (1991) 457; BGBl 1990, II, 889)
          Art. 12 615

1994
Mar. 2   Framework Agreement for Federation (Bosnia and Herzegovina) 77-9

1995
Dec. 14   Dayton Peace Agreements (35 ILM (1996) 75) 89-93
          Art. I 90
          Art. III 93
          Art. VII 90, 203
          Art. X 26, 79, 93, 201-2
          Annex 4 (Constitution of Bosnia and Herzegovina) 90-2, 132
          Annex II 91-3
          Annex 6 202-3

Human rights—*Jus cogens* character of certain human rights norms—Prohibition of genocide—Genocide Convention, 1948 — Status — Nature of rights and obligations under Genocide Convention—Character as obligations *erga omnes*

International Court of Justice—Jurisdiction—Principles on which jurisdiction based—Whether Court should adopt strict approach to jurisdiction—Disputes clause in multi-lateral treaty—Genocide Convention, 1948, Article IX—Jurisdiction *ratione personae*—Whether Convention in force between claimant and respondent — Date at which Convention must be in force—Jurisdiction *ratione materiae* —Scope of Convention—Nature of disputes covered by Article IX—Jurisdiction *ratione temporis*—Admissibility

International Court of Justice—Counter-claims—Rules of Court, Article 80—Definition of counter-claim—Requirement of direct connection between counter-claim and original claim—Meaning—Connection in fact and in law—Discretion of Court—Procedure—Whether Court obliged to hold oral proceedings on admissibility of counter-claim

International criminal law—Genocide—Genocide Convention, 1948—Definition—Nature of obligations under Genocide Convention — Whether conferring rights and imposing responsibility upon States

International organizations—United Nations—Admission of new member—Significance—Admission of Bosnia and Herzegovina as member—Whether establishing Statehood of Bosnia and Herzegovina—Recognition of President of Bosnia and Herzegovina

Recognition—Of States and governments—Significance—Whether establishing that entity is a State—Whether signifying acceptance of claim to succession—Recognition of particular individual as Head of State—Significance of non-recognition—Whether treaty in force between States which do not recognize one another—Subsequent act of mutual recognition — Dayton–Paris Agreement between Bosnia and Herzegovina, Croatia and Federal Republic of Yugoslavia

State responsibility—Acts of State organs—Relationship between State responsibility and individual criminal

responsibility — Genocide — Genocide Convention, 1948—
Whether State can be responsible for genocide contrary
to the Convention — Whether dispute regarding alleged
responsibility of State for genocide falling within Article IX
of the Convention—Prohibition of genocide as obligation
owed *erga omnes*—Significance

State succession—Dissolution of State—Socialist Federal
Republic of Yugoslavia — Emergence of Bosnia and
Herzegovina as State — Treaty obligations of former
Yugoslav State — Genocide Convention, 1948 — Whether
Bosnia and Herzegovina succeeding to obligations of
former Yugoslavia—Concept of automatic succession to
certain treaties—Whether part of customary international
law—Date on which Bosnia and Herzegovina became party
to Genocide Convention

States—Existence—Admission to United Nations—Circumstances in which State created—Significance of recognition
and non-recognition

Treaties—Application—Genocide Convention, 1948—Nature
of rights and obligations—Interpretation—Succession of
new States

War and armed conflict—Character of conflict—Conflict in
Bosnia and Herzegovina—Whether internal or international
—Allegations of genocide—Whether affected by character
of conflict

CASE CONCERNING APPLICATION OF THE CONVENTION ON THE PREVENTION
AND PUNISHMENT OF THE CRIME OF GENOCIDE

(BOSNIA AND HERZEGOVINA v. YUGOSLAVIA)[1]

[1] The Republic of Bosnia and Herzegovina was represented by HE Mr Muhamed Sacirbey, Ambassador and Permanent Representative of the Republic of Bosnia and Herzegovina to the United Nations, as Agent; Mr Phon van den Biesen, Attorney in Amsterdam, as Deputy-Agent, Counsel and Advocate; Mr Thomas M. Franck, Professor at the School of Law and Director, Center for International Studies, New York University, Mr Alain Pellet, Professor, University of Paris X-Nanterre and Institute of Political Studies, Paris, and Ms Brigitte Stern, Professor, University of Paris I (Panthéon-Sorbonne), as Counsel and Advocates; Mr Khawar M. Qureshi, Member of the English Bar, Lecturer in Law, King's College, London, Ms Vasvija Vidović, Minister-Counsellor, Embassy of Bosnia and Herzegovina in the Netherlands, Representative of the Republic of Bosnia and Herzegovina at the International Criminal Tribunal for the former Yugoslavia, and Mr Marc Weller, Assistant Director of Studies, Centre for International Studies, University of Cambridge, Member of the Faculty of Law of the University of Cambridge, as Counsel; Mr Pierre Bodeau, Research Assistant/Tutor, University of Paris X-Nanterre, Mr

International Court of Justice

Preliminary Objections. 11 *July* 1996

(Bedjaoui, *President*; Schwebel, *Vice-President*; Oda, Guillaume, Shahabuddeen, Weeramantry, Ranjeva, Herczegh, Shi, Koroma, Vereshchetin, Ferrari Bravo and Parra-Aranguren, *Judges*; Lauterpacht[2] and Kreća,[3] *Judges ad hoc*)

Order on Counter-claims. 17 *December* 1997

(Schwebel, *President*; Weeramantry, *Vice-President*; Oda, Bedjaoui, Guillaume, Herczegh, Shi, Fleischhauer, Koroma, Vereshchetin, Parra-Aranguren and Kooijmans, *Judges*; Lauterpacht and Kreća, *Judges ad hoc*)

SUMMARY:[4] *The facts*:—Bosnia and Herzegovina had been one of the six republics constituting the Socialist Federal Republic of Yugoslavia ("SFRY"). It declared itself independent on 6 March 1992 and was admitted as a member of the United Nations on 22 May 1992. During 1991 and 1992 three other republics (Croatia, Macedonia and Slovenia) also declared themselves independent of the SFRY. The two remaining republics (Serbia and Montenegro) announced that they would continue in federation under the name of the Federal Republic of Yugoslavia. The population of Bosnia and Herzegovina comprised Muslims, Serbs and Croats. Following the declaration of independence, hostilities occurred between Bosnian Government forces and Serb and Croat forces throughout most of Bosnia and Herzegovina. These hostilities did not cease until the conclusion of the General Framework Agreement for Peace ("the Dayton–Paris Agreement") which was signed by the Republic of Bosnia and Herzegovina, the Republic of Croatia and the Federal Republic of Yugoslavia on 14 December 1995.[5]

Michiel Pestman, Attorney in Amsterdam, and Mr Thierry Vaissière, Research Student, Cedin-Paris I (Panthéon-Sorbonne), as Counsellors; and Mr Hervé Ascencio, Research Assistant/Tutor, University of Paris X-Nanterre, Ms Marieke Drenth, Ms Froana Hoff, Mr Michael Kellogg, Mr Harold Kocken, Ms Nathalie Lintvelt, Mr Sam Muller, Mr Joop Nijssen, and Mr Eelco Szabó, as Assistants.
    The Federal Republic of Yugoslavia was represented by Mr Rodoljub Etinski, Chief Legal Adviser, Ministry of Foreign Affairs of the Federal Republic of Yugoslavia, Professor of International Law, Novi Sad University, and Mr Djordje Lópičić, Chargé d'Affaires, Embassy of the Federal Republic of Yugoslavia in the Netherlands, as Agents; Mr Ian Brownlie, CBE, FBA, QC, Chichele Professor of Public International Law, University of Oxford, Mr Miodrag Mitić, Assistant Federal Minister for Foreign Affairs of the Federal Republic of Yugoslavia (Ret.), and Mr Eric Suy, Professor, Catholic University of Louvain (K.U. Leuven), formerly Under-Secretary-General and Legal Counsel of the United Nations, as Counsel and Advocates; and Mr Stevan Djordjević, Professor of International Law, Belgrade University, Mr Shabtai Rosenne, Member of the Israel Bar, and Mr Gavro Perazić, Professor of International Law, Podgorica University, as Counsel.
[2] Judge *ad hoc* designated by Bosnia and Herzegovina.
[3] Judge *ad hoc* designated by Yugoslavia.
[4] The summary was prepared by Professor Christopher Greenwood.
[5] 35 ILM (1996) 75.

On 20 March 1993, the Republic of Bosnia and Herzegovina ("Bosnia and Herzegovina") filed an Application instituting proceedings against the Federal Republic of Yugoslavia (Serbia and Montenegro) ("Yugoslavia") in which it accused Yugoslavia of violations of the Genocide Convention and other international agreements.[6] Bosnia and Herzegovina also requested provisional measures of protection.[7] Bosnia and Herzegovina maintained that Yugoslavia had been involved in the hostilities in Bosnia and Herzegovina and was responsible for acts of genocide which it maintained had been committed against the people of Bosnia and Herzegovina.[8]

Bosnia and Herzegovina initially maintained that the Court had jurisdiction under Article IX of the Convention on the Prevention and Punishment of the Crime of Genocide, 1948 ("the Genocide Convention"), which provides that:

> Disputes between the Contracting Parties relating to the interpretation, application or fulfilment of the present Convention, including those relating to the responsibility of a State for genocide or for any of the other acts enumerated in Article III, shall be submitted to the International Court of Justice at the request of any of the parties to the dispute.

The SFRY had been a party to the Genocide Convention. On 27 April 1992 Yugoslavia formally declared that it would abide by all the international commitments assumed by the SFRY. On 29 December 1992 Bosnia and Herzegovina deposited with the Secretary-General of the United Nations a Notice of Succession, declaring that it wished to accede to the Genocide Convention with effect from 6 March 1992. The Secretary-General formally notified the parties to the Genocide Convention of this Notice on 18 March 1993.

Subsequently, Bosnia and Herzegovina also sought to rely upon the Treaty of Saint Germain-en-Laye, 1919,[9] on the customary and conventional laws of war and international humanitarian law, on a letter dated 8 June 1992 from the Presidents of the republics of Serbia and Montenegro to the President of the Arbitration Commission of the International Conference for Peace in Yugoslavia[10] and the doctrine of *forum prorogatum*. In its second Provisional Measures Order of 13 September 1993 the Court doubted whether its jurisdiction could be founded upon any of these additional bases for jurisdiction. The Memorial of Bosnia and Herzegovina concentrated upon the Genocide Convention[11] but did not abandon reliance upon the additional bases for jurisdiction.

---

[6] The relevant part of the Application is set out at p. 13 below.

[7] The Court indicated provisional measures in its Order of 8 April 1993 (95 *ILR* 1). A further Order in respect of requests for provisional measures of protection advanced by both Parties was given on 13 September 1993 (95 *ILR* 1).

[8] See the relevant passage from the Memorial of Bosnia and Herzegovina, set out at p. 15 below.

[9] Treaty between the Allied and Associated Powers (the United States of America, the British Empire, France, Italy and Japan) and the Kingdom of the Serbs, Croats and Slovenes, signed at Saint Germain-en-Laye on 10 September 1919.

[10] The relevant part of this letter appears at p. 31 below. For consideration of this letter by the Arbitration Commission, see *Interlocutory Decision (Opinions Nos 8, 9 and 10)* of 4 July 1992, 92 *ILR* 194.

[11] See p. 15 below.

Preliminary Objections Proceedings

Yugoslavia submitted preliminary objections to the jurisdiction of the Court.[12] With regard to the question of jurisdiction under the Genocide Convention, Yugoslavia contended that:

(1) The Court lacked jurisdiction *ratione personae*, because Bosnia and Herzegovina had not established itself as an independent State in accordance with the principle of self-determination and had not, therefore, become a party to the Genocide Convention.

(2) The Court lacked jurisdiction *ratione materiae*, because:

(a) the conflict in Bosnia and Herzegovina was an internal conflict in which Yugoslavia took no part. Nor did Yugoslavia exercise jurisdiction over any part of Bosnia and Herzegovina; and

(b) the Application was based upon a fundamentally erroneous interpretation of the Genocide Convention and contained allegations of State responsibility which fell outside the scope of the Convention.

(3) Even if the Court did possess jurisdiction, that jurisdiction was limited *ratione temporis* and did not exist in respect of events occurring before Yugoslavia recognized Bosnia and Herzegovina on 14 December 1995. Alternatively, the relevant date was the date on which the Genocide Convention entered into force between Bosnia and Herzegovina and Yugoslavia. Since the Notification of Succession deposited by Bosnia and Herzegovina on 29 December 1992 operated as an instrument of accession, the Convention entered into force for Bosnia and Herzegovina on 29 March 1993 (three months after the Notice). If, however, Bosnia and Herzegovina was held to have become a party to the Genocide Convention by operation of the principle of State succession, the relevant date was either 18 March 1993, when the Notification of Succession was communicated to other Parties, or 29 December 1992, the date on which the Notification was given to the depositary. The Notification could not operate retrospectively.

Yugoslavia also challenged the additional grounds for jurisdiction advanced by Bosnia and Herzegovina and the admissibility of the Application.

Held (in the Judgment of 11 July 1996):—(i) (by thirteen votes to two) the Court had jurisdiction under Article IX of the Genocide Convention; (ii) (by fourteen votes to one) the Court did not have jurisdiction under any of the other instruments relied upon by Bosnia and Herzegovina; and (iii) (by thirteen votes to two) the Application was admissible.

(1) (by fourteen votes to one) The objection to the jurisdiction *ratione personae* of the Court was rejected. The Genocide Convention was a treaty in force between Bosnia and Herzegovina and Yugoslavia.

(a) When the Federal Republic of Yugoslavia was proclaimed on 27 April 1992, it was announced that the Federal Republic would abide by all the treaty commitments of the SFRY. Since the SFRY had been party to the Genocide Convention, that Convention was in force for Yugoslavia when the Application was filed on 20 March 1993 (p. 23).

---

[12] Those objections are set out in the form in which they were originally submitted at p. 17 below. The preliminary objections in the form in which they were advanced by Yugoslavia at the oral hearings are set out at p. 19.

(b) Bosnia and Herzegovina had been admitted to membership of the United Nations by decisions of the Security Council and the General Assembly on 22 May 1992. It was not necessary to decide whether Bosnia and Herzegovina automatically succeeded to the Genocide Convention, since it had undoubtedly succeeded by the date of the Application (pp. 24-5).

(c) Nor was it necessary to determine the effect of non-recognition upon treaty relations between Bosnia and Herzegovina and Yugoslavia prior to 14 December 1995. Even if the Genocide Convention was not applicable between the two States prior to that date, it was applicable now. Since Bosnia and Herzegovina could always bring a fresh Application, the Court would not determine that it lacked jurisdiction on the ground that there might have been no treaty basis for jurisdiction between the two States at the date the Application was filed (pp. 25-7).

Per Judges Shahabuddeen, Weeramantry and Parra-Aranguren: The special nature of the Genocide Convention meant that it was a treaty to which the succession of States was automatic when new States emerged from the dissolution of a State which had been a party to the Convention. This conclusion followed from the fact that the Convention did not impose obligations over and above those which existed under customary international law and from the need to avoid a hiatus in succession to obligations under the Convention (pp. 46-9 and 51-67).

(2) (by eleven votes to four) Yugoslavia's objection to jurisdiction *ratione materiae* was rejected. There was a dispute, within the scope of Article IX of the Genocide Convention, between the two States.

(a) The fact that Article I of the Genocide Convention[13] provided that genocide was a crime whether committed in time of peace or in time of war clearly indicated that the Convention was applicable whenever the acts to which it referred were committed, irrespective of the nature of the conflict in the course of which they were committed (pp. 27-8).

(b) The question whether or not Yugoslavia had taken part in the conflict in Bosnia and Herzegovina was a matter in dispute between the parties and fell to be resolved at the merits stage (p. 28).

(c) The rights and obligations enshrined in the Convention were rights and obligations *erga omnes*. The obligation of each State to prevent and punish the crime of genocide was not territorially limited by the Convention (pp. 28-9).

(d) Article IX conferred jurisdiction in respect of "the responsibility of a State for genocide". No distinction was drawn between responsibility for failure to prevent and punish and responsibility for the actual perpetration of genocide. Nor did the provisions which contemplated the criminal responsibility of "rulers" or "public officials" exclude the responsibility of the State for the acts of its organs (pp. 29-30).

Per Judge Oda (dissenting): The Genocide Convention was essentially directed not to the rights and obligations of States but to the protection of the rights and obligations of individuals and groups of persons. Bosnia and Herzegovina had failed to show in its Application that it was alleging that Yugoslavia had violated Bosnia and Herzegovina's rights under the

[13] See p. 28 below.

Convention. It was doubtful whether the Court was the appropriate forum for the resolution of this case. The Court should maintain a strict position regarding its jurisdiction (pp. 38-43).

Per Judges Shi and Vereshchetin (dissenting from part of the reasoning): The Genocide Convention was primarily directed towards the punishment of persons committing genocide and genocidal acts and to the prevention of such crimes by individuals, not towards State responsibility (pp. 44-5).

(3) (by fourteen votes to one) Yugoslavia's objection to jurisdiction *ratione temporis* was rejected. Article IX did not contain any clause the object or effect of which was to limit the jurisdiction of the Court *ratione temporis*, nor did the parties assert such a limitation at the time of becoming party to the Convention or on signature of the Dayton–Paris Agreement. The Court therefore had jurisdiction to give effect to the Convention with regard to the relevant facts which had occurred since the beginning of the conflict in Bosnia and Herzegovina (p. 30).

(4) (by fourteen votes to one) None of the additional bases for jurisdiction advanced by Bosnia and Herzegovina could be accepted. The letter to the President of the Arbitration Commission did not amount to a binding undertaking by the Presidents of Serbia and Montenegro unconditionally to accept the unilateral submission to the Court of a wide range of legal disputes. The Court saw no reason to depart from the view in its second provisional measures decision[14] that the other instruments relied on by Bosnia and Herzegovina did not confer jurisdiction on the Court. Nor had Yugoslavia given consent to a wider jurisdiction under the doctrine of *forum prorogatum* (pp. 30-4).

Per Judge *ad hoc* Lauterpacht: The Court could have found that it had jurisdiction on the basis of *forum prorogatum* (p. 35).[15]

Per Judge Shahabuddeen: The decision of the Court regarding *forum prorogatum* was correct. That doctrine was, in any event, irrelevant to the question of jurisdiction under Article IX of the Genocide Convention (pp. 49-51).

(5) (by thirteen votes to two) The objections to the admissibility of the Application were rejected. The fact that the conflict in Bosnia and Herzegovina might have been a civil war did not preclude the Court from adjudicating upon allegations of violations of the Genocide Convention. Notwithstanding Yugoslavia's claim that Mr Alija Izetbegović had not been the lawful President of Bosnia and Herzegovina and that the decision to commence proceedings had not been validly taken, Mr Izetbegović had been internationally recognized as Head of State, in particular by the United Nations. Under international law, every Head of State was presumed to be able to act on behalf of the State and its international relations (pp. 34-5).

---

[14] 95 *ILR* 1.

[15] Judge *ad hoc* Lauterpacht discussed this question in his Separate Opinion in the second provisional measures case: 95 *ILR* 1 at 136-9.

Per Judge *ad hoc* Kreća (dissenting): (1) The Court had failed to resolve the essential question whether Bosnia and Herzegovina at the time of filing the Application and Bosnia and Herzegovina after the Dayton–Paris Agreement were one and the same. The proclamation of Bosnia and Herzegovina as an independent State had been a substantial breach of the norms on equal rights and self-determination of peoples. Accordingly, there had been no *de jure* succession by Bosnia and Herzegovina to the rights and obligations of the SFRY (pp. 70-102 and 115-74).

(2) The fact that the decision to institute proceedings was taken in violation of the internal law of Bosnia and Herzegovina was of great importance. At the time of filing the Application, Mr Izetbegović was not the Head of State of Bosnia and Herzegovina and had no authority to act on behalf of Bosnia and Herzegovina (pp. 102-15).

(3) (a) The conflict in Bosnia and Herzegovina was *sui generis* and could not be classified as wholly internal in character, although elements of civil war were present. The *jus cogens* character of the prohibition of genocide meant that it was a universal norm which bound States in all parts of the world. However, the fact that the norm prohibiting genocide was a norm of *jus cogens* did not imply that the obligation of States to prevent and punish genocide was not territorially limited. On the contrary, respect for the territorial integrity of States, iself a norm of *jus cogens*, meant that the obligations of States under the Genocide Convention had to be performed within their own territories (pp. 174-7).

(b) A State could not be responsible for genocide under the Genocide Convention, which was concerned with the responsibility of individuals, not States. A dispute regarding alleged State responsibility for genocide did not, therefore, come within Article IX of the Genocide Convention (pp. 177-82).

(4) The concept of "automatic succession" to certain types of treaty was not yet part of customary international law and existed solely at the level of *lex ferenda* (pp. 183-204).

Counter-claims Order

Following the dismissal of its preliminary objections, Yugoslavia filed its Counter-Memorial on 22 July 1997. The Counter-Memorial included counter-claims.[16] In its counter-claims, Yugoslavia asked the Court to adjudge and declare that Bosnia and Herzegovina had been guilty of genocide against the Serb population of Bosnia and Herzegovina and of other violations of the Genocide Convention. Bosnia and Herzegovina maintained that the counter-claims did not meet the requirements of Article 80(1) of the Rules of Court[17] on the ground that they were not sufficiently directly connected with the subject-matter of Bosnia and Herzegovina's claim.

Held (*in the Order of 17 December 1997*) (by thirteen votes to one):—The counter-claims were admissible as such and formed part of the current proceedings.

---

[16] The counter-claims are set out at pp. 210-11 below.

[17] Article 80(1) provides that:

A counter-claim may be presented provided that it is directly connected with the subject-matter of the claim of the other party and that it comes within the jurisdiction of the Court.

(1) A counter-claim had a dual character. It was an autonomous legal act, the object of which was to submit a new claim to the Court and thus to widen the subject-matter of the dispute. It was, however, linked to the principal claim and reacted to it. A respondent State was allowed to submit a counter-claim, instead of pursuing its claim in separate proceedings, for reasons of procedural economy and to allow the Court to have an overview of the respective claims and to decide them in a consistent way. A respondent was not entitled to use a counter-claim as a means of referring to an international court claims which exceeded the limits of that court's jurisdiction as recognized by the parties (pp. 216-17).

(2) The Rules of Court did not, however, define what was meant by "directly connected" and it was therefore for the Court, in its sole discretion, to determine whether the counter-claim was sufficiently connected to the principal claim, taking account of the particular aspects of each case. That task involved an assessment of the degree of connection between the claim and the counter-claim both in fact and in law (p. 218).

(3) In the present case, the claim and the counter-claims rested on facts of the same nature and forming part of the same factual complex. Moreover, Yugoslavia intended to rely on certain identical facts both for its defence and for its counter-claims. The fact that the Genocide Convention was not based upon reciprocity of obligations did not preclude the Yugoslav counter-claims being directly connected with the Bosnia and Herzegovina claim (pp. 218-20).

Per Judge *ad hoc* Kreća: A claim made by a respondent State which fulfilled the requirements of Article 80(1) of the Rules of Court was automatically to be treated as a counter-claim and joined to the original proceedings. In the present case, the existence of a legal connection between the claim and the counter-claims was obvious; both were inseparably connected to the Genocide Convention (pp. 222-31).

Per Judge Koroma: The Court should not allow a counter-claim to be used as the means of delaying the administration of justice, especially in a case which involved such grave issues. If the Rules of Court appeared to place restraints on the Court, the Court should either exercise its discretion in the interests of the good administration of justice or propose that the Rules be reviewed (pp. 231-6).

Per Judge *ad hoc* Lauterpacht: In accordance with Article 80(3) of the Rules[18] the Court should have held oral proceedings before ruling on the admissibility of the counter-claims. It was not necessary, for the purposes of establishing a direct connection within Article 80(1), that a counter-claim in respect of genocide be directly connected to the individual and specific acts forming the basis of the principal claim, provided that the counter-claim related to acts affected by the same treaty and occurring in the course of the same conflict. While it was open to the Court, even in a case in which the requirements of Article 80(1) were met, to order a separate trial of a counter-claim, the present case was not suitable for such separation (pp. 236-44).

---

[18] See p. 237 below.

Per Vice-President Weeramantry (dissenting): The Yugoslav allegations were not properly characterized as counter-claims within the meaning of Article 80 of the Rules and should have been the subject of separate proceedings. The delay which the counter-claims would create would have led the Court to exercise its discretion against joining them to the original claim. The involvement of Croatia in the counter-allegations also suggested that joinder was inappropriate (pp. 244-53).

The Judgment on Preliminary Objections, the Order on Counter-claims and the Declarations, Separate Opinions and Dissenting Opinions of Judges are set out as follows:

	page
Judgment on Preliminary Objections	10
Declaration of Judge Oda	38
Joint declaration of Judges Shi and Vereshchetin	44
Declaration of Judge *ad hoc* Lauterpacht	45
Separate Opinion of Judge Shahabuddeen	46
Separate Opinion of Judge Weeramantry	51
Separate Opinion of Judge Parra-Aranguren	66
Dissenting Opinion of Judge *ad hoc* Kreća	68
Order on Counter-claims	206
Declaration of Judge *ad hoc* Kreća	222
Separate Opinion of Judge Koroma	231
Separate Opinion of Judge *ad hoc* Lauterpacht	236
Dissenting Opinion of Vice-President Weeramantry	244

The text of the Order on Counter-claims commences at p. 206. The following is the text of the Judgment on Preliminary Objections:

THE COURT,   **[597**

composed as above,

after deliberation,

delivers the following Judgment:

1. On 20 March 1993, the Government of the Republic of Bosnia and Herzegovina (hereinafter called "Bosnia and Herzegovina") filed in the Registry of the Court an Application instituting proceedings against the Government of

598] the Federal Republic of Yugoslavia (hereinafter called "Yugoslavia") in respect of a dispute concerning alleged violations of the Convention on the Prevention and Punishment of the Crime of Genocide (hereinafter called "the Genocide Convention"), adopted by the General Assembly of the United Nations on 9 December 1948, as well as various matters which Bosnia and Herzegovina claims are connected therewith. The Application invoked Article IX of the Genocide Convention as the basis of the jurisdiction of the Court.

2. Pursuant to Article 40, paragraph 2, of the Statute, the Application was immediately communicated to the Yugoslav Government by the Registrar; pursuant to paragraph 3 of that Article, all States entitled to appear before the Court were notified of the Application.

3. Pursuant to Article 43 of the Rules of Court, the Registrar addressed the notification provided for in Article 63, paragraph 1, of the Statute to all the States which appeared to be parties to the Genocide Convention on the basis of the information supplied by the Secretary-General of the United Nations as depositary; he also addressed to the Secretary-General the notification provided for in Article 34, paragraph 3, of the Statute.

4. On 20 March 1993, immediately after the filing of its Application, Bosnia and Herzegovina submitted a request for the indication of provisional measures under Article 41 of the Statute. On 31 March 1993, the Agent of Bosnia and Herzegovina filed in the Registry, invoking it as an additional basis of the jurisdiction of the Court in the case, the text of a letter dated 8 June 1992, addressed to the President of the Arbitration Commission of the International Conference for Peace in Yugoslavia by the Presidents of the Republics of Montenegro and Serbia.

On 1 April 1993, Yugoslavia submitted written observations on Bosnia and Herzegovina's request for provisional measures, in which, in turn, it recommended the Court to order the application of provisional measures to Bosnia and Herzegovina.

By an Order dated 8 April 1993, the Court, after hearing the Parties, indicated certain provisional measures with a view to the protection of rights under the Genocide Convention.

5. By an Order of 16 April 1993, the President of the Court fixed 15 October 1993 as the time-limit for the filing of the Memorial of Bosnia and Herzegovina and 15 April 1994 as the time-limit for the filing of the Counter-Memorial of Yugoslavia.

6. Since the Court included upon the Bench no judge of the nationality of the Parties, each of them exercised its right under Article 31, paragraph 3, of the Statute of the Court to choose a judge *ad hoc* to sit in the case: Bosnia and Herzegovina chose Mr. Elihu Lauterpacht, and Yugoslavia chose Mr. Milenko Kreća.

7. On 27 July 1993, Bosnia and Herzegovina submitted a new request for the indication of provisional measures; and, by a series of subsequent communications, it stated that it was amending or supplementing that request, as well as, in some cases, the Application, including the basis of jurisdiction relied on therein. By letters of 6 August and 10 August 1993, the Agent of Bosnia and Herzegovina indicated that his Government was relying, as additional bases of the jurisdiction of the Court in the case, on, respectively, the Treaty between the Allied and Associated Powers and the Kingdom of the Serbs, Croats and Slovenes on the Protection of Minorities, signed at Saint-Germain-en-Laye on

10 September 1919, and on customary and conventional international laws of **[599**
war and international humanitarian law; and, by a letter of 13 August 1993,
the Agent of Bosnia and Herzegovina confirmed his Government's desire to
rely, on the same basis, on the aforementioned letter from the Presidents of
Montenegro and Serbia, dated 8 June 1992 (see paragraph 4 above).

On 10 August 1993, Yugoslavia also submitted a request for the indication of
provisional measures; and, on 10 August and 23 August 1993, it filed written
observations on Bosnia and Herzegovina's new request, as amended or supple-
mented.

By an Order dated 13 September 1993, the Court, after hearing the Parties,
reaffirmed the measures indicated in its Order of 8 April 1993 and declared that
those measures should be immediately and effectively implemented.

8. By an Order dated 7 October 1993, the Vice-President of the Court, at the
request of Bosnia and Herzegovina, extended to 15 April 1994 the time-limit for
the filing of the Memorial; the time-limit for the filing of the Counter-Memorial
was extended, by the same Order, to 15 April 1995. Bosnia and Herzegovina
duly filed its Memorial within the extended time-limit thus fixed.

9. By an Order dated 21 March 1995, the President of the Court, at the
request of Yugoslavia, extended to 30 June 1995 the time-limit for the filing of
the Counter-Memorial. Within the extended time-limit thus fixed, Yugoslavia,
referring to Article 79, paragraph 1, of the Rules of Court, raised preliminary
objections concerning, respectively, the admissibility of the Application and the
jurisdiction of the Court to entertain the case. Accordingly, by an Order dated
14 July 1995, the President of the Court, noting that, by virtue of Article 79,
paragraph 3, of the Rules of Court, the proceedings on the merits were suspended, fixed 14 November 1995 as the time-limit within which Bosnia and
Herzegovina could present a written statement of its observations and submissions on the preliminary objections raised by Yugoslavia. Bosnia and Herzegovina filed such a statement within the time-limit so fixed, and the case
became ready for hearing in respect of the preliminary objections.

10. By a letter dated 2 February 1996, the Agent of Yugoslavia submitted to
the Court, "as a document relevant to the case", the text of the General Framework Agreement for Peace in Bosnia and Herzegovina and the annexes thereto
(collectively "the peace agreement"), initialled in Dayton, Ohio, on 21 November 1995 and signed in Paris on 14 December 1995 (hereinafter called the
"Dayton-Paris Agreement").

11. Pursuant to Article 53, paragraph 2, of the Rules of Court, the Court
decided to make the pleadings and documents annexed thereto accessible to the
public on the opening of the oral proceedings.

12. Public hearings were held between 29 April and 3 May 1996 at which the
Court heard the oral arguments and replies of:

For Yugoslavia: Mr. Rodoljub Etinski,
                             Mr. Miodrag Mitić,
                             Mr. Djordje Lopičić,
                             Mr. Eric Suy,
                             Mr. Ian Brownlie,
                             Mr. Gavro Perazić.

600] *For Bosnia and Herzegovina:* H.E. Mr. Muhamed Sacirbey,
Mr. Phon van den Biesen,
Mr. Alain Pellet,
Ms Brigitte Stern,
Mr. Thomas M. Franck.

*

13. In the Application, the following requests were made by Bosnia and
Herzegovina:

"Accordingly, while reserving the right to revise, supplement or amend
this Application, and subject to the presentation to the Court of the relevant evidence and legal arguments, Bosnia and Herzegovina requests the
Court to adjudge and declare as follows:

(a) that Yugoslavia (Serbia and Montenegro) has breached, and is con-
tinuing to breach, its legal obligations toward the People and State of
Bosnia and Herzegovina under Articles I, II *(a)*, II *(b)*, II *(c)*,
II *(d)*, III *(a)*, III *(b)*, III *(c)*, III *(d)*, III *(e)*, IV and V of the
Genocide Convention;

(b) that Yugoslavia (Serbia and Montenegro) has violated and is continuing to violate its legal obligations toward the People and State of
Bosnia and Herzegovina under the four Geneva Conventions of
1949, their Additional Protocol I of 1977, the customary international laws of war including the Hague Regulations on Land Warfare
of 1907, and other fundamental principles of international humanitarian law;

(c) that Yugoslavia (Serbia and Montenegro) has violated and continues
to violate Articles 1, 2, 3, 4, 5, 6, 7, 8, 9, 10, 11, 12, 13, 15, 16, 17, 18,
19, 20, 21, 22, 23, 25, 26 and 28 of the Universal Declaration of
Human Rights with respect to the citizens of Bosnia and Herzegovina;

(d) that Yugoslavia (Serbia and Montenegro), in breach of its obligations under general and customary international law, has killed,
murdered, wounded, raped, robbed, tortured, kidnapped, illegally
detained, and exterminated the citizens of Bosnia and Herzegovina,
and is continuing to do so;

(e) that in its treatment of the citizens of Bosnia and Herzegovina,
Yugoslavia (Serbia and Montenegro) has violated, and is continuing
to violate, its solemn obligations under Articles 1 (3), 55 and 56 of
the United Nations Charter;

(f) that Yugoslavia (Serbia and Montenegro) has used and is continuing
to use force and the threat of force against Bosnia and Herzegovina
in violation of Articles 2 (1), 2 (2), 2 (3), 2 (4), and 33 (1), of the
United Nations Charter;

(g) that Yugoslavia (Serbia and Montenegro), in breach of its obligations under general and customary international law, has used and is
using force and the threat of force against Bosnia and Herzegovina;

(h) that Yugoslavia (Serbia and Montenegro), in breach of its obligations under general and customary international law, has violated
and is violating the sovereignty of Bosnia and Herzegovina by:

— armed attacks against Bosnia and Herzegovina by air and land;

— aerial trespass into Bosnian airspace;   **[60**
— efforts by direct and indirect means to coerce and intimidate the Government of Bosnia and Herzegovina;

(i) that Yugoslavia (Serbia and Montenegro), in breach of its obligations under general and customary international law, has intervened and is intervening in the internal affairs of Bosnia and Herzegovina;

(j) that Yugoslavia (Serbia and Montenegro), in recruiting, training, arming, equipping, financing, supplying and otherwise encouraging, supporting, aiding, and directing military and paramilitary actions in and against Bosnia and Herzegovina by means of its agents and surrogates, has violated and is violating its express charter and treaty obligations to Bosnia and Herzegovina and, in particular, its charter and treaty obligations under Article 2 (4) of the United Nations Charter, as well as its obligations under general and customary international law;

(k) that under the circumstances set forth above, Bosnia and Herzegovina has the sovereign right to defend Itself and its People under United Nations Charter Article 51 and customary international law, including by means of immediately obtaining military weapons, equipment, supplies and troops from other States;

(l) that under the circumstances set forth above, Bosnia and Herzegovina has the sovereign right under United Nations Charter Article 51 and customary international law to request the immediate assistance of any State to come to its defence, including by military means (weapons, equipment, supplies, troops, etc.);

(m) that Security Council resolution 713 (1991), imposing a weapons embargo upon the former Yugoslavia, must be construed in a manner that shall not impair the inherent right of individual or collective self-defence of Bosnia and Herzegovina under the terms of United Nations Charter Article 51 and the rules of customary international law;

(n) that all subsequent Security Council resolutions that refer to or reaffirm resolution 713 (1991) must be construed in a manner that shall not impair the inherent right of individual or collective self-defence of Bosnia and Herzegovina under the terms of United Nations Charter Article 51 and the rules of customary international law;

(o) that Security Council resolution 713 (1991) and all subsequent Security Council resolutions referring thereto or reaffirming thereof must not be construed to impose an arms embargo upon Bosnia and Herzegovina, as required by Articles 24 (1) and 51 of the United Nations Charter and in accordance with the customary doctrine of *ultra vires*;

(p) that pursuant to the right of collective self-defence recognized by United Nations Charter Article 51, all other States parties to the Charter have the right to come to the immediate defence of Bosnia and Herzegovina — at its request — including by means of immediately providing it with weapons, military equipment and supplies, and armed forces (soldiers, sailors, airpeople, etc.);

[602]   *(q)* that Yugoslavia (Serbia and Montenegro) and its agents and surrogates are under an obligation to cease and desist immediately from its breaches of the foregoing legal obligations, and is under a particular duty to cease and desist immediately:

— from its systematic practice of so-called 'ethnic cleansing' of the citizens and sovereign territory of Bosnia and Herzegovina;

— from the murder, summary execution, torture, rape, kidnapping, mayhem, wounding, physical and mental abuse, and detention of the citizens of Bosnia and Herzegovina;

— from the wanton devastation of villages, towns, districts, cities, and religious institutions in Bosnia and Herzegovina;

— from the bombardment of civilian population centres in Bosnia and Herzegovina, and especially its capital, Sarajevo;

— from continuing the siege of any civilian population centres in Bosnia and Herzegovina, and especially its capital, Sarajevo;

— from the starvation of the civilian population in Bosnia and Herzegovina;

— from the interruption of, interference with, or harassment of humanitarian relief supplies to the citizens of Bosnia and Herzegovina by the international community;

— from all use of force — whether direct or indirect, overt or covert — against Bosnia and Herzegovina, and from all threats of force against Bosnia and Herzegovina;

— from all violations of the sovereignty, territorial integrity or political independence of Bosnia and Herzegovina, including all intervention, direct or indirect, in the internal affairs of Bosnia and Herzegovina;

— from all support of any kind — including the provision of training, arms, ammunition, finances, supplies, assistance, direction or any other form of support — to any nation, group, organization, movement or individual engaged or planning to engage in military or paramilitary actions in or against Bosnia and Herzegovina;

(r) that Yugoslavia (Serbia and Montenegro) has an obligation to pay Bosnia and Herzegovina, in its own right and as *parens patriae* for its citizens, reparations for damages to persons and property as well as to the Bosnian economy and environment caused by the foregoing violations of international law in a sum to be determined by the Court. Bosnia and Herzegovina reserves the right to introduce to the Court a precise evaluation of the damages caused by Yugoslavia (Serbia and Montenegro)."

14. In the written proceedings, the following submissions were presented by the Parties:

On behalf of the Government of Bosnia and Herzegovina,
in the Memorial:

"On the basis of the evidence and legal arguments presented in this Memorial, the Republic of Bosnia and Herzegovina,

Requests the International Court of Justice to adjudge and declare,   **[603**

1. That the Federal Republic of Yugoslavia (Serbia and Montenegro), directly, or through the use of its surrogates, has violated and is violating the Convention on the Prevention and Punishment of the Crime of Genocide, by destroying in part, and attempting to destroy in whole, national, ethnical or religious groups within the, but not limited to the, territory of the Republic of Bosnia and Herzegovina, including in particular the Muslim population, by

— killing members of the group;
— causing deliberate bodily or mental harm to members of the group;
— deliberately inflicting on the group conditions of life calculated to bring about its physical destruction in whole or in part;
— imposing measures intended to prevent births within the group;

2. That the Federal Republic of Yugoslavia (Serbia and Montenegro) has violated and is violating the Convention on the Prevention and Punishment of the Crime of Genocide by conspiring to commit genocide, by complicity in genocide, by attempting to commit genocide and by incitement to commit genocide;

3. That the Federal Republic of Yugoslavia (Serbia and Montenegro) has violated and is violating the Convention on the Prevention and Punishment of the Crime of Genocide by aiding and abetting individuals and groups engaged in acts of genocide;

4. That the Federal Republic of Yugoslavia (Serbia and Montenegro) has violated and is violating the Convention on the Prevention and Punishment of the Crime of Genocide by virtue of having failed to prevent and to punish acts of genocide;

5. That the Federal Republic of Yugoslavia (Serbia and Montenegro) must immediately cease the above conduct and take immediate and effective steps to ensure full compliance with its obligations under the Convention on the Prevention and Punishment of the Crime of Genocide;

6. That the Federal Republic of Yugoslavia (Serbia and Montenegro) must wipe out the consequences of its international wrongful acts and must restore the situation existing before the violations of the Convention on the Prevention and Punishment of the Crime of Genocide were committed;

7. That, as a result of the international responsibility incurred for the above violations of the Convention on the Prevention and Punishment of the Crime of Genocide, the Federal Republic of Yugoslavia (Serbia and Montenegro) is required to pay, and the Republic of Bosnia and Herzegovina is entitled to receive, in its own right and as *parens patriae* for its citizens, full compensation for the damages and losses caused, in the amount to be determined by the Court in a subsequent phase of the proceedings in this case.

The Republic of Bosnia and Herzegovina reserves its right to supplement or amend its submissions in the light of further pleadings.

The Republic of Bosnia and Herzegovina also respectfully draws the attention of the Court to the fact that it has not reiterated, at this point, several of the requests it made in its Application, on the formal assumption that the Federal Republic of Yugoslavia (Serbia and Montenegro) has

[604] accepted the jurisdiction of this Court under the terms of the Convention on the Prevention and Punishment of the Crime of Genocide. If the Respondent were to reconsider its acceptance of the jurisdiction of the Court under the terms of that Convention — which it is, in any event, not entitled to do — the Government of Bosnia and Herzegovina reserves its right to invoke also all or some of the other existing titles of jurisdiction and to revive all or some of its previous submissions and requests."

On behalf of the Government of Yugoslavia,
in the preliminary objections:

"The Federal Republic of Yugoslavia asks the Court to adjudge and declare:

First preliminary objection

A.1. Whereas civil war excludes the existence of an international dispute,

the Application of the so-called Republic of Bosnia and Herzegovina is not admissible.

Second preliminary objection

A.2. Whereas Alija Izetbegović did not serve as the President of the Republic at the time when he granted the authorization to initiate proceedings and whereas the decision to initiate proceedings was not taken by the Presidency nor the Government as the competent organs, the authorization for the initiation and conduct of proceedings was granted in violation of a rule of internal law of fundamental significance and, consequently,

the Application by the so-called Republic of Bosnia and Herzegovina is not admissible.

Third preliminary objection

B.1. Whereas the so-called Republic of Bosnia and Herzegovina has by its acts on independence flagrantly violated the duties stemming from the principle of equal rights and self-determination of peoples and for that reason the Notification of Succession, dated 29 December 1992, of the Applicant to the 1948 Convention on the Prevention and Punishment of the Crime of Genocide has no legal effect,

Whereas the so-called Republic of Bosnia and Herzegovina has not become a State party to the 1948 Convention on the Prevention and Punishment of the Crime of Genocide in accordance with the provisions of the Convention itself,

the so-called Republic of Bosnia and Herzegovina is not a State party to the 1948 Convention on the Prevention and Punishment of the Crime of Genocide and consequently

the Court has no jurisdiction over this case.

Fourth preliminary objection

B.2. Whereas the so-called Republic of Bosnia and Herzegovina has been recognized in contravention of the rules of international law and that

it has never been established in the territory and in the form in which it **[605**
pretends to exist ever since its illegal declaration of independence, and that
there are at present four States in existence in the territory of the former
Yugoslav Republic of Bosnia and Herzegovina, the so-called Republic of
Bosnia and Herzegovina is not a party to the 1948 Convention on the Prevention and Punishment of the Crime or Genocide, and consequently,

the Court has no jurisdiction over this case.

Fifth preliminary objection

C. Whereas the case in point is an internal conflict between four sides in
which the Federal Republic of Yugoslavia is not taking part and whereas
the Federal Republic of Yugoslavia did not exercise any jurisdiction over
the disputed areas in the period under review,

Whereas the Memorial of the Applicant State is based upon a fundamentally erroneous construction of the 1948 Convention on the Prevention
and Punishment of the Crime of Genocide and, in consequence the claims
contained in the 'Submissions' are based on allegations of State responsibility which fall outside the scope of the Convention and of its compromissory clause,

there is no international dispute under Article IX of the 1948 Convention on the Prevention and Punishment of the Crime of Genocide and,
consequently,

the Court has no jurisdiction over this case.

If the Court does not accept any of the above-mentioned preliminary
objections:

Sixth preliminary objection

D.1. Without prejudice to the above exposed preliminary objections,
whereas the Notification of Succession, dated 29 December 1992, whereby
the so-called Republic of Bosnia and Herzegovina expressed the intention
to enter into the 1948 Convention on the Prevention and Punishment of
the Crime of Genocide can only produce the effect of accession to the
Convention,

the Court has jurisdiction over this case as of 29 March 1993 and, thus,
the Applicant's claims pertaining to the alleged acts or facts which
occurred prior to that date do not fall within the jurisdiction of the
Court.

In case the Court refuses to adopt the preliminary objection under D.1:

Seventh preliminary objection

D.2. Without prejudice to the sixth preliminary objection, if the Applicant State's Notification of Succession, dated 29 December 1992, is construed on the basis that it has the effect that the Applicant State became a
party to the 1948 Genocide Convention from 6 March 1992, according to
the rule of customary international law, the 1948 Convention on the Prevention and Punishment of the Crime of Genocide would not be operative
between the parties prior to 29 December 1992 and, accordingly, this would

[606] not confer jurisdiction on the Court in respect of events occurring prior to 29 December 1992 and consequently,

the Applicant's claims pertaining to the alleged acts or facts which occurred prior to 29 December 1992 do not fall within the jurisdiction of the Court.

The Federal Republic of Yugoslavia reserves its right to supplement or amend its submissions in the light of further pleadings."

On behalf of the Government of Bosnia and Herzegovina,

in the written statement containing its observations and submissions on the preliminary objections:

"In consideration of the foregoing, the Government of the Republic of Bosnia and Herzegovina requests the Court:

— to reject and dismiss the Preliminary Objections of Yugoslavia (Serbia and Montenegro); and
— to adjudge and declare:

  (i) that the Court has jurisdiction in respect of the submissions presented in the Memorial of Bosnia and Herzegovina; and
  (ii) that the submissions are admissible."

15. In the oral proceedings, the following submissions were presented by the Parties:

On behalf of the Government of Yugoslavia[1],

at the hearing on 2 May 1996:

"The Federal Republic of Yugoslavia asks the Court to adjudge and declare:

First preliminary objection

Whereas the events in Bosnia and Herzegovina to which the Application refers constituted a civil war, no international dispute exists within the terms of Article IX of the 1948 Convention on the Prevention and Punishment of the Crime of Genocide, consequently,

the Application of Bosnia and Herzegovina is not admissible.

Second preliminary objection

Whereas Mr. Alija Izetbegović did not serve as the President of the Republic at the time when he granted the authorization to initiate proceedings and whereas the decision to initiate proceedings was not taken either by the Presidency or the Government as the competent organs, the authorization for the initiation and conduct of proceedings was granted in violation of the rules of internal law of fundamental significance, consequently,

the Application by Bosnia and Herzegovina is not admissible.

Third preliminary objection

Whereas Bosnia and Herzegovina has not established its independent

---

[1] The Government of Yugoslavia relinquished its fourth preliminary objection.

statehood in conformity with the principle of equal rights and self- [607] determination of peoples and for that reason could not succeed to the 1948 Convention on the Prevention and Punishment of the Crime of Genocide,

Whereas Bosnia and Herzegovina has not become a party to the 1948 Convention on the Prevention and Punishment of the Crime of Genocide in accordance with the provisions of the Convention itself,

Bosnia and Herzegovina is not a party to the 1948 Convention on the Prevention and Punishment of the Crime of Genocide, consequently,

the Court lacks the competence over the case.

Fifth preliminary objection

Whereas the case in point is an internal conflict between three sides in which the Federal Republic of Yugoslavia was not taking part and whereas the Federal Republic of Yugoslavia did not exercise any jurisdiction within the region of Bosnia and Herzegovina at the material time,

Whereas the Memorial of the Applicant State is based upon a fundamentally erroneous interpretation of the 1948 Convention on the Prevention and Punishment of the Crime of Genocide and, in consequence, the claims contained in the 'Submissions' are based on allegations of State responsibility which fall outside the scope of the Convention and of its compromissory clause,

there is no international dispute under Article IX of the 1948 Convention on the Prevention and Punishment of the Crime of Genocide, consequently,

the Court lacks the competence over the case.

If the Court does not accept any of the above-mentioned preliminary objections:

Sixth preliminary objection

Without prejudice to the above exposed preliminary objections, whereas the two Parties recognized each other on 14 December 1995, the 1948 Convention on the Prevention and Punishment of the Crime of Genocide was not operative between them prior to 14 December 1995, consequently,

the Court lacks the competence before 14 December 1995 over the case.

Alternatively and without prejudice to the preliminary objections formulated above, whereas the Notification of Succession, dated 29 December 1992, whereby Bosnia and Herzegovina expressed the intention to enter into the 1948 Convention on the Prevention and Punishment of the Crime of Genocide can only produce the effect of accession to the Convention,

the Court lacks competence before 29 March 1993 over the case and, thus, the Applicant's claims pertaining to the alleged acts or facts which occurred prior to that date do not fall within the competence of the Court.

In case the Court refuses to adopt the above preliminary objections:

[608] *Seventh preliminary objection*

If the Applicant State's Notification of Succession, dated 29 December 1992, is construed as having an effect of the Applicant State becoming a party to the 1948 Convention on the Prevention and Punishment of the Crime of Genocide from 6 March 1992 and whereas the Secretary-General of the United Nations sent to the parties of the said Convention the Note dated 18 March 1993, informing of the said succession, according to the rules of general international law, the 1948 Convention on the Prevention and Punishment of the Crime of Genocide would not be operative between the Parties prior to 18 March 1993 and, whereas this would not confer the competence on the Court in respect of events occurring prior to 18 March 1993, consequently,

> the Applicant's claims pertaining to the alleged acts or facts which occurred prior to 18 March 1993 do not fall within the competence of the Court.

As a final alternative:

If the Applicant State's Notification of Succession, dated 29 December 1992, is construed as having the effect of the Applicant State becoming a party to the Convention on the Prevention and Punishment of the Crime of Genocide from 6 March 1992, according to the rules of general international law, the 1948 Convention on the Prevention and Punishment of the Crime of Genocide would not be operative between the Parties prior to 29 December 1992, and, whereas this would not confer competence on the Court in respect of events occurring prior to 29 December 1992, consequently,

> the Applicant's claims pertaining to the alleged acts or facts which occurred prior to 29 December 1992 do not fall within the competence of the Court.

Objections on alleged additional bases of jurisdiction

In view of the claim of the Applicant to base the jurisdiction of the Court under Articles 11 and 16 of the Treaty between Allied and Associated Powers and the Kingdom of Serbs, Croats and Slovenes, signed at Saint-Germain-en-Laye on 10 September 1919, the Federal Republic of Yugoslavia asks the Court

> to reject the said claim,

— because the Treaty between Allied and Associated Powers and the Kingdom of Serbs, Croats and Slovenes signed at Saint-Germain-en-Laye on 10 September 1919 is not in force; and alternatively
— because the Applicant is not entitled to invoke the jurisdiction of the Court according to Articles 11 and 16 of the Treaty.

In view of the claim of the Applicant to establish the jurisdiction of the Court on the basis of the letter of 8 June 1992, sent by the Presidents of the two Yugoslav Republics, Serbia and Montenegro, Mr. Slobodan Milošević and Mr. Momir Bulatović, to the President of the Arbitration Commission of the Conference on Yugoslavia, the Federal Republic of Yugoslavia asks the Court

> to reject the said claim,

— because the declaration contained in the letter of 8 June 1992 cannot **[609]** be understood as a declaration of the Federal Republic of Yugoslavia according to the rules of international law; and

— because the declaration was not in force on 31 March 1993 and later.

In view of the claim of the Applicant State to establish the jurisdiction of the Court on the basis of the doctrine of *forum prorogatum*, the Federal Republic of Yugoslavia asks the Court

to reject the said claim,

— because the request for indication of provisional measures of protection does not imply a consent to the jurisdiction of the Court; and

— because the conditions for the application of the doctrine of *forum prorogatum* are not fulfilled."

On behalf of the Government of Bosnia and Herzegovina,
at the hearing on 3 May 1996:

"Considering what has been stated by Bosnia and Herzegovina in all of its previous written submissions, considering what has been stated by the representatives of Bosnia and Herzegovina in the course of this week's oral proceedings, the Government of Bosnia and Herzegovina respectfully requests the Court,

1. to adjudge and declare that the Federal Republic of Yugoslavia has abused its right to raise preliminary objections as foreseen in Article 36, paragraph 6, of the Statute of the Court and to Article 79 of the Rules of Court;

2. to reject and dismiss the preliminary objections of the Federal Republic of Yugoslavia; and

3. to adjudge and declare:

 (i) that the Court has jurisdiction on the various grounds set out in our previous written submissions and as further demonstrated during the present pleadings in respect of the submissions presented in the Memorial of Bosnia and Herzegovina; and

 (ii) that the submissions are admissible."

* * *

16. Bosnia and Herzegovina has principally relied, as a basis for the jurisdiction of the⁻Court in this case, on Article IX of the Genocide Convention. The Court will initially consider the preliminary objections raised by Yugoslavia on this point. It takes note, first, of the withdrawal by Yugoslavia, during the oral proceedings, of its fourth preliminary objection, which therefore need no longer be dealt with. In its third objection, Yugoslavia, on various grounds, has disputed the contention that the Convention binds the two Parties or that it has entered into force between them; and in its fifth objection, Yugoslavia has objected, for various reasons, to the argument that the dispute submitted by Bosnia

[610] and Herzegovina falls within the provisions of Article IX of the Convention. The Court will consider these two alleged grounds of lack of jurisdiction in turn.

*

17. The proceedings instituted before the Court are between two States whose territories are located within the former Socialist Federal Republic of Yugoslavia. That Republic signed the Genocide Convention on 11 December 1948 and deposited its instrument of ratification, without reservation, on 29 August 1950. At the time of the proclamation of the Federal Republic of Yugoslavia, on 27 April 1992, a formal declaration was adopted on its behalf to the effect that:

> "The Federal Republic of Yugoslavia, continuing the State, international legal and political personality of the Socialist Federal Republic of Yugoslavia, shall strictly abide by all the commitments that the Socialist Federal Republic of Yugoslavia assumed internationally."

This intention thus expressed by Yugoslavia to remain bound by the international treaties to which the former Yugoslavia was party was confirmed in an official Note of 27 April 1992 from the Permanent Mission of Yugoslavia to the United Nations, addressed to the Secretary-General. The Court observes, furthermore, that it has not been contested that Yugoslavia was party to the Genocide Convention. Thus, Yugoslavia was bound by the provisions of the Convention on the date of the filing of the Application in the present case, namely, on 20 March 1993.

18. For its part, on 29 December 1992, Bosnia and Herzegovina transmitted to the Secretary-General of the United Nations, as depositary of the Genocide Convention, a Notice of Succession in the following terms:

> "the Government of the Republic of Bosnia and Herzegovina, having considered the Convention on the Prevention and Punishment of the Crime of Genocide, of December 9, 1948, to which the former Socialist Federal Republic of Yugoslavia was a party, wishes to succeed to the same and undertakes faithfully to perform and carry out all the stipulations therein contained with effect from March 6, 1992, the date on which the Republic of Bosnia and Herzegovina became independent".

On 18 March 1993, the Secretary-General communicated the following Depositary Notification to the parties to the Genocide Convention:

> "On 29 December 1992, the notification of succession by the Government of Bosnia and Herzegovina to the above-mentioned Convention was deposited with the Secretary-General, with effect from 6 March 1992, the date on which Bosnia and Herzegovina assumed responsibility for its international relations."

19. Yugoslavia has contested the validity and legal effect of the Notice **[611]** of 29 December 1992, contending that, by its acts relating to its accession to independence, the Republic of Bosnia and Herzegovina had flagrantly violated the duties stemming from the "principle of equal rights and self-determination of peoples". According to Yugoslavia, Bosnia and Herzegovina was not, for this reason, qualified to become a party to the convention. Yugoslavia subsequently reiterated this objection in the third preliminary objection which it raised in this case.

The Court notes that Bosnia and Herzegovina became a Member of the United Nations following the decisions adopted on 22 May 1992 by the Security Council and the General Assembly, bodies competent under the Charter. Article XI of the Genocide Convention opens it to "any Member of the United Nations"; from the time of its admission to the Organization, Bosnia and Herzegovina could thus become a party to the Convention. Hence the circumstances of its accession to independence are of little consequence.

20. It is clear from the foregoing that Bosnia and Herzegovina could become a party to the Convention through the mechanism of State succession. Moreover, the Secretary-General of the United Nations considered that this had been the case, and the Court took note of this in its Order of 8 April 1993 (*Application of the Convention on the Prevention and Punishment of the Crime of Genocide, Provisional Measures, I.C.J. Reports 1993*, p. 16, para. 25).[19]

21. The Parties to the dispute differed as to the legal consequences to be drawn from the occurrence of a State succession in the present case. In this context, Bosnia and Herzegovina has, among other things, contended that the Genocide Convention falls within the category of instruments for the protection of human rights, and that consequently, the rule of "automatic succession" necessarily applies. Bosnia and Herzegovina concluded therefrom that it became a party to the Convention with effect from its accession to independence. Yugoslavia disputed any "automatic succession" of Bosnia and Herzegovina to the Genocide Convention on this or any other basis.

22. As regards the nature of the Genocide Convention, the Court would recall what it stated in its Advisory Opinion of 28 May 1951 relating to the *Reservations to the Convention on the Prevention and Punishment of the Crime of Genocide*:[20]   .

> "In such a convention the contracting States do not have any interests of their own; they merely have, one and all, a common interest, namely, the accomplishment of those high purposes which are the *raison d'être* of the convention. Consequently, in a convention of this type one cannot speak of individual advantages or disadvantages to States, or of the maintenance of a perfect contractual balance between rights and duties." (*I.C.J. Reports 1951*, p. 23.)

[[19] 95 *ILR* 1 at 18.]   [[20] 18 *ILR* 364.]

[612] The Court subsequently noted in that Opinion that:

> "The object and purpose of the Genocide Convention imply that it was the intention of the General Assembly and of the States which adopted it that as many States as possible should participate. The complete exclusion from the Convention of one or more States would not only restrict the scope of its application, but would detract from the authority of the moral and humanitarian principles which are its basis." (*I.C.J. Reports 1951*, p. 24.)

23. Without prejudice as to whether or not the principle of "automatic succession" applies in the case of certain types of international treaties or conventions, the Court does not consider it necessary, in order to decide on its jurisdiction in this case, to make a determination on the legal issues concerning State succession in respect to treaties which have been raised by the Parties. Whether Bosnia and Herzegovina automatically became party to the Genocide Convention on the date of its accession to independence on 6 March 1992, or whether it became a party as a result — retroactive or not — of its Notice of Succession of 29 December 1992, at all events it was a party to it on the date of the filing of its Application on 20 March 1993. These matters might, at the most, possess a certain relevance with respect to the determination of the scope *ratione temporis* of the jurisdiction of the Court, a point which the Court will consider later (paragraph 34 below).

24. Yugoslavia has also contended, in its sixth preliminary objection, that, if the Notice given by Bosnia and Herzegovina on 29 December 1992 had to be interpreted as constituting an instrument of accession within the meaning of Article XI of the Genocide Convention, it could only have become effective, pursuant to Article XIII of the Convention, on the 90th day following its deposit, that is, 29 March 1993.

Since the Court has concluded that Bosnia and Herzegovina could become a party to the Genocide Convention as a result of a succession, the question of the application of Articles XI and XIII of the Convention does not arise. However, the Court would recall that, as it noted in its Order of 8 April 1993, even if Bosnia and Herzegovina were to be treated as having acceded to the Genocide Convention, which would mean that the Application could be said to be premature by nine days when filed on 20 March 1993, during the time elapsed since then, Bosnia and Herzegovina could, on its own initiative, have remedied the procedural defect by filing a new Application. It therefore matters little that the Application had been filed some days too early. As will be indicated in the following paragraphs, the Court is not bound to attach the same degree of importance to considerations of form as they might possess in domestic law.

25. However, in the oral proceedings Yugoslavia submitted that, even supposing that Bosnia and Herzegovina had been bound by the Convention in March 1993, it could not, at that time, have entered into force

between the Parties, because the two States did not recognize one another **[613**
and the conditions necessary to found the consensual basis of the Court's
jurisdiction were therefore lacking. However, this situation no longer
obtains since the signature, and the entry into force on 14 December
1995, of the Dayton-Paris Agreement, Article X of which stipulates that:

> "The Federal Republic of Yugoslavia and the Republic of Bosnia
> and Herzegovina recognize each other as sovereign independent
> States within their international borders. Further aspects of their
> mutual recognition will be subject to subsequent discussions."

26. For the purposes of determining its jurisdiction in this case, the
Court has no need to settle the question of what the effects of a situation
of non-recognition may be on the contractual ties between parties to a
multilateral treaty. It need only note that, even if it were to be assumed
that the Genocide Convention did not enter into force between the Parties
until the signature of the Dayton-Paris Agreement, all the conditions are
now fulfilled to found the jurisdiction of the Court *ratione personae*.
It is the case that the jurisdiction of the Court must normally be
assessed on the date of the filing of the act instituting proceedings. However, the Court, like its predecessor, the Permanent Court of International Justice, has always had recourse to the principle according to
which it should not penalize a defect in a procedural act which the applicant could easily remedy. Hence, in the case concerning the *Mavrommatis Palestine Concessions*, the Permanent Court said: [21]

> "Even if the grounds on which the institution of proceedings was
> based were defective for the reason stated, this would not be an
> adequate reason for the dismissal of the applicant's suit. The Court,
> whose jurisdiction is international, is not bound to attach to matters
> of form the same degree of importance which they might possess in
> municipal law. Even, therefore, if the application were premature
> because the Treaty of Lausanne had not yet been ratified, this cir-
> cumstance would now be covered by the subsequent deposit of the
> necessary ratifications." (*P.C.I.J., Series A, No. 2*, p. 34.)

The same principle lies at the root of the following *dictum* of the Permanent Court of International Justice in the case concerning *Certain German Interests in Polish Upper Silesia*: [22]

> "Even if, under Article 23, the existence of a definite dispute were
> necessary, this condition could at any time be fulfilled by means of
> unilateral action on the part of the applicant Party. And the Court
> cannot allow itself to be hampered by a mere defect of form, the
> removal of which depends solely on the Party concerned." (*P.C.I.J.,
> Series A, No. 6*, p. 14.)

The present Court applied this principle in the case concerning the
Northern Cameroons (*I.C.J. Reports 1963*, p. 28), as well as *Military and* [23]

[[21] 2 *Ann Dig* 312.]   [[22] 3 *Ann Dig* 426.]   [[23] 35 *ILR* 353.]

[614] *Paramilitary Activities in and against Nicaragua (Nicaragua v. United* [24] *States of America)* when it stated: "It would make no sense to require Nicaragua now to institute fresh proceedings based on the Treaty, which it would be fully entitled to do." (*I.C.J. Reports 1984*, pp. 428-429, para. 83.)

In the present case, even if it were established that the Parties, each of which was bound by the Convention when the Application was filed, had only been bound as between themselves with effect from 14 December 1995, the Court could not set aside its jurisdiction on this basis, inasmuch as Bosnia and Herzegovina might at any time file a new application, identical to the present one, which would be unassailable in this respect.

In the light of the foregoing, the Court considers that it must reject Yugoslavia's third preliminary objection.

*

27. In order to determine whether it has jurisdiction to entertain the case on the basis of Article IX of the Genocide Convention, it remains for the Court to verify whether there is a dispute between the Parties that falls within the scope of that provision. Article IX of the Convention is worded as follows:

> "Disputes between the Contracting Parties relating to the interpretation, application or fulfilment of the present Convention, including those relating to the responsibility of a State for genocide or for any of the other acts enumerated in article III, shall be submitted to the International Court of Justice at the request of any of the parties to the dispute."

It is jurisdiction *ratione materiae*, as so defined, to which Yugoslavia's fifth objection relates.

28. In their final form, the principal requests submitted by Bosnia and Herzegovina are for the Court to adjudge and declare that Yugoslavia has in several ways violated the Genocide Convention; to order Yugoslavia to cease the acts contrary to the obligations stipulated in the Convention; and to declare that Yugoslavia has incurred international responsibility by reason of those violations, for which it must make appropriate reparation. While Yugoslavia has refrained from filing a Counter-Memorial on the merits and has raised preliminary objections, it has nevertheless wholly denied all of Bosnia and Herzegovina's allegations, whether at the stage of proceedings relating to the requests for the indication of provisional measures, or at the stage of the present proceedings relating to those objections.

29. In conformity with well-established jurisprudence, the Court accordingly notes that there persists

> "a situation in which the two sides hold clearly opposite views concerning the question of the performance or non-performance of certain treaty obligations" (*Interpretation of Peace Treaties with*

[²⁴ 76 *ILR* 1 at 104.]

Bulgaria, Hungary and Romania, First Phase, Advisory Opinion, **[615**
I.C.J. Reports 1950, p. 74) [25]

and that, by reason of the rejection by Yugoslavia of the complaints
formulated against it by Bosnia and Herzegovina, "there is a legal dispute" between them (*East Timor (Portugal* v. *Australia), I.C.J. Reports* [26]
1995, p. 100, para. 22).

30. To found its jurisdiction, the Court must, however, still ensure
that the dispute in question does indeed fall within the provisions of
Article IX of the Genocide Convention.

Yugoslavia disputes this. It contests the existence in this case of an
"international dispute" within the meaning of the Convention, basing
itself on two propositions: first, that the conflict occurring in certain
parts of the Applicant's territory was of a domestic nature, Yugoslavia
was not party to it and did not exercise jurisdiction over that territory at
the time in question; and second, that State responsibility, as referred to
in the requests of Bosnia and Herzegovina, was excluded from the scope
of application of Article IX.

31. The Court will begin with a consideration of Yugoslavia's first
proposition.

In doing so, it will start by recalling the terms of Article I of the Genocide Convention, worded as follows:

> "The Contracting Parties confirm that genocide, whether commit-
> ted in time of peace or in time of war, is a crime under international
> law which they undertake to prevent and to punish."

The Court sees nothing in this provision which would make the applicability of the Convention subject to the condition that the acts contemplated by it should have been committed within the framework of a
particular type of conflict. The contracting parties expressly state therein
their willingness to consider genocide as "a crime under international
law", which they must prevent and punish independently of the context
"of peace" or "of war" in which it takes place. In the view of the Court,
this means that the Convention is applicable, without reference to the circumstances linked to the domestic or international nature of the conflict,
provided the acts to which it refers in Articles II and III have been perpetrated. In other words, irrespective of the nature of the conflict forming
the background to such acts, the obligations of prevention and punishment which are incumbent upon the States parties to the Convention
remain identical.

As regards the question whether Yugoslavia took part — directly or
indirectly — in the conflict at issue, the Court would merely note that the
Parties have radically differing viewpoints in this respect and that it cannot, at this stage in the proceedings, settle this question, which clearly
belongs to the merits.

Lastly, as to the territorial problems linked to the application of the
Convention, the Court would point out that the only provision relevant

[[25] 17 *ILR* 331.]   [[26] 105 *ILR* 226.]

[616] to this, Article VI, merely provides for persons accused of one of the acts prohibited by the Convention to "be tried by a competent tribunal of the State in the territory of which the act was committed . . .". It would also recall its understanding of the object and purpose of the Convention, as set out in its Opinion of 28 May 1951, cited above:

> "The origins of the Convention show that it was the intention of the United Nations to condemn and punish genocide as 'a crime under international law' involving a denial of the right of existence of entire human groups, a denial which shocks the conscience of mankind and results in great losses to humanity, and which is contrary to moral law and to the spirit and aims of the United Nations (Resolution 96 (I) of the General Assembly, December 11th 1946). The first consequence arising from this conception is that the principles underlying the Convention are principles which are recognized by civilized nations as binding on States, even without any conventional obligation. A second consequence is the universal character both of the condemnation of genocide and of the co-operation required 'in order to liberate mankind from such an odious scourge' (Preamble to the Convention)." (*I.C.J. Reports 1951*, p. 23.)

It follows that the rights and obligations enshrined by the Convention are rights and obligations *erga omnes*. The Court notes that the obligation each State thus has to prevent and to punish the crime of genocide is not territorially limited by the Convention.

32. The Court now comes to the second proposition advanced by Yugoslavia, regarding the type of State responsibility envisaged in Article IX of the Convention. According to Yugoslavia, that Article would only cover the responsibility flowing from the failure of a State to fulfil its obligations of prevention and punishment as contemplated by Articles V, VI and VII; on the other hand, the responsibility of a State for an act of genocide perpetrated by the State itself would be excluded from the scope of the Convention.

The Court would observe that the reference in Article IX to "the responsibility of a State for genocide or for any of the other acts enumerated in Article III", does not exclude any form of State responsibility.

Nor is the responsibility of a State for acts of its organs excluded by Article IV of the Convention, which contemplates the commission of an act of genocide by "rulers" or "public officials".

33. In the light of the foregoing, the Court considers that it must reject the fifth preliminary objection of Yugoslavia. It would moreover observe that it is sufficiently apparent from the very terms of that objection that the Parties not only differ with respect to the facts of the case, their imputability and the applicability to them of the provisions of the Genocide Convention, but are moreover in disagreement with respect to the meaning and legal scope of several of those provisions, including Article IX. For the Court, there is accordingly no doubt that there exists a dispute between them relating to "the interpretation, application or

fulfilment of the . . . Convention, including . . . the responsibility of a [617] State for genocide . . .", according to the form of words employed by that latter provision (cf. *Applicability of the Obligation to Arbitrate under Section 21 of the United Nations Headquarters Agreement of 26 June 1947, Advisory Opinion, I.C.J. Reports 1988,* pp. 27-32). [27]

*

34. Having reached the conclusion that it has jurisdiction in the present case, both *ratione personae* and *ratione materiae* on the basis of Article IX of the Genocide Convention, it remains for the Court to specify the scope of that jurisdiction *ratione temporis.* In its sixth and seventh preliminary objections, Yugoslavia, basing its contention on the principle of the non-retroactivity of legal acts, has indeed asserted as a subsidiary argument that, even though the Court might have jurisdiction on the basis of the Convention, it could only deal with events subsequent to the different dates on which the Convention might have become applicable as between the Parties. In this regard, the Court will confine itself to the observation that the Genocide Convention — and in particular Article IX — does not contain any clause the object or effect of which is to limit in such manner the scope of its jurisdiction *ratione temporis,* and nor did the Parties themselves make any reservation to that end, either to the Convention or on the occasion of the signature of the Dayton-Paris Agreement. The Court thus finds that it has jurisdiction in this case to give effect to the Genocide Convention with regard to the relevant facts which have occurred since the beginning of the conflict which took place in Bosnia and Herzegovina. This finding is, moreover, in accordance with the object and purpose of the Convention as defined by the Court in 1951 and referred to above (see paragraph 31). As a result, the Court considers that it must reject Yugoslavia's sixth and seventh preliminary objections.

* *

35. After the filing of its Application, Bosnia and Herzegovina invoked various additional bases of jurisdiction of the Court in the present case. Even though, in both the written and oral proceedings, it relied essentially upon Article IX of the Genocide Convention, Bosnia and Herzegovina indicated that it was maintaining its claims in relation to those additional grounds of jurisdiction. In particular, it specified at the hearing that while it was renouncing "all the claims [set forth in its Application] which are not directly linked to the genocide committed or abetted by Yugoslavia", those additional bases could nonetheless

> "present a degree of interest, enabling the Court to make findings on some of the means used by Yugoslavia to perpetrate the genocide of which it stands accused, and particularly its recourse to a war of

[27 82 *ILR* 225.]

[618] aggression during which it seriously violated the 1949 Geneva Conventions and the 1977 Protocols I and II";

and Bosnia and Herzegovina went on to say that "The Court might proceed in this way on the basis of Article IX alone", explaining that

> "The possibility of relying on other bases of jurisdiction . . . would at least . . . avoid futile arguments between the Parties as to whether such conduct is or is not linked 'with sufficient directness' to the Convention."

36. Yugoslavia, for its part, contended during the proceedings that the Court could not take account of such additional grounds as could have been referred to in the Application but to which no reference was in fact made. However, in its final submissions, it did not reiterate that objection and asked the Court, for the reasons there given, to declare that it lacked jurisdiction on those grounds.

*

37. As the Court has indicated above (see paragraph 4), the Agent of Bosnia and Herzegovina filed in the Registry, on 31 March 1993, the text of a letter dated 8 June 1992 that was addressed to the President of the Arbitration Commission of the International Conference for Peace in Yugoslavia by Mr. Momir Bulatović, President of the Republic of Montenegro, and Mr. Slobodan Milosević, President of the Republic of Serbia. According to the English translation of that letter provided by Bosnia and Herzegovina, they expressed the following views, *inter alia:*

> "FR Yugoslavia holds the view that all legal disputes which cannot be settled by agreement between FR Yugoslavia and the former Yugoslav republics should be taken to the International Court of Justice, as the principal judicial organ of the United Nations.

> Accordingly, and in view of the fact that all the issues raised in your letter are of a legal nature, FR Yugoslavia proposes that in the event that agreement is not reached among the participants in the Conference, these questions should be adjudicated by the International Court of Justice, in accordance with its Statute."

The Court finds that, given the circumstances in which that letter was written and the declarations that ensued, it could not be taken as expressing an immediate commitment by the two Presidents, binding on Yugoslavia, to accept unconditionally the unilateral submission to the Court of a wide range of legal disputes. It thus confirms the provisional conclu-
[28] sion which it had reached in this regard in its Orders of 8 April (*I.C.J.*
[29] *Reports 1993*, pp. 16-18, paras. 27-32) and 13 September 1993 (*I.C.J. Reports 1993*, pp. 340-341, para. 32); besides, no fundamentally new argument has been presented to it on this matter since that time. It fol-

[[28] 95 *ILR* 1 at 18.]   [[29] 95 *ILR* 1 at 43.]

lows that the Court cannot find in that letter an additional basis of juris- **[619]** diction in the present case.

38. The Court has likewise recalled above (see paragraph 7) that, by a communication dated 6 August 1993, the Agent of Bosnia and Herze- govina indicated that his Government intended likewise to submit, as an additional basis of jurisdiction, the Treaty between the Allied and Asso- ciated Powers (the United States of America, the British Empire, France, Italy and Japan) and the Kingdom of the Serbs, Croats and Slovenes, that was signed at Saint-Germain-en-Laye on 10 September 1919 and entered into force on 16 July 1920. Chapter I of that Treaty concerns the protection of minorities and includes an Article 11 according to which:

> "The Serb-Croat-Slovene State agrees that any Member of the Council of the League of Nations shall have the right to bring to the attention of the Council any infraction, or any danger of infraction, of any of these obligations, and that the Council may thereupon take such action and give such directions as it may deem proper and effective in the circumstances.
>
> The Serb-Croat-Slovene State further agrees that any difference of opinion as to questions of law or fact arising out of these Articles between the Serb-Croat-Slovene State and any one of the Principal Allied and Associated Powers or any other Power, a member of the Council of the League of Nations, shall be held to be a dispute of an international character under Article 14 of the Covenant of the League of Nations. The Serb-Croat-Slovene State hereby consents that any such dispute shall, if the other party thereto demands, be referred to the Permanent Court of International Justice. The deci- sion of the Permanent Court shall be final and shall have the same force and effect as an award under Article 13 of the Covenant."

Chapter II, which concerns succession in respect of treaties, trade, the treatment of foreign vessels and freedom of transit, includes an Article 16 which provides, *inter alia*, that

> "All rights and privileges accorded by the foregoing Articles to the Allied and Associated Powers shall be accorded equally to all States Members of the League of Nations."

Bosnia and Herzegovina substantially contends that, by the effect of those two provisions, any Member of the League of Nations could refer to the Permanent Court a dispute to which Article 11 applied; that the General Assembly of the United Nations has taken the place of the Council of the League of Nations in respect of such matters; and that Bosnia and Herzegovina, as a Member of the United Nations, may now, by operation of Article 37 of the Statute, seise the present Court of its dispute with Yugoslavia, on the basis of the 1919 Treaty.

The Court considers that, in so far as Yugoslavia is now bound by the

[620] 1919 Treaty as successor to the Kingdom of the Serbs, Croats and Slovenes, its obligations under that Treaty would be limited to its present territory; it notes that Bosnia and Herzegovina has put forward no claim in its Application concerning the treatment of minorities in Yugoslavia. In these circumstances, the Court is unable to uphold the 1919 Treaty as a basis on which its jurisdiction in this case could be founded. On this point as well, the Court thus confirms the provisional conclusion reached in its Order of 13 September 1993 (*I.C.J. Reports 1993*, pp. 339-[30] 340, paras. 29-31); besides, no fundamentally new argument has been presented on this matter either, since that time.

39. As the Court has also recalled above (see paragraph 7), Bosnia and Herzegovina, by a letter from its Agent dated 10 August 1993, further invoked as an additional basis of jurisdiction in the present case

"the Customary and Conventional International Laws of War and International Humanitarian Law, including but not limited to the Four Geneva Conventions of 1949, their First Additional Protocol of 1977, the Hague Regulations on Land Warfare of 1907, and the Nuremberg Charter, Judgment, and Principles".

As it has already pointed out in its Order of 13 September 1993 (*I.C.J. Reports 1993*, p. 341, para. 33), the Court can find no provision relevant to its jurisdiction in any of the above-mentioned instruments. It notes, in addition, that the Applicant has made no further reference to this basis of jurisdiction as such.

40. Lastly, at a later stage of the proceedings, Bosnia and Herzegovina advanced two related arguments aimed at basing the Court's jurisdiction in this case on still other grounds.

According to the first of those arguments, Yugoslavia, by various aspects of its conduct in the course of the incidental proceedings set in motion by the requests for the indication of provisional measures, had acquiesced in the jurisdiction of the Court on the basis of Article IX of the Genocide Convention. As the Court has already reached the conclusion that it has jurisdiction on the basis of that provision, it need no longer consider that question.

According to the second argument, as Yugoslavia, on 1 April 1993, itself called for the indication of provisional measures some of which were aimed at the preservation of rights not covered by the Genocide Convention, it was said, in accordance with the doctrine of *forum prorogatum (stricto sensu)*, to have given its consent to the exercise by the Court, in the present case, of a wider jurisdiction than that provided for in Article IX of the Convention. Given the nature of both the provisional measures subsequently requested by Yugoslavia on 9 August 1993 — which were aimed exclusively at the preservation of rights conferred by

[[30] 95 *ILR* 1 at 43.]

the Genocide Convention — and the unequivocal declarations whereby **[621]**
Yugoslavia consistently contended during the subsequent proceedings
that the Court lacked jurisdiction — whether on the basis of the Genocide Convention or on any other basis — the Court finds that it must
confirm the provisional conclusion that it reached on that subject in its
Order of 13 September 1993 (*I.C.J. Reports 1993*, pp. 341-342, para. 34).
The Court does not find that the Respondent has given in this case a
"voluntary and indisputable" consent (see *Corfu Channel, Preliminary* [31]
Objection, Judgment, 1948, I.C.J. Reports 1947-1948, p. 27) which would
confer upon it a jurisdiction exceeding that which it has already acknowledged to have been conferred upon it by Article IX of the Genocide
Convention.

*

41. It follows from the foregoing that the Court is unable to uphold
any of the additional bases of jurisdiction invoked by the Applicant and
that its only jurisdiction to entertain the case is on the basis of Article IX
of the Genocide Convention.

* * *

42. Having ruled on the objections raised by Yugoslavia with respect
to its jurisdiction, the Court will now proceed to consider the objections
of Yugoslavia that relate to the admissibility of the Application.

*

43. According to the first preliminary objection of Yugoslavia, the
Application is said to be inadmissible on the ground that it refers to
events that took place within the framework of a civil war, and there is
consequently no international dispute upon which the Court could make
a finding.
   This objection is very close to the fifth objection which the Court has
already considered (paragraphs 27-33). In responding to the latter objection, the Court has in fact also answered this. Having noted that there
does indeed exist between the Parties a dispute falling within the provisions of Article IX of the Genocide Convention — that is to say an international dispute —, the Court cannot find that the Application is inadmissible on the sole ground that, in order to decide the dispute, it would
be impelled to take account of events that may have occurred in a context
of civil war. It follows that the first objection of Yugoslavia must be
rejected.
44. According to the second objection of Yugoslavia, the Application
is inadmissible because, as Mr. Alija Izetbegović was not serving as President of the Republic — but only as President of the Presidency — at the

[[31] 15 *Ann Dig* 349.]

622] time at which he granted the authorization to initiate proceedings, that authorization was granted in violation of certain rules of domestic law of fundamental significance. Yugoslavia likewise contended that Mr. Izetbegović was not even acting legally at that time as President of the Presidency.

The Court does not, in order to rule on that objection, have to consider the provisions of domestic law which were invoked in the course of the proceedings either in support of or in opposition to that objection. According to international law, there is no doubt that every Head of State is presumed to be able to act on behalf of the State in its international relations (see for example the Vienna Convention on the Law of Treaties, Art. 7, para. 2 *(a)*). As the Court found in its Order of 8 April [32] 1993 (*I.C.J. Reports 1993*, p. 11, para. 13), at the time of the filing of the Application, Mr. Izetbegović was recognized, in particular by the United Nations, as the Head of State of Bosnia and Herzegovina. Moreover, his status as Head of State continued subsequently to be recognized in many international bodies and several international agreements — including the Dayton-Paris Agreement — bear his signature. It follows that the second preliminary objection of Yugoslavia must also be rejected.

*

45. The Court concludes from the foregoing that the Application filed by Bosnia and Herzegovina on 20 March 1993 is admissible.

* * *

46. The Court has taken note of the withdrawal of the fourth preliminary objection of Yugoslavia and has rejected the other preliminary objections. In conclusion, the Court emphasizes that in so doing it does not consider that Yugoslavia has, in presenting those objections, abused its rights to do so under Article 36, paragraph 6, of the Statute of the Court and Article 79 of the Rules of Court. The Court rejects the request made to that end by Bosnia and Herzegovina in its final submissions. The Court must, in each case submitted to it, verify whether it has jurisdiction to deal with the case, and, if necessary, whether the Application is admissible, and such objections as are raised by the Respondent may be useful to clarify the legal situation. As matters now stand, the preliminary objections presented by Yugoslavia have served that purpose. Having established its jurisdiction under Article IX of the Genocide Convention, and having concluded that the Application is admissible, the Court may now proceed to consider the merits of the case on that basis.

* * *

[[32] 95 *ILR* 1 at 18.]

47. For these reasons,   **[623**

THE COURT,

(1) Having taken note of the withdrawal of the fourth preliminary objection raised by the Federal Republic of Yugoslavia,

Rejects

(a) by fourteen votes to one,

the first, second and third preliminary objections;

IN FAVOUR: *President* Bedjaoui; *Vice-President* Schwebel; *Judges* Oda, Guillaume, Shahabuddeen, Weeramantry, Ranjeva, Herczegh, Shi, Koroma, Vereshchetin, Ferrari Bravo, Parra-Aranguren; *Judge* ad hoc Lauterpacht;

AGAINST: *Judge* ad hoc Kreća;

(b) by eleven votes to four,

the fifth preliminary objection;

IN FAVOUR: *President* Bedjaoui; *Vice-President* Schwebel; *Judges* Guillaume, Shahabuddeen, Weeramantry, Ranjeva, Herczegh, Koroma, Ferrari Bravo, Parra-Aranguren; *Judge* ad hoc Lauterpacht;

AGAINST: *Judges* Oda, Shi, Vereshchetin; *Judge* ad hoc Kreća;

(c) by fourteen votes to one,

the sixth and seventh preliminary objections;

IN FAVOUR: *President* Bedjaoui; *Vice-President* Schwebel; *Judges* Oda, Guillaume, Shahabuddeen, Weeramantry, Ranjeva, Herczegh, Shi, Koroma, Vereshchetin, Ferrari Bravo, Parra-Aranguren; *Judge* ad hoc Lauterpacht;

AGAINST: *Judge* ad hoc Kreća;

(2) *(a)* by thirteen votes to two,

Finds that, on the basis of Article IX of the Convention on the Prevention and Punishment of the Crime of Genocide, it has jurisdiction to adjudicate upon the dispute;

IN FAVOUR: *President* Bedjaoui; *Vice-President* Schwebel; *Judges* Guillaume, Shahabuddeen, Weeramantry, Ranjeva, Herczegh, Shi, Koroma, Vereshchetin, Ferrari Bravo, Parra-Aranguren; *Judge* ad hoc Lauterpacht;

AGAINST: *Judge* Oda; *Judge* ad hoc Kreća;

(b) By fourteen votes to one,

Dismisses the additional bases of jurisdiction invoked by the Republic of Bosnia and Herzegovina;

IN FAVOUR: *President* Bedjaoui; *Vice-President* Schwebel; *Judges* Oda, Guillaume, Shahabuddeen, Weeramantry, Ranjeva, Herczegh, Shi, Koroma, Vereshchetin, Ferrari Bravo, Parra-Aranguren; *Judge* ad hoc Kreća;

AGAINST: *Judge* ad hoc Lauterpacht;

624]   (3) By thirteen votes to two,

Finds that the Application filed by the Republic of Bosnia and Herzegovina on 20 March 1993 is admissible.

IN FAVOUR: *President* Bedjaoui; *Vice-President* Schwebel; *Judges* Guillaume, Shahabuddeen, Weeramantry, Ranjeva, Herczegh, Shi, Koroma, Vereshchetin, Ferrari Bravo, Parra-Aranguren; *Judge* ad hoc Lauterpacht;

AGAINST: *Judge* Oda; *Judge* ad hoc Kreća.

Done in French and in English, the French text being authoritative, at the Peace Palace, The Hague, this eleventh day of July, one thousand nine hundred and ninety-six, in three copies, one of which will be placed in the archives of the Court and the others transmitted to the Government of the Republic of Bosnia and Herzegovina and the Government of the Federal Republic of Yugoslavia, respectively.

(Signed) Mohammed BEDJAOUI,
President.

(Signed) Eduardo VALENCIA-OSPINA,
Registrar.

Judge ODA appends a declaration to the Judgment of the Court; Judges SHI and VERESHCHETIN append a joint declaration to the Judgment of the Court; Judge *ad hoc* LAUTERPACHT appends a declaration to the Judgment of the Court.

Judges SHAHABUDDEEN, WEERAMANTRY and PARRA-ARANGUREN append separate opinions to the Judgment of the Court.

Judge *ad hoc* KREĆA appends a dissenting opinion to the Judgment of the Court.

(Initialled) M.B.
(Initialled) E.V.O.

DECLARATION OF JUDGE ODA   [625

1. I feel some disquiet at being dissociated from the great majority of the Court, particularly in view of my abhorrence of the appalling events which took place in Bosnia and Herzegovina in 1992-1993. It is, however, as a matter of legal conscience that I present my position that the Court should dismiss the Application filed by Bosnia and Herzegovina on 20 March 1993.

The main reason for my negative vote is my conviction that the Court lacks jurisdiction *ratione materiae*, as the Applicant, in its Application, did not assert the existence of a dispute with the Respondent under the Genocide Convention which could have led to the Court being seised of the present case.

*

2. Bosnia and Herzegovina, which relies upon Article IX of the Genocide Convention as a basis for the Court's jurisdiction, has requested the Court to adjudge and declare principally that Yugoslavia (Serbia and Montenegro (hereinafter called "Yugoslavia")) has breached its legal obligations towards Bosnia and Herzegovina under the Genocide Convention, that Yugoslavia must immediately desist from its breaches of these obligations, and that Yugoslavia has to make reparation for the damages to persons and property and to the Bosnian economy and environment that have been caused by its violations of international law.

In my view, however, Bosnia and Herzegovina, in its Application, has not given any indication of opposing views regarding the *application or interpretation* of the Genocide Convention which may have existed at the time of filing of the Application, which alone can enable the Court to find that there is a dispute with Yugoslavia under that Convention.

3. If any dispute were to be unilaterally submitted to the Court by one of the Contracting Parties to a treaty pursuant to the compromissory clause of that treaty, this would mean in essence that the dispute had arisen because of (i) the alleged *failure* of another Contracting Party *to fulfil the obligations imposed by that treaty* — a failure for which it is responsible — and (ii) the *infringement of the rights bestowed upon the former State by that treaty* due to that failure. The failure of the other State is itself a violation of the treaty but such a violation alone cannot be interpreted as constituting a dispute between the applicant State and the respondent State relating to that treaty unless it can

626] be shown to have infringed such rights of the former State as are protected thereby.

*

4. The Genocide Convention is unique in having been adopted by the General Assembly in 1948 at a time when — due to the success of the Nuremberg Trials — the idea prevailed that an international criminal tribunal should be established for the punishment of criminal acts directed against human rights, including genocide; it is essentially directed *not* to the rights and obligations of States *but* to the protection of rights of individuals and groups of persons which have become recognized as universal.

To be sure, the Contracting Parties to the Convention defined genocide as "a crime under international law" (Art. I). The Convention binds the Contracting Parties to punish persons responsible for those acts, whoever they may be, and is thus directed to the punishment of persons committing genocide and genocidal acts (Art. IV). The Contracting Parties undertake "to enact, in accordance with their respective Constitutions, the necessary legislation to give effect to the provisions of the present Convention" (Art. V).

As persons committing genocide or genocidal acts may possibly be "constitutionally responsible rulers [or] public officials" (Art. IV), the Convention contains a specific provision which allows "[a]ny Contracting Party [to] call upon the competent organs of the United Nations to take such action under the Charter of the United Nations as they consider appropriate for the prevention and suppression of [those acts]" (Art. VIII) and contemplates the establishment of an international penal tribunal (Art. VI).

Genocide is defined as "a crime under international law which [the Contracting Parties] undertake to prevent and to punish" (Art. I). Even if this general clause (which was subjected to criticism at the Sixth Committee in 1948 when it was felt by some delegates that it should have been placed in the preamble, but *not* in the main text) is to be interpreted as meaning specifically that the Contracting Parties are obliged "to prevent and to punish" genocide or genocidal acts, these legal obligations are borne in a general manner *erga omnes* by the Contracting Parties in their relations with all the other Contracting Parties to the Convention — or, even, with the international community as a whole — but are *not* obligations in relation to any specific and particular signatory Contracting Party.

The failure of any Contracting Party "to prevent and to punish" such a crime may only be rectified and remedied through (i) resort to a competent organ of the United Nations (Art. VIII) or (ii) resort to an international penal tribunal (Art. VI), but *not* by invoking the responsibility of States in inter-State relations before the International Court of Justice. This constitutes a unique character of the Convention which was pro-

duced in the post-war period in parallel with the emergence of the con- [627
cept of the protection of human rights and humanity.

5. In this regard, some explanation of the dispute settlement provision of the Convention (Art. IX) may be pertinent. It reads as follows:

> "Disputes between the Contracting Parties relating to the interpretation, application or fulfilment of the present Convention, including those relating to the responsibility of a State for genocide or for any of the other acts enumerated in article III, shall be submitted to the International Court of Justice at the request of any of the parties to the dispute"

and is unique as compared with the compromissory clauses found in other multilateral treaties which provide for submission to the International Court of Justice of such disputes between the Contracting Parties as relate to the *interpretation or application* of the treaties in question.

The construction of Article IX of the Genocide Convention is very uncertain as it incorporates specific references to "[d]isputes . . . relating to . . . fulfilment of the Convention" and to "disputes relating to the responsibility of a State for genocide or [genocidal acts]" — references which can hardly be understood in any meaningful sense as a compromissory clause.

The original draft of the Genocide Convention was drawn up by an *Ad Hoc* Committee on Genocide in the ECOSOC in April-May 1948, and contained an orthodox type of compromissory clause (*Official Records of the Economic and Social Council, Third Year, Seventh Session, Supplement No. 6*), which read:

> "Disputes between the High Contracting Parties relating to the *interpretation or application* of this Convention shall be submitted to the International Court of Justice, *provided that* no dispute shall be submitted to the International Court of Justice involving an issue which has been referred to and is pending before or has been passed upon by a competent international criminal tribunal." (Emphasis added.)

When this draft was taken up by the Sixth Committee of the General Assembly in its Third Session in October 1948, the addition of the two aforementioned references was proposed (*Official Records of the General Assembly, Third Session, Sixth Committee,* Annexes, p. 28: A/C6/258) without, in my view, the drafters having a clear picture of the new type of convention to be adopted. While some delegates understood that "fulfilment" would not be different from "application", a proposal to delete "fulfilment" from the additions was rejected by 27 votes to 10, with 8 abstentions. However, another deletion of the words "including [disputes] relating to the responsibility of a State for genocide or [genocidal

628] acts]" was also rejected but only by 19 votes to 17, with 9 abstentions (*Official Records of the General Assembly, Third Session, Sixth Committee*, SR.104, p. 447). The *travaux préparatoires* of the Convention seem to confirm that there was some measure of confusion among the drafters, reflecting in particular the unique nature of their task in the prevailing spirit of the times.

How can one then interpret this reference to the "responsibility of a State"? As far as I know such a reference has never been employed in any other treaty thereafter. It seems to be quite natural to assume that that reference would not have had any meaningful sense or otherwise would not have added anything to the clause providing for the submission to the Court of disputes relating to the *interpretation or application* of the Convention, because, in general, any inter-State dispute covered by a treaty *per se* always relates to the responsibility of a State and the singling-out of a reference to the responsibility of a State does not have any sense with regard to a compromissory clause.

*

6. In order to seise the Court of the present case, Bosnia and Herzegovina would certainly have had to show that applying the Genocide Convention to the situation in the area of the former Yugoslavia, Yugoslavia could indeed have been responsible for the failure of the fulfilment of the Convention in relation to Bosnia and Herzegovina. But, more particularly, Bosnia and Herzegovina would have to show that Yugoslavia has breached the rights of *Bosnia and Herzegovina as a Contracting Party* (which by definition is a State) that should have been protected under the Convention. This, however, has not been shown in the Application and in fact the Convention is not intended to protect the rights of Bosnia and Herzegovina as a State. Yugoslavia might have been responsible for certain instances of genocide or genocidal acts committed by its public officials or surrogates in the territory of Bosnia and Herzegovina, but this fact alone does not mean that there is a "dispute" between the States relating to the responsibility of a State, as Yugoslavia did not violate the rights bestowed upon Bosnia and Herzegovina by the Convention. I would like to repeat and to emphasize that what should be protected by the Convention is *not* the particular rights of any individual State (Bosnia and Herzegovina in this case) *but* the status of human beings with human rights and the universal interest of the individual in general.

7. What Bosnia and Herzegovina did in its Application was to point to certain *facts* tantamount to genocide or genocidal acts which had allegedly ·been committed within its territory by the Government of Yugoslavia or by its agents or surrogates, and to submit *claims* alleged to have arisen out of these acts. This cannot be taken to indicate the

existence of an inter-State dispute relating to the responsibility of a State **[629** which could have been made a basis for the Court's jurisdiction.

Bosnia and Herzegovina certainly might have claimed "reparations for any damages to persons and property as well as to the Bosnian economy and environment caused by the . . . violations of international law" (Application, para. 135 *(r)*) — *not* under the Genocide Convention but *only* as a general issue of international law. (Bosnia and Herzegovina states that the claims to reparation for damages have been caused by the violations of *international law, not* by the Genocide Convention.) If this is the case, whether the present Court has jurisdiction over such claims under the Genocide Convention is quite a different problem and is irrelevant to the present case.

8. After all, Bosnia and Herzegovina does not appear to allege that it has a dispute with Yugoslavia relating to the interpretation or application of the Genocide Convention, although only such a dispute — and not the commission of genocide or genocidal acts which certainly are categorized as a crime under international law — can constitute a basis of the Court's jurisdiction under the Convention.

*

9. Looking at the new concept of genocide emerging with the Second World War and the corresponding preparation of the Genocide Convention — a new type of treaty to deal with the rights of individuals as a whole, but not with the rights and obligations in the inter-State relations — I question whether the International Court of Justice is the appropriate forum for the airing of the questions relating to genocide or genocidal acts which Bosnia and Herzegovina has raised in the current proceedings. I am inclined to doubt whether international law, the Court, or the welfare of the unfortunate individuals concerned will actually benefit from the consideration of cases of this nature by the Court.

The establishment of an international penal tribunal as contemplated in the Convention is now, after half a century, about to be put into effect by the United Nations General Assembly thanks to the work of the International Law Commission. In addition, one month before the Application of Bosnia and Herzegovina in this case, it was decided on 22 February 1993 by Security Council resolution 808 (1993), that the International Criminal Tribunal for the Former Yugoslavia would be established "for the prosecution of persons responsible for serious violations of international humanitarian law committed in the territory of the former Yugoslavia since 1991" and that Tribunal established on 25 May 1993 pursuant to Security Council resolution 827 (1993) is presently in operation.

10. I would like to add one thing and that is that the Court should maintain a very strict position in connection with its jurisdiction. The

630] consensus of the sovereign States in dispute essentially constitutes the basis of that jurisdiction. Were we ever to relax the basic conditions, I would expect to see a flood of cases pouring into this judicial institution, the task of which is mainly the settlement of international disputes. Genocide is precisely the sort of issue that should be settled by any other appropriate organ of the United Nations as suggested in Article VIII of the Convention, or by the international penal tribunal under Article VI. This is, as I repeat, the main idea of the Genocide Convention.

I admit that the extremely vague and uncertain provision of Article IX of the Genocide Convention may leave room for the Court to allow itself to be seised of the present case, but consider that such a conclusion would be based on a misinterpretation of the real spirit of the Genocide Convention. Moreover, note should be taken in parallel of the repeated resolutions taken by the Security Council or the statements made by the President of the Security Council concerning Yugoslavia (which were made prior to the Dayton-Paris Agreement) and the current work of the International Criminal Tribunal for the Former Yugoslavia for the determination of criminal responsibility.

11. Finally, I would like to add that my vote against the decision on the jurisdiction of the Court does not in any way prejudge the position I may take during the merits phase with regard to my legal evaluation concerning the allegations of genocide committed in the former Yugoslavia which are covered by the Application of Bosnia and Herzegovina of 20 March 1993.

(Signed) Shigeru ODA.

JOINT DECLARATION   [631
OF JUDGES SHI AND VERESHCHETIN

We have voted in favour of paragraphs 1 *(a)*, *(c)*, 2 and 3 of the *dispositif* because we are persuaded that Article IX of the Convention on the Prevention and Punishment of the Crime of Genocide affords an arguable legal basis for the Court's jurisdiction in this case. However, we regret that we were unable to vote for paragraph 1 *(b)* as we are disquieted by the statement of the Court, in paragraph 32 of the Judgment, that Article IX of the Genocide Convention "does not exclude any form of State responsibility". It is this disquiet that we wish briefly to explain.

The Convention on Genocide is essentially and primarily directed towards the punishment of persons committing genocide or genocidal acts and the prevention of the commission of such crimes by individuals. The *travaux préparatoires* show that it was during the last stage of the elaboration of the Convention that, by a very slim majority of 19 votes to 17 with 9 abstentions, the provision relating to the responsibility of States for genocide or genocidal acts was included in the dispute settlement clause of Article IX, without the concurrent introduction of necessary modifications into other articles of the Convention. As can be seen from the authoritative commentary to the Convention, published immediately after its adoption, "there were many doubts as to the actual meaning" of the reference to the responsibility of States (Nehemiah Robinson, *The Genocide Convention. Its Origin and Interpretation*, 1949, p. 42). As to the creation of a separate civil remedy applicable as between States, the same author observes that "since the Convention does not specifically refer to reparation, the parties to it did not undertake to have accepted the Court's compulsory jurisdiction in this question" (*ibid.*, p. 43).

In substance, the Convention remains an instrument relating to the criminal responsibility of individuals. The Parties undertake to punish persons committing genocide, "whether they are constitutionally responsible rulers, public officials or private individuals", and to enact the necessary legislation to this effect (Arts. IV and V). Persons charged with genocide or genocidal acts are to be tried "by a competent tribunal of the State in the territory of which the act was committed, or by such international penal tribunal as may have jurisdiction . . ." (Art. VI). Such a tribunal was established (after the filing of the Application) specifically for the prosecution of persons responsible for serious violations of humanitarian law committed in the territory of the former Yugoslavia since 1991.

632]   The determination of the international community to bring *individual perpetrators* of genocidal acts to justice, irrespective of their ethnicity or the position they occupy, points to the most appropriate course of action. We share the view expressed by Britain's Chief Prosecutor at Nuremberg, Hartley Shawcross, in a recent article in which he declared that

> "There can be no reconciliation unless individual guilt for the appalling crimes of the last few years replaces the pernicious theory of collective guilt on which so much racial hatred hangs." (*International Herald Tribune*, 23 May 1996, p. 8.)

Therefore, in our view, it might be argued that this Court is perhaps not the proper venue for the adjudication of the complaints which the Applicant has raised in the current proceedings.

While we consider that Article IX of the Genocide Convention, to which both the Applicant and the Respondent are parties, affords a basis for the jurisdiction of the Court to the extent that the subject-matter of the dispute relates to "the interpretation, application or fulfilment" of the Convention, and having, for this reason, voted for this Judgment, we nevertheless find ourselves obliged to express our concern over the above-mentioned substantial elements of this case.

(Signed)   SHI Jiyuong.

(Signed)   Vladlen S. VERESHCHETIN.

633]   DECLARATION OF JUDGE LAUTERPACHT

I respectfully concur in operative paragraphs 1, 2 *(a)* and 3 of the Judgment of the Court, but regret that I am unable to vote in favour of paragraph 2 *(b)* in so far as it reflects (as stated in paragraph 40 of the Judgment) a decision of the Court that the conduct of the Federal Republic of Yugoslavia does not "confer upon [the Court] a jurisdiction *exceeding that which it has already acknowledged to have been conferred upon it by Article IX of the Genocide Convention*" (emphasis added). Although the point is now at the very margins of this case, I do not wish to convey any impression of acting in a manner inconsistent with what I said on the question of *forum prorogatum* in paragraphs 24-37 of my separate opinion of 13 September 1993 relating to the Further Requests for the Indication of Provisional Measures (*I.C.J. Reports 1993*, p. 325, pp. 416-442).[1]

(Signed)   Elihu LAUTERPACHT.

[1 95 *ILR* 1 at 134.]

SEPARATE OPINION OF JUDGE SHAHABUDDEEN   [634

I would like to explain my support for the judgment of the Court on two points, namely, treaty succession and *forum prorogatum*.

Treaty Succession

The course taken by the Court in its judgment makes it unnecessary to consider whether Bosnia and Herzegovina was a party to the Genocide Convention as from the date of its independence. However, as this point was closely argued and is the subject of some attention, I propose to say a word on it.

I think that the more general arguments as to succession to treaties may be put aside in favour of an approach based on the special characteristics of the Genocide Convention. In the case of the *Reservations to the Convention on the Prevention and Punishment of the Crime of Genocide*, the Court likewise considered that the "solution of [the] problems" [1] which arose there "must be found in the special characteristics of the Genocide Convention" (*I.C.J. Reports 1951*, p. 23). The fact that the Genocide Convention provided for the possibility of cessation or denunciation did not affect its special character as found by the Court. It observed:

> "The origins of the Convention show that it was the intention of the United Nations to condemn and punish genocide as 'a crime under international law' involving a denial of the right of existence of entire human groups, a denial which shocks the conscience of mankind and results in great losses to humanity, and which is contrary to moral law and to the spirit and aims of the United Nations (Resolution 96 (I) of the General Assembly, December 11th, 1946). The first consequence arising from this conception is that the principles underlying the Convention are principles which are recognized by civilized nations as binding on States, even without any conventional obligation. A second consequence is the universal character both of the condemnation of genocide and of the co-operation required 'in order to liberate mankind from such an odious scourge' (Preamble to the Convention). The Genocide Convention was therefore intended by the General Assembly and by the contracting parties to be definitely universal in scope." *(Ibid.)*

Thus, the universality of the Convention attached both to the principles underlying the Convention and to "the co-operation required 'in

[¹ 18 *ILR* 364.]

635] order to liberate mankind from such an odious scourge'". Obviously, universality as regards co-operation could not be achieved without universality of participation. The Court recognized this when it noted "the clearly universal character of the United Nations under whose auspices the Convention was concluded, and the very wide degree of participation envisaged by Article XI of the Convention" (*I.C.J. Reports 1951*, p. 21). In a famous passage, it said:

> "The objects of such a convention must also be considered. The Convention was manifestly adopted for a purely humanitarian and civilizing purpose. It is indeed difficult to imagine a convention that might have this dual character to a greater degree, since its object on the one hand is to safeguard the very existence of certain human groups and on the other to confirm and endorse the most elementary principles of morality. In such a convention the contracting States do not have any interests of their own; they merely have, one and all, a common interest, namely, the accomplishment of those high purposes which are the *raison d'être* of the convention. Consequently, in a convention of this type one cannot speak of individual advantages or disadvantages to States, or of the maintenance of a perfect contractual balance between rights and duties. The high ideals which inspired the Convention provide, by virtue of the common will of the parties, the foundation and measure of all its provisions." (*Ibid.*, p. 23.)

It added:

> "The object and purpose of the Genocide Convention imply that it was the intention of the General Assembly and of the States which adopted it that as many States as possible should participate." (*Ibid.*, p. 24.)

If the arguments of Yugoslavia are correct, they lead in one way or another, so far as a successor State such as Bosnia and Herzegovina is concerned, to the introduction of an inescapable time-gap in the protection which the Genocide Convention previously afforded to all of the "human groups" comprised in the former Socialist Federal Republic of Yugoslavia. There could be many long and single days during such a time-gap when, for all practical purposes, that protection is no longer heard of. It is difficult to appreciate how the inevitability of such a break in protection could be consistent with a Convention the object of which was "on the one hand . . . to safeguard the very existence of certain human groups and on the other to confirm and endorse the most elementary principles of morality".

I think that the object and purpose of the Genocide Convention required parties to observe it in such a way as to avoid the creation of such a break in the protection which it afforded. The Convention could not be read as meaning that a party, which was bound under the Convention to apply its jurisdictional provisions for the protection of the "human

groups" inhabiting a given area, was allowed to regard itself as liberated **[636**
from those provisions in relation to a successor State by reason of the
fact that that particular area was now comprised within the territory of
the successor State; such a party would continue to be bound by those
provisions in relation to other parties in respect of the same "human
groups" while being inconsistently free in relation to the successor State
within whose territory breaches of the Convention are allegedly being
perpetrated by it.

To effectuate its object and purpose, the Convention would fall to be
construed as implying the expression of a unilateral undertaking by each
party to the Convention to treat successor States as continuing as from
independence any status which the predecessor State had as a party to
the Convention. The necessary consensual bond is completed when the
successor State decides to avail itself of the undertaking by regarding
itself as a party to the treaty. It is not in dispute that, one way or another,
Yugoslavia is a party to the Convention. Yugoslavia has therefore to be
regarded as bound by a unilateral undertaking to treat Bosnia and Herzegovina (being a successor State) as having been a party to the Convention
as from the date of its independence.

It may be said that this approach presents existing parties with problems of retroactivity and uncertainty of status of successor States in so far
as the precise position taken by the latter may not emerge until some time
after the dates of their independence. The answer is, I think, provided by
recourse to the jurisprudence of the Court in the *Right of Passage over
Indian Territory* case: the problems in question would be the result of the [2]
scheme of the Genocide Convention which parties to the Convention
accepted when they accepted the Convention. Since Yugoslavia considers
itself a party to the Convention, it is bound by the scheme. Consequently,
it has to regard Bosnia and Herzegovina as a party to the Convention as
from the date of its independence irrespective of possible difficulties.

The foregoing conclusion is reinforced by the following consideration.
The Court would be correct in accepting the generally prevailing view
that even Yugoslavia is not a continuation of the international personal-
ity of the previous Socialist Federal Republic of Yugoslavia but is a new
State and therefore itself a successor State. If, as no one disputes, Yugo-
slavia is correct in regarding itself as having always been a party to the
Convention, this by parity of reasoning applies equally to the case of
Bosnia and Herzegovina.

*

Touching on the wider problem concerning State succession to human
rights treaties, I am not persuaded, for present purposes, to draw too
sharp a distinction between the Genocide Convention (and in particular

[² 31 *ILR* 23.]

[637] its jurisdictional provisions) considered as a measure intended to prevent and punish conduct detrimental to the integrity of certain "human groups" and human rights treaties *stricto sensu*: basically they are all concerned with the rights of the human being — in the case of the Genocide Convention, with some of the most important human rights of all. The origins of the Convention lay in "the intention of the United Nations to condemn and punish genocide as 'a crime under international law' involving a denial of the right of existence of entire human groups"; consequently, the "object" of the Convention was to "safeguard the very existence of certain human groups". That object could not be achieved unless it included the safeguarding of the right to life in certain circumstances, ultimately through the jurisdictional provisions of the Convention. One writer, not unreasonably, described the Convention as "the first human rights instrument adopted by the United Nations" (Matthew Lippman, "The Drafting of the 1948 Convention on the Prevention and Punishment of the Crime of Genocide", *Boston University International Law Journal*, 1985, Vol. 3, p. 1).

But to say that a treaty is a human rights treaty, while providing a possible foundation, does not necessarily indicate a precise juridical mechanism for treating it as being automatically succeeded to by a successor State consistently with the consensual character of treaty relationships. It is possible that such a juridical mechanism is furnished by drawing on the above-mentioned argument and proposing more generally that the effectuation of the object and purpose of such treaties, inclusive of the desideratum of avoiding operational gaps, will support a construction being placed upon them to the effect that they constitute the expression of a unilateral undertaking by existing parties to treat successor States as parties with effect from the date of emergence into independence. As suggested above, the consensual bond is completed when the successor State avails itself of the undertaking by deciding to regard itself as a party to the treaty.

This could provide an answer to the question whether there is automatic succession in the case of human rights treaties in general. However, I do not propose to express a definite opinion at this point on this complex and much disputed question. The construction referred to suffices, in my view, to answer the question in the case of the Genocide Convention in the light of the specific features of this particular instrument.

FORUM PROROGATUM

The Court has correctly held that, in the circumstances of the case, this doctrine does not enable jurisdiction to be founded on bases additional to that provided by Article IX of the Genocide Convention. As to jurisdiction under that provision, I agree with the Court in taking the position, as I think it has, that the question of the applicability of the doctrine need **[638** not be considered. Counsel for Bosnia and Herzegovina submitted — rightly, I think — that the question which arose in the case of that provision was not one of *forum prorogatum*, but one as to whether Yugoslavia had acquiesced in the view that that provision was applicable. There is a distinction between acceptance of the jurisdiction provided for by the jurisdictional provision of a treaty on the basis that the provision itself does not apply and acceptance of the proposition that the jurisdictional provision itself applies. In the first case, the acceptance is the only basis of jurisdiction; in the second case, it is not, being merely an admission that the treaty applies. The latter is how I understood the position taken by counsel for Bosnia and Herzegovina (see CR 96/8, pp. 75-76, 79-80, 81-82, and CR 96/11, p. 52).

Moreover, I agree with what I understood to be also the position taken by counsel for Bosnia and Herzegovina, that is to say, that the doctrine of *forum prorogatum* does not come into play where the same jurisdiction exists under an applicable title of jurisdiction; *ex hypothesi*, the doctrine may be imported only where the jurisdiction in question does not otherwise exist (CR 96/8, p. 82). In this case, the Court having found that Article IX of the Genocide Convention applies as a treaty provision between the parties, there is neither need nor basis for having recourse to the doctrine in question in order to attract the jurisdiction provided for under that provision.

The positions so taken by counsel for Bosnia and Herzegovina accord with the fact that, in paragraph 34 of its Order of 13 September 1993, the Court did not understand that a question of *forum prorogatum* had been raised in respect of Article IX of the Convention; that understanding is retained in paragraph 40 of today's Judgment. The Court's understanding is consistent with the course of the arguments during both of the two previous phases of the case, namely, those of 1-2 April 1993 and those of 25-26 August 1993. (For the stage at which — towards the end of the second phase of the case — and for the circumstances in which the question of *forum prorogatum* was first raised, see *I.C.J. Reports 1993*, pp. 416-420, separate opinion of Judge *ad hoc* Lauterpacht.)[3]

By way of comparison, it may be observed that in the *Corfu Channel* [4] case the plea of *forum prorogatum* was raised, without loss of time, by the United Kingdom both in its written observations and in its oral arguments (see *I.C.J. Reports 1947-1948*, pp. 26 ff.; and *I.C.J. Pleadings, Corfu Channel*, Vol. II, pp. 15-18, particularly para. 9 *(g)* at p. 18, and Vol. III, pp. 36, 56 ff., 66 and 69). In the case of the *Anglo-Iranian Oil Co.*, the initiative was likewise taken, and taken immediately, by the [5] United Kingdom, even though its contentions were not upheld (see *I.C.J. Reports 1952*, pp. 112-114, and *I.C.J. Pleadings, Anglo-Iranian Oil Co.*, pp. 517-518, 540, 544, 553-556, 594, 626, 630 ff.). Immediacy of response is important in appraising the understanding of the parties; *forum pro-*

[3 95 *ILR* 1 at 134.]   [4 15 *Ann Dig* 349.]   [5 19 *ILR* 507.]

639] *rogatum* rests ultimately on the same consensual foundations which underpin the jurisdiction of the Court.

These considerations support what I believe to be the position taken by the Court, that is to say, that Bosnia and Herzegovina is not relying — and correctly, I think — on *forum prorogatum* in relation to Article IX of the Genocide Convention.

(Signed) Mohamed SHAHABUDDEEN.

[640]   SEPARATE OPINION OF JUDGE WEERAMANTRY

TABLE OF CONTENTS

	Page
THE ISSUE OF AUTOMATIC SUCCESSION TO THE GENOCIDE CONVENTION	52
THEORIES RELATING TO STATE SUCCESSION	52
THE "CLEAN SLATE" PRINCIPLE	54
(a) Historical antecedents of the clean slate principle	54
(b) Theoretical bases of the clean slate principle	55
(c) Necessary exceptions to the clean slate principle	56
REASONS FAVOURING VIEW OF AUTOMATIC SUCCESSION TO THE GENOCIDE CONVENTION	56
1. It is not centred on individual State interests	56
2. It transcends concepts of State sovereignty	57
3. The rights it recognizes impose no burden on the State	58
4. The obligations imposed by the Convention exist independently of conventional obligations	58
5. It embodies rules of customary international law	59
6. It is a contribution to global stability	59
7. The undesirability of a hiatus in succession to the Genocide Convention	60
8. The special importance of human rights guarantees against genocide during periods of transition	61
9. The beneficiaries of the Genocide Convention are not third parties in the sense which attracts the *res inter alios acta* principle	62
10. The rights conferred by the Convention are non-derogable	62
INTERNATIONAL PRESSURE FOR RECOGNITION OF THE PRINCIPLE OF AUTOMATIC SUCCESSION	64

THE ISSUE OF AUTOMATIC SUCCESSION   **[641**
TO THE GENOCIDE CONVENTION

I agree with the majority of my colleagues that the Court does have jurisdiction in this case. However, this case raises the important issue of automatic succession to the Genocide Convention, which has not been developed in the Court's Judgment. I believe it warrants consideration.

One of the principal concerns of the contemporary international legal system is the protection of the human rights and dignity of every individual. The question of succession to the Genocide Convention raises one of the most essential aspects of such protection.

The topic which I wish to address in this opinion is the continuing applicability of the Convention to the populations to which it has applied. When a convention so significant for the protection of human life has been entered into by a State, and that State thereafter divides into two or more successor States, what is the position of its subjects in the interim period that elapses before the formal recognition of the successor States, or before the new State's formal accession to treaties such as the Genocide Convention? I think this situation should not be passed by without attention, especially having regard to the fact that the foundations for a consideration of this matter are to be found in the Court's Opinion in the earlier case on genocide which came before it over forty years ago (*Reservations to the Convention on the Prevention and Punishment of the Crime of Genocide, Advisory Opinion, I.C.J. Reports 1951,* p. 15).[1]

Another reason calling for attention to this topic is the fact that the international community is passing through a historical period, when, throughout the world, the phenomenon is being experienced of the splintering of States. This has occurred with particular intensity especially after the end of the Cold War. It is vitally important that the principle of protection of populations against human rights abuses and atrocities should be strengthened in every manner available under current legal principles; and the clarification of the law relating to State succession to a humanitarian treaty so important as the Genocide Convention is eminently such an area.

Bosnia has contended that there is automatic succession to this treaty, and Yugoslavia denies this proposition. This problem leads into the intricate field of State succession to treaties — a field in which there has been much difference of juristic opinion, and in which many competing theories strive for recognition.

THEORIES RELATING TO STATE SUCCESSION

State succession is one of the oldest problems of international law. As Oscar Schachter reminds us, this problem goes all the way back

[¹ 18 *ILR* 364.]

[642] to Aristotle who, in his *Politics*, gave his mind to the question of continuity when "the State is no longer the same" [1].

On this problem, the views of jurists have varied between the two poles of universal succession (these were among the earliest theories, taking their conceptual position largely from the analogy of the Roman law of testamentary succession, involving a total succession to the deceased), and of total negativism, involving a complete denial of succession (based upon the conceptual analogy of a personal contract). It is not necessary for present purposes to refer to the various theories lying between these two extremes.

The circumstances of international life have demonstrated that neither of these absolutist theories is adequate to cover all situations that might arise and that any workable theory lies somewhere between these poles [2]. Quite clearly, whichever of these positions one might lean towards, some exceptions must necessarily be admitted.

The question for consideration in this case is whether, even on the basis of the negativist theory that treaties of the predecessor State are not binding, a necessary exception must exist in relation to treaties such as the Genocide Convention. Much guidance is to be had on this question from the consideration of automatic succession to human rights and humanitarian treaties in general. The discussions and literature on this matter suggest a principle of automatic succession to a large range of such treaties. This opinion does not seek to deal with all human rights and humanitarian treaties, but uses principles worked out in the context of such treaties to reach the conclusion that they apply *a fortiori* to the Genocide Convention which, in consequence, is a treaty to which there is automatic State succession according to the contemporary principles of international law.

---

[1] Oscar Schachter, "State Succession: The Once and Future Law", *Virginia Journal of International Law*, 1992-1993, Vol. 33, p. 253, citing Aristotle, *The Politics*, Book III, Chap. 1. While analysing the constituent elements of a State — territory, government and population — Aristotle refers, *inter alia*, to the question of the continuity of contractual obligations after a change in the State.

[2] A number of studies view multilateral treaties as an exception to the clean slate principle — see Ian Brownlie, *Principles of Public International Law*, 4th ed., 1990, p. 670; D. P. O'Connell, *State Succession in Municipal Law and International Law*, 1967, Vol. II, pp. 212-219. The latest edition of Oppenheim, while observing that there is more room than with regard to treaties generally for the new State, on separation, to be considered bound by multilateral treaties of a law-making nature, singles out treaties of a humanitarian character as especially attracting this view (*Oppenheim's International Law*, 9th ed., Jennings and Watts (eds.), 1992, Vol. 1, s. 64, pp. 222-223). However, the definition of multilateral treaties presents a problem and, for the purposes of the present opinion, it is not necessary to enter into this field.

THE "CLEAN SLATE" PRINCIPLE

(a) *Historical Antecedents of the Clean Slate Principle*

The principle that a new State ought not in general to be fettered with treaty obligations which it has not expressly agreed to assume after it has attained statehood (the clean slate principle) is of considerable historical and theoretical importance. New States ought not, in principle, to be burdened with treaty-based responsibilities without their express consent.

With the sudden advent into the international community of nearly eighty newly independent States in the late fifties and early sixties, there was a realization among them, in the words of Julius Stone, that:

"their authority or their territory or both are burdened with debts, concessions, commercial engagements of various kinds or other obligations continuing on from the earlier colonial regime . . ."[3].

For example, in Nigeria, 300 treaties negotiated by Britain were said to be applicable to the country[4].

Other newly emerging countries soon became conscious of the dangers to their autonomy involved in this principle, and what came to be known as the Nyerere Doctrine emerged under which none of the colonial treaties became applicable unless the new State, within a specified period of time, notified its accession to such treaties[5]. In the language of Jenks, in relation to State succession to colonial treaties, "The psychology of newly won independence is a formidable reality."[6]

This was not, however, the only historical reality that favoured the clean slate theory. There were numerous older precedents, of which a few illustrative examples may be mentioned. Following the Franco-Prussian war and the transfer of Alsace-Lorraine, French treaties applicable to the

---

[3] Julius Stone, "A Common Law for Mankind?", *International Studies*, 1960, Vol. 1, pp. 430-431. See also E. G. Bello, "Reflections on Succession of States in the Light of the Vienna Convention on Succession of States in Respect of Treaties 1978", *German Yearbook of International Law*, 1980, Vol. 23, p. 298; D. P. O'Connell, *State Succession, op. cit.*, p. 116.

[4] By exchange of letters between the Prime Minister and the United Kingdom High Commission on the very day of independence, the Federation assumed all rights and obligations entered into "on their behalf" before independence, and undertook to keep such agreements in force until the Government of Nigeria could consider whether they required modification or renegotiation in any respect (E. G. Bello, *op. cit.*, p. 298).

[5] *Ibid.*, pp. 298-299.

[6] C. Wilfred Jenks, "State Succession in Respect of Law-Making Treaties", *British Year Book of International Law*, 1952, Vol. 29, p. 108.

644] provinces had, in general[7], to cease to have effect and be replaced by German treaties. Again, British jurists, facing the problem of annexation of colonial territories, tended towards the view that "the treaties of the expunged legal person died with it"[8], so that they received those colonies free of the burden of prior treaties. At the United Nations Conference on Succession of States in Respect of Treaties[9], several other examples were referred to, among them the situation resulting from the termination of the Austro-Hungarian Empire, when Czechoslovakia and Poland emerged as independent States with a clean slate in regard to treaties of the former Austro-Hungarian Empire, except for certain multilateral treaties[10].

The clean slate theory was thus the result of many historical trends[11], and had received favour at one time or another from both emerging and established nations.

(b) *Theoretical Bases of the Clean Slate Principle*

Theoretically, the clean slate principle can be justified on several powerful bases — the principle of individual State autonomy, the principle of self-determination, the principle of *res inter alios acta*, and the principle that there can be no limitations on a State's rights, except with its consent. Newly independent States should not have to accept as a *fait accompli* the contracts of predecessor States, for it is self-evident that the new State must be free to make its own decisions on such matters.

The clean slate principle could also be described as an important corollary to the principle of self-determination, which is of cardinal importance in modern international law. The principle of self-determination could be emptied of an important part of its content if prior treaties automatically bind the new State.

One of the bases of the negativist view is that treaties entered into by the predecessor State are *res inter alios acta*. Castrén, dealing specially with the case of division of a pre-existing State into new States, observes:

> "When a State is dismembered into new independent States, its *treaties* as a rule become null and void without descending to the new States. Treaties are generally personal in so far as they presuppose, in addition to the territory, also the existence of a certain

---

[7] An exception was, however, in regard to ecclesiastical law, where Napoleon's Concordat with the Holy See continued to apply.

[8] D. P. O'Connell, "Reflections on the State Succession Convention", *Zeitschrift für ausländisches öffentliches Recht und Völkerrecht*, 1979, Vol. 39, p. 735.

[9] Vienna, 4 April-6 May 1977, and 31 July-23 August 1978.

[10] *Official Records*, Vol. III, p. 92, para. 14.

[11] O'Connell, "Reflections on the State Succession Convention", *op. cit.*, p. 735.

sovereign over the territory. To the succeeding State, the treaties **[645** concluded by the former State are *res inter alios acta.*"[12]

Basic concepts of State sovereignty also require that any curtailment of the sovereign authority of a State requires the express consent of the State.

If there is to be, in a given case, a deviation from the clean slate principle, sufficiently cogent reasons should exist to demonstrate that the new State's sovereignty is not being thereby impaired. The question needs therefore to be examined as to whether there is any impairment of State sovereignty implicit in the application of the principle of automatic succession to any given treaty.

(c) *Necessary Exceptions to the Clean Slate Principle*

Human rights and humanitarian treaties involve no loss of sovereignty or autonomy of the new State, but are merely in line with general principles of protection that flow from the inherent dignity of every human being which is the very foundation of the United Nations Charter.

At the same time, it is important that the circle of exceptions should not be too widely drawn. Conceivably some human rights treaties may involve economic burdens, such as treaties at the economic end of the spectrum of human rights. It is beyond the scope of this opinion to examine whether all human rights and humanitarian treaties should be exempted from the clean slate principle. It is sufficient for the purposes of this opinion to note a variety of reasons why it has been contended that human rights and humanitarian treaties in general attract the principle of automatic succession. These reasons apply with special force to treaties such as the Genocide Convention or the Convention against Torture, leaving no room for doubt regarding automatic succession to such treaties. The international community has a special interest in the continuity of such treaties.

REASONS FAVOURING VIEW OF AUTOMATIC SUCCESSION
TO THE GENOCIDE CONVENTION

1. *It Is Not Centred on Individual State Interests*

This Court, in its earlier consideration of the Genocide Convention, drew pointed attention to the difference between a humanitarian treaty

---

[12] E. Castrén, "Obligations of States Arising from the Dismemberment of Another State", *Zeitschrift für ausländisches öffentliches Recht und Völkerrecht*, 1950-1951, Vol. 13, p. 754 (emphasis added); cited by M. G. Maloney in *Virginia Journal of International Law*, 1979-1980, Vol. 19, p. 892.

646] such as the Genocide Convention, and a convention aimed at protecting the interests of a State. The Court stated in its Opinion on *Reservations to the Convention on the Prevention and Punishment of the Crime of* [2]*Genocide* that:

> "In such a convention the contracting States do not have any interests of their own; they merely have, one and all, a common interest, namely, the accomplishment of those high purposes which are the *raison d'être* of the convention. Consequently, in a convention of this type one cannot speak of individual advantages or disadvantages to States, or of the maintenance of a perfect contractual balance between rights and duties." (*I.C.J. Reports 1951*, p. 23.)

Charles De Visscher has remarked on the contrast

> "between the frailty of agreements of merely individual interest, dependent as these are upon transitory political relations, and the relative stability of conventions dictated by concern for order or respect for law" [13].

He has also remarked in this context that the growing part played by multilateral treaties in the development of international law should count in favour of the transmission rather than disappearance of the obligations they create [14].

Human rights and humanitarian treaties do not represent an exchange of interests and benefits between contracting States in the conventional sense, and in this respect may also be distinguished from the generality of multilateral treaties, many of which are concerned with the economic, security or other interests of States. Human rights and humanitarian treaties represent, rather, a commitment of the participating States to certain norms and values recognized by the international community.

Stated another way, the personality of the sovereign is not the essence of such an agreement. Multilateral treaties are most often concluded with the object of protecting and benefiting the international community as a whole, and for the maintenance of world order and co-operation, rather than of protecting and advancing one particular State's interests.

2. It Transcends Concepts of State Sovereignty

The Genocide Convention does not come to an end with the dismemberment of the original State, as it transcends the concept of State sovereignty. An important conceptual basis denying continuity to treaties is that the recognition of the continuity of the predecessor State's treaties would be an intrusion upon the sovereignty of the successor State. This-

---

[13] *Theory and Reality in Public International Law*, revised ed., 1968, translated from the French by P. E. Corbett, p. 179.
[14] *Ibid.*

would be so if it were a matter confined within the ambit of a State's sov- **[647**
ereignty. But with human rights and humanitarian treaties, we are in a
sphere which reaches far beyond the narrow confines of State sovereignty, and enters the domain of universal concern.

In its ongoing development, the concept of human rights has long
passed the stage when it was a narrow parochial concern between sovereign and subject. We have reached the stage, today, at which the
human rights of anyone, anywhere, are the concern of everyone, every-
where. The world's most powerful States are bound to recognize them,
equally with the weakest, and there is not even the semblance of a suggestion in contemporary international law that such obligations amount to a
derogation of sovereignty.

3. The Rights It Recognizes Impose No Burden on the State

Moreover, a State, in becoming party to the Convention, does not give
away any of its rights to its subjects. It does not burden itself with any
new liability. It merely confirms its subjects in the enjoyment of those
rights which are theirs by virtue of their humanity. Human rights are
never a gift from the State and hence the State, in recognizing them, is
not imposing any burden upon itself. We have long passed the historical
stage when a sovereign, granting to his subjects what we would today call
a human right, could claim their gratitude for surrendering to them what
was then considered to be a part of his absolute and undoubted rights as
a sovereign. Human rights treaties are no more than a formal recognition
by the sovereign of rights which already belong to each of that sovereign's subjects. Far from being largesse extended to them by their sovereign, they represent the entitlement to which they were born.

Quite contrary to the view that human rights treaties are a burden on
the new State, it could indeed be asserted that the adherence by a new
State to a system which is universally accepted, whereby the new State
becomes part of that system, is indeed a benefit to the new State, in sharp
contrast to the position of disadvantage in which it would place itself if it
stood outside that system.

4. The Obligations Imposed by the Convention Exist Independently of Conventional Obligations

This Court observed in *Reservations to the Convention on the Prevention and Punishment of the Crime of Genocide*, "the principles underlying [3]
the [Genocide] Convention are principles which are recognized by civilized nations as binding on States, even without any conventional obligation" (*I.C.J. Reports 1951*, p. 23). The same may be said of all treaties
concerning basic human rights.

[³ 18 *ILR* 364.]

648]   The Court referred also in the same Opinion to the universal character of the condemnation of genocide. This condemnation has its roots in the convictions of humanity, of which the legal rule is only a reflection. The same could likewise be said of many of the basic principles of human rights and humanitarian law.

5. It Embodies Rules of Customary International Law

The human rights and humanitarian principles contained in the Genocide Convention are principles of customary international law. These principles continue to be applicable to both sovereign and subjects, irrespective of changes in sovereignty, for the new sovereign, equally with the old, is subject to customary international law. The customary rights which the subjects of that State enjoy continue to be enjoyed by them, whoever may be their sovereign. The correlative duties attach to the sovereign, whoever he may be. The position is no different when those customary rights are also embodied in a treaty.

This factor may indeed be seen in wider context as essential to the evolution of international law into a universal system. Among writers who have stressed this aspect in relation to multilateral treaties are Wilfred Jenks, who observed:

> "It is generally admitted that a new State is bound by existing rules of customary international law. This principle has, indeed, been of fundamental importance in the development of international law into a world-wide system . . . It is not clear why, now that the rules established by multipartite legislative instruments constitute so large a part of the operative law of nations, a new State should be regarded as starting with a clean slate in respect of rules which have a conventional rather than a customary origin." [15]

In regard to such a matter as genocide, there can be no doubt that the treaty is of fundamental importance to the development of the operative law of nations.

6. It Is a Contribution to Global Stability

The strengthening of human rights protections in accordance with universally held values is a matter of universal concern and interest.

The promotion and encouragement of respect for human rights is, according to Article 1 (3) of the United Nations Charter, one of the Purposes of the United Nations, and the reaffirmation of faith in fundamental human rights and the dignity and worth of the human person are

---

[15] W. Jenks, *op. cit.*, p. 107.

among the foremost objects that the peoples of the United Nations set **[649**
before themselves "to save succeeding generations from the scourge of
war".

Genocide attacks these concepts at their very root and, by so doing,
strikes at the foundations of international stability and security.

A State's guarantees of human rights to its subjects in terms of even
such a Covenant as the International Covenant on Civil and Political
Rights are thus a matter which does not concern that State alone, but
represent a contribution to human dignity and global stability — as distinguished, for example, from a commercial or trading treaty. This aspect
is all the more self-evident in a treaty of the nature of the Genocide Convention.

At the United Nations Conference on State Succession on 22 April
1977, the Soviet Union drew attention to a letter by the International
Committee of the Red Cross to the Chairman of the International Law
Commission to the effect that no State had ever claimed to be released
from any obligation under the Geneva Conventions. In this connection,
the representative of the Soviet Union observed that, "Such a practice
had not created difficulties for newly independent States"[16]. He also
observed:

> "Thus treaties of a universal character were of paramount impor-
> tance for the whole international community, and particularly for
> newly independent States. It was therefore in the interests of not
> only newly independent States but also of the international commu-
> nity as a whole that a treaty of universal character should not cease
> to be in force when a new State attained independence." [17]

7. *The Undesirability of a Hiatus in Succession to the Genocide Convention*

If the contention is sound that there is no principle of automatic succession to human rights and humanitarian treaties, the strange situation
would result of the people within a State, who enjoy the full benefit of a
human rights treaty, such as the International Covenant on Civil and
Political Rights, and have enjoyed it for many years, being suddenly
deprived of it as though these are special privileges that can be given or
withdrawn at the whim or fancy of Governments. Populations once protected cease to be protected, may be protected again, and may again
cease to be protected, depending on the vagaries of political events. Such
a legal position seems to be altogether untenable, especially at this stage
in the development of human rights.

---

[16] 24th meeting, 22 April 1977, *Official Records*, Vol. I, p. 164, para. 5.
[17] *Ibid.,* p. 163, para. 2.

650]   Jenks observes, "It is not a matter of perpetuating the dead hand of the past, but of avoiding a legal vacuum."[18] This vacuum could exist over "hundreds of thousands of square miles and millions of citizens . . ."[19]. He also refers to:

> "the uncertainty, confusion and practical inconvenience of a legal vacuum which may be gravely prejudicial not only to the interests of other States concerned but equally to the interests of the new State itself and its citizens"[20].

The undesirability of such a result becomes more evident still if the human rights treaty under consideration is one as fundamental as the Genocide Convention. If the principle set out earlier is not clearly recognized, the international legal system would be endorsing the curious result that people living under guarantees that genocide will not be committed against them will suddenly be deprived of that guarantee, *precisely at the time they need it most* — when there is instability in their State. The anomaly of a grant followed by a withdrawal of the benefits, of such a Covenant as the International Covenant for Civil and Political Rights, becomes compounded in the case of the Genocide Convention, and the result is one which, in my view, international law does not recognize or endorse at the present stage of its development.

Furthermore, there may be circumstances where, after a new State has proclaimed its independence, the accession of that State to statehood may itself be delayed by the non-recognition of a breakaway State by the State from which it breaks away. In such a situation, where advent of the new State to statehood is deliberately delayed by action of the former State, there can be no accession to the treaty by the breakaway State for a considerable time. During that period, it seems unreasonable that the citizens of that breakaway State should be deprived of such protection as the Convention may give them, against acts of genocide by the State from which the secession has occurred, as well as by the State that has seceded. The longer the delay in recognition, the longer then would the period be during which those citizens are left unprotected. Such a result seems to me to be totally inconsistent with contemporary international law — more especially in regard to a treaty protecting such universally recognized rights as the Genocide Convention.

8. The Special Importance of Human Rights Guarantees against Genocide during Periods of Transition

To the strong conceptual position resulting from the foregoing considerations, there must be added the practical imperatives that result from

---

[18] Jenks, *op. cit.*, p. 109.
[19] *Ibid.*
[20] *Ibid.*

a realistic view of the international situation occurring in the process of the **[651**
dismemberment of a State, with all the political, social and military turmoil
that is known only too well to accompany that process in modern times.

It would in fact be most dangerous to view the break-up of a State as
clearing the decks of the human rights treaties and obligations of the
predecessor State. It is dangerous even to leave the position unclear,
and that is why I have felt impelled to state my opinion upon this all-
important matter.

All around us at the present time, the break-up of States has often been
accompanied by atrocities of the most brutal and inhuman kind, practised on a scale that defies quantification. To leave a lacuna in the continuity of the law or any vagueness in the perception of that continuity
would be fraught with danger to the most cherished values of civilization.

If the principle of continuity in relation to succession of States, adopted
in Article 34 (1) in the 1978 Vienna Convention on Succession of States
in Respect of Treaties, is to apply to any treaties at all, the Genocide
Convention must surely be among such treaties.

Furthermore, humanitarian treaties formulate principles that are an
established part of the law of war. The law of war applies, of course, even
in regard to an internal war (*vide* Geneva Convention 1977, Protocol II).
The applicability of the principles underlying these treaties, among which
the Genocide Convention may also be reckoned, becomes particularly
important in times of internal turmoil. Such treaties cannot be suspended
sine die during times of internal unrest such as accompany the break-up
of a State, when they are most needed.

9. *The Beneficiaries of the Genocide Convention Are Not Third Parties in the Sense Which Attracts the* Res Inter Alios Acta *Principle*

The beneficiaries of the Genocide Convention, as indeed of all human
rights treaties, are not strangers to the State which recognizes the rights
referred to in the Convention. The principle that *res inter alios acta* are
not binding, an important basis of the clean slate rule, does not therefore
apply to such conventions. There is no vesting of rights in extraneous
third parties or in other States, and no obligation on the part of the State
to recognize any rights of an external nature. Far from being a transaction *inter alios*, such treaties promote the highest internal interests
which any State can aspire to protect.

10. *The Rights Conferred by the Convention Are Non-derogable*

The rights and obligations guaranteed by the Genocide Convention are
non-derogable, for they relate to the right to life, the most fundamental

652] of human rights, and an integral part of the irreducible core of human rights. It relates not merely to the right to life of one individual, but to that right *en masse*.

Moreover, under the Genocide Convention, the obligation of States is not merely to refrain from committing genocide, but to *prevent* and *punish* acts of genocide. The failure by a successor régime to assume and discharge this obligation would be altogether incompatible with State obligations as recognized in contemporary international law.

Another possible line of enquiry, not necessary for the determination of the present matter, is the analogy between a treaty vesting human rights, and a dispositive treaty vesting property rights. From the time of Vattel[21], such a dispositive treaty, as for example a treaty recognizing a servitude, has been looked upon as vesting rights irrevocably in the party to whom they were granted; and those rights, once vested, could not be taken away. Perhaps in comparable fashion, human rights, once granted, become vested in the persons enjoying them in a manner comparable, in their irrevocable character, to vested rights in a dispositive treaty[22].

This interesting legal hypothesis need not detain us here as the conclusion I have reached is amply supported by the other principles discussed.

* * *

Some of the reasons set out above, even considered individually, are cogent enough to demonstrate the applicability of automatic succession to the Genocide Convention (and indeed to a wide range of human rights and humanitarian treaties). Taken cumulatively, they point strongly to the clear incompatibility with international law of the contention that the Genocide Convention ceases to apply to the subjects of a State upon the division of that State.

---

[21] See E. de Vattel, *The Law of Nations or Principles of Natural Law*, C. Fenwick (trans.), 1916, p. 169, referred to in *Virginia Journal of International Law*, 1979-1980, Vol. 19, p. 888, note 16.

[22] On the possible extension to human rights of the doctrine of acquired rights which has traditionally been applied to dispositive treaties and property rights, see Malcolm N. Shaw, "State Succession Revisited", *Finnish Yearbook of International Law*, 1994, Vol. 5, p. 82; Rein Mullerson, "The Continuity and Succession of States, by Reference to the Former USSR and Yugoslavia", *International and Comparative Law Quarterly*, 1993, Vol. 42, pp. 490-491. See also the statement at the Human Rights Committee of one of its members referring to these rights as "acquired rights" which were not "diluted" when a State was divided (Serrano Caldera, CCPR/C/SR.1178/Add.1, 5 November 1992, p. 9).

In the discussions that took place at the United Nations Conference on Succession of States in Respect of Treaties, this aspect of a need to prevent a hiatus occurring in the process of succession of States received emphasis from several States. The position was well summarized by one delegate who, while pointing out that the "essence of the problem was to strike a balance between continuity and the freedom of choice which was the basis of the 'clean slate' principle"[23], stated that, in the case of multilateral treaties, the need for continuity was pressing. He described as an "international vacuum" the situation that could arise if this were not the case, and spoke of this as "a lacuna inconvenient both to the newly independent State and to the international community"[24].

This question has also been considered in some depth by the Commission on Human Rights and by the Human Rights Committee.

At its forty-ninth session, the Commission on Human Rights adopted resolution 1993/23 of 5 March 1993, entitled "Succession of States in respect of international human rights treaties". This resolution encouraged successor States to confirm officially that they continued to be bound by international obligations under relevant human rights treaties. The special nature of human rights treaties was further confirmed by the Commission in its resolution 1994/16 of 25 February 1994, and the Commission, in that resolution, reiterated its call to successor States which had not yet done so to confirm to appropriate depositories that they continued to be bound by obligations under international human rights treaties.

The Committee on Human Rights, at its forty-seventh session (March-April 1993), stated that all the people within the territory of a former State party to the Covenant remained entitled to the guarantees under the Covenant.

It is worthy of note also that during the fifth meeting of persons chairing the human rights treaty bodies, held from 19 to 23 September 1994:

"The chairpersons emphasized, however, that they were of the view that successor States were automatically bound by obligations under international human rights instruments from the respective date of independence and that observance of the obligations should

---

[23] Mr. Shahabuddeen, speaking for Guyana, 23rd Meeting, 21 April 1977, *Official Records*, Vol. I, p. 163.
[24] *Ibid.*, p. 162. See, also, Sweden, Mr. Hellners, 26th meeting, 25 April 1977, *ibid.*, p. 177.

[654]   not depend on a declaration of confirmation made by the Government of the successor State." [25]

The *Ad Hoc* Committee on Genocide also made the important point that the crime of genocide generally entails the complicity or direct involvement of Governments [26], and national courts are likely to be reluctant or ineffective in adjudicating claims of State-sponsored genocide [27] — hence the importance of Article IX.

All of these views, though not authoritative in themselves, serve to underline the principle here under discussion. These are all committees with special experience of handling problems in the human rights area, and the force of their conviction of the necessity of such a rule emphasizes how vital it is in actual practice.

If such should be the principle suggested, in regard to human rights conventions such as the Covenant on Civil and Political Rights, one can be left in little doubt regarding its essentiality in regard to conventions such as the Genocide Convention.

A clarification of this principle is one of the ways in which international law can respond to the needs of international society.

In the words of Jenks, written in the context of State succession to treaties:

> "if our legal system fails to respond to the widely felt and urgent needs of a developing international society, both its authority as a legal system and the prospect of developing a peaceful international order will be gravely prejudiced" [28].

* * *

All of the foregoing reasons combine to create what seems to me to be a principle of contemporary international law that there is automatic State succession to so vital a human rights convention as the Genocide Convention. Nowhere is the protection of the quintessential human right — the right to life — more heavily concentrated than in that Convention.

Without automatic succession to such a Convention, we would have a situation where the worldwide system of human rights protections con-

---

[25] E/CN.4/1995/80, 28 November 1994, p. 4.

[26] United Nations, *Official Records of the Economic and Social Council, Ad Hoc* Committee on Genocide, Sixth Session, 4th meeting, United Nations doc. E/AC.25/SR.4 (1948), pp. 3-5, cited in M. Lippman, "The 1948 Convention on the Prevention and Punishment of the Crime of Genocide: Forty-five Years Later", *Temple International and Comparative Law Journal*, 1994, Vol. 8, p. 70.

[27] *Ibid.*

[28] Jenks, *op. cit.*, p. 110.

tinually generates gaps in the most vital part of its framework, which **[655** open up and close, depending on the break-up of the old political authorities and the emergence of the new. The international legal system cannot condone a principle by which the subjects of these States live in a state of continuing uncertainty regarding the most fundamental of their human rights protections. Such a view would grievously tear the seamless fabric of international human rights protections, endanger peace, and lead the law astray from the Purposes and Principles of the United Nations, which all nations, new and old, are committed to pursue.

(Signed) Christopher Gregory WEERAMANTRY.

SEPARATE OPINION OF JUDGE PARRA-ARANGUREN   **[656**

While endorsing the operative paragraphs in the Judgment, I have decided to append this separate opinion to emphasize the following points that I consider of great importance:

1. The fact that Bosnia and Herzegovina became a party to the Genocide Convention was expressly admitted by Yugoslavia on 10 August 1993 when requesting the Court to indicate the following provisional measures:

> "The Government of the so-called Republic of Bosnia and Herzegovina should immediately, *in pursuance of its obligation under the Convention on the Prevention and Punishment of the Crime of Genocide of December 1948*, take all measures within its power to prevent commission of the crime of genocide against the Serb ethnic group." (Emphasis added.)

Therefore, Yugoslavia admitted that Bosnia and Herzegovina was a party to the Genocide Convention and consequently that the Court has jurisdiction on the basis of its Article IX; a declaration that is particularly important because it was made almost two months after the Secretary-General of the United Nations received, on 15 June 1993, the communication from Yugoslavia objecting to the notification of succession made by Bosnia and Herzegovina in respect of the Genocide Convention.

2. The declaration made by Bosnia and Herzegovina expressing its wish to succeed to the Convention with effect from 6 March 1992, the date on which it became independent, is wholly in conformity with the humanitarian nature of the Genocide Convention, the non-performance of which may adversely affect the people of Bosnia and Herzegovina. In

my opinion the Judgment should have remarked on and developed this point, taking into account that the importance of maintaining the application of such conventions of humanitarian character had already been recognized by the Court in its Advisory Opinion of 21 June 1971, when determining "the legal consequences for States of the continued presence of South Africa in Namibia, notwithstanding Security Council resolution 276 (1970)"; resolution that had declared invalid and illegal all acts taken by the Government of South Africa on behalf of or concerning Namibia after the termination of the Mandate. In that case it was recalled that member States were under an obligation to abstain from entering into treaty relations with South Africa in all cases in which the **657]** Government of South Africa purported to act on behalf of or concerning Namibia; and immediately after the Court added:

> "With respect to existing bilateral treaties, member States must abstain from invoking or applying those treaties or provisions of treaties concluded by South Africa on behalf of or concerning Namibia which involve active intergovernmental co-operation. With respect to multilateral treaties, however, the same rule cannot be applied to certain general conventions such as those of a humanitarian character, the non-performance of which may adversely affect the people of Namibia." (*Legal Consequences for States of the Continued Presence of South Africa in Namibia (South West Africa)* [1]*notwithstanding Security Council Resolution 276 (1970), I.C.J. Reports 1971*, p. 55, para. 122.)

Similar ideas are sustained by Article 60, paragraph 5, of the 1969 Vienna Convention on the Law of Treaties when providing that its rules on termination or suspension of a treaty as a consequence of its breach

> "do not apply to provisions relating to the protection of the human person contained in treaties of a humanitarian character, in particular to provisions prohibiting any form of reprisals against persons protected by such treaties".

It is not easy to understand why the same conclusion was not accepted by the Court in this case relating to the application of the Genocide Convention.

(*Signed*) Gonzalo PARRA-ARANGUREN.

DISSENTING OPINION OF JUDGE KREĆA

TABLE OF CONTENTS

Paragraphs

INTRODUCTION

FIRST PRELIMINARY OBJECTION

Basic approach to the meaning of the first preliminary objection   1
Concept of the State *ab intra*   3-4
Application of the constituent element of the concept to Bosnia
  and Herzegovina   5-26

  Meaning of the Dayton Agreement in the establishment of
    Bosnia and Herzegovina within the administrative bounda-
    ries of that former Yugoslav federal unit   22-25
  Recognition of Bosnia and Herzegovina   26

SECOND PRELIMINARY OBJECTION

Relevance of internal law *in concreto*   27
Was the President of the Presidency of Bosnia and Herzegovina
  authorized to personally accredit a "General Agent with
  extraordinary and plenipotentiary powers to the Court"?   28-29
Could Mr. Izetbegović have performed the function of Presi-
  dent of the Presidency *ex constitutione* after 20 December
  1992?   30-37
Legal qualification of the matter   38-39

THIRD PRELIMINARY OBJECTION

Sedes materiae of the third preliminary objection   40
Relevance of international law to the birth of States (concept of
  the State *ab extra*)   41-44
The legality of the proclamation of Bosnia and Herzegovina's
  independence in the light of the internal law of the Socialist
  Federal Republic of Yugoslavia   45-67

  Relevance of the internal law of the Socialist Federal Repub-
    lic of Yugoslavia   45-46
  Constitutional concept of the Yugoslav State — constitu-
    tional concept of Bosnia and Herzegovina   47-58
  Promulgation of Bosnia and Herzegovina as a sovereign State   59-67

Legality of the proclamation of independence of Bosnia and
  Herzegovina in the light of international law   68-81
Relation between the legality of the birth of a State and succes-
  sion with respect to international treaties   82-89
Is Yugoslavia a party to the Genocide Convention?   90-97

[659] FIFTH PRELIMINARY OBJECTION

Principal legal questions raised by Yugoslavia's fifth prelimi-
nary objection   99
Qualification of the conflict in Bosnia and Herzegovina   100
Legal nature of the rights and obligations of States under the
Convention   101
Does the Genocide Convention contain the principle of univer-
sal repression?   102
Could a State be responsible for genocide?   103-104
The scope of Article IX of the Convention   105

SIXTH PRELIMINARY OBJECTION

General approach to the issue raised by Yugoslavia's sixth pre-
liminary objection   106-107
Legal nature of the Genocide Convention   108
Institute of "automatic succession" — *lex lata* or *lex ferenda*? 109-111

Principles underlying the Convention as a part of the *corpus
juris cogentis*   112-114
Notification of succession — whether it is capable *per se* of
expressing consent to be bound by the treaty?   115-118
Is the Dayton Agreement a basis for the application of the
Genocide Convention between Yugoslavia and Bosnia and
Herzegovina?   119

SEVENTH PRELIMINARY OBJECTION

Scope of Article IX of the Convention *ratione temporis* —
retroactivity or non-retroactivity?   120

In spite of my respect for the Court, I am compelled, with deep regret, to avail myself of the right to express a dissenting opinion.

As each objection appears to be designed as a separate whole, I shall treat the objections raised by Yugoslavia separately, in such a way as to ensure that the conclusions drawn therefrom will serve as a proper basis for my general conclusion concerning the jurisdiction of the Court and the admissibility of Bosnia and Herzegovina's claim.

FIRST PRELIMINARY OBJECTION

1. My approach to the meaning of the first preliminary objection is essentially different from that of the Court. Prior to deciding whether *in concreto* there is an international dispute within the terms of Article IX of the Genocide Convention, it is necessary, in my opinion, to resolve the dilemma of whether Bosnia and Herzegovina at the time when the Application, as well as the Memorial, were submitted, and Bosnia and Herzegovina as it exists today when this case is being heard, are actually one and the same State. This question represents, in my opinion, a typical example of what Judge Fitzmaurice in his separate opinion in the *Northern Cameroons* case[1] described as objections "which can and strictly should be taken in *advance* of any question of competence", for it opens the way for the *persona standi in judicio* of Bosnia and Herzegovina.

If they are the same State, then the issue raised by the preliminary objection is in order. In the event that they are not, the situation is in my opinion clear — there is no dispute concerning Article IX of the Convention — hence, *placitum aliud personale.*

In this regard, the issue raised by the first preliminary objection is not an issue of admissibility *stricto sensu*, but a mixture, in its own right, of admissibility and jurisdiction *ratione personae.*

2. The aforementioned question is directly linked with the concept of an international dispute, the substance of which consists of two cumulative elements — the material, and the formal. The generally accepted definition of the dispute which the Court gave in the *Mavrommatis Palestine Concessions* case[2] represents, in fact, only the material element of the concept of "international dispute". In order to qualify "a disagreement over a point of law or fact, a conflict of legal views or of interests", which is evident in this specific case, as an "international dispute", another, formal element is indispensable, i.e., that the parties in the "disagreement or conflict" be States in the sense of international public law.

---

[1] *I.C.J. Reports 1963*, p. 105. [35 *ILR* 353.]
[2] *P.C.I.J., Series A, No. 2*, p. 11. [2 *Ann Dig* 398.]

661] Article IX of the Genocide Convention stipulates the competence of the Court for the "disputes between the Parties". The term "Parties", as it obviously results from Article XI of the Convention, means States, either members or non-members of the United Nations.

The term "State" is not used either *in abstracto* in the Genocide Convention, or elsewhere; it means a concrete entity which combines in its personality the constituting elements of a State, determined by the international law. The pretention of an entity to represent a State, and even recognition by other States, is not, in the eyes of the law, sufficient on its own to make it a State within the meaning of international law.

From the very beginning of the proceedings before the Court, Yugoslavia challenged the statehood of Bosnia and Herzegovina. It is true that, as the Court noted, Yugoslavia explicitly withdrew this preliminary objection. However substantial arguments against the statehood of Bosnia and Herzegovina at the relevant time were indicated by Yugoslavia in support of its third objection. *Exempli causa*, Yugoslavia emphasized that "[t]he central organs of the Government of this Republic controlled a very small part of the territory of Bosnia and Herzegovina . . . In fact four states existed in the territory of the former Socialist Republic of Bosnia and Herzegovina . . ."[3]. The third objection of Yugoslavia may in substance be reduced to the assertion that Bosnia and Herzegovina, in the light of relevant legal rules, "has not established its independent statehood" within the administrative boundaries of that former federal unit. This was an additional reason for the Court to take its stand on the aforementioned question, not only in order to be able to take the decision on the first preliminary objection of Yugoslavia, but also in order to decide whether, and to what extent, it was competent in this case.

The response to the question whether Bosnia and Herzegovina, at the relevant points in time, was constituted as a State within the administrative boundaries of the federal unit of Bosnia and Herzegovina has, in my opinion, a definite affect on the succession to the Genocide Convention. To be bound by the Genocide Convention is only one of the forms of "replacement of one State by another in the responsibility for international relations of the territory". The word "territory" refers to the space in which the newly formed State exercises *summa potestas*, the space within which it is constituted as a State in the sense of the relevant norms of international law. It need hardly be said that there is no legal basis that would enable one State to assume contractual obligations in the name of another State or States, whether recognized or not. Bosnia and Herzegovina explicitly claims — and, what is more, its entire Memorial is based on that claim — that it is acting in the name of the whole of the former federal unit of Bosnia and Herzegovina, i.e., that Bosnia and Herze-

---

[3] CR 96/5, p. 35.

govina is the successor State in relation to the entire territory of that [662] former federal unit. Hence, in my opinion, it is essential that the Court, in defining the factual and legal state of affairs in the territory of Bosnia and Herzegovina at the relevant points in time, should precisely determine the scope of its jurisdiction.

Finally, in its scope, the answer to the question of the State identity of Bosnia and Herzegovina is, in my view, also relevant with regard to the Yugoslav claim stated in the fifth preliminary objection according to which the case "in point is an international conflict between three sides in which FRY was not taking part".

Having in mind the foregoing, and even in the event that Yugoslavia has not made such an assertion, the Court is not relieved of the obligation to do so. As established in the Judgment on the *Appeal Relating to the Jurisdiction of the ICAO Council*:

> "The Court must however always be satisfied that it has jurisdiction, and must if necessary go into that matter *proprio motu*. The real issue raised by the present case was whether, in the event of a party's failure to put forward a jurisdictional objection as a preliminary one, that party might not thereby be held to have acquiesced in the jurisdiction of the Court."[4]

3. (*The concept of the State* ab intra.) The concept of the State *ab intra* defines the State as an isolated, static phenomenon on the basis of its constituent elements. The State so defined is usually understood to be an entity comprised cumulatively of a permanent population, an established territory and sovereign authority. Not infrequently, other elements of the State are also cited but they do not merit the qualification of constituent elements. They are by their nature either derived elements (*exempli causa*, "capacity to enter into relations with other States") or they reflect exclusivistic concepts which are ontologically in contradiction with the democratic nature of positive international law ("degree of civilization such as enables it to observe the principles of international law", etc.).

As far as the nature of the cited constituent elements of the State are concerned, they are legal facts. As legal facts they have two dimensions.

The qualification "constituent elements of the State" reflects the static, phenomenological dimension of the concept of the State. It proceeds from the State as a fact, i.e., phenomenologically, and focuses on the basic constituent elements of its static being.

In the case of the emergence of new States, the constituent elements of the concept of the State lose their phenomenological characteristics — since in that case, there is no State as an entity — and are transformed into *prerequisites* for the emergence of a State. In other words, for a cer-

---

[4] *I.C.J. Reports 1972*, p. 52. [48 *ILR* 331.]

663] tain entity to become a State it must cumulatively fulfil conditions which are, in the material sense, identical with the constituent elements of a State in the static, phenomenological sense.

4. What is the mutual relationship among the basic constituent elements of the State? From the formal standpoint, the question may appear to be superfluous, as by its very wording it suggests the only possible answer and that is that they are elements that function cumulatively. However, the question does have a logic of its own if one views it as relating to the value relationship among the cumulative elements or, in other words, if one views, within the concept of the State comprised of the three cited elements, their mutual relationship *ab intra*.

With the reservation that the value relationship among the cited elements is to some extent determined in advance by the cumulative nature of the elements, some conclusions can nonetheless be drawn. First, there is no doubt that a certain value relationship, if not even a hierarchy, does exist. Suffice it to note that territory and population are immanent to some non-State entities as well. It is also beyond doubt that the element of sovereignty is peculiar to the State alone. Thirdly — and this is the *differentia specifica* between States and other, non-State entities — sovereignty is in a sense a qualifying condition, a condition of special value, for sovereign authority is not only one of the constituent elements of the State, but it is at the same time an element which gives concrete substance to the rather abstract and broad concepts of "territory" and "population" and, in so doing, links them to the concept of the State in the sense of international law. Evidently, for a "territory" to be "State territory" it must be subject to sovereign authority. Without it a "territory" is not a State territory but it is something else (*res nullius*, trusteeship territory, *res communis omnium*, common heritage of mankind and the like).

5. Were the constituent elements of a State in existence in the case of Bosnia and Herzegovina at the relevant point in time?

6. There is no doubt that Bosnia and Herzegovina had a "permanent population" if we use the term in the technical sense, i.e., in the sense of a group of individuals who were linked to the relevant territory by their way of life.

However, within the system of positive international law, the term "permanent population" acquires a different meaning. In a system that recognizes the fundamental significance of the norms of equal rights and self-determination of peoples (see paras. 67-68, 71 below), the concept of a "permanent population", at least when referring to a territory inhabited by several peoples, cannot have only the cited technical meaning. In that case, if one is to be able to speak of a "permanent population" in view of the norm on equal rights and self-determination of peoples, there has to be a minimum of consensus among the peoples regarding the conditions of their life together.

In Bosnia and Herzegovina that minimum did not exist. The Referendum of 29 February and 1 March 1992, in relation to the national plebiscite of the Serb people in Bosnia and Herzegovina of 9-10 November **[664** 1991, showed that the "permanent population" of the federal unit of Bosnia and Herzegovina was divided into the Muslim-Croat peoples on the one hand and the Serb people on the other. The unification of the communes with a majority Croat population into the Croatian Community of Herceg-Bosna on 19 November 1991 and especially the formation of the independent State community of Herceg-Bosna on 4 July 1992, symbolized the complete divergence of options among the three peoples of Bosnia and Herzegovina. In an entity in which *summa potestas* is a constituent element of special importance and bearing in mind how it was distributed in Bosnia and Herzegovina, there are strong grounds to claim that in Bosnia and Herzegovina there were in fact three "permanent populations".

7. The use of the term "defined territory" implies defined and settled boundaries in accordance with the rules of positive international law. As a condition for the existence of a State, "defined and settled boundaries" do not have absolute value — in practice a State has been considered to have been constituted even when all its boundaries were not defined. However, it is essential that "there is a consistent band of territory which is undeniably controlled by the Government of the alleged State"[5]. The rule is that the boundaries be established by international treaty or, exceptionally, on the basis of the principle of effectiveness.

The question whether Bosnia and Herzegovina had "defined and settled boundaries" has a two-fold meaning: material and in terms of time.

8. In the material sense, the relevant question is whether one can equate administrative-territorial boundaries within a composite State and frontiers between States in the sense of international law?

The answer can only be negative both from the standpoint of the internal law of the Socialist Federal Republic of Yugoslavia (SFRY) and from the standpoint of international law.

As far as the internal law of SFRY is concerned, suffice it to note the provisions of Article 5 (1) of the SFRY Constitution which stipulated *expressis verbis* that the "territory of SFRY is unified" and that it is "composed of the territories of the Socialist Republics". That the "boundaries" between the federal units were merely lines of administrative division is also evidenced by the fact that they were not directly established by any legal act. They were determined indirectly, via the territories of the communes which comprised a certain federal unit so that they were, in a sense, the aggregation of communal borders. Thus, the Constitution of Bosnia and Herzegovina stipulated in Article 5: "[t]he territory of SR Bosnia-Herzegovina is composed of the areas of the communes".

---

[5] M. N. Shaw, *International Law*, 1986, p. 127.

665]   The administrative nature of the boundaries of the federal units in SFRY was also recognized by the Arbitration Commission of the Conference on Yugoslavia whose opinions are used by the Applicant as its main argument. In Opinion No. 3, it described the boundaries between the Yugoslav federal units as "demarcation lines"[6].

In the light of international law, the terms "frontier" or "State border lines" are reserved for States with international personality. More particularly, whereas the SFRY was a State in terms of public international law and of the United Nations Charter, the republics were the component parts of Yugoslavia and, in the context of the legal nature of a federation, they were the component parts of a single State *in foro externo* and of a composite State *in foro interno* since the federation is distinguished by the parallel existence of a federal and a republican government organization in a manner and on a scale established under the Constitution and the law.

9. From the standpoint of time, the question is posed differently — were the administrative-territorial boundaries of Bosnia and Herzegovina transformed into borders in the sense of international law, *tractu temporis*, from the moment the "sovereignty and independence" of Bosnia and Herzegovina was proclaimed?

The possibility of such a transformation exists in principle. "Nonborders" can become "borders" in the same way in which "borders" are constituted, that is by agreement or, exceptionally, on the basis of the principle of effectiveness.

Examples of such a transformation are the cases of the Soviet Republics and the Czech Republic and Slovakia. In the Yugoslav case, such a transformation implied two things: first, that a decision on the dissolution of SFRY or a state-legal restructuring had been taken by the highest organ of authority through an appropriate procedure and, second, that in either case, the establishment of Bosnia and Herzegovina as an independent State had been envisaged. The relevant facts imposed such a solution. First, Bosnia and Herzegovina was not an authentic constituent of the Yugoslav State. Such a status was enjoyed, among others, by the peoples of Bosnia and Herzegovina (paras. 48-60 below). Further, being a derivative entity of the constitutional law of Yugoslavia without the right to secession, Bosnia and Herzegovina's existence depended on the existence of Yugoslavia. *Consequently, even under the hypothesis that the dissolution of SFRY had taken place, this would not in itself signify the transformation of Bosnia and Herzegovina into an independent State within its administrative boundaries. Legally, the hypothetical dissolution would necessarily have had to result in the political and legal reconstruc-*

---

[6] The Conference for Peace in Yugoslavia, Arbitration Commission, Opinion No. 3, para. 2 (3). [92 *ILR* 170.]

tion of the space of Bosnia and Herzegovina on the basis of the norm on **[66€**
equal rights and self-determination of peoples.

Bosnia and Herzegovina did not accept the "Concept for the future
organization of the State", proposed by a working group comprising representatives of all the Republics, as a basis for further talks involving the
republican presidents and the State Presidency, which, *inter alia*, included
a "Proposed Procedure for dissociation from Yugoslavia" on the basis of
the self-determination of peoples. This part of the "Concept" which was
drawn up to deal with the constitutional crisis in SFRY in a peaceful and
democratic manner, respecting the relevant norms of international law
and the internal law of SFRY, envisaged a corresponding solution for the
borders as well. On the basis of the draft amendment to the SFRY Constitution, the "Concept" stipulated the obligation of the Federal Government to "*c.* prepare proposals for the territorial demarcation and the
frontiers of the future states and other issues of importance for formulating the enactment on withdrawal"[7].

What remains therefore, is the principle of effectiveness as a possible
basis for the transformation of the administrative-territorial boundaries
of the federal unit of Bosnia and Herzegovina into international borders.
As this principle implies the effective, actual exercise of sovereign authority, and considering the scope of that authority of the central government
in Sarajevo (see para. 18 below), it is beyond doubt that the mentioned
transformation of boundaries on the basis of the principle of effectiveness did not occur.

10. The Arbitration Commission of the Conference on Yugoslavia
whose opinion Bosnia and Herzegovina uses as argument, states with
respect to the relevant question:

> "[e]xcept where otherwise agreed, the former boundaries become
> borders protected by international law. This conclusion follows from
> the principle of respect for the territorial status quo and, in particu-
> lar, from the principle of *uti possidetis* . . . [which] though initially
> applied in settling decolonization issues in America and Africa, is
> today recognized as a general principle, as stated by the Interna-
> tional Court of Justice in its Judgment of 22 December 1986 in the
> case between Burkina Faso and Mali (*Frontier Dispute*, (1986) *I.C.J.
> Reports* 554 at 565):[1]

'Nevertheless the principle is not a special rule which pertains

---

[7] *Focus*, Special Issue, January 1992, p. 33.
[[1] 80 *ILR* 440 at 459.]

667]   solely to one specific system of international law. It is a general
principle, which is logically connected with the phenomenon of
the obtaining of independence, wherever it occurs. Its obvious
purpose is to prevent the independence and stability of the new
States being endangered by fratricidal struggles.'"[8]

Such reasoning is not legally tenable.

First, the phrase "territorial status quo" in this specific case is a *contraditio in adiecto*. It does have a logical and legal sense in the international order, in the mutual relations between States as persons in international law. The territorial status quo in the United Nations system is a terminological substitute for the principle of respecting a State's territorial integrity, and strictly speaking, it refers to States in the sense of international law and not to the integral parts of a federation. *In foro interno*, the "territorial status quo" is of qualified significance for a State's own territorial organization as a matter which falls within the domain of strictly internal jurisdiction *(domaine réservé)*. So, since the creation of Yugoslavia in 1918, the internal administrative territorial boundaries have been drawn three times: first in 1918 within the Kingdom of the Serbs, Croats and Slovenes with a division of the country into 32 regions; next in 1929, in the Kingdom of Yugoslavia, with the organization of nine *Banovinas* as administrative units; and then in the period between 1943 and the early post-war years during the formation of Federal Yugoslavia and its six republics. *Consequently, the expression "territorial status quo" in municipal law can only be considered as a kind of legal metaphor for a rule of national law which would prohibit changing administrative boundaries.*

Second, reference to the Judgment of the International Court of Justice in the *Frontier Dispute* case cannot have effect in this concrete case not only because the relevant part of the Judgment is not cited *in extenso*[9], but also because the meaning of the Judgment as a whole differs significantly.

Outside the colonial context to which the reasoning of the Court applies in the *Frontier Dispute* case, the principle of *uti possidetis* in positive international law can only have the meaning which corresponds to the original meaning of that principle as expressed in the formula *"uti possidetis, ita posideatur"*, i.e., the meaning of the principle of effectiveness.

11. With regard to the qualification of the borders of Bosnia and Herzegovina, it is interesting to examine the "Framework Agreement for the Federation" concluded on 2 March 1994 in Washington. Chapter I (Establishment) of the "Framework Agreement for the Federation" stipulates, *inter alia*, that:

---

[8] The Conference for Peace in Yugoslavia, Arbitration Commission, Opinion No. 3, para. 2 (4). [92 *ILR* 170.]

[9] The part of the Judgment which the Commission has cited ends with the words: *"provoked by the challenging of frontiers following the withdrawal of the administering power"* (para. 20; emphasis added). See paragraphs 19, 20, 23 of the *Frontier Dispute* Judgment, *I.C.J. Reports 1986*, pp. 564-565, 566.

> "Bosniacs and Croats, as constituent peoples (along with others) [668
> and citizens of the Republic of Bosnia and Herzegovina, in the exer-
> cise of their sovereign rights, transform the internal structure of the
> territories with a majority of Bosniac and Croat population in the
> Republic of Bosnia and Herzegovina into a Federation, which is
> composed of federal units with equal rights and responsibilities."

Though the "Framework Agreement" makes no mention of frontiers,
there is no doubt that its contents, in the context of relevant norms of
international law, has definite implications with respect to the borders of
Bosnia and Herzegovina.

The "Framework Agreement" represents a tacit renunciation of the
concept of a unified Bosnia and Herzegovina and thereby of the administrative boundaries of Bosnia and Herzegovina as international frontiers. In particular, it is clear that by this Agreement, the political representatives of the Croat and Muslim peoples in Bosnia and Herzegovina
agreed to constitute a federal State which would have confederal links
with Croatia. The Constitution of the Federation was undoubtedly
derived from the norm of equal rights and self-determination of the Muslim and Croat peoples in Bosnia and Herzegovina even though this norm
is not explicitly mentioned in the Agreement. Such a conclusion is warranted by the qualification that the Federation was constituted on the
basis of "the exercise of sovereign rights . . . [of] Bosniacs and Croats as
constituent peoples". True, the Agreement proceeds from the "sovereignty and territorial integrity of the Republic of Bosnia and Herzegovina" but this syntagm in the context of the relevant facts has more of
a declarative than a material significance. The "Framework Agreement"
defines the territory of Bosnia and Herzegovina as "territories with a
majority of Bosniac and Croat populations in the Republic of Bosnia
and Herzegovina". In relation to the parts of Bosnia and Herzegovina
inhabited by a majority Serb population, the "Framework Agreement" says:

> "[t]he decisions on the constitutional status of the territories of the
> Republic of Bosnia and Herzegovina with a majority of Serbian
> population shall be made in the course of negotiations toward a
> peaceful settlement and at the International Conference on the
> Former Yugoslavia".

It is therefore beyond question that:

(a) the "Framework Agreement" envisages the constitution of a Muslim-Croat Federation on the territory of Bosnia and Herzegovina;
(b) those territories of Bosnia and Herzegovina that are inhabited by a
majority Serb people are left out of the territories of the Federation;
(c) representatives of the Muslim-Croat Federation are acting and are
accepted in international affairs, including international organizations, as representatives of an autonomous, independent State;

669] *(d)* the "Framework Agreement" links the decision on the status of "territories of Bosnia and Herzegovina with a majority Serb population" to the "course of negotiations toward a peaceful settlement and at the International Conference on the Former Yugoslavia". In view of the rules of general international law on the decision-making procedure which, it goes without saying, apply also to the International Conference on the Former Yugoslavia, the conclusion that imposes itself is that the material-legal meaning of the "Framework Agreement" with respect to the borders of Bosnia and Herzegovina is that the Federation, constituted as a result of the will of two out of the three constituent peoples of Bosnia and Herzegovina, renounced the administrative borders of Bosnia and Herzegovina as State borders of the Federation leaving open the possibility of those borders being changed on the basis of decisions taken "in the course of negotiations toward a peaceful settlement and at the International Conference on the Former Yugoslavia".

12. It was the Dayton Agreement which transformed the administrative Boundaries of Bosnia and Herzegovina into international borders. Article 10 of the Agreement stipulates that "[t]he Federal Republic of Yugoslavia and the Republic of Bosnia and Herzegovina recognize each other as sovereign independent States within their international borders".

13. Regardless of theoretical definitions of sovereignty and the distinctions based on them regarding its manifestations, it is evident that the sovereignty of States implies:

(i) *suprema potestas* — "by which is meant that the State has over it no other authority than that of international law"[10]. The equals-mark that is being placed between *suprema potestas* and independence[11] is indicative of a substantial fact — that the entity purporting to be a State in the sense of international public law takes vital political decisions autonomously and independently of third States. A State in the international legal sense cannot and must not comply with alien political decisions regardless of whether such compliance has a formal or informal basis. Therein lies the meaning of the qualification according to which "the first condition for statehood is that there must exist a government actually independent of any other State"[12].

(ii) *summa potestas* — in the sense of the exercise of real, factual authority on the territory of the State. The intention to establish genuine authority is no more than a political project, an intellectual construction that has not materialized. That intention has to be realized and this implies, *inter alia*, the existence of an institutional network suit-

---

[10] *Customs Régime between Germany and Austria, Advisory Opinion, 1931, P.C.I.J., Series A/B, No. 41*, separate opinion of Judge Anzilotti, p. 57. [6 *Ann Dig* 26.]

[11] *Island of Las Palmas* case, *Reports of International Arbitral Awards*, Vol. II, p. 838. [4 *Ann Dig* 103.]

[12] H. Lauterpacht, *Recognition in International Law*, 1949, p. 26.

able for and capable of implementing its decisions throughout the [670
State territory. Hence, *summa potestas* is a mere figure of speech
"until a stable political organisation has been created, and until public authorities become strong enough to assert themselves throughout
the territory of the State"[13].

These two segments of sovereignty constitute an organic whole. As for
their mutual relationship, *summa potestas* has the character of a prior
assumption as, for an entity to constitute an independent State, it is
essential that it should have come into existence as a State — from the
theoretical standpoint *suprema potestas* is the qualifying condition of
existence of an independent State, the *differentia specifica* between independent and dependent States.

14. The question whether Bosnia and Herzegovina had *summa potestas* within the administrative boundaries of Bosnia and Herzegovina
must be linked to a certain time frame. For the purpose of this specific
question, two points in time are relevant:

(a) the moment of the proclamation of a "sovereign and independent
       Bosnia"; and,
(b) the moment at which proceedings were brought against the Federal
       Republic of Yugoslavia before the International Court of Justice.

Did the Applicant at these relevant points in time have a "stable political organization" within the administrative boundaries of Bosnia and
Herzegovina on the one hand and were its "public authorities strong
enough to assert themselves throughout the territory" of Bosnia and
Herzegovina on the other?

15. According to the assertions of the Applicant, Bosnia and Herzegovina was proclaimed a "sovereign and independent Bosnia" on 6 March
1992 when the results of the referendum held on 29 February and
1 March 1992 were officially promulgated. *It is beyond dispute that, at
that point in time, the Applicant did not have a "stable political organization" throughout the territory of Bosnia and Herzegovina nor were
its "public authorities strong enough to assert themselves throughout the
territory" of Bosnia and Herzegovina. More particularly, prior to the
proclamation of "sovereign and independent Bosnia" within the administrative boundaries of Bosnia and Herzegovina two de facto States — the
Republic of Srpska and the Croatian Community of Herceg-Bosna —
had been formed.*

The Croatian Community of Herceg-Bosna was founded on 9 November 1991 (and it was proclaimed an independent State community under
the same name on 4 July 1992), whereas the Republic of the Serb people
of Bosnia and Herzegovina was formed by a Declaration of the Assembly

---

[13] Legal Aspects of the Aaland Island Question, Report of the International Committee
of Jurists, *Official Journal of the League of Nations*, Special Supp. No. 3, p. 3 (1920).

671] of the Serb people issued in January 1992 (it changed its name to the Republic of Srpska on 7 April of the same year[14]).

The common denominator of both units is that they represent the institutionalization of authority in regions in which, in the main, the parties of the Serb and Croatian peoples of Bosnia and Herzegovina won a majority at the first multi-party elections held on 18 and 19 November 1990[15] and under the direct influence of the substantive differences that had emerged among the national parties of the three constituent peoples with respect to the future status of the federal unit of Bosnia and Herzegovina. Those differences appeared in a clear and unambiguous form already at the time of the outbreak of the constitutional crisis in SFRY with the proclamation of the "sovereignty and independence" of the federal units of Slovenia and Croatia, and culminated when the "Platform on the Status of Bosnia and Herzegovina and the Future Set-Up of the Yugoslav Community" was adopted by the then rump Assembly of Bosnia and Herzegovina on 14 October 1991.

The "Platform on the Status of Bosnia and Herzegovina" *inter alia* qualified Bosnia and Herzegovina as a "democratic sovereign State" which would advocate the adoption of a "Convention on the mutual recognition of the sovereignty, inviolability and unchangeability of the borders of the present-day republics"[16].

The practical effect of the "Platform on the Status" was the dissolution of the *state-legal body of the federal unit of Bosnia and Herzegovina*, hence the powers vested in its organs according to the federal Constitution and the Constitution of Bosnia and Herzegovina *via facti* were itself taken over by the three ethnic communities.

16. *(Republika Srpska.)* The Assembly of the Serb people of Bosnia and Herzegovina at its session held on 9 January 1992 adopted a "Declaration on the Proclamation of the Republic of the Serb People of Bosnia and Herzegovina" in the areas

> "of the Serb autonomous regions and areas and other ethnic Serb communities in Bosnia-Herzegovina, including the areas where the Serb people has remained a minority as a result of genocide against it during World War Two and further to the outcome of the plebiscite held on November 9 and 10, 1991 at which the Serb people voted to remain in the common State of Yugoslavia"[17].

---

[14] *Official Gazette of the Socialist Republic of Bosnia and Herzegovina*, No. 42 of 19 December 1991.
[15] *Ibid.*
[16] *Ibid.*, No. 32 of 16 October 1991.
[17] *Official Gazette of the Serb People of Bosnia and Herzegovina*, No. 2/92.

The Declaration stipulated, *inter alia*, that: **[672**

> "[p]ending the election and constitution of new organs and institu-
> tions to be established under the Constitution of the Republic, the
> functions of the State organs in the Republic shall be discharged by
> the present Assembly of the Serb people in Bosnia-Herzegovina and
> by the Council of Ministers" (Art. VI);

and that

> "[t]he federal regulations, along with those of the former Bosnia-
> Herzegovina, except those found by the Serb People's Assembly to
> be contrary to the Federal Constitution, shall remain in force pend-
> ing the promulgation of the Republic's Constitution, its laws and
> other regulations" (Art. VIII).

The Assembly of the Serb People in Bosnia and Herzegovina, at its
session held on 29 February 1992, adopted the "Constitution of the
Republic of Srpska" on the basis of the

> "inalienable and intransferable natural right of the Serb people to
> self-determination, self-organization and association, on the basis of
> which it may freely determine its political status and ensure eco-
> nomic, social and cultural development".

The formal acts were accompanied by the actual assumption of authority in the territories of the communes.

The armed forces of the Republic of Srpska was at first composed of
territorial defence units in the communes and of other armed formations.
The Army of the Republic of Srpska was formed on 13 May 1992[18].

The Army of the Republic of Srpska, from its formation, operated
autonomously as the military force of the proclaimed State. Clear
confirmation of this is to be found in the above-mentioned report of the
Secretary-General:

> "The Bosnia and Herzegovina Presidency had initially been reluc-
> tant to engage in talks . . . with the leadership of the 'Serbian Repub-
> lic of Bosnia and Herzegovina' and insisted upon direct talks with
> the Belgrade authorities instead. A senior Yugoslav Peoples' Army
> (JNA) representative from Belgrade, General Nedeljko Bosković,
> has conducted discussions with the Bosnia and Herzegovina Presi-
> dency, *but it has become clear that his word is not binding on the
> commander of the army of the 'Serb Republic of Bosnia and Herze-
> govina', General Mladić — it is also clear that the emergence of Gen-
> eral Mladić and the forces under his command as independent actors*

---

[18] Report of the Secretary-General pursuant to paragraph 4 of the Security Council
resolution 752/1992, doc. S/24049, 30 May 1992, para. 2.

673]   *beyond the control of JNA* greatly complicates the issues raised in
paragraph 4 of the Security Council Resolution 752 (1992)."[19]

In addition, Republic Srpska had its own legislative, executive and judicial organs.

17. *(Croatian community of Herceg-Bosna.)* Herceg-Bosna, the State of the Croatian people in Bosnia and Herzegovina, was proclaimed on 4 July 1992. With the exception of certain territorial changes, this act only formalized the situation created in November 1991 when the Croatian Community of Herceg-Bosna was created. From the very beginning, this functioned *de facto* as a State.

Herceg-Bosna had its own armed force. The Decree on the armed forces of the Croatian Community of Herceg-Bosna stipulated that the armed forces constitute a unified whole comprising the "regular and reserve forces"[20]. Confirmation of the existence of the autonomous armed forces of Herceg-Bosna is to be found also in the "Report of the Secretary-General pursuant to paragraph 4 of Security Council resolution 752 (1992)" (see para. 18 below). The Government in Sarajevo did not deny this fact either. A letter addressed by Hadzo Efendić as "Acting Prime Minister" to C. Vance and Lord Owen, the Co-Chairmen of the Conference on Former Yugoslavia on 29 April 1993, says *inter alia*:

> "With the purpose of realizing the agreement from item 5 of the Common Statement made by Messrs Alija Izetbegović and Mato Boban at the meeting held in Zagreb on April 24, 1993 . . . we would like to ask you to undertake activities aimed at establishing a separate, independent international commission for establishing the facts on violations of international humanitarian law and war crimes committed over the civilian population *during the renewed conflicts between the Army of the R B-H and HVO in Central Bosnia and some other parts of the Republic of Bosnia and Herzegovina.*"[21]

In addition to its armed forces, Herceg-Bosna had its own executive, legislative and judicial organs.

Supreme authority was vested in the Presidency, composed of representatives of the Croat people in Bosnia and Herzegovina, headed by the President of the Presidency. The Croatian representatives withdrew from the joint organs of the Applicant and moved to Mostar which was pro

---

[19] Doc. S/2409, 30 May 1992, paras. 8-9 (emphasis added).

[20] *Borba*, Belgrade, 6 July 1992.

[21] Letter dated 29 April 1993 from Acting Prime Minister Hadzo Efendić addressed to "Cyrus Vance, Lord David Owen, Co-chairmen of The Conference on Former Yugoslavia".

claimed the capital of the State[22]. Herceg-Bosna appropriated all the **[674**
matériel of JNA as well as all the property of the organs and bodies of
the former federation. Public, State enterprises were formed in the sectors
of agriculture, forestry and mining, the Post, Telegram and Telephone
Service (PTT) and publishing[23].

It was determined that the Law on Regular Courts would be applied
even under conditions of war, and military tribunals were set up in the
zones of military operations, as autonomous departments of the main
military tribunals.

18. In my opinion there can be no doubt that at the moment of the
proclamation of "sovereign and independent Bosnia" the authorities in
Sarajevo which had been recognized by the international community as
the authorities of the whole of Bosnia and Herzegovina did not by a long
way exercise *summa potestas* on the territories within the administrative
demarcation lines of the federal unit of Bosnia and Herzegovina.

A "[s]table political organization of sovereign and independent
Bosnia" simply did not exist at either of the relevant points in time. What
is more, even *before the proclamation of Bosnia and Herzegovina as a
"sovereign and independent" State, the unified administrative, judicial and
legislative apparatus of the federal unit of Bosnia and Herzegovina had
ceased to function. It follows from the relevant facts that the proclamation of the Republic of the Serb People and of the Croatian Community of
Herceg-Bosna merely formalized the dissolution of the state apparatus of
the federal unit of Bosnia and Herzegovina and its replacement by the
appropriate structures of the three ethnic communities.* That process
embraced both the civilian and military structures of authority. This is
evidenced also in the Report of the Secretary-General pursuant to paragraph 4 of Security Council resolution 752 (1992). In paragraphs 5 and
10 the Report refers to the existence of "the army of the so-called 'Serbian Republic of Bosnia and Herzegovina'", and the "territorial Defence
of Bosnia and Herzegovina which is under the political control of the
Presidency of that Republic" and "local [Croat] Territorial Defence".
The "[s]table political organization of sovereign and independent Bosnia", was not created even after the proclamation of independence so
that it is obvious that the organs of the Applicant were not "strong
enough to assert themselves throughout the territory" of Bosnia and
Herzegovina.

This obvious fact is confirmed also in the "Report on the situation of
human rights in the territory of the former Yugoslavia submitted by
Mr. T. Mazowiecki, Special Rapporteur of the Commission on Human

---

[22] Letter from the President of the Government of the Republic of Bosnia-Herzegovina
to the Secretary-General of the United Nations, 13 May 1993.
[23] *Borba*, Belgrade, 6 July 1992.

675] Rights, pursuant to paragraph 14 of Commission Resolution 1992/S-1/1 of August 1992". The "Report" states, *inter alia*, that

"[m]uch of the territory of Bosnia and Herzegovina is not under the control of the recognized Government. Most observers agree that the Serbian Republic of Bosnia and Herzegovina, an unrecognized government proclaimed *when* Bosnia and Herzegovina declared its independence from Yugoslavia against the wishes of the Serbian population, controls between 50 and 70 per cent of the territory . . . It ['Serbian Republic of Bosnia and Herzegovina'] is comprised of four 'autonomous regions', one of which, Banja Luka, was visited by the Special Rapporteur.

According to the information received, the law applied within the 'Serbian Republic of Bosnia and Herzegovina' is the law of the Federal Republic of Yugoslavia, as modified by the local legislatures." [24]

All that needs to be added is that the "Serbian Republic of Bosnia and Herzegovina" was not proclaimed "when Bosnia and Herzegovina declared its independence" since the "Serbian Republic of Bosnia and Herzegovina" was proclaimed on 9 January 1992 while the rump Parliament of Bosnia and Herzegovina proclaimed the independence of Bosnia and Herzegovina on 6 March of the same year.

The "Report of the Secretary-General pursuant to paragraph 4 of Security Council resolution 752 (1992)" states that:

"International observers do not, however, doubt that portions of Bosnia and Herzegovina are under the control of Croatian military units, whether belonging to the local Territorial Defence, to paramilitary groups or to the Croatian Army." [25]

This in fact refers to the territories of the communes comprising the Croatian Community of Herceg-Bosna formed on 9 November 1991, that is before the proclamation of "sovereign and independent Bosnia".

The territory within which the organs of the Applicant exercised real, effective authority comprised in fact:

"Three separate regions are under the control of the Government of Bosnia and Herzegovina, namely, part of the capital, Sarajevo; the region known as Bihac, adjacent to the border with Croatia in North-West Bosnia, and parts of central Bosnia and Herzegovina." [26]

---

[24] Doc. E/CN.4/1992/S-1/9, 9.18 (emphasis added).

[25] Doc. S/24049, p. 4, para. 10.

[26] Report on the human rights in the territory of the former Yugoslavia, submitted by Mr. T. Mazowiecki, Special Rapporteur of the Commission on Human Rights, pursuant to paragraph 14 of Commission Resolution 1992/S-1/1 of 14 August 1992, doc. E/CN.4/1992/S-1/9, p. 18.

19. *The timing of the constitution of the Republic of Srpska and of* [676
*Herceg-Bosna, on the one hand, and of the Applicant State, on the other,
points to the conclusion that the constitution of the Republic of Srpska
and of Herceg-Bosna cannot be qualified as armed rebellion against the
central authority, as there simply was no central authority at the time, but
only as the emergence of several States in the circumstance of the constitutional and State crisis of the Yugoslav federation.*

The assumed existence of a Muslim-Croat central authority in Bosnia
and Herzegovina had no factual grounds from the very beginning of the
crisis as convincingly evidenced by the war that broke out between Croat
and Muslim forces in 1993. In a letter addressed to the Chairman of the
European Affairs Subcommittee of the Senate Foreign Affairs Committee of the United States of America, on 24 February 1993, the Prime
Minister of Bosnia and Herzegovina, the Croatian representative in the
joint Croat-Muslim Government, M. Akmadzić, described Mr. Izetbegović and Mr. Silajdzić "only as one Muslim member of the Presidency"
(see para. 37 below). Indicative of the situation in the joint Croat-Muslim
Government in Bosnia and Herzegovina is the letter of the Prime Minister addressed to the Secretary-General of the United Nations on 7 May
1993 which says, *inter alia*:

"*On 7 May 1993 I was informed by public media that Mr. Hadzo
Efendić sent Your Excellency a letter in the capacity of Acting Prime
Minister.*

Therefore, I would like to inform Your Excellency that *Mr. Hadzo
Efendić was not elected as a member of the Government*, nor as Vice-
President of the Government and especially was not elected as Acting President of the Government of the Republic of Bosnia-Herzegovina. Mr. Hadzo Efendić was not elected based upon my proposal.
This is the only legal course of election that is in accordance with the
valid acts and regulations of the Republic of Bosnia-Herzegovina.

I am informing Your Excellency that *no individual can sign documents of the Government of the Republic of Bosnia-Herzegovina in
the capacity of the President of the Government other than myself.*
As a result of this, *I request Your Excellency not to consider any
document of the President of the Government of the Republic of
Bosnia-Herzegovina as valid unless it is signed by myself.*

My office is temporarily in Mostar where I am performing my
duties as President of the Government of the Republic of Bosnia-
Herzegovina." [27]

Therefore, in the territory of Bosnia and Herzegovina in the relevant
period the following institutions were functioning:

---

[27] Letter dated 7 May 1993 addressed to "United Nations Secretary-General, His
Excellency Dr. Boutros-Boutros Ghali from Milo Akmadzić, President of the Government of the Republic of Bosnia-Herzegovina" (emphasis added).

677] *(a)* the State organs of the so-called central authorities (Croat-Muslim alliance), which formally collapsed with the outbreak of the armed conflict between the Muslims and the Croats and was transformed into Muslim authority. The latter then split up in September 1993 into the Government in Sarajevo and the authorities of the Autonomous Province of Western Bosnia;

(b) the State organs of the Republic of Srpska;

(c) the State organs of Herceg-Bosna; and

(d) as of March 1994, also the State organs of the newly formed Federation which, however, functioned only on paper.

20. Mr. Jadranko Prlić, Prime Minister of the Croatia Republic of Herceg-Bosna and Hercegovina, testified to the fact that the promotion of Croat-Muslim Federation in Bosnia and Herzegovina was a mere proclamation. In an interview given to the *Slobodna Dalmacija* daily newspaper of 18 December 1995, answering the question about the functions of the Minister of Defence in the Government of the Federation and the Republic, Mr. Prlić, who initialled the Dayton Treaties on behalf of the Croat-Muslim Federation, replied as follows:

> "it should be said that *all the time two states and two armies were in existence*. But, there was a certain form of coordination and a result was achieved, primarily thanks to the support of the Croat army and Croat state"[28].

When asked until when Herceg-Bosna would function he replied as follows:

> "No deadline could be set. That will depend on the overall process. When all the rights of the Croat people are ensured and then the Federation becomes capable of taking over those functions that Herceg-Bosna has, then Herceg-Bosna will be reshaped, probably into a political community."[29]

The words of the Croat President Tudjman, one of the participants in the Dayton Conference, imply that revival of the Federation was one of the aims of the Conference. In the Report on the state of the Croatian State and Nations in 1995, Mr. Tudjman mentioned, *inter alia*, that:

> "The international proponents attach special significance to the Federation, within their concept of peace and new order in this area, as testified by the fact that *the Agreement on implementation of B-H Federation*, signed by the representatives of Croatian and Muslim-

---

[28] *Slobodna Dalmacija*, Split, 18 December 1995 (emphasis added).
[29] *Ibid.*

Boshniak people, was endorsed by representatives of USA, Euro- **[678** pean Union and Germany."[30]

It seems that only the Dayton Agreement and the political will that gave birth to them, encouraged serious steps towards actual constitution of the Muslim-Croat Federation.

On 14 January 1996, a couple of months after the signing of the Dayton Agreement and almost two years after the proclamation of the Croat-Muslim Federation, the "Presidency of the Croatian Democratic Union for B-H" adopted a decision on the establishment of the Croatian community of Herceg-Bosna as a political, economic and cultural community of Croatian people in Bosnia and Herzegovina. *Within its option for a thorough implementation of the Dayton Agreement*, the Presidency of the Croat Democratic Community (HDZ) of Bosnia and Herzegovina also passed a resolution on the progressive transfer of the function of executive authority of the Croatian Republic of Herceg-Bosna to the authorities of the Federation of Bosnia and Herzegovina. Members of the HDZ Presidency of Bosnia and Herzegovina also called on *the Muslim counterpart in the Federation to start transferring the authority to the organs of the Federation*[31].

The Government of the Federation was established as late as 31 January 1996. President of the Federation Mr. K. Zubak, in his address to the Constitutional Assembly stressed, *inter alia*, that *"by transferring authority from the Republic to the Government of the Federation the functions of Herceg-Bosna will be transferred to the Federation"*[32].

As *Le Monde* reported:

"The Croat separatists in Bosnia announced on Saturday 15 June that they were forming a new government for their 'independent State of Herzeg-Bosna'. In principle, all the institutions of this self-proclaimed State should have disappeared with the advent of the institutions of the Croat-Muslim Federation."[33]

Hence, the political project of promotion of Muslim-Croat Federation in Bosnia and Herzegovina, incorporated in the Washington Agreement of 1993, has not materialized. Muslim and Croat State entities continued to function after the agreement as *de facto* States, which from time to time kept entering into a sort of political and military co-ordination for the sake of pragmatic political aims. But that co-operation was, according to its inherent characteristics, a co-operation between State entities.

---

[30] *Vjesnik*, Zagreb, 2 January 1996 (emphasis added).
[31] *Vecernji List*, Zagreb, 15 January 1996.
[32] *Borba*, Belgrade, 1 February 1996 (emphasis added).
[33] *Le Monde*, Tuesday 18 June 1996/3. *[Translation by the Registry.]*

[679]   *In the light of the Dayton Agreement, promotion of the Federation is a political and contractual obligation, thus in view of the present state of affairs, it could be said that the Federation is a State entity* in statu nascendi.

The qualification "self-proclaimed" which is usually attached to the Republic of Srpska and Herceg-Bosna can hardly have any legal effect. According to its original, grammatical meaning, it denotes the obvious fact that no-one can "proclaim" a newly emerging State except itself — in that sense every newly emerging State is "self-proclaimed". The heart of the matter is therefore, not whether a new State is "self-proclaimed" or is proclaimed by a second or third party, but whether the proclamation is based on fact and the law.

This qualification can have legal meaning only within the reasoning of constitutive theory on the recognition of States as a condition of their emergence or in the neoconstitutive practice of the application of the ruling, declarative theory.

21. Bosnia and Herzegovina as a State within the administrative borders of the former federal administrative unit, bearing the name of the former federal unit, could only be discussed, so to speak, after the enforcement of the Dayton Agreements. A precise qualification of Bosnia and Herzegovina in these terms may be given only after a global analysis of the contents of the above-mentioned Agreements.

22. The "Dayton Agreements" as a collective name for a series of agreements, are endowed with ambivalent legal faculties.

In formal terms, the fundamental part of the Agreements should be the General Framework Agreement for Peace in Bosnia and Herzegovina. Such a conclusion is imposed by the fact that other agreements were qualified as annexes to the General Framework Agreement (Agreement on the Military Aspects of the Peace Settlement; Agreement on Regional Stabilization; Agreement on Inter-Entity Boundary Line and Related Issues; Agreement on Elections; Agreement on Arbitration; Agreement on Human Rights; Agreement on Refugees and Displaced Persons; Agreement on the Commission to Preserve National Monuments; Agreement on the Establishment of Bosnia and Herzegovina Public Corporations; Agreement on Civilian Implementation; Agreement on International Police Task Force), with the exception of the Agreement on Initialling the General Framework Agreement for Peace in Bosnia and Herzegovina. The contents of the General Framework Agreement, on the one hand, and the rest of the Agreements, drawn up in the form of annexes, on the other, suggest that the main commitments conducive to a comprehensive settlement to bring an end to the tragic conflict in the region, as stated in the General Framework Agreement, are contained in those annexes.

The General Framework Agreement, by its nature, is a specific combination of elements of political declarations and elements relative to guarantees which resemble an international treaty, *stricto sensu*, conceived as an act creating reciprocal rights and obligations of the parties thereto. The elements characteristic of political declarations are reflected in

the provisions in a series of the General Framework Agreement **[680**
Articles (Arts. II, III, IV, V, VI, VII and IX) whereby the parties only wel-
come and endorse arrangements stipulated in the Annexes to the General
Framework Agreement. The only Articles of the General Framework
Agreement binding on the parties in a way suitable to international
treaties, *stricto sensu*, are Articles I and VII. True, most of the Articles
mentioned above include a standard form of words providing that
"[t]he parties shall fully respect and promote fulfilment of the commitments made" but the meaning of such a wording, in terms of the contents of
Article I of the General Framework Agreement and the nature of those
commitments is, at least when SFY and Croatia are referred to, more of a
sort of a guarantee that the parties to the Agreements, specified as Annexes,
will implement the undertakings, rather than constituting a binding obligation. Particularly significant in that regard, apart from the above-mentioned
standard wording in the Annexes, is the Agreement on Initialling the General Framework Agreement for Peace in Bosnia and Herzegovina. By that
Agreement, which is not formally an annex to the General Framework
Agreement, "[t]he Parties [the Republic of Bosnia and Herzegovina, the
Republic of Croatia and the Federal Republic of Yugoslavia], and the Entities that they represent, commit themselves to signature of these Agreements" (Art. I). It provides that the very implementation of the General
Framework Agreement and its Annexes is to be entrusted to the Joint
Interim Commission composed of representatives of the Bosnia and Herzegovina Federation, Republic Srpska, Bosnia-Herzegovina Republic. The
position of the Bosnia-Herzegovina Republic, as a contracting party, is specific in this context, as the Republic of Bosnia and Herzegovina, by virtue
of Article I (3) of the Constitution "*shall* consist of the two Entities, the
Federation of Bosnia and Herzegovina and the Republic Srpska (hereinafter 'the Entities')" (emphasis added). Hence the entities figuring in the
structure of the Dayton Agreements, in Annex 4 to the Agreements, are the
parties; therefore, in the light of relevant conditions for constitution of the
Bosnia-Herzegovina Republic as a State within the administrative borders
of that former federal unit, it follows that the Bosnia-Herzegovina Republic
guarantees the obligations of the entities to constitute it. This discrepancy
results from the premise of an unbroken legal personality of Bosnia and
Herzegovina under international law as a State — which is of dubious legal
validity (see para. 23 below).

Hence it may be said that the Annexes constitute the essential substance of the Dayton Agreements, while the General Framework Agreement, as implied by its very name, constitutes a legal-political framework
integrating the regulatory contents of the Annexes. The parties to the
"General Framework Agreement" are, as stated in the Preamble, "[t]he
Republic of Bosnia and Herzegovina, the Republic of Croatia and the
Federal Republic of Yugoslavia". The parties to the Agreement's Annexes
are, however, different. The Republic of Bosnia and Herzegovina, the
Federation of Bosnia and Herzegovina and the Republic of Srpska are,
either alone or together with Croatia and Yugoslavia, parties to most of

681] the Annexes. The three aforementioned parties signed the Agreement on the Military Aspects of the Peace Settlement; Agreement on Inter-Entity Boundary Line and Related Issues; Agreement on Elections; Agreement on Refugees and Displaced Persons; Agreement on Commission to Preserve National Monuments; and Agreement on International Police Task Force. Together with the Republic of Croatia and the Federal Republic of Yugoslavia, the three parties figure as parties to the Agreement on Regional Stabilization and the Agreement on Civilian Implementation of the Peace Settlement. The Federation of Bosnia and Herzegovina and the Republic of Srpska are parties to the Agreement on Establishment of Bosnia and Herzegovina Public Corporations and the Agreement on Arbitration. The Constitution of the Republic of Bosnia and Herzegovina is also an integral part of the Dayton Agreements. It is designed in the form of Annex 4 of the Agreement and is approved by respective declarations of the Republic of Bosnia and Herzegovina, the Federation of Bosnia and Herzegovina and the Republic Srpska.

23. *In the light of the contents of the Dayton Agreements and in particular in the light of the current state of affairs, Bosnia and Herzegovina may be qualified in terms of international law as a State* in statu nascendi. At the time of the entry into force of the Dayton Agreements, the Republic of Bosnia and Herzegovina, as a State within the administrative borders of the former Yugoslav federal unit of the same name, possessed literally no relevant attribute of a State in terms of international law. More particularly:

(a) The Republic of Bosnia and Herzegovina has no central State authorities to this day. Annex 4 (Constitution of Bosnia and Herzegovina) to the Dayton Agreements stipulates in Articles IV, V, VI and VII joint authorities in the form of a Parliamentary Assembly, a Presidency, a Council of Ministers, a Constitutional Court and a Central Bank, but the Constitution is conditioned upon "free, fair, and democratic elections" as a basis for a representative government[34]. In keeping with the provision of Article 4 of "Transitional Arrangements", joined in the form of Annex II to the Constitution, "[u]ntil superseded by applicable agreement or law, governmental offices, institutions, and other bodies of Bosnia and Herzegovina will operate in accordance with applicable law"[35]. Systematically interpreted, the above-mentioned provision implies that governmental offices, institutions and other bodies of the entities in the territory of Bosnia and Herzegovina "will operate in accordance with applicable law";

(b) The Republic of Bosnia and Herzegovina up to the present time has possessed no coherent legislation of its own. True, the Constitution of the Republic as a supreme legal act has come into force but

---

[34] Preamble of the Agreement on Elections, doc. A/50/790-S/1995/999, p. 53.
[35] *Ibid.*, p. 76.

"[a]ll laws, regulations and judicial rules of procedure in effect **[682**
within the territory of Bosnia and Herzegovina when the Constitution enters into force shall remain in effect to the extent not
inconsistent with the Constitution, until otherwise determined by
a competent governmental body of Bosnia and Herzegovina"[36];

(c) The Republic of Bosnia and Herzegovina has no single judicial system or administrative procedure. This fact is also formally endorsed
by Article 3 of the "Transitional Arrangements", which states:

"[a]ll proceedings in courts or administrative agencies functioning
within the territory of Bosnia and Herzegovina when the Constitution enters into force shall continue in or be transferred to other
courts or agencies in Bosnia and Herzegovina in accordance with
any legislation governing the competence of such courts or
agencies"[37];

(d) The Republic of Bosnia and Herzegovina has no armed force of its
own. Moreover, a joint army is not an institution of a central
authority, since it does not figure as one of the responsibilities of the
Peace Settlement and the Agreement on Regional Stabilization,
which are relevant in this matter. By their wording and their content
they resemble the agreements among sovereign, independent States
on confidence and security building measures, rather than agreements among entities within one State. The main purpose of the
obligations entered into under the Agreement on the Military
Aspects of the Peace Settlement relate to the establishment of a
durable cessation of hostilities, which implies that

"[n]either Entity shall threaten or use force against the other
Entity, and under no circumstances shall any armed forces of
either Entity enter into or stay within the territory of the other
Entity without the consent of the government of the latter and of
the Presidency of Bosnia and Herzegovina"

and that "lasting security and arms control measures . . . . which aim
to promote a permanent reconciliation between all Parties" are to be
established[38]. The Agreement on Regional Stabilization, however,
provided for a general obligation of establishment of progressive
measures for regional stability and arms control by achieving balances and stable defence force levels at the constant numbers consistent with the parties' respective security and the need to avoid an
arms race in the region[39];

---

[36] Doc. A/50/790-S/1995/999, Transitional Arrangements, Art. 2, p. 76.
[37] *Ibid.*, Art. 3.
[38] *Ibid.*, Art. I (2) *(a)*, *(c)*, p. 8.
[39] *Ibid.*, p. 2.

683] *(e)* The Republic of Bosnia and Herzegovina does not have its own police force. The competence of the police forces of the entities is limited *ratione loci*. Only the International Police Task Force, established under the corresponding Agreement marked as Annex 11, is authorized, in keeping with its tasks laid down in Article III of the Agreement, to act throughout the Republic of Bosnia and Herzegovina.

Of the relevant conditions for statehood of Bosnia and Herzegovina within its administrative borders, only the condition concerning the contractually determined administrative borders of Bosnia and Herzegovina as the internationally recognized ones, has been fully met[40].

24. *In the light of the foregoing it may be said that the relevant factual and legal status of Bosnia and Herzegovina as a State within the administrative borders of the same ex-federal unit, may be defined as a political project of the organized international community, whose materialization was transformed by the Dayton Agreements into a binding obligation of the parties to the Agreements.* The fact that this is more a contractual obligation to establish Bosnia and Herzegovina as a State than a consecration of the current state of affairs is testified to by the nature of the Constitution of the Republic of Bosnia and Herzegovina. As it stands, it is not, *stricto sensu*, a constitution, that is, an act of the internal constitution-making authority, but is an international treaty incorporating the text of the Constitution. The term "party" denotes a State which has consented to be bound by the treaty and for which the treaty is in force[41]. By virtue of Article 2 *(a)* of the Convention on the Law of Treaties,

> "'treaty' means an international agreement concluded between States in written form and governed by international law, whether embodied in a single instrument or in two or more related instruments and whatever its particular designation".

In other words, underlying the title "Constitution of Bosnia and Herzegovina" is a treaty of two State entities — the Federation of Bosnia and Herzegovina and the Republika Srpska — to establish a State within the administrative borders of the former federal unit of Bosnia and Herzegovina, since "[e]very State possesses capacity to conclude treaties"[42].

Moreover, the personality of one of the parties — the Federation of Bosnia and Herzegovina — possesses elements of political fiction that considerably outweigh the real attributes of statehood (see para. 19 above). Hence, in a broader context, the global contractual obligation to establish Bosnia and Herzegovina within its administrative borders also covers the materialization of a separate contractual obligation undertaken by

---

[40] Article X of the General Framework Agreement for Peace in Bosnia and Herzegovina.
[41] Convention on the Law of Treaties, 1969, Art. 2 (9).
[42] *Ibid.*, Art. 6.

the Croat and Muslim state entities in Bosnia and Herzegovina under **[684**
the Washington agreement — the obligation to form the Federation of
Bosnia and Herzegovina.

At present, an absence of the crucial State elements in terms of international law makes Bosnia and Herzegovina within its administrative borders a State sui generis: *a combination of a contractual relationship of two entities with a strongly installed element of an international protectorate.* This status is expressed at two levels, that is

(a) the factual level, as reflected in the position of IFOR. These forces are, by definition, a "multinational military Implementation Force"[43] deployed to Bosnia and Herzegovina to "help ensure compliance with the provisions of this Agreement"[44]. IFOR is not only one armed force which shall "have complete and unimpeded freedom of movement by ground, air, and water throughout Bosnia and Herzegovina"[45] but is even authorized to "take such actions as required, including the use of necessary force, to ensure compliance with this Annex, and to ensure its own protection"[46];

(b) the legal level, since particularly relevant provisions of Article VI of the Constitution of Bosnia and Herzegovina (Constitutional Court), which is an inherently adjudicative body which has "exclusive jurisdiction to decide any dispute that arises under this Constitution between the Entities or between Bosnia and Herzegovina and an Entity or Entities, or between institutions of Bosnia and Herzegovina"[47]. Paragraph 1 of the above-mentioned Article provides for the composition of the Court in the following way:

> "The Constitutional Court of Bosnia and Herzegovina shall have nine members.
>
> *(a)* Four members shall be selected by the House of Representatives of the Federation, and two members by the Assembly of the Republika Srpska. The remaining three members shall be selected by the President of the European Court of Human Rights after consultation with the Presidency."[48]

It is, therefore, beyond any doubt that the election of one-third of the members of the court is not in any way influenced by the Presidency of the Republic of Bosnia and Herzegovina or by any other organ of the

---

[43] Article 1 of the Agreement on the Military Aspects of the Peace Settlement, doc. A/50/790/S/1995/999, p. 7.
[44] *Ibid.*
[45] *Ibid.*, p. 19.
[46] *Ibid.*, p. 8.
[47] *Ibid.*, p. 71.
[48] *Ibid.*, p. 70.

685] Republic or Entities, in practical terms, given the fact that consultation *per definitionem* has no binding force.

The provisions relating to the competence of the International Police Task Force can be mentioned among others. The competences of these forces cover, *inter alia*, the "monitoring, observing and inspecting [of] law enforcement activities and facilities, including associated judicial organizations, structures, and proceedings"[49]. The real range of these powers in the context of *suprema potestas* of the Republic of Bosnia and Herzegovina becomes clear in view of the provisions of Article VII of the Agreement which defines law enforcement agencies as those involved in law enforcement, criminal investigations, public and State security, or detention or judicial activities[50].

The elements of international protectorate moreover possess a twofold significance. On the one hand, they are, especially when the composition of the Constitutional Court is concerned, an integral part of the State structure of Bosnia and Herzegovina, construed by the Dayton Agreements, while on the other, they serve to guarantee enforcement obligations entered into by the entities under the agreements.

25. There is an essential analogy between the Republic of Bosnia and Herzegovina and Finland after its proclamation of independence on 4 December 1917. Since the Permanent Court of International Justice did not exist at the time, an opinion on the status of Finland was requested of the International Committee of Jurists. In its Report the Committee noted, *inter alia*, that:

> "Certain elements essential to the existence of a state, even some elements of fact, were lacking for a fairly considerable period. Political and social life was disorganized; the authorities were not strong enough to assert themselves, civil war was rife; further the Diet, the legality of which had been disputed by a large section of the people, had been dispersed by the revolutionary party . . . the armed camps and the police were divided into two opposing forces . . . It is, therefore, difficult to say at what exact date the Finnish Republic, in the legal sense of the term, actually became a definitely constituted sovereign state. This certainly did not take place until stable political organization had been created, and until the public authorities had become strong enough to assert themselves throughout the territories of the state without the assistance of foreign troops."[51]

As Warren Christopher, the United States Secretary of State, noted:

---

[49] Article III.1 *(a)* of the Agreement on International Police Task Force, doc. A/50/790/S/1995/999, p. 118.

[50] *Ibid.*, Art. VII, p. 120.

[51] Report by the International Committee of Jurists (Larnoude (President), Struycken, Huber), *Official Journal of the League of Nations*, Spec. Supp. No. 3 (1920), p. 8.

"Without elections, there will be no unified Bosnia state, no **[686** national constitution or judiciary and little hope for greater coopera-tion among Bosnia's diverse communities." [52]

26. The recognition of Bosnia and Herzegovina is frequently, explicitly or implicitly, used as an argument in support of the existence of Bosnia and Herzegovina as a sovereign and independent State within the admin-istrative boundaries of the former Yugoslav federal unit.

Such an approach is somewhat surprising, since "the State exists by itself *(par lui-même)* and the recognition of a State is nothing else than a declaration of this existence, recognized by the States from which it ema-nates" [53].

This is specially so, having in mind that "the practice of States shows that the act of recognition is still regarded as essentially a political deci-sion, *which each State decides in accordance with its own free apprecia-tion of the situation*" [54].

It is reasonable to suppose that, merely by relying on these facts, the learned scholar is able to conclude that "[r]ecognition is still in the lan-guage of diplomats but it does not belong to the language of law" [55].

It is true that the position of Bosnia and Herzegovina is a specific one, since it has been recognized by practically the whole international com-munity. This fact serves as the basis for the thesis that

"recognition, along with membership of international organizations, bears witness to these States' conviction that the political entity so recognized is a reality and confers on it certain rights and obliga-tions under international law" [56].

This, in doctrinal terms, elegant thesis highlights among other things, the ambivalent nature of the institute of recognition of States. In the spirit of the ruling, declarative theory, the recognition of States should be a statement of the factual situation formed *leges artis* in harmony with the relevant legal rules on the emergence of new States. The "States' con-viction that the political entity . . . is a reality" clearly need not corre-spond to the factual situation. "Conviction", *per definitionem*, is not a

---

[52] "Without Elections, There Will Be No Unified Bosnian State", *International Herald Tribune*, 15-16 June 1996, p. 6.
[53] Deutsche Continental Gas-Gesselschaft *v.* Polish State, 5 AD 11 at p. 15 (1929-1930).
[54] United Nations Secretariat Memorandum of February 1950 concerning the question of representation of Members in the United Nations, United Nations doc. S/1466, *SCOR*, 5th Year, Supp. for Jan./May 1950, p. 19.

[55] L. Henkin, "General Course on Public International Law", *Recueil des cours de l'Académie de droit international de La Haye,* Vol. 216, 1989, p. 31.
[56] Statement of the Government of the Republic of Bosnia and Herzegovina on Pre-liminary Objections, para. 4.14.

[687] factual condition but its subjective expression — hence it is necessary *ad casum* to carry out an investigation so as to establish the precise meaning of the phrase "States' conviction" and to see whether or not it is based on fact or law. *A contrario*, the whole problem would be shifted to the domain of the rule of "majority opinion", so that fact would be what the majority considers it to be.

Having that in mind, it is, generally speaking, necessary from the standpoint of law to examine in each individual case whether the relevant legal criteria for recognition are met.

Concerning Bosnia and Herzegovina, it is obvious that, as an assumed State in the administrative boundaries of that former Yugoslav federal unit, it could be ranked among the circle of States only as a new State. Hence, it is necessary to see which criteria are relevant for the recognition of new States.

The essence of those criteria may be taken to be expressed in paragraph 100 (Minimum Requirements for Recognition of New States) of the *Restatement of the Law*:

> "Before recognizing an entity as a new state, the recognizing state is required to make a determination, reasonably based upon fact, that the entity:
>
> *(a)* has a defined territory and population;
> *(b)* is under the control of a regime that satisfies the minimum requirements for recognition as a government under [paragraph] 101;
> *(c)* has the capacity to engage in foreign relations;
> *(d)* shows reasonable indications that the requirements of Clauses *(a)-(c)* will continue to be satisfied."[57]

Paragraph 101 stipulates:

> "Before recognizing a revolutionary regime as a government of a state, the recognizing state is required to make a determination, reasonably based upon fact, that the regime
>
> *(a)* is in control of the territory and population of the state; or
> *(b)* is in control of a substantial part of the territory and population of the state and shows reasonable promise that it will succeed in displacing the previous government in the territory of the state."[58]

The cited criteria are, as a whole, applicable to the case of Bosnia and Herzegovina. In such an assessment, it is decisive that

---

[57] American Law Institute, *Restatement of the Law, Second, Foreign Relations Law of the United States*, 1965, p. 321.
[58] *Ibid.*, p. 322.

"Recognition of a government becomes a problem for decision **[688**
only if an abnormal change of government is involved, i.e., one in
violation of the existing constitution of a state." [59]

Bosnia and Herzegovina did not meet the relevant criteria for recognition
in the static or dynamic sense. More particularly, at the time of recognition, not only did it not have a "defined territory and population" (see
paras. 6-9 above) nor, in particular, "control of a substantial part of
the territory and population" (see para. 18 above) but there were no
"reasonable indications" that it could fulfil those requirements in the
future without active external support. Even Bosnia and Herzegovina
itself in the "Second Request for Indication of Provisional Measures of
Protection" of 27 July 1993 notes at the end of its submission: "[t]his will
be the last opportunity that this Court shall have to save . . . [the] State
of Bosnia and Herzegovina" (p. 55). The "Minimum Requirements for
the Recognition of New States", as presented, should definitely be
complemented with legal requirements as well since "the development of
self-determination [is] an additional criterion of statehood, denial of
which" would obviate statehood [60].

These additional criteria strengthen the grounds for the conclusion
that the recognition of Bosnia and Herzegovina was granted on an exclusively political basis. Also, the "Guidelines on the recognition of new
States in Eastern Europe and in the Soviet Union", on the basis of which
Bosnia and Herzegovina was recognized by the European Community
and its member States, and the discussions in the United Nations Organization at the time of the admission of Bosnia and Herzegovina, indicate
that in the realm of law, recognition was granted on the grounds of the
right of peoples to self-determination even though, in this particular case,
its application is at the very least doubtful (see paras. 44-76 below).
    In other words, the recognition of Bosnia and Herzegovina as an inde-
pendent State was inspired more by the interests of national politics and
opportuneness than by the existence of relevant legal principles in regard
to this matter. The recognition of Bosnia and Herzegovina was, essentially, one of the instruments for the realization of the political concept
on the settlement of the Yugoslav crisis, an instrument which reflected
the internal logic of that concept independently of the relevant legal rules.
The instrumental nature of the recognition in the Yugoslav case was
pointed out by Ambassador Brown:

    "Lord Carrington, who chaired the Conference on Yugoslavia . . .
    believed that recognition was an important weapon in bringing the

---

[59] American Law Institute, *Restatement of the Law, Second, Foreign Relations Law of
the United States*, p. 323.
[60] M. N. Shaw, *International Law*, 2nd ed., 1986, p. 132.

689] sides together. Recognition could be an incentive for cooperation or a sanction for lack of cooperation." [61]

This is particularly conspicuous in the "Declaration on Yugoslavia" of 16 December 1991 which together with the "Guidelines on the recognition of new States in Eastern Europe and the Soviet Union", passed on the same day by the EC Ministerial Council, served as a basis for the recognition of Bosnia and Herzegovina by the European Community and its member States.

By their Declaration, the EC and its member States invited

> *"all Yugoslav Republics to state by 23 December whether:*
> — *they wish to be recognized as independent States;*
> — they accept the commitments contained in the above-mentioned guidelines;
> — *they accept the provisions laid down in the Draft Convention —* especially those in Chapter II on human rights and rights of national or ethnic groups — *under consideration by the Conference on Yugoslavia."* [62]

Bosnia and Herzegovina therefore, together with the other federal units of SFRY, *was invited to state whether it wished to be recognized as an independent State.* The invitation was made at a time when the desire for independence had still not been expressed in the appropriate way in Bosnia and Herzegovina. The referendum on the status of Bosnia and Herzegovina at which two out of the three peoples of Bosnia and Herzegovina declared themselves in favour of the "sovereignty and independence of Bosnia and Herzegovina" was not held until March 1992. It is hard to assume that such an invitation, extended by a body which had offered its good services and mediation in dealing with the Yugoslav crisis, could have had no effect on the political options taken in Bosnia and Herzegovina, particularly if the invitation to recognition is linked with the terms for recognition which, *inter alia*, included the acceptance of "the provisions laid down in the Draft Convention . . . under consideration by the Conference on Yugoslavia". The key provision of the "Draft Convention" which the Conference Chairman Lord Carrington presented to the Conference on 23 October 1991 is contained in Article I which reads:

> "The new relations between the Republics will be based on the following:
> *(a)* sovereign and independent Republics with an international personality for those which wish it;

---

[61] E. G. Brown, "Force and Diplomacy in Yugoslavia: the U.S. Interest", *American Foreign Policy Newsletter*, Vol. 15, No. 4, August 1993, p. 2.

[62] European Political Co-operation, Press Release, 17 December 1991 (emphasis added).

(b) a free association of the Republics with an international per- [690
sonality as envisaged in this Convention;

(c) comprehensive arrangements, including supervisory mecha-
nisms for the protection of human rights and special status for
certain groups and areas;

. . . .

(d) in the framework of general settlement, recognition of the independence, within the existing borders, unless otherwise agreed,
of those Republics wishing it."

The relevant circumstances show that there existed a connection
between recognition and the dismemberment of the SFRY along the
seams of the administrative division into federal units as provided for by
Article 1 *(a)* of the Draft Convention. That concept, which included the
automatic substitution for the personality of the SFRY of the personality
of the federal units, reflected the value judgment of the "Declaration on
Yugoslavia" of 16 December 1991, on the basis of which its contents
were designed. There can be no other explanation for certain formulations contained in the Declaration — *exempli causa,* those according to
which the European Community and its member States "will not recognize entities which are the result of aggression". Aggression *per definitionem* is the

"use of armed force *by a state* against the sovereignty, territorial
integrity or political independence of *another state,* or in any other
manner inconsistent with the Charter of the United Nations"[63].

In fact, there are certain indications that the presentation of the Draft
Convention by the providers of good offices and mediators was the
expression of a political decision on the transformation of Yugoslav federal units into sovereign States. The EPC statement of 6 October 1991
emphasized that

"it was agreed that a political solution should be sought in the perspective of recognition of the independence of those republics wishing it, at the end of the negotiating process conducted in good faith
and involving all parties".

A further indication is the actual title of the document — the term "Convention" denotes an *"agreement between states in the sense of international law".* The Convention on the Law of Treaties (1969), *lex lata* in
this area, stipulates in Article 2 that a "Treaty" represents "an international agreement concluded between States in written form and governed
by international law . . . whatever its particular designation". Article 6 of
the Convention stipulates that "[e]very State possesses capacity to conclude treaties".

---

[63] Art. 1, General Assembly resolution 3314 (XXIX) of 14 December 1974 (emphasis
added).

691]   Testifying to such a nature of the recognition of independence of the
Yugoslav federal units is the linkage of recognition with practical political aims. The United States-European Community Declaration on the
recognition of the Yugoslav republics states *inter alia*:

> "The Community and its member States and the United States
> have agreed to coordinate their approaches to completing the pro-
> cess of recognizing those Yugoslav republics that seek independence.
>
> . . . .
>
> (i) that the United States will, in this context, give rapid and posi-
> tive consideration to the requests for recognition by Croatia and
> Slovenia *in such a way as to support the dual-track approach
> based on the deployment of the UN peacekeeping force and the
> European Community Peace Conference chaired by Lord Car-
> rington.*
> (ii) that positive consideration should be given to the requests for
> recognition of the other two republics, contingent on the resolu-
> tion of the remaining European Community questions relating
> to those two republics. In this context, they strongly urge all
> parties in Bosnia-Herzegovina to adopt without delay constitu-
> tional arrangements that will provide for a peaceful and harmo-
> nious development of this republic within its existing borders.
> The Community and its member States and the United States
> also agree strongly to oppose any effort to undermine the sta-
> bility and territorial integrity of those two republics."

In connection with the recognition of Bosnia and Herzegovina as an
independent State within the administrative boundaries of the former
federal unit, at least two conclusions have to be drawn:

(a) phenomenologically, in this case, the recognition of Bosnia and
Herzegovina did not follow the natural logic of the legal process of
recognition, namely, that it should be a passive acknowledgment of
the establishment of the State. In the case of Bosnia and Herzegovina, the recognition, as testified to by developments, was one of
the instruments for the establishment of Bosnia and Herzegovina as
a State within its administrative boundaries. The recognizing States,
by recognizing Bosnia and Herzegovina, actually demonstrated their
intention to create it or to participate in its creation;
(b) legally, the recognition of Bosnia and Herzegovina within its administrative boundaries represented the recognition of a non-existent
State. It was granted exclusively on the basis of political considerations since, at the moment of recognition, Bosnia and Herzegovina
did not fulfil the minimum requirements for recognition as a new
State.

Moreover, having in mind the importance of self-determination of peoples **[692**
as a criterion in the decision regarding statehood[64], it may be concluded
that the admission of Bosnia and Herzegovina to the United Nations was
an act of diplomacy which runs counter to the established practice of the
Organization in that regard.

SECOND PRELIMINARY OBJECTION

27. The position of the Court regarding the second preliminary objection raised by Yugoslavia is based on two premises:

(i) that it "does not, in order to rule on that objection, have to consider
     the provisions of domestic law which were invoked in the course of
     the proceedings either in support of or in opposition to that objec-
     tion", since "[a]ccording to international law, there is no doubt that
     every Head of State is presumed to be able to act on behalf of the
     State in its international relations", and
(ii) that, "Mr. Izetbegović was recognized, in particular by the United
     Nations, as the Head of State" and that "his status as Head of State
     continued subsequently to be recognized in many international
     bodies and several international agreements" (Judgment, para. 44).

My views on the matter are very different. The Application like that of
Bosnia and Herzegovina instituting proceedings before the Court constitutes a typical unilateral act of the State producing legal consequences for
the mutual relations among the parties to the Genocide Convention.
Hence the Court is authorized to consider the relevant provisions of Bosnia and Herzegovina's constitutional law, as well as other cases in which
the application of a norm of international law was dependent upon internal law) (*exempli causa*, the *Western Griqualand Diamond Deposits* case
(1871) (*2 Recueil des arbitrages internationaux 1856-72*, pp. 676-705
(1923)); *Cleveland Award* (1888) (2 Moore, *International Arbitrations
1945-68)*; the case concerning *Free Zones of Upper Savoy and the Dis-* [2]
trict of Gex (1932) *(P.C.I.J., Series A/B, No. 46)*; the *Fisheries* case
(I.C.J. Reports 1951, pp . 125-126); the *Nottebohm* case (*I.C.J. Reports* [3]
1955, p. 4); the case concerning the *Application of the Convention of 1902
Governing the Guardianship of Infants (I.C.J. Reports 1958*, pp. 62-66), [4]
etc.). In other words, this is not a case of conflict between internal and
international law, as, *exempli causa*, in the *Certain German Interests in* [5]
Polish Upper Silesia or *S.S. "Wimbledon"* cases, but a matter in which [6]
these two laws are in co-ordination, dependent on each other.

In concreto, Yugoslavia claims that Mr. A. Izetbegović could not have
issued an authorization for instituting proceedings before the Court in
the present case since:

---

[64] J. Dugard, *Recognition and the United Nations*, 1987, p. 79.
[[2] 6 *Ann Dig* 431.]   [[4] 25 *ILR* 242.]   [[6] 2 *Ann Dig* 4.]
[[3] 22 *ILR* 349.]   [[5] 3 *Ann Dig* 5.]

693] (i) the issue of such authorization was not within the scope of the competence of the President of the Presidency of Bosnia and Herzegovina, and

(ii) at the relevant point in time, Mr. Izetbegović was not, according to the Constitution of Bosnia and Herzegovina, the President of the Presidency.

It is indisputable that both claims are based primarily on the internal law of Bosnia and Herzegovina so that diagnosing solutions established by the constitutional law of Bosnia and Herzegovina with respect to both questions is essential, albeit in different ways, for the application of the relevant norms of international law. This is indirectly recognized by Bosnia and Herzegovina itself in its request to the Court to:

> "take cognizance of the following facts which establish that President Izetbegović *was duly appointed President* of the Presidency of Bosnia and Herzegovina and that *he exercised his functions in accordance with the relevant constitutional procedures"*[65].

In the point under (i) the relevant general legal principle as expressed in Article 46 of the Convention on the Law of Treaties (1969) seeks to strike a relative balance between international and internal law in the form of a modified internationalistic theory (Head of State Theory). The only way for the Court to decide whether this general legal principle is applicable in this specific case is by entering into an examination of the internal law of Bosnia and Herzegovina with a view to establishing whether, when Mr. Izetbegović granted the authorization to institute proceedings before the Court the internal law of Bosnia and Herzegovina was violated.

The point under (ii) also cannot be resolved without an examination of the internal law of Bosnia and Herzegovina.

There is no denying, as is noted by Bosnia and Herzegovina, that "[n]o rule of international law . . . requires the structure of a State to follow any particular pattern"[66]. It is also beyond dispute that international law, being sovereign and independent of internal law, determines the circle of persons that represent the State in international affairs (this holds good regardless of the fact that the circle of persons representing the State *in foro externo* is determined on the basis of virtually identical constitutional regulations). However, *sedes materiae* the point under (ii) raised in the second preliminary objection *does not question the right of Mr. Alija Izetbegović, as Head of State, and in conformity with international law, to issue an authorization for the institution of proceedings before the Court but rather questions whether Mr. Izetbegović was, at the relevant point in time, i.e., at the time of issuing of the authorization in question,*

---

[65] Statement of the Government of the Republic of Bosnia and Herzegovina, p. 42.
[66] Case concerning the *Western Sahara, Advisory Opinion, I.C.J. Reports 1975*, p. 43. [59 *ILR* 13 at 30.]

the Head of State. The only way to answer this question raised in the **[694** second preliminary objection is by examining the internal, constitutional law of Bosnia and Herzegovina. *A contrario*, the relevant norm of international law would be the one determining not only the pattern of the structure of a State but also the modalities of the Constitution and the duration of that structural pattern.

28. On the second day of the hearing regarding the first request for the indication of provisional measures, the Agent of Bosnia and Herzegovina pointed out *inter alia* that:

> "*President Izetbegović personally accredited* . . . Ambassador Sacirbey, who appeared before you yesterday, and me as General Agents with Extraordinary and Plenipotentiary Powers to the Court on behalf of Bosnia and Herzegovina."[67]

That the statements of the then Agent of Bosnia and Herzegovina correspond to the factual situation is confirmed by the text of the act on the appointment of

> "H.E. Muhamed Sacirbey, our Ambassador and Permanent Representative to the United Nations, and Francis A. Boyle, Professor of International Law at the University of Illinois College . . . to be our General Agents with Extraordinary and Plenipotentiary Powers to institute, conduct and defend against any and all legal proceedings on our behalf before the International Court of Justice."

The text of this act was signed, as stated in the act, by "Alija Izetbegović, President of the Republic of Bosnia and Herzegovina". The title "President of the Republic of Bosnia and Herzegovina" indicates unequivocally the personal nature of President Izetbegović's accreditation — particularly so as, contrary to the practice of the Presidency of Bosnia and Herzegovina, it is not stated in the text that it is an act of the Presidency[68]. The fact that the act was written "on the official stationery of the Presidency" cannot, in my opinion, be taken as proof that the act was issued in the name of the Presidency of Bosnia and Herzegovina. The use of official stationery is only prima facie grounds for the assumption that what is written on it is an act of the organ whose name appears in the heading. The assumption is refutable as official stationery is only the external sign of identification of its owner, incorporates the decision of

---

[67] CR 93/13, p. 38 (emphasis added).
[68] *Exempli causa*, the Decree on the change of name of the Socialist Republic of Bosnia and Herzegovina (Statement of the Government of the Republic of Bosnia and Herzegovina on Preliminary Objections, Annexes, Vol. I, Ann. 2.12) was issued by the "Presidency of the Socialist Republic of Bosnia and Herzegovina at a session held on April 8, 1992", and signed by the "President of the Presidency of SR B-H Alija Izetbegović". An identical example is the Decision on the proclamation of an imminent threat of war passed on the same day, as well as all the other published acts of the Presidency of Bosnia and Herzegovina.

595] the organ as well, and depends on whether in each concrete case the formal and material conditions for issuing the act written on the official stationery have been met. *A contrario* it would be absurd to assume that every text written on the official stationery of an organ constitutes *ipso facto* an act of that organ.

In concreto, the question may be posed whether the stationery on which Mr. Izetbegović gave the authorization for instituting proceedings before the Court is without any doubt the only official stationery of the Presidency of the Republic of Bosnia and Herzegovina. The grounds for raising this question are provided by the fact that the word "Presidency" on the stationery heading is found underneath the name of the State — "Republic of Bosnia and Herzegovina" — and above the word "President". The word "Presidency" can also be taken to indicate the head-quarters of the President, particularly as Mr. Izetbegović is described as the "President of the Republic of Bosnia and Herzegovina". The name of the collective Head of State, according to the Constitution of Bosnia and Herzegovina, is not the "Presidency" but the "Presidency of the Republic of Bosnia and Herzegovina" [69].

Of particular importance is the fact that in contravention of Article 10 of the Operating Procedure of the Presidency and its customary practice, the letter signed by Mr. Alija Izetbegović does not feature any stamp (either the small or the large one) of the Presidency of Bosnia and Herzegovina.

These several points provide convincing evidence that in this concrete case we are dealing with a "personal accreditation" by Mr. Izetbegović.

Was President Izetbegović authorized on the basis of the internal law of the Applicant to personally accredit a "General Agent with extraordinary and plenipotentiary powers to the Court"?

29. The function of the "President of the Republic of Bosnia and Herzegovina" is not established by the Constitution of Bosnia and Herzegovina. Chapter X of the Constitution speaks of the "Presidency of the Republic of Bosnia and Herzegovina" as the organ "representing the Republic of Bosnia and Herzegovina" [70]. The Presidency of the Republic of Bosnia and Herzegovina is the collective Head of State "that operates and decides collectively at meetings and bears collective responsibility for its work" [71].

The Presidency of the Republic of Bosnia and Herzegovina taken as a whole, as a collegium, is the organ of representation according to the Constitution. The President of the Presidency as the *primus inter pares* does not exercise any independent political powers. The enactments within the terms of reference of the Presidency of the Republic of Bosnia

---

[69] Chapter X of the Constitution of Bosnia and Herzegovina.

[70] Article 219 (1) of the Constitution of Bosnia and Herzegovina.

[71] Article 3 of the Rules of Procedure of the Presidency of the Socialist Republic of Bosnia and Herzegovina, *Official Gazette of the Socialist Republic of Bosnia and Herzegovina*, No. 36 (1990).

and Herzegovina (decrees, decisions and conclusions as well as regulations [69€
with the effect of law in cases stipulated by the Constitution) are adopted
by the Presidency of the Republic of Bosnia and Herzegovina as a whole[72].

The President of the Presidency, on behalf of the Presidency, represents the Presidency[73]. Of particular interest among the functions of the
President of the Presidency listed in Article 22 of the Operating Procedure is the function to "sign acts passed by the Presidency".

Consequently, Mr. Izetbegović, as the President of the Presidency, was
not authorized to "personally accredit[ed] . . . [a] General Agent with
Extraordinary and Plenipotentiary Powers to the Court on behalf of
Bosnia and Herzegovina".

30. Yugoslavia claims in its previous objection that at the time at
which the authorization for instituting proceedings before the Court was
issued (20 March 1993), Mr. Izetbegović "did not serve as the President
of the Republic" and that the "authorization for the initiation and conduct of proceedings was granted in violation of rules of internal law of
fundamental significance"[74].

Bosnia and Herzegovina, on the other hand, finds that

"on 20 March 1993, the time of filing of the present case in the International Court of Justice, the President of the Presidency exercised
their functions lawfully, in accordance with the relevant constitutional provisions, including those relating to a state of war or emergency. As President of the Presidency, President Izetbegović is legally
entitled to represent the Republic of Bosnia and Herzegovina internationally in this matter."[75]

The dispute is over the question whether Mr. Izetbegović could have
performed the function of President of the Presidency *ex constitutione*
after 20 December 1992. It is indisputable that Mr. A. Izetbegović
assumed the function of President of the Presidency of the Socialist
Republic of Bosnia and Herzegovina in December 1990, in conformity
with the relevant constitutional provisions. The term of office was
extended by a year, also in conformity with Amendment LI (para. 4,
point 6) to the Constitution of the Socialist Republic of Bosnia and
Herzegovina which stipulated:

"The President of the Presidency is elected by the Presidency from
among its members for a period of one year and he may be re-
elected for another, consecutive year on one occasion."

The Constitution therefore prohibited the exercise of the function of the
President of the Presidency for more than two years or two consecutive

[72] Article 49 of the Operating Procedure.
[73] Article 21 of the Operating Procedure.
[74] Preliminary Objections of Yugoslavia, p. 141, para. A.2.
[75] Statement of the Government of the Republic of Bosnia and Herzegovina on Preliminary Objections, p. 47, para. 2.19.

697] terms. This prohibition was absolute in the original text of the Constitution of the Socialist Republic of Bosnia and Herzegovina as, in respect to the President of the Presidency, no exceptions were envisaged even in the case of a "state of war or imminent threat of war". That such an interpretation is correct is corroborated by Article 358 of the Constitution:

> "In the event of a state of war or imminent threat of war *the mandate of the Members of the Presidency of SR B-H shall be continued until such time as the conditions for election of the new Members of the Presidency are met.*" (Emphasis added.)

The prohibition was modified by Amendment LI (par. 4 (8)) to the Constitution of the Socialist Republic of Bosnia and Herzegovina according to which:

> "In the event of a state of war or imminent threat of war, the mandate of Members of the Presidency and the President shall be continued until such time as the conditions for election of new Members of the Presidency are met." [76]

This amendment extends *ratione personae* the range of the exception established for members of the Presidency by Article 358 of the Constitution of the Socialist Republic of Bosnia and Herzegovina to include the President of the Presidency. The main elements of the solutions contained in Amendment LI are:

(a) the continuation of the term of office is linked to the eventuality of a "state of war or imminent threat of war";

(b) the prohibition of a third consecutive mandate is not abolished, but the continuation of a mandate is envisaged in the cited cases;

(c) the continuation of the mandate is limited by appropriate "conditions for the election of new Members of the Presidency", not by the termination of the "state of war or imminent threat of war".

Bosnia and Herzegovina also refers to Article 220 of the Consolidated Constitution of the Republic of Bosnia and Herzegovina adopted on 24 February 1993, which reads:

> "In the event of war or a state of emergency, the mandate of the Members of the Presidency and of the President shall be continued until such time as the conditions for new elections for the Presidency are met."

In my opinion, the consolidated text of the Constitution cannot, in this particular case, be accepted as a relevant legal basis.

More particularly, a consolidated text in Yugoslav constitutional practice was a strictly legal-technical procedure whereby the text of a norma-

---

[76] *Official Gazette of the Socialist Republic of Bosnia and Herzegovina*, No. 13 of 21 April 1989, p. 338.

tive act, the Constitution or laws, was adjusted to its purpose and to **[698**
the requirements of practical implementation. It excluded even minor
material-legal changes in the text of the act and was for the most part
reduced to a procedure of renumeration of segments of the normative act.
Hence, in Yugoslav constitutional practice, the consolidated text of a
normative act could not be referred to in formal proceedings including
court proceedings.

In comparison with the contents of Amendment LI, Article 220 of the
consolidated text of the Constitution of the Republic of Bosnia and
Herzegovina constitutes a modification of the Constitution. The prolongation of the term of office of the Members and the President of the
Presidency in Amendment LI (para. 4 (8)) is linked to a case "of war or
imminent threat of war" whereas in Article 220 of the consolidated text
the basis for the prolongation is a case "of war or a state of emergency".
Hence, it may be concluded that the form of consolidation of the text
actually conceals a modification of the Constitution.

The Presidency of Bosnia and Herzegovina, as stated in the preamble
to the Constitution, adopted a decision to establish a consolidated text of
the Constitution of the Republic of Bosnia and Herzegovina, and was
not authorized by the Constitution to effect any changes to the Constitution, this being within the exclusive competence of the Assembly of Bosnia and Herzegovina[77]. The Presidency as well as the Government of the
Republic, each of the Assembly Chambers and at least 30 Assembly
Deputies, appear as the only possible proponents of proposals to amend
the Constitution[78]. Changes in the Constitution of the Republic of Bosnia and Herzegovina may only be made in the form of Constitutional
Amendments or Constitutional Laws[79].

It follows from the above that Article 220 of the Consolidated Constitution of the Republic of Bosnia and Herzegovina, in the section in which
the continuation of the term of office of Members and the President of
the Presidency is linked also to a "state of emergency", constitutes a
modification of the Constitution of the Republic of Bosnia and Herzegovina, and that the change was effected, both formally and materially,
contra constitutionem.

31. Consequently, what remains to be seen is whether, in the light of
the provisions of Article 358 of the Bosnia and Herzegovina Constitution
as amended by Amendment LI (4 (8)), the established conditions had
been met for the continuation of the mandate of the President of the
Presidency of the Republic of Bosnia and Herzegovina after 20 December 1992, i.e., after the expiry of his second consecutive term.

The relevant provision of Bosnia and Herzegovina's Constitution stipulated that the "mandate of the President shall be continued" in the event

---

[77] Article 268 (3), (4) of the Constitution.
[78] Article 268 (1) of the Constitution.
[79] Article 268 (5) of the Constitution.

699] of "war or imminent threat of war". In other words, "war or imminent threat of war" constituted the material, constitutional basis for the automatic continuation of the mandate of the President of the Presidency.

The fulfilment of this requirement *ex constitutione* implies that the decision on the existence of "war or imminent threat of war" was taken by the competent organ in line with established constitutional procdure.

32. The Presidency of the Socialist Republic of Bosnia and Herzegovina, at its session of 8 April 1992, passed a "Decision on the proclamation of an imminent threat of war" in the territory of Bosnia and Herzegovina. The decision was taken, as stated in the preamble

"in conformity with the provisions of Amendments LI and LXXII to the Constitution of the Socialist Republic of Bosnia and Herzegovina and upon the proposal of the Assembly of the Socialist Republic of Bosnia and Herzegovina".

It follows from this statement:

(a) that the "Decision" was taken upon the proposal of the Assembly of the Socialist Republic of Bosnia and Herzegovina, and,

(b) that the Presidency took the "Decision" on the basis of Amendments LI and LXXII to the Constitution of the Socialist Republic of Bosnia and Herzegovina.

33. The competences of the Assembly of the Socialist Republic of Bosnia and Herzegovina were established by Article 314 of the Constitution of the Socialist Republic of Bosnia and Herzegovina (see para. 36 below). The unequivocal conclusion to be drawn from the text of that Article is that the submission of the proposal on the proclamation of the imminent threat of war was not within the terms of reference of the Assembly of the Socialist Republic of Bosnia and Herzegovina. Article 314 was modified by Amendment LXXI adopted on 31 July 1990. In the part relating to the competences of the Assembly adopted at a joint session of all the Assembly Chambers, the Amendment stipulated:

"5. The Chambers of the Assembly of SR B-H at their joint session may:

— decide on changes to the Constitution of the Socialist Republic of Bosnia and Herzegovina;

— proclaim the Constitution of the Socialist Republic of Bosnia and Herzegovina and any changes thereto;

— make proposals, express opinions and approve any changes to the Constitution of the Socialist Federal Republic of Yugoslavia;

— approve changes to the borders of the Socialist Federal Republic of Yugoslavia;

— decide on modifications of the borders of the Socialist Republic **[700**
    of Bosnia and Herzegovina;
— review foreign policy issues;
— decide on the prolongation of the mandates of deputies to the
    Assembly of SR B-H and those of aldermen serving in the
    assemblies of the communes and assemblies of municipalities;
— pass the social plan of Bosnia and Herzegovina, the budget and
    final accounts of the budget of SR B-H;

— call a Republic-wide referendum;
— decide on the floating of Republic-wide public lons;

— decide on debts or other obligations of the Republic;
— decide on whether to entrust affairs within the competence of the
    Republic to a municipal community as a separate socio-political
    community;
— elect and relieve of office: the President and Vice-President of the
    Assembly of SR B-H; the member of the Presidency of SFRY
    from SR B-H; the President, Vice-President and members of the
    Government of SR B-H; the President and Judges of the Con-
    stitutional Court of Bosnia and Herzegovina; the President and
    Judges of the Supreme Court of Bosnia and Herzegovina; the
    President and members of the working bodies of the Assembly of
    SR B-H;

— elect and relieve of office members of the Delegation of the
    Assembly of SR B-H in the Chamber of Republics and Provinces
    of the Assembly of SFRY;

— appoint and relieve of office: ministers; the Governor of the
    National Bank of Bosnia and Herzegovina; the Public Prosecu-
    tor of the Republic, the Public Attorney of the Republic and the
    Secretary General of the Assembly of SR B-H;
— adopt the Rules of Procedure of the Assembly of SR B-H;

The Chambers of the Assembly of SR B-H may decide to review
at a joint session other matters within the common terms of reference of the Assembly of SR B-H." [80]

Consequently, the submission of the proposal to proclaim an "imminent
threat of war" was not within the competence of the Assembly of the

---

[80] *Official Gazette of the Socialist Republic of Bosnia and Herzegovina*, No. 21 of
31 July 1990.

701] Socialist Republic of Bosnia and Herzegovina exercised at a joint session of all the Assembly Chambers nor was it envisaged by the amended version of Article 314 of the Applicant's Constitution. *A fortiori*, the same conclusion applies to the competences of the Assembly exercised at sessions of individual Assembly Chambers.

34. It is only the consolidated text of the Constitution of the Republic of Bosnia and Herzegovina that contains a provision according to which the Assembly of the Republic of Bosnia and Herzegovina, *inter alia*, "decides on war and peace"[81]. This provision, however, cannot be considered as relevant in this specific case for two main reasons. Firstly, by its nature it constitutes a revision of the Constitution carried out *contra constitutionem* in the form of a consolidation of the text of the Constitution — hence, the arguments presented in reference to Article 220 of the Consolidated Constitution apply *per analogiam* (see para. 30 above). Secondly, the Consolidated Constitution of the Republic of Bosnia and Herzegovina was passed in February 1993, i.e., almost a year after the adoption of the "Decision on the proclamation of imminent threat of war", so that with respect to this concrete case it is irrelevant.

35. The preamble to the "Decision on the proclamation of an imminent threat of war" states, *inter alia*, that it was taken "in accordance with the provisions of Amendments LI and LXXII to the Constitution of SR B-H". In the wording of this Decision, therefore, Amendments LI and LXXII appear as a concrete constitutional basis. The contents of Amendment LXXII can hardly be linked to the "Decision on the proclamation of imminent threat of war", as this Amendment actually abrogates Amendment XVII to the Constitution of the Socialist Republic of Bosnia and Herzegovina by stipulating that: "The provisions of Amendment XVII to the Constitution of SR B-H on the Council of the Republic shall cease to be valid."[82] Prima facie, there is a link between Amendment LI and the "Decision on the proclamation of imminent threat of war", since the subject of the Amendment was the establishment of the competences of the Presidency of the Socialist Republic of Bosnia and Herzegovina. Amendment LI stipulated that:

"1. The Presidency of the Socialist Republic of Bosnia and Herzegovina:

(1) represents the Socialist Republic of Bosnia and Herzegovina;

(2) reviews questions relating to the implementation of adopted policies in the areas of all peoples' defence, state security, social self-protection and international co-operation and proposes to the Assembly of SR Bosnia and Herzegovina the passage of appropriate

---

[81] Article 206 (5) of the consolidated text.
[82] *Official Gazette of the Socialist Republic of Bosnia and Herzegovina*, No. 21 of 31 July 1990.

measures to implement those policies and, in the event of an emer- **[702]** gency preventing or seriously hamering the realization of the social order as established by the Constitution, proposes to the Assembly of SR Bosnia and Herzegovina the adoption of necessary measures to overcome the intervening disturbances;

(3) establishes the defence plan of the Republic and provides appropriate guide-lines in conformity with the law;
(4) in accordance with the positions and proposals of the Assembly of SR Bosnia and Herzegovina reviews matters related to the participation of the Socialist Republic of Bosnia and Herzegovina in the establishment and implementation of the foreign policy of the Socialist Federal Republic of Yugoslavia, to co-operation between the Republic and other Republics and Autonomous Provinces in the area of international co-operation within the framework of the adopted foreign policy of SFRY and international treaties, and, on the basis of prior consultations within the Republic, proposes candidates for appointment as heads of diplomatic missions and informs the Presidency of SFRY and the Assembly of SR Bosnia and Herzegovina of its proposals;

(5) establishes, on the basis of prior consultations within the Republic, proposals for candidates for the appointment as President and Judges of the Constitutional Court of Bosnia and Herzegovina;
(6) establishes on the basis of prior consultations in the Republic, the proposal of candidates for appointment as members of the Council of the Republic;
(7) establishes proposals for decorations conferred by the SFRY Presidency and confers decorations and other marks of honour of the Republic in conformity with the law;

(8) pardons offenders, in conformity with the law;
(9) adopts the Rules of Procedure of the Presidency." [83]

In the light of the established competences of the Presidency of the Socialist Republic of Bosnia and Herzegovina, prima facie, any acceptance of Amendment LI as a possible constitutional basis for passing the "Decision on the proclamation of imminent threat of war" is out of the question. Amendment LI gives no authorization whatsoever to the Presidency to proclaim an imminent threat of war upon its own initiative or upon the proposal of any other organ. In its paragraph 2, the said Amendment establishes the competences of the Presidency "in the event of extraordinary conditions preventing or seriously hampering the reali-

---

[83] *Official Gazette of the Socialist Republic of Bosnia and Herzegovina*, No. 21 of 31 July 1990.

703] zation of the constitutionally established order", but those conditions could hardly include the proclamation of imminent threat of war. On the one hand the term "extraordinary conditions" is far broader than the term "imminent threat of war". In Yugoslav constitutional terminology, the term "extraordinary conditions" served to denote a state of affairs provoked by natural disasters (Article 364 of the Constitution of the Socialist Republic of Bosnia and Herzegovina enunciates as "extraordinary conditions" events like "natural disaster, epidemics"). All powers linked to a state of war or imminent threat of war were entirely in the hands of federal organs. On the other hand, even on the hypothesis that the competences of the Presidency on the basis of paragraph 2 of Amendment LI included the question of "imminent threat of war", the procedure by which the "Decision on the proclamation of imminent threat of war" was passed could only be qualified as formally unconstitutional, as the cited paragraph of Amendment LI stipulates the right of the Presidency in the case of extraordinary conditions "to propose to the Assembly of SR B-H that it take necessary measures to eliminate the existing disturbances". Hence, the Presidency was not authorized to *"take necessary measures to remove the existing disturbances"* (emphasis added) but only *to propose* to the Assembly the taking of such measures. The prerequisites for such a procedure existed as, judging from the text of the preamble of the "Decision", the Assembly had convened when it made the proposal for the proclamation of an imminent threat of war.

36. Consequently, bearing in mind that on the basis of Article 358 of the Constitution of Bosnia and Herzegovina as amended by Amendment LI (4 (8)) "war or imminent threat of war" was the constitutional condition for the automatic continuation of the mandate of the President of the Presidency and that in the light of the relevant provisions of Article 314 of the Constitution of SR Bosnia and Herzegovina as amended by Amendment LXXI and Amendment LI, the "Decision on the proclamation of imminent threat of war" was passed in contravention of the Constitution by an unauthorized organ, the mandate of Mr. Alija Izetbegović as President of the Presidency could not have been automatically continued after 20 December 1992.

37. The letter addressed by the Prime Minister of Bosnia and Herzegovina to the Secretary-General of the United Nations on 1 March 1993, i.e., 20 days before Mr. Alija Izetbegović issued the authorization for the institution of proceedings before the Court, reads *inter alia*:

"I also advised . . . that the mandate of Mr. Alija Izetbegović as President of the Presidency had expired. This is to demonstrate the immediate need for the international community to assist not only in protecting Bosnia and Herzegovina's sovereignty and territorial integrity but also in assuring that the country is governed in accordance with its democratic and constitutional principles. I should be

grateful if you would have the text of the present letter and its annex [704
circulated as a document of the General Assembly, under agenda
item 143 and of the Security Council."[84]

The Annex of this letter is "Letter dated 24 February 1993 from the
Prime Minister of Bosnia and Herzegovina to the Chairman of the European Affairs Subcommittee of the Senate Foreign Affairs Committee of
the United States of America", and states *inter alia*:

> "Furthermore, please be advised that the mandate of Mr. Alija
> Izetbegović as President of the Presidency of the Republic of Bosnia
> and Herzegovina expired on 20 December 1992. He is presently
> without constitutional authority to act in that capacity. The Presi-
> dency, and not the President alone, is the representative body of the
> Republic of Bosnia and Herzegovina. Only the Presidency can invoke
> constitutional emergency powers, not the President alone. The Presi-
> dent is merely *primus inter pares*. Like Mr. Silajdzić, Mr. Izetbegović
> does not speak for the Presidency as a whole with respect to the cur-
> rent stage of the Vance/Owen talks, but only as one Muslim member
> of the Presidency."[85]

In this connection, Mr. R. Zacklin, Director and Deputy to the Under-
Secretary-General in charge of the Office of Legal Affairs, in a letter
addressed to the Registrar of the International Court of Justice on
25 March 1993, stressed *inter alia* that:

> "Mr. Izetbegović participated in the general debate of the last
> session of the General Assembly as President of Bosnia-Herzegovina
> and no communication has been made to the United Nations since
> then advising us that he is no longer the President. In the United
> Nations and in the International Conference on the former Yugo-
> slavia, Mr. Izetbegović has been regarded and continues to be
> regarded as the President of Bosnia-Herzegovina."[86]

Can the fact that "[i]n the United Nations and in the International
Conference on the former Yugoslavia, *Mr. Izetbegović has been regarded
and continues to be regarded as the President of Bosnia-Herzegovina*"
change the legal order established by the Constitution of Bosnia and
Herzegovina?

The answer to this question can only be negative, as if this were not the
case, we would find ourselves in the absurd situation of attributing to the
institution of recognition, which is in practice an eminently political act,
constitutional powers, the power to change the internal political structure
of a State. Another conclusion may be drawn however — that the inter-

---

[84] Doc. A/47/899-S/25360, 5 March 1995.
[85] *Ibid.*
[86] Letter dated 25 March 1993 addressed to E. Valencia-Ospina, Registrar, International Court of Justice, from R. Zacklin, United Nations Director and Deputy to the
Under-Secretary-General in charge of the Office of Legal Affairs.

705] national community organized within the United Nations was in legal error *(error juris)*, judging from the meaning of the formulations used in the aforementioned letter, with regard to the nature of the institution of Head of State in the constitutional system of Bosnia and Herzegovina.

38. In the light of the relevant provisions of Bosnia and Herzegovina's internal law, it is evident that Mr. Alija Izetbegović was without constitutional authority to act in the capacity of President of the Presidency of Bosnia and Herzegovina as of 21 December 1991. The relevance of that fact cannot be denied in the domain of international law, as, in my view, we are faced with a general legal principle according to which:

"the act of an official cannot juridically be set up as an act of State unless it was within the sphere of competency of that official. The act of an incompetent official is not an act of the State."[87]

39. This general principle is also expressed in Article 8 of the Convention on the Law of Treaties (1969).

A measure taken by an official outside the sphere of competence of that official is by definition a non-existent measure, a measure limited to the factual sphere as it is devoid of legal effect. In that respect the qualification contained in the commentary on Article 8 of the Convention on the Law of Treaties is applicable *per analogiam*:

"where a person lacking any authority to represent the State in this connection purported to express its consent to be bound by a treaty, the true legal position was that his act was not attributable to the State and that, in consequence, there was no question of any consent having been expressed by it . . . the unauthorized act of the representative is without legal effect"[88].

THIRD PRELIMINARY OBJECTION

40. The *sedes materiae* of the third preliminary objection lies in the statement that Bosnia and Herzegovina's proclamation of sovereignty and independence was effected in an illegal manner in flagrant breach of the principle of equal rights and self-determination of peoples; hence, no succession of the Applicant to the Genocide Convention of 1948 could have been possible.

The Court finds, quite simply, that

"Bosnia and Herzegovina became a Member of the United Nations following the decisions adopted on 22 May 1992 by the Security

---

[87] The Presiding Commissioner of the France-Mexican Mixed Claims Commission [7] (1924) in the *Caire* case (1929), cited in Bin Cheng, *General Principles of Law as Applied by International Courts and Tribunals*, 1953, p. 205.

[88] Draft Articles on the Law of Treaties with commentaries adopted by the ILC at its Eighteenth Session, UNCLT, First and Second Sessions, Vienna, 26 March-24 May 1968 and 9 April-22 May 1969, *Official Records*, p. 13, para. 1.

[[7] 5 *Ann Dig* 146.]

Council and the General Assembly, bodies competent under the **[706** Charter",

and indicates that

"Article XI of the Genocide Convention opens it to 'any Member of the United Nations'; from the time of its admission to the Organization, Bosnia and Herzegovina could thus become a party to the Convention. Hence the circumstances of its accession to independence are of little consequence." (Para. 19 of the Judgment.)

In my opinion, the legality of Bosnia and Herzegovina's birth is far from being a fact in the light of the relevant legal rules. It implicitly relies on the concept of the so-called "process of dissolution" of Yugoslavia, elaborated in the Opinions of the Arbitration Commission of the Conference on Yugoslavia, which is not a legal term *stricto sensu*. This concept is most aptly seen as a sort of metaphor where a State figures as a kind of vessel from which its vital substance is trickling away and which, through the will of an imaginary creator, is being transformed into the tissue of a new State organism.

(This is eloquently shown by the position taken by the Arbitration Commission in relation to the date of succession of States in the Yugoslav case. In its Opinion No. 11, the Commission took [8] the view:

"That the date upon which the States stemming from the Socialist Federal Republic of Yugoslavia succeeded the Socialist Federal Republic of Yugoslavia are:

— 8 October 1991 in the case of the Republic of Croatia and the Republic of Slovenia,
— 17 November 1991 in the case of the former Yugoslav Republic of Macedonia,
— 6 March 1992 in the case of the Republic of Bosnia and Herzegovina" (International Conference on the Former Yugoslavia, Arbitration Commission, Opinion No. 11, para. 10).

Thus the Commission claims that the succession here occurred in the relations between the SFRY as the predecessor-State and the newly-independent republics as the successor-States. In other words, it did not take place *uno ictu*; rather, what is known as succession is in fact a set of successions which occurred one after another between 8 October 1991 and 27 April 1992. The succession of Slovenia and Croatia has not destroyed the international legal personality of the SFRY as the predecessor-State. *A contrario*, Macedonia could not exit from the SFRY and succeed SFRY at the same time. *The same applies to Bosnia and Herzegovina*, because this former federal unit, in the Commission's view, also succeeded SFRY. Such an approach of the Commission could reasonably be explained by *"the complex interaction between*

707] *the deliberations of the Arbitration Commission and the political decisions of the EC institutions and member States [which] is noteworthy"*
(Conference on Yugoslav Arbitration Commission: Opinions on Questions Arising from the Dissolution of Yugoslavia, Introductory Note
by Maurizio Ragazzi, *International Legal Materials,* 1992, p. 1490). In
the light of the above, there exists a clear connection between such
qualification and the content of Article 1 *(a)* of the Draft Convention
submitted by President of the Conference proposing that "[n]ew relations between the Republics will be based on the following: *(a)* sovereign and independent Republics with an international personality for
those who wish it, etc.")

Of utmost importance is the fact that there exists a substantial connection, in fact a causal connection, between the legality of the birth of a State
and the status of a successor State in legal terms (see paras. 81-88 below).

In order to reach a conclusion as to whether Bosnia and Herzegovina
was established in the legal way, it is necessary to examine both the relevant norms of international law and the internal law of SFRY. The relevance of the internal law of SFRY to that effect derives from the specific
nature of the norm of equal rights and self-determination of peoples in
multi-ethnic States (see paras. 44-46 above).

A. Relevance of International Law
to the Birth of States

41. A reply in the matter of relevance is often sought in the option for
one of the two mutually exclusive qualifications: birth of States as *questio
facti* or as *questio juris.* Neither of these qualifications, taken on its own
merits and individually, really corresponds to the actual state of affairs,
in view of their oversimplification and untenable.segregation. The first
suggests that international law is indifferent to the issue of the birth of
States, that they are created in a legal vacuum, a sort of legal vacant
space, in a free interaction of power and opportunity elements. The
second, however, reduces the birth of States to legalistic procedures, to
a matter of the mere will of an imaginary international legislator, materi-
alled in the form of a State, independently of real social processes. In the
final analysis, the first statement reduces international law relative to the
birth of States to an *ex post* rationalization of actual developments and
thereby to its own negation, while the second takes a completely opposite
course, elevating international law to the level of a maker, a creator of
social phenomena.

The fundamental defect in the option for either of the two mutually **[708**
exclusive explanations is the confusion of two dimensions involved in the
birth of States: the socio-political and the legal. As it is indisputable that
birth of States is a matter of realistic social processes from a socio-political standpoint, so it is that the birth of States takes place in the environment of the international community. Thus, international law cannot
abdicate from the regulation of such a crucial issue of international life.
Shaw is right in observing that:

> "[t]he relationship . . . between factual and legal criteria is a crucial
> shifting one. Whether the birth of a new state is primarily a question
> of fact or law and how the interaction between the criteria of effec-
> tiveness and other relevant legal principles may be reconciled are
> questions of considerable complexity and significance." [89]

42. Since its inception international law has never been or could have
been indifferent to the question of the birth of States. The substance and
nature of its rules have undergone modifications depending on the
achieved degree of advancement of international law. *Grosso modo*, the
rules of international law concerning the birth of States may be classified
into two groups:

— the first would comprise the rules of international law defining the State
  ab intra, as a legal fact within the system of international law. In other
  words, these rules of international law define *what a State is*. The very
  definition is static and narrowed down to an enumeration of the constituent elements of a State. On the whole, such a definition of a State is
  founded on the principle of effectiveness and by this means international
  law specifies the static, categorial meaning of the concept of a State.

— the second group would comprise the rules defining a State *ab extra*,
  from the point of view of other relevant rules of international law.
  While definition *ab intra* starts from a State as an isolated, static phenomenon, definition *ab extra* locates the State in the system of international law, linking its birth and functioning in the international community to other legal rules. In expressing the dynamic side of a concrete
  issue concerning a certain State, the notion of a State *ab extra* includes,
  in fact, principles and norms fundamental to the birth of States.
  Those principles have accompanied practically the whole period of existence of international law. The birth of States, since the Westphalian
  Peace Accord in 1648, has been justified by a principle-like balance of
  power, legitimacy and interpretation of the "Holy Alliance", the quasi-
  legislative competences of super-powers, the principle of nationality,
  and, during the twentieth century, the self-determination of peoples.

---

[89] M. N. Shaw, *International Law*, 2nd ed., 1986, p. 126.

709] It may be said that the above principles basically derive from the concept of legality.

43. It should be kept in mind, however, that the nature of the legality concept has been changing with the development of international law. That concept was based, for quite some time, upon subjective, eliminatory criteria, which recognized, in a community that tolerated uncontrolled resort to force and even to war, the property of a legislative factor, meaning legality no more than in the formal sense of the word. Determined *ad casum*, on the basis of the fulfilment of formal and procedural requirements, that legality was not *stricto sensu* legality, as measured by the norms of a more developed internal law, but rather a political decision in a more acceptable guise.

A basis for a radical change of attitude to the question of legality is provided by the hierarchical division of international law according to the criterion of the legal merit of its norms. The division of international law into "lower" and "higher" law opened the way towards the conceptualization of peremptory norms of general international law *(jus cogens)*, effected by Articles 53 and 64 of the Convention on the Law of Treaties of 1969. As Judge Ammoun put it in his separate opinion in the *Barcelona Traction* case (Second Phase, 1970):

> "through an already lengthy practice of the United Nations, the concept of *jus cogens* obtained a greater degree of effectiveness, by ratifying, as an imperative norm of international law, the principles appearing in the preamble to the Charter"[90].

Jus cogens creates grounds for a global change in relations of State sovereignty to the legal order in the international community and for the establishment of conditions in which the rule of law can prevail over the free will of States. As an objective, non-eliminatory norm, it constitutes a material basis, a criterion for challenging the legality of individual acts in the international community. Therefore, it essentially limits the impact of effectiveness in international law. Effectiveness in a system with a defined concept of legality may be legally accepted only in cases in which it does not conflict with the norms that serve as criteria of legality. Within the co-ordinates of the *de jure* order *effectiveness versus legality* is an incorrect approach, because to accept effectiveness as a rule

> "would indeed be to apply a hatchet to the very roots of the law of nations and to cover with its spurious authority an infinitive series of international wrongs and disregard for international obligations"[91].

---

[90] *I.C.J. Reports 1970*, p. 304. [46 *ILR* 1 at 178.]
[91] J. H. W. Verzijl, *International Law in Historical Perspective*, I, 1968, p. 293.

44. The concept of a material, homogeneous legality is unavoidably [710] reflected in the matter of the birth of States. This is suggested by an as yet insufficiently advanced and stabilized international practice. Let us take the case of Southern Rhodesia. In that case, the criterion of effectiveness was fully met, as the white, minority government, exercised effective rule over the territory. But, in spite of that, United Nations Security Council resolution 217 of 20 November 1965 established that the declaration of independence had "no legal validity" and national government had been proclaimed by "illegal authorities". Such an attitude towards Southern Rhodesia, which on the basis of the *ab intra* criterion, was a State beyond any doubt, was governed by the intention "to allow the people of Southern Rhodesia to determine their own future consistent with the objectives of General Assembly resolution 1514 (XV)" (1960)[92]. United Nations General Assembly resolution 1514 of 14 December 1960, entitled "Declaration on the Granting of Independence to Colonial Countries and Peoples" established, *inter alia*, that

> "All peoples have the right to self-determination. By virtue of that right they freely determine their political status and freely pursue their economic, social and cultural development." (Para. 2.)

In that way the practice of States confirmed that:

> "in the case of an entity seeking to become a state and accepted by the international community as being entitled to exercise the right of self-determination, it may well be necessary to demonstrate that the internal requirements of the principle have not been offended. One cannot define this condition too rigorously in view of state practice to date, but it would appear to be a sound proposition that systematic and institutionalised discrimination might invalidate a claim to statehood."[93]

However, it would be an overstatement to assert that the introduction of the concept of material legality created a harmonious unity between the *ab intra* and *ab extra* definitions of a State. This has not been achieved due to the chronic institutional insufficiency of the international order which, acting in the environment of a primarily political community — which is what the international community virtually is — often leads to the prevalence of policy over law. Hence, the discrepancy between international law and international order, since norms have not always been applied as they should have been in view of their substance, but more or less under the influence of non-legal, political views. Indisputably, the achievement of the aforementioned harmony constitutes not only an aim of but also a condition for the establishment of international order as a *de jure* order in this particular context.

---

[92] Security Council resolution 217 (1965), 20 November 1965, para. 7.
[93] M. N. Shaw, *op. cit.*, p. 132.

711]   *B. The Legality of the Proclamation of Bosnia and Herzegovina's*
Independence in the Light of the Internal Law of the Socialist Federal
Republic of Yugoslavia

1. Relevance of the internal law of the Socialist Federal Republic of
Yugoslavia in this particular case

45. The original international legal norm of self-determination of peoples is both incomplete and imperfect, at least when it concerns subjects entitled to self-determination in multi-ethnic States and their exercise of external self-determination infringing upon the territorial integrity of a State. Given its incompleteness, the original norm of self-determination of peoples is rendered inapplicable in its respective parts to certain practical situations and constitutes a sort of decorative, empty normative structure. Interested entities often refer to it, but it can function only outside the legal domain, as a convenient cover for an eminently political strategy, based on opportuneness and the balance of power.

This implies a need to see the norm of the right to external self-determination in the States composed of more than one people as a complex norm consisting of two parts: on the one hand, original international legal norms of the right of peoples to external self-determination, and, on the other, relevant parts of the internal law of the given State. In this context, the original international legal norm of the right of peoples has the role of a general, permissive norm, which assumes an operative character, the property of a norm which may become effective in the event that the internal law of a multi-ethnic State has stipulated the right to external self-determination if it defines the entitlement to it, as well as the procedure for its exercise. In other words, the relevant provisions of internal law are *ad casum* an integral part of the norm of the right of peoples to external self-determination. Only in this way does the original international legal norm of the right to external self-determination become applicable at the level of the fundamental premise of the rule of law.

The necessity for such a relationship between international and internal laws is rightfully suggested by the following:

> "If the rule of law is to be made effective in world affairs it must cover a wide range of increasingly complex transactions which are governed partly by international and partly by municipal law . . . It is therefore important that international courts and tribunals should be in a position, when adjudicating upon complex international transactions, to apply simultaneously the relevant principles and rules of international law and the provisions of any system of municipal law which may be applicable to the particular transaction . . . One of the essential functions of international law and international organisation is to promote the rule of law within as well as among nations, for only on the basis of the rule of law within nations can the rule of law among nations develop and be made

secure. International courts and tribunals can contribute to this [71?
result more effectively if the extent to which the interpretation and
application of municipal law in the course of their work is a normal
and necessary incident of international adjudication on complex
transactions is more fully understood." [94]

Positive international law free of Manicheanism and the antagonistic
burden of dualistic-monistic theoretical controversy has firmly embarked
upon this course. One can think of a long list of rules of positive international law that rest on the symbiosis of an international norm containing both implicit and explicit references to the internal law and the
respective norms of that internal law. To illustrate, Article 46 of the Convention on the Law of Treaties (1969) stipulates that a State may invoke
the fact that its consent to be bound by a treaty has been expressed in
violation of its internal law regarding competence to conclude treaties as
invalidating its consent in a case where that "violation was manifest and
concerned a rule of its internal law of fundamental importance". Or in
the law of the sea, where the subject of protection and preservation of the
marine environment is entirely regulated on the basis of a symbiosis of
international and internal laws. *Exempli causa*, Article 207 (1) (Pollution
from Land-Based Sources) of the Convention on the Law of the Sea
stipulates:

> "States shall adopt laws and regulations to prevent, reduce and
> control pollution of the marine environment from land-based sources
> . . ., taking into account internationally agreed rules, standards and
> recommended practices and procedures."

Reliance on internal law as a criterion for undertaking international
acts is not unknown in the diplomatic practice of States. One can mention the practice of the United States inaugurated by President Wilson
according to which a new test of "constitutionality" making the "coming
into power" of a new government by constitutional means is a prerequisite for recognition of that government by the United States[95].

46. Thus, in the present case, this is not a matter of a conflict between
a norm of international and a norm of internal law, a type of case adjudicated by several international courts (*Greco-Bulgarian "Communities"*, [9]
P.C.I.J., Series B, No. 17, p. 32; *Free Zones of Upper Savoy and the
District of Gex, P.C.I.J., Series A, No. 22*, p. 167; *Treatment of Polish* [10]
*Nationals and Other Persons of Polish Origin or Speech in the Danzig
Territory, P.C.I.J., Series A/B, No. 44*, p. 24), but rather of the applica- [11]
tion of an international norm of a complex structure, namely a norm that
incorporates relevant norms of internal law relating to external self-

---

[94] C. Wilfred Jenks, *The Prospects of International Adjudication*, 1964, p. 547.
[95] M. Whiteman, *Digest of International Law*, Vol. 2, p. 69.
[[9] 5 *Ann Dig* 4.]   [[10] 5 *Ann Dig* 461.]   [[11] 6 *Ann Dig* 209.]

713] determination. I am of the view that, in this case, the reasoning of the Court in the case concerning *Brazilian Loans* (1929) is relevant.

In the *Brazilian Loans* case the Court pointed out, *inter alia*, that

"[o]nce the Court has arrived at the conclusion that it is necessary to apply the municipal law of a particular country, there seems no doubt that it must seek to apply it as it would be applied in that country. It would not be applying the municipal law of a country if it were to apply it in a manner different from that in which that law would be applied in the country in which it is in force.

It follows that the Court must pay the utmost regard to the decisions of the municipal courts of a country, for it is with the aid of their jurisprudence that it will be enabled to decide what are the rules which, in actual fact, are applied in the country the law of which is recognized as applicable in a given case. If the court were obliged to disregard the decisions of municipal courts, the result would be that it might in certain circumstance apply rules other than those actually applied; this would seem to be contrary to the whole theory on which the application of municipal law is based.

Of course, the Court will endeavour to make a just appreciation of the jurisprudence of municipal courts. If this is uncertain or divided, it will rest with the Court to select the interpretation which it considers most in conformity with the law. To compel the Court to disregard that jurisprudence would not be in conformity with its function when applying municipal law." [96]

2. *Constitutional concept of the Yugoslav State — constitutional concept of Bosnia and Herzegovina as a federal unit*

47. In order to elucidate the constitutional concept of the Yugoslav State and that of Bosnia and Herzegovina as a federal unit, I will quote some relevant provisions of the constitutions of the Yugoslav State that suggest a conclusion on its nature and, more specifically, on the status of its peoples.

48. The first constitution of the Yugoslav State — the constitution of the Kingdom of Serbs, Croats and Slovenes, promulgated on 28 June 1921, stipulated that the Kingdom "is a state of Serbs, Croats and Slovenes, a constitutional, parliamentary and hereditary monarchy. The official state name is: Kingdom of Serbs, Croats and Slovenes." Article 3 of the Constitution provided that the "official language of the Kingdom will be Serb-Croat-Slovenian".

49. The Constitution of the Kingdom of Yugoslavia of 3 September 1931, did not indicate *expressis verbis* its constitutive peoples. They were

---

[96] *P.C.I.J., Series A, No. 21*, p. 124. [5 *Ann Dig* 466.]

mentioned only indirectly, as, for example, in the provision of Article 3 of [714 the Constitution stipulating that the "official language of the Kingdom [shall be] Serbian-Croat-Slovenian".

50. The resolution constituting Yugoslavia on the federal principle, approved by the Second Conference of the Anti-Fascist Council of National Liberation of Yugoslavia on 29 November 1943, said, *inter alia*,

> "By virtue of *the right of each people to self-determination includ-ing the right to separation or unification with other peoples*, . . . the Anti-Fascist Council of National Liberation of Yugoslavia, passes the following
>
> RESOLUTION
>
> . . . .
>
> (2) To effectuate the principle of sovereignty of the peoples of Yugoslavia, . . . Yugoslavia is being constructed and will be con-structed on the federal principle which will secure full equality to *Serbs, Croats, Slovenians, Macedonians and Montenegrans, id est peoples of Serbia, Croatia, Slovenia, Macedonia, Montenegro and Bosnia and Herzegovina . . ."* [97]

51. The first Constitution of the federal Yugoslavia of 1946 in its Article 1 defined the Federal Peoples' Republic of Yugoslavia as

> "a federal peoples' State in the form of a Republic, a community of equal peoples, who have expressed their will, based on the right to self-determination, including the right to separation, to live together in a federal State".

52. In the second Constitution of 1963, the Federation was defined as a:

> "Federal state of freely unified and equal peoples and a socialist democratic community based on the rule of working people and self-government."

The Constitution of the Socialist Republic of Bosnia and Herzegovina of 1963, laid down in its Basic Principles, *inter alia*, that,

> "Linked throughout their common history by their living together, by their aspirations and struggle for freedom and social progress, *Serbs, Muslims and Croats*, overcoming the attempts of foreign powers and local reactionary forces, have come together for the first time in freedom, equality and brotherhood in their Republic, which became the political and social form of both their unity and mutual equality and their *equality with the other peoples of Yugoslavia with*

---

[97] Decision on building up Yugoslavia on the federal principle, *Official Gazette of DFJ*, No. 1/1945 (emphasis added).

715] *whom they voluntarily entered a common state on the basis of the right to self-determination, including the right to separation:* the Federal Peoples' Republic of Yugoslavia thereby secured full equality and conditions of comprehensive national development, material and cultural progress for an overall socialist transformation." (Emphasis added.)

Article 1 of the Constitution of Bosnia and Herzegovina qualified it as "a state socialist democratic community of peoples of Bosnia and Herzegovina based on the rule of working people and self-government".

53. The Constitution of the SFRY of 1974 begins with Chapter I of the Basic Principles, which was worded as follows:

"The peoples of Yugoslavia, starting from the right of each nation to self-determination, including the right to secession, on the grounds of their will freely expressed in the joint struggle of all peoples and nationalities in the national liberation war and socialist revolution . . . have created a socialist federal community of working people — the Socialist Federal Republic of Yugoslavia . . .".

In Chapter VII of the Basic Principles, it is stated, *inter alia*, that the Socialist Federal Republic of Yugoslavia upholds:

"— the right of each people freely to determine and build its social and political order by ways and means freely chosen;
— the right of people to self-determination and national independence and the right to wage a liberation war, in pursuit of these causes;
— regard for generally accepted norms of international law".

The Constitution of the SFRY in its operative part, defined it as a

"federal State, a state community of freely united peoples and their socialist Republics . . . based on the rule and self-management of the working class and of all working people and the socialist self-managed democratic community of working people and citizens and equal peoples and nationalities" (Art. 1 of the Constitution).

54. The Constitution of 1974 of the Socialist Republic of Bosnia and Herzegovina laid down in its Article 1:

"The Socialist Republic of Bosnia and Herzegovina is a socialist democratic State and socialist self-managed democratic community of working people and citizens, *peoples of Bosnia and Herzegovina — Muslims, Serbs and Croats,* with the members of other peoples and nationalities, who live in it, *based on* the rule and self-manage-

ment of the working class and all working people and *on sovereignty* [716
and equality of the peoples of Bosnia and Herzegovina and the members of other nations and nationalities, living in it.

    The Socialist Republic of Bosnia and Herzegovina is an integral
part of the Socialist Federal Republic of Yugoslavia." (Emphasis
added.)

Article 2 of the Constitution of Bosnia and Herzegovina stipulates:

    "Working people and citizens, *peoples of Bosnia and Herzegovina
— Serbs, Croats and Muslims* and members of other nations and
nationalities *shall exercise their sovereign rights in the Socialist
Republic of Bosnia and Herzegovina*, except for those rights which
the Constitution of the SFRY has designated to be exercised in the
Socialist Federal Republic of Yugoslavia in the common interest of
working people and citizens, peoples and nationalities." (Emphasis
added.)

The Preamble says, *inter alia*, that

    "peoples of Bosnia and Herzegovina — *Muslims, Serbs and Croats*
. . . along with workers and other working people and citizens
and peoples and nationalities in other socialist republics and socialist autonomous provinces of the Socialist Republic of Yugoslavia achieved significant success in . . . advancing . . . unity and
equality . . ."

and further states that

    "the social and political order of Bosnia and Herzegovina is based
on the principles laid down in the SFRY constitution by the peoples
and nationalities and working people of Yugoslavia".

The Basic Principles of the Constitution stipulate that

    "*The peoples of Bosnia and Herzegovina — Serbs, Muslims and
Croats* . . . with other peoples and nationalities of Yugoslavia, . . .
*based on the right to self-determination including the right to seces-
sion, have voluntarily come together in the common State — the
Socialist Federal Republic of Yugoslavia*, and have thereby secured
full equality and the conditions for comprehensive national development . . ." (Chapter I of the Basic Principles.)

Chapter II of the same Basic Principles stipulates, *inter alia*, that

    "*the peoples of Bosnia and Herzegovina — Croats, Serbs and Mus-
lims* and members of other peoples and nationalities shall *exercise
within the Socialist Republic of Bosnia and Herzegovina*, as a State
and self-managed community, *their sovereign rights and* further their
class and *national interests.*" (Emphasis added.)

717] It is made particularly clear that

> "Starting from the principles . . . of respect for freedom and inde-
> pendence of peoples, active peaceful coexistence, openness to the
> world and the need for the development of comprehensive inter-
> national cooperation, the Socialist Republic of Bosnia and Herze-
> govina shall participate, on an equal footing with other republics
> and autonomous provinces, in the exercise of the foreign policy of
> the Socialist Republic of Yugoslavia." (Chapter X of the Basic Prin-
> ciples.)

On 31 July 1990 the Assembly of the Socialist Republic of Bosnia and
Herzegovina approved Amendments LIX-LXXX to the Constitution of
the Socialist Republic of Bosnia and Herzegovina (*Official Gazette of the
Socialist Republic of Bosnia and Herzegovina*, No. 21 of 31 July 1990).
Amendment LX replaced paragraph 1 of Article 1 of the Constitution
of the Socialist Republic of Bosnia and Herzegovina and reads as
follows:

> "1. The Socialist Republic of Bosnia and Herzegovina is *a demo-
> cratic sovereign state of equal citizens, peoples of Bosnia and Herze-
> govina — Muslims, Serbs and Croats* and members of other peoples
> and nationalities living in it."

Amendment LI stipulates that:

> "All peoples and nationalities will be guaranteed proportionate
> representation in the assemblies of socio-political communities,
> bodies elected by them in the Presidency of SR B-H and in other
> State organs" (this amendment is added to Article 3 of the Consti-
> tution of the Socialist Republic of Bosnia and Herzegovina).

Paragraph 10 of Amendment LXX stipulates that:

> "The Assembly of SR Bosnia and Herzegovina shall form a Coun-
> cil to deal with the question of the exercise of the equality of peoples
> and nationalities of Bosnia and Herzegovina. Members of the Coun-
> cil will be appointed from the ranks of deputies — members of the
> nations of Bosnia and Herzegovina — Muslims, Serbs and Croats in
> equal proportion, and respective number of deputies from the ranks
> of other peoples and nationalities and others who live in Bosnia and
> Herzegovina. The *Council shall reach its decision by a consensus of
> the members of all nations and nationalities.* The Council shall spe-
> cifically discuss the issues relating to the equality of languages and
> alphabets; the organization and activities of cultural institutions of
> particular importance for the expression and affirmation of the
> national specificities of individual peoples and nationalities and *the
> promulgation of regulations to implement constitutional provisions
> expressly determining the principles of equality among peoples and
> nationalities.*" (Emphasis added.)

55. A consistently undeniable fact, underlying the broad spectrum of **[718** changes that have affected the Yugoslav State since its inception in 1918, was a point of departure, explicit or implicit, of all constitutional solutions: *that is that Yugoslavia has primarily been a community of peoples since its birth.*

The subject of changes was the number of constitutive, State-making peoples. At the moment of its inception in 1918, Yugoslavia was a community of three constitutive peoples (Serbs, Croats and Slovenes). The Federal Constitution of 1946 recognized the status of constitutive peoples of Macedonians and Montenegrans, who used to be taken to be parts of the Serbian national *corps*. Finally, the Constitution of 1963 included Muslims in the ranks of constitutive peoples.

56. Since the formation of the Yugoslav State as a federation this *constant has governed fully, and without any reservation, the federal unit of Bosnia and Herzegovina.* Hence, the widely used but somewhat literary qualification of Bosnia and Herzegovina as the "small Yugoslavia", where the essential characteristics of the Yugoslav federation are expressed in a narrow margin.

Federal Yugoslavia was formed under the resolution of the Second Conference of the Anti-Fascist Council of National Liberation of Yugoslavia in 1943, as a community of sovereign and equal peoples, while subsequent constitutional intervention created republics, as federal units. Thus, like the rest of the republics, Bosnia and Herzegovina was formally brought into being by its Constitution of 1946, although temporary authorities had been created since the adoption of the resolution establishing Yugoslavia as a federal State.

In the light of both the federal Constitution of 1946 and the republican Constitution promulgated the same year, Bosnia and Herzegovina was formed as a State of Serb and Croat peoples. Muslims participated in the formation of the Yugoslav federation and in Bosnia and Herzegovina itself as an integral part of the Serb or Croat peoples, or more precisely as the Serbs or Croats of Muslim religion, not as a constitutive people, endowed with the right to self-determination.

57. The constitutional solutions of 1963 changed the constitutional position of Muslims, promoting them into a constitutive people. In keeping with this change Bosnia and Herzegovina was defined by its republican Constitution of 1963 as the "state socialist democratic union of peoples of Bosnia and Herzegovina . . .". The Basic Principles of the Constitution named as "peoples of Bosnia and Herzegovina": "the Serbs, Muslims and Croats". This status was reserved for the Muslims in the constitutional regulations of 1974.

In other words, the Muslims were turned into a constitutive nation *ex post*, after Bosnia and Herzegovina had been formed, on the basis of the exercised right to self-determination of Serbs and Croats, as a federal unit

719] within the Yugoslav federation. Does this fact influence the scope and quality of the rights of Muslims as a constitutive nation? The reply can only be in the negative. Having been granted the status of a constitutive nation, the Muslims came into possession of absolutely equal rights in the same way as Serbs and Croats in Bosnia and Herzegovina. The full equality of rights of constitutive peoples was accentuated *in continuo* by all constitutional solutions, whether federal or in Bosnia and Herzegovina, between 1946 and 1974. This was effected not only by the use of corresponding terms (*exempli causa*, "the right of each people"; "full equality"; "sovereignty and equality of peoples") but by inversion in quoting the names of peoples, strikingly present in the constitutions of Bosnia and Herzegovina, so as to stress both in substance and diction the full equality of constitutive peoples. *In concreto*, equality is both an explicit and implicit reference to the right of "each nation to self-determination including the right to secession or unification with other peoples".

58. *In the light of constitutional solutions and consequent legal and political practice resulting in the qualification of Bosnia and Herzegovina as a federation of nations, personal federation* sui generis *was the closest to the actual state of affairs.* Such a qualification was justified by several facts of fundamental importance.

Firstly, in the light of both norms and facts, Bosnia and Herzegovina was a community of three peoples. The Republic of Bosnia and Herzegovina was not, unlike the rest of the Yugoslav republics, a genuine, original form of the State personality of the Yugoslav State, but was created *ex post*, as a relevant form of internal administrative and territorial division of the State in the federal phase of its existence. *Ratione valorem*, Bosnia and Herzegovina was not only constituted but also functioned, in political and legal terms, as a community of peoples. It suffices to point to the composition of the bodies of authority in the Socialist Republic of Bosnia and Herzegovina. The issue of cadres in Bosnia and Herzegovina was governed by the "Social compact on personal policy in SR of Bosnia and Herzegovina"[98]. Article 7 (3) thereof bound the signatories of the compact to secure:

> "the proportionate and, in particular, adequate representation of peoples and nationalities on the assemblies of socio-political communities, state organs and bodies of socio-political organizations in the Republic and election to posts with a term of office of one or two years from among the ranks of all the peoples".

---

[98] *Official Gazette of the Socialist Republic of Bosnia and Herzegovina*, No. 34 of 8 November 1982.

Such a solution was also legally sanctioned. Article 170a of the Law on [720 the Changes and Amendments of the Law on State Administration[99] stipulated that any

"Official as head of an administrative agency and his deputy may be recalled before the end of their respective terms if so required by eligibility criteria for the equal representation of peoples . . . of Bosnia and Herzegovina in State administration and in pursuance of personnel policy".

An identical provision is contained in Article 175a of the same law relating to high political officials.

The above facts suggest that Bosnia and Herzegovina was phenomenologically only apparently a federal unit, while substantively and materially it was a union of its constitutive peoples.

Secondly, *the SFRY Constitution of 1974 and the Constitution of the Socialist Republic of Bosnia and Herzegovina promulgated the same year, defined the right to self-determination as a subjective, collective right of peoples.* Such a provision was consigned in earlier constitutions. It derives from the very nature of the matter. The subject entitled to self-determination is, by definition, a people. It is yet another question that, on the one hand, the right to self-determination is exercised on the territory in question, and that, on the other, in the circumstances of a territorialized international community the consequences of the exercised right to self-determination are territorialized. Overlapping of the right to self-determination and territorialization occurs, as a rule, in single-people communities, and it follows that formulations which recognize the right to a territorial entity are colloquial formulations. However, in multi-ethnic communities composed of peoples provided with equal rights, a territory is exclusively an area where equal rights of self-determination are exercised.

Thirdly, *Bosnia and Herzegovina, as a federal unit, was not equipped with a right to self-determination that would include the right to secession.*

Fourthly, *Bosnia and Herzegovina likewise possessed none of the classic attributes of statehood which are characteristic of federal units in modern federations.* Although a "constitutive element of the federation" Bosnia and Herzegovina was, in the structure of Yugoslav federalism like other federal units, designed — both constitutionally and legally — in a specific way. After 1963, it had dichotomic properties: on the one hand, it possessed the powers characteristic of most of the other federal units in contemporary federations, and, on the other, it represented the socialist

---

[99] *Official Gazette of the Socialist Republic of Bosnia and Herzegovina*, No. 10 of 28 March 1991.

721] self-managed democratic community of working people and citizens, peoples of Bosnia and Herzegovina — Muslims, Serbs and Croats — and members of other peoples and nationalities living in it, based on the rule and self-management of the working class and all working people, and the sovereignty and equality of peoples of Bosnia and Herzegovina (Article 1 of the Constitution of the Socialist Republic of Bosnia and Herzegovina of 1974). That dichotomy of Bosnia and Herzegovina's personality within the Yugoslav constitutional system is a result of a fundamental ideological overtone of the premise that a State, as a class creation, is a passing historical phenomenon, incompatible with the nature of a socialist society and consequently doomed to wither away. "De-etatization" was the main motto of the Yugoslav constitutional approach after the introduction of self-management as a basic social relationship — society *versus* State was the fundamental political orientation which operated even in the domain of legal norms. "De-etatization" gave birth to "working people and peoples" so that federalism was no longer "governmental" but "sociopolitical". Mutual relations between the parts of the dichotomy of Bosnia and Herzegovina attributed more weight to the part representing the self-managing community. This is clearly suggested by the constitutional positioning of self-management and the ensuing social ownership over the means of production, as the basic social relationship (Chapter II of the Basic Principles of the Constitution of the Socialist Republic of Bosnia and Herzegovina of 1974). Hence, *exempli causa* Bosnia and Herzegovina itself is defined as the "socialist self-managed democratic community" (Article 1 of the Constitution of the Socialist Republic of Bosnia and Herzegovina of 1974), while "the Assembly is an organ of socialist self-management and the highest deliberative body in the domain of rights and obligations of the socio-political community" (Article 136 of the Constitution of Bosnia and Herzegovina).

The fact that Bosnia and Herzegovina is essentially a community of peoples has been confirmed by the consolidated text of the Constitution of Bosnia and Herzegovina adopted in March 1993 after the proclamation of the sovereignty and independence of that federal unit as well as by a series of instruments on the international plane. Article 1 of that consolidated text defines the Republic of Bosnia and Herzegovina as a "sovereign and independent state . . . of the peoples of Bosnia and Herzegovina — Moslems, Serbs, Croats and members of other peoples living in it". The precise sense of that wording may be ascertained when one takes into account the interpretative provision of Article 269 of the refined text of the Constitution (Transitional Final Provisions). Article 269 provides that:

> "The term used in the Constitution 'members of other peoples who live in the Republic' or 'members of other peoples who live in it' denotes the nationalities of national minorities in Bosnia and Herzegovina."

The above-mentioned text of the Constitution likewise conserved the substantial characteristics of Bosnia and Herzegovina as a personal federation. On the basis of the principle of the "equality of the peoples [722 of Bosnia and Herzegovina" it is stipulated that:

> "In the assemblies of the socio-political communities, and in the bodies elected by them of the Presidency of the Republic of Bosnia and Herzegovina, proportional representation shall be guaranteed to the peoples of Bosnia and Herzegovina and to the other peoples living in it." [100]

All the plans for the constitutional arrangements of Bosnia and Herzegovina submitted during the negotiations about the peaceful solution of the conflict in Bosnia and Herzegovina start from the qualification of Bosnia and Herzegovina as a community of peoples.

In the draft "Constitutional Structure for Bosnia and Hercegovina", submitted by the Co-Chairmen on 27 October 1992, and on 16 November specifically endorsed by the Security Council (resolution 787 (1992) para. 1) (the so-called Vance-Owen Plan), it is said, *inter alia*, that: *"(c)* The constitution is to recognize three 'constituent peoples', as well as groups of 'others'" [101]. Article 1 of Chapter 1 of the "Constitutional Arrangements of the Union of Republic of Bosnia and Herzegovina" submitted by the Co-Chairmen Owen and Stoltenberg in September 1993, envisaged that:

> "[t]he Union of Republic of Bosnia and Hercegovina is composed of three Constituent Republics and encompasses three constituent peoples: the Muslims, Serbs and Croats, as well as a group of other peoples" [102].

In the Preamble to Annex 4 of the Dayton Agreement "Bosniacs, Croats, and Serbs" are qualified as constituent peoples (A/50/790/S/1995/999, p. 59). So it can be said that the fact that Bosnia and Herzegovina is essentially a community of peoples is recognized on an international plane.

3. The promulgation of Bosnia and Herzegovina as a sovereign State

59. In the part of the Memorial entitled: "The International Status of Bosnia and Herzegovina", *"(a)* The alleged absence of statehood of Bosnia and Herzegovina", the Applicant, summing up its views of the subject matter, states:

> "The existence of the main elements in this respect has been summed up by the Arbitration Commission in its Opinion No. 11 of 16 July 1993:

---

[100] Article 3 (1.3) of the refined text of the Constitution of the Republic of Bosnia and Herzegovina.
[101] ICFY/6, Annex I, S/25403.

[102] Agreement relating to Bosnia and Herzegovina, ICFY, Appendix I.

723] 'in a referendum held on 29 February and 1 March 1992, the majority of people of the Republic have expressed themselves in favour of a sovereign and independent Bosnia, the result of the referendum was officially promulgated on 6 March, and since that date, notwithstanding the dramatic events that have occurred in Bosnia and Herzegovina, the constitutional authorities of the Republic have acted like those of sovereign state in order to maintain its territorial integrity and their full and exclusive powers'." [103]

60. Two conditions should have been met to make the promulgation of sovereignty and independence of Bosnia and Herzegovina legally perfect, in the light of internal law of SFRY, as follows:

first, that Yugoslav law should have provided for the right to secession of federal units; and

second, that the procedure prescribed by the Constitution and law should have been observed, for,

"[w]hether the federation dissolves into two or more states also brings into focus the doctrine of self-determination in the form of secession. Such a dissolution may be the result of an amicable and constitutional agreement or may occur pursuant to a forceful exercise of secession. In the latter case, international legal rules may be pleaded in aid, but the position would seem to be that (apart from recognised colonial situations) there is no right of self-determination applicable to independent states that would justify the resort to secession." [104]

61. The Yugoslav federal units possessed no right to secession (*jus secessionis*), beyond any doubt. The right to self-determination was absolutely reserved for constitutive nations (see paras. 48-56 above).

In the part relating to external self-determination, the provisions of the SFRY constitution offer the conclusion that the right to external self-determination had been fully exercised.

To begin with "the right to self-determination, including the right to secession" was formulated in the past tense in the SFRY Constitution, as in all previous constitutions of the federal Yugoslavia. Then, the right in question was located in the Basic Principles of the Constitution and there was no mention of it in the operative provisions of the Constitution. Finally, neither the Constitution nor the law envisaged any procedure for an exercise of the right to self-determination. In other words, the constitutive nations of Yugoslavia exercised the right to external self-determination at the time of the formation of the federal Yugoslavia. Once they had decided to live in a common State they dispensed with that right, which from that time on constituted a legal merit of existence of the com-

[103] Memorial, para. 4.2.1.10.
[104] M. N. Shaw, *International Law*, 1986, p. 139.

mon state, its *validus titulus*, but not a living, topical right to be resorted **[724** to at will. This does not mean, however, that the issue of the right to external self-determination was closed for good. It could, like other issues, have been redefined in the guaranteed constitutional procedure.

The Constitutional Court of Yugoslavia, as the main agent securing constitutionality and legality in the constitutional system of SFRY, underscored in its decision I U No. 108/1-91 (*Official Gazette of SFRY*, No. 83/91) that, *inter alia*:

> "this right [right to self-determination including the right to secession] may be exercised *only under conditions and in a manner to be determined in conformity with the SFRY constitution and the right of peoples of self-determination including the right to secession —* under an enactment promulgated by the SFRY Assembly or in agreement among the peoples of Yugoslavia and their republics" (emphasis added).

Therefore, in the light of the relevant provisions of the SFRY Constitution, the ruling of the Constitutional Court of Yugoslavia reads as follows:

> "any enactment of a republic that declares the republic to be a sovereign and independent state — is an unconstitutional change of the state order of Yugoslavia, i.e., an act of secession, which, by virtue of the decision of the Constitutional Court of Yugoslavia can have no legal effect" [105].

The proposal to resolve the controversies surrounding the exercise of the right to external self-determination *constitutione artis*, namely via a corresponding constitutional revision, was contained in the "Concept for the Future Organization of the State proposed by a Working Group comprising Representatives of all the Republics as a basis for further Talks between the Republican President and the State Presidency".
Starting from the basic premise that

> "The Yugoslav state community, séen as a federal state of equal citizens and equal peoples and their republics [footnote commentary: Kasim Trnka from Bosnia and Herzegovina proposed that the republics be placed first] and as a democratic state, will be founded on human and civil rights and liberties, the rule of law and social justice",

---

[105] Reply of the Constitutional Court of Yugoslavia to the question of Lord Carrington whether it was a matter of dissolution or secession — referred to by the Arbitration Commission of ICFY, No. SU 365/91.

725] the "Concept" contains a part entitled "Proposed Procedure for Disassociation from Yugoslavia" which reads:

"In connection with initiatives in certain republics for secession from Yugoslavia, that is, the 'disunion' of the country, and in view of the general demand for a peaceful, democratic and constitutional resolution of the constitutional crisis, the question of procedure arises with regard to the possible realization of these initiatives.

The aim of the initiatives is the withdrawal of certain republics from the Socialist Federal Republic of Yugoslavia. *They are based on the permanent and inalienable right of peoples to self-determination and should be constitutionally regulated.*

The right of peoples to self-determination, as one of the universal rights of modern law, is set out in the basic principles of the SFRY Constitution.

However, the realization of the right of peoples to secession, which includes the possibility of certain republics' withdrawal from the SFRY, is not regulated by the SFRY Constitution. It is therefore necessary to amend the SFRY Constitution in order to create a basis for exercising this right.

Revision of the SFRY Constitution on these lines should be based on the democratic nature of the entire process of statement of views, the equality of the Yugoslav nations, the protection of fundamental human and civil rights and freedoms, and the principle of the peaceful resolution of all disputes.

In keeping with the above, appropriate amendments should be made to the SFRY Constitution which would in a general manner regulate the procedure for the execution of the right of peoples to secession and thereby the withdrawal of certain republics from the SFRY.

The amendments to the SFRY Constitution should express the following commitments:

1. The right to launch the initiative for a certain republic to withdraw from the SFRY is vested in the Assembly of the respective republic, except if otherwise regulated by the republican constitution.

2. A decision on the initiative is taken at a referendum at which the free, direct and secret voting of all citizens of the republic is ensured.

3. During the preparations for the referendum, the public and voters will be informed objectively and on time of the importance and the consequences of the referendum.

4. The referendum will be monitored by representatives of the Assembly of Yugoslavia and, possibly, representatives of other republics and interested international institutions.

5. A decision will be deemed adopted if it receives more than one [726 half of the votes of all registered voters.

6. *In republics populated by members of several Yugoslav nations, the necessary majority will be established for each Yugoslav nation separately. If one nation votes against, all settlements in which this nation is predominant and which border on the remaining territory of Yugoslavia and can constitute its territorial compactness will remain part of the SFRY.*

7. If the result of the referendum is negative, the same initiative may be launched after the expiry of a period of five years.

8. The Assembly of the republic will inform the public and the Assembly of Yugoslavia of the result of the referendum, and will submit to the Assembly of Yugoslavia a proposal to adopt a constitutional enactment on the withdrawal of the respective republic from the SFRY, in accordance with the will of the people expressed at the referendum.

9. The Assembly of Yugoslavia acknowledges the legality and legitimacy of the expressed will of the people and members of nations, and instructs the Federal Government to carry out the necessary preparations for the adoption of the enactment on withdrawal from the SFRY.

In this context, the Federal Government is obligated to:

(a) prepare a proposal for the division of jointly created values and the property of the federation (movable and immovable property) in the country and abroad registered as the property of the federation; international obligations and claims; assets of the National Bank of Yugoslavia; foreign currency, commodity and monetary reserves of the federation, property of the Yugoslav People's Army, archives of Yugoslavia, certain infrastructure facilities, licences and other rights and obligations ensuing from ratified international conventions. The Federal Government proposal would also include issues relating to citizenship, pension and other rights of citizens and the like. This requires the establishment of common responsibility for the obligations and guarantees of the SFRY toward foreign countries;

(b) propose to the Assembly of Yugoslavia the manner of the election and authorization of a parity body or committee which will prepare a proposal for the division of rights and obligations and submit it to the Assembly of Yugoslavia;

(c) prepare proposals for the territorial demarcation and the frontiers of the future states and other issues of importance for formulating the enactment on withdrawal.

10. On the basis of the Federal Government proposals regarding material and territorial issues, the Assembly of Yugoslavia will

727]   formulate, with the consent of the republican assemblies, a constitutional enactment (constitutional law) on withdrawal from the SFRY which, among other things, establishes:

— citizens' right of choice (term and manner in which citizens will state their choice in the event of territorial changes), and the obligation to ensure just compensation for change of residence);

— the obligation to provide judicial protection of the rights of citizens, legal entities and members of certain nations (compensation for damages resulting directly from the execution of the right to withdrawal, etc.);

— the obligation to harmonize certain laws and other enactments with changes in the structure of the SFRY;

— supervision and control of the enforcement of determined obligations;

— other issues which must be resolved by the time of the definitive disassociation (judiciary, environment protection, joint ventures and the like);

— the transitional period and the moment of disassociation from the SFRY." [106]

However, Bosnia and Herzegovina did not accept the proposed "Concept", as clearly demonstrated by the arrangements for the referendum on "sovereign and independent Bosnia".

62. The promulgation of Bosnia and Herzegovina as a "sovereign and independent Bosnia" was, according to item 4.2.1.10 of the Memorial, composed of two elements, two actions:

(1) a referendum held on 29 February and 1 March 1992, when the majority of people of the Republic expressed themselves in favour of a sovereign and independent Bosnia; and

(2) the official promulgation of the results of the referendum on 6 March 1992. The sovereignty and independence of Bosnia were constituted on that date, in view of the fact that according to Bosnia and Herzegovina:

> "*Since that date* notwithstanding the dramatic events that have occurred in Bosnia-Herzegovina, the constitutional authorities of the Republic have acted like those of sovereign State in order to maintain its territorial integrity and thus full and exclusive powers." (Emphasis added.)

A correct interpretation of the above-quoted statement of Bosnia and Herzegovina leads one to the conclusion that Bosnia and Herzegovina

---

[106] *Focus*, Special Issue, January 1992, pp. 31-33.

has been constituted as "sovereign and independent Bosnia" since the [728
date of promulgation of the referendum results. In other words, the
promulgation of the results of the referendum held on 29 February and
1 March had a constitutive, State-making character.

63. The referendum of 29 February and 1 March asked the following:

> "Are you for a sovereign and independent Bosnia and Herze-
> govina, a State of equal citizens, peoples of Bosnia and Herzegovina
> — Muslims, Serbs and Croats and members of other peoples living
> in it?"

The referendum was called in order to "determine the status of Bosnia
and Herzegovina". The decision to call the referendum was taken by virtue of Article 152 of the Constitution of the Socialist Republic of Bosnia
and Herzegovina, the provision of item 5, line 9, of Amendment LXXI to
the Constitution of the Socialist Republic of Bosnia and Herzegovina
and the provisions of Articles 3 and 26 of the Law on Referendum[107].

There can be no doubt that the Assembly of the Socialist Republic of
Bosnia and Herzegovina had the authority to call a referendum, in the
light of the above-mentioned facts — both a preliminary referendum, i.e.,
a referendum for preliminary voting, and a subsequent one for the confirmation of laws, regulations and other enactments.

64. It is questionable, however, whether the Assembly of the Socialist
Republic of Bosnia and Herzegovina was entitled to call a referendum in
order to determine the status of Bosnia and Herzegovina.

Starting from a general provision that "the Assembly of SR Bosnia
and Herzegovina is exercising its rights and responsibilities on the basis
of and within the constitution and law"[108] and abiding by the relevant
rule on the relationship between the constitution and law, we now turn to
Article 314 of the Constitution of the Socialist Republic of Bosnia and
Herzegovina which stipulates the competences of the Assembly of the
Socialist Republic of Bosnia and Herzegovina:

> "The Assembly of SR Bosnia and Herzegovina shall:
>
> (1) Decide on the changes of the Constitution of the Socialist
> Republic of Bosnia and Herzegovina; submit a proposal or opinion,
> or issue an approval of the changes to the Constitution of the
> SFRY;
>
> (2) Determine the policy and decide on other fundamental issues
> of relevance to the political, economic, social and cultural develop-
> ment of the Republic;
>
> (3) Consider the issues of common interest to the organizations of
> associated labour and other self-managed organizations and com-

---

[107] *Official Gazette of the Socialist Republic of Bosnia and Herzegovina*, No. 29 (1977)
and 24 (1991).
[108] Article 313 of the Constitution of the Socialist Republic of Bosnia and Herzegovina.

729] munities and harmonize their relations and interests; encourage self-management agreements and social compacts;

(4) Consider the issues in the sphere of foreign policy and international relations: approve the negotiation of international treaties in cases stipulated by the SFRY Constitution;

(5) Determine the proposals, or approve arrangements for relationships to be decided on by the Assembly of the Socialist Federal Republic of Yugoslavia on the merit of a proposal, namely agreement by the republic assemblies;

(6) Adopt the social plan of Bosnia and Herzegovina, the budget of the Republic, the balance sheet, the republican global balance of resources and the land development plan of Bosnia and Herzegovina; pass the laws and other regulations and general enactments; issue authentic interpretations of republican laws;

(7) Decide on modifications of republican borders;

(8) Determine the system of national defence in the Republic;

(9) Grant amnesty for criminal offences stipulated in the law of the Republic;

(10) Decide on the indebtedness of the Republic and on calling public loans in the Republic;

(11) Establish work organizations;

(12) Call a republican referendum;

(13) Determine the policy of enforcement of republican laws and other regulations and general enactments and obligations of the organs and organizations in the Republic and enforcement of the federal and republican laws;

(14) Supervise politically the performances of the Executive Council and republican bodies of authority and their organizations and issue general guidelines; supervise politically the holders of public and other social functions, reporting to the Assembly;

(15) Hear the opinions and proposals of the Constitutional Court of Bosnia and Herzegovina concerning the protection of constitutionality and legality;

(16) Hear the reports of the republican judiciary on law enforcement and their performance and issue position papers on these reports;

(17) Exercise public surveillance;

(18) Elect and recall the president and members of the Presidency of the Socialist Republic of Bosnia and Herzegovina and the members of the Presidency of the Socialist Federal Republic of Yugoslavia;

(19) Elect and recall the delegation of the Assembly to the Chamber of Republics and Provinces in the SFRY Assembly;

(20) Elect and recall the President and Vice-President of the [730
Assembly, members of commissions, committees and of other bodies
of the Assembly;

(21) Elect and recall the President and members of the Executive
Council, the President and Judges of the Constitutional Court of
Bosnia and Herzegovina, the President and Judges of the Supreme
Court of Bosnia and Herzegovina and other courts stipulated by law
and members of the Council of the Republic;

(22) Appoint and recall republican Secretaries and other execu-
tives of the republican bodies of authority and organizations acting
in the spheres of interest of the Republic; the republican Social
Attorney of Self-management, the Secretary-General and secretaries
of the Assembly, the Republican prosecutor, the Governor of the
National Bank of Bosnia and Herzegovina and other officials, members of decision-making bodies and members of managing bodies of
the organizations stipulated as such by this constitution and the law;

(23) Decide on the extension of terms of office of the delegates to
the assemblies of socio-political communities;

(24) Perform other functions laid down in the present Constitution.

The Assembly may pass declarations, resolutions and recommendations."

The provision of paragraph 12 of Article 134 of the Constitution entitling
the Assembly "to call a referendum" means that the Assembly is to call
the referendum on issues falling within its competence. The need for such
an interpretation is found in the Law on Referendum which says that the
"Assembly of SR Bosnia and Herzegovina may call a referendum on
issues falling within its purview" (Art. 26 of the Law). The formulation of
the referendum question clearly indicates the intention of *changing* the
status of Bosnia and Herzegovina in terms of public law. The *ratio* of the
referendum was to transform Bosnia and Herzegovina from a federal
unit within the Yugoslav federation into "sovereign and independent
Bosnia" as the referendum question reads. If this were not the case, the
referendum would have been devoid of any purpose in view of the fact
that certain elements of statehood inherent to the Yugoslav model of
federalism were accorded to Bosnia and Herzegovina at the time when
the referendum was called.

The purpose of the referendum question was, in the strictly formal
legal context, to determine the status of Bosnia and Herzegovina in terms
of public law. Hence, the purpose of referendum was contrary both to the
Constitution of Bosnia and Herzegovina and the Constitution of SFRY.
More particularly, the Constitution of Bosnia and Herzegovina stipulates
in Article 1 (2) that the Socialist Republic of Bosnia and Herzegovina is
a part of SFRY. The Constitution of SFRY defined the federation as "a
federal state . . . of socialist republics" (Art. 1 of the Constitution), one
member of which, besides other republics, was the Republic of Bosnia
and Herzegovina (Art. 5 (1) of the Constitution) and provided that the

731] "frontier of the SFRY cannot be changed without the consent of all the republics" (Art. 5 (3) of the Constitution). Obviously, in terms of the relevant constitutional regulations, the very fact of calling a referendum on the status of Bosnia and Herzegovina constituted a potential threat to the territorial integrity of SFRY protected by the SFRY Constitution, or more particularly, an act incriminated by the Penal Code of SFRY.

The very promulgation of the "sovereignty and independence" of Bosnia and Herzegovina on the basis of the referendum held, constituted a threat to the territorial integrity of the SFRY.

65. The act of launching a referendum in order to "determine the status of Bosnia and Herzegovina" was formally and materially unconstitutional.

Elements of formal unconstitutionality are demonstrated by the fact that the Assembly of the Socialist Republic of Bosnia and Herzegovina called a referendum which fell outside its constitutionally and legally limited jurisdiction. *In concreto*, this is a case of specific non-competence, because the organ otherwise competent to call a referendum, having called a referendum on the "status of Bosnia and Herzegovina", had acted *ultra vires*. At the same time, calling a referendum on the "status of Bosnia and Herzegovina" constituted an unconstitutional act in the material sense (material unconstitutionality), because the building of Bosnia and Herzegovina as a "sovereign and independent" State, taken *per se*, was contrary to the SFRY Constitution. More particularly, the "sovereignty and independence of Bosnia" means an automatic modification of the State frontiers of SFRY, while by virtue of the SFRY Constitution the State territory is but one (Art. 5 (1) of the Constitution) and "the frontier of SFRY cannot be changed without the consent of all republics" (Art. 5 (3) of the Constitution). Moreover, calling a referendum was materially unconstitutional in terms of the Constitution of Bosnia and Herzegovina itself. Amendment LXX to the Constitution of the Socialist Republic of Bosnia and Herzegovina established, in its paragraph 10, a Council entrusted with the exercise of the right to equality of nations and nationalities of Bosnia and Herzegovina. The mandate of the Council is *inter alia* to "consider in particular the questions relating to . . . the promulgation of regulations ensuring the materialization of constitutional provisions which provide explicitly for the principle of equality of peoples and nationalities". The Council is composed of an

"equal number of deputies from among the ranks of members of peoples of Bosnia and Herzegovina — Muslims, Serbs and Croats, and a corresponding number of deputies members of other people and nationalities and the others who live in Bosnia and Herzegovina",

who are to take decisions "on the merit of agreement of members from among the ranks of all peoples and nationalities".

The *ratio legis* of Amendment LXX (10) certainly lies in ensuring and **[73?** guaranteeing the equality of peoples. The significance attached to the Council, within the constitutional system of Bosnia and Herzegovina, is amply demonstrated in paragraph 10, which says that

> "in questions of interest to the exercise of equality of peoples and nationalities in B-H, at the proposal of the Council, the Assembly shall decide, by means of a specific procedure set out in the Rules of Order of the Assembly of the Socialist Republic Bosnia and Herzegovina, by a two-thirds majority of the total number of deputes".

The Council was designed by the Constitution as an unavoidable instance, a forum where deliberations were concentrated and proposals originated for the equality of peoples. In view of these facts, the proposal to call a referendum on the "status of Bosnia and Herzegovina" must have been an issue for consideration by the Council, as this is the question that directly infringed upon "the principles of equality among peoples and nationalities".

The circle of formal and material unconstitutionality encompasses also the act of "official promulgation of the results of the referendum on March 6, 1992". The qualification of "official promulgation" invokes, *mutatis mutandis*, the relevance of the facts corroborating the formal and material unconstitutionality of calling the referendum on the status of Bosnia and Herzegovina.

The referendum on the "status of Bosnia and Herzegovina" falls into the category of the so-called preliminary referenda in the constitutional regulation of the Socialist Republic of Bosnia and Herzegovina, since the purpose had been a preliminary voting of citizens on the relevant issue of the status of Bosnia and Herzegovina. That is why the "official promulgation of the results of a referendum" is, actually, a legal act. More particularly, voting of citizens in a referendum is no decision in formal terms, irrespective of whether the result of the voting is or is not binding on the organ which called the referendum. The result of the referendum is a material condition for decision-making in formal terms and this is, in the present case, the nature of the "official promulgation".

Such a legal nature of the "official promulgation" of a federal unit of Bosnia and Herzegovina as a "sovereign and independent" State constitutes an additional aspect of material unconstitutionality in respect to the relevant decisions of the Constitution of the Socialist Republic of Bosnia and Herzegovina. More particularly, Article 252 of that Constitution stipulated that the:

> "[s]acred and inalienable right and responsibility of peoples and nationalities . . . of Bosnia and Herzegovina is to safeguard and foster freedom, independence, sovereignty, *territorial unity and the constitutionally established social system of the SFRY and the Socialist Republic Bosnia and Herzegovina*" (emphasis added).

733] Item 7 of Amendment LXIX to the Constitution of the Socialist Republic of Bosnia and Herzegovina provided that: "Political organizations and acts aimed at the forceful change of the constitutionally established system, and *threats to the territorial unity and independence of SFRY*" (emphasis added) are prohibited. Both of the constitutional provisions mentioned above include "territorial unity" as a constitutionally protected object while "official promulgation" is a form of direct threat to that object.

66. The referendum for determination of the status of Bosnia and Herzegovina was called in the form of a referendum of citizens. This fact derives from the method of voting at the referendum, which remained undisputed by Bosnia and Herzegovina, as it stated in its Memorial, in the context of the promulgation of its sovereignty and independence (Memorial, para. 4.2.1.10), *inter alia*, that "the majority of the people of the Republic" voted positively on the referendum question. The use of the term "people" in the singular undoubtedly suggests that Bosnia and Herzegovina is also of the view that this was but a civic referendum.

Was a civic referendum, in the form of a direct expression of the will of citizens, quite apart from the questions elaborated in items 5 and 6, a good way in which to decide the "status of Bosnia and Herzegovina"? Civic referendum is, *per definitionem*, a form of the exercise of national sovereignty, that is to say, the rule of the people as *Demos*. Since three peoples exist in Bosnia and Herzegovina and are provided with the right to self-determination, it is indisputable, irrespective of the reasons stated in paragraphs 5 and 27 of this opinion, that the form of civic referendum is absolutely inadequate to express the will of each of the three peoples. In some sort of ultimately strained hypothesis that "sovereign and independent Bosnia" was voted for by such a majority of citizens embodying the majority of each of the members of the three peoples, it might be said that a civic referendum consummated the national referendum, although *per se* it was not such a referendum. But that was not the case, as is known. In view of the fact that all the three peoples of Bosnia and Herzegovina are, by virtue of the Constitution of Bosnia and Herzegovina, "sovereign and equal", a national referendum is only relevant for the direct exercise of the right to self-determination. A separate exercise of the right to self-determination could have been anticipated by means of a corresponding decision taken by elected representatives of the three peoples of Bosnia and Herzegovina, particularly as in 1990, democratic multiparty elections were held in Bosnia and Herzegovina. Maps of constituencies correctly mirrored the ethnic structure of Bosnia and Herzegovina since the national parties of the three peoples individually gathered practically all the votes of their national *corps*.

The referendum was an inadequate form of voting on the "status of Bosnia and Herzegovina" not only because of the reasons relating to its constitutionality and essential inability to express the will of the three peoples of Bosnia and Herzegovina, but because of the very provisions of the Law on Referendum on the basis of which it was held.

The provisions of the Law on Referendum of Bosnia and Herzegovina [734
taken *per se* are certainly not formulated so as to imply the possibility
of deciding "on the status of Bosnia and Herzegovina" by means of a
referendum, as designed by the Law.

Apart from the general provisions on calling the referendum already
discussed in paragraph 5 of this opinion, the provisions concerning the
method of decision-making and the individuals participating in the
voting are also of relevance.

Article 33 of the Law stipulates that the

> "decision on referendum is to be taken by a majority vote of all
> working people and citizens registered as voters in the territory
> or part of the territory of SR of Bosnia and Herzegovina where the
> referendum is called".

The decision at the referendum is to be taken by majority vote. Leaving aside the issue of the legality of a referendum, a logical question
arises, i.e., whether a valid issue, such as "the status of Bosnia and Herzegovina", may possibly be decided by simple majority. The rational reason
underlying this question relates to the fact that the Constitution of the
Socialist Republic of Bosnia and Herzegovina stipulated voting of at
least two-thirds of the total number of voters of the Socialist Republic of
Bosnia and Herzegovina on the question of a change of borders of the
Socialist Republic of Bosnia and Herzegovina (Amendment LXII to Article 5 of the Constitution[109]). In other words, the constitutional requirement for the correction of indirectly determined lines of administrative
division within the federation was a two-thirds majority, while the Law on
Referendum required a simple majority for the decision on the status of
Bosnia and Herzegovina in terms of public law. This is, in my view, sufficient proof that the legislator did not, when passing the Law on Referendum (either irrespective of the Constitution of the Socialist Republic of
Bosnia and Herzegovina or just relying on the Constitution of the Socialist
Republic of Bosnia and Herzegovina), have in mind a referendum of that
kind. More particularly, it is difficult to imagine that the legislator would
lay down much stricter requirements for a referendum on the change of
borders, which in the practice of the Yugoslav federal units was nothing
but a couple of hectares of pasture lands, forests or villages, than
for a referendum on the fateful, existential question of the very federal
unit.

The Law on Referendum also stipulated that "all working people and
citizens included in voters' lists in the territory, namely that part of territory of SR B-H where referendum shall take place", shall have the right
to vote in the referendum (Art. 33 of the Law). Such a provision raises
the question about who in fact was voting at the referendum. The provision entitling "all working people and citizens" to vote means that the
criterion of eligibility to vote was not citizenship in the republic. The only

---

[109] *Official Gazette of the Socialist Republic of Bosnia and Herzegovina*, No. 21 (1990).

735] criterion was residence, since it was a condition of enlistment for voting. Hence, the right to vote in the referendum was, for instance, accorded to Slovenes or Macedonians, who had a residence in Bosnia and Herzegovina, while Muslims or Serbs, citizens of Bosnia and Herzegovina, who resided in another republic were deprived of that right.

67. Finally, from the standpoint of the Constitutional law of SFRY, it would be hard to imagine a more meritorious judgment on the legal evaluation of the referendum on the "status of Bosnia and Herzegovina" than the one handed down by the Constitutional Court of Yugoslavia as the main proponent of constitutionality and legality in the constitutional system of SFRY (Art. 375 of the SFRY Constitution). The Constitutional Court of Yugoslavia never took up the referendum on the status of Bosnia and Herzegovina as a separate issue. However, it made several rulings on the analogous acts of federal units which had promulgated "sovereignty and independence" before Bosnia and Herzegovina. Apart from the actual decisions of the Constitutional Court of Yugoslavia in the concrete cases, we shall quote from relevant parts of the explanations of those decisions since they extend beyond the framework of the concrete issue in formal and material terms, on which the court ruled. In other words they constitute a meritorious legal evaluation of the highest judicial instance in SFRY on the relevant question. In ruling I U No. 108/1-91 (*Official Gazette of SFRY*, No. 83/91), the Constitutional Court pointed out, *inter alia*, that

"The right of peoples of Yugoslavia to self-determination, including the right to secession, may not, in the view of the Constitutional Court of Yugoslavia, be exercised by unilateral acts of the peoples of Yugoslavia, namely enactments of the Assemblies of the republics within the Socialist Federal Republic of Yugoslavia . . . Although the procedure for the exercise of the right to self-determination including the right to secession is not provided for by the SFRY Constitution, this does not mean that the right can be exercised on the basis of unilateral acts on self-determination and secession. No people and, more particularly, no assembly of a republic can, by means of a unilateral act, decide on the exercise of that right before the procedure and conditions governing the procedure have been jointly determined for the exercise of that right.

A unilateral promulgation of sovereignty and independence of republics making up the Socialist Federal Republic of Yugoslavia implies, in the opinion of the Constitutional Court of Yugoslavia, an infringement upon the provisions of the SFRY Constitution concerning the composition of the Socialist Federal Republic of Yugoslavia and of the frontiers of Yugoslavia as a federal state and state community of voluntarily united peoples and their socialist republics."

It is worth mentioning that the above ruling was approved in the course **[736**
of the court deliberations in full composition as provided for in
Article 381 of the SFRY Constitution and in the presence of both judges
from Bosnia and Herzegovina.

C. *Legality of the Proclamation of Independence of Bosnia and Herzegovina in the Light of International Law*

68. In a series of international instruments starting with the United
Nations Charter and continuing via the Declaration on the Granting of
Independence to Colonial Countries and Peoples (1960), and the Covenants on Human Rights (1966), to the Declaration on Principles of
International Law concerning Friendly Relations and Co-operation
among States in Accordance with the Charter of the United Nations
(1974), the equal rights and self-determination of peoples has been of
essential universal value of the democratic *ordre public* embodied in the
United Nations Charter, and raised to a positive norm of general international law with the character of *jus cogens*[110]. In the case concerning
East Timor, the Court in its Judgment stated *inter alia*: [12]

> "In the Court's view, . . . the right of peoples to self-determina-
> tion, as it is evolved from the Charter and from United Nations
> practice, has an *erga omnes* character . . . the principle of self-deter-
> mination of peoples has been recognized by the United Nations
> Charter and in the jurisprudence of the Court (see *Legal Conse-
> quences for States of the Continued Presence of South Africa in
> Namibia (South West Africa) notwithstanding Security Council
> Resolution 276 (1970), Advisory Opinion, I.C.J. Reports 1971,* [13]
> pp. 31-32, paras. 52-53; *Western Sahara, Advisory Opinion, I.C.J.* [14]
> *Reports 1975,* pp. 31-33, paras. 54-59); it is one of the essential prin-
> ciples of contemporary international law."[111]

---

[110] J. J. Caicedo Perdomo, "La teoria del *ius cogens* en derecho internacional a la luz de
la Convención de Viena sobre el derecho de los tratados", *Revista de la Academia colom-
bina de jurisprudencia*, January-June 1975, pp. 216-274; L. Alexidze, "Legal Nature of *jus
cogens* in Contemporary International Law", *Recueil des cours de l'Académie de droit
international de La Haye*, Vol. 172, 1981, p. 262; Bedjaoui notes that "Among those principles, 'the right of complete independence' and 'the right of self-determination' are considered to be inalienable and must accordingly be recognized immediately and unconditionally" *[translation by the Registry]:* "Non-alignement et droit international", *ibid.*,
Vol. 151, 1976, p. 421. M. Šahović, "Codification of the Legal Principles of Coexistence
and the Development of Contemporary International Law", in *Principles of International
Law Concerning Friendly Relations and Cooperation*, 1972, p. 23; draft rules on International Responsibility; the list of international crimes covers also "*(b)* a serious breach of
an international obligation of essential importance of safeguarding the right of self-determination of peoples" (Art. 19), Fifth Report on State Responsibility, *Yearbook of the
International Law Commission*, 1976, Vol. II, Part Two, p. 75).
[111] *I.C.J. Reports 1995*, p. 102.

[12] 105 *ILR* 226.]   [13] 49 *ILR* 2.]   [14] 59 *ILR* 13 at 30.]

737] 69. Equal rights and self-determination of peoples is a complex norm in terms of structure.

On the one hand, the very phrase "equal rights and self-determination of peoples" is a link, an amalgam of a general legal principle ("equal rights") and the norm on the self-determination of peoples. "Equal rights" in the above phrase, as a normative substitute for "equality of States", has a broader meaning because it defines, in a broader form, the relationship of each people taken individually to the sum of rights recognized to peoples under international law. Its virtual meaning lies in a prohibition of any distinction between peoples and the respective rights recognized to them. In other words, the principle of "equal rights" defines the scope of the norms of international law that relate to the status of peoples. The right to self-determination does, however, have an immediate material substance as

> "all peoples have the right freely to determine, without external interference, their political status and to pursue their economic, social and cultural development and every State has the duty to respect this right in accordance with the provisions of the Charter" (para. 1 of the Declaration on Principles).

On the other hand, the norm on "equal rights and self-determination of peoples" is incomplete, less than full norm in view of its application. More particularly, it contains no definition of the notion of "people" and no such definition, as an institutional mechanism authorized to define what a "people" is, can be found to exist in the international law in force. That is why the only way to make the norms on "equal rights and self-determination of peoples" operational and effective is to take the norms of internal law which define "peoples", as relevant (paras. 44-45 above). The norms of internal law can likewise be relevant in the event of an exercise of external self-determination in States comprising more than one people, in view of the nature of the prohibition of violations of territorial integrity and political unity.

70. Certain strong arguments support the assertation that the proclamation of Bosnia and Herzegovina as a "sovereign and independent" State within its administrative borders was a violation of the fundamental entitlement to equal rights and self-determination of peoples.

On the assumption that other relevant processes and material requirements were in place (paras. 59-63 above), the merit of the proclamation of Bosnia and Herzegovina as a "sovereign and independent" State, could only relate to the converging will of the three peoples in Bosnia and Herzegovina. However, there was an evident divergence in the basic political stances of the representatives of these three peoples. While the will of the Muslim political leadership was expressed in the Draft Declaration on the Sovereign Bosnia and Herzegovina since February 1991, which has been, at least temporarily, accepted by Croat political leaders,

the political leadership of Bosnian Serbs insisted on the preservation of [73**
Bosnia and Hezegovina as a federal unit within the Yugoslav federation.

The referendum of 29 February and 1 March 1992 was not an expression of equal rights and self-determination of the three peoples of Bosnia
and Herzegovina, whether in terms of its form (see para. 64 above) or its
substance. Although absolutely inappropriate in form, its substance could,
however, be qualified at best as the *de facto* self-determination of the
Muslim and Croat peoples in Bosnia and Herzegovina. A national plebiscite of the Serbian people in Bosnia and Herzegovina was organized in
the form of referendum on 9 and 10 November 1991, "in the areas of the
Serbian autonomous regions and other Serbian ethnic enclaves in Bosnia
and Herzegovina", where 96.4 per cent of citizens voted for an independent State within the Yugoslav federation (*Politika*, 11 and 13 November
1991).

Relevant circumstances concerning the referendum of 29 February and
1 March 1992 reveal the *intention* to have the decision on the legal status
of Bosnia and Herzegovina taken independently of the norm on equal
rights and self-determination of peoples.

In the first place, Mr. Alija Izetbegović stated the following at a press
conference in Sarajevo on 30 January 1991:

> "If Slovenia and Croatia secede from the present Federation,
> I will consider that I no longer have any authority to conduct further
> talks on a new Yugoslavia. I will propose *that a referendum* be held
> of all citizens of Bosnia and Herzegovina — not of individual
> peoples — to decide on the independence and sovereignty of
> Bosnia-Herzegovina." [112]

Secondly, Bosnia and Herzegovina's submissions mentioned more than
once the *"People of the Republic"* (*exempli causa*, paras. 5, 31, 114, 134,
135, 136 of the Application instituting proceedings filed in the Registry of
the Court on 20 March 1993; Memorial, paras. 4.2.1.10; 4.2.2.19). Thus
in paragraph 4.2.1.10 it was written that the referendum on the sovereignty of Bosnia and Herzegovina was based on the will of the "majority
of *people* of the Republic" (emphasis added).

This proves that the merit of the relevant decision was not the will of
the three peoples of Bosnia and Herzegovina to "determine their political
status", but was rather the will, in the light of facts and law, of an imaginary *"people* of Bosnia and Herzegovina". The objective meaning of the
phrase "people of Bosnia and Herzegovina" in the given context lies in a
denial of the existence of the three peoples of Bosnia and Herzegovina,

---

[112] Referendum on the independence of Bosnia and Herzegovina, *The Politika Daily*,
31 January 1991 (emphasis added).

739] thereby denying the relevance of the norm on equal rights and self-determination of peoples.

Thirdly, the reference of Bosnia and Herzegovina to the opinion of the Arbitration Commission as advisory body of the Conference on Yugoslavia is reasonably connected to the standpoint of the Commission on the issue of self-determination of Serbian people in Bosnia and Herzegovina. In reply to the question raised by Lord Carrington, Chairman of the Conference on Peace in Yugoslavia: "As a constituent people of Yugoslavia, do the Serbian Populations(s) in . . . Bosnia-Herzegovina enjoy the right to self-determination?", the Commission, *inter alia*, stressed:

> "that the Serbian population of Bosnia-Herzegovina . . . is entitled to all the minority rights accorded to minorities and ethnic groups under international law and under the provisions of the draft Convention of the Conference on Yugoslavia of 4 November 1991, to which the Republics of Bosnia-Herzegovina . . . have undertaken to give effect" [113].

In other words, a construction of the Commission on independence of Bosnia and Herzegovina which served as basis for the policy of recognition of Bosnia and Herzegovina has been derived independently of a cogent norm on equal rights and self-determination of peoples, since one of the constituent peoples of Bosnia and Herzegovina has been treated as a "minority and ethnic group".

71. The right to self-determination is composed of two rights: the right to internal and the right to external self-determination. These two rights are an organic unity expressing dialectics in the development of the idea of self-determination.

The right to internal self-determination is materialized in the institutional environment of a sovereign, independent State. It is reduced to the right of each State freely, without external interference, to choose the form of its social system (political self-determination) and the right to free disposal of its natural wealth and resources. So construed, a right to internal self-determination embodies the ideas of sovereignty and democracy.

The right to external self-determination means the right to choose the institutional framework for the continuous exercise of internal self-determination. Statehood is thus not the necessary and automatic outcome of the exercise of the right to external self-determination, since that right could be expressed not only by the "establishment of a sovereign and independent State" but by "free association or integration with an independent State or the emergence into any other political status freely determined by a people".

---

[113] The Conference on Yugoslavia, Arbitration Commission, Opinion No. 2, para. 4. [92 *ILR* 167.]

72. The question of fundamental importance in this context is whether **[740**
the right to external self-determination is universal or limited in scope?

It seems indisputable that *in abstracto* the right to self-determination is
a norm of universal scope. A limitation of the scope of the right to self-
determination would mean tacit partial derogation from it. Universality
is an inherent characteristic of both aspects of the right to self-determination — internal and external self-determination. It is clearly and
undoubtedly indicated by the wording that self-determination belongs
to "all peoples" (Art. 1 of both Covenants on Human Rights (1966) and
Declaration on Principles of International Law regarding Friendly Relations and Co-operation among States (1970)). Were that not the case, the
right to self-determination would relate not to the "equal rights" of
peoples but to an "unequal right".

The fact that in the Court's practice (Advisory Opinion in the *Namibia* [15]
case, *I.C.J. Reports 1971*, p. 31; *Western Sahara* case, *I.C.J. Reports
1975*, pp. 12, 31), the right to external self-determination has been linked [16]
to non-self-governing territories cannot be interpreted as a limitation of
the scope of the right to self-determination *ratione personae*, but as an
application of universal law *ad casum*.

73. However, there is no automatic equation between universality and
non-limitation of the right to self-determination. In the exercise of the
right to self-determination there are limits determined by the very norm
of self-determination of peoples and limitations deriving from other
norms in the system of international law.

These limitations affect the right to self-determination in its entirety,
i.e., their subject matter is both internal and external self-determination.

Exempli causa, when it comes to internal self-determination, it is evident that in the context of political self-determination, the subject right
includes no option for a social system based on racial discrimination or
segregation. More particularly, the right to self-determination, *ex definitione*, is a general permissive norm, a norm comprising categorical
authorization. The exercise of that authorization is effected, however,
within the system of international law, which is to say that it encounters
limits in categorical prohibitions contained in other cogent norms (*in
concreto*, in the norm prohibiting racial discrimination).

The basic constraint affecting the exercise of external self-determination derives from the very norm on equal rights and self-determination of
peoples. The right to self-determination shall not

> "be construed as authorizing or encouraging any action which could
> dismember or impair, totally or in part, the territorial integrity or
> political unity of sovereign and independent States conducting them-
> selves in compliance with the principle of equal rights and self-

[[15] 49 *ILR* 2.]   [[16] 59 *ILR* 13 at 30.]

determination of peoples . . . and . . . possessed of a government representing the whole people belonging to the territory without distinction as to race, creed or colour" [114].

The above-mentioned constraint on the exercise of external self-determination in a narrow sense, within the meaning of the norm on equal rights and self-determination of peoples, reveals the relevance of the norm on territorial integrity and political unity of a State. Being linked to the exercise of the right to self-determination to which "peoples" are entitled, this limitation protects the territorial integrity and political unity of a State from any action that might be undertaken *within the State* — unlike the ban on the use of force and threat of force in *international relations among States* which safeguard its territorial integrity and political unity against an *external* action.

74. As Henkin pointed out "[i]t is accepted that self-determination . . . does not include a right of secession for a people from an existing State" [115].
The rule applies equally to federations:

> "[w]hether the federation dissolves into two or more States also brings into focus the doctrine of self-determination in the form of secession. Such a dissolution may be the result of an amicable and constitutional agreement or may occur pursuant to a forceful exercise of secession. In the latter case, international legal rules may be pleaded in aid, but the position would seem to be that (apart from recognised colonial situations) there is no right of self-determination applicable to independent states that would justify the resort to secession." [116]

In other words, that is to say that in the existing States made up of several peoples, the norm of equal rights and self-determination establishes prohibition of the exercise of external self-determination, since it naturally represents an action which "dismembers or impairs totally or in part, the territorial integrity or political unity". The addressee of that prohibition is a people equipped with the right to self-determination; in view of the fact that

> "[s]ecessionist claims *involve*, first and *foremost*, disputed claims to territory . . . The two supposedly competing principles of people and territory actually work in tandem." [117]

---

[114] Declaration of Principles, para. 7.
[115] L. Henkin, "General Course of Public International Law", *Recueil des cours de l'Académie de droit international de La Haye*, Vol. 216, 1989, p. 243.
[116] M. N. Shaw, *International Law*, 1986, p. 139.
[117] L. Brilmayer, "Secession and Self-Determination", *Yale Journal of International Law*, Vol. 16, 1991, p. 178 (emphasis added).

75. The basis of prohibition lies in the conflict of two norms of the [742
same legal rank — the norm of self-determination and the norm of territorial integrity. The latter, *tractu temporis*, has become an integral
ingredient of the sovereign equality of States (point *(d)* of the Principle
of Sovereign Equality of States in the Declaration on Principles of International Law), a cogent norm *per se*, so that the aforementioned conflict
is impossible to resolve on the grounds of hierarchy of norms of international law. Apart from this practical justification, such a solution has a
principled one, i.e., no one is more qualified than a State, as a sovereign
political unit, to decide on its fate when it finds itself caught between two
substantially opposing norms and when its decision does not affect the
rights of third States.

76. According to paragraph 7 of the Declaration on Principles of
International Law, the prohibition of dismemberment or impairment in
the territorial integrity or political unity concerns the States

"conducting themselves in compliance with principles of equal rights
and self-determination of peoples . . . and possessed of government
representing the whole people belonging to the territory without distinction as to race, creed or colour".

The stated provisions contain two criteria: the first is the conduct of the
State in compliance with the principle of equal rights and self-determination of peoples, and the second is the criterion of representatives of a
government with the view to ensuring the representation of the whole
people without discrimination as to race, creed or colour. By its nature,
the second criterion is general. In this concrete case, it should also be
interpreted as an absence of discrimination among peoples who comprised the SFRY.

How does this relate to the application of the two legal criteria in the
case of the Yugoslav federation?
77. The self-determination of peoples has been more than a statement
in constitutional and legal documents of the federal Yugoslavia. It was a
constitutive principle of the Yugoslav State. Equally, in the Yugoslav
constitutional law, "national equality" or "equality of peoples" went
hand in hand with the right to self-determination.

The 1974 Constitution of the SFRY qualified equality of peoples
explicitly as one of the major constitutional principles (the first section of
the Basic Principles) and developed it into several provisions in the
operative, normative part of the Constitution (e.g., Arts. 1, 244, 245).
Article 245, devoted to the relations within the Federation, stipulated
that: "In SFRY peoples . . . enjoy equality."

743]   The equality of peoples in the composition of the State authorities of SFRY was ensured in two ways:

(i) via constitutional provisions on the equal representation of republics and provinces, namely the joint representation of republics in the federal bodies. Both chambers of the SFRY Assembly, the general representation (Federal Chamber) and the federal house (Chamber of Republics and Provinces) were formed according to the classical principle of parity (Arts. 284 and 291 of the SFRY Constitution). The same principle applied to the collective Head of State — Presidency of the SFRY (Amendment XLI, point 1, to the SFRY Constitution). Care was taken, in appointing members of the Federal Executive Council (Government of SFRY) to ensure an equal representation of republics and an adequate representation of provinces (Amendment XLIII to the SFRY Constitution). The principle of equal representation of republics was applied in the courts (Constitutional Court and Federal (Supreme) Court).

(ii) Social compacts on the policy of recruitment of cadres determined eligibility criteria in which national origin was placed high on the list in multi-ethnic communities.

The personnel picture in the highest State bodies in SFRY in 1990, immediately prior to proclamation of declaration of independence in some federal units, was as follows:

President of the Presidency of SFRY: Croat; Vice-President: Serb;
Prime Minister of the Federal Government: Croat; Vice-premiers: Serb and Slovene;
President of the Parliament: Muslim from Bosnia and Herzegovina. The latest Federal cabinet comprised five Croats; three Serbs; one Muslim; one Serb from Bosnia; three Slovenes; one Montenegran; one Yugoslav; one Albanian; one Hungarian; and two Macedonians.

In the light of the aforementioned facts, one cannot but conclude that the State organs of SFRY represented all the Yugoslav peoples.

78. As to Bosnia and Herzegovina's view on the subject-matter, it never questions the representativeness of the SFRY bodies in principle, but points out that, by the proclamation of independence of some federal units, that representativeness had disappeared and, moreover, "the common federal bodies on which all the Yugoslav republics where represented no longer exist; no body of that type has functioned

since" (Memorial, para. 4.2.1.26). The claim rests on a general thesis [74:
that

> "in the case of a federal-type State, which embraces communities
> that possess a degree of autonomy and, moreover, participate in the
> exercise of political power within the framework of institutions com-
> mon to the Federation, the existence of the State implies that the
> federal organs represent the components of the Federation and wield
> effective power"[118].

In the case of Yugoslavia, "common federal bodies" ceased to exist
due to referendum on independence in three republics, and in "Bosnia
and Herzegovina, by a sovereignty resolution adopted by Parliament
on October 14th, 1991, whose validity has been contested by the Serbian
community of the Republic of Bosnia and Herzegovina"[119],

> "The composition and workings of the essential organs of the
> Federation, be they the Federal Presidency, the Federal Council, the
> Council of the Republics and the Provinces, the Federal Executive
> Council, the Constitutional Court or the Federal Army, no longer
> meet the criteria of participation and representativeness inherent in a
> federal state."[120]

This claim could be hardly taken as legally meritorious. The lack of
credibility of the above claim, both in its general and in specific meaning,
is evidenced by the following.

79. The wording "the federal organs represent the components of the
Federation" has two possible meanings. First, that the Federation, via its
organs, represents federal units. Such a meaning of the above wording is
logically implied by the fact that a federation is, by definition, a higher,
superior power in relation to its constituent parts and that the organs of
the whole represent the parts constituting it, and, secondly, that federal
organs by their very composition represent federal units — in other
words they are a sort of institutional aggregate of the representativeness
of federal units.

The claim of Bosnia and Herzegovina, supported by the Opinion of the
Commission, is evidently aimed in that direction. In the light of the com-
parative practice of the federation and constitution of the SFRY, those
claims are groundless. As a rule, federal organs represent the federal
State as a whole (*exempli causa*: United States President; United States
House of Representatives; executive and judicial organs in almost all

---

[118] International Conference on Peace in Yugoslavia, Arbitration Commission,
Opinion No. 1, para. 1 *(d)*. [92 *ILR* 162.]
[119] *Ibid.*, para. 2 *(a)*.
[120] *Ibid.*, para. 2 *(b)*.

745] federal States) and only the federal chamber is *bicameral*, representing parts of the federation (United States Senate, Canada or Brazil, German Bundesrat, National Council in Switzerland, etc.).

Also, the relevant solution in the SFRY Constitution ranged within the framework of that generally accepted practice in federal States. With the exception of the Council of Republics and Provinces, all federal organs in SFRY represented the federation as a whole. Delegates in the Federal Council represented "self-managing organizations and communities and socio-political organizations" and *were elected* in the republics and provinces (Art. 129 of the SFRY Constitution); members of the Federal Executive Council and officials did not, moreover, represent republics/provinces and an explicit constitutional provision prohibited them from accepting guidelines and orders from republics and provinces (Art. 362). The President and Members of the SFRY Presidency, President and Members of the Constitutional Court and other federal officials used to take an oath to the effect that they would foster the sovereignty, independence and integrity of the SFRY, abide by the Constitution of the Federation (Art. 397), so that they were not representatives of the republics/provinces under the Constitution.

80. It follows that there is no legal connection between an actual refusal to participate in the federal organs and the existence of these organs in the eyes of law. This is evidenced by the Yugoslav case. No federal organ has been dissolved or wound up on the grounds of wilful absence and individual resignations on the part of certain federal officials.

The Constitution of the SFRY of 27 April 1992, as well as the constitutional law and its implementation, were approved by the SFRY Assembly. By virtue of that law, all the supreme federal organs continued to act pending the election of new organs (Art. 2 of the Law). The SFRY Presidency acted until the election of the President of the Republic (15 June 1992) and the Federal Executive Council acted until the formation of a new federal government (14 July 1992).

Participation in the activities of federal organs and the duties of the elected representatives were construed with the intention of endowing the resulting decisions of the federation with objective legal personalities in terms of national and international law, in the general interest. The wilful abstention of federal officials elected in Bosnia and Herzegovina was seen

as constituting an abuse of the law[121]. The consequences of an abuse of [74
law affect those who resort to it, in line with the general legal principle
*nullus commodum capere de sua injuria propria et ex delicto non oritur
actio*.

81. Bosnia and Herzegovina's reasoning has been tacitly based on an
inverted liberalistic idea of consent as a fundamental of the legitimacy of
a State. The original idea, that a legitimate government must stem from
the consent of the governed, is interpreted in Bosnia and Herzegovina's
approach as implying that stepping out of the State organs entails a loss
of legitimacy of the government and constitutes the right to opt out of an
existing State.

In fact,

"actual consent is not necessary to political legitimacy . . . Separatists cannot base their arguments upon a right to opt out because no
such right exists in democratic theory.

Government by the consent of the governed does not necessarily
encompass a right to opt out. It only requires that within the existing
political unit a right to participate through electoral processes be
available. Moreover, participatory rights do not entail a right to
secede. On the contrary, they suggest that the appropriate solution
for dissatisfied groups rests in their full inclusion in the polity, with
full participation in its decision-making processes."[122]

82. Does the "Existence of the state impl[y] that the federal organs . . .
yield effective power"?

The exercise of effective power is *per definitionem* the purpose of the
existence of State organs irrespective of whether the State is unitary or
federal. *In concreto*, the question is whether an evident crisis in the functioning of State organs of the Federation led to their ceasing to exist? To
equate the constitutional crisis in SFRY and the non-existence of federal
organs is legally unacceptable. The scope of the effectiveness, quantity
and quality of State organs is a variable category, because it demonstrates an actual, political state of affairs. In principle, there are situations in which State organs do in fact cease from exercising power (e.g.,
cases of military occupation, civil war and, to a certain extent, various
forms of constitutional crises), but do not cease to exist. State organs as

---

[121] The Constitutional Court of Yugoslavia stated in its Decision II U. No. 122/91 that
the abstention of federal officials from work in federal organs represents "an unconstitutional change of the composition of the common federal state" (*Official Gazette of SFRY*,
No. 89/91). That decision was approved by the Constitutional Court in its full composition and with the participation of both judges from Bosnia and Herzegovina.

[122] L. Brilmayer, "Secession and Self-determination: A Territorial Interpretation",
Yale Journal of International Law, 1991, Vol. 16, pp. 184-185.

747] elements of State organization cease to exist when the State on whose behalf they are acting ceases to exist.

D. The Relationship between the Legality of the Birth of a State and Succession with Respect to International Treaties

83. Bosnia and Herzegovina claims that it is a "successor State" because:

(a) "succession of States" means the "replacement of one State by another in the responsibility for the international relations of territory", according to the very widely accepted definition given in both Vienna Conventions on Succession of States of 1978 and 1983; and

(b) "it is obvious that Bosnia and Herzegovina has replaced the former SFRY for the international relations of what was the Federal Republic of Bosnia and Herzegovina before the dissolution of former Yugoslavia" (Memorial, para. 4.2.1.26).

On the contrary, the position of Yugoslavia in the subject-matter is that "the so-called Republic of Bosnia and Herzegovina has not become a State party to that 1948 Convention on the Prevention and Punishment of the Crime of Genocide in accordance with the provisions of the Convention itself" (Submissions, B.1) because:

(a) "The Applicant State cannot enter into the international treaties of the predecessor State on the basis of succession because it flagrantly violated the principle of equal rights and self-determination of peoples" (Preliminary Objections, para. B.1.2.39);

(b) "As the Applicant State has violated the obligations deriving from the principle of equal rights and self-determination of peoples, the Vienna Convention on the Succession of States in Respect of Treaties could not apply to this case even if it had come into force" (*ibid.*, para. B.1.3.5); and

(c) "Notification of succession is a manner of entry into treaties of the predecessor State in cases where the new State has based its existence upon the principle of equal rights and self-determination of peoples. In this particular case, the Applicant State has based its existence on the violation of duties deriving from the principle of equal rights and self-determination of peoples, and thus cannot make use of the notification of succession as a method of entry into the international treaties of its predecessor State." (*Ibid.*, para. B.1.4.11.)

The essence of this objection by Yugoslavia is that because of its

"flagrant violation of the principle of equal rights and self-determination [74]
of peoples", Bosnia and Herzegovina was not a successor State and
hence could not have acquired the capacity of State party to the 1948
Convention on Genocide on the grounds of succession.

To make a valid conclusion on the merits of the objection, it is
necessary to answer the question of whether there is a connection between
succession of States and legality of territorial changes.

84. The answer to this question implies a precise definition of the concept of succession. The term "succession" is used in a broad, imprecise
meaning.

> "Succession of States means both the territorial change itself — in
> other words, the fact that within a given territory one State replaces
> another — and the succession of one of those States to the rights and
> obligations of the other, i.e., the State whose territory has passed to
> the successor States." [123]

It can be seen that the term "succession" means two things: *(a)* territorial change itself; and *(b)* transmission of rights and obligations from
predecessor State to successor State(s).

The distinction between succession taken in terms of territorial change
(de facto succession) and succession as transmission of derived rights and
obligations from predecessor State to successor State(s) *(de jure* succession) is drawn also by the Convention on Succession of States in respect
of Treaties, referred to by Bosnia and Herzegovina in order to prove its
status of "Successor State". This Convention in its Article 2 *(b)* (Use of
Terms) defines "succession of States" as "the replacement of one State by
another in the responsibility for the international relations of the territory". At the same time, Article 6 (Cases of Succession of States Covered
by the Present Convention) specifies that the Convention "applies only to
the effects of a succession of States occurring in conformity with the
international law and, in particular, the principles of international law
embodied in the Charter of the United Nations". Relations between
Article 2 *(b)* and Article 6 of the Convention are precisely defined in
the Comment to Article 2 of the Draft Articles on Succession of States in
respect of Treaties on the basis of which Article 2 of the Convention on
Succession of States in respect of Treaties was adopted. This Comment,
inter alia, says:

> "the term ['succession'] is used as referring exclusively to *the fact of*
> *replacement* of one State by another in the responsibility for inter-

---

[123] H. Kelsen, *Dictionnaire de la terminologie du droit international*, Vol. 42, p. 314.
Thus O'Connell, *The Law of State Succession*, 1956, pp. 3, 6; K. Zemanek, "Die Wiener
Konvention über die Staatennachfolge in Veträge", *Festschrift für Alfred Verdross*, 1980,
p. 719; M. Jones, "State Succession in Matter of Treaties", *British Year Book of International Law*, 1947, Vol. 24, pp. 360-361.

national relations of territory leaving aside any connotation of inheritance of rights or obligations on the occurrence of that event" [124].

Such a definition of succession corresponds to the basic concept of "succession of States" which emerged from the study of the topic by the International Law Commission. More particularly:

> "The approach to succession adopted by the Commission after its study of the topic of succession in respect of *treaties* is based upon drawing a clear distinction between, on the one hand, the fact of replacement of one State by another in the responsibility for the international relations of a territory and, on the other, the transmission of treaty rights and obligations from the predecessor to the successor State . . .
> In order to make clear the distinction between the fact of replacement of one State by another and the transmission of rights and obligations, the Commission inserted in article 2 a provision defining the meaning of the expression 'succession of States' for the purpose of the draft. Under this provision the expression 'succession of States' is used throughout the articles to denote simply a change in the responsibility for the international relations of a territory, thus leaving aside from the definition all questions of the rights and obligations as a legal incident of that change." [125]

This distinction was necessary as

> "the difficulty stemmed from the fact that the expression 'succession' was not qualified in the definitions of it given in art. 2 (1, *b*). From that paragraph it might be deduced that the convention was also intended to apply to unlawful successions" [126].

Because of that,

> "art. 6 was the most important saving clause of the draft articles, since it safeguarded the legality of all provisions of the future conventions by limiting their application to the effects of lawful succession . . . the provisions of the future convention would not apply to

---

[124] Draft Articles on Succession of States in respect of Treaties, *Yearbook of the International Law Commission*, 1972, Vol. II, p. 231, para. 3; identical interpretation was quoted *in extenso* in the comment to Article 2 of the Draft Articles on Succession of States in respect of State Property, Archives and Debts, *ibid.*, Vol. II, Part Two, p. 21.

[125] *Yearbook of the International Law Commission*, 1972, Vol. II, p. 226, paras. 29-30.
[126] Sette-Camara, *UNCSS*, First Session, p. 53, para. 11.

unlawful transfers which were contrary to the will of people and to **[75◀**
the principle of self-determination"[127].

Therefore, "succession of States" in terms of "replacement of one State
by another in the responsibility for the international relations of territory" "does not mean *ipso facto* a juridical substitution of the acquiring
State in the complex rights and duties possessed by the previous sovereign"[128] or, in the present case, entry into the international treaties of
SFRY as a predecessor State. The condition thereto is that the "replacement of one State by another" occurred "in conformity with international law, in particular, with the principles of international law embodied in the Charter of the United Nations".

85. A provision concerning territorial changes to be effected "in conformity with international law and, in particular, with the principles of
international law embodied in the Charter of the United Nations" has a
declarative impact. So,

"even if the article did not appear in the convention, that instrument
would apply only to lawful succession from the point of view of the
principles of international law especially those embodied in the UN
Charter, which was the keystone of all international conventions"[129].

The principle underlying the provision of Article 6 of the Convention on
Succession of States in respect of Treaties is a self-evident principle, axio-
matic to any legal order *stricto sensu*. It is *ratione materiae* a narrowed
projection of the general concept of lawfulness of acts, an application of
the concept of lawfulness to the questions of succession. In view of the
material significance of lawfulness for the very existence of a *de jure*
order, the rule making provisions of any codification applicable only to
the facts occurring and situations established in conformity with international law is a general presumption, a self-explanatory matter[130]. The
reason for a universal provision of legality led the Commission separately
to specify the rule limiting the application of the provisions of the Convention to the cases of lawful succession:

"Other members, however, were of the opinion that in regard,
particularly, to transfers of territory it was desirable to underline

---

[127] Tabibi, *UNCSS*, First Session, p. 54, para. 20.

[128] O'Connell, *op. cit.*, p. 3.
[129] Ushakov, *UNCSS*, First Session, pp. 54-55, para. 24.

[130] "to admit that, apart from well-defined exceptions, an unlawful act, or its immediate
consequences, may become *suo vigore* a source of legal right for the wrongdoer, is to
introduce into a legal system a contradiction which cannot be solved except by
denial of its legal character. International law does not and cannot form an exception to that imperative alternative." (H. Lauterpacht, *Recognition in International
Law*, 1947, p. 421.)

751]   that only transfers occurring in conformity with international law should fall within the concept of 'succession of States' for the purpose of the present articles. Since, to specify the element of conformity with the international law with reference to one category of succession of States might give rise to misunderstandings as to the position regarding that element on other categories of succession of States, the Commission decided to include amongst the general articles a provision safeguarding the question of lawfulness of the succession of States dealt with in the present articles. Accordingly, article 6 provides that the present articles relate only to the effects of a succession of States occurring in conformity with international law." [131]

86. Notification of succession is only a technical means by which the successor State expresses its consent to be considered bound by the treaty whose original party is the predecessor State. Hence, to make a notification of succession produce its intended legal effects, the actual succession must have been lawful. The criterion of lawfulness of the succession is "international law and, in particular, the principles of international law embodied in the Charter of the United Nations".

In the present case, and with regard to the position of Bosnia and Herzegovina, of special importance are the principles of territorial integrity and political unity, and of equal rights and self-determination of peoples.

The specific relevance of those principles for the matter of succession is a logical consequence of the nature of changes activating the institution of succession and the role of equal rights and self-determination of peoples in constituting new States. Hence, these principles of the United Nations Charter have been particularly accentuated. The Special Rapporteur, Mr. Mohammed Bedjaoui, stated in his proposal concerning lawfulness of succession that,

> "The conditions for succession of States shall include respect for general international law and the provisions of the United Nations Charter concerning the territorial integrity of States and the right of peoples to self-determination." [132]

The Preamble to the Convention on Succession of States in respect of Treaties "recall[s] that respect for the territorial integrity and political independence of any State is required by the Charter of the United

---

[131] *UNCSS*, First Session, p. 236, para. 1.

[132] Fifth Report on succession in respect of matters other than treaties, doc. A/CN.4/259, *Yearbook of the International Law Commission*, 1972, Vol. II, p. 66, para. 28.

Nations". That wording confirms that the existence of territorial integrity [752] and political independence derive from the United Nations Charter and, hence, binds the States irrespective of the Convention.

87. The proclamation of Bosnia and Herzegovina as a "sovereign and independent state" constitutes, in my view, a substantial breach of the cogent norm on equal rights and self-determination of peoples in both the formal and material sense.

A substantial breach in the formal sense is reflected in the following:

(a) the procedure of proclamation of Bosnia and Herzegovina was conducted in an unconstitutional way, contrary to the relevant provisions of its own Constitution and that of the SFRY;

(b) self-determination in the subject case was *de facto* conceived as a right of a territory within a sovereign, independent State, rather than as a right of peoples.

The breach of the norm on equal rights and self-determination of peoples in a material sense is reflected in the following:

(a) the proclamation of independence of a federal unit of Bosnia and Herzegovina, in violation of relevant provisions of the internal law of the SFRY and of Bosnia and Herzegovina, endangered the territorial integrity and political unity of SFRY, in contravention of the provision of paragraph 7 of the Declaration on Principles;

(b) the proclamation of the independence of Bosnia and Herzegovina within its administrative borders was not based on the equal rights and self-determination of all three peoples of Bosnia and Herzegovina.

Therefore, the proclamation of the independence of Bosnia and Herzegovina was not in conformity with the relevant principles of equal rights and self-determination of peoples, and territorial integrity and political unity and, as such, has no merit for lawful succession in terms of the succession of Bosnia and Herzegovina with respect to the Convention on Prevention and Punishment of the Crime of Genocide.

88. By its nature, the proclamation of Bosnia and Herzegovina's independence was an act of secession. Bosnia and Herzegovina does not contest that assertion of Yugoslavia. It is taken from paragraph 3.22 of the Statement of Bosnia and Herzegovina which reads:

"whether or not Bosnia, at the time of its secession, had a *right* to self-determination is irrelevant because: (1) it is now a recognized, sovereign State, and (2) even if, *arguendo*, it were supposed that it had no *right* to self-determination in international law, international law certainly did not *prohibit* its achieving the status of an independent State at the occasion of the disintegration of the Former

753] Socialist Federal Republic of Yugoslavia." (Statement of the Government of the Republic of Bosnia and Herzegovina on Preliminary Objections, p. 60.)

89. Secession is, *per definitionem*, "the creation of a State by the use or threat of force and without the consent of the former sovereign"[133]. Therefore it is understandable that the

"United Nations Charter does not recognize the term or concept of 'secession', for this concept is profoundly at odds with the spirit and normative principles of the Charter. The Charter raises respect for territorial integrity to the rank of a constitutional norm, a norm of *jus cogens*. On January 1, 1970, the UN Secretary-General made the following statement:

'So, as far as the question of secession of a particular section of a Member State is concerned, the United Nations' attitude is unequivocal. As an international organization, the United Nations has never accepted and does not accept, and I do not believe it will ever accept, the principle of secession of a part of a Member State.'"[134]

The Security Council has characterized secession as illegal. In its resolution 169 (1961) on the Congo, the Security Council, *inter alia*,

"*strongly deprecate[d]* the secessionist activities illegally carried out by the provincial administration of Katanga with the aid of external resources and manned by foreign mercenaries . . . and

Declare[d],

. . . .

(d) that all secessionist activities against the Republic of Congo are contrary to the *Loi fondamentale*".

The implicit characterization of secession as an illegal act under international law can be found in paragraph 7 of the "Declaration of Principles of International Law Concerning Friendly Relations among States" which stipulates, *inter alia*, that the right to self-determination shall not be construed as

"authorizing or encouraging any action which could dismember or impair, totally or in part, the territorial integrity or political unity of sovereign and independent States".

On the regional, European level, such a characterization of secession is contained in the Declaration on Principles Guiding Relations between

---

[133] J. Crawford, *The Creation of States in International Law*, 1979, p. 247.
[134] United Nations, *Monthly Chronicle*, Vol. 7, p. 36 (February 1970).

Participating States contained in the Conference on Security and Co- [75⁴
operation in Europe (CSCE) Final Act adopted on 1 August 1975 at
Helsinki:

> "[t]he participating States regard as inviolable all one another's fron-
> tiers as well as the frontiers of all States in Europe and therefore they
> will refrain now and in future from assaulting these frontiers".

On the other hand, an explicit condemnation of secession can be found in
the general principles of law recognized by civilized nations as a formal
source of international law pursuant to Article 38 *(c)* of the Statute
of the International Court of Justice. Secession is deemed to be a most
serious crime by the national legislations of civilized nations. More particularly, an inside assault on the territorial integrity of a country
or an attempted assault, including preparatory actions, are categorized
as one of the gravest of crimes in virtually all the criminal codes of
civilized nations.

90. The admission of Bosnia and Herzegovina to the United Nations
cannot convalidate substantial legal defects in its establishment as an
independent State, especially because of the need to draw a sharp distinction between

> "secession in pursuance of, and in violation of, self-determination.
> Where the territory in question is a self-determination unit it may be
> presumed that any secessionary government possesses the general
> support of the people: secession in such a case, where self-determi-
> nation is forcibly denied, will be presumed to be in furtherance of, or
> at least not inconsistent with, the application of self-determination
> to the territory in question." [135]

There is not much doubt that the admission of Bosnia and Herzegovina to the United Nations has given general, political support to Bosnia and Herzegovina. However that political support does not, and could
not, be interpreted as a subsequent convalidation of illegality of Bosnia
and Herzegovina's birth. Even if the General Assembly had such an
intention in mind when admitting Bosnia and Herzegovina to the membership of the United Nations, such an outcome was legally impossible,
since such an act implied a derogation from the self-determination of
peoples which has the character of *jus cogens*. Norms of *jus cogens* do
not tolerate derogation, so any concurrent régime or situation, whether it
be established by way of a bilateral or unilateral act, cannot acquire legal
force due to the peremptoriness of *jus cogens* — more specifically, this act
or acts remains in the sphere of simple facts. One could say that this is a
classic example of application of the general principle of law expressed in

---

[135] J. Crawford, *op. cit.*, p. 258; see also, separate opinion of Judge Ammoun, *Western
Sahara, I.C.J. Reports 1975*, pp. 99-100. [59 *ILR* 1 at 30.]

755] the maxim *quidquid ab initio vitiosus est, non potest tractu temporis convalescere.*

In my opinion, therefore, the meaning of the admission of Bosnia and Herzegovina to the United Nations is confined to the recognition of Bosnia and Herzegovina as a fact, and has no impact on the legality of its birth. Such a conclusion corresponds to the fact that

> "[r]ecognition by the UN means that a State (or its government) will be invited to important international conferences, allowed to accede to numerous international treaties and to become a Member of several international organizations and to send observers to others" [136].

91. By rejecting Yugoslavia's third preliminary objection, the Court has responded to one side of the question of its jurisdiction *ratione personae*. The other side of the question relates to the status of Yugoslavia as a party to the Genocide Convention. I am in agreement with the Court's finding that Yugoslavia is a party to the Genocide Convention but I disagree with the Court's reasoning leading to that finding.

With regard to Yugoslavia's status as a party to the Genocide Convention, the Court states that:

> "it has not been contested that Yugoslavia was party to the Genocide Convention [and] . . . was bound by the provisions of the Convention on the date of the filing of the Application in the present case . . ." (para. 17 of the Judgment).

The Court bases this conclusion on the following:

(a) "that it has not been contested that Yugoslavia was party to the Genocide Convention", and

(b) that

> "[a]t the time of the proclamation of the Federal Republic of Yugoslavia, on 27 April 1992, a formal declaration was adopted on its behalf to the effect that:
>
> > 'The Federal Republic of Yugoslavia, continuing the State, international legal and political personality of the Socialist Federal Republic of Yugoslavia, shall strictly abide by all the commitments that the Socialist Federal Republic of Yugoslavia assumed internationally.'
>
> This intention thus expressed by Yugoslavia to remain bound by the international treaties to which the former Yugoslavia was party was confirmed in an official Note of 27 April 1992 from the Permanent Mission of Yugoslavia to the United Nations, addressed to the Secretary-General." (Para. 17 of the Judgment.)

---

[136] H. G. Schermers, *International Constitutional Law*, 1980, p. 929.

I agree with the Court that Yugoslavia is a party to the Genocide Con- **[756**
vention but its reasoning regarding the effect of the formal declaration
issued on 27 April 1992 does not appear to be tenable.

92. A logical meaning of the pronouncement that "it has not been contested that Yugoslavia was party to the Genocide Convention" is that
Yugoslavia is a party to the Genocide Convention because its status as a
party has not been contested.

It is true that the proceedings on preliminary objections are substantially based on the initiative of the parties. However, that does not mean
that the parties have the right to determine the jurisdiction of the Court.

By a decision on preliminary objections, the Court might be said to
achieve two mutually connected and interdependent objectives:

(a) the direct objective is that the Court decides on the objection in the
form of a judgment "by which it shall either uphold the objection,
reject it, or declare that the objection does not possess, in the
circumstances of the case, an exclusively preliminary character"
(Art. 79 (7) of the Rules of Court);

(b) the indirect objective is to ascertain or confirm its jurisdiction. In the
light of this objective, preliminary objections raised by a party are
only a tool, a procedurally designed instrument for the establishment of the jurisdiction of the Court, *suo nomine et suo vigore*, for
according to its Statute it is under an obligation to do so — not
proprio motu but *ex officio*. For,

> "[t]he Court is the guardian of its Statute. It is not within its
> power to abandon . . . a function which by virtue of an express
> provision of the Statute is an essential safeguard of its compulsory
> jurisdiction. This is so in particular in view of the fact that the
> principle enshrined in Article 36 (6) of the Statute is declaratory of
> one of the most firmly established principles of international arbi-
> tral and judicial practice. *That principle is that, in the matter of its
> jurisdiction, an international tribunal, and not the interested party,
> has the power of decision whether the dispute before it is covered
> by the instrument creating its jurisdiction.*" [137]

93. The participants in the Joint Session of the SFRY Assembly, the
National Assembly of the Republic of Serbia and the Assembly of the
Republic of Montenegro have declared, *inter alia*, by a Declaration made
on 27 April 1992:

> "The Federal Republic of Yugoslavia, continuing the State, inter-
> national, legal and political personality of the Socialist Federal

---

[137] *Interhandel, Preliminary Objections, Judgment, I.C.J. Reports 1959*, dissenting
opinion of Sir Hersch Lauterpacht, p. 104 (emphasis added). [27 *ILR* 475 at 542.]

757]   Republic of Yugoslavia, shall strictly abide by all the commitments that the SFR of Yugoslavia assumed internationally in the past.

At the same time, it shall be ready to fully respect the rights and interests of the Yugoslav Republics which declared independence. The recognition of the newly-formed States will follow after all the outstanding questions negotiated within the conference on Yugoslavia have been regulated.

Remaining bound by all obligations to international organizations and institutions whose member it is, the Federal Republic of Yugoslavia shall not obstruct the newly-formed States to join these organizations and institutions, particularly the United Nations and its specialized agencies.

The Diplomatic and Consular Missions of the Federal Republic of Yugoslavia shall continue without interruption to perform their functions of representing and protecting the interests of Yugoslavia.

They shall also extend consular protection to all nationals of the SFR Yugoslavia whenever they request them to do so until a final regulation of their nationality status.

The Federal Republic of Yugoslavia recognized, at the same time, the full continuity of the representation of foreign States by their diplomatic and consular mission in its territory." [138]

This declaration, *per se*, cannot be qualified as a basis for being bound by the Genocide Convention, at least on account of the two basic reasons, one being of a formal and the other of a material nature.

The formal reason resides in the nature of the declarations in the constitutional system of Yugoslavia. The declarations of the Assembly in the constitutional system of Yugoslavia have, since its foundation, represented general political acts of the representative body, which have as their subject the questions which are not subject to legal regulations or are not included within the competence of the representative body [139]. As political acts, they are not binding, so they do not contain legal sanctions for the case of non-observance.

The "Participants to the Joint Session of the SFRY Assembly, the National Assembly of the Republic of Serbia and the Assembly of the Republic of Montenegro, and the Federal Assembly itself" are not organs

---

[138] Constitution of the Federal Republic of Yugosavia, Belgrade, 1992, pp. 57-58.

[139] M. Snuderl, *Constitutional Law*, Ljubljana, 1957, Vol. II, p. 47; A. Fira, *Constitutional Law*, Belgrade, 1977, p. 381.

of foreign representation authorized to appear on behalf of the State in [758
international relations, so that, the measures they adopt, even when
legally binding, cannot be put into effect by one-sided acts of State
organs which have such authority. The material reason concerns the
content of the Declaration. The statement that the Federal Republic of
Yugoslavia "shall strictly abide by all the commitments that the SFR
Yugoslavia assumed internationally" is not given in the Declaration *in
abstracto*, in the form of an unconditional, generalized acceptance of the
commitments that the SFRY assumed internationally in the past, but as
a declarative expression of the premise that the FR of Yugoslavia is
"continuing the State, international, legal and political personality of the
Socialist Federal Republic of Yugoslavia". This fact is not contested by
Bosnia and Herzegovina, for it asserts that

> "it is on the basis of this alleged 'continuity' that Yugoslavia (Serbia
> and Montenegro) considers itself to be bound by all international
> commitments undertaken by the former SFRY" (Memorial,
> para. 4.2.2.11).

According to the Declaration, the FR of Yugoslavia does not assume the
obligations of the SFRY, but *"remains bound by all obligations to international organizations and institutions of which it is a member"* (emphasis
added).

At the meeting of the Federal Chamber of the Assembly of the SFRY
held on 27 April 1992, which proclaimed the Constitution of the Federal
Republic of Yugoslavia, the President of the Assembly of Serbia emphasized, in his introductory speech, *inter alia*, that:

> "[t]he adoption of one-sided acts by some of the republics on their
> secession from Yugoslavia and the international recognition of those
> republics in the administrative borders of the former Yugoslavia
> republics forced the Yugoslav peoples who want to continue to live
> in Yugoslavia to rearrange the relations in it"

and that "Serbia and Montenegro do not recognize that Yugoslavia is
abolished and does not exist"[140]. Another opening speaker, the President
of the Assembly of Montenegro emphasized that Serbia and Montenegro
were "the only states which brought their statehood with them on the
creation of Yugoslavia, and decided to constitutionally rearrange the
former Yugoslavia"[141].

Moreover, even if the intention of the FR of Yugoslavia to assume

---

[140] *Politika*, Belgrade, 28 April 1992, p. 6.
[141] *Ibid.* (emphasis added).

759] formally the obligations of the SFRY were built into the Declaration, the Declaration, as the external textual expression of such an intention, could hardly represent anything more than a political proclamation which should be operationalized, in the absence of rules on automatic succession, in accordance with the relevant rules of the Law of Treaties on the expression of consent to be bound by a treaty.

94. Whereas after the adoption of its Constitution on 27 April 1992, Yugoslavia did not express its consent to be bound by the Genocide Convention in the way prescribed by Article XI of the Convention and nor did it send to the Secretary-General of the United Nations the notification of succession, it is obvious that the only possible legal basis on which Yugoslavia could be considered a party to the Genocide Convention is the legal identity and continuity of the SFRY in the domain of multilateral treaties.

In the practice of the Secretary-General as depositary of multilateral treaties, Yugoslavia figures also, after the territorial changes which took place in the period 1991-1992, as a party to the multilateral treaties deposited with the Secretary-General, although the FR of Yugoslavia did not express its acceptance to be bound by concrete treaties in the ways fixed by the treaties, nor did it address to the Secretary-General as depositary the appropriate notifications of succession. The date when the FR of Yugoslavia expressed its acceptance to be bound is mentioned as the day on which it was bound by that specific instrument. *Exempli causa*, in the "Multilateral Treaties Deposited with the Secretary-General" for 1992, and in the list of "Participants" of the Convention on the Prevention and Punishment of the Crime of Genocide, "Yugoslavia" is included, and the 29 August 1950 is mentioned as the date of the acceptance of the obligation — the date on which the SFRY ratified that Convention. Identical dates are also found in the issues of the "Multilateral Treaties Deposited with the Secretary-General" for 1993 and 1994. Such a model is applied, *mutatis mutandis*, to other multilateral conventions deposited with the Secretary-General of the United Nations.

Therefore, it is indisputable that the practice of the Secretary-General as the depositary of the multilateral treaties consistently qualifies Yugoslavia as a party to these multilateral treaties on the basis of the acceptance of those treaties expressed by the SFRY.

95. On the basis of existing practice, the "Summary of Practice of the Secretary-General as depositary of Multilateral Treaties" concludes:

"The independence of a new successor State, which then exercises its sovereignty on its territory, is of course without effect as concerns the treaty rights and obligations of the predecessor State as concerns it own (remaining) territory. Thus, after the separation of parts of the territory of the Union of Soviet Socialist Republics (which

became independent States), the Union of Soviet Socialist Republics **[760**
(as the Russian Federation) continued to exist as a predecessor
State, and all its treaty rights and obligations continued in force in
respect of its territory . . . The same applies to the Federal Republic
of Yugoslavia (Serbia and Montenegro), which remains as the predecessor State upon separation of parts of the territory of the former
Yugoslavia. General Assembly resolution 47/1 of 22 September 1992,
to the effect that the Federal Republic of Yugoslavia could not automatically continue the membership of the former Yugoslavia in the
United Nations (see para. 89 above), was adopted within the framework of the United Nations and the context of the Charter of the
United Nations, and not as an indication that the Federal Republic
of Yugoslavia was not to be considered a predecessor State." [142]

On the other side, a

"different situation occurs when the predecessor State disappears.
Such was the case when the Czech Republic and Slovakia were
formed after the separation of their territories from Czechoslovakia,
which ceased to exist. Each of the new States is then in the position
of a succeeding State." [143]

Such a practice is completely in accordance with the interpretation of
the range of resolution 47/1 of the General Assembly of the United
Nations which, otherwise, serves as the basis of the contentions that
Yugoslavia, by the mere fact of territorial changes lost, *ipso facto*, the
status of party to multilateral conventions.

In the letter from the United Nations Office of Legal Affairs of
16 April 1993, it is stated, *inter alia*, that

"the status of Yugoslavia as a party to treaties was not affected by
the adoption of the General Assembly resolution 47/1 of 22 September 1992. By that resolution, the General Assembly decided that the
Federal Republic of Yugoslavia (Serbia and Montenegro) shall not
participate in the work of the General Assembly. It did not address
Yugoslavia's status as a party to treaties."

96. Regarding the qualification mentioned in paragraph 297 of the
"Summary", the Permanent Representative of the United States to the
United Nations in her letter addressed to the Secretary-General dated
5 April 1996 (doc. A/51/95; S/1996/251, 8 April 1996) protested against

---

[142] ST/LEG.8, p. 89, para. 297 (emphasis added).
[143] *Ibid.*, para. 298.

761] such a qualification. Four days later, on 9 April 1996, the Legal Counsel of the United Nations issued "Errata" (doc. LA41TR/220) which, *inter alia*, deleted the qualification of the FR of Yugoslavia as a predecessor State contained in paragraph 297 of the "Summary". Protests against such a qualification of Yugoslavia were also expressed in the letters addressed to the Secretary-General by the Permanent Representative of Germany to the United Nations (doc. A/50/929; S/1996/263, 11 April 1996) and by the Chargé d'Affaires *ad interim* of the Permanent Mission of Guinea on behalf of the Organization of the Islamic Conference (OIC) and the Contact Group on Bosnia and Herzegovina (doc. A/50/930; S/1996/260, 12 April 1996). Both of the latter letters were, however, dated 10 April 1996, i.e., after the "Errata" had been prepared and published.

The formal circumstances of this concrete question make, in my opinion, both the objections and the "Errata" of the Legal Counsel of the United Nations irrelevant. More particularly,

(a) The subject-matter of the objections submitted in the letters of the permanent representatives of three member States of the Organization are "views" and "interpretations" of the legal position of Yugoslavia as a predecessor State expressed in the "Summary of Practice of the Secretary-General as depositary of multilateral treaties", or, to put it more precisely, in paragraphs 297 and 298 of that document. In other words, the above-mentioned objections do not concern the practice of the Organization and of its organs in the concrete matter as an objective fact, but relate to the interpretation of that practice presented in the "Summary".

(b) "Errata" *per definitionem* represents "a mis-statement or misprint in something that is published or written"[144].

Leaving aside the question of whether the "errata" are well founded in this specific case, it is obvious that the document concerns the relevant parts of the "*Summary* of Practice of the Secretary-General" (emphasis added). A "Summary" by itself does not have the value of an autonomous document, a document which determines or constitutes something. It is just the condensed expression, the external lapidary assertion of a fact which exists outside it and independently from it. In that sense, the Introduction to the "Summary of the Practice of the Secretary-General as depositary of multilateral treaties" says, *inter alia*, that "the purpose of the present summary is to highlight the main features of the practice followed by the Secretary-General in this field" (p. 1).

Therefore, the errata in this specific case do not question the relevance of the practice of the Secretary-General as the depositary of

---

[144] *Webster's Third New International Dictionary*, 1966, p. 772.

multilateral treaties. This practice is, in relation to the status of the **[76:**
FR of Yugoslavia as party to the multilateral treaties, uniform and
without exceptions, so that it has no pressing need of a "summary"
which would "highlight [its] main features";

(c) The fact that the term "Federal Republic" is not used before or after
the name "Yugoslavia" cannot, in my opinion, be taken as proof
that it does not concern the FR of Yugoslavia. The name "Yugoslavia" designates the Yugoslav State, regardless of the factual and
legal changes which it experienced during its existence, which were
also reflected in its name. For example, at the time when Yugoslavia
entered into the obligations under the Convention on the Prevention
and Punishment of the Crime of Genocide — in August 1950 — the
full name of the Yugoslav State was "Federal People's Republic of
Yugoslavia". Yugoslavia is, on the basis of legal identity and continuity, a party to the conventions which bound — in the era of the
League of Nations — the Yugoslav State which was called, at that
time, the "Kingdom of Serbs, Croats and Slovenes".

It follows that the terms such as the "former Yugoslavia" or the
"Federal Republic of Yugoslavia (Serbia and Montenegro)" *per se*
have no other meaning except the epistemiological one. In relation
to the SFRY, the Kingdom of Serbs, Croats and Slovenes represents
the "former Yugoslavia", just as the "Democratic Federal Yugoslavia", constituted at Session II of the Anti-Fascist Assembly of the
People's Liberation of Yugoslavia on 29 November 1943, represents
the "former Yugoslavia" in relation to the Federal People's Republic of Yugoslavia established by the 1946 Constitution. The conventional nature of such terms is also seen in the practice of the
principal organs of the United Nations with respect to the use of the
name "Federal Republic of Yugoslavia (Serbia and Montenegro)".
Since 22 November 1995, the Security Council uses in its resolutions
1021 and 1022 the term "Federal Republic of Yugoslavia" instead
of the former "Federal Republic of Yugoslavia (Serbia and Montenegro)" without any express decision and in a legally unchanged
situation in relation to the one in which it, like other organs of the
United Nations, employed the term "Federal Republic of Yugoslavia (Serbia and Montenegro)". The fact that this change in the
practice of the Security Council appeared on the day following
the initialling of the Peace Agreement in Dayton, gives a strong
basis for the conclusion that the concrete practice is not based on
objective, legal criteria but rather on political criteria.

97. The practice of the Secretary-General as the depositary of multilateral treaties corresponds to the general legal principle that a diminution of territory does not of itself affect the legal personality of the State.

763] This principle of international law is deeply rooted in international practice[145]. As early as 1925, the arbitrator, Professor Borel, held in the *Otta*-
[17] *man Debt Arbitration* that, notwithstanding both the territorial losses and the revolution, "in international law, the Turkish Republic was deemed to continue the international personality of the former Turkish Empire"[146]. In the practice of the United Nations, it is expressed in the opinion given by the United Nations Secretariat regarding the secession of Pakistan from India in which it was stated that "[t]he territory which breaks off, Pakistan, will be a new State; . . . the portion which separated was considered a new State; the remaining portion continued as an existing State with all the rights and duties which it had before"[147]. A possible exception cited is the case in which territorial changes affect the "territorial nucleus" of a State[148], which did not happen in the case of Yugoslavia since the "territorial nucleus" has been preserved[149].

98. It is noteworthy to underline that the practice of the Court is identical to the practice of the Secretary-General as depositary of multilateral treaties. The *Yearbook 1993-1994* of the International Court of Justice says that:

"On 31 July 1994, the following 184 States were Members of the United Nations:

State	Date of Admission
. . . .	. . . .
Yugoslavia	. Original Member."[150]

An identical formulation is also found in the previous issue[151]. On the basis of Article 93 (1) of the Charter of the United Nations, all Members of the United Nations are *ipso facto* parties to the Statute.

Such a practice of the Court is in full agreement with the interpretation of the scope of resolution 47/1 of the General Assembly given in a letter which the Under-Secretary-General and the Legal Counsel of the United Nations addressed on 29 September 1992 to the permanent representa-

---

[145] D. Anzilotti, this is one of the most certain rules in international law: "nessun principio più sicuro di questo nel diritto internazionale", "La formazione del Regno d'Italia nei guardi del diritto internazionale", *Revista di diritto internazionale*, 1912, p. 9.

[146] Cited in K. Marek, *Identity and Continuity of States in Public International Law*, 1954, p. 40.
[147] United Nations Press Release PM/473, 12 August 1947 (*Yearbook of the International Law Commission*, Vol. II, p. 101).
[148] Hall, *A Treatise on International Law*, 1924, p. 22; American Society of International Law, Panel on "State Succession and Relations with Federal States", Gold Room, Rayburn House Office Building, Washington, D.C., E. Williamson, United States State Department, 1 April 1992, p. 10.
[149] M. Akehurst, *A Modern Introduction to International Law*, 1984, p. 147.
[150] *I.C.J. Yearbook 1993-1994*, No. 48, p. 67.
[151] *I.C.J. Yearbook 1992-1993*, No. 47, p. 59.
[17 *3 Ann Dig* 78.]

tives of Bosnia and Herzegovina and Croatia to the United Nations and [76⁴ which asserts, *inter alia*, that "the resolution does not terminate nor suspend Yugoslavia's membership in the Organization"[152].

FIFTH PRELIMINARY OBJECTION

99. Three principal legal questions are raised by Yugoslavia's fifth preliminary objection, and relate to:

(a) the qualification of the conflict in Bosnia and Herzegovina;
(b) the territorial or non-territorial nature of the obligations of States under the Genocide Convention; and
(c) the type of the State responsibility referred to in Article IX of the Convention.

100. Having in mind the territorial nature of the obligations of States under the Genocide Convention, the qualification of the conflict in Bosnia and Herzegovina is of considerable importance. Even if this question is closely linked to the merits, this does not prevent the Court from

> "mak[ing] a summary survey of the merits to the extent necessary to satisfy itself that the case discloses claims that are reasonably arguable or issues that are reasonably contestable; in other words, that these claims or issues are rationally grounded on one or more principles of law, the application of which may resolve the dispute. The essence of this preliminary survey of the merits is that the question of jurisdiction or admissibility under consideration is to be determined not on the basis of whether the applicant's claim is right but exclusively on the basis whether it discloses a right to have the claim adjudicated."[153]

In my opinion, the conflict in Bosnia and Herzegovina cannot be qualified as "civil war" or "internal conflict" exclusively as Yugoslavia asserts. That assertion is only partly correct.

The armed conflict in Bosnia and Herzegovina was a special, *sui generis* conflict, in which elements of civil war and international armed conflict were intermingled.

Elements of civil war were obviously present in the armed conflict in Bosnia and Herzegovina; however, according to my opinion, they could in no way be seen as its dominant characteristic. They were especially

---

[152] United Nations, General Assembly, A/47/485, 30 September 1992, Annex.

[153] *Nuclear Tests, I.C.J. Reports 1974,* joint dissenting opinion of Judges Onyeama, Dillard, Jiménez de Aréchaga and Sir Humphrey Waldock, p. 364. [57 *ILR* 348 at 398.]

765] expressed in the period of constitutional crisis before the proclamation of the independence of Bosnia and Herzegovina by the incomplete parliament of Bosnia and Herzegovina. The passive, preparatory stage of that war consisted especially of the acts of creation of national militias as early as in 1991, while the active phase of the war started with attacks against the organs of the central federal authorities, especially against the units of the Yugoslav People's Army.

After the proclamation of sovereignty and independence of Bosnia and Herzegovina by the incomplete parliament of Bosnia and Herzegovina, the civil war became, in my opinion, an international armed conflict, in which one side consisted of a fictitious, *de jure* recognized State — the Republic of Bosnia and Herzegovina — and the other side consisted of two *de facto* States not recognized by the international community — Republika Srpska and Herzeg-Bosna. This was *bellum omnium contra omnes*, which is eloquently shown by the war between the Muslim authorities in Sarajevo and Herzeg-Bosna in 1993, and by the war between the authorities in Sarajevo and the alternative Muslim Autonomous Region of Western Bosnia, proclaimed in September 1993.

101. The relevant passage of the Court's Judgment relating to the nature of the rights and obligations of States under the Convention reads as follows:

> "the rights and obligations enshrined by the Convention are rights and obligations *erga omnes*. The Court notes that the obligation each State thus has to prevent and to punish the crime of genocide is not territorially limited by the Convention." (Para. 31 of the Judgment.)

In my opinion, it is necessary to draw a clear distinction, on the one hand, between the legal nature of the norm prohibiting genocide, and, on the other, the implementation or enforcement of that norm.

The norm prohibiting genocide, as a norm of *jus cogens*, establishes obligations of a State toward the international community as a whole, hence by its very nature it is the concern of all States. As a norm of *jus cogens* it does not have, nor could it possibly have, a limited territorial application with the effect of excluding its application in any part of the international community. In other words, the norm prohibiting genocide as a universal norm binds States in all parts of the world.

As an absolutely binding norm prohibiting genocide, it binds all subjects of international law even without any conventional obligation. To that effect, and only to that effect, the concrete norm is of universal applicability (a norm *erga omnes*), and hence "non-territorality" as another pole of limited territorial application may be taken as an element of the very being of a cogent norm of genocide prohibition.

The position is different, however, when it comes to the implementation or enforcement of the norm of genocide prohibition. The norm prohibiting genocide, like other international legal norms, is applicable by

States not in an imaginary space, but in an area of the territoralized inter- **[766**
national community. And, as was pointed out by the Permanent Court of
International Justice in the *"Lotus"* case:

> "Now the first and foremost restriction imposed by international
> law upon a State is that — failing the existence of a permissive rule
> to the contrary — it may not exercise its power in any form in the
> territory of another State. In this sense jurisdiction is certainly terri-
> torial; it cannot be exercised by a State outside its territory except by
> virtue of a permissive rule derived from international custom or
> from a convention.
>
> . . . .
>
> In these circumstances, all that can be required of a State is that it
> should not overstep the limits which international law places upon
> its jurisdiction; within these limits, its title to exercise jurisdiction
> rests in its sovereignty." [154]

A territorial jurisdiction conceived in this way suggests, as a general
rule, the territorial character of the State's obligation in terms of implementation of an international legal norm, both in prescriptive and enforcement terms. If this were not the case, norm on territorial integrity and
sovereignty, also having the character of *jus cogens*, would be violated.

102. What is the status of the Genocide Convention? With respect to
the obligation of prevention of the crime of genocide, the Convention
does not contain the principle of universal repression. It has firmly opted
for the territorial principle of the obligation of prevention and

> "the only action relating to crimes committed outside the territory of
> the Contracting Party is by organs of the United Nations within the
> scope of the general competence" [155].

Accordingly,

> "the States are . . . obliged to punish persons charged with the com-
> mission of acts coming under the Convention insofar as they were
> committed in their territory" [156].

Article VII of the draft Genocide Convention, prepared by the Secretary-General, was based on the concept of universal repression [157]. In its
draft Convention the *Ad Hoc* Committee on Genocide replaced the text
of Article VII, hence "the principle of universal repression was rejected
by the Committee by 4 votes (among which were France, the United

---

[154] *"Lotus"*, Judgment No. 9, P.C.I.J., Series A, No. 10, pp. 18-19. [4 *Ann Dig* 153.]
[155] N. Robinson, *The Genocide Convention, Its Origin and Interpretation*, 1949, pp. 13-14.
[156] *Ibid.*, p. 31.
[157] Doc. E1447, p. 8.

767] States of America and the Union of Soviet Socialist Republics) against 2
with 1 abstention"[158].

An unfavourable position regarding the principle of universal punishment emerges also from declarations and reservations concerning the Genocide Convention[159], Communication of Governments[160] and by non-governmental organizations that have a consultative status with the Economic and Social Council[161].

The Special Rapporteur concluded that

> "since no international criminal court has been established, the question of universal punishment should be reconsidered, if it is decided to prepare new international instruments for the prevention and punishment of genocide"[162].

The intention of the drafters of the Convention to establish territorial obligations of States under the Convention clearly and irrefutably stems from the provisions of Article XII of the Convention which reads:

> "Any Contracting Party may at any time, by notification addressed to the Secretary-General of the United Nations, *extend the application of the present Convention to all or any of the territories for the conduct of whose foreign relations that Contracting Party is responsible*." (Emphasis added.)

It is obvious that, if this were not the case, the said Article would be deprived of all sense and logic.

103. Could a State be responsible for genocide? The Court finds, when it refers to "the responsibility of a State for genocide or for any of the other acts enumerated in Article III", that Article IX does not exclude any form of State responsibility, nor is

> "the responsibility of a State for acts of its organs excluded by Article IV of the Convention, which contemplates the commission of an act of genocide by 'rulers' or 'public officials'" (para. 32 of the Judgment).

Such a position does not appear, in my opinion, to be tenable.

Article IV of the Genocide Convention, which stipulates criminal responsibility for genocide or the other acts enumerated in Article III of the Convention, has a twofold meaning:

(a) a positive meaning, starting from the principle of individual guilt, since Article IV establishes as criminally responsible "persons . . .

---

[158] See Study of the Question of the Prevention and Punishment of the Crime of Genocide, prepared by N. Ruhashyankiko, Special Rapporteur, doc. E/CN.4/Sub.2/416, 4 July 1978, p. 49.
[159] *Ibid.*, pp. 51-52.
[160] *Ibid.*, pp. 52-55.
[161] *Ibid.*, p. 55.
[162] *Ibid.*, p. 56.

whether they are constitutionally appointed rulers, public officials or **[768**
private individuals". This rule represents *lex lata*, because:

> "international practice since the Second World War has con-
> stantly applied the principle of individual criminal responsibility
> for crimes of international law, including those of genocide"[163],

(b) a negative meaning — contained in the exclusion of criminal responsibility of States, governments or State authorities and the rejection
of the application of the doctrine of the act of the State in this
matter. Such a solution is expressed in the positive international law.
The International Law Commission, when elaborating the Draft
Code of Offences against the Peace and Security of Mankind, concluded, *inter alia*, in relation to the content *ratione personae* of the
Draft Code that:

> "With regard to the content *ratione personae*, the Commission
> took the view that its efforts at this stage should be devoted exclu-
> sively to the criminal responsibility of *individuals*. This approach
> was dictated by the uncertainty still attaching to the problem of
> criminal responsibility of States . . . True, the criminal responsi-
> bility of individuals does not eliminate the international responsi-
> bility of States for the acts committed by persons acting as organs
> or agents of the State. But, such responsibility is of a different
> nature and falls within the traditional concept of State responsi-
> bility . . . the question of international criminal responsibility
> should be limited, at least at the present stage, to that of
> individuals."[164]

The resolution built into Article IV of the Genocide Convention represents an expression of a broader understanding of the inability to establish
the criminal responsibility of legal persons *(societas delinquere non potest)*.

The understanding is based on the premise that a criminal offence as a
phenomenon is reduced to a human action, that is to say, to a physical
act or to its omission. Since States are legal entities of an abstract character, persons without a physical body and incapable of criminal liability,
they thus cannot be guilty as perpetrators of criminal acts.

It is hardly necessary to state that the interest of safeguarding the
essential values of the international community involves the issue of
criminal responsibility of a State as illustrated, *inter alia*, by the Draft

---

[163] Study of the Question of the Prevention and Punishment of the Crime of Genocide,
prepared by Mr. N. Ruhashyankiko, Special Rapporteur, doc. E/CN.4/Sub.2/415, 4 July
1978, p. 36, para. 151.
[164] Report of the International Law Commission on the work of its thirty-sixth session
(7 May to 27 July 1984 (doc. A/39/10), *Yearbook of the International Law Commission*,
1984, Vol. II, Part Two, p. 11, para. 32.

769] Code of Offences against the Peace and Security of Mankind[165]. Theoretically, the issue of criminal responsibility of a State may be situated within the framework of a pure model of a State authority or State as the offender, namely in the framework of collective, simultaneous responsibility of a State as a legal person and physical personality, as its political representative.

However, the above are just projects which, irrespective of their relevance, have not yet found a place within positive international law. This fact *per se*, irrrespective of the circumstances of a concrete case, renders the Court, as an authority implementing *positive law* to subject cases, incapable of taking such projects into account or accepting them as relevant. If this were not the case, the Court would step away from its fundamental judicial function and penetrate into the legislative or quasi-legislative area[166].

104. Even in the hypothesis that, *tractu temporis*, since the Genocide Convention came into force, criminal responsibility for genocide or for any of the other acts enumerated in Article III has been extended to States as well, the relevance of such a change to the subject case could be highly questionable.

The rationale of such a question is the nature of the compromissory clause contained in Article IX of the Genocide Convention. The establishment of jurisdiction of the Court for disputes concerning the interpretation, application or fulfilment of the Convention is undoubtedly precedent to the general rule of an optional character of the Court's jurisdiction in international law. This fact has a dual meaning — legal and meta-legal. In legal terms, precedent has to be strictly interpreted[167], particularly when it comes to the restriction of the sovereign rights of States. In this case, the jurisdiction of the Court is founded in relation to disputes "relating to the interpretation, application or fulfilment of the *present Convention*" (emphasis added). In other words, the Court has, on the basis of Article IX of the Convention, jurisdiction to settle disputes relating to the *relevant provisions of the Convention* but not such disputes concerning the rules as might possibly exist outside its frame.

Meta-legal meaning resides in the fact that the extension of the Court's jurisdiction beyond the provisions of Article IX of the Convention would, in normal reasoning, inhibit the States in other cases. An evident readiness of States to accept the binding jurisdiction of the

---

[165] *Yearbook of the International Law Commission*, 1976, Vol. II, Part Two, pp. 7-18.

[166] "the enormity of the crime of genocide can hardly be exaggerated, and any treaty for its repression deserves the most generous interpretation; but the Genocide Convention is an instrument which is intended to produce legal effects by creating legal obligations between the parties to it" (*Reservations to the Convention on the Prevention and Punishment of the Crime of Genocide, Advisory Opinion, I.C.J. Reports 1951*, joint dissenting opinion of Judges Guerrero, Sir Arnold McNair, Read and Hsu Mo, p. 47). [18 *ILR* 364.]

[167] *P.C.I.J., Series A, No. 7*, p. 76.

Court on a broad basis would be strengthened by such a move on the [770 part of the Court.

105. Article IX of the Convention stipulates that:

> "Disputes between the Contracting Parties relating to the interpre-
> tation, application or fulfilment of the present Convention, including
> those relating to the responsibility of a State for genocide or for any
> of the other acts enumerated in article III, shall be submitted to the
> International Court of Justice at the request of any of the parties to
> the dispute."

If one attempts to determine the genuine meaning of the wording "responsibility of a State for genocide or for any of the other acts enumerated in
article III", several elements are of crucial importance.

(a) Article IX by its nature is a standard compromissory clause. As a
procedural provision, it aims at determining the jurisdiction of the Court
within the co-ordinates of "interpretation, application or fulfilment" of
the material provisions of the Convention. Hence, interpretations of
Article IX of the Convention may not *in concreto* go beyond the provisions on individual criminal responsibility stipulated in Article IV of the
Convention (see para. 101 above). As is forcefully expressed in the joint
separate opinion of Judges Sir Percy Spender and Sir Gerald Fitzmaurice
in the *South West Africa* case:

> "The principle of interpretation directed to giving provisions their
> maximum effect cannot legitimately be employed in order to intro-
> duce what would amount to a revision of those provisions." [168]

(b) The wording "responsibility of a State for genocide or for any of
the other acts enumerated in article III" is abstract and broad in its
vagueness, particularly in terms of the convention on criminal law "in
which care should be taken to avoid giving the State a fictitious legal
character, a procedure which should only be used in civil or commercial
matters" [169]. What is more, the wording "responsibility of a State" is
incorporated into the procedural provisions of the Genocide Convention.
It is not used, however, in the operative part of the Convention to denote
a possible consequence of committing the crime of genocide. The reason
for such a solution is obviously to be traced in the option for individual
criminal responsibility for genocide or related punishable acts.

For, as Manley Hudson concludes:

> "The article goes further, however, in 'including' among such dis-
> putes 'those relating to the responsibility of a State for genocide or
> any of the other acts enumerated in Article III'. As no other provi-
> sion in the Convention deals expressly with State responsibility, it is

---

[168] *I.C.J. Reports 1962*, p. 468. [37 *ILR* 3.]
[169] N. Ruhashyankiko, *op. cit.*, p. 82, para. 314.

771]   difficult to see how a dispute concerning such responsibility can be *included* among disputes relating to the interpretation or application or fulfilment of the Convention. In view of the undertaking of the parties in Article I to prevent genocide, it is conceivable that a dispute as to State responsibility may be a dispute as to fulfilment of the Convention. Yet read as a whole, the Convention refers to the punishment of individuals only; the punishment of a State is not adumbrated in any way, and it is excluded from Article V by which the parties undertake to enact punitive legislation. Hence the 'responsibility of a State' referred to in Article IX is not criminal liability." [170]

The genuine meaning of the wording "responsibility of a State" should hence be traced within the responsibility for the obligations entered into by the parties under the Convention. Primary responsibilities of the parties have been stipulated in Articles V and VI, and covering:

— an obligation to enact necessary legislation to give effect to the provisions of the Convention; and
— the obligation of instituting legal proceedings for punishable acts provided for by Article III of the Convention against persons charged in a competent tribunal of the State in the territory of which the act was committed.

Obligations of the Contracting Parties "to enact . . . the necessary legislation" and to punish persons who commit genocide and related acts constitute a form of international responsibility of the State, responsibility towards crucial interest of the international community as a whole, built into the norm prohibiting genocide.

Given the nature of these obligations, one could hardly disagree with the Special Rapporteur, Mr. N. Ruhashyankiko, that "at the present stage in the development of international criminal law, the State can bear only political responsibility for international crimes" [171], or perhaps, in more precise terms, the State can bear primarily political responsibility for a failure to perform obligations concerning the prohibition and punishment of international crimes.

(c) The qualification of a State as a responsible entity for the crime of genocide as a primarily political responsibility is not *a priori* exclusive of the civil responsibility of a State. The civil responsibility of a State in the matter of genocide may assume two forms of expression:

---

[170] M. M. Whiteman, *Digest of International Law*, 1968, p. 857.
[171] Study of the Question of the Prevention and Punishment of the Crime of Genocide, prepared by Mr. N. Ruhashyankiko, Special Rapporteur, doc. E/CN.4/Sub.2/416, 4 July 1978, p. 38, para. 159.

(i) civil responsibility for the crime of genocide committed in its own [772
State territory; and
(ii) civil responsibility for the crime of genocide committed in the territory of another State.

In the eventuality contemplated by (i) above, it would be civil responsibility under internal law which is to be considered and adjudicated in its
entirety by the internal judicial authorities of a contracting party.

A case falling under (ii) above would be different in terms of quality.
Leaving aside the conditions in which a State may be responsible for
genocide perpetrated in the territory of another State, civil responsibility
would be characterized by two stages. The first stage would comprise a
claim for reparations to the competent authorities of the State responsible for genocide and adjudicated in the procedure established by its own
internal law. The second stage would involve an international litigation
for the reparation of losses incurred by genocide, the parties to it being
the State responsible for genocide and the State on whose territory genocide was perpetrated. In other words, it would be a case of the typical
international civil responsibility of a State. Given the fact that the
national, ethnic, racial or religious group, as an object safeguarded from
the crime of genocide, has no *locus standi* in the Court, the State on
whose territory the crime has been perpetrated should espouse the cause
of the "national, ethnic, racial or religious" group after having exhausted
local legal remedies.

I am convinced that the Genocide Convention provided for no international civil responsibility of States for the crime of genocide. Such a standing of the Convention on the matter of international responsibility may of
course be qualified in more than one way, but it is difficult to infer any
conclusion on the force of the concept of international civil responsibility
within the fibre of the Convention, unless one strays into the area of legal
construction. It is easy to accept the view that the international civil
responsibility of States for the crime of genocide would strengthen the
effectiveness of prohibition of the crime of genocide. However, in the
present case, the question is reduced to the qualification of positive
law concerning responsibility for genocide and not to the qualification
of optimal solutions *in abstracto*. As suggested by Special Rapporteur
Whitaker

> "when the Convention is revised consideration shall be given to
> including provisions for a State responsibility for genocide together
> with reparations" [172].

---

[172] Review of further development in fields which the sub-commission has been concerned with, revised and updated report on the question of the prevention and punishment of the crime of genocide, prepared by Mr. V. Whitaker (E/CN.4/Sub.2/1985/6, 2 July
1985, p. 26, para. 54.

106. With regard to the sixth preliminary objection raised by Yugoslavia, the Court finds that:

> "Bosnia and Herzegovina could become a party to the Convention through the mechanism of State succession. Moreover, the Secretary-General of the United Nations considered that this had been the case" (para. 20 of the Judgment)

and that

> "the Court does not consider it necessary, in order to decide on its jurisdiction in this case, to make a determination on the legal issues concerning State succession in respect to treaties which have been raised by the Parties. Whether Bosnia and Herzegovina automatically became party to the Genocide Convention on the date of its accession to independence on 6 March 1992, or whether it became a party as a result — retroactive or not — of its Notice of Succession of 29 December 1992, at all events it was a party to it on the date of the filing of its Application on 20 March 1993." (Para. 23 of the Judgment.)

107. I must say that, in my view, the opposite is the case. No one denies that Bosnia and Herzegovina "could become a party to the Convention through the mechanism of State succession". *However, the real question is not whether Bosnia and Herzegovina "could have become a party", for every new State has in principle that possibility, but whether it became a party to the Convention through the succession mechanism.* The fact that the Secretary-General "considered that this had been the case" is not of decisive importance, as the scope of depositary functions is clearly defined in positive international law. As stated in the Commentary to Article 77 (Functions of Depositaries) of the Convention on the Law of Treaties:

> a depositary has *a certain duty* to examine whether signatures, instruments and reservations are in conformity with any applicable provisions of the treaty or of the present articles, and if necessary to bring the matter to the attention of the State in question. *That is, however, the limit of the depositary's duty in this connexion. It is no part of the functions to adjudicate on the validity of an instrument or reservation."* [173]

In other words it is firmly established that "the depositary *is not invested*

---

[173] UNCLT, First and Second Sessions, Vienna, 26 March-24 May 1968 and 9 April-22 May 1969, *Official Records* Documents of the Conference, p. 89, para. 4 (emphasis added).

with any competence to adjudicate upon or to determine matters arising in [774] *connexion with the performance of its functions"* [174].

In my opinion, the Court had to consider whether Bosnia and Herzegovina had become a party to the Convention on the basis of succession, at least vis-à-vis Yugoslavia, for two reasons:

— in the formal sense, there exists a dispute between Bosnia and Herzegovina and Yugoslavia in that the positions of the parties to the dispute in relation to "automatic succession" are radically opposed. While Bosnia and Herzegovina considers automatic succession to be a feature of positive international law and therefore contends that "it *has automatically succeeded* to the Genocide Convention" [175], Yugoslavia denies this, claiming that "the 'clean slate' rule has been and remains in force as a rule of customary international law for new States" [176].

(It should be noted that expressions such as "automatic succession to the Genocide Convention" or "has automatically succeeded to the Genocide Convention" are not sufficiently precise and are, consequently, incorrect. The objects of succession are not treaties as legal acts but concern the status of the parties to the concrete treaty and/or the rights and obligations stipulated by that treaty. If treaties as legal acts were the object of succession, then succession would also apply to treaties whose obligation has been performed, for they are as valid as before, albeit merely of historical interest, which is clearly not the case.)

— in the material sense, as Bosnia and Herzegovina did not express its consent to be bound by the Convention in the way prescribed by Article XI of the Convention, the rules of succession are the only possible basis on which Bosnia and Herzegovina could be considered a party to the Genocide Convention.

108. The Genocide Convention, by its nature, is a convention in the field of international criminal law. This is something which results from the very nature of the matter, and which hardly needs arguing. A convention which has, as its subject, the definition and punishment of genocide as a crime under international law, and whose provisions are implemented through national criminal legislation, could hardly be defined in a different way. Another consideration is that in a community like the international community, many conventions and other international legal acts have a direct or indirect humanitarian meaning. Such a meaning of

---

[174] UNCLT, First and Second Sessions, Vienna, 26 March-24 May 1968 and 9 April-22 May 1969, *Official Records*, Documents of the Conference, p. 89, para. 8 (emphasis added).

[175] Statement of the Government of the Republic of Bosnia and Herzegovina on Preliminary Objections, 14 November 1995, para. 6.9 at p. 111 (emphasis added).

[176] Preliminary Objections of the Federal Republic of Yugoslavia, para. B.1.4.10.

775] international legal acts results unavoidably from the fact that, in the final analysis, the international community is *genus humanum*, that in a system whose original and basic subjects are abstract beings, the individual represents the final addressee of the legal rules. However, it could not be concluded from that that the Genocide Convention is a humanitarian convention, a convention which belongs to humanitarian law, because that term denotes the rules contained in conventions and international customs whose subject is "to reduce or limit the suffering of individuals, and to circumscribe the area within which the savagery of armed conflicts is permissible" [177] (in that sense it should be noted that the full name of the Geneva Conference of 1974-1977 which adopted Protocols I and II was "Diplomatic Conference on the Reaffirmation and Development of International Humanitarian Law Applicable in Armed Conflicts").

The qualification of a convention or of other international legal acts as "humanitarian", on the basis of the direct or indirect significance of that convention for the legal status of individuals, would make the predominant part of international law a "humanitarian law". *Exempli causa*, the "humanitarian law" understood in such a way would include the instruments which regulate the position of the minorities, the right of peoples to self-determination, the conventions which punish acts of terrorism, and, in general, all conventions in the field of international criminal law.

The term "humanitarian convention" or "convention of humanitarian character" is used, so it seems, in order to stress the importance of the convention. However, terms like "humanitarian convention", "convention on human rights", etc., do not, logically speaking, denote the legal force of the convention, but rather its appurtenance to a *species*, in the system of international law. The importance of a convention may rather be expressed by other qualifications — in this concrete case by the qualification according to which the Genocide Convention represents a "general multilateral convention of universal interest".

109. Article 34 (Succession of States in Cases of Separation of Parts of a State) of the Convention on Succession in respect of Treaties (1978) stipulates *inter alia*:

> "1. When a part or parts of the territory of a State separate to form one or more States, whether or not the predecessor State continues to exist:
>
> *(a)* any treaty in force at the date of the succession of States in respect of the entire territory of the predecessor State continues in force in respect of each successor State so formed".

The relevant provision of the cited Article has been formulated in terms of automatic succession. Theoretically, it corresponds to the concept of

---

[177] J. G. Starke, *Introduction to International Law*, 1989, p. 553.

universal succession based on a strict analogy with the notion of inheri- [77
tance in civil law and/or the concept on legal succession (substitution +
continuation) according to which "the successor State under international law succeeds to its predecessor's rights and obligations, which
become its own" *[translation by the Registry]* [178].

In concreto, the fundamental question is the qualification of the term
"automatic succession" as stipulated by Article 34 of the Convention on
Succession in respect of Treaties (1978), i.e., does it constitute *lex lata*, a
part of positive international law — or not?

110. The answer to the fundamental question thus posed implies:

(a) a qualification of the solution established by Article 34 (1) of the
Convention from the standpoint of treaty law;

(b) a qualification of that solution from the standpoint of the practice
of States prior to the adoption of the Convention on Succession in
respect of Treaties;

(c) a qualification of the practice of States after the Convention was
adopted at the diplomatic conference in Vienna in August 1978.

Article 34 (Succession of States in Cases of Separation of Parts of a
State) is an integral part of the Convention on Succession in respect of
Treaties, hence the rule contained in it is a treaty rule and shares the fate
of the Convention itself. Article 49 (Entry into Force) of the Convention
stipulates that:

"1. The present Convention shall enter into force on the thirtieth
day following the date of deposit of the fifteenth instrument of ratification or accession."

Since the condition for the coming into force of the Convention has not
been fulfilled, the Convention has not become a part of the positive legal
milieu. Consequently, the rule contained in Article 34 (1) is in a state of
lex ferenda.

The rule contained in Article 34 (1) could, naturally, be *lex lata* outside
the framework of the Convention as an expression of existing customary
law. Does this rule merit the qualification of a customary rule?

The generally held view of customary law, endorsed by this Court [179], is
that the creation of a rule of customary international law postulates:
"two constitutive elements: (1) a general practice of States, and (2) the
acceptance by States of the general practice as law" [180].

An analysis of practice in cases of separation of parts of a State when

---

[178] "Der Nachfolger des Völkerrechts aber tritt in Rechte und Pflichten seines Vor-
gängers so ein, als wären es seine eigenen" (H. M. Huber, *Beiträge zu einer Lehre von der
Staatensuccession*, Berlin, 1897, p. 14).

[179] *Exempli causa, North Sea Continental Shelf* cases, *I.C.J. Reports 1969*, p. 44,
para. 77. [41 *ILR* 29.]

[180] G. Schwarzenberger, *A Manual of International Law*, 1967, p. 32.

777] the predecessor State continues to exist suggests two principal conclusions:

(a) In quantitative terms it is difficult, if not impossible, to speak of a generalized practice in this respect. As the ILC loyally notes in its commentary on Article 33 (Succession of States in Cases of Separation of Parts of a State) and Article 34 (Position of a State Continues after Separation of Part of Its Territory) of its Draft: "During the United Nations period cases of separation resulting in the creation of a newly independent State . . . have been comparatively few." [181] Previous practice does not substantively affect the argument because "[b]efore the era of the United Nations, colonies were considered as being in the fullest sense territories of the colonial power", hence, "some of the earlier precedents usually cited . . . in cases of secession concerned secession of colonies" [182]. One could rather, and with greater justification, speak of a certain number of precedents;

(b) These precedents in the qualitative sense have in common an identical position regarding treaties of the predecessor State — new States were neither bound nor entitled *ipso jure* to the continuance of pre-independence treaties. In relation to the period prior to the foundation of the United Nations,

> "[t]he majority of writers take the view, supported by State practice, that a newly independent State begins its life with a clean slate, except in regard to 'local' or 'real' obligations" [183].

The practice in the United Nations era is presented in the commentary on Article 33 of the Draft (Article 34 of the Convention) with the cases of Pakistan and Singapore. The case of Pakistan is qualified as the application of the principle that on separation such a State has a "clean slate" in the sense that it is not under any *obligation* to accept the continuance in force of its predecessor's treaties [184]. As far as Singapore is concerned, in spite of the "devolution agreement" of 1965, it "adopted a posture similar to that of other newly independent States", that is, "[w]hile ready to continue Federation treaties in force, Singapore regarded that continuance as a matter of mutual consent" [185].

---

[181] Draft Articles on Succession of States in respect of Treaties with commentaries adopted by the International Law Commission at its twenty-sixth session, United Nations Conference on Succession of States in respect of Treaties, 1977 session and resumed session 1978, *Official Records*, Vol. III, Documents of the Conference, p. 92, para. 17.

[182] *Ibid.*, p. 91, para. 12.

[183] *Ibid.*, p. 41, para. 3.

[184] *Ibid.*, p. 92, para. 17.

[185] *Ibid.*, pp. 93-99, para. 18.

The ILC viewed the case of Pakistan as a "special one"[186] probably [77?] because it prompted a legal opinion of the United Nations Secretariat. The relevant part of the opinion reads:

"1. From the viewpoint of international law, the situation is one in which part of an existing State breaks off and becomes a new State. On this analysis there is no change in the international status of India; it continues as a State with all treaty rights and obligations of membership in the United Nations. The territory which breaks off, Pakistan, will be a new State, it will not have the treaty rights and obligations of the old State . . .

In international law the situation is analogous to the separation of the Irish Free State from Britain, and of Belgium from the Netherlands. In these cases the portion which separated was considered a new State; the remaining portion continued as an existing State with all the rights and duties which it had before."[187]

This legal opinion was given in connection with the concrete issue concerning Pakistan's position in relation to the Charter of the United Nations, but its wording and argumentation clearly indicate that it was designed as an opinion of principle. In any event, there are clear indications that States interpreted it as a principled position of the United Nations with regard to the relationship of a part of a State territory which breaks off and becomes a new State, to the treaty rights and obligations of the old State[188].

111. It would appear that the main methodological approach of the Commission in drafting Article 34 of the Convention was based on the drawing of a distinction between two things:

(a) the obligation of the new State to continue to apply the treaties of its predecessor to its territory after the succession of States; and,

---

[186] United Nations Conference on Succession of States in respect of Treaties, 1977 session and resumed session 1978, *Official Records*, Vol. III, Documents of the Conference, p. 92, para. 17.

[187] Legal opinion of 8 August 1947 by the Assistant Secretary-General for Legal Affairs, approved and made public by the Secretary-General in United Nations Press Release PM/473, 12 August 1947 (*Yearbook of the International Law Commission*, 1962, Vol. II, p. 101.

[188] In the *note verbale* of its Permanent Mission to the United Nations received on 11 September 1963, the Government of Afghanistan bases its assertion that "Pakistan is not a successor to British treaty rights because Pakistan is a new State" precisely on the argument that the Secretary-General of the United Nations "denied the right of succession" to Pakistan — United Nations, *Legislative Series*, Materials on Succession of States, 1967 (ST/LEG/SER.B/14), p. 2, para. 3 *(a)* and footnote 1.

779] *(b)* the right of the new State to consider itself a party to those treaties in its own name after the succession of States[189].

The Commission proceeded explicitly from this distinction in formulating the provisions of Article 15 of the Draft Convention which stipulates that:

"A newly independent State is not bound to maintain in force, or to become a party to, any treaty by reason only of the fact that at the date of the succession of States the treaty was in force in respect of the territory to which the succession of States relates."

If the Commission was guided by the practice of States in formulating the provisions of Articles 15 and 33 of the Draft (Articles 16 and 34 of the Convention) then a complete analogy has to be applied when one is determining the consequences of succession in the case of the creation of a newly independent State by secession from the metropolis and the creation of a State by the separation of parts of an existing State. In particular, in the period prior to the United Nations era, cases of "secession" concerned the "secession of colonies"[190]. In other words this is a virtually uniform practice, the practice in the case of Pakistan and Singapore, the only cases cited in the commentary to Article 33 of the Draft to illustrate the practice during the United Nations period, being characterized as the "clean slate" rule.

Making a distinction between the consequences of succession in the case of a newly independent State the territory of which immediately before the date of succession was a dependent territory, and the case of a new State formed by separation of a part of an existing State, and establishing different rules for these two cases — "clean slate" in the former and "automatic continuity" in the latter — the Convention undoubtedly went beyond the sphere of codification of existing practice and entered the sphere of progressive development.

The provision on "automatic continuity" could hardly be justified in a convention on succession even in the event that the new States, following the logic of the right to consider themselves as parties to the treaties in their own name after the succession of States, had uniformly accepted the rights and obligations stemming from the treaties of the predecessor State.

The very fact that we are dealing with the *right* of the new State "to consider itself a party to the treaties *in its own name*" (emphasis added), a right that has been operationalized in conformity with the rules of

---

[189] See Commentary to Article 15, Position in respect of the Treaties of the Predecessor State of the Draft Articles, United Nations Conference on Succession of States in respect of Treaties, 1977 session and resumed session 1978, *Official Records*, Vol. III, Documents of the Conference, p. 40, para. 2.

[190] *Ibid.*, p. 91, para. 12.

treaty law based on the fundamental principle of consent, eliminates, [78**
within the logic of codification of existing practice, the construction on
"automatic continuity" which is, by its meaning, an *obligation*. What
could be open to debate as we are dealing with a right or authorization is
whether that right or authorization, depending on the nature of the practice, is an ordinary or categorical authorization *(jus cogens)*. Even the
uniform exercise of a right does not provide grounds for transforming the
right into an obligation. *Per analogiam*, if on the basis of the authorizing
norm contained in Article 33 of the Convention on the Law of the Sea
(1982) a large majority of States were to proclaim a contiguous zone, that
would not mean that the establishment of the zone would constitute an
obligation of States. The consequences of such a practice would be the
constitution of customary rules on the right of States to proclaim exclusive economic zones or *in concreto* the customary rule on the *right* of the
successor State "to consider itself as a party to the predecessor State's
treaties in its own name".

It is therefore not difficult to agree with the opinion of the Expert Con-
sultant of the Conference, Sir Francis Vallat, that

> "[t]he rule [in Article 2 — Succession of States in Case of Separation
> of Parts of a State] was not based either on established practice or on
> precedent, it was a matter of the progressive development of inter-
> national law rather than of codification" [191].

It was noted that, in the case of Article 34 of the Convention

> "the International Law Commission abandoned the 'clean slate'
> principle and introduced, on the contrary, a rule of continuity. It
> was clear that in doing so it had been aware of the fact that it was
> not simply reflecting the present state of the law, but was proposing
> progressive development. For 'clean slate' was part of general inter-
> national law and would continue to be so, whatever solution was
> adopted in the Convention." [192]

Multilateral law-making conventions do not represent an exception since:

> "Succession to multilateral law-making conventions after separa-
> tion or secession is a right, not an obligation. Multilateral law-mak-
> ing conventions establish a body of rules of international law. They
> do not create subjective rights of individual states. In case of succes-
> sion no acquired right of a third party need be protected, by making
> it the successor's responsibility to perform it. No automatic change

---

[191] *Summary Records*, Committee of the Whole, 48th Meeting, 8 August 1978, p. 105,
para. 10.
[192] Ritter, *The UN Conference on Succession in Respect of Treaties, Vienna, 31 July-
23 August 1978*, pp. 52-55.

781] of attribution; in other words: no automatic succession, therefore, takes place."[193]

Finally, it is also worth examining the practice of States following the adoption on 22 August 1978 of the Convention on Succession in respect of Treaties, which was open for signature until 28 February 1979. Article 46 (Signature) of Chapter VII of the Convention stipulates

> "The present Convention shall be open for signature by all States until 28 February 1979 at the Federal Ministry for Foreign Affairs of the Republic of Austria, and subsequently, until 31 August 1979, at the United Nations Headquarters in New York."

The position of States regarding the Convention could hardly, even given a maximum degree of benevolence, be described as satisfactory. In the almost twenty years since the Convention was opened to ratification and accession, only 13 States have deposited instruments of ratification, accession or succession, so that not even the obviously modest requirement of 15 instruments of ratification or accession for the Convention to enter into effect has been fulfilled. This fact — *volens nolens* — is indicative of the attitude of States towards the Convention, regardless of the fact that the number of ratifications or accessions cannot, in itself, be considered conclusive with regard to the acceptance of the rules contained in a Convention which has not come into force. The practice of new States which have emerged since 1993 clearly shows that automatic succession is not accepted as a positive rule (Multilateral Treaties Deposited with the Secretary-General, Status as at 31 December 1993).

112. It follows from the above that the rule on automatic succession of multilateral treaties — *lex ferenda*, as matters now stand — has not been accepted in positive international law. However, it would be wrong to conclude from this that a new State begins life in the international community as a *tabula rasa*, a newborn in a legal vacuum deprived of all treaty rights and obligations. Such a state of affairs would be in contradiction with the very idea of an organized, *de jure* international community, an idea which does not recognize or tolerate the existence of any entity which is not directly or indirectly subject to the rule of law.

Moreover, treaty rights and obligations are subject to the division of rights and obligations effected in the well-known dictum of the Court in the [18] case concerning *Barcelona Traction, Light and Power Company, Limited:*

> "[a]n essential distinction should be drawn between the obligations of a State toward the international community as a whole, and those

---

[193] K. Zemanek, "State Succession after Decolonization", *Recueil des cours de l'Académie de droit international de La Haye*, Vol. 116, 1965, p. 233.
[[18] 46 *ILR* 1.]

arising vis-à-vis another State . . . By their very nature, the former **[78**
are the concern of all States." [194]

(Modern international law does not take the classical view according to which only custom, as a formal source, may *originally* constitute a norm of general international law, whereas a rule created by treaty, *per definitionem*, represents a particular norm which may possibly acquire the status of a norm of general international law *tractu temporis* by means of custom. This view played its part when the international community was primitive and undeveloped and when constructions like this were required to fill in the vast gaps in the positive law. Today such a concept is untenable both in theory and from the standpoint of positive law.

Theoretically, if it is rightly considered that the basis of the binding nature of general international law is the "will of the international community as a whole", general custom and comprehensive multilateral treaties are only the instrumentalization of that will. Their mutual relationship in value terms is determined by the inherent capacity of both sources to express that will. Any other approach implicitly introduces dualism into the foundation of the binding nature of international law for it is obvious that neither general custom nor general multilateral treaties imply unanimity, the agreement of all States. Therefore, to recognize custom as having an exclusive role in the generation of general international law is tantamount to a metaphysical joke (Lauterpacht speaks of "the mysterious phenomenon of customary international law which is deemed to be a source of law only on condition that it is in accordance with law" ("Sovereignty over Submarine Areas", 27 *British Year Book of International Law* 376, p. 394 (1950)); he also raises the question of "why custom is binding. The answer, beyond which it is in law not possible to go, is that it is the will of the international community that international law, in its various manifestations, shall be binding" (H. Lauterpacht, *International Law*, Collected Papers, 1, General Works, 1970, p. 58).

In positive legal terms, the capacity of general multilateral treaties to generate norms *jus cogens superveniens* has been established by the Convention on the Law of Treaties. The commentary on Article 50 of the Draft (Article 53 of the Convention) says *inter alia*: "a modification of a rule of *jus cogens* would today most probably be effected through a general multilateral treaty" — *Yearbook of the International Law Commission,* 1966, Vol. II, p. 248, para. 4. If a general multilateral treaty is capable of creating a norm of *jus cogens*, as the most perfect part of international law, then *a fortiori* it is capable of generating a norm of general international law.)

---

[194] *I.C.J. Reports 1970*, p. 32.

783]   General multilateral treaties adopted in the interest of the international community, being the instrumental form of expression of the will of the international community as a whole, operate *erga omnes* independently of contractual approval. The Genocide Convention is a case in point. As indicated by the International Court of Justice in its Advisory Opinion concerning *Reservations to the Convention on the Prevention and Punish-* [19] *ment of the Crime of Genocide*, proceeding from the qualification of genocide as "a denial of the right of existence of entire human groups" which "is contrary to moral law and to the spirit and aims of the United Nations", "the principles underlying the Convention . . . are recognized by civilized nations as binding on States, *even without any conventional obligation*" [195].

Hence, the principles underlying the Genocide Convention are part of the *corpus juris cogentis*. Any new State is *a priori* subject to these rules since they express the universal interest of the international community as a whole [196].

113. The cited opinion of the Court raises a question of fundamental importance for these concrete proceedings — the question of the relationship between the principles underlying the Genocide Convention and the provisions of the Genocide Convention. This question has two dimensions — a quantitative and a qualitative one. The quantitative dimension of the question has to do with the relationship between underlying principles and the provisions of the Convention, i.e., whether those principles apply to the Convention as a whole. The answer to this question can, in my opinion, only be negative. The fundamental principles of international law underlying the Genocide Convention are manifested only in the substantive provisions of the Convention, the provisions defining its object and purpose. The transitional and final provisions of the Convention, to which should be added the procedural provisions regarding methods of settling disputes, are not such as to warrant being described as expressing the spirit and letter of the fundamental principles of international law. This is corroborated not only by the possibility of expressing reservations regarding these provisions but also by the effect of termination carried out in accordance with Article XIV of the Convention.

In qualitative terms the relationship between the "principles underlying the Convention" and the substantive provisions of the Convention is rele-

---

[195] *I.C.J. Reports 1951*, p. 23 (emphasis added).

[196] It might be concluded that, having in mind that nature of the principles underlying the Genocide Convention, the then Secretary-General Hammarsjköld warned the Congo authorities during United Nations operations in that country that the principles of the Convention must be held to govern even a new State like the Congo and to apply to subordinate political authorities within the Congo State (Annual Report of the Secretary-General 1960-1961, General Assembly, 16th Sess., Supp. No. 1, p. 11; Waldock, "General Course on Public International Law", *Recueil des cours de l'Académie de droit international de La Haye*, Vol. 106, 1962, p. 228).

[[19] 18 *ILR* 364.]

vant from the standpoint of whether the legal effect of those principles **[784** covers the substantive provisions of the Convention. These provisions of the Convention are the normative concretization of the "principles under-lying the Convention", the transformation of the general — for practical purposes inoperable — categorical imperative into a series of concrete, particular categorical imperatives in the form of specific substantive pro-visions of the Convention.

In other words, the substantive provisions of the Genocide Conven-tion, as the concretization of those principles, are interpretative in nature so that they share the cogent nature of the principles underlying the Con-vention.

If this were not the case, these lofty principles "recognized by civilized States as binding on States" would remain in the air, as a kind of monu-ment to good intentions which never came to fruition.

For, if the provisions of the Genocide Convention were not a concre-tization of the principles underlying the Convention, the international community would be faced with insurmountable legal obstacles in the pursuit of its intention to eliminate the crime of genocide. Thus, *exempli causa*, non-party States would not be bound by the Convention's provi-sions which determine the substance of the crime of genocide or by the obligation to prevent and punish the crime of genocide.

114. In other words, Bosnia and Herzegovina as a new State is *a priori* bound by the substantive provisions of the Genocide Convention even without any conventional obligation. By formal accession to the Geno-cide Convention, with respect to the substantive provisions of the Con-vention, Bosnia and Herzegovina would merely confirm in contractual form the obligations by which it was bound independently of its will, obligations which are beyond the autonomous will of States.

The legal effect of accession to the Convention lies, primarily, in a commitment to those rules of the Convention which do not have a cogent nature, i.e., rules of a procedural nature such as *exempli causa*, the rules contained in Articles VIII, IX, XIV, XV or XVI of the Con-vention.

115. "Automatic succession" and "notification of succession" are mutually exclusive. The effect of automatic succession would consist of the automatic, *ipso jure* transfer of treaty rights and obligations from the predecessor State to the successor State. In that case, therefore, the suc-cession does not occur as a result of the will of the successor but on the basis of the norm of international law which stipulates the transfer of treaty rights and obligations as a consequence of the replacement of one State by another in the responsibility for the international relations of territory. "Notification of succession" has a rational and legal justifica-tion only in cases in which the transfer of treaty rights and obligations or the modalities of that transfer depend on the will of the successor since, *ex definitione*, it represents "any notification, however phrased or named, made by a successor State *expressing its consent to be considered as*

85] *bound by the treaty*"[197]. In other words, it is applied in cases when the successor State is not bound, by norms of objective international law, to continue to apply the treaties of its predecessor to its territory after the succession of States but is entitled, according to the relevant norm, to consider itself as a party to the treaties in its own name.

116. In this connection, the question is whether "notification of succession" is appropriate, *per se*, for expressing consent to be bound by treaty. The legitimacy of this question relies on two facts:

(i) the connection that exists between the rules on succession with respect to international treaties and the rules of treaty law, and
(ii) the meaning of the instrument of "notification of succession".

It is natural that the succession of States with respect to treaties has the closest links with the law of treaties itself and could be regarded as dealing with particular aspects of participation in treaties, the conclusion of treaties and the application of treaties.

Special Rapporteur Humphrey Waldock described these links as follows:

> "the Commission could not do otherwise than examine the topic of succession with respect to treaties within the general framework of the law of treaties . . . the principles and rules of the law of treaties seemed to provide a surer guide to the problems of succession with respect to treatis than any general theories of succession"[198].

Or as stated by O'Connell,

> "The effect of change of sovereignty on treaties is not a manifestation of some general principle or rule of State succession, but rather a matter of treaty law and interpretation."[199]

The determination of "notification of succession" given in Article 2 *(g)* of the Convention on Succession in respect of Treaties, as well as the practice of States in the matter, cast serious doubts as to the possibility of "notification of succession" as an instrument, *per se*, that acts as a means of binding by treaty.

The Convention on the Law of Treaties (1969) stipulates in Article 11 (Means of Expressing Consent To Be Bound by a Treaty):

> "The consent of a State to be bound by a treaty may be expressed by signature, exchange of instruments constituting a treaty, ratifica-

---

[197] Article 2 *(g)* of the Convention on Succession of States in respect of Treaties (emphasis added).

[198] *Yearbook of the International Law Commission*, 1968, p. 131, para. 52.

[199] D. P. O'Connell, *The Law of State Succession*, 1956, p. 15.

tion, acceptance, approval or accession, or by any other means if so **[78** agreed."

The formulation of Article 11 of the Convention on the Law of Treaties does not exclude the *possibility* of notification of succession being understood as a means of expressing approval to be bound by a treaty. The operationalization of this possibility implies, however, the agreement of the parties for, in the light of treaty law as expressed in Article 11 of the Convention, "notification of succession" undoubtedly comes under *"any other means"* of expressing consent to be bound by a treaty but is conditioned by the phrase "if so agreed". From this viewpoint, *"notification of succession" as a unilateral act of the State, constitutes a basis for a collateral agreement in simplified form between the new State and the individual parties to its predecessor's treaties.* Thus "notification of succession" actually represents an abstract, generalized form of the new State's consent to be bound by the treaties of the predecessor State — a form of consent which is, in each particular case, realized in conformity with the general rule of the law of treaties on expression of consent to be bound by a treaty contained in Article 11 of the Convention on the Law of Treaties and prescribed by provisions of the concrete Treaty.

An exception to the general rule according to which consent of the successor State to be bound by a treaty has to be expressed *ad casum* in conformity with Article 11 of the Convention on the Law of Treaties could be envisaged in the event that, outside and independently of the Convention, there exists a generally accepted rule according to which "notification of succession" is considered a specific means of binding new States by treaties. Grounds for such an interpretation are also provided by Article 73 of the Convention on the Law of Treaties: "The provisions of the present Convention shall not prejudge any question that may arise in regard to a treaty from a succession of States . . ."

There is no real evidence that such a rule exists. The Convention on the Law of Treaties which is, by its nature, a combination of codification and progressive development, does not make any mention in its Article 11 (Means of Expressing Consent To Be Bound by a Treaty) of "notification of succession" as such a means. This is particularly conspicuous in view of the fact that Article 11 is built on the premise of deformalization of the means of expressing consent to be bound by a treaty. The reason for such a state of affairs lies, in my opinion, in the still outstanding basic questions regarding the succession of States with respect to treaties.

"Notification of succession" can only have two basic meanings:

(a) it can represent a confirmation that the new State is bound by treaty and, in that case, it has only a declarative effect; and

(b) it can represent an instrument, however phrased or named, expressing consent of a successor State to be bound by the treaty.

787]   In the case of *(a)* above, the basic norm on the succession of States with respect to treaties is automatic succession — the rights and obligations stemming from treaties *ipso jure*, that are transferred from the predecessor State to the successor State by the very act of territorial change. In this case, "notification of succession" is essentially unnecessary. It would merely be information that a territorial change had occurred and that, as a result, the rule on the automatic transfer of rights and obligations stipulated by treaty had been activated.

In the case under *(b)* above, "notification of succession" is a means of expressing consent to be bound by a treaty. Since succession *per se* is not and cannot be an independent method of expressing consent to be bound by a treaty, except under the hypothesis of automatic succession, it follows that "notification of succession" can only be a descriptive notion, a collective term for various forms of expression of consent of a new State to be bound by a treaty.

The practice of States in the area of succession with respect to treaties is predominantly linked to the gaining of independence of former colonies from the metropolis. It is characterized by diversity and the absence of clear and precise rules. If any tendency can be said to be prevalent, it is that "a great many new States could be classified in a variety of 'pick and choose' categories"[200] which is by its meaning close to the "clean slate" concept. However, regardless of whether they have accepted the Nyerere formula and laid down a specified period for the review of treaties, which period would automatically lapse if not taken up by the new State before its expiry, or the Zambia formula, which assumed the continued application of many pre-independence treaties, but which laid down an unlimited period of review to determine which had lapsed or which had in practice been adopted if the new States considered them suited to their needs. Those new States adopted such treaties by sending appropriate notes to the depositary. The position on specific treaties was expressed in the form of "acceptance", "accession", and the like[201]. There are not many examples of the acceptance of a treaty by a successor expressed in the form of an instrument that could be called a "notification of succession". "Notification of succession" is rather a synthetic, collective term denoting various forms of new States being bound by the treaties of the predecessor State, and was developed primarily in the practice of the United Nations Secretary-General as the depositary of multilateral treaties. The term implies the existence of a rule of general international law on the transfer of rights and obligations stemming from multilateral treaties to which the predecessor State is a party, to the successor State which does not correspond to the actual state of affairs since:

---

[200] Kearney, *Yearbook of the International Law Commission,* 1968, Vol. I, p. 136.
[201] See *United Nations Legislative Series,* Materials on Succession of States (ST/LEG/SER.B/14), 1967, pp. 42 (11); 181; 224-229.

"In spite of some evidence to the contrary, emanating mainly from **[788**
diplomatic rather than legal sources, it is submitted that the general
principle is that newly established States which do not result from a
political dismemberment and cannot fairly be said to involve political continuity with any predecessor, start with a clean slate in the
matter of treaty obligation, save in so far as obligations may be
accepted by them in return for the grant of recognition to them or
for other reasons, and except as regards the purely local or 'real'
obligations of the State formerly exercising sovereignty over the territory of the new State." [202]

The practice of new States following the adoption of the Convention
on Succession in respect of Treaties is heterogeneous but is clearly not
heading in the direction of establishment of "notification of succession"
as a specific means of binding new States by the treaties of the predecessor State.

117. Article XI of the Genocide Convention stipulates:

"The present Convention shall be open until 31 December 1949
for signature on behalf of any Member of the United Nations and of
any non-member State to which an invitation to sign has been
addressed by the General Assembly.

The present Convention shall be ratified, and the instruments of
ratification shall be deposited with the Secretary-General of the
United Nations.

After 1 January 1950 the present Convention may be acceded to
on behalf of any Member of the United Nations and of any non-
member State which has received an invitation as aforesaid.

Instruments of accession shall be deposited with the Secretary-
General of the United Nations."

It follows unequivocally from the cited Article that ratification and
accession are the relevant means of expressing States' consent to be
bound by the Genocide Convention. In its notification of succession of
29 December 199, Bosnia and Herzegovina states:

"The Government of the Republic of Bosnia and Herzegovina,
having considered the Convention on the Prevention and Punishment of the Crime of Genocide of 9 December 1948 to which the
former Socialist Federal Republic of Yugoslavia was a party *wishes
to succeed to the same* and undertakes faithfully to perform and
carry out all the stipulations therein contained with effect from

---

[202] McNair, *Law of Treaties*, 1961, p. 601.

789]   6 March 1992, the date on which the Republic of Bosnia and Herzegovina became independent." (Emphasis added.)

The Secretary-General of the United Nations, acting in his capacity as
depositary, communicated the following:

> "On 29 December 1992, the *notification of succession* by the Gov-
> ernment of Bosnia and Herzegovina to the above-mentioned [Geno-
> cide] Convention was deposited with the Secretary-General, with
> effect from 6 March 1992, the date on which Bosnia and Herze-
> govina assumed responsibility for its international relations." [203]

On 15 June 1993, the Secretary-General received from the Government
of Yugoslavia the following communication:

> "Considering the fact that the replacement of sovereignty on the
> part of the territory of the Socialist Federal Republic of Yugoslavia
> previously comprising the Republic of Bosnia and Herzegovina was
> carried out contrary to the rules of international law, the Govern-
> ment of the Federal Republic of Yugoslavia herewith states that it
> does not consider the so-called Republic of Bosnia and Herzegovina
> a party to the [said Convention] but does consider that the so-called
> Republic of Bosnia and Herzegovina is bound by the obligation to
> respect the norms on preventing and punishing the crime of genocide
> in accordance with general international law irrespective of the Con-
> vention on the Prevention and Punishment of the Crime of Geno-
> cide."

118. On the basis of the above general considerations as well as those
relating directly to the "notification of succession" of Bosnia and Herzegovina, the following relevant conclusions can, in my view, be drawn:

The "notification of succession" of Bosnia and Herzegovina is not fully
in harmony with the practice of States as expressed in the relevant provisions of the Convention on Succession in respect of Treaties. More particularly, the concept of "notification of succession" was developed in the
practice of States specifically in connection with decolonization.

(The expression itself is rather imprecise. In United Nations practice
such notifications are called — "declarations" (see Introduction to the
Multilateral Treaties Deposited with the Secretary-General, Status as
at 31 December 1991, and cited by the Court in paragraph 6 of the
Order of 8 April 1993, note 4). "Notification" of a function is a rather
loose qualification of the practice of States, in the form of a "note"
without the suffix "of succession" (see United Nations, *Legislative
Series*, Materials on Succession of States (ST/LEG/SER.B/14), 1967,
pp. 225-228), to declare themselves bound uninterruptedly by multi-

---

[203] Communication from the Secretary-General of the United Nations dated 18 March
1993 (reference C.N.451.1992.Treaties-5 (Depositary Notification)), entitled "Succession
by Bosnia and Herzegovina" (emphasis added).

lateral treaties concluded on their behalf by the parent State before the [79₵
new State emerged to full sovereignty or to deposit their own instruments of acceptance of such treaties, effective from the date of deposit
of the new instrument. It would therefore be more opportune to speak
of a "declaration of entry into the treaty". Furthermore, the mentioned
"notes", as a rule, represented a form of realization of conventional
obligations assumed by "devolution agreements".)

The Genocide Convention does not envisage "notification of succession" as a means of expression of consent to be bound by the treaty so
that in the concrete case at hand agreement would be required between
Bosnia and Herzegovina and the individual parties to the Convention on
acceptance of a "notification of succession" as a means of expressing consent to be bound by the Convention [204]. Yugoslavia, as a party to the
Convention, submitted its reservation stating that it "does not consider
the so-called Republic of Bosnia and Herzegovina a party [to the said
Convention]" because the "replacement of sovereignty on the part of the
territory of SFRY previously comprising the Republic of Bosnia and
Herzegovina was carried out contrary to the rules of international law".
Yugoslavia, by this reservation, disputed the status of the successor State
of Bosnia and Herzegovina because the "replacement of one State by
another in the responsibility . . ." constitutes only one, factual aspect of
succession or, more precisely, a territorial change which provokes the
question of succession in a legal sense. Hence the conclusion that follows
is that no appropriate collateral agreement was reached between Bosnia
and Herzegovina and Yugoslavia, so that notification of succession by
Bosnia and Herzegovina does not have, vis-à-vis Yugoslavia, the legal
effect of consent to be bound by the Genocide Convention. This was
pointed out at the 965th meeting of the International Law Commission
by Tabibi: "Succession with respect to treaties did not take place without
an express provision of the treaty or the express consent of the other
party." [205]

119. The Court implicitly takes the view that on the basis of the Dayton Agreement the Genocide Convention became applicable as between
Bosnia and Herzegovina and Yugoslavia. Such a conclusion stems from
its pronouncement that

"even if it were to be assumed that the Genocide Convention did not
enter into force between the Parties until the signature of the

---

[204] "In the absence of provisions which set specific conditions for succession or which
otherwise restrict succession, the Secretary-General is guided by the participation
clauses of the treaties as well as by the general principles governing the participation
of States" ("Summary of Practice of the Secretary-General as Depositary of Multilateral Treaties" (ST/LEG.8), p. 89, para. 297).

[205] *Yearbook of the International Law Commission,* 1968, Vol. I, p. 132, para. 64.

791]   Dayton-Paris Agreement, all the conditions are now fulfilled to found the jurisdiction of the Court *ratione personae*" (para. 26 of the Judgment).

In my opinion, such an interpretation is untenable.

Yugoslavia argues that the "Genocide Convention became applicable between the Parties to this case as from the signature of the Dayton Agreement of 1995" and that "it was only under the Dayton Agreement (particularly Annex 6 . . .) that the Parties in contention accepted the applicability of the Genocide Convention" [206]. It is a fact that in the absence of recognition, the contractual *nexus* between Bosnia and Herzegovina and Yugoslavia could not be established in the framework of the Genocide Convention. A mutual recognition of two States is the general condition for the establishment of the bilateral contractual *nexus*, since a contractual relationship between States represents a relationship *intuitu personae*.

Yugoslavia and Bosnia and Herzegovina recognized each other by Article X of the General Framework Agreement for Peace in Bosnia and Herzegovina [207]. Article X of the General Framework Agreement stipulates, *inter alia*, that

> "The Federal Republic of Yugoslavia and the Republic of Bosnia and Herzegovina recognize each other as sovereign independent States within their international borders."

In normal circumstances, the mutual recognition *per se* results in the establishment of the contractual *nexus* in the framework of a multilateral agreement between the countries which recognize each other, or between the State which extends recognition and the State which is being recognized. For reservations regarding the status of a party to the agreement of a State which is not recognized, are expressed, as a rule, in order not to establish a tacit collateral agreement between that State and the recognizing State, an agreement which represents *per se* a *de facto* recognition.

The circumstances in this concrete case could not be termed normal. In the notification addressed to the Secretary-General of the United Nations on 15 June 1993, Yugoslavia emphasized that "it does not consider the so-called Bosnia and Herzegovina a party to that [Genocide Convention]" since, in its opinion,

> "the replacement of sovereignty on the part of the territory of the Socialist Federal Republic of Yugoslavia previously comprising the Republic of Bosnia and Herzegovina was carried out contrary to the rules of International Law".

In other words, Yugoslavia challenges, by the notification referred to, the legality of the genesis of Bosnia and Herzegovina as a State. It could, of course, be said that a recognition, as a rule, convalidates the defects in

---

[206] CR 96/6, p. 23.
[207] Doc. A/50/790, S/1995/999, 30 November 1995, p. 4.

the genesis of a State. Such a conclusion could be drawn from the very **[79**
nature of the recognition of the new State, since "To recognize a political
community as a state is to declare that it fulfils the conditions of statehood as required by International Law." [208] This specific case could be
qualified as an exception from the general rule, for two basic reasons:

Primo, Yugoslavia insisted, even after the signature of the Dayton
Agreement, that Bosnia and Herzegovina was constituted in an illegal
way. A clear and unequivocal proof of that is the content of the third
objection. The fact that Yugoslavia withdrew, during the procedure, its
fourth preliminary objection which concerned the factual non-existence
of Bosnia and Herzegovina in the administrative borders of that former
federal unit, but continued to argue that Bosnia and Herzegovina was
constituted *contra legem*, leads one to the conclusion that the recognition
of Bosnia and Herzegovina by Yugoslavia in the Dayton Agreement had
only the function of acknowledging

> "as a fact . . . the independence of the body claiming to be a State
> and . . . declar[ing] the recognizing State's readiness to accept the
> normal consequences of that fact, namely, the usual courtesies of
> international intercourse" [209]

while keeping its attitude towards the legality of the constitution of
Bosnia and Herzegovina as an independent State.

Secundo, in its third preliminary objection Yugoslavia claims, *inter
alia*, that the norm on the "equal rights and self-determination of peoples"
is a peremptory norm of general international law *(jus cogens)*. If that
argument could be proved to be correct, then the recognition, even if
conceived and designed as convalidation, would be without legal effect,
since the norms of *jus cogens* as the absolute, unconditional imperative,
cannot be derogated by *inter se* agreements.

Outside the context of recognition, the Dayton Agreement does not
touch the relations between the Federal Republic of Yugoslavia and the
Republic of Bosnia and Herzegovina as parties to the Genocide Convention. The allegation that "under the Dayton Agreement (particularly
Annex 6 . . .) . . . the Parties in contention accepted the applicability of
the Genocide Convention" [210] has no foothold in the text of the Dayton
Agreement.

Annex 6 of the Dayton Agreement, which is invoked as the basis of the
application of the Genocide Convention in this specific case, represents,
in fact, the "Agreement on Human Rights", whose parties are — the

---

[208] H. Lauterpacht, *Recognition in International Law*, 1947, p. 6.
[209] L. Brierly, *The Law of Nations*, 1963, p. 138.
[210] CR 96/6, p. 24.

793] Republic of Bosnia and Herzegovina, the Federation of Bosnia and Herzegovina, and Republika Srpska. The only connection between Yugoslavia and Annex 6 consists in the fact that Yugoslavia, together with the Republic of Croatia and the Republic of Bosnia and Herzegovina, by virtue of Article VII of the General Framework Agreement

> "agree to and shall fully comply with the provisions concerning human rights set forth in Chapter One of the Agreement at Annex 6, as well as the provisions concerning refugees and displaced persons set forth in Chapter One of the Agreement at Annex 7".

Chapter One of the Agreement on Human Rights contains a list of individual, mainly classical, personal and political rights and liberties which the "Parties [the Republic of Bosnia and Herzegovina, the Federation of Bosnia and Herzegovina and Republika Srpska] shall secure to all persons within their jurisdiction" (Art. I of the Agreement). Article VII of the General Framework Agreement is the contractual confirmation, phrased in a general way, of the obligation of the respect of basic human rights and freedoms enumerated in Article I of the Agreement on Human Rights, which the parties to the General Framework Agreement are bound to respect as parties to the instruments which contain them, and in some cases as cogent rules, independently of their acceptance. Therefore, the purpose of Article VII of the General Framework Agreement is rather in the field of political reasoning, the reasoning which starts from the need to engage politically the subjects outside Bosnia and Herzegovina in the implementation of the Dayton Agreement, and less as imposing concrete obligations regarding human rights as contained in Chapter One of the Agreement on Human Rights.

In other words, in this specific case, the recognition as a general condition for the establishment of the bilateral contractual *nexus* is not sufficient to enable me to consider the Genocide Convention applicable in the relations between Yugoslavia and Bosnia and Herzegovina. It results from the circumstances of the case that, for that purpose, a qualifactory condition is also indispensable, and that condition would consist of the absence of the notification of Yugoslavia addressed to the Secretary-General of the United Nations on 15 June 1993, which represents, by its material meaning, a reservation made by Yugoslavia with the effect of preventing the establishment of the mentioned *nexus*, and in the absence of the fourth preliminary objection regarding the legality of the constitution of Bosnia and Herzegovina as a State. Therefore, the mutual recognition given in the form of Article 7 of the General Framework Agreement may be qualified as the recognition of the creation of Bosnia and Herzegovina in the factual sense of the word, but with a reservation regarding the legality of its constitution. With respect to the fulfilment of this qualificative condition in the relations between Yugoslavia and Bosnia and Herzegovina, the provision given *in fine* of Article X of the Agreement is relevant, and reads "[f]urther aspects of their mutual recognition will be subject to subsequent discussions".

120. The position of the Court regarding its jurisdiction *ratione temporis* can be summarized by the following part of paragraph 34 of the Judgment, in which it finds:

"that the Genocide Convention — and in particular Article IX — does not contain any clause the object or effect of which is to limit in such manner the scope of its jurisdiction *ratione temporis*, and nor did the Parties themselves make any reservation to that end, either to the Convention or on the occasion of the signature of the Dayton-Paris Agreement. The Court thus finds that it has jurisdiction in this case to give effect to the Genocide Convention with regard to the relevant facts."

Concerning the jurisdiction of the Court *ratione temporis*, the situation is, in my opinion, clear — according to the rule of general international law, expressed in paragraph 3 of Article 24 (Entry into Force) of the Convention on the Law of Treaties:

"When the consent of a State to be bound by a treaty is established on a date after the treaty has come into force, the treaty enters into force for that State on that date, unless the treaty otherwise provides."

Article IX of the Genocide Convention is a procedural provision of the Convention and, being an integral part of it, shares the Convention's destiny or, to put it more precisely, the destiny of its contractual provisions. Consequently, if the Convention does not have a retroactive effect — and it obviously does not — then its Article IX likewise has no such effect. So, as the general rule of non-retroactivity stipulates, the Convention is applied to the events and situations which took place after it had come into effect in relation to Bosnia and Herzegovina or, in the circumstances of the present case, when the Convention became applicable between Bosnia and Herzegovina and Yugoslavia.

The analogy which the Court has drawn between this case and *Mavrommatis Palestine Concessions* (para. 26 of the Judgment) does not [20] seem convincing. One can rather speak of an analogy between this case and the *Ambatielos* case to the effect that: [21]

"To accept this theory would mean giving retroactive effect to Article 29 of the Treaty of 1926, whereas Article 32 of this Treaty states *that the Treaty, which must mean all the provisions of the Treaty*, shall come into force immediately upon ratification. Such a conclusion might have been rebutted if there had been any special clause or any special object necessitating retroactive interpretation. *There is no such clause or object in the present case. It is therefore impossible to hold that any of its provisions must be deemed to have been in force earlier.*" [211]

---

[211] *Ambatielos, Preliminary Objections, Judgment, I.C.J. Reports 1952*, p. 40 (emphasis added).

[[20] 3 *Ann Dig* 204.]   [[21] 19 *ILR* 416.]

795]   For, as it is clearly stated in the commentary on Article 24 of the Convention on the Law of Treaties:

> *"when a jurisdictional clause is attached to the substantive clauses of a treaty* as a means of securing their due application, the *non-retro-activity principle may operate to limit* ratione temporis *the application of the jurisdictional clause.* Thus in numerous cases under the European Convention for the Protection of Human Rights and Fundamental Freedoms, the European Commission of Human Rights had held that it is incompetent to entertain complaints regarding alleged violations of human rights said to have occurred prior to the entry into force of the Convention with respect to the State in question."[212]

* * *

On the basis of the foregoing, I take the liberty of concluding that, in my opinion, the relevant conditions for the entertainment of the case by the Court, relating both to jurisdiction and to admissibility, have not been met.

(Signed) Milenko KREĆA.

[Report: *ICJ Reports 1996,* p. 595]

---

[212] Draft Articles on the Law of Treaties with commentaries, adopted by the ICL at its Eighteenth Session, UNCLT, First and Second Sessions, Vienna, 26 March-24 May 1968 and 9 April-22 May 1969, *Official Records*, p. 32, para. 2.

[The following is the text of the Order on Counter-claims:]

The International Court of Justice,

composed as above,

after deliberation,

having regard to Article 48 of the Statute of the Court and to Articles 31, 44, 45 and 80 of the Rules of Court,

makes the following Order:

1. Whereas, on 20 March 1993, the Government of the Republic of Bosnia and Herzegovina (hereinafter called "Bosnia and Herzegovina") filed in the Registry of the Court an Application instituting proceedings against the Government of the Federal Republic of Yugoslavia (hereinafter called "Yugoslavia") in respect of a dispute concerning alleged violations of the Convention on the Prevention and Punishment of the Crime of Genocide (hereinafter called "the Genocide Convention"), adopted by the General Assembly of the United Nations on 9 December 1948, as well as various matters which Bosnia and Herzegovina claims are connected therewith; whereas, in its Application, Bosnia and Herzegovina invoked Article IX of the Genocide Convention as the basis of the jurisdiction of the Court; and, whereas at the end of its Application, it set out its claims as follows:

Accordingly, while reserving the right to revise, supplement or amend this Application, and subject to the presentation to the Court of the relevant evidence and legal arguments, Bosnia and Herzegovina requests the Court to adjudge and declare as follows:

(a) that Yugoslavia (Serbia and Montenegro) has breached, and is continuing to breach, its legal obligations toward the People and State of Bosnia and Herzegovina under Articles I, II(a), II(b), II(c), II(d), III(a), III(b), III(c), III(d), III(e), IV and V of the Genocide Convention;

(b) that Yugoslavia (Serbia and Montenegro) has violated and is continuing to violate its legal obligations toward the People and State of Bosnia and Herzegovina under the four Geneva Conventions of 1949, their Additional Protocol I of 1977, the customary international laws of war including the Hague Regulations on Land Warfare of 1907, and other fundamental principles of international humanitarian law;

(c) that Yugoslavia (Serbia and Montenegro) has violated and continues to violate Articles 1, 2, 3, 4, 5, 6, 7, 8, 9, 10, 11, 12, 13, 15, 16, 17, 18, 19, 20, 21, 22, 23, 25, 26 and 28 of the Universal Declaration of Human Rights with respect to the citizens of Bosnia and Herzegovina;

(d) that Yugoslavia (Serbia and Montenegro), in breach of its obligations under general and customary international law, has killed, murdered, wounded, raped, robbed, tortured, kidnapped, illegally detained, and exterminated the citizens of Bosnia and Herzegovina, and is continuing to do so;

(e) that in its treatment of the citizens of Bosnia and Herzegovina, Yugoslavia (Serbia and Montenegro) has violated, and is continuing to violate, its solemn obligations under Articles 1(3), 55 and 56 of the United Nations Charter;

(f) that Yugoslavia (Serbia and Montenegro) has used and is continuing to use force and the threat of force against Bosnia and Herzegovina in violation of Articles 2(1), 2(2), 2(3), 2(4), and 33(1) of the United Nations Charter;

(g) that Yugoslavia (Serbia and Montenegro), in breach of its obligations under general and customary international law, has used and is using force and the threat of force against Bosnia and Herzegovina;

(h) that Yugoslavia (Serbia and Montenegro), in breach of its obligations under general and customary international law, has violated and is violating the sovereignty of Bosnia and Herzegovina by:

armed attacks against Bosnia and Herzegovina by air and land; aerial trespass into Bosnian airspace; efforts by direct and indirect means to coerce and intimidate the Government of Bosnia and Herzegovina;

(i) that Yugoslavia (Serbia and Montenegro), in breach of its obligations under general and customary international law, has intervened and is intervening in the internal affairs of Bosnia and Herzegovina;

(j) that Yugoslavia (Serbia and Montenegro), in recruiting, training, arming, equipping, financing, supplying and otherwise encouraging, supporting, aiding, and directing military and paramilitary actions in and against Bosnia and Herzegovina by means of its agents and surrogates, has violated and is violating its express charter and treaty obligations to Bosnia and Herzegovina and, in particular, its charter and treaty obligations under Article 2(4) of the United Nations Charter, as well as its obligations under general and customary international law;

(k) that under the circumstances set forth above, Bosnia and Herzegovina has the sovereign right to defend Itself and its People under United Nations Charter Article 51 and customary international law, including by means of immediately obtaining military weapons, equipment, supplies and troops from other States;

(l) that under the circumstances set forth above, Bosnia and Herzegovina has the sovereign right under United Nations Charter Article 51 and customary international law to request the immediate assistance of any State to come to its defence, including by military means (weapons, equipment, supplies, troops, etc.);

(m) that Security Council Resolution 713 (1991), imposing a weapons embargo upon the former Yugoslavia, must be construed in a manner that shall not impair the inherent right of individual or collective self-defence of Bosnia and Herzegovina under the terms of United Nations Charter Article 51 and the rules of customary international law;

(n) that all subsequent Security Council Resolutions that refer to or reaffirm Resolution 713 (1991) must be construed in a manner that shall not impair the inherent right of individual or collective self-defence of Bosnia and Herzegovina under the terms of United Nations Charter Article 51 and the rules of customary international law;

(o) that Security Council Resolution 713 (1991) and all subsequent Security

Council Resolutions referring thereto or reaffirming thereof must not be construed to impose an arms embargo upon Bosnia and Herzegovina, as required by Articles 24(1) and 51 of the United Nations Charter and in accordance with the customary doctrine of *ultra vires*;

(p) that pursuant to the right of collective self-defence recognized by United Nations Charter Article 51, all other States parties to the Charter have the right to come to the immediate defence of Bosnia and Herzegovina —at its request—including by means of immediately providing It with weapons, military equipment and supplies, and armed forces (soldiers, sailors, air people, etc.);

(q) that Yugoslavia (Serbia and Montenegro) and its agents and surrogates are under an obligation to cease and desist immediately from its breaches of the foregoing legal obligations, and is under a particular duty to cease and desist immediately:

from its systematic practice of so-called 'ethnic cleansing' of the citizens and sovereign territory of Bosnia and Herzegovina; from the murder, summary execution, torture, rape, kidnapping, mayhem, wounding, physical and mental abuse, and detention of the citizens of Bosnia and Herzegovina; from the wanton devastation of villages, towns, districts, cities, and religious institutions in Bosnia and Herzegovina; from the bombardment of civilian population centres in Bosnia and Herzegovina, and especially its capital, Sarajevo; from continuing the siege of any civilian population centres in Bosnia and Herzegovina, and especially its capital, Sarajevo; from the starvation of the civilian population in Bosnia and Herzegovina; from the interruption of, interference with, or harassment of humanitarian relief supplies to the citizens of Bosnia and Herzegovina by the international community; from all use of force—whether direct or indirect, overt or covert—against Bosnia and Herzegovina, and from all threats of force against Bosnia and Herzegovina; from all violations of the sovereignty, territorial integrity or political independence of Bosnia and Herzegovina, including all intervention, direct or indirect, in the internal affairs of Bosnia and Herzegovina; from all support of any kind—including the provision of training, arms, ammunition, finances, supplies, assistance, direction or any other form of support—to any nation, group, organization, movement or individual engaged or planning to engage in military or paramilitary actions in or against Bosnia and Herzegovina;

(r) that Yugoslavia (Serbia and Montenegro) has an obligation to pay Bosnia and Herzegovina, in its own right and as *parens patriae* for its citizens, reparations for damages to persons and property as well as to the Bosnian economy and environment caused by the foregoing violations of international law in a sum to be determined by the Court. Bosnia and Herzegovina reserves the right to introduce to the Court a precise evaluation of the damages caused by Yugoslavia (Serbia and Montenegro);

2. Whereas, on 20 March 1993, immediately after the filing of its Application, Bosnia and Herzegovina submitted a request for the indication of provisional measures under Article 41 of the Statute; whereas, on 1 April 1993, Yugoslavia submitted written observations on Bosnia and Herzegovina's request for provisional measures, in which, in turn, it recommended the Court to order the application of

provisional measures to Bosnia and Herzegovina; and whereas, by an Order dated 8 April 1993,[1] the Court indicated certain provisional measures with a view to the protection of rights under the Genocide Convention; and whereas, on 27 July 1993, Bosnia and Herzegovina submitted a new request for the indication of provisional measures; whereas, on 10 August 1993, Yugoslavia also submitted a request for the indication of provisional measures; and whereas, the Court, by an Order dated 13 September 1993,[2] reaffirmed the measures indicated in its Order of 8 April 1993 and declared that those measures should be immediately and effectively implemented;

3. Whereas, on 15 April 1994, within the time-limit laid down, as extended by Order of the Vice-President of the Court on 7 October 1993, Bosnia and Herzegovina filed its Memorial at the end of which it presented its submissions as follows:

On the basis of the evidence and legal arguments presented in this Memorial, the Republic of Bosnia and Herzegovina,

Requests the International Court of Justice to adjudge and declare,

1. That the Federal Republic of Yugoslavia (Serbia and Montenegro), directly, or through the use of its surrogates, has violated and is violating the Convention on the Prevention and Punishment of the Crime of Genocide, by destroying in part, and attempting to destroy in whole, national, ethnical or religious groups within the, but not limited to the, territory of the Republic of Bosnia and Herzegovina, including in particular the Muslim population, by:

killing members of the group; causing deliberate bodily or mental harm to members of the group; deliberately inflicting on the group conditions of life calculated to bring about its physical destruction in whole or in part; imposing measures intended to prevent births within the group;

2. That the Federal Republic of Yugoslavia (Serbia and Montenegro) has violated and is violating the Convention on the Prevention and Punishment of the Crime of Genocide by conspiring to commit genocide, by complicity in genocide, by attempting to commit genocide and by incitement to commit genocide;

3. That the Federal Republic of Yugoslavia (Serbia and Montenegro) has violated and is violating the Convention on the Prevention and Punishment of the Crime of Genocide by aiding and abetting individuals and groups engaged in acts of genocide;

4. That the Federal Republic of Yugoslavia (Serbia and Montenegro) has violated and is violating the Convention on the Prevention and Punishment of the Crime of Genocide by virtue of having failed to prevent and to punish acts of genocide;

5. That the Federal Republic of Yugoslavia (Serbia and Montenegro) must immediately cease the above conduct and take immediate and effective steps to ensure full compliance with its obligations under the Convention on the Prevention and Punishment of the Crime of Genocide;

6. That the Federal Republic of Yugoslavia (Serbia and Montenegro) must wipe out the consequences of its international wrongful acts and must restore

[1 95 *ILR* 1 at 18.]   [2 95 *ILR* 1 at 43.]

the situation existing before the violations of the Convention on the Prevention and Punishment of the Crime of Genocide were committed;

7. That, as a result of the international responsibility incurred for the above violations of the Convention on the Prevention and Punishment of the Crime of Genocide, the Federal Republic of Yugoslavia (Serbia and Montenegro) is required to pay, and the Republic of Bosnia and Herzegovina is entitled to receive, in its own right and as *parens patriae* for its citizens, full compensation for the damages and losses caused, in the amount to be determined by the Court in a subsequent phase of the proceedings in this case.

The Republic of Bosnia and Herzegovina reserves its right to supplement or amend its submissions in the light of further pleadings.

The Republic of Bosnia and Herzegovina also respectfully draws the attention of the Court to the fact that it has not reiterated, at this point, several of the requests it made in its Application, on the formal assumption that the Federal Republic of Yugoslavia (Serbia and Montenegro) has accepted the jurisdiction of this Court under the terms of the Convention on the Prevention and Punishment of the Crime of Genocide. If the Respondent were to reconsider its acceptance of the jurisdiction of the Court under the terms of that Convention—which it is, in any event, not entitled to do—the Government of Bosnia and Herzegovina reserves its right to invoke also all or some of the other existing titles of jurisdiction and to revive all or some of its previous submissions and requests;

4. Whereas, on 26 June 1995, within the time-limit laid down for the filing of the Counter-Memorial, as extended by Order of the President of the Court dated 21 March 1995, Yugoslavia, referring to Article 79, paragraph 1, of the Rules of Court, raised preliminary objections concerning, respectively, the admissibility of the Application and the jurisdiction of the Court to hear the case; and whereas, by its Judgment dated 11 July 1996, the Court dismissed these preliminary objections and found, on the one hand, that on the basis of Article 9 of the Genocide Convention it had jurisdiction to adjudicate upon the dispute and, on the other hand, that the Application was admissible;

5. Whereas, on 22 July 1997, within the new time-limit laid down by Order of the President of the Court dated 23 July 1996, Yugoslavia filed its Counter-Memorial; whereas in the introduction to that Counter-Memorial, Yugoslavia indicated that it "included counter-claims"; and, whereas at the end of the Counter-Memorial, it presented its submissions as follows:

The Federal Republic of Yugoslavia requests the International Court of Justice to adjudge and declare:

1. In view of the fact that no obligations established by the 1948 Convention on the Prevention and Punishment of the Crime of Genocide have been violated with regard to Muslims and Croats since the acts alleged by the Applicant have not been committed at all, or not to the extent and in the way alleged by the Applicant, or if some have been committed, there was absolutely no intention of committing genocide, and/or they have not been directed

specifically against the members of one ethnic or religious group, i.e., they have not been committed against individuals just because they belong to some ethnic or religious group, consequently, they cannot be qualified as acts of genocide or other acts prohibited by the 1948 Convention on the Prevention and Punishment of the Crime of Genocide, and/or

2. In view of the fact that the acts alleged by the Applicant in its submissions cannot be attributed to the Federal Republic of Yugoslavia, since they have not been committed by the organs of the Federal Republic of Yugoslavia, since they have not been committed on the territory of the Federal Republic of Yugoslavia, since they have not been committed by the order or under control of the organs of the Federal Republic of Yugoslavia, since there is no other ground[s] based on the rules of international law to consider them as acts of the Federal Republic of Yugoslavia, therefore the Court rejects all claims of the Applicant, and

3. Bosnia and Herzegovina is responsible for the acts of genocide committed against the Serbs in Bosnia and Herzegovina and for other violations of the obligations established by the 1948 Convention on the Prevention and Punishment of the Crime of Genocide, because it has incited acts of genocide by the "Islamic Declaration", and in particular by the position contained in it that "there can be no peace or coexistence between 'Islamic faith' and 'non-Islamic' social and political institutions", because it has incited acts of genocide by the "Novi Vox", paper of the Muslim youth, and in particular by the verses of a "Patriotic Song" which read as follows:

Dear mother, I'm going to plant willows,
We'll hang Serbs from them.
Dear mother, I'm going to sharpen knives,
We'll soon fill pits again.

because it has incited acts of genocide by the paper "Zmaj od Bosne", and in particular by the sentence in an article published in it that "Each Muslim must name a Serb and take oath to kill him"; because public calls for the execution of Serbs were broadcast on radio "Hajat" and thereby acts of genocide were incited; because the armed forces of Bosnia and Herzegovina, as well as other organs of Bosnia and Herzegovina, have committed acts of genocide and other acts prohibited by the 1948 Convention on the Prevention and Punishment of the Crime of Genocide, against the Serbs in Bosnia and Herzegovina, which have been stated in Chapter Seven of the Counter-Memorial; because Bosnia and Herzegovina has not prevented the acts of genocide and other acts prohibited by the 1948 Convention on the Prevention and Punishment of the Crime of Genocide, against the Serbs on its territory, which have been stated in Chapter Seven of the Counter-Memorial.

4. Bosnia and Herzegovina has the obligation to punish the persons held responsible for the acts of genocide and other acts prohibited by the 1948 Convention on the Prevention and Punishment of the Crime of Genocide.

5. Bosnia and Herzegovina is bound to take necessary measures so that the said acts would not be repeated in the future.

6. Bosnia and Herzegovina is bound to eliminate all consequences of the violation of the obligations established by the 1948 Convention on the Prevention and Punishment of the Crime of Genocide and provide adequate compensation;

6. Whereas, by a letter dated 28 July 1997, the Deputy Agent of Bosnia and Herzegovina informed the Registrar that "the Applicant [was] of the opinion that the Counter-Claims submitted by the Respondent . . . [did] not meet the criterion of Article 80, paragraph 1, of the Rules of Court and should therefore not be joined to the original proceedings"; and the Deputy Agent specified that, when the President of the Court met the Agents of the Parties under Article 31 of the Rules of Court, Bosnia and Herzegovina would ask for "an early date to hear the Parties according to Article 80, paragraph 3, of the Rules of Court";

7. Whereas, on 22 September 1997, the President of the Court held a meeting with the Agents of the Parties in order to ascertain their views as to the further proceedings in the case; whereas the two Agents accepted that their respective Governments submit written observations on the question of the admissibility of the Yugoslav counter-claims; and whereas they contemplated that their governments then be heard orally on the question;

8. Whereas, by a letter dated 26 September 1997, on the instructions of the Court, the Registrar invited the Government of Bosnia and Herzegovina to specify in writing, not later than 10 October 1997, the legal basis on which it maintained that the counter-claims made by the Respondent did not meet the criterion laid down in Article 80, paragraph 1, of the Rules of Court; and whereas, in that letter, the Registrar specified that the Yugoslav Government would in turn be invited to submit its views on the question within two weeks of Bosnia and Herzegovina filing its observations; and whereas the Registrar sent a copy of that letter to Yugoslavia the same day;

9. Whereas, by a letter from its Deputy Agent dated 9 October 1997 and received in the Registry on 10 October 1997, Bosnia and Herzegovina submitted its observations on the Respondent's counter-claims to the Court; and whereas, by a letter dated 10 October 1997, the Registrar communicated a copy of those observations to the Yugoslav Government advising it that it might make known its own observations on the question within a time-limit expiring on 24 October 1997; and whereas on the same day the Registrar informed the Government of Bosnia and Herzegovina of this;

10. Whereas, in its written observations, Bosnia and Herzegovina maintains that "the alleged 'counter-claim' presented by Yugoslavia is not in accordance with the provisions of Article 80 of the Rules of Court"; and whereas it specifies that, although the counter-claim was presented in the Counter-Memorial and comes within the jurisdiction of the Court, conversely, it is not "directly connected . . . with the subject-matter of the initial proceedings";

11. Whereas, in order to establish the absence of such a connection

in this case, Bosnia and Herzegovina invokes first the structure and content of Yugoslavia's Counter-Memorial; whereas it argues that the Counter-Memorial is divided into two completely autonomous parts, one in which Yugoslavia "attempts to reply to the accusations made in the Memorial of Bosnia and Herzegovina" and the other in which "Yugoslavia claims that Bosnia and Herzegovina itself is responsible for violations of the Genocide Convention"; whereas it argues that "the facts put before the Court by Yugoslavia, in the form of its 'counter-claim', are totally different from those on which the initial claim of Bosnia and Herzegovina is based" and whereas "the examination of each of the two sets of facts would be of no help in the judicial analysis of the other set and could not affect its outcome in any way whatsoever"; and whereas it asserts that, since Yugoslavia does not ask the Court, in its submissions in its Counter-Memorial, to find that there is any "kind of relationship, a legally significant one" to be established between the two claims, it recognizes in reality that "the judicial outcome of the one cannot determine or influence the outcome of the other in any manner whatsoever";

12. Whereas Bosnia and Herzegovina observes that, moreover, given the specific nature of the obligations embodied in the Genocide Convention, Yugoslavia could not have adopted any other position; whereas it points to the *erga omnes* and non-reciprocal nature of those obligations; and whereas it infers from this that, within the system of the Convention, "no place remains for the logic of reciprocity", so that "it cannot be envisaged that the judicial finding of a violation of the Convention committed by a State could in the event be influenced by the fact that a second violation—of which the State in question is allegedly the victim—had been perpetrated";

13. Whereas, for the purposes of confirming that its contentions are well-founded, Bosnia and Herzegovina refers to scholarly opinion and infers from it that the counter-claim must, on the one hand, aim "to 'counter' the principal claim, i.e., to oppose it in order to block it or to reduce its effects" and, on the other hand, claim "something more", in particular "a judgment against the applicant in the principal proceedings"; and whereas it submits that this is not the case as regards the Yugoslav "counter-claim" since, even if the allegation set out therein against Bosnia and Herzegovina were founded, "this could not in any way result in the total or partial dismissal (or 'neutralization') of Bosnia and Herzegovina's original claim, nor—of course—in 'something more'";

14. Whereas Bosnia and Herzegovina refers also to the jurisprudence of the Court and of its predecessor; whereas it indicates that "a study of what happens in practice reveals no case of a counter-claim which did not have the objective of countering the principal claim, either to make it fail, or to reduce its scope and effects" and it submits that

Yugoslavia's so-called "counter-claim" is not really one at all: in submitting its counter-claim the other Party does not counter the initial claim, but formulates a second, autonomous dispute relating to other facts, the settlement of which could in no way influence the solution of the first dispute brought before the Court by Bosnia and Herzegovina;

15. Whereas, Bosnia and Herzegovina also maintains that when, as is the case here, a "counter-claim" raises a question which is independent of the initial claim, any joinder of these claims must be avoided on the grounds that this could have detrimental effects, on the one hand, on equality of the Parties—since the Applicant could only respond once in writing, in its Reply, to the counter-claim—and, on the other hand, on the rights and interests of third States—since those third States would not be informed of the counter-claim;

16. Whereas at the end of its written observations Bosnia and Herzegovina argues that "the 'counter-claim' submitted by Yugoslavia in its Counter-Memorial is therefore not admissible, since any direct connection with the subject-matter of Bosnia and Herzegovina's original claim is totally lacking" whereas, it "requests the Court to decide—having heard the Parties as provided for in Article 80, paragraph 3, of the Rules of Court—that the 'counter-claim' in question should not be joined to the principal claim"; and whereas it "recognizes that Yugoslavia, should it so desire, may always submit to the Court an application instituting proceedings through the normal channels";

17. Whereas, by a communication from its Agent dated 23 October 1997 and received in the Registry on 24 October 1997, Yugoslavia submitted to the Court its observations on the admissibility of the counter-claims set out in its Counter-Memorial, taking account of the observations submitted by Bosnia and Herzegovina; and whereas, by a letter dated 24 October 1997, the Registrar sent a copy of the observations of the Yugoslav Government to the Government of Bosnia and Herzegovina, informing it that, on the one hand, the Court would decide the remainder of the procedure on the basis of the documents presently before it and, on the other hand, that the Agents of the Parties would be advised of that decision in due course; and whereas, on the same day, the Registrar transmitted the same information to the Yugoslav Government;

18. Whereas, in its written observations, Yugoslavia points out that the original claim and the counter-claim are based on the same legal ground, that is to say the Genocide Convention and the general rules of State responsibility; whereas it submits that:

The disputed facts of the claim and counter-claim are the facts of the same tragic conflict, i.e., civil war in Bosnia and Herzegovina, which happened in a single territorial and temporal setting, based on the same historical background and within the framework of the same political development;

and from this it infers "all relevant facts which form the basis of claim and counter-claim are interrelated in such a way as to make a factual and legal connection relevant to the issue";

19. Whereas Yugoslavia maintains that "there is a direct connection between Part Two of the Counter-Memorial, i.e., the counter-claim, and Part One of the Counter-Memorial, the defence of the Respondent"; whereas the counter-claim and the subject-matter of the claim "are directly connected"; whereas "the facts on which the counter-claim is based and which are contained in Part Two . . . of the Counter-Memorial are of crucial importance to answer the question of attribution to the Respondents of acts alleged by the Applicant"; and whereas the facts on which the counter-claim is based "are also relevant for qualification of the acts alleged by the Applicant as crimes of genocide";

20. Whereas, in its written observations, Yugoslavia, refers, *inter alia*, to

some identical facts . . . presented as a basis for denying the allegation of the Applicant which are, according to its view relevant for attribution of alleged acts to the Respondent and as a basis for the counter-claim;

and whereas it explains in particular that "acts of direct and public incitement to commit genocide against the Serbs" for which it asks the Court to establish the responsibility of Bosnia and Herzegovina, operate also as a defence against the accusation made in the principal claim, in so far as such acts "strongly influenced the attitude of the Serb people in Bosnia and Herzegovina" and "are very relevant for deciding on whether the Serb people acted under the orders of the Yugoslav authorities . . . or spontaneously to protect itself";

21. Whereas Yugoslavia moreover states that it "agrees with the Applicant that a breach of the Genocide Convention cannot serve as an excuse for another breach of the same Convention", but "the two Parties are in dispute over existence of a breach of the Genocide Convention, i.e., genocide against the Muslim and non-Serb population"; whereas it notes that "for different reasons, the Respondent denies the existence of crimes of genocide against the Muslim and non-Serb population" and specifies that "one of the very relevant reasons is the absence of intent to commit genocide"; it maintains that "the facts presented by Part Two . . . of the Counter-Memorial, which constitute the basis for the counter-claim, i.e., crimes of genocide committed against the Serb people in Bosnia and Herzegovina are part and parcel of the circumstances of the situation" and are relevant "for identifying the motives and intentions of individuals who committed crimes vis-à-vis Muslims"; and whereas it submits that these facts, for which it asks the Court to establish the responsibility of Bosnia and Herzegovina, "served for proper qualification of the acts alleged by the Applicant";

22. Whereas Yugoslavia alleges moreover that the Applicant, when it "referred to *positions doctrinales* and *la jurisprudence internationale* regarding the direct connection between the counter-claim and subject-matter of the claim . . . failed to reach the end of development of the construction of Article 80, paragraph 1, of the Rules of Court"; whereas it submits that "careful study of the practice of the Court reveals an important development of understanding of the said paragraph", the Court having "departed from this [original] position" according to which "a counter-claim is directly connected with the subject-matter of the claim of the other Party when it serves for a rejection of the claim and for obtaining a judgment on the responsibility of the other Party"; and whereas it notes that academic writings have after all emphasized "the lack of rigidity" which characterizes the treatment of counter-claims;

23. Whereas Yugoslavia also observes that "it seems that the Applicant is of the opinion that a counter-claim has to be limited exclusively to facts presented in [the main] claim"; whereas in order to establish that "this opinion is not based on the law", it invokes Article 49, paragraph 2, of the Rules of Court according to which "[the] Counter-Memorial shall contain . . . any additional facts, if necessary"; whereas it infers from this that "if the Respondent is entitled to submit new facts by a Counter-Memorial, it can certainly do it by a counter-claim"; and whereas it notes that in the present case, the additional facts invoked as a basis for the counter-claim are, in any event, "relevant for rejection of [the] claim";

24. Whereas at the end of its written observations Yugoslavia submits that "the counter-claim is directly connected with the subject-matter of the claim and the counter-claim meets the conditions of Article 80, paragraphs 1 and 2, of the Rules of Court"; and whereas it accordingly requests the Court "to reject all requests of Bosnia and Herzegovina submitted by its letter of 9 October 1997";

25. Whereas, having received full and detailed written observations from each of the Parties, the Court is sufficiently well informed of the positions they hold with regard to the admissibility of the claims presented as counter-claims by Yugoslavia in its Counter-Memorial; and whereas, accordingly, it does not appear necessary to hear the Parties otherwise on the subject;

26. Whereas it is now necessary to consider whether the Yugoslav claims in question constitute "counter-claims" within the meaning of Article 80 of the Rules of Court and, if so, whether they fulfil the conditions set out in that provision;

27. Whereas it is established that a counter-claim has a dual character in relation to the claim of the other party; whereas a counter-claim is independent of the principal claim in so far as it constitutes a separate "claim", that is to say an autonomous legal act the object of which is to submit a new claim to the Court, and,

whereas at the same time, it is linked to the principal claim, in so far as, formulated as a "counter" claim, it reacts to it; whereas the thrust of a counter-claim is thus to widen the original subject-matter of the dispute by pursuing objectives other than the mere dismissal of the claim of the Applicant in the main proceedings—for example, that a finding be made against the Applicant; and, whereas in this respect, the counter-claim is distinguishable from a defence on the merits;

28. Whereas, in Article 80 of its Rules, the Court did not confer a different meaning on the expression "counter-claim"; whereas the inclusion of Article 80 in Section D ("Incidental Proceedings") of Part III ("Proceedings in Contentious Cases") of the Rules of Court, and the provisions set out in that Article show that it does not apply to mere defences on the merits which the Court must hear in the normal exercise of its functions to decide the Applicant's claims; and whereas the need to differentiate between counter-claims and defences in the scheme of the Rules of Court is moreover sufficiently clear from the jurisprudence of the Court:

Whereas, moreover, if the Iranian Government considers the alleged activities of the United States in Iran legally to have a close connection with the subject-matter of the United States Application, it remains open to that Government under the Court's Statute and Rules to present its own arguments to the Court regarding those activities either by way of defence in a Counter-Memorial or by way of a counter-claim filed under Article 80 of the Rules of Court . . . (*United States Diplomatic and Consular Staff in Tehran, Provisional Measures*, Order of 15 December 1979, *ICJ Reports 1979*, p. 15, para. 24);[3]

29. Whereas in the present case, although Submissions 1 and 2 in the Counter-Memorial of Yugoslavia relate exclusively to the dismissal of the claims of Bosnia and Herzegovina, Submissions 3 to 6, on the contrary, set out separate claims seeking relief beyond the dismissal of the claims of Bosnia and Herzegovina; and whereas such claims constitute "counter-claims" within the meaning of Article 80 of the Rules of Court;

30. Whereas, however, a claim should normally be made before the Court by means of an application instituting proceedings; whereas, although it is permitted for certain types of claim to be set out as incidental proceedings, that is to say, within the context of a case which is already in progress, this is merely in order to ensure better administration of justice, given the specific nature of the claims in question; whereas, as far as counter-claims are concerned, the idea is essentially to achieve a procedural economy whilst enabling the Court to have an overview of the respective claims of the Parties and to

decide them more consistently; and whereas the admissibility of the counter-claims must necessarily relate to the aims thus pursued and be subject to conditions designed to prevent abuse;

31. Whereas the Respondent cannot use a counter-claim as a means of referring to an international court claims which exceed the limits of its jurisdiction as recognized by the Parties; and whereas the Respondent cannot use that means either to impose on the Applicant any claim it chooses, at the risk of infringing the Applicant's rights and of compromising the proper administration of justice; and whereas it is for that reason that paragraph 1 of Article 80 of the Rules of Court requires that the counter-claim "comes within the jurisdiction of the Court" and "that it is directly connected with the subject-matter of the claim of the other party";

32. Whereas in the present case it is not disputed that the Yugoslav counter-claims were "made in the Counter-Memorial of the Party presenting it, and . . . appear as part of the submissions of that Party", in accordance with Article 80, paragraph 2, of the Rules of Court; and whereas, although Bosnia and Herzegovina recognizes that these claims meet the jurisdictional requirement set out in paragraph 1 of that Article, it denies that they meet the requirement of being directly connected with the subject-matter of the claim, also set out in that Article;

33. Whereas the Rules of Court do not define what is meant by "directly connected"; whereas it is for the Court, in its sole discretion, to assess whether the counter-claim is sufficiently connected to the principal claim, taking account of the particular aspects of each case; and whereas, as a general rule, the degree of connection between the claims must be assessed both in fact and in law;

34. Whereas, in the present case, it emerges from the Parties' submissions that their respective claims rest on facts of the same nature; whereas they form part of the same factual complex since all those facts are alleged to have occurred on the territory of Bosnia and Herzegovina and during the same period; and whereas Yugoslavia states, moreover, that it intends to rely on certain identical facts in order both to refute the allegations of Bosnia and Herzegovina and to obtain judgment against that State;

35. Whereas Bosnia and Herzegovina was right to point to the *erga omnes* character of the obligations flowing from the Genocide Convention (see *Application of the Convention on the Prevention and Punishment of the Crime of Genocide (Bosnia and Herzegovina v. Yugoslavia)*, Judgment of 11 July 1996, para. 31),[4] and the Parties rightly recognized that in no case could one breach of the Convention serve as an excuse for another; and whereas, however, the argument drawn from the absence of reciprocity in the scheme of the Convention is not determinative as

[4 See p. 29 above.]

regards the assessment of whether there is a legal connection between the principal claim and the counter-claim, in so far [as] the two Parties pursue, with their respective claims, the same legal aim, namely the establishment of legal responsibility for violations of the Genocide Convention;

36. Whereas in its Orders of 8 April and 13 September 1993,[5] the Court considered the requests for the indication of provisional measures made by each of the Parties; and whereas, in its Order of 13 September 1993, it stated, *inter alia*, as follows:

45. Whereas the measure requested by Yugoslavia would be appropriate to protect rights under the Genocide Convention, which are accordingly within the prima facie jurisdiction of the Court; whereas, on the evidence and information available to it, the Court must also recognize the existence of some risk to the persons whose protection Yugoslavia seeks; whereas however the question for the Court is whether the circumstances are such as to "require" the indications of provisional measures, in accordance with Article 41 of the Statute;

46. Whereas by paragraph 52A of its Order of 8 April 1993 the Court, having indicated that Yugoslavia should take all measures within its power to prevent genocide, indicated what "in particular" were the appropriate measures to be taken by Yugoslavia in the circumstances of the case, where the risk was of genocide not on Yugoslav territory but in Bosnia-Herzegovina; whereas furthermore, as the Court noted in paragraph 45 of its Order of 8 April 1993, both Yugoslavia and Bosnia-Herzegovina are under a clear obligation to do all in their power to prevent the commission of any acts of genocide, and by paragraph 52B of that Order the Court indicated that both Bosnia-Herzegovina and Yugoslavia should not take any action and should ensure that no action is taken which might aggravate or extend the existing dispute over the prevention or punishment of the crime of genocide, or render it more difficult of solution; whereas the Court does not find that the circumstances, as they now present themselves to the Court, are such as to require a more specific indication of measures addressed to Bosnia-Herzegovina so as to recall to it both its undoubted obligations under the Genocide Convention, and the need to refrain from action of the kind contemplated by paragraph 52B of the Court's Order of 8 April 1993;

37. Whereas in the light of the foregoing, the Court considers that the counter-claims submitted by Yugoslavia are directly connected with the subject-matter of Bosnia and Herzegovina's claims; and whereas, as counter-claims, they are therefore admissible and form part of the present proceedings;

38. Whereas a decision given on the admissibility of a counter-claim taking account of the requirements of Article 80 of the Rules of Court in no way prejudges any question with which the Court would have to deal during the remainder of the proceedings;

[5 95 *ILR* 1 at 18 and 43.]

39. Whereas in order to protect the rights which third States entitled to appear before the Court derive from the Statute, the Court instructs the Registrar to transmit a copy of this Order to them;

40. Whereas when, in accordance with the provisions of its Rules, the Court decides, in the interests of the proper administration of justice, to rule on the respective claims of the Parties in a single set of proceedings, it must not, for all that, lose sight of the interest of the Applicant to have its claims decided within a reasonable time-period;

41. Whereas, during the meeting which the President of the Court held on 22 September 1997 with the Agents of the Parties (see paragraph 7 above), the Agent of Bosnia and Herzegovina indicated that his Government requested that the case be decided as soon as possible, was opposed to any further exchange of written pleadings on the merits and asked the Court immediately to set a date for the opening of the oral proceedings; whereas the Agent of Yugoslavia, conversely, made it known that, if the proceedings were to go forward, his Government wished to have a second round of written pleadings on the merits; whereas the two Agents were invited to express their views as to suitable time-limits to be fixed for the filing of further pleadings in the event that the Court decided that their submission was necessary; and whereas the Agent of Bosnia and Herzegovina specified, *inter alia*, that his Government would be in a position to present a Reply six months from the date of filing of the Counter-Memorial of Yugoslavia —that is, no later than 23 January 1998— whether or not the Reply had to respond to the counter-claims made by Yugoslavia in its Counter-Memorial;

42. Whereas, taking into account the conclusions it has reached above regarding the admissibility of the Yugoslav counter-claims, the Court considers that it is necessary for Bosnia and Herzegovina to file a Reply and for Yugoslavia to file a Rejoinder relating to the claims of both Parties; and whereas it is necessary moreover, in order to ensure strict equality between the Parties, to reserve the right of Bosnia and Herzegovina to present its views in writing a second time on the Yugoslav counter-claims, in an additional pleading which may be the subject of a subsequent Order;

43. For these reasons,

THE COURT,

(A) by thirteen votes to one,

Finds that the counter-claims submitted by Yugoslavia in its Counter-Memorial are admissible as such and form part of the current proceedings;

IN FAVOUR: *President* Schwebel; *Judges* Oda, Bedjaoui, Guillaume, Herczegh, Shi, Fleischhauer, Koroma, Vereshchetin, Parra-Aranguren, Kooijmans; *Judges* ad hoc Lauterpacht, Kreća;

AGAINST: *Vice-President* Weeramantry;

(B) by thirteen votes to one,

Directs Bosnia and Herzegovina to submit a Reply and Yugoslavia to submit a Rejoinder relating to the claims of both Parties and fixes the following dates, accepted by the Parties, as time-limits for the filing of these pleadings:

For the Reply of Bosnia and Herzegovina, 23 January 1998;

For the Rejoinder of Yugoslavia, 23 July 1998;

IN FAVOUR: *President* Schwebel; *Judges* Oda, Bedjaoui, Guillaume, Herczegh, Shi, Fleischhauer, Koroma, Vereshchetin, Parra-Aranguren, Kooijmans; *Judges* ad hoc Lauterpacht, Kreća;

AGAINST: *Vice-President* Weeramantry;

and

Reserves the subsequent procedure for further decision.

Done in French and in English, the French text being authoritative, at the Peace Palace, The Hague, this seventeenth day of December, one thousand nine hundred and ninety-seven, in three copies, one of which will be placed in the archives of the Court and the others transmitted to the Government of the Republic of Bosnia and Herzegovina and the Government of the Federal Republic of Yugoslavia, respectively.

(*Signed*) Stephen M. SCHWEBEL,
President.

(*Signed*) Eduardo VALENCIA-OSPINA,
Registrar.

Judge *ad hoc* KREĆA appends a declaration to the Order of the Court.

Judge KOROMA and Judge *ad hoc* LAUTERPACHT append separate opinions to the Order of the Court.

Vice-President WEERAMANTRY appends a dissenting opinion to the Order of the Court.

(*Initialled*) S.M.S.
(*Initialled*) E.V.O.

DECLARATION OF JUDGE *AD HOC* KREĆA

Although I voted in favour of the operative parts of the Court's Order, I shall also make some observations on and amplifications to some aspects of the concept of a counter-claim and its application to this particular case.

1. The Order essentially qualifies a counter-claim as "independent", "an autonomous legal act" (para. 27) though, it seems to me, this is with a certain amount of caution (*reservatio mentalis*). That is to say, the Court states that the "counter-claim is independent of the principal claim in so far as it constitutes a separate 'claim'" (*ibid.*). The fact that the Applicant's claim is being qualified as the "principal" claim determines the counter-claim, by the logic of *argumentum a contrario*, as a non-principal claim, a lesser claim. It follows that the counter-claim is a response or, to put it another way, a secondary claim. Such qualification is exact in a very limited sense only.

It is created by the fact that the Respondent submits the claim against the Applicant in the litigation which had already been instituted against the Respondent. Therefore, the counter-claim (if we view the litigation exclusively as a series of acts which, according to a certain logic, follow each other, at certain time intervals) looks like a non-autonomous act, a secondary claim. However, if we consider the litigation in the only correct way, as a tripartite relationship in which all participants in the proceedings—the Applicant, the Respondent and the Court—have certain rights and obligations (Bulgarus: *Procesus est actus trium personarum—actoris, rei judicus*), then we inevitably come to the conclusion that the counter-claim represents an autonomous claim made by the Respondent which, in the circumstances of the procedure in the case, is strongly connected to the claim. This link is the basis for the integration of two proceedings into one single proceeding.

The fact that the counter-claim is submitted after the establishment of the basic jurisdictional link does not mean, *ipso facto*, that the "counter-claim" is merely the reaction to the "claim" which established that link. The proof of that assertion lies in the very fact that the "counter-claim" changes the positions in the litigation of the parties to the dispute—the Respondent becomes the Applicant and vice versa. The very nature of the counter-claim—a claim which may be joined to the original claim or which amounts to the presentation of a fresh claim—implies the very opposite. In fact, as a rule a counter-claim has not a defensive but an offensive character except in cases of claims for compensation or preliminary claims.

Therefore, it seems to me that the autonomous nature of the counter-claim (its other characteristic being self-sufficiency) suggests that in relation to the counter-claim, the Applicant's claim is not the "principal" claim, but simply the initial or original claim.

2. It seems to me that the Court has been trying to pinpoint the relevant issues of a conceptual nature as a result of the incompleteness and lack of precision of Article 80 of the Rules of Court.

2.1. Article 80 of the Rules of Court tacitly proceeds from the assumption that a counter-claim is a general legal notion. One cannot explain in any other way the fact that neither the Statute of the International Court of Justice nor the Rules of Court define counter-claims; moreover, the text of the Statute does not contain the word "counter-claim" at all. Examining the notion of counter-claim in the light of Article 40 of the Rules of Court of 1922, Anzilotti says:

> Il existe, en effet, une notion de la demande reconventionnelle qui, en substance, est commune à toutes les législations, même si les règles qui concrétisent cette notion diffèrent dans chacune de ces législations: d'un ensemble de règles distinctes en leur forme, mais ayant un contenu commun, il est bien possible d'abstraire ce contenu en un concept lequel est ensuite concrétisé en règles propres d'un autre droit. (D. Anzilloti, "La demande reconventionnelle et procédure internationale", *Journal du droit international*, Tome 57, 1930, p. 867.)

This concise wording expresses the substance of the *philosophie juridique synthétique* according to which legal notions have two aspects: logical and extensive. The logical aspect or the generic notion means a general notion which is familiar to all branches of law. On the other hand, the extensive side or the extensive notion is reduced to a set of legal prescriptions (*praescriptiones*) which makes the general notion specific within the limits of a given legal order (see T. Givanovitch, *Système de la Philosophie juridique synthétique*, Paris 1927-1970).

The logical and the extensive aspects of the legal notion are in a state of dynamic unity—by adopting specific rules (*praescriptiones*) one enriches and crystallizes the logical, generic part of a legal notion which serves as a model and guiding rule for specific rules in appropriate branches of the law.

However, it seems to me that the concretization of the general notion in Article 80 of the Rules of Court has not been correctly carried out.

Article 80 of the Rules of Court deals with the abstract term "counter-claim". The interpretation of the wording in Article 80 allows for the conclusion that every claim made by the Respondent is a counter-claim. For instance, paragraph 1 of Article 80 stipulates:

A counter-claim may be presented provided that it is directly connected with the subject-matter of the claim of the other party and that it comes within the jurisdiction of the Court.

It follows that there are two types of counter-claim: counter-claims which "may be presented" and counter-claims which "may not be presented". In other words, every claim made by the Respondent may represent a counter-claim, with the only difference being that while a counter-claim which fulfils the conditions set out in that provision "may be presented", those which do not fulfil them "may not be presented". As an abstract term, the expression "counter-claim" used in Article 80 unites procedural and material meanings of the counter-claim. Contrary to Article 80 of the Rules of Court, the proposition put forward by four members of the Court (Judges Negulesco, Wang, Schücking and Fromageot) at the private meeting held by the Court on 29 May 1934 elegantly removed that dichotomy. That proposition, as quoted by the then President from a document circulated by Judges Negulesco, Wang, Schücking and Fromageot (see *PCIJ, Series D, No 2,* 4th Add., p. 263) reads:

No claim may be included in the Counter-Case as a counter-claim unless it is directly connected with the subject of the application filed by the other party, and unless it comes within the jurisdiction of the Court.

Certain elements of that dichotomy are not alien to this Order either. Paragraph 26 of the Order reads "it is now necessary to consider whether the Yugoslav claims . . . constitute 'counter-claims' within the meaning of Article 80 of the Rules of Court and, if so, whether they fulfil the conditions set out in that provision". Does that mean that the "Yugoslav claims in question constitute 'counter-claims'" before it has been established whether "they fulfil the conditions set out in that provision"?

2.2. In this connection, two relevant questions emerge:

(i) If the Respondent's claim fulfils the conditions stipulated in paragraph 1 of Article 80 of the Rules of Court, is it *ipso facto* a counter-claim within the meaning of Article 80 of the Rules of Court, i.e., is it automatically joined to the original claim or does the Court deliberate upon its joinder?

Article 80 of the Rules of Court has been built upon the notion of permissive joinder. Such a conclusion indisputably follows from the wording of paragraph 1 of the Article which stipulates that "[a] counter-claim may be presented" provided that the counter-claim fulfils two conditions: (a) that it is directly connected with the subject-matter of the claim of the other party, and (b) that it comes within the jurisdiction of the Court. Therefore, the Respondent is entitled to submit a counter-claim, the submission of which is subject to the aforementioned conditions. It may be concluded from this that a claim made by the Respondent which fulfils the conditions stipulated in paragraph 1 of Article 80 of the Rules of Court is *ipso facto* a counter-claim within the meaning of Article 80, and that it is automatically joined to the original proceedings. This is also suggested by the wording of paragraph 2 of Article 80 which provides that "[a] counter-claim shall be made in the Counter-Memorial . . . and shall appear as part of the submissions of that party."

Is that conclusion also valid in cases covered by paragraph 3 of Article 80 of the Rules of Court?

From the interpretation of the wording, it appears that, in the event of doubt as to the connection between the questions presented by way of counter-claim and the subject-matter of the claim of the other party, joinder of the counter-claim to the original proceedings is not automatically carried out, but is to be decided upon by the Court. The Court would therefore not be obliged to decide to join the claim of the Respondent to the original proceedings even if the conditions stipulated in paragraph 1 of Article 80 of Rules of Court were fulfilled, i.e., if the "direct connection" were not in doubt.

That option is hardly acceptable. Essentially, there is a possibility that some undetermined and, from the procedural point of view, unarticulated notion of doubt may alter the legal nature of the counter-claim incorporated into the basis of Article 80 of the Rules of Court.

"In the event of doubt"—is the doubt sufficient? Here we can distinguish two basic situations:

(a) when the Court evaluates, *proprio motu*, the existence of a "connection", doubt appears to be the psychological motive for the Court to assess the existence of the connection and to adopt a corresponding decision;

(b) where there is doubt on the Applicant's side in the original proceedings, that is obviously not sufficient on its own. It represents only the psychological, mental basis for the initiation of an appropriate action in the litigation. In substance, that is an objection, although the form in which it appears and the name given to it by the Applicant are not important. The importance lies in the material nature of the Applicant's reaction to the Respondent's "counter-claim". In this particular case, the Applicant set out its approach to the admissibility of the "counter-claim" in the form of "observations", although they were in fact objections. For, if the Applicant has a "doubt", and does not express that doubt in an appropriate way, then the doubt itself is legally irrelevant. I understand the true meaning of paragraph 3 of

Article 80 to be that it suspends the automatic joinder of the Respondent's claim to the original proceedings until the doubt as to the relevant connection between the question presented by way of counter-claim and the subject-matter of the initial Applicant's claim is removed. Objections may be raised to this interpretation that it does not accord with the wording of paragraph 3 according to which "the Court shall . . . decide whether or not the question thus presented shall be joined to the original proceedings". This failure to accord may prove relevant if the decision of the Court that "the question thus presented shall be joined to the original proceedings" is understood as a decision which has a declaratory effect only. It seems to me that this is a way to preserve the original nature of the counter-claim, which is essentially the Respondent's right to increase the dimensions of a lawsuit by having his claims included in it under certain conditions. *A contrario*, from a right of the Respondent, the counter-claim is transformed into a question which the Court decides in its sole discretion, independently of the conditions stipulated in paragraph 1 of Article 80 of the Rules of Court. Such transformation reduces the complex character of the counter-claim to a question of procedural economy. It hardly needs saying that the very nature of the counter-claim does not allow such a reduction. The right to make a counter-claim derives from the principle of the equality of the parties on the one hand and the principle of material truth on the other hand. A counter-claim however does not only allow for better administration of justice in respect of procedural economy, but also in respect of the complex solution of conflicting relations between the Parties and the prevention of different trials (*ne variae judicetur*).

Such interpretation of paragraph 3 of Article 80 of the Rules of Court has a direct influence on the subject of the Court's decision in the event of a doubt as to the connection between the question presented by way of counter-claim and the subject-matter of the claim of the other party. If a claim made by the Respondent which fulfils the "direct connection" condition stipulated in paragraph 1 of Article 80 of the Rules of Court is qualified *ipso facto* as a counter-claim, then the Court, in proceedings instituted according to paragraph 3 of Article 80, could not decide upon the admissibility of the counter-claim, but only upon the existence of a direct connection between counter-claims submitted by the Respondent and the subject-matter of the Applicant's claims. If it finds that there exists such a connection, then this means, as was stated by the Permanent Court in the *Factory at Chorzów case* (*Merits, Judgment No 13, 1928, PCIJ, Series A, No 17*, p. 38),[6] that the material condition required by the Rules as regards counter-claims is fulfilled, which implies joinder of the counter-claim to the original proceedings.

[[6] 4 *Ann Dig* 499.]

(ii) Is the Court fully master of the proceedings conducted on the basis of paragraph 3 of Article 80 of the Rules of Court?

This question results from the fact that, in this particular case, the Court did not hear the Parties. The decision of the Court not to conduct hearings seems rational to me, because it rests upon the founded belief that, through the written observations of the Parties, it obtained a complete picture of all relevant matters, which enabled it to exercise its jurisdiction, on the basis of Article 80 of the Rules of Court.

Unfortunately, it should be said in the interest of truth that paragraph 3 of Article 80 of the Rules of Court does not favour such rational determination by the Court.

Paragraph 3 of Article 80 stipulates in imperative wording that, *inter alia*, "the Court shall, after hearing the parties, decide whether or not the question thus presented shall be joined to the original proceedings". It is highly doubtful whether the exchange of written statements by the parties may be a substitute for "hearing", since "hearing" as a term of the procedure before the Court denotes, in the sense of Article 43, paragraph 5, and Article 51 of the Statute, oral proceedings before the Court. The exchange of written statements by the parties would suffice for hearing the parties under Article 68 of the 1972 Rules of Court which, instead of the phrase "after hearing the parties", contained the phrase "after due examination", a phrase leaving room for liberal interpretation. It appears that paragraph 3 of Article 80 of the Rules of Court does not permit liberal interpretation.

For as Rosenne says, the phrase "after hearing the parties" means that:

in future there will always be some oral proceedings in the event of doubt . . . as to the connection between the question presented by way of counter-claim and the subject-matter of the claim of the other party. (S. Rosenne, *Procedure in the International Court, A Commentary on the 1978 Rules of the International Court of Justice*, 1983, p. 171.)

There are reasonable grounds for assuming that in future the Court may find itself in a situation where it has to choose between submission to rigid rules or flexibility, which opens the path to better administration of justice. Consequently, a revision of paragraph 3 of Article 80 of the Rules of Court seems desirable to me, in order that the rational determination of the Court might not be at variance with the, in this case unnecessarily, rigid rule of procedure.

3. In proceedings based on paragraph 3 of Article 80 of the Rules of Court the question of "direct connection" is of the utmost importance.

The term "direct connection" itself firmly establishes Anzilotti's thesis that "la demande principale et la demande reconventionnelle sont autonomes, mais réunies dans un même rapport de procédure"

(D. Anzilotti, "La demande reconventionnelle en procédure internationale", *Journal du droit international*, Tome 57, 1930, p. 875).
Although somewhat broad and vague, it obviously does not mean
identity or coincidence of the subject-matter of the application and the
subject-matter of the counter-claim. For such a qualification, the
meaning of the word "connection" is of basic importance (in this
phrase, the word "direct" is only a condition of qualification, a factor
which defines the quality of "connection", as the main element of the
phrase). A "connection" in the sense of a relationship or link may exist
only between things which exist separately, in themselves, things
having the properties of autonomy and apartness. *A contrario*, the
question of either direct or indirect "connection" may not even be
asked, for there are no such things between which the relationship or
link is established. One thing cannot have a "connection" with itself,
for in that case it would not be a separate thing, but just a relationship
between things.

In qualifying the meaning of the term "direct connection" the Court
has, in accordance with widespread opinion, assumed that "direct
connection" represents connection in law and in fact. The Order
determines, *inter alia*, that "as a general rule, the degree of connection
between the claims must be assessed both in fact and in law" (para.
33). However, what is particularly significant is the fact that the Court,
in weighing the relevance of "connection in law" and "connection in
fact", gives tacit preponderance to "connection in law". The Court
states *inter alia* that

it emerges from the Parties' submissions that their respective claims rest on
facts of the same nature; whereas they form part of the same factual complex
since all those facts are alleged to have occurred on the territory of Bosnia
and Herzegovina and during the same period.

That means that the Court found that there was a direct connection
between Yugoslavia's counter-claim and Bosnia and Herzegovina's
original claim, despite the fact that Yugoslavia did not rely on identical
facts in its counter-claim.

In my opinion, such a standpoint of the Court is valid and justified.
It is possible to assume that in some cases, the links between the "claim"
and the "counter-claim" in fact and in law are not equal, therefore one
may ask the question whether the link in law is sufficient to constitute a
"direct connection" in the sense of Article 80, and vice versa? In other
words, whether we could, conditionally speaking, establish a certain
kind of hierarchy in the mutual relationship between "connection in
law" and "connection in fact", meaning that one of these "connections"
is more important, that it is preponderant over the other. Logically
speaking, "connection in law" should be preponderant, if for no other

reason than that, out of a single event, parties may initiate actions which are not complementary. In fact, "connection in law" may appear as *differentia specifica* between "counter-claim" and "cross-claim".

The standpoint that legal connection can always be considered to be a direct connection between the subject-matter of the claim and that of the counter-claim has support in the case-law of the Court. In the *Case concerning the Diversion of Water from the Meuse* (1937),[7] the Belgian counter-claim concerned questions different from those initiated by the Netherlands in its claim (*PCIJ, Series A/B, No 70*, pp. 5-6).

The Netherlands Government asked the Court to adjudge and declare that:

(a) the construction by Belgium of works which render it possible for a canal situated below Maestricht to be supplied with water taken from the Meuse elsewhere than at that town is contrary to the Treaty of May 12th, 1863;

(b) the feeding of the Belgian section of the Zuid-Willemsvaart, of the Campine Canal, of the Hasselt branch of that canal and of the branch leading to Beverloo Camp, as also of the Turnhout Canal, through the Neerhaeren Lock with water taken from the Meuse elsewhere than at Maestricht, is contrary to the said Treaty;

(c) Belgium's project of feeding a section of the Hasselt Canal with water taken from the Meuse elsewhere than at Maestricht is contrary to the said Treaty;

(d) Belgium's project of feeding the section of the canal joining the Zuid-Willemsvaart to the Scheldt between Herenthals (Viersel) and Antwerp with water taken from the Meuse elsewhere than at Maestricht is contrary to the said Treaty.

In its Counter-Memorial the Belgian Government asserted (1) that the Netherlands Government had committed a breach of the Treaty of 1863 by constructing the Borgharen barrage on the Meuse below Maastricht; (2) that the Juliana Canal constructed by the Netherlands alongside the Meuse below Maastricht from Limmel to Maasbracht, was subject, as regards its water supply, to the same Treaty.

Therefore, there were two independent claims. What made those claims directly connected for the purpose of the Court procedure was their legal basis. All questions arising from the Netherlands' claim and from Belgium's counter-claim directly concerned the interpretation and application of the Treaty of 12 May 1863 or, to be precise, whether various actions of the Parties were in accordance with the relevant provisions of the Treaty. This fact led the Court to conclude that the counter-claim "is directly connected with the principal claim" and that "it was permissible to present it in the Counter-Memorial" (*PCIJ, Series A/B, No 70*, p. 28).

[7 *8 Ann Dig* 444.]

The Court's reasoning was limited to that framework also in the *Factory at Chorzów case (Merits)*,[8] the *Asylum case*[9] and in the provisional measures phase of the *Case concerning United States Diplomatic and Consular Staff in Tehran*.[10]

A preponderance of the "connection in law" over the strictly understood "facts of case" (if the word "fact" is meant in *lato sensu*, it includes law as well) is, in my opinion, a normal consequence of the relativity of the facts of the case. It is therefore justified to pose the question whether it has to do with "facts" or subjective perceptions of facts. Another well-respected authority on the counter-claim issue, Miaya de la Muela, justly observes:

La reconvención se basa en unos hechos constitutivos diferentes con los alegados por el actor para su pretensión, aunque con el grado de conexidad entre ambos conjuntos de hechos que exija el sistema procesal respectivo. Su diferencia de la excepción está en que la última se basa en hechos, casi siempre no alegados por el actor, pero que pretenden ser impeditivos o extintivos de los efectos producidos por los alegados en la demande. (A. Miaja de la Muela, "La reconvención ante el Tribunal internacional de Justicia", *Estudios de derecho procesal en honor de Niceto Alcalá-Zamora y Castillo, Boletín mejicano de derecho comparado*, No 24, 1975, p. 757.)

This is why, what are usually called the "facts" of the case should be understood as a "factual complex" or the "factual background" as an objective basis, the main features of which are represented as the facts of the case by the parties.

4. In this particular case, the existence of a "connection in law" is obvious. It results directly from the findings of the Court in the Judgment adopted on the occasion of the Respondent's preliminary objections. By its Judgment on the preliminary objections, the Court established the legal relationship between the Respondent and the Applicant on the one hand, and the Genocide Convention, on the other. The preliminary objections represented, according to their legal nature, a kind of counter-claim—a "preliminary" counter-claim—the basic purpose of which was to establish a relevant legal relationship between the parties in the litigation.

Questions initiated both in the Memorial and the Counter-Memorial are organically and inseparably connected to the Genocide Convention. The *sedes materiae* of the dispute between Bosnia and Herzegovina and the Federal Republic of Yugoslavia resides in the qualification of the acts ascribed by the Parties to each other, from the standpoint of the relevant provisions of the Convention. Moreover, in contrast to the factographic side of the *Case of the Diversion of Water from the Meuse*,[11] in which Belgium put forward questions of fact different

[8 *4 Ann Dig* 258.]   [10 61 *ILR* 502 at 513.]
[9 17 *ILR* 280.]   [11 8 *Ann Dig* 444.]

from those mentioned by the Netherlands in its claim, there exists, in this particular case, a partial coincidence regarding the factual questions set out in the claim of Bosnia and Herzegovina, and in the counter-claim of the Federal Republic of Yugoslavia, but the Parties interpret them in different, in fact in diametrically opposed, ways.

As regards the form and reasoning, there are no substantial differences between the Memorial and the Counter-Memorial. Even a prima facie assessment shows that there is a substantial similarity regarding the form and content of the Memorial and Counter-Memorial, which frequently coincide, so that phenomenologically, regardless of the order of the submission of the documents, one could describe the Counter-Memorial as the inversion of the Memorial, and vice versa.

In such a state of affairs, Yugoslavia's counter-claim exceeds the usual framework of counter-claims encountered by the Court. That is to say, the substantial concentration of the Memorial and Counter-Memorial on the relevant event—the armed conflict in Bosnia and Herzegovina, and its consequences, and the opposing claims of the Parties which derive from different assessments of the factual and legal sides of that event, makes it possible to conclude that there is genuinely no distinction between the Applicant and the Respondent. The positions of the Parties in this dispute could be compared to the positions of Parties in the case of a territorial dispute, both Parties putting forward rival claims. So that, as was pointed out by the arbitrator Max Huber in the *Island of Palmas case* (1928),[12] "each party is called upon to establish the arguments on which it relies in support of its claim . . . over the object in dispute" (*RIAA, Vol. II*, p. 837).

(*Signed*) Milenko KREĆA.

SEPARATE OPINION OF JUDGE KOROMA

It is not without considerable misgivings that I have voted in favour of the Court's Order, not least, because of my concern regarding its effect and perceived effect on the sound administration of justice particularly in a case where allegations of grave breaches of the Genocide Convention and other massive violation[s] of human rights have been made.

On 20 March 1993, the Government of Bosnia and Herzegovina instituted proceedings against the Government of Yugoslavia in respect of a matter concerning the Application of the Convention on the Prevention and Punishment of the Crime of Genocide as well as various matters which Bosnia and Herzegovina claims are connected

[12 *Ann Dig* 3.]

thereto. Bosnia and Herzegovina invoked Article IX of the said Convention as the basis of the Court's jurisdiction. Immediately thereafter it submitted a request for the indication of provisional measures under Article 41 of the Statute of the Court.

On 1 April 1993, Yugoslavia submitted written observations on Bosnia and Herzegovina's request for provisional measures and in turn requested the Court to order the application of provisional measures to Bosnia-Herzegovina.

By an Order dated 8 April 1993,[13] the Court granted interim measures of protection in the light of the gravity and urgency of the situation, so as to prevent irreparable damage to rights under the Genocide Convention. In reaching this decision, the Court appeared to have also taken into consideration the serious allegations of genocide that were made, the humanitarian aspect of the case as well as the need to ensure that Bosnia and Herzegovina survived as a State. On 27 July 1993, Bosnia and Herzegovina submitted a new request for the indication of provisional measures. On 10 August, Yugoslavia also submitted a request for the indication of provisional measures. By an Order dated 13 September 1993,[14] the Court reaffirmed the measures indicated in its Order of 8 April 1993, declared that those measures should be immediately and effectively implemented and noted that:

great suffering and loss of life had been sustained by the population of Bosnia-Herzegovina in circumstances which shock the conscience of mankind and flagrantly conflict with moral law and the spirit and aim of the United Nations (*ICJ Reports 1993*, p. 348).

The Court also observed that since its previous Order:

the grave risk which the Court then apprehended of action being taken which may aggravate or extend the existing dispute over the prevention and punishment of the crime of genocide, or render it more difficult of solution, has been deepened by the persistence of conflicts on the territory of Bosnia-Herzegovina and the commission of heinous acts in the course of those conflicts (*ibid.* p. 348).

Following this reaffirmation of the Court's previous Order, on 15 April 1994 within the time-limit laid down at its request, Bosnia and Herzegovina filed its Memorial and made the following submissions:

On the basis of the evidence and legal arguments presented in this Memorial, the Republic of Bosnia and Herzegovina,

Requests the International Court of Justice to adjudge and declare, [*inter alia*],

[[13] 95 *ILR* 1 at 18.]   [[14] 95 *ILR* 1 at 43.]

1. That the Federal Republic of Yugoslavia (Serbia and Montenegro), directly, or through the use of its surrogates, has violated and is violating the Convention on the Prevention and Punishment of the Crime of Genocide, by destroying in part, and attempting to destroy in whole, national, ethnical or religious groups within the, but not limited to the, territory of the Republic of Bosnia and Herzegovina, including in particular the Muslim population, by killing members of the group; causing deliberate bodily or mental harm to members of the group; deliberately inflicting on the group conditions of life calculated to bring about its physical destruction in whole or in part; imposing measures intended to prevent births within the group.

[. . .]

4. That the Federal Republic of Yugoslavia (Serbia and Montenegro) has violated and is violating the Convention on the Prevention and Punishment of the Crime of Genocide by virtue of having failed to prevent and to punish acts of genocide.

On 21 March 1995, Yugoslavia invoked Article 79, paragraph 1, of the Rules of Court, and raised preliminary objections concerning, respectively, the admissibility of the Application and the jurisdiction of the Court to hear the case. By its Judgment dated 11 July 1996, the Court dismissed the preliminary objections and found that on the basis of Article IX of the Genocide Convention it had jurisdiction to adjudicate upon the dispute and that the Application was admissible.

In the light of the foregoing, it thus took more than three years after the institution of proceedings alleging grave violations of the Genocide Convention for the Court to be in a position to declare that it had jurisdiction to adjudicate upon the matter and that the Application was admissible. As has been recognized above, in its consideration of and decision to grant interim measures of protection, the Court must have realized the urgency of the matter as well as the need to protect the rights of the individuals. This together with its consideration and its disposal of the preliminary objections raised by the Respondent were all in accordance with the Statute and Rules of Court. However, one could not have failed to observe that it took more than three years from the commencement of proceedings for the Court to be in a position even to declare that it is entitled to exercise its jurisdiction in a matter of such grave importance which had been submitted to it for consideration. Three years to found that it is competent to hear a matter in which the Court itself had noted the sustaining of "great suffering and loss of life" and "in circumstances which shock the conscience of mankind and flagrantly conflict with moral law and the spirit and aims of the United Nations" (*ICJ Reports 1993*, p. 348)! It had, moreover, in its Order of 8 April 1993 indicated that the Respondent should take all measures within its power to prevent genocide and that both Yugoslavia and Bosnia and Herzegovina were under a clear obligation to do all in their power to prevent the commission of any acts of genocide.

Following the Court's finding that it was entitled to exercise its jurisdictional function and that the Application was admissible, on 22 July 1997, Yugoslavia, within the time-limit laid down by the Court, filed its Counter-Memorial which "included counter-claims" in accordance with Article 80, paragraph 2, of the Rules of Court. The Yugoslav claims are also based on the 1948 Genocide Convention. However, and as recounted in the Order, the acts which Yugoslavia alleges Bosnia and Herzegovina committed in breach of the Convention are different from those it is accused of by Bosnia and Herzegovina. Furthermore the acts described in the Yugoslav claims are acts which were allegedly committed outside its territory against persons over whom it has no jurisdiction (in fact, these are acts which it is alleged were perpetrated on the territory of Bosnia and Herzegovina against part of its population); conversely, the acts charged by Bosnia and Herzegovina in its original claims are acts which are alleged to have been committed on its own territory and against some of its own nationals.

When the Counter-Memorial of Yugoslavia was sent to Bosnia and Herzegovina on 28 July 1997, Bosnia and Herzegovina indicated that it would not only request "a short time-limit to be set for the next phase of the proceedings, but also . . . an early date to hear the Parties according to Article 80, paragraph 3, of the Rules of Court". Bosnia and Herzegovina contends that the counter-claims submitted by the Respondent on 22 July 1997 do not meet the criterion set out in Article 80, paragraph 1, of the Rules of Court, that they should therefore not be joined to the original proceedings and that, should Yugoslavia so desire, it could always submit to the Court an application instituting proceedings through the normal channels.

Yugoslavia, for its part, submitted that the counter-claims are directly connected with the subject-matter of Bosnia and Herzegovina's claim, are based on the same legal ground and fulfil the conditions laid down in Article 80, paragraphs 1 and 2, of the Rules of Court. It requested the Court to reject the requests of Bosnia and Herzegovina that the counter-claim did not fulfil the criterion laid down in the Rules of Court.

It was against this background that the Court considered this matter and came to the conclusion that part of the submissions of the Counter-Memorial of Yugoslavia constitute "counter-claims" within the meaning of Article 80 of the Rules of Court. The Court therefore found the counter-claims admissible and decided that they should be joined to the original proceedings. In accordance with this decision the Court directed Bosnia and Herzegovina to submit a Reply and Yugoslavia a Rejoinder relating to the claims of the two Parties and fixed the following dates as time-limits for the filing of these pleadings:

For the reply of Bosnia and Herzegovina—23 January 1998.
For the Rejoinder of Yugoslavia—23 June 1998.
The Court also reserved the remainder of the proceedings.

After this latest decision, it is now four years after proceedings were instituted alleging grave breaches of the Genocide Convention and, even by dint of the Rules of Court regarding pleadings, the matter has still not reached a stage when it is ready for oral hearings. The admissibility and joinder of the counter-claims to the original claim in this matter thus have the effect of further prolonging what is otherwise a matter requiring urgent consideration by the Court in the interests of the sound administration of justice.

As the Court itself has acknowledged, the idea of a counter-claim is essentially to achieve procedural economy whilst enabling the Court to have an overview of the respective claims of both Parties and to decide them more consistently. However, and as the Court has also pointed out, the admissibility of the counter-claims must of necessity relate to the aims thus pursued and be subject to conditions designed to prevent abuse, thus when in the interests of the proper administration of justice the Court is required to rule on the respective claims of the Parties in one sole set of proceedings, the Court must not, for all that, lose sight of the interests of the main Applicant to have its claim decided within a reasonable time period.

From this perspective, one cannot view with equanimity or fail to be concerned by the effect the Court's decision to join the counter-claims to the original Application at this stage would appear to have on the sound and proper administration of justice, and in particular on the interests of the Applicant to have its claim decided within a reasonable time-frame.

As we have noted above, this is not to say that all the steps taken so far, by both Parties and the Court, have not been in accordance with the Statute and Rules of Court. That the Court should maintain its judicial impartiality and objectivity at all times and ensure that the arguments of both sides to this dispute are given a fair hearing is beyond question. Nonetheless, the Court, in considering and applying Article 80, paragraph 3, of the Rules, should have carried out this exercise in such a way as to prevent further delay in this matter since that delay could give the appearance of further extending the gestation period of this case and the delay of justice.

Article 80, paragraph 3, of the Rules of Court provides as follows:

3. In the event of doubt as to the connection between the question presented by way of counter-claim and the subject-matter of the claim of the other party the Court shall, after hearing the parties, decide whether or not the question thus presented shall be joined to the original proceedings.

It is also my considered view that in exercising its discretion under this provision and before reaching its decision, the Court should have granted oral hearings to the Parties especially since, even according to the Parties' own submissions, their respective claims do not stem from the same facts, although those facts form part of the same factual complex in the eyes of the Court. The Order, *inter alia*, states that a counter-claim cannot be used to impose on the Applicant any claim the Respondent may choose, since this could entail the risk of infringing the Applicant's rights and of compromising the proper administration of justice. It therefore seems to me that the Court, in exercising its discretion under this provision, should have done so in such a way as to avoid further delay in such a serious matter and to avoid running the risk that its Order on the Respondent's claims might appear to compromise the proper administration of justice. I am convinced that this was not the Court's intention. However, in my view since the issue of counter-claims is not often visited by the Court, particularly where the Court is called upon to make a ruling, and since the Rules of Court aim, among other things, to simplify and expedite the procedure of the Court, it is perhaps now not untimely for the relevant provisions of the Rules to be reviewed, and if necessary, adapted to a changing world as well as to the pace of events.

(Signed) Abdul G. KOROMA.

SEPARATE OPINION OF JUDGE *AD HOC* LAUTERPACHT

1. This opinion is written in implementation of my statement made at the provisional measures stage of this case regarding the role of an *ad hoc* judge:

He has, I believe, the special obligation to endeavour to ensure that, so far as is reasonable, every relevant argument in favour of the party that has appointed him has been fully appreciated in the course of collegial consideration and, ultimately, is reflected—though not necessarily accepted—in any separate or dissenting opinion that he may write. (*Application of the Convention on the Prevention and Punishment of the Crime of Genocide, Provisional Measures, Order of 13 September 1993, ICJ Reports 1993*, p. 409, para. 6.)[15]

2. The problem before the Court at this stage of the case is one of the admissibility of counter-claims filed by the Government of the Federal Republic of Yugoslavia ("Yugoslavia" hereinafter). While I agree with the Court's Order in so far as it relates to the admissibility

[[15] 95 *ILR* 1 at 127.]

of the counter-claims, I have been concerned about the fact that the
Court has not given the Parties the opportunity to develop their
respective positions in oral argument.

PROCEDURE

3. The justification for oral proceedings lies in Article 80, paragraph
3, of the Rules of Court which provides that:

In the event of doubt as to the connection between the question presented by
way of counter-claim and the subject-matter of the claim of the other party
the Court shall, after hearing the parties, decide whether or not the question
thus presented shall be joined to the original proceedings.

4. The Court has taken the view that the requirement of "hearing
the parties" can, in the present case, be satisfied by giving each of
them the opportunity of presenting its views in writing. The position
taken by the Court is supported by its practice in respect of some, but
not all, other matters covered by a similar requirement, for example,
the nomination of *ad hoc* judges. Article 35, paragraph 4, of the Rules
provides that:

In the event of any objection or doubt, the matter shall be decided by the
Court, if necessary after hearing the parties.

Again, in relation to the problem of appointing an *ad hoc* judge that
arises when two or more parties may be in the same interest, Article
36, paragraph 2, provides that "the matter may be decided by the
Court, if necessary after hearing the parties". Likewise, Article 56,
paragraph 2, relating to the authorization of the production of
documents after the closure of the written proceedings, contains a
similar formula, as does Article 67. In regard to these matters, the
practice of the Court has been merely to give the parties the opportunity
to present their views in writing.

5. Even so, that interpretation is not one that immediately springs to
mind in respect of so substantial an issue as the admissibility of
counter-claims. It is to be recalled that the Rule on counter-claims
(Art. 80) appears immediately after the rule on preliminary objections
(Art. 79) and that both are classed together in Section D of the Rules,
under the heading "Incidental Proceedings". A similar requirement of
hearing the parties appears also in Article 79, paragraph 7, and has
regularly been met by the holding of oral proceedings. Even if the
Court retains a discretion to decide in a given case that such
proceedings need not be held, the present case is one in which the
relative merits and the complexity of the issues involved would

certainly have warranted giving the parties the additional opportunity of commenting orally on each other's arguments and the Court the opportunity of the more extended consideration of the matter that would have been involved in the holding of a hearing and in the deliberations that would then have followed—the more so as such a step would also have met the expressed expectations of the Parties.

6. The degree to which the decision of the Court not to hold such oral proceedings departs from the opinion of, amongst others, the most learned commentator on the Court's procedure may be gathered from the terms in which the question is discussed by Professor Rosenne in the latest edition of his major work. As regards Article 80, paragraph 3, of the Rules he writes:

> Paragraph 3 corresponds to the last sentence in the previous Rules, with the substitution of "after hearing the parties" for "after due examination". This means that in future there will always be some oral proceedings in the event of doubt—by whom is not stated—as to the connection between the question presented by way of counter-claim and the subject-matter of the claim of the other party. (*The Law and Practice of the International Court 1920-1996*, 3rd edn, 1997, vol. III, p. 1273.)

7. It is, therefore, to be hoped that when the Rules of Court next come to be revised, the opportunity will be taken to eliminate the cause of the present division of opinion by ensuring that the word "hearing" is used consistently to convey the idea of oral proceedings and that when the Court intends to retain a discretion to determine that the exchanges between representatives of the parties are to be limited to written proceedings, it will adhere to such wording as is used elsewhere in the Rules (e.g. Arts. 46, para. 1, 53, paras. 1 and 2, 55 and 58, para. 2), namely "after ascertaining the views of the parties" or, as in Article 76, paragraph 3, after affording "the parties an opportunity of presenting their observations on the subject" or, as in Article 79, paragraph 3, "the other party may present a written statement of its observations".

THE ADMISSIBILITY OF THE COUNTER-CLAIMS

8. The present consideration by the Court of the question of counter-claims is occasioned by the filing by Yugoslavia on 23 July 1997 of an extensive Counter-Memorial. This falls into two parts. The first part, of nearly 350 pages, may be described in general terms as containing "defences". The second part, consisting of over 700 pages, sets out factually Yugoslavia's allegations of genocide by Bosnia and Herzegovina ("Bosnia" hereinafter) against the Serbs in Bosnia and Herzegovina. Apart from a statement in the Introduction to the Counter-Memorial that it "includes counterclaims" and the inclusion

as one of the three Submissions at the close of the Counter-Memorial of an elaboration of the statement that "Bosnia and Herzegovina is responsible for the acts of genocide committed against the Serbs in Bosnia and Herzegovina", the Counter-Memorial contains no discussion of the legal aspects of the counter-claims. But even though the Counter-Memorial contains no reference to Article 80 of the Rules of Court and no argument that the matters covered in Part II of that pleading are "directly connected with the subject-matter of the claim" of Bosnia, it would have been unrealistic not to recognize that Part for what it is. Accordingly, on 28 July 1997, Bosnia addressed a letter to the Court expressing the opinion that the counter-claims "did not meet the criteria of Article 80, paragraph 1, of the Rules of Court and should therefore not be joined to the original proceedings". Having then been requested by the Court to specify in writing "the legal ground on which this opinion is based", Bosnia responded on 9 October 1997 with a letter to the Court in which it contended that the Yugoslav counter-claim was not admissible since, by reference to Article 80, paragraph 1, of the Rules of Court, "any direct connection with the subject-matter of Bosnia and Herzegovina's original claim is totally lacking". Through conceding that both claim and counter-claim are based on the same legal ground—the Genocide Convention— Bosnia contended that the two sets of allegations had nothing to do with one another:

[it] is evident that the alleged victims are not the same . . . nor are the material perpetrators of the alleged atrocities the same . . . This means, then, that if the two claims were joined in the same proceedings before the Court, it would in any event have to verify separately the facts alleged *ex adverso* and consider separately whether, in regard to the Genocide Convention, they constitute unlawful conduct attributed, respectively, to one or the other Party . . . (Letter to the Registrar from the Deputy-Agent of Bosnia and Herzegovina dated 9 October 1997, para. 3.)

9. Bosnia also requested the Court to decide that the counter-claim should not be joined to the principal claim, but expressly acknowledged that Yugoslavia was free to submit to the Court a separate application instituting proceedings in the normal way.

10. Yugoslavia, for its part, responded that there is a direct connection between Part II of its Counter-Memorial, i.e., the counter-claim, and the Bosnian claim. Yugoslavia pointed out, first, that the claim and counter-claim are based on the same legal grounds, namely the Genocide Convention and general rules of State responsibility. Secondly, it contended:

The disputed facts of the claim and counter-claim are the facts of the same tragic conflict, i.e. civil war in Bosnia and Herzegovina, which happened in a single territorial and temporal setting, based on the same historical background and within the framework of the same political development. Due to that reason as well as to the same legal ground of the claim and counter-claim, all relevant facts which form the basis of claim and counter-claim are interrelated in such a way to make a factual and legal connection relevant to the issue. (Statement of Yugoslavia concerning the admissibility of the counter-claim, 23 October 1997, para. 4.)

11. It thus appears that Bosnia supports what may be called a "restrictive" interpretation of the requirement of "direct connection", while Yugoslavia advances a "broad" one. For Bosnia there must be an identity of the alleged victims as there must be of the material perpetrators; the judicial analysis of the facts in the counter-claim must have a relationship to, or must be of help in, the examination of the facts in the principal claim. For Yugoslavia it is sufficient that the counter-claim "raised the question of genocide of the Serbs as one relevant to contradicting facts presented by the Applicant as being relevant for attributing alleged acts to the Respondent".

12. In the present case, the choice between these two approaches must depend to a large extent on the nature of the concept "genocide". Can what we conceive of as amounting to genocide be constituted by a single act of a horrific nature? Or can it only be constituted by a series of acts which, while individually being no more than murder or causing serious bodily harm to individuals or such like, are, when viewed cumulatively, evidence of a pattern of activity amounting to genocide?

13. The second alternative seems logically to be the more cogent. A single murder or other horrific act cannot be genocide. Only a series or accumulation of such acts, if they reveal collectively the necessary intent and are directed against a group identifiable in the manner foreseen in Article II of the Convention, will serve to constitute genocide —whereupon liability for the individual component crimes, as well as for the special crime of genocide, will fall not only upon the individuals directly responsible but also upon the State to which their acts are attributable.

14. Approached thus, it is not possible to require that the facts underlying a counter-claim in respect of genocide must have their direct connection with the individual and specific acts forming the basis of the principal claim of genocide. It is sufficient that the acts invoked as constituting the basis of the counter-claim should be directly connected with the principal claim by reason of their occurrence in the course of the same conflict. Indeed, it may be suggested that the policy underlying the prohibition of genocide favours this broader view since the particular obligations of respect for human rights embodied in the Genocide Convention are ones which rest with equal weight upon all persons involved. It is upon this basis that I agree with the conclusion of the Court that the Yugoslav counter-claim is admissible.

15. It is not necessary to repeat here the Court's analysis of its own jurisprudence, but it is appropriate to mention the support for this approach to be derived from the treatment of the analogous problem within national legal systems when counter-claims are brought against plaintiff States which would, were they sued directly as defendants, be able to plead State immunity. One may recall pertinent statements of two particularly distinguished United States judges. The first was made by J. Manton, of the United States Court of Appeals, Second Circuit:

Claims arising out of the same transaction may be set off against a sovereign. The same transaction does not necessarily mean occurring at the same time. In *Moore* v. *New York Cotton Exchange* . . . the court said that the transaction may comprehend a series of many occurrences depending not so much upon the immediateness of their connection as upon their logical relationship. (*United States* v. *National City Bank of New York* (1936) 83 F 2d, p. 236; 8 *Annual Digest of Public International Law Cases*, p. 218, at p. 220.)

16. The second contribution was by Justice Frankfurter in the Supreme Court of the United States in a case in which the principal claim was by the Republic of China for the recovery of a deposit made in the defendant Bank by the Shanghai-Nanking Railway Administration, an official agency of the State. The Bank counter-claimed on defaulted Treasury Notes of the Republic of China owned by it. Justice Frankfurter said:

It is recognized that a counterclaim based on the subject matter of a sovereign's suit is allowed to cut into the doctrine of immunity. This is proof positive that the doctrine is not absolute, and that considerations of fair play must be taken into account in its application. But the limitation of "based on the subject matter" is too indeterminate, indeed too capricious, to mark the bounds of the limitations on the doctrine of sovereign immunity. There is great diversity among courts on what is and what is not a claim "based on the subject matter of the suit" or "growing out of the same transaction" . . . No doubt the present counterclaims cannot fairly be deemed to be related to the Railway Agency's deposit of funds except insofar as the transactions between the Republic of China and the petitioner may be regarded as aspects of a continuous business relationship. The point is that the ultimate thrust of the consideration of fair dealing which allows a setoff or counterclaim based on the same subject matter reaches the present situation. (*National City Bank of New York* v. *Republic of China, et al.* (1955) 348, US 356; 22 *International Law Reports*, p. 210, at p. 215.)

17. Nothing in Article 9 (counter-claims) of the Draft Articles on Jurisdictional Immunities of States and their Property, adopted in 1991 by the International Law Commission of the United Nations, suggests that codification of the subject has led to any materially different conclusion:

A State instituting a proceeding before a court of another State cannot invoke immunity from the jurisdiction of the court in respect of any counter-claim arising out of the same legal relationship or facts as the principal claim. (*Yearbook of the International Law Commission, 1991*, vol. II, Part Two, p. 30.)

18. But determination that the Yugoslav counter-claim is directly connected with the subject-matter of the Bosnian claim cannot be the end of the matter. Each case must be looked at in the light of its own particular facts. The Court has an inherent power and duty to ensure the orderly and effective administration of justice. Cases should be heard with all deliberate speed. To these ends the Court enjoys a significant measure of discretion. It is not controlled by the letter of Article 80 of its Rules. It should be recalled that, in contrast with many of the Rules of the Court, Article 80 does not have its source in any obligatory provision of the Court's Statute. In Article 80 the Court is not laying down a procedure for the implementation of its statutory duty; it is only exercising the general power conferred on it by Article 30 of the Statute to "frame rules for carrying out its functions". The Court has seen the consideration of counter-claims as a possible aspect of its functions and so, of its own initiative, it has framed certain rules. But it is not rigidly or perpetually bound by these Rules. It is free, and, indeed, obliged, to apply them reasonably and to adjust their application to the circumstances of the case before it.

19. It would, therefore, have been open to the Court to have exercised its discretion in the present case by declining to join the otherwise admissible counter-claims to the principal claims. The principal factor that could have been invoked to justify the separation of the treatment of the claims and counter-claims is the immense additional complexity to which the treatment of the counter-claims simultaneously with the claims is bound to give rise. As stated above, a claim of genocide involves the establishment of a pattern or accumulation of individual crimes. Bosnia has in its Memorial alleged six categories of offences: the use of concentration camps; killing; torture; rape; expelling of people and destruction of property, homes, places of worship and cultural objects; and the creation of destructive living conditions—shelling, starvation and intimidation of the population. Yugoslavia has responded in detail to each of these allegations in Part I (the "defence" section) of its Counter-Memorial, as well as adding in Part II a detailed catalogue of the crimes alleged to have been committed by Bosnians and Croats against Serbians. The assessment of the allegations and responses, if approached other than on a fairly general level (a matter on which it is not appropriate to express any view at this stage of the case), could take months of hearings and deliberation. The annexes adduced by Bosnia in support of this part of its case are some 15 cm thick; and those adduced by Yugoslavia in connection

with Part I of its Counter-Memorial are some 18 cm thick, while those adduced in support of Yugoslavia's counter-claims add about a further 14.5 cm. The bulk of paper in a case is not always a good guide to its true simplicity or complexity, but it is safe to say that nothing in the materials presented by the two Parties in this case suggests that the task that will eventually face the Court when it comes to the merits will be other than an extremely heavy one.

20. The question is, however, whether the Court could exercise its discretion to defer the consideration of the material contained in the Yugoslav counter-claim until after it has disposed of the Bosnian claim without improperly depriving Yugoslavia of its right to deploy those defences that the latter thinks are necessary as a response to the Bosnian claim. The answer in this case is no. It appears from the Yugoslav Statement of 23 October 1997 in reply to Bosnia's Statement of 9 October 1997 that Yugoslavia considers that the material it has advanced in Part II of its Counter-Memorial (the "counter-claim" part) is also an essential ingredient of its defence to the principal Bosnian claim. It is impossible for the Court at this stage of the case to attempt to assess the extent to which the material in Part II of the Yugoslav Counter-Memorial is or is not proper for use as a defence to the Bosnian principal claim. Also, the Court cannot disregard the possibility that the Yugoslav Counter-Memorial is advancing a *tu quoque* argument.

21. One fact which might have affected the admissibility of the Yugoslav counter-claim is that some of the allegations of genocidal conduct are levelled not only against Bosnians but also against Croats, thus seemingly bringing into the case the question of the liability of a State not party to the proceedings. The Yugoslav Counter-Memorial does not grapple with the implications of this fact. However, the number of situations in which allegations are made against Croats would appear, at the present stage at any rate, to be too small to lead the Court to treat this feature by itself as sufficient to exclude the admissibility of the counter-claims [as] a whole.

22. In short, reluctant though one may feel to see the complexity of this case magnified by the incorporation of the Yugoslav counter-claim, there appears to be no convincing basis on which it may be excluded—though the possibility is not to be excluded that some satisfactory solution might have been found if the Court had agreed to oral proceedings on this interlocutory, but nevertheless important, aspect of the case.

23. In conclusion, it is essential to appreciate that the difficulties which confront the Court are not of its own making nor, indeed, of the making of the Parties. The closer one approaches the problems posed by the operation of the judicial settlement procedure contemplated by Article IX of the Genocide Convention, the more one is obliged to recognize that these problems are of an entirely different kind from

those normally confronting an international tribunal of essentially civil, as opposed to criminal, jurisdiction. The difficulties are systemic and their solution cannot be rapidly achieved, whether by the Court or, perhaps more appropriately, by the Parties to the Genocide Convention.

(Signed) Elihu LAUTERPACHT.

DISSENTING OPINION OF VICE-PRESIDENT WEERAMANTRY

The jurisprudence of the Court in regard to counter-claims is not well developed. There is no definition of the term "counter-claim" in the Rules, nor in the Court's decisions and, as has been noted in this connection:

lack of rigidity is a feature of the manner in which States and the Court approach counter-claims. Some difficulty, indeed, is seen in extracting any general principles from these cases, unless it be that each case is to be treated on its merits. (Shabtai Rosenne, *The Law and Practice of the International Court, 1920-1996*, 3rd edn, 1997, vol. III, p. 1276.)

The Court's Order in this case ventures into new legal territory (the development of the topic of counter-claims in international law has tended to be somewhat slender—see A. D. Renteln, "Encountering Counterclaims", 15 *Denver Journal of International Law and Policy* (1986-7), pp. 379, 384-5, and the references therein. See, however, M. Pellonpää and D. D. Caron, *The UNCITRAL Arbitration Rules as Interpreted and Applied*, 1994, pp. 348-55; and G. H. Aldrich, *The Jurisprudence of the Iran–United States Claims Tribunal*, 1996, pp. 110-20, for a detailed discussion of counter-claims before that Tribunal) and I have some concerns with the direction it takes, and with its juristic and practical implications.

It is therefore with much regret that I find myself unable to concur in the decision of my colleagues. I deeply appreciate the reasoning, so well stated in the Order, in regard to the expression "directly connected" as appearing in Article 80 of the Rules of Court but, in my view, the consideration of the matter in hand calls for a close examination of some other aspects as well.

My concerns may very broadly be formulated under three heads:

(a) the meaning of the term "counter-claim";

(b) the discretion of the Court in determining whether to accept a counter-claim; and

(c) the involvement of a third State in the matters raised by the counter-claims.

Before dealing with these, I would like to make a few preliminary observations.

It is common ground in this case that a breach of the Genocide Convention cannot be pleaded as an excuse or justification for another breach of the same Convention. Nobody has sought to argue otherwise, nor is any such argument even remotely conceivable.

Yet the question whether offences under the Convention are of such a nature that they can be used to counter each other arises, in the present case, in the context of the provision regarding counter-claims in Article 80 of the Rules of Court. That Article needs to be analysed to ascertain whether its provisions are such as to enable it to accommodate, as a "counter-claim", the allegations that Yugoslavia seeks to join to the hearing of the original claim of Bosnia and Herzegovina.

An analysis of Article 80, paragraph 1, of these Rules, dealing with the presentation of a counter-claim, reveals three prerequisites to the presentation of a counter-claim.

In the first place, the matter in question must fall within the category of a "counter-claim". If it does not, further inquiry is unnecessary, for without a "counter-claim", the Article is not brought into operation.

Secondly, if it is in fact a counter-claim, it must be directly connected with the subject-matter of the claim of the other party.

Thirdly, it must come within the jurisdiction of the Court.

However, even if all these prior requisites are satisfied, joinder is not automatic, for the language of Article 80 only states that a counter-claim "may be presented", provided the prescribed requisites are present. Whether that counter-claim will be accepted must still depend on the undoubted discretion of the Court as the master of its own procedure. There are many circumstances relevant to the exercise of that discretion, as will appear later in this opinion. Thus a fourth requisite that must be satisfied before the counter-claim is accepted is that the Court's discretion must be exercised in the respondent's favour.

The first requisite presents a problem, in the absence of an authoritative definition of a counter-claim, for the purposes of the Court's jurisprudence (in other contexts, such as arbitration under the UNCITRAL Rules, there have been attempts at a more precise delineation of the term). We are thrown back upon what may be considered as the general and natural meaning of the term, and upon such general principles as we can gather from scrutinizing counter-claims as they are understood in legal systems across the world. Needless to say, a party's characterization of its claim as a counter-claim is not determinative of this matter. It is a judicial question for determination by the Court. The question must first be asked whether the claim that is presented is a counter-claim such as is recognized in ordinary legal phraseology.

(a) *The Meaning of the Term "Counter-Claim"*

To my mind, a counter-claim is what its name implies—that it is a legal claim or factual situation alleged by the respondent that counters the claim set up by the applicant. The mere fact that it is a claim made by the respondent in the same proceedings is not enough. The mere fact that it pays back the plaintiff in the same coin, so to speak, does not make it a counter-claim. The juristic concept of a counter-claim has more to it than mere parallelism or reciprocity. There must be some point of intersection between the claims, which makes one exert an influence upon the judicial consequence of the other.

The ordinary meaning of the expression "counter-claim" lends support to this view. The *Concise Oxford Dictionary* (9th edn, 1995, p. 306) gives two meanings to the expression. The first is "a claim made against another claim". Under this definition, the two claims in question should, in principle, be capable of being opposable to each other—whether by way of diminution of responsibility, or by monetary set-off, or in any other legally recognized manner. Failing this, one cannot be a counter-claim to the other.

The other meaning given to "counter-claim" is that it is "a claim made by a defendant in a suit against the plaintiff". This meaning emphasizes another aspect, namely, that such claims are envisaged only in civil proceedings, for these expressions—"plaintiff", "defendant" and "suit"—are quite clearly set in the context of civil claims. Crimes, by their very nature, do not fit within this definition.

Black's Law Dictionary, on the same lines, gives a short definition of a counter-claim for the Anglo-American system as:

A claim presented by a defendant in opposition to or deduction from the claim of the plaintiff. Fed.R. Civil P. 13. If established, such will defeat or diminish the plaintiff's claim. (*Black's Law Dictionary*, 6th edn, 1990, p. 349.)

The understanding of the word "counter-claim" by those who inspired the drafting of Article 40 of the Rules in 1922 is also illuminating. To quote a verbatim record of the discussion at the 1922 preliminary session:

M. WEISS (translation).—Are there not cases where a counter-claim may be regarded as a defence to the principal claim?

M. ANZILOTTI (translation).—That is what we call a plea of counter-claim, but that would be a question to be decided by the Court in the particular case. (*PCIJ, Series D, No 2, 4th Add.*, p. 262.)

The counter-claim was thus, according to the understanding of President Anzilotti, a claim which operated, at least *inter alia*, as a defence to the principal claim.

Another aspect of counter-claims, stressed by various writers on the subject, is that their object goes beyond the mere dismissal of the principal claim, to obtain something more. (See D. Anzilotti, "La demande reconventionnelle en procédure internationale", *Journal du droit international*, vol. 57 (1930), p. 867. See, to the same effect, Georges Scelle, *Report on Arbitration Proceedings*, submitted to the International Law Commission in 1949, *YILC, 1950*, vol. II, p. 137.) This suggests that while the essential character of a counter-claim is to impinge on the original claim and thus weaken or destroy it, it may even go further. The attack upon the original claim would appear, however, to be one of its basic characteristics. Having regard to President Anzilotti's prominent contribution to the discussion leading to the drafting of the Rules of the Permanent Court of International Justice, his observations must carry great weight in our understanding of the rule relating to joinder of counter-claims as it presently stands.

At the meeting of the Permanent Court held on 28 May 1934 to consider Article 39 of the Rules then prevailing, which dealt *inter alia* with a counter-case presented by the respondent, Mr Fromageot observed that the best definition of a counter-claim would be "a claim directly dependent on the facts of the main action" (*ibid.*, p. 112), and Mr Negulesco that, in using the expression "direct connection", the authors of the new text had in mind what was termed in English "the counter-claim", but had wished to exclude the cross action (*PCIJ, Series D, No 2, 4th Add.*, p. 264).

A leading article on the subject, written shortly after the 1936 Rules, probably captures the contemporary understanding of these Rules, when it observes specifically that:

counter-claim proceedings should have the objective of neutralizing the principal claim by means of a counter-attack, of having the principal claim dismissed, and this objective necessarily includes requesting a judgment against the applicant in the principal proceedings (R. Genet, "Les demandes reconventionnelles et la procédure de la CPJI", *Revue de droit international et de législation comparée*, vol. 19 (1938), p. 175; Registry translation, cited by Bosnia).

As to the words "une demande reconventionnelle", appearing in the French version of the Rules, it is useful to recall that at the same 1922 session, when the proposal to add "une demande reconventionnelle" was discussed, Lord Finlay observed: "There might be une demande reconventionnelle which, though in form a demand, was really in the nature of a defence to the proceedings" (*PCIJ, Series D, No 2, 4th Add.*, p. 262).

I note also the statement in the *Corpus Juris Secundum* that "reconvention, in the civil law, is equivalent in general to a counter-claim; it is a demand that a defendant in a suit is permitted to engraft on the main action" (vol. LXXX, p. 16.) The *Corpus* goes on to mention that "reconvention", "reconventional demand", and "demanding reconvention" are civil law terms.

Analogies in domestic jurisprudence are plentiful. The party responding to a claim for relief seeks, by presenting the counter-claim, to negate the claim or to reduce or mitigate it. The principal object of the exercise is to whittle down or destroy the claim presented. The party seeks alleviation of the legal consequences of its own action through reliance on countervailing circumstances constituting a claim, though of course it may seek more.

A claim that is autonomous and has no bearing on the determination of the initial claim does not thus qualify as a counter-claim. Especially would this be so of a vast catalogue of criminal acts which is advanced as a "counter-claim" to a vast catalogue of similar criminal acts alleged by the applicant. The juristic thread which is necessary to link the two as claim and counter-claim is lacking, for neither the second catalogue nor any component item thereof is an answer to the first catalogue or any of its component items. The two stand separate and distinct, as two separate and independent subjects of inquiry.

The Inapplicability of the Concept to Criminal Offences

Indeed, the concept of a counter-claim is a concept of the civil, as opposed to the criminal, law, for while civil acts and claims may be set off one against another, the intrinsic nature of a criminal wrong prevents the set off of one criminal act against another. The impact of crime stretches far beyond the party actually injured, and the concept of one crime being set off or used as a counter-claim to another crime is totally alien to modern jurisprudence, domestic or international.

A murder cannot be set off against another murder, nor a rape against a rape. Crimes must be viewed against the jurisprudential background of the interests and rights of the community. Civil claims, by way of contrast, are viewed against the background of the rights of the individuals concerned. Moreover, civil claims, which are often quantified in monetary terms, are inherently capable of being set off one against the other. When the individual claimant is thus satisfied, the matter is at an end. In the field of crime, however, the wrong done to the community cannot be ended in this fashion by a set-off of one act of criminality against the other. Least of all can crime be counter-claimed against crime. Legitimate defences and extenuating circumstances may naturally be pleaded as an undoubted right of the respondent, but always within the scope of their proper function—such as denial of facts, denial of responsibility, mitigation of offence, and the like— never as a counter-claim which offsets or neutralizes the crime in the sense in which a counter-claim does in a civil context.

What I have observed thus far applies *a fortiori* to the international crime of genocide. An act of genocide by the applicant cannot be a counter-claim to an act of genocide by the respondent. Each act stands untouched by the other, in drawing upon itself the united condemnation of the international community.

On more than one occasion, this Court has stressed this aspect of genocide in the strongest terms. In its Advisory Opinion on *Reservations to the Convention on the Prevention and Punishment of the Crime of Genocide*,[16] it observed:

In such a convention, the contracting States do not have any interests of their own; they merely have, one and all, a common interest, namely, the accomplishment of those high purposes which are the *raison d'être* of the convention. Consequently, in a convention of this type one cannot speak of individual advantages or disadvantages to States, or of the maintenance of a perfect contractual balance between rights and duties. (*ICJ Reports 1951*, p. 23.)

The Genocide Convention takes us beyond the realm of crimes against any particular State, and into the realm of crimes against humanity, where the notion of balancing of individual State interests is unthinkable. This Court has therefore stressed more than once the *erga omnes* character of the rights and obligations flowing from the Convention, which makes the wrongdoers responsible to the international community as a whole (*Barcelona Traction, Light and Power Company, Limited, ICJ Reports 1970*, p. 32, para. 33;[17] *Application of the Convention on the Prevention and Punishment of the Crime of Genocide, Preliminary Objections, ICJ Reports 1996*, p. 22, para. 31).[18]

As Bosnia and Herzegovina argues, Yugoslavia's Counter-Memorial is in two parts. One part consists of a reply to the accusations contained in Bosnia and Herzegovina's Memorial. It consists, *inter alia*, of evidence and materials of the sort which a Court must necessarily take into account in determining the principal claim—material which every respondent to a charge of crime has an undoubted right to place before the Court. This material must, of course, be considered by the Court within the ambit of the present proceedings.

The second part, however, which is twice as voluminous, treads different ground. It proceeds from the defensive to the offensive and alleges that the complainant itself is guilty of the very same category of offences with which the Respondent is charged. An accused person is always entitled to make such allegations in separate proceedings if they can be proved, but not as a counter-claim to the original charge. The facts may be relevant by way of mitigation of the original charge, but not as the substance of an independent claim.

These allegations cannot therefore be considered to be a counter-claim within the meaning of Article 80, enabling it to be heard within the framework of the current case.

[[16] 18 *ILR* 364.]   [[17] 46 *ILR* 1 at 178.]   [[18] See p. 28 above.]

The Respondent pleads that the facts presented in Part Two, Chapter VII of the Counter-Memorial, "i.e., crimes of genocide committed against the Serb people in Bosnia and Herzegovina are part and parcel of the circumstances of the situation" (Statement of Yugoslavia concerning the admissibility of the counter-claim, 23 October 1997, p. 20, para. 6.4). Even if this be so, they still remain separate acts of genocide. Even on the assumption that the acts of genocide alleged against Bosnia and Herzegovina are proved, the acts of genocide alleged against Yugoslavia do not lose their gravity.

The "counter-claim" of genocide necessarily depends on other facts than the genocide alleged by Bosnia, for the alleged murderers are different, the victims are different, the motivations are different, and the times and venues are not coincidental. In short, a separate fact-finding process is required for the inquiry into the claim and the inquiry into the "counter-claim". Each of these inquiries must be independently pursued, and will require independent evidence to be placed before the Court. The judicial conclusions reached in the one do not dilute or magnify the conclusions reached in the other.

(b) *The Discretion of the Court*

Circumstances exist in the present case which, in my view, should incline the Court, even if all the other prerequisites are satisfied, to use its discretion against the joinder of the Respondent's application to that of the Applicant.

In the first place, the case of the Applicant has been pending before this Court since 1993, and now, at the end of 1997, when the case is nearly ripe for hearing, the Applicant is entitled to an expeditious disposal of this matter. What is sought to be introduced by way of a counter-claim four years later, which is in reality another claim of the same magnitude as the claim of the Applicant, will necessarily have the effect of further delaying the hearing of the Applicant's claim.

Furthermore, not only will there be delay in bringing the allegations of the Respondent to a state of readiness for hearing, but the actual process of hearing will itself be prolonged. The claim of Bosnia and Herzegovina is complex enough already, with vast numbers of allegations of fact to be probed and proved. That itself is a task which would probably require several weeks, if not months, of hearing. To combine this massive set of allegations with a fresh set of allegations of like magnitude will considerably lengthen the time necessary for the hearing of the case. Delay in actual hearing, added to delay in preparation for hearing, could well defeat the ends of justice.

I note in this connection, the stress laid by the *International Encyclopedia of Comparative Law* (in its volume on "Civil Procedure" which surveys the cross action in numerous jurisdictions) upon the importance of the principle that the decision on the principal action should not be delayed by consideration of the cross action. In dealing with what it describes as, "The cross-action in cases of connexity of claim and counter-claim", it refers, with approval, to a procedure available in Germany, "by which plaintiff's well-founded, ripe complaint can proceed to judgment without regard to the cross action", thus stressing the importance of not permitting a principal claim, which is ripe for hearing, to be delayed by a cross or counter-claim (*International Encyclopedia of Comparative Law*, vol. XVI, "*Civil Procedure*", Mauro Cappelletti (ed.), pp. 66-7).

Moreover, in hearing the case, the Court would be moving from one set of allegations to the other, and would not be able to reach a conclusion upon the case presented to it until it has heard the entire case against the Applicant. There will not be that concentration upon the subject-matter of either claim which would be requisite for the proper determination of a matter of this degree of complexity.

The Court will, in fact, be making one case out of two separate cases, each involving voluminous evidence in regard to a multitude of criminal acts, and, in the process, imposing an enormous procedural burden upon itself, with little corresponding benefit to either Party. It may be noted that the second part of the Yugoslavian Counter-Memorial, containing the allegations on which the "counter-claim" is based, runs to over 700 pages of material aimed at proving that Bosnia and Herzegovina was itself guilty of violations of the Genocide Convention. These 700 pages of allegations will need separate verification, quite independently of the verification required for the several allegations that are the substance of Bosnia and Herzegovina's claim.

After hearing the extensive evidence that will no doubt be offered by the Applicant, the Court would have to reserve its conclusions thereon until it heard the extensive evidence which would similarly be offered by the Respondent. From a practical point of view, this would hamper the process of decision-making upon the first set of facts for so long a period, that the impressions created by them upon the minds of the Judges may well lose their freshness and immediacy. This can be very damaging to the process of fact-finding in a long drawn out inquiry.

There is also a question of principle involved here, because if this Application should be allowed, it could open the door to parties who seek to delay proceedings against themselves to file, when the case is nearly ready for hearing, what is, in effect, another case against the applicant, with a view to delaying the proceedings against itself. Where such an application comes years after the original claim, this could have damaging effects upon the due administration of international justice.

The claim of the Respondent, now put forward four years after the Applicant's claim, could always be heard by way of separate proceedings, if it were instituted as such. No prejudice is thereby caused to the Respondent, who can urge in such proceedings whatever contention, and adduce whatever evidence, it can in the present case.

The situation contemplated by Article 80 is quite distinct from that contemplated by Article 47 of the Rules which permits two or more separate cases to be joined. Had Yugoslavia filed a separate case on the subject-matter it now advances in its counter-claim, and had an Order of joinder seemed appropriate by reason of common background, similar circumstances, judicial economy, or other cogent reason, such an Order could well have been a course available to the Court and the Parties.

However, that is not the situation we face here. A different claim has been filed within the ambit of the same case.

In exercising its discretion, the Court also needs to bear in mind another aspect touching on the "equality of arms" of the Parties before it.

However great may be the magnitude of its subject-matter, the respondent to the counter-claim, namely the original applicant, has in general only one opportunity to state its position on the allegations made against itself, whereas the respondent to the original claim has the opportunity not only to file a counter-memorial, but also to file a rejoinder. When cases of this magnitude are joined, in the fashion requested by the Respondent in the present proceedings, this aspect of inequality can weigh rather heavily upon its adversary, especially in a case such as the present.

Indeed, this aspect attracted the attention of Mr Negulesco, at the meeting of the Permanent Court of 28 May 1934, already referred to. Mr Negulesco observed that:

in a normal case before the Court, each party could file two written documents and could address the Court twice orally. On the contrary, in the case of counter-claims, the existing system, according to which the respondent raised a counter-claim in the Counter-Case only, allowed the applicant to file a single written document—the Reply—in regard to the claim, whereas the respondent could refer to the matter a second time, in his Rejoinder. M. Negulesco raised the question whether this inequality between the parties in the written proceedings in regard to a counter-claim was not inconsistent with the spirit of the Statute. (*PCIJ, Series D, No 2, Add. 4*, p. 262.)

The Court has, in the present case, taken note of this aspect, in paragraph 38 of the Order, by providing Bosnia and Herzegovina with the right to provide its views a second time in an additional pleading, but this is an aspect that needs to be borne in mind whenever future counter-claims are involved. Moreover, it is an aspect that makes for further delay in bringing the conjoint case to a trial-ready state.

All these are circumstances that bear upon the exercise of the Court's discretion in deciding whether to join a counter-claim to the original claim, even if all the other requisites are satisfied. In my view, they should have inclined the Court to use its discretion against joinder.

(c) *The Involvement of a Third State*

Another consideration which I view as militating strongly against the Respondent's contention that its claim against Bosnia and Herzegovina should be joined to Bosnia and Herzegovina's claim against itself, is that the alleged counter-claim also involves the conduct of Croatia. A "counter-claim" between the immediate parties to litigation is one thing. But a counter-claim involving a third party is another. Both convenience and judicial economy could be adversely affected by the joinder to a claim of a "counter-claim" involving a third party.

Furthermore, from the standpoint of practical considerations, this introduces yet another element of delay. Croatia would have to be given notice of its involvement and would be entitled to file its response to whatever allegations are made against it. It would need time to do so, in addition to such time as is already involved in the joinder of the two claims. New witnesses may well be necessary, thus adding further complications to the already difficult task imposed on the Court of examining the allegations made by each Party against the other.

For these reasons, I consider that the joinder of a claim involving a third party, namely, Croatia, militates against the spirit and purpose of the Court's procedural provisions relating to counter-claims—and particularly so in the circumstances of this case.

The considerations outlined above persuade me to the view that, in the present case, the course which would have been more in accordance with legal principle and practical convenience would have been to proceed to the hearing and completion of the Application of Bosnia and Herzegovina, leaving to Yugoslavia its undoubted right to make its counter-claim the subject of a separate proceeding. This rather long-delayed Application would then be brought to completion, and the way cleared for the hearing of the counter-claim as a case by itself which, in my view, it undoubtedly is. Both Parties would then have had the benefit of an expeditious hearing and a concentration of the Court's attention upon their respective claims and allegations, uncluttered by voluminous evidence extraneous to the particular subject-matter of each case.

(*Signed*) Christopher Gregory WEERAMANTRY.

[Report: Not yet published]

Human rights—Right to life—Nuclear weapons—Testing of nuclear weapons—Whether French nuclear tests in the South Pacific constituting a threat to life—Whether residents of islands near test area victims of violations of the International Covenant on Civil and Political Rights, 1966

International tribunals — United Nations Human Rights Committee—Competence—Admissibility of communication —Requirement that author of communication be a victim of a violation—Matter simultaneously brought before two human rights tribunals

BORDES AND TEMEHARO *v.* FRANCE

(*Communication No 645/1995*)

United Nations Human Rights Committee.[1]   22 *July* 1996

SUMMARY: *The facts:*—The authors were all citizens residing in Papeete, Tahiti, French Polynesia. In June 1995, the French President had announced that France intended to conduct a series of underground nuclear tests on the atolls of Mururoa and Fangataufa in the South Pacific. In July 1995, the authors submitted a communication to the Committee contending that the decision by the French President was in clear violation of international law. Thereafter, France carried out six underground nuclear tests between September 1995 and the beginning of 1996.

The authors claimed that the French authorities had failed to take sufficient measures to protect their life and security and had been unable to show that the underground nuclear tests did not constitute a danger to the health of the inhabitants of the South Pacific and to the environment, as well as that the contamination of the food chain would threaten human life indirectly. Finally, the authors argued that French domestic remedies were ineffective, and that due to the urgent nature of their case, they could not be expected to await the outcome of judicial procedures before the French tribunals.

France challenged the admissibility of the communication on grounds that the authors did not qualify as victims within the meaning of the Optional Protocol of the International Covenant on Civil and Political Rights, 1966 and that purely theoretical and hypothetical violations did not suffice to make them victims. France also contended that its reservation to Article 5(2)(a) of

---

[1] The members of the Committee in 1996, with the country of nationality of each member placed in parentheses, were: Francisco José Aguilar Urbina (Costa Rica), Nisuke Ando (Japan), Prafullachandra Natwarlal Baghwati (India), Tamás Bán (Hungary), Marco Tulio Bruni Celli (Venezuela), Thomas Buergenthal (United States of America), Christine Chanet (France), Omran El Shafei (Egypt), Elizabeth Evatt (Australia), Laurel Francis (Jamaica), Rosalyn Higgins (United Kingdom), Eckart Klein (Germany), David Kretzmer (Israel), Rajsoomer Lallah (Mauritius), Andreas V. Mavrommatis (Cyprus), Cecilia Médina Quiroga (Chile), Fausto Pocar (Italy) and Julio Prado Vallejo (Ecuador).

Pursuant to Rule 85 of the Rules of Procedure, Committee member Christine Chanet (France) did not participate in the examination of the present communication.

the Optional Protocol rendered the communication inadmissible because two of the authors, Ms Bordes and Mr Tauira, were co-authors of a complaint of "the same matter" made in August 1995 before the European Commission of Human Rights, thereby also excluding the Committee's competence in respect of the present case. France further contended that the authors' claim was inadmissible *ratione materiae* and on grounds of non-exhaustion of domestic remedies.

Held:—(1) The Committee discontinued consideration of Mr Tauira's complaint as he had withdrawn his communication from consideration by the Committee on 18 August 1995. Ms Bordes had withdrawn her application to the European Commission of Human Rights on 17 August 1995 before any decision by the European Commission had been adopted. As the authors of the case before the European Commission and of the present case were therefore not identical, it was not necessary to examine whether the French reservation to Article 5, paragraph 2(a) applied to the present case (p. 261).

(2) The Committee observed that the authors had not substantiated their claim that the conduct of nuclear tests between September 1995 and the beginning of 1996 placed them in a position in which they could have justifiably claimed to be victims whose right to life and to family life had then been violated or had been under a real threat of violation. Furthermore, the Committee could not ascertain the validity or correctness of the authors' contention that the nuclear tests would further deteriorate the geological structure of the atolls on which the tests were carried out and thereby increase the likelihood of an accident of catastrophic proportions (p. 262).

(3) As the authors could not claim to be victims within the meaning of the Optional Protocol, the Committee declared the communication inadmissible. However, the Committee reiterated that "it was evident that the designing, testing, manufacture, possession and deployment of nuclear weapons were among the greatest threats to the right to life which confront mankind today" (p. 262).

The following is the text of the views of the Committee:

Decision on admissibility

1. The authors of the communication are Vaihere Bordes, Noël Narii Tauira and John Temeharo, all French citizens residing in Papeete, Tahiti, French Polynesia. All claim to be victims of violations by France of Articles 6 and 17 of the International Covenant on Civil and Political Rights. The authors are represented by counsel.

Facts and claim

2.1 On 13 June 1995, French President Jacques Chirac announced that France intended to conduct a series of underground nuclear tests on the atolls of Mururoa and Fangataufa in the South Pacific. The authors challenge the decision of President Chirac, which they claim is in clear violation of international law. They contend that the tests represent a threat to their right to life and their right not to be subjected to arbitrary interference with their privacy and their family life. After the submission of the communication, six underground nuclear tests were carried out between 5 September 1995 and the beginning of 1996. According to the State Party, these underground tests would be the last to be carried out by France, as President Chirac has announced France's intention to accede to the Comprehensive Nuclear Test Ban Treaty, which is scheduled to be adopted in Geneva in late 1996.

2.2 The authors recall the General Comments of the Human Rights Committee on the right to life, in particular General Comment 14[23] on nuclear weapons, and add that numerous studies show the danger to life caused by nuclear tests, on account of the direct effects of the radiation on the health of individuals living in the test area, which manifests itself in an increased number of cancer and leukaemia cases, as well as genetical risks. Indirectly, human life is said to be threatened through the contamination of the food chain.

2.3 According to the authors, the French authorities have failed to take sufficient measures to protect their life and security. They claim that the authorities have not been able to show that the underground nuclear tests do not constitute a danger to the health of the inhabitants of the South Pacific and to the environment. They therefore request the Committee to ask France, under Rule 86 of the Rules of Procedure, not to carry out any nuclear tests until an independent international commission has found that the tests are indeed without risks and do not violate any of the rights protected under the Covenant. Both during the 54th and 55th sessions, the Committee decided not to grant interim protection under Rule 86.

2.4 With regard to the requirement of exhaustion of domestic remedies, the authors contend that because of the urgent nature of their cases, they cannot be expected to await the outcome of judicial procedures before the French tribunals. It is further argued that domestic remedies are ineffective in practice, and would fail to offer the authors any protection or any remedy.

State Party's submission on the admissibility of the complaint

3.1 In its submission under Rule 91 of the Rules of Procedure, dated 22 January 1996, the State Party challenges the admissibility of the communication on several grounds.

3.2 The State Party argues that, in the first instance, the authors do not qualify as "victims" within the meaning of Articles 1 and 2 of the Optional Protocol. In this context, it refers to the arguments developed in its submission to the European Commission of Human Rights in a case (No 28024/95) virtually identical to that before the Committee introduced before that body. The State Party provides a detailed description of the geology of the atoll of Mururoa, where most of the underground tests are carried out, and of the techniques developed for the conduct of the tests. These techniques, the State Party notes, are designed to provide a maximum of security and to minimize the risks of radioactive contamination of the environment and atmosphere. It dismisses the authors' argument that earlier underground tests in the 1970s and incidents said to have occurred during those tests have led to fissures in the atoll's geology and, thereby, increases the risk of radiation escaping from the underground shafts where the nuclear devices are tested, through a process known as "venting".

3.3 The State Party further rejects the argument that the tests expose the population of the islands surrounding the testing area to an increased risk of radiation. It recalls that the level of radioactivity at Mururoa is identical to that measured over and at other islands and atolls in the South Pacific and is, for example, less than that measured in metropolitan France: thus, the level of Caesium 137 measured in French Polynesia in 1994 was one third of the level measured in France and in the northern hemisphere at the same date where, it is noted, the emissions resulting from the nuclear accident which occurred at Chernobyl (Ukraine) in 1985 are still clearly measurable.

3.4 Similar considerations apply to the alleged and expected contamination of the food chain through the nuclear tests. The State Party refutes the authors' argument that they run a risk of contamin- ation through consumption of agricultural products produced and fish caught in proximity of the testing area. It points out that all serious scientific studies on the environmental effects of underground nuclear tests have concluded that whatever radioactive elements reach the surface of the lagoon at Mururoa or Fangataufa are subsequently diluted by the ocean to levels which are perfectly innocuous for the marine fauna and flora and, *a fortiori*, for human beings. In the same vein, the State Party rejects as unfounded and unsubstantiated the authors' contention that the incidence of cases of cancer has risen in French Polynesia *as a result* of French nuclear tests in the area.

3.5 The State Party notes that it has granted access to the testing area to several independent commissions of inquiry in the past, including, in 1982, a mission led by the internationally recognized vulcanologist Haroun Tazieff, in 1983, a mission of experts from New Zealand, Australia and Papua New Guinea, one by J. Y. Cousteau in 1987, etc. That the monitoring of the environmental effects of the tests carried out by the French authorities has been serious and of high quality has, *inter alia*, been confirmed by the Lawrence Livermore Laboratory (California) and the International Laboratory of Marine Radioactivity in Monaco.

3.6 In the light of the above, the State Party affirms that the authors have failed to discharge the burden of proof that they are "victims" within the meaning of Article 1 of the Optional Protocol. It notes that the authors cannot argue that the risk to which they might be exposed through the nuclear tests would be such as to render imminent a violation of their rights under Articles 6 and 17 of the Covenant. Purely theoretical and hypothetical violations, however, do not suffice to make them "victims" within the meaning of the Optional Protocol.

3.7 Subsidiarily, the State Party contends that the communication is inadmissible under Article 5, paragraph 2(a), of the Optional Protocol, since two of the authors, Ms Bordes and Mr Tauira, are co-authors of the complaint which was placed before the European Commission of Human Rights and registered by that body in August 1995 (case No 28204/95). The State Party recalls its reservation to Article 5, paragraph 2(a), pursuant to which the Committee "shall not have competence to consider a communication from an individual if the same matter is being examined or has already been considered under another procedure of international investigation or settlement". As the case which was examined by the European Commission and declared inadmissible on 4 December 1995 in fact concerned the alleged unlawfulness of the French nuclear tests and thus the "same matter", the Committee's competence in respect of the present case is said to be excluded.

3.8 Equally subsidiarily, the State Party submits that the complaint is inadmissible on the basis of non-exhaustion of domestic remedies. It refers to its arguments developed before the European Commission of Human Rights on this point: thus, the authors *could* have filed a complaint before the *Conseil d'Etat* and argued that President Chirac's decision to resume nuclear tests constituted an abuse of (executive) power (. . . *recours pour excès de pouvoir*). Contrary to what the authors affirm, such a recourse could not *a priori* be deemed futile or ineffective. Furthermore, the State Party notes that as the authors essentially invoke the potential risks which the tests entail for their health and the environment, they should have requested compensation from the competent authorities, which they failed to do. If their request had been rejected, they could have filed a complaint before the administrative tribunals, invoking the State's no fault responsibility (*responsabilité sans faute*).

3.9 Finally, the State submits that the authors' claim is incompatible *ratione materiae* with Articles 6 and 17 of the Covenant. For the State Party, Article 6 only applies in the event of a real and immediate threat to the right to life, which presents itself with some degree of certainty; such is not the case in the authors' situation. Similar considerations apply to Article 17, where the prohibited unlawful interference with private or family life is a real and effective interference, and not the risk of a purely hypothetical interference.

4.1 In her comments, dated 8 April 1996, counsel for the authors contends that the risk of adverse effects of the nuclear tests already carried out on the authors' life, health and environment is real and serious. She deplores the absence of an independent international investigation into the impacts of the programmed and concluded tests. She criticizes the lack of transparency of the French authorities, which are said to even misrepresent the *true* number of underground nuclear tests carried out on Mururoa and Fangataufa since the 1970s. She further points out that even the reports invoked by the State Party itself (see paragraph 3.5 above) contain passages which caution that the danger of escape of radioactive particles (Caesium 134, Iodium 131) from the underground shafts and consequently contamination of the atmosphere is real; however, the State Party has chosen to invoke only those conclusions favourable to its position.

4.2 Counsel argues that the tests do have adverse impacts on the marine environment in the testing area, and from there have repercussions on the whole region's ecosystem, by propagation of radiation through the food chain (especially fish). She notes that a July 1995 report prepared by *Médecins Sans Frontières* rightly criticizes the absence of medical supervision of the population of French Polynesia in the aftermath of the nuclear tests.

4.3 It is submitted that the nuclear tests carried out will, with some degree of probability, increase the incidence of cases of cancer among inhabitants of French Polynesia. Counsel concedes that it is too early to gauge the extent of the contamination of the ecosystem, the marine environment and the food chain by radiation, as cancers may take ten to thirty years to develop and manifest themselves; the same is true for genetical malformations. She notes that some reports have revealed the presence of Iodium 131 in significant quantities in the lagoon of Mururoa after the tests, and surmises that the discovery of Caesium 134 in the lagoon's waters is an indicator of the leaky nature of the underground shafts, from which more radioactivity is likely to escape in the future. Finally, negative effects are expected from the poisoning of fish in the South Pacific by a toxic substance found on algae growing on dead coral reefs, and which trigger a disease known as ciguatera: there is said to be a correlation between the conduct of nuclear tests in the South Pacific and the increase in poisoning of fish and of human beings by ciguatera.

4.4 On the basis of the above, counsel argues that the authors *do* qualify as victims within the meaning of Article 1 of the Optional Protocol. The risks to the health of Mr Temeharo and Ms Bordes are said to be significant, clearly exceeding the threshold of purely hypothetical threats. The evaluation of the threats to the authors' rights under Articles 6 and 17 can only be, according to counsel, made during evaluation of the *merits* of the authors' claims. For purposes of admissibility, the burden of proof is said to have been discharged, as the authors have made prima facie substantiated allegations.

4.5 Counsel denies that the communication is inadmissible under Article 5, paragraph 2(a), of the Optional Protocol. She notes that Ms Bordes withdrew her complaint from the European Commission of Human Rights by letter of 17 August 1995; conversely, Mr Tauira withdrew his complaint from consideration by the Human Rights Committee by letter of 18 August 1995. Counsel further contends that the French reservation to Article 5, paragraph 2(a), of the Optional Protocol, is inapplicable in the present case: in this context, she affirms that the reservation only applies if the "same matter" has been the subject of a decision *on the merits* by another instance of international investigation or settlement. In the instant case, the European Commission of Human Rights declared the case presented to it inadmissible, without entering into a debate on the merits of the authors' claims.

4.6 Counsel submits that the authors should be deemed to have complied with the requirement of exhaustion of domestic remedies, since available judicial remedies are clearly ineffective. In this context, she notes that President Chirac's decision to resume nuclear tests in the South Pacific is not susceptible of judicial control: this is said to be confirmed by the jurisprudence of the French *Conseil d'Etat*, the highest administrative tribunal. Thus, in a judgment handed down in 1975,[2] the *Conseil d'Etat* had already held that the establishment of a security zone around the nuclear testing areas in the South Pacific were governmental decisions (*acte de gouvernement*) which could not be dissociated from France's international relations and were not susceptible of control by national tribunals. The same considerations are applicable to the present case. Counsel further notes that the French section of Greenpeace challenged the resumption of nuclear tests before the *Conseil d'Etat*: by judgment of 29 September 1995, the *Conseil d'Etat* dismissed the complaint, on the basis of the "act of government" theory.[3]

4.7 Counsel reiterates that the authors' complaints are compatible *ratione materiae* with Articles 6 and 17 of the Covenant. As far as Article 6 is concerned, she recalls that the Human Rights Committee has consistently, including in General Comment 6[16] on Article 6, argued that the right to life must not be interpreted restrictively, and that States should adopt positive measures to protect this right. In the context of examination of periodic State reports, for example, the Committee has frequently enquired into States Parties' policies relating to measures to reduce infant mortality or improve life expectancy and policies relating to the protection of the environment or of public health. Counsel emphasizes that the Committee itself has stated, in its General Comment 14[21] of 2 November 1984, that the development, testing, possession and deployment of nuclear weapons constitutes one of the most serious threats to the right to life.

[2] Judgment in the case of *Sieur Paris de Bollardière*, 11 July 1975 [74 *ILR* 95].
[3] *Association Greenpeace France*, judgment of 29 September 1995 [106 *ILR* 231].

4.8 As far as the authors' claim under Article 17 is concerned, counsel notes that the risks to the authors' family life are real: thus, the danger that they lose a member of their family through cancer, leukaemia, ciguatera, etc., increases as long as measures are not taken to prevent the escape of radioactive material set free by the underground tests into the atmosphere and environment. This is said to constitute an unlawful interference with the authors' right to their family life.

Issues and proceedings before the Committee

5.1 Before considering any claims contained in a communication, the Human Rights Committee must, in accordance with Rule 87 of its Rules of Procedure, decide whether or not it is admissible under the Optional Protocol to the Covenant.

5.2 The Committee notes that Mr Tauira withdrew his communication from consideration by the Committee by letter dated 18 August 1995, so as to enable him to present his case to the European Commission of Human Rights. In his respect, therefore, the Committee discontinues consideration of his complaint. Conversely, Ms Bordes withdrew her application to the European Commission by telefax of 17 August 1995, before any decision was adopted by the European Commission of Human Rights. Given, therefore, that the authors of the case which was before the European Commission and of the present case are not identical, the Committee need not examine whether the French reservation to Article 5, paragraph 2(a), of the Optional Protocol, applies in the present case.

5.3 In the initial communication, the authors challenge President Chirac's decision to resume nuclear underground tests on Mururoa and Fangataufa as a violation of their rights under Articles 6 and 17 of the Covenant. In subsequent letters, they reformulate their claim in that the actual conduct of tests has increased the risks to their lives and for their families.

5.4 The Committee has noted the State Party's contention that the authors do not qualify as "victims" within the meaning of Article 1 of the Optional Protocol. It recalls that for a person to claim to be a victim of a violation of a right protected by the Covenant, he or she must show either that an act or omission of a State Party has already adversely affected his or her enjoyment of such right, or that there is a real threat of such result.[4]

5.5 The issue in the present case therefore is whether the announcement and subsequent conduct of underground nuclear tests by France on Mururoa and Fangataufa resulted in a violation of their right to life and their right to their family life, specific to Ms Bordes and Mr

---

[4] See, e.g., decision on Communication No 429/1990 (*EW et al.* v. *The Netherlands*), adopted on 8 April 1993, paragraph 6.2.

Temeharo, or presented an imminent threat to their enjoyment of such rights. The Committee observes that, on the basis of the information presented by the parties, the authors have not substantiated their claim that the conduct of nuclear tests between September 1995 and the beginning of 1996 did not place them in a position in which they could justifiably claim to be victims whose right to life and to family life was then violated or was under a real threat of violation.

5.6 Finally, as to the authors' contention that the nuclear tests will further deteriorate the geological structure of the atolls on which the tests are carried out, further fissurate the limestone caps of the atolls, etc., and thereby increase the likelihood of an accident of catastrophic proportions, the Committee notes that this contention is highly controversial even in concerned scientific circles; it is not possible for the Committee to ascertain its validity or correctness.

5.7 On the basis of the above considerations and after careful examination of the arguments and materials before it, the Committee is not satisfied that the authors can claim to be victims within the meaning of Article 1 of the Optional Protocol.

5.8 In the light of the above, the Committee need not address the other inadmissibility grounds that have been adduced by the State Party.

5.9 Although the authors have not shown that they are "victims" within the meaning of Article 1 of the Optional Protocol, the Committee wishes to reiterate, as it observed in its General Comment 14[23], that "it is evident that the designing, *testing*, manufacture, possession and deployment of nuclear weapons are among the greatest threats to the right to life which confront mankind today".[5]

6. The Human Rights Committee therefore decides:

(a) that the communication is inadmissible under Article 1 of the Optional Protocol;

(b) that this decision shall be communicated to the State Party, to the authors and to their counsel.

[Adopted in English, French and Spanish, the English text being the original version. Subsequently to be issued also in Arabic, Chinese and Russian as part of the Committee's annual report to the General Assembly.]

[Report: Doc. CCPR/C/57/D/645/1995]

---

[5] General Comment 14[23], adopted on 2 November 1984.

Human rights—Right to property—Confiscation of property in Hungary during Communist period—Confiscation based on racial factors—Post-Communist legislation providing for compensation but not for restitution of property — Whether violation of owner's rights under International Covenant on Civil and Political Rights, 1966

SOMERS v. HUNGARY

(*Communication No 566/1993*)

United Nations Human Rights Committee.[1]   23 *July* 1996

SUMMARY: *The facts*:—The author was an Australian citizen of Hungarian origin. In 1951, the author's parents and a relative had been arrested by the Hungarian Communist state security police and all the family's property and assets had been confiscated by the Hungarian Government. A report dated 1952 confirmed the arrest and confiscation of the property due to their Jewish background and political beliefs. Although the author had received nominal monetary compensation under Hungarian legislation of 1991 (Act XXV) and 1992 (Act XXVI) concerning compensation for expropriation under the former Communist period, he had been unable to recover his family's property.

In 1993, the author submitted a communication to the Human Rights Committee, contending that the new legislation had failed to distinguish between cases where the expropriation had been the consequence of breaches of the International Covenant on Civil and Political Rights, 1966 and the majority of cases where the expropriation had been the result of the nationalization of private property during the Communist regime. The author also claimed that the new legislation was discriminatory and that, by rejecting restitution in favour of nominal monetary compensation, the legislation also gave continuing effect to these expropriations regardless of whether they had been linked, in the past, to violations of the Covenant. As victims of political persecution under the former Communist regime, the author claimed that he and his mother faced particular disadvantages under Hungarian law and practice because the tenants currently occupying the residential property in Hungary enjoyed an option to buy their home from the Hungarian Government on a priority basis. Hungary argued that the communication was inadmissible *ratione temporis*, as the events had occurred prior to the date of entry into force of the Optional Protocol for Hungary.

In March 1995, the communication was declared admissible in so far as it appeared to raise issues under Article 26 of the Covenant.

Held:—There had been no breach of Article 26, nor of any other provision of the Covenant.

---

[1] For the composition of the Committee, see p. 254, note 1. Pursuant to Rule 85 of the Rules of Procedure, Committee member Tamás Bán (Hungary) did not participate in the examination of the communication.

(1) Although the right to property was not protected under the Covenant, confiscation of private property or failure by a State Party to pay compensation for such confiscation could still have entailed a breach of the Covenant if the relevant act or omission had been based on discriminatory grounds in violation of Article 26 of the Covenant (pp. 274-5).

(2) The Hungarian legislation of 1991 (Act XXV) contained objective compensation criteria which were applied equally and without discrimination to individuals in the author's situation. As there was no right to property under the Covenant, it did not protect the right to restoration of confiscated property. Furthermore, if a State Party provided compensation for nationalization or expropriation on equal terms, it did not discriminate against those whose property had been expropriated or nationalized. The compensation criteria in the 1991 legislation were both objective and reasonable (pp. 275-6).

(3) The criteria for the privatization of former State-owned residential property in the 1993 legislation (Act LXXVIII) were objective. The fact that the current tenants of former State-owned property were given priority in the privatization sale of such property was not unreasonable. Furthermore, if the former owners were compensated on equal and non-discriminatory terms, the interplay between the 1991 and 1993 legislation could be deemed compatible with Article 26 of the Covenant. The privatization legislation had not been applied in a discriminatory manner with respect to the author's case (p. 276).

The following is the text of the views of the Committee:

Views under Article 5, paragraph 4, of the Optional Protocol

1. The author of the communication is Ivan Somers, an Australian citizen of Hungarian origin currently residing in Edgecliff, New South Wales, Australia. He submits the complaint on his and his mother's behalf, and alleges violations by Hungary of Articles 14, 18, 19, 21, 22, 24 and 26 of the International Covenant on Civil and Political Rights. The Optional Protocol entered into force for Hungary on 7 December 1988.

The facts as submitted by the author

2.1 In March 1951, the author's parents and his maternal grandmother were arrested by the Hungarian communist state security police (AVH). They were taken to the AVH headquarters in Budapest, interrogated over a period of four weeks and forced to sign false confessions which, according to the author, had been prepared well in advance. The author's parents were then interned, without trial, at the prison of Kistarcsa, on the pretext that they had failed to inform on the author's grandmother, who had allegedly given a parcel of clothing to a Russian officer, to take to her son then living in Vienna.

2.2 According to the author, the true reason for the arrest only became known in 1992, when he was able to obtain a copy of a report drawn up in 1952 by the local branch of the AVH in the town where his parents had lived (Reference No 23-5354/52). This report had been addressed to the AVH headquarters in Budapest.

2.3 The report charged the author's parents with being opponents to the Communist Party. It identified the author's father as an influential member of the Social Democratic Party, which was then being "liquidated". The report further singled out his parents as members of the local Jewish community with alleged "Zionist connections". The author submits that in the early 1950s, any such accusation was sufficient to cause someone's imprisonment without trial.

2.4 The author refers in particular to paragraph 3 of the report, which confirms that following his parents' arrest, all the family's property and assets were confiscated by the local governmental authorities. These expropriations pre-date the nationalization of private property in Hungary. The difference is said to be demonstrated by the fact that in spite of the nationalization of land and property under the Communist regime, many Hungarians were allowed to keep their home. In the case of the author's parents, however, their home in a two-storey apartment building in the town of Szekesfehervar, which belonged to the father of Mr Somers, was confiscated and immediately occupied by the secretary of the local branch of the Communist Party.

2.5 The author's mother and grandmother were released in August 1953, following an amnesty decreed after the death of Stalin. His father died in prison under circumstances that, to date, remain largely unexplained.

2.6 Since 1953, the author's mother has made numerous attempts to recuperate her former home. These attempts have continued after she emigrated to Australia. Local government authorities in Hungary have rejected her claim, despite a gradual move, in Hungary, to restitute property seized under the Communist regime to their former owners.

The complaint

3.1 In 1991, the Hungarian Parliament was called upon to consider the status of properties expropriated during the Communist period. In adopting new legislation, the State Party has failed, in the author's opinion, to distinguish between such cases where the expropriation was the consequence of breaches of the Covenant and the majority of cases where the expropriation had been the result of the national-ization of private property.

3.2 It is submitted that by rejecting restitution of property in favour of what amounts to no more than nominal monetary compensation—worth approximately 2 per cent of the current market value of the property seized by the State—the new legislation gives continuing effect to these expropriations, regardless of whether they were linked, in the past, to violations of the Covenant.

3.3 The author submits that his family's assets were seized by the State Party in violation of Articles 14, 18, 19, 21, 22, 24 and 26 of the Covenant (i.e. before the widespread nationalization programme in Hungary). He contends that the only proper course for Hungary would be to restitute those assets which were obtained by the State through extra-legal or illegal means. The current Government's failure to restitute property obtained by such means is said to amount to its endorsing Covenant breaches committed during the Communist period.

The State Party's observations and the author's comments
4.1 In its submission under Rule 91 of the Rules of Procedure, dated 31 March 1994, the State Party contends that as the events complained of occurred prior to the date of entry into force of the Optional Protocol for Hungary, the communication should be deemed inadmissible *ratione temporis*. In this context, the State Party refers to the 1969 Vienna Convention on the Law of Treaties, and in particular to its Article 28 laying down the principle of non-retroactivity of treaties.

4.2 The State Party emphasizes that it has always expressed "its deepest sympathy with victims of violations of human rights committed under the previous regime . . . It has been and remains committed to provide these victims with moral support and, in accordance with the relevant legislative acts, financial compensation to the victims."

5.1 In his comments, Mr Somers reiterates that his parents were expropriated and persecuted on the basis of their social background and their political beliefs. He provides a certificate dated 6 July 1993 from the Hungarian Indemnification and Compensation Authority, in which the State Party acknowledges that his mother was wrongfully imprisoned; a letter dated 7 July 1993 from the same Authority acknowledges that the death of his father had resulted from the unlawful action of government agents.

5.2 To the author, the political nature of the expropriation of his family's home and assets is demonstrated by the fact that it occurred prior to the adoption of Law-Decree No 4 of 1952 on the nationalization of private property. He adds that by Act 1027 of 1963, the then Government of Hungary allowed a number of former owners of real estate to request the annulment of an expropriation order, with the possibility of restitution. To the application of the author's mother, the authorities replied, however, that she did not come within the scope of application of Act 1027 and that, as a former internee, her former house in Szekesfehervar could not be restituted to her.

5.3 In 1991, the Constitutional Court of Hungary (*Alkotmánybiroság*) quashed Law-Decree 4 of 1952 as unconstitutional. The author notes, however, that the decision apparently did *not* affect expropriations carried out pursuant to the Decree.

5.4 Regarding the State Party's *ratione temporis* argument, the author reiterates that his case refers to action taken by the State Party since the ratification of the Covenant and the Optional Protocol. He notes that in contrast to legislation adopted in the former Czechoslovakia and in Germany, where the rightful owners of property formerly seized by the State may claim restitution, Hungarian legislation passed in 1991 (Act XXV) and in 1992 (Act XXVI) merely recognizes the right of owners to nominal compensation and excludes restitution, except for the property of religious orders. Accordingly, the legislation is said to sanction the State Party's continued ownership of property confiscated during the Communist period.

5.5 Mr Somers contends that as victims of political persecution under the former regime, he and his mother face particular disadvantages under current Hungarian law and practice relating to the privatization of (State) property. He explains that the tenants currently occupying residential property in Hungary enjoy an option to buy their home from the local government authority on a priority basis.

5.6 The author submits that by restricting the rights of former owners, including those dispossessed on account of political persecution, to compensation, the 1991 legislation has enabled the Hungarian Government to reap substantial profits from the sale, at current market prices, of property seized under the Communist regime. Moreover, owners are barred from claiming even the proceeds of the sale of their property by the State. He encloses a letter dated 21 June 1994 from a Government agency acting on behalf of the City Council of Szekesfehervar, which states that notwithstanding the proceedings before the Human Rights Committee, the agency will proceed with the sale of the author's family home.

5.7 The author further points out that the 1991 legislation does not distinguish between nationalization of private property by legislation from confiscation of the property of former political prisoners, such as the author's parents. He notes that the 1991 legislation obliges the State to pay compensation in the form of vouchers, whose value is calculated by reference to an (arbitrarily chosen) amount per square metre of the building. Under the legislation, he received vouchers with a face value of Forint 333,000 in full settlement for his parents' former home, an amount equivalent to approximately US $3,330. The author adds that these vouchers traded on the Hungarian stock exchange for only 42 per cent of their face value (the equivalent of US $1,400) and have since become worthless, as they have ceased to be listed due to lack of demand.

5.8 The discriminatory nature of the regulation is said to be further demonstrated by the fact that the current occupants of residential properties who enjoy a "buy first option" may insist that the *total* face value of the vouchers circulated in accordance with the 1991 and 1992 legislation on partial compensation is set off against the purchase price of their home. The author therefore concludes that under the *current* legislation, he is in a substantially worse position than someone who, though dispossessed of legal ownership by the 1952 Law Decree, was able to remain in his/her home as a tenant.

5.9 The author rejects as "totally inconsistent with the State Party's current status as a party to the Covenant and the Protocol" the possibility that it may now derive potential financial benefits from the sale of his family's property. He requests the Committee to seek restitution of his property or, alternatively, the *full proceeds* of its sale.

The Committee's admissibility decision

6.1 During its 53rd session, the Committee considered the admissibility of the communication. It noted the author's claim relating to the confiscation of his family's property in 1951 and observed that irrespective of the fact that these events occurred prior to the entry into force of the Optional Protocol for Hungary, the right to property was not protected under the Covenant. The allegation concerning a violation of the author's and his mother's right to property *per se* was thus inadmissible *ratione materiae*, under Article 3 of the Optional Protocol.

6.2 Regarding the author's claims under Articles 14, 18, 19, 21, 22 and 24, the Committee noted that the author had failed to substantiate, for purposes of admissibility, how State Party action prior to the entry into force of the Optional Protocol for Hungary had continued to produce effects which *in themselves* would constitute a violation of any of these rights after the entry into force. These claims were deemed inadmissible *ratione temporis*.

6.3 As to the author's further complaint that legislation on compensation for expropriation during the Communist period adopted in 1991 and 1992 (i.e. *after* the entry into force of the Optional Protocol for Hungary) was discriminatory, in that it placed himself and his mother, as victims of political persecution during the Communist period, in a significantly more unfavourable position than those expropriated under Law Decree 4 of 1952, the Committee noted that the State Party had not addressed this point and merely argued that *all* of the claims are inadmissible *ratione temporis*. It recalled that the State Party's obligations under the Covenant applied as of the date of entry into force for the State Party. There was, however, another issue as to when the Committee's competence to consider complaints about violations of the Covenant under the Optional Protocol was: it was the Committee's jurisprudence under the Optional Protocol that it cannot consider alleged violations of the Covenant which occurred before the entry into force of the Protocol for the State Party, unless the violations complained of continue after the entry into force of the Protocol. A continuing violation must be interpreted as an affirmation, by act or clear implication, of the previous violations of the State Party.

6.4 It was correct that Mr Somers and his mother did not fall under the terms of the State Party's 1991-1992 legislation concerning compensation for expropriation during the Communist period. The Committee noted that this was the crux of their claim under Article 26: they considered that the omission of a clearly cognizable group of individuals—i.e. those who were expropriated on the basis of political opinion and/or social origin prior to the Law Decree of 1952—from the scope of this legislation constituted discrimination contrary to Article 26, and that their situation should have been addressed in relevant legislative provisions. It concluded that this issue was based on acts of the State Party which occurred after the entry into force of the Optional Protocol for Hungary and believed that it required examination under Article 26 of the Covenant.

6.5 On 15 March 1995, the Committee therefore declared the communication admissible in so far as it appeared to raise issues under Article 26 of the Covenant.

State Party's observations on the merits and author's comments thereon

7.1 In its submission under Article 4, paragraph 2, of the Optional Protocol, dated 31 January 1996, the State Party recalls that for compensation for expropriation under the former Communist regime, three Parliament Acts have thus far been enacted. Of these,[2] only Act XXV of 1991 is relevant to the author's case. Its Section 1, Subsection 2, stipulates that compensation is due to those individuals whose property had been seized through application of regulations enacted after 8 June 1949. Compensation is partial, and its sum total must be calculated on the basis of a chart contained in Section 4, Subsection 2, of the Act. Regarding the modalities of compensation, Section 5, Subsection 1, provides that compensation vouchers will be issued for the total amount of compensation. Under Subsection 2, these vouchers are bearer securities, transferable, and their face value is the sum total of debt owed by the State. Under Section 7, Subsection 1, the State must ensure that bearers of such vouchers may use them under the conditions laid down in the Act (a) for purchasing property etc. sold during privatization of State property, or (b) for obtaining farmland.

7.2 As to privatization legislation, the State Party indicates that in as far as the author's case is concerned, Act LXXVIII of 1993 on the privatization of residential property is relevant. Its Section 45 confers on tenants of apartments in State or local government ownership the right to purchase the property they occupy. The State Party emphasizes that the right to purchase an apartment is conferred upon tenants

---

[2] Act XXV of 1991, Act XXVI of 1992, Act XXXII of 1992.

irrespective of his/her being a past victim of violation of the right to property or other rights. Nor is the right to buy the apartment dependent on the tenant's other status, such as residence or citizenship; it is immaterial whether the tenant was or was not the owner of the property he/she currently rents before the extensive nationalization of property in the 1940s and 1950s. The *only* criterion for eligibility to buy the property is that the buyer is currently the tenant.

7.3 As to the claim under Article 26, the State Party dismisses the author's contention that as victims of political persecution under the former political regime, he and his mother face specific disadvantages since, contrary to tenants currently occupying property and enjoy[ing] an option to buy the same from the Government at attractive prices, they cannot do the same. It notes that the reason why the author and his mother cannot recover their old property is factual not legal, as they are not tenants of any residential property in State or local government ownership. In the State Party's view, the difference in treatment of two different groups of people—tenants and non-tenants —and the difference in treatment of these two groups by law is based on objective criteria and is reasonable in the sense that tenants have, in the practice of the Hungarian tenancy system, always contributed financially to the maintenance of their apartments or invested money in those apartments so as to increase their comfort. The difference in treatment thus cannot be said to constitute prohibited discrimination.

7.4 In respect of the author's claim that, in the 1991 and 1992 legislation on compensation for past violations of property rights, Hungary failed to distinguish between cases in which expropriation was the result of breaches of the ICCPR and the majority of cases where expropriation had resulted from the nationalization of private property, the State Party points out that at the material time (i.e. in the early 1950s), no clear-cut distinction between confiscation or national-ization on political or other grounds existed in Hungary: at the time, nationalization provided for by law and confiscation pronounced by court or administrative orders served a political end, namely to dispossess the wealthy and others considered as opponents of the regime. Thus, in the State Party's opinion, the author's starting point is incorrect. In this context, it notes that the transfer of the author's parents' home into State property was, contrary to Mr Somers' assertion, precisely based on Law Decree 4 of 1952, entitled "[O]n the transfer of certain buildings into State ownership". The extract from the land register and decision No 21-1122543-00 15598 on the author's compensation show that Mr Somers' father was dispossessed on the basis of Law Decree No 4.

7.5 The State Party argues that the wording of Section 1 of this Law Decree clearly shows that the Decree was motivated by the intention to dispossess owners of real estate on political grounds. As Mr Somers

SOMERS *v.* HUNGARY 271

was compensated for the deprivation of his father's property pursuant to Law Decree 4, the State Party argues that it cannot be said that the author suffered harm since the legislation on compensation failed to take into account that his father had been dispossessed of his property as a result of political persecution. Hence, this claim is said to be unfounded.

7.6 The State Party concedes that the value of the vouchers the author was given as compensation was indeed lower than the value of his father's home. But, the State Party adds, Hungarian compensation legislation only provides for partial compensation of past grievances, as full compensation cannot be granted owing to the "huge number of claims and the difficult economic situation of the country". Such exceptions as exist to this rule do not in any event apply to the author's case. The calculation of compensation due is based on objective criteria: pursuant to Section 4 of Act XXV of 1991, the same criteria are applied to all applicants. Moreover, all decisions on compensation are subject to appeal if the applicant believes that the law was not applied correctly to his case. The State Party notes that on the basis of available information, the author did not appeal against the decision on compensation.

7.7 As to the allegation that the Hungarian compensation legislation is discriminatory because those who are authorized to buy the residential property they occupy can set off the total face value of the vouchers against the purchase price whereas the author, as a non-tenant, cannot do so, the State notes that while this possibility is indeed provided for under Section 7, Subsection 1, of Act XXV of 1991, there can be no question of prohibited discriminatory treatment. In the State Party's view, the author simply compares two groups of people without in fact taking into account the substantial difference between the situation of the two groups—i.e. those who are the tenants of the apartment against the purchase price of which vouchers can be set off, and those who are neither occupants nor tenants of any apartment in State or local government ownership. For the State Party, "not taking into account this difference leads to an arbitrary comparison of two situations under Article 26 of the Covenant". An issue under Article 26 would only arise if Hungarian law treated occupants or tenants of State-owned dwellings differently, allowing some to set off vouchers and denying others the possibility to do so. As this is not the author's situation, the State Party concludes that he is not discriminated against, as he is not the tenant of any residential property to be sold under the privatization legislation.

7.8 In conclusion, and by reference to paragraph 13 of the Committee's General Comment 18[37] on Article 26,[3] the State Party

---

[3] The General Comment states that not every differentiation in treatment constitutes discrimination, if the differentiation criteria are reasonable and objective and if the aim is to achieve a legitimate purpose under the Covenant.

argues that the Hungarian legislation on compensation of past grievances and on privatization of residential property, as well as their application to the author's case, is in compliance with the provisions of Article 26 of the Covenant.

8.1 In his comments, the author notes that the State Party itself admits that confiscation of residential property under the former regime violated the Covenant, as the nationalization legislation and confiscation orders served the purpose of dispossessing the wealthy and opponents to the regime (see paragraph 7.4 above). That being the case, the State Party should have provided an "effective remedy" to the victims of such violations. The author refers to the Committee's Views on communication 516/1992,[4] where it was held that the appropriate remedy in respect of unlawful compensation of property "may be compensation if the property in question cannot be returned". He recalls that his communication referred *inter alia* to Hungary's failure (in contrast to laws adopted by Germany or the Czech Republic and Slovakia) to return property confiscated from individuals during the Communist period. No explanations were offered by the State Party about its failure to return residential property to its rightful owners: Mr Somers observes that the State Party still *could*, if it wanted, return his father's home to him, subject to the protection of the current tenants, as the property exists and former ownership is not disputed.

8.2 As to the amount of compensation awarded by the State Party, the author recalls that the sum payable for notional losses in excess of Hungarian Forint (HUF) 200,000 (approx. US $2,000) is progressively reduced by applying the compensation scale in Section 4, Subsection 2, of Act XXV of 1991. Compensation is reduced to 10 per cent for any part of the loss over HUF 500,000. For the author, this "scale of compensation" displays the same ideological prejudice as Law Decree 4 of 1952, i.e. to dispossess the wealthy and others considered opponents of the regime. The negative effect on someone in Mr Somers' situation, it is pointed out, is compounded by the fact that there is no compensation in respect of the land component of the property, loss of income from rent, or confiscation of the contents of someone's home. That compensation is paid in vouchers rather than cash, and that only "current tenants" of residential property in State ownership may use vouchers to buy property, contrary to the former owners of the property who were displaced from it in violation of their rights, is said to further underline the discriminatory nature of the compensation legislation.

8.3 Mr Somers challenges the justification of the State Party's argument that the face value of the vouchers given to him is lower than the value of his late father's property because of the "difficult

⁴ *Simunek et al.* v. *Czech Republic*, Views adopted on 19 July 1995.

economic situation of the country". He notes that Hungary's economic situation is no worse than that of the Czech Republic or Slovakia, which have restituted property to their rightful owners: the State Party's obligation to provide for adequate compensation arises from the State Party's refusal to restitute property it confiscated. Its current economic situation is irrelevant considering that the income it has derived from the property since 1952, i.e. net proceeds from rent for more than four decades and the proceeds from the privatization sale of the property, is sufficient to cover adequate compensation. Mr Somers deplores that the State Party has failed to address this part of his claim.

8.4 The author rejects the State Party's contention that he did not appeal against the compensation decision as misleading, since the 1991 legislation (Act XXV) does not provide for an avenue of appeal in respect of the criteria used to calculate the amount of the author's compensation.

8.5 Mr Somers asserts that the State Party "conveniently ignores" his claim that as victims of political persecution during the Communist period, he and his mother are faced with addition[al]—discriminatory—disadvantages under the 1991 and 1993 legislation. Thus, Act XXV of 1991 gives no remedy or compensation for the violation inherent in his and his mother's removal from their apartment. Moreover, Section 45 of Act LXXVIII of 1993 gives continuing effect to this removal by restricting the participation in the privatization of all State-owned residential property to "current tenants". The discriminatory effect of Section 45 is allegedly reinforced by Section 7, Subsection 1, of Act XXV of 1991, which confers on "current tenants" of residential property an exclusive right to use compensation vouchers introduced under the 1991 legislation to purchase the property from the local authority.

8.6 The author dismisses as absurd the State Party's contention that it is both fair and reasonable that current tenants should participate in the privatization of residential property on a priority basis as tenants have contributed to the maintenance and improvement of their apartments during their tenancy. To the author, this is tantamount to the State Party in fact confirming the violations that continue to affect him and his mother *as a result of political persecution* during the Communist period, as the sole reason for their not being the tenants or occupants of their apartment is their removal from said apartment in 1951 and the sequence of violations which finally made them leave Hungary. The author moreover recalls that his late father's entitlement to the apartment was not based on tenancy; hence, to stipulate tenancy as a precondition for entitlement to participation in the privatization of the apartment is wholly unreasonable.

8.7 In respect of the latter argument, the author explains that there are two kinds of residential property in Hungary: unencumbered freehold properties and properties "affected", i.e. encumbered by the rights of current tenants. In practice, under Act LXXVIII of 1993, current tenants of State-owned property can buy their apartment/ home from the local authority for less than half the current unencumbered freehold value of the property. As the author cannot, under Section 45 of Act LXXVIII of 1993, participate in the privatization of residential property, he would have, in order to buy an apartment comparable to the one he and his family occupied in 1951, [to] pay the unencumbered freehold value, that is approximately double the amount paid for the property by the current tenants. This is said to be another discriminatory element in the State Party's legislation.

8.8 The author summarizes the discriminatory elements and disadvantages he and his mother are facing under the 1991 and 1993 legislation as follows:

(a) absence of any remedy in respect of the unlawful deprivation of their right to occupy their apartment, i.e. forced displacement from their home;

(b) absence of any remedy in respect of the confiscation of the contents of their apartment;

(c) exclusion, under Section 45 of Act LXXVIII of 1993, from the right to participate in the privatization of residential property;

(d) exclusion, under Section 7, Subsection 1, of Act XXV of 1991, from the right to use the compensation vouchers they received as nominal compensation for the expropriation of the author's father's home to purchase residential property;

(e) and, because of the exclusions referred to in (c) and (d) above, the authors were forced to sell their compensation vouchers on the Hungarian stock exchange where they traded for less than half of their face value.

The author suggests that so as to redress the discrimination inherent in his exclusion, under the 1993 legislation, from any right to participate in the privatization of their former home, the State Party should award them (at least) the full proceeds of the sale of their former apartment.

Examination on the merits

9.1 The Human Rights Committee has considered the present communication in the light of all the information made available to it by the parties, as provided in Article 5, paragraph 1, of the Optional Protocol.

9.2 The present communication was declared admissible only in so far as it may raise issues under Article 26 of the Covenant. As the Committee explained in its admissibility decision, the right to property as such is not protected under the Covenant. However, confiscation of private property or failure by a State Party to pay compensation for such confiscation could still entail a breach of the Covenant if the relevant act or omission was based on discriminatory grounds in violation of Article 26 of the Covenant.

9.3 The principal issue before the Committee is whether the application of Act XXV of 1991 and of Act LXXVIII of 1993 to the author and his mother resulted in a violation of their right to equality before the law and to equal protection of the law. The author contends that these laws, in their effect, confirm the earlier discriminatory confiscation of his father's property. The Committee notes that the confiscation itself is not at issue here, but rather the alleged discriminatory effect of the compensation law on the author and his mother.

9.4 The Committee must first determine whether the application of the State Party's compensation legislation, regulated by Act XXV of 1991, to the authors' case, was discriminatory. As noted in the previous paragraph, the *only* issue is whether the award of less than full compensation for the loss of the author's property, under Act XXV of 1991, is contrary to Article 26. The Committee observes that Act XXV contains objective compensation criteria, which are applied equally and without discrimination to individuals in the author's situation.

9.5 As to whether the compensation criteria and calculation tables for compensation in Act XXV are reasonable, the Committee has noted the author's argument that the value of the bearer securities in [the] form of vouchers he received as compensation differs de facto, depending on whether the bearer is the tenant of State-owned residential property or not, as only the former can use the vouchers under the conditions of Section 7, Subsection 1, of the Act (i.e. may offset them fully against the purchase price of the property). On the basis of the material available to it, the Committee does not share this reading of Section 7 of Act XXV.

9.6 The corollary of the fact that the Covenant does not protect the right to property is that there is no right, as such, to have (expropriated or nationalized) property restituted. If a State Party to the Covenant provides compensation for nationalization or expropriation on equal terms, it does not discriminate against those whose property was expropriated or nationalized. The Committee is of the opinion that Section 7 of Act XXV of 1991 provides for compensation on equal terms. Under Section 7(1), individuals compensated by vouchers but not tenants of any residential property may set off the full face value of their vouchers against the price of *any* property, shares or business shares sold during the privatization of former State-owned property. This means that *if* the author wanted to buy former State-owned residential property, he would be able to offset the full face value of the vouchers he received. Similarly, *if* he decided to invest in other property, such as business shares of former State-owned companies, he would also be able to offset the full face value of the vouchers. *Only* if he wanted to redeem his vouchers on the open market because he is not interested in any property other than his former apartment will he receive less than the nominal value of the vouchers.

9.7 On the basis of the considerations in paragraphs 9.5 and 9.6 above, the Committee considers that the compensation criteria in Act XXV are both objective *and* reasonable.

9.8 The Committee has further examined whether Article 9 of Act XXV of 1991 and the privatization legislation of 1993 (Act LXXVIII) are compatible with the requirements of Article 26. Under Section 9 of Act XXV, if the tenant does not exercise himself/herself the "buy first option" to purchase the residential property he/she occupies, the former owner of the property may purchase it and, in so doing, may offset the full value of the vouchers he/she received against the purchase price. As in the case of Act XXV, the criteria for the privatization of former State-owned property in Act LXXVIII of 1993 are objective. The State Party has justified the (exclusionary) require-ment that current tenants of former State-owned residential property have a "buy first option" even vis-à-vis the former owner of the property with the argument that tenants contribute to the maintenance of the property through improvements of their own. The Committee does not consider that the fact of giving the current tenants of former State-owned property priority in the privatization sale of such property is in itself unreasonable; the interests of the "current tenants", who may have been occupying the property for years, are deserving of protection. If the former owners are, moreover, compensated on equal and non-discriminatory terms (paragraph 9.6), the interplay between Act XXV of 1991 and of Act LXXVIII of 1993 can be deemed compatible with Article 26 of the Covenant; with respect to the application of the privatization legislation to the author's case, the Committee does not dispose of sufficient elements to conclude that its criteria were applied in a discriminatory manner.

10. The Human Rights Committee, acting under Article 5, paragraph 4, of the Optional Protocol to the International Covenant on Civil and Political Rights, is of the view that the facts as found by the Committee do not reveal a breach of Article 26 or of any other provision of the Covenant.

[Adopted in English, French and Spanish, the English text being the original version. Subsequently to be issued also in Arabic, Chinese and Russian as part of the Committee's annual report to the General Assembly.]

[Report: Doc. CCPR/C/57/D/566/1993]

Human rights—Right to a fair trial—Trial of terrorist suspect before special criminal court—Ireland—Whether court possessing sufficient independence — Procedures followed — Whether communication inadmissible — Inadmissibility *ratione temporis*—Trial occurring before entry into force of human rights instruments for Respondent State—Concept of continuing violation—Requirement of exhaustion of domestic remedies

International tribunals—United Nations Human Rights Committee — Competence — Domestic remedies rule — Failure to exhaust domestic remedies—Whether communication inadmissible *ratione temporis*—Date of entry into force of International Covenant on Civil and Political Rights, 1966 and Optional Protocol for Respondent State

HOLLAND v. IRELAND

(*Communication No 593/1994*)

United Nations Human Rights Committee.[1]   25 *October* 1996

SUMMARY: *The facts:*—The author, an Irish citizen, was arrested in April 1989 under Section 30 of the Offences Against the State Act 1939 and charged with possession of explosives for unlawful purposes. Shortly thereafter, together with four co-defendants, he was tried by a Special Criminal Court, found guilty and sentenced to ten years' imprisonment. In May 1990 the Court of Appeal reduced his sentence. He was released in September 1994. At his trial before the Special Criminal Court the author had pleaded guilty, allegedly on the advice of his lawyer that he would have otherwise risked a heavier sentence. The author maintained that there was no evidence against him other than an uncorroborated police statement containing an admission.

On 8 June 1994 the author submitted a communication to the Human Rights Committee, claiming that his trial had been unfair, as the Special Criminal Court was not an independent and impartial tribunal and therefore violated Article 14(1) of the International Covenant on Civil and Political Rights, 1966. He complained that the Government of Ireland decided which cases would go before the Special Courts, and the members of these courts were not necessarily members of the judiciary. The author also claimed that he was discriminated against within the prison system as he "fought for his rights".

Ireland argued that the communication was inadmissible *ratione temporis*, as the author's complaint related largely to his trial in June 1989, before the Covenant and its Optional Protocol entered into force for Ireland (on 8 March 1990). Ireland also argued that the communication was inadmissible

[1] For the composition of the Committee, see p. 254, note 1.

for failure to exhaust domestic remedies, and outlined a number of possible avenues that the author could have pursued. The author countered, *inter alia*, that he had not previously been in a position to challenge the matters now being contested, as he was a layman relying on his legal advisers, who had let him down.

In a further submission on the author's claim of discrimination within the prison system, Ireland then argued that decisions as to where the author would serve his sentence were made largely on the basis of his personal and family circumstances and, in any event, did not amount to discrimination. Ireland maintained that the author's communication was inadmissible under Article 3 of the Optional Protocol to the Covenant, and further that it was inadmissible for non-exhaustion of domestic remedies as the author could have challenged his place of imprisonment and his referral to the Special Criminal Court. In response, the author commented, *inter alia*, that his main complaint was the illegality of the Special Criminal Court in that it had been established without Ireland making an application under Article 4(3) of the Covenant.

Held:—(1) The author's communication was not inadmissible *ratione temporis*, as the alleged violations in this case continued, or had continuing effects, after the date at which the Covenant entered into force for Ireland (p. 285).

(2) The communication was inadmissible on the ground of failure to exhaust domestic remedies. The author had not appealed against his conviction, nor objected to the nature of the Special Court at the time, despite being represented by legal counsel throughout. Further, he had not taken proceedings to address the alleged discriminatory treatment of him while he was in prison (pp. 285-6).

The following is the text of the views of the Committee:

Decision on admissibility

1. The author of the communication is Patrick Holland, an Irish citizen, born on 12 March 1939, at the time of submission of the communication serving a prison term in Ireland. He claims to be a victim of a violation by Ireland of Articles 14 and 26 of the Covenant. Both the Covenant and the Optional Protocol entered into force for Ireland on 8 March 1990.

The facts as submitted by the author

2.1 The author was arrested on 6 April 1989 under Section 30 of the Offences against the State Act 1939 and charged with possession of explosives for unlawful purposes. He was tried on 27 June 1989 by a Special Criminal Court, together with four co-defendants, found guilty and sentenced to ten years' imprisonment. On appeal against sentence, the Court of Appeal, on 21 May 1990, reduced the sentence to seven years' imprisonment, considering that the judgment of the Special

Court might give the impression that he was convicted of a more serious charge, namely of possession of explosives for enabling others to endanger life. The author was released from prison on 27 September 1994.

2.2 At the trial before the Special Criminal Court, the author pleaded guilty of the charge, allegedly because his lawyer had told him that "in this court, they are going to believe the police" and that his sentence would be heavier if he would plead not guilty. In this context, the author states that one of his co-accused who pleaded not guilty was indeed sentenced to a longer term of imprisonment.

2.3 The author submits that there was no evidence against him, but that the police claimed that he had admitted to them that he knew about the explosives in his house. No tape recording of the author's alleged confession was provided; he did not sign any confession.

2.4 The author explains that in April 1989, an acquaintance of his, AM, stayed with him in his house, having come from England to inquire into the possibilities of renting a restaurant or pub. On 3 April 1989, they were joined by PW, a friend of AM, who had come to Dublin to attend a court hearing. The author states that he did not know PW before, but that he allowed him to stay at his house. The author, who had his own printing business, worked most of the time, only coming home to sleep or eat. At lunchtime on 6 April 1989, the police raided his house, and arrested him, AM and PW and a fourth acquaintance, a former colleague, who was visiting the author. Explosives were found in a black bag, but the author denies having had knowledge of their presence.

The complaint

3.1 The author claims that the trial against him was unfair, because the Special Criminal Court does not constitute an independent and impartial tribunal, in violation of Article 14, paragraph 1, of the Covenant. In this connection, the author explains that the Irish constitution permits the establishment of "special courts" for the trial of offences in cases where it is determined that the ordinary courts are inadequate to secure the effective administration of justice and the preservation of public peace and order. The author points out that it is the Government who decides which cases are to be brought before a special court. The author quotes from Section 39 of the Offences against the State Act, which provides that members of special courts are appointed and removed at will by the Government. The remuneration, if any, is determined by the Ministry for Finance. Members of special courts need not be members of the judiciary; barristers and solicitors of at least seven years' standing and high-ranking officers of the Defence Forces may also be appointed.

3.2 The author contends that the special courts represent a threat to the equality of treatment of those accused of crimes, because the independence of the members of such courts is not protected. In this context, the author refers to the judgment in his case, which appeared to sentence him for a more serious offence [than] that for which he had been charged.

3.3 The author further alleges that he was discriminated against in the prison system because he "fought for his rights" through the courts in order to have his proper entitlement to parole established. He states that two of his co-accused, who received the same sentence, were moved to an open prison in 1992 and early 1993, whereas the author was only moved to an open prison in the beginning of 1994. The author points out that regular weekend home visits are allowed from an open prison, whereas he was unable to obtain permission to visit his sister in hospital before she died on 22 December 1993; he was granted parole from 22 to 27 December 1993, after she had already died.

State Party's submission and the author's comments

4.1 By submission of 5 December 1994, the State Party argues that the communication is inadmissible *ratione temporis*, since the substance of the author's complaint relates to his trial in the Special Criminal Court on 27 June 1989, that is before the entry into force of the Covenant and its Optional Protocol for Ireland.

4.2 The State Party further argues that the communication is inadmissible for failure to exhaust domestic remedies. The State Party notes that the essence of the author's claim is that he did not receive a fair trial before an independent and impartial tribunal and that he claims that he was innocent of the offences with which he was charged. However, the author withdrew his plea of not guilty, leaving the trial court with no option but to accept his acknowledgement and sentence him accordingly. The State Party submits that he might have been acquitted, had he pleaded not guilty. It contests the author's suggestion that persons tried in the Special Criminal Courts are invariably convicted.

4.3 The State Party further submits that the author failed to request the judges of the Special Court to disqualify themselves on the grounds that they were not independent and impartial. In this connection, the State Party notes that the author, in fact, has not alleged any bias against the judges of the Court which tried him. His argument seems to be that by virtue of the method of appointment and dismissal of the members of the Court a lack of independence and impartiality could arise, not that it did.

4.4 The State Party explains that the Special Court is subject to control through judicial review by the High Court. A person who alleges a breach of the constitution or of natural justice can seek an order from the High Court quashing a decision by the Special Criminal

Court or prohibiting it from acting contrary to the Constitution or to the rules of natural justice. If the author would have had reason to argue that he had not received a fair trial in the Special Court, he could therefore have sought an order of judicial review from the High Court, which he failed to do.

4.5 In this context, the State Party refers to the Supreme Court's decision in the *Eccles* case,[2] where it was held that the Government could not lawfully terminate the appointment of individual members of the Special Court for disagreeing with their decisions. The Court found that whereas the express constitutional guarantees of judicial independence did not apply to the Special Court, it enjoyed a derived guarantee of independence in carrying out its function.

4.6 The State Party also argues that it would have been open to the author to argue at the hearing of his appeal that his conviction was defective by reason of lack of independence of the judges. The State Party notes that the author, however, failed to appeal against his conviction and made no allegation that the Special Court was biased or lacked independence.

4.7 Further, the State Party argues that the author has not shown that he is personally a victim of the violation alleged. The State Party refers to the author's argument that under the applicable legislation the independence of the court cannot be guaranteed. The State Party submits that this is an argument of an *actio popularis*, since the author does not argue that the judges who tried him did in fact lack independence or that they were biased against him, nor does he specify any shortcoming in the proceedings. In this context, the State Party refers to the decision by the European Commission on Human Rights in the *Eccles* case,[3] which found that the Special Court was independent within the meaning of Article 6 of the European Convention.

4.8 The State Party explains that Article 38 of the Constitution provides that special courts may be established by law for the trial of offences in cases where it may be determined in accordance with such law that the ordinary courts are inadequate to secure the effective administration of justice and the preservation of public peace and order. The Offences against the State Act 1939 provides for the establishment of such special courts, if the Government is satisfied that the ordinary courts are inadequate to secure the effective administration of justice and the preservation of public peace and order and publishes a proclamation accordingly. Any such Government proclamation may be annulled by resolution of the Lower House of Parliament. A Special Criminal Court was first established in 1939 and remained in existence until 1962. In 1972, due to the situation arising from the troubles in Northern Ireland, the Special Criminal Court was re-established.

[2] *Eccles* v. *Ireland* [1985] IR 545.
[3] *Eccles et al.* v. *Ireland*, Application No 12839/87, decision of 9 December 1988.

4.9 Section 39 of the Offences against the State Act regulates the appointment of members to the Court. The State Party underlines that with few exceptions the members of the Special Criminal Court since 1972 have been judges of ordinary courts at the times of their appointment, and that since 1986 the Court has been comprised only of serving judges. No members of the Defence Forces have been appointed to the Court since its establishment in 1972.

4.10 Section 40 of the Act provides that the determination of the Special Criminal Court is to be according to the opinion of the majority and that individual opinions are not to be disclosed. Pursuant to Section 44 of the Act convictions or sentences of a Special Criminal Court are subject to appeal to the Court of Criminal Appeal in the same.way as convictions and sentences of the Central Criminal Court. There are no rules of evidence applying to the Special Criminal Court which do not apply to the ordinary courts, apart from provisions permitting the taking of evidence on commission in Northern Ireland.

4.11 Finally, the State Party informs the Committee that the Court before which the author was tried consisted of a judge of the High Court, a judge of the Circuit Court and a District Justice. The State Party adds that it is not aware of any challenge to the members' personal impartiality and independence.

5.1 On 8 February 1995, the author provided his comments on the State Party's submission. He reiterates that members of the Special Court can be dismissed at will by the Government and that there is therefore no guarantee for their independence and impartiality.

5.2 As to the State Party's argument that his communication is inadmissible for non-exhaustion of domestic remedies because he withdrew his plea of not guilty, the author explains that after he had pleaded not guilty, his barrister asked the Court for a short recess. He then came to see him and advised him to plead guilty, since he was before the Special Criminal Court and a not guilty plea would result in a twelve years' sentence. Consequently, he pleaded guilty.

5.3 As regards the State Party's argument that he failed to ask the judges of the trial court to disqualify themselves, that he failed to have the trial proceedings quashed by judicial review and that he failed to appeal against his conviction or to raise the alleged lack of independence of the court as a ground of appeal, the author states that he could not have done any of these things because his own defence counsel had already told him to plead guilty and he himself had not yet learned about United Nations human rights treaties. The author recalls that as a layman he was depending on his legal advisers, who let him down and never raised these issues. In this connection, the author states that he knows of a lot of people who stood up and did not recognize the court and then were sentenced for that alone.

Further submission from the State Party

6.1 Upon request of the Committee, the State Party, in a further submission of 2 July 1996, comments on the admissibility of the author's claim that he had been discriminated against in the prison system, and explains the legislation and practice surrounding the decision to bring the author's case before the Special Criminal Court.

6.2 As regards the author's claim that he is a victim of discrimination, the State Party confirms that the two co-accused who were sentenced to six years' imprisonment were moved to an open prison prior to the completion of their sentences and that the author and one other co-accused remained in a closed institution until their release. The State Party explains further that the co-accused moved to an open prison received the standard 25 per cent remission of their sentences and were released about six months early. The third co-accused spent the duration of his sentence in a high security facility and was released thirty-six days prior to his release date.

6.3 The State Party explains that the author was considered for a transfer to an open prison, but that, since the author had friends and relatives in Dublin, and all the open facilities were outside the Dublin area, it was decided that it would be better if he stayed in a closed institution in Dublin. The author was offered early release from 27 June 1994, that is three months prior to his release date. However, he declined to leave prison as he had nowhere to live. He was subsequently released on 22 September 1994, four days early.

6.4 The State Party submits that transfers from a closed to an open prison are benefits accorded certain prisoners on the basis of their records, home addresses and other relevant considerations, but that it is not a right to which all prisoners are equally entitled. Reference is made to the Judgment of the European Court of Human Rights in the *Ashingdane* case[4] (14/1983/70/106).

6.5 It is further submitted that the author was not treated differently from others, but that the decision to keep the author in a closed institution in Dublin was taken, as were the decisions to transfer two of his co-accused to an open institution outside Dublin, by reference to their personal and family circumstances and were intended to facilitate communication between the detainees and persons close to them. Moreover, it is submitted that, might the Committee nevertheless find that the author was treated differently, this treatment was based on reasonable and objective criteria and did not amount to discrimination.

6.6 The State Party argues that the communication is inadmissible under Article 3 of the Optional Protocol, for being incompatible with the provisions of the Covenant. Further, it is argued that the author's claim is inadmissible for non-exhaustion of domestic remedies, since it

[4 81 *ILR* 107.]

was open to the author to seek judicial review of the order made by the Minister of Justice to transfer him to Whatefield Detention Centre in Dublin and not to an open prison. It was also open to the author to institute proceedings for alleged breach of constitutional rights, since the Constitution in Article 10.1 protects the right of all citizens to be held equal before the law. It is submitted that the author never availed himself of any of the remedies open to him.

7.1 As regards the procedures of deciding whether a case will be tried before a Special Criminal Court, the State Party explains that the Director of Public Prosecutions decides in accordance with law whether a case will be tried by the ordinary Criminal Courts or by the Special Criminal Court under Part V of the Offences against the State Act. The Director is independent of the Government and the police in the discharge of his functions. The Offences against the State Act provides for certain offences to be scheduled under that Act. Where a person is charged with a scheduled offence, the Director of Public Prosecutions, under Section 47(1) of the Act, may have that person brought before the Special Criminal Court to be tried on such offence. The author was charged with possession of explosive substances for an unlawful object, a scheduled indictable offence in accordance with Section 47(1) of the Act.

7.2 A panel of nine judges, appointed by the Government and all being judges of the High Court, Circuit Court or District Court, is available to hear cases in the Special Criminal Court. The designation of members to hear a case is exclusively a matter for the judges of the panel to decide. The State Party strongly refutes any suggestion that the judges of the Special Criminal Court lack independence or would have been biased against the author.

7.3 The State Party explains that the decision to charge the author with the offence in question, as well as the decision to refer the author's case to the Special Criminal Court, was based on an assessment of the available evidence that was made known to the Director of Public Prosecutions by the Irish police.

7.4 The State Party explains that the institution of the Special Criminal Court can be challenged since it is subject to constitutional scrutiny. It is also possible to challenge the constitutionality of various aspects of the legislation relating to the Special Criminal Court. Several such challenges have been undertaken. The author however did not attempt to initiate any proceedings in this respect.

7.5 The State Party explains that it is also possible to challenge the referral of a case to the Special Criminal Court through judicial review of the Director of Public Prosecutions' decision. However, the relevant case-law all relates to situations where the accused had been charged with a non-scheduled offence and the Director decided that he or she be tried before the Special Criminal Court. In availing himself of this remedy, the author would have had to show that the Director of Public Prosecutions had acted with *mala fides*.

7.6 The State Party reiterates that the communication should be declared inadmissible.

Author's comments on the State Party's submission

8.1 In his comments on the State Party's submission, the author emphasizes that his main complaint is that the Special Criminal Court was illegal, because it was set up without making an application under Article 4, paragraph 3, of the Covenant. He contends that there is no escaping a conviction before the Special Court and reiterates that when he pleaded not guilty, his solicitor told him that his sentence would be lower with a guilty plea, upon which he changed his plea.

8.2 The author reiterates that he was not allowed to leave prison in time to visit his dying sister in December 1993, but that he was only given leave after she died, to attend her funeral.

Issues and proceedings before the Committee

9.1 Before considering any claim contained in a communication, the Human Rights Committee must, in accordance with Rule 87 of its Rules of Procedure, decide whether or not it is admissible under the Optional Protocol to the Covenant.

9.2 The Committee has taken note of the State Party's argument that the communication is inadmissible *ratione temporis*. The Committee refers to its prior jurisprudence and reiterates that it is precluded from considering a communication if the alleged violations occurred before the entry into force of the Covenant for the State Party concerned, *unless* the alleged violations continue or have continuing effects which in themselves constitute a violation. The Committee notes that, although the author was convicted and sentenced at first instance in June 1989, that is before the entry into force of the Covenant for Ireland, his appeal was dismissed on 21 May 1990, that is after the entry into force of the Covenant for Ireland, and his imprisonment lasted until August 1994. In the circumstances, the Committee is not precluded *ratione temporis* from considering the author's communication.

9.3 As regards the author's claim that he did not receive a fair trial because he was tried before a Special Criminal Court, which was established in violation of Article 14 of the Covenant, the Committee notes that the author pleaded guilty to the charge against him, that he failed to appeal his conviction, and that he never raised any objections with regard to the impartiality and independence of the Special Court. In this context, the Committee notes that the author was represented by legal counsel throughout and that it appears from the file that he made use of his right to petition the High Court with regard to other issues but did not raise the aforesaid issue. In the circumstances, the

Committee finds that the author has failed to fulfil the requirement of Article 5, paragraph 2(b), of the Optional Protocol, to exhaust available domestic remedies.

9.4 As regards the author's claim that he was discriminated against because he was not transferred to an open prison at the same time as his co-accused, the Committee notes that the State Party has argued, and the author has not denied, that it would have been open to the author to seek judicial review of this decision. In the circumstances, the Committee considers that this claim is also inadmissible under Article 5, paragraph 2(b), of the Optional Protocol, for non-exhaustion of domestic remedies.

10. The Human Rights Committee therefore decides:

(a) that the communication is inadmissible;

(b) that this decision shall be communicated to the State Party and to the author.

[Adopted in English, French and Spanish, the English text being the original version.]

[Report: Doc. CCPR/C/58/D/593/1994]

Human rights — Right to a fair trial — Non-disclosure of prosecution evidence to the defence—Effects—Circumstances in which it is appropriate for international human rights tribunal to question conduct of trial—Actions of defence counsel — International Covenant on Civil and Political Rights, 1966, Article 14

Human rights—Torture, inhuman and degrading treatment —Prison conditions—'Death row' phenomenon—Whether length of time convicted person held on death row amounts to inhuman treatment — Failure of State to investigate conditions in prison—International Covenant on Civil and Political Rights, 1966, Articles 7 and 10

International tribunals — United Nations Human Rights Committee—Procedure—Admissibility of communication —Failure of State to challenge admissibility—Time allowed

to State to provide information on steps taken to give effect to views of Committee

ADAMS v. JAMAICA

(Communication No 607/1994)

United Nations Human Rights Committee.[1]   30 *October* 1996

SUMMARY: *The facts:*—The author of the communication, a Jamaican citizen, was convicted of murder on the grounds that he induced an unidentified gunman to shoot a security guard, although the gunman in fact killed another person. The author was initially sentenced to death, but, in November 1994, after the present communication had been submitted, his sentence was commuted. His appeal to the Court of Appeal in Jamaica and his petition for leave to appeal to the Judicial Committee of the Privy Council had both been dismissed.

During the course of the trial, the security guard referred to an incriminating comment made by the author, although he had not referred to this comment at the preliminary inquiry, nor had it been disclosed to the defence prior to the murder trial. The author claimed that non-disclosure of the security guard's statement to the defence prior to the trial had violated the author's rights under Article 14(1), (2), (3)(b) and (e) of the International Covenant on Civil and Political Rights, 1966. The author also contended that, had he known of the security guard's evidence, he would have called certain witnesses to testify on his behalf. In addition, the author maintained that the trial judge, in his summing up, had misdirected the jury as to the proper approach to be taken on the evidence and that this failure amounted to a denial of justice. The author also claimed that he had been seriously ill-treated during pre-trial detention and while in prison. Complaints about his ill-treatment had been made, among others, to the Jamaica Council for Human Rights and the Parliamentary Ombudsman of Jamaica. The author had also been held on death row for over three and a half years before his death sentence had been commuted, and he claimed this violated the decision of the Privy Council in *Pratt and Morgan.*[2] The author claimed that his ill-treatment, his extended stay on death row and the general conditions in which he was held amounted to violations of Articles 7 and 10(1) of the Covenant.

In its observations, Jamaica did not specifically address the admissibility of the communication but disputed its merits. Jamaica maintained that the non-disclosure of the security guard's statement could have been challenged by counsel at the trial; that the author's witnesses were available to him, had he chosen to call them; and that the alleged misdirection to the jury by the trial judge was a matter for the appellate courts, rather than the Committee. Jamaica therefore denied that Article 14 had been violated. As regarded the

---

[1] For the composition of the Committee, see p. 254, note 1. Pursuant to Rule 85 of the Rules of Procedure, Committee member Laurel Francis (Jamaica) did not participate in the examination of the communication.

[2] *Pratt and Morgan* v. *Attorney-General of Jamaica*, 98 *ILR* 335.

claim of ill-treatment, Jamaica noted that the author was taken to a doctor while in police custody, and undertook to investigate the author's treatment in prison. Jamaica contended, as regarded the "death row phenomenon", that *Pratt and Morgan* had not established that incarceration on death row for a specific period of time constituted cruel and inhuman treatment. Each case had to be examined on its own facts.

Held:—(1) The author had exhausted domestic remedies for the purposes of the Optional Protocol. Further, Jamaica had not addressed the admissibility of the communication but had commented on the merits, and the Committee therefore proceeded to examine the case on its merits (p. 297).

(2) As regarded allegations of irregularities in the court proceedings, particularly the judge's instructions to the jury, such matters were largely for the Jamaican appellate courts. In that respect, therefore, the communication was inadmissible under Article 3 of the Optional Protocol (p. 297).

(3) The Committee found admissible the remaining claims of the author (p. 297).

(4) There had not been a violation of Articles 7 and 10 as regarded the length of the author's detention on death row, since, without further compelling circumstances, this did not *per se* constitute cruel, inhuman or degrading treatment in violation of Article 7 of the Covenant (pp. 297-8).

(5) There had been a violation of Articles 7 and 10(1) of the Covenant as regarded the author's treatment both during pre-trial detention and later in prison. Jamaica had not denied the author's allegation of ill-treatment in detention, and had promised to investigate his allegation concerning his treatment in prison, but had failed to do so (p. 298).

(6) However, there had been no violation of Article 14 in relation to the non-disclosure of the security guard's statement, or the absence at the author's trial of his alibi witnesses. Counsel had chosen not to address those issues, and the Committee would not question counsel's professional judgment, except where it was obviously incompatible with the interests of justice (pp. 298-9).

The Committee gave Jamaica ninety days in which to provide it with information on measures taken to give effect to the Committee's views (p. 299).

The following is the text of the views of the Committee:

Views under Article 5, paragraph 4, of the Optional Protocol

1. The author of the communication is Michael Adams, a Jamaican citizen who, at the time of submission of his complaint, was awaiting execution at St Catherine District Prison, Jamaica. He claims to be a victim of violations by Jamaica of Articles 7, 10, paragraph 1, and 14, paragraphs 1, 2, 3(b) and (e), of the International Covenant on Civil and Political Rights. He is represented by counsel. The author's death sentence was commuted on 14 November 1994.

The facts as submitted by the author

2.1 On 7 March 1991, the author was convicted of murder in the Kingston Home Circuit Court and sentenced to death. He applied for leave to appeal against conviction and sentence; on 24 February 1992, the Court of Appeal of Jamaica, treating the application for leave to appeal as the hearing of the appeal, dismissed the author's appeal. On 4 November 1993, the author's petition for special leave to appeal to the Judicial Committee of the Privy Council was dismissed. With this, it is submitted, all domestic remedies have been exhausted. On 14 November 1994, the author was re-classified as a non-capital offender.

2.2 The author was convicted on the basis of common design. The case for the prosecution was that, on 3 May 1990, the author induced an unidentified man (the gunman) with whom he was allegedly working in concert, to shoot a security guard, one Charles Wilson; the gunman however killed another person, one Alvin Scarlett.

2.3 On the morning of 3 May 1990, Mr Wilson was on duty at the entrance gate to the dump of a bottling plant compound on the Spanish Town Road, Kingston. At approximately 8.00 a.m., he allowed two trucks to enter the dump from the compound. Several men climbed on the first truck. During the trial, Charles Wilson testified that he had seen two men, one of whom he identified in court as the author, sitting by the side of the dump's enclosure; the author followed the second truck down to the dump on foot. Fifteen minutes later, the second truck returned, with Alvin Scarlett, one Carlton McKie and the author; it stopped at the gate, and the three men unloaded some pallets. As the truck slowly entered the compound, Mr Wilson began closing the gate, he heard a gunshot and felt a pain in his hand. He saw the other man, who had been by the fence with the author, pointing a gun at him. Mr Wilson was unable to draw his own gun because of the hand injury. He testified that he saw the author, who had been out of sight, walk around the truck, saying to the gunman: "Shot the guard boy, let we get his gun." He then escaped, pursued by the author and the gunman. While running, he heard three more gunshots. The two men then gave up chasing him, and he saw their backs as they ran back towards the dump.

2.4 Mr Wilson claimed that he had first seen the author three years earlier, when he was working as a security guard at a biscuit factory, and that the author used to ask him for biscuits. He had seen him once before at the dump, but had not spoken to him.

2.5 Carlton McKie testified that, while unloading the pallets, he saw a man firing at the guard, and Alvin Scarlett, who was standing in the back of the truck, fell on his back. He had then seen the author on the other side of the truck, and that the author and the gunman had pursued the guard for some distance, and then ran back towards the dump. Mr McKie further testified that he had known the author for about one year, and that during this period he had often seen the author at the dump.

2.6 Blandford Davies, the investigating officer of the Hunts Bay Police Station, testified that, on 4 May 1990, he obtained a warrant for the author's arrest; on 4 June 1990, he saw the author at the Police Station, and arrested and charged him with the murder of Alvin Scarlett. Under arrest, the author claimed to be innocent.

2.7 The case for the defence was based on sworn evidence given by the author. He denied having been waiting by the side of the enclosure together with another man, and testified that he had gone down to the dump with a group of men. As they reached the premises of the bottling plant, the truck was about to pass the gate, and he and six other men had climbed on board. On returning from the dump, he and Mr Scarlett, whom he had known for four years, unloaded the pallets. The author said he heard a gunshot while he was on the other side of the truck and could not see Mr Wilson; he could not say from which direction the gunshot came. He further stated that he and others ran away, that he did not speak to anyone, and that he was not aware of anyone running in front of him. He heard several more shots and ran home. Later, he returned to the premises of the bottling plant to retrieve the pallets; he learned that Alvin Scarlett had been killed. The author denied ever having said "Shot the guard boy, let we get his gun", or having chased Charles Wilson; he stated that he had seen Mr Wilson at the premises of the bottling plant prior to 3 May 1990, but denied ever having seen him at the biscuit factory.

2.8 The trial transcript reveals that Mr Wilson first mentioned the author's utterance "Shot the guard boy, let we get his gun" in a written statement to the police; he did not repeat it during the preliminary enquiry at the Gun Court but did mention it again during the trial, during the examination-in-chief by crown counsel. It further appears that the author's attorney (who had not represented him at the preliminary enquiry) was not aware of the written statement and, when cross-examining Mr Wilson, challenged that the author had ever said those words. In re-examination, crown counsel showed the written police statement to the author's attorney and requested the judge to admit it in evidence; with reference to established jurisprudence he argued that if a statement made by a witness during examination-in-chief is challenged on the basis that it is a recent concoction, it is open to the prosecution to tender a written statement made previously, to show that the statement was in fact made. The author's attorney opposed the admission of the written statement as an exhibit, on the ground that it was self-serving, self-corroborating evidence of the witness. The judge, however, allowed the statement to be admitted in evidence to rebut the suggestion of recent fabrication.

The complaint

3.1 It is claimed that the non-disclosure of the statement to the defence prior to the trial violated the author's rights under Article 14, paragraphs 1, 2, 3(b) and (e), of the Covenant.

3.2 In this respect, counsel quotes from a letter received from the author's previous representative in Jamaica: "I think the point which turned the scales against Michael Adams was the statement by the witness Wilson that he had told the police that Adams said: . . . shoot the guard boy mek we get fi him gun. Wilson did not say that at the preliminary enquiry. That was a material difference and that statement ought to have been made available to the defence to ensure a fair trial. If that statement had been disclosed, the cross-examination of Charles Wilson would not have been conducted as it was. In light of this, did Adams receive a fair trial?"

3.3 Counsel points to the Committee's General Comment on Article 14 of the Covenant, where it observed in respect of the right of an accused person to have adequate time and facilities for the preparation of his defence that: ". . . the facilities must include access to documents and other evidence which the accused requires to prepare his case". It is submitted that, while the author's attorney in Jamaica affirms that he had sufficient time to prepare the case and was allowed to cross-examine witnesses on the same terms as the prosecution, this could *not* have been the situation with regard to Mr Wilson. Counsel reiterates that, had the statement been disclosed to the defence, the attorney's cross-examination of the witness would have been different, and that, consequently, the author was denied adequate facilities for the preparation of his defence as guaranteed by Article 14, paragraph 3(b). He adds that, without prior knowledge of the statement, further cross-examination by counsel was not as effective as it should have been and was limited by the judge in its scope, amounting to a violation of Article 14, paragraph 3(e). It is further submitted that the defence was therefore unable to rebut the witness' allegations, contrary to Article 14, paragraph 2, and that, consequently, the author was denied the right to a fair trial (Article 14, paragraph 1).

3.4 In support of these claims, counsel refers to the Committee's Views on Communication No 283/1988 (*Aston Little* v. *Jamaica*). He also refers to an affidavit taken by Ms Shelagh Anne Simmons, who visited Mr Adams at St Catherine District Prison from 29 August to 5 September 1994, which states that: "I told my lawyer, . . . that there were witnesses willing to give evidence on my behalf, but he said that the prosecution had so little evidence against me that witnesses would not be needed. The witnesses were people who were on the scene when the crime took place. . . . They can verify that I was never a party to the murder I am charged for. The witnesses were Alfred Campbell . . ., a man I know as 'Willy' . . ., and a girl called

'Reenie' . . ." Counsel points out that, if Mr Wilson's statement to the police had been disclosed to the author's attorney, it is likely that he would have called the witnesses mentioned by the author to testify on his behalf. Thus, it is submitted, by denying adequate time and facilities for the preparation of the defence, there has also been a violation of Article 14, paragraph 3(e), in that the author was unable to obtain the testimony of witnesses on his behalf.

3.5 In affidavits dated 10 September 1994 from the three witnesses mentioned by the author, it appears that all of them, on separate occasions, tried to give statements to the police, specifically to the investigating officer. The witnesses claim that they were "warned off". In this respect, reference is made to a recent judgment of the Court of Appeal of the United Kingdom.[3] Counsel submits that, although DPP or the author's attorney had not specifically requested that statements be taken from the three above-mentioned witnesses, the investigating officer was under a duty to investigate and to take statements from witnesses willing to testify on the author's behalf. The failure of the Jamaican police, and in particular of the investigating officer, to obtain statements from alibi witnesses is said to amount to a violation of Article 14, paragraphs 1 and 2.

3.6 Counsel further claims that the trial judge, in his summing up, misdirected the jury as to the proper approach to be taken on the evidence, which amounted to a denial of justice. He submits that, by allowing the prosecution to tender in evidence the statement Charles Wilson had made to the police, the judge inevitably led the jury to a finding of guilty. In directing the jury on how to use the statement, the judge failed to clarify sufficiently that the statement should not be used to determine whether the remark "shot the guard boy, let we get his gun" was true, but was simply relevant to the credibility of Mr Wilson as a witness. In addition, he effectively directed the jury not to consider whether Mr Wilson was mistaken. Further, the judge effectively directed the jury that, by accepting that the statement was made, it was inevitable to conclude that the author must have had the necessary intention to participate in the joint enterprise, at the time the gunman shot Alvin Scarlett. Moreover, during the summing up, the trial judge repeatedly used the phrase "Shoot the guard boy . . .", as opposed to the phrase "shot the guard boy . . .", used by Mr Wilson in court and in his statement to the police. Counsel points out that, in doing so, the judge misrepresented the evidence and encouraged the jury to interpret the word "shot" as "shoot".

3.7 Counsel submits that the author is a victim of a violation of Articles 7 and 10, paragraph 1, because of ill-treatment by the police

---

[3] *Ivan Fergus* (1994) 98 Cr App R (failure of the police to carry out the instructions of the Crown Prosecution Service to take statements from alibi witnesses contributed to the miscarriage of justice).

after his arrest. The author claims that he spent about six months in custody on a shooting charge before being charged for murder. After his arrest, he was first detained at the Spanish Town Police Station, and then transferred to the Hunts Bay Police Station. He claims that, there, he "sustained beatings to my back, chest, neck and foot bottom by policemen, namely Bobby Williams, R. Scott and Detective Corporal Davis, who led these beatings on me which caused me to pass blood in my urine and damage to my nerves. I was beaten over a two week period, twice daily. I was denied visitors or medical treatment by the police. . . . Whenever the police went out in search of men who they say committed the crime without finding them, they always come and beat up on me for information I knew nothing about. I told my lawyer about the beatings, but nothing was done about it."

3.8 The author's claims of ill-treatment by the police appear to be corroborated by the testimony of his aunt, Janet Gayle, who stated in an affidavit dated 10 September 1994, that: "On a visit to Michael at the police station, he informed me that when he was being questioned . . ., he stated his innocence and was then beaten by the investigating officers. He said he was beaten at least three or four times a week. When I visited him, I noted that he had open wounds and scars. Michael told me that after one beating he 'blacked out' and was taken to a doctor and then back to the police station." She stated that she thought that the trial lawyer was unaware of the author's ill-treatment. She further stated that: "Michael never suffered from epilepsy prior to his beatings while detained. I think he was diagnosed as suffering from epilepsy about one year after the murder trial. Michael has told me that he first 'blacked out' after the first beating he received while detained at Spanish Town Police Station. He has also said that he has had episodes of blackout in prison. These have normally occurred after being beaten in prison. In fact, one time I went to visit Michael in prison but was late and the visiting hours had finished. I then went to visit a friend who was in Spanish Town Hospital and to my surprise and horror I saw Michael there with his head cut open and bleeding. . . . Michael is currently on medication for his epilepsy and if he stops the medication he suffers from fits. He is now dependent on that medication. . . . I think that the beatings trigger the epilepsy fits." Although Janet Gayle refers to the actions of the police at Spanish Town Police Station, the author has confirmed that the beatings actually took place at Hunts Bay Police Station and not at the Spanish Town Police Station.

3.9 In a letter of 18 February 1994 to London counsel, the author explains that: "On several occasions the police . . . took me out of the cell and carried me to the guard room where [they] beat me with pieces of 2 x 4 boards, iron pipes and a pickaxe stick. I sustained several cuts on my head, swollen to my arms and my legs. Internal injury indicative of lots of blood in my urine, and whenever I cough, blood came from my stomach. Several cuts on my back. I was also beaten on the soles of my feet. As a result of being locked away for more than a month, being not able to speak to anyone, I did not go to report the issue of the beatings to anyone before I was taken to Court, and in Court, I was not allowed to speak to anyone throughout the trial."

3.10 Furthermore, on 19 July 1993, Ms Simmons, a human rights worker from England, made a report to the Jamaica Council for Human Rights on behalf of the author; she stated that on 24 June 1993, the author was viciously assaulted by a warder at St Catherine District Prison and, as a result, spent three and a half days in the Spanish Town Hospital suffering from head injuries.

3.11 On 20 July 1993, counsel filed a complaint, on the author's behalf, with the Parliamentary Ombudsman of Jamaica, requesting an investigation into the incidents. He also requested the Jamaica Council for Human Rights to ensure that the Ombusman in fact investigate the matter. On 4 August 1993, the office of the Ombudsman informed counsel that "the complaint would receive the most prompt attention possible". On 3 February and 5 July 1994, counsel requested the Ombudsman about the outcome of the investigations, if any. He states that to date no reply has been forthcoming from the office of the Ombudsman. The Jamaica Council for Human Rights also sent an urgent action request to the Director of the World Organization against Torture on 1 October 1993. In addition, Father Brian Massie SJ, Chaplain of St Catherine District Prison, wrote to the Prison Superintendent on 23 July 1993, requesting that the author's allegations be investigated, and that a brief report be made available to the Board of Visitors' meeting. On 30 March 1994, Father Massie contacted counsel, explaining that nothing substantial had been done.

3.12 The affidavit taken by Ms Simmons refers to the fact that, on each of her visits to the author, a warder was present, and that the author told her that he felt uneasy about openly answering questions on his maltreatment by the prison warders, for fear of reprisals. Ms Simmons adds that she was herself on one day subjected to thirty minutes of humiliating treatment by the Superintendent and certain members of his staff, and that her visits to the author were restricted. The Jamaica Council for Human Rights sought to raise the matter with the Commissioner of Correctional Services, but the author preferred that no further action be taken, fearing reprisals from warders. It is submitted that the requirements of the *UN Standard Minimum Rules for the Treatment of Prisoners* were not met during the author's detention at the Hunts Bay Police Station and at St Catherine District Prison, and that the treatment to which he was subjected on 24 June 1993, the inadequate medical treatment he received, as well as the continuing fear of reprisals, amount to violations of Articles 7 and 10, paragraph 1.

3.13 Counsel points out that the author has been held on death row for three years and seven months, prior to the commutation of his death sentence to life imprisonment as a result of the reclassification process. Reference is made to the decision of the Judicial Committee of the Privy Council in the case of *Pratt and Morgan*,[4] where it was held, *inter alia*, that it should be possible for the State Party to complete the entire domestic appeals process within approximately two years. It is submitted that the delay in the author's case, during which he had to face the agony of execution, amounts to a violation of Articles 7 and 10, paragraph 1.

3.14 Finally, reference is made to the findings of a delegation of Amnesty International, which visited St Catherine District Prison in November 1993. It was observed, *inter alia*, that the prison is holding more than twice the capacity for which it was constructed in the nineteenth century, and that the facilities provided by the State are scant: no mattresses, other bedding or furniture in the cells; no integral sanitation in the cells; broken plumbing, piles of refuse and open sewers; no artificial lighting in the cells and only small air vents through which natural light can enter; almost no employment opportunities available to inmates; no doctor attached to the prison so that medical problems are generally treated by warders who receive very limited training. It is submitted that the particular impact of these general conditions upon the author [was] that he was confined to his cell for twenty-two hours a day. He spent most of the day isolated from other men, with nothing to keep him occupied. Much of the time he spent in enforced darkness. He further complained about pains in his chest and about being unable to digest any food, but had not seen a doctor as of 29 August 1994. The conditions under which the author was detained at St Catherine District Prison are said to amount to cruel, inhuman and degrading treatment within the meaning of Articles 7 and 10, paragraph 1.

The State Party's information and observations on admissibility and the author's comments thereon

4.1 In a submission, dated 1 June 1995, the State Party does not specifically address the admissibility and offers observations on the merits of the case.

4.2 With regard to the claim that the non-disclosure of the statement given by Mr Wilson to the police constituted a violation of Article 14, paragraph 3(b), the State Party contends that counsel could challenge

---

[4] *Earl Pratt and Ivan Morgan* v. *Attorney-General of Jamaica*; PC Appeal No 10 of 1993, judgment delivered on 2 November 1993 [98 *ILR* 335].

the defence witnesses' statement at the trial and was therefore not left without any course of action through which to protect his client's interests. It further contends that these matters relate to questions of evidence which, according to the Committee's own jurisprudence, are best left to the appellate courts to decide.

4.3 With respect to the claim that the author was unable to cross-examine witnesses on the same terms as the prosecution, the State Party refers to the comments given by the author's lawyer in Jamaica to London counsel and contends that the former's opinion constitutes strong evidence as to the events which occurred, which belie the claim under Article 14, paragraph 3(b).

4.4 The State Party denies that there was a violation of Article 14, paragraph 3(e). It submits that the author's witnesses were available to him, had he chosen to call them.

4.5 With regard to the alleged misdirections to the jury by the trial judge, the State Party contends that this is an issue of evaluation of facts and evidence which is for the appellate courts, rather than the Committee, to decide.

4.6 As to the allegations that the author was ill-treated in police detention, the State Party argues that it is significant that Mr Adams did not bring this to the attention of his counsel, and that the author's aunt admits that he was taken to a doctor. With respect to the author's allegation that he was ill-treated in prison, the State Party informs that it will investigate the matter and inform the Committee as soon as the results of the investigation are available. No further information had been received as of 1 March 1996.

4.7 As to the "death row phenomenon" claim, the State Party contends that the Privy Council's decision in *Earl Pratt and Ivan Morgan* v. *Attorney-General of Jamaica* is not an authority for the proposition that incarceration on death row for a specific period of time constitutes cruel and inhuman treatment. Each case must be examined on its own facts, in accordance with applicable legal principles. In support of its argument, the State Party refers to the Committee's Views in the case of *Pratt and Morgan*, where it was held that delays in judicial proceedings did not *per se* constitute cruel, inhuman or degrading treatment.

5.1 In his comments counsel reaffirms that his client is a victim of violations of Articles 14, paragraphs 1, 2, 3(b) and (e). He considers that the non-disclosure of the statement to the defence denied the author the possibility to examine witnesses on equal terms, by eliminating the possibility of rebutting the allegation and effectively denying him a fair trial. With regard to the availability of the defence witnesses, these were "frightened off" by the investigation officer; consequently, and contrary to the State Party's affirmation, they were not "available" to the author.

5.2 Counsel notes that the State Party does not deny the ill-treatment the author was subjected to during detention and at St Catherine District Prison.

Admissibility consideration and examination of merits

6.1 Before considering any claim contained in a communication, the Human Rights Committee must, in accordance with Rule 87 of its [Rules of] Procedure, decide whether or not it is admissible under the Optional Protocol to the Covenant.

6.2 The Committee observes that with the dismissal of the author's petition for special leave to appeal by the Judicial Committee of the Privy Council on 4 November 1993, the author exhausted domestic remedies for purposes of the Optional Protocol. In this context, it notes that the State Party has not specifically addressed the admissibility of the case and has formulated comments on the merits. The Committee recalls that Article 4, paragraph 2, of the Optional Protocol stipulates that the receiving State shall submit its written observations on the merits of a communication within six months of the transmittal of the communication to it for comments on the merits. The Committee reiterates that this period may be shortened, in the interest of justice, if the State Party so wishes. The Committee further notes that counsel for the author does not object to the examination of the case on the merits at this stage.

6.3 With respect to allegations about irregularities in the court proceedings, in particular improper instructions from the judge to the jury on the evaluation of evidence, such as the statement given by Mr Wilson to the police, the Committee recalls that it is generally for the courts of States Parties to the Covenant to evaluate the facts and evidence in a particular case; similarly, it is for the appellate courts and not for the Committee to review specific instructions to the jury by the judge in a trial by jury, unless it can be ascertained that the instructions to the jury were clearly arbitrary or amounted to a denial of justice, or that the judge manifestly violated his obligation of impartiality. The author's allegations do not show that the judge's instructions suffered from such defects. In this respect, therefore, the communication is inadmissible as incompatible with the provisions of the Covenant, pursuant to Article 3 of the Optional Protocol.

7. In respect of the author's remaining claims, the Committee decides that the case is admissible and proceeds, without further delay, to an examination of the substance of his claims, in the light of all the information made available to it by the parties, as required by Article 5, paragraph 1, of the Optional Protocol.

8.1 With regard to the author's claim that the length of his detention on death row amounts to a violation of Articles 7 and 10 of the Covenant, the Committee refers to its prior jurisprudence that detention on death row does not *per se* constitute cruel, inhuman or degrading treatment in violation of Article 7 of the Covenant, in the absence of some further compelling circumstances.[5] The Committee observes that the author has not shown how the length of his detention on death row affected him as to raise an issue under Articles 7 and 10 of the Covenant. While it would be desirable for appeal proceedings to be conducted as expeditiously as possible, in the circumstances of the present case, the Committee concludes that a delay of three years and seven months does not constitute a violation of Articles 7 and 10, paragraph 1.

8.2 With regard to the author's allegation that he was ill-treated the Committee considers that there are two separate issues, the ill-treatment the author suffered during pre-trial detention and later at St Catherine District Prison. With respect to the ill-treatment during pre-trial detention the Committee notes that the State Party has not denied the ill-treatment but has simply stated that the author received medical attention. With regard to the author's alleged ill-treatment at St Catherine District Prison, the Committee notes that the author has made very precise allegations, which he documented in complaints to the Parliamentary Ombudsman of Jamaica and to the Jamaica Council for Human Rights. The State Party has promised to investigate these claims, but has failed to forward to the Committee its findings, almost ten months after promising to do so. In the circumstances, the Committee finds that the author's claims concerning the treatment he was subjected to both during pre-trial detention and at St Catherine Prison have been substantiated and concludes that Articles 7 and 10, paragraph 1, of the Covenant have been violated.

8.3 The author has alleged a violation of Article 14, paragraphs 1, 2, 3(b) and (e), in that the non-disclosure, by the prosecution, of the statement made by Mr Wilson to the police, denied him the possibility of cross-examining witnesses on the same terms as the prosecution, and thus denied him adequate facilities for the preparation of his defence. The Committee, however, notes that even though counsel objected to its submission into evidence, from the record it appears that he did not request an adjournment or even ask for a copy of the statement. The Committee considers therefore that the claim has not been substantiated, and consequently there is no violation of the Covenant in this respect.

8.4 The author contends that he was unable to obtain the attendance and examination of witnesses on his behalf on equal terms as witnesses against him, as the witnesses were "warned off" by the police. The State Party has not explained why statements were not taken from three potential alibi witnesses, who had on different occasions

[5] See the Committee's Views on communication No 588/1994 (*Errol Johnson* v. *Jamaica*), adopted on 22 March 1996, paragraphs 8.2 to 8.5.

indicated their willingness to testify on behalf of the author, as attested to by affidavits signed by all three of them. However, the Committee considers that as the witnesses were available to the author, it was counsel's professional choice not to call them. The Committee reaffirms its standard jurisprudence where it has held that it is not for the Committee to question counsel's professional judgment, unless it was or should have been manifest to the judge that the lawyer's behaviour was incompatible with the interests of justice. In the instant case, there is no reason to believe that counsel was not using his best judgment. In the circumstances, the Committee finds that the facts before it do not reveal a violation of the Covenant.

9. The Human Rights Committee, acting under Article 5, paragraph 4, of the Optional Protocol to the International Covenant on Civil and Political Rights, is of the view that the facts before it disclose violations of Articles 7 and 10, paragraph 1, of the Covenant.

10. Pursuant to Article 2, paragraph 3(a), of the Covenant, the author is entitled to an effective remedy, entailing compensation.

11. Bearing in mind that by becoming a State Party to the Optional Protocol, the State Party has recognized the competence of the Committee to determine whether there has been a violation of the Covenant or not and that, pursuant to Article 2 of the Covenant, the State Party has undertaken to ensure to all individuals within its territory and subject to its jurisdiction the rights recognized in the Covenant and to provide an effective and enforceable remedy in case a violation has been established, the Committee wishes to receive from the State Party, within ninety days, information about the measures taken to give effect to the Committee's Views.

[Adopted in English, French and Spanish, the English text being the original version. Subsequently to be issued also in Arabic, Chinese and Russian as part of the Committee's annual report to the General Assembly.]

[Report: Doc. CCPR/C/58/D/607/1994]

**Human rights — Minorities — International Covenant on
Civil and Political Rights, 1966, Article 27—Sami reindeer
herdsmen in Finland—Whether rights violated by legislation
on logging and by road-building programmes—Consultation
of Sami herdsmen by Government of Finland—Limited
impact of Government plans for logging and road-building
on culture of the Sami**

**International tribunals—United Nations Human Rights
Committee — Competence — Procedure — Request for
indication of interim measures**

J. LÄNSMAN et al. v. FINLAND

(Communication No 671/1995)

United Nations Human Rights Committee.[1]   30 October 1996

SUMMARY: *The facts*:—The authors of the communication, Finnish citizens
of ethnic Sami origin, claimed to be victims of a violation by Finland of their
right, as members of a minority group, to enjoy their culture in accordance
with Article 27 of the International Covenant on Civil and Political Rights,
1966. The authors were reindeer breeders who argued that Finland's plans to
approve logging and to construct roads in the north of Finland would have
adverse consequences for Sami reindeer herding. The authors invoked *Ilmari
Länsman et al* v. *Finland*[2] as a warning to Finland against taking new measures
that would affect the living conditions of local Sami. They claimed they had
exhausted domestic remedies, having unsuccessfully taken their case through
various stages of appeal in Finland.

In their initial communication of 28 August 1995, the authors also referred
to the Committee's views on *Ivan Kitok* v. *Sweden*[3] and *Ominayak* v. *Canada*,[4] and
they cited other relevant legal documents. They requested interim measures
of protection to prevent irreparable damage. Finland argued against the
request for interim measures on the ground, *inter alia*, that this case was not
sufficiently serious to result in irreparable damage that was a threat to life or
physical integrity.

On 14 March 1995 the Committee declared the communication admissible
and set aside the request for interim measures. In its observations on the
merits, Finland argued, *inter alia*, that Sami reindeer herdsmen were fully
consulted in decisions on logging and related activities, and that Finnish
courts had taken Article 27 of the Covenant into account and nonetheless
rejected the authors' claims. Finland accepted that the Sami community
formed an ethnic community within the terms of Article 27 and that
protection of their "culture" incorporated traditional means of livelihood, but

---

[1] For the composition of the Committee, see p. 254, note 1.
[2] Communication No 511/1992.
[3] Communication No 197/1985, 96 *ILR* 637.
[4] Communication No 167/1984, 96 *ILR* 667.

only to the extent that these were essential to the culture and necessary for its survival. In this case, the impact of the contested activities on Sami culture was limited, and had to be reconciled with other interests such as forestry. Finland contended that the authors were raising before the Committee the "threshold" for measures that could constitute a "denial" under Article 27, and this matter had already been dealt with by the domestic courts.

In response, the authors disputed Finland's observations on the limited magnitude and nature of the logging. They also denied that there was "effective participation" by them in the logging plans, and claimed that they sought from the Committee its interpretation of Article 27 of the Covenant, not a "reassessment of the evidence".

Held:—(1) The crucial question was whether the logging that had already taken place in the specified area and logging approved for the future was such that it would deny the authors the right to enjoy their culture in that area (p. 317).

(2) The logging activities carried out, as well as those approved, did not constitute a denial of the authors' right to enjoy their culture, since, *inter alia*, the herdsmen were consulted in the logging plans, and the Finnish authorities and courts took into account the requirements of Article 27. Moreover, future logging activities did not appear to threaten the survival of reindeer husbandry (p. 317).

(3) Nonetheless, if large-scale future logging plans were approved in the contested area, or the effects of logging already planned were more serious than currently envisaged, this might constitute a violation of the authors' right, under Article 27, to enjoy their culture. Finland had to bear in mind that while different activities affecting the natural environment might not violate this Article, such activities taken together might do so (p. 318).

(4) There had been no breach of Article 27 of the Covenant in this case (p. 318).

The following is the text of the views of the Committee:

Views under Article 5, paragraph 4, of the Optional Protocol

1. The authors of the communication (dated 28 August 1995) are Jouni E. Länsman, Jouni A. Länsman, Eino A. Länsman and Marko Torikka, all members of the Muotkatunturi Herdsmen's Committee. The authors claim to be victims of a violation by Finland of Article 27 of the International Covenant on Civil and Political Rights. They are represented by counsel.

The facts as submitted by the authors
2.1 The authors are reindeer breeders of Sami ethnic origin; they challenge the plans of the Finnish Central Forestry Board to approve logging and the construction of roads in an area covering about 3,000 hectares of the area of the Muotkatunturi Herdsmen's Committee. The members of the Muotkatunturi Herdsmen's Committee occupy

areas in the north of Finland, covering a total of 225,000 hectares, of which one fifth is suitable for winter herding. The 3,000 hectares are situated within these winter herding lands.

2.2 The authors point out that the question of ownership of the lands traditionally used by the Samis remains unsettled.

2.3 The activities of the Central Forestry Board were initiated in late October 1994, but stopped on 10 November 1994 by an injunction of the Supreme Court of Finland (*Korkein oikeus*). According to the authors, a representative of the Central Forestry Board has recently stated that the activities will resume before the winter; they express concern that the logging will resume in October or November 1995, since the injunction issued by the Supreme Court lapsed on 22 June 1995.

2.4 The disputed area is situated close to the Angeli village near the Norwegian border, and to the Muotkatunturi Herdsmen's Committee's slaughterhouse and location for annual roundup of reindeer. The authors affirm that some 40 per cent of the total number of the reindeer owned by the Muotkatunturi Herdsmen's Committee feed on the disputed lands during winter. The authors observe that the area in question consists of old untouched forests, which means that both the ground and the trees are covered with lichen. This is of particular importance due to its suitability as food for young calves and its utility as "emergency food" for elder reindeer during extreme weather conditions. The authors add that female reindeer give birth to their calves in the disputed area during springtime, because the surroundings are quiet and undisturbed.

2.5 The authors note that the economic viability of reindeer herding continues to decline, and that Finnish Sami reindeer herdsmen have difficulties competing with their Swedish counterparts, since the Swedish Government subsidizes the production of reindeer meat. Moreover, traditional Finnish Sami reindeer herdsmen in the north of Finland have difficulties competing with the reindeer meat producers in the south of the Sami Homeland, who use fencing and feeding with hay, methods very distinct from the nature-based traditional Sami methods.

2.6 The authors observe that logging is not the only activity with adverse consequences for Sami reindeer herding. They concede that the dispute concerns a specific geographic area and the logging and construction of roads in the area. However, they believe that other activities, such as quarrying, that have already taken place, and such logging as has taken place or will take place, as well as any future mining (for which licences have already been granted by the Ministry of Trade and Industry), on the total area traditionally used by the Samis, should be taken into consideration when considering the facts of their new case. In this context, the authors refer to the Central Forestry Board's submission to the Inari Court of First Instance (*Inarin kihlakunnanoikeus*) of 28 July 1993, where the Board expressed its intention of logging, by the year 2005, a total of 55,000 cubic metres of wood from 1,100 hectares of forests in the western parts of the winter herding lands of the Muotkatunturi Herdsmen's Committee. The authors observe that logging has already been carried out in other parts of the winter herding lands, in particular in the Paadarskaidi area in the south-east.

2.7 The authors reiterate that the situation is very difficult for Samis in the north of Finland, and that any new measure causing adverse effects on reindeer herding in the Angeli area would amount to a denial of the local Samis' right to enjoy their own culture. In this context, the authors invoke paragraph 9.8 of the Views in case No 511/1992, which they interpret as a warning to the State Party regarding new measures that would affect the living conditions of local Samis.

2.8 As to the requirement of exhaustion of domestic remedies, the authors filed a complaint, invoking Article 27 of the Covenant, with the Inari Court of First Instance (*Inarin kihlakunnanoikeus*). The authors asked the Court to prohibit any logging or construction of roads on a limited geographic area. The Court declared the case admissible but decided against the authors on the merits on 20 August 1993. According to the Court, the disputed activities would have caused *some* adverse effects for a limited period of time, but only to a minor degree.

2.9 The authors then appealed to the Rovaniemi Court of Appeal (*Rovaniemen hovioikeus*) which, after oral hearings, delivered judgment on 16 June 1994. The Appeal Court found that the adverse consequences of the disputed activities were much more severe than the Court of First Instance had held. Still, two judges of the three-member panel came to the conclusion that the adverse effects for reindeer herding did not amount to a "denial of right to enjoy their culture" within the meaning of Article 27 of the Covenant. The Court of Appeal considered that it had not been proven "that logging in the land specified in the petition and road construction . . . would prevent them from enjoying in community with other members of their group the Sami culture by practising reindeer herding". The third judge dissented, arguing that logging and construction of roads should be prohibited and stopped. The authors sought leave to appeal before the Supreme Court (*Korkein oikeus*), pointing out that they were satisfied with the establishment of the facts by the Court of Appeal, and asking the Supreme Court to review only the issue of whether the adverse consequences of the activities amounted to a "denial" of the authors' rights under Article 27 of the Covenant. On 23 September 1994, the Supreme Court granted leave to appeal, without ordering interim measures of protection. On 10 November 1994, however, it ordered the Central Forestry Board to suspend the activities that had been initiated in late October 1994. On

22 June 1995, the Supreme Court confirmed the Court of Appeal's judgment in its entirety and withdrew the interim injunction. The authors contend that no further domestic remedies are available to them.

The complaint

3.1 The authors claim that the facts as described violate their rights under Article 27, and invoke the Committee's Views on the cases of *Ivan Kitok* v. *Sweden* (Communication No 197/1985),[5] *Ominayak* v. *Canada* (Communication No 167/1984)[6] and *Ilmari Länsman et al.* v. *Finland* (Communication No 511/1992), as well as ILO Convention No 169 on the rights of indigenous and tribal people in independent countries, the Committee's General Comment No 23[50] on Article 27, and the United Nations Draft Declaration on Indigenous Peoples.

3.2 Finally, the authors, who contend that logging and road construction might resume in October or November 1995 and is therefore imminent, request interim measures of protection under Rule 86 of the Rules of Procedure, so as to prevent irreparable damage.

Further submissions by the parties

4.1 On 15 November 1995, the communication was transmitted to the State Party under Rule 91 of the Committee's Rules of Procedure. Pursuant to Rule 86 of the Rules of Procedure, the State Party was requested to refrain from adopting measures which would cause irreparable harm to the environment which the authors claim is vital to their culture and livelihood. The State Party was requested, if it contended that the request for interim protection was not appropriate in the circumstances of the case, to so inform the Committee's Special Rapporteur for New Communications and to give reasons for its contention. The Special Rapporteur would then reconsider the appropriateness of maintaining the request under Rule 86.

4.2 By further submission of 8 December 1995, the authors note that the Upper Lapland Branch of the Central Forestry Board started logging in the area specified in the present communication on 27 November 1995. The logging activities are scheduled to continue until the end of March 1996: the target is to cut some 13,000 cubic metres of wood. Between 27 November and 8 December 1995, some 1,000 cubic metres had been cut over an area covering 20 hectares. Given this situation, the authors request the Committee to reiterate the request under Rule 86 and urge the State Party to discontinue logging immediately.

4.3 On the other hand, a group of Sami forestry officials from the Inari area who earn their living from forestry and wood economy, by

[⁵ 96 *ILR* 637.]   [⁶ 96 *ILR* 667.]

submission of 29 November 1995 addressed to the Committee, contend that forestry as practised today does *not* hamper reindeer husbandry, and that both reindeer husbandry and forestry can be practised simultaneously in the same areas. This assessment was confirmed by the Supreme Court of Finland in a judgment of 22 June 1995. If forestry activities in the Inari area were to be forbidden, Sami groups practising two different professions would be subject to unequal treatment.

4.4 In a submission dated 15 December 1995, the State Party contends that interim measures of protection should be issued restrictively, and only in serious cases of human rights violations where the possibility of irreparable damage is real, e.g. when the life or physical integrity of the victim is at stake. In the State Party's opinion, the present communication does not reveal circumstances pointing to the possibility of irreparable damage.

4.5 The State Party notes that the present logging area covers an area of not more than 254 hectares, out of a total of 36,000 hectares of forest owned by the State and available for reindeer husbandry to the Muotkatunturi Herdsmen's Committee. This area includes the surface of the Lemmenjoki National Park, which obviously is off-limits for any logging activity. The logging area consists of small separate surfaces treated by "seed tree felling", for natural regeneration. "Virgin forest areas" are left untouched in between the logged surfaces.

4.6 The State Party notes that the Finnish Central Forestry Board had, in a timely manner and before beginning logging activities, negotiated with the Muotkatunturi Reindeer Husbandry Association, to which the authors also belong; this Association had not opposed the logging plans and schedule. The letter referred to in paragraph 4.3 above demonstrates, to the State Party, the need for coordination of various and diverging interests prevalent in the way of life of the Sami minority. The State Party finally observes that some of the authors have logged their privately owned forests; this is said to demonstrate the "non-harmfulness" of logging in the area in question.

4.7 In the light of the above, the State Party regards the request under Rule 86 of the Rules of Procedure as inappropriate in the circumstances of the case, and requests the Committee to set aside the request under Rule 86. Notwithstanding, it undertakes not to elaborate further logging plans in the area in question, and to decrease the current amount of logging by 25 per cent, while awaiting the Committee's final decision.

4.8 The State Party concedes that the communication is admissible and pledges to formulate its observations on the merits of the claim as soon as possible.

The Committee's admissibility decision

5.1 During its 56th session, the Committee considered the admissibility of the communication. It noted the State Party's argument that the request for interim measures of protection in the case should be set aside, and that the communication met all admissibility criteria. It nonetheless examined whether the communication met the admissibility criteria under Articles 2, 3 and 5, paragraphs 2(a) and (b), of the Optional Protocol, concluded that it did, and that the authors' claim under Article 27 should be examined on its merits.

5.2 On 14 March 1996, therefore, the Committee declared the communication admissible and set aside the request for interim measures of protection.

State Party's observations on the merits and counsel's comments thereon

6.1 In its submission under Article 4, paragraph 2, of the Optional Protocol, the State Party supplements and corrects the facts as presented by the authors. It recalls that part of the Muotkatunturi Herdsmen's Committee's herding area belongs to the Lemmenjoki National Park, an area of pine-dominated forest suitable for reindeer herding during wintertime. As to the consultation process between National Forest and Park Service (hereafter NFPS—formerly called the Central Forestry Board) and local Sami reindeer herders, its notes that the representatives of the NFPS had contacted the chairman of the reindeer owners' association, JS, who in turn invited the representatives of the NFPS to the extraordinary meeting of the Muotkatunturi Herdsmen's Committee on 16 July 1993. Planned logging activities were discussed and amendments agreed upon during the meeting: i.e. reverting to use of winter roads and exclusion of the northern part of the logging area. The records of the Inari District Court (28 July 1993) show that two opinions were presented during the meeting: one in support of and one against the authors. The Muotkatunturi Herdsmen's Committee did not make statements directed against the NFPS.

6.2 The State Party further recalls that some Sami are forest owners and practise forest management, whereas others are employed by the NFPS in functions related to forest management. It emphasizes that the authors' comparison of surface areas to be logged is not illustrative, as it does not relate to forest management practices. Instead, it would be preferable to compare plans of the NFPS with plans for logging of private forests in the Angeli area: thus, the NFPS plans logging activities covering 900 hectares by the year 2005, whereas the regional plan for private forests of the Angeli area (years 1994-2013) includes forest regeneration of 1,150 ha by using the seed tree method.

6.3 The State Party recalls that the authors' claims were thoroughly examined by the domestic courts (i.e. the Inari District Court, the Rovaniemi Court of Appeal and the Supreme Court). At every instance, the court had before it extensive documentation, on the basis of which the case was examined *inter alia* in the light of Article 27 of the Covenant. All three instances rejected the authors' claims explicitly by reference to Article 27. The State Party adds that the requirements of Article 27 were consistently taken into account by the State Party's authorities in their application and implementation of the national legislation and the measures in question.

6.4 In the above context, the State Party contends that, given that the authors conceded before the Supreme Court that the Court of Appeal of Rovaniemi had correctly established the facts, they are in fact asking the Committee to assess and evaluate once again the facts in the light of Article 27 of the Covenant. The State Party submits that the national judge is far better positioned than an international instance to examine the case in all of its aspects. It adds that the Covenant has been incorporated into Finnish law by Act of Parliament, and that its provisions are directly applicable before all Finnish authorities. There is thus no need to argue, as the authors chose to do, that the Finnish courts refrain from interpreting the Covenant's provisions and to wait for the Committee to express itself on "borderline cases and new developments". In the same vein, there is no ground for the authors' argument that the interpretation of Article 27 of the Covenant by the Supreme Court and Court of Appeal is "minimalist" or "passive".

6.5 The State Party acknowledges that the Sami community forms an ethnic community within the meaning of Article 27 of the Covenant, and that the authors, as members of that community, are entitled to protection under the provision. It reviews the Committee's jurisprudence on Article 27 of the Covenant, including the Views on cases Nos 167/1984 (*B. Ominayak and members of the Lubicon Lake Band* v. *Canada*),[7] 197/1985 (*Kitok* v. *Sweden*)[8] and 511/1992 (*I. Länsman* v. *Finland*) and concedes that the concept of "culture" within the meaning of Article 27 covers reindeer husbandry, as an essential component of the Sami culture.

6.6 The State Party also admits that "culture" within the meaning of Article 27 provides for protection of the traditional means of livelihood for national minorities, *in so far as they are essential to the culture and necessary for its survival*. Not every measure or its consequences, which in some way modify the previous conditions, can be construed as a prohibited interference with the right of minorities to enjoy their own culture. This line of reasoning has been followed by the Parliamentary Committee for Constitutional Law, which has stated that Finland's obligations under international conventions mean that reindeer husbandry exercised by the Sami must not be subjected to unnecessary restrictions.

[7 96 *ILR* 667.]   [8 96 *ILR* 637.]

6.7 The State Party refers to the Committee's General Comment on Article 27,[9] which acknowledges that the protection of rights under Article 27 is directed to ensuring "the survival and continued development of the cultural, religious and social identity of the minorities concerned" (paragraph 9). It further invokes the *ratio decidendi* of the Committee's Views on case No 511/1992 (*I. Länsman et al.* v. *Finland*), where it was held that States Parties may understandably wish to encourage economic development and allow economic activity, and that measures which have a certain limited impact on the way of life of persons belonging to a minority will not necessarily amount to a violation of Article 27. The State Party argues that the present communication is in many respects similar to case No 511/1992, i.e. (1) the responsibility for the contested activities lies once again with the State Party; (2) the contested measures merely have a certain limited impact; (3) economic activities and conduct of reindeer husbandry have been reconciled in an appropriate manner; and (4) earlier logging and future logging plans were explicitly taken into consideration in the resolution of the case by the domestic courts.

6.8 In addition, the State Party points to the solution of a comparable case by the Supreme Court of Norway, where submersion of a small land area after construction of a hydroelectric dam had been challenged by local Samis. In that case, too, the decisive point for the Supreme Court was the factual extent of the interference with the interests of the local Sami, which was deemed to be too small to raise issues of minority protection under international law. The Supreme Court's reasoning was subsequently endorsed by the European Commission of Human Rights. The State Party concludes that the Committee's case-law shows that not all measures imputable to the State amount to a denial of the rights under Article 27: this principle is said to apply in the present case.

6.9 Still in relation to the authors' argument that different rights and interests cannot be reconciled, and that the right of the Sami to practise reindeer herding should have precedence over the practice of other rights, such as the right to log forests, the State Party asserts that the interests of both forestry and reindeer management can be and have been taken into account and reconciled when measures related to forestry management were or are being planned. This is generally done by the NFPS. The reconciliation is not only possible in the area referred to by the authors and in the entire region in which reindeer husbandry is practised, but it is also a significant issue, as reindeer husbandry is practised in the entire area inhabited by the Sami. It is noted that this type of reconciliation was explicitly approved by the Committee in its Views on case No 511/1992 (paragraph 9.8), where it was admitted that "economic activities must, in order to comply

[9] General Comment No 23[50], adopted in April 1994.

with Article 27, be carried out in a way that enables the authors to continue to benefit from reindeer husbandry". The State Party adds that measures related to forestry management can benefit the reindeer husbandry in many cases, and that many herdsmen simultaneously practise forestry.

6.10 In the State Party's view, the authors merely raise before the Committee the same issues they had been raising before the domestic courts: i.e. what type of measures in the areas concerned trigger the "threshold" beyond which measures must be regarded as a "denial", within the meaning of Article 27, of the Samis' right to enjoy their own culture. Before the local courts, the impairments to reindeer husbandry caused by logging and road construction were deemed to be below this threshold. In the State Party's opinion, the authors have failed to adduce new grounds which would enable the Committee to assess the "threshold" issue in any other way than the domestic courts.

6.11 In this context, the State Party argues that if the concept of "denial" within the meaning of Article 27 is interpreted as widely as by the authors, this would in fact give the Sami reindeer herders the right to reject all such activities which are likely to interfere with reindeer husbandry even to a small extent: "[t]his kind of right of veto with respect to small-size reasonable legal activities of the landowners and other land users would be simultaneously given to the herdsmen practising husbandry and would thus have a significant influence on the decision-making system". Simultaneously, legislation governing the exploitation of natural resources as well as the existing plans for land use would become "almost useless". This, the State Party emphasizes, cannot be the purpose and object of the Covenant and of Article 27. It should further be noted that since the Samis' right to practise reindeer husbandry is not restricted to the State-owned area, the Committee's decision will have serious repercussions on how private individuals may use and exploit land they own in the area of reindeer husbandry.

6.12 In the State Party's opinion, the Committee's insistence on the principle of "effective participation of members of minority communities in decisions which affect them",[10] [a] principle which was reiterated in the Views on case No 511/1992, was fully applied in the instant case. The area in which interests of forestry management and reindeer husbandry co-exist and possibly conflict forms part of the area of the Muotkatunturi Herdsmen's Committee (the legal entity responsible for matters relating to reindeer husbandry). The State Party and the Herdsmen's Committee have had continuous negotiation links, in a framework in which interests of forestry and reindeer husbandry are reconciled. The State Party contends that the experiences with this negotiation process have been good, and that it guarantees the Samis' right to conduct reindeer husbandry in

[10] General Comment No 23[50], paragraph 7.

accordance with Article 27. The NFPS has been in constant contact with the Muotkatunturi Herdsmen's Committee, of which the authors are members.

6.13 The State Party explains that reindeer management has been partly transformed into an activity that uses the possibilities offered by forestry management. Herdsmen use roads constructed for the purpose of forestry management: it is recalled that in the privately owned forests in the area of the Muotkatunturi Herdsmen's Committee, logging has been carried out by those practising reindeer husbandry. Furthermore, the State Party notes, forestry management practised by Samis does not differ from the way other private forest owners practise forestry management. If the forestry and logging methods used in areas administered by the NFPS are compared with the logging methods used in privately owned forests and by Samis, the lighter methods of forestry management used by the NFPS and manual logging are more mindful of the interests of reindeer husbandry than logging in privately owned forests carried out by machines. The NFPS intends to carry out manual logging, a more natural method than the mechanical logging which was carried out in privately owned forests in the Angeli area in the winter of 1993-1994. Manual logging is moreover closer to the traditional way of life and the culture of the Sami, and its effects on them thus lighter.

6.14 The State Party concludes that the authors' concern[s] over the future of reindeer husbandry have been taken into account in an appropriate way in the present case. While the logging and tracks in the ground will temporarily have limited adverse effects on the winter pastures used by the reindeer, it has not been shown, in the State Party's opinion, that the consequences would create considerable and long-lasting harm, which would prevent the authors from continuing reindeer husbandry in the area under discussion on its present scale. The authors are not, accordingly, denied their right to enjoy their own culture within the meaning of Article 27 of the Covenant.

7.1 In their comments, the authors begin by noting that logging in the Pyhäjärvi area, a part of the area specified in their complaint, was completed in March 1996. Adverse consequences of the logging for reindeer are said to be mostly of a long-term nature. The authors and other reindeer herdsmen have however already observed that the reindeer use neither the logging area nor "virgin forest areas" in between the logging areas as pasture. During the winter of 1996, therefore, a considerable part of the winter herding lands of the Muotkatunturi Herdsmen's Committee has been inaccessible for the reindeer. This has caused the reindeer herders much extra work and additional expenses, in comparison to previous years.

7.2 According to the authors, some of the negative consequences of the logging will only materialize after several years or even decades.

For example, one particularly difficult winter during which a solid ice layer would prevent reindeer from digging lichen through the snow may cause the starvation of many reindeer, because of the absence of their natural emergency resource, i.e. the lichen growing on old trees. If storms send down the remaining trees, there is a distinct danger of large areas becoming totally treeless, thereby causing a permanent reduction in the surface of winter herding lands for the Muotkatunturi Herdsmen's Committee.

7.3 Counsel observes that because the economic benefit from reindeer herding is low, many reindeer herdsmen have had to look for additional sources of income. This development has been accelerated as most herding committees have been forced to cut the number of their herds. The necessity to reduce the herds has been caused by the scarcity of herding lands and the poor condition of existing, over-used herding lands. In such a situation, suitable winter herding areas are a truly critical resource, which determine the scale of reductions in the number of reindeer belonging to each herdsmen's committee. The authors themselves developed other economic activities besides reindeer herding in order to survive. They work as butchers for other herdsmen's committees, work for private local landowners or conduct small-scale logging within their own private forests. All, however, would prefer to work solely in reindeer herding.

7.4 As to the extent of the logging already carried out, counsel transmits four photographs, including aerial photographs, which are said to provide a clear understanding of the nature and impact of the logging: very few trees remain in logged areas of up to 20 hectares, and all old trees, rich with lichen, have been cut.

7.5 The authors dismiss as misleading the State Party's observations on the magnitude and nature of the logging, as the 254 ha mentioned by the State Party relate only to logging already completed. The NFPS however plans to continue logging in the area specified in the complaint. If comparisons are made with a larger area, the authors recall the long-lasting and extensive logging, in Paadarskaidi, another part of the winter herding area of the Muotkatunturi Herdsmen's Committee. The consequences of logging activities in Paadarskaidi are said to be alarming, since the reindeer simply have abandoned this area. The authors also challenge the State Party's comments on the logging methods and submit that so-called seed-tree felling is also harmful for reindeer herding, as the animals do not use such forests for a number of reasons. In addition, there is the danger that storms fell the seed trees and the area gradually becomes treeless.

7.6 Counsel emphasizes that if two of the authors have sought additional income from forestry, this has not been of their free choice and in no way indicates that logging would be part of the Sami way of life. He criticizes the State Party's observations which use this argument against the authors, rather than taking it as a serious indicator of developments which endanger the Sami culture and the Sami way of life. It is submitted that the State Party's attempt to explain "manual logging" as being close to the traditional way of life and culture of the Sami is totally unfounded and distorts the facts.

7.7 The authors point specifically to the magnitude of the different logging projects in the area. Of a total of 255,000 ha area of the Muotkatunturi Herdsmen's Committee, some 36,000 ha are forests administered by the NFPS. The most suitable winter herding lands of the Muotkatunturi Herdsmen's Committee are located within these State-administered areas, deep in the forests. Privately owned forests cover some 14,600 ha and are owned by 111 separate owners. Most of the privately owned forests do not exceed 100 ha and are typically located along the main roads. They are accordingly, much less suitable for reindeer herding as for example the strategically important winter herding areas identified by the authors in the present case.

7.8 The authors challenge the State Party's affirmation that there was "effective participation" of the Muotkatunturi Herdsmen's Committee and themselves in the negotiation process. Rather, they assert, there was no negotiation process and no real consultation of the local Sami when the State forest authority prepared its logging plans. At most, the Chairman of the Muotkatunturi Herdsmen's Committee was *informed* of the logging plans. In the authors' opinion, the facts as established by the Finnish courts do not support the State Party's contention. The Sami furthermore are generally dissatisfied with the way the State forest authorities exercise their powers as "landowners". On 16 December 1995, the Sami Parliament discussed the experiences of Sami consultation in relation to logging plans by the State Party forest authorities. The resolution adopted notes, *inter alia*, that it is "[t]he opinion of the Sami Parliament that the present consultation system between the Central Forestry Board and reindeer management does not function in a satisfactory way . . .".

7.9 As far as logging in the Angeli area is concerned, the authors note that, even under the terms of the State Party's submission, the "negotiations" only proceeded after the authors had instituted court proceedings in order to prevent the logging. The local Sami "had become coincidentally aware" of existing logging plans, upon which the authors instituted court proceedings. The authors contend that what the State Party refers to as "negotiations" with local reindeer herdsmen amounts to little more than invitations extended to the chairmen of the herdsmen's committees to annual forestry board meetings, during which they are informed of short-term logging plans. This process, the authors emphasize, involves no real consultation of the Sami. They express their desire to have a more significant influence on the decision-making processes leading to logging activities within their homelands, and refute the State Party's view on the perceived good experiences with the existing consultation process (see paragraph 6.12 above).

7.10 Concerning the State Party's argument that the authors in fact seek a re-evaluation, by the Committee, of evidence already thoroughly examined and weighed by the local courts, the authors affirm that the only contribution they seek from the Committee is the interpretation of Article 27, not any "reassessment of the evidence", as suggested by the Government. They dismiss as irrelevant the observations of the State Party on the role of the national judge (see paragraph 6.4 above).

7.11 As to the State Party's comments referred to in paragraph 6.7 above, the authors largely agree with the former's points relating to the Government's responsibility for interference with Sami rights and the weighing of all relevant activities and their impact by the local courts. They strongly disagree with the State Party's second point, namely that the measures agreed to and carried out only have a limited impact. In the first *Länsman* case, the Committee could limit its final assessment to activities which had already been concluded. The present case not only concerns such logging as has already been conducted, but all future logging within the geographical area specified in the complaint. Thus, the winter herding lands in question in the present case are of strategical importance to the local Sami: logging causes long-lasting or permanent damage to reindeer herding, which does not end when the activity itself is concluded. Therefore, the "limited impact" of quarrying on Mt Riutusvaara, which was at the basis of the first case,[11] cannot be used as a yardstick for the determination of the present case, where the adverse consequences of logging are said to be of an altogether different magnitude.

7.12 The authors equally disagree with the State Party's contention that there was an appropriate reconciliation between the interests of reindeer herdsmen and economic activities, noting that the logging plans were drawn up without the authors' participation or of the local Sami in general.

7.13 The authors challenge the State Party's assessment of the impact of the logging activities already carried out on the author's ability to continue reindeer herding. They believe that the logging which has taken place and, more so, further envisaged logging, will prevent them from continuing to benefit from reindeer husbandry. The Government's optimistic assessment is contrasted with that of the Rovaniemi Court of Appeal, which admitted that the logging would cause "considerable" and "long-lasting" harm to the local Sami. However, the domestic courts did not prohibit the planned logging activities, because they set the threshold for the application of

[11] Views on case No 511/1992 (*I. Länsman et al.* v. *Finland*), adopted 26 October 1994.

Article 27 in the necessity of "giving up reindeer herding", and not in terms of "continuing to benefit from reindeer husbandry".[12]

7.14 In addition to the above, the authors provide information on recent developments concerning Sami rights in Finland. While the development has been positive with respect to constitutional amendments and the formally recognized rule of the Sami Parliament, it has been negative and insecure in other respects, i.e. in relation to the economic well-being of the Sami who live mostly from reindeer herding and associated activities. The authors further refer to a case currently pending before the Supreme Administrative Court of Finland, relating to mining claims staked by Finnish and foreign companies within the Sami homeland. The principal legal basis for the administrative appeals by Sami in this case was Article 27 of the Covenant; by decision of 15 May 1996, the Supreme Administrative Court quashed 104 claims which had previously been approved by the Ministry for Trade and Industry, and referred the companies' claim applications back to the Ministry for reconsideration. A decision on the merits of the case remains outstanding.

7.15 The authors conclude that, overall, the logging already conducted by the State Party's forestry authorities within the area specified in the communication has caused "immediate adverse consequences to the authors, and to the Sami reindeer herdsmen in the Angeli area and the Muotkatunturi Herdsmen's Committee in general". The logging will, and further logging envisaged by the State Party's authorities would, result in considerable, long-lasting and even permanent adverse effect to them. To the authors, this conclusion has been well documented and also been confirmed by the judgments of the Rovaniemi Court of Appeal and of the Supreme Court in the case.

8.1 In additional comments dated 27 June 1996, the State Party dismisses as groundless the authors' explanations concerning the perceived economic unsuitability of some parts of the logging area. It notes that as far as the possibility of loss of reindeer calves after the harsh winter of 1996 is concerned, possible losses are due to the exceptionally late arrival of spring and the deep cover of snow which has lasted an unusually long time. The situation has been identical for the *whole* reindeer herding area, and since losses are expected *all* over the reindeer herding area, supplementary feeding of reindeer has been increased accordingly. The State Party observes that it is not measures related to forestry management, but the extent of reindeer management that has been the reason for the need to reduce the number of reindeer; continuous over-grazing of herding areas is a well-known fact. Finally, the State Party considers it to be "self-evident" that selective seed-tree felling is a milder procedure than clear felling.

---

[12] See Note 3, paragraph 9.8.

8.2 As regards logging conducted by the authors themselves, the State Party notes that private landowners have independent authority in matters concerning the logging of their own forests. It would be difficult to understand that reindeer owners would carry out logging if its consequences for reindeer herding and for Sami culture were as harmful as the authors contend.

8.3 The State Party reaffirms, once again, that the processes through which reindeer associations or herdsmen participate in decisions affecting them are effective. The very issue of "effective participation" was discussed in a meeting between the NFPS, the Association of Herdsmen's Committees and different herdsmen's committees on 19 February 1996 in Ivalo. In this meeting, the negotiation system described by the State Party in its submission under Article 4(2) of the Optional Protocol was considered useful. The State Party also argues that contrary to the authors' assertion, the Muotkatunturi Herdsmen's Committee did *not* react negatively to the plans for logging initially submitted by the NFPS. The State Party regrets that the authors have tended to invoke its comments and observations only partially, thereby distorting the true content of the Finnish Government's remarks.

8.4 As to the impact of logging activities on the authors' ability to carry out reindeer herding, the State Party once more refers to the reasoning of the Rovaniemi Court of Appeal, which concluded that it had not "been proven that logging in the land specified in the petition and road construction for any other reasons mentioned by [the authors] would prevent them from enjoying, in community with other members of their group, the Sami culture by practising reindeer herding". For the State Party, this conclusion is fully compatible not only with the wording of Article 27 of the Covenant but also paragraphs 9.6 and 9.8 of the Committee's Views in the first *Länsman* case: accordingly, these measures do not create such considerable and long-lasting harm to prevent the authors from continuing reindeer herding even temporarily.

9.1 In additional comments dated 1 July 1996, the authors take issue with some of the State Party's observations referred to in paragraph 8.1 above. In particular, they challenge the Government's assertion that selective seed-tree felling is a milder procedure than clear felling, and submit that in the extreme climatic conditions of the area in question, so-called "selective felling", which leaves no more than eight to ten trees per hectare, has the same consequences as clear felling. Moreover, the negative effect on reindeer herding is the same due to the growing impact of storms, the remaining trees might fall.

9.2 The authors submit that if the Government invokes the argument that the effects of selective cutting are milder than in the case of clear felling, the only conclusion should be that all further logging in the area in question should be postponed until objective and scientific findings show that the forest in the area already logged—the Pyhäjärvi area—has recovered. The authors further note that the Government's submission is patently mistaken if it states that "logging does not concern the Pyhäjärvi winter feeding area", since the area already logged is called "Pyhäjärvi" even by the NFPS itself and is located in the winter feeding area of the Muotkatunturi Herdsmen's Committee.

9.3 On the issue of "effective participation", the authors contend that meetings such as the one of 19 February 1996 referred to by the State Party (see paragraph 8.3 above) do *not* serve as a proper vehicle for effective participation. This was reconfirmed by the Sami Parliament on 14 June 1996, when it once again stated that the NFPS does not cooperate with the herdsmen's committees in a satisfactory manner. The authors deny that they have in any way distorted the contents of the State Party's earlier submissions, the conclusions of the Rovaniemi Court of Appeal, or of the Committee's Views in the first *Länsman* case.

Examination of the merits

10.1 The Human Rights Committee has considered the present communication in the light of all the information provided by the parties, as required to do under Article 5, paragraph 1, of the Optional Protocol. The issue to be determined is whether logging of forests in an area covering approximately 3,000 hectares of the area of the Muotkatunturi Herdsmen's Committee (of which the authors are members)—i.e. such logging as has already been carried out and future logging—violates the authors' rights under Article 27 of the Covenant.

10.2 It is undisputed that the authors are members of a minority within the meaning of Article 27 of the Covenant and as such have the right to enjoy their own culture. It is also undisputed that reindeer husbandry is an essential element of their culture; that some of the authors practise other economic activities in order to gain supplementary income does not change this conclusion. The Committee recalls that economic activities may come within the ambit of Article 27 if they are an essential element of the culture of an ethnic community.[13]

10.3 Article 27 requires that a member of a minority shall not be denied the right to enjoy his culture. Measures whose impact amounts to a denial of the right are incompatible with the obligations under Article 27. As noted by the Committee previously in its Views on case No 511/1992, however, measures that have a certain limited impact on the way of life and the livelihood of persons belonging to a minority will not necessarily amount to a denial of the rights under Article 27.

[13] Cf. Views on case No 197/1985 (*Kitok* v. *Sweden*) [96 *ILR* 637], Views adopted 27 July 1988, paragraph 9.2; on case No 511/1992 (*I. Länsman et al.* v. *Finland*), adopted 26 October 1994, paragraph 9.1.

10.4 The crucial question to be determined in the present case is whether the logging that has already taken place within the area specified in the communication, as well as such logging as has been approved for the future and which will be spread over a number of years, is of such proportions as to deny the authors the right to enjoy their culture in that area. The Committee recalls the terms of paragraph 7 of its General Comment on Article 27, according to which minorities or indigenous groups have a right to the protection of traditional activities such as hunting, fishing or reindeer husbandry, and that measures must be taken "to ensure the effective participation of members of minority communities in decisions which affect them".

10.5 After careful consideration of the material placed before it by the parties, and duly noting that the parties do not agree on the long-term impact of the logging activities already carried out and planned, the Committee is unable to conclude that the activities carried out as well as approved constitute a denial of the authors' right to enjoy their own culture. It is uncontested that the Muotkatunturi Herdsmen's Committee, to which the authors belong, *was* consulted in the process of drawing up the logging plans and in the consultation, the Muotkatunturi Herdsmen's Committee did not react negatively to the plans for logging. That this consultation process was unsatisfactory to the authors and was capable of greater interaction does not alter the Committee's assessment. It transpires that the State Party's authorities *did* go through the process of weighing the authors' interests and the general economic interests in the area specified in the complaint when deciding on the most appropriate measures of forestry management, i.e. logging methods, choice of logging areas and construction of roads in these areas. The domestic courts considered specifically whether the proposed activities constituted a denial of Article 27 rights. The Committee is not in a position to conclude, on the evidence before it, that the impact of logging plans would be such as to amount to a denial of the authors' rights under Article 27 or that the finding of the Court of Appeal affirmed by the Supreme Court, misinterpreted and/or misapplied Article 27 of the Covenant in the light of the facts before it.

10.6 As far as future logging activities are concerned, the Committee observes that on the basis of the information available to it, the State Party's forestry authorities have approved logging on a scale which, while resulting in additional work and extra expenses for the authors and other reindeer herdsmen, does not appear to threaten the survival of reindeer husbandry. That such husbandry is an activity of low economic profitability is not, on the basis of the information available, a result of the encouragement of other economic activities by the State Party in the area in question, but of other, external, economic factors.

10.7 The Committee considers that *if* logging plans were to be approved on a scale larger than that already agreed to for future years in the area in question or if it could be shown that the effects of logging already planned were more serious than can be foreseen at present, then it may have to be considered whether it would constitute a violation of the authors' right to enjoy their own culture within the meaning of Article 27. The Committee is aware, on the basis of earlier communications, that other large-scale exploitations touching upon the natural environment, such as quarrying, are being planned and implemented in the area where the Sami people live. Even though in the present communication the Committee has reached the conclusion that the facts of the case do not reveal a violation of the rights of the authors, the Committee deems it important to point out that the State Party must bear in mind when taking steps affecting the rights under Article 27, that though different activities in themselves may not constitute a violation of this article, such activities, taken together, may erode the rights of Sami people to enjoy their own culture.

11. The Human Rights Committee, acting under Article 5, paragraph 4, of the Optional Protocol to the International Covenant on Civil and Political Rights, is of the view that the facts as found by the Committee do not reveal a breach of Article 27 of the Covenant.

[Adopted in English, French and Spanish, the English text being the original version. Subsequently to be issued also in Arabic, Chinese and Russian as part of the Committee's annual report to the General Assembly.]

[Report: Doc. CCPR/C/58/D/671/1995]

Human rights—Right to respect for family and private life —Right of entry to 'own country'—Alien long-term resident in State threatened with deportation on account of criminal convictions—Family resident in State—Whether State could be regarded as alien's 'own country' for purposes of Covenant—Whether violation of rights under International Covenant on Civil and Political Rights, 1966, Articles 7, 9, 12, 13, 17 and 23

International tribunals — United Nations Human Rights Committee—Procedure—Interim measures—Request for stay of deportation

STEWART *v.* CANADA

(*Communication No 538/1993*)

United Nations Human Rights Committee.[1]   1 *November* 1996.

SUMMARY: *The facts:*—The author, a British citizen resident in Canada, was, at the time he submitted his communication, facing deportation from Canada. Born in 1960, he had emigrated to Canada at the age of seven with his family and had lived there since then. His parents, younger brother, ex-wife and young children all lived in Canada. His older brother had been deported to the United Kingdom in 1992. Between 1978 and 1991 the author had been convicted of forty-two criminal offences, most of which were petty offences. In 1990, the Canadian Government ordered that the author be deported from Canada on account of his criminal convictions. It was only when he had been contacted by the immigration officials in this matter that he had realized he was not a citizen of Canada. His appeals to the domestic courts against deportation were dismissed. The author maintained that if he were to be deported, readmission to Canada would be extremely difficult if not impossible. The author sought interim measures of protection from deportation while the Committee considered his communication.

The author claimed violations of Articles 7, 9, 12, 13, 17 and 23 of the International Covenant on Civil and Political Rights, 1966. He argued, in relation to Article 23, that Canada did not provide clear and adequate legislative recognition of the protection of the family. Further, Canada, in breach of Article 17, did not protect aliens from interference with their private lives. The author also argued that Article 12(4) applied to his situation, since Canada was his "own country". He contended that, broadly interpreted, Article 9 applied to his deprivation of liberty, and that enforcement of the deportation order would violate Article 7.

On 26 April 1993 the Special Rapporteur on New Communications requested Canada's views on admissibility, and also asked Canada to refrain, in the interim, from deporting the author. Canada sought clarification of the basis on which the Special Rapporteur called for interim measures and asked for withdrawal of this request, since there were no special circumstances that could cause irreparable harm to the author. Canada argued that the author's claims were not substantiated.

As regarded the admissibility of this communication, the Committee noted that domestic remedies had been exhausted. Claims under Articles 7, 9 and 13 of the Covenant had not been substantiated, and were therefore not admissible. The Committee found admissible the claim under Articles 12(4), 17 and 23. In relation to the Special Rapporteur's request for interim

[1] For the composition of the Committee, see p. 254, note 1.

measures, the Committee commented that "irreparable damage" to the victim could not be determined generally, although the essential criterion was irreversibility of the consequences. In deportation cases, the Committee would need to know an author could return, in the event of a finding in his favour on the merits.

Held:—(1) (Mrs Chanet and Mr Prado Vallejo dissenting) The communication was admissible in so far as it raised issues under Articles 12(4), 17 and 23 (pp. 330-1, 334).

Per Mrs Chanet and Mr Prado Vallejo (dissenting): If the author was disqualified from acquiring nationality the Committee should have rejected the communication at its admissibility stage, since any application of Article 12(4) of the Covenant was thereby precluded. The Committee should decide the "own country" question on a case-by-case basis, or establish and publish criteria in order to avoid contradictions in admissibility decisions (pp. 343-4).

(2) If Article 12(4) had applied to the author, Canada would have been precluded from deporting him (p. 335).

(3) (Mr Klein and Mr Francis concurring; Ms Evatt, Ms Médina Quiroga, Mrs Chanet and Messrs Prado Vallejo and Baghwati dissenting) The concept of "his own country" in Article 12(4) applied to individuals who were nationals, and to certain categories of individuals who were not nationals in a formal sense and were also not "aliens" within the meaning of Article 13. The latter categories were individuals who had special ties to a particular country without being mere aliens, such as: nationals who had been stripped of their nationality contrary to international law; individuals whose country of nationality had been incorporated into or transferred to another national entity whose nationality was being denied them; or stateless persons arbitrarily denied the rights to acquire nationality in their country of residence. Further, when the country of immigration facilitated acquiring its nationality, and the immigrant refrained from doing do, the country of origin did not become "his own country" within the meaning of Article 12(4). By not acquiring Canadian nationality the author had remained an alien, and he did not belong to a category of non-national entitled to the protection of Article 12(4). Canada could not therefore be the author's "own country" and Article 12(4) had not been violated (pp. 335-7).

Per Mr Klein (concurring): The relationship between Articles 12(4) and 13 was not exclusive, and non-nationals covered by Article 12(4) might be deemed to be "aliens". Article 13 applied to the procedural aspects of all cases where an alien was to be expelled, while Article 12(4) might bar deportation, including of aliens, for substantive reasons (pp. 337-8).

Per Mr Francis (concurring): The author was both an alien lawfully resident in Canada and an "own country" resident under Article 12 of the Covenant. His expulsion under Article 13 had not been in violation of Article 12(4) (pp. 338-9).

Per Mrs Evatt and Ms Médina Quiroga (dissenting): The author could claim the protection of Article 12(4). That article could apply to an alien whose links with a State were sufficiently well established to support a finding that it was his "own country". The author had established Canada as his own country, and the decision to deport him, with its consequences, could be considered arbitrary if the grounds relied on were unreasonable when weighed against his connections with the country. In the circumstances of the case, the decision to deport the author was arbitrary and violated Article 12(4) of the Covenant (pp. 340-3).

Per Mrs Chanet (dissenting): Given that Canada might not have been considered as the author's "own country", the Committee should have rejected the communication at the admissibility stage under Article 12(4) of the Covenant (pp. 343-4).

Per Mr Baghwati (dissenting): Since this case would have an impact on huge numbers of immigrants and refugees, human rights in this context should have been liberally construed. Article 12(4) protected everyone against arbitrary deportation from his own country. It applied to a broad category of individuals, such as the author, who had special ties or claims to a given country, and therefore considered it their "own country". Such individuals did not lose the protection of Article 12(4) by failing to acquire formally the nationality of that country. Canada's decision to deport the author because of his criminal record was arbitrary in that it was disproportionate to the harm sought to be prevented. There was therefore a violation of Article 12(4) of the Covenant in this case (pp. 344-9).

(4) The obvious human problems raised by the deportation of the author would not have arisen had he been deported earlier. However, the Committee did not wish to establish a principle that could encourage States to deport immigrants on their first brush with the law, lest they become entitled to the protection of Article 12(4) (p. 336).

(5) (Mrs Evatt and Ms Médina Quiroga dissenting) Although the author's deportation would interfere with his family relations, this interference was neither arbitrary nor unlawful. There was therefore no violation of Articles 17 and 23 of the Covenant (p. 337).

Per Mrs Evatt and Ms Médina Quiroga (dissenting): The decision to deport the author was arbitrary and therefore also a violation of his rights under Articles 17 and 23 of the Covenant (p. 343).

The following is the text of the views of the Committee:

Views under Article 5, paragraph 4, of the Optional Protocol

1. The author of the communication is Charles Edward Stewart, a British citizen born in 1960. He has resided in Ontario, Canada, since the age of seven, and currently faces deportation from Canada. He claims to be a victim of violations by Canada of Articles 7, 9, 12, 13, 17 and 23 of the International Covenant on Civil and Political Rights. He is represented by counsel.

The facts as submitted by the author

2.1 The author was born in Scotland in December 1960. At the age of seven, he emigrated to Canada with his mother; his father and older brother were already, at the time, living in Canada. The author's parents have since separated, and the author lives together with his mother and with his younger brother. His mother is in poor health, and his brother is mentally disabled and suffers from chronic epilepsy. His older brother was deported to the United Kingdom in 1992, because of a previous criminal record. This brother apart, all of the author's relatives reside in Canada; the author himself has two young twin children, who live with their mother, from whom the author divorced in 1989.

2.2 The author claims that for most of his life, he considered himself to be a Canadian citizen. He claims that it was only when he was contacted by immigration officials because of a criminal conviction that he realized that, legally, he was only a permanent resident, as his parents had never requested Canadian citizenship for him during his youth. It is stated that between September 1978 and May 1991, the author was convicted on forty-two occasions, mostly for petty offences and traffic offences. Two convictions were for possession of marijuana seeds and of a prohibited martial arts weapon. One conviction was for assault with bodily harm, committed in September 1984, on the author's former girlfriend. Counsel indicates that most of her client's convictions are attributable to her client's substance abuse problems, in particular alcoholism. Since his release on mandatory supervision in September 1990, the author has participated in several drug and alcohol rehabilitation programmes. He has further received medical advice to control his alcohol abuse and, with the exception of one relapse, has remained alcohol-free.

2.3 It is stated that although the author cannot contribute much financially to the subsistence of his family, he does so whenever he is able to and helps his ailing mother and retarded brother around the home.

2.4 In 1990, an immigration enquiry was initiated against the author pursuant to Section 27, paragraph 1, of the Immigration Act. Under this provision, a permanent resident in Canada must be ordered deported from Canada if an adjudicator in an immigration enquiry is satisfied that the defendant has been convicted of certain specified offences under the Immigration Act. On 20 August 1990, the author was ordered deported on account of his criminal convictions. He appealed the order to the Immigration Appeal Division. The Board of the Appeal Division heard the appeal on 15 May 1992, dismissing it by judgment of 21 August 1992, which was communicated to the author on 1 September 1992.

2.5 On 30 October 1992, the author complained to the Federal Court of Appeal for an extension of the time limit for applying for leave to appeal. The Court first granted the request but subsequently dismissed the application for leave to appeal. There is no further appeal or application for leave to appeal from the Federal Court of Appeal to the Supreme Court of Canada, or to any other domestic tribunal. Thus, no further effective domestic remedy is said to be available.

2.6 If the author is deported, he would not be able to return to Canada without the express consent of the Canadian Minister of Employment and Immigration, under the terms of Sections 19(1)(i) and 55 of the Immigration Act. A re-application for emigration to Canada would not only require ministerial consent but also that the author fulfil all the other statutory admissibility criteria for immigrants. Furthermore, because of his convictions, the author would be barred from readmission to Canada under Section 19(2)(a) of the Act.

2.7 As the deportation order against the author could now be enforced at any point in time, counsel requests the Committee to seek from the State Party interim measures of protection, pursuant to Rule 86 of the Rules of Procedure.

The complaint

3.1 The author claims that the above facts reveal violations of Articles 7, 9, 12, 13, 17 and 23 of the Covenant. He claims that in respect of Article 23, the State Party has failed to provide for clear legislative recognition of the protection of the family. In the absence of such legislation which ensures that family interests would be given due weight in administrative proceedings such as, for example, those before the Immigration and Refugee Board, he claims, there is a prima facie issue as to whether Canadian law is compatible with the requirement of protection of the family.

3.2 The author also refers to the Committee's General Comment on Article 17, according to which "interference [with home and privacy] can only take place on the basis of law, which itself must be compatible with the provisions, aims and objectives of the Covenant". He asserts that there is no law which ensures that his legitimate family interests or those of the members of his family would be addressed in deciding on his deportation from Canada; there is only the vague and general discretion given to the Immigration Appeal Division to consider all the circumstances of the case, which is said to be insufficient to ensure a balancing of his family interests and other legitimate State aims. In its decision, the Immigration Appeal Division allegedly did not give any weight to the disabilities of the author's mother and brother; instead, it ruled that "taking into account that the appellant does not have anyone depending on him and there being no real attachment to and no real support from anyone, the Appeal Division sees insufficient circumstances to justify the appellant's presence in this country".

3.3 According to the author, the term "home" should be interpreted broadly, encompassing the (entire) community of which an individual is a part. In this sense, his "home" is said to be Canada. It is further submitted that the author's privacy must include the fact of being able to live within this community without arbitrary or unlawful interference.

To the extent that Canadian law does not protect aliens against such interference, the author claims a violation of Article 17.

3.4 The author submits that Article 12, paragraph 4, is applicable to his situation since, for all practical purposes, Canada is his own country. His deportation from Canada would result in an absolute statutory bar from re-entering Canada. It is noted in this context that Article 12(4) does not indicate that everyone has the right to enter his country of nationality or of birth but only "his own country". Counsel argues that the UK is no longer the author's "own country", since he left it at the age of seven and his entire life is now centred upon his family in Canada—thus, although not Canadian in a formal sense, he must be considered *de facto* a Canadian citizen.

3.5 The author affirms that his allegations under Articles 17 and 23 should also be examined in the light of other provisions, especially Articles 9 and 12. While Article 9 addresses deprivation of liberty, there is no indication that the *only* concept of liberty is one of physical freedom. Article 12 recognizes liberty in a broader sense: the author believes that his deportation from Canada would violate "his liberty of movement within Canada and within his community", and that it would not be necessary for one of the legitimate objectives enumerated in Article 12, paragraph 3.

3.6 The author contends that the enforcement of the deportation order would amount to cruel, inhuman and degrading treatment within the meaning of Article 7 of the Covenant. He concedes that the Committee has not yet decided whether the permanent separation of an individual from his/her family and/or close relatives and the effective banishment of a person from the only country he ever knew and in which he grew up may amount to cruel, inhuman and degrading treatment; he submits that this is an issue to be determined on its merits.

3.7 In this connection, the author recalls that (a) he has resided in Canada since the age of seven; (b) at the time of issue of the deportation order all members of his immediate family resided in Canada; (c) while his criminal record is extensive, it does by no means reveal that he is a danger to public safety; (d) he has taken voluntary steps to control his substance-abuse problems; (e) deportation from Canada would effectively and permanently sever all his ties in Canada; and (f) the prison terms served for various convictions already constitute adequate punishment and the reasoning of the Immigration Appeal Division, by emphasizing his criminal record, amounts to the imposition of additional punishment.

The Special Rapporteur's request for interim measures of protection and State Party's reaction

4.1 On 26 April 1993, the Special Rapporteur on New Communications transmitted the communication to the State Party, requesting it, under Rule 91 of the Rules of Procedure, to provide information and observations on the admissibility of the communication. Under Rule 86 of the Rules of Procedure, the State Party was requested not to deport the author to the United Kingdom while his communication was under consideration by the Committee.

4.2 In a submission dated 9 July 1993 in reply to the request for interim measures of protection, the State Party indicates that although the author would undoubtedly suffer personal inconvenience should he be deported to the United Kingdom, there are no special or compelling circumstances in the case that would appear to cause irreparable harm. In this context, the State Party notes that the author is not being returned to a country where his safety or life would be in jeopardy; furthermore, he would not be barred once and for all from readmission to Canada. Secondly, the State Party notes that although the author's social ties with his family may be affected, his complaint makes it clear that his family has no financial or other objective dependence on him: the author does not contribute financially to his brother, has not maintained contact with his father for seven or eight years and, after the divorce from his wife in 1989, apparently has not maintained any contact with his wife or children.

4.3 The State Party submits that the application of Rule 86 should *not* impose a general rule on States Parties to suspend measures or decisions at a domestic level unless there are special circumstances where such a measure or decision might conflict with the effective exercise of the author's right of petition. The fact that a complaint has been filed with the Committee should not automatically imply that the State Party is restricted in its power to implement a deportation decision. The State Party argues that considerations of State security and public policy must be considered prior to imposing restraints on a State Party to implement a decision lawfully taken. It therefore requests the Committee to clarify the criteria at the basis of the Special Rapporteur's decision to call for interim measures of protection and to consider withdrawing the request for interim protection under Rule 86.

4.4 In her comments, dated 15 September 1993, counsel challenges the State Party's arguments related to the application of Rule 86. She contends that deportation would indeed bar the author's readmission to Canada forever. Furthermore, the test of what may constitute "irreparable harm" to the petitioner should not be considered by reference to the criteria developed by the Canadian courts where, it is submitted, the test for irreparable harm in relation to family has become one of almost exclusive financial dependency, but by reference to the Committee's own criteria.

4.5 Counsel submits that the communication was filed precisely *because* Canadian courts, including the Immigration Appeal Division, do not recognize family interests beyond financial dependency of family

326   UNITED NATIONS HUMAN RIGHTS COMMITTEE

members. She adds that it is the very test applied by the Immigration Appeal Division and the Federal Court which is at issue before the Human Rights Committee: it would defeat the effectiveness of any order the Committee might make in the author's favour in the future if the Rule 86 request were to be cancelled now. Finally, counsel contends that it would be unjustified to apply a "balance of convenience" test in determining whether or not to invoke Rule 86, as this test is inappropriate where fundamental human rights are at issue.

State Party's admissibility observations and counsel's comments

5.1 In its submission under Rule 91, dated 14 December 1993, the State Party contends that the author has failed to substantiate his allegations of violations of Articles 7, 9, 12 and 13 of the Covenant. It recalls that international and domestic human rights law clearly states that the right to remain in a country and not to be expelled from it is confined to nationals of that State. These laws recognize that any such rights possessed by non-nationals are available only in certain circumstances and are more limited than those possessed by nationals. Article 13 of the Covenant "delineates the scope of that instrument's application in regard to the right of an alien to remain in the territory of a State party . . . Article 13 directly regulates only the procedure and not the substantive grounds for expulsion. Its purpose is clearly to prevent *arbitrary* expulsions. [The provision] aims to ensure that the *process* of expelling such a person complies with what is laid down in the State's domestic law and that it is not tainted by bad faith or the abuse of power." Reference is made to the Committee's Views in case No 58/1979, *Maroufidou* v. *Sweden*.[2]

5.2 The State Party submits that the application of the Immigration Act in the instant case satisfied the requirements of Article 13. In particular, the author was represented by counsel during the inquiry before the immigration adjudicator, was given the opportunity to present evidence as to whether he should be permitted to remain in Canada, and to cross-examine witnesses. Based on evidence adduced during the inquiry, the adjudicator issued a deportation order against the author. The State Party explains that the Immigration Appeal Board to which the author complained is an independent and impartial tribunal with jurisdiction to consider any ground of appeal that involved a question of law or fact, or mixed law and fact. It also has jurisdiction to consider an appeal on humanitarian grounds that an individual should not be removed from Canada. The Board is said to have carefully considered and weighed all the evidence presented to it, as well as the circumstances of the author's case.

5.3 While the State Party concedes that the right to remain in a country might exceptionally fall within the scope of application of the

[[2] 62 *ILR* 278.]

Covenant, it is submitted that there are no such circumstances in the case: the decision to deport Mr Stewart is said to be "justified by the facts of the case and by Canada's duty to enforce public interest statutes and protect society. Canadian courts have held that the most important objective for a government is to protect the security of its nationals. This is consistent with the view expressed by the Supreme Court of Canada that the executive arm of government is pre-eminent in matters concerning the security of its citizens . . . and that the most fundamental principle of immigration law is that non-citizens do not have an unqualified right to enter or remain in the country."

5.4 The State Party argues that both the decision to deport Mr Stewart and to uphold the deportation order met with the requirements of the Immigration Act, and that these decisions were in accordance with international standards; there are no special circumstances which would "trigger the application of the Covenant to justify the complainant's stay in Canada". Furthermore, there is no evidence of abuse of power by Canadian authorities and in the absence of such an abuse, "it is inappropriate for the Committee to evaluate the interpretation and application by those authorities of Canadian law".

5.5 As to the alleged violation of Articles 17 and 23 of the Covenant, the State Party argues that its immigration laws, regulations and policies are compatible with the requirements of these provisions. In particular, Section 114(2) of the Immigration Act allows for the exemption of persons from *any* regulations made under the Act or the admission into Canada of persons where there exist compassionate or humanitarian considerations. Such considerations include the existence of family in Canada and the potential harm that would result if a member of the family were removed from Canada.

5.6 A general principle of Canadian immigration programmes and policies is that dependants of immigrants into Canada are eligible to be granted permanent residence at the same time as the principal applicant. Furthermore, where family members remain outside Canada, the Immigration Act and ancillary regulations facilitate reunification through family class and assisted relative sponsorships: "[r]eunification in fact occurs as a result of such sponsorships in almost all cases".

5.7 In the light of the above, the State Party submits that any effects which a deportation may have on the author's family in Canada would occur further to the application of legislation that is compatible with the provisions, aims and objectives of the Covenant: "In the case at hand, humanitarian and compassionate grounds, which included family considerations, were taken into account during the proceedings before the immigration authorities and were balanced against Canada's duty and responsibility to protect society and to properly enforce public interest statutes".

5.8 In conclusion, the State Party affirms that Mr Stewart has failed to substantiate violations of rights protected under the Covenant and is in fact claiming a right to remain in Canada. He is said to be in fact seeking to establish an avenue under the Covenant to claim the right not to be deported from Canada: this claim is incompatible *ratione materiae* with the provisions of the Covenant and inadmissible under Article 3 of the Optional Protocol.

6.1 In her comments, counsel notes that the State Party wrongly conveys the impression that the author had two full hearings before the immigration authorities, which took into account all the specific factors in his case. She observes that the immigration adjudicator conducting the inquiry " has no equitable jurisdiction". Once he is satisfied that the person is the one described in the initial report, that this person is a permanent resident of Canada, and that he has been convicted of a criminal offence, a removal order is mandatory. Counsel contends that the adjudicator "may not take into account any other factors and has no statutory power of discretion to relieve against any hardship caused by the issuance of the removal order".

6.2 As to the discretionary power, under Section 114(2) of the Immigration Act, to exempt persons from regulatory requirements and to facilitate admission on humanitarian grounds, counsel notes that this power is *not* used to relieve the hardship of a person and his/her family caused by the removal of a permanent resident from Canada: "[T]he Immigration Appeal Division exercises a quasi-judicial statutory power of discretion after a full hearing, and it has been seen as inappropriate for the Minister or his officials to in fact 'overturn' a negative decision . . . by this body."

6.3 Counsel affirms that the humanitarian and compassionate discretion delegated to the Minister by the Immigration Regulations can in any event hardly be said to provide an effective mechanism to ensure that family interests are balanced against other interests. In recent years, Canada is said to have routinely separated families or attempted to separate families where the interests of young children were at stake: thus, "the best interests of children are not taken into account in this administrative process".

6.4 Counsel submits that Canada ambiguously conveys the impression that family class and assisted relative sponsorships are almost always successful. This, according to her, may be true of family class sponsorships, but it is clearly not the case for assisted relative sponsorships, since assisted relative applicants must meet all the selection criteria for independent applicants. Counsel further dismisses as " patently wrong" the State Party's argument that the Court, upon application for judicial review of a deportation order, may balance the hardship caused by removal against the public interest. The Court, as it has articulated repeatedly, cannot balance these interests, is limited to strict judicial review, and cannot substitute its own decision for that of the decision maker(s), even if it would have reached a different conclusion on the facts: it is limited to quashing a decision because of jurisdictional error, a breach of natural justice or fairness, an error of law, or an erroneous finding of fact made in a perverse or in a capricious manner (Sec. 18(1) Federal Court Act).

6.5 As to the compatibility of the author's claims with the Covenant, counsel notes that Mr Stewart is not claiming an absolute right to remain in Canada. She concedes that the Covenant does not *per se* recognize a right of non-nationals to enter or remain in a State. Nonetheless, it is submitted that the Covenant's provisions cannot be read in isolation but are inter-related: accordingly, Article 13 must be read in the light of other provisions.

6.6 Counsel acknowledges that the Committee has held that Article 13 provides for procedural and not for substantive protection; however, procedural protection cannot be interpreted in isolation from the protection provided under other provisions of the Covenant. Thus, legislation governing expulsion cannot discriminate on any of the grounds listed in Article 26; nor can it arbitrarily or unlawfully interfere with family, privacy and home (Article 17).

6.7 As to the claim under Article 17, counsel notes that the State Party has only set out the provisions of the Immigration Act which provide for family reunification—provisions which she considers inapplicable to the author's case. She adds that Article 17 imposes positive duties upon States Parties, and that there is no law in Canada which would recognize family, privacy or home interests in the context raised in the author's case. Furthermore, while she recognizes that there is a process provided by law which grants to the Immigration Appeal Division a general discretion to consider the personal circumstances of a permanent resident under order of deportation, this discretion does not recognize or encompass consideration of fundamental interests such as integrity of the family. Counsel refers to the case of *Sutherland* as another example of the failure to recognize that integrity of the family is an important and protected interest. For counsel, there "can be no balancing of interests if . . . family . . . interests are not recognized as fundamental interests for the purpose of balancing. The primary interest in Canadian law and jurisprudence is the protection of the public . . ."

6.8 Concerning the State Party's contention that a "right to remain" may only come within the scope of application of the Covenant under exceptional circumstances, counsel claims that the process whereby the author's deportation was decided and confirmed proceeded without recognition or cognizance of the author's rights under Articles 7, 9, 12, 13, 17 or 23. While it is true that Canada has a duty to ensure that society is protected, this legitimate interest must be balanced against other protected individual rights.

6.9 Counsel concedes that Mr Stewart was given an opportunity, before the Immigration Appeal Division, to present all the circumstances of his case. She concludes, however, that domestic legislation and jurisprudence do not recognize that her client will be subjected to a breach of his fundamental rights if he were deported. This is because such rights are not and need not be considered given the way immigration legislation is drafted. Concepts such as home, privacy, family or residence in one's own country, which are protected under the Covenant, are foreign to Canadian law *in the immigration context*. The overriding concern in view of removal of a permanent resident, without distinguishing long-term residents from recently arrived immigrants, is national security.

The Comittee's admissibility decision

7.1 Before considering any claims contained in a communication, the Human Rights Committee must, in acordance with Rule 87 of its Rules of Procedure, decide whether or not it is admissible under the Optional Protocol to the Covenant.

7.2 The Committee noted that it was uncontested that there were no further domestic remedies for the author to exhaust, and that the requirements of Article 5, paragraph 2(b), of the Optional Protocol had been met.

7.3 Inasmuch as the author's claims under Articles 7 and 9 of the Covenant are concerned, the Committee examined whether the conditions of Articles 2 and 3 of the Optional Protocol were met. In respect of Articles 7 and 9, the Committee did not find, on the basis of the material before it, that the author had substantiated, for purposes of admissibility, his claim that deportation to the United Kingdom and separation from his family would amount to cruel or inhuman treatment within the meaning of Article 7, or that it would violate his right to liberty and security of person within the meaning of Article 9, paragraph 1. In this respect, therefore, the Committee decided that the author had no claim under the Covenant, within the meaning of Article 2 of the Optional Protocol.

7.4 As to Article 13, the Committee noted that the author's deportation was ordered pursuant to a decision adopted in accordance with the law, and that the State Party had invoked arguments of protection of society and national security. It was not apparent that this assessment was reached arbitrarily. In this respect, the Committee found that the author had failed to substantiate his claim, for purposes of admissibility, and that this part of the communication was inadmissible under Article 2 of the Optional Protocol.

7.5 Concerning the claim under Article 12, the Committee noted the State Party's contention that no substantiation in support of this claim had been adduced, as well as counsel's contention that Article

12, paragraph 4, was applicable to Mr Stewart's case. The Committee noted that the determination of whether Article 12, paragraph 4, was applicable to the author's situation required a careful analysis of whether Canada could be regarded as the author's "country" within the meaning of Article 12, and, if so, whether the author's deportation to the United Kingdom would bar him from re-entering "his own country", and, in the affirmative, whether this would be done arbitrarily. The Committee considered that there was no *a priori* indication that the author's situation could *not* be subsumed under Article 12, paragraph 4, and therefore concluded that this issue should be considered on its merits.

7.6 As to the claims under Articles 17 and 23 of the Covenant, the Committee observed that the issue whether a State was precluded, by reference to Articles 17 and 23, from exercising a right to deport an alien otherwise consistent with Article 13 of the Covenant, should be examined on the merits.

7.7 The Committee noted the State Party's request for clarifications of the criteria that formed the basis of the Special Rapporteur's request for interim protection under Rule 86 of the Committee's Rules of Procedure, as well as the State Party's request that the Committee withdraw its request under Rule 86. The Committee observed that what may constitute "irreparable damage" to the victim within the meaning of Rule 86 cannot be determined generally. The essential criterion is indeed the irreversibility of the consequences, in the sense of the inability of the author to secure his rights, should there later be a finding of a violation of the Covenant on the merits. The Committee may decide, in any given case, not to issue a request under Rule 86 where it believes that compensation would be an adequate remedy. Applying these criteria to deportation cases, the Committee would require to know that an author would be able to return, should there be a finding in his favour on the merits.

8. On 18 March 1994 the Committee declared the communication admissible in so far as it might raise issues under Articles 12, paragraph 4, 17 and 23 of the Covenant.

State Party's observations and author's comments

9.1 In its submission of 24 February 1995, the State Party argues that Mr Stewart "has never acquired an unconditional right to remain in Canada as his country". Moreover, his deportation will not operate as an absolute bar to his re-entry to Canada. A humanitarian review in the context of a future application to re-enter Canada as an immigrant is a viable administrative procedure that does not entail a reconsideration of the judicial decision of the Immigration Appeal Board.

9.2 Articles 17 and 23 of the Covenant cannot be interpreted as being incompatible with a State Party's right to deport an alien, provided that the conditions of Article 13 of the Covenant are observed. Under Canadian law everyone is protected against arbitrary or unlawful interference with privacy, family and home as required by Article 17. The State Party submits that when a decision to deport an alien is taken after a full and fair procedure in accordance with law and policy, which are not themselves inconsistent with the Covenant, and in which the demonstrably important and valid interests of the State are balanced with the Covenant rights of the individual, such a decision cannot be found to be arbitrary. In this context the State Party submits that the conditions established by law on the continued residency of non-citizens in Canada are reasonable and objective and the application of the law by Canadian authorities is consistent with the provisions of the Covenant, read as a whole.

9.3 The State Party points out that the proposed deportation of Mr Stewart is not the result of a summary decision by Canadian authorities, but rather of careful deliberation of all factors concerned, pursuant to full and fair procedures compatible with Article 13 of the Covenant, in which Mr Stewart was represented by counsel and submitted extensive argument in support of his claim that deportation would unduly interfere with his privacy and family life. The competent Canadian tribunals considered Mr Stewart's interests and weighed them against the State's interest in protecting the public. In this context the State Party refers to the Convention relating to the Status of Refugees, which gives explicit recognition to the protection of the public against criminals and those who are security risks; it is submitted that these considerations are equally relevant in interpreting the Covenant. Moreover, Canada refers to the Committee's General Comment No 15 on "The position of aliens under the Covenant", which provides that "It is for the competent authorities of the State party, in good faith and in the exercise of their powers, to apply and interpret the domestic law, observing, however, such requirements under the Covenant as equality before the law." It also refers to the Committee's Views in communication No 58/1979, *Maroufidou* v. *Sweden*,[3] in which the Committee held that the deportation of Ms Maroufidou did not entail a violation of the Covenant, because she was expelled in accordance with the procedure laid down by the State's domestic law and there had been no evidence of bad faith or abuse of power. The Committee held that in such circumstances, it was not within its competence to re-evaluate the evidence or to examine whether the competent authorities of the State had correctly interpreted and applied its law, unless it was manifest that they had acted in bad faith or had abused their power. In this communication there has been no suggestion of bad faith or abuse of power. It is

[³ 62 *ILR* 278.]

therefore submitted that the Committee should not substitute its own findings without some objective reason to think that the findings of fact and credibility by Canadian decision-makers were flawed by bias, bad faith or other factors which might justify the Committee's intervention in matters that are within the purview of domestic tribunals.

9.4 As to Canada's obligation under Article 23 of the Covenant to protect the family, reference is made to relevant legislation and practice, including the Canadian Constitution and the Canadian Charter on Human Rights. Canadian law provides protection for the family which is compatible with the requirements of Article 23. The protection required by Article 23, paragraph 1, however, is not absolute. In considering his removal, the competent Canadian courts gave appropriate weight to the impact of deportation on his family in balancing these against the legitimate State interests to protect society and to regulate immigration. In this context the State Party submits that the specific facts particular to his case, including his age and lack of dependants, suggest that the nature and quality of his family relationships could be adequately maintained through correspondence, telephone calls and visits to Canada, which he would be at liberty to make pursuant to Canadian immigration laws.

9.5 The State Party concludes that deportation would not entail a violation by Canada of any of Mr Stewart's rights under the Covenant.

10.1 In her submission dated 16 June 1995, counsel for Mr Stewart argues that by virtue of his long residence in Canada, Mr Stewart is entitled to consider Canada to be "his own country" for purposes of Article 12, paragraph 4, of the Covenant. It is argued that this provision should not be subject to any restrictions and that the denial of entry to a person in Mr Stewart's case would be tantamount to exile. Counsel reviews and criticizes relevant Canadian case-law, including the 1992 judgment in *Chiarelli* v. *MEI*, in which the loss of permanent residence was likened to a breach of contract; once the contract is breached, removal can be effected. Counsel maintains that permanent residence in a country and family ties should not be dealt with as in the context of commercial law.

10.2 As to Mr Stewart's ability to return to Canada following deportation, author's counsel points out that because of his criminal record, he would face serious obstacles in gaining readmission to Canada as a permanent resident and would have to meet the selection standards for admission to qualify as an independent immigrant, taking into account his occupational skills, education and experience. As to the immigration regulations, he would require a pardon from his prior criminal convictions, otherwise he would be barred from readmission as a permanent resident.

10.3 With regard to persons seeking permanent resident status in Canada, counsel refers to decisions of the Canadian immigration authorities that have allegedly not given sufficient weight to extenuating circumstances. Counsel further complains that the exercise of discretion by judges is not subject to review on appeal.

10.4 As to a violation of Articles 17 and 23 of the Covenant, author's counsel points out that family, privacy and home are not concepts incorporated into the provisions of the Immigration Act. Therefore, although the immigration authorities can take into account family and other factors, they are not obliged by law to do so. Moreover, considerations of dependency have been limited to the aspect of financial dependency, as illustrated in decisions in the *Langner* v. *MEI*, *Toth* v. *MEI* and *Robinson* v. *MEI* cases.

10.5 It is argued that the Canadian authorities did not sufficiently take into account Mr Stewart's family situation in their decisions. In particular, counsel objects to the evaluation by Canadian courts that Mr Stewart's family bonds were tenuous, and refers to the unofficial transcript of the deportation hearings, in which Mr Stewart stressed the emotionally supportive relationship that he had with his mother and brother. Mr Stewart's mother confirmed that he helped her in caring for her youngest son. Counsel further criticizes the reasoning of the Immigration Appeal Division in the Stewart decision, which allegedly put too much emphasis on financial dependency: "The appellant has a good relationship with his mother who has written in support of him. But the appellant's mother has always lived independently of him and has never been supported by him. The appellant's younger brother is in a program for the disabled and is therefore taken care of by social services. As a matter of fact, there is no one depending on the appellant for sustenance and support . . ." Counsel argues that emphasis on the financial aspect of the relationship does not take into account the emotional family bond and submits in support of her argument the report of Dr Irwin Silverman, a psychologist, summarizing the complexity of human relationships. Moreover counsel cites from a book by Jonathan Bloom-Fesbach, *The Psychology of Separation and Loss*, outlining the long-term effects of breaking the family bond.

10.6 Counsel rejects the State Party's argument that proper balancing has taken place between State interests and individual human rights.

Issues and proceedings before the Committee

11.1 This communication was declared admissible in so far as it might raise issues under Articles 12, paragraph 4, 17 and 23 of the Covenant.

11.2 The Committee has considered the communication in the light of all the information made available to it by the parties, as provided in Article 5, paragraph 1, of the Optional Protocol.

12.1 The question to be decided in this case is whether the

expulsion of Mr Stewart violates the obligations Canada has assumed under Articles 12, paragraph 4, 17 and 23 of the Covenant.

12.2 Article 12, paragraph 4, of the Covenant provides: "No one shall be arbitrarily deprived of the right to enter his own country." This article does not refer directly to expulsion or deportation of a person. It may, of course, be argued that the duty of a State Party to refrain from deporting persons is a direct function of this provision and that a State Party that is under an obligation to allow entry of a person is also prohibited from deporting that person. Given its conclusion regarding Article 12, paragraph 4, that will be explained below, the Committee does not have to rule on that argument in the present case. It will merely assume that if Article 12, paragraph 4, were to apply to the author, the State Party would be precluded from deporting him.

12.3 It must now be asked whether Canada qualifies as being Mr Stewart's "country". In interpreting Article 12, paragraph 4, it is important to note that the scope of the phrase "his own country" is broader than the concept "country of his nationality", which it embraces and which some regional human rights treaties use in guaranteeing the right to enter a country. Moreover, in seeking to understand the meaning of Article 12, paragraph 4, account must also be had of the language of Article 13 of the Covenant. That provision speaks of "an alien lawfully in the territory of a State party" in limiting the rights of States to expel an individual categorized as an "alien". It would thus appear that "his own country" as a concept applies to individuals who are nationals and to certain categories of individuals who, while not nationals in a formal sense, are also not "aliens" within the meaning of Article 13, although they may be considered as aliens for other purposes.

12.4 What is less clear is who, in addition to nationals, is protected by the provisions of Article 12, paragraph 4. Since the concept "his own country" is not limited to nationality in a formal sense, that is, nationality acquired on birth or by conferral, it embraces, at the very least, an individual who, because of his special ties to or claims in relation to a given country, cannot there be considered to be a mere alien. This would be the case, for example, of nationals of a country who have there been stripped of their nationality in violation of international law and of individuals whose country of nationality has been incorporated into or transferred to another national entity whose nationality is being denied them. In short, while these individuals may not be nationals in the formal sense, neither are they aliens within the meaning of Article 13. The language of Article 12, paragraph 4, permits a broader interpretation, moreover, that might embrace other categories of long-term residents, particularly stateless persons arbitrarily deprived of the right to acquire the nationality of the country of such residence.

12.5 The question in the present case is whether a person who enters a given State under that State's immigration laws, and subject to the conditions of those laws, can regard that State as his own country when he has not acquired its nationality and continues to retain the nationality of his country of origin. The answer could possibly be positive were the country of immigration to place unreasonable impediments on the acquiring of nationality by new immigrants. But when, as in the present case, the country of immigration facilitates acquiring its nationality, and the immigrant refrains from doing so, either by choice or by committing acts that will disqualify him from acquiring that nationality, the country of immigration does not become "his own country" within the meaning of Article 12, paragraph 4, of the Covenant. In this regard it is to be noted that while in the drafting of Article 12, paragraph 4, of the Covenant the term "country of nationality" was rejected, so was the suggestion to refer to the country of one's permanent home.

12.6 Mr Stewart is a British national both by birth and by virtue of the nationality of his parents. While he has lived in Canada for most of his life he never applied for Canadian nationality. It is true that his criminal record might have kept him from acquiring Canadian nationality by the time he was old enough to do so on his own. The fact is, however, that he never attempted to acquire such nationality. Furthermore, even had he applied and been denied nationality because of his criminal record, this disability was of his own making. It cannot be said that Canada's immigration legislation is arbitrary or unreasonable in denying Canadian nationality to individuals who have criminal records.

12.7 This case would not raise the obvious human problems Mr Stewart's deportation from Canada presents were it not for the fact that he was not deported much earlier. Were the Committee to rely on this argument to prevent Canada from now deporting him, it would establish a principle that might adversely affect immigrants all over the world whose first brush with the law would trigger their deportation lest their continued residence in the country convert them into individuals entitled to the protection of Article 12, paragraph 4.

12.8 Countries like Canada, which enable immigrants to become nationals after a reasonable period of residence, have a right to expect that such immigrants will in due course acquire all the rights and assume all the obligations that nationality entails. Individuals who do not take advantage of this opportunity and thus escape the obligations nationality imposes can be deemed to have opted to remain aliens in Canada. They have every right to do so, but must also bear the consequences. The fact that Mr Stewart's criminal record disqualified him from becoming a Canadian national cannot confer on him greater rights than would be enjoyed by any other alien who, for whatever reasons, opted not to become a Canadian national. Individuals in these situations must be distinguished from the categories of persons described in paragraph 12.4 above.

12.9 The Committee concludes that as Canada cannot be regarded as Mr Stewart's "country", for the purposes of Article 12, paragraph 4, of the Covenant, there could not have been a violation of that article by the State Party.

12.10 The deportation of Mr Stewart will undoubtedly interfere with his family relations in Canada. The question is, however, whether the said interference can be considered either unlawful or arbitrary. Canada's Immigration Law expressly provides that the permanent residency status of a non-national may be revoked and that that person may then be expelled from Canada if he or she is convicted of serious offences. In the appeal process the Immigration Appeal Division is empowered to revoke the deportation order "having regard to all the circumstances of the case". In the deportation proceedings in the present case, Mr Stewart was given ample opportunity to present evidence of his family connections to the Immigration Appeal Division. In its reasoned decision the Immigration Appeal Division considered the evidence presented but it came to the conclusion that Mr Stewart's family connections in Canada did not justify revoking the deportation order. The Committee is of the opinion that the interference with Mr Stewart's family relations that will be the inevitable outcome of his deportation cannot be regarded as either unlawful or arbitrary when the deportation order was made under law in furtherance of a legitimate State interest and due consideration was given in the deportation proceedings to the deportee's family connections. There is therefore no violation of Articles 17 and 23 of the Covenant.

13. The Human Rights Committee, acting under Article 5, paragraph 4, of the Optional Protocol to the International Covenant on Civil and Political Rights, is of the view that the facts before the Committee do not disclose a violation of any of the provisions of the International Covenant on Civil and Political Rights.

[Adopted in English, French and Spanish, the English text being the original version. Subsequently to be issued also in Arabic, Chinese and Russian as part of the Committee's annual report to the General Assembly.]

A. *Individual opinion by Eckart Klein (concurring)*

Being in full agreement with the finding of the Committee that the facts of the case disclose neither a violation of Article 12, paragraph 4, nor of Articles 17 and 23 of the Covenant, for the reasons given in the view, I cannot accept the way how the relationship between Article 12, paragraph 4, and Article 13 has been determined. Although this issue is not decisive for the outcome of the present case, it could become relevant for the consideration of other communications, and I therefore feel obliged to clarify this point.

The view suggests that there is a category of persons who are not "nationals in the formal sense", but are also not "aliens within the meaning of Article 13" (paragraph 12.4). While I clearly accept that the scope of Article 12, paragraph 4, is not entirely restricted to nationals but may embrace other persons as pointed out in the view, I nevertheless think that this category of persons—not being nationals, but still covered by Article 12, paragraph 4—may be deemed to be "aliens" in the sense of Article 13. I do not believe that Article 13 deals only with *some* aliens. The wording of the article is clear and provides for no exceptions, and aliens are all non-nationals. The relationship between Article 12, paragraph 4, and Article 13 is not exclusive. Both provisions may come into play together.

I therefore hold that Article 13 applies in all cases where an alien is to be expelled. Article 13 deals with the procedure of expelling aliens, while Article 12, paragraph 4, and, under certain circumstances, also other provisions of the Covenant may bar deportation for substantive reasons. Thus, Article 12, paragraph 4, may apply even though it concerns a person who is an "alien".

Eckart Klein [signed]
[Original: English]

B. *Individual opinion by Laurel B. Francis (concurring)*

This opinion is given against the background of my recorded views during the Committee's preliminary consideration of this case quite early in the session when I stated *inter alia* that (a) Mr Stewart was an "own country" resident under Article 12 of the Covenant and (b) his expulsion under Article 13 was *not* in violation of Article 12, paragraph 4.

I will as far as possible avoid a discursive format in relation to the Committee's decision adopted on 1 November with respect to the question whether the expulsion of Mr Stewart from Canada (under Article 13 of the Covenant) violates the State Party's obligation under Articles 12, paragraph 4, 17 and 23 of the Covenant.

I should like to submit that:

1. Firstly, I concur with the reasons given by the Committee at paragraph 12.10 and the decision taken that there was no violation of Articles 17 and 23 of the Covenant.

2. But, secondly, I do not agree with the Committee's restricted application of his "own country" concept at the fourth sentence of

paragraph 12.3 of the Committee's decision under reference ("That provision speaks of an 'alien lawfully in the territory of a State party' in limiting the rights of States to expel an individual categorized as an 'alien'.") Does it preclude the expulsion of *unlawful* aliens? Of course not—falling as they do under another legal regime. I have made this point in order to suggest that the legal significance in relation to "an alien lawfully in the territory of a State party" as appears in the first line of Article 13 of the Covenant, is related to the first line of Article 12: "everyone lawfully in the territory of a State", which includes aliens but, it may be borne in mind that in respect of a compatriot of Mr Stewart lawfully in Canada on a visitor's visa (not being a permanent resident of Canada) he would not normally have acquired "own country" status as Mr Stewart had, and would be indifferent to the application of Article 12, paragraph 4. But Mr Stewart would certainly be concerned as indeed he has been.

3. Thirdly, were it intended to restrict the application of Article 13 to exclude aliens lawfully in the territory of a State Party who had acquired "own country" status, such exclusion would have been specifically provided in Article 13 itself and not left to the interpretation of the scope of Article 12, paragraph 4, which incontestably applies to nationals and other persons contemplated in the Committee's text.

4. In regard to "own country" status in its submission of 24 February 1995 the State Party argues that "Mr Stewart has never acquired an *unconditional*[1] right to remain in Canada as his 'own country'. Moreover his deportation will not operate as an absolute bar to his re-entry to Canada. A humanitarian review in the context of the future application to re-enter Canada as an immigrant is a viable administrative procedure that does not entail reconsideration of the judicial decision of the Immigration Appeal Board" (see 9.1)[2].

Implicit in the foregoing is the admission that the State Party recognizes Mr Stewart's status as a permanent resident in Canada as his "own country". It is that *qualified* right applicable to such status which facilitated the decision to expel Mr Stewart.

But for the foregoing statement attributable to the State Party we could have concluded that the decision taken to expel Mr Stewart terminated his "own country" status in regard to Canada but in light of such statement the "own country" status remains only suspended at the pleasure of the State Party.

---

[1] Emphasis mine (see 9.1).
[2] See also paragraph 4.2 statements attributable to the State Party, including the following " . . . furthermore, he would not be barred once and for all from re-admission to Canada".

On the basis of the foregoing analysis, I am unable to support the decision of the Committee that Mr Stewart had at no time acquired "own country" status in Canada.

Laurel B. Francis [signed]
[Original: English]

C. *Individual opinion by Elizabeth Evatt and Cecilia Médina Quiroga, co-signed by Francisco José Aguilar Urbina (dissenting)*

1. We are unable to agree with the Committee's conclusion that the author cannot claim the protection of Article 12, paragraph 4.

2. A preliminary issue is whether the arbitrary deportation of a person from his/her own country should be equated with arbitrary deprivation of the right to enter that country, in circumstances where there has as yet been no attempt to enter or re-enter the country. The Committee does not reach a conclusion on this issue; it merely assumes that if Article 12, paragraph 4, were to apply to the author, the State would be precluded from deporting him (paragraph 12.2). The effect of the various proceedings taken by Canada, and the orders made, is that the author's right of residence has been taken away and his deportation ordered. He can no longer enter Canada as of right, and the prospects of his ever being able to secure permission to enter for more than a short period, if at all, seem remote. In our view, the right to enter a country is as much a prospective as a present right, and the deprivation of that right can occur, as in the circumstances of this case, whether or not there has been any actual refusal of entry. If a State Party is under an obligation to allow entry of a person it is prohibited from deporting that person. In our opinion the author has been deprived of the right to enter Canada, whether he remains in Canada awaiting deportation or whether he has already been deported.

3. The author's communication under Article 13 was found inadmissible, and no issue arises for consideration under that provision. The Committee's view is, however, that Article 12, paragraph 4 applies only to persons who are nationals, or who, while not nationals in a formal sense are also not aliens within the meaning of Article 13 (paragraph 12.3). Two consequences appear to follow from this view. The first one is that the relationship between an individual and a State may be not only that of national or alien (including stateless) but may also fall into a further, undefined, category. We do not think this is supported either by Article 12 of the Covenant or by general international law. As a consequence of the Committee's view it would also appear to follow that a person could not claim the protection of both Articles 13 and 12, paragraph 4. We do not agree. In our view Article 13 provides a minimum level of protection in respect of

expulsion for any alien, that is any non-national, lawfully in a State. Furthermore, there is nothing in the language of Article 13 which suggests that it is intended to be the exclusive source of rights for aliens, or that an alien who is lawfully within the territory of a State may not also claim the protection of Article 12, paragraph 4, if he or she can establish that it is his/her own country. Each provision should be given its full meaning.

4. The Committee attempts to identify the further category of individuals who could make use of Article 12, paragraph 4, by stating that a person cannot claim that a State is his or her own country, within the meaning of Article 12, paragraph 4, unless that person is a national of that State, or has been stripped of his or her nationality, or denied nationality by that State in the circumstances described (paragraph 12.4). The Committee is also of the view that unless unreasonable impediments have been placed in the way of an immigrant acquiring nationality, a person who enters a given State under its immigration laws, and who had the opportunity to acquire its nationality, cannot regard that State as his own country when he has failed to acquire its nationality (paragraph 12.5).

5. In our opinion, the Committee has taken too narrow a view of Article 12, paragraph 4, and has not considered the *raison d'être* of its formulation. Individuals cannot be deprived of the right to enter "their own country" because it is deemed unacceptable to deprive any person of close contact with his family, or his friends or, put in general terms, with the web of relationships that form his or her social environment. This is the reason why this right is set forth in Article 12, which addresses individuals lawfully within the territory of a State, not those who have formal links to that State. For the rights set forth in Article 12, the existence of a formal link to the State is irrelevant; the Covenant is here concerned with the strong personal and emotional links an individual may have with the territory where he lives and with the social circumstances obtaining in it. This is what Article 12, paragraph 4, protects.

6. The object and purpose of the right set forth in Article 12, paragraph 4, are reaffirmed by its wording. Nothing in it or in Article 12 generally suggests that its application should be restricted in the manner suggested by the Committee. While a person's "own country" would certainly include the country of nationality, there are factors other than nationality which may establish close and enduring connections between a person and a country, connections which may be stronger than those of nationality. After all, a person may have several nationalities, and yet have only the slightest or no actual connections of home and family with one or more of the States in question. The words "his own country" on the face of it invite consideration of such matters as long-standing residence, close

personal and family ties and intentions to remain (as well as to the absence of such ties elsewhere). Where a person is not a citizen of the country in question, the connections would need to be strong to support a finding that it is his "own country". Nevertheless our view is that it is open to an alien to show that there are such well-established links with a State that he or she is entitled to claim the protection of Article 12, paragraph 4.

7. The circumstances relied on by the author to establish that Canada is his own country are that he had lived in Canada for over thirty years, was brought up in Canada from the age of seven, had married and divorced there. His children, mother, handicapped brother continue to reside there. He had no ties with any other country, other than that he was a citizen of the UK; his elder brother had been deported to the UK some years before. The circumstances of his offences are set out in paragraph 2.2; as a result of these offences it is not clear if the author was ever entitled to apply for citizenship. Underlying the connections mentioned is the fact that the author and his family were accepted by Canada as immigrants when he was a child and that he became in practical terms a member of the Canadian community. He knows no other country. In all the circumstances, our view is that the author has established that Canada is his own country.

8. Was the deprivation of the author's right to enter Canada arbitrary? In another context, the Committee has taken the view that "arbitrary" means unreasonable in the particular circumstances, or contrary to the aims and objectives of the Covenant (General Comment on Article 17). That approach also appears to be appropriate in the context of Article 12, paragraph 4. In the case of citizens, there are likely to be few if any situations when deportation would not be considered arbitrary in the sense outlined. In the case of an alien such as the author, deportation could be considered arbitrary if the grounds relied on to deprive him of his right to enter and remain in the country were, in the circumstances, unreasonable, when weighed against the circumstances which make that country his "own country".

9. The grounds relied on by the State Party to justify the expulsion of the author are his criminal activities. It must be doubted whether the commission of criminal offences alone could justify the expulsion of a person from his own country, unless the State could show that there are compelling reasons of national security or public order which require such a course. The nature of the offences committed by the author do not lead readily to that conclusion. In any event, Canada can hardly claim that these grounds were compelling in the case of the author when it has in another context argued that the author might well be granted an entry visa for a short period to enable him to visit his family. Furthermore, while the deportation proceedings were not

unfair in procedural terms, the issue which arose for determination in those proceedings was whether the author could show reasons against his deportation, not whether there were grounds for taking away his right to enter "his own country". The onus was put on the author rather than on the State. In these circumstances, we conclude that the decision to deport the author was arbitrary, and thus a violation of his rights under Article 12, paragraph 4.

10. We agree with the Committee that the deportation of the author will undoubtedly interfere with his family relations in Canada (paragraph 12.10), but we cannot agree that this interference is not arbitrary, since we have come to the conclusion that the decision to deport the author—which is the cause of the interference with the family—was arbitrary. We have to conclude, therefore, that Canada has also violated the author's rights under Articles 17 and 23.

Elizabeth Evatt [signed]
Cecilia Médina Quiroga [signed]
Francisco José Aguilar Urbina [signed]
[Original: English]

D. *Individual opinion by Christine Chanet, co-signed by Julio Prado Vallejo (dissenting)*

I do not share the Committee's position with regard to the Stewart case, in which it concludes that, "as Canada cannot be regarded as Mr Stewart's 'own country'", there has been no violation by Canada of Article 12, paragraph 4, of the Covenant.

My criticism concerns the approach taken to the case on this point:

—assuming that wrongful acts disqualified the author from acquiring nationality and that, as a consequence, Canada may consider that it is not his own country, that conclusion should have led the Committee to reject the communication at the admissibility stage, since its awareness of that impediment should have precluded any application of Article 12, paragraph 4, of the Covenant.

—there is nothing either in the Covenant itself or in the *travaux préparatoires* about the "own country" concept; the Committee must, therefore, either decide the question on a case-by-case basis or establish criteria and make them known to States and authors, thus avoiding any contradiction with admissibility decisions; if a person is unable to acquire the nationality of a country owing to legal impediments, then regardless of any other criteria or factual circumstances, the communication should not be declared admissible under Article 12, paragraph 4, of the Covenant.

I agree with the substance of the individual opinion formulated by Ms Evatt and Ms Médina Quiroga.

Christine Chanet [signed]
Julio Prado Vallejo [signed]
[Original: French]

E. *Individual opinion by Prafullachandra Baghwati (dissenting)*

I entirely agree with the separate opinion prepared by Mrs Elizabeth Evatt and Mrs Cecilia Médina Quiroga, but having regard to the importance of the issues involved in the case, I am writing a separate opinion. This separate opinion may be read as supplementary to the opinion of Mrs Evatt and Mrs Médina Quiroga with which I find myself wholly in agreement.

This is not a case of one single individual. Its decision will have an impact on the lives of tens of thousands of immigrants and refugees. This case has therefore caused me immense anxiety. If the view taken by the majority of the Committee is right, people who have forged close links with a country not only through long residence but having regard to various other factors, who have adopted a country as their own, who have come to regard a country as their home country, would be left without any protection. The question is: are we going to read human rights in a generous and purposive manner or in a narrow and constricted manner? Let us not forget that basically, human rights in the International Covenant are rights of the individual against the State; they are protections against the State and they must therefore be construed broadly and liberally. This backdrop must be kept in mind when we are interpreting Article 12, paragraph 4.

First let me dispose of the argument with regard to Article 13. The Committee has declared the communication under Article 13 inadmissible and therefore it does not call for consideration. Coming to Article 12, paragraph 4, it raises three issues. The first is whether Article 12, paragraph 4, covers a case of deportation or is it confined only to right of entry; the second is as to what is the meaning and connotation of the words "his own country" and whether Canada could be said to be the author's own country; and the third is what are the criteria for determining whether an action alleged to be violative of Article 12, paragraph 4, is arbitrary and whether the action of Canada in deporting the author was arbitrary. I may point out at the outset that if the action of Canada was, on the facts, not arbitrary, there would be no violation of Article 12, paragraph 4, even if the other two elements were satisfied, namely, that Article 12, paragraph 4, covers deportation and Canada was the author's own country within the meaning of Article 12, paragraph 4, and it would in that event not be necessary to consider whether or not these two elements were satisfied. But since the majority of the members of the Committee have rested their opinion on the interpretation of the words "his own country" and taken the view, in my opinion wrongly, that Canada could not be said to be the author's own country, I think it necessary to consider all the three elements of Article 12, paragraph 4.

I am of the view that on a proper interpretation, Article 12, paragraph 4, protects everyone against arbitrary deportation from his own country. There are two reasons in support of this view. In the first place, unless Article 12, paragraph 4, is read as covering a case of deportation, a national of a State would have no protection against expulsion or deportation under the Covenant. Suppose the domestic law of a State empowers the State to expel or deport a national for certain specific reasons which may be totally irrelevant, fanciful or whimsical. Can it be suggested for a moment that the Covenant does not provide protection to a national against expulsion or deportation under such domestic law? The only article of the Covenant in which this protection can be found is Article 12, paragraph 4. It may be that under international law, a national cannot be expelled from his country of nationality. I am not familiar with all aspects of international law and I am therefore not in a position to affirm or disaffirm this proposition. But, be as it may, a law can be made by a State providing for expulsion of a national. It may conflict with a principle of international law, but that would not invalidate the domestic law. The principle of international law would not afford protection to the person concerned against domestic law. The only protection such a person would have is under Article 12, paragraph 4. We should not read Article 12, paragraph 4, in a manner which would leave a national unprotected against expulsion under domestic law. In fact, there are countries where there is domestic law providing for expulsion even of nationals and Article 12, paragraph 4, properly read, provides protection against arbitrary expulsion of a national. The same reasoning would apply also in a case where a non-national is involved. Article 12, paragraph 4, must therefore be read as covering expulsion or deportation.

Moreover, it is obvious that if a person has a right to enter his own country and he/she cannot be *arbitrarily* prevented from entering his/her own country, but he/she can be arbitrarily expelled, it would make non-sense of Article 12, paragraph 4. Suppose a person is expelled from his own country arbitrarily because he/she has no protection under Article 12, paragraph 4, and immediately after expulsion, he/she seeks to enter the country. Obviously he/she cannot be prevented because Article 12, paragraph 4, protects his/her entry. Then what is the sense of expelling him? We must therefore read Article 12, paragraph 4, as embodying, by necessary implication, protection against arbitrary expulsion from one's own country.

That takes me to the second issue. What is the scope and ambit of "his own country"? There is a general acceptance that "his own country" cannot be equated with "country of nationality" and I will not therefore spend any time on it. It is obvious that the expression "his own country" is wider than "country of nationality" and that is conceded by the majority view. "His own country" includes "country of nationality and something more". What is that "something more"? The majority view accepts that the concept "his own country" embraces, at the very least, "an individual who, because of his special ties to or claims in relation to a given country cannot there be considered to be a mere alien". I am in full agreement with this view. But then, the majority proceeds to delimit this concept by confining it to the following three illustrative cases:

(1) where nationals of a country have been stripped of their nationality in violation of international law,

(2) where the country of nationality of individuals has been incorporated into or transferred to another national entity whose nationality is being denied to them and

(3) stateless persons arbitrarily deprived of their right to acquire the nationality of the country of their residence.

It is the view of the majority that "while these individuals may not be nationals in the formal sense, neither are they aliens within the meaning of Article 13" and they fall within Article 12, paragraph 4.

There are two observations I would like to make in connection with this view of the majority. The majority view argues that Articles 12, paragraph 4, and 13 are mutually exclusive. It is observed by the majority in the view of the Committee that "'his own country' as a concept applies to individuals who are nationals and to certain categories of individuals who, while not nationals in a formal sense, are also not 'aliens' within the meaning of Article 13, though they may be considered as aliens for other purposes". Thus, according to the majority view, an individual falling within Article 12, paragraph 4, would not be an "alien" within the meaning of Article 13. I too subscribe to the same view. But there my agreement with the view of the majority ends. The question is: who is protected by Article 12, paragraph 4? Who falls within its protective wing? I may again repeat, in agreement with the majority view, that Article 12, paragraph 4, embraces, at the very least, an individual who, because of his special ties to or claims in relation to a given country cannot there be considered to be an alien. This is a correct test but I fail to understand why its application should be limited to the three kinds of cases referred to by the majority. These three kinds of cases would certainly be covered by this test but there may be many more which would also answer this test. I do not see any valid reason why they should be excluded except a predetermination by the majority that they should not be regarded as fulfilling this test, because that would affect the immigration policies of the developed countries. Take for example, a large number of Africans or Latin Americans or Indians who are settled in the UK, but who have not acquired UK citizenship. Their children, born and brought up in the UK would not have even visited their country of nationality. If you ask them: "which is your own country?", they would unhesitatingly say: "UK". Can you say that only India or some country in Africa or Latin America which they have never visited and with which they have no links at all is the only country which they can call their own country? I agree that mere length of residence would not be a determinative test but length of residence may be a factor coupled with other factors. The totality of factors would have to be taken into account for the purpose of determining whether the country in question is a country which the person concerned has adopted as his own country or is a country with which he has special ties or the most intimate connection or link in order to be regarded as "his own country" within the meaning of Article 12, paragraph 4.

Before I part with the discussion of this point, I must refer to one other illogicality in which the majority appears to have fallen. The majority seems to suggest that where the country of immigration places unreasonable impediments on the acquiring of nationality by a new immigrant, it might be possible to say that for the new immigrant who has not acquired the nationality of the country of immigration and continues to retain the nationality of his country of origin, the country of immigration may be regarded as "his own country". There are at least two objections against the validity of this view. In the first place, it is the sovereign right of a State to determine under what conditions it will grant nationality to a non-national. It is not for the Committee to pass judgment whether the conditions are reasonable or not and whether the conditions are such as to impose unreasonable impediments on the acquisition of nationality by a new immigrant nor is the Committee competent to enquire whether the action of the State in rejecting the application of a new immigrant for nationality is reasonable or not. Secondly, I fail to see what is the difference between the two situations: one, where an application for nationality is made and is unreasonably refused and the other, where an application for nationality is not made at all. In both cases, the new immigrant would continue to be a non-national and if in one case, special ties or intimate connection or link with the country of immigration would render such country "his own country", there is no logical or relevant reason why it should not have the same consequence or effect in the other case.

I fail to understand what is the basis on which the majority states that countries like Canada have a *right* to expect that immigrants within due course acquire all the rights and assume all the obligations that nationality entails. I agree that individuals who do not take advantage of the opportunity to apply for nationality must bear the consequences of not being nationals. But the question is: what are these consequences? Do they entail exclusion from the benefit of Article 12, paragraph 4? That is the question which has to be answered and it cannot be *assumed*, as the majority seems to have done, that the consequence is exclusion from the benefit of Article 12, paragraph 4. Throughout the decision of the Committee, I find that the majority starts with the predetermination that in the case of the author, Canada cannot be regarded as "his own country" even though he has special ties and most intimate connection and link with Canada and he has always regarded Canada as his own country, and then tries to justify this conclusion by holding that there were no unreasonable impediments in the way of the author acquiring Canadian nationality but the author did not take advantage of the opportunity to apply for Canadian nationality and must therefore bear the consequence of Canada not being regarded as his own country and therefore of being deprived of the benefit of Article 12, paragraph 4. If I may repeat, the fact that the author did not apply for Canadian nationality in a situation where there were no unreasonable impediments in such acquisition, cannot have any bearing on the question whether Canada could or could not be regarded as "his own country". It is because the author is not a Canadian national that the question has arisen and it is begging the question to say that Canada could not be regarded as "his own country" because he did not or could not acquire Canadian nationality.

It is undoubtedly true that on this view, both the UK and Canada would be "his own country" for the author. One would be the country of nationality while the other would be, what I may call, the country of adoption. It is quite conceivable that an individual may have two countries which he can call his own: one may be a country of his nationality and the other, a country adopted by him as his own country. I am therefore inclined to take the view, on the facts as set out in the communication, that Canada was the author's own country within the meaning of Article 12, paragraph 4, and he could not be arbitrarily expelled or deported from Canada by the Government of Canada.

That leaves the question whether the expulsion or deportation of the author could be said to be arbitrary. On this question, I recall the Committee's jurisprudence that the concept of arbitrariness must not be confined to procedural arbitrariness but must include substantive arbitrariness as well and it must not be equated with "against the law" but must be interpreted broadly to include such elements as inappropriateness or excessiveness or disproportionateness. Where an action taken by the State Party against a person is excessive or disproportionate to the harm sought to be prevented, it would be unreasonable and arbitrary. Here, in the present case, the author is sought to be expelled on account of his recidivist tendency. He has committed around forty offences including theft and robbery for which he has been punished. The question is whether it is *necessary*, in all the circumstances of the case, to expel or deport him in order to protect the society from his criminal propensity or whether this object can be achieved by taking a lesser action than expulsion or deportation. The element of proportionality must be taken into account. I think that if this test is applied, the action of Canada in seeking to expel or deport the author would appear to be arbitrary, particularly in the light of the fact that the author has succeeded in controlling alcohol abuse and no offence appears to have been committed by him since May 1991. If the author commits any more offences, he can be adequately punished and imprisoned and if, having regard to his past criminal record, a sufficiently heavy sentence of imprisonment is passed against him, it would act as a deterrent against any further criminal activity on his part and in any event, he would be put out of action during the time that he is in prison. This is the kind of action which would be taken against a national in order to protect the society and *qua* a national, it would be regarded as adequate. I do not see why it should not be regarded as adequate *qua* a person who is not a national but who has adopted Canada as his own country or come to regard Canada as his own country. I am of the view that the action of expulsion or deportation of the author from Canada resulting in completely uprooting him from his home, family and moorings, would be excessive and disproportionate to the harm sought to be prevented and hence must be regarded as arbitrary.

I would therefore hold that in the present case, there is violation of Article 12, paragraph 4, of the Covenant. On this view, it becomes unnecessary to consider whether there is also violation of Articles 17 and 23 of the Covenant.

Prafullachandra Baghwati [signed]
[Original: English]

[Report: Doc. CCPR/C/58/D/538/1993]

Human rights—Right to a fair trial—International Covenant on Civil and Political Rights, 1966, Article 14—Capital case—Appeal—Conduct of defence counsel on appeal—Duty of Court to take exceptional care in capital case—Commutation of death sentence—Sufficient remedy for violation of Article 6 but not for violation of Article 14

PRICE *v.* JAMAICA

(*Communication No 572/1994*)

United Nations Human Rights Committee.[1]   6 *November* 1996

SUMMARY: *The facts:*—The author of the communication, a Jamaican citizen, was convicted of murder by a court in Jamaica. He submitted that, on his appeal to the Court of Appeal on the grounds of unfair trial and insufficient evidence to warrant a conviction, he did not receive a fair trial in accordance with Article 14(3)(d) of the International Covenant on Civil and Political Rights, 1966. The legal aid lawyers conducting the appeal did not consult with the author before the hearing and counsel for the author advised the Court of Appeal during the hearing that he could find no grounds for the appeal to be allowed. The author claimed that he would have asked for different legal aid counsel had he known that counsel would not put forward grounds of appeal. Further, the author claimed that the failure of the Court of Appeal to produce a written judgment in his case constituted a violation of Article 14(3)(c) and (5) of the Covenant, since this failure effectively barred him from appealing to the Judicial Committee of the Privy Council.

Jamaica argued that the communication should be declared inadmissible, since the author had failed to exhaust domestic remedies (appeal to the Privy Council or constitutional motion to the Supreme Court). Counsel for the author replied that there were no effective domestic remedies open to the author as there were no grounds for petition to the Privy Council, and a constitutional motion could not be pursued since legal aid was unavailable. In its observations on the merits, Jamaica maintained that the communication was inadmissible for non-exhaustion of domestic remedies. Concerning the alleged breach of Article 14(3)(d), Jamaica contended it had a duty only to provide competent legal aid counsel to poor persons, and this duty did not extend to the manner in which counsel represented the accused.

Held:—(1) This matter appeared to raise an issue under Article 14(3)(b), but the Committee could not examine it as counsel had never raised this claim (p. 354).

(2) While Article 14(3)(d) did not entitle the accused to select legal aid counsel, the Court should have ensured that counsel's conduct of the appeal was not incompatible with the interests of justice. In a capital case, when

---

[1] For the composition of the Committee, see p. 254, note 1. Pursuant to Rule 85 of the Rules of Procedure, Committee member Laurel Francis (Jamaica) did not participate in the examination of the communication.

counsel for the accused considered that the appeal had no merit, the Court should check that counsel had so informed the accused in order that he could consider his remaining options. The author had not been effectively represented on his appeal, and Article 14(3)(d) had been violated (p. 354).

(3) Since the author had been sentenced to death without effective representation on appeal in accordance with Article 14, there had also been a violation of Article 6. However, Jamaica had commuted the author's death sentence, and this constituted sufficient remedy for the violation of Article 6(2) in this case (p. 354).

(4) Since there had been a violation of Article 14(3)(d), the author was entitled to an appropriate remedy. Jamaica had also to ensure that similar events did not occur in future (p. 355).

(5) The Committee gave Jamaica ninety days in which to provide it with information about measures taken to give effect to the Committee's views (p. 355).

The following is the text of the views of the Committee:

Views under Article 5, paragraph 4, of the Optional Protocol

1. The author of the communication is Mr Hezekiah Price, a Jamaican citizen, currently imprisoned at the General Penitentiary, Kingston, Jamaica, serving a life term. The author claims to be a victim of a violation by Jamaica of Article 14, paragraphs 3(c), (d) and 5, of the International Covenant on Civil and Political Rights. He is represented by counsel.

The facts as submitted by the author

2.1 The author was arrested on 19 June 1983 and charged with the murder of his common-law wife earlier that same day. On 26 January 1984, after a trial in the St Catherine Circuit Court, he was found guilty of murder and sentenced to death.

2.2 The author's application for leave to appeal was dismissed by the Court of Appeal on 29 November 1985. A note of oral judgment was delivered on 6 October 1987. At the beginning of 1989 the author's sentence was commuted to life imprisonment.

2.3 The prosecution's case was based on evidence given by eye-witnesses, who had heard the author and his common-law wife quarrelling. They testified that when the author and his wife came out of the house, he held her by the arm, beat her with the flat of a machete, and when she had fallen on the ground, he killed her with several sharp blows of the machete. The author then walked to the police station to give himself up. The case for the accused was based on self-defence. The judge also put the defence of provocation before the jury.

The complaint

3.1 The author claims that he did not have a fair trial. More particularly he claims that his right under Article 14, paragraph 3(d), was violated. An application for leave to appeal was filed with the Court of Appeal on the grounds of unfair trial and insufficient evidence to warrant a conviction. The legal aid lawyers who were instructed to conduct the appeal did not consult with the author before the hearing. Moreover, it appears from the note of the oral judgment that counsel for the author advised the Court of Appeal during the hearing that he could find no grounds for the appeal to be allowed. The author claims that, had he known that counsel would not put forward any grounds of appeal, he would have asked to have different legal aid counsel assigned to his case.

3.2 The author also claims that the failure of the Court of Appeal to produce a written judgment in his case constitutes a violation of Article 14, paragraphs 3(c) and 5, since this failure effectively barred him from appealing to the Judicial Committee of the Privy Council.

The State Party's observations on admissibility and author's comments thereon

4. By submission of 11 November 1994, the State Party argues that the communication is inadmissible under Article 5, paragraph 2(b), of the Optional Protocol, because the author has failed to exhaust domestic remedies. It notes that the author may still appeal to the Judicial Committee of the Privy Council by way of petition for special leave to appeal. The State Party adds that the author may still apply for constitutional redress; in this context, it notes that the rights invoked by the author and protected by Article 14, paragraph 3(c) and (d), are coterminous with Sections 20(6) and 110 of the Jamaican Constitution. Pursuant to Section 25 of the Constitution, it is open to the author to seek redress for the alleged violations of his rights by way of a constitutional motion to the Supreme Court.

5. In his comments, dated 30 January 1995, the author's counsel states that he has been advised by leading counsel that there were no grounds upon which to petition the Privy Council, and concludes there are no effective domestic remedies that the author should still exhaust. He further states that, since legal aid is not made available for constitutional motions, a constitutional motion does not constitute an effective remedy in this case.

The Committee's admissibility decision

6.1 During its 54th session, the Committee considered the admissibility of the communication. The Committee found that the formal requirements of admissibility under Article 5, paragraph 2(a) and (b), of the Optional Protocol had been met.

6.2 The Committee considered that author's counsel had failed, for purposes of admissibility, to present sufficient elements that would substantiate a possible violation of Article 14, paragraph 3(c). In particular, author's counsel had not argued that, in the specific circumstances of Mr Price's case, an earlier written judgment or note of oral judgment would have led to a different result.

6.3 The Committee considered that the author and his counsel had sufficiently substantiated, for purposes of admissibility, a possible violation of Article 14, paragraph 3(d). The Committee recalled its jurisprudence that "measures must be taken to ensure that counsel, once assigned, provides effective representation in the interests of justice. This includes consulting with, and informing, the accused if he intends to withdraw an appeal or to argue before the appeal court that the appeal has no merits."[2] The Committee found that this part of the communication needed to be examined on the merits.

6.4 The Committee considered that the author and his counsel had failed to substantiate for purposes of admissibility, that the communication raised issues under Article 14, paragraph 5, of the Covenant.

6.5 On 21 July 1995, therefore, the Human Rights Committee declared the communication admissible inasmuch as it appeared to raise issues under Article 14, paragraph 3(d), of the Covenant.

State Party's observations on the merits and counsel's comments thereon

7.1 In its submission under Article 4, paragraph 2, of the Optional Protocol, dated 19 February 1996, the State Party reiterates that the communication is inadmissible for non-exhaustion of domestic remedies.

7.2 On the alleged breach of Article 14, paragraph 3(d), because counsel did not argue the author's appeal, the State Party contends that it has a duty to provide competent legal aid counsel to represent poor persons, thereafter the manner in which counsel represents the accused cannot be attributed to the State Party.

8. In his comments on the State Party's submission, counsel rebuts the State Party's contention that domestic remedies are still open to the author and reiterates that the State Party is responsible for the quality of legal aid counsel, and refers to the Committee's jurisprudence.

Examination on the merits

9.1 The Human Rights Committee has considered the present communication in the light of all the information made available to it by the parties, as required under Article 5, paragraph 1, of the Optional Protocol.

9.2 Counsel has claimed that Mr Price was not effectively represented on appeal, and the Committee notes that the Court of Appeal

[2] Communication No 253/1987 (*Kelly* v. *Jamaica*), Views adopted on 8 April 1991, paragraph 5.10.

Judgment shows that Mr Price's legal aid counsel for appeal conceded at the hearing that there was no merit in the appeal. The Committee notes that the matter would appear also to raise an issue under Article 14, paragraph 3(b), of the Covenant, but that it is precluded from examining whether such a violation has occurred, as this claim was never raised by counsel. The Committee recalls its earlier jurisprudence[3] that while Article 14, paragraph 3(d), does not entitle the accused to choose counsel provided to him free of charge, the Court should ensure that the conduct of the appeal by the lawyer is not incompatible with the interests of justice. While it is not for the Committee to question counsel's professional judgment, the Committee considers that in a capital case, when counsel for the accused concedes that there is no merit in the appeal, the Court should ascertain whether counsel has consulted with the accused and informed him accordingly. The Committee is of the opinion that Mr Price should have been informed that his counsel was not going to argue any grounds in support of the appeal so that he could have considered any remaining options open to him. In the circumstances, the Committee finds that Mr Price was not effectively represented on appeal, in violation of Article 14, paragraph 3(d), of the Covenant.

9.3 The Committee is of the opinion that the imposition of a sentence of death upon conclusion of a trial in which the provisions of the Covenant have not been respected constitutes, if no further appeal against the sentence is possible, a violation of Article 6 of the Covenant. As the Committee noted in its General Comment 6[16], the provision that a sentence of death may be imposed only in accordance with the law and not contrary to the provisions of the Covenant implies that "the procedural guarantees therein prescribed must be observed, including the right to a fair hearing by an independent tribunal, the presumption of innocence, the minimum guarantees for the defence, and the right to review of the conviction and sentence by a higher tribunal". In the present case, since the final sentence of death was passed without having observed the requirement of effective represent-ation on appeal as set out in Article 14, it must be concluded that the right protected by Article 6 of the Covenant has been violated. The Committee notes that the State Party has commuted the author's death sentence and considers that this constitutes sufficient remedy for the violation of Article 6, paragraph 2, in this case.

10. The Human Rights Committee, acting under Article 5, paragraph 4, of the Optional Protocol to the International Covenant on Civil and Political Rights, is of the view that the facts before it disclose a violation of Article 14, paragraph 3(d), of the Covenant.

---

[3] See *inter alia* the Committee's Views in respect of communications Nos 459/1991 (*Osborne Wright and Eric Harvey* v. *Jamaica*), adopted on 27 October 1995, paragraph 10.5 and 461/1991 (*George Graham and Arthur Morrison* v. *Jamaica*), adopted on 25 March 1996, paragraph 10.5.

11. Pursuant to Article 2, paragraph 3(a) of the Covenant, the author is entitled to an appropriate remedy. The State Party is under an obligation to ensure that similar events do not occur in the future.

12. Bearing in mind, that by becoming a State Party to the Optional Protocol, the State Party has recognized the competence of the Committee to determine whether there has been a violation of the Covenant or not and that, pursuant to Article 2 of the Covenant, the State Party has undertaken to ensure to all individuals within its territory and subject to its jurisdiction the rights recognized in the Covenant and to provide an effective and enforceable remedy in case a violation has been established, the Committee wishes to receive from the State Party, within ninety days, information about the measures taken to give effect to the Committee's Views.

[Adopted in English, French and Spanish, the English text being the original version. Subseqently to be issued also in Arabic, Chinese and Russian as part of the Committee's annual report to the General Assembly.]

[Report: Doc. CCPR/C/58/D/572/1994]

Human rights—Freedom of expression—Restrictions on freedom of expression—Conditions—Requirement that any restriction be provided by law, address a legitimate aim and be necessary for the achievement of that aim—French legislation prohibiting the denial of certain offences connected with the Holocaust — Whether a violation of International Covenant on Civil and Political Rights, 1966, Article 19

International tribunals—United Nations Human Rights Committee — Competence — Domestic remedies rule — Committee not empowered to question in the abstract the compatibility of national law with the Covenant —

Committee confined to investigating the communications submitted to it

FAURISSON *v.* FRANCE

(*Communication No 550/1993*)

United Nations Human Rights Committee.[1]   8 *November* 1996

SUMMARY: *The facts*:—The author of the communication had dual French and British citizenship and resided in France. Without invoking specific provisions of the International Covenant on Civil and Political Rights, 1966, he claimed to be a victim of violations by France. The author was an academic who, in the course of his work, had cast doubt on the occurrence of certain events during the Holocaust, arguing, *inter alia*, that the gas chambers at Nazi concentration camps were not used for extermination purposes. He alleged that he had been attacked and threatened as a result of his opinions, and that French authorities had not successfully prosecuted his assailants. On 13 July 1990 France had passed the "Gayssot Act", making it an offence to contest the existence of crimes against humanity, as defined in the 1945 Charter of the International Military Tribunal at Nuremberg. The author contended that this Act promoted the Nuremberg trial and judgment to dogma, immune from challenge. A French magazine then published an interview with the author, in which he expressed his views on the Holocaust and on the Gayssot Act. The author and the editor of the magazine were subsequently subject to a private criminal prosecution brought by former French resistance fighters and deportees to German concentration camps. On 18 April 1991 they were convicted and fined. On appeal to the Court of Appeal of Paris their conviction was upheld and their fine increased. The author could have appealed to the Court of Cassation, but claimed he could not afford the legal fees and that, in the political climate, such an appeal would have been futile.

In his communication of 2 January 1993 to the United Nations Human Rights Committee, the author contended that the Gayssot Act curtailed his right to freedom of expression and academic freedom, and that it targeted him personally. He also questioned the impartiality in his case of the Court of Appeal and stated that, as a result of the magazine interview, he was facing more than one private criminal action, in violation of the principle *ne bis in idem*. Further, he was still subject to serious threats and assaults. France responded that the *ratio legis* of the Gayssot Act was to fill a gap in the available criminal sanctions, by criminalizing the acts of those "revisionists" negating the existence of certain crimes against humanity. France also contended that the author's communication was inadmissible for non-exhaustion of domestic remedies, rejecting the author's criticisms of the Court

---

[1] For the composition of the Committee, see p. 254, note 1. Pursuant to Rule 85 of the Committee's Rules of Procedure, Committee members Christine Chanet (France) and Thomas Buergenthal (United States) did not participate in the consideration of the case. A statement made by Mr Buergenthal can be found at p. 373.

of Cassation. Further, regarding the alleged violation of Article 14(7) of the Covenant, French law upheld the principle of *ne bis in idem*, and any action taken against the author in breach of this principle would be annulled by the courts.

The author replied that his co-accused, the editor of the magazine, had appealed to the Court of Cassation, which had dismissed his appeal in December 1994. He maintained that his complaint primarily concerned the infringement, by the Gayssot Act, of his right to freedom of opinion, and of academic research, rather than freedom of expression. He also provided details of the cases pending against him in breach of Article 14(7) of the Covenant.

The Committee decided that the complaint was admissible under Article 19 as it raised issues regarding the author's freedom of expression, opinion and academic research. Although he had not exhausted domestic remedies, his co-accused had done so on the same facts and therefore the author had no effective domestic remedy. The Committee found inadmissible the author's complaints of violation of the principle of *ne bis in idem*, and of the alleged partiality of the Court of Appeal.

Held:—(1) Although the terms of the Gayssot Act were such that they might, in certain circumstances, lead to decisions or measures incompatible with the Covenant, the task of the Committee was not to criticize, in the abstract, laws enacted by States Parties, but to make decisions on the communications brought before it (p. 372).

(2) Any restriction on the right to freedom of expression must meet certain conditions. It must be provided by law, it must address one of the aims set out in paragraph 3(a) and (b) of Article 19, and it must be necessary to achieve a legitimate purpose (p. 372).

(3) The restriction on the author's freedom of expression was provided by law in the form of the Gayssot Act. The jurisprudence of the Committee was that the restrictive law must be in compliance with the Covenant. In the present case, the author was convicted not for holding and expressing his opinion in general, but for violating the rights and reputation of others. In the author's case, the Gayssot Act therefore complied with the Covenant (p. 372).

(4) The restriction was permissible under Article 19(3)(a) of the Covenant, as its aim was to encourage respect for the reputation of the Jewish community, and Article 19(3)(a) might relate to the interests of a community as a whole (p. 373).

(5) The restriction was necessary under Article 19(3) of the Covenant as France contended that the Gayssot Act was necessary in the struggle against racism and anti-semitism, and no argument had been put forward undermining the validity of this argument (p. 373).

(6) There had been no violation of Article 19(3) of the Covenant (p. 373).

Per Mr Ando (concurring): The Gayssot Act could threaten the right to freedom of expression. It might be better to replace this Act with specific legislation prohibiting well-defined acts of anti-semitism, or a general provision protecting the rights or reputations of others (p. 374).

Per Mrs Evatt, Mr Kretzmer and Mr Klein (concurring): The main issue was whether the restriction on the author's freedom of expression was *necessary* for the respect of the *rights* of others in terms of Article 19(3)(a) of the

Covenant. The scope of the restriction imposed on freedom of expression must be proportional to the value which the restriction served to protect. Although certain restrictions imposed by the Gayssot Act generally did not meet the proportionality test, in the specific circumstances of the author's case the restrictions did meet this test and were necessary (pp. 374-7).

Per Ms Médina Quiroga (concurring): Although the Gayssot Act itself might violate Article 19 of the Covenant, the French court which tried the author had interpreted the Act so as to adapt it to France's international obligations regarding freedom of expression (pp. 377-8).

Per Mr Lallah (concurring): The creation of the offence provided for in the Gayssot Act, as applied to the author's case, fell more appropriately within the powers of France under Article 20(2). There was no difficulty in invoking Article 20(2) despite the fact that the author's communication was declared admissible only with regard to Article 19. Recourse to restrictions permissible under Article 19(3) tended to destroy the existence of this valuable right (pp. 378-80).

Per Mr Baghwati (concurring): The restriction on freedom of expression imposed by the Gayssot Act satisfied all three elements required by Article 19(3) and was not inconsistent with Article 19(2) of the Covenant. Hence the conviction of the author under the Gayssot Act did not violate his freedom of expression (pp. 380-3).

The following is the text of the views of the Committee:

Views under Article 5, paragraph 4, of the Optional Protocol

1. The author of the communication, dated 2 January 1993, is Robert Faurisson, born in the United Kingdom in 1929 and with dual French/British citizenship, currently residing in Vichy, France. He claims to be a victim of violations of his human rights by France. The author does not invoke specific provisions of the Covenant.

The facts as submitted by the author

2.1 The author was a professor of literature at the Sorbonne University in Paris until 1973 and at the University of Lyons until 1991, when he was removed from his chair. Aware of the historical significance of the Holocaust, he has sought proof of the methods of killings, in particular by gas asphyxiation. While he does not contest the use of gas for purposes of disinfection, he doubts the existence of gas chambers for extermination purposes (*"chambres à gaz homicides"*) at Auschwitz and in other Nazi concentration camps.

2.2 The author submits that his opinions have been rejected in numerous academic journals and ridiculed in the daily press, notably in France; nonetheless, he continues to question the existence of extermination gas chambers. As a result of public discussion of his opinions and the polemics accompanying these debates, he states that, since 1978, he has become the target of death threats and that on eight occasions he has been physically assaulted. On one occasion in 1989, he claims to have suffered serious injuries, including a broken jaw, for which he was hospitalized. He contends that although these attacks were brought to the attention of the competent judicial authorities, they were not seriously investigated and none of those responsible for the assaults has been arrested or prosecuted. On 23 November 1992, the Court of Appeal of Riom followed the request of the prosecutor of the *Tribunal de Grande Instance* of Cusset and decreed the closure of the proceedings (*ordonnance de non-lieu*) which the authorities had initiated against X.

2.3 On 13 July 1990, the French legislature passed the so-called "Gayssot Act", which amends the law on the Freedom of the Press of 1881 by adding an Article 24 *bis*; the latter makes it an offence to contest the existence of the category of crimes against humanity as defined in the London Charter of 8 August 1945, on the basis of which Nazi leaders were tried and convicted by the International Military Tribunal at Nuremberg in 1945-1946. The author submits that, in essence, the "Gayssot Act" promotes the Nuremberg trial and judgment to the status of dogma, by imposing criminal sanctions on those who dare to challenge its findings and premises. Mr Faurisson contends that he has ample reason to believe that the records of the Nuremberg trial can indeed be challenged and that the evidence used against Nazi leaders is open to question, as is, according to him, the evidence about the number of victims exterminated at Auschwitz.

2.4 In substantiation of the claim that the Nuremberg records cannot be taken as infallible, he cites, by way of example, the indictment which charged the Germans with the Katyn massacre, and refers to the introduction by the Soviet prosecutor of documents purporting to show that the Germans had killed the Polish prisoners of war at Katyn (Nuremberg document USSR-054). The Soviet authorship of this crime, he points out, is now established beyond doubt. The author further notes that, among the members of the Soviet Katyn (Lyssenko) Commission, which had adduced proof of the purported German responsibility for the Katyn massacre, were Professors Burdenko and Nicolas, who also testified that the Germans had used gas chambers at Auschwitz for the extermination of four million persons (Document USSR-006). Subsequently, he asserts, the estimated number of victims at Auschwitz has been revised downward to approximately one million.

2.5 Shortly after the enactment of the "Gayssot Act", Mr Faurisson was interviewed by the French monthly magazine *Le Choc du Mois*, which published the interview in its Number 32 issue of September 1990. Besides expressing his concern that the new law constituted a threat to freedom of research and freedom of expression, the author reiterated his personal conviction that there were no homicidal gas chambers for the extermination of Jews in Nazi concentration camps. Following the publication of this interview, eleven associations of French resistance fighters and of deportees to German concentration camps filed a private criminal action against Mr Faurisson and Patrice Boizeau, the editor of the magazine *Le Choc du Mois*. By judgment of 18 April 1991, the 17th *Chambre Correctionnelle du Tribunal de Grande Instance de Paris* convicted Messrs Faurisson and Boizeau of having committed the crime of *"contestation de crimes contre l'humanité"* and imposed on them fines and costs amounting to FF 326,832.

2.6 The conviction was based, *inter alia*, on the following Faurisson statements:

. . . No one will have me admit that two plus two make five, that the earth is flat, or that the Nuremberg Tribunal was infallible. I have excellent reasons not to believe in this policy of extermination of Jews or in the magic gas chamber . . .

I would wish to see that 100 per cent of all French citizens realize that the myth of the gas chambers is a dishonest fabrication (*"est une gredinerie"*), endorsed by the victorious powers of Nuremberg in 1945-46 and officialized on 14 July 1990 by the current French Government, with the approval of the "court historians".

2.7 The author and Mr Boizeau appealed their conviction to the Court of Appeal of Paris (Eleventh Chamber). On 9 December 1992, the Eleventh Chamber, under the Presidency of Mrs Françoise Simon, upheld the conviction and fined Messrs Faurisson and Boizeau a total of FF 374,045.50. This sum included compensation for immaterial damage to the eleven plaintiff associations. The Court of Appeal did, *inter alia*, examine the facts in the light of Articles 6 and 10 of the European Convention of Human Rights and Fundamental Freedoms and concluded that the court of first instance had evaluated them correctly. The author adds that, in addition to this penalty, he incurred considerable additional expenses, including attorney's fees for his defence and hospitalization costs as a result of injuries sustained when he was assaulted by members of Bétar and Tagar on the first day of the trial.

2.8 The author observes that the "Gayssot Act" has come under attack even in the French National Assembly. Thus, in June 1991, Mr Jacques Toubon, a member of Parliament for the *Rassemblement pour la République* (RPR) and currently the French Minister of Justice, called for the abrogation of the Act. Mr Faurisson also refers to the criticism of the Gayssot Act by Mrs Simone Veil, herself an Auschwitz survivor, and by one of the leading legal representatives of a Jewish association. In this context, the author associates himself with a suggestion put forward by Mr Philippe Costa, another French citizen tried under

Article 24 *bis* and acquitted by the Court of Appeal of Paris on 18 February 1993, to the effect that the Gayssot Act be replaced by legislation specifically protecting all those who might become victims of incitement to racial hatred and in particular to anti-semitism, without obstructing historical research and discussion.

2.9 Mr Faurisson acknowledges that it would still be open to him to appeal to the Court of Cassation; he claims, however, that he does not have the FF 20,000 of lawyers' fees which such an appeal would require, and that in any event, given the climate in which the trial at first instance and the appeal took place, a further appeal to the Court of Cassation would be futile. He assumes that even if the Court of Cassation were to quash the judgments of the lower instances, it would undoubtedly order a re-trial, which would produce the same results as the initial trial in 1991.

The complaint

3.1 The author contends that the "Gayssot Act" curtails his right to freedom of expression and academic freedom in general, and considers that the law targets him personally ("lex Faurissonia"). He complains that the incriminated provision constitutes unacceptable censorship, obstructing and penalizing historical research.

3.2 In respect of the judicial proceedings, Mr Faurisson questions, in particular, the impartiality of the Court of Appeal (Eleventh Chamber). Thus, he contends that the President of the Chamber turned her face away from him throughout his testimony and did not allow him to read any document in court, not even excerpts from the Nuremberg verdict, which he submits was of importance for his defence.

3.3 The author states that, on the basis of separate private criminal actions filed by different organizations, both he and Mr Boizeau are being prosecuted for the same interview of September 1990 in two other judicial instances which, at the time of submission of the communication, were scheduled to be heard in June 1993. This he considers to be a clear violation of the principle *ne bis in idem*.

3.4 Finally, the author submits that he continues to be subjected to threats and physical aggressions to such an extent that his life is in danger. Thus, he claims to have been assaulted by French citizens on 22 May 1993 in Stockholm, and again on 30 May 1993 in Paris.

State Party's submission on the question of admissibility and author's comments thereon

4.1 In its submission under Rule 91, the State Party provides a chronological overview of the facts of the case and explains the *ratio legis* of the law of 13 July 1990. In this latter context, it observes that the law in question fills a gap in the panoply of criminal sanctions, by criminalizing the acts of those who question the genocide of the Jews and the existence of gas chambers. In the latter context, it adds that the so-called "revisionist" theses had previously escaped any criminal qualification, in that they could not be subsumed under the prohibition of (racial) discrimination, of incitement to racial hatred, or glorification of war crimes or crimes against humanity.

4.2 The State Party further observes that in order to avoid making it an offence to manifest an opinion ("*délit d'opinion*"), the legislature chose to determine precisely the material element of the offence, by criminalizing only the negation ("*contestation*"), by one of the means enumerated in Article 23 of the Law on the Freedom of the Press of 1881, of one or several of the crimes against humanity in the sense of Article 6 of the Statute of the International Military Tribunal. The role of the judge seized of allegations of facts that might be subsumed under the new law is *not* to intervene in an academic or an historical debate, but to ascertain whether the contested publications of words negate the existence of crimes against humanity recognized by international judicial instances. The State Party points out that the Law of 13 July 1990 was noted with appreciation by the Committee on the Elimination of Racial Discrimination in March 1994.

4.3 The State Party submits that the communication is inadmissible on the basis of non-exhaustion of domestic remedies in so far as the alleged violation of Mr Faurisson's freedom of expression is concerned, as he did not appeal his case to the Court of Cassation. It recalls the Committee's jurisprudence that mere doubts about the effectiveness of available remedies do not absolve an author from availing himself of them. Furthermore, it contends that there is no basis for the author's doubt that recourse to the Court of Cassation could not provide him with judicial redress.

4.4 In this context, the State Party notes that while the Court of Cassation indeed does not examine facts and evidence in a case, it *does* ascertain whether the law was applied correctly to the facts, and can determine that there was a violation of the law, of which the Covenant is an integral part (Article 55 of the French Constitution of 4 June 1958). Article 55 stipulates that international treaties take precedence over domestic laws, and according to a judgment of the Court of Cassation of 24 May 1975, domestic laws contrary to an international treaty shall not be applied, even if the internal law was adopted *after* the conclusion of the treaty. Thus, the author remained free to invoke the Covenant before the Court of Cassation, as the Covenant takes precedence over the Law of 13 July 1990.

4.5 As to the costs of an appeal to the Court of Cassation, the State Party notes that pursuant to Articles 584 and 585 of the Code of Criminal Procedure, it is not mandatory for a convicted person to be represented by counsel before the Court of Cassation. Furthermore, it observes that legal aid would be available to the author, upon sufficiently motivated request, in accordance with the provisions of Law 91-647 of 10 July 1991 (especially para. 10 thereof). The author did not file any such request, and in the absence of information about his financial resources, the State Party contends that nothing would allow the conclusion that an application for legal aid, had it been filed, would not have been granted.

4.6 Concerning the alleged violation of Article 14, paragraph 7, the State Party underlines that the principle of "*ne bis in idem*" is firmly anchored in French law, which has been confirmed by the Court of Cassation in numerous judgments (see in particular Article 6 of the Code of Criminal Procedure).

4.7 Thus, if new complaints and criminal actions against the author were entertained by the courts, for facts already judged by the Court of Appeal of Paris on 9 December 1992, then, the State Party affirms, the prosecutor and the court would have to invoke, *ex officio*, the principle of "*non bis in idem*" and thereby annul the new proceedings.

4.8 The State Party dismisses the author's allegation that he was a target of other criminal procedures based on the same facts as manifestly abusive, in the sense that the sole existence of the judgment of 9 December 1992 is sufficient to preclude further prosecution. In any event, the State Party argues that Mr Faurisson failed to produce any proof of such prosecution.

5.1 In his comments on the State Party's submission, the author argues that the editor-in-chief of the magazine *Le Choc*, which published the disputed interview in September 1990, *did* appeal to the Court of Cassation; on 20 December 1994, the Criminal Chamber of the Court of Cassation dismissed the appeal. The author was informed of this decision by registered letter of 21 February 1995 from the Registry of the Court of Appeal of Paris.

5.2 Mr Faurisson reiterates that assistance of legal counsel in proceedings before the Court of Cassation is, if not necessarily required by law, indispensable in practice: if the Court may only determine whether the law was applied correctly to the facts of a case, the accused must have specialized legal knowledge himself so as to follow the hearing. On the question of legal aid, the author simply notes that such aid is generally not granted to individuals with the salary of a university professor, even if this salary is, in his own situation, severely reduced by an avalanche of fines, punitive damages and other legal fees.

5.3 The author observes that he invokes less a violation of the right to freedom of expression, which *does* admit of some restrictions, but of his right to freedom of opinion and to doubt, as well as freedom of academic research. The latter, he contends, may not, by its very nature, be subjected to limitations. However, the Law of 13 July 1990, unlike comparable legislation in Germany, Belgium, Switzerland or

Austria, *does limit* the freedom to doubt and to carry out historical research in strict terms. Thus, it elevates to the rank of infallible dogma the proceedings and the verdict of the International Military Tribunal sitting at Nuremberg. The author notes that the proceedings of the Tribunal, its way of collecting and evaluating evidence, and the personalities of the judges themselves have been subjected to trenchant criticism over the years, to such an extent that one could call the proceedings a *"mascarade"* (. . . *"la sinistre et déshonorante mascarade judiciaire de Nuremberg"*).

5.4 The author dismisses as absurd and illogical the *ratio legis* adduced by the State Party, in that it even prohibits historians from *proving*, rather than negating, the existence of the Shoah or the mass extermination of Jews in the gas chambers. He contends that in the way it was drafted and is applied, the law endorses the orthodox Jewish version of the history of the Second World War once and for all.

5.5 As to the alleged violation of Article 14, paragraph 7, the author reaffirms that one and the same interview published in one and the same publication resulted in three (distinct) proceedings before the XVIIth Criminal Chamber of the *Tribunal de Grande Instance* of Paris. These cases were registered under the following registry codes: (1) P. 90 302 0325/0; (2) P. 90 302 0324/1; and (3) P. 90 271 0780/1. On 10 April 1992, the Tribunal decided to suspend the proceedings *inasmuch as the author was concerned* for the last two cases, pending a decision on the author's appeal against the judgment in the first case. The proceedings remained suspended after the judgment of the Court of Appeal, until the dismissal of the appeal filed by the journal *Le Choc du Mois* by the Court of Cassation on 20 December 1994. Since then, the procedure in the last two cases has resumed, and hearings took place on 27 January and 19 May 1995. Another hearing was scheduled for 17 October 1995.

The Committee's admissibility decision

6.1 During its fifty-fourth session, the Committee considered the admissibility of the communication. It noted that, at the time of the submission of the communication on 2 January 1993, the author had not appealed the judgment of the Court of Appeal of Paris (Eleventh Chamber) of 9 December 1992 to the Court of Cassation. The author argued that he did not have the means to secure legal representation for that purpose and that such an appeal would, at any rate, be futile. As to the first argument, the Committee noted that it was open to the author to seek legal aid, which he did not. As to the latter argument the Committee referred to its constant jurisprudence that mere doubts about the effectiveness of a remedy do not absolve an author from resorting to it. At the time of submission, therefore, the communication did not meet the requirement of exhaustion of domestic remedies set out in Article 5, paragraph 2(b), of the Optional Protocol. In the meantime, however, the author's co-accused, the Editor-in-Chief of the magazine *Le Choc*, which published the disputed interview in September 1990, had appealed to the Court of Cassation, which, on 20 December 1994, dismissed the appeal. The judgment delivered by the Criminal Chamber of the Court of Cassation reveals that the court concluded that the law was applied correctly to the facts, that the law was constitutional and that its application was not inconsistent with the French Republic's obligations under international human rights treaties, with specific reference to the provisions of Article 10 of the European Convention on Human Rights, which provisions protect the right to freedom of opinion and expression in terms which are similar to the terms used in Article 19 of the International Covenant on Civil and Political Rights for the same purpose. In the circumstances, the Committee held that it would not be reasonable to require the author to have recourse to the Court of Cassation on the same matter. That remedy could no longer be seen as an effective remedy within the meaning of Article 5, paragraph 2(b), of the Optional Protocol, i.e. a remedy that would provide the author with a reasonable prospect of judicial redress. The communication, therefore, no longer suffered from the initial bar of non-exhaustion of domestic remedies, in so far as it appeared to raise issues under Article 19 of the Covenant.

6.2 The Committee considered that the author had sufficiently substantiated, for purposes of admissibility, his complaint about alleged violations of his right to freedom of expression, opinion and of academic research. These allegations should, accordingly, be considered on their merits.

6.3 On the other hand, the Committee found that the author had failed, for purposes of admissibility, to substantiate his claim that his right not to be tried twice for the same offence had been violated. The facts of the case did not reveal that he had invoked that right in the proceedings that were pending against him. The Committee noted the State Party's submission that the prosecutor and the court would be obliged to apply the principle of *"non bis in idem"* if invoked and to annul the new proceedings if they related to the same facts as those judged by the Court of Appeal of Paris on 9 December 1992. The author, therefore, had no claim in this respect under Article 2 of the Optional Protocol.

6.4 Similarly, the Committee found that the author had failed, for purposes of admissibility, to substantiate his claims related to the alleged partiality of judges on the Eleventh Chamber of the Court of Appeal of Paris and the alleged reluctance of the judicial authorities to investigate aggressions to which he claims to have been subjected. In this respect, also, the author had no claim under Article 2 of the Optional Protocol.

6.5 On 19 July 1995, therefore, the Human Rights Committee declared the communication admissible inasmuch as it appeared to raise issues under Article 19 of the Covenant.

State Party's observations on the merits and author's comments thereon

7.1 In its submission under Article 4, paragraph 2, of the Optional Protocol, the State Party considers that the author's claim should be dismissed as incompatible *ratione materiae* with the provisions of the Covenant, and subsidiarily as manifestly ill-founded.

7.2 The State Party once again explains the legislative history of the "Gayssot Act". It notes, in this context, that anti-racism legislation adopted by France during the 1980s was considered insufficient to prosecute and punish, *inter alia*, the trivialization of Nazi crimes committed during the Second World War. The Law adopted on 13 July 1990 responded to the preoccupations of the French legislator *vis-à-vis* the development, for several years, of "revisionism", mostly through individuals who justified their writings by their (perceived) status as historians, and who challenged the existence of the Shoah. To the Government, these revisionist theses constitute "a subtle form of contemporary anti-semitism" ("... *constituent une forme subtile de l'antisémitisme contemporain*") which, prior to 13 July 1990, could not be prosecuted under any of the existing provisions of French criminal legislation.

7.3 The legislator thus sought to fill a legal vacuum, while attempting to define the new provisions against revisionism in as precise a manner as possible. The former Minister of Justice, Mr Arpaillange, had aptly summarized the position of the then Government by stating that it was impossible *not* to devote oneself fully to the fight against racism, adding that racism did not constitute an opinion but an aggression, and that every time racism was allowed to express itself publicly, the public order was immediately and severely threatened. It was exactly *because* Mr Faurisson expressed his anti-semitism through the publication of his revisionist theses in journals and magazines and thereby tarnished the memory of the victims of Nazism, that he was convicted in application of the Law of 13 July 1990.

7.4 The State Party recalls that Article 5, paragraph 1, of the Covenant allows a State Party to deny any group or individual any right to engage in activities aimed at the destruction of any of the rights and freedoms recognized in the Covenant; similar wording is found in Article 17 of the European Convention on Human Rights and Fundamental Freedoms. The State Party refers to a case examined by the European Commission of Human Rights[2] which in its opinion presents many similarities with the present case and whose *ratio decidendi* could be used for the determination of Mr Faurisson's case. In

---

[2] Cases Nos 8348/78 and 8406/78 (*Glimmerveen and Hagenbeek* v. *The Netherlands*), declared inadmissible on 11 October 1979.

this case, the European Commission observed that Article 17 of the European Convention concerned essentially those rights which would enable those invoking them to exercise activities which effectively aim at the destruction of the rights recognized by the Convention (". . . *vise essentiellement les droits qui permettraient, si on les invoquait, d'essayer d'en tirer le droit de se livrer effectivement à des activités visant à la destruction des droits ou libertés reconnus dans la Convention*"). It held that the authors, who were prosecuted for possession of pamphlets whose content incited to racial hatred and who had invoked their right to freedom of expression, could not invoke Article 10 of the European Convention (the equivalent of Article 19 of the Covenant), as they were claiming this right in order to exercise activities contrary to the letter and the spirit of the Convention.

7.5 Applying these arguments to the case of Mr Faurisson, the State Party notes that the tenor of the interview with the author which was published in *Le Choc* (in September 1990) was correctly qualified by the Court of Appeal of Paris as falling under the scope of application of Article 24 *bis* of the Law of 29 July 1881, as modified by the Law of 13 July 1990. By challenging the reality of the extermination of Jews during the Second World War, the author incites his readers to anti-semitic behaviour (". . . *conduit ses lecteurs sur la voie de comportements antisémites*") contrary to the Covenant and other international conventions ratified by France.

7.6 To the State Party, the author's judgment on the *ratio legis* of the Law of 13 July 1990, as contained in his submission of 14 June 1995 to the Committee, i.e. that the law casts in concrete the orthodox Jewish version of the history of the Second World War, clearly reveals the demarche adopted by the author: under the guise of historical research, he seeks to accuse the Jewish people of having falsified and distorted the facts of the Second World War and thereby having created the myth of the extermination of the Jews. That Mr Faurisson designated a former Chief Rabbi (*Grand rabbin*) as the author of the Law of 13 July 1990, whereas the Law is of parliamentary origin, is another illustration of the author's methods to fuel anti-semitic propaganda.

7.7 On the basis of the above, the State Party concludes that the author's "activities", within the meaning of Article 5 of the Covenant, clearly contain elements of racial discrimination, which is prohibited under the Covenant and other international human rights instruments. The State Party invokes Article 26 and in particular Article 20, paragraph 2, of the Covenant, which stipulates that "any advocacy of national, racial or religious hatred that constitutes incitement to discrimination, hostility or violence shall be prohibited by law". Furthermore, the State Party recalls that it is a party to the International Convention on the Elimination of All Forms of Racial

Discrimination; under Article 4 of this Convention, States Parties "shall declare an offence punishable by law all dissemination of ideas based on racial superiority or hatred" (para. 4(a)). The Committee on the Elimination of Racial Discrimination specifically welcomed the adoption of the Law of 13 July 1990 during the examination of the periodic report of France in 1994. In the light of the above, the State Party concludes that it merely complied with its international obligations by making the (public) denial of crimes against humanity a criminal offence.

7.8 The State Party further recalls the decision of the Human Rights Committee in case No 104/1981,[3] where the Committee had held that "the opinions which Mr T seeks to disseminate through the telephone system clearly constitute the advocacy of racial or religious hatred which Canada has an obligation under Article 20(2) of the Covenant to prohibit", and that the claim of the author based on Article 19 was inadmissible as incompatible with the provisions of the Covenant. This reasoning, the State Party submits, should be applied to the case of Mr Faurisson.

7.9 On a subsidiary basis, the State Party contends that the author's claim under Article 19 is manifestly without merits. It notes that the right to freedom of expression laid down in Article 19 of the Covenant is not without limits (cf. Article 19, para. 3), and that French legislation regulating the exercise of this right is perfectly consonant with the principles laid down in Article 19; this has been confirmed by a decision of the French Constitutional Court of 10 and 11 October 1984.[4] In the instant case, the limitations on Mr Faurisson's right to freedom of expression flow from the Law of 13 July 1990.

7.10 The State Party emphasizes that the text of the Law of 13 July 1990 reveals that the offence of which the author was convicted is defined in precise terms and is based on objective criteria, so as to avoid the creation of a category of offences linked merely to expression of opinions ("*délit d'opinion*"). The committal of the offence necessitates (a) the denial of crimes against humanity, as defined and recognized internationally, and (b) that these crimes against humanity have been adjudicated by judicial instances. In other words, the Law of 13 July 1990 does not punish the expression of an opinion, but the denial of a historical reality universally recognized. The adoption of the provision was necessary in the State Party's opinion, not only to protect the rights and the reputation of others, but also to protect public order and morals.

7.11 In this context, the State Party recalls once more the virulent terms in which the author, in his submission of 14 June 1995 to the

[3] Communication No 104/1981 (*JRT and the WG Party* v. *Canada*), declared inadmissible 6 April 1983, para. 8(b).
[4] No 84-181 D.C. of 10 and 11 October 1984, Rec. p. 78.

Committee, had criticized the judgment of the International Tribunal of Nuremberg, dismissing it as a sinister and dishonouring judicial sham ("... *la sinistre et déshonorante mascarade judiciaire de Nuremberg*"). In so doing, he not only challenged the validity of the judgment of the Nuremberg Tribunal, but also unlawfully attacked the reputation and the memory of the victims of Nazism.

7.12 In support of its arguments, the State Party refers to decisions of the European Commission of Human Rights addressing the interpretation of Article 10 of the European Convention (the equivalent of [Article] 19 of the Covenant). In a case decided on 16 July 1982,[5] which concerned the prohibition, by judicial decision, of display and sale of brochures arguing that the assassination of millions of Jews during the Second World War was a Zionist fabrication, the Commission held that "it was neither arbitrary nor unreasonable to consider the pamphlets displayed by the applicant as a defamatory attack against the Jewish community and against each individual member of this community. By describing the historical fact of the assassination of millions of Jews, a fact which was even admitted by the applicant himself, as a lie and zionist swindle, the pamphlets in question not only gave a distorted picture of the relevant historical facts but also contained an attack on the reputation of all those . . . described as liars and swindlers . . ." The Commission further justified the restrictions on the applicant's freedom of expression, arguing that the "restriction was . . . not only covered by a legitimate purpose recognized by the Convention (namely the protection of the reputation of others), but could also be considered as necessary in a democratic society. Such a society rests on the principles of tolerance and broad-mindedness which the pamphlets in question clearly failed to observe. The protection of these principles may be especially indicated *vis-à-vis* groups which have historically suffered from discrimination . . ."

7.13 The State Party notes that identical considerations transpire from the judgment of the Court of Appeal of Paris of 9 December 1992, which confirmed the conviction of Mr Faurisson, by reference, *inter alia*, to Article 10 of the European Convention and to the International Convention on the Elimination of All Forms of Racial Discrimination. It concludes that the author's conviction was fully justified, not only by the necessity of securing respect for the judgment of the International Military Tribunal at Nuremberg, and through it the memory of the survivors and the descendants of the victims of Nazism, but also by the necessity of maintaining social cohesion and public order.

8.1 In his comments, the author asserts that the State Party's observations are based on a misunderstanding: he concedes that the

[5] Case No 9235/81 (*X* v. *Federal Republic of Germany*), declared inadmissible 16 July 1982.

freedoms of opinion and of expression indeed have some limits, but
that he invokes less these freedoms than the freedom to doubt and the
freedom of research which, to his mind, do not permit any restrictions.
The latter freedoms are violated by the Law of 13 July 1990 which
elevates to the level of only and unchallengeable truth what a group of
individuals, judges of an international military tribunal, had decreed in
advance as being authentic. Mr Faurisson notes that the Spanish and
United Kingdom Governments have recently recognized that anti-
revisionist legislation of the French model is a step backward both for
the law and for history.

8.2 The author reiterates that the desire to fight anti-semitism
cannot justify *any* limitations on the freedom of research on a subject
which is of obvious interest to Jewish organizations: the author
qualifies as "exorbitant" the "privilege of censorship" from which the
representatives of the Jewish community in France benefit. He observes
that no other subject he is aware of has ever become a virtual taboo
for research, following a request by another political or religious
community. To him, no law should be allowed to prohibit the
publication of studies on any subject, under the pretext that there is
nothing to research on it.

8.3 Mr Faurisson asserts that the State Party has failed to provide
the slightest element of poof that his own writings and theses constitute
a "subtle form of contemporary anti-semitism" (see para. 7.2 above) or
incite the public to anti-semitic behaviour (see para. 7.5 above). He
accuses the State Party of hubris in dismissing his research and
writings as "pseudo-scientific" ("*prétendument scientifique*"), and adds that
he does not *deny* anything but merely challenges what the State Party
refers to as a "universally recognized reality" ("*une réalité universellement
reconnue*"). The author further observes that the revisionist school has,
over the past two decades, been able to dismiss as doubtful or wrong
so many elements of the "universally recognized reality" that the
impugned law becomes all the more unjustifiable.

8.4 The author denies that there is *any* valid legislation which would
prevent him from challenging the verdict and the judgment of the
International Tribunal at Nuremberg. He challenges the State Party's
argument that the basis for such prohibition precisely *is* the Law of 13
July 1990 as pure tautology and *petitio principis*. He further notes that even
French jurisdictions have admitted that the procedures before and
decisions of the International Tribunal could justifiably be criticized.[6]

8.5 The author observes that on the occasion of a recent revisionist
affair (case of Roger Garaudy), the vast majority of French intellectuals
as well as representatives of the French League for Human Rights
have publicly voiced their opposition to the maintenance of the Law of
13 July 1990.

[6] Cf. Seventeenth Criminal Chamber, *Tribunal Correctionnel de Paris*, 18 April 1991.

8.6 As to the violations of his right to freedom of expression and opinion, the author notes that this freedom remains severely limited: thus, he is denied the right of reply in the major media, and judicial procedures in his case are tending to become closed proceedings (". . . *mes procès tendent à devenir des procès à huis-clos*"). Precisely *because* of the applicability of the Law of 13 July 1990, it has become an offence to provide column space to the author or to report the nature of his defence arguments during his trials. Mr Faurisson notes that he sued the newspaper *Libération* for having refused to grant him a right of reply; he was convicted in first instance and on appeal and ordered to pay a fine to the newspaper's director. Mr Faurisson concludes that he is, in his own country, "buried alive".

8.7 Mr Faurisson argues that it would be wrong to examine his case and his situation purely in the light of legal concepts. He suggests that his case should be examined in a larger context: by way of example, he invokes the case of Galileo, whose discoveries *were* true, and any law, which would have enabled his conviction, would have been by its very nature wrong or absurd. Mr Faurisson contends that the Law of 13 July 1990 was hastily drafted and put together by three individuals and that the draft law did not pass muster in the National Assembly when introduced in early May 1990. He submits that it was only after the profanation of the Jewish cemetery at Carpentras (Vaucluse) on 10 May 1990 and the alleged "shameless exploitation" ("*exploitation nauséabonde*") of this event by the then Minister of the Interior, P. Joxe, and the President of the National Assembly, L. Fabius, that the Law passed. If adopted under such circumstances, the author concludes, it cannot but follow that it must one day disappear, just as the "myth" of the gas chambers at Auschwitz.

8.8 In a further submission dated 3 July 1996 the State Party explains the purposes pursued by the Act of 13 July 1990. It points out that the introduction of the Act was in fact intended to serve the struggle against anti-semitism. In this context the State Party refers to a statement made by the then Minister of Justice, Mr Arpaillange, before the Senate characterizing the denial of the existence of the Holocaust as the contemporary expression of racism and anti-semitism.

8.9 In his comments of 11 July 1996 made on the State Party's submission the author reiterates his earlier arguments; *inter alia* he again challenges the "accepted" version of the extermination of the Jews, because of its lack of evidence. In this context he refers for example to the fact that a decree ordering the extermination has never been found, and it has never been proven how it was technically possible to kill so many people by gas-asphyxiation. He further recalls that visitors to Auschwitz have been made to believe that the gas chamber they see there is authentic, whereas the authorities know that it is a reconstruction, built on a different spot than the original is said to have been. He concludes that as a historian, interested in the facts, he is not willing to accept the traditional version of events and has no choice but to contest it.

Examination of the merits

9.1 The Human Rights Committee has considered the present communication in the light of all the information made available to it by the parties, as it is required to do under Article 5, paragraph 1, of the Optional Protocol.

9.2 The Committee takes note of public debates in France, including negative comments made by French parliamentarians on the Gayssot Act, as well as of arguments put forward in other, mainly European, countries which support and oppose the introduction of similar legislations.

9.3 Although it does not contest that the application of the terms of the Gayssot Act, which, in their effect, make it a criminal offence to challenge the conclusions and the verdict of the International Military Tribunal at Nuremberg, may lead, under different conditions than the facts of the instant case, to decisions or measures incompatible with the Covenant, the Committee is not called upon to criticize in the abstract laws enacted by States Parties. The task of the Committee under the Optional Protocol is to ascertain whether the conditions of the restrictions imposed on the right to freedom of expression are met in the communications which are brought before it.

9.4 Any restriction on the right to freedom of expression must cumulatively meet the following conditions: it must be provided by law, it must address one of the aims set out in paragraph 3(a) and (b) of Article 19, and must be necessary to achieve a legitimate purpose.

9.5 The restriction on the author's freedom of expression was indeed provided by law, i.e. the Act of 13 July 1990. It is the constant jurisprudence of the Committee that the restrictive law itself must be in compliance with the provisions of the Covenant. In this regard the Committee concludes, on the basis of the reading of the judgment of the 17th *Chambre correctionnelle du Tribunal de grande instance de Paris* that the finding of the author's guilt was based on his following two statements: ". . . I have excellent reasons not to believe in the policy of extermination of Jews or in the magic gas chambers . . . I wish to see that 100 per cent of the French citizens realize that the myth of the gas chambers is a dishonest fabrication." His conviction therefore did not encroach upon his right to hold and express an opinion in general, rather the court convicted Mr Faurisson for having violated the rights and reputation of others. For these reasons the Committee is satisfied that the Gayssot Act, as read, interpreted and applied to the author's case by the French courts, is in compliance with the provisions of the Covenant.

9.6 To assess whether the restrictions placed on the author's freedom of expression by his criminal conviction were applied for the purposes provided for by the Covenant, the Committee begins by noting, as it did in its General Comment 10, that the rights for the protection of which restrictions on the freedom of expression are permitted by Article 19, paragraph 3, may relate to the interests of other persons or to those of the *community as a whole*. Since the statements made by the author, read in their full context, were of a nature as to raise or strengthen anti-semitic feelings, the restriction served the respect of the Jewish community to live free from fear of an atmosphere of anti-semitism. The Committee therefore concludes that the restriction of the author's freedom of expression was permissible under Article 19, paragraph 3(a), of the Covenant.

9.7 Lastly the Committee needs to consider whether the restriction of the author's freedom of expression was necessary. The Committee noted the State Party's argument contending that the introduction of the Gayssot Act was intended to serve the struggle against racism and anti-semitism. It also noted the statement of a member of the French Government, the then Minister of Justice, which characterized the denial of the existence of the Holocaust as the principal vehicle for anti-semitism. In the absence in the material before it of any argument undermining the validity of the State Party's position as to the necessity of the restriction, the Committee is satisfied that the restriction of Mr Faurisson's freedom of expression was necessary within the meaning of Article 19, paragraph 3, of the Covenant.

10. The Human Rights Committee, acting under Article 5, paragraph 4, of the Optional Protocol to the International Covenant on Civil and Political Rights, is of the view that the facts as found by the Committee do not reveal a violation by France to Article 19, paragraph 3, of the Covenant.

[Adopted in English, French and Spanish, the English text being the original version. Subsequently to be issued also in Arabic, Chinese and Russian as part of the Committee's annual report to the General Assembly.]

A. *Statement by Mr Thomas Buergenthal*

As a survivor of the concentration camps of Auschwitz and Sachsenhausen whose father, maternal grandparents and many other family members were killed in the Nazi Holocaust, I have no choice but to recuse myself from participating in the decision of this case.

Thomas Buergenthal [signed]
[Original: English]

B. *Individual opinion by Nisuke Ando (concurring)*

While I do not oppose the adoption of the Views by the Human Rights Committee in the present case, I would like to express my concern about the danger that the French legislation in question, the Gayssot Act, might entail. As I understand it, the Act criminalizes the negation ("contestation" in French), by one of the means enumerated in Article 23 of the Law on the Freedom of the Press of 1881, of one or several of the crimes against humanity in the sense of Article 6 of the Statute of the International Military Tribunal of Nuremberg (see para. 4.2). In my view the term "negation" ("contestation"), if loosely interpreted, could comprise various forms of expression of opinions and thus has a possibility of threatening or encroaching the right to freedom of expression, which constitutes an indispensable prerequisite for the proper functioning of a democratic society. In order to eliminate this possibility it would probably be better to replace the Act with a specific legislation prohibiting well-defined acts of anti-semitism or with a provision of the criminal code protecting the rights or reputations of others in general.

Nisuke Ando [signed]
[Original: English]

C. *Individual opinion by Elizabeth Evatt and David Kretzmer, co-signed by Eckart Klein (concurring)*

1. While we concur in the view of the Committee that in the particular circumstances of this case the right to freedom of expression of the author was not violated, given the importance of the issues involved we have decided to append our separate, concurring, opinion.

2. Any restriction on the right to freedom of expression must cumulatively meet the following conditions: it must be provided by law, it must address one of the aims set out in paragraph 3(a) and (b) of Article 19, and it must be necessary to achieve that aim. In this case we are concerned with the restriction on the author's freedom of expression arising from his conviction for his statements in the interview published in *Le Choc du Mois*. As this conviction was based on the prohibition laid down in the Gayssot Act, it was indeed a restriction provided by law. The main issue is whether the restriction has been shown by the State Party to be necessary, in terms of Article 19, paragraph 3(a), for respect of the rights or reputations of others.

3. The State Party has argued that the author's conviction was justified "by the necessity of securing respect for the judgment of the International Military Tribunal at Nuremberg, and through it the memory of the survivors and the descendants of the victims of

Nazism". While we entertain no doubt whatsoever that the author's statements are highly offensive both to Holocaust survivors and to descendants of Holocaust victims (as well as to many others), the question under the Covenant is whether a restriction on freedom of expression in order to achieve this purpose may be regarded as a restriction *necessary* for the respect of the *rights* of others.

4. Every individual has the right to be free not only from discrimination on grounds of race, religion and national origins, but also from incitement to such discrimination. This is stated expressly in Article 7 of the Universal Declaration of Human Rights. It is implicit in the obligation placed on States Parties under Article 20, paragraph 2, of the Covenant to prohibit by law any advocacy of national, racial or religious hatred that constitutes incitement to discrimination, hostility or violence. The crime for which the author was convicted under the Gayssot Act does not expressly include the element of incitement, nor do the statements which served as the basis for the conviction fall clearly within the boundaries of incitement, which the State Party was bound to prohibit, in accordance with Article 20, paragraph 2. However, there may be circumstances in which the right of a person to be free from incitement to discrimination on grounds of race, religion or national origins cannot be fully protected by a narrow, explicit law on incitement that falls precisely within the boundaries of Article 20, paragraph 2. This is the case where, in a particular social and historical context, statements that do not meet the strict legal criteria of incitement can be shown to constitute part of a *pattern* of incitement against a given racial, religious or national group, or where those interested in spreading hostility and hatred adopt sophisticated forms of speech that are not punishable under the law against racial incitement, even though their effect may be as pernicious as explicit incitement, if not more so.

5. In the discussion in the French Senate on the Gayssot Act the then Minister of Justice, Mr Arpaillange, explained that the said law, which, *inter alia*, prohibits denial of the Holocaust, was needed since Holocaust denial is a contemporary expression of racism and anti-semitism. Furthermore, the influence of the author's statements on racial or religious hatred was considered by the Paris Court of Appeal, which held that by virtue of the fact that such statements propagate ideas tending to revive Nazi doctrine and the policy of racial discrimination, they tend to disrupt the harmonious coexistence of different groups in France.

6. The notion that in the conditions of present-day France, Holocaust denial may constitute a form of incitement to anti-semitism cannot be dismissed. This is a consequence not of the mere challenge to well-documented historical facts, established both by historians of different persuasions and backgrounds as well as by international and domestic

tribunals, but of the context, in which it is implied, under the guise of impartial academic research, that the victims of Nazism were guilty of dishonest fabrication, that the story of their victimization is a myth and that the gas chambers in which so many people were murdered are "magic".

7. The Committee correctly points out, as it did in its General Comment 10, that the right for the protection of which restrictions on freedom of expression are permitted by Article 19, paragraph 3, may relate to the interests of a community as a whole. This is especially the case in which the right protected is the right to be free from racial, national or religious incitement. The French courts examined the statements made by the author and came to the conclusion that his statements were of a nature as to raise or strengthen anti-semitic tendencies. It appears therefore that the restriction on the author's freedom of expression served to protect the right of the Jewish community in France to live free from fear of incitement to anti-semitism. This leads us to the conclusion that the State Party has shown that the aim of the restrictions on the author's freedom of expression was to respect the right of others, mentioned in Article 19, paragraph 3. The more difficult question is whether imposing liability for such statements was necessary in order to protect that right.

8. The power given to States Parties under Article 19, paragraph 3, to place restrictions on freedom of expression, must not be interpreted as licence to prohibit unpopular speech, or speech which some sections of the population find offensive. Much offensive speech may be regarded as speech that impinges on one of the values mentioned in Article 19, paragraph 3(a) or (b) (the rights or reputations of others, national security, *ordre public*, public health or morals). The Covenant therefore stipulates that the purpose of protecting one of those values is not, of itself, sufficient reason to restrict expression. The restriction must be *necessary* to protect the given value. This requirement of necessity implies an element of proportionality. The scope of the restriction imposed on freedom of expression must be proportional to the value which the restriction serves to protect. It must not exceed that needed to protect that value. As the Committee stated in its General Comment 10, the restriction must not put the very right itself in jeopardy.

9. The Gayssot Act is phrased in the widest language and would seem to prohibit publication of *bona fide* research connected with matters decided by the Nuremberg Tribunal. Even if the purpose of this prohibition is to protect the right to be free from incitement to anti-semitism, the restrictions imposed do not meet the proportionality test. They do not link liability to the intent of the author, nor to the tendency of the publication to incite to anti-semitism. Furthermore, the legitimate object of the law could certainly have been achieved by a less drastic provision that would not imply that the State Party had

attempted to turn historical truths and experiences into legislative dogma that may not be challenged, no matter what the object behind that challenge, nor its likely consequences. In the present case we are not concerned, however, with the Gayssot Act, *in abstracto,* but only with the restriction placed on the freedom of expression of the author by his conviction for his statements in the interview in *Le Choc du Mois.* Does this restriction meet the proportionality test?

10. The French courts examined the author's statements in great detail. Their decisions, and the interview itself, refute the author's argument that he is only driven by his interest in historical research. In the interview the author demanded that historians "particularly Jewish historians" ("les historiens, en particulier juifs") who agree that some of the findings of the Nuremberg Tribunal were mistaken be prosecuted. The author referred to the "magic gas chamber" ("la magique chambre à gaz") and to "the myth of the gas chambers" ("le mythe des chambres à gaz"), that was a "dirty trick" ("une gredinerie") endorsed by the victors in Nuremberg. The author has, in these statements, singled out Jewish historians over others, and has clearly implied that the Jews, the victims of the Nazis, concocted the story of gas chambers for their own purposes. While there is every reason to maintain protection of *bona fide* historical research against restriction, even when it challenges accepted historical truths and by so doing offends people, anti-semitic allegations of the sort made by the author, which violate the rights of others in the way described, do not have the same claim to protection against restriction. The restrictions placed on the author did not curb the core of his right to freedom of expression, nor did they in any way affect his freedom of research; they were intimately linked to the value they were meant to protect—the right to be free from incitement to racism or anti-semitism; protecting that value could not have been achieved in the circumstances by less drastic means. It is for these reasons that we joined the Committee in concluding that, in the specific circumstances of the case, the restrictions on the author's freedom of expression met the proportionality test and were necessary in order to protect the rights of others.

Elizabeth Evatt [signed]
David Kretzmer [signed]
Eckart Klein [signed]
[Original: English]

D. *Individual opinion by Cecilia Médina Quiroga (concurring)*

1. I concur with the Committee's opinion in this case and wish to associate myself with the individual opinion formulated by Ms Evatt and Mr Kretzmer as being the one that most clearly expresses my own thoughts.

2. I would like to add that a determining factor for my position is the fact that, although the wording of the Gayssot Act might, in application, constitute a clear violation of Article 19 of the Covenant, the French court which tried Mr Faurisson interpreted and applied that Act in the light of the provisions of the Covenant, thereby adapting the Act to France's international obligations with regard to freedom of expression.

Cecilia Médina Quiroga [signed]
[Original: Spanish]

E. *Individual opinion by Rajsoomer Lallah (concurring)*

1. I have reservations on the approach adopted by the Committee in arriving at its conclusions. I also reach the same conclusions for different reasons.

2. It is perhaps necessary to identify, in the first place, what restrictions or prohibitions a State Party may legitimately impose, by law, on the right to freedom of expression or opinion, whether under Article 19, paragraph 3, or 20, paragraph 2, of the Covenant; and, secondly, where the non-observance of such restrictions or prohibitions is criminalized by law, what are the elements of the offence that the law must, in its formulation, provide for so that an individual may know what these elements are and so that he may be able to defend himself, in respect of those elements, by virtue of the fundamental right to a fair trial by a Court conferred upon him under Article 14 of the Covenant.

3. The Committee, and indeed my colleagues Evatt and Kretzmer whose separate opinion I have had the advantage of reading, have properly analysed the purposes for which restrictions may legitimately be imposed under Article 19, paragraph 3, of the Covenant. They have also properly underlined the requirement that the restrictions must be necessary to achieve those purposes. I need not add anything further on this particular aspect of the matter.

4. In so far as restrictions or prohibitions in pursuance of Article 20, paragraph 2, are concerned, the element of necessity is merged with the very nature of the expression which may legitimately be prohibited by law, that is to say, the expression must amount to advocacy of national, racial or religious hatred that constitutes incitement to discrimination, hostility or violence.

5. The second question as to what the law must provide for, in its formulation, is a more difficult one. I would see no great difficulty in the formulation of a law which prohibits, in the very terms of Article 20, paragraph 2, the advocacy of national, racial or religious hatred that constitutes incitement to discrimination, hostility or violence. The

formulation becomes more problematic for the purposes of Article 19, paragraph 3. Because, here, it is not, as is the case under Article 20, paragraph 2, the particular expression that may be restricted but rather the adverse effect that the expression must necessarily have on the specified objects or interests which paragraphs (a) and (b) are designed to protect. It is the prejudice to these objects or interests which becomes the material element of the restriction or prohibition and, consequently, of the offence.

6. As my colleagues Evatt and Kretzmer have noted, the Gayssot Act is formulated in the widest terms and would seem to prohibit publication of *bona fide* research connected with principles and matters decided by the Nuremberg Tribunal. It creates an absolute liability in respect of which no defence appears to be possible. It does not link liability either to the intent of the author nor to the prejudice that it causes to respect for the rights or reputations of others as required under Article 19, paragraph 3(a), or to the protection of national security or of public order or of public health or morals as required under Article 19, paragraph 3(b).

7. What is significant in the Gayssot Act is that it appears to criminalize, in substance, any challenge to the conclusions and the verdict of the Nuremberg Tribunal. In its effects, the Act criminalizes the bare denial of historical facts. The assumption, in the provisions of the Act, that the denial is necessarily anti-semitic or incites anti-semitism is a parliamentary or legislative judgment and is not a matter left to adjudication or judgment by the courts. For this reason, the Act would appear, in principle, to put in jeopardy the right of any person accused of a breach of the Act to be tried by an independent court.

8. I am conscious, however, that the Act must not be read *in abstracto* but in its application to the author. In this regard, the next question to be examined is whether any deficiencies in the Act, in its application to the author, were or were not remedied by the courts.

9. It would appear, as also noted by my colleagues Evatt and Kretzmer, that the author's statements on racial or religious hatred were considered by the French courts. Those courts came to the conclusion that the statements propagated ideas tending to revive Nazi doctrine and the policy of racial discrimination. The statements were also found to have been of such a nature as to raise or strengthen anti-semitic tendencies. It is beyond doubt that, on the basis of the findings of the French courts, the statements of the author amounted to the advocacy of racial or religious hatred constituting incitement, at the very least, to hostility and discrimination towards people of the Jewish faith which France was entitled under Article 20, paragraph 2, of the Covenant to proscribe. In this regard, in considering this aspect of the matter and reaching the conclusions which they did, the French courts would appear to have, quite properly, arrogated back to themselves

the power to decide a question which the Legislature had purported to decide by a legislative judgment.

10. Whatever deficiencies, therefore, which the Act contained were, in the case of the author, remedied by the courts. When considering a communication under the Optional Protocol what must be considered is the action of the State as such, irrespective of whether the State had acted through its legislative arm or its judicial arm or through both.

11. I conclude, therefore, that the creation of the offence provided for in the Gayssot Act, as it has been applied by the courts to the author's case, falls more appropriately, in my view, within the powers of France under Article 20, paragraph 2, of the Covenant. The result is that there has, for this reason, been no violation by France under the Covenant.

12. I am aware that the communication of the author was declared admissible only with regard to Article 19. I note, however, that no particular article was specified by the author when submitting his communication. And, in the course of the exchange of observations by both the author and the State Party, the substance of matters relevant to Article 20, paragraph 2, were also mooted or brought in issue. I would see no substantive or procedural difficulty in invoking Article 20, paragraph 2.

13. Recourse to restrictions that are, in principle, permissible under Article 19, paragraph 3, bristles with difficulties, tending to destroy the very existence of the right sought to be restricted. The right to freedom of opinion and expression is a most valuable right and may turn out to be too fragile for survival in the face of the too frequently professed necessity for its restriction in the wide range of areas envisaged under paragraphs (a) and (b) of Article 19, paragraph 3.

Rajsoomer Lallah [signed]
[Original: English]

F. *Individual opinion by Prafullachandra Baghwati* (concurring)

The facts giving rise to this communication have been set out in detail in the majority opinion of the Committee and it would be an idle exercise for me to reiterate the same over again. I will, instead, proceed straight away to deal with the question of law raised by the author of the communication. The question is whether the conviction of the author under the Gayssot Act was violative of Article 19, paragraph 2, of the International Covenant on Civil and Political Rights.

Article 19, paragraph 2, declares that everyone shall have the right to freedom of expression which includes freedom to impart information and ideas of all kinds through any media, but restrictions can be imposed on this freedom under Article 19, paragraph 3, provided such restrictions cumulatively meet the following conditions: (1) they must be provided for by law, (2) they must address one of the aims enumerated in paragraph 3(a) and 3(b) of Article 19 and (3) they must be *necessary* to achieve a legitimate purpose, this last requirement introducing the principle of proportionality.

The Gayssot Act was passed by the French Legislature on 13 July 1990 amending the Law on the Freedom of the Press by adding an Article 24 *bis* which made it an offence to contest the existence of the category of crimes against humanity as defined in the London Charter of 8 August 1945 on the basis of which Nazi leaders were tried and convicted by the International Military Tribunal at Nuremberg in 1945-46. The Gayssot Act thus provided restriction on freedom of expression by making it an offence to speak or write denying the existence of the Holocaust or of gas asphyxiation of Jews in gas chambers by Nazis. The author was convicted for breach of the provisions of the Gayssot Act and it was therefore breach of this restriction on which the finding of guilt recorded against him was based. The offending statements made by the author on which his conviction was based were the following:

. . . No one will have me admit that two plus two make five, that the earth is flat or that the Nuremberg trial was infallible. I have excellent reasons not to believe in this policy of extermination of Jews or in the magic gas chamber . . .

I would wish to see that 100 per cent of all French citizens realize that the myth of the gas chambers is a dishonest fabrication ('est une gredinerie'), endorsed by the victorious powers of Nuremberg in 1945-46 and officialized on 14 July 1990 by the current French Government with the approval of the Court historians.

These statements were clearly in breach of the restriction imposed by the Gayssot Act and were therefore plainly covered by the prohibition under the Gayssot Act. But the question is whether the restriction imposed by the Gayssot Act which formed the basis of the conviction of the author, satisfied the other two elements in Article 19, paragraph 3, in order to pass the test of permissible restriction.

The second element in Article 19, paragraph 3, requires that the restriction imposed by the Gayssot Act must address one of the aims enumerated in paragraph 3(a) and (b) of Article 19. It must be necessary (a) for respect of the rights or reputations of others or (b) for the protection of national security or of public order (*ordre public*) or of public health or morals. It would be difficult to bring the restriction under paragraph 3(b) because it cannot be said to be necessary for any of the purposes set out in paragraph 3(b). The only question to which it is necessary to address oneself is whether the restriction can be said to be necessary for respect of the rights and reputations of others so as to be justifiable under paragraph 3(a).

Now if a law were merely to prohibit any criticism of the functioning of the International Military Tribunal at Nuremberg or any denial of a historical event simpliciter, on pain of penalty, such law would not be justifiable under paragraph 3(a) of Article 19 and it would clearly be inconsistent under Article 19, paragraph 2. But, it is clear from the submissions made by the State Party and particularly, the submission made on 3 July 1996 that the object and purpose of imposing restriction under the Gayssot Act on freedom of expression was to prohibit or prevent insidious expression of anti-semitism. According to the State Party:

the denial of the Holocaust by authors who qualify themselves as revisionists could only be qualified as an expression of racism and the principal vehicle of anti-semitism.

the denial of the genocide of the Jews during World War Two fuels debates of a profoundly anti-semitic character, since it accuses the Jews of having fabricated themselves the myth of their extermination.

Thus, according to the State Party, the necessary consequence of denial of extermination of Jews by asphyxiation in the gas chamber was fuelling of anti-semitic sentiment by the clearest suggestion that the myth of the gas chamber was a dishonest fabrication by the Jews and it was in fact so articulated by the author in his offending statement.

It is therefore clear that the restriction on freedom of expression imposed by the Gayssot Act was intended to protect the Jewish community against hostility, antagonism and ill-will which would be generated against them by statements imputing dishonest fabrication of the myth of gas chamber and extermination of Jews by asphyxiation in the gas chamber. It may be noted, as observed by the Committee in its General Comment 10, that the rights for the protection of which restrictions on the freedom of expression are permitted by Article 19, paragraph 3(a), may relate to the interests of other persons or to those of the *community as a whole*. Since the statement made by the author, read in the context of its necessary consequence, was calculated or was at least of such a nature as to raise or strengthen anti-semitic feelings and create or promote hatred, hostility or contempt against the Jewish community as dishonest fabricators of lies, the restriction imposed on such statement by the Gayssot Act was intended to serve the purpose of respect for the right and interest of the Jewish community to live free from fear of an atmosphere of anti-semitism, hostility or contempt. The second element required for the applicability of Article 19, paragraph 3, was therefore satisfied.

That takes me to a consideration of the question whether the third element could be said to have been satisfied in the present case. Was the restriction on the author's freedom of expression imposed under the Gayssot Act necessary for respect of the rights and interests of the Jewish community? The answer must obviously be in the affirmative. If the restriction on freedom of expression in the manner provided under the Gayssot Act had not been imposed and statements denying the Holocaust and the extermination of Jews by asphyxiation in the gas chamber had not been made penal, the author and other revisionists like him could have gone on making statements similar to the one which invited the conviction of the author and the *necessary consequence and fall-out* of such statements would have been, in the context of the situation prevailing in Europe, promotion and strengthening of anti-semitic feelings, as emphatically pointed out by the State Party in its submissions. Therefore, the imposition of restriction by the Gayssot Act was necessary for securing respect for the rights and interests of the Jewish community to live in society with full human dignity and free from an atmosphere of anti-semitism.

It is therefore clear that the restriction on freedom of expression imposed by the Gayssot Act satisfied all the three elements required for the applicability of Article 19, paragraph 3, and was not inconsistent with Article 19, paragraph 2, and consequently, the conviction of the author under the Gayssot Act was not violative of his freedom of expression guaranteed under Article 19, paragraph 2. I have reached this conclusion under the greatest reluctance because I firmly believe that in a free democratic society, freedom of speech and expression is one of the most prized freedoms which must be defended and upheld at any cost and this should be particularly so in the land of Voltaire. It is indeed unfortunate that in the world of today, when science and technology have advanced the frontiers of knowledge and mankind is beginning to realize that human happiness can be realized only through interdependence and cooperation, the threshold of tolerance should be going down. It is high time man should realize his spiritual dimension and replace bitterness and hatred by love and compassion, tolerance and forgiveness.

I have written this separate opinion because, though I agree with the majority conclusion of no violation, the process of reasoning through which I have reached this conclusion is a little different from the one which has found favour with the majority.

Prafullachandra Baghwati [signed]
[Original: English]

[Report: Doc. CCPR/C/58/D/550/1993]

Economics, trade and finance — Trade in services —
Broadcasting — Australia–New Zealand Closer Economic
Relations Trade Agreement in force 1 January 1983—Trade
in Services Protocol in force 1 January 1989—Articles 4 and
5(1) of Protocol—Equal access and treatment for New
Zealand film and television industry in Australian
market—Australia's treaty obligations

Relationship of international law and municipal law —
Treaties—Effect in municipal law—Broadcasting Services
Act 1992 (Cth)—Section 122 of Act empowering Australian
Broadcasting Authority to determine Australian Content
Standard—Section 160(d) of Act requiring Australian Broad-
casting Authority to perform its obligations in manner
consistent with Australia's treaty obligations—Clause 9 of
Standard favouring Australian television programmes—
Whether Clause 9 of Standard conflicting with Articles 4
and 5 of Protocol — Interpretation and compatibility of
Sections 122 and 160 of Act—Whether Clause 9 of Standard
made in breach of Act—Validity of Standard—The law of
Australia

PROJECT BLUE SKY INC. AND OTHERS *v.* AUSTRALIAN
BROADCASTING AUTHORITY[1]

Australia, High Court.   28 *April* 1998

(Brennan CJ; McHugh, Gummow, Kirby and Hayne JJ)

SUMMARY: *The facts:*—The respondent, the Australian Broadcasting Authority
("the ABA"), was empowered by Section 122 of the Broadcasting Services Act
1992 (Cth)[2] to determine the Australian content of television programmes.[3]
Section 160(d) of the Act[4] obliged the ABA to perform its functions in a
manner consistent with Australia's treaty obligations. In December 1995 the
ABA set the Australian Content Standard ("the Standard"), Clause 9 of
which required that at least 50 per cent of all television programmes
broadcast between 1 January 1996 and 31 December 1997[5] be Australian.

[1] The appellants were represented by R. J. Ellicott QC, D. M. Yates and A. J. Silink and the
solicitors were Minter Ellison. The respondent was represented by R. V. Gyles QC and N. E.
Abadee and the solicitor was the Australian Government Solicitor. S. J. Gageler appeared as
amicus curiae on behalf of the Australian Film Commission and other interested parties and the
solicitors were Fisher Grogan.
[2] For the text of Section 122, see p. 389 below.
[3] To qualify as Australian, programmes had to be identifiably Australian in their content,
creation or production.
[4] For the text of Section 160, see p. 386 below.
[5] That is, programmes broadcast between 6 a.m. and midnight. The Australian content was
to be increased to 55 per cent from 1 January 1998. For the text of Clause 9 of the Standard, see
p. 387 below.

On 1 January 1989 the Protocol on Trade in Services ("the Protocol") to the Australia–New Zealand Closer Economic Relations Trade Agreement ("the Trade Agreement") had come into force. Under Articles 4 and 5(1) of this Protocol[6] New Zealand nationals were to receive access rights in the market and treatment no less favourable than that accorded to Australian persons and to services provided by them.

The appellant ("Blue Sky"), a New Zealand film company, challenged the validity of the Standard. Blue Sky claimed that the ABA had not fulfilled its obligation under Section 160 of the Act, in that it had not performed its functions in a manner consistent with Australia's obligations under the Protocol. It contended that, by reason of Articles 4 and 5(1) of the Protocol, Australia was under an obligation not to create or maintain any legal impediment that would adversely affect the capacity of the New Zealand film and television industry to compete equally with the Australian industry in the Australian market for the broadcasting of film and television products.

The Federal Court held that the Standard was invalid to the extent that it failed to be consistent with the Protocol. The Full Court of the Federal Court set aside the declaration of the trial judge, and upheld the validity of the Standard on the ground that Section 122, a specific provision, overrode Section 160, a general provision. Blue Sky appealed to the High Court of Australia.

Held:—The appeal was allowed.

Per McHugh, Gummow, Kirby and Hayne JJ: (1) As it was accepted between the Parties that Clause 9 of the Standard was in conflict with Articles 4 and 5 of the Protocol, it was necessary to ascertain whether Clause 9 was in breach of Section 160(d) of the Act and, if so, whether Clause 9 was invalid (p. 403).

(2) Although the Standard related to the Australian content of programmes within the literal meaning of Section 122(2)(b) of the Act, it was the duty of a court to give the words of a statutory provision their legal meaning, that is, the meaning intended for them by the legislature. The legal meaning often, but not always, corresponded with the literal meaning (pp. 405-6).

(3) Although Sections 122 and 160 of the Act were interlocking provisions, Section 160 was dominant and provided the conceptual framework within which the ABA was to carry out its functions. To give Section 122 its literal meaning would result in the authorization of standards inconsistent with Australia's treaty obligations. Accordingly, the legal meaning of Section 122, read together with Section 160, was that the ABA was to determine standards relating to the Australian content of programmes but only in so far as those standards were consistent with the directions in Section 160. As the Trade Agreement and Protocol were agreements within the meaning of Section 160(d), Section 122 imposed upon the ABA an obligation to ensure that the Standard which it determined was not inconsistent with those agreements (p. 407).

(4) Clause 9 of the Standard was made in contravention of Article 122(4) as it breached Articles 4 and 5 of the Protocol. In requiring at least 50 per cent of programmes to be Australian, the Standard was denying the equal access and treatment guaranteed to New Zealand in the Protocol (p. 408).

[6] For the text of Articles 4 and 5(1) of the Protocol, see p. 387 below.

(5) Although in breach of the Act, the making of Clause 9 of the Standard was within the powers granted to the ABA. As Section 160 regulated the exercise of functions already conferred on the ABA, there was a strong indication that an act done in breach of that section was not intended to be invalid. Such invalidation would have resulted in much inconvenience to those members of the public who had acted in reliance on the conduct of the ABA (pp. 410-14).

Per Brennan CJ: (1) In order to determine whether Section 122(2)(b) of the Act was inconsistent with Section 160(d) of the Act, it was necessary to ascertain the meaning of the terms "standard" and "the Australian content of programs" used in Section 122(2)(b) (pp. 389-91).

(2) A transmission quota for programmes was a standard which was designed to ensure that broadcasting licensees broadcast programmes of Australian content. Given that the legislative history of the relevant provisions of the Act did not provide any assistance, the meaning of "Australian content" was to be ascertained from the statutory context (pp. 391-3).

(3) According to its statutory context, "Australian content" was the matter in a programme in which Australian ideas found expression. The ABA was thus empowered by Section 122(1)(a) of the Act to determine a transmission quota for programmes in which Australian ideas found expression and the manner in and extent to which such programmes must contain Australian ideas. There was no foundation for the proposition that the term could be used to classify programmes by reference to their provenance. As such, the basis for classifying programmes in the determination of the Standard was impermissible and the Standard invalid (pp. 393-5).

(4) Even if the ABA was empowered to determine and prescribe a transmission quota for programmes having an Australian provenance, the Standard was still invalid as it did not conform with the Protocol (pp. 395-9).

The following is the text of the judgment of the Court:

[1] Brennan CJ. The Australian Broadcasting Authority (the ABA) has a **[49**
number of "primary functions" which are listed in s 158 of the Broadcasting Services Act 1992 (Cth) (the Act), including, inter alia:

> (h) to assist broadcasting service providers to develop codes of practice that, as far as possible, are in accordance with community standards; and
> (i) to monitor compliance with those codes of practice; and
> (j) to develop program standards relating to broadcasting in Australia; and
> (k) to monitor compliance with those standards.

Section 159 allows for "additional functions" which may be conferred on it by the Act or another Act. Section 160 imposes general obligations on the ABA in these terms:

> The ABA is to perform its functions in a manner consistent with:
> (a) the objects of this Act and the regulatory policy described in section 4; and
> (b) any general policies of the Government notified by the Minister under section 161; and
> (c) any directions given by the Minister in accordance with this Act; and

(d) Australia's obligations under any convention to which Australia is a party or any agreement between Australia and a foreign country.

In these proceedings, the appellants (to whom I shall refer as "Blue Sky"), which have the objective of encouraging the profitable growth of the New Zealand film and television industry, challenge the validity of a standard determined by the ABA on the ground that the ABA has not performed its function consistently with Australia's obligations under an "agreement between Australia and a foreign country". The agreement relied on is the Protocol on Trade in Services to the Australia New Zealand Closer Economic Relations Trade Agreement. The Protocol came into force on 1 January 1989. Article 4 of the Protocol reads as follows:

493]   Each Member State shall grant to persons of the other Member State and services provided by them access rights in its market no less favourable than those allowed to its own persons and services provided by them.

Article 5(1) reads as follows:

Each Member State shall accord to persons of the other Member State and services provided by them treatment no less favourable than that accorded in like circumstances to its persons and services provided by them.

[2]   Blue Sky contends that, by reason of Arts 4 and 5(1), Australia is under an obligation not to create or maintain any legal impediment which would adversely affect the capacity of the New Zealand film and television industry to compete equally with the Australian industry in the Australian market for the broadcasting of film and television products.

[3]   The impugned standard, known as the Australian Content Standard, was determined by the ABA on 15 December 1995 in purported exercise of the power conferred on the ABA by s 122(1)(a) of the Act. Part 5 of the Australian Content Standard, headed "Transmission Quota" contains but one clause: cl 9, headed "Australian transmission quota". Clause 9 reads:

(1) Subject to subclause (3), until the end of 1997, Australian programs must be at least 50% of all programming broadcast between 6.00am and midnight in a year that was made without financial assistance from the television production fund.

(2) Subject to subclause (3), from the beginning of 1998, Australian programs must be at least 55% of all programming broadcast between 6.00am and midnight in a year that was made without financial assistance from the television production fund.

(3) If an Australian program:

  (a) is first release sports coverage; and

  (b) begins before midnight and ends on the next day;

the part of the program broadcast between midnight and 2.00am is taken to have been broadcast between 6.00am and midnight.

The quotas specified in cl 9 guarantee minimum periods between 6 am and midnight during which Australian programs are to be broadcast. New Zealand programs are left to compete with all other programs (including Australian programs) for the remainder of the periods between 6 am and midnight. Even if New Zealand programs were successful in obtaining transmission for the entire 50% of the relevant periods which, until the end of 1997, were available after the Australian program quota was satisfied, the Australian Content Standard would preclude their achieving more than 45% from the beginning of 1998. The definition of an Australian program is contained in cl 7 which reads:

(1) A program is an Australian program if:

(a) it is produced under the creative control of Australians who ensure an Australian perspective, as only evidenced by the program's compliance with subclause (2), subclause (3) or subclause (4); and

(b) it was made without financial assistance from the television production fund.

(2) A program is an Australian program if:

(a) the Minister for Communications and the Arts has issued a final certificate under section 124ZAC of Division 10BA of Part III of the Income Tax Assessment Act 1936 in relation to the program; and

(b) the certificate is in force.

(3) A program is an Australian program if it has been made pursuant to an agreement or arrangement between the Government of Australia or an authority of the Government of Australia and the Government of another country or an authority of the Government of another country.

(4) Subject to subclause (5), a program is an Australian program if: **[49**

(a) the producer of the program is, or the producers of the program are, Australian (whether or not the program is produced in conjunction with a co-producer, or an executive producer, who is not an Australian); and

(b) either:

(i) the director of the program is, or the directors of the program are, Australian; or

(ii) the writer of the program is, or the writers of the program are, Australian; and

(c) not less than 50% of the leading actors or on-screen presenters appearing in the program are Australians; and

(d) in the case of a drama program — not less than 75% of the major supporting cast appearing in the program are Australians; and

(e) the program:

(i) is produced and post-produced in Australia but may be filmed anywhere; and

(ii) in the case of a news, current affairs or sports program that is filmed outside Australia, may be produced or post produced outside Australia if to do otherwise would be impractical.

(5) If an Australian program:

(a) is comprised of segments which, if they were individual programs, would not comply with subclause (4); and

(b) is not a news, current affairs or sports program;

only those segments that, if they were individual programs, would comply with subclause (4) are taken to be Australian programs.

[4] The Australian Content Standard thus provides a minimum quota for the transmission of programs made in compliance with subcl (2), (3) or (4) of cl 7, that is, programs classified by the circumstances in which they were made. It is the provenance of a program, not its subject matter, which determines whether it is an "Australian program" for the purposes of the Australian Content Standard. The Australian Content Standard gives a competitive advantage to programs having an Australian provenance over programs having a corresponding New Zealand provenance. Thus the Australian Content Standard appears not to be consistent with Australia's obligations under Arts 4 and 5(1) of the Protocol.

[5] In the Federal Court, Davies J made a declaration that the Australian Content Standard "is invalid to the extent to which it fails to be consistent with the Protocol". The consequential order that his Honour made was in these terms:

(2) The court orders that unless the Standard is revoked or varied in accordance with law by the respondent on or before 31 December 1996, the Standard is set aside with effect from 31 December 1996.

On appeal to the Full Court of the Federal Court a majority (Wilcox and Finn JJ, Northrop J dissenting) upheld the validity of the ABA's Standard. The Full Court allowed the appeal and dismissed Blue Sky's application.[1] Pursuant to a grant of special leave, Blue Sky appeals against the Full Court's orders and seeks in lieu thereof a declaration that the Australian Content Standard is invalid.

The issues

[6]   The power of the ABA to determine standards is conferred by s 122 which reads:

495]   (1) The ABA must, by notice in writing:
  (a) determine standards that are to be observed by commercial television broadcasting licensees; and
  (b) determine standards that are to be observed by community television broadcasting licensees.
  (2) Standards under subsection (1) for commercial television broadcasting licensees are to relate to:
  (a) programs for children; and
  (b) the Australian content of programs.
  (3) Standards under subsection (1) for community television broadcasting licensees are to relate to programs for children.
  (4) Standards must not be inconsistent with this Act or the regulations.

The standards which may be determined in exercise of the power conferred by s 122 are limited to standards relating to the matters specified in paras (a) and (b) of subs (2) — relevantly, "the Australian content of programs".

[7]   The majority of the Full Court pointed out[2] that the term "Australian content" is not defined by s 122 or by any other provision in the Act. The connotation which their Honours attributed to "Australian" was "something particular to this country". Then, noting that "a New Zealand program is not an Australian program", their Honours reasoned that:[3]

> If the ABA specified the "Australian content" of television programs in such a way as to allow any of that required content to be satisfied by New Zealand programs, however they might be defined, it would fail to carry out its statutory task ... The only standard the ABA could set, consistent with the Protocol, would be one that allowed for there to be no Australian content programs at all, provided that New Zealand programs were broadcast in lieu of programs having Australian content. While one may be able to describe this as determining a standard, it is not one that puts into effect the statutory obligation to determine a standard that relates to the Australian content of programs.

[8]   Herein lies a difficulty. The proposition that a New Zealand program does not, or cannot, satisfy the "Australian content" requirement of a standard to be determined under s 122 is not self-evident. No doubt the proposition depends on the meaning to be attributed to "Australian content" in s 122, a question to which

1. (1996) 71 FCR 465 at 484; 141 ALR 397 at 415
2. (1996) 71 FCR 465 at 482; 141 ALR 397 at 413
3. (1996) 71 FCR 465 at 482; 141 ALR 397 at 413

I shall return. The proposition led their Honours to the conclusion[4] that, in enacting ss 122 and 160:

> Parliament has given the ABA two mutually inconsistent instructions. It has said, first, that the ABA is to provide for preferential treatment of Australian programs, but, second, that it is to do so even-handedly as between Australia and New Zealand.

Holding that there was an irreconcilable conflict between s 122(2)(b) and s 160(d), the majority regarded s 122(2)(b) as a special provision overriding the general provision in s 160(d).[5] Accordingly, the validity of the Australian Content Standard was upheld.

[9]   In argument, Blue Sky attacked the reasoning of the majority but chiefly upon grounds which appear to assume that a standard prescribing a transmission quota for "Australian programs" as defined by cl 7 of the Australian Content Standard is a standard relating to the "Australian content" of programs within the meaning of that term in s 122(2)(b). On that assumption and on the further [496] assumption that "Australian content" excluded non-Australian content, New Zealand programs could not satisfy either the Australian Content Standard or any other standard determined under s 122(1). Allowing that to be so, the argument relied on the wide import of the words "relate to" in s 122(2). The width of that phrase was said to permit the prescription of transmission quotas for Australian programs in terms which, in obedience to s 160(d), would also provide equal transmission quotas for New Zealand programs.[6] It was also submitted that a standard would "relate to" Australian content and would be valid if it prescribed Australian content without excluding non-Australian content.

[10]   Before any inconsistency can be found between s 122(2)(b) and s 160(d), it is necessary to ascertain the meaning of the terms used in the former provision. What is a "standard" and what is "Australian content"? The parties and the interveners made their submissions principally on the basis that Australian content could be seen or heard only in a program having an Australian provenance. The adoption of that common basis is understandable.

[11]   First, it is in the interveners' interests to assert that Australian content is to be found only in programs having an Australian provenance. If that be correct, s 122(2) authorises the determination of a standard that, by safeguarding Australian content, safeguards programs having an Australian provenance.

[12]   Secondly, the commercial interests represented by Blue Sky presumably recognise that the content of programs made in New Zealand or by New Zealanders will not be recognisably Australian or will be less likely to be recognisably Australian than programs having an Australian provenance. Blue Sky did not seek to have the Australian Content Standard set aside on the ground that the power to determine standards could be used only to prescribe the content of programs, whatever the provenance of those programs might be. However,

---

4. (1996) 71 FCR 465 at 483; 141 ALR 397 at 414
5. (1996) 71 FCR 465 at 484; 141 ALR 397 at 414
6. An example was proffered of a standard which prescribed 10% or more solely for Australian programs, an equal percentage solely for New Zealand programs but a minimum 50% for Australian and New Zealand programs combined. The ABA submitted that such a standard would be an invalid prescription of New Zealand content and would diminish the minimum Australian content which the ABA had found to be appropriate.

Mr Ellicott QC, senior counsel for Blue Sky, accepted that to confine "Australian content" to what could be seen and heard in a program and to deny that the term includes the provenance of a program removes any possibility of inconsistency between s 122(2)(b) and s 160(d). In the course of argument, counsel submitted:

> Obviously, if a standard could be devised which had no reference to — I have called them trade-related matters — then it may be that there was no need to be concerned about the international obligation.
>
> ... May I say this ... *if a standard was confined to content in the sense of subject matter, then anybody in the world could make or produce with whatever actors or writers, etc, they wanted to such films.* Therefore, it could be argued everybody would be on a level playing field in relation to such a standard and there may not be any specific requirements for the application of s 160(d).
>
> In other words, all I am positing is that it is quite possible, fully consistent with our argument, that you may have a case where a standard satisfies s 122 and is consistent with s 160(d), even though it does not have to mention New Zealand films or other films if they have a most favoured nation situation [emphasis added].

But Blue Sky was not willing to advance that as the true construction of "Australian content", perhaps because it was thought that success on that ground **197]** might yield little commercial benefit. This seems to have been recognised by counsel who observed that "my clients might in another matter want to say otherwise".

[13] However, the interests of persons concerned in the litigation and the assumptions made in the rival submissions cannot divert the court from its duty to construe the statute. "Judges are more than mere selectors between rival views", said Lord Wilberforce in *Saif Ali v Sydney Mitchell & Co*,[7] "they are entitled to and do think for themselves".

[14] Thirdly, the ABA relied on the legislative history relating to program standards in an attempt to show that "Australian content" in s 122(2)(b) requires the involvement of Australians in the making of the program and that cl 7 of the Australian Content Standard conforms with the historical understanding.

[15] The issues for determination can now be stated:

1. Is a transmission quota for programs of a particular description a "standard"?

2. What is the meaning of "the Australian content of programs"?

3. Is the Australian Content Standard consistent with s 160(d)?

4. If not, is the Australian Content Standard valid?

1. Is a transmission quota a standard?

[16] A standard in the context of something "to be observed by commercial television broadcasting licensees" is a measure of performance to which licensees must attain. As the standard must relate to "the Australian content of programs", a standard to be observed by broadcasting licensees is a standard which is calculated to ensure that they broadcast programs of Australian content. A transmission quota for programs is a standard of that kind.

---

7. [1980] AC 198 at 212

2. "The Australian content of programs"

(a) Legislative history

[17]　The Broadcasting Act 1942 (Cth) (the 1942 Act) which was repealed by the Act defined[8] "program standard" as "a standard or condition determined by the Tribunal in the performance of its function under paragraph 16(1)(d)". Section 16(1)(d) of the 1942 Act[9] defined one of the functions of the Australian Broadcasting Tribunal constituted under that Act to be the determination of "standards to be observed by licensees in respect of the broadcasting of programs and in respect of programs to be broadcast". The definition did not provide a description of the kind of programs which might be selected in determining a standard. A standard was determined by the tribunal under the 1942 Act known as (TPS)14 which contained a transmission quota for Australian programs and other provisions designed to ensure the broadcasting of programs in the making of which Australians played a substantial part or which featured Australians[10] or the accomplishments of Australians. When the Act — that is, the 1992 Act — was introduced, transitional provisions were introduced by the Broadcasting Services (Transitional Provisions and Consequential Amendments) Act 1992 (Cth) (the [498 Transitional Act). Section 21 of the Transitional Act affected the continuance of (TPS)14, the relevant provisions of the section reading as follows:

(1) In subsection (2), a reference to a program standard is a reference to a program standard that was in force immediately before the commencement of this Act under paragraph 16(1)(d) of the Broadcasting Act.

(2) A program standard or a part of a program standard that related to programs for children or the level of Australian content of programs is taken, after that commencement, to be a standard determined by the ABA under paragraph 122(1)(a) of the new Act.

(3) For the purposes of subsection (2), the provisions of section 114 of the Broadcasting Act are taken to be program standards in force under the Broadcasting Act relating to the level of Australian content of programs.

. . .

(8) A program standard relating to a matter referred to in subsection (2) ceases to be in force upon the determination by the ABA under paragraph 122(1)(a) of the new Act of a program standard relating to that matter.

. . .

[18]　The ABA submits that the parliament must have understood that the continuance of (TPS)14 and the continued operation of s 114 of the 1942 Act meant that the standard which the ABA was to determine under s 122(2)(b) was a standard governing the minimum use or the preferential use of Australian programs. Thus, so the argument ran, the Australian Content Standard was within the power conferred on the ABA by s 122.

[19]　The argument fails to take account of the text of s 21(2) of the Transitional Act and s 122(2) of the 1992 Act. Section 21 of the Transitional Act does not

---

8. s 4(1)
9. See s 99(2) of the 1942 Act and ss 123(2) and 125 as well as s 122 of the 1992 Act
10. Section 114 of the 1942 Act required the Australian Broadcasting Corporation and commercial broadcasting licensees under that Act to use the services of Australians, as far as possible, "in the production and presentation of radio and television programs"

continue the entirety of a standard determined under the 1942 Act. Subsection (2) provides that only a program standard or only that part of a program standard under the 1942 Act which related to "programs for children or the level of Australian content of programs" should be taken to be a standard determined under s 122(1)(a) of the 1992 Act. Section 21 of the Transitional Act textually follows the terms of s 122(2) of the 1992 Act. To ascertain what part of (TPS)14 was continued in operation when the 1992 Act commenced operation, it is necessary to construe the text of s 122(2) which accords with s 21 of the Transitional Act. To assume that (TPS)14 continued in undiminished force in order to illuminate the meaning of the words which governed whether and to what extent it was continued in force is a fallacy: it assumes the operation of a statute in order to discover its meaning.

[20] However, the scope of s 21(2) of the Transitional Act is fictionally extended by subs (3) which requires the provisions of s 114 of the 1942 Act be taken to be a program standard in force under the 1942 Act "relating to the level of Australian content of programs". That deeming provision, which expired pursuant to subs (8), cannot illuminate the meaning of "Australian content" except in one respect. It indicates that preferential provisions such as those contained in s 114 of the 1942 Act would not fall within the concept of "a standard relating to the Australian content of programs" if there were no deeming provision.

[21] Thus the legislative history of the relevant provisions of the 1992 Act sheds no light on the meaning of s 122(2)(b). It remains for this court to ascertain the meaning of "Australian content" in s 122(2)(b) from the statutory context and to determine whether the Australian Content Standard, so far as it prescribes a transmission quota for programs having an Australian provenance, relates to the Australian content of programs.

(b) The meaning derived from the statutory context

[22] The term "program" in relation to a broadcasting service is defined by the Act[11] to mean:

    (a) matter the primary purpose of which is to entertain, to educate or to inform an audience; or

    (b) advertising or sponsorship matter, whether or not of a commercial kind.

The "content" of a "program" is what a program contains. The Act calls that content "matter": it is what the broadcast audience sees or hears. "Australian" is the adjective describing the matter contained in the program; but the matter contained in a program is not its provenance. The content of a program for broadcast may be difficult to define in a statute, for it has to do with the communication of sights and sounds that convey ideas and the classification of an idea as "Australian" is a rather elusive concept. But that is not to deny the reality of Australian ideas; they are identifiable by reference to the sights and sounds that depict or evoke a particular connection with Australia, its land, sea and sky, its people, its fauna and its flora. They include our national or regional symbols, our topography and environment, our history and culture, the achievements and failures of our people, our relations with other nations, peoples and cultures and the contemporary issues of particular relevance or interest to Australians. The conferring of power on the ABA to determine a standard relating to the Australian content of programs accords with one of the objects prescribed by the Act, namely, "to promote the role of broadcasting services in developing and reflecting a sense of Australian identity, character and cultural diversity".[12]

[23] The "Australian content of a program" is the matter in a program in which Australian ideas find expression. The ABA is empowered by s 122(1)(a) to determine a transmission quota for programs in which Australian ideas find expression and the manner in which and the extent to which such programs must contain Australian ideas.

[24] Also, s 125 empowers the ABA to determine standards in relation to a matter referred to in s 123(2) if a code of practice governing such a matter has not been registered or is not operating to provide appropriate community safeguards. The "matters" referred to in s 123(2) are all concerned with the content of programs to be broadcast, the last of which is expressed[13] as "such other matters relating to program content as are of concern to the community". That "content" is a term which connotes what is to be seen and heard in a program is confirmed by the provisions of s 129. That section ensures that the ABA's power to determine standards does not empower the ABA to require the approval by it of programs before broadcasting except in relation to children's programs. The purpose of the provision seems to be to deny the ABA general power to require a program, other than children's programs, to be seen and heard by the ABA before broadcasting.

[25] A distinct regime applies in respect of "Australian drama programs" which might be broadcast by subscription television broadcasting licensees. The [50◀ definition of "Australian drama program" in s 6 draws a distinction between the provenance of a drama program and its content. That definition selects Australian provenance and Australian content as alternative criteria of Australian drama programs. These are the programs for which a minimum expenditure requirement is imposed on subscription television broadcasting licensees by s 102. Although s 215 includes a minimum expenditure requirement as an item to be reviewed by the minister when the minister reviews "the operation of the condition relating to Australian content on subscription television broadcasting licensees", the circumstance that either criterion will identify a program as an Australian drama program does not mean that "Australian content" includes Australian provenance. The "condition" relating to Australian content is prescribed[14] by paras (b), (e), (f) and (g) of cl 10(1) in Sch 2 to the Act. All of these paragraphs relate to the matter to be broadcast, not the provenance of the programs broadcast.

[26] The provisions of the Act uniformly point to one meaning of "the Australian content of programs", namely, the Australian matter contained in a program. There is neither historical nor textual foundation for the proposition that the term can be used to classify programs by reference to their provenance. The

---

12. s 3(e)
13. s 123(2)(l)
14. By virtue of s 99

determination of the Australian Content Standard adopts an impermissible basis for classifying programs as the subject of a standard under s 122. It follows that I would hold the Australian Content Standard to be invalid, but for a reason other than the reason advanced by Blue Sky and debated by the ABA and the interveners.

3. Is the Australian Content Standard consistent with s 160(d)?

[27]   If, contrary to my view, s 122(2)(b) empowered the ABA to determine and prescribe a transmission quota for programs having an Australian provenance, is it consistent with s 160(d)?

[28]   Section 160 defines four categories of constraint on the ABA's performance of its functions. The "objects of this Act" in para (a) are to be collected from the terms of the Act. As the particular terms of the Act would prevail over the general requirements of s 160 in any event, the "objects of this Act" requirement in para (a) — but not "regulatory policy" — must prevail over the other requirements in s 160. The "objects of this Act" in para (a) and "Australia's obligations" in para (d) prescribe existing constraints on the ABA's performance of its functions; the constraints imposed by paras (b) and (c) await the notification of general policies or the giving of directions and the constraint of "regulatory policy" awaits the formulation of that policy. As there is nothing which suggests that parliament contemplated that the four categories of constraints might be inconsistent or incompatible one with another, the policies which may be formulated under para (a) or notified under para (b) and the directions which may be given under para (c) must be consistent with the objects of the Act and with para (d). So construed, there could be no conflict between the constraint created by the objects of the Act or by para (d) and any of the other constraints imposed by s 160. If there were any conflict between "the objects of this Act" and s 160(d) the former would prevail but no such conflict appears in the present case. Section 160(d) therefore prescribes a manner in which the ABA must perform its statutory functions. It has effect according to its tenor.

[29]   Of course, the ascertainment of Australia's obligations under "any convention to which Australia is a party or any agreement between Australia and a foreign country" may be difficult to ascertain, especially if those obligations are mutually inconsistent. Counsel for the interveners pointed to a number of international instruments which indicate that the conventions and international agreements to which Australia is a party create obligations which, if not mutually inconsistent, at least throw doubt on the proposition that Arts 4 and 5(1) of the Protocol entitle Australian and New Zealand makers of programs to share the market between them and equally. Clearly parliament did not contemplate that the constraints imposed by s 160(d) could be mutually inconsistent for the entirety of Australia's obligations had to be observed by the ABA in the performance of its functions.

[30]   Here, Arts 4 and 5(1) express unequivocally Australia's obligations under an agreement "between Australia and a foreign country". Whether or not Australia's obligations under other agreements or conventions restrict the proportion of a market available to Australian and New Zealand service providers, Arts 4 and 5(1) of the Protocol impose an obligation on Australia to extend to New Zealand service providers market access and treatment no less

favourable to New Zealand service providers than the market access and treatment available to Australian service providers. As there is nothing to show that Arts 4 and 5(1) do not truly impose obligations on Australia, s 160(d) has the effect of requiring the ABA to perform its functions in a manner consistent with Arts 4 and 5(1).

[31]   On the hypothesis that the prescription of a transmission quota for programs having an Australian provenance could be supported by an exercise of power conferred by s 122, s 160(d) directs the ABA not to exercise its power so as to breach Australia's international obligations. On that hypothesis, a majority of this court, reading s 122 with s 160, holds that:[15]

> the legal meaning of s 122 is that the ABA must determine standards relating to the Australian content of programs but only to the extent that those standards are consistent with the directions in s 160.

Given the hypothesis, I would respectfully agree. And, as Australian program makers are given an advantage over the New Zealand program makers by cll 7 and 9 of the Australian Content Standard, I would hold those clauses to be inconsistent with s 160(d).

4. Is the Australian Content Standard valid?

[32]   Although I apprehend that, on the hypothesis stated, the majority and I would hold cll 7 and 9 to be inconsistent with s 160(d) of the Act, my analysis of the consequences is radically different. I must explain the basis on which I proceed.

[33]   The supposed conflict between s 122 and s 160(d) which a majority of the Federal Court held to exist was not textual; it was operational. There is no textual inconsistency between s 122 and s 160. And an operational conflict could arise only if s 122 conferred a power which required the ABA to determine a standard inconsistent with Australia's obligations under an agreement with another [50 country. Were that the situation, s 122 would prevail because, on that construction of s 122, it would express the parliament's direction to the ABA to exercise the power it confers in a particular way while s 160 expresses a direction as to the way in which the ABA's functions generally were to be exercised. One of the "objects of this Act" would be expressed by s 122. The special direction contained in s 122 would prevail over the general direction contained in s 160(d).[16] However, as it is not possible to construe s 122 as containing a direction to the ABA to determine a standard inconsistent with Australia's obligations under an agreement with another country, there is no textual inconsistency between the two provisions. Nor is there any operational inconsistency as it is open to the ABA so to formulate a determination as to afford the same protection to the makers of New Zealand programs as that afforded to the makers of Australian programs. Therefore this question arises: what is the effect of an obligation owed by Australia under an agreement with a foreign country on the ambit of the power conferred on the ABA by s 122?

---

15. *Project Blue Sky Inc v Australian Broadcasting Authority* (1998) 153 ALR 510 at [80]
16. *Smith v R* (1994) 181 CLR 338 at 348; 125 ALR 385; *Refrigerated Express Lines (A'asia) Pty Ltd v Australian Meat and Live-stock Corp* (1980) 29 ALR 333 at 347

[34] A provision conferring a general power and a provision prescribing the manner in which the repository of that power must exercise it have to be read together. In *Colquhoun v Brooks*,[17] Lord Herschell said:

> It is beyond dispute, too, that we are entitled and indeed bound when construing the terms of any provision found in a statute to consider any other parts of the Act which throw light upon the intention of the legislature and which may serve to shew that the particular provision ought not to be construed as it would be if considered alone and apart from the rest of the Act.

When the parliament confers a power and statutorily directs the manner of its exercise, "[t]he ambit of the power must be ascertained by the character of the statute and the nature of the provisions it contains": *Morton v Union Steamship Co of New Zealand Ltd*.[18] Therefore a provision conferring the power must be so construed as to conform with a provision governing the manner of its exercise. The authority conferred on the repository of a general power cannot be exercised in conflict with a provision which governs the manner of its exercise;[19] the constraint on the exercise of the power defines the ambit of the power granted. A purported exercise of a power in breach of the provision which governs the manner of its exercise is invalid, since there is no power to support it.

[35] If a statutory instrument is invalid by reason of conflict between the terms of the instrument and a statutory direction as to the manner in which the power to make the instrument may be exercised, the source of the invalidity is the restricted ambit of the power, not the absence of some act or occurrence extrinsic to the statute. A statutory direction as to the manner in which a power may be exercised is not a condition upon the existence of the power or a mere direction as to the doing of some preliminary or collateral act. It is a delimitation of the power itself.

[36] If the power exercised by a repository is within the ambit of the power reposed, there can be no unlawfulness on the part of the repository in exercising it. Either there is power available for exercise in the manner in which the repository has exercised it and the exercise is lawful or there is no power available for exercise in the manner in which the repository has purported to exercise it and the purported exercise is invalid.

[37] A provision which directs the manner of the exercise of a power is quite different from a provision which prescribes an act or the occurrence of an event as a condition on the power — that is, a provision which denies the availability of the power unless the prescribed act is done or the prescribed event occurs. In one case, power is available for exercise by the repository but the power available is no wider than the direction as to the manner of its exercise permits; in the other case, no power is available for exercise by the repository unless the condition is satisfied.[20] A provision which prescribes such a condition has traditionally been

---

17. (1889) 14 App Cas 493 at 506
18. (1951) 83 CLR 402 at 410
19. *Shanahan v Scott* (1957) 96 CLR 245 at 250; *Clyne v DCT* (1984) 154 CLR 589 at 597-8; 55 ALR 143; *Shop Distributive and Allied Employees Association v Minister for Industrial Affairs (SA)* (1995) 183 CLR 552 at 561; 129 ALR 191; *Harrington v Lowe* (1996) 136 ALR 42 at 49; 70 ALJR 495 at 500-1; *Utah Construction & Engineering Pty Ltd v Pataky* [1966] AC 629 at 640; *Willocks v Anderson* (1971) 124 CLR 293 at 298-9
20. See, for example, *Spicer v Holt* [1977] AC 987

described as mandatory because non-compliance is attended with invalidity. A purported exercise of a power when a condition has not been satisfied is not a valid exercise of the power.

[38] A third kind of provision must be distinguished from provisions which restrict the ambit of the power and provisions which prescribe conditions on its availability for exercise. A provision may require the repository or some other person to do or to refrain from doing something (sometimes within a period prescribed by the statute) before the power is exercised but non-compliance with the provision does not invalidate a purported exercise of the power:[21] the provision does not condition the existence of the power.[22] Such a provision has often been called directory, in contradistinction to mandatory, because it simply directs the doing of a particular act (sometimes within a prescribed period) without invalidating an exercise of power when the act is not done or not done within the prescribed period. The description of provisions as either mandatory or directory provides no test by which the consequences of non-compliance can be determined; rather, the consequences must be determined before a provision can be described as either mandatory or directory.

[39] The terms of the statute show whether a provision governs the manner of exercise of a general power, or is a condition on a power, or merely directs the doing or refraining from doing an act before a power is exercised. The distinction between conditions on a power and provisions which are not conditions on a power is sometimes difficult to draw, especially if the provision makes substantial compliance with its terms a condition.[23] Then an insubstantial non-compliance with the same provision seems to give the provision a directory quality, although in truth such a provision would have a dual application: substantial [50 non-compliance is a condition; insubstantial non-compliance is not.[24]

[40] The question whether a breach of a provision prescribing the doing of some act before a power is exercised invalidates a purported exercise of the power[25] is not, in my respectful opinion, relevant to the present case. We are here concerned not with the availability of a power or the classification of a provision as mandatory or directory but with a provision which determines the ambit of a power which was available for exercise by the ABA.

[41] The purpose of construing the text of a statute is to ascertain therefrom the intention of the enacting parliament. When the validity of a purported exercise of

21. *Osborne v Commonwealth* (1911) 12 CLR 321 at 336-7; *Buchanan v Commonwealth* (1913) 16 CLR 315 at 329
22. See, for example, *Clayton v Heffron* (1960) 105 CLR 214 at 246-8; *Simpson v Attorney-General* [1955] NZLR 271; *Wang v Commissioner of Inland Revenue* [1994] 1 WLR 1286; [1995] 1 All ER 367
23. *Scurr v Brisbane City Council* (1973) 133 CLR 242 at 255-6; 1 ALR 420; *Grunwick Processing Laboratories Ltd v Advisory, Conciliation and Arbitration Service* [1978] AC 655 at 691-2; cf *R v Inner London Betting Licensing Committee; Ex parte Pearcy* [1972] 1 WLR 421; [1972] 1 All ER 932
24. Wade and Forsyth, *Administrative Law*, 7th ed (1994) p 253
25. *Montreal Street Railway Co v Normandin* [1917] AC 170 at 175; *Victoria v Commonwealth and Connor* (1975) 134 CLR 81 at 161-2, 178-9; 7 ALR 1; *Tasker v Fullwood* [1978] 1 NSWLR 20 at 23-4; *London & Clydeside Estates Ltd v Aberdeen District Council* [1980] 1 WLR 182 at 201-2; [1979] 3 All ER 876 at 892-3; *TVW Enterprises Ltd v Duffy (No 3)* (1985) 8 FCR 93 at 102; 62 ALR 63 at 71

a statutory power is in question, the intention of the parliament determines the scope of a power as well as the consequences of non-compliance with a provision prescribing what must be done or what must occur before a power may be exercised. If the purported exercise of the power is outside the ambit of the power or if the power has been purportedly exercised without compliance with a condition on which the power depends, the purported exercise is invalid. If there has been non-compliance with a provision which does not affect the ambit or existence of the power, the purported exercise of the power is valid. To say that a purported exercise of a power is valid is to say that it has the legal effect which the parliament intended an exercise of the power to have.

[42] Here, s 160(d) is a provision which directs the manner of the exercise of the powers conferred on the ABA under the Act, including (so far as is relevant) the power conferred by s 122(1)(a). If the ABA purports to exercise its powers in breach of the injunction contained in s 122(4) and s 160(d), to that extent the purported exercise of the power is invalid and the purported standard (or the non-conforming provisions thereof) is invalid and of no effect. The standard cannot be saved by some notion that s 160(d) is "directory". The Act empowers the ABA to determine a program standard that relates to the Australian content of programs only to the extent that the standard is consistent with Australia's obligations under Arts 4 and 5(1) of the Protocol. On the hypothesis that the Australian Content Standard authorises the determination of a standard prescribing a transmission quota for programs having an Australian provenance, cl 9 does not conform with Arts 4 and 5(1). It is therefore invalid.

[43] On either view of the meaning of "Australian content" I would allow the appeal. Allowing the appeal, I would set aside the order of the Full Court of the Federal Court and in lieu thereof order that the appeal to that court be dismissed. The respondent must pay the costs.

[44] **McHugh, Gummow, Kirby and Hayne JJ.** The question in this appeal is whether a program standard,[26] known as the Australian Content Standard, made by the respondent, the Australian Broadcasting Authority (ABA), is invalid. The appellants contend that it is invalid because it gives preference to Australian television programs contrary to Australia's obligations under the Australia New Zealand Closer Economic Relations Trade Agreement (the Trade Agreement) and the Trade in Services Protocol to the Trade Agreement (the Protocol).

[45] The appeal is brought against an order of the Full Court of the Federal Court of Australia (Wilcox and Finn JJ, Northrop J dissenting)[27] which set aside an order made by Davies J in the Federal Court.[28] The order made by Davies J declared that the Australian Content Standard was invalid to the extent that it was inconsistent with the Trade Agreement and the Protocol.

[46] The appellants are companies involved in the New Zealand film industry.

---

26. "Program standards" are defined by s 6 of the Broadcasting Services Act 1992 (Cth) to mean "standards determined by the ABA relating to the content or delivery of programs"

27. *Australian Broadcasting Authority v Project Blue Sky Inc* (1996) 71 FCR 465 at 484; 141 ALR 397 at 415

28. The order of Davies J was made in *Project Blue Sky Inc v Australian Broadcasting Authority* (Fed C, 26 August 1996, unreported). The reasons for judgment but not the order are reported in *Project Blue Sky Inc v Australian Broadcasting Authority* (1996) 68 FCR 455; 148 ALR 412

The ABA was established by the Broadcasting Services Act 1992 (Cth) (the Act)[29] to supervise and control television and radio broadcasting in Australia. Section 158 sets out its primary functions. They include:

> (j) to develop program standards relating to broadcasting in Australia; and
> (k) to monitor compliance with those standards.

The legislation

[47]   Section 4(1) of the Act declares that parliament "intends that different levels of regulatory control be applied across the range of broadcasting services according to the degree of influence that different types of broadcasting services are able to exert in shaping community views in Australia".

[48]   Three of the objects of the Act are:[30]

> (d) to ensure that Australians have effective control of the more influential broadcasting services; and
> (e) to promote the role of broadcasting services in developing and reflecting a sense of Australian identity, character and cultural diversity; and
>   . . .
> (g) to encourage providers of commercial and community broadcasting services to be responsive to the need for a fair and accurate coverage of matters of public interest and for an appropriate coverage of matters of local significance.

[49]   Section 160 declares that:

> The ABA is to perform its functions in a manner consistent with:
> (a) the objects of this Act and the regulatory policy described in section 4; and
> (b) any general policies of the Government notified by the Minister under section 161; and
> (c) any directions given by the Minister in accordance with this Act; and
> (d) Australia's obligations under any convention to which Australia is a party or any agreement between Australia and a foreign country.[31]

[50]   The appellants contend that para (d) of s 160 required the ABA in determining program standards to comply with the Trade Agreement and the Protocol. They contend that, because the Protocol requires equality of treatment and access to markets, the Australian Content Standard is invalid because it gives television programs made by Australians preferential treatment over programs made by New Zealand nationals.

[51]   The Act imposes a specific obligation on the ABA to determine program standards to be observed by commercial television broadcasting licensees in respect of the Australian content of television programs. Section 122 states:

---

29. s 154
30. s 3
31. A number of federal statutes and regulations have provisions similar to s 160(d). See Air Services Act 1995 (Cth) s 9(3); Australian Postal Corporation Act 1989 (Cth) s 28(c); Chemical Weapons (Prohibition) Act 1994 ss 22, 95; Civil Aviation Act 1988 (Cth) s 11; Customs Act 1901 (Cth) s 269SK; Customs (Prohibited Exports) Regulations reg 13CA(2); Endangered Species Protection Act 1992 (Cth) s 171; Extradition (Ships and Fixed Platforms) Regulations regs 6(2), 7(2); Hazardous Waste (Regulation of Exports and Imports) Regulations reg 7(2); Navigation Act 1912 (Cth) s 422; Nuclear Non-Proliferation (Safeguards) Act 1987 (Cth) s 70(1); Ozone Protection Act 1989 (Cth) s 45(5); Sea Installations Act 1987 (Cth) s 13; Telecommunications Act 1997 (Cth) s 366

(1) The ABA must, by notice in writing:

    (a) determine standards that are to be observed by commercial television broadcasting licensees; and

    (b) determine standards that are to be observed by community television broadcasting licensees.

(2) Standards under subsection (1) for commercial television broadcasting licensees are to relate to:

    (a) programs for children; and

    (b) the Australian content of programs.

(3) Standards under subsection (1) for community television broadcasting licensees are to relate to programs for children.

(4) Standards must not be inconsistent with this Act or the regulations.

[52] Section 6 defines "program" in relation to a broadcasting service to mean:

    (a) matter the primary purpose of which is to entertain, to educate or to inform an audience; or

    (b) advertising or sponsorship matter, whether or not of a commercial kind.

[53] Before determining, varying or revoking a standard, the ABA must "seek public comment on the proposed standard or the variation or revocation".[32] Decisions by the ABA with respect to standards are not decisions under the Act which may be reviewed under s 204 by the Administrative Appeals Tribunal. Instead, the Act gives the Houses of Parliament authority to alter a standard. Section 128(1) provides that, upon either of the Houses of Parliament agreeing to an amendment of a standard which has been determined, the standard has effect as amended from the 28th day after the date on which the other House agrees to the amendment.

[54] The Act also provides for the allocation of commercial television broadcasting licences and the conditions of such licences[33] include[34] a requirement that the licensee comply with program standards determined by the ABA. Breaches of licence conditions are offences[35] and may lead to cancellation of a licence by the ABA.[36]

[55] Pursuant to the power conferred by s 122, the ABA determined the Australian Content Standard on 15 December 1995. It was to become operative from 1 January 1996. Clause 3 declares:

507]   The object of this Standard is to promote the role of commercial television in developing and reflecting a sense of Australian identity, character and cultural diversity by supporting the community's continued access to television programs produced under Australian creative control.

[56] Clause 4 declares:

This Standard:

    (a) sets minimum levels of Australian programming to be broadcast on commercial television; and

---

32. s 126
33. Set out in Sch 2 of the Act
34. Subcl 7(1)(b) of Sch 2
35. s 139(1)
36. s 143

    (b) requires minimum amounts of first release Australian drama, documentary and children's programs ... to be broadcast on commercial television; and

    (c) requires preschool programs broadcast on commercial television to be Australian programs.

[57]   Clause 5 defines "Australian" to mean "a citizen or permanent resident of Australia". Clauses 5 and 7 define "an Australian program" as one that was "produced under the creative control of Australians who ensure an Australian perspective, as only evidenced by the program's compliance with subclause (2), subclause (3) or subclause (4)" and which was made without financial assistance from a fund administered by the Australian Film Commission. A program complies with subcl (2) if the Minister for Communications and the Arts has issued a final certificate under s 124ZAC of the Income Tax Assessment Act 1936 (Cth). Such a certificate can only be given with respect to a film which has a significant Australian content.[37] A program complies with subcl (3) if it was made pursuant to an agreement between the Australian Government or an Australian government authority and the government or a government authority of another country. A program complies with subcl (4) if it meets certain criteria ensuring that Australians are primarily responsible for the making of the program and that Australia is the country where the program is produced or post-produced unless that production "would be impractical".

[58]   Clause 9, which is the critical clause for the purposes of this appeal, declares:

    (1) Subject to subclause (3), until the end of 1997, Australian programs must be at least 50% of all programming broadcast between 6.00am and midnight in a year that was made without financial assistance from the television production fund.

    (2) Subject to subclause (3), from the beginning of 1998, Australian programs must be at least 55% of all programming broadcast between 6.00am and midnight in a year that was made without financial assistance from the television production fund.

    (3) If an Australian program:

      (a) is first release sports coverage; and

      (b) begins before midnight and ends on the next day;

    the part of the program broadcast between midnight and 2.00am is taken to have been broadcast between 6.00am and midnight.

[59]   Clauses 10 and 11 deal with Australian drama program requirements, an Australian drama program being defined in cl 5 as an Australian program that meets certain criteria. Clauses 12, 13, 14 and 15 deal with the Australian content of children's programs. Clause 16 requires that at least 10 hours of first release Australian documentary programs be broadcast each year by a licensee.

[60]   The objects specified in s 3 of the Act make it clear that a primary purpose of the Act is to ensure that Australian television is controlled by Australians for the benefit of Australians. The objects require that the Act should be administered [50**?** so that broadcastings reflect a sense of Australian identity, character and cultural diversity, that Australians will effectively control important broadcasting services and that those services will provide an appropriate coverage of matters of local significance. However, the direction in s 160(d) contains the potential for conflict with the objects of the Act because it requires the ABA to perform its functions

---

37. See the definition of "Australian film" in s 124ZAA of the Income Tax Assessment Act 1936 (Cth)

in a manner consistent with Australia's obligations under any convention to which Australia is a party or under any agreement between Australia and a foreign country. It is not difficult to imagine treaties entered into between Australia and a foreign country which may be utterly inconsistent with those objects.

[61] Furthermore, s 160(b) and s 160(c) respectively require the ABA to perform its functions in accordance with "any general policies of the Government notified by the Minister under section 161" and with "any directions given by the Minister in accordance with this Act". These provisions also contain the potential for conflicts with the objects of the Act. However, arguably, the minister cannot notify policies or give directions which attempt "to widen the purposes of the Act, to add new and different means of carrying them out or to depart from or vary the plan which the legislature has adopted to attain its ends".[38]

[62] It is not necessary in this case, however, to decide which of the directions in s 160 is to prevail if, in a particular case, two or more applicable directions are inconsistent with each other. Nothing in the objects of the Act requires the ABA to give preferential treatment to Australian over New Zealand nationals in determining "standards that are to be observed by commercial television broadcasting licensees".[39] Nor were we referred to any notified policy or ministerial direction to that effect.

The Trade Agreement and the Protocol

[63] The Trade Agreement came into force on 1 January 1983. Its object was the expansion of free trade between Australia and New Zealand. In August 1988, the Protocol was signed. It came into effect on 1 January 1989.

[64] Article 4 of the Protocol states:

Each Member State shall grant to persons of the other Member State and services provided by them access rights in its market no less favourable than those allowed to its own persons and services provided by them.

[65] Article 5 states:

Each Member State shall accord to persons of the other Member State and services provided by them treatment no less favourable than that accorded in like circumstances to its persons and services provided by them.

[66] It was common ground between the parties that the provisions of cl 9 of the Australian Content Standard are in conflict with the provisions of Arts 4 and 5 of the Protocol. That being so, two questions arise: (1) is cl 9 of the Australian Content Standard in breach of s 160(d) of the Act; (2) if it is, is cl 9 invalid?

509] The Federal Court

[67] At first instance in the Federal Court, Davies J made a declaration that the Australian Content Standard was invalid to the extent to which it failed to be

---

38. *Shanahan v Scott* (1957) 96 CLR 245 at 250; *Peppers Self Service Stores Pty Ltd v Scott* (1958) 98 CLR 606 at 610. See also *Morton v Union Steamship Co of New Zealand Ltd* (1951) 83 CLR 402 at 410; *Banks v Transport Regulation Board (Vic)* (1968) 119 CLR 222 at 235; *Waters v Public Transport Corp* (1991) 173 CLR 349 at 369, 380-1; 103 ALR 513
39. s 122(1)(a)

consistent with the Protocol.[40] His Honour also ordered[41] that "unless the Standard is revoked or varied in accordance with law by [the ABA] on or before 31 December 1996, the Standard is set aside with effect from 31 December 1996".

[68]   On appeal, the Full Court set aside the orders of Davies J.[42] In a joint judgment Wilcox and Finn JJ held[43] that there was "an irreconcilable conflict between the special provision constituted by s 122(2)(b) of the Act and the general provision of s 160(d), as applied to the [Trade Agreement]" and that s 122(2)(b) must prevail. Northrop J dissented. His Honour was of the opinion that there was no irreconcilable conflict between the two sections. He held[44] that the ABA had failed to comply with the obligations imposed upon it by ss 160(d) and 122(4) of the Act and that the Australian Content Standard was invalid.

Conflicting statutory provisions should be reconciled so far as is possible

[69]   The primary object of statutory construction is to construe the relevant provision so that it is consistent with the language and purpose of all the provisions of the statute.[45] The meaning of the provision must be determined "by reference to the language of the instrument viewed as a whole".[46] In *Commissioner for Railways (NSW) v Agalianos*,[47] Dixon CJ pointed out that "the context, the general purpose and policy of a provision and its consistency and fairness are surer guides to its meaning than the logic with which it is constructed". Thus, the process of construction must always begin by examining the context of the provision that is being construed.[48]

[70]   A legislative instrument must be construed on the prima facie basis that its provisions are intended to give effect to harmonious goals.[49] Where conflict appears to arise from the language of particular provisions, the conflict must be alleviated, so far as possible, by adjusting the meaning of the competing provisions to achieve that result which will best give effect to the purpose and language of those provisions while maintaining the unity of all the statutory provisions.[50] Reconciling conflicting provisions will often require the court "to determine which is the leading provision and which the subordinate provision, and which must give way to the other".[51] Only by determining the hierarchy of [510

---

40. *Project Blue Sky Inc v Australian Broadcasting Authority* (Fed C, 26 August 1996, unreported)
41. Fed C, 26 August 1996, unreported
42. *Australian Broadcasting Authority v Project Blue Sky Inc* (1996) 71 FCR 465 at 484; 141 ALR 397 at 415
43. (1996) 71 FCR 465 at 484; 141 ALR 397 at 414
44. (1996) 71 FCR 465 at 475; 141 ALR 397 at 406
45. See *Taylor v Public Service Board (NSW)* (1976) 137 CLR 208 at 213; 10 ALR 211 per Barwick CJ
46. *Cooper Brookes (Wollongong) Pty Ltd v FCT* (1981) 147 CLR 297 at 320; 35 ALR 151 per Mason and Wilson JJ. See also *South West Water Authority v Rumble's* [1985] AC 609 at 617 per Lord Scarman, "in the context of the legislation read as a whole"
47. (1955) 92 CLR 390 at 397
48. *Toronto Suburban Railway Co v Toronto Corp* [1915] AC 590 at 597; *Minister for Lands (NSW) v Jeremias* (1917) 23 CLR 322 at 332; *K & S Lake City Freighters Pty Ltd v Gordon & Gotch Ltd* (1985) 60 ALR 509; 157 CLR 309 at 312 per Gibbs CJ, 315 per Mason J, 321 per Deane J
49. *Ross v R* (1979) 141 CLR 432 at 440; 25 ALR 137 per Gibbs J
50. See *Australian Alliance Assurance Co Ltd v Attorney-General of Queensland* [1916] St R Qd 135 at 161 per Cooper CJ; *Minister for Resources v Dover Fisheries* (1993) 43 FCR 565 at 574; 116 ALR 54 at 63 per Gummow J
51. *Institute of Patent Agents v Lockwood* [1894] AC 347 at 360 per Lord Herschell LC

the provisions will it be possible in many cases to give each provision the meaning which best gives effect to its purpose and language while maintaining the unity of the statutory scheme.

[71]   Furthermore, a court construing a statutory provision must strive to give meaning to every word of the provision.[52] In *Commonwealth v Baume*[53] Griffith CJ cited *R v Berchet*[54] to support the proposition that it was "a known rule in the interpretation of statutes that such a sense is to be made upon the whole as that no clause, sentence, or word shall prove superfluous, void, or insignificant, if by any other construction they may all be made useful and pertinent".

The Australian Content Standard was authorised by the literal meaning of s 122

[72]   The Australian Content Standard made on 15 December 1995 is plainly a standard that relates to "the Australian content of programs" within the literal and grammatical meaning of s 122(2)(b) of the Act. The term "Australian content" is not defined by s 122 or by the Act. But, given the history of the term, there can be no doubt that the standard made on 15 December 1995 relates to the "Australian content of programs" within the literal meaning of s 122(2)(b) of the Act.

[73]   Immediately prior to the commencement of the Act "TPS 14 (Australian Content of Television Programs)"[55] was in force. Section 21 of the Broadcasting Services (Transitional Provisions and Consequential Amendments) Act 1992 (Cth) (the Transitional Provisions Act) deemed TPS 14 to be a standard determined by the ABA under s 122(1)(a) of the Act. It also provided that the provisions of s 114 of the Broadcasting Act 1942 (Cth) were to be taken to be program standards in force under that Act relating to the level of Australian content of programs and were continued in force.

[74]   Clause 1 of TPS 14 declared that the objective of that standard was:

to encourage programs which:

(a) are identifiably Australian;
(b) recognise the diversity of cultural backgrounds represented in the Australian community;
(c) are developed for an Australian audience; and
(d) are produced with Australian creative control.

[75]   Clause 21 provided that:

Not less that 35% of the time occupied by programs broadcast by a licensee between the hours of 6.00am and midnight, averaged over the calendar year commencing 1 January 1990, shall be devoted to the broadcasting of Australian programs, including repeats. The percentage requirement shall increase to:

(a) 40% for the calendar year commencing 1 January 1991;
(b) 45% for the calendar year commencing 1 January 1992;
(c) 50% for the calendar year commencing 1 January 1993 and for each calendar year thereafter.

---

52. *Commonwealth v Baume* (1905) 2 CLR 405 at 414 per Griffith CJ, 419 per O'Connor J; *Chu Kheng Lim v Minister for Immigration, Local Government and Ethnic Affairs* (1992) 176 CLR 1 at 12-13; 110 ALR 97 per Mason CJ
53. (1905) 2 CLR 405 at 414
54. (1688) 1 Show KB 106; 89 ER 480
55. "TPS": Television Program Standard

[76] Other clauses in TPS 14 spelt out the criteria for determining whether **[51**
programs qualified for the transmission quota referred to in cl 21. Thus, cl 23
relevantly provided:

> (a) Programs other than drama will qualify in full for the transmission quota if they
>   are:
>   (i)   designed for and relevant to Australian society;
>   (ii)   under Australian creative control; and
>   (iii)(A) are shot in Australia and all elements of the program have been designed
>   and produced by Australians for an Australian audience; or
>   (B)   are produced in Australia for an Australian audience but some elements
>   of the program have been made by non-Australians (eg news, current
>   affairs and today programs); or
>   (C)   are shot overseas but with substantial Australian production involvement
>   (eg Australian travel documentaries and sporting events covered on site
>   by Australian interviewers and commentators).

It is unnecessary to set out the criteria for other programs to qualify as Australian
programs for the purpose of cl 21 of TPS 14. It is enough to say that to qualify
they had to be identifiably Australian either in their content or in their creation or
production.

[77] Against the background of TPS 14 and its continuation into force by the
Transitional Provisions Act, it is clear that the Australian Content Standard was
authorised by the literal meaning of s 122(2)(b).

The legal meaning of s 122

[78] However, the duty of a court is to give the words of a statutory provision
the meaning that the legislature is taken to have intended them to have.
Ordinarily, that meaning (the legal meaning) will correspond with the
grammatical meaning of the provision. But not always. The context of the words,
the consequences of a literal or grammatical construction, the purpose of the
statute or the canons of construction[56] may require the words of a legislative
provision to be read in a way that does not correspond with the literal or
grammatical meaning. In *Statutory Interpretation*, Mr Francis Bennion points
out:[57]

> The distinction between literal and legal meaning lies at the heart of the problem of
> statutory interpretation. An enactment consists of a verbal formula. Unless defectively
> worded, this has a grammatical meaning in itself. The unwary reader of this formula
> (particularly if not a lawyer) may mistakenly conclude that the grammatical meaning is
> all that is of concern. If that were right, there would be little need for books on statutory
> interpretation. Indeed, so far as concerns law embodied in statute, there would scarcely
> be a need for law books of any kind. Unhappily this state of being able to rely on
> grammatical meaning does not prevail in the realm of statute law; nor is it likely to. In
> some cases the grammatical meaning, when applied to the facts of the instant case, is
> ambiguous. Furthermore there needs to be brought to the grammatical meaning of an
> enactment due consideration of the relevant matters drawn from the context (using that
> term in its widest sense). Consideration of the enactment in its context may raise factors
> that pull in different ways. For example the desirability of applying the clear literal

---

56. For example, the presumption that, in the absence of unmistakable and unambiguous language,
    the legislature has not intended to interfere with basic rights, freedoms or immunities: *Coco v
    R* (1994) 179 CLR 427 at 437; 120 ALR 415
57. 3rd ed (1997) pp 343-4

meaning may conflict with the fact that this does not remedy the mischief that parliament intended to deal with [footnotes omitted].

§12][79]   The express words of s 160 require the ABA to carry out its functions in accordance with the directions given by that section. Section 160 therefore provides the conceptual framework in which the functions conferred by s 158 are to be carried out. The function specified in s 158(j) encompasses the direction in s 122 to "determine standards" to be observed by commercial and community television broadcasting licensees. The carrying out of the directions in s 122 is therefore one of the functions of the ABA.

[80]   If s 122(1) and (2) were given their grammatical meaning, without regard to the provisions of s 160, they would authorise the making of standards which were inconsistent with Australia's obligations under international conventions or under its agreements with foreign countries. However, the express words of s 122(4) and the mandatory direction in s 160 show that the grammatical meaning of s 122(1) and (2) is not the legal meaning of those subsections. When s 122 is read with s 160, the legal meaning of s 122 is that the ABA must determine standards relating to the Australian content of programs but only to the extent that those standards are consistent with the directions in s 160. If, by reason of an obligation under a convention or agreement with a foreign country, it is impossible to make an Australian content standard that is consistent with that obligation, the ABA is precluded by s 160 from making the standard, notwithstanding the literal command of s 122(1) and (2). Accordingly, in making the Australian Content Standard in December 1995, the ABA was under an obligation to ensure that the Standard was not inconsistent with the Trade Agreement or the Protocol.

[81]   The majority judges in the Full Court in the present case were therefore in error in holding that the relationship of s 160 and s 122 is that of a general and a special provision. They are interlocking provisions, with s 160 — the dominant provision — directing how the function conferred by s 122 is to be carried out. The power conferred by s 122 must therefore be exercised within the framework imposed by s 160.

An Australian content standard must be consistent with the Trade Agreement and the Protocol

[82]   The Trade Agreement and the Protocol are agreements "between Australia and a foreign country" within the meaning of s 160(d). They fall within the ordinary grammatical meaning of that paragraph. Moreover, the explanatory memorandum that accompanied the bill that became the Act stated that cl 160:[58]

> Requires the ABA to perform its functions in a manner consistent with various matters, including Australia's international obligations or agreements such as Closer Economic Relations with New Zealand.

Accordingly, s 122 prohibits the ABA from making a standard that is inconsistent with the Trade Agreement or the Protocol.

[83]   No doubt it is a curious feature of the 1992 legislation that, despite the

58. *Australian Broadcasting Authority v Project Blue Sky Inc* (1996) 71 FCR 465 at 483; 141 ALR 397 at 414

enactment of s 160(d) of the Act, s 21 of the Transitional Provisions Act maintained TPS 14 in force notwithstanding that its provisions were inconsistent with the Protocol and that, for present purposes, its provisions are substantially the same as the Australian Content Standard. However, the continuation in force of TPS 14 provides no ground for holding that s 122 authorises standards that are in conflict with Australia's obligations under the Trade Agreement or the [51]Protocol. The continuation of TPS 14 was probably a stop-gap measure, designed to protect Australian interests, until the ABA promulgated a new standard that was consistent with Australia's international obligations including those under the Trade Agreement and the Protocol. Certainly, the Minister for Transport and Communications was aware that the provisions of TPS 14 might be in conflict with Australia's obligations under the Protocol. In a letter dated 2 December 1992 to the chairperson of the ABA, the minister, after referring to s 160 and the Trade Agreement, said:

> Having consulted with the Minister for Trade and Overseas Development, I am aware that Australia's present treatment of New Zealand produced programming in Australian content Standard TPS 14 may be in breach of Australia's Services Protocol obligations. I would hope that the ABA can quickly reconsider the Australian content standard.

[84] Clause 9 of the Australian Content Standard published in December 1995 is plainly in breach of Australia's obligations under Arts 4 and 5 of the Protocol. That is because cl 9 requires Australian programs to constitute 50% (rising to 55%) of programming broadcasts made between 6 am and midnight. Consequently, Australian programs have an assured market of at least 50% of broadcasting time while New Zealand programs have to compete with all other programs including Australian programs for the balance of broadcasting time. New Zealand programs therefore have less favourable access rights to the market for television programs than Australian programs have. As a result, cl 9 of the Australian Content Standard is in breach of Art 4 (access rights of persons and services to a market to be no less favourable) and Art 5 (treatment of persons and services to be no less favourable) of the Protocol and was therefore made in contravention of s 122(4).

[85] It would seem to follow from the conclusion that cl 9 is in breach of the Act that other provisions of the Standard such as cll 10-16, which have a similar effect to cl 9, were also made in breach of s 122(4). However, the court heard no detailed submissions on the validity of cll 10-16. For the purpose of the present case, it is unnecessary to come to any fixed view about the validity of these clauses. It is sufficient to hold that cl 9 was made in breach of the Act.

[86] However, it does not follow that cl 9 of the Standard is void and of no force or effect. A group of Australian companies and persons who were given leave to appear in the proceedings as amici curiae, submitted to the court that, on its proper construction, s 160(d) did not impose any duty on the ABA that would result in the invalidity of any act done in breach of that paragraph. Before turning to this submission, however, it is necessary to discuss the conclusion of the majority judges in the Full Court that, because of the Trade Agreement and the Protocol, in enacting ss 122 and 160:[59]

---

59. *Australian Broadcasting Authority v Project Blue Sky Inc* (1996) 71 FCR 465 at 483; 141 ALR 397 at 414

Parliament has given the ABA two mutually inconsistent instructions. It has said, first, that the ABA is to provide for preferential treatment of Australian programs, but, secondly, that it is to do so even-handedly as between Australia and New Zealand.

[87] With great respect to their Honours, the parliament has done no such thing. The parliament has not said that the ABA must give preferential treatment to Australian programs. It has said that the ABA must determine standards that "relate to ... the Australian content of programs".[60] The words "relate to" are "extremely wide".[61] They require the existence of a connection or association[62] between the content of the Standard and the Australian content of programs. What constitutes a sufficient connection or association to form the required relationship is a matter for judgment depending on the facts of the case. No doubt the association or connection must be a relevant one in the sense that it cannot be accidental or so remote that the Standard has no real effect or bearing on the Australian content of programs. But, without attempting to provide an exhaustive definition, once the Standard appears to prohibit, regulate, promote or protect the Australian content of television broadcasts the required relationship will exist. Furthermore, the fact that the Standard also deals with matters other than the Australian content of programs will not necessarily negate the existence of a relevant relationship. A standard can relate to the Australian content of programs although it also regulates other matters.[63] Section 158(j) gives the ABA power to develop program standards relating to broadcasting including those standards referred to in s 122. There is nothing in the Act to prevent the ABA from utilising the power conferred by s 158(j) to determine program standards in a general way and at the same time carry out its obligation to determine the Australian content of programs.

[88] Nor is there anything in the Act — including the combined effect of s 160 and the Trade Agreement — which prevents the ABA from determining a standard relating to the Australian content of programs in cases where preferential treatment cannot be given to Australian programs. The phrase "the Australian content of programs" in s 122 is a flexible expression that includes, inter alia, matter that reflects Australian identity, character and culture. A program will contain Australian content if it shows aspects of life in Australia or the life, work, art, leisure or sporting activities of Australians or if its scenes are or appear to be set in Australia or if it focuses on social, economic or political issues concerning Australia or Australians. Given the history of the concept of Australian content as demonstrated by the provisions of TPS 14, a program must also be taken to contain Australian content if the participants, creators or producers of a program are Australian. Nothing in the notion of the Australian content of programs requires, however, that a standard made pursuant to s 122

---

60. s 122(2)(b)
61. *Tooheys Ltd v Commissioner of Stamp Duties (NSW)* (1961) 105 CLR 602 at 620 per Taylor J
62. *Perlman v Perlman* (1984) 155 CLR 474 at 484; 51 ALR 317. See also *R v Ross-Jones; Ex parte Beaumont* (1979) 141 CLR 504 at 510; 23 ALR 179; *R v Ross-Jones; Ex parte Green* (1984) 156 CLR 185 at 196-7; 56 ALR 609; *O'Grady v Northern Queensland Co Ltd* (1990) 169 CLR 356 at 367, 376; 92 ALR 213
63. cf *Herald and Weekly Times Ltd v Commonwealth* (1966) 115 CLR 418 at 434; *Murphyores Incorporated Pty Ltd v Commonwealth* (1976) 136 CLR 1 at 11, 19-20; 9 ALR 199; *Commonwealth v Tasmania* (1983) 158 CLR 1 at 151; 46 ALR 625 (the *Tasmanian Dam* case)[7]
[[7] 68 *ILR* 266.]

must give preference to Australian programs. Nor does the phrase "the Australian content of programs" in s 122 require that such programs should be under Australian creative control.

[89]   Absent s 160(d), a standard containing cl 9 and similar clauses of the Australian Content Standard would plainly be valid. But it is a fallacy to suppose that a standard that does not provide preference for Australian programs is not a standard that relates to the Australian content of programs. The ABA has complete authority to make a standard that relates to the Australian content of programs as long as the standard does not discriminate against persons of New Zealand nationality or origin or the services that they provide or against the [51! members of any other nationality protected by agreements similar to those contained in the Protocol. Subject to s 160, the form that standard takes is a matter for the ABA.

[90]   It is of course true that one of the objects of the Act is "to promote the role of broadcasting services in developing and reflecting a sense of Australian identity, character and cultural diversity".[64] But this object can be fulfilled without requiring preference to be given to Australian programs over New Zealand programs. Thus, the ABA could determine a standard that required that a fixed percentage of programs broadcast during specified hours should be either Australian or New Zealand programs or that Australian and New Zealand programs should each be given a fixed percentage of viewing time. Such a standard would relate to the Australian content of programs even though it also dealt with the New Zealand content of programs. In any event, the existence of the object referred to in s 3(e) cannot control the dominating effect of s 160(d). That paragraph and s 122(4) insist that any program made under s 122 must be consistent with Australia's agreements with foreign countries. The Trade Agreement and the Protocol constitute such an agreement.

Does the failure to comply with s 160 mean that cl 9 of the Australian Content Standard is invalid?

[91]   An act done in breach of a condition regulating the exercise of a statutory power is not necessarily invalid and of no effect. Whether it is depends upon whether there can be discerned a legislative purpose to invalidate any act that fails to comply with the condition. The existence of the purpose is ascertained by reference to the language of the statute, its subject matter and objects, and the consequences for the parties of holding void every act done in breach of the condition. Unfortunately, a finding of purpose or no purpose in this context often reflects a contestable judgment. The cases show various factors that have proved decisive in various contexts, but they do no more than provide guidance in analogous circumstances. There is no decisive rule that can be applied;[65] there is not even a ranking of relevant factors or categories to give guidance on the issue.

[92]   Traditionally, the courts have distinguished between acts done in breach of an essential preliminary to the exercise of a statutory power or authority and acts done in breach of a procedural condition for the exercise of a statutory power or

---

64. s 3(e)
65. *Howard v Bodington* (1877) 2 PD 203 at 211 per Lord Penzance

authority. Cases falling within the first category are regarded as going to the jurisdiction of the person or body exercising the power or authority.[66] Compliance with the condition is regarded as mandatory, and failure to comply with the condition will result in the invalidity of an act done in breach of the condition.[67] Cases falling within the second category are traditionally classified

16] as directory rather than mandatory. In *Pearse v Morrice*,[68] Taunton J said "a clause is directory where the provisions contain mere matter of direction and nothing more". In *R v Loxdale*,[69] Lord Mansfield CJ said "[t]here is a known distinction between circumstances which are of the essence of a thing required to be done by an Act of Parliament, and clauses merely directory". As a result, if the statutory condition is regarded as directory, an act done in breach of it does not result in invalidity.[70] However, statements can be found in the cases to support the proposition that, even if the condition is classified as directory, invalidity will result from non-compliance unless there has been "substantial compliance" with the provisions governing the exercise of the power.[71] But it is impossible to reconcile these statements with the many cases which have held an act valid where there has been no substantial compliance with the provision authorising the act in question. Indeed in many of these cases, substantial compliance was not an issue simply because, as Dawson J pointed out in *Hunter Resources Ltd v Melville*[72] when discussing the statutory provision in that case:

> substantial compliance with the relevant statutory requirement was not possible. Either there was compliance or there was not.

[93] In our opinion, the Court of Appeal of New South Wales was correct in *Tasker v Fullwood*[73] in criticising the continued use of the "elusive distinction between directory and mandatory requirements"[74] and the division of directory

66. See, for example, *R v Loxdale* (1758) 1 Burr 445; 97 ER 394; *Bowman v Blyth* (1856) 7 El & Bl 26; 119 ER 1158; *Thwaites v Wilding* (1883) 12 QBD 4; *Edwards v Roberts* [1891] 1 QB 302; *Parisienne Basket Shoes Pty Ltd v Whyte* (1938) 59 CLR 369; *R v Murray; Ex parte Proctor* (1949) 77 CLR 387; *Sutherland Shire Council v Finch* (1970) 123 CLR 657; *Victoria v Commonwealth and Connor* (1975) 134 CLR 81; 7 ALR 1; *Mark v Australian Broadcasting Tribunal* (1991) 32 FCR 476; 108 ALR 209
67. *Townsend's Case* (1554) 1 Plowden 111; 75 ER 173; *Stradling v Morgan* (1560) 1 Plowden 199; 75 ER 305; *Maloney v McEacharn* (1904) 1 CLR 77; *SS Constructions Pty Ltd v Ventura Motors Pty Ltd* [1964] VR 229; *Public Prosecutor v Oie Hee Koi* [1968] AC 829; *Cullimore v* [8] *Lyme Regis Corp* [1962] 1 QB 718; *Sandvik Australia Pty Ltd v Commonwealth* (1989) 89 ALR 213
68. (1834) 2 Ad & E 84 at 96; 111 ER 32 at 37
69. (1758) 1 Burr 445 at 447; 97 ER 394 at 395
70. *Stallwood v Tredger* (1815) 2 Phill Ecc 287; 161 ER 1147; *R v Leicester* (1827) 7 B & C 6; 108 ER 627; *Catterall v Sweetman* (1845) 9(1) Jur 951; *R v Lofthouse* (1866) LR 1 QB 433; *Montreal Street Railway Co v Normandin* [1917] AC 170 at 174-5; *Clayton v Heffron* (1960) 105 CLR 214 at 247; *Australian Broadcasting Corp v Redmore Pty Ltd* (1989) 166 CLR 454; 84 ALR 199
71. *Woodward v Sarsons* (1875) LR 10 CP 733 at 746-7; *Caldow v Pixell* (1877) 2 CPD 562 at 566-7; *Scurr v Brisbane City Council* (1973) 133 CLR 242 at 255-6; 1 ALR 420
72. (1988) 164 CLR 234 at 249; 77 ALR 8 at 18
73. [1978] 1 NSWLR 20 at 23-4. See also *Victoria v Commonwealth and Connor* (1975) 134 CLR 81 at 161-2; 7 ALR 1 per Gibbs J
74. *Australian Capital Television Pty Ltd v Minister for Transport and Communications* (1989) 86 ALR 119 at 146 per Gummow J
[8 42 *ILR* 441.]

acts into those which have substantially complied with a statutory command and those which have not. They are classifications that have outlived their usefulness because they deflect attention from the real issue which is whether an act done in breach of the legislative provision is invalid. The classification of a statutory provision as mandatory or directory records a result which has been reached on other grounds. The classification is the end of the inquiry, not the beginning.[75] That being so, a court, determining the validity of an act done in breach of a statutory provision, may easily focus on the wrong factors if it asks itself whether compliance with the provision is mandatory or directory and, if directory, whether there has been substantial compliance with the provision. A better test for determining the issue of validity is to ask whether it was a purpose of the legislation that an act done in breach of the provision should be invalid. This has been the preferred approach of courts in this country in recent years, particularly in New South Wales.[76] In determining the question of purpose, regard must be [51] had to "the language of the relevant provision and the scope and object of the whole statute".[77]

An act done in breach of s 160 is not invalid

[94]   Section 160 proceeds on the hypothesis that the ABA has power to perform certain functions and directs that it "is to perform" those functions "in a manner consistent with" the four matters set out in the section. In the present case, for example, s 158(j) as well as s 122 authorised the making of a standard relating to the Australian content of television programs. Thus, the making of an Australian content standard was not outside the powers granted to the ABA[78] even though, as we have concluded, cl 9 of the Standard was made in breach of the Act. The fact that s 160 regulates the exercise of functions already conferred on the ABA rather than imposes essential preliminaries to the exercise of its functions strongly indicates that it was not a purpose of the Act that a breach of s 160 was intended to invalidate any act done in breach of that section.

[95]   That indication is reinforced by the nature of the obligations imposed by s 160. Not every obligation imposed by the section has a rule-like quality which can be easily identified and applied. Thus, s 160 requires the functions of the ABA to be performed in a manner consistent with:

* the objects of the Act and the regulatory policy described in s 4;
* any general policies of the government notified by the minister under s 161;

---

75. *McRae v Coulton* (1986) 7 NSWLR 644 at 661; *Australian Capital Television* (1989) 86 ALR 119 at 147
76. *Hatton v Beaumont* [1977] 2 NSWLR 211 at 213, 226; *Attorney-General (NSW); Ex rel Franklins Stores Pty Ltd v Lizelle Pty Ltd* [1977] 2 NSWLR 955 at 965; *Tasker v Fullwood* [1978] 1 NSWLR 20 at 24; *National Mutual Fire Insurance Co Ltd v Commonwealth* [1981] 1 NSWLR 400 at 408; *TVW Enterprises Ltd v Duffy (No 3)* (1985) 8 FCR 93 at 102; 62 ALR 63 at 71; *McRae v Coulton* (1986) 7 NSWLR 644 at 661 and see *Australian Broadcasting Corp v Redmore Pty Ltd* (1989) 166 CLR 454 at 457-60; 84 ALR 199; *Yates Security Services Pty Ltd v Keating* (1990) 25 FCR 1 at 24-6; 98 ALR 68 at 90-2. See also two recent decisions of the Court of Appeal of the Supreme Court of the Northern Territory: *Johnston v Paspaley Pearls Pty Ltd* (1996) 110 NTR 1 at 5; *Collins Radio Constructions Inc v Day* (1997) 116 NTR 14 at 17; and *Wang v Commissioner of Inland Revenue* [1994] 1 WLR 1286 at 1294, 1296; [1995] 1 All ER 367 at 375, 377
77. *Tasker v Fullwood* [1978] 1 NSWLR 20 at 24
78. cf *Mark v Australian Broadcasting Tribunal* (1991) 32 FCR 476; 108 ALR 209

• any directions[79] given by the minister in accordance with the Act.

In particular situations, it is almost certain that there will be room for widely differing opinions as to whether or not a particular function has been carried out in accordance with these policies or general directions. When a legislative provision directs that a power or function be carried out in accordance with matters of policy, ordinarily the better conclusion is that the direction goes to the administration of a power or function rather than to its validity.[80]

[96] Furthermore, while the obligations of Australia under some international conventions and agreements are relatively clear, many international conventions and agreements are expressed in indeterminate language[81] as the result of compromises made between the contracting State parties.[82] Often their **18]** provisions are more aptly described as goals to be achieved rather than rules to be obeyed. The problems that might arise if the performance of any function of the ABA carried out in breach of Australia's international obligations was invalid are compounded by Australia being a party to about 900 treaties.[83]

[97] Courts have always accepted that it is unlikely that it was a purpose of the legislation that an act done in breach of a statutory provision should be invalid if public inconvenience would be a result of the invalidity of the act.[84] Having regard to the obligations imposed on the ABA by s 160, the likelihood of that body breaching its obligations under s 160 is far from fanciful, and, if acts done in breach of s 160 are invalid, it is likely to result in much inconvenience to those members of the public who have acted in reliance on the conduct of the ABA.

[98] Among the functions of the ABA, for example, are the allocation and renewal of licences[85] and the design and administration of price-based systems for the allocation of commercial television and radio broadcasting licences.[86] It is hardly to be supposed that it was a purpose of the legislature that the validity of a licence allocated by the ABA should depend on whether or not a court ultimately ruled that the allocation of the licence was consistent with a general direction, policy or treaty obligation falling within the terms of s 160. This is particularly so, given that the "general policies of the Government notified by the Minister under section 161" unlike the "directions given by the Minister in accordance with this Act"[87] are not required to be publicly recorded and that even those with experience in public international law sometimes find it difficult to ascertain the extent of Australia's obligations under agreements with other

---

79. Except as otherwise specified in the Act, the directions are to be only of a general nature (s 162)
80. cf *Broadbridge v Stammers* (1987) 16 FCR 296 at 300; 76 ALR 339 at 343
81. Bennion, *Statutory Interpretation*, 2nd ed (1992) p 461
82. *Applicant A v Minister for Immigration and Ethnic Affairs* (1997) 142 ALR 331 at 352; 71 ALJR 381 at 397
83. *Minister for Immigration and Ethnic Affairs v Teoh* (1995) 183 CLR 273 at 316; 128 ALR 353 [9]
84. *Montreal Street Railway Co v Normandin* [1917] AC 170 at 175; *Clayton v Heffron* (1960) 105 CLR 214 at 247; *TVW Enterprises Ltd v Duffy (No 3)* (1985) 8 FCR 93 at 104-5; 62 ALR 63 at 73-4
85. s 158(c)
86. s 158(e)
87. See s 162(2) which required the minister to "cause a copy of each direction given to the ABA to be published in the *Gazette* as soon as practicable after giving the direction"

[[9] 104 *ILR* 460.]

countries. In many cases, licensees would have great difficulty in ascertaining whether the ABA was acting consistently with the obligations imposed by s 160. Expense, inconvenience and loss of investor confidence must be regarded as real possibilities if acts done in breach of s 160 are invalid.

[99]   Because that is so, the best interpretation of s 160 is that, while it imposes a legal duty on the ABA, an act done in breach of its provisions is not invalid.

[100]   In a case like the present, however, the difference between holding an act done in breach of s 160 is invalid and holding it is valid is likely to be of significance only in respect of actions already carried out by, or done in reliance on the conduct of, the ABA. Although an act done in contravention of s 160 is not invalid, it is a breach of the Act and therefore unlawful. Failure to comply with a directory provision "may in particular cases be punishable".[88] That being so, a person with sufficient interest is entitled to sue for a declaration that the ABA has acted in breach of the Act and, in an appropriate case, obtain an injunction restraining that body from taking any further action based on its unlawful action.

Order   [51

[101]   The appeal to this court from the Full Court of the Federal Court should be allowed with costs. However, that court was correct in allowing the appeal from the orders of Davies J because his Honour had held that the Australian Content Standard was invalid to the extent that it was inconsistent with the Trade Agreement and the Protocol. Order (1) of the Full Court's orders should therefore stand. In lieu of the orders made by the Full Court, however, there should be substituted the following orders:

(1) The appeal be allowed and the orders made by Davies J set aside.

(2) The court declares that cl 9 of the Australian Content Standard (the Standard) determined by the appellant on 15 December 1995 was unlawfully made.

(3) The appellant pay the costs of the appeal and of the proceedings before Davies J.

(4) Each party has liberty to apply further, as it may be advised.

(5) Without limiting the generality of order (4), the respondents have liberty to apply for such further or other orders as they may be entitled to arising from the alleged failure of a clause of the Standard to comply with Australia's obligations under the Australia New Zealand Closer Economic Relations Trade Agreement and the Trade in Services Protocol to that agreement.

(6) There be no order in relation to the costs of the interveners.

Order

(1) Appeal allowed.

(2) The respondent pay the appellants' costs of this appeal.

(3) In lieu of the orders of the Full Court of the Federal Court of 12 December 1996, substitute the following orders:

---

88. *Simpson v Attorney-General* [1955] NZLR 271 at 281; *Montreal Street Railway Co v Normandin* [1917] AC 170 at 175

(1) The appeal be allowed and the orders made by Davies J set aside.
(2) The court declares that cl 9 of the Australian Content Standard (the Standard) determined by the appellant on 15 December 1995 was unlawfully made.
(3) The appellant pay the costs of the appeal and of the proceedings before Davies J.
(4) Each party has liberty to apply further, as it may be advised.
(5) Without limiting the generality of order (4), the respondents have liberty to apply for such further or other orders as they may be entitled to arising from the alleged failure of a clause of the Standard to comply with Australia's obligations under the Australia New Zealand Closer Economic Relations Trade Agreement and the Trade in Services Protocol to that agreement.
(6) There be no order in relation to the costs of the interveners.

[Report: (1998) 153 ALR 490]

State immunity—Jurisdictional immunity—Expropriation — Foreign company — Claim against foreign State for damages — Policy of "Zairianization" operated by State of Zaire—Claim in Belgian courts to recover compensation payable under the law of Zaire—Whether State of Zaire entitled to invoke immunity from jurisdiction—Whether "Zairianization" of foreign-owned companies constituting an act of sovereignty — Whether recourse to procedure established by Zairian Government for recovery of compensation constituting an ordinary commercial act—The law of Belgium

SA BIOCARE v. GÉCAMINES (ZAIRE) AND REPUBLIC OF ZAIRE

Belgium, Civil Court of Brussels (Second Chamber).   16 *March* 1989

(Thiry, *President*)

SUMMARY: *The facts:*—The plaintiff company Biocare brought a claim against a Zairian State-owned company, Gécamines, for compensation payable under the law of Zaire for the loss of its shareholding in a company incorporated in Zaire, which had been expropriated and transferred to

Gécamines pursuant to the "Zairianization" decree, adopted by the President of Zaire in 1973. At first instance, it was held that the Belgian courts had no jurisdiction over the claim. On appeal, the plaintiff company argued that, since the defendant company had an office in Belgium, the debt could be claimed there. The State of Zaire, intervening, argued that it was entitled to jurisdictional immunity from the claim.

Held:—The appeal was dismissed.

(1) While proceedings could be instituted against foreign companies in Belgium if they had established a registered office or subsidiary there, such proceedings could not be brought where, as here, they had no connection with operations carried out by the company concerned in Belgium.

(2) The "Zairianization" decree was unquestionably an act of sovereignty to which jurisdictional immunity applied. However, the proceedings before the Belgian courts did not challenge the principle of "Zairianization" but rather concerned the procedure adopted by the agency established by the Government of Zaire to recover compensation on behalf of those individuals and bodies whose property had been expropriated. The recourse to that procedure, which could be used by private individuals, constituted an ordinary commercial act beyond the scope of jurisdictional immunity, which only covered those acts relating to the political life of the State.

The following is the text of the relevant part of the judgment of the Court:

The judge at first instance held that he had no jurisdiction and consequently no competence over these proceedings . . .

The appellant company objects to that decision, asks for it to be quashed, and submits that the Belgian courts should hold that they are competent in these proceedings . . . The appellant company accordingly asks this Court to hold that those proceedings are admissible and well founded, and to order the respondents to pay compensation for expropriation ("Zairianization") in the amount of 347,157,030 Belgian francs . . .

The appellant company alleges that, on the territory of the Kingdom of Belgium, it was the victim of the "Zairianization" [expropriation], decided upon by the President of the Republic of Zaire on 30 November 1973, of the African Company Minoteries de Kakontwe, of which it held almost the complete share capital, and it claims compensation for that loss.

The appellant specifies that, pursuant to Zairian Law No 78.003 of 20 January 1978, concerning measures for the recovery of sums payable to the State by those acquiring assets subjected to Zairianization by expropriation of their assets on 30 November 1973, equitable compensation is payable by the Zairian company Gécamines which acquired the shares in SARL Minoteries de Kakontwe . . .

[The Court then examined in detail whether it was competent to exercise jurisdiction over the claim from the standpoint of Article 635 of the Judicial Code, which provided that proceedings could be brought against foreigners before the Belgian courts if the foreigner in question was domiciled or resident in Belgium or had a registered office there. The appellant argued that the respondent company Gécamines had an office in Belgium so that the proceedings were admissible. The Court considered the application of the doctrine of choice of domicile with regard to companies in relation to Article 635 and concluded that the conditions for its application were not satisfied in this case because the debt claimed and the policy of Zairianization had no connection with the operation of the respondent's office established in Belgium.

The Court rejected the appellant's contention that, since it no longer exercised any activity in Zaire, it would be impossible to pay the debt claimed to it in that country. On the contrary, the Court considered that it would be perfectly possible for the compensation claimed to be paid into an account in Zaire in the name of the appellant and subsequently for the funds to be transferred to Belgium or elsewhere. Accordingly, since it could not be argued that the debt claimed was necessarily payable in Belgium in accordance with ordinary commercial practice, the Belgian courts had no jurisdiction over the claim. The Court continued:]

The Republic of Zaire criticizes the judgment under appeal for failing to respond to submissions which primarily raised the issue of immunity from jurisdiction.

The respondent considers that the ground based on incompetence and lack of jurisdiction must be examined before the plea of lack of territorial competence because a plea of jurisdictional immunity is a plea in bar which takes precedence over any other grounds.

The respondent Republic of Zaire points out that international territorial competence is a matter for private international law whereas State immunity is governed by public international law and that pleas based on public international law, in particular where they concern matters of jurisdiction, must be examined before pleas based on private international law.

The Republic of Zaire is unquestionably correct when it states that the decree of "Zairianization" is an act performed *jure imperii* which is exclusively a matter for the sovereignty of the State of Zaire and is not subject to the jurisdiction of the Belgian courts. Nevertheless, it must be pointed out that the action brought against the State of Zaire does not bring into question the principle of Zairianization and immunity for an act performed *jure imperii* but, rightly or wrongly and it is for the trial court to decide that question, relates to the action by the State of

Zaire in establishing an agency governed by public law, the Office for the Management of Public Debt (OGEDEP) to recover compensation on behalf of individuals and legal bodies whose property was expropriated.

This procedure, which could be used by private individuals, constitutes an ordinary commercial act outside the scope of immunity which concerns only those acts relating to the political life of the State.

Accordingly, the judge at first instance . . . was correct in deciding that . . . in the proceedings against the State of Zaire . . . Article 635 of the Judicial Code was inapplicable and the Court therefore had no jurisdiction over the claim against that State.

For these reasons the Court confirms the judgment under appeal.

[Report: *JT* 1989, p. 548 (in French)]

State immunity—Jurisdictional immunity—Employee of cultural and information centre of foreign State—Contract of employment—Dismissal—Claim for damages in lieu of notice—Whether foreign State entitled to jurisdictional immunity—Whether contract of employment concluded *jure imperii* or *jure gestionis*—Proper method of service of writ on a foreign State—The law of Belgium

FRANÇOIS *v.* STATE OF CANADA

Belgium, Labour Court of Brussels (First Chamber).   23 *May* 1989

(Dekeyser, *Vice-President*)

SUMMARY: *The facts*:—The plaintiff was employed as a technician at the Cultural and Information Centre of the Canadian Embassy in Brussels from 1978 to 1986. Following his dismissal he claimed that the indemnity offered to him in lieu of notice, in accordance with the provisions of Belgian law, was inadequate. Canada invoked jurisdictional immunity.

Held:—Jurisdictional immunity was denied and the claim was allowed in part.

(1) The defendant State had acted *jure gestionis* in concluding the contract of employment with the plaintiff. It was significant in this regard that, in

terminating the contract, the defendant State had allocated an indemnity in lieu of notice, making express reference to Belgian law.

(2) In accordance with the Belgian Judicial Code, service abroad on a foreign State was accomplished by the handing over of the writ to the postal services in the State of the forum, for delivery by registered post, with a receipt being issued.

The following is the text of the judgment of the Court:

The purpose of these proceedings is to obtain judgment against the defendant for payment of the sum of 191,175 Belgian francs as compensation in lieu of notice . . . with interest and costs.

The facts

The claimant entered into the service of the defendant on 1 October 1978 as a technician at the Cultural and Information Centre of the Embassy of Canada in Brussels, under a letter of engagement of 1 August 1978.

By a letter of 19 June 1986, his contract was terminated with effect from 30 June 1986 subject to the payment of an indemnity in lieu of notice of nine months' salary. On 26 June 1986, counsel for the claimant asked for an additional three months' salary.

Lack of jurisdiction

The defendant raises the lack of jurisdiction of the Court in application of the principle of the jurisdictional immunity of States.

The defendant State is entitled in principle to jurisdictional immunity, but such immunity is not absolute. A distinction must be made between acts performed within the framework of public power, which involve the sovereignty of the defendant State, and those acts performed within the framework of its private administration. It is necessary to determine whether the foreign State acted as a private person or on the basis of its *imperium*. Only in the latter case will it enjoy jurisdictional immunity (cf. Labour Court of Brussels, 1 February 1980, *JTT* 1980, p. 274 with references cited there; *Rupture du contrat de travail, chronique de jurisprudence, 1982-84, JTT* 1986, p. 103).

In this case the contract between the parties is a contract of employment which relates to the private administration of the defendant State. It is not a governmental act and its sovereignty is not involved. The State acted merely as an ordinary private person without bringing its public power into play.

Furthermore, it is very significant that in terminating the contract of employment, the defendant State allocated an indemnity in lieu of notice, making express reference to Belgian law.

The period of limitation

The defendant State also relies upon the fact that the proceedings are time-barred, since they were brought more than a year after the termination of the contract.

The defendant takes into consideration the date on which the writ was served upon it, that is to say the State of Canada, having been notified by the Belgian Embassy in Ottawa on 14 August 1987. The defendant State takes the view that service abroad is only regarded as having been made when the Belgian diplomatic authorities forward the writ to the authority designated by the sending State.

The claimant State, on the basis of Section 40 of the Judicial Code, takes the critical date as 24 June 1987, which was the date when the court official (*huissier de justice*), by registered post and having obtained a receipt, sent two copies of the writ to the Belgian Ministry of Foreign Affairs. That Ministry is responsible for forwarding the writ to its addressee, in this case the Canadian Ministry for External Relations.

Section 40 of the Judicial Code puts an end to this controversy. According to this provision, service of a judicial act abroad is accomplished when a copy of the act is sent by the *huissier de justice* by registered post, without prejudice to other methods of transmission agreed between Belgium and the State of the addressee. *Service is regarded as accomplished by the handing over of the act to the postal services with a receipt being issued for the letter . . .*

In this case, a postal receipt has been produced.

The Court has no knowledge, and the defendant State has not produced any document in this regard, of any international agreement between Belgium and Canada providing for the service of judicial acts by a method of transmission which would take precedence over that laid down by Section 40 of the Judicial Code, that is to say the delivery of the act to the postal services.

These proceedings are therefore not time-barred.

The indemnity in lieu of notice

Taking account of the seniority of the claimant (who has been employed for nine years and nine months), his function as a technician, his annual salary of 764,700 Belgian francs and his age (thirty-two years), the period of notice given to him should have been ten months.

Since an indemnity of only nine months was paid, an additional indemnity of one month is due. That amounts to 63,725 Belgian francs.

For these reasons, the Court declares that the claim is admissible and partially well founded.

[Report: *Jurisprudence des juridictions du travail de Bruxelles* 1989, p. 274 (in French)]

State immunity — Jurisdictional immunity — Chauffeur employed by embassy of foreign State—Contract of employment—Dismissal—Claim for damages for unjustifiable dismissal—Whether foreign State entitled to jurisdictional immunity—Whether fact that employee is a foreign national is material—Relevance of European Convention on State Immunity, 1972, Article 5(1) — Whether applicable as codification of customary international law even though defendant State not a party—The law of Belgium

KINGDOM OF MOROCCO *v.* DR

Belgium, Labour Court of Brussels (Sixth Chamber).   6 *November* 1989

(Thomas, *President*)

SUMMARY: *The facts:*—The respondent, a Portuguese national, was employed as a chauffeur by the Embassy of Morocco. In October 1985 he was dismissed with one month's notice. He brought proceedings claiming compensation for unjustifiable dismissal and Morocco invoked jurisdictional immunity. At first instance the plea of immunity was rejected and Morocco appealed.

Held:—Jurisdictional immunity was denied and the claim was allowed.

(1) In concluding and subsequently terminating a contract of employment, the appellant State had not exercised its public power but had rather performed an ordinary commercial act in the same manner as a private individual. The nationality of the individual had no bearing on the rules applicable to contracts of employment executed in Belgium.

(2) This conclusion was confirmed by Article 5(1) of the European Convention on State Immunity, 1972. Although Morocco was not a party to the Convention, Article 5(1) enshrined a rule of customary international law which was binding on non-parties to the Convention.

The following is the text of the judgment of the Court:

I. *With regard to jurisdiction ratione materiae*
The judge at first instance (Labour Court of Brussels, 2 April 1987) correctly considered that a distinction has always been made in the case-law between acts of public power and commercial acts, even where a foreign State is the defendant.

The Court of Cassation decided as early as 1903 that where a State did not exercise its public power but acted in the same manner as an individual might, as an ordinary private person, any dispute arising from such an act between a Belgian citizen and a foreign State was subject to the jurisdiction of the Belgian courts (Court of Cassation, 11 June 1903, *Pas.*, I, p. 294; also for the same approach see Labour Court of Brussels, 1 February 1980[1] and 25 April 1983, *JTT* 1984, p. 277).[2]

[1 82 *ILR* 100.]   [2 82 *ILR* 118.]

It is not relevant to point out that the respondent is not Belgian but Portuguese. The nationality of the employee has no bearing on the laws applicable to contracts of employment executed in Belgium. Furthermore, since the entry of Portugal into the European Community, the argument is of no relevance.

In this case, the appellant performed an ordinary commercial act.

The appellant also argues that the judge at first instance was wrong to justify his jurisdiction by reference to the European Convention of 16 May 1972, ratified by the Law of 19 July 1975, since the Kingdom of Morocco is not a signatory to that Convention.

Article 5 of that Convention provides that: "A Contracting State cannot claim immunity from jurisdiction of a court of another Contracting State if the proceedings relate to a contract of employment between the State and an individual where the work has to be performed on the territory of the State of the forum."

The judge at first instance correctly concluded that while, in this case, the Convention to which Morocco is not a party cannot, of itself, bind the Court, there is nothing to prevent it from applying as a rule of law or codified custom (see the note to the judgment referred to above of 25 April 1983 and Verhoeven, "Jurisprudence belge relative au droit international", *RBDI*, 1978-9, p. 717). Furthermore, the Explanatory Memorandum to the Draft Law approving that Convention is explicit in this regard, when it states that "it is Belgian and Italian jurisprudence which must be credited with having initiated the theory of restrictive or relative immunity. First mentioned by the Court of Appeal of Brussels in 1840, this theory was approved by the Court of Cassation in 1903. Since then, it has been applied on numerous occasions in Belgian case-law."

It results from these considerations that this Court has jurisdiction over the case.

II. *The facts*

In the document headed "decision" of 23 March 1984, the appellant engaged the respondent as a caretaker with effect from 1 March 1984. From 1 April 1985, he was employed as a chauffeur.

By a letter of 25 October 1985, the employee was informed that: "You are dismissed with effect from today. Accordingly, one month's notice is given to you from 25 October to 24 November 1985 inclusive." By a letter of 30 October 1985, the employee protested over the legality of this notice. By a "decision" of 31 October 1985, the appellant informed the employee "that his functions were terminated with effect from 25 November 1985". By a letter of 5 November 1985, counsel for the employee concluded that the "decision" taken on 31 October 1985 without proper notice was an act equivalent to a breach of contract and that the employee reserved his rights as to the future.

III. *Compensation for breach of contract*
On 25 October 1985 the appellant, without concern for the applicable legal provisions, thought that he was entitled to put an end to the contract by giving notice that it would terminate exactly one month later.

On 31 October 1985, the appellant confirmed that the contract would terminate on 25 November while the employee could no longer perform his functions from 31 October.

[This Court considers] that this termination of the contract is improper and the appellant is therefore entitled to compensation.

IV. *Wrongful dismissal*
Having regard to Section 63 of the Law of 3 July 1978, an employer becomes liable to pay special compensation if he cannot prove that he dismissed his employee for reasons inherent in his aptitude for the job, or his conduct, or service requirements. The burden of proof rests upon the employer.

In order to satisfy this legal requirement, the appellant State seeks to demonstrate that it dismissed the employee because the latter, taking the Embassy car without permission, was involved in two accidents on 24 July 1984 and 17 July 1985. The appellant therefore places the problem at the level of the conduct or driving ability of the employee.

Even if the respondent had a traffic accident on 24 July 1984, whilst employed as Embassy chauffeur, it cannot be concluded, as the appellant argues, that his functions as chauffeur were only exercised from 1 April 1985.

The accidents invoked do not in any way demonstrate that the appellant acted reasonably in dismissing its chauffeur. Inevitably, the occupational hazard of the job and traffic conditions exposed the respondent to the risk of accidents. The fact that, in this case, accidents occurred, in no way demonstrates negligence or repeated carelessness such as to justify the view that dismissal was necessary. Furthermore, it is hardly appropriate to speak of an accident in the first case because the chauffeur was stationary at a traffic light when his vehicle was lightly hit from behind by another driver, when he was lightly pressing the brake . . .

It is more reasonable to take the view that the appellant is trying to show in a bad light facts which it is inappropriate to regard as proper grounds for dismissal.

Furthermore, on 16 October 1985, when the Ambassador of Morocco was transferred, he gave an eloquent testimonial for the services performed by the respondent, without any reservation.

Accordingly, since the appellant State has brought no proof of its grounds for dismissal, special compensation is payable . . .

[Report: *Chronique de droit social* 1992, p. 334 (in French)]

International organizations—Immunity—Attachment and execution—Arbitration—Award in favour of former employee of international organization—Enforceability of award— Rejection by arbitral body of plea of jurisdictional immunity by international organization — Whether automatically implying no immunity from execution of award — Bank account of international organization—Whether immune from execution—Whether any presumption that funds in such an account are allocated for the mission of the organization — Waiver of immunity — Conditions — Headquarters Agreement between Belgium and the Centre for Industrial Development, 1978, Articles 1, 3 and 5—Whether court order of *exequatur* for award necessarily excluding immunity from execution—The law of Belgium

CENTRE FOR INDUSTRIAL DEVELOPMENT *v.* NAIDU

Belgium, Civil Court of Brussels (Jurisdiction for Attachments).   27 *May* 1991

(Gruwez, *President*)

SUMMARY: *The facts:*—The Centre for Industrial Development ("the Centre") was an international institution established by the Third Lomé (ACP–EC) Convention in 1986 to promote the creation of industrial undertakings in the ACP (African, Caribbean and Pacific) States. Mr Naidu was a former employee who invoked an arbitration procedure against the Centre following his dismissal. The Arbitral Tribunal considered and rejected a plea of jurisdictional immunity by the Centre, concluding that the contract of employment was governed by private law, that arbitration was incumbent upon the Centre and that it had in any case waived its immunity. The Tribunal made an award of compensation in favour of Mr Naidu and the Belgian courts subsequently granted an *exequatur* for the award and a conservatory attachment in execution of funds held in a Belgian bank account in the name of the Centre. The Centre appealed to the Belgian courts for the vacation of the attachment.

According to the Headquarters Agreement between Belgium and the Centre of 1978, the property of the Centre was immune from execution, except in the case of a specific waiver, and the Centre could designate those accounts and funds which were necessary for the performance of its operations (Articles 1, 3 and 5). Pursuant to Decision No 4/86 of the ACP–EC Council of Ministers, establishing Staff Rules for the Centre, decisions taken by the arbitral body were binding for the parties and, so far as necessary, enforceable in relation to the competent authorities of the signatory States and the institutions provided for by the Convention.

Held:—The attachment should be vacated.

(1) Immunity from jurisdiction was not synonymous with immunity from execution. The first was derived from the nature of the acts performed by the

person in question whereas the second was derived from the nature of the assets at issue, having regard to their allocated purpose. So far as funds held in the name of an international organization were concerned, they were in principle specifically allocated for the objects for which the organization had been created, and consequently they were covered by immunity from execution. It was not necessary to demonstrate that the funds were allocated for the performance of the mission of the organization.

(2) An order of *exequatur* was merely a preliminary step prior to execution and immunity from execution could constitute a bar to its enforcement. Such an order could therefore be blocked by a grant of immunity from execution. Waiver of such immunity could not be presumed and the specific waiver required by the Headquarters Agreement could not arise in a general manner.

The following is the text of the judgment of the Court:

The object of these proceedings is to obtain the vacation of the attachment in execution, enforced on 31 October 1990 by the court officer (*huissier de justice*) H. Cleopater at the request of Hari Krishnan Naidu, of funds in the hands of SA Banque Bruxelles Lambert ("BBL") held in the account of the Centre for Industrial Development ("the Centre"), an international institution created by the Lomé Convention.

1. *The facts*
The relevant facts of this case, based on an examination of the files and written submissions of the parties, are as follows:

The decision, pursuant to which an attachment in execution has been obtained, is an arbitral award of 5 April 1990 rendered between the parties, Naidu as the claimant and the Centre as the defendant in default. That award rules on compensation payable by the Centre to Naidu following his dismissal by the Centre. The total amount payable is 6,903,520 Belgian francs plus interest at 8 per cent from 23 October 1987 and the costs of the arbitration. The Arbitral Tribunal examined the grounds invoked by the Centre for its failure to enter an appearance: jurisdictional immunity (based on the contention that the dispute was not subject to arbitration) and the improper composition of the Tribunal. These grounds were rejected by the Tribunal which thereby declared that it was competent. The reasoning of the Arbitral Tribunal (inseparably bound up with the *dispositif*) was as follows:

—First, since the dispute concerned the performance of an international contract governing relations of private law, in this case a contract of employment concluded according to the forms and within the framework of private law, jurisdictional immunity could not be invoked by a party which would normally benefit from it, particularly as in this case that party had waived its immunity and furthermore arbitration was in fact incumbent upon the Centre;

—Secondly, the parties not having chosen the law applicable to the arbitral proceedings, an examination of the connecting factors involved in the dispute necessarily resulted in the conclusion that Belgian law was applicable.

By an order of 17 April 1990, the award was rendered enforceable in accordance with Section 1710 of the Judicial Code. On 16 May 1990 the order and the award were notified to the Centre together with a notice to pay the amounts due. On 15 June 1990 the Centre lodged an objection to the order of *exequatur* and requested the annulment of the arbitral award. That case is now pending before the court of first instance of Brussels.

On 25 June 1990 Mr Naidu, having been authorized by the judge with jurisdiction over attachments in *ex parte* proceedings, obtained a conservatory attachment of funds in the hands of the BBL in the name of the Centre.

On 3 October 1990, the judge with jurisdiction over attachments held that the objection to the attachment lodged by the Centre was admissible and well founded, and the Court ordered the vacation of the attachment . . . The following facts appear from that decision, which are inseparably linked to the *dispositif*:

—First, it appears both from general principles of law and the applicable provisions (the First Lomé Convention, Decision No 2/76 of the ACP–EC Council of Ministers of 14 July 1976 and the Headquarters Agreement between the Kingdom of Belgium and the Centre, signed in Brussels on 29 November 1978 and approved by the Law of 9 February 1981, *MB*, 31 March 1981) that the Centre is endowed with legal personality, notwithstanding the fact that Decision No 2/76 was published neither in the *Moniteur Belge* nor in the Official Journal of the European Communities (OJEC);

—Secondly, the publicity given to the Third Lomé Convention and its final act are sufficient to justify their being relied upon against third parties. That publicity consists of the publication of the Convention (OJEC, 31 March 1986) as well as Regulation No 714/90 adopted on 5 March 1990 by the Council of the European Communities (OJEC, 30 March 1990) concerning the application of Decision No 2/90 of the ACP–EC Council of Ministers taken by the ACP–EC Committee of Ambassadors and concerning transitional measures effective from 1 March 1990, as well as Regulation No 714/90 which provides that Decision No 2/90 is applicable in the Community until 28 February 1991. The decision of the ACP–EC Committee for Industrial Cooperation, on the basis of Article 3 of Decision No 2/90, to extend the mandates of Mr Akinrele as director and Mr Mosgard as assistant director from 1 July 1990 to 30 September 1990 (as well as the delegation of powers by the ACP–EC Council of Ministers to the Committee of Ambassadors) and their competence as organs of the Centre, can therefore be relied upon against third parties;

—Finally, the ground based on the contention that the Centre was entitled to immunity from execution was superfluous and therefore not examined.

In his decision of 3 October 1990, the judge with responsibility for attachments noted that, on 18 June 1990, the Centre lodged an application for the suspension of the effects of the order for an *exequatur* for the arbitral award. This Court takes note that, in these proceedings, that procedural act has not been relied upon.

On 31 October 1990, Mr Naidu obtained the attachment in execution of funds held by BBL for the account of the Centre, as security for the debt at issue on the basis of the *dispositif* of the arbitral award. The attachment was notified on 7 November 1990 to the Centre through the services of the Minister for Foreign Affairs. On 29 November 1990 the judge with jurisdiction over attachments made certain procedural orders. On 30 November 1990 the Minister for Foreign Affairs transmitted to the competent court officer the receipt of notification signed by the Centre on 28 November 1990. On 13 December 1990, Mr Naidu served notice on BBL to transfer the funds to him.

On 12 December 1990, the Centre entered a third party opposition to the attachment in execution.

2. [The Court summarized the arguments of the parties and continued:]

3. *In law*

[The Court first considered the scope of the present proceedings, pointing out that it had no jurisdiction to re-examine the clear terms of an arbitral award which had acquired the force of *res judicata* covering both the award and its grounds, and for which an *exequatur* had been granted. The Arbitral Tribunal had examined and rejected an argument put forward by the Centre based on its alleged immunity from jurisdiction. The ground now invoked by the applicant Centre, that the Arbitral Tribunal had no jurisdiction, was therefore inadmissible. Equally, the ground invoked by the respondent Mr Naidu, that the applicant Centre had no legal personality, had already been rejected and the force of *res judicata* also applied to that decision so that this ground was also inadmissible. The Court continued:]

On immunity from execution

The relevant facts are not contested:

—The Centre was ordered to pay certain sums to Mr Naidu by an arbitral award rendered on 5 April 1990, for which an *exequatur* was granted by an order of 17 April 1990.

—Pursuant to the Third Lomé Convention, the Centre "shall contribute to the creation and consolidation of industrial undertakings of the ACP States". The tasks assigned to the Centre are to commission studies, to supply information, and to identify and evaluate potential industrial projects . . .

In accordance with the Headquarters Agreement between the Kingdom of Belgium and the Centre of 29 November 1978, approved by the Law of 9 February 1981 (*MB*, 31 March 1981), "A specific waiver (on the part of the Centre) is necessary for every measure of execution" (Article 1); "Except to the extent necessary for enquiries . . . the property and assets of the Centre shall not be the subject of any form of requisition, sequestration or other form of seizure or distraint, even for the purposes of national defence or the public good" (Article 3); and "The Centre can designate all those accounts and funds which are necessary for the performance of its operations in accordance with its objects" (Article 5).

Pursuant to Decision No 4/86 of the ACP–EC Council of Ministers of 24 March 1986 fixing the rules applicable to staff of the Centre, "Decisions taken by the arbitral body shall be binding for the parties and, so far as necessary, shall be enforceable in relation to the competent authorities of the Member States of the Community or the ACP States as well as for the institutions and organs provided for by the Convention" (Article 36).

Arguments of the parties

The respondent Naidu argues that, by Decision No 4/86, the Centre waived its immunity from execution in this case and that, in the alternative, it must nevertheless be considered that since immunity from execution is only relative and only applicable by reference to the allocated purpose of the funds in question, whether *jure imperii* or *jure gestionis*, the attachment was therefore enforced against assets which were not immune.

The applicant Centre contests the validity of both these arguments.

In law

Both immunity from jurisdiction and immunity from execution, even if it is accepted that the persons entitled to the benefit of those immunities are not subject to legal process, must nevertheless be justified within the framework of the law and accordingly they cannot be considered as absolute.

Immunity from jurisdiction is not synonymous with immunity from execution. The first is derived from the nature of the acts performed by the person, whereas the second is derived from the nature of the assets of the person in question, having regard to their allocated purpose. A decision on one type of immunity does not determine the decision on the other. While it is appropriate to adopt the criteria of *jure imperii* and *jure gestionis*, it is nevertheless necessary to interpret them having regard to the type of immunity at issue.

In this case, we are not concerned with a State or analogous authority whose funds cannot all be regarded as public, but rather with an international institution whose funds held in its name are in principle specifically allocated for the object for which it was created.

Consequently it must be stated that the subject of enforcement in this case, a bank account subjected to attachment in the hands of BBL, is in principle covered by immunity. It is not necessary to demonstrate to the respondent Naidu why funds allocated by an entity for its staff are necessary for the performance of its mission, where it is a service mission, except in order to consider the question, which has not been raised here, as to whether all the staff are employed for the purposes of the mission given to the entity.

The order of *exequatur* is merely a preliminary step prior to execution, whose enforcement may come up against the immunity of the assets subjected thereto.

An order granting an *exequatur* is therefore not synonymous with execution.

The respondent Naidu has not produced any specific waiver which, pursuant to the Headquarters Agreement, is necessary for any measure of execution against the Centre.

Waiver cannot be presumed and a specific waiver cannot arise in a general manner.

It is therefore necessary to state that the funds subjected to attachment in this case are covered by immunity.

The ground based by the claimant Centre on immunity from execution is therefore well founded so that it is unnecessary to examine any other grounds relied upon.

The application for the vacation of the attachment lodged by the claimant Centre is therefore admissible and well founded and it is evidently therefore not appropriate to grant the counter-claim of the respondent Naidu for damages for vexatious proceedings . . .

For these reasons . . . (Order in accordance with the above-mentioned grounds).

[Report: *Revue régionale de droit* 1992, p. 86 (in French)]

State immunity—Jurisdictional immunity—Language teacher employed in consular section of embassy of foreign State— National of employing State—Contract of employment— Dismissal—Claim for damages for breach of contract— Whether foreign State entitled to jurisdictional immunity— Whether fact that employee a national of the employing State is relevant—Relevance of European Convention on State Immunity, 1972, Article 5(2)—Whether applicable as codification of customary international law even though defendant State not a party—The law of Belgium

DE QUEIROZ *v.* STATE OF PORTUGAL

Belgium, Labour Court of Brussels (Fourth Chamber). 22 *September* 1992

(Gustot, *President*; Werquin, *Ministère Public*)

SUMMARY: *The facts:*—The appellant, a Portuguese national, was employed as a language teacher by the consular section of the Portuguese Embassy from 1976 to 1990, when he was dismissed. He brought proceedings against his employer claiming damages for breach of contract. The respondent State did not enter an appearance but the court of first instance raised, *ex officio*, the issue of jurisdictional immunity and held that Portugal was entitled to immunity from the proceedings in accordance with Article 5(2) of the European Convention on State Immunity, 1972. Portugal had signed but not ratified the Convention. Nevertheless the court of first instance held that Article 5(2) enshrined a rule of customary international law that where the proceedings related to a contract of employment between a State and an individual, who was a national of the employing State, that State could claim immunity. De Queiroz appealed.

Held:—The appeal was allowed. The Belgian courts were competent to exercise jurisdiction over the claim.

(1) According to the rules of customary international law, the contract between the parties was governed by private law since the State of Portugal, in hiring the appellant to teach Portuguese language and culture, had not performed an act of sovereignty. Since Portugal had signed but not ratified the European Convention on State Immunity, only those of its provisions which were declaratory of customary international law (such as Article 5(1)) were applicable to the employment relationship at issue.

(2) Article 5(2) of the Convention did not reproduce a pre-existing rule of customary international law since it referred to a connecting factor based on the nationality of the employee, which negated the theory of restrictive immunity based on the distinction between acts of sovereignty performed *jure imperii* and commercial acts performed *jure gestionis*.

The text of the judgment of the Court commences on the following page.

The judgment under appeal was rendered on 28 May 1991, in default of appearance by the respondent, by the Labour Court of Brussels.

Facts
The appellant, the original plaintiff, was employed as a language teacher by the consular section of the Portuguese Embassy from 19 October 1976 to 31 August 1990.

A copy of form C4, sent to him on 18 September 1990, mentioned as the reason for his unemployment "termination of contract". The employer mentioned is the Embassy of Portugal, consular section . . .

De Queiroz was immediately allocated unemployment benefit on an interim basis.

At first instance, the plaintiff claimed compensation for breach of contract (1,127,963 Belgian francs). The judge held that he had no jurisdiction over the claim and the defendant did not enter an appearance.

The Labour Court found that the plaintiff had the same nationality as the employing State. Accordingly Article 5(2) of the European Convention on State Immunity of 16 May 1972 (the so-called Basle Convention) was applicable.

While it was true that Portugal had neither signed nor ratified that Convention, the Court held that this provision merely reproduced an existing rule of customary international law and that "the binding force of its provisions extends beyond the contracting parties to the Convention and affects all those who are regularly subject to the codified rules of custom".

The appellant has asked for that judgment to be quashed and for his original claim equal to fifteen months' salary to be reinstated.

Once again the respondent has not entered an appearance.

In law
Jurisdiction of the Belgian courts
The proceedings concern the non-performance of an obligation arising in Belgium. Proceedings can be instituted against a foreigner before the Belgian courts, even by another foreigner (Article 635(3) of the Judicial Code).

The respondent, in default of appearance, has not raised a plea of immunity from jurisdiction.

The court of first instance considered, however, that this ground should be raised *ex officio*, on the basis that jurisdictional immunity deprived it of competence by reason of the nationality of the plaintiff (by application of Article 5(2) of the European Convention on State Immunity of 16 May 1972, approved by the Law of 19 July 1975).

That Convention establishes as a basic rule (Article 5(1)) that

A Contracting State cannot claim immunity from the jurisdiction of a court of another Contracting State if the proceedings relate to a contract of employment between the State and an individual where the work has to be performed on the territory of the State of the forum.

By way of derogation, Article 5(2) of the Convention provides that

Paragraph 1 shall not apply where:
(a) the individual is a national of the employing State at the time when the proceedings are brought . . .

That is the position in this case.

Portugal signed the European Convention on State Immunity on 10 May 1979 but has not ratified it.

The judge at first instance stressed "that it is accepted where a treaty merely reproduces a pre-existing custom that the binding force of its provisions extends beyond the contracting parties and affects all those who are regularly subject to the custom as codified" (see the references to the doctrine contained in the judgment).

According to the court of first instance, "the provisions of the Convention constitute evidence of the codification of a pre-existing rule of customary law".

The appellant argues that Article 5(2) is merely a derogation from the general rule contained in Article 5(1) and must therefore be interpreted restrictively. Accordingly, that rule should not be applied to non-contracting States.

The appellant also argues that the employing State cannot exempt itself from the jurisdiction of the State of the forum where the employment law of that State confers exclusive jurisdiction on its courts (Article 627(9) of the Judicial Code).

Furthermore, the Portuguese Code of Procedure in Employment Matters provides that actions based on a contract of employment brought by an employee against his employer must be submitted to the court of the place where the contract was performed (Section 14 of Decree-Law 272 A 81 approving the Portuguese Code of Procedure in Employment Matters).

The *Ministère public*, in his long and detailed submissions, points out with regard to the non-ratification by Portugal of the European Convention on State Immunity of 16 May 1972, that Article 38(2) of the Statute of the International Court of Justice states that "international custom, as evidence of a general practice accepted as law" is also a source of law and obligation for States in their mutual relations (Rousseau, *Droit international public*, vol. I, *Introduction et sources*, 1971, p. 307 no 259).

Both the decisions of international tribunals and international treaties contribute to the formation of customary law. However, it is difficult to determine in a codifying convention those parts which are devoted to custom and those parts which create new rules.

In this case it is necessary to determine whether Article 5 of the European Convention on State Immunity of 16 May 1972 constitutes codification of a rule of customary law.

A study of the practice of the Member States of the Council of Europe on immunity questions reveals a certain disparity of attitude between the States concerned. Some States opt for absolute immunity (United Kingdom . . .), whereas others have an uncertain position or opt for restrictive immunity (France, Belgium, Germany, Italy . . .).

Belgian jurisprudence refuses to recognize immunity where the sovereignty of a State has not been engaged, even if the State itself has acted, thereby making a distinction between *jus gestionis* and *jus imperii*. According to this theory, it is necessary to make a distinction dependent upon the capacity in which the State has acted.

Where a State exercises rights in a commercial context by participating as a civil party in relations governed by private law, that State is no longer entitled to invoke immunity (De Visscher and Verhoeven, "L'immunité de l'Etat étranger dans la jurisprudence belge et le projet de Convention du Conseil de l'Europe", in *L'immunité de juridiction et d'exécution des Etats*, Brussels, 1971, p. 46).

The courts consider that the public or private character of the action of the State at issue is determined by the nature of the act, without in principle any consideration of the purpose pursued by the foreign State.

The question of whether the act at issue is an act of public authority or a commercial act is dependent upon whether the act constitutes an exercise of sovereignty or is merely part of a procedure capable of being used by ordinary individuals (see . . . judicial decisions: Labour Court of Brussels, 25 April 1983, *JTT* 1984, p. 271. . .;[1] Labour Court of Brussels, 6 November 1989, *RG* 20.524, *Kingdom of Morocco* v. *DR*;[2] Labour Court of Brussels, 26 June 1985, *RG* 16.736, *Air Algérie*; Labour Court of Brussels, 23 May 1989, *François* v. *Canada*, *JJTB* 1989, p. 274).[3]

Article 5(1) of the European Convention on State Immunity, referred to above, constitutes an application of the theory of restrictive immunity, enshrining the non-application of immunity to ordinary commercial acts.

This provision constitutes a codification of a pre-existent custom or rather the crystallization of a rule of customary law in formation (see the judgments cited above of the Labour Court of Brussels, 25 April 1983, *JTT* 1984, p. 277[4] and 6 November 1989.[5]

[1 82 *ILR* 118.]   [3 See p. 418 above.]   [5 See p. 421 above.]
[2 See p. 421 above.]   [4 82 *ILR* 118.]

The same does not apply in respect of Article 5(2) of the European Convention on State Immunity, as the *Ministère public* correctly pointed out in his opinion, as follows:

Derogations from the rule enshrined in paragraph (1), by acceptance of a connecting factor linked to the nationality of the employee, represent a total departure from the principles established by the restrictive theory of immunity, which they bring into question in a manner contrary to Belgian jurisprudence, and they certainly do not reproduce a pre-existing custom.

This opinion is based upon the commentary of Salmon (*Le projet de Convention du Conseil de l'Europe sur l'immunité des Etats*, 1971, p. 92) and an examination of the explanatory memorandum to the Law ratifying the Convention . . .

In this case the contract between the parties is an employment contract establishing relations governed by private law. The respondent did not perform an act of sovereignty and acted as a private person.

The State of Portugal, in hiring the appellant by means of a contract of employment to teach Portuguese language and culture in Belgium, did not behave as a public authority in the exercise of its political sovereignty.

This Court shares the opinion of the *Ministère public* that, since Portugal has signed but not ratified the European Convention on State Immunity of 16 May 1972, that Convention is not applicable to these proceedings except in relation to those of its provisions which are declaratory of customary international law (Article 5(1)).

Paragraph 2 of Article 5 does not reproduce a pre-existing rule of customary law since it refers to a connecting factor based on the nationality of the employee, which negates the theory of restrictive immunity based on the distinction between acts of sovereignty performed *jure imperii* and commercial acts performed *jure gestionis*.

The Court is therefore competent to exercise jurisdiction over these proceedings.

. . .

For these reasons the Court, having heard *Ministère public* Werquin at the public hearing on 23 June 1992, and having considered his written opinion with which this judgment concurs:

Holds that the appeal is admissible;

Declares the appeal well founded;

Quashes the judgment under appeal;

Ruling anew, holds that the original claim is well founded and

Declares that it is competent to exercise jurisdiction over the claim.

[Report: *Pas* 1992, II, p. 104 (in French)]

NOTE.—In an earlier judgment of the same chamber of the Labour Court of Brussels in *Collée* v. *Gécamines Commerciale*, the plaintiff was employed under a fixed-term contract by Sozacom, a State-owned company in Zaire. In January 1983 he was dismissed on the ground that a work permit application made on his behalf by the company had been refused. He claimed damages and the company disputed the jurisdiction of the Belgian courts on the grounds, *inter alia*, of jurisdictional immunity. The Court, referring to earlier case-law, rejected the plea of jurisdictional immunity on the ground that, in terminating a contract of employment of the type at issue, the company had not performed an act of public power (*jure imperii*) but rather an ordinary commercial act (*jure gestionis*). The Court therefore held that it was competent to exercise jurisdiction and ordered the company to pay the amount claimed (judgment of 30 March 1990, *Journal des tribunaux du travail* 1991, p. 9 (in French)).

State immunity — State entity — Whether endowed with independent legal personality—Whether entitled to invoke jurisdictional immunity — American Battle Monuments Commission — Locally recruited employee — Dispute concerning contract of employment—Whether Commission entitled to invoke jurisdictional immunity from proceedings before municipal courts—United States of America–Belgium Agreement of 27 November 1958 concerning American Military Cemeteries—Provision for immunity from civil jurisdiction—Whether Agreement may be relied upon against individuals in the absence of its publication

Treaties — Effect on third parties — Requirement of publication — Treaty affecting rights and obligations of third parties—Whether treaty can be invoked against third parties in the absence of publication—The law of Belgium

VAESSEN *v.* AMERICAN BATTLE MONUMENTS COMMISSION

Belgium, Labour Court of Verviers. 3 *December* 1997

(Barth, *President*)

SUMMARY: *The facts:*—Vaessen, a Belgian national, was employed from April 1978 as a visitors' guide at the United States military cemetery of

Henri-Chapelle. Following a series of warnings for failures in the performance of his duties, he was summarily dismissed in June 1982 for having absented himself from his post without authorization. He sued his employers, the American Battle Monuments Commission, for compensation for unlawful dismissal. The defendants claimed that they were entitled to jurisdictional immunity pursuant to an Agreement of 27 November 1958 between the United States of America and Belgium concerning American military cemeteries.[1]

Held:—The action was admissible but unfounded.

(1) If an international agreement affected the rights or obligations of individuals, its publication was necessary. Consequently an international agreement which had not been published in its entirety could not be relied upon against individuals. In the case at issue, the Agreement relied upon deprived a worker of his right to bring proceedings before the Belgian court. Accordingly, since it had not been demonstrated that the Agreement had been published, it could not be relied upon against the plaintiff.

(2) The defendant was a body with its own legal personality, independent of the Government of the United States, and had so acted in concluding and terminating the contract of employment at issue in this case. Consequently the proceedings had been properly instituted against the defendant.

The following is the text of the judgment of the Court:

In law

The Court has considered the file of the proceedings *RG* 0368/96, which are in the proper form, and in particular the summons served on 6 September 1992 . . .

The attempt at conciliation provided for by Article 734 of the Judicial Code has failed.

The Court has heard the submissions of the parties made at the public hearing on 3 September 1997.

The Court has considered the provisions of the Law of 15 June 1935 on the use of languages in judicial matters as well as the Judicial Code.

The action is admissible since it was brought in accordance with the correct legal forms and time limit, and the plaintiff has the capacity and interest to institute the proceedings.

1. *The facts*

The plaintiff was hired for the first time by the defendant in April 1978. He was employed until 17 September 1979 as a guide at the American Cemetery of Henri-Chapelle.

On that date the plaintiff was dismissed with immediate effect for serious fault in the following terms: "We consider that your being absent from your post at 3 p.m. on Sunday afternoon, 16 September 1979, without permission and without informing anyone, at a time

---

[1] The text of the provisions of the Agreement relied upon is printed at pp. 438-9 below.

when you were alone in charge of the American Cemetery of Henri-Chapelle, constitutes serious fault justifying your dismissal without notice."

The facts were not disputed but, following various initiatives by Mr Vaessen, he was re-employed on 22 October 1979. The principal responsibility with which he was entrusted was to greet and receive visitors to the cemetery, to respond to their questions and to escort them to the graves. Mr Vaessen was also charged with the administration of the cemetery office.

His trial period was extended by three months and subsequently, having regard to his behaviour, a new reprimand was addressed to him on 26 March 1980. This was presented as a final warning following his behaviour towards other members of staff and failures in the performance of his work.

On 8 December 1980 a new warning was addressed to Mr Vaessen. He was reprimanded in particular for not having respected the times for raising the flag as well as for failing to remove the snow from a path on 6 December 1980 in order to allow visitors to gain access to the museum without danger.

On 30 January 1981 Mr Vaessen received a new and final warning putting him on notice that any new failure in the future would result in his dismissal. He was reprimanded in particular for the manner in which he had dealt with correspondence, which included typing errors, and failure to record correctly the addressee of letters . . .

On 2 June 1982 Mr Hubai, the superintendent who was the most senior person working at the cemetery, requested Mr Vaessen to return by 1.45 p.m. Nevertheless the plaintiff went to the post office at Aubel after lunch. He claims that he received prior authorization to do so from the deputy superintendent, which the latter denies.

By a letter of 3 June 1982, Mr Vaessen was dismissed with immediate effect for serious fault, without compensation or notice, in the following terms:

1. . . .
2. On 2 June 1982 I informed you twice, in the presence of the deputy superintendent, that your presence was of particularly crucial importance that afternoon (after 1.45 p.m.), because of unexpected preparations for the forthcoming commemorative ceremony. You were clearly informed that the deputy superintendent would be absent, obtaining films, drinks, etc. . . . At the same time I clearly and explicitly explained the necessity for me to go to meet local council officials at Plombières, to discuss "last minute" arrangements for that ceremony.
3. Contrary to my instructions, you deliberately disobeyed me and abandoned your post, in a government vehicle, at approximately 2.35 p.m. A number of employees as well as a "trip ticket" vehicle have established that you left the site without "any qualified personnel" for a period of approximately 35 minutes.

4. The deliberate abandonment, contrary to instructions, of this important and frequently visited cemetery, constitutes serious fault justifying your instant dismissal. You were well aware of this fact since, as early as 17 September 1979, you had been relieved of your duties for the same reason, the abandonment of your post.

5. Furthermore, on 1 June 1982, in the presence of the deputy superintendent, you were reprimanded for having on numerous occasions (see the letter of reprimand of 16 November 1981) displayed non-professional conduct and inadequacies in the performance of your duties, including "solving" crossword puzzles and passing your time reading personal papers during working hours, as well as spreading false rumours in the neighbouring village . . .

6. I repeat that your bad faith and continuous signs of lack of maturity, in conjunction with your failure to comply with the rules and regulations of the American Battle Monuments Commission and the American Military Cemetery of Henri-Chapelle, justify your instant dismissal.

The plaintiff considers that he was dismissed because the superintendent wished to be rid of someone who annoys him and whom he did not consider sufficiently accommodating. In the summons of 6 September 1982 he claims:

—459,910 Belgian francs as compensation in lieu of notice equivalent to ten months' salary;

—77,265 Belgian francs for additional holiday pay;

—64,387 Belgian francs for additional holiday pay to be added to the compensation in lieu of notice;

—275,946 Belgian francs as compensation for wrongful dismissal equivalent to six months' salary.

2. *In law*

A. *Lack of jurisdiction of the Belgian courts*

The defendant raises *in limine litis* the immunity from civil jurisdiction to which it claims to be entitled pursuant to the Agreement signed in Brussels on 27 November 1958 between the Government of the United States of America and the Belgian Government concerning American Military Cemeteries.

That Agreement provides:

Article 5(2)

The Government of the United States of America may have recourse to local Belgian workers as necessary, provided only that it complies with Belgian laws concerning social security and pays the contributions fixed by Belgian legislation or by the collective agreements drawn up by joint industrial councils.

Article 7(1a)

The Government of the United States of America may designate one or more institutions to carry out the provisions of this Agreement and shall notify the Belgian Government of the institution or institutions thus designated.

Article 7(2)

Every institution designated in accordance with Article 7(1) above shall enjoy, in Belgium, immunity from civil jurisdiction for acts performed by it pursuant to this Agreement.

The plaintiff argues, however, that the Agreement cannot be relied upon against him for lack of publication.

P. de Visscher in "Observations sur l'avertissement parlementaire aux traités et accords internationaux et sur leur publication" (*JT* 1974, p. 150) considers:

The principle contained in Article 129 of the Constitution is applicable to treaties and international agreements to the extent that the provisions of a treaty only have "binding" force for individuals if they have been published "in the manner determined by the law". This principle was enunciated in a judgment of the Court of Cassation of 11 December 1953 (*Pas.* 1954, I, 299; *RCJB* 1954, 85 with note by Mast; see also *Cass.* 18.11.1957, *Pas.* 1958, I, 290; for the previous jurisprudence see Masquelin, *RPDB sub Traité internationaux*, Nos 205 & 218 and Salmon, *JT* 1971, 511, note 18 to his commentary on the conflict between international treaties and domestic law in Belgium following the judgment rendered by the Court of Cassation on 27 May 1971). This principle was implemented in Article 8 of the Law of 31 May 1961 concerning the use of languages in legislative measures, the publication and the entry into force of legal and regulatory texts. The obligation of publication is deduced from the natural requirements of the notion of binding force, as understood in the domestic legal order, so that it only concerns treaties whose provisions, or certain of them, are capable, directly or indirectly, of creating rights for individuals (see the opinion of the Legislative Section of the *Conseil d'Etat* of 17 February 1964, *DP Ch.* 1953-1964, No 773/1, p. 5 following which Article XXXV of the GATT Agreement of 30 October 1960 was published (*MB* 4.11.1964)). Treaties which impose obligations only on the contracting States can frequently create rights for the benefit of individuals, standstill rules, for example. They can also give rise to objective legal situations which individuals can invoke in disputes concerning their own rights (for example, frontier treaties). This applies in particular where the situation created by a treaty "conditions the existence or the scope of a subjective right established by the domestic legal order or by another rule of international law" (P. de Visscher, *RBDJ*, 1965, p. 137; see also Salmon, *op. cit.* with references referred to there) thus having an effect on the rights and obligations of individuals.

According to M. Melchior, in his written course on public international law distributed to undergraduate students at the University of Liège (pp. 203 ff.), "it appears that at a very minimum publication is necessary pursuant to the Law of 1961 where a treaty is capable of being invoked against individuals or of imposing obligations upon them".

On 19 March 1991 (*Pas.* 1981, p. 779) the Court of Cassation decided that the fact that it has not been published in its entirety means that an international treaty cannot be relied upon against individuals.

In the case submitted to this Court, the Agreement of 27 November 1958, which deprives a worker of his right to bring proceedings against his employer before the Belgian courts, unquestionably has repercussions on the legal position of the plaintiff. The publication of that Agreement is therefore a condition *sine qua non* for its ability to be relied upon against the plaintiff. The defendant has not demonstrated that the Agreement in question was published.

The Agreement signed in Brussels on 27 November 1958 between the Government of the United States of America and the Belgian Government concerning American Military Monuments cannot therefore be relied upon against the plaintiff.

B. *The legal personality of the defendant*

The defendant argues that it does not have legal personality and that it is not authorized or empowered to accept service of a writ.

According to the defendant, the plaintiff should have served the writ on the Government of the United States of America.

This Court considers, however, that the documents issued by the defendant mention its own name without any reference to it acting on behalf of the American Government. This applies to:
 (a) the letter of dismissal of 17 September 1979;
 (b) the contract of employment of 22 October 1979;
 (c) the letter of dismissal of 3 June 1982;
 (d) the form C4;
 (e) . . .
The Court concludes that the defendant is a body with its own legal personality (V. Simonart, *La personnalité morale en droit privé comparé*, Bruylant, 1995, No 396 ff.)

C. *Whether the summons is in the proper form*

In the light of the above considerations, the Court considers that the defendant must be considered as being endowed in Belgium with legal personality.

It is therefore necessary to establish whether a Belgian legal body was properly summoned in France to appear before a Belgian court.

The summons in this case was sent by registered post on 6 September 1982 by the Belgian court officer (*huissier*) to his French counterpart, who delivered the summons through a policeman to the defendant. The defendant was represented at both the hearing on 14 September 1983 and the full hearing on 3 September 1997.

This procedure is certainly in conformity with Article 10(6) of the Hague Convention of 15 November 1965, as well as Article IV of the Protocol annexed to the Brussels Convention of 27 September 1968 (cf. *Les Conventions de Bruxelles et de La Haye en matière civile et commerciale*, La Chartre, p. 72; "La signification des actes judiciaires entre la

Belgique, la RFA et la France", R. Ledoux, *JTT* 1979, p. 385). The summons is therefore in the proper form.

2. *On the merits*

A. *Compensation for breach of contract, wrongful dismissal and loss of additional vacation pay*

It is not disputed that the plaintiff received an instruction from the superintendent to be present at the cemetery on the afternoon of 2 June 1982. Nor is it disputed that the plaintiff nevertheless went to the post office in Aubel on that afternoon.

This insubordination, taken in conjunction with the previous dismissal for leaving his post without permission, constitutes a serious reason within the meaning of Article 35 of the Law on Contracts of Employment. This position is not affected by the alleged authorization given by the deputy superintendent. In fact:

—The notion of authorization implies that the initiative came from the plaintiff, that is to say a request which went against the order previously given.

—Even if the authorization was given, which is formally denied and has not been proved by the plaintiff, it would have emanated from a subordinate agent (the deputy superintendent) and would not therefore be such as to override an order given by a person of superior rank in the hierarchy.

The claim is therefore unfounded.

B. *Additional sum payments in lieu of holidays*

Of the eighteen pages consisting of the summons, submissions, further submissions and rejoinders deposited over a period of fifteen years, the plaintiff justifies this claim simply on the basis that: "At the time of his dismissal, his gross remuncration was 45,991 Belgian francs per month and the plaintiff considers that he was also entitled to paid holidays in 1981 and 1982 (additional lump sum payments in lieu of holidays)."

The defendant, far from accepting this claim, makes no reference to it in its submissions but nevertheless asks in the operative part of its defence for all parts of the claim to be rejected.

The claim is therefore contested.

Since the plaintiff has failed to justify his claim, it must be rejected.

For these reasons the Court, having reserved judgment,

Ruling publicly and finally in the dispute between the parties:

Holds that the action is admissible but unfounded;

Rejects the plaintiff's claim and orders the plaintiff to pay the costs;

Fixes the costs as 7,380 Belgian francs for the defendant and 7,064 Belgian francs for the plaintiff in accordance with the submissions of 8 April 1983.

[Report: Unpublished (in French)]

States—Conduct of foreign relations—Diplomatic relations —Decision by receiving State that foreign diplomat is *persona non grata*—Notification of such decision to sending State pursuant to Vienna Convention on Diplomatic Relations, 1961, Article 9(1)—Whether justiciable in courts of receiving State — Whether constituting an *acte de gouvernement*

Diplomatic relations—Diplomatic agent—Notification by receiving State that diplomat is *persona non grata*—Vienna Convention on Diplomatic Relations, 1961, Article 9(1)— Whether such notification justiciable in municipal courts— Scope of obligation of sending State to recall diplomat in such circumstances—The law of Belgium

T *v.* BELGIUM

Belgium, Conseil d'Etat.   9 *April* 1998

(Vanhaeverbeek, *President*)

SUMMARY: *The facts*:—T, a Congolese national who was financial attaché at the Embassy of the Democratic Republic of the Congo, applied for the temporary suspension of a decision by which the Belgian State, acting pursuant to Article 9(1) of the Vienna Convention on Diplomatic Relations, 1961, had declared him *persona non grata* and asked him to leave Belgian territory within eight days. The reason for this decision was that the applicant had systematically failed to pay domestic rent over a number of years, despite repeated legal proceedings and warnings, and had also failed to comply with a court judgment ordering him to vacate the premises in question by a certain date.

Held:—The application was rejected as inadmissible.

(1) A request for the recall of a diplomat, provided for by the Vienna Convention, which could be made at any time and without the receiving State having to explain its decision, involved the exercise of a discretionary power by the receiving State. Such a request was a matter between States. By reason of its nature, the act by which the receiving State informed the sending State that a member of its diplomatic staff was *persona non grata* was not subject to judicial review.

(2) Whenever a member of diplomatic staff was declared *persona non grata*, it was for the sending State to recall the person affected or to terminate his functions for the mission. A request made by the receiving State for a member of a diplomatic mission to leave its territory had necessarily to be followed by a decision of the sending State with regard to the diplomat concerned. The *Conseil d'Etat* had no jurisdiction over any act emanating from a foreign State.

The text of the decision of the *Conseil d'Etat* commences on the opposite page.

This is an application lodged on 3 April 1998 by T, a Congolese national, in which he seeks the suspension under the procedure for cases of extreme urgency of the execution of a decision by which the respondent declared him *persona non grata* and asked him, together with his family, to leave Belgian territory before 4 April 1998.

The *Conseil d'Etat* has considered the application lodged on the same day by the same applicant for interim measures whereby the Ministry for Foreign Affairs would be required to vacate the measure taken against the applicant provisionally . . .

The facts necessary for an examination of the request for suspension as a matter of extreme urgency are as follows:

1. The applicant is a diplomat who initially represented the Republic of Zaire and now represents the Democratic Republic of the Congo, as a financial attaché. He was accredited in this capacity on 28 September 1989.

2. The applicant established his home in a rented property in Vilvorde from 3 October 1989. Since he systematically failed to pay his rent, his financial privileges were suspended on 3 June 1997.

3. By a judgment rendered after hearing the parties by the justice of the peace of Vilvorde on 26 June 1997, the applicant was ordered, along with his wife, to make payment of the provisional sum of 1,600,000 Belgian francs in arrears of rent up to June 1997, a penalty for re-letting the property of 86,700 Belgian francs and a penalty for continued occupation, equal to the rent of 28,900 Belgian francs per month. The Court rescinded the lease on 1 July 1997 and ordered the defendants to leave the premises by 15 July 1997 at the latest, under penalty of expulsion. No appeal was lodged against this judgment which was served on 5 August 1997 and which has now become final.

4. On 19 January 1998 the applicant notified the Protocol Department that he was ready "in accordance with the judgment rendered to vacate the house which he had rented by 31 March 1998".

5. On 2 March 1998 the applicant forwarded to the respondent a rental agreement between him and Sofidis for an apartment situated in Brussels with the lease to take effect from 1 March 1998.

6. By a *Note verbale* of 26 March 1998, the applicant was declared *persona non grata* in application of Article 9 of the Vienna Convention on Diplomatic Relations, 1961. That Note, which the respondent party considers it is not authorized to produce by reason of its confidential nature, is produced by the applicant in an annexe to his application.

The Note, which is the act attacked in these proceedings, is drawn up as follows:

The Minister for Foreign Affairs, External Trade and Development Cooperation presents his compliments to the Embassy of the Democratic Republic of the Congo and has the honour to refer to his *Note verbale* No 451 of 29 January 1998 concerning in particular the case of T.

The Ministry notes that, despite the very clear request in that Note addressed to Mr T, Attaché at the Embassy, kindly to comply before the end of the month of February 1998 with the final judgment rendered in Vilvorde on 26 June 1997, which ordered him together with others to vacate the dwelling which he was occupying at 321, Henrik I Lei in Vilvorde, the latter has still not vacated that house.

In application of Article 9 of the Vienna Convention on Diplomatic Relations, 1961, the Ministry for Foreign Affairs has decided to declare Mr T, Attaché at the Embassy of the Democratic Republic of the Congo, *persona non grata.*

Consequently Mr T and his family are requested to leave Belgian territory before 4 April 1998. If they continue to reside in Belgium after that date, the Belgian authorities will cease to recognize Mr T as a member of the staff of the diplomatic mission of the Democratic Republic of the Congo in Brussels. The immunities and privileges of Mr T and his family will therefore automatically cease to have effect at that date.

The Ministry for Foreign Affairs deeply regret having found it necessary to take such a step but considers that it has given sufficient warning to Mr T and demonstrated considerable patience in this matter. The Ministry stresses that the measure taken against Mr T does not in any way contradict the firm desire of the Belgian authorities to maintain the best possible relations with the Democratic Republic of the Congo.

The Ministry for Foreign Affairs, External Trade and Development Cooperation takes this opportunity to renew to the Embassy of the Democratic Republic of the Congo assurances of its highest esteem.

The respondent party raises a plea of lack of competence according to which "the act by which the Kingdom of Belgium, in the exercise of its sovereignty as a State, declares a diplomat *persona non grata*, and consequently requests him to leave Belgian territory, is an act of State (*acte de gouvernement*) which is not subject to review by the *Conseil d'Etat.* It concerns exclusively the diplomatic relations which the Belgian State maintains with other Powers, whose diplomats are their organs. The declaration is therefore addressed to the head of the mission to which the diplomat belongs and not to the diplomat himself, on whom it is not served."

As worded, the plea raised by the respondent party concerns both the competence of the *Conseil d'Etat* and the interest of the applicant in obtaining the suspension of the act being challenged. With regard to the latter point, even if the act in question is not addressed to him, the applicant nevertheless has an interest in asking for the suspension of an act which affects him personally and, in declaring him *persona non grata*, unquestionably prejudices his position by reason of its serious consequences with regard to the effect on his status as a diplomat.

At the hearing, the applicant stated that he no longer maintained his request with regard to the decision of the respondent party declaring him *persona non grata.* He still requests, however, with regard to the request that he should leave Belgian territory prior to 4 April 1998, that he should be given sufficient time to organize his departure and allow his children to complete the current school year.

The two parts of the decision being challenged are linked to each other on this point. The request to leave Belgian territory follows directly from the status of the applicant as *persona non grata* so that his request for partial suspension cannot be upheld.

The decision being challenged was taken in application of Article 9(1) of the Vienna Convention on Diplomatic Relations of 18 April 1961 which provides as follows:

The receiving State may at any time and without having to explain its decision, notify the sending State that the head of the mission or any member of the diplomatic staff of the mission is *persona non grata* or that any other member of the staff is not acceptable. In any such case, the sending State shall, as appropriate, either recall the person concerned or terminate his functions with the mission. A person may be declared *non grata* or not acceptable before arriving in the territory of the receiving State.

The request for the recall of a diplomat provided for by the Vienna Convention, which may be made at any time and without the receiving State having to explain its decision, involves the exercise of a discretionary power by the receiving State. Such a request is a matter for the relations between States. By reason of its nature, the act by which the receiving State informs the sending State that a member of its diplomatic staff is *persona non grata* is not subject to review by the *Conseil d'Etat* for *ultra vires*.

Whenever a member of diplomatic staff is declared *persona non grata* it is for the sending State to recall the person affected or to terminate his functions for the mission. A request made by the receiving State for a member of a diplomatic mission to leave its territory must necessarily be followed by a subsequent decision of the sending State. The decision of the receiving State, which in itself has no legal effect, cannot be subjected to review by the *Conseil d'Etat*. Equally, the *Conseil d'Etat* has no jurisdiction over any act emanating from a foreign State. The application for suspension is therefore inadmissible.

The provisional measures requested must suffer the same fate as the request for suspension, by application of Article 18(1) of the Co-ordinated Laws concerning the *Conseil d'Etat*. The application for provisional measures brought before the *Conseil d'Etat* is inadmissible.

The *Conseil d'Etat* decides:

The requests for suspension for reasons of extreme urgency and for interim measures are rejected . . .

[Report: *Jurisprudence de Liège, Mons et Bruxelles* 1998, p. 1549 (in French)]

NOTE.—It appears that this is the first decision in which the Belgian *Conseil d'Etat* has recognized the theory of act of State (*acte de gouvernement*).

Human rights—Property rights—Recognition of indigenous land rights—Legal rights of the Gitksan and Wet'suwet'en aboriginal peoples over territory in British Columbia — Whether aboriginal peoples possessing aboriginal title — Whether aboriginal peoples having right to self-government — Relationship between aboriginal rights and aboriginal title—Aboriginal rights encompassing aboriginal title— Nature and content of aboriginal title—*Sui generis* character of aboriginal title—Proof of aboriginal title—Relevance of oral history evidence of use and occupation of territory— Relevance of aboriginal perspectives — Common law aboriginal title—Effect of Section 35(1) of Constitution Act 1982 recognizing and affirming existing aboriginal rights— Nature and scope of constitutional protection afforded by Section 35(1) of Constitution Act 1982 — Whether any limitation to aboriginal rights—Whether aboriginal rights absolute—Whether infringement of aboriginal rights by government permissible—Test of justification

Territory — Title — Occupation of Canada by aboriginal peoples before assertion of British sovereignty—Source of aboriginal title—Relevance of Royal Proclamation of 1763 —Requirements for proof of aboriginal title—Relevance of physical fact of occupation—Common law principle that occupation proving possession of land in law—Whether claimants occupying land prior to British sovereignty — Whether continuity between present and pre-sovereignty occupation—Whether occupation was exclusive—Whether aboriginal title surviving colonization—Fiduciary obligation of Crown to aboriginal peoples — Reconciling aboriginal interests with sovereignty of the Crown—Section 91(24) of Constitution Act 1867—Whether Federal Government having exclusive jurisdiction over aboriginal rights — British Columbia joining Confederation in 1871—Whether British Columbia having power to extinguish aboriginal rights after 1871—The law of Canada

Delgamuukw and Others *v.* The Queen in Right of British Columbia and Others; First Nations Summit and Others, Interveners[1]

---

[1] Stuart Rush QC, Peter Grant, Michael Jackson, Louise Mandell and David Paterson represented the appellants, respondents on cross-appeal, the Gitksan Hereditary Chiefs and others.

Marvin R. V. Storrow QC, Joanne R. Lysyk and Joseph C. McArthur represented the appellants, respondents on cross-appeal, the Wet'suwet'en Hereditary Chiefs and others.

Joseph J. Arvay QC, Mark G. Underhill and Brenda Edwards represented the respondent, appellant on cross-appeal, The Queen in right of British Columbia.

Canada, Supreme Court.   11 December 1997

(Lamer CJC; La Forest, L'Heureux-Dubé, Sopinka,[2] Cory, McLachlin
and Major JJ)

SUMMARY: *The facts*:—The appellants, hereditary chiefs representing two
aboriginal peoples, the Gitksan[3] and Wet'suwet'en,[4] claimed aboriginal title
over an area of more than 58,000 square kilometres in north-western British
Columbia.[5] While acknowledging that the land could only be alienated to the
Crown which possessed underlying title, the appellants maintained that their
aboriginal title was equivalent to an inalienable fee simple and encompassed
the exclusive right to occupy, use and enjoy the lands as they had done since
time immemorial. Their claim was further based on the Royal Proclamation,
1763,[6] and Section 35(1) of the Constitution Act 1982 which granted recognition
and affirmation to the existing aboriginal and treaty rights of the aboriginal
peoples of Canada. In addition, the appellants claimed the right to self-
government in accordance with their aboriginal laws, and damages for loss of
lands or resources.

The respondents maintained that Section 35(1) of the Constitution Act
1982 only constitutionalized individual aboriginal rights and not aboriginal
title which, at most, encompassed the right to exclusive use and occupation of
land in order to engage in those activities constituting aboriginal rights. The
Province of British Columbia, which had joined the Canadian Confederation
in 1871, counter-claimed for a declaration that the appellants had no right or
interest in the territory or, in the alternative, that their cause of action ought
to be against the Federal Government.

The trial judge in the British Columbia Supreme Court, McEachern CJ,
dismissed the chiefs' original individual claims for ownership, jurisdiction and
aboriginal rights in the territory. He granted a declaration that the chiefs
were entitled to use unoccupied or vacant land subject to the general law of
the Province, and dismissed the claim for damages as well as British Columbia's
counter-claim. He rejected oral history evidence of attachment to the land as
insufficient to establish occupancy to support their claims of ownership.

Graham Garton QC, Judith Bowers QC, Murray T. Wolf and Geoffrey S. Lester represented
the respondent, Attorney-General of Canada.
Arthur Pape, Harry A. Slade, Peter Hogg and Jean Teillet represented intervener, First
Nations Summit. Jack Woodward and Albert C. Peeling represented intervener, Westbank First
Nation. Marvin R. V. Storrow QC, Joanne R. Lysyk and Joseph C. McArthur represented
interveners, Musqueam Nation and others. J. Keith Lowes represented interveners, B.C.
Cattlemen's Association and others. Charles F. Willms represented intervener, Skeena Cellulose
Inc. J. Edward Gouge QC and Jill M. Marks represented intervener, Alcan Aluminium Ltd.
[2] Sopinka J took no part in the judgment.
[3] The Gitksan people numbered approximately 4,000 to 5,000 persons most of whom lived in
the territory claimed, generally the watersheds of the north and central Skeena, Nass and Babine
Rivers and their tributaries.
[4] The Wet'suwet'en people numbered approximately 1,500 to 2,000 persons most of whom
lived in the territory claimed, mainly in the watersheds of the Bulkley and parts of the
Fraser–Nechako River systems and their tributaries.
[5] Other aboriginal peoples also lived on the claimed territory, notably the Carrier-Sekani and
Nishga peoples, along with a non-aboriginal population of approximately 30,000 persons.
[6] For the relevant parts of the text of the Royal Proclamation, 1763, see p. 534.

Aboriginal customs and rules were held to be too flexible and uncertain to warrant jurisdiction or sovereignty over the territory in question. Although at the date of British sovereignty the chiefs had established non-exclusive aboriginal sustenance rights, all aboriginal rights to the land had been extinguished by colonial enactments before British Columbia entered the Confederation. Permission to use vacant Crown lands for lawful purposes, until the land was dedicated to another purpose, was thus based solely upon the fiduciary obligation of the Crown. As all aboriginal rights had been extinguished, Section 35(1) of the Constitution Act 1982 had no application.

The chiefs appealed to the British Columbia Court of Appeal. They amended their claims, but not their pleadings, from ownership and jurisdiction to aboriginal title and self-government over the territory in question, and from individual claims into two communal claims. British Columbia cross-appealed. Both appeals were dismissed. While declaring that the chiefs did have unextinguished non-exclusive aboriginal rights, the Court upheld the trial judge's conclusion that the chiefs did not have ownership or the right to the exclusive use or possession of the land.

The appellants appealed and British Columbia cross-appealed to the Supreme Court of Canada.

Held:—The appeal was allowed in part and the cross-appeal dismissed. A new trial was ordered.

Per Lamer CJC (Cory, McLachlin and Major JJ concurring): (1) The replacement by the appellants of the original claims for ownership and jurisdiction over the territory with claims for aboriginal title and self-government on appeal was permissible given the uncertainty surrounding the nature and content of aboriginal rights under common law and under Section 35(1) of the Constitution Act 1982 at that time. The amalgamation of the individual claims into two communal claims without formal amendment to the pleadings did, however, necessitate a new trial. The amendment prejudiced the respondents, because collective claims had not been in issue at the trial (pp. 478-9).

(2) Although, as a general rule, the Supreme Court would not interfere with findings of fact made at trial, the dismissal of oral histories as evidence of occupation and use of the claimed territory was a serious error that warranted appellate intervention and a new trial. Although common law doctrine, aboriginal rights were *sui generis* and, as such, required a unique approach to evidence which accorded due weight to the perspective of aboriginal peoples while at the same time not straining the Canadian legal and constitutional structure (pp. 479-91).

(3) In order to give guidance to the judge at the new trial, it was appropriate to consider the content of aboriginal title, the nature of protection afforded to it by Section 35(1) of the Constitution Act 1982, and requirements for its proof which were all disputed by the parties (p. 491).

(4) Aboriginal title was a *sui generis* interest in land, distinct from fee simple and other "normal" proprietary interests. Although inalienable to any third party other than the Crown, aboriginal title was nevertheless a proprietary interest which amounted to more than a licence to use and occupy the land. Its source was the occupation of Canada by aboriginal peoples before the

assertion of British sovereignty, the physical fact of occupation proving possession of its lands according to the common law principle. The Royal Proclamation of 1763 had merely recognized the title. Aboriginal title thus survived colonization and could only be understood by reference to both common law and pre-existing systems of aboriginal law. The title could only be held communally and not by individual members of an aboriginal nation (pp. 491-3).

(5) Aboriginal title encompassed the right of exclusive use and occupation of the land. Use of the land was not confined to specific activities tied to aboriginal practices, customs and traditions. Aboriginal title therefore extended beyond aboriginal rights. This was evidenced in Canadian jurisprudence on aboriginal title, the legal principles governing aboriginal interest in reserve lands, including Section 18 of the Indian Act, and the Indian Oil and Gas Act. The content of aboriginal title did, however, contain an inherent limitation that lands held pursuant to title could not be used in a manner that was irreconcilable with the nature of the claimant's attachment to those lands. This limitation revealed another aspect of the *sui generis* character of aboriginal title and resulted from the continuity of the physical and cultural relationship between an aboriginal community and its land (pp. 493-500).

(6) Aboriginal title at common law was protected in its full form by Section 35(1) of the Constitution Act 1982. Recognized under the common law prior to 1982, this aboriginal right was not created but merely constitutionalized by Section 35(1). An aboriginal right did not, however, have to exist at common law in order to warrant the recognition and protection of Section 35(1). Although a species of aboriginal right, aboriginal title was distinct from other aboriginal rights in that it arose where the connection of a group with a piece of land was of central significance to their distinctive culture and it conferred the right to the land itself and was not defined merely in terms of activities (pp. 500-3).

(7) In order for claimants to prove aboriginal title it was necessary that (i) the land was occupied prior to the establishment of sovereignty, (ii) there was continuity between present and pre-sovereignty occupation if present occupation was relied on as proof of occupation pre-sovereignty, and (iii) at the establishment of sovereignty, that occupation was exclusive. Occupation at the time of sovereignty was necessary if there was to be an underlying title belonging to the Crown upon which aboriginal title was a burden. Under common law, occupation or possession was sufficient to establish aboriginal title and the assumption of sovereignty provided a certain date at which to assess occupation. If conclusive evidence of pre-sovereignty occupation was unavailable, present occupation was acceptable as proof provided that there was continuity in occupation. The nature of occupation did not have to be the same provided that uses of the land were not inconsistent with continued use by future generations of aboriginals. Proof of exclusivity, as with proof of occupancy, was to be established by giving equal weight to both the common law and the aboriginal perspectives (pp. 503-11).

(8) Aboriginal rights, including aboriginal title, recognized and affirmed by Section 35(1) of the Constitution Act 1982 were not, however, absolute. Infringement of those rights by the Federal Government and provincial governments was possible if it satisfied the test of justification, that is, if it

furthered a compelling and substantial legislative objective and if it was consistent with the special fiduciary relationship between the Crown and aboriginal peoples. An objective was compelling and substantial if it was directed towards the recognition of the prior occupation of North America by aboriginal peoples or the reconciliation of aboriginal prior occupation with the assertion of the sovereignty of the Crown, that is, if it was consistent with the purposes underlying the recognition and affirmation of aboriginal rights by Section 35(1). Fiduciary duty has been interpreted and applied, according to the context, in various ways. These include the priority given to aboriginal rights, the limitation on infringement, the award of compensation for expropriation and consultation with the affected aboriginal group. Infringement of aboriginal title could be justified by a broad range of legislative objectives, such as the development of agriculture, mining and the protection of the environment (pp. 511-17).

(9) Whether the appellants had made out a claim to self-government was a question to be determined at the new trial (p. 517).

(10) The Federal Government had exclusive jurisdiction over lands reserved for Indians, including aboriginal rights, by virtue of Section 91(24) of the Constitution Act 1867. This precluded provincial laws concerning aboriginal rights and their extinguishment. Although provincial laws of general application also applied to Indians living on reserves, such laws could not extinguish aboriginal rights because they failed to show the requisite clear and plain intent and because Section 91(24) of the Constitution Act 1867 protected this core of federal jurisdiction over aboriginal rights through the operation of the doctrine of interjurisdictional immunity. Neither did Section 88 of the Indian Act, which allowed the application of provincial laws to Indians, permit the extinguishment of aboriginal rights. Apart from lacking the necessary clear and plain intent, its explicit reference to treaty rights indicated that the provision was not intended to undermine aboriginal rights. Therefore, after joining the Confederation in 1871, British Columbia had no power to extinguish aboriginal rights, either under its own jurisdiction or through the operation of Section 88 of the Indian Act. Those rights thus existed in 1982 and could be afforded the protection of Section 35(1) of the Constitution Act 1982 (pp. 518-23).

(11) Given that aboriginal title conferred a right to use and occupy land to the exclusion of non-aboriginals and other aboriginal nations alike, it was advisable that any other aboriginal nations with claims to the land in question intervene in any new litigation. The ordering of a new trial was not, however, to be interpreted as an encouragement to litigate further. Negotiations undertaken in good faith were the preferred solution to the problem of reconciling the pre-existence of aboriginal societies with the sovereignty of the Crown (pp. 523-4).

Per La Forest J (L'Heureux-Dubé and McLachlin JJ concurring): (1) Although arguing the acquisition of an absolute interest in the claimed territory, the appellants sought to prove general occupation of the claimed land as opposed to the required governance and control. It was this substantial defect in the pleadings, rather than a technical one, that rendered a new trial necessary (pp. 527-8).

(2) The aboriginal right of possession was derived from the historic use and occupation of ancestral lands by aboriginal peoples. A *sui generis* interest in land, aboriginal title was distinct from fee simple ownership and could not be described in terms of traditional property law. It was a personal interest, alienable only to the Crown which was under a fiduciary obligation to treat aboriginal peoples fairly (pp. 528-9).

(3) The recognition of a general right to occupy and possess ancestral lands for a variety of uses was to be distinguished from the recognition of a discrete right to engage in an aboriginal activity in a particular area. The nature of aboriginal title was generally to be defined without reference to statutory provisions and regulations concerning reserve lands (pp. 529-30).

(4) It was necessary that the nature of an aboriginal claim to land was identified precisely with regard to particular practices, customs and traditions as the court would examine the occupation and use of the land as part of the aboriginal society's traditional way of life. The area claimed by the aboriginal people had to be specific and their occupation and use of it continuous. Aboriginal title was established at the time of the assertion of sovereignty over the land by the Crown, although continuity could still exist where the present occupation of one area was connected to the pre-sovereignty occupation of another area. Prior occupation could also be proved by evidence of present occupation. Continued occupation and use of land was sufficient proof that the land was of central significance to the aboriginal people (pp. 530-2).

(5) The Royal Proclamation of 1763, although not the sole source of aboriginal title in Canada, evidenced that British policy towards aboriginal peoples was based on respect for their right to occupy ancestral lands by reserving vast tracts of territory for indigenous use (pp. 532-3).

(6) Aboriginal rights, although recognized and affirmed under Section 35(1) of the Constitution Act 1982, were not absolute. They could be infringed by government regulation if the test of justification under Section 35(1) was satisfied. Infringements were permissible if pursuant to valid legislative objectives, such as the general economic development of the interior of British Columbia, but these objectives were also subject to the accommodation of aboriginal peoples' interests. Such accommodation included adequate notification and consultation of aboriginal peoples and fair compensation. In developing vast tracts of land, the government was expected to consider the economic well-being of all Canadians, not forgetting the aboriginal peoples. The legal right of aboriginal peoples to occupy and possess certain lands, as confirmed by Section 35(1) of the Constitution Act 1982, mandated basic fairness commensurate with the honour and good faith of the Crown (pp. 533-5).

(7) There was insufficient evidence for the Court to make any determination with regard to the issue of self-government (p. 535).

(8) The respondent, British Columbia, had no authority to extinguish aboriginal rights either under the Constitution Act 1867 or by virtue of Section 88 of the Indian Act (p. 535).

(9) The case was best solved by a process of negotiation and reconciliation that properly considered the complex and competing interests at stake (p. 535).

The following is the text of the judgments delivered in the Court:

LAMER C.J.C. (CORY and MAJOR JJ. concurring):— [20]
I. INTRODUCTION

[1] This appeal is the latest in a series of cases in which it has fallen to this Court to interpret and apply the guarantee of existing aboriginal rights found in s. 35(1) of the *Constitution Act, 1982*. Although that line of decisions, commencing with *R. v. Sparrow*, [1990] 1 S.C.R. 1075, 70 D.L.R. (4th) 385, proceeding through the *Van der Peet* trilogy (*R. v. Van der Peet*, [1996] 2 S.C.R. 507, 137 D.L.R. (4th) 289, *R. v. N.T.C. Smokehouse Ltd.*, [1996] 2 S.C.R. 672, 137 D.L.R. (4th) 528, and *R. v. Gladstone*, [1996] 2 S.C.R. 723, 137 D.L.R. (4th) 648), and ending in *R. v. Pamajewon*, [1996] 2 S.C.R. 821, 138 D.L.R. (4th) 204 *sub nom. R. v. Gardner; R. v. Jones, R. v. Adams*, [1996] 3 S.C.R. 101, 138 D.L.R. (4th) 657, and *R. v. Côté*, [1996] 3 S.C.R. 139, 138 D.L.R. (4th) 385, have laid down the jurisprudential framework for s. 35(1), this appeal raises a set of interrelated and novel questions which revolve around a single issue — the nature and scope of the constitutional protection afforded by s. 35(1) to common law aboriginal title.

[2] In *Adams*, and in the companion decision in *Côté*, I considered and rejected the proposition that claims to aboriginal rights must also be grounded in an underlying claim to aboriginal title. But I held, nevertheless, that aboriginal title was a distinct species of aboriginal right that was recognized and affirmed by s. 35(1). Since aboriginal title was not being claimed in those earlier appeals, it was unnecessary to say more. This appeal demands, however, that the Court now explore and elucidate the implications of the constitutionalization of aboriginal title. The first is the specific content of aboriginal title, a [202] question which this Court has not yet definitively addressed, either at common law or under s. 35(1). The second is the related question of the test for the proof of title, which, whatever its content, is a right *in land*, and its relationship to the definition of the aboriginal rights

recognized and affirmed by s. 35(1) in *Van der Peet* in terms of *activities*. The third is whether aboriginal title, as a right in land, mandates a modified approach to the test of justification first laid down in *Sparrow* and elaborated upon in *Gladstone*.

[3] In addition to the relationship between aboriginal title and s. 35(1), this appeal also raises an important practical problem relevant to the proof of aboriginal title which is endemic to aboriginal rights litigation generally — the treatment of the oral histories of Canada's aboriginal peoples by the courts. In *Van der Peet*, I held that the common law rules of evidence should be adapted to take into account the *sui generis* nature of aboriginal rights. In this appeal, the Court must address what specific form those modifications must take.

[4] Finally, given the existence of aboriginal title in British Columbia, this Court must address, on cross-appeal, the question of whether the province of British Columbia, from the time it joined Confederation in 1871, until the entrenchment of s. 35(1) in 1982, had jurisdiction to extinguish the rights of aboriginal peoples, including aboriginal title, in that province. Moreover, if the province was without this jurisdiction, a further question arises — whether provincial laws of general application that would otherwise be inapplicable to Indians and Indian lands could nevertheless extinguish aboriginal rights through the operation of s. 88 of the *Indian Act*, R.S.C. 1985, c. I-5.

II. Facts

[5] At the British Columbia Supreme Court, McEachern C.J. heard 374 days of evidence and argument. Some of that evidence was not in a form which is familiar to common law courts, including oral histories and legends. Another significant part was the evidence of experts in genealogy, linguistics, archeology, anthropology, and geography.

[6] The trial judge's decision (reported at [1991] 3 W.W.R. 97, 79 D.L.R. (4th) 185) is nearly 400 pages long, with another 100 pages of schedules. Although I am of the view that there must be a new

trial, I nevertheless find it useful to summarize some of the relevant [20:
facts, so as to put the remainder of the judgment into context.

A. The Claim at Trial

[7] This action was commenced by the appellants, who are all
Gitksan or Wet'suwet'en hereditary chiefs, who, both individually
and on behalf of their "Houses" claimed separate portions of 58,000
square kilometres in British Columbia. For the purpose of the claim,
this area was divided into 133 individual territories, claimed by the
71 Houses. This represents all of the Wet'suwet'en people, and all
but 12 of the Gitksan Houses. Their claim was originally for "ownership" of the territory and "jurisdiction" over it. (At this Court, this
was transformed into, primarily, a claim for aboriginal title over the
land in question.) The province of British Columbia counterclaimed
for a declaration that the appellants' have no right or interest in and
to the territory or alternatively, that the appellants' cause of action
ought to be for compensation from the Government of Canada.

B. The Gitksan and Wet'suwet'en People

(1) Demography

[8] The Gitksan consist of approximately 4,000 to 5,000 persons,
most of whom now live in the territory claimed, which is generally
the watersheds of the north and central Skeena, Nass and Babine
Rivers and their tributaries. The Wet'suwet'en consist of approximately 1500 to 2000 persons, who also predominantly live in the
territory claimed. This territory is mainly in the watersheds of the
Bulkley and parts of the Fraser-Nechako River systems and their tributaries. It lies immediately east and south of the Gitksan.

[9] Of course, the Gitksan and Wet'suwet'en are not the only people living in the claimed territory. As noted by both McEachern C.J.
at trial (at p. 440) and Lambert J.A. on appeal ([1993] 5 W.W.R. 97 at
p. 243, 104 D.L.R. (4th) 470), there are other aboriginals who live in
the claimed territory, notably the Carrier-Sekani and Nishga peoples.
Some of these people have unsettled land claims overlapping with
the territory at issue here. Moreover, there are also numerous non-
aboriginals living there. McEachern C.J. found that, at the time of
the trial, the non-aboriginal population in the territory was over 30,000.

(2) History

[10] There were numerous theories of the history of the Gitksan
and Wet'suwet'en peoples before the trial judge. His conclusion from

204] the evidence was that their ancestors migrated from Asia, probably through Alaska, and spread south and west into the areas which they found to be liveable. There was archeological evidence, which he accepted, that there was some form of human habitation in the territory and its surrounding areas from 3500 to 6000 years ago, and intense occupation of the Hagwilget Canyon site (near Hazelton), prior to about 4000 to 3500 years ago. This occupation was mainly in or near villages on the Skeena River, the Babine River or the Bulkley River, where salmon, the staple of their diet, was easily obtainable. The other parts of the territory surrounding and between their villages and rivers were used for hunting and gathering for both food and ceremonial purposes. The scope of this hunting and gathering area depended largely on the availability of the required materials in the areas around the villages. Prior to the commencement of the fur trade, there was no reason to travel far from the villages for anything other than their subsistence requirements.

(3) North American Exploration

[11] There was little European influence in western Canada until the arrival of Capt. Cook at Nootka on Vancouver Island in 1778, which led to the sea otter hunt in the north Pacific. This influence grew with the establishment of the first Hudson's Bay trading post west of the Rockies (although east of the territories claimed) by Simon Fraser in 1805-1806. Trapping for the commercial fur trade was not an aboriginal practice, but rather one influenced by European contact. The trial judge held that the time of direct contact between the aboriginal peoples in the claimed territory was approximately 1820, after the trader William Brown arrived and Hudson's Bay had merged with the North West Company.

(4) Present Social Organization

[12] McEachern C.J. set out a description of the present social organization of the appellants. In his opinion, this was necessary because "one of the ingredients of aboriginal land claims is that they arise from long-term communal rather than personal use or possession of land" (at p. 147). The fundamental premise of both the Gitksan and the Wet'suwet'en people is that they are divided into clans and Houses. Every person born of a Gitksan or Wet'suwet'en woman is automatically a member of his or her mother's House and clan. There are four Gitksan and four Wet'suwet'en clans, which are subdivided into houses. Each house has one or more Hereditary Chief as its

titular head, selected by the elders of their house, as well as possibly **[20!**
the Head Chief of the other Houses of the clan. There is no head
chief for the clans, but there is a ranking order of precedence within
communities or villages, where one House or clan may be more prominent than others.

[13] At trial, the appellants' claim was based on their historical
use and "ownership" of one or more of the territories. The trial judge
held that these are marked, in some cases, by physical and tangible
indicators of their association with the territories. He cited as examples totem poles with the Houses' crests carved, or distinctive regalia.
In addition, the Gitksan houses have an "adaawk" which is a collection of sacred oral tradition about their ancestors, histories and
territories. The Wet'suwet'en each have a "kungax" which is a spiritual song or dance or performance which ties them to their land.
Both of these were entered as evidence on behalf of the appellants
(see my discussion of the trial judge's view of this evidence, *infra*).

[14] The most significant evidence of spiritual connection between
the Houses and their territory is a feast hall. This is where the Gitksan
and Wet'suwet'en people tell and re-tell their stories and identify their
territories to remind themselves of the sacred connection that they
have with their lands. The feast has a ceremonial purpose, but is also
used for making important decisions. The trial judge also noted the
Criminal Code prohibition on aboriginal feast ceremonies, which
existed until 1951.

III. JUDGMENTS BELOW

A. SUPREME COURT OF BRITISH COLUMBIA

(1) General Principles

[15] The trial judge began his analysis by considering the significant cases in this area: *St. Catharines Milling and Lumber Co. v. The
Queen* (1887), 13 S.C.R. 577, *Calder v. Attorney General of British
Columbia*, [1973] S.C.R. 313, 34 D.L.R. (3d) 145, *Baker Lake v.* [7]
Minister of Indian Affairs and Northern Development, [1980] 1 F.C.
518, 107 D.L.R. (3d) 513, *Guerin v. The Queen*, [1984] 2 S.C.R. 335,
13 D.L.R. (4th) 321, *R. v. Sioui*, [1990] 1 S.C.R. 1025, 70 D.L.R.
(4th) 427, and *Sparrow, supra*. On the basis of this jurisprudence, he
set out four propositions of law. First, aboriginal interests arise out of
occupation or use of specific land for aboriginal purposes for an
indefinite or long, long time before the assertion of sovereignty. Second, aboriginal interests are communal, consisting of subsistence

206] activities and are not proprietary. Third, at common law, aboriginal rights exist at the pleasure of the Crown and may be extinguished when the intention of the Crown is clear and plain. This power reposed with the Imperial Crown during the colonial period. Upon Confederation the province obtained title to all Crown land in the province subject to the "Interests" of the Indians. Finally, unextinguished aboriginal rights are not absolute. Crown action and aboriginal rights may, in proper circumstances, be reconciled. Generally speaking, aboriginal rights may be regulated by the Crown only when such regulation operates to interfere with aboriginal rights pursuant to legitimate Crown objectives which can honourably be justified, without undue interference with such rights. Moreover, when regulating, government must be mindful of the appropriate level of priority which aboriginal rights have over competing, inconsistent activities.

[16] With respect to the appellants' claims, McEachern C.J. divided his analysis into three parts: (1) jurisdiction over the territory; (2) ownership of the territory; and (in the alternative) (3) particular aboriginal rights over the territory. In the ownership claim, the appellants asserted they were "absolutely entitled to occupy and possess the individual territories" claimed (at p. 126). The claim to jurisdiction was understood by the trial judge as comprising jurisdiction over land and people in the territory, and amounted to aboriginal sovereignty, a right to "govern the territory free of provincial control in all matters where their aboriginal laws conflict with the general law" (at p. 128). Although the claim advanced at trial was advanced by individual chiefs on behalf of themselves or their House members, the trial judge held that since aboriginal rights are communal in nature, any judgment must be for the benefit of the Gitksan and Wet'suwet'en people generally.

(2) Aboriginal Ownership

[17] McEachern C.J. started from the proposition, for which he cited *St. Catharines Milling*, that aboriginal rights are not proprietary in nature, but rather "personal and usufructuary", and dependent upon the good will of the Sovereign. He was satisfied that at the date of British sovereignty, the appellants' ancestors were living in their villages on the great rivers, in a form of communal society. He was satisfied that they were occupying or possessing fishing sites and the

adjacent lands, as their ancestors had done for the purpose of hunting [20?
and gathering that which they required for sustenance. However, he
was not satisfied that they owned the territory in its entirety in any
sense that would be recognized by the law.

[18] There were several specific claims of the plaintiffs as to their
uses of the land before the assertion of sovereignty. He concluded
that the appellants' ancestors lived within the territory, but predominantly at the village sites. He accepted, at p. 372, that they harvested
the resources of the lands, but that there was only evidence of
"commonsense subsistence practices . . . entirely compatible with
bare occupation for the purposes of subsistence". He was not persuaded that there was any system of governance or uniform custom
relating to land outside the villages. He refused to accept that the
spiritual beliefs exercised within the territory were necessarily common to all the people or that they were universal practices. He was
not persuaded that the present institutions of the plaintiffs' society
were recognized by their ancestors. Rather, he found, at p. 373, that
"they more likely acted as they did because of survival instincts". He
stated that the maintenance and protection of the boundaries were
unproven because of the numerous intrusions into the territory by
other peoples. The oral histories, totem poles and crests were not
sufficiently reliable or site specific to discharge the plaintiff's burden of proof. Although McEachern C.J. recognized the social
importance of the feast system and the fact that it evolved from earlier practices, he did not accept its role in the management and
allocation of lands, particularly after the fur trade. McEachern C.J.
concluded, at p. 383, that "I cannot infer from the evidence that the
Indians possessed or controlled any part of the territory, other than
for village sites and for aboriginal use in a way that would justify a
declaration equivalent to ownership".

[19] Although he was of the opinion that the status of the villages
and their immediate surrounding area may be different from the territory as a whole, they were already predominantly reserve lands.
Hence, the question of the Gitksan and Wet'suwet'en people's rights
to these particular lands did not need to be dealt with. Moreover,
to the extent that there were hunting grounds not included on those
lands, McEachern C.J. believed he had no jurisdiction to extend their
boundaries.

208] *(3) Aboriginal Sovereignty*

[20] McEachern C.J. interpreted the appellants' claim for "jurisdiction" as a claim to govern the territories in question. This would include the right to enforce existing aboriginal law, as well as make and enforce new laws, as required for the governance of the people and their land. Most notably, this would also include a right to supersede the laws of British Columbia if the two were in conflict. McEachern C.J. rejected the appellants' claim for a right of self-government, relying on both the sovereignty of the Crown at common law, and what he considered to be the relative paucity of evidence regarding an established governance structure. First, he stated, at p. 386, that when British Columbia was united with Canada, "all legislative jurisdiction was divided between Canada and the province, and there was no room for aboriginal jurisdiction or sovereignty which would be recognized by the law or the courts". Second, he characterized the Gitksan and Wet'suwet'en legal system, at p. 379, as a "most uncertain and highly flexible set of customs which are frequently not followed by the Indians themselves". He continued, at pp. 379-80, stating:

> I heard many instances of prominent Chiefs conducting themselves other than in accordance with these rules, such as logging or trapping on another chief's territory, although there always seemed to be an aboriginal exception which made almost any departure from aboriginal rules permissible. In my judgment, these rules are so flexible and uncertain that they cannot be classified as laws.

As a result of the flexibility and uncertainty of the customs and rules, McEachern C.J. rejected the appellant's claim to jurisdiction or sovereignty over the territories.

(4) Aboriginal Rights

[21] After rejecting the appellants' claim for ownership of and jurisdiction over the disputed territories, McEachern C.J. turned to the possibility that the appellants nevertheless have aboriginal rights exercisable therein. He set out, at p. 388, the four part test from *Baker Lake* for an aboriginal right:

> 1. That they [the plaintiffs] and their ancestors were members of an organized society.
>
> 2. That the organized society occupied the specific territory over which they assert the aboriginal title.
>
> 3. That the occupation was to the exclusion of other organized societies.
>
> 4. That the occupation was an established fact at the time sovereignty was asserted by England.

McEachern C.J. noted that the requirement for an organized society [20!
had been satisfied, even though he did not believe the appellants'
ancestors had institutions and governed themselves. However, he held
that no specific level of sophistication ought to be required in satisfy-
ing this requirement. He then stated that there was evidence that the
ancestors of the plaintiffs occupied specific locations in the territory
(the villages) and they used surrounding lands. Although there was
evidence that the Gitksan and Wet'suwet'en would not have been
able to keep invaders or traders out of their territory, no other organized societies had established themselves in the core areas on any
permanent basis. Moreover, he noted at the outset of his reasons on this
point that he was uncertain about the requirement for exclusivity.

[22] The activities that were to be protected were only those carried on at the time of contact or European influence and that were
still carried on at the time of sovereignty. This included "all sustenance practices and the gathering of those products of the land and
waters of the territory I shall define which they practised and used
before exposure to European civilization (or sovereignty) for subsistence or survival" (at p. 391). This did not include trapping for the
fur trade, or other land-based commercial enterprise. McEachern C.J.
ultimately concluded, at p. 395 that "the plaintiffs have established,
as of the date of British sovereignty, the requirements for continued
residence in their villages, and for non-exclusive aboriginal sustenance rights within [certain] portions of the territory".

(5) Extinguishment and Fiduciary Duties

[23] McEachern C.J. started with the proposition, at pp. 396-97,
that the law "never recognized that the settlement of new lands depended upon the consent of the Indians". All aboriginal rights existed
at the pleasure of the Crown, and could be extinguished by unilateral
act. He accepted the "clear and plain" intention test for extinguishment, but took the view that it need not be express or even mention
aboriginal rights, if the intention can be identified by necessary implication. An example of such implied extinguishment might be a fee
simple grant to a third party, or a grant of a lease, licence, permit or
other tenure inconsistent with continuing aboriginal interest.

[24] McEachern C.J. held that any aboriginal rights to the land
had been extinguished. The extinguishment arose out of certain colonial enactments which demonstrated an intention to manage Crown
lands in a way that was inconsistent with continuing aboriginal rights.

[210] He stated, at p. 411, that "the Crown with full knowledge of the local situation fully intended to settle the colony and to grant titles and tenures unburdened by any aboriginal interests". Crown grantees who received land in colonial times were clearly intended to receive the land free from any aboriginal encumbrances. Moreover, this intention to extinguish did not only apply to lands that had actually been granted to third parties, but rather all Crown land in B.C. However, it should be noted that he was careful to distinguish between land and fishing rights. Since McEachern C.J. was of the view that all aboriginal title to the territories in question had been extinguished during colonial times, it was not necessary to consider whether the province had the power to extinguish aboriginal rights after Confederation.

[25] Notwithstanding the complete extinguishment of all aboriginal rights in land, McEachern C.J. held, at p. 417, that the Crown was under a fiduciary obligation to continue to allow native persons to use vacant crown lands for lawful purposes until the land "is dedicated to another purpose". This is not an aboriginal "right", to which s. 35 can be applied, since any such "rights" over the land had been extinguished. However, he held that where the Crown extinguishes an aboriginal right, and makes a promise regarding use of Crown land at the same time, this creates the same fiduciary obligation as if the aboriginal people had surrendered the land to the Crown. In articulating guidelines for the application of the Crown's fiduciary obligation, McEachern C.J. made it clear that the Crown must be free to direct resource management in the province in the best interests of both the aboriginal and non-aboriginal persons in the province. However, Crown authorities should always keep the "aboriginal interests of the plaintiffs very much in mind" (at p. 423) in developing policies for the territory, and should ensure that aboriginal activities on the land are not unduly impaired.

(6) Damages

[26] Since the plaintiffs failed to establish that existing ownership, jurisdiction, or aboriginal rights had been breached, the claim for damages for wrongful appropriation of their territory was dismissed by McEachern C.J.

(7) Lands Subject to Aboriginal Rights at Sovereignty

[27] McEachern C.J. felt it necessary to delineate the boundaries of the lands that were subject to aboriginal rights at the time of

sovereignty in case he was wrong that these rights had been extin- [211]
guished. He considered the evidence regarding the external boundary
of the territory, and the internal boundaries therein. He found numerous inconsistencies, and generally did not find it to be reliable. He
rejected the boundaries as put forth by the appellants.

[28] Nevertheless, since he had held that the Gitksan and
Wet'suwet'en had aboriginal sustenance rights over part of the land,
he had to delineate their boundaries. He put forth three alternatives,
and ultimately chose "Map 5" (at p. 400). This area recognized that
the plaintiffs' ancestors likely used more distant areas in the territory.
However, McEachern C.J. was not persuaded of such use in either
the northernmost or southernmost portions of the territory. The northern boundary was drawn through the centre of the Skeena River, with
20 miles on the north side of the river being added. The southern
boundary was drawn following some of the internal boundaries, but
excluding several of the southern Wet'suwet'en individual territories. He selected this alternative because it worked less injustice for
the Wet'suwet'en who lived more spread out and less concentrated
near the rivers. However, he cut off the north and south portions of
the claimed territory because he did not have confidence in the presence of the Gitksan or Wet'suwet'en in the areas north or south of the
boundaries he drew.

(8) Other Matters

[29] McEachern C.J. concluded his reasons by rejecting the province's argument that the plaintiffs' aboriginal rights to some of the
lands had been abandoned. He did not think courts should be quick
to treat aboriginal lands as abandoned. He could not say with confidence which lands should be abandoned, and which should not, even
though there was clearly declining aboriginal use of some of the lands.
He also stressed that the onus of demonstrating abandonment rested
with the province and that they had not discharged that onus. He also
rejected the argument that the plaintiffs had waived their rights by
accepting and using reserves and by conforming to the general law
of the province. The honour of the Crown precluded the province
from relying on this defence.

(9) Final Order

[30] In result, therefore, McEachern C.J. dismissed the action
against Canada, dismissed the plaintiffs' claims for ownership and

[212] jurisdiction and for aboriginal rights in the territory, granted a declaration that the plaintiffs were entitled to use unoccupied or vacant land subject to the general law of the province, dismissed the claim for damages and dismissed the province's counterclaim. No order for costs was made.

B. BRITISH COLUMBIA COURT OF APPEAL

(1) Judgment of Macfarlane J.A. (Taggart J.A. concurring)

[31] Macfarlane J.A. set out the following propositions of law which he indicated were the starting points for analysing aboriginal [8] rights in land, which he garnered from *Baker Lake, Calder, Guerin,* [9]*Sparrow*, and *Mabo v. Queensland* (1992), 107 A.L.R. 1 (H.C.). First, such rights arise from historic occupation and possession of the aboriginal peoples' tribal lands. Second, they arise by operation of law and do not depend on a grant from the Crown. Third, they are not absolute, but they are subject to regulation and extinguishment. Fourth, they are *sui generis* communal rights. Fifth, they cannot be alienated other than to the Crown. Finally, they are related to aboriginal activities which formed an integral part of traditional Indian life prior to sovereignty.

(a) Ownership Rights

[32] Examining the appellants' ownership claim, Macfarlane J.A. agreed that an exclusive right to occupy land is required to support a claim akin to ownership. He noted that the use of the term "ownership" (which was used by the plaintiffs in their pleadings) was unfortunate, since *Guerin* specifically held that the aboriginal interest does not amount to beneficial ownership. In his view, the trial judge properly applied the law to the plaintiffs' claim of ownership. Similarly, he found no merit in the appellants' challenge to the trial judge's findings of fact on a number of points. Although some of the areas of the evidence were cause for concern, he concluded that the issues required an interpretation of the evidence as a whole and that it would be inappropriate for this court to intervene and substitute its opinions for that of the trial judge. Hence, he did not disturb the judge's conclusion with regard to ownership of the territory, nor his conclusion that any interest which the appellants have in the land is not proprietary.

(b) Aboriginal Sustenance Rights

[33] Macfarlane J.A. canvassed the trial judge's findings regarding aboriginal sustenance rights. He noted that McEachern C.J.'s error in requiring a "time-depth" of a long time prior to contact in order to

establish the rights did not affect his view of the territorial limits of **[213]**
the right. He agreed with the trial judge's application of the *Baker
Lake* test. In particular, he viewed the significant question to be
whether the practices were integral to aboriginal society or had only
resulted from European influences. Macfarlane J.A. concluded that
it would be inappropriate to intervene and substitute his view for that
of the trial judge with respect to the weight of the evidence. Hence, if
the appellants succeeded on the appeal with respect to extinguishment, they were entitled to sustenance rights in the area as identified
by McEachern C.J. on Map 5.

(c) Jurisdiction

[34] Macfarlane J.A. essentially agreed with the trial judge with
respect to his analysis of the jurisdiction, or sovereignty issue. He
characterized the claim as the right to control and manage the use of
lands and resources in the territory, as well as the right to govern the
people within the territory, to the possible exclusion of laws of general application within the province. He stated that the Gitksan and
Wet'suwet'en people do not need a court declaration to permit internal self-regulation, if they consent to be governed. However, the rights
of self-government encompassing a power to make general laws governing the land, resources, and people in the territory are legislative
powers which cannot be awarded by the courts. Such jurisdiction is
inconsistent with the *Constitution Act, 1867* and its division of powers. When the Crown imposed English law on all the inhabitants of
the colony and when British Columbia entered Confederation, the
aboriginal people became subject to Canadian (and provincial) legislative authority. For this reason, the claim to jurisdiction failed.

(d) Extinguishment

[35] Macfarlane J.A. began by noting that treaty-making is the
most desirable way to resolve aboriginal land issues. However, he
noted that prior to 1982, the rights of aboriginal people could be extinguished by the unilateral act of the sovereign, without the consent
of the aboriginal people. Intention to extinguish must be clear and
plain. Although express language is not strictly necessary, the honour of the Crown requires its intentions to be either express or
manifested by unavoidable implication. Unavoidable implication
should not be easily found — it occurs only where the interpretation
of the instrument permits no other result. This, in turn, depends on
the nature of the aboriginal interest and of the impugned grant.

214]   [36] Macfarlane J.A. disagreed with the trial judge that the colonial instruments manifested the required clear and plain intention to extinguish all aboriginal interests in land. The purpose of the colonial instruments in question was to facilitate an orderly settlement of the province, and to give the Crown control over grants to third parties. It is not inevitable, upon a reading of the statutory scheme, that the aboriginal interest was to be disregarded. They did not foreclose the possibility of treaties or of co-existence of aboriginal and Crown interests. Similarly, even fee simple grants to third parties do not necessarily exclude aboriginal use. For example, uncultivated vacant land held in fee simple does not necessarily preclude the exercise of hunting rights. Moreover, it is clear that, at common law, two or more interests in land less than fee simple can co-exist. However, since the record was not sufficiently specific to permit the detailed analysis of such issues, Macfarlane J.A. suggested that these issues be dealt with in negotiation. He concluded that extinguishment by a particular grant needed to be determined on a case by case basis.

[37] Macfarlane J.A. considered the constitutional power of the province to extinguish aboriginal rights after 1871, and in particular, whether valid provincial legislation could extinguish aboriginal rights in land by incidental effect. After 1871, the exclusive power to legislate in relation to "Indians, and Lands reserved for the Indians" was given to the federal government by virtue of s. 91(24) of the *Constitution Act, 1867*. Valid provincial legislation may apply to Indians, so long is it is a law of general application and not one that affects their Indianness, their status, or their core values (*Four B Manufacturing Ltd. v. United Garment Workers*, [1980] 1 S.C.R. 1031, 102 D.L.R. (3d) 385; *Natural Parents v. Superintendent of Child Welfare*, [1976] 2 S.C.R. 751, 60 D.L.R. (3d) 148; *Dick v. The Queen*, [1985] 2 S.C.R. 309, 23 D.L.R. (4th) 33). However, the proposition that provincial laws could extinguish Indian title by incidental effect must be examined in light of federal authority relating to Indians and of the aboriginal perspective. The traditional homelands of aboriginal people are integral to their traditional way of life and their self-concept. If the effect of provincial legislation were to strip the aboriginal people of the use and occupation of their traditional homelands, it would be an impermissible intrusion into federal jurisdiction, as such a law would "trench on the very core of the subject matter of s. 91(24)" (at p. 169). Hence, he concluded that provincial legislatures do not have

the constitutional competence to extinguish common law aboriginal [215
rights. Moreover, extinguishment by adverse dominion could only
be accomplished by the federal government. Similarly, s. 88 of the
Indian Act did not assist the province. Laws of general application
which do not affect the "core of Indianness" apply by their own force.
However, provincial laws which do affect that core rely on s. 88,
which referentially incorporates them into federal law. For s. 88 of
the *Indian Act* to give the province authority to extinguish aboriginal
rights, it would have to show a clear and plain intention to do so.
Since no such intention exists in s. 88 in particular or the *Indian Act*
in general, it cannot authorize outright extinguishment. However, it
may authorize provincial regulation of and interference with aboriginal rights. Of course, now the operation of such regulations are now
subject to s. 35 of the *Constitution Act, 1982*.

(e) Relief Allowed

[38] Macfarlane J.A. granted a declaration that the plaintiffs' aboriginal rights were not all extinguished by the colonial instruments
enacted prior to British Columbia's entry into Confederation in 1871.
He also granted a declaration that the appellants have unextinguished,
non-exclusive aboriginal rights, formerly protected at common law,
and now protected under s. 35(1) of the *Constitution Act, 1982*. These
rights are not ownership or property rights, and are located within
the area indicated on Map 5. Their characteristics may vary depending on the particular context in which the rights are said to exist, and
are dependent on the specific facts of each case.

[39] Macfarlane J.A. did not grant a declaration with respect to
jurisdiction over land and resources or people within the territory,
leaving this to negotiation. He also did not interfere with the decision
of the trial judge that the claim for damages must be dismissed. He
noted that the parties wished to negotiate the precise location, scope,
content and consequences of the aboriginal rights which the trial judge
has held may be exercised in that part of the territory, the approxi-
mate area of which is illustrated on Map 5. However, no order of the
court was required to permit the parties to enter into such negotiations.

[40] Finally, Macfarlane J.A. stated that he would not give effect
to the alternative declarations sought by the province relating to the
alleged extinguishment of aboriginal rights by grants of fee simple
and of lesser interests in the period from 1871-1982. The province

16] did not have the power after 1871 to extinguish aboriginal rights. However, some provincial land and resource laws affecting aboriginal rights may be given force as federal laws through the operation of s. 88 of the *Indian Act*. The effect of fee simple and lesser grants on the particular aboriginal rights would require a detailed and complete analysis, which neither the record nor the submissions permitted. He made no order for costs, adopting the reasons of the trial judge.

(2) Wallace J.A. (concurring)

(a) Scope of Appellate Review

[41] Wallace J.A. considered the appropriate principles for appellate review of a trial judge's findings of fact. An appellate court should find error on the part of the trial judge with respect to those aspects of the finding of facts which involve questions of credibility or weight to be given the evidence of a witness only if it is established that the trial judge made some "palpable and overriding error" which affected his assessment of the material facts. Such an error exists in three situations: firstly, when it can be demonstrated there was no evidence to support a material finding of fact of the trial judge; secondly, when the trial judge wrongly overlooked admissible evidence relevant and material to the issue before the court; or thirdly, where the trial judge's finding of fact cannot be supported as reasonable. In reversing the trial judge for "palpable and overriding error" the Court of Appeal must designate the specific error and state why the nature of the error justifies reversing the trial judge's finding of fact. Wallace J.A. held that these principles applied to the trial judge's determination of the nature and territorial scope of the aboriginal activities, the question of jurisdiction and control over the territory, and the weight to be attributed to the evidence of the various witnesses.

(b) General Principles

[42] Wallace J.A. stated that aboriginal rights of occupation and use originate in the Indians' historic occupation and use of their tribal lands, and is recognized by the common law. Unlike the trial judge, he recognized that these rights may resemble a proprietary title, not unlike those in western property law systems, or they may be restricted to certain uses of the land. He set out the requirements for establishing aboriginal rights, varying from the *Baker Lake* test used by the trial judge. In Wallace J.A.'s formulation of the test, the practices supporting the rights in question had to be integral to the

claimants' distinctive and traditional society or culture. Moreover, [21⁴
he resolved the trial judge's concerns about the requirement of exclusivity as follows: if the plaintiffs claim exclusive occupation and
use, the traditional occupation had to be to the exclusion of other
organized societies.

(c) Aboriginal Ownership

[43] Wallace J.A. considered there to be reasonable support for
the trial judge's conclusions regarding the nature and scope of the
appellants' interest in the territory. The standard of occupation required to support the claim of ownership depended on the nature of
the interest. The appellants' claim was to manage the lands and natural resources. This suggests exclusive control and possession of the
territory, requiring the appellants to demonstrate exclusive possession. Since they could not do so, he concluded that the trial judge
correctly dismissed their claim for ownership.

(d) Aboriginal Rights of Occupation and Use of Traditional Lands

[44] Even if the appellants' claim were characterized as a claim
for aboriginal title, rather than ownership, Wallace J.A. agreed with
the criteria applied by the trial judge: the occupation of specific territory, the exclusion of other organized societies, occupation at the time
of British sovereignty and long-time aboriginal practices. Applying
these principles to the trial judge's findings of fact, Wallace J.A. concluded that the appellants had not established a manifest or palpable
error in concluding that the appellants' rights were non-exclusive,
and confined to user rights. However, he was of the view was that the
court was not in a position to express an opinion on the specific territorial scope of these rights.

(e) Aboriginal Jurisdiction or Self-Government

[45] Wallace J.A. agreed that the claim for "jurisdiction" was for
an undefined form of government over land and people in the territory, which would be paramount as against provincial laws in the
case of a conflict. Wallace J.A. held, at p. 225, that this claim was
"incompatible with every principle of parliamentary sovereignty which
vested in the Imperial Parliament in 1846". Moreover, British Columbia's entry into Canada in 1871 exhaustively distributed legislative
power between the province and the federal government. Section 35
of the *Constitution Act, 1982* could not revive and protect any sovereignty rights which the Gitksan and Wet'suwet'en may have had.

18]   *(f) Extinguishment*

[46] Wallace J.A. agreed with Macfarlane J.A. on this issue. He set out the test ("clear and plain intention") and decided that the rights of use and occupation discussed above had not been extinguished.

(g) Miscellaneous

[47] Wallace J.A. agreed that the appellants' damages claim should be dismissed, without deciding whether damages might be payable for wrongful interference with the Gitksan's and Wet'suwet'en's non-exclusive aboriginal rights in the territory. He also considered the appellants' claim that the appeal be adjourned in part for two years, during which time the parties would attempt to negotiate an agreement regarding the geographic parameters of the claimed territory. The court would retain jurisdiction to determine issues or refer them to the trial court if the parties failed to reach an agreement during the two-year period. However, he noted that the role of the Court of Appeal is not to tailor its judgment to facilitate negotiation. The Court of Appeal is restricted to declaring the legal status of rights claimed, on the basis of the trial record.

(3) Lambert J.A. (dissenting)

(a) General Principles

[48] Lambert J.A. considered at length the leading cases with regard to aboriginal rights in British Columbia. He set out a number of conclusions. He recognized that aboriginal title and aboriginal rights are *sui generis*, and not easily explicable in terms of ordinary western jurisprudential analysis or common law concepts. He noted that aboriginal title is a form of aboriginal rights, and is therefore protected by s. 35. All rights arise from the practices, customs and traditions which form an integral part of the distinctive culture of the aboriginal people, and were part of the social fabric of aboriginal society at the time of the arrival of the first Europeans. This co-existed with the settlors' common law rights from the time of contact until sovereignty. After that time, aboriginal rights that continued as part of the social fabric of the aboriginal society were protected by both their own internal institutions and the common law.

[49] Lambert J.A. believed that aboriginal rights were not frozen at the time of contact. Rather, they must be permitted to maintain contemporary relevance in relation to the needs of the holders of the rights as those needs change along with the changes in overall

society. The rights may be individual, or they may be collective, de- **[21**
pending on how they were and are treated by aboriginal people.
Moreover, they do not come from aboriginal practice dating from
time immemorial. Rather, they come, under the doctrine of continuity, from the practices, customs and traditions of the aboriginal people.

[50] Aboriginal rights are neither abrogated by the fact that similar rights may be held by non-aboriginal people nor because the holders
of the rights participate in the wage or cash economy. A right to occupy,
possess, use and enjoy land to the exclusion of all others does not
mean that it must be confined to the activities carried on in 1846, or
that its exercise requires a renunciation of the contemporary world.

(b) Extinguishment

[51] Lambert J.A. considered the test for extinguishment from
Calder, and expressly rejected Judson J.'s views. He derived the au- [10]
thority to do so from the way in which extinguishment was dealt
with in *Sparrow*. In considering implicit extinguishment, he stated
that it will only be held to occur where no other conclusion is possible from the particular instrument or conduct. It could not take place
through adverse dominion. In the case of an inconsistency between a
Crown grant of land and aboriginal title, the title should not necessarily give way in the absence of a clear and plain intention to
extinguish. In any case, no grants or other interests were granted in
the territory prior to 1871, and after that date, the British Columbia
legislature had no power to legislate to extinguish, by adverse dominion, or otherwise. Lambert J.A. recognized, at p. 312, that because
of s. 91(24) of the *Constitution Act, 1867*, and the doctrine of
interjurisdictional immunity, provincial legislation could not affect
"Indians in their Indianness". This included aboriginal rights, since
they are an integral part of aboriginal culture. This is not affected by
s. 88 of the *Indian Act*.

[52] Lambert J.A. applied the same principles to a consideration
of whether the right to self-government had been extinguished. Neither the assertion of sovereignty nor the colonial enactments
mentioned by the trial judge were sufficient to extinguish aboriginal
rights in the claimed territory. He saw no incompatibility between
statements that the Crown owned the land of the province and the
notion that aboriginal title was a burden on the Crown's radical title.
Moreover, there was no "inescapable inference" that the colonial

[[10] 73 *ILR* 56.]

20] enactments were intended to extinguish aboriginal interests. If this were the case, aboriginal peoples would instantly become trespassers on any lands not reserved for them as soon as the Crown took title. Finally, the evidence that the aboriginal peoples of northern British Columbia surrendered their title under Treaty No. 8 also suggested that they had title interests to surrender.

(c) Findings at Trial

[53] Lambert J.A. considered the factual findings made by the trial judge and made a number of general observations. First, if a finding of fact is necessary to the decision in the case, it should be given more deference than a fact which is merely made in the course of the decision or for some incidental reason. Second, findings of historical fact based on historical or anthropological evidence given by historians and anthropologists should be given only the kind of weight that other historians or anthropologists might have given them. These social scientists do not always agree, circumstances change, and new material is discovered and interpreted. Third, the appellants' oral evidence should be weighed, like all evidence, against the weight of countervailing evidence and not against an absolute standard so long as it is enough to support an air of reality. Fourth, with the election of an NDP government in British Columbia in 1991, the province reconsidered its legal stance in this case. As such, it invited the court to confirm the existence of aboriginal rights of unspecified content over unspecified areas and to permit the parties to negotiate the precise content and the precise areas. In Lambert J.A.'s view, the Crown, by adopting the position that it wished to negotiate the content and territorial scope of aboriginal rights, must be taken to have waived the argument that the findings of the trial judge must stand and that any aboriginal rights held by the Gitksan and Wet'suwet'en peoples must be confined to non-exclusive sustenance rights over the area covered by Map 5. In short, reliance on the findings of fact of the trial judge is entirely inconsistent with negotiation.

[54] Nonetheless, Lambert J.A. was of the view that the findings of fact with respect to boundaries and with respect to the scope and content of aboriginal rights, including both rights in land and rights of self-government, cannot stand even in accordance with the usual principles governing the consideration of findings of fact, because they are flawed by errors of law.

[55] With regard to the ownership claim, Lambert J.A. identified **[22**
the following errors in the trial judge's reasons. In his view, the trial
judge erred: (1) in not treating the ownership claim as a claim to
aboriginal title and applied incorrect legal standards as a result; (2) in
treating the claim to aboriginal title as a claim to a proprietary interest in land; (3) in applying a test of indefinite or long, long time use
and occupation before the assertion of sovereignty; (4) in treating
evidence of commercial interaction with the first Europeans as not
being evidence of aboriginal practices; (5) in treating the rights to
trap as being the exercise of rights other than aboriginal rights; (6) in
rejecting evidence about commercial trapping and the evidence of
Dr. Ray, a historical geographer who gave evidence at trial; (7) in
rejecting possession, occupation, use, and enjoyment in a social sense
as sufficient to establish aboriginal title; (8) in treating the test of
possession and occupation as being whether there was a law which
would have required a trespasser to depart; (9) in considering that
aboriginal rights cannot be held jointly by more than one people;
(10) in not concluding that aboriginal title could rest on occupation,
possession, use, and enjoyment of land even though that occupation
may have diminished in the period after contact; (11) in his treatment
of blanket extinguishment of aboriginal title; and (12) in concluding
that all aboriginal rights had been extinguished by the colonial instruments. These errors of law led to an incorrect conclusion on the
part of the trial judge about the existence of aboriginal title. His findings of fact can be reconsidered on appellate review.

[56] With regard to the jurisdiction claim, Lambert J.A. stated that
the trial judge erred: (1) in treating the claim to jurisdiction as a claim
to govern territory and assert sovereignty over the territory; (2) in
trying to define the appellants' claim in terms of the answers given
by one witness in cross-examination; (3) in concluding that the claim
to jurisdiction must fail because the nature of aboriginal self-
government and self-regulation was such that it does not produce a
set of binding and enforceable laws; and (4) in considering that the
existence of a legislative institution is an essential part of the existence of an aboriginal right to self-government. Because of these errors
of law, the trial judge's conclusions were wrong.

[57] With regard to the claim to aboriginal rights, Lambert J.A.
was of the view that the trial judge erred: (1) in not treating the

22] evidence of occupation, possession, use, and enjoyment of the territory in an organized way by the appellants for their purposes, but particularly for sustenance, as being sufficient to establish aboriginal title to much of the land within the territory; (2) in separating commercial practices of aboriginal people from other practices and saying that commercial practices were not aboriginal practices; (3) in not considering the evidence of trading practices with neighbouring peoples; (4) in his treatment of the question of exclusivity both in relation to aboriginal title and sustenance rights; and (5) in considering participation in the wage or cash economy in relation to the existence (or non-existence) of aboriginal title. Again, given these errors of law, Lambert J.A. asserted that an appellate court had jurisdiction to intervene and set aside the trial judge's findings.

(d) Substituted Findings

[58] In light of these errors, Lambert J.A. substituted his own findings of fact for those of the trial judge. In his view, the evidence established that in 1846, the Gitksan and Wet'suwet'en peoples occupied, possessed, used and enjoyed their traditional ancestral lands in accordance with their own practices, customs and traditions which were an integral part of their distinctive culture. Those ancestral lands extend throughout the claimed territory, well beyond the area indicated in Map 5. In areas where there were no conflicting claims to user rights, the appellants rights should be characterized as aboriginal title. In areas of shared occupancy and use, the appellants' title would be shared-exclusive aboriginal title. In areas where the Gitksan and Wet'suwet'en people did not occupy, possess or use the land as an integral part of their culture, they would not have title, but may have aboriginal sustenance rights. These rights were not extinguished through any blanket extinguishment in the colonial period. Precise legislation related to a specific area may have extinguished some rights. However, no such legislation was before the court. The geographic scope of the rights was a matter to be negotiated between the parties, and failing negotiation, needed to be determined by a new trial

[59] Lambert J.A. also concluded that in 1846, the appellants' ancestors had rights of self-government and self-regulation, which rested on the practices, customs and traditions of those people which formed an integral part of their distinctive cultures. It is true that the rights

may have been diminished by the assertion of British sovereignty, [22:
but those rights that continue are protected by s. 35 of the *Constitution Act, 1982.*

[60] Turning to aboriginal sustenance rights, Lambert J.A. stated
that they are entirely encompassed within aboriginal title in those
areas where Gitksan and Wet'suwet'en aboriginal title exists. They
also may exist in areas outside of title lands. In areas where such
rights were shared by a number of peoples, the appellants' rights may
be limited to specific sustenance activities as opposed to exclusive or
shared-exclusive use and occupation.

(e) Other Issues

[61] With regard to the *Royal Proclamation, 1763*, R.S.C. 1985,
App. II, No. 1, Lambert J.A. expressed no views on its application or
effect in the claimed territory and its inhabitants. With regard to infringement or denial of the appellants' rights in the claimed territory,
Lambert J.A. concluded that the evidence in the case did not permit a
proper consideration of the issues. Each infringement or denial would
have to be examined in relation to the specific circumstances.

(f) Disposition

[62] Lambert J.A. would have allowed the appeal, and made a
number of declarations. First, he would declare that the Gitksan and
Wet'suwet'en peoples had, at the time of the assertion of British sovereignty in 1846, aboriginal title to occupy, possess, use and enjoy
all or some of the land within the claimed territory. The land covered
by aboriginal title at that time extended far beyond village sites and
the immediate areas surrounding. Second, he would declare that the
Gitksan and Wet'suwet'en peoples may have had aboriginal sustenance rights, including hunting, fishing, gathering, and similar rights
over any parts of the land within the claimed territory to which aboriginal title did not extend. He would also declare that the aboriginal
title and the aboriginal sustenance rights described may have been
exclusive to the Gitksan in certain areas and exclusive to the
Wet'suwet'en in others, and in some they may have shared with each
other, or other aboriginal peoples, or non-aboriginals.

[63] Lambert J.A. would have also declared that the appellants'
ancestors had, at the time of the assertion of British sovereignty in
1846, aboriginal rights of self-government and self-regulation relating to their own organized society, its members, its institutions and

224] its sustenance rights. These rights were recognized by, incorporated into, and protected by the common law after 1846. They have not been extinguished by any form of blanket extinguishment. Hence, they exist in modern form, subject only to specific extinguishment of the specific title or specific sustenance right in a specific area. However, the right of aboriginal self-government did not include any rights that were inconsistent with British sovereignty, any rights that are repugnant to natural justice, equity and good conscience, and have not been modified to overcome that repugnancy, and any rights which are contrary to the part of the common law that applied to the territory, the Gitksan and Wet'suwet'en peoples and their institutions.

[64] Lambert J.A. would also declare that these aboriginal title rights, aboriginal rights of self-government and self-regulation, and aboriginal sustenance rights may have been subject, after 1846 to specific extinguishment by the clear and plain extinguishing intention of the Sovereign Power, legislatively expressed by Parliament. Any specific extinguishment of specific rights might have been express or implicit, and, if implicit, it may have been brought about by the legislation itself (implied extinguishment) or by acts authorized by the legislation (extinguishment by adverse dominion), provided the intention to extinguish was contained within the legislative expression and was clear and plain. Instances of such specific extinguishment could not be decided on this appeal.

[65] Lambert J.A. would declare that the present aboriginal rights of self-government and self-regulation of the Gitksan and Wet'suwet'en peoples, exercisable in relation to their aboriginal title, would include the specific rights claimed in this appeal by the plaintiffs in relation to aboriginal title. He would also declare that the present aboriginal rights of self-government and self-regulation of the Gitksan and Wet'suwet'en peoples would include rights of self-government and self-regulation exercisable through their own institutions to preserve and enhance their social, political, cultural, linguistic and spiritual identity.

[66] Finally, Lambert J.A. would remit a number of questions back to trial. These include the question of the territorial boundaries for both title and sustenance rights; the degree of exclusivity or shared exclusivity which the appellants hold, on both the territories over which they have title and the territories over which they have sustenance rights; the scope and content of the sustenance rights; the scope

and content of the rights to self-government and self-regulation; and **[22**:
all questions relating to the plaintiffs' entitlement to damages and the
quantum of damages. He would have also awarded the plaintiffs their
costs, both in the Court of Appeal, and at trial.

(4) Hutcheon J.A. (dissenting in part)

(a) Rights to Land

[67] Hutcheon J.A. agreed with the trial judge that the *Royal Proclamation, 1763* did not apply to the territory or its inhabitants.
Nonetheless, the policy reflected in the Proclamation was, generally
speaking, acceptance of aboriginal rights to land. Moreover, Hutcheon
J.A. concluded on the basis of *Calder* and *Sparrow* that the colonial [11]
enactments did not extinguish the aboriginal rights in the claimed
territory. He found it unnecessary to decide whether a grant in fee
simple extinguishes aboriginal title or whether entitlement to compensation arises in such circumstances.

(b) Nature of the Rights

[68] Hutcheon J.A. accepted that aboriginal rights to land existed
prior to 1846 over the claimed territory. He found it sufficient to say,
at p. 389, that aboriginal rights can "compete on an equal footing"
with proprietary interests. Additionally, he noted that these rights are
collective, inalienable except to the Crown, and extend to the traditional territory of the particular people.

(c) Territory

[69] Hutcheon J.A. disagreed with the trial judge's conclusion that
the appellants' ancestors occupied or controlled only the villages in
the territory and the immediately surrounding areas. In Hutcheon
J.A.'s view, the trial judge misapprehended the legal test for occupation and disregarded the independent evidence which showed that
the territory occupied or controlled by the appellants extended far
beyond the villages.

(d) Self-Regulation

[70] The traditions of the Gitksan and Wet'suwet'en peoples existed long before 1846 and continued thereafter. They included the
right to names and titles, the use of masks and symbols in rituals, the
use of ceremonial robes, and the right to occupy and control places
of economic importance. The traditions also included the institution
of the clans and the Houses in which membership descended through
the mother and the feast system. They regulated marriage and

[[11] 73 *ILR* 56.]

26] relations with neighbouring societies. The right to practise these traditions was not lost, although the *Indian Act* and provincial laws have affected the appellants' right to self-regulation. Only negotiations will define with greater specificity the areas and terms under which the appellants and the federal and provincial governments will exercise jurisdiction in respect of the appellants, their institutions, and laws.

(e) Disposition

[71] Hutcheon J.A. would have allowed the appeal and have made a number of declarations. First, he would declare that all of the aboriginal rights of the appellants were not extinguished before 1871. Second, the appellants continue to have existing aboriginal rights to undefined portions of land within the claimed territory. Third, the appellants have rights of self-regulation exercisable through their own institutions to preserve and enhance their social, political, cultural, linguistic and spiritual identity. He would have remitted the outstanding matters to the Supreme Court of British Columbia, and stayed the proceedings for two years from the date of the judgment, or such shorter or longer period, in order for the parties to agree about the lands in respect of which the appellants have aboriginal rights, the scope of such rights on and to such lands, the scope of the right of self-regulation, and the appellants' entitlement to and quantum of damages. Hutcheon J.A. would have awarded the appellants their costs throughout the proceedings.

IV. Issues

[72] The following are the principal issues which must be addressed in this appeal. As will become apparent in my analysis, some of these issues in turn raise a number of sub-issues which I will address as well:

A. Do the pleadings preclude the Court from entertaining claims for aboriginal title and self-government?

B. What is the ability of this Court to interfere with the factual findings made by the trial judge?

C. What is the content of aboriginal title, how is it protected by s. 35(1) of the *Constitution Act, 1982*, and what is required for its proof?

D. Has a claim to self-government been made out by the appellants?

E. Did the province have the power to extinguish aboriginal rights after 1871, either under its own jurisdiction or through the operation of s. 88 of the *Indian Act*?

V. ANALYSIS   [22

A. DO THE PLEADINGS PRECLUDE THE COURT FROM ENTERTAINING CLAIMS
   FOR ABORIGINAL TITLE AND SELF-GOVERNMENT?

[73] In their pleadings, the appellants, 51 Chiefs representing most
of the houses of the Gitksan and Wet'suwet'en nations, originally
advanced 51 individual claims on their own behalf and on behalf of
their houses for "ownership" and "jurisdiction" over 133 distinct territories which together comprise 58,000 square kilometres of
northwestern British Columbia. On appeal, that original claim was
altered in two different ways. First, the claims for ownership and
jurisdiction have been replaced with claims for aboriginal title and
self-government, respectively. Second, the individual claims by each
house have been amalgamated into two communal claims, one advanced on behalf of each nation. However, there were no formal
amendments to the pleadings to this effect, and the respondents accordingly argue that claims which are central to this appeal are not
properly before the Court. Furthermore, the respondents argue that
they have suffered prejudice as a result because they might have conducted the defence quite differently had they known the case to meet.

[74] I reject the respondents' submission with respect to the substitution of aboriginal title and self-government for the original claims
of ownership and jurisdiction. Although it is true that the pleadings
were not formally amended, the trial judge, at p. 158, did allow a *de
facto* amendment to permit "a claim for aboriginal rights other than
ownership and jurisdiction". Had the respondents been concerned
about the prejudice arising from this ruling, they could have appealed
accordingly. However, they did not, and, as a result, the decision of
the trial judge on this point must stand.

[75] Moreover, in my opinion, that ruling was correct because it
was made against the background of considerable legal uncertainty
surrounding the nature and content of aboriginal rights, under both
the common law and s. 35(1). The content of common law aboriginal
title, for example, has not been authoritatively determined by this
Court and has been described by some as a form of "ownership". As
well, this case was pleaded prior to this Court's decision in *Sparrow*,
supra, which was the first statement from this Court on the types of
rights that come within the scope of s. 35(1). The law has rapidly
evolved since then. Accordingly, it was just and appropriate for the

28] trial judge to allow for an amendment to pleadings which were framed when the jurisprudence was in its infancy.

[76] However, no such amendment was made with respect to the amalgamation of the individual claims brought by the 51 Gitksan and Wet'suwet'en Houses into two collective claims, one by each nation, for aboriginal title and self-government. Given the absence of an amendment to the pleadings, I must reluctantly conclude that the respondents suffered some prejudice. The appellants argue that the respondents did not experience prejudice since the collective and individual claims are related to the extent that the territory claimed by each nation is merely the sum of the individual claims of each house; the external boundaries of the collective claims therefore represent the outer boundaries of the outer territories. Although that argument carries considerable weight, it does not address the basic point that the collective claims were simply not in issue at trial. To frame the case in a different manner on appeal would retroactively deny the respondents the opportunity to know the appellants' case.

[77] This defect in the pleadings prevents the Court from considering the merits of this appeal. However, given the importance of this case and the fact that much of the evidence of individual territorial holdings is extremely relevant to the collective claims now advanced by each of the appellants, the correct remedy for the defect in pleadings is a new trial, where, to quote the trial judge at p. 368, "[i]t will be for the parties to consider whether any amendment is required in order to make the pleadings conform with the evidence." Moreover, as I will now explain, there are other reasons why a new trial should be ordered.

B. What Is the Ability of This Court to Interfere with the Factual Findings Made by the Trial Judge?

(1) General Principles

[78] I recently reviewed the principles governing the appellate review of findings of fact in *Van der Peet, supra*. As a general rule, this Court has been extremely reluctant to interfere with the findings of fact made at trial, especially when those findings of fact are based on an assessment of the testimony and credibility of witnesses. Unless there is a "palpable and overriding error", appellate courts should not substitute their own findings of fact for those of the trial judge. The leading statement of this principle can be found in *Stein v. The Ship*

"Kathy K", [1976] 2 S.C.R. 802 at p. 808, 62 D.L.R. (3d) 1, *per* **[22**
Ritchie J.:

> These authorities are not to be taken as meaning that the findings of fact made
> at trial are immutable, but rather that they are not to be reversed unless it can
> be established that the learned trial judge made some palpable and overriding
> error which affected his assessment of the facts. While the Court of Appeal is
> seized with the duty of re-examining the evidence in order to be satisfied that
> no such error occurred, it is not, in my view, a part of its function to substitute
> its assessment of the balance of probability for the findings of the judge who
> presided at the trial.

The same deference must be accorded to the trial judge's assessment
of the credibility of expert witnesses: see *N.V. Bocimar S.A. v. Century Insurance Co. of Canada*, [1987] 1 S.C.R. 1247, 39 D.L.R. (4th)
465.

[79] The policy reason underlying this rule is protection of "[t]he
autonomy and integrity of the trial process" (*Schwartz v. Canada*,
[1996] 1 S.C.R. 254 at p. 278, 133 D.L.R. (4th) 289), which recognizes that the trier of fact, who is in direct contact with the mass of
the evidence, is in the best position to make findings of fact, particularly those which turn on credibility. Moreover, *Van der Peet* clarified
that deference was owed to findings of fact even when the trial judge
misapprehended the law which was applied to those facts, a problem
which can arise in quickly evolving areas of law such as the jurisprudence surrounding s. 35(1).

[80] I recently held, in *Van der Peet*, that these general principles
apply to cases litigated under s. 35(1). On the other hand, while accepting the general principle of non-interference, this Court has also
identified specific situations in which an appeal court can interfere
with a finding of fact made at trial. For example, appellate intervention is warranted "where the courts below have misapprehended or
overlooked material evidence": see *Chartier v. Attorney General of
Quebec*, [1979] 2 S.C.R. 474 at p. 493, 104 D.L.R. (3d) 321. In cases
involving the determination of aboriginal rights, appellate intervention is also warranted by the failure of a trial court to appreciate the
evidentiary difficulties inherent in adjudicating aboriginal claims
when, first, applying the rules of evidence and, second, interpreting
the evidence before it. As I said in *Van der Peet*, at para. 68:

> In determining whether an aboriginal claimant has produced evidence sufficient to demonstrate that her activity is an aspect of a practice, custom or
> tradition integral to a distinctive aboriginal culture, *a court should approach*

230]   *the rules of evidence, and interpret the evidence that exists,* with a conscious-
ness of the special nature of aboriginal claims, and of the evidentiary difficulties
in proving a right which originates in times where there were no written records
of the practices, customs and traditions engaged in. *The courts must not un-
dervalue the evidence presented by aboriginal claimants simply because that
evidence does not conform precisely with the evidentiary standards that would
be applied in, for example, a private law torts case.* [Emphasis added.]

[81] The justification for this special approach can be found in the
nature of aboriginal rights themselves. I explained in *Van der Peet*
that those rights are aimed at the reconciliation of the prior occupation of North America by distinctive aboriginal societies with the
assertion of Crown sovereignty over Canadian territory. They attempt
to achieve that reconciliation by "their bridging of aboriginal and
non-aboriginal cultures" (at para. 42). Accordingly, "a court must
take into account the perspective of the aboriginal people claiming
the right . . . while at the same time taking into account the perspective of the common law" such that "[t]rue reconciliation will, equally,
place weight on each" (at paras. 49 and 50).

[82] In other words, although the doctrine of aboriginal rights is a
common law doctrine, aboriginal rights are truly *sui generis*, and
demand a unique approach to the treatment of evidence which accords due weight to the perspective of aboriginal peoples. However,
that accommodation must be done in a manner which does not strain
"the Canadian legal and constitutional structure" (at para. 49). Both
the principles laid down in *Van der Peet* — first, that trial courts must
approach the rules of evidence in light of the evidentiary difficulties
inherent in adjudicating aboriginal claims, and second, that trial courts
must interpret that evidence in the same spirit — must be understood
against this background.

[83] A concrete application of the first principle can be found in
Van der Peet itself, where I addressed the difficulties inherent in demonstrating a continuity between current aboriginal activities and the
pre-contact practices, customs and traditions of aboriginal societies.
As I reiterate below, the requirement for continuity is one component
of the definition of aboriginal rights (although, as I explain below, in
the case of title, the issue is continuity from sovereignty, not contact). However, given that many aboriginal societies did not keep
written records at the time of contact or sovereignty, it would be ex-
ceedingly difficult for them to produce (at para. 62) "conclusive

evidence from pre-contact times about the practices, customs and **[231**
traditions of their community". Accordingly, I held that (at para. 62):

> The evidence relied upon by the applicant and the courts may relate to aborigi-
> nal practices, customs and traditions *post-contact*; it simply needs to be directed
> at demonstrating which aspects of the aboriginal community and society have
> their origins *pre-contact*. [Emphasis added.]

**The same considerations apply when the time from which title is
determined is sovereignty**

[84] This appeal requires us to apply not only the first principle in
Van der Peet but the second principle as well, and adapt the laws of
evidence so that the aboriginal perspective on their practices, customs and traditions and on their relationship with the land, are given
due weight by the courts. In practical terms, this requires the courts
to come to terms with the oral histories of aboriginal societies, which,
for many aboriginal nations, are the only record of their past. Given
that the aboriginal rights recognized and affirmed by s. 35(1) are
defined by reference to pre-contact practices or, as I will develop
below, in the case of title, pre-sovereignty occupation, those histories play a crucial role in the litigation of aboriginal rights.

[85] A useful and informative description of aboriginal oral his-
tory is provided by the *Report of the Royal Commission on Aboriginal
Peoples* (Ottawa: The Commission, 1996), vol. 1 (*Looking Forward,
Looking Back*) at p. 33:

> The Aboriginal tradition in the recording of history is neither linear nor
> steeped in the same notions of social progress and evolution [as in the non-
> Aboriginal tradition]. Nor is it usually human centred in the same way as in
> the western scientific tradition, for it does not assume that human beings are
> anything more than one — and not necessarily the most important — element
> of the natural order of the universe. Moreover, the Aboriginal historical tradi-
> tion is an oral one, involving legends, stories and accounts handed down through
> the generations in oral form. It is less focussed on establishing objective truth
> and assumes that the teller of the story is so much a part of the event being
> described that it would be arrogant to presume to classify or categorize the
> event exactly or for all time.
>
> In the Aboriginal tradition the purposes of repeating oral accounts from the
> past is broader than the role of written history in western societies. It may be
> to educate the listener, to communicate aspects of culture, to socialize people
> into a cultural tradition, or to validate the claims of a particular family to au-
> thority and prestige. . . .
>
> Oral accounts of the past include a good deal of subjective experience.
> They are not simply a detached recounting of factual events but, rather, are

"facts enmeshed in the stories of a lifetime". They are also likely to be rooted in particular locations, making reference to particular families and communities. This contributes to a sense that there are many histories, each characterized in part by how a people see themselves, how they define their identity in relation to their environment, and how they express their uniqueness as a people.

[86] Many features of oral histories would count against both their admissibility and their weight as evidence of prior events in a court that took a traditional approach to the rules of evidence. The most fundamental of these is their broad social role not only "as a repository of historical knowledge for a culture" but also as an expression of "the values and mores of . . . [that] culture": Clay McLeod, "The Oral Histories of Canada's Northern People, Anglo-Canadian Evidence Law, and Canada's Fiduciary Duty to First Nations: Breaking Down the Barriers of the Past" (1992), 30 Alta. L. Rev. 1276 at p. 1279. Dickson J. (as he was then) recognized as much when he stated in *Kruger v. The Queen*, [1978] 1 S.C.R. 104 at p. 109, 75 D.L.R. (3d) 434, that "[c]laims to aboriginal title are woven with history, legend, politics and moral obligations". The difficulty with these features of oral histories is that they are tangential to the ultimate purpose of the fact-finding process at trial the determination of the historical truth. Another feature of oral histories which creates difficulty is that they largely consist of out-of-court statements, passed on through an unbroken chain across the generations of a particular aboriginal nation to the present-day. These out-of-court statements are admitted for their truth and therefore conflict with the general rule against the admissibility of hearsay.

[87] Notwithstanding the challenges created by the use of oral histories as proof of historical facts, the laws of evidence must be adapted in order that this type of evidence can be accommodated and placed on an equal footing with the types of historical evidence that courts are familiar with, which largely consists of historical documents. This is a long-standing practice in the interpretation of treaties between the Crown and aboriginal peoples: *Sioui, supra*, at p. 1068; *R. v. Taylor* (1981), 62 C.C.C. (2d) 227 (Ont. C.A.) at p. 232. To quote Dickson C.J., given that most aboriginal societies "did not keep written records", the failure to do so would "impose an impossible burden of proof" on aboriginal peoples, and "render nugatory" any rights that they have (*Simon v. The Queen*, [1985] 2 S.C.R. 387 at p. 408, 24 D.L.R. (4th) 390). This process must be undertaken on a case-by-case

basis. I will take this approach in my analysis of the trial judge's **[23:**
findings of fact.

[88] On a final note, it is important to understand that even when a
trial judge has erred in making a finding of fact, appellate intervention does not proceed automatically. The error must be sufficiently
serious that it was "overriding and determinative in the assessment
of the balance of probabilities with respect to that factual issue"
(*Schwartz, supra*, at p. 281).

(2) Application of General Principles

(a) General Comments

[89] The general principle of appellate non-interference applies
with particular force in this appeal. The trial was lengthy and very
complex. There were 318 days of testimony. There were a large
number of witnesses, lay and expert. The volume of evidence is enormous. To quote the trial judge at pp. 116-17:

> A total of 61 witnesses gave evidence at trial, many using translators from
> their native Gitksan or Wet'suwet'en language; "word spellers" to assist the
> official reporters were required for many witnesses; a further 15 witnesses
> gave their evidence on commission; 53 territorial affidavits were filed; 30
> deponents were cross-examined out of court; there are 23,503 pages of tran-
> script evidence at trial; 5898 pages of transcript of argument; 3,039 pages of
> commission evidence and 2,553 pages of cross-examination on affidavits (all
> evidence and oral arguments are conveniently preserved in hard copy and on
> diskettes); about 9,200 exhibits were filed at trial comprising, I estimate, well
> over 50,000 pages; the plaintiffs' draft outline of argument comprises 3,250
> pages, the province's 1,975 pages, and Canada's over 1,000 pages; there are
> 5,977 pages of transcript of argument in hard copy and on diskettes. All par-
> ties filed some excerpts from the exhibits they referred to in argument. The
> province alone submitted 28 huge binders of such documents. At least 15 bind-
> ers of reply argument were left with me during that stage of the trial.

The result was a judgment of over 400 pages in length.

[90] It is not open to the appellants to challenge the trial judge's
findings of fact merely because they disagree with them. I fear that a
significant number of the appellants' objections fall into this category.
Those objections are too numerous to list in their entirety. The bulk
of these objections, at best, relate to alleged instances of misappre-
hension or oversight of material evidence by the trial judge. However,
the respondents have established that, in most situations, there was
some contradictory evidence that supported the trial judge's conclusion. The question, ultimately, was one of weight, and the appellants
have failed to demonstrate that the trial judge erred in this respect.

234]   [91] One objection that I would like to mention specifically, albeit in passing, is the trial judge's refusal to accept the testimony of two anthropologists who were brought in as expert witnesses by the appellants. This aspect of the trial judge's reasons was hotly contested by the appellants in their written submissions. However, I need only reiterate what I have stated above, that findings of credibility, including the credibility of expert witnesses, are for the trial judge to make, and should warrant considerable deference from appellate courts.

[92] On the other hand, the appellants have alleged that the trial judge made a number of serious errors relating to the treatment of the oral histories of the appellants. Those oral histories were expressed in three different forms: (i) the adaawk of the Gitksan, and the kungax of the Wet'suwet'en; (ii) the personal recollections of members of the appellant nations, and (iii) the territorial affidavits filed by the heads of the individual houses within each nation. The trial judge ruled on both the admissibility of, and the weight to be given to, these various forms of oral history without the benefit of my reasons in *Van der Peet*, as will become evident in the discussion that follows.

(b) Adaawk and Kungax

[93] The adaawk and kungax of the Gitksan and Wet'suwet'en nations, respectively, are oral histories of a special kind. They were described by the trial judge, at p. 164, as a "sacred 'official' litany, or history, or recital of the most important laws, history, traditions and traditional territory of a House". The content of these special oral histories includes its physical representation totem poles, crests and blankets. The importance of the adaawk and kungax is underlined by the fact that they are "repeated, performed and authenticated at important feasts". At those feasts, dissenters have the opportunity to object if they question any detail and, in this way, help ensure the authenticity of the adaawk and kungax. Although they serve largely the same role, the trial judge found that there are some differences in both the form and content of the adaawk and the kungax. For example, the latter is "in the nature of a song which is intended to represent the special authority and responsibilities of a chief . . .". However, these differences are not legally relevant for the purposes of the issue at hand.

[94] It is apparent that the adaawk and kungax are of integral importance to the distinctive cultures of the appellant nations. At trial,

they were relied on for two distinct purposes. First, the adaawk was **[235**
relied on as a component of and, therefore, as proof of the existence
of a system of land tenure law internal to the Gitksan, which covered
the whole territory claimed by that appellant. In other words, it was
offered as evidence of the Gitksan's historical use and occupation of
that territory. For the Wet'suwet'en, the kungax was offered as proof
of the central significance of the claimed lands to their distinctive
culture. As I shall explain later in these reasons, both use and occupation, and the central significance of the lands occupied, are relevant
to proof of aboriginal title.

[95] The admissibility of the adaawk and kungax was the subject
of a general decision of the trial judge handed down during the course
of the trial regarding the admissibility of all oral histories (incorrectly indexed as *Uukw v. R.*, [1987] 6 W.W.R. 155, 40 D.L.R. (4th)
685 *sub nom. Delgamuukw v. British Columbia* (B.C.S.C.)). Although
the trial judge recognized that the evidence at issue was a form of
hearsay, he ruled it admissible on the basis of the recognized exception that declarations made by deceased persons could be given in
evidence by witnesses as proof of public or general rights: see Michael
Newman Howard, Peter Crane and Daniel A. Hochberg, *Phipson on
Evidence*, 14th ed. (London: Sweet & Maxwell, 1990), at p. 736. He
affirmed that earlier ruling in his trial judgment, correctly in my view,
by stating, at p. 180 that the adaawk and kungax were admissible
"out of necessity as exceptions to the hearsay rule" because there
was no other way to prove the history of the Gitksan and Wet'suwet'en
nations.

[96] The trial judge, however, went on to give these oral histories
no independent weight at all. He held, at p. 180, that they were only
admissible as "direct evidence of the facts in issue . . . in a few cases
where they could constitute confirmatory proof of early presence in
the territory". His central concern that the adaawk and kungax could
not serve "as evidence of detailed history, or land ownership, use or
occupation". I disagree with some of the reasons he relied on in support of this conclusion.

[97] Although he had earlier recognized, when making his ruling
on admissibility, that it was impossible to make an easy distinction
between the mythological and "real" aspects of these oral histories,
he discounted the adaawk and kungax because they were not

236] "literally true", confounded "what is fact and what is belief", "included some material which might be classified as mythology", and projected a "romantic view" of the history of the appellants. He also cast doubt on the authenticity of these special oral histories (at p. 181) because, *inter alia*, "the verifying group is so small that they cannot safely be regarded as expressing the reputation of even the Indian community, let alone the larger community whose opportunity to dispute territorial claims would be essential to weight". Finally, he questioned (at p. 181) the utility of the adaawk and kungax to demonstrate use and occupation because they were "seriously lacking in detail about the specific lands to which they are said to relate".

[98] Although he framed his ruling on weight in terms of the specific oral histories before him, in my respectful opinion, the trial judge in reality based his decision on some general concerns with the use of oral histories as evidence in aboriginal rights cases. In summary, the trial judge gave no independent weight to these special oral histories because they did not accurately convey historical truth, because knowledge about those oral histories was confined to the communities whose histories they were and because those oral histories were insufficiently detailed. However, as I mentioned earlier, these are features, to a greater or lesser extent, of all oral histories, not just the adaawk and kungax. The implication of the trial judge's reasoning is that oral histories should never be given any independent weight and are only useful as confirmatory evidence in aboriginal rights litigation. I fear that if this reasoning were followed, the oral histories of aboriginal peoples would be consistently and systematically undervalued by the Canadian legal system, in contradiction of the express instruction to the contrary in *Van der Peet* that trial courts interpret the evidence of aboriginal peoples in light of the difficulties inherent in adjudicating aboriginal claims.

(c) Recollections of Aboriginal Life

[99] The trial judge also erred when he discounted the "recollections of aboriginal life" offered by various members of the appellant nations. I take that term to be a reference to testimony about personal and family history that is not part of an adaawk or a kungax. That evidence consisted of the personal knowledge of the witnesses and declarations of witnesses' ancestors as to land use. This history had been adduced by the appellants in order to establish the requisite degree of use and occupation to make out a claim to ownership and,

for the same reason as the adaawk and kungax, is material to the **[237** proof of aboriginal title.

[100] The trial judge limited the uses to which the evidence could be put. He reasoned, at p. 177, that this evidence, at most, established "without question, that the plaintiff's immediate ancestors, for the past 100 years or so" had used land in the claimed territory for aboriginal purposes. However, the evidence was insufficiently precise to demonstrate that the more distant ancestors of the witnesses had engaged in specific enough land use "far enough back in time to permit the plaintiffs to succeed on issues such as internal boundaries". In the language of *Van der Peet*, the trial judge effectively held that this evidence did not demonstrate the requisite continuity between present occupation and past occupation in order to ground a claim for aboriginal title.

[101] In my opinion, the trial judge expected too much of the oral history of the appellants, as expressed in the recollections of aboriginal life of members of the appellant nations. He expected that evidence to provide definitive and precise evidence of pre-contact aboriginal activities on the territory in question. However, as I held in *Van der Peet*, this will be almost an impossible burden to meet. Rather, if oral history cannot conclusively establish pre-sovereignty (after this decision) occupation of land, it may still be relevant to demonstrate that current occupation has its origins prior to sovereignty. This is exactly what the appellants sought to do.

(d) Territorial Affidavits

[102] Finally, the trial judge also erred in his treatment of the territorial affidavits filed by the appellant chiefs. Those affidavits were declarations of the territorial holdings of each of the Gitksan and Wet'suwet'en houses and, at trial, were introduced for the purposes of establishing each House's ownership of its specific territory. Before this Court, the appellants tried to amalgamate these individual claims into collective claims on behalf of each nation and the relevance of the affidavits changed accordingly. I have already held that it is not open to the appellants to alter fundamentally the nature of their claim in this way on appeal. Nevertheless, the treatment of the affidavits is important because they will be relevant at a new trial to the existence and nature of the land tenure system within each nation and, therefore material to the proof of title.

238]   [103] The affidavits rely heavily on the declarations of deceased persons of use or ownership of the lands, which are a form of oral history. But those declarations are a kind of hearsay and the appellants therefore argued that the affidavits should be admitted through the reputation exception to the hearsay rule. Although he recognized, at p. 438, that the territorial affidavits were "the best evidence [the appellants] could adduce on the question of internal boundaries", the trial judge held that this exception did not apply and refused to admit the declarations contained in the affidavits.

[104] I am concerned by the specific reasons the trial judge gave for refusing to apply the reputation exception. He questioned the degree to which the declarations amounted to a reputation because they were largely confined to the appellants' communities. The trial judge asserted that neighbouring aboriginal groups whose territorial claims conflicted with those of the appellants, as well as non-aboriginals who potentially possessed a legal interest in the claimed territory, were unaware of the content of the alleged reputation at all. Furthermore, the trial judge reasoned that since the subject-matter of the affidavits was disputed, its reliability was doubtful. Finally, the trial judge questioned, at p. 441, the "independence and objectivity" of the information contained in the affidavits, because the appellants and their ancestors (at p. 440) "have been actively discussing land claims for many years".

[105] Although he regretted this finding, the trial judge felt bound to apply the rules of evidence because it did not appear to him (at p. 442) "that the Supreme Court of Canada has decided that the ordinary rules of evidence do not apply to this kind of case". The trial judge arrived at this conclusion, however, without the benefit of *Van der Peet*, where I held that the ordinary rules of evidence must be approached and adapted in light of the evidentiary difficulties inherent in adjudicating aboriginal claims.

[106] Many of the reasons relied on by the trial judge for excluding the evidence contained in the territorial affidavits are problematic because they run against this fundamental principle. The requirement that a reputation be known in the general community, for example, ignores the fact that oral histories, as noted by the Royal Commission on Aboriginal Peoples, generally relate to particular locations, and refer to particular families and communities and may, as a result,

be unknown outside of that community, even to other aboriginal na- **[23**
tions. Excluding the territorial affidavits because the claims to which
they relate are disputed does not acknowledge that claims to aboriginal rights, and aboriginal title in particular, are almost always disputed
and contested. Indeed, if those claims were uncontroversial, there
would be no need to bring them to the courts for resolution. Casting
doubt on the reliability of the territorial affidavits because land claims
had been actively discussed for many years also fails to take account
of the special context surrounding aboriginal claims, in two ways.
First, those claims have been discussed for so long because of British
Columbia's persistent refusal to acknowledge the existence of aboriginal title in that province until relatively recently, largely as a direct
result of the decision of this Court in *Calder, supra*. It would be per- [12]
verse, to say the least, to use the refusal of the province to acknowledge
the rights of its aboriginal inhabitants as a reason for excluding evidence which may prove the existence of those rights. Second, this
rationale for exclusion places aboriginal claimants whose societies
record their past through oral history in a grave dilemma. In order for
the oral history of a community to amount to a form of reputation,
and to be admissible in court, it must remain alive through the discussions of members of that community; those discussions are the
very basis of that reputation. But if those histories are discussed too
much, and too close to the date of litigation, they may be discounted
as being suspect, and may be held to be inadmissible. The net effect
may be that a society with such an oral tradition would never be able
to establish a historical claim through the use of oral history in court.

(e) Conclusion

[107] The trial judge's treatment of the various kinds of oral histories did not satisfy the principles I laid down in *Van der Peet*. These
errors are particularly worrisome because oral histories were of critical importance to the appellants' case. They used those histories in
an attempt to establish their occupation and use of the disputed territory, an essential requirement for aboriginal title. The trial judge, after
refusing to admit, or giving no independent weight to these oral histories, reached the conclusion that the appellants had not demonstrated
the requisite degree of occupation for "ownership". Had the trial judge
assessed the oral histories correctly, his conclusions on these issues
of fact might have been very different.

[[12] 73 *ILR* 56.]

240] [108] In the circumstances, the factual findings cannot stand. However, given the enormous complexity of the factual issues at hand, it would be impossible for the Court to do justice to the parties by sifting through the record itself and making new factual findings. A new trial is warranted, at which the evidence may be considered in light of the principles laid down in *Van der Peet* and elaborated upon here. In applying these principles, the new trial judge might well share some or all of the findings of fact of McEachern C.J.

C. WHAT IS THE CONTENT OF ABORIGINAL TITLE, HOW IS IT PROTECTED BY S. 35(1), AND WHAT IS REQUIRED FOR ITS PROOF?

(1) Introduction

[109] The parties disagree over whether the appellants have established aboriginal title to the disputed area. However, since those factual issues require a new trial, we cannot resolve that dispute in this appeal. But factual issues aside, the parties also have a more fundamental disagreement over the content of aboriginal title itself, and its reception into the Constitution by s 35(1). In order to give guidance to the judge at the new trial, it is to this issue that I will now turn.

[110] I set out these opposing positions by way of illustration and introduction because I believe that all of the parties have characterized the content of aboriginal title incorrectly. The appellants argue that aboriginal title is tantamount to an inalienable fee simple, which confers on aboriginal peoples the rights to use those lands as they choose and which has been constitutionalized by s. 35(1). The respondents offer two alternative formulations: first, that aboriginal title is no more than a bundle of rights to engage in activities which are themselves aboriginal rights recognized and affirmed by s. 35(1), and that the *Constitution Act, 1982*, merely constitutionalizes those individual rights, not the bundle itself, because the latter has no independent content; and second, that aboriginal title, at most, encompasses the right to exclusive use and occupation of land in order to engage in those activities which are aboriginal rights themselves, and that s. 35(1) constitutionalizes this notion of exclusivity.

[111] The content of aboriginal title, in fact, lies somewhere in between these positions. Aboriginal title is a right in land and, as such, is more than the right to engage in specific activities which may be themselves aboriginal rights. Rather, it confers the right to use land for a variety of activities, not all of which need be aspects of practices, customs and traditions which are integral to the distinctive

cultures of aboriginal societies. Those activities do not constitute the **[24**
right *per se*; rather, they are parasitic on the underlying title. However, that range of uses is subject to the limitation that they must not
be irreconcilable with the nature of the attachment to the land which
forms the basis of the particular group's aboriginal title. This inherent limit, to be explained more fully below, flows from the definition
of aboriginal title as a *sui generis* interest in land, and is one way in
which aboriginal title is distinct from a fee simple.

(2) Aboriginal title at common law

(a) General features

[112] The starting point of the Canadian jurisprudence on aboriginal title is the Privy Council's decision in *St. Catherine's Milling and
Lumber Co. v. The Queen* (1888), 14 App. Cas. 46, which described
aboriginal title as a "personal and usufructuary right" (at p. 54). The
subsequent jurisprudence has attempted to grapple with this definition, and has in the process demonstrated that the Privy Council's
choice of terminology is not particularly helpful to explain the various dimensions of aboriginal title. What the Privy Council sought to
capture is that aboriginal title is a *sui generis* interest in land. Aboriginal title has been described as *sui generis* in order to distinguish it
from "normal" proprietary interests, such as fee simple. However, as
I will now develop, it is also *sui generis* in the sense that its characteristics cannot be completely explained by reference either to the
common law rules of real property or to the rules of property found
in aboriginal legal systems. As with other aboriginal rights, it must
be understood by reference to both common law and aboriginal
perspectives.

[113] The idea that aboriginal title is *sui generis* is the unifying
principle underlying the various dimensions of that title. One dimension is its *inalienability*. Lands held pursuant to aboriginal title cannot
be transferred, sold or surrendered to anyone other than the Crown
and, as a result, is inalienable to third parties. This Court has taken
pains to clarify that aboriginal title is only "personal" in this sense,
and does not mean that aboriginal title is a non-proprietary interest
which amounts to no more than a licence to use and occupy the land
and cannot compete on an equal footing with other proprietary interests: see *Canadian Pacific Ltd. v. Paul*, [1988] 2 S.C.R. 654 at
p. 677, 53 D.L.R. (4th) 487.

242]   [114] Another dimension of aboriginal title is its *source*. It had originally been thought that the source of aboriginal title in Canada was the *Royal Proclamation, 1763*: see *St. Catherine's Milling*. However, it is now clear that although aboriginal title was recognized by the Proclamation, it arises from the prior occupation of Canada by aboriginal peoples. That prior occupation, however, is relevant in two different ways, both of which illustrate the *sui generis* nature of aboriginal title. The first is the physical fact of occupation, which derives from the common law principle that occupation is proof of possession in law: see Kent McNeil, *Common Law Aboriginal Title* (Oxford: Clarendon Press, 1989), at p. 7. Thus, in *Guerin, supra*, Dickson J. described aboriginal title, at p. 376, as a "legal right derived from the Indians' historic occupation and possession of their tribal lands". What makes aboriginal title *sui generis* is that it arises from possession *before* the assertion of British sovereignty, whereas normal estates, like fee simple, arise afterward: see Kent McNeil, "The Meaning of Aboriginal Title", in Michael Asch, ed., *Aboriginal and Treaty Rights in Canada* (Vancouver: U.B.C. Press, 1997), 135, at p. 144. This idea has been further developed in *Roberts v. Canada*, [1989] 1 S.C.R. 322, 57 D.L.R. (4th) 197, where this Court unanimously held at p. 340 that "aboriginal title pre-dated colonization by the British and survived. British claims to sovereignty" (also see *Guerin, supra*, at p. 378). What this suggests is a second source for aboriginal title the relationship between common law and pre-existing systems of aboriginal law.

[115] A further dimension of aboriginal title is the fact that it is held *communally*. Aboriginal title cannot be held by individual aboriginal persons; it is a collective right to land held by all members of an aboriginal nation. Decisions with respect to that land are also made by that community. This is another feature of aboriginal title which is *sui generis* and distinguishes it from normal property interests.

(b) The content of aboriginal title

[116] Although cases involving aboriginal title have come before this Court and Privy Council before, there has never been a definitive statement from either court on the *content* of aboriginal title. In *St. Catherine's Milling*, the Privy Council, as I have mentioned, described the aboriginal title as a "personal and usufructuary interest", but declined to explain what that meant because it was not

"necessary to express any opinion on the point" (at p. 55). Similarly, **[24?** in *Calder, Guerin,* and *Paul,* the issues were the extinguishment of, [13] the fiduciary duty arising from the surrender of, and statutory easements over land held pursuant to, aboriginal title, respectively; the content of title was not at issue and was not directly addressed.

[117] Although the courts have been less than forthcoming, I have arrived at the conclusion that the content of aboriginal title can be summarized by two propositions: first, that aboriginal title encompasses the right to exclusive use and occupation of the land held pursuant to that title for a variety of purposes, which need not be aspects of those aboriginal practices, customs and traditions which are integral to distinctive aboriginal cultures; and second, that those protected uses must not be irreconcilable with the nature of the group's attachment to that land. For the sake of clarity, I will discuss each of these propositions separately.

Aboriginal title encompasses the right to use the land held pursuant to that title for a variety of purposes, which need not be aspects of those aboriginal practices, cultures and traditions which are integral to distinctive aboriginal cultures

[118] The respondents argue that aboriginal title merely encompasses the right to engage in activities which are aspects of aboriginal practices, customs and traditions which are integral to distinctive aboriginal cultures of the aboriginal group claiming the right and, at most, adds the notion of exclusivity; i.e., the exclusive right to use the land for those purposes. However, the uses to which lands held pursuant to aboriginal title can be put are not restricted in this way. This conclusion emerges from three sources: (i) the Canadian jurisprudence on aboriginal title, (ii) the relationship between reserve lands and lands held pursuant to aboriginal title, and (iii) the *Indian Oil and Gas Act,* R.S.C. 1985, c. I-7. As well, although this is not legally determinative, it is supported by the critical literature. In particular, I have profited greatly from Professor McNeil's article, "The Meaning of Aboriginal Title", *supra.*

(i) Canadian jurisprudence on aboriginal title

[119] Despite the fact that the jurisprudence on aboriginal title is somewhat underdeveloped, it is clear that the uses to which lands held pursuant to aboriginal title can be put is not restricted to the practices, customs and traditions of aboriginal peoples integral to

[[13] 73 *ILR* 56.]

244] distinctive aboriginal cultures. In *Guerin*, for example, Dickson J. described aboriginal title as "an interest in land" which encompassed "a legal right to occupy and possess certain lands" (at p. 382). The "right to occupy and possess" is framed in broad terms and, significantly, is not qualified by reference to traditional and customary uses of those lands. Any doubt that the right to occupancy and possession encompasses a broad variety of uses of land was put to rest in *Paul*, where the Court went even further and stated that aboriginal title was "more than the right to enjoyment and occupancy" (at p. 688). Once again, there is no reference to aboriginal practices, customs and traditions as a qualifier on that right. Moreover, I take the reference to "more" as emphasis of the broad notion of use and possession.

(ii) Reserve Land

[120] Another source of support for the conclusion that the uses to which lands held under aboriginal title can be put are not restricted to those grounded in practices, customs and traditions integral to distinctive aboriginal cultures can be found in *Guerin*, where Dickson J. stated at p. 379 that the same legal principles governed the aboriginal interest in reserve lands and lands held pursuant to aboriginal title:

> It does not matter, in my opinion, that the present case is concerned with the interest of an Indian Band in a reserve rather than with unrecognized aboriginal title in traditional tribal lands. *The Indian interest in the lands is the same in both cases*. . . . [Emphasis added.]

[121] The nature of the Indian interest in reserve land is very broad, and can found in s. 18 of the *Indian Act*, which I reproduce in full:

> 18(1) Subject to this Act, reserves are held by Her Majesty for the *use and benefit* of the respective bands for which they were set apart, and subject to this Act and to the terms of any treaty or surrender, the Governor in Council may determine whether any purpose for which lands in a reserve are used or are to be used is for the use and benefit of the band.
>
> (2) The Minister may authorize the use of lands in a reserve for the purpose of Indian schools, the administration of Indian affairs, Indian burial grounds, Indian health projects or, with the consent of the council of the band, *for any other purpose for the general welfare of the band*, and may take any lands in a reserve required for those purposes, but where an individual Indian, immediately prior to the taking, was entitled to the possession of those lands, compensation for that use shall be paid to the Indian, in such amount as may be agreed between the Indian and the Minister, or, failing agreement, as may be determined in such manner as the Minister may direct. [Emphasis added.]

The principal provision is s. 18(1), which states that reserve lands are held "for the use and benefit" of the bands which occupy them; those

uses and benefits, on the face of the *Indian Act*, do not appear to be **[245**
restricted to practices, customs and traditions integral to distinctive
aboriginal cultures. The breadth of those uses is reinforced by s. 18(2),
which states that reserve lands may be used "for any other purpose
for the general welfare of the band". The general welfare of the band
has not been defined in terms of aboriginal practices, customs and
traditions, nor in terms of those activities which have their origin
pre-contact; it is a concept, by definition, which incorporates a reference to the present-day needs of aboriginal communities. On the basis
of *Guerin*, lands held pursuant to aboriginal title, like reserve lands,
are also capable of being used for a broad variety of purposes.

(iii) Indian Oil and Gas Act

[122] The third source for the proposition that the content of aboriginal title is not restricted to practices, customs, and traditions which
are integral to distinctive aboriginal cultures is the *Indian Oil and
Gas Act*. The overall purpose of the statute is to provide for the exploration of oil and gas on reserve lands through their surrender to
the Crown. The statute presumes that the aboriginal interest in reserve land includes mineral rights, a point which this Court
unanimously accepted with respect to the *Indian Act* in *Blueberry
River Indian Band v. Canada (Department of Indian Affairs and Northern Development)*, [1995] 4 S.C.R. 344, 130 D.L.R. (4th) 193. On
the basis of *Guerin*, aboriginal title also encompass mineral rights,
and lands held pursuant to aboriginal title should be capable of exploitation in the same way, which is certainly not a traditional use for
those lands. This conclusion is reinforced by s. 6(2) of the Act, which
provides:

> 6(2) Nothing in this Act shall be deemed to abrogate the rights of Indian
> people or preclude them from negotiating for oil and gas benefits in those
> areas in which land claims have not been settled.

The areas referred to in s. 6(2), at the very least, must encompass
lands held pursuant to aboriginal title, since those lands by definition
have not been surrendered under land claims agreements. The presumption underlying s. 6(2) is that aboriginal title permits the
development of oil and gas reserves.

[123] Although this is not determinative, the conclusion that the
content of aboriginal title is not restricted to those uses with their
origins in the practices, customs and traditions integral to distinctive

246] aboriginal societies has wide support in the critical literature: Jocelyn
Gagne, "The Content of Aboriginal Title at Common Law: A Look at
the Nishga Claim" (1982-83), 47 Sask. L. Rev. 309 at pp. 336-37;
Kent McNeil, *Common Law Aboriginal Title*, *supra*, at p. 242; Kent
McNeil, "The Meaning of Aboriginal Title", *supra*, at pp. 143-150;
William Pentney, "The Rights of the Aboriginal Peoples of Canada
in the *Constitution Act, 1982* Part II — Section 35: The Substantive
Guarantee" (1988), 22 U.B.C. L. Rev. 207 at pp. 221; *Report of the
Royal Commission on Aboriginal Peoples*, vol. 2, *Restructuring the
Relationship*, at pp. 561; Brian Slattery, "The Constitutional Guaran-
tee of Aboriginal and Treaty Rights" (1982-83), 8 Queen's L.J. 232
at pp. 268-9; Brian Slattery, *Ancestral Lands, Alien Laws: Judicial
Perspectives on Aboriginal Title* (Saskatoon: University of Saskatch-
ewan Native Law Centre, 1983) at pp. 34; Brian Slattery,
"Understanding Aboriginal Rights", *supra*, at pp. 746-48.

[124] In conclusion, the content of aboriginal title is not restricted
to those uses which are elements of a practice, custom or tradition
integral to the distinctive culture of the aboriginal group claiming the
right. However, nor does aboriginal title amount to a form of inalienable fee simple, as I will now explain.

  *(c) Inherent Limit: Lands held pursuant to aboriginal title cannot
    be used in a manner that is irreconcilable with the nature of the
    attachment to the land which forms the basis of the group's claim
    to aboriginal title*

[125] The content of aboriginal title contains an inherent limit that
lands held pursuant to title cannot be used in a manner that is irreconcilable with the nature of the claimants' attachment to those lands.
This limit on the content of aboriginal title is a manifestation of the
principle that underlies the various dimensions of that special interest in land — it is a *sui generis* interest that is distinct from "normal"
proprietary interests, most notably fee simple.

[126] I arrive at this conclusion by reference to the other dimensions of aboriginal title which are *sui generis* as well. I first consider
the source of aboriginal title. As I discussed earlier, aboriginal title
arises from the prior occupation of Canada by aboriginal peoples.
That prior occupation is relevant in two different ways: first, because
of the physical fact of occupation, and second, because aboriginal
title originates in part from pre-existing systems of aboriginal law.

However, the law of aboriginal title does not only seek to determine **[247** the historic rights of aboriginal peoples to land; it also seeks to afford legal protection to prior occupation in the present-day. Implicit in the protection of historic patterns of occupation is a recognition of the importance of the continuity of the relationship of an aboriginal community to its land over time.

[127] I develop this point below with respect to the test for aboriginal title. The relevance of the continuity of the relationship of an aboriginal community with its land here is that it applies not only to the past, but to the future as well. That relationship should not be prevented from continuing into the future. As a result, uses of the lands that would threaten that future relationship are, by their very nature, excluded from the content of aboriginal title.

[128] Accordingly, in my view, lands subject to aboriginal title cannot be put to such uses as may be irreconcilable with the nature of the occupation of that land and the relationship that the particular group has had with the land which together have given rise to aboriginal title in the first place. As discussed below, one of the critical elements in the determination of whether a particular aboriginal group has aboriginal title to certain lands is the matter of the occupancy of those lands. Occupancy is determined by reference to the activities that have taken place on the land and the uses to which the land has been put by the particular group. If lands are so occupied, there will exist a special bond between the group and the land in question such that the land will be part of the definition of the group's distinctive culture. It seems to me that these elements of aboriginal title create an inherent limitation on the uses to which the land, over which such title exists, may be put. For example, if occupation is established with reference to the use of the land as a hunting ground, then the group that successfully claims aboriginal title to that land may not use it in such a fashion as to destroy its value for such a use (e.g., by strip-mining it). Similarly, if a group claims a special bond with the land because of its ceremonial or cultural significance, it may not use the land in such a way as to destroy that relationship (e.g., by developing it in such a way that the bond is destroyed, perhaps by turning it into a parking lot).

[129] It is for this reason also that lands held by virtue of aboriginal title may not be alienated. Alienation would bring to an end the

248] entitlement of the aboriginal people to occupy the land and would terminate their relationship with it. I have suggested above that the inalienability of aboriginal lands is, at least in part, a function of the common law principle that settlers in colonies must derive their title from Crown grant and, therefore, cannot acquire title through purchase from aboriginal inhabitants. It is also, again only in part, a function of a general policy "to ensure that Indians are not dispossessed of their entitlements": see *Mitchell v. Peguis Indian Band*, [1990] 2 S.C.R. 85 at p. 133, 71 D.L.R. (4th) 193. What the inalienability of lands held pursuant to aboriginal title suggests is that those lands are more than just a fungible commodity. The relationship between an aboriginal community and the lands over which it has aboriginal title has an important non-economic component. The land has an inherent and unique value in itself, which is enjoyed by the community with aboriginal title to it. The community cannot put the land to uses which would destroy that value.

[130] I am cognizant that the *sui generis* nature of aboriginal title precludes the application of "traditional real property rules" to elucidate the content of that title (*St. Mary's Indian Band v. Cranbrook (City)*, [1997] 2 S.C.R. 657, 147 D.L.R. (4th) 385 at para. 14). Nevertheless, a useful analogy can be drawn between the limit on aboriginal title and the concept of equitable waste at common law. Under that doctrine, persons who hold a life estate in real property cannot commit "wanton or extravagant acts of destruction" (E.H. Burn, *Cheshire and Burn's Modern Law of Real Property*, 14th ed. (London: Butterworths, 1988), at p. 264) or "ruin the property" (Robert E. Megarry and H.W.R. Wade, *The Law of Real Property*, 4th ed. (London: Stevens, 1975) at p. 105). This description of the limits imposed by the doctrine of equitable waste capture the kind of limit I have in mind here.

[131] Finally, what I have just said regarding the importance of the continuity of the relationship between an aboriginal community and its land, and the non-economic or inherent value of that land, should not be taken to detract from the possibility of surrender to the Crown in exchange for valuable consideration. On the contrary, the idea of surrender reinforces the conclusion that aboriginal title is limited in the way I have described. If aboriginal peoples wish to use their lands in a way that aboriginal title does not permit, then they

must surrender those lands and convert them into non-title lands to **[249**
do so.

[132] The foregoing amounts to a general limitation on the use of lands held by virtue of aboriginal title. It arises from the particular physical and cultural relationship that a group may have with the land and is defined by the source of aboriginal title over it. This is not, I must emphasize, a limitation that restricts the use of the land to those activities that have traditionally been carried out on it. That would amount to a legal strait-jacket on aboriginal peoples who have a legitimate legal claim to the land. The approach I have outlined above allows for a full range of uses of the land, subject only to an overarching limit, defined by the special nature of the aboriginal title in that land.

(d) Aboriginal title under s. 35(1) of the Constitution Act, 1982

[133] Aboriginal title at common law is protected in its full form by s. 35(1). This conclusion flows from the express language of s. 35(1) itself, which states in full: "[t]he *existing* aboriginal and treaty rights of the aboriginal peoples of Canada are hereby recognized and affirmed" (emphasis added). On a plain reading of the provision, s. 35(1) did not create aboriginal rights; rather, it accorded constitutional status to those rights which were "existing" in 1982. The provision, at the very least, constitutionalized those rights which aboriginal peoples possessed at common law, since those rights existed at the time s. 35(1) came into force. Since aboriginal title was a common law right whose existence was recognized well before 1982 (e.g., *Calder, supra*), s. 35(1) has constitutionalized it in its full form.

[134] I expressed this understanding of the relationship between common law aboriginal rights, including aboriginal title, and the aboriginal rights protected by s. 35(1) in *Van der Peet*. While explaining the purposes behind s. 35(1), I stated that "it must be remembered that s. 35(1) did not create the legal doctrine of aboriginal rights; aboriginal rights existed and were recognized under the common law" (at para. 28). Through the enactment of s. 35(1), "a pre-existing legal doctrine was elevated to constitutional status" (at para. 29), or in other words, s. 35(1) had achieved "the constitutionalization of those rights" (at para. 29).

[135] Finally, this view of the effect of s. 35(1) on common law aboriginal title is supported by numerous commentators: Patrick

250] Macklem, "First Nations Self-Government and the Borders of the Canadian Legal Imagination" (1991), 36 McGill L.J. 382 at pp. 447-48; Kent McNeil, "The Constitutional Rights of the Aboriginal Peoples of Canada" (1982), 4 Sup. Ct. L. Rev. 255 at pp. 256-57; James O'Reilly, "La Loi constitutionnelle de 1982 droit des autochtones" (1984), 25 C. de D. 125 at p. 137; William Pentney, "The Rights of the Aboriginal Peoples of Canada in the *Constitution Act, 1982* Part II — Section 35: The Substantive Guarantee", *supra*, at pp. 220-21; Douglas Sanders, "The Rights of the Aboriginal Peoples of Canada" (1983), 61 Can. Bar Rev. 314 at p. 329; Douglas Sanders, "Pre-Existing Rights: The Aboriginal Peoples of Canada", in Gérald-A. Beaudoin and Ed Ratushny, eds., *The Canadian Charter of Rights and Freedoms*, 2nd ed. (Toronto: Carswell, 1989), at pp. 731-32; Brian Slattery, "The Constitutional Guarantee of Aboriginal Treaty Rights", *supra*, at p. 254; Brian Slattery, *Ancestral Lands, Alien Laws: Judicial Perspectives on Aboriginal Title*, *supra*, at p. 45.

[136] I hasten to add that the constitutionalization of common law aboriginal rights by s. 35(1) does not mean that those rights exhaust the content of s. 35(1). As I said in *Côté, supra*, at para. 52:

> [s]ection 35(1) would fail to achieve its noble purpose of preserving the integral and defining features of distinctive aboriginal societies if it only protected those defining features which were fortunate enough to have received the legal recognition and approval of European colonizers.

I relied on this proposition in *Côte* to defeat the argument that the possible absence of aboriginal rights under French colonial law was a bar to the existence of aboriginal rights under s. 35(1) within the historic boundaries of New France. But it also follows that the existence of a particular aboriginal right at common law is not a *sine qua non* for the proof of an aboriginal right that is recognized and affirmed by s. 35(1). Indeed, none of the decisions of this Court handed down under s. 35(1) in which the existence of an aboriginal right has been demonstrated has relied on the existence of that right at common law. The existence of an aboriginal right at common law is therefore sufficient, but not necessary, for the recognition and affirmation of that right by s. 35(1).

[137] The acknowledgement that s. 35(1) has accorded constitutional status to common law aboriginal title raises a further question — the relationship of aboriginal title to the "aboriginal rights" protected by s. 35(1). I addressed that question in *Adams*,

supra, where the Court had been presented with two radically differ- [**251**
ent conceptions of this relationship. The first conceived of aboriginal
rights as being "inherently based in aboriginal title to the land" (at
para. 25), or as fragments of a broader claim to aboriginal title. By
implication, aboriginal rights must rest either in a claim to title or the
unextinguished remnants of title. Taken to its logical extreme, this
suggests that aboriginal title is merely the sum of a set of individual
aboriginal rights, and that it therefore has no independent content.
However, I rejected this position for another that aboriginal title is
"simply one manifestation of a broader-based conception of aboriginal rights" (at para. 25). Thus, although aboriginal title is a species of
aboriginal right recognized and affirmed by s. 35(1), it is distinct
from other aboriginal rights because it arises where the connection
of a group with a piece of land "was of a central significance to their
distinctive culture" (at para. 26).

[138] The picture which emerges from *Adams* is that the aboriginal rights which are recognized and affirmed by s. 35(1) fall along a
spectrum with respect to their degree of connection with the land. At
the one end, there are those aboriginal rights which are practices,
customs and traditions that are integral to the distinctive aboriginal
culture of the group claiming the right. However, the "occupation
and use of the land" where the activity is taking place is not "sufficient to support a claim of title to the land" (at para. 26). Nevertheless,
those activities receive constitutional protection. In the middle, there
are activities which, out of necessity, take place on land and indeed,
might be intimately related to a particular piece of land. Although an
aboriginal group may not be able to demonstrate title to the land, it
may nevertheless have a site-specific right to engage in a particular
activity. I put the point this way in *Adams*, at para. 30:

> Even where an aboriginal right exists on a tract of land to which the aboriginal
> people in question do not have title, that right may well be site specific, with
> the result that it can be exercised only upon that specific tract of land. For
> example, *if an aboriginal people demonstrates that hunting on a specific tract
> of land was an integral part of their distinctive culture then, even if the right
> exists apart from title to that tract of land, the aboriginal right to hunt is none-
> theless defined as, and limited to, the right to hunt on the specific tract of land.*
> [Emphasis added.]

At the other end of the spectrum, there is aboriginal title itself. As
Adams makes clear, aboriginal title confers more than the right to
engage in site-specific activities which are aspects of the practices,

252] customs and traditions of distinctive aboriginal cultures. Site-specific rights can be made out even if title cannot. What aboriginal title confers is the right to the land itself.

[139] Because aboriginal rights can vary with respect to their degree of connection with the land, some aboriginal groups may be unable to make out a claim to title, but will nevertheless possess aboriginal rights that are recognized and affirmed by s. 35(1), including site-specific rights to engage in particular activities. As I explained in *Adams*, this may occur in the case of nomadic peoples who varied "the location of their settlements with the season and changing circumstances" (at para. 27). The fact that aboriginal peoples were non-sedentary, however (at para. 27)

> . . . does not alter the fact that nomadic peoples survived through reliance on the land prior to contact with Europeans and, further, that many of the practices, customs and traditions of nomadic peoples that took place on the land were integral to their distinctive cultures.

(e) Proof of aboriginal title

(i) Introduction

[140] In addition to differing in the degree of connection with the land, aboriginal title differs from other aboriginal rights in another way. To date, the Court has defined aboriginal rights in terms of *activities*. As I said in *Van der Peet* (at para. 46):

> . . . in order to be an aboriginal right an *activity* must be an element of a practice, custom or tradition integral to the distinctive culture of the aboriginal group claiming the right. [Emphasis added.]

Aboriginal title, however, is a *right to the land* itself. Subject to the limits I have laid down above, that land may be used for a variety of activities, none of which need be individually protected as aboriginal rights under s. 35(1). Those activities are parasitic on the underlying title.

[141] This difference between aboriginal rights to engage in particular activities and aboriginal title requires that the test I laid down in *Van der Peet* be adapted accordingly. I anticipated this possibility in *Van der Peet* itself, where I stated that (at para. 74):

> *Aboriginal rights arise from the prior occupation of land, but they also arise from the prior social organization and distinctive cultures of aboriginal peoples on that land.* In considering whether a claim to an aboriginal right has been made out, courts must look at both the relationship of an aboriginal claimant to the land *and* [emphasis in original] at the practices, customs and traditions

arising from the claimant's distinctive culture and society. Courts must not **[253**
focus so entirely on the relationship of aboriginal peoples with the land that
they lose sight of the other factors relevant to the identification and definition
of aboriginal rights. [Emphasis added.]

Since the purpose of s. 35(1) is to reconcile the prior presence of
aboriginal peoples in North America with the assertion of Crown
sovereignty, it is clear from this statement that s. 35(1) must recognize and affirm both aspects of that prior presence — first, the
occupation of land, and second, the prior social organization and distinctive cultures of aboriginal peoples on that land. To date the
jurisprudence under s. 35(1) has given more emphasis to the second
aspect. To a great extent, this has been a function of the types of
cases which have come before this Court under s. 35(1) — prosecutions for regulatory offences that, by their very nature, proscribe
discrete types of activity.

[142] The adaptation of the test laid down in *Van der Peet* to suit
claims to title must be understood as the recognition of the first aspect of that prior presence. However, as will now become apparent,
the tests for the identification of aboriginal rights to engage in particular activities and for the identification of aboriginal title share
broad similarities. The major distinctions are first, under the test for
aboriginal title, the requirement that the land be integral to the distinctive culture of the claimants is subsumed by the requirement of
occupancy, and second, whereas the time for the identification of
aboriginal rights is the time of first contact, the time for the identification of aboriginal title is the time at which the Crown asserted
sovereignty over the land.

(ii) The test for the proof of aboriginal title

[143] In order to make out a claim for aboriginal title, the aboriginal group asserting title must satisfy the following criteria: (i) the
land must have been occupied prior to sovereignty, (ii) if present
occupation is relied on as proof of occupation pre-sovereignty, there
must be a continuity between present and pre-sovereignty occupation, and (iii) at sovereignty, that occupation must have been exclusive.

The land must have been occupied prior to sovereignty

[144] In order to establish a claim to aboriginal title, the aboriginal group asserting the claim must establish that it occupied the lands
in question at the *time at which the Crown asserted sovereignty over*

254] *the land subject to the title.* The relevant time period for the establishment of title is, therefore, different than for the establishment of aboriginal rights to engage in specific activities. In *Van der Peet*, I held, at para. 60 that "[t]he time period that a court should consider in identifying whether the right claimed meets the standard of being integral to the aboriginal community claiming the right is the period prior to contact. . . ." This arises from the fact that in defining the central and distinctive attributes of pre-existing aboriginal societies it is necessary to look to a time prior to the arrival of Europeans. Practices, customs or traditions that arose solely as a response to European influences do not meet the standard for recognition as aboriginal rights.

[145] On the other hand, in the context of aboriginal title, sovereignty is the appropriate time period to consider for several reasons. First, from a theoretical standpoint, aboriginal title arises out of prior occupation of the land by aboriginal peoples and out of the relationship between the common law and pre-existing systems of aboriginal law. Aboriginal title is a burden on the Crown's underlying title. However, the Crown did not gain this title until it asserted sovereignty over the land in question. Because it does not make sense to speak of a burden on the underlying title before that title existed, aboriginal title crystallized at the time sovereignty was asserted. Second, aboriginal title does not raise the problem of distinguishing between distinctive, integral aboriginal practices, customs and traditions and those influenced or introduced by European contact. Under common law, the act of occupation or possession is sufficient to ground aboriginal title and it is not necessary to prove that the land was a distinctive or integral part of the aboriginal society before the arrival of Europeans. Finally, from a practical standpoint, it appears that the date of sovereignty is more certain than the date of first contact. It is often very difficult to determine the precise moment that each aboriginal group had first contact with European culture. I note that this is the approach has support in the academic literature: Brian Slattery, "Understanding Aboriginal Rights", *supra*, at p. 742; Kent McNeil, *Common Law Aboriginal Title*, *supra*, at p. 196. For these reasons, I conclude that aboriginals must establish occupation of the land from the date of the assertion of sovereignty in order to sustain a claim for aboriginal title. McEachern C.J. found, at pp. 233-34, and the parties

did not dispute on appeal, that British sovereignty over British Co- **[255**
lumbia was conclusively established by the *Oregon Boundary Treaty*
of 1846. This is not to say that circumstances subsequent to sovereignty may never be relevant to title or compensation; this might be
the case, for example, where native bands have been dispossessed of
traditional lands after sovereignty.

[146] There was a consensus among the parties on appeal that proof
of historic occupation was required to make out a claim to aboriginal
title. However, the parties disagreed on how that occupancy could be
proved. The respondents assert that in order to establish aboriginal
title, the occupation must be the physical occupation of the land in
question. The appellant Gitksan nation argue, by contrast, that aboriginal title may be established, at least in part, by reference to
aboriginal law.

[147] This debate over the proof of occupancy reflects two diver-
gent views of the source of aboriginal title. The respondents argue, in
essence, that aboriginal title arises from the physical reality at the
time of sovereignty, whereas the Gitksan effectively take the position that aboriginal title arises from and should reflect the pattern of
land holdings under aboriginal law. However, as I have explained
above, the source of aboriginal title appears to be grounded both in
the common law and in the aboriginal perspective on land; the latter
includes, but is not limited to, their systems of law. It follows that
both should be taken into account in establishing the proof of occupancy. Indeed, there is precedent for doing so. In *Baker Lake, supra*,
Mahoney J. held that to prove aboriginal title, the claimants needed
both to demonstrate their "physical presence on the land they occupied" (at p. 561) and the existence "among [that group of] . . . a
recognition of the claimed rights . . . by the regime that prevailed
before" (at p. 559).

[148] This approach to the proof of occupancy at common law is
also mandated in the context of s. 35(1) by *Van der Peet*. In that
decision, as I stated above, I held at para. 50 that the reconciliation of
the prior occupation of North America by aboriginal peoples with
the assertion of Crown sovereignty required that account be taken of
the "aboriginal perspective while at the same time taking into account the perspective of the common law" and that "[t]rue
reconciliation will, equally, place weight on each". I also held that

256] the aboriginal perspective on the occupation of their lands can be gleaned, in part, but not exclusively, from their traditional laws, because those laws were elements of the practices, customs and traditions of aboriginal peoples: at para. 41. As a result, if, at the time of sovereignty, an aboriginal society had laws in relation to land, those laws would be relevant to establishing the occupation of lands which are the subject of a claim for aboriginal title. Relevant laws might include, but are not limited to, a land tenure system or laws governing land use.

[149] However, the aboriginal perspective must be taken into account alongside the perspective of the common law. Professor McNeil has convincingly argued that at common law, the fact of physical occupation is proof of possession at law, which in turn will ground title to the land: *Common Law Aboriginal Title, supra,* at p. 73; also see Cheshire and Burn, *Modern Law of Real Property, supra,* at p. 28; and Megarry and Wade, *The Law of Real Property, supra,* at p. 1006. Physical occupation may be established in a variety of ways, ranging from the construction of dwellings through cultivation and enclosure of fields to regular use of definite tracts of land for hunting, fishing or otherwise exploiting its resources: see McNeil, *Common Law Aboriginal Title, supra,* at pp. 201-202. In considering whether occupation sufficient to ground title is established, "one must take into account the group's size, manner of life, material resources, and technological abilities, and the character of the lands claimed": Brian Slattery, "Understanding Aboriginal Rights", at pp. 758.

[150] In *Van der Peet,* I drew a distinction between those practices, customs and traditions of aboriginal peoples which were "an aspect of, or took place in" the society of the aboriginal group asserting the claim and those which were "a central and significant part of the society's culture" (at para. 55). The latter stood apart because they "made the culture of that society distinctive . . . it was one of the things which truly made the society what it was" (at para. 55). The same requirement operates in the determination of the proof of aboriginal title. As I said in *Adams,* a claim to title is made out when a group can demonstrate "that their connection with the piece of land . . . was of central significance to their distinctive culture" (at para. 26).

[151] Although this remains a crucial part of the test for aboriginal rights, given the occupancy requirement in the test for aboriginal title, I cannot imagine a situation where this requirement would

actually serve to limit or preclude a title claim. The requirement ex- [257
ists for rights short of title because it is necessary to distinguish
between those practices which were central to the culture of claimants and those which were more incidental. However, in the case of
title, it would seem clear that any land that was occupied pre-sovereignty, and which the parties have maintained a substantial connection
with since then, is sufficiently important to be of central significance
to the culture of the claimants. As a result, I do not think it is necessary to
include explicitly this element as part of the test for aboriginal title.

> *If present occupation is relied on as proof of occupation pre-*
> *sovereignty, there must be a continuity between present and*
> *pre-sovereignty occupation*

[152] In *Van der Peet*, I explained that it is the pre-contact practices, customs and traditions of aboriginal peoples which are
recognized and affirmed as aboriginal rights by s. 35(1). But I also
acknowledged it would be "next to impossible" (at para. 62) for an
aboriginal group to provide conclusive evidence of its pre-contact
practices, customs and traditions. What would suffice instead was
evidence of post-contact practices, which was "directed at demonstrating which aspects of the aboriginal community and society have
their origins pre-contact" (at para. 62). The same concern, and the
same solution, arises with respect to the proof of occupation in claims
for aboriginal title, although there is a difference in the time for determination of title. Conclusive evidence of pre-sovereignty
occupation may be difficult to come by. Instead, an aboriginal community may provide evidence of present occupation as proof of
pre-sovereignty occupation in support of a claim to aboriginal title.
What is required, in addition, is a *continuity* between present and
pre-sovereignty occupation, because the relevant time for the determination of aboriginal title is at the time before sovereignty.

[153] Needless to say, there is no need to establish "an unbroken
chain of continuity" (*Van der Peet*, at para. 65) between present and
prior occupation. The occupation and use of lands may have been
disrupted for a time, perhaps as a result of the unwillingness of European colonizers to recognize aboriginal title. To impose the
requirement of continuity too strictly would risk "undermining the
very purposes of s. 35(1) by perpetuating the historical injustice suffered by aboriginal peoples at the hands of colonizers who failed to
respect" aboriginal rights to land (*Côté, supra*, at para. 53). In *Mabo*, [14]

[[14] 112 *ILR* 457.]

258] *supra*, the High Court of Australia set down the requirement that there must be "substantial maintenance of the connection" between the people and the land. In my view, this test should be equally applicable to proof of title in Canada.

[154] I should also note that there is a strong possibility that the precise nature of occupation will have changed between the time of sovereignty and the present. I would like to make it clear that the fact that the nature of occupation has changed would not ordinarily preclude a claim for aboriginal title, as long as a substantial connection between the people and the land is maintained. The only limitation on this principle might be the internal limits on uses which land that is subject to aboriginal title may be put, i.e., uses which are inconsistent with continued use by future generations of aboriginals.

At sovereignty, occupation must have been exclusive

[155] Finally, at sovereignty, occupation must have been exclusive. The requirement for exclusivity flows from the definition of aboriginal title itself, because I have defined aboriginal title in terms of the right to *exclusive* use and occupation of land. Exclusivity, as an aspect of aboriginal title, vests in the aboriginal community which holds the ability to exclude others from the lands held pursuant to that title. The proof of title must, in this respect, mirror the content of the right. Were it possible to prove title without demonstrating exclusive occupation, the result would be absurd, because it would be possible for more than one aboriginal nation to have aboriginal title over the same piece of land, and then for all of them to attempt to assert the right to exclusive use and occupation over it.

[156] As with the proof of occupation, proof of exclusivity must rely on both the perspective of the common law and the aboriginal perspective, placing equal weight on each. At common law, a premium is placed on the factual reality of occupation, as encountered by the Europeans. However, as the common law concept of possession must be sensitive to the realities of aboriginal society, so must the concept of exclusivity. Exclusivity is a common law principle derived from the notion of fee simple ownership and should be imported into the concept of aboriginal title with caution. As such, the test required to establish exclusive occupation must take into account the context of the aboriginal society at the time of sovereignty. For example, it is important to note that exclusive occupation can be demonstrated even if other aboriginal groups were present, or frequented

the claimed lands. Under those circumstances, exclusivity would be **[259** demonstrated by "the intention and capacity to retain exclusive control" (McNeil, *Common Law Aboriginal Title, supra,* at p. 204). Thus, an act of trespass, if isolated, would not undermine a general finding of exclusivity, if aboriginal groups intended to and attempted to enforce their exclusive occupation. Moreover, as Professor McNeil suggests, the presence of other aboriginal groups might actually reinforce a finding of exclusivity. For example, "[w]here others were allowed access upon request, the very fact that permission was asked for and given would be further evidence of the group's exclusive control" (at p. 204).

[157] A consideration of the aboriginal perspective may also lead to the conclusion that trespass by other aboriginal groups does not undermine, and that presence of those groups by permission may reinforce, the exclusive occupation of the aboriginal group asserting title. For example, the aboriginal group asserting the claim to aboriginal title may have trespass laws which are proof of exclusive occupation, such that the presence of trespassers does not count as evidence against exclusivity. As well, aboriginal laws under which permission may be granted to other aboriginal groups to use or reside even temporarily on land would reinforce the finding of exclusive occupation. Indeed, if that permission were the subject of treaties between the aboriginal nations in question, those treaties would also form part of the aboriginal perspective.

[158] In their submissions, the appellants pressed the point that requiring proof of exclusive occupation might preclude a finding of joint title, which is shared between two or more aboriginal nations. The possibility of joint title has been recognized by American courts: *United States v. Sante Fe Pacific Railroad Co.,* 314 U.S. 339 (1941). I would suggest that the requirement of exclusive occupancy and the possibility of joint title could be reconciled by recognizing that joint title could arise from shared exclusivity. The meaning of shared exclusivity is well-known to the common law. Exclusive possession is the right to exclude others. Shared exclusive possession is the right to exclude others except those with whom possession is shared. There clearly may be cases in which two aboriginal nations lived on a particular piece of land and recognized each other's entitlement to that land but nobody else's. However, since no claim to joint title has been asserted here, I leave it to another day to work out all the

260] complexities and implications of joint title, as well as any limits that another band's title may have on the way in which one band uses its title lands.

[159] I should also reiterate that if aboriginals can show that they occupied a particular piece of land, but did not do so exclusively, it will always be possible to establish aboriginal rights short of title. These rights will likely be intimately tied to the land and may permit a number of possible uses. However, unlike title, they are not a right to the land itself. Rather, as I have suggested, they are a right to do certain things in connection with that land. If, for example, it were established that the lands near those subject to a title claim were used for hunting by a number of bands, those shared lands would not be subject to a claim for aboriginal title, as they lack the crucial element of exclusivity. However, they may be subject to site-specific aboriginal rights by all of the bands who used it. This does not entitle anyone to the land itself, but it may entitle all of the bands who hunted on the land to hunting rights. Hence, in addition to shared title, it will be possible to have shared, non-exclusive, site-specific rights. In my opinion, this accords with the general principle that the common law should develop to recognize aboriginal rights (and title, when necessary) as they were recognized by either *de facto* practice or by the aboriginal system of governance. It also allows sufficient flexibility to deal with this highly complex and rapidly evolving area of the law.

(f) Infringements of aboriginal title: the test of justification

(i) Introduction

[160] The aboriginal rights recognized and affirmed by s. 35(1), including aboriginal title, are not absolute. Those rights may be infringed, both by the federal (e.g., *Sparrow*) and provincial (e.g., *Côté*) governments. However, s. 35(1) requires that those infringements satisfy the test of justification. In this section, I will review the Court's nascent jurisprudence on justification and explain how that test will apply in the context of infringements of aboriginal title.

(ii) General Principles

[161] The test of justification has two parts, which I shall consider in turn. First, the infringement of the aboriginal right must be in furtherance of a legislative objective that is compelling and substantial. I explained in *Gladstone* that compelling and substantial objectives were those which were directed at either one of the

purposes underlying the recognition and affirmation of aboriginal [261
rights by s. 35(1), which are (at para. 72):

> . . . the recognition of the prior occupation of North America by aboriginal
> peoples or . . . the reconciliation of aboriginal prior occupation with the asser-
> tion of the sovereignty of the Crown.

I noted that the latter purpose will often "be most relevant" (at
para. 72) at the stage of justification. I think it important to repeat
why (at para. 73) that is so:

> Because . . . distinctive aboriginal societies exist within, and are part of, a
> broader social, political and economic community, over which the Crown is
> sovereign, there are circumstances in which, in order to pursue objectives of
> compelling and substantial importance to that community as a whole (taking
> into account the fact that aboriginal societies are part of that community),
> some limitation of those rights will be justifiable. *Aboriginal rights are a nec-*
> *essary part of the reconciliation of aboriginal societies with the broader*
> *political community of which they are part; limits placed on those rights are,*
> *where the objectives furthered by those limits are of sufficient importance to*
> *the broader community as a whole, equally a necessary part of that reconcili-*
> *ation.* [Emphasis added; "equally" emphasized in original.]

The conservation of fisheries, which was accepted as a compelling
and substantial objective in *Sparrow*, furthers both of these purposes,
because it simultaneously recognizes that fishing is integral to many
aboriginal cultures, and also seeks to reconcile aboriginal societies
with the broader community by ensuring that there are fish enough
for all. But legitimate government objectives also include "the pursuit of economic and regional fairness" and "the recognition of the
historical reliance upon, and participation in, the fishery by non-
aboriginal groups" (para. 75). By contrast, measures enacted for relatively unimportant reasons, such as sports fishing without a significant
economic component (*Adams, supra*) would fail this aspect of the
test of justification.

[162] The second part of the test of justification requires an assessment of whether the infringement is consistent with the special
fiduciary relationship between the Crown and aboriginal peoples.
What has become clear is that the requirements of the fiduciary duty
are a function of the "legal and factual context" of each appeal
(*Gladstone, supra*, at para. 56). *Sparrow* and *Gladstone*, for example, interpreted and applied the fiduciary duty in terms of the idea of
priority. The theory underlying that principle is that the fiduciary
relationship between the Crown and aboriginal peoples demands that

262] aboriginal interests be placed first. However, the fiduciary duty does not demand that aboriginal rights always be given priority. As was said in *Sparrow, supra*, at pp. 1114-15:

> The nature of the constitutional protection afforded by s. 35(1) *in this context* demands that there be a link between the question of justification and the allocation of priorities in the fishery. [Emphasis added.]

Other contexts permit, and may even require, that the fiduciary duty be articulated in other ways (at p. 1119):

> Within the analysis of justification, there are further questions to be addressed, depending on the circumstances of the inquiry. These include the questions of whether there has been as little infringement as possible in order to effect the desired result; whether, in a situation of expropriation, fair compensation is available; and, whether the aboriginal group in question has been consulted with respect to the conservation measures being implemented.

Sparrow did not explain when the different articulations of the fiduciary duty should be used. Below, I suggest that the choice between them will in large part be a function of the nature of the aboriginal right at issue.

[163] In addition to variation in the *form* which the fiduciary duty takes, there will also be variation in degree of scrutiny required by the fiduciary duty of the infringing measure or action. The degree of scrutiny is a function of the nature of the aboriginal right at issue. The distinction between *Sparrow* and *Gladstone*, for example, turned on whether the right amounted to the exclusive use of a resource, which in turn was a function of whether the right had an internal limit. In *Sparrow*, the right was internally limited, because it was a right to fish for food, ceremonial and social purposes, and as a result would only amount to an exclusive right to use the fishery in exceptional circumstances. Accordingly, the requirement of priority was applied strictly to mean that (at p. 1116) "any allocation of priorities after valid conservation measures have been implemented must give top priority to Indian food fishing".

[164] In *Gladstone*, by contrast, the right to sell fish commercially was only limited by supply and demand. Had the test for justification been applied in a strict form in *Gladstone*, the aboriginal right would have amounted to an exclusive right exploit the fishery on a commercial basis. This was not the intention of *Sparrow*, and I accordingly modified the test for justification, by altering the idea of priority in the following way (at para. 62):

> . . . the doctrine of priority requires that the government demonstrate that, in **[263**
> allocating the resource, it has taken account of the existence of aboriginal
> rights and allocated the resource in a manner respectful of the fact that those
> rights have priority over the exploitation of the fishery by other users. This
> right is at once both procedural and substantive; at the stage of justification
> the government must demonstrate both that the process by which it allocated
> the resource and the actual allocation of the resource which results from that
> process reflect the prior interest of aboriginal rights holders in the fishery.

After *Gladstone*, in the context of commercial activity, the priority
of aboriginal rights is constitutionally satisfied if the government had
taken those rights into account and has allocated a resource "in a
manner respectful" (at para. 62) of that priority. A court must be satisfied that "the government has taken into account the existence and
importance of [aboriginal] rights" (at para. 63) which it determines
by asking the following questions (at para. 64):

> Questions relevant to the determination of whether the government has granted
> priority to aboriginal rights holders are . . . questions such as whether the
> government has accommodated the exercise of the aboriginal right to partici-
> pate in the fishery (through reduced licence fees, for example), whether the
> government's objectives in enacting a particular regulatory scheme reflect the
> need to take into account the priority of aboriginal rights holders, the extent of
> the participation in the fishery of aboriginal rights holders relative to their
> percentage of the population, how the government has accommodated differ-
> ent aboriginal rights in a particular fishery (food *versus* commercial rights, for
> example), how important the fishery is to the economic and material well-
> being of the band in question, and the criteria taken into account by the
> government in, for example, allocating commercial licences amongst differ-
> ent users.

(iii) Justification and Aboriginal Title

[165] The general principles governing justification laid down in
Sparrow, and embellished by *Gladstone*, operate with respect to infringements of aboriginal title. In the wake of *Gladstone*, the range
of legislative objectives that can justify the infringement of aboriginal title is fairly broad. Most of these objectives can be traced to the
reconciliation of the prior occupation of North America by aboriginal peoples with the assertion of Crown sovereignty, which entails
the recognition that "distinctive aboriginal societies exist within, and
are a part of, a broader social, political and economic community"
(at para. 73). In my opinion, the development of agriculture, forestry,
mining, and hydroelectric power, the general economic development
of the interior of British Columbia, protection of the environment or

264] endangered species, the building of infrastructure and the settlement of foreign populations to support those aims, are the kinds of objectives that are consistent with this purpose and, in principle, can justify the infringement of aboriginal title. Whether a particular measure or government act can be explained by reference to one of those objectives, however, is ultimately a question of fact that will have to be examined on a case-by-case basis.

[166] The manner in which the fiduciary duty operates with respect to the second stage of the justification test — both with respect to the standard of scrutiny and the particular form that the fiduciary duty will take — will be a function of the nature of aboriginal title. Three aspects of aboriginal title are relevant here. First, aboriginal title encompasses the right to *exclusive* use and occupation of land; second, aboriginal title encompasses *the right to choose* to what uses land can be put, subject to the ultimate limit that those uses cannot destroy the ability of the land to sustain future generations of aboriginal peoples; and third, that lands held pursuant to aboriginal title have an inescapable *economic component*.

[167] The exclusive nature of aboriginal title is relevant to the degree of scrutiny of the infringing measure or action. For example, if the Crown's fiduciary duty requires that aboriginal title be given priority, then it is the altered approach to priority that I laid down in *Gladstone* which should apply. What is required is that the government demonstrate (at para. 62) "both that the process by which it allocated the resource and the actual allocation of the resource which results from that process reflect the prior interest" of the holders of aboriginal title in the land. By analogy with *Gladstone*, this might entail, for example, that governments accommodate the participation of aboriginal peoples in the development of the resources of British Columbia, that the conferral of fee simples for agriculture, and of leases and licences for forestry and mining reflect the prior occupation of aboriginal title lands, that economic barriers to aboriginal uses of their lands (e.g., licensing fees) be somewhat reduced. This list is illustrative and not exhaustive. This is an issue that may involve an assessment of the various interests at stake in the resources in question. No doubt, there will be difficulties in determining the precise value of the aboriginal interest in the land and any grants, leases or licences given for its exploitation. These difficult economic considerations obviously cannot be solved here.

[168] Moreover, the other aspects of aboriginal title suggest that **[265**
the fiduciary duty may be articulated in a manner different than the
idea of priority. This point becomes clear from a comparison between
aboriginal title and the aboriginal right to fish for food in *Sparrow*.
First, aboriginal title encompasses within it a right to choose to what
ends a piece of land can be put. The aboriginal right to fish for food,
by contrast, does not contain within it the same discretionary component. This aspect of aboriginal title suggests that the fiduciary
relationship between the Crown and aboriginal peoples may be satisfied by the involvement of aboriginal peoples in decisions taken with
respect to their lands. There is always a duty of consultation. Whether
the aboriginal group has been consulted is relevant to determining
whether the infringement of aboriginal title is justified, in the same
way that the Crown's failure to consult an aboriginal group with respect to the terms by which reserve land is leased may breach its
fiduciary duty at common law: *Guerin*. The nature and scope of the
duty of consultation will vary with the circumstances. In occasional
cases, when the breach is less serious or relatively minor, it will be
no more than a duty to discuss important decisions that will be taken
with respect to lands held pursuant to aboriginal title. Of course, even
in these rare cases when the minimum acceptable standard is consultation, this consultation must be in good faith, and with the intention
of substantially addressing the concerns of the aboriginal peoples
whose lands are at issue. In most cases, it will be significantly deeper
than mere consultation. Some cases may even require the full consent of an aboriginal nation, particularly when provinces enact hunting
and fishing regulations in relation to aboriginal lands.

[169] Second, aboriginal title, unlike the aboriginal right to fish
for food, has an inescapably economic aspect, particularly when one
takes into account the modern uses to which lands held pursuant to
aboriginal title can be put. The economic aspect of aboriginal title
suggests that compensation is relevant to the question of justification
as well, a possibility suggested in *Sparrow* and which I repeated in
Gladstone. Indeed, compensation for breaches of fiduciary duty are
a well-established part of the landscape of aboriginal rights: *Guerin*.
In keeping with the duty of honour and good faith on the Crown, fair
compensation will ordinarily be required when aboriginal title is infringed. The amount of compensation payable will vary with the nature
of the particular aboriginal title affected and with the nature and

266] severity of the infringement and the extent to which aboriginal interests were accommodated. Since the issue of damages was severed from the principal action, we received no submissions on the appropriate legal principles that would be relevant to determining the appropriate level of compensation of infringements of aboriginal title. In the circumstances, it is best that we leave those difficult questions to another day.

D. Has a Claim to Self-Government Been Made Out by the Appellants?

[170] In the courts below, considerable attention was given to the question of whether s. 35(1) can protect a right to self-government, and if so, what the contours of that right are. The errors of fact made by the trial judge, and the resultant need for a new trial, make it impossible for this Court to determine whether the claim to self-government has been made out. Moreover, this is not the right case for the Court to lay down the legal principles to guide future litigation. The parties seem to have acknowledged this point, perhaps implicitly, by giving the arguments on self-government much less weight on appeal. One source of the decreased emphasis on the right to self-government on appeal is this Court's judgment *Pamajewon*. There, I held that rights to self-government, if they existed, cannot be framed in excessively general terms. The appellants did not have the benefit of my judgment at trial. Unsurprisingly, as counsel for the Wet'suwet'en specifically concedes, the appellants advanced the right to self-government in very broad terms, and therefore in a manner not cognizable under s. 35(1).

[171] The broad nature of the claim at trial also led to a failure by the parties to address many of the difficult conceptual issues which surround the recognition of aboriginal self-government. The degree of complexity involved can be gleaned from the *Report of the Royal Commission on Aboriginal Peoples*, which devotes 277 pages to the issue. That report describes different models of self-government, each differing with respect to their conception of territory, citizenship, jurisdiction, internal government organization, etc.. We received little in the way of submissions that would help us to grapple with these difficult and central issues. Without assistance from the parties, it would be imprudent for the Court to step into the breach. In these circumstances, the issue of self-government will fall to be determined at trial.

E. Did the Province Have the Power to Extinguish Aboriginal [26?
   Rights after 1871, either under Its Own Jurisdiction or through
   the Operation of s. 88 of the Indian Act?

(1) Introduction

[172] For aboriginal rights to be recognized and affirmed by s.
35(1), they must have existed in 1982. Rights which were extinguished
by the sovereign before that time are not revived by the provision. In
a federal system such as Canada's, the need to determine whether
aboriginal rights have been extinguished raises the question of which
level of government has jurisdiction to do so. In the context of this
appeal, that general question becomes three specific ones. First, there
is the question whether the province of British Columbia, from the
time it joined Confederation in 1871, until the entrenchment of s.
35(1) in 1982, had the jurisdiction to extinguish the rights of aboriginal peoples, including aboriginal title, in that province. Second, if
the province was without such jurisdiction, another question arises —
whether provincial laws which were not in pith and substance aimed
at the extinguishment of aboriginal rights could have done so nevertheless if they were laws of general application. The third and final
question is whether a provincial law, which could otherwise not extinguish aboriginal rights, be given that effect through referential
incorporation by s. 88 of the *Indian Act*.

(2) Primary Jurisdiction

[173] Since 1871, the exclusive power to legislate in relation to
"Indians, and Lands reserved for Indians" has been vested with the
federal government by virtue of s. 91(24) of the *Constitution Act,
1867*. That head of jurisdiction, in my opinion, encompasses within
it the exclusive power to extinguish aboriginal rights, including aboriginal title.

"Lands reserved for the Indians"

[174] I consider the second part of this provision first, which confers jurisdiction to the federal government over "Lands reserved for
the Indians". The debate between the parties centred on whether that
part of s. 91(24) confers jurisdiction to legislate with respect to aboriginal title. The province's principal submission is that "Lands
reserved for the Indians" are lands which have been specifically set
aside or designated for Indian occupation, such as reserves. However, I must reject that submission, because it flies in the face of the

268] judgment of the Privy Council in *St. Catherine's Milling*. One of the issues in that appeal was the federal jurisdiction to accept the surrender of lands held pursuant to aboriginal title. It was argued that the federal government, at most, had jurisdiction over "Indian Reserves". Lord Watson, speaking for the Privy Council, rejected this argument, stating that had the intention been to restrict s. 91(24) in this way, specific language to this effect would have been used. He accordingly held that (at p. 59):

> ... the words actually used are, according to their natural meaning, sufficient to include all lands reserved, upon any terms or conditions, for Indian occupation.

Lord Watson's reference to "all lands" encompasses not only reserve lands, but lands held pursuant to aboriginal title as well. Section 91(24), in other words, carries with it the jurisdiction to legislate in relation to aboriginal title. It follows, by implication, that it also confers the jurisdiction to extinguish that title.

[175] The province responds by pointing to the fact that underlying title to lands held pursuant to aboriginal title vested with the provincial Crown pursuant to s. 109 of the *Constitution Act, 1867*. In its submission, this right of ownership carried with it the right to grant fee simples which, by implication, extinguish aboriginal title, and so by negative implication excludes aboriginal title from the scope of s. 91(24). The difficulty with the province's submission is that it fails to take account of the language of s. 109, which states in part that:

> 109. All Lands, Mines, Minerals and Royalties belonging to the several Provinces of Canada ... at the Union ... shall belong to the several Provinces ... subject to any Trusts existing in respect thereof, and to any Interest other than that of the Province in the same.

Although that provision vests underlying title in provincial Crowns, it qualifies provincial ownership by making it subject to the "any Interest other than that of the Province in the same". In *St. Catherine's Milling*, the Privy Council held that aboriginal title was such an interest, and rejected the argument that provincial ownership operated as a limit on federal jurisdiction. The net effect of that decision, therefore, was to separate the ownership of lands held pursuant to aboriginal title from jurisdiction over those lands. Thus, although on surrender of aboriginal title the province would take absolute title, jurisdiction to accept surrenders lies with the federal government. The same can [26? be said of extinguishment — although on extinguishment of aboriginal title, the province would take complete title to the land, the jurisdiction to extinguish lies with the federal government.

[176] I conclude with two remarks. First, even if the point were not settled, I would have come to same conclusion. The judges in the court below noted that separating federal jurisdiction over Indians from jurisdiction over their lands would have a most unfortunate result — the government vested with primary constitutional responsibility for securing the welfare of Canada's aboriginal peoples would find itself unable to safeguard one of the most central of native interests — their interest in their lands. Second, although the submissions of the parties and my analysis have focussed on the question of jurisdiction over aboriginal title, in my opinion, the same reasoning applies to jurisdiction over any aboriginal right which relates to land. As I explained earlier, *Adams* clearly establishes that aboriginal rights may be tied to land but nevertheless fall short of title. Those relationships with the land, however, may be equally fundamental to aboriginal peoples and, for the same reason that jurisdiction over aboriginal title must vest with the federal government, so too must the power to legislate in relation to other aboriginal rights in relation to land.

"Indians"

[177] The extent of federal jurisdiction over Indians has not been definitively addressed by this Court. We have not needed to do so because the *vires* of federal legislation with respect to Indians, under the division of powers, has never been at issue. The cases which have come before the Court under s. 91(24) have implicated the question of jurisdiction over Indians from the other direction — whether provincial laws which on their face apply to Indians intrude on federal jurisdiction and are inapplicable to Indians to the extent of that intrusion. As I explain below, the Court has held that s. 91(24) protects a "core" of Indianness from provincial intrusion, through the doctrine of interjurisdictional immunity.

[178] It follows, at the very least, that this core falls within the scope of federal jurisdiction over Indians. That core, for reasons I will develop, encompasses aboriginal rights, including the rights that

270] are recognized and affirmed by s. 35(1). Laws which purport to extinguish those rights therefore touch the core of Indianness which lies at the heart of s. 91(24), and are beyond the legislative competence of the provinces to enact. The core of Indianness encompasses the whole range of aboriginal rights that are protected by s. 35(1). Those rights include rights in relation to land; that part of the core derives from s. 91(24)'s reference to "Lands reserved for the Indians". But those rights also encompass practices, customs and traditions which are not tied to land as well; that part of the core can be traced to federal jurisdiction over "Indians". Provincial governments are prevented from legislating in relation to both types of aboriginal rights.

(3) Provincial Laws of General Application

[179] The vesting of exclusive jurisdiction with the federal government over Indians and Indian lands under s. 91(24), operates to preclude provincial laws in relation to those matters. Thus, provincial laws which single out Indians for special treatment are *ultra vires*, because they are in relation to Indians and therefore invade federal jurisdiction: see *R. v. Sutherland*, [1980] 2 S.C.R. 451, 113 D.L.R. (3d) 374. However, it is a well established principle that (*Four B Manufacturing Ltd., supra*, at p. 1048):

> The conferring upon Parliament of exclusive legislative competence to make laws relating to certain classes of persons does not mean that the totality of these persons' rights and duties comes under primary federal competence to the exclusion of provincial laws of general application.

In other words, notwithstanding s. 91(24), provincial laws of general application apply *proprio vigore* to Indians and Indian lands. Thus, this Court has held that provincial labour relations legislation (*Four B*) and motor vehicle laws (*R. v. Francis*, [1988] 1 S.C.R. 1025, 51 D.L.R. (4th) 418), which purport to apply to all persons in the province, also apply to Indians living on reserves.

[180] What must be answered, however, is whether the same principle allows provincial laws of general application to extinguish aboriginal rights. I have come to the conclusion that a provincial law of general application could not have this effect, for two reasons. First, a law of general application cannot, by definition, meet the standard which has been set by this Court for the extinguishment of aboriginal rights without being *ultra vires* the province. That standard was laid down in *Sparrow, supra*, at p. 1099, as one of "clear and

plain" intent. In that decision, the Court drew a distinction between [27]
laws which extinguished aboriginal rights, and those which merely
regulated them. Although the latter types of laws may have been "necessarily inconsistent" with the continued exercise of aboriginal rights,
they could not extinguish those rights. While the requirement of clear
and plain intent does not, perhaps, require that the Crown "use language which refers expressly to its extinguishment of aboriginal
rights" (*Gladstone, supra*, at para. 34), the standard is still quite high.
My concern is that the only laws with the sufficiently clear and plain
intention to extinguish aboriginal rights would be laws in relation to
Indians and Indian lands. As a result, a provincial law could never,
proprio vigore, extinguish aboriginal rights, because the intention to
do so would take the law outside provincial jurisdiction.

[181] Second, as I mentioned earlier, s. 91(24) protects a core of
federal jurisdiction even from provincial laws of general application,
through the operation of the doctrine of interjurisdictional immunity.
That core has been described as matters touching on "Indianness" or
the "core of Indianness" (*Dick, supra*, at pp. 326 and 315; also see
Four B, supra, at p. 1047 and *Francis, supra*, at pp. 1028-29). The
core of Indianness at the heart of s. 91(24) has been defined in both
negative and positive terms. Negatively, it has been held to not include labour relations (*Four B*) and the driving of motor vehicles
(*Francis*). The only positive formulation of Indianness was offered
in *Dick*. Speaking for the Court, Beetz J. assumed, but did not decide, that a provincial hunting law did not apply *proprio vigore* to the
members of an Indian band to hunt and because those activities were
"at the centre of what they do and who they are" (*supra*, at p. 320).
But in *Van der Peet*, I described and defined the aboriginal rights that
are recognized and affirmed by s. 35(1) in a similar fashion, as protecting the occupation of land and the activities which are integral to
the distinctive aboriginal culture of the group claiming the right. It
follows that aboriginal rights are part of the core of Indianness at the
heart of s. 91(24). Prior to 1982, as a result, they could not be extinguished by provincial laws of general application.

(4) Section 88 of the Indian Act

[182] Provincial laws which would otherwise not apply to Indians
proprio vigore, however, are allowed to do so by s. 88 of the *Indian
Act*, which incorporates by reference provincial laws of general

272] application: *Dick, supra,* at pp. 326-27; *Derrickson v. Derrickson,* [1986] 1 S.C.R. 285 at p. 297, 26 D.L.R. (4th) 175; *Francis, supra,* at pp. 1030-31. However, it is important to note, in Professor Hogg's words, that s. 88 does not "invigorate" provincial laws which are invalid because they are in relation to Indians and Indian lands (*Constitutional Law of Canada,* 3rd ed. (Scarborough, Ont.: Carswell, 1992), at p. 676; also see *Dick, supra,* at p. 322). What this means is that s. 88 extends the effect of provincial laws of general application which cannot apply to Indians and Indian lands because they touch on the Indianness at the core of s. 91(24). For example, a provincial law which regulated hunting may very well touch on this core. Although such a law would not apply to aboriginal people *proprio vigore,* it would still apply through s. 88 of the *Indian Act,* being a law of general application. Such laws are enacted to conserve game and for the safety of all.

[183] The respondent B.C. Crown argues that since such laws are *intra vires* the province, and applicable to aboriginal persons, s. 88 could allow provincial laws to extinguish aboriginal rights. I reject this submission, for the simple reason that s. 88 does not evince the requisite clear and plain intent to extinguish aboriginal rights. The provision states in full:

> 88. Subject to the terms of any treaty and any other Act of Parliament, all laws of general application from time to time in force in any province are applicable to and in respect of Indians in the province, except to the extent that those laws are inconsistent with this Act or any order, rule, regulation, or by-law made thereunder, and except to the extent that those laws make provision for any matter for which provision is made by or under this Act.

I see nothing in the language of the provision which even suggests the intention to extinguish aboriginal rights. Indeed, the explicit reference to treaty rights in s. 88 suggests that the provision was clearly not intended to undermine aboriginal rights.

VI. CONCLUSION AND DISPOSITION

[184] For the reasons I have given above, I would allow the appeal in part, and dismiss the cross-appeal. Reluctantly, I would also order a new trial.

[185] I conclude with two observations. The first is that many aboriginal nations with territorial claims that overlap with those of the appellants did not intervene in this appeal, and do not appear to have

done so at trial. This is unfortunate, because determinations of abo- [273
riginal title for the Gitksan and Wet'suwet'en will undoubtedly affect
their claims as well. This is particularly so because aboriginal title
encompasses an *exclusive* right to the use and occupation of land,
i.e., to the *exclusion* of both non-aboriginals and members of other
aboriginal nations. It may, therefore, be advisable if those aboriginal
nations intervened in any new litigation.

[186] Finally, this litigation has been both long and expensive, not
only in economic but in human terms as well. By ordering a new
trial, I do not necessarily encourage the parties to proceed to litigation and to settle their dispute through the courts. As was said in
Sparrow, at p. 1105, s. 35(1) "provides a solid constitutional base
upon which subsequent negotiations can take place". Those negotiations should also include other aboriginal nations which have a stake
in the territory claimed. Moreover, the Crown is under a moral, if not
a legal, duty to enter into and conduct those negotiations in good
faith. Ultimately, it is through negotiated settlements, with good faith
and give and take on all sides, reinforced by the judgments of this
Court, that we will achieve what I stated in *Van der Peet, supra*, at
para. 31, to be a basic purpose of s. 35(1) — "the reconciliation of
the pre-existence of aboriginal societies with the sovereignty of the
Crown".'Let us face it, we are all here to stay.

SCHEDULE 1
Appellants

DELGAMUUKW, also known as Earl Muldoe, suing on his own behalf and on behalf
of all the members of the Houses of Delgamuukw and Haaxw

GISDAY WA, also known as Alfred Joseph, suing on his own behalf and on behalf of
all the members of the House of Gisday Wa

NII KYAP, also known as Gerald Gunanoot, suing on his own behalf and on behalf
of all the members of the House of Nii Kyap

LELT, also known as Lloyd Ryan, suing on his own behalf and on behalf of all the
members of the Houses of Lelt and Haak'w

ANTGULILBIX, also known as Mary Johnson, suing on her own behalf and on behalf
of all the members of the House of Antgulilbix

TENIMGYET, also known as Arthur Matthews, Jr., suing on his own behalf and on
behalf of all the members of the House of Tenimgyet

GOOHLAHT, also known as Lucy Namox, suing on her own behalf and on behalf of
all of the members of the Houses of Goohlaht and Samooh

KLIIYEM LAX HAA, also known as Eva Sampson, suing on her own behalf and on
behalf of all the members of the Houses of Kliiyem Lax Haa and Wii'mugulsxw

GWIS GYEN, also known as Stanley Williams, suing on his own behalf and on behalf
of all the members of the House of Gwis Gyen

274] Kweese, also known as Florence Hall, suing on her own behalf and on behalf of all the members of the House of Kweese

Djogaslee, also known as Walter Wilson, suing on his own behalf and on behalf of all the members of the House of Djogaslee

Gwagl'lo, also known as Ernest Hyzims, suing on his own behalf and on behalf of all the members of the Houses of Gwagl'lo and Duubisxw

Gyolugyet, also known as Mary McKenzie, suing on her own behalf and on behalf of all the members of the House of Gyolugyet

Gyetm Galdoo, also known as Sylvester Green, suing on his own behalf and on behalf of all the members of the Houses of Gyetm Galdoo and Wii'Goob'l

Haak Asxw, also known as Larry Wright, suing on his own behalf and on behalf of all the members of the House of Haak Asxw

Geel, also known as Walter Harris, suing on his own behalf and on behalf of all the members of the House of Geel

Haalus, also known as Billy Morrison, suing on his own behalf and on behalf of all the members of the House of Haalus

Wii Hlengwax, also known as Herbert Burke, suing on his own behalf and on behalf of all the members of the House of Wii Hlengwax

Luutkudziiwus, also known as Ben McKenzie, Sr., suing on his own behalf and on behalf of all the members of the House of Luutkudziiwus

Ma'uus, also known as Jeffrey Harris, Jr., suing on his own behalf and on behalf of all the members of the House of Ma'uus

Miluu Lak, also known as Alice Jeffery, suing on her own behalf and on behalf of all the members of the Houses of Miluu Lak and Haiwas

Nika Teen, also known as James Woods, suing on his own behalf and on behalf of all the members of the House of Nika Teen

Skiik'm Lax Ha, also known as John Wilson, suing on his own behalf and on behalf of all the members of the House of Skiik'm Lax Ha

Wii Minosik, also known as Robert Stevens, suing on his own behalf and on behalf of all the members of the House of Wii Minosik

Gwinin Nitxw, also known as Solomon Jack, suing on his own behalf and on behalf of all the members of the House of Gwinin Nitxw

Gwoimt, also known as Kathleen Wale, suing on her own behalf and on behalf of all the members of the Houses of Gwoimt and Tsabux

Luus, also known as Jeffrey Harris, suing on his own behalf and on behalf of all the members of the House of Luus

Niist, also known as David Blackwater, suing on his own behalf and on behalf of all the members of the Houses of Niist and Baskyelaxha

Spookw, also known as Steven Robinson, suing on his own behalf and on behalf of all the members of the Houses of Spookw and Yagosip

Wii Gaak, also known as Neil Sterritt, Sr., suing on his own behalf and on behalf of all the members of the House of Wii Gaak

Dawamuxw, also known as Charlie Clifford, suing on his own behalf and on behalf of all the members of the House of Dawamuxw

Gitludahl, also known as Peter Muldoe, suing on his own behalf and on behalf of all the members of the Houses of Gitludahl and Wiigyet

GUXSAN, also known as Herbert Wesley, suing on his own behalf and on behalf of [275 all the members of the House of Guxsan

HANAMUXW, also known as Joan Ryan, suing on her own behalf and on behalf of all the members of the House of Hanamuxw

YAL, also known as George Turner, suing on his own behalf and on behalf of all the members of the House of Yal

GWIIYEEHL, also known as Chris Skulsh, suing on his own behalf and on behalf of all the members of the House of Gwiiyeehl

SAKXUM HIGOOKX, also known as Vernon Smith, suing on his own behalf and on behalf of all the members of the House of Sakxum Higookx

MA DEEK, also known as James Brown, suing on his own behalf and on behalf of all the members of the House of Ma Deek

WOOS, also known as Roy Morris, suing on his own behalf and on behalf of all the members of the House of Woos

KNEDEBEAS, also known as Sarah Layton, suing on her own behalf and on behalf of all the members of the House of Knedebeas

SMOGELGEM, also known as Leonard George, suing on his own behalf and on behalf of all the members of the House of Smogelgem

KLO UM KHUN, also known as Patrick Pierre, suing on his own behalf and on behalf of all the members of the House of Klo Um Khun

HAG WIL NEGH, also known as Ron Mitchell, suing on his own behalf and on behalf of all the members of the House of Hag Wil Negh

WAH TAH KEG'HT, also known as Henry Alfred, suing on his own behalf and on behalf of all the members of the House of Wah Tah Keg'ht

WAH TAH KWETS, also known as John Namox, suing on his own behalf and on behalf of all the members of the House of Wah Tah Kwets

WOOSIMLAXHA, also known as Victor Mowatt, suing on his own behalf and on behalf of all the members of the House of Gutginuxw

XSGOGIMLAXHA, also known as Vernon Milton, suing on his own behalf and on behalf of all the members of the House of Xsgogimlaxha

WIIGYET, also known as Roy Wesley, suing on his own behalf and on behalf of all the members of the House of Wiigyet

WII ELAAST, also known as Jim Angus, Jr., suing on his own behalf and on behalf of all the members of the Houses of Wii Elaast and Amagyet

GAXSBGABAXS, also known as Gertie Watson, suing on her own behalf and on behalf of all the members of the House of Gaxsbgabaxs

WIGETIMSCHOL, also known as Dan Michell, suing on his own behalf and on behalf of all the members of the House of Namox

SCHEDULE 2

Those Intervening with the Musqueam Nation

Delbert Guerin
Gail Y. Sparrow
Jim Kew
Larry Grant
Leona M. Sparrow

276] Mary Charles
Myrtle McKay
Nolan Charles
Susan A. Point
Chief George Guerin

SCHEDULE 3

Those Intervening with the B.C. Cattlemen's Association

B.C. Chamber of Commerce
B.C. Wildlife Federation
Business Council of British Columbia
Council of Tourist Associations
Fisheries Council of British Columbia
Guideoutfitters Association of British Columbia
Mining Association of British Columbia
Pacific Fishermen's Defence Alliance

[187] LA FOREST J. (L'HEUREUX-DUBÉ J. concurring):—I have read the reasons of the Chief Justice, and while I agree with his conclusion, I disagree with various aspects of his reasons and in particular, with the methodology he uses to prove that aboriginal peoples have a general right of occupation of certain lands (often referred to as "aboriginal title").

[188] I begin by considering why a new trial is necessary in this case. It is true, as the Chief Justice points out, that the amalgamation of the appellants' individual claims represents a defect in the pleadings and, technically speaking, this prevents us from considering the merits of the case. However, in my view, there is a more substantive problem with the pleadings in this case. Before this Court, the appellants sought a declaration of "aboriginal title" but attempted, in essence, to prove that they had complete control over the territory in question. The appellants effectively argued on appeal, as they did at trial, that by virtue of their social and land tenure systems—consisting of Chief authority, Houses, feasts, crests, and totem poles—they acquired an absolute interest in the claimed territory, including ownership of and jurisdiction over the land. The problem with this approach is that it requires proof of governance and control as opposed to proof of general occupation of the affected land. Only the latter is the *sine qua non* of "aboriginal title". It follows that what the appellants sought by way of declaration from this Court and what they set out to prove by way of the evidence were two different matters. In light of this substantive defect in the pleadings, a new trial

should be ordered to permit a reassessment of the matter on the basis **[277** of these reasons.

[189] In my view, the foundation of "aboriginal title" was succinctly described by Judson J. in *Calder v. Attorney General of British Columbia*, [1973] 1 S.C.R. 313, 34 D.L.R. (3d) 145, where, at [15] p. 328, he stated: "the fact is that when the settlers came, the Indians were there, organized in societies and occupying the land as their forefathers had done for centuries. This is what Indian title means. . . ." Relying in part on Judson J.'s remarks, Dickson J. (as he then was) wrote in *Guerin v. The Queen*, [1984] 2 S.C.R. 335 at p. 382, 13 D.L.R. (4th) 321, that aboriginal peoples have a "legal right to occupy and possess certain lands, the ultimate title to which is in the Crown". As well, in *Canadian Pacific Ltd. v. Paul*, [1988] 2 S.C.R. 654, 53 D.L.R. (4th) 487, this Court stated, at p. 678: "The inescapable conclusion from the Court's analysis of Indian title up to this point is that the Indian interest in land is truly *sui generis*. It is more than the right to enjoyment and occupancy although . . . it is difficult to describe what more in traditional property law terminology." More recently, Judson J.'s views were reiterated in *R. v. Van der Peet*, [1996] 2 S.C.R. 507, 137 D.L.R. (4th) 289. There Lamer C.J. wrote for the majority, at para. 30, that the doctrine of aboriginal rights (one aspect of which is "aboriginal title") arises from "one simple fact: when Europeans arrived in North America, aboriginal peoples *were already here*, living in communities on the land, and participating in distinctive cultures, as they had done for centuries" (emphasis in original).

[190] It follows from these cases that the aboriginal right of possession is derived from the historic occupation and use of ancestral lands by aboriginal peoples. Put another way, "aboriginal title" is based on the continued occupation and use of the land as part of the aboriginal peoples' traditional way of life. This *sui generis* interest is not equated with fee simple ownership; nor can it be described with reference to traditional property law concepts. The best description of "aboriginal title", as set out above, is a broad and general one derived from Judson J.'s pronouncements in *Calder, supra*. Adopting the same approach, Dickson J. wrote in *Guerin, supra*, that the aboriginal right of occupancy is further characterized by two principal features. First, this *sui generis* interest in the land is personal in

[[15] 73 *ILR* 56.]

278] that it is generally inalienable except to the Crown. Second, in dealing with this interest, the Crown is subject to a fiduciary obligation to treat aboriginal peoples fairly. Dickson J. went on to conclude, at p. 382, that "[a]ny description of Indian title which goes beyond these two features is both unnecessary and potentially misleading". I share his views and am therefore reluctant to define more precisely the "right [of aboriginal peoples] to live on their lands as their fore-fathers had lived"; see *Calder, supra*, at p. 328.

[191] The approach I adopt, in defining the aboriginal right of occupancy, is also a highly contextual one. More specifically, I find it necessary to make a distinction between: (1) the recognition of a general right to occupy and possess ancestral lands; and (2) the rec-ognition of a discrete right to engage in an aboriginal activity in a particular area. I defined the latter in *R. v. Côté*, [1996] 3 S.C.R. 139, 138 D.L.R. (4th) 385, at para. 97, as "the traditional use, by a tribe of Indians, that has continued from pre-contact times of a particular area for a particular purpose". The issue in *Côté*, as in *Van der Peet*, was whether the use of a particular fishing spot was really an aspect of the aboriginal peoples' way of life in pre-contact times; see also in the *Van der Peet* trilogy *R. v. Gladstone*, [1996] 2 S.C.R. 723, 137 D.L.R. (4th) 648, and *R. v. N.T.C. Smokehouse Ltd.*, [1996] 2 S.C.R. 672, 137 D.L.R. (4th) 528. In all those cases, the fishing rights as-serted by the aboriginal claimants were not associated with a more general occupancy of the affected land. By contrast, the present case deals with a general claim to occupy and possess vast tracts of terri-tory (58,000 square kilometres). This type of generalized land claim is not merely a bundle of discrete aboriginal rights to engage in spe-cific activities. Rather, it is, as the Chief Justice states, at para. 111, "the right to use the land for a variety of activities, not all of which need be aspects of practices, customs and traditions which are inte-gral to the distinctive cultures of aboriginal societies". These land-based activities are, of course, related to the aboriginal soci-ety's habits and mode of life.

[192] I note, as well, that in defining the nature of "aboriginal title", one should generally not be concerned with statutory provi-sions and regulations dealing with reserve lands. In *Guerin, supra*, this Court held that the interest of an Indian band in a reserve is de-rived from, and is of the same nature as, the interest of an aboriginal

society in its traditional tribal lands. Accordingly, the Court treated **[279**
the aboriginal interest in reserve lands as one of occupation and possession while recognizing that the underlying title to those lands was
in the Crown. It was not decided in *Guerin, supra,* and it by no means
follows, that specific statutory provisions governing reserve lands
should automatically apply to traditional tribal lands. For this reason, I am unable to assume that specific "reserve" provisions of the
Indian Act, R.S.C. 1985, c. I-5, and the *Indian Oil and Gas Act,* R.S.C.
1985, c. I-7, apply to huge tracts of land which are subject to an
aboriginal right of occupancy.

[193] I turn next to this Court's decision in *Van der Peet, supra,*
where the Chief Justice identified a number of factors essential to the
recognition of aboriginal rights under s. 35(1) of the *Constitution
Act, 1982.* As I have already indicated, the *Van der Peet* trilogy dealt
with activity-based discrete rights and, more specifically, with fishing activities that were carried out in the face of statutory prohibitions.
By contrast, the present case deals with a generalized claim over vast
tracts of territory, a claim which is itself the foundation for particular
rights and activities. Moreover, I agree with the appellants that this
generalized claim should not be defined as merely a compendium of
aboriginal rights, each of which must meet the test set out in *Van der
Peet, supra.* Nonetheless, I am of the view that the "key" factors
identified in *Van der Peet,* namely precision, specificity, continuity,
and centrality are still met by my approach in the present case.

[194] First, it is clear that the nature of an aboriginal claim must
be identified *precisely* with regard to particular practices, customs
and traditions. As already mentioned, when dealing with a claim of
"aboriginal title", the court will focus on the occupation and use of
the land as part of the aboriginal society's *traditional way of life.* In
pragmatic terms, this means looking at the manner in which the society used the land *to live,* namely to establish villages, to work, to get
to work, to hunt, to travel to hunting grounds, to fish, to get to fishing
pools, to conduct religious rites, etc. These uses, although limited to
the aboriginal society's traditional way of life, may be exercised in a
contemporary manner; see *R. v. Sparrow,* [1990] 1 S.C.R. 1075 at
p. 1099, 70 D.L.R. (4th) 385.

[195] Second, it is self-evident that an aboriginal society asserting
the right to live on its ancestral lands must *specify* the area which

280] has been continuously used and occupied. That is, the general boundaries of the occupied territory should be identified. I recognize, however, that when dealing with vast tracts of territory it may be impossible to identify geographical limits with scientific precision. Nonetheless, this should not preclude the recognition of a general right of occupation of the affected land. Rather, the drawing of exact territorial limits can be settled by subsequent negotiations between the aboriginal claimants and the government.

[196] Some would also argue that specificity requires *exclusive* occupation and use of the land by the aboriginal group in question. The way I see it, exclusivity means that an aboriginal group must show that a claimed territory is indeed its ancestral territory and not the territory of an unconnected aboriginal society. On the other hand, I recognize the possibility that two or more aboriginal groups may have occupied the same territory and used the land communally as part of their traditional way of life. In cases where two or more groups have accommodated each other in this way, I would not preclude a finding of joint occupancy. The result may be different, however, in cases where one dominant aboriginal group has merely permitted other groups to use the territory or where definite boundaries were established and maintained between two aboriginal groups in the same territory.

[197] Third, as indicated above, the aboriginal right of possession is based on the *continued* occupation and use of traditional tribal lands. The Chief Justice concludes that the relevant time period for the establishment of "aboriginal title" is the time at which the Crown asserted sovereignty over the affected land. I agree that in the context of generalized land claims, it is more appropriate, from a practical and theoretical standpoint, to consider the time of sovereignty as opposed to the time of first contact between an aboriginal society and Europeans. However, I am also of the view that the date of sovereignty may not be the only relevant moment to consider. For instance, there may have been aboriginal settlements in one area of the province but, after the assertion of sovereignty, the aboriginal peoples may have all moved to another area where they remained from the date of sovereignty until the present. This relocation may have been due to natural causes, such as the flooding of villages, or

to clashes with European settlers. In these circumstances, I would **[281**
not deny the existence of "aboriginal title" in that area merely
because the relocation occurred post-sovereignty. In other words, continuity may still exist where the present occupation of one area is
connected to the pre-sovereignty occupation of another area.

[198] Also, on the view I take of continuity, I agree with the Chief
Justice that it is not necessary for courts to have conclusive evidence
of pre-sovereignty occupation. Rather, aboriginal peoples claiming a
right of possession may provide evidence of present occupation as
proof of prior occupation. Further, I agree that there is no need to
establish an unbroken chain of continuity and that interruptions in
occupancy or use do not necessarily preclude a finding of "title". I
would go further, however, and suggest that the presence of two or
more aboriginal groups in a territory may also have an impact on
continuity of use. For instance, one aboriginal group may have ceded
its possession to subsequent occupants or merged its territory with
that of another aboriginal society. As well, the occupancy of one aboriginal society may be connected to the occupancy of another society
by conquest or exchange. In these circumstances, continuity of use
and occupation, extending back to the relevant time, may very well
be established; see Brian Slattery, "Understanding Aboriginal Rights"
(1987), 66 Can. Bar Rev. 727 at p. 759.

[199] Fourth, if aboriginal peoples continue to occupy and use the
land as part of their traditional way of life, it necessarily follows that
the land is of *central significance* to them. As already suggested,
aboriginal occupancy refers not only to the presence of aboriginal
peoples in villages or permanently settled areas. Rather, the use of
adjacent lands and even remote territories to pursue a traditional mode
of life is also related to the notion of occupancy. Viewed in this light,
occupancy is part of aboriginal culture in a broad sense and is, therefore, absorbed in the notion of distinctiveness. To use the language
of *Van der Peet*, proof of occupancy is proof of centrality.

[200] I would also add that my approach regarding the nature of
aboriginal occupancy is supported by the terms of the *Royal Proclamation, 1763*, R.S.C. 1985, App. II, No. 1. Although the Proclamation
is not the sole source of "aboriginal title" in this country, it bears
witness to the British policy towards aboriginal peoples which was

282] based on respect for their right to occupy their ancestral lands; see *R. v. Sparrow, supra*, at p. 1103. Specifically, the Proclamation provides:

> And We do further declare it to be Our Royal Will and Pleasure, for the present as aforesaid, to reserve under our Sovereignty, Protection, and Dominion, for the use of the said Indians, all the Lands and Territories not included within the Limits of Our said Three new Governments, or within the Limits of the Territory granted to the Hudson's Bay Company, as also all the Lands and Territories lying to the Westward of the Sources of the Rivers which fall into the Sea from the West and North West as aforesaid.

In clear terms vast tracts of territory (including large portions of the area now comprising Ontario, Quebec, and the prairie provinces) were reserved for aboriginal peoples. These huge tracts of land were by no means limited to villages or permanent settlements but were reserved more generally as "Hunting Grounds" and "for the use of the said Indians". Aboriginal peoples had the right to possess the lands reserved for them and "not be molested or disturbed in the Possession" of such territory. In essence, the rights set out in the Proclamation—which were applied in principle to aboriginal peoples across the country—underlie the view I have taken of aboriginal occupancy; see *R. v. Wesley*, [1932] 4 D.L.R. 774 (Alta. S.C., App. Div.) at p. 787, and *R. v. Sikyea* (1964), 43 D.L.R. (2d) 150 (N.W.T.C.A.), affirmed *Sikyea v. The Queen*, [1964] S.C.R. 642, 50 D.L.R. (2d) 80.

[201] The analysis thus far has focussed on the nature of the aboriginal right to occupy and possess certain lands—a right recognized and affirmed under s. 35(1) of the *Constitution Act, 1982*. Nonetheless, as Dickson C.J. and I wrote in *Sparrow, supra*, at p. 1109: "Rights that are recognized and affirmed are not absolute." Thus, government regulation can infringe upon aboriginal rights if it meets the test of justification under s. 35(1). It is important to emphasize as well that the approach adopted under s. 35(1) is a highly contextual one. This is also clear from the reasons I wrote jointly with Dickson C.J. in *Sparrow, supra*, at p. 1111:

> We wish to emphasize the importance of context and a case-by-case approach to s. 35(1). Given the generality of the text of the constitutional provision, and especially in light of the complexities of aboriginal history, society and rights, the contours of a justificatory standard must be defined in the specific context of each case.

[202] In the context of the present case, I agree with the Chief Justice that the general economic development of the interior of

British Columbia, through agriculture, mining, forestry, and hydro- [28:
electric power, as well as the related building of infrastructure and
settlement of foreign populations are valid legislative objectives that,
in principle, satisfy the first part of the justification analysis.

[203] Under the second part of the justification test, these legislative objectives are subject to accommodation of the aboriginal peoples'
interests. This accommodation must always be in accordance with
the honour and good faith of the Crown. Moreover, when dealing
with a generalized claim over vast tracts of land, accommodation is
not a simple matter of asking whether licences have been fairly allocated in one industry, or whether conservation measures have been
properly implemented for a specific resource. Rather, the question of
accommodation of "aboriginal title" is much broader than this. Certainly, one aspect of accommodation in this context entails notifying
and consulting aboriginal peoples with respect to the development of
the affected territory. Another aspect of accommodation is fair compensation. More specifically, in a situation of expropriation, one asks
whether fair compensation is available to the aboriginal peoples; see
Sparrow, *supra*, at p. 1119. Indeed, the treatment of "aboriginal title"
as a compensable right can be traced back to the *Royal Proclamation, 1763*. The relevant portions of the Proclamation are as follows:

> . . . such Parts of Our Dominions and Territories as, *not having been ceded to
> or purchased by Us, are reserved to them* [aboriginal peoples] or any of them,
> as their Hunting Grounds. . . .

> We do, with the Advice of our Privy Council strictly enjoin and require,
> that *no private Person do presume to make any purchase from the said Indians
> of any Lands* reserved to the said Indians . . . but that, *if at any Time any of the
> Said Indians should be inclined to dispose of the said Lands, the same shall be
> Purchased only for Us*, in Our Name. . . . [Emphasis added.]

Clearly, the Proclamation contemplated that aboriginal peoples would
be compensated for the surrender of their lands; see also Slattery,
supra, at pp. 751-52. It must be emphasized, nonetheless, that fair
compensation in the present context is not equated with the price of a
fee simple. Rather, compensation must be viewed in terms of the
right and in keeping with the honour of the Crown. Thus, generally
speaking, compensation may be greater where the expropriation relates to a village area as opposed to a remotely visited area. I add that
account must be taken of the interdependence of traditional uses to
which the land was put.

284]   [204] In summary, in developing vast tracts of land, the government is expected to consider the economic well being of *all* Canadians. But the aboriginal peoples must not be forgotten in this equation. Their legal right to occupy and possess certain lands, as confirmed by s. 35(1) of the *Constitution Act, 1982*, mandates basic fairness commensurate with the honour and good faith of the Crown.

[205] With regard to the issue of self-government, I conclude, as does the Chief Justice, that there was insufficient evidence before this Court to make any determination regarding this aspect of the appellants' claim.

[206] As for the issue raised on the cross-appeal, I agree with the Chief Justice's conclusion. The respondent province had no authority to extinguish aboriginal rights either under the *Constitution Act, 1867* or by virtue of s. 88 of the *Indian Act*.

[207] On a final note, I wish to emphasize that the best approach in these types of cases is a process of negotiation and reconciliation that properly considers the complex and competing interests at stake. This point was made by Lambert J.A. in the Court of Appeal, [1993] 5 W.W.R. 97 at pp. 379-80, 104 D.L.R. (4th) 470:

> So, in the end, *the legal rights of the Indian people will have to be accommodated within our total society by political compromises and accommodations based in the first instance on negotiation and agreement and ultimately in accordance with the sovereign will of the community as a whole.* The legal rights of the Gitksan and Wet'suwet'en peoples, to which this law suit is confined, and which allow no room for any approach other than the application of the law itself, and the legal rights of all aboriginal peoples throughout British Columbia, form only one factor in the ultimate determination of what kind of community we are going to have in British Columbia and throughout Canada in the years ahead. [Emphasis added.]

(See also *Report of the Royal Commission on Aboriginal Peoples*, vol. 2, Part 2 (1996) at pp. 561-62.)

[208] Accordingly, I would allow the appeal in part and order a new trial on the basis of the principles set out in these reasons. I would also dismiss the cross-appeal.

[209] McLACHLIN J.:—I concur with the Chief Justice. I add that I am also in substantial agreement with the comments of Justice La Forest.

Appeal allowed in part; cross-appeal dismissed.

[Report: (1998) 153 DLR (4th) 193]

**Human rights — Self-determination — Scope and extent —
Right to self-determination in the context of an existing
State—Whether part of the population of an existing State
capable of constituting a "people" for the purpose of the
right of self-determination — Internal and external self-
determination—Whether international law recognizes a
right of unilateral secession for part of the population of an
existing State—Quebec—Whether population of Quebec or
part thereof a "people"—Whether population of Quebec
enjoying internal self-determination — Declaration of
Principles of Friendly Relations between States 1970**

**Recognition — Of States — Of right of people to self-
determination — Recognition as condonation of unlawful
act—Whether likelihood of recognition of breakaway State
means that there is a right to create such a State**

**Relationship of international law and municipal law—In
general—Whether Supreme Court of Canada entitled to
answer question regarding application of international
law—International law as part of the law of Canada—Right
of self-determination under Canadian law and international
law**

**States — Creation and dissolution — Self-determination of
groups within State — Whether conferring a right of
unilateral secession — Relationship between right of self-
determination and respect for territorial integrity of State
—The law of Canada**

RE REFERENCE BY THE GOVERNOR IN COUNCIL CONCERNING CERTAIN
QUESTIONS RELATING TO THE SECESSION OF QUEBEC FROM CANADA[1]

[1] The following counsel appeared in the case:
For the Attorney-General of Canada: L. Yves Fortier QC, Pierre Bienvenu, Warren J. Newman, Jean-Marc Aubry QC, and Mary Dawson QC.
For the *amicus curiae*: André Joli-Coeur, Michel Paradis, Louis Masson, André Binette, Clément Samson, Martin Bédard and Martin St-Amant.
For the Attorney-General of Manitoba (intervener): Donna J. Miller QC, and Deborah L. Carlson.
For the Attorney-General of Saskatchewan (intervener): Graeme G. Mitchell and John D. Whyte QC.
For the Minister of Justice of the Northwest Territories (intervener): Bernard W. Funston.
For the Minister of Justice of the Yukon Territory (intervener): Stuart J. Whitley QC and Howard L. Kushner.
For Kitigan Zibi Anishinabeg (intervener): Agnès Laporte and Richard Gaudreau.
For the Grand Council of the Crees (Eeyou Estchee) (intervener): Claude-Armand Sheppard, Paul Joffe and Andrew Orkin.
For Makivik Corporation (intervener): Peter W. Hutchins and Carol Hilling.
For the Chiefs of Ontario (interveners): Michael Sherry.

Canada, Supreme Court.   20 August 1998

(Lamer CJC; L'Heureux-Dubé, Gonthier, Cory, McLachlin, Iacobucci, Major, Bastarache and Binnie JJ)

SUMMARY: *The facts*:—The Governor in Council of Canada referred to the Supreme Court of Canada three questions regarding the possible secession of Quebec, one of the Canadian provinces, from Canada.[2] The three questions were:

(1) Under the Constitution of Canada, can the National Assembly, Legislature or Government of Quebec effect the secession of Quebec from Canada unilaterally?

(2) Does international law give the National Assembly, Legislature or Government of Quebec the right to effect the secession of Quebec from Canada unilaterally? In this regard, is there a right to self-determination under international law that would give the National Assembly, Legislature or Government of Quebec the right to effect the secession of Quebec from Canada unilaterally?

(3) In the event of a conflict between domestic and international law on the right of the National Assembly, Legislature or Government of Quebec to effect the secession of Quebec from Canada unilaterally, which would take precedence?

The Government of Quebec did not take part in the proceedings before the Court. The Court appointed an *amicus curiae* to represent the interests of Quebec. The *amicus* took a preliminary objection to the jurisdiction of the Court, *inter alia* on the ground that the questions posed were hypothetical and that Question 2 raised an abstract question of pure international law which it was beyond the competence of the Court to answer.

Held:—*The Jurisdiction of the Court*

The Court had jurisdiction to answer the questions posed and it was appropriate for the Court to exercise that jurisdiction in the present case.

(1) The Supreme Court Act, Section 53, which made provision for the reference by the Governor in Council of questions on which the Court's opinion was sought, was consistent with the Constitution Act. The questions posed fell within the scope of Section 53 (pp. 540-4).

For the Minority Advocacy and Rights Council (intervener): Raj Anand and M. Kate Stephenson.

For the *Ad Hoc* Committee of Canadian Women on the Constitution (intervener): Mary Eberts and Anne Bayefsky.

For Guy Bertrand (intervener): Guy Bertrand and Patrick Monahan.

For Roopnarine Singh, Keith Owen Henderson, Claude Leclerc, Kenneth O'Donnell and Van Hoven Petteway (interveners): Stephen A. Scott.

Vincent Pouliot (intervener) appeared in person.

[2] The reference was made under the Supreme Court Act 1985, Section 53(1), which gave the Governor in Council the power to refer to the Supreme Court important questions of law and fact concerning the interpretation of the Constitution Acts and the powers of the Federal and provincial governments and parliaments, irrespective of whether the particular power in question has been, or is proposed to be, exercised.

(2) In answering Question 2, the Court would not be purporting to act as an international tribunal; its answer would not bind any other State or any international tribunal which might subsequently consider this, or a similar, question. The fact that Question 2 raised an issue of international law did not preclude the Court from answering the question. The Court could look to international law in order to determine the rights or obligations of an actor within the Canadian legal system. In the present case, the question posed was not one of "pure" international law but sought to determine the legal rights and obligations of institutions within the Canadian legal system (pp. 545-6).

(3) The questions raised were justiciable (pp. 546-9).

Question 1
Under the Constitution, the secession of a province was not something which could be achieved unilaterally but only on the basis of negotiation between that province, the Federal Government and the other provinces.

(1) Even where the population of a province voted for independence by a clear majority, it was necessary to take account of other principles of the Canadian Constitution, in particular federalism, the rule of law, the protection of minorities and the operation of democracy in the other provinces and in Canada as a whole. It followed that the Constitution did not give Quebec a unilateral right of secession. To hold otherwise would be to allow a unilateral act by one province to alter governance in a manner which was not compatible with the Constitution (pp. 549-70).

(2) Nevertheless, the democratic principle on which the Constitution was based meant that a clear majority for secession in Quebec would require the other provinces and the Federal Government to enter into negotiations on the basis of good faith, in order to attempt to reconcile the rights and obligations of two legitimate majorities, namely that in Quebec and that in Canada as a whole (pp. 570-5).

(3) It was for the political authorities to determine what constituted a sufficiently clear majority and to settle the political process of negotiation. The Court would have no role with regard to the political aspects of constitutional negotiations (pp. 575-8).

Question 2
Neither the population of Quebec nor the provincial institutions possessed a right of unilateral secession under international law. International law did not grant a specific right to secede, nor did it specifically prohibit secession.

(1) The right of a people to self-determination was now firmly established as a right under international law (pp. 580-2).

(2) It was clear that a "people" might include only a portion of the population of an existing State. Nevertheless, while much of the population of Quebec shared many of the characteristics of a "people", such as a common language and culture, it was not necessary in the present case to determine whether or not the population of Quebec constituted a "people" within the meaning of international law (p. 583).

(3) The right to self-determination was normally fulfilled through internal self-determination, the pursuit of a people's political, economic, social and

cultural development within the framework of an existing State. A right to external self-determination, which might take the form of the assertion of a right to unilateral secession, arose only in the most extreme cases and only under carefully defined circumstances. Accordingly, there was no necessary incompatibility between the maintenance of the territorial integrity of existing States and the right of a people to self-determination. A State whose government represented the whole of the people or peoples resident within its territory, on a basis of equality and without discrimination, and which respected the principles of self-determination in its internal arrangements, was entitled to the protection under international law of its territorial integrity (pp. 584-5).

(4) The right to external self-determination clearly existed in the case of a colonial people and of a people which was subject to alien subjugation, domination or exploitation. It was possible that such a right also existed where the ability of a people to exercise its right of internal self-determination was totally frustrated, although it was not clear that this proposition reflected an existing international law standard. Even if it did, however, the situation in Canada was entirely different. Canada was a sovereign and independent State conducting itself in compliance with the principle of equal rights and self-determination of peoples and thus possessed of a government representing the whole people of the territory without distinction. The population of Quebec enjoyed extensive autonomy and members of that population were prominent in all aspects of Canadian national life (pp. 585-8).

(5) The fact that a unilateral secession by Quebec might be followed by the recognition of the newly proclaimed State by other States did not mean that there was a right of secession in international law (pp. 589-91).

Question 3
Since there was no conflict between international law and Canadian law, it was unnecessary to answer Question 3 (p. 591).

The following is the text of the judgment of the Court:

393] I. INTRODUCTION

[1] This Reference requires us to consider momentous questions that go to the heart of our system of constitutional government. The observation we made more than a decade ago in *Reference re Manitoba Language Rights*, [1985] 1 S.C.R. 721, 19 D.L.R. (4th) 1 (*Manitoba Language Rights Reference*), at p. 728, applies with equal force here: as in that case, the present one "combines legal and constitutional questions of the utmost subtlety and complexity with

political questions of great sensitivity". In our view, it is not poss- [394
ible to answer the questions that have been put to us without a consideration of a number of underlying principles. An exploration of
the meaning and nature of these underlying principles is not merely
of academic interest. On the contrary, such an exploration is of
immense practical utility. Only once those underlying principles
have been examined and delineated may a considered response to
the questions we are required to answer emerge.

[2] The questions posed by the Governor in Council by way of
Order in Council P.C. 1996-1497, dated September 30, 1996, read
as follows:

1.   Under the Constitution of Canada, can the National Assembly, legislature
      or government of Quebec effect the secession of Quebec from Canada
      unilaterally?

2.   Does international law give the National Assembly, legislature or gov-
      ernment of Quebec the right to effect the secession of Quebec from
      Canada unilaterally? In this regard, is there a right to self-determination
      under international law that would give the National Assembly, legisla-
      ture or government of Quebec the right to effect the secession of Quebec
      from Canada unilaterally?

3.   In the event of a conflict between domestic and international law on the
      right of the National Assembly, legislature or government of Quebec to
      effect the secession of Quebec from Canada unilaterally, which would
      take precedence in Canada?

[3] Before turning to Question 1, as a preliminary matter, it is
necessary to deal with the issues raised with regard to this Court's
reference jurisdiction.

II. THE PRELIMINARY OBJECTIONS TO THE COURT'S REFERENCE
    JURISDICTION

[4] The *amicus curiae* argued that s. 101 of the *Constitution Act,
1867* does not give Parliament the authority to grant this Court the
jurisdiction provided for in s. 53 of the *Supreme Court Act*, R.S.C.,
1985, c. S-26. Alternatively, it is submitted that even if Parliament
were entitled to enact s. 53 of the *Supreme Court Act*, the scope of
that section should be interpreted to exclude the kinds of questions
the Governor in Council has submitted in this Reference. In particular, it is contended that this Court cannot answer Question 2, since
it is a question of "pure" international law over which this Court has
no jurisdiction. Finally, even if this Court's reference jurisdiction is
constitutionally valid, and even if the questions are within the

395] purview of s. 53 of the *Supreme Court Act*, it is argued that the three questions referred to the Court are speculative, of a political nature, and, in any event, are not ripe for judicial decision, and therefore are not justiciable.

[5] Notwithstanding certain formal objections by the Attorney General of Canada, it is our view that the *amicus curiae* was within his rights to make the preliminary objections, and that we should deal with them.

A. *The Constitutional Validity of Section 53 of the Supreme Court Act*

[6] In *Re References by Governor-General in Council* (1910), 43 S.C.R. 536, affirmed on appeal to the Privy Council, [1912] A.C. 571, 3 D.L.R. 509 (*sub nom. Attorney-General for Ontario v. Attorney-General for Canada*), the constitutionality of this Court's special jurisdiction was twice upheld. The Court is asked to revisit these decisions. In light of the significant changes in the role of this Court since 1912, and the very important issues raised in this Reference, it is appropriate to reconsider briefly the constitutional validity of the Court's reference jurisdiction.

[7] Section 3 of the *Supreme Court Act* establishes this Court both as a "general court of appeal" for Canada and as an "additional court for the better administration of the laws of Canada". These two roles reflect the two heads of power enumerated in s. 101 of the *Constitution Act, 1867*. However, the "laws of Canada" referred to in s. 101 consist only of *federal* law and statute: see *Quebec North Shore Paper Co. v. Canadian Pacific Ltd.*, [1977] 2 S.C.R. 1054 at pp. 1065-66, 71 D.L.R. (3d) 111. As a result, the phrase "additional courts" contained in s. 101 is an insufficient basis upon which to ground the special jurisdiction established in s. 53 of the *Supreme Court Act*, which clearly exceeds a consideration of federal law alone (see, *e.g.*, s. 53(2)). Section 53 must therefore be taken as enacted pursuant to Parliament's power to create a "general court of appeal" for Canada.

[8] Section 53 of the *Supreme Court Act* is *intra vires* Parliament's power under s. 101 if, in "pith and substance", it is legislation in relation to the constitution or organization of a "general court of appeal". Section 53 is defined by two leading characteristics — it establishes an original jurisdiction in this Court and imposes a duty on the Court to render advisory opinions.

Section 53 is therefore constitutionally valid only if (1) a "general [39 $\mathbb{C}$
court of appeal" may properly exercise an original jurisdiction; and
(2) a "general court of appeal" may properly undertake other legal
functions, such as the rendering of advisory opinions.

(1) May a Court of Appeal Exercise an Original Jurisdiction?

[9] The words "general court of appeal" in s. 101 denote the status of the Court within the national court structure and should not be
taken as a restrictive definition of the Court's functions. In most
instances, this Court acts as the exclusive ultimate appellate court in
the country, and, as such, is properly constituted as the "general
court of appeal" for Canada. Moreover, it is clear that an appellate
court can receive, on an exceptional basis, original jurisdiction not
incompatible with its appellate jurisdiction.

[10] The English Court of Appeal, the U.S. Supreme Court and
certain courts of appeal in Canada exercise an original jurisdiction
in addition to their appellate functions. See *De Demko v. Home
Secretary*, [1959] A.C. 654 (H.L.), at p. 660; *Re Forest and
Registrar of Court of Appeal of Manitoba* (1977), 77 D.L.R. (3d)
445 (Man. C.A.), at p. 453; U.S. Constitution, art. III, § 2. Although
these courts are not constituted under a head of power similar to
s. 101, they certainly provide examples which suggest that there is
nothing inherently self-contradictory about an appellate court exercising original jurisdiction on an exceptional basis.

[11] It is also argued that this Court's original jurisdiction is
unconstitutional because it conflicts with the original jurisdiction of
the provincial superior courts and usurps the normal appellate process. However, Parliament's power to establish a general court of
appeal pursuant to s. 101 is plenary, and takes priority over the
province's power to control the administration of justice in
s. 92(14). See *Attorney-General for Ontario v. Attorney-General for
Canada*, [1947] A.C. 127, [1947] 1 D.L.R. 801 (P.C.). Thus, even if
it could be said that there is any conflict between this Court's reference jurisdiction and the original jurisdiction of the provincial
superior courts, any such conflict must be resolved in favour of
Parliament's exercise of its plenary power to establish a "general
court of appeal" provided, as discussed below, advisory functions
are not to be considered inconsistent with the functions of a general
court of appeal.

397]   *(2) May a Court of Appeal Undertake Advisory Functions?*

[12] The *amicus curiae* submits that:

> [TRANSLATION] Either this constitutional power [to give the highest court in the federation jurisdiction to give advisory opinions] is expressly provided for by the Constitution, as is the case in India (*Constitution of India*, art. 143), *or it is not provided for therein and so it simply does not exist.* This is what the Supreme Court of the United States has held. [Emphasis added.]

[13] However, the U.S. Supreme Court did not conclude that it was unable to render advisory opinions because no such *express power* was included in the U.S. Constitution. Quite the contrary, it based this conclusion on the *express limitation* in art. III, § 2, restricting federal court jurisdiction to actual "cases" or "controversies". See, *e.g.*, *Muskrat v. United States*, 219 U.S. 346 (1911), at p. 362. This section reflects the strict separation of powers in the American federal constitutional arrangement. Where the "case or controversy" limitation is missing from their respective state constitutions, some American state courts *do* undertake advisory functions (*e.g.*, in at least two states — Alabama and Delaware — advisory opinions are authorized, in certain circumstances, by statute: see Ala. Code 1975 § 12-2-10; Del. Code Ann. tit. 10, § 141 (1996 Supp.)).

[14] In addition, the judicial systems in several European countries (such as Germany, France, Italy, Spain, Portugal and Belgium) include courts dedicated to the review of constitutional claims; these tribunals do not require a concrete dispute involving individual rights to examine the constitutionality of a new law — an "abstract or objective question" is sufficient. See L. Favoreu, "American and European Models of Constitutional Justice", in D. S. Clark, ed., *Comparative and Private International Law: Essays in Honor of John Henry Merryman on His Seventieth Birthday* (1990), 105, at p. 113. The European Court of Justice, the European Court of Human Rights, and the Inter-American Court of Human Rights also all enjoy explicit grants of jurisdiction to render advisory opinions. See *Treaty establishing the European Community*, Art. 228(6); Protocol No. 2 of the *Convention for the Protection of Human Rights and Fundamental Freedoms*, Europ. T.S. No. 5, p. 36; *Statute of the Inter-American Court of Human Rights*, Art. 2. There is no plausible basis on which to conclude that a court is, by its nature, inherently precluded from undertaking another legal function in tandem with its judicial duties.

[15] Moreover, the Canadian Constitution does not insist on a [39£
strict separation of powers. Parliament and the provincial legislatures may properly confer other legal functions on the courts, and
may confer certain judicial functions on bodies that are not courts.
The exception to this rule relates only to s. 96 courts. Thus, even
though the rendering of advisory opinions is quite clearly done outside the framework of adversarial litigation, and such opinions are
traditionally obtained by the executive from the law officers of the
Crown, there is no constitutional bar to this Court's receipt of jurisdiction to undertake such an advisory role. The legislative grant of
reference jurisdiction found in s. 53 of the *Supreme Court Act* is
therefore constitutionally valid.

B. The Court's Jurisdiction Under Section 53

[16] Section 53 provides in its relevant parts as follows:

> 53(1) The Governor in Council may refer to the Court for hearing and con-
> sideration important questions of law or fact concerning
>
>> (a) the interpretation of the *Constitution Acts*;
>>
>>   . . . . .
>>
>> (d) the powers of the Parliament of Canada, or of the legislatures of the
>> provinces, or of the respective governments thereof, whether or not
>> the particular power in question has been or is proposed to be exer-
>> cised.
>
> (2) The Governor in Council may refer to the Court for hearing and con-
> sideration important questions of law or fact concerning any matter, whether
> or not in the opinion of the Court *ejusdem generis* with the enumerations con-
> tained in subsection (1), with reference to which the Governor in Council sees
> fit to submit any such question.
>
> (3) Any question concerning any of the matters mentioned in subsections
> (1) and (2), and referred to the Court by the Governor in Council, shall be con-
> clusively deemed to be an important question.

[17] It is argued that even if Parliament were entitled to enact
s. 53 of the *Supreme Court Act*, the questions submitted by the
Governor in Council fall outside the scope of that section.

[18] This submission cannot be accepted. Question 1 is directed,
at least in part, to the interpretation of the *Constitution Acts*, which
are referred to in s. 53(1)(a). Both Question 1 and Question 2 fall
within s. 53(1)(d), since they relate to the powers of the legislature
or government of a Canadian province. Finally, all three questions
are clearly "important questions of law or fact concerning any matter" so that they must come within s. 53(2).

399]   [19] However, the *amicus curiae* has also raised some specific
concerns regarding this Court's jurisdiction to answer Question 2.
The question, on its face, falls within the scope of s. 53, but the concern is a more general one with respect to the jurisdiction of this
Court, as a domestic tribunal, to answer what is described as a question of "pure" international law.

[20] The first contention is that in answering Question 2, the
Court would be exceeding its jurisdiction by purporting to act as an
international tribunal. The simple answer to this submission is that
this Court would not, in providing an advisory opinion in the context of a reference, be purporting to "act as" or substitute itself for
an international tribunal. In accordance with well-accepted principles of international law, this Court's answer to Question 2 would
not purport to bind any other state or international tribunal that
might subsequently consider a similar question. The Court nevertheless has jurisdiction to provide an advisory opinion to the
Governor in Council in its capacity as a national court on legal questions touching and concerning the future of the Canadian federation.

[21] Second, there is a concern that Question 2 is beyond the
competence of this Court, as a domestic court, because it requires
the Court to look at international law rather than domestic law.

[22] This concern is groundless. In a number of previous cases, it
has been necessary for this Court to look to international law to
determine the rights or obligations of some actor within the
Canadian legal system. For example, in *Reference re Powers to
Levy Rates on Foreign Legations and High Commissioners'
Residences*, [1943] S.C.R. 208, [1943] 2 D.L.R. 481, the Court was
required to determine whether, taking into account the principles of
international law with respect to diplomatic immunity, a municipal
council had the power to levy rates on certain properties owned by
foreign governments. In two subsequent references, this Court used
international law to determine whether the federal government or a
province possessed proprietary rights in certain portions of the territorial sea and continental shelf (*Reference re Ownership of
[3] Offshore Mineral Rights of British Columbia*, [1967] S.C.R. 792, 65
D.L.R. (2d) 353; *Reference re Newfoundland Continental Shelf*,
[1984] 1 S.C.R. 86, 5 D.L.R. (4th) 385 *sub nom. Reference re:
Seabed and Subsoil of the Continental Shelf Offshore
Newfoundland*).[4]

[3] 43 *ILR* 93.]   [4] 86 *ILR* 593.]

[23] More importantly, Question 2 of this Reference does not ask **[400** an abstract question of "pure" international law but seeks to determine the legal rights and obligations of the National Assembly, legislature or government of Quebec, institutions that clearly exist as part of the Canadian legal order. As will be seen, the *amicus curiae* himself submitted that the success of any initiative on the part of Quebec to secede from the Canadian federation would be governed by international law. In these circumstances, a consideration of international law in the context of this Reference about the legal aspects of the unilateral secession of Quebec is not only permissible but unavoidable.

C. *Justiciability*

[24] It is submitted that even if the Court has jurisdiction over the questions referred, the questions themselves are not justiciable. Three main arguments are raised in this regard:

(1) the questions are not justiciable because they are too "theoretical" or speculative;

(2) the questions are not justiciable because they are political in nature;

(3) the questions are not yet ripe for judicial consideration.

[25] In the context of a reference, the Court, rather than acting in its traditional adjudicative function, is acting in an advisory capacity. The very fact that the Court may be asked hypothetical questions in a reference, such as the constitutionality of proposed legislation, engages the Court in an exercise it would never entertain in the context of litigation. No matter how closely the procedure on a reference may mirror the litigation process, a reference does not engage the Court in a disposition of rights. For the same reason, the Court may deal on a reference with issues that might otherwise be considered not yet "ripe" for decision.

[26] Though a reference differs from the Court's usual adjudicative function, the Court should not, even in the context of a reference, entertain questions that would be inappropriate to answer. However, given the very different nature of a reference, the question of the appropriateness of answering a question should not focus on whether the dispute is formally adversarial or whether it disposes of cognizable rights. Rather, it should consider whether the dispute is appropriately addressed by a court of law. As we stated in *Reference*

401] *re Canada Assistance Plan (B.C.)*, [1991] 2 S.C.R. 525 at p. 545, 83 D.L.R. (4th) 297:

> While there may be many reasons why a question is non-justiciable, in this appeal the Attorney General of Canada submitted that to answer the questions would draw the Court into a political controversy and involve it in the legislative process. In exercising its discretion whether to determine a matter that is alleged to be non-justiciable, *the Court's primary concern is to retain its proper role within the constitutional framework of our democratic form of government* . . . In considering its appropriate role the Court must determine whether the question is purely political in nature and should, therefore, be determined in another forum *or whether it has a sufficient legal component to warrant the intervention of the judicial branch.* [Emphasis added.]

Thus the circumstances in which the Court may decline to answer a reference question on the basis of "non-justiciability" include:

(i) if to do so would take the Court beyond its own assessment of its proper role in the constitutional framework of our democratic form of government or

(ii) if the Court could not give an answer that lies within its area of expertise: the interpretation of law.

[27] As to the "proper role" of the Court, it is important to underline, contrary to the submission of the *amicus curiae*, that the questions posed in this Reference do not ask the Court to usurp any democratic decision that the people of Quebec may be called upon to make. The questions posed by the Governor in Council, as we interpret them, are strictly limited to aspects of the legal framework in which that democratic decision is to be taken. The attempted analogy to the U.S. "political questions" doctrine therefore has no application. The legal framework having been clarified, it will be for the population of Quebec, acting through the political process, to decide whether or not to pursue secession. As will be seen, the legal framework involves the rights and obligations of Canadians who live outside the province of Quebec, as well as those who live within Quebec.

[28] As to the "legal" nature of the questions posed, if the Court is of the opinion that it is being asked a question with a significant extralegal component, it may interpret the question so as to answer only its legal aspects; if this is not possible, the Court may decline to answer the question. In the present Reference the questions may clearly be interpreted as directed to legal issues and, so interpreted, the Court is in a position to answer them.

[29] Finally, we turn to the proposition that even though the ques-   [402
tions referred to us are justiciable in the "reference" sense, the Court
must still determine whether it should exercise its discretion to
refuse to answer the questions on a pragmatic basis.

[30] Generally, the instances in which the Court has exercised its
discretion to refuse to answer a reference question that is otherwise
justiciable can be broadly divided into two categories. First, where
the question is too imprecise or ambiguous to permit a complete or
accurate answer: see, *e.g., McEvoy v. New Brunswick (Attorney
General)*, [1983] 1 S.C.R. 704, 148 D.L.R. (3d) 25; *Reference re
Waters and Water-Powers*, [1929] S.C.R. 200, [1929] 2 D.L.R. 481;
Reference re Goods and Services Tax, [1992] 2 S.C.R. 445, 94
D.L.R. (4th) 51; *Reference re Remuneration of Judges of the
Provincial Court of Prince Edward Island*, [1997] 3 S.C.R. 3, 150
D.L.R. (4th) 577 *sub nom. Reference re: Provincial Court Act and
Public Sector Pay Reduction Act (P.E.I.), s. 10 (Provincial Judges
Reference)*, at para. 256. Second, where the parties have not pro-
vided sufficient information to allow the Court to provide a
complete or accurate answer: see, *e.g., Hirsch v. Protestant Board of
School Commissioners of Montreal*, [1926] S.C.R. 246, [1926] 2
D.L.R. 8 *(Reference re Education System in Montreal)*; *Reference re
Authority of Parliament in Relation to the Upper House*, [1980] 1
S.C.R. 54, 102 D.L.R. (3d) 1 *sub nom. Reference re: Legislative
Authority of Parliament to Alter or Replace the Senate (Senate
Reference)*; *Provincial Judges Reference*, at para. 257.

[31] There is no doubt that the questions posed in this Reference
raise difficult issues and are susceptible to varying interpretations.
However, rather than refuse to answer at all, the Court is guided by
the approach advocated by the majority on the "conventions" issue
in *Reference re Resolution to Amend the Constitution*, [1981] 1
S.C.R. 753, 125 D.L.R. (3d) 1 *(Patriation Reference)*, at pp. 875-76:

> If the questions are thought to be ambiguous, this Court should not, in a
> constitutional reference, be in a worse position than that of a witness in a trial
> and feel compelled simply to answer yes or no. Should it find that a question
> might be misleading, or should it simply wish to avoid the risk of misunder-
> standing, the Court is free either to interpret the question . . . or it may qualify
> both the question and the answer . . .

The Reference questions raise issues of fundamental public importance. It cannot be said that the questions are too imprecise or
ambiguous to permit a proper legal answer. Nor can it be said that

[403] the Court has been provided with insufficient information regarding the present context in which the questions arise. Thus, the Court is duty bound in the circumstances to provide its answers.

III. Reference Questions

A. *Question 1*

> Under the Constitution of Canada, can the National Assembly, legislature or government of Quebec effect the secession of Quebec from Canada unilaterally?

(1) Introduction

[32] As we confirmed in *Reference re Objection by Quebec to a Resolution to Amend the Constitution*, [1982] 2 S.C.R. 793 at p. 806, 140 D.L.R. (3d) 385 *sub nom. Quebec (Attorney General) v. Canada (Attorney General)*, "The *Constitution Act, 1982* is now in force. Its legality is neither challenged nor assailable." The "Constitution of Canada" certainly includes the constitutional texts enumerated in s. 52(2) of the *Constitution Act, 1982*. Although these texts have a primary place in determining constitutional rules, they are not exhaustive. The Constitution also "embraces unwritten, as well as written rules", as we recently observed in the *Provincial Judges Reference, supra*, at para. 92. Finally, as was said in the *Patriation Reference, supra*, at p. 874, the Constitution of Canada includes

> the global system of rules and principles which govern the exercise of constitutional authority in the whole and in every part of the Canadian state.

These supporting principles and rules, which include constitutional conventions and the workings of Parliament, are a necessary part of our Constitution because problems or situations may arise which are not expressly dealt with by the text of the Constitution. In order to endure over time, a constitution must contain a comprehensive set of rules and principles which are capable of providing an exhaustive legal framework for our system of government. Such principles and rules emerge from an understanding of the constitutional text itself, the historical context, and previous judicial interpretations of constitutional meaning. In our view, there are four fundamental and organizing principles of the Constitution which are relevant to addressing the question before us (although this enumeration is by no means exhaustive): federalism; democracy; constitutionalism and the rule of law; and respect for minorities. The foundation and substance of these principles are addressed in the following

paragraphs. We will then turn to their specific application to the first [404]
reference question before us.

(2) Historical Context: The Significance of Confederation

[33] In our constitutional tradition, legality and legitimacy are
linked. The precise nature of this link will be discussed below.
However, at this stage, we wish to emphasize only that our constitutional history demonstrates that our governing institutions have
adapted and changed to reflect changing social and political values.
This has generally been accomplished by methods that have ensured
continuity, stability and legal order.

[34] Because this Reference deals with questions fundamental to
the nature of Canada, it should not be surprising that it is necessary
to review the context in which the Canadian union has evolved. To
this end, we will briefly describe the legal evolution of the
Constitution and the foundational principles governing constitutional amendments. Our purpose is not to be exhaustive, but to
highlight the features most relevant in the context of this Reference.

[35] Confederation was an initiative of elected representatives of
the people then living in the colonies scattered across part of what
is now Canada. It was not initiated by Imperial *fiat*. In March 1864,
a select committee of the Legislative Assembly of the Province of
Canada, chaired by George Brown, began to explore prospects for
constitutional reform. The committee's report, released in June
1864, recommended that a federal union encompassing Canada East
and Canada West, and perhaps the other British North American
colonies, be pursued. A group of Reformers from Canada West, led
by Brown, joined with Etienne P. Taché and John A. Macdonald in
a coalition government for the purpose of engaging in constitutional
reform along the lines of the federal model proposed by the committee's report.

[36] An opening to pursue federal union soon arose. The leaders
of the maritime colonies had planned to meet at Charlottetown in
the fall to discuss the perennial topic of maritime union. The
Province of Canada secured invitations to send a Canadian delegation. On September 1, 1864, 23 delegates (five from New
Brunswick, five from Nova Scotia, five from Prince Edward Island,
and eight from the Province of Canada) met in Charlottetown. After
five days of discussion, the delegates reached agreement on a plan
for federal union.

[405]   [37] The salient aspects of the agreement may be briefly outlined. There was to be a federal union featuring a bicameral central legislature. Representation in the Lower House was to be based on population, whereas in the Upper House it was to be based on regional equality, the regions comprising Canada East, Canada West and the Maritimes. The significance of the adoption of a federal form of government cannot be exaggerated. Without it, neither the agreement of the delegates from Canada East nor that of the delegates from the maritime colonies could have been obtained.

[38] Several matters remained to be resolved, and so the Charlottetown delegates agreed to meet again at Quebec in October, and to invite Newfoundland to send a delegation to join them. The Quebec Conference began on October 10, 1864. Thirty-three delegates (two from Newfoundland, seven from New Brunswick, five from Nova Scotia, seven from Prince Edward Island, and twelve from the Province of Canada) met over a two and a half week period. Precise consideration of each aspect of the federal structure preoccupied the political agenda. The delegates approved 72 resolutions, addressing almost all of what subsequently made its way into the final text of the *Constitution Act, 1867*. These included guarantees to protect French language and culture, both directly (by making French an official language in Quebec and Canada as a whole) and indirectly (by allocating jurisdiction over education and "Property and Civil Rights in the Province" to the provinces). The protection of minorities was thus reaffirmed.

[39] Legally, there remained only the requirement to have the Quebec Resolutions put into proper form and passed by the Imperial Parliament in London. However, politically, it was thought that more was required. Indeed, Resolution 70 provided that "The Sanction of the Imperial and *Local Parliaments* shall be sought for the Union of the Provinces on the principles adopted by the Conference". (Cited in J. Pope, ed., *Confederation: Being a Series of Hitherto Unpublished Documents Bearing on the British North America Act* (1895), at p. 52 (emphasis added).)

[40] Confirmation of the Quebec Resolutions was achieved more smoothly in central Canada than in the Maritimes. In February and March 1865, the Quebec Resolutions were the subject of almost six weeks of sustained debate in both houses of the Canadian legislature. The Canadian Legislative Assembly approved the Quebec

Resolutions in March 1865 with the support of a majority of mem- [406
bers from both Canada East and Canada West. The governments of
both Prince Edward Island and Newfoundland chose, in accordance
with popular sentiment in both colonies, not to accede to the Quebec
Resolutions. In New Brunswick, a general election was required
before Premier Tilley's pro-Confederation party prevailed. In Nova
Scotia, Premier Tupper ultimately obtained a resolution from the
House of Assembly favouring Confederation.

[41] Sixteen delegates (five from New Brunswick, five from
Nova Scotia, and six from the Province of Canada) met in London
in December 1866, to finalize the plan for Confederation. To this
end, they agreed to some slight modifications and additions to the
Quebec Resolutions. Minor changes were made to the distribution
of powers, provision was made for the appointment of extra sena-
tors in the event of a deadlock between the House of Commons and
the Senate, and certain religious minorities were given the right to
appeal to the federal government where their denominational school
rights were adversely affected by provincial legislation. The British
North America Bill was drafted after the London Conference with
the assistance of the Colonial Office, and was introduced into the
House of Lords in February 1867. The Act passed third reading in
the House of Commons on March 8, received royal assent on March
29, and was proclaimed on July 1, 1867. The Dominion of Canada
thus became a reality.

[42] There was an early attempt at secession. In the first
Dominion election in September 1867, Premier Tupper's forces
were decimated: members opposed to Confederation won 18 of
Nova Scotia's 19 federal seats, and in the simultaneous provincial
election, 36 of the 38 seats in the provincial legislature. Newly-
elected Premier Joseph Howe led a delegation to the Imperial
Parliament in London in an effort to undo the new constitutional
arrangements, but it was too late. The Colonial Office rejected
Premier Howe's plea to permit Nova Scotia to withdraw from
Confederation. As the Colonial Secretary wrote in 1868:

> "The neighbouring province of New Brunswick has entered into the union in
> reliance on having with it the sister province of Nova Scotia; and vast obliga-
> tions, political and commercial, have already been contracted on the faith of a
> measure so long discussed and so solemnly adopted . . . I trust that the
> Assembly and the people of Nova Scotia will not be surprised that the Queen's
> government feel that they would not be warranted in advising the reversal of

407] a great measure of state, attended by so many extensive consequences already in operation." [Quoted in H. Wade MacLauchlan, "Accounting for Democracy and the Rule of Law in the Quebec Secession Reference" (1997), 76 Can. Bar Rev. 155, at p. 168.]

The interdependence characterized by "vast obligations, political and commercial", referred to by the Colonial Secretary in 1868, has, of course, multiplied immeasurably in the last 130 years.

[43] Federalism was a legal response to the underlying political and cultural realities that existed at Confederation and continue to exist today. At Confederation, political leaders told their respective communities that the Canadian union would be able to reconcile diversity with unity. It is pertinent, in the context of the present Reference, to mention the words of George-Etienne Cartier (cited in J.C. Bonenfant, "Les Canadiens français et la naissance de la Confédération", [1952] C.H.A.R. 39, at p. 42):

> "[TRANSLATION] When we are united, he said, we shall form a political nationality independent of the national origin or the religion of any individual. There are some who regretted that there was diversity of races and who expressed the hope that this distinctive character would disappear. The idea of unity of races is a utopia; it is an impossibility. A distinction of this nature will always exist, just as dissimilarity seems to be in the order of the physical, moral and political worlds. As to the objection based on this fact, that a large nation cannot be formed because Lower Canada is largely French and Catholic and Upper Canada is English and Protestant and the interior provinces are mixed, it constitutes, in my view, reasoning that is futile in the extreme . . . In our own federation, we will have Catholics and Protestants, English, French, Irish and Scots and everyone, through his efforts and successes, will add to the prosperity and glory of the new confederation. We are of different races, not so that we can wage war on one another, but in order to work together for our well-being."

The federal-provincial division of powers was a legal recognition of the diversity that existed among the initial members of Confederation, and manifested a concern to accommodate that diversity within a single nation by granting significant powers to provincial governments. The *Constitution Act, 1867* was an act of nation-building. It was the first step in the transition from colonies separately dependent on the Imperial Parliament for their governance to a unified and independent political state in which different peoples could resolve their disagreements and work together toward common goals and a common interest. Federalism was the political mechanism by which diversity could be reconciled with unity.

[44] A federal-provincial division of powers necessitated a writ- **[408** ten constitution which circumscribed the powers of the new Dominion and Provinces of Canada. Despite its federal structure, the new Dominion was to have "a Constitution similar in Principle to that of the United Kingdom" (*Constitution Act, 1867*, preamble). Allowing for the obvious differences between the governance of Canada and the United Kingdom, it was nevertheless thought important to thus emphasize the continuity of constitutional principles, including democratic institutions and the rule of law; and the continuity of the exercise of sovereign power transferred from Westminster to the federal and provincial capitals of Canada.

[45] After 1867, the Canadian federation continued to evolve both territorially and politically. New territories were admitted to the union and new provinces were formed. In 1870, Rupert's Land and the Northwest Territories were admitted and Manitoba was formed as a province. British Columbia was admitted in 1871, Prince Edward Island in 1873, and the Arctic Islands were added in 1880. In 1898, the Yukon Territory and in 1905, the provinces of Alberta and Saskatchewan were formed from the Northwest Territories. Newfoundland was admitted in 1949 by an amendment to the. *Constitution Act, 1867*. The new territory of Nunavut was carved out of the Northwest Territories in 1993 with the partition to become effective in April 1999.

[46] Canada's evolution from colony to fully independent state was gradual. The Imperial Parliament's passage of the *Statute of Westminster, 1931* (U.K.), 22 & 23 Geo. 5, c. 4, confirmed in law what had earlier been confirmed in fact by the Balfour Declaration of 1926, namely, that Canada was an independent country. Thereafter, Canadian law alone governed in Canada, except where Canada expressly consented to the continued application of Imperial legislation. Canada's independence from Britain was achieved through legal and political evolution with an adherence to the rule of law and stability. The proclamation of the *Constitution Act, 1982* removed the last vestige of British authority over the Canadian Constitution and re-affirmed Canada's commitment to the protection of its minority, aboriginal, equality, legal and language rights, and fundamental freedoms as set out in the *Canadian Charter of Rights and Freedoms*.

409]   [47] Legal continuity, which requires an orderly transfer of authority, necessitated that the 1982 amendments be made by the Westminster Parliament, but the legitimacy as distinguished from the formal legality of the amendments derived from political decisions taken in Canada within a legal framework which this Court, in the *Patriation Reference*, had ruled were in accordance with our Constitution. It should be noted, parenthetically, that the 1982 amendments did not alter the basic division of powers in ss. 91 and 92 of the *Constitution Act, 1867*, which is the primary textual expression of the principle of federalism in our Constitution, agreed upon at Confederation. It did, however, have the important effect that, despite the refusal of the government of Quebec to join in its adoption, Quebec has become bound to the terms of a Constitution that is different from that which prevailed previously, particularly as regards provisions governing its amendment, and the *Canadian Charter of Rights and Freedoms*. As to the latter, to the extent that the scope of legislative powers was thereafter to be constrained by the *Charter*, the constraint operated as much against federal legislative powers as against provincial legislative powers. Moreover, it is to be remembered that s. 33, the "notwithstanding clause", gives Parliament and the provincial legislatures authority to legislate on matters within their jurisdiction in derogation of the fundamental freedoms (s. 2), legal rights (ss. 7 to 14) and equality rights (s. 15) provisions of the *Charter*.

[48] We think it apparent from even this brief historical review that the evolution of our constitutional arrangements has been characterized by adherence to the rule of law, respect for democratic institutions, the accommodation of minorities, insistence that governments adhere to constitutional conduct and a desire for continuity and stability. We now turn to a discussion of the general constitutional principles that bear on the present Reference.

(3) Analysis of the Constitutional Principles

(a) Nature of the Principles

[49] What are those underlying principles? Our Constitution is primarily a written one, the product of 131 years of evolution. Behind the written word is an historical lineage stretching back through the ages, which aids in the consideration of the underlying constitutional principles. These principles inform and sustain the

constitutional text; they are the vital unstated assumptions upon **[410** which the text is based. The following discussion addresses the four foundational constitutional principles that are most germane for resolution of this Reference: federalism, democracy, constitutional- ism and the rule of law, and respect for minority rights. These defining principles function in symbiosis. No single principle can be defined in isolation from the others, nor does any one principle trump or exclude the operation of any other.

[50] Our Constitution has an internal architecture, or what the majority of this Court in *OPSEU v. Ontario (Attorney General)*, [1987] 2 S.C.R. 2 at p. 57, 41 D.L.R. (4th) 1, called a "basic consti- tutional structure". The individual elements of the Constitution are linked to the others, and must be interpreted by reference to the structure of the Constitution as a whole. As we recently emphasized in the *Provincial Judges Reference*, certain underlying principles infuse our Constitution and breathe life into it. Speaking of the rule of law principle in the *Manitoba Language Rights Reference, supra*, at p. 750, we held that "the principle is clearly implicit in the very nature of a Constitution". The same may be said of the other three constitutional principles we underscore today.

[51] Although these underlying principles are not explicitly made part of the Constitution by any written provision, other than in some respects by the oblique reference in the preamble to the *Constitution Act, 1867*, it would be impossible to conceive of our constitutional structure without them. The principles dictate major elements of the architecture of the Constitution itself and are as such its lifeblood.

[52] The principles assist in the interpretation of the text and the delineation of spheres of jurisdiction, the scope of rights and obli- gations, and the role of our political institutions. Equally important, observance of and respect for these principles is essential to the ongoing process of constitutional development and evolution of our Constitution as a "living tree", to invoke the famous description in *Edwards v. Attorney-General for Canada*, [1930] A.C. 124 at p. 136, [1930] 1 D.L.R. 98 *sub nom. Re Section 24 of the B.N.A. Act* (P.C.). As this Court indicated in *New Brunswick Broadcasting Co. v. Nova Scotia (Speaker of the House of Assembly)*, [1993] 1 S.C.R. 319, 100 D.L.R. (4th) 212, Canadians have long recognized the existence and importance of unwritten constitutional principles in our system of government.

411]   [53] Given the existence of these underlying constitutional principles, what use may the Court make of them? In the *Provincial Judges Reference, supra,* at paras. 93 and 104, we cautioned that the recognition of these constitutional principles (the majority opinion referred to them as "organizing principles" and described one of them, judicial independence, as an "unwritten norm") could not be taken as an invitation to dispense with the written text of the Constitution. On the contrary, we confirmed that there are compelling reasons to insist upon the primacy of our written constitution. A written constitution promotes legal certainty and predictability, and it provides a foundation and a touchstone for the exercise of constitutional judicial review. However, we also observed in the *Provincial Judges Reference* that the effect of the preamble to the *Constitution Act, 1867* was to incorporate certain constitutional principles by reference, a point made earlier in *Fraser v. Public Service Staff Relations Board,* [1985] 2 S.C.R. 455 at pp. 462-63, 23 D.L.R. (4th) 122. In the *Provincial Judges Reference,* at para. 104, we determined that the preamble "invites the courts to turn those principles into the premises of a constitutional argument that culminates in the filling of gaps in the express terms of the constitutional text".

[54] Underlying constitutional principles may in certain circumstances give rise to substantive legal obligations (have "full legal force", as we described it in the *Patriation Reference, supra,* at p. 845), which constitute substantive limitations upon government action. These principles may give rise to very abstract and general obligations, or they may be more specific and precise in nature. The principles are not merely descriptive, but are also invested with a powerful normative force, and are binding upon both courts and governments. "In other words", as this Court confirmed in the *Manitoba Language Rights Reference, supra,* at p. 752, "in the process of Constitutional adjudication, the Court may have regard to unwritten postulates which form the very foundation of the Constitution of Canada". It is to a discussion of those underlying constitutional principles that we now turn.

(b) Federalism

[55] It is undisputed that Canada is a federal state. Yet many commentators have observed that, according to the precise terms of the *Constitution Act, 1867,* the federal system was only partial.

See, *e.g.*, K. C. Wheare, *Federal Government* (4th ed., 1963), at [41?
pp. 18-20. This was so because, on paper, the federal government
retained sweeping powers which threatened to undermine the autonomy of the provinces. Here again, however, a review of the written
provisions of the Constitution does not provide the entire picture.
Our political and constitutional practice has adhered to an underlying principle of federalism, and has interpreted the written
provisions of the Constitution in this light. For example, although
the federal power of disallowance was included in the *Constitution
Act, 1867*, the underlying principle of federalism triumphed early.
Many constitutional scholars contend that the federal power of disallowance has been abandoned (*e.g.*, P. W. Hogg, *Constitutional
Law of Canada* (4th ed., 1997), at p. 120).

[56] In a federal system of government such as ours, political
power is shared by two orders of government: the federal government on the one hand, and the provinces on the other. Each is
assigned respective spheres of jurisdiction by the *Constitution Act,
1867*. See, *e.g.*, *Liquidators of the Maritime Bank of Canada v.
Receiver-General of New Brunswick*, [1892] A.C. 437 (P.C.), at
pp. 441-42. It is up to the courts "to control the limits of the respective sovereignties": *Northern Telecom Canada Ltd. v. Com-
munication·Workers of Canada*, [1983] 1 S.C.R. 733 at p. 741, 147
D.L.R. (3d) 1. In interpreting our Constitution, the courts have
always been concerned with the federalism principle, inherent in the
structure of our constitutional arrangements, which has from the
beginning been the lodestar by which the courts have been guided.

[57] This underlying principle of federalism, then, has exercised
a role of considerable importance in the interpretation of the written
provisions of our Constitution. In the *Patriation Reference, supra*,
at pp. 905-9, we confirmed that the principle of federalism runs
through the political and legal systems of Canada. Indeed, Martland
and Ritchie JJ., dissenting in the *Patriation Reference*, at p. 821,
considered federalism to be "the dominant principle of Canadian
constitutional law". With the enactment of the *Charter*, that proposition may have less force than it once did, but there can be little
doubt that the principle of federalism remains a central organiza-
tional theme of our Constitution. Less obviously, perhaps, but
certainly of equal importance, federalism is a political and legal
response to underlying social and political realities.

413]   [58] The principle of federalism recognizes the diversity of the component parts of Confederation, and the autonomy of provincial governments to develop their societies within their respective spheres of jurisdiction. The federal structure of our country also facilitates democratic participation by distributing power to the government thought to be most suited to achieving the particular societal objective having regard to this diversity. The scheme of the *Constitution Act, 1867*, it was said in *Re the Initiative and Referendum Act*, [1919] A.C. 935 at p. 942, 48 D.L.R. 18 (P.C.), was:

> . . . not to weld the Provinces into one, nor to subordinate Provincial Governments to a central authority, but to establish a central government in which these Provinces should be represented, entrusted with exclusive authority only in affairs in which they had a common interest. Subject to this each Province was to retain its independence and autonomy and to be directly under the Crown as its head.

More recently, in *Haig v. Canada*, [1993] 2 S.C.R. 995 at p. 1047, 105 D.L.R. (4th) 577, the majority of this Court held that differences between provinces "are a rational part of the political reality in the federal process". It was referring to the differential application of federal law in individual provinces, but the point applies more generally. A unanimous Court expressed similar views in *R. v. S. (S.)*, [1990] 2 S.C.R. 254, at pp. 287-88.

[59] The principle of federalism facilitates the pursuit of collective goals by cultural and linguistic minorities which form the majority within a particular province. This is the case in Quebec, where the majority of the population is French-speaking, and which possesses a distinct culture. This is not merely the result of chance. The social and demographic reality of Quebec explains the existence of the province of Quebec as a political unit and indeed, was one of the essential reasons for establishing a federal structure for the Canadian union in 1867. The experience of both Canada East and Canada West under the *Union Act, 1840* (U.K.), 3 & 4 Vict., c. 35, had not been satisfactory. The federal structure adopted at Confederation enabled French-speaking Canadians to form a numerical majority in the province of Quebec, and so exercise the considerable provincial powers conferred by the *Constitution Act, 1867* in such a way as to promote their language and culture. It also made provision for certain guaranteed representation within the federal Parliament itself.

[60] Federalism was also welcomed by Nova Scotia and New [41⁴ Brunswick, both of which also affirmed their will to protect their individual cultures and their autonomy over local matters. All new provinces joining the federation sought to achieve similar objectives, which are no less vigorously pursued by the provinces and territories as we approach the new millenium.

(c) Democracy

[61] Democracy is a fundamental value in our constitutional law and political culture. While it has both an institutional and an individual aspect, the democratic principle was also argued before us in the sense of the supremacy of the sovereign will of a people, in this case potentially to be expressed by Quebecers in support of unilateral secession. It is useful to explore in a summary way these different aspects of the democratic principle.

[62] The principle of democracy has always informed the design of our constitutional structure, and continues to act as an essential interpretive consideration to this day. A majority of this Court in *OPSEU v. Ontario, supra,* at p. 57, confirmed that "the basic structure of our Constitution, as established by the *Constitution Act, 1867,* contemplates the existence of certain political institutions, including freely elected legislative bodies at the federal and provincial levels". As is apparent from an earlier line of decisions emanating from this Court, including *Switzman v. Elbling,* [1957] S.C.R. 285, 7 D.L.R. (2d) 337; *Saumur v. City of Quebec,* [1953] 2 S.C.R. 299, [1953] 4 D.L.R. 641; *Boucher v. The King,* [1951] S.C.R. 265, [1951] 2 D.L.R. 369; and *Reference re Alberta Statutes,* [1938] S.C.R. 100, [1938] 2 D.L.R. 81, the democracy principle can best be understood as a sort of baseline against which the framers of our Constitution, and subsequently, our elected representatives under it, have always operated. It is perhaps for this reason that the principle was not explicitly identified in the text of the *Constitution Act, 1867* itself. To have done so might have appeared redundant, even silly, to the framers. As explained in the *Provincial Judges Reference, supra,* at para. 100, it is evident that our Constitution contemplates that Canada shall be a constitutional democracy. Yet this merely demonstrates the importance of underlying constitutional principles that are nowhere explicitly described in our constitutional texts. The representative and democratic nature of our political institutions was simply assumed.

415] [63] Democracy is commonly understood as being a political system of majority rule. It is essential to be clear what this means. The evolution of our democratic tradition can be traced back to the *Magna Carta* (1215) and before, through the long struggle for Parliamentary supremacy which culminated in the English *Bill of Rights* in 1688-89, 1 Will. & Mar. sess. 2, c. 2, the emergence of representative political institutions in the colonial era, the development of responsible government in the 19th century, and eventually, the achievement of Confederation itself in 1867. "[T]he Canadian tradition", the majority of this Court held in *Reference re Provincial Electoral Boundaries (Sask.)*, [1991] 2 S.C.R. 158 at p. 186, 81 D.L.R. (4th) 16 *sub nom. Reference re: Electoral Boundaries Commission Act, ss. 14, 20 (Sask.)*, is "one of evolutionary democracy moving in uneven steps toward the goal of universal suffrage and more effective representation". Since Confederation, efforts to extend the franchise to those unjustly excluded from participation in our political system — such as women, minorities and aboriginal peoples — have continued, with some success, to the present day.

[64] Democracy is not simply concerned with the process of government. On the contrary, as suggested in *Switzman v. Elbling*, *supra*, at p. 306, democracy is fundamentally connected to substantive goals, most importantly, the promotion of self-government. Democracy accommodates cultural and group identities: *Reference re Provincial Electoral Boundaries*, at p. 188. Put another way, a sovereign people exercises its right to self-government through the democratic process. In considering the scope and purpose of the *Charter*, the Court in *R. v. Oakes*, [1986] 1 S.C.R. 103, 26 D.L.R. (4th) 200, articulated some of the values inherent in the notion of democracy (at p. 136):

> The Court must be guided by the values and principles essential to a free and democratic society which I believe to embody, to name but a few, respect for the inherent dignity of the human person, commitment to social justice and equality, accommodation of a wide variety of beliefs, respect for cultural and group identity, and faith in social and political institutions which enhance the participation of individuals and groups in society.

[65] In institutional terms, democracy means that each of the provincial legislatures and the federal Parliament is elected by popular franchise. These legislatures, we have said, are "at the core of the system of representative government": *New Brunswick Broadcasting*, *supra*, at p. 387. In individual terms, the right to vote

in elections to the House of Commons and the provincial legisla- [416
tures, and to be candidates in those elections, is guaranteed to
"Every citizen of Canada" by virtue of s. 3 of the *Charter*.
Historically, this Court has interpreted democracy to mean the process of representative and responsible government and the right of
citizens to participate in the political process as voters (*Reference re
Provincial Electoral Boundaries, supra*) and as candidates (*Harvey
v. New Brunswick (Attorney General)*, [1996] 2 S.C.R. 876, 137
D.L.R. (4th) 142). In addition, the effect of s. 4 of the *Charter* is to
oblige the House of Commons and the provincial legislatures to
hold regular elections and to permit citizens to elect representatives
to their political institutions. The democratic principle is affirmed
with particular clarity in that section 4 is not subject to the notwithstanding power contained in s. 33.

[66] It is, of course, true that democracy expresses the sovereign
will of the people. Yet this expression, too, must be taken in the context of the other institutional values we have identified as pertinent
to this Reference. The relationship between democracy and federalism means, for example, that in Canada there may be different and
equally legitimate majorities in different provinces and territories
and at the federal level. No one majority is more or less "legitimate"
than the others as an expression of democratic opinion, although, of
course, the consequences will vary with the subject matter. A federal
system of government enables different provinces to pursue policies
responsive to the particular concerns and interests of people in that
province. At the same time, Canada as a whole is also a democratic
community in which citizens construct and achieve goals on a
national scale through a federal government acting within the limits
of its jurisdiction. The function of federalism is to enable citizens to
participate concurrently in different collectivities and to pursue
goals at both a provincial and a federal level.

[67] The consent of the governed is a value that is basic to our
understanding of a free and democratic society. Yet democracy in
any real sense of the word cannot exist without the rule of law. It is
the law that creates the framework within which the "sovereign
will" is to be ascertained and implemented. To be accorded legitimacy, democratic institutions must rest, ultimately, on a legal
foundation. That is, they must allow for the participation of, and
accountability to, the people, through public institutions created

[417] under the Constitution. Equally, however, a system of government cannot survive through adherence to the law alone. A political system must also possess legitimacy, and in our political culture, that requires an interaction between the rule of law and the democratic principle. The system must be capable of reflecting the aspirations of the people. But there is more. Our law's claim to legitimacy also rests on an appeal to moral values, many of which are imbedded in our constitutional structure. It would be a grave mistake to equate legitimacy with the "sovereign will" or majority rule alone, to the exclusion of other constitutional values.

[68] Finally, we highlight that a functioning democracy requires a continuous process of discussion. The Constitution mandates government by democratic legislatures, and an executive accountable to them, "resting ultimately on public opinion reached by discussion and the interplay of ideas" (*Saumur v. City of Quebec, supra*, at p. 330). At both the federal and provincial level, by its very nature, the need to build majorities necessitates compromise, negotiation, and deliberation. No one has a monopoly on truth, and our system is predicated on the faith that in the marketplace of ideas, the best solutions to public problems will rise to the top. Inevitably, there will be dissenting voices. A democratic system of government is committed to considering those dissenting voices, and seeking to acknowledge and address those voices in the laws by which all in the community must live.

[69] The *Constitution Act, 1982* gives expression to this principle, by conferring a right to initiate constitutional change on each participant in Confederation. In our view, the existence of this right imposes a corresponding duty on the participants in Confederation to engage in constitutional discussions in order to acknowledge and address democratic expressions of a desire for change in other provinces. This duty is inherent in the democratic principle which is a fundamental predicate of our system of governance.

(d) Constitutionalism and the Rule of Law

[70] The principles of constitutionalism and the rule of law lie at the root of our system of government. The rule of law, as observed in *Roncarelli v. Duplessis*, [1959] S.C.R. 121 at p. 142, 16 D.L.R. (2d) 689, is "a fundamental postulate of our constitutional structure". As we noted in the *Patriation Reference, supra*, at pp. 805-6, "[t]he 'rule of law' is a highly textured expression, importing many

things which are beyond the need of these reasons to explore but [418] conveying, for example, a sense of orderliness, of subjection to known legal rules and of executive accountability to legal authority". At its most basic level, the rule of law vouchsafes to the citizens and residents of the country a stable, predictable and ordered society in which to conduct their affairs. It provides a shield for individuals from arbitrary state action.

[71] In the *Manitoba Language Rights Reference, supra,* at pp. 747-52, this Court outlined the elements of the rule of law. We emphasized, first, that the rule of law provides that the law is supreme over the acts of both government and private persons. There is, in short, one law for all. Second, we explained, at p. 749, that "the rule of law requires the creation and maintenance of an actual order of positive laws which preserves and embodies the more general principle of normative order". It was this second aspect of the rule of law that was primarily at issue in the *Manitoba Language Rights Reference* itself. A third aspect of the rule of law is, as recently confirmed in the *Provincial Judges Reference, supra,* at para. 10, that "the exercise of all public power must find its ultimate source in a legal rule". Put another way, the relationship between the state and the individual must be regulated by law. Taken together, these three considerations make up a principle of profound constitutional and political significance.

[72] The constitutionalism principle bears considerable similarity to the rule of law, although they are not identical. The essence of constitutionalism in Canada is embodied in s. 52(1) of the *Constitution Act, 1982,* which provides that "[t]he Constitution of Canada is the supreme law of Canada, and any law that is inconsistent with the provisions of the Constitution is, to the extent of the inconsistency, of no force or effect". Simply put, the constitutionalism principle requires that all government action comply with the Constitution. The rule of law principle requires that all government action must comply with the law, including the Constitution. This Court has noted on several occasions that with the adoption of the *Charter,* the Canadian system of government was transformed to a significant extent from a system of Parliamentary supremacy to one of constitutional supremacy. The Constitution binds all governments, both federal and provincial, including the executive branch (*Operation Dismantle Inc. v. The Queen,* [1985] 1 S.C.R. 441 at

[419] p. 455, 18 D.L.R. (4th) 481). They may not transgress its provisions; indeed, their sole claim to exercise lawful authority rests in the powers allocated to them under the Constitution, and can come from no other source.

[73] An understanding of the scope and importance of the principles of the rule of law and constitutionalism is aided by acknowledging explicitly why a constitution is entrenched beyond the reach of simple majority rule. There are three overlapping reasons.

[74] First, a constitution may provide an added safeguard for fundamental human rights and individual freedoms which might otherwise be susceptible to government interference. Although democratic government is generally solicitous of those rights, there are occasions when the majority will be tempted to ignore fundamental rights in order to accomplish collective goals more easily or effectively. Constitutional entrenchment ensures that those rights will be given due regard and protection. Second, a constitution may seek to ensure that vulnerable minority groups are endowed with the institutions and rights necessary to maintain and promote their identities against the assimilative pressures of the majority. And third, a constitution may provide for a division of political power that allocates political power amongst different levels of government. That purpose would be defeated if one of those democratically elected levels of government could usurp the powers of the other simply by exercising its legislative power to allocate additional political power to itself unilaterally.

[75] The argument that the Constitution may be legitimately circumvented by resort to a majority vote in a province-wide referendum is superficially persuasive, in large measure because it seems to appeal to some of the same principles that underlie the legitimacy of the Constitution itself, namely, democracy and self-government. In short, it is suggested that as the notion of popular sovereignty underlies the legitimacy of our existing constitutional arrangements, so the same popular sovereignty that originally led to the present Constitution must (it is argued) also permit "the people" in their exercise of popular sovereignty to secede by majority vote alone. However, closer analysis reveals that this argument is unsound, because it misunderstands the meaning of popular sovereignty and the essence of a constitutional democracy.

[76] Canadians have never accepted that ours is a system of sim- **[420]** ple majority rule. Our principle of democracy, taken in conjunction with the other constitutional principles discussed here, is richer. Constitutional government is necessarily predicated on the idea that the political representatives of the people of a province have the capacity and the power to commit the province to be bound into the future by the constitutional rules being adopted. These rules are "binding" not in the sense of frustrating the will of a majority of a province, but as defining the majority which must be consulted in order to alter the fundamental balances of political power (including the spheres of autonomy guaranteed by the principle of federalism), individual rights, and minority rights in our society. Of course, those constitutional rules are themselves amenable to amendment, but only through a process of negotiation which ensures that there is an opportunity for the constitutionally defined rights of all the parties to be respected and reconciled.

[77] In this way, our belief in democracy may be harmonized with our belief in constitutionalism. Constitutional amendment often requires some form of substantial consensus precisely because the content of the underlying principles of our Constitution demand it. By requiring broad support in the form of an "enhanced majority" to achieve constitutional change, the Constitution ensures that minority· interests must be addressed before proposed changes which would affect them may be enacted.

[78] It might be objected, then, that constitutionalism is therefore incompatible with democratic government. This would be an erroneous view. Constitutionalism facilitates — indeed, makes possible — a democratic political system by creating an orderly framework within which people may make political decisions. Viewed correctly, constitutionalism and the rule of law are not in conflict with democracy; rather, they are essential to it. Without that relationship, the political will upon which democratic decisions are taken would itself be undermined.

(e) Protection of Minorities

[79] The fourth underlying constitutional principle we address here concerns the protection of minorities. There are a number of specific constitutional provisions protecting minority language, religion and education rights. Some of those provisions are, as we have recognized on a number of occasions, the product of historical

[421] compromises. As this Court observed in *Reference re Bill 30, An Act to Amend the Education Act (Ont.)*, [1987] 1 S.C.R. 1148 at p. 1173, 40 D.L.R. (4th) 18, and in *Reference re Education Act (Que.)*, [1993] 2 S.C.R. 511 at pp. 529-30, 105 D.L.R. (4th) 266, the protection of minority religious education rights was a central consideration in the negotiations leading to Confederation. In the absence of such protection, it was felt that the minorities in what was then Canada East and Canada West would be submerged and assimilated. See also *Greater Montreal Protestant School Board v. Quebec (Attorney General)*, [1989] 1 S.C.R. 377 at pp. 401-2, 57 D.L.R. (4th) 521, and *Adler v. Ontario*, [1996] 3 S.C.R. 609, 140 D.L.R. (4th) 385. Similar concerns animated the provisions protecting minority language rights, as noted in *Société des Acadiens du Nouveau-Brunswick Inc. v. Association of Parents for Fairness in Education, Grand Falls District 50 Branch*, [1986] 1 S.C.R. 549 at p. 564, 27 D.L.R. (4th) 406.

[80] However, we highlight that even though those provisions were the product of negotiation and political compromise, that does not render them unprincipled. Rather, such a concern reflects a broader principle related to the protection of minority rights. Undoubtedly, the three other constitutional principles inform the scope and operation of the specific provisions that protect the rights of minorities. We emphasize that the protection of minority rights is itself an independent principle underlying our constitutional order. The principle is clearly reflected in the *Charter*'s provisions for the protection of minority rights. See, *e.g.*, *Reference re Public Schools Act (Man.), s. 79(3), (4) and (7)*, [1993] 1 S.C.R. 839, 100 D.L.R. (4th) 723, and *Mahe v. Alberta*, [1990] 1 S.C.R. 342, 68 D.L.R. (4th) 69.

[81] The concern of our courts and governments to protect minorities has been prominent in recent years, particularly following the enactment of the *Charter*. Undoubtedly, one of the key considerations motivating the enactment of the *Charter*, and the process of constitutional judicial review that it entails, is the protection of minorities. However, it should not be forgotten that the protection of minority rights had a long history before the enactment of the *Charter*. Indeed, the protection of minority rights was clearly an essential consideration in the design of our constitutional structure even at the time of Confederation: *Senate Reference, supra*, at

p. 71. Although Canada's record of upholding the rights of minori- **[422]** ties is not a spotless one, that goal is one towards which Canadians have been striving since Confederation, and the process has not been without successes. The principle of protecting minority rights continues to exercise influence in the operation and interpretation of our Constitution.

[82] Consistent with this long tradition of respect for minorities, which is at least as old as Canada itself, the framers of the *Constitution Act, 1982* included in s. 35 explicit protection for existing aboriginal and treaty rights, and in s. 25, a non-derogation clause in favour of the rights of aboriginal peoples. The "promise" of s. 35, as it was termed in *R. v. Sparrow*, [1990] 1 S.C.R. 1075 at p. 1083, 70 D.L.R. (4th) 385, recognized not only the ancient occupation of land by aboriginal peoples, but their contribution to the building of Canada, and the special commitments made to them by successive governments. The protection of these rights, so recently and arduously achieved, whether looked at in their own right or as part of the larger concern with minorities, reflects an important underlying constitutional value.

(4) The Operation of the Constitutional Principles in the Secession Context

[83] Secession is the effort of a group or section of a state to withdraw itself from the political and constitutional authority of that state, with a view to achieving statehood for a new territorial unit on the international plane. In a federal state, secession typically takes the form of a territorial unit seeking to withdraw from the federation. Secession is a legal act as much as a political one. By the terms of Question 1 of this Reference, we are asked to rule on the legality of unilateral secession "under the Constitution of Canada". This is an appropriate question, as the legality of unilateral secession must be evaluated, at least in the first instance, from the perspective of the domestic legal order of the state from which the unit seeks to withdraw. As we shall see below, it is also argued that international law is a relevant standard by which the legality of a purported act of secession may be measured.

[84] The secession of a province from Canada must be considered, in legal terms, to require an amendment to the Constitution, which perforce requires negotiation. The amendments necessary to

423] achieve a secession could be radical and extensive. Some commentators have suggested that secession could be a change of such a magnitude that it could not be considered to be merely an amendment to the Constitution. We are not persuaded by this contention. It is of course true that the Constitution is silent as to the ability of a province to secede from Confederation but, although the Constitution neither expressly authorizes nor prohibits secession, an act of secession would purport to alter the governance of Canadian territory in a manner which undoubtedly is inconsistent with our current constitutional arrangements. The fact that those changes would be profound, or that they would purport to have a significance with respect to international law, does not negate their nature as amendments to the Constitution of Canada.

[85] The Constitution is the expression of the sovereignty of the people of Canada. It lies within the power of the people of Canada, acting through their various governments duly elected and recognized under the Constitution, to effect whatever constitutional arrangements are desired within Canadian territory, including, should it be so desired, the secession of Quebec from Canada. As this Court held in the *Manitoba Language Rights Reference*, *supra*, at p. 745: "[t]he Constitution of a country is a statement of the will of the people to be governed in accordance with certain principles held ·as fundamental and certain prescriptions restrictive of the powers of the legislature and government". The manner in which such a political will could be formed and mobilized is a somewhat speculative exercise, though we are asked to assume the existence of such a political will for the purpose of answering the question before us. By the terms of this Reference, we have been asked to consider whether it would be constitutional in such a circumstance for the National Assembly, legislature or government of Quebec to effect the secession of Quebec from Canada *unilaterally*.

[86] The "unilateral" nature of the act is of cardinal importance and we must be clear as to what is understood by this term. In one sense, any step towards a constitutional amendment initiated by a single actor on the constitutional stage is "unilateral". We do not believe that this is the meaning contemplated by Question 1, nor is this the sense in which the term has been used in argument before us. Rather, what is claimed by a right to secede "unilaterally" is the

right to effectuate secession without prior negotiations with the [424 other provinces and the federal government. At issue is not the legality of the first step but the legality of the final act of purported unilateral secession. The supposed juridical basis for such an act is said to be a clear expression of democratic will in a referendum in the province of Quebec. This claim requires us to examine the possible juridical impact, if any, of such a referendum on the functioning of our Constitution, and on the claimed legality of a unilateral act of secession.

[87] Although the Constitution does not itself address the use of a referendum procedure, and the results of a referendum have no direct role or legal effect in our constitutional scheme, a referendum undoubtedly may provide a democratic method of ascertaining the views of the electorate on important political questions on a particular occasion. The democratic principle identified above would demand that considerable weight be given to a clear expression by the people of Quebec of their will to secede from Canada, even though a referendum, in itself and without more, has no direct legal effect, and could not in itself bring about unilateral secession. Our political institutions are premised on the democratic principle, and so an expression of the democratic will of the people of a province carries weight, in that it would confer legitimacy on the efforts of the government of Quebec to initiate the Constitution's amendment process in order to secede by constitutional means. In this context, we refer to a "clear" majority as a qualitative evaluation. The referendum result, if it is to be taken as an expression of the democratic will, must be free of ambiguity both in terms of the question asked and in terms of the support it achieves.

[88] The federalism principle, in conjunction with the democratic principle, dictates that the clear repudiation of the existing constitutional order and the clear expression of the desire to pursue secession by the population of a province would give rise to a reciprocal obligation on all parties to Confederation to negotiate constitutional changes to respond to that desire. The amendment of the Constitution begins with a political process undertaken pursuant to the Constitution itself. In Canada, the initiative for constitutional amendment is the responsibility of democratically elected representatives of the participants in Confederation. Those representatives may, of course, take their cue from a referendum, but in legal terms,

425] constitution-making in Canada, as in many countries, is undertaken by the democratically elected representatives of the people. The corollary of a legitimate attempt by one participant in Confederation to seek an amendment to the Constitution is an obligation on all parties to come to the negotiating table. The clear repudiation by the people of Quebec of the existing constitutional order would confer legitimacy on demands for secession, and place an obligation on the other provinces and the federal government to acknowledge and respect that expression of democratic will by entering into negotiations and conducting them in accordance with the underlying constitutional principles already discussed.

[89] What is the content of this obligation to negotiate? At this juncture, we confront the difficult interrelationship between substantive obligations flowing from the Constitution and questions of judicial competence and restraint in supervising or enforcing those obligations. This is mirrored by the distinction between the legality and the legitimacy of actions taken under the Constitution. We propose to focus first on the substantive obligations flowing from this obligation to negotiate; once the nature of those obligations has been described, it is easier to assess the appropriate means of enforcement of those obligations, and to comment on the distinction between legality and legitimacy.

[90] The conduct of the parties in such negotiations would be governed by the same constitutional principles which give rise to the duty to negotiate: federalism, democracy, constitutionalism and the rule of law, and the protection of minorities. Those principles lead us to reject two absolutist propositions. One of those propositions is that there would be a legal obligation on the other provinces and federal government to accede to the secession of a province, subject only to negotiation of the logistical details of secession. This proposition is attributed either to the supposed implications of the democratic principle of the Constitution, or to the international law principle of self-determination of peoples.

[91] For both theoretical and practical reasons, we cannot accept this view. We hold that Quebec could not purport to invoke a right of self-determination such as to dictate the terms of a proposed secession to the other parties: that would not be a negotiation at all. As well, it would be naive to expect that the substantive goal of secession could readily be distinguished from the practical details of

secession. The devil would be in the details. The democracy princi- [426
ple, as we have emphasized, cannot be invoked to trump the
principles of federalism and rule of law, the rights of individuals and
minorities, or the operation of democracy in the other provinces or
in Canada as a whole. No negotiations could be effective if their
ultimate outcome, secession, is cast as an absolute legal entitlement
based upon an obligation to give effect to that act of secession in the
Constitution. Such a foregone conclusion would actually undermine
the obligation to negotiate and render it hollow.

[92] However, we are equally unable to accept the reverse proposition, that a clear expression of self-determination by the people of
Quebec would impose *no* obligations upon the other provinces or
the federal government. The continued existence and operation of
the Canadian constitutional order cannot remain indifferent to the
clear expression of a clear majority of Quebecers that they no longer
wish to remain in Canada. This would amount to the assertion that
other constitutionally recognized principles necessarily trump the
clearly expressed democratic will of the people of Quebec. Such a
proposition fails to give sufficient weight to the underlying constitutional principles that must inform the amendment process,
including the principles of democracy and federalism. The rights of
other provinces and the federal government cannot deny the right of
the government of Quebec to pursue secession, should a clear
majority of the people of Quebec choose that goal, so long as in
doing so, Quebec respects the rights of others. Negotiations would
be necessary to address the interests of the federal government, of
Quebec and the other provinces, and other participants, as well as
the rights of all Canadians both within and outside Quebec.

[93] Is the rejection of both of these propositions reconcilable?
Yes, once it is realized that none of the rights or principles under discussion is absolute to the exclusion of the others. This observation
suggests that other parties cannot exercise their rights in such a way
as to amount to an absolute denial of Quebec's rights, and similarly,
that so long as Quebec exercises its rights while respecting the
rights of others, it may propose secession and seek to achieve it
through negotiation. The negotiation process precipitated by a decision of a clear majority of the population of Quebec on a clear
question to pursue secession would require the reconciliation of various rights and obligations by the representatives of two legitimate

427] majorities, namely, the clear majority of the population of Quebec, and the clear majority of Canada as a whole, whatever that may be. There can be no suggestion that either of these majorities "trumps" the other. A political majority that does not act in accordance with the underlying constitutional principles we have identified puts at risk the legitimacy of the exercise of its rights.

[94] In such circumstances, the conduct of the parties assumes primary constitutional significance. The negotiation process must be conducted with an eye to the constitutional principles we have outlined, which must inform the actions of *all* the participants in the negotiation process.

[95] Refusal of a party to conduct negotiations in a manner consistent with constitutional principles and values would seriously put at risk the legitimacy of that party's assertion of its rights, and perhaps the negotiation process as a whole. Those who quite legitimately insist upon the importance of upholding the rule of law cannot at the same time be oblivious to the need to act in conformity with constitutional principles and values, and so do their part to contribute to the maintenance and promotion of an environment in which the rule of law may flourish.

[96] No one can predict the course that such negotiations might take. The possibility that they might not lead to an agreement amongst the parties must be recognized. Negotiations following a referendum vote in favour of seeking secession would inevitably address a wide range of issues, many of great import. After 131 years of Confederation, there exists, inevitably, a high level of integration in economic, political and social institutions across Canada. The vision of those who brought about Confederation was to create a unified country, not a loose alliance of autonomous provinces. Accordingly, while there are regional economic interests, which sometimes coincide with provincial boundaries, there are also national interests and enterprises (both public and private) that would face potential dismemberment. There is a national economy and a national debt. Arguments were raised before us regarding boundary issues. There are linguistic and cultural minorities, including aboriginal peoples, unevenly distributed across the country who look to the Constitution of Canada for the protection of their rights. Of course, secession would give rise to many issues of great complexity and difficulty. These would have to be resolved within the

overall framework of the rule of law, thereby assuring Canadians **[428**
resident in Quebec and elsewhere a measure of stability in what
would likely be a period of considerable upheaval and uncertainty.
Nobody seriously suggests that our national existence, seamless in
so many aspects, could be effortlessly separated along what are now
the provincial boundaries of Quebec. As the Attorney General of
Saskatchewan put it in his oral submission:

> A nation is built when the communities that comprise it make commit-
> ments to it, when they forego choices and opportunities on behalf of a nation
> . . . when the communities that comprise it make compromises, when they
> offer each other guarantees, when they make transfers and perhaps most point-
> edly, when they receive from others the benefits of national solidarity. The
> threads of a thousand acts of accommodation are the fabric of a nation.

[97] In the circumstances, negotiations following such a referendum would undoubtedly be difficult. While the negotiators would
have to contemplate the possibility of secession, there would be no
absolute legal entitlement to it and no assumption that an agreement
reconciling all relevant rights and obligations would actually be
reached. It is foreseeable that even negotiations carried out in conformity with the underlying constitutional principles could reach an
impasse. We need not speculate here as to what would then transpire. Under the Constitution, secession requires that an amendment
be negotiated.

[98] The respective roles of the courts and political actors in dis-
charging the constitutional obligations we have identified follows
ineluctably from the foregoing observations. In the *Patriation
Reference*, a distinction was drawn between the law of the
Constitution, which, generally speaking, will be enforced by the
courts, and other constitutional rules, such as the conventions of the
Constitution, which carry only political sanctions. It is also the case,
however, that judicial intervention, even in relation to the *law* of the
Constitution, is subject to the Court's appreciation of its proper role
in the constitutional scheme.

[99] The notion of justiciability is, as we earlier pointed out in
dealing with the preliminary objection, linked to the notion of
appropriate judicial restraint. We earlier made reference to the discussion of justiciability in *Reference re Canada Assistance Plan*,
supra, at p. 545:

> In exercising its discretion whether to determine a matter that is alleged to be
> non-justiciable, the Court's primary concern is to retain its proper role within
> the constitutional framework of our democratic form of government.

[429] In *Operation Dismantle, supra*, at p. 459, it was pointed out that justiciability is a "doctrine . . . founded upon a concern with the appropriate role of the courts as the forum for the resolution of different types of disputes". An analogous doctrine of judicial restraint operates here. Also, as observed in *Canada (Auditor General) v. Canada (Minister of Energy, Mines and Resources)*, [1989] 2 S.C.R. 49 at p. 91, 61 D.L.R. (4th) 604 (the *Auditor General's* case):

> There is an array of issues which calls for the exercise of judicial judgment on whether the questions are properly cognizable by the courts. Ultimately, such judgment depends on the appreciation by the judiciary of its own position in the constitutional scheme.

[100] The role of the Court in this Reference is limited to the identification of the relevant aspects of the Constitution in their broadest sense. We have interpreted the questions as relating to the constitutional framework within which political decisions may ultimately be made. Within that framework, the workings of the political process are complex and can only be resolved by means of political judgments and evaluations. The Court has no supervisory role over the political aspects of constitutional negotiations. Equally, the initial impetus for negotiation, namely a clear majority on a clear question in favour of secession, is subject only to political evaluation, and properly so. A right and a corresponding duty to negotiate secession cannot be built on an alleged expression of democratic will if the expression of democratic will is itself fraught with ambiguities. Only the political actors would have the information and expertise to make the appropriate judgment as to the point at which, and the circumstances in which, those ambiguities are resolved one way or the other.

[101] If the circumstances giving rise to the duty to negotiate were to arise, the distinction between the strong defence of legitimate interests and the taking of positions which, in fact, ignore the legitimate interests of others is one that also defies legal analysis. The Court would not have access to all of the information available to the political actors, and the methods appropriate for the search for truth in a court of law are ill-suited to getting to the bottom of constitutional negotiations. To the extent that the questions are political in nature, it is not the role of the judiciary to interpose its own views on the different negotiating positions of the parties, even were it invited to do so. Rather, it is the obligation of the elected representatives to give concrete form to the discharge of their constitutional

obligations which only they and their electors can ultimately assess. **[430** The reconciliation of the various legitimate constitutional interests outlined above is necessarily committed to the political rather than the judicial realm, precisely because that reconciliation can only be achieved through the give and take of the negotiation process. Having established the legal framework, it would be for the democratically elected leadership of the various participants to resolve their differences.

[102] The non-justiciability of political issues that lack a legal component does not deprive the surrounding constitutional framework of its binding status, nor does this mean that constitutional obligations could be breached without incurring serious legal repercussions. Where there are legal rights there are remedies, but as we explained in the *Auditor General*'s case, *supra*, at p. 90, and *New Brunswick Broadcasting*, *supra*, the appropriate recourse in some circumstances lies through the workings of the political process rather than the courts.

[103] To the extent that a breach of the constitutional duty to negotiate in accordance with the principles described above undermines the legitimacy of a party's actions, it may have important ramifications at the international level. Thus, a failure of the duty to undertake negotiations and pursue them according to constitutional principles may undermine that government's claim to legitimacy which is generally a precondition for recognition by the international community. Conversely, violations of those principles by the federal or other provincial governments responding to the request for secession may undermine their legitimacy. Thus, a Quebec that had negotiated in conformity with constitutional principles and values in the face of unreasonable intransigence on the part of other participants at the federal or provincial level would be more likely to be recognized than a Quebec which did not itself act according to constitutional principles in the negotiation process. Both the legality of the acts of the parties to the negotiation process under Canadian law and the perceived legitimacy of such action, would be important considerations in the recognition process. In this way, the adherence of the parties to the obligation to negotiate would be evaluated in an indirect manner on the international plane.

[104] Accordingly, the secession of Quebec from Canada cannot be accomplished by the National Assembly, the legislature or

[431] government of Quebec unilaterally, that is to say, without principled negotiations, and be considered a lawful act. Any attempt to effect the secession of a province from Canada must be undertaken pursuant to the Constitution of Canada, or else violate the Canadian legal order. However, the continued existence and operation of the Canadian constitutional order cannot remain unaffected by the unambiguous expression of a clear majority of Quebecers that they no longer wish to remain in Canada. The primary means by which that expression is given effect is the constitutional duty to negotiate in accordance with the constitutional principles that we have described herein. In the event secession negotiations are initiated, our Constitution, no less than our history, would call on the participants to work to reconcile the rights, obligations and legitimate aspirations of all Canadians within a framework that emphasizes constitutional responsibilities as much as it does constitutional rights.

[105] It will be noted that Question 1 does not ask how secession could be achieved in a constitutional manner, but addresses one form of secession only, namely unilateral secession. Although the applicability of various procedures to achieve lawful secession was raised in argument, each option would require us to assume the existence of facts that at this stage are unknown. In accordance with the usual rule of prudence in constitutional cases, we refrain from pronouncing on the applicability of any particular constitutional procedure to effect secession unless and until sufficiently clear facts exist to squarely raise an issue for judicial determination.

(5) Suggested Principle of Effectivity

[106] In the foregoing discussion we have not overlooked the principle of effectivity, which was placed at the forefront in argument before us. For the reasons that follow, we do not think that the principle of effectivity has any application to the issues raised by Question 1. A distinction must be drawn between the right of a people to act, and their power to do so. They are not identical. A right is recognized in law: mere physical ability is not necessarily given status as a right. The fact that an individual or group can act in a certain way says nothing at all about the legal status or consequences of the act. A power may be exercised even in the absence of a right to do so, but if it is, then it is exercised without legal foundation. Our Constitution does not address powers in this sense. On

the contrary, the Constitution is concerned only with the rights and [432] obligations of individuals, groups and governments, and the structure of our institutions. It was suggested before us that the National Assembly, legislature or government of Quebec could unilaterally effect the secession of that province from Canada, but it was not suggested that they might do so as a matter of law; rather, it was contended that they simply could do so as a matter of fact. Although under the Constitution there is no right to pursue secession unilaterally, that is secession without principled negotiation, this does not rule out the possibility of an unconstitutional declaration of secession leading to a *de facto* secession. The ultimate success of such a secession would be dependent on effective control of a territory and recognition by the international community. The principles governing secession at international law are discussed in our answer to Question 2.

[107] In our view, the alleged principle of effectivity has no constitutional or legal status in the sense that it does not provide an *ex ante* explanation or justification for an act. In essence, acceptance of a principle of effectivity would be tantamount to accepting that the National Assembly, legislature or government of Quebec may act without regard to the law, simply because it asserts the power to do so. So viewed, the suggestion is that the National Assembly, legislature or government of Quebec could purport to secede the province unilaterally from Canada in disregard of Canadian and international law. It is further suggested that if the secession bid was successful, a new legal order would be created in that province, which would then be considered an independent state.

[108] Such a proposition is an assertion of fact, not a statement of law. It may or may not be true; in any event it is irrelevant to the questions of law before us. If, on the other hand, it is put forward as an assertion of law, then it simply amounts to the contention that the law may be broken as long as it can be broken successfully. Such a notion is contrary to the rule of law, and must be rejected.

B. *Question 2*

> Does international law give the National Assembly, legislature or government of Quebec the right to effect the secession of Quebec from Canada unilaterally? In this regard, is there a right to self-determination under international law that would give the National Assembly, legislature or government of Quebec the right to effect the secession of Quebec from Canada unilaterally?

433]   [109] For reasons already discussed, the Court does not accept the contention that Question 2 raises a question of "pure" international law which this Court has no jurisdiction to address. Question 2 is posed in the context of a Reference to address the existence or non-existence of a right of unilateral secession by a province of Canada. The *amicus curiae* argues that this question ultimately falls to be determined under international law. In addressing this issue, the Court does not purport to act as an arbiter between sovereign states or more generally within the international community. The Court is engaged in rendering an advisory opinion on certain legal aspects of the continued existence of the Canadian federation. International law has been invoked as a consideration and it must therefore be addressed.

[110] The argument before the Court on Question 2 has focused largely on determining whether, under international law, a positive legal right to unilateral secession exists in the factual circumstances assumed for the purpose of our response to Question 1. Arguments were also advanced to the effect that, regardless of the existence or non-existence of a positive right to unilateral secession, international law will in the end recognize effective political realities — including the emergence of a new state — as facts. While our response to Question 2 will address considerations raised by this alternative argument of "effectivity", it should first be noted that the existence of a positive legal entitlement is quite different from a prediction that the law will respond after the fact to a then existing political reality. These two concepts examine different points in time. The questions posed to the Court address legal rights in advance of a unilateral act of purported secession. While we touch below on the practice governing the international recognition of emerging states, the Court is as wary of entertaining speculation about the possible future conduct of sovereign states on the international level as it was under Question 1 to speculate about the possible future course of political negotiations among the participants in the Canadian federation. In both cases, the Reference questions are directed only to the *legal* framework within which the political actors discharge their various mandates.

(1) Secession at International Law

[111] It is clear that international law does not specifically grant component parts of sovereign states the legal right to secede

unilaterally from their "parent" state. This is acknowledged by the [434] experts who provided their opinions on behalf of both the *amicus curiae* and the Attorney General of Canada. Given the lack of specific authorization for unilateral secession, proponents of the existence of such a right at international law are therefore left to attempt to found their argument: (i) on the proposition that unilateral secession is not specifically prohibited and that what is not specifically prohibited is inferentially permitted; or (ii) on the implied duty of states to recognize the legitimacy of secession brought about by the exercise of the well-established international law right of "a people" to self-determination. The *amicus curiae* addressed the right of self-determination, but submitted that it was not applicable to the circumstances of Quebec within the Canadian federation, irrespective of the existence or non-existence of a referendum result in favour of secession. We agree on this point with the *amicus curiae*, for reasons that we will briefly develop.

(a) Absence of a Specific Prohibition

[112] International law contains neither a right of unilateral secession nor the explicit denial of such a right, although such a denial is, to some extent, implicit in the exceptional circumstances required for secession to be permitted under the right of a people to self-determination, *e.g.*, the right of secession that arises in the exceptional situation of an oppressed or colonial people, discussed below. As will be seen, international law places great importance on the territorial integrity of nation states and, by and large, leaves the creation of a new state to be determined by the domestic law of the existing state of which the seceding entity presently forms a part (R.Y. Jennings, *The Acquisition of Territory in International Law* (1963), at pp. 8-9). Where, as here, unilateral secession would be incompatible with the domestic Constitution, international law is likely to accept that conclusion subject to the right of peoples to self-determination, a topic to which we now turn.

(b) The Right of a People to Self-determination

[113] While international law generally regulates the conduct of nation states, it does, in some specific circumstances, also recognize the "rights" of entities other than nation states — such as the right of a *people* to self-determination.

[114] The existence of the right of a people to self-determination is now so widely recognized in international conventions that the

[435] principle has acquired a status beyond "convention" and is considered a general principle of international law (A. Cassese, *Self-determination of peoples: A legal reappraisal* (1995), at pp. 171-72; K. Doehring, "Self-Determination", in B. Simma, ed., *The Charter of the United Nations: A Commentary* (1994), at p. 70).

[115] Article 1 of the *Charter of the United Nations*, Can. T.S. 1945 No. 7, states in part that one of the purposes of the United Nations (U.N.) is:

Article 1

. . . . .

2. To develop friendly relations among nations based on respect for the principle of equal rights and self-determination of peoples, and to take other appropriate measures to strengthen universal peace;

[116] Article 55 of the U.N. *Charter* further states that the U.N. shall promote goals such as higher standards of living, full employment and human rights "[w]ith a view to the creation of conditions of stability and well-being which are necessary for peaceful and friendly relations among nations based on respect for the principle of equal rights and self-determination of peoples".

[117] This basic principle of self-determination has been carried forward and addressed in so many U.N. conventions and resolutions that, as noted by Doehring, *supra*, at p. 60:

The sheer number of resolutions concerning the right of self-determination makes their enumeration impossible.

[118] For our purposes, reference to the following conventions and resolutions is sufficient. Article 1 of both the U.N.'s *International Covenant on Civil and Political Rights*, 999 U.N.T.S. 171, and its *International Covenant on Economic, Social and Cultural Rights*, 993 U.N.T.S. 3, states:

1. All peoples have the right of self-determination. By virtue of that right they freely determine their political status and freely pursue their economic, social and cultural development.

[119] Similarly, the U.N. General Assembly's *Declaration on Principles of International Law Concerning Friendly Relations and Co-operation Among States in Accordance with the Charter of the United Nations*, GA Res. 2625 (XXV), 24 October 1970, states:

By virtue of the principle of equal rights and self-determination of peoples enshrined in the Charter of the United Nations, all peoples have the right freely to determine, without external interference, their political status and to

pursue their economic, social and cultural development, and every State has **[436**
the duty to respect this right in accordance with the provisions of the Charter.

[120] In 1993, the U.N. World Conference on Human Rights
adopted the *Vienna Declaration and Programme of Action*, A/Conf.
157/24, 25 June 1993, that reaffirmed Article 1 of the two above-
mentioned covenants. The U.N. General Assembly's *Declaration on
the Occasion of the Fiftieth Anniversary of the United Nations*, GA
Res. 50/6, 9 November 1995, also emphasizes the right to self-
determination by providing that the U.N.'s member states will:

1. . . .

> Continue to reaffirm the right of *self-determination of all peoples*, taking
> into account the particular situation of peoples under colonial or other
> forms of alien domination or foreign occupation, and recognize the right
> of peoples to take legitimate action in accordance with the Charter of the
> United Nations to realize their inalienable right of self-determination.
> *This shall not be construed as authorizing* or encouraging any action that
> would dismember or impair, totally or in part, the *territorial integrity or
> political unity of sovereign and independent States* conducting them-
> selves in compliance with the principle of equal rights and
> self-determination of peoples and thus possessed of a Government repre-
> senting the whole people belonging to the territory without distinction of
> any kind. [Emphasis added.]

[121] The right to self-determination is also recognized in other
international legal documents. For example, the *Final Act of the
Conference on Security and Co-operation in Europe*, 14 I.L.M.
1292 (1975) (*Helsinki Final Act*), states (in Part VIII):

> The participating States will respect the equal rights of peoples and *their
> right to self-determination*, acting at all times in conformity with the purposes
> and principles of the Charter of the United Nations and with the relevant
> norms of international law, including those relating to territorial integrity of
> States.
>
> By virtue of the principle of equal rights and self-determination of peoples,
> all peoples always have the right, in full freedom, to determine, when and as
> they wish, their internal and external political status, without external inter-
> ference, and to pursue as they wish their political, economic, social and
> cultural development. [Emphasis added.]

[122] As will be seen, international law expects that the right to
self-determination will be exercised by peoples within the framework of existing sovereign states and consistently with the
maintenance of the territorial integrity of those states. Where this is
not possible, in the exceptional circumstances discussed below, a
right of secession may arise.

(i) Defining "Peoples"

[123] International law grants the right to self-determination to "peoples". Accordingly, access to the right requires the threshold step of characterizing as a people the group seeking self-determination. However, as the right to self-determination has developed by virtue of a combination of international agreements and conventions, coupled with state practice, with little formal elaboration of the definition of "peoples", the result has been that the precise meaning of the term "people" remains somewhat uncertain.

[124] It is clear that "a people" may include only a portion of the population of an existing state. The right to self-determination has developed largely as a human right, and is generally used in documents that simultaneously contain references to "nation" and "state". The juxtaposition of these terms is indicative that the reference to "people" does not necessarily mean the entirety of a state's population. To restrict the definition of the term to the population of existing states would render the granting of a right to self-determination largely duplicative, given the parallel emphasis within the majority of the source documents on the need to protect the territorial integrity of existing states, and would frustrate its remedial purpose.

[125] While much of the Quebec population certainly shares many of the characteristics (such as a common language and culture) that would be considered in determining whether a specific group is a "people", as do other groups within Quebec and/or Canada, it is not necessary to explore this legal characterization to resolve Question 2 appropriately. Similarly, it is not necessary for the Court to determine whether, should a Quebec people exist within the definition of public international law, such a people encompasses the entirety of the provincial population or just a portion thereof. Nor is it necessary to examine the position of the aboriginal population within Quebec. As the following discussion of the scope of the right to self-determination will make clear, whatever be the correct application of the definition of people(s) in this context, their right of self-determination cannot in the present circumstances be said to ground a right to unilateral secession.

(ii) Scope of the Right to Self-determination

[126] The recognized sources of international law establish that the right to self-determination of a people is normally fulfilled

through *internal* self-determination — a people's pursuit of its [438
political, economic, social and cultural development within the
framework of an existing state. A right to *external* self-
determination (which in this case potentially takes the form of the
assertion of a right to unilateral secession) arises in only the most
extreme of cases and, even then, under carefully defined circumstances. *External* self-determination can be defined as in the
following statement from the *Declaration on Friendly Relations*,
supra, as:

> The establishment of a sovereign and independent State, the free associa-
> tion or integration with an independent State or the emergence into any other
> political status freely determined by a *people* constitute modes of implement-
> ing the right of self-determination by *that people*. [Emphasis added.]

[127] The international law principle of self-determination has
evolved within a framework of respect for the territorial integrity of
existing states. The various international documents that support the
existence of a people's right to self-determination also contain parallel statements supportive of the conclusion that the exercise of
such a right must be sufficiently limited to prevent threats to an
existing state's territorial integrity or the stability of relations
between sovereign states.

[128] The *Declaration on Friendly Relations*, *supra*, *Vienna
Declaration*, *supra*, and *Declaration on the Occasion of the Fiftieth
Anniversary of the United Nations*, *supra*, are specific. They state,
immediately after affirming a people's right to determine political,
economic, social and cultural issues, that such rights are *not* to:

> ... be construed as authorizing or encouraging any action which would dis-
> member or *impair, totally or in part, the territorial integrity or political unity
> of sovereign and independent States conducting themselves in compliance
> with the principle of equal rights and self-determination of peoples* as
> described above and thus possessed of a government representing the whole
> people belonging to the territory without distinction. [Emphasis added.]

[129] Similarly, while the concluding document of the Vienna
Meeting in 1989 of the Conference on Security and Co-operation in
Europe on the follow-up to the *Helsinki Final Act* again refers to
peoples having the right to determine "their internal and *external*
political status" (emphasis added), that statement is immediately
followed by express recognition that the participating states will at
all times act, as stated in the *Helsinki Final Act*, "in conformity with
the purposes and principles of the Charter of the United Nations and

[439] with the relevant norms of international law, *including those relat -
ing to territorial integrity of states"* (emphasis added). Principle 5
of the concluding document states that the participating states
(including Canada):

> . . . confirm their commitment strictly and effectively to observe the principle
> of the territorial integrity of States. They will refrain from any violation of this
> principle and thus from any action aimed by direct or indirect means, in con-
> travention of the purposes and principles of the Charter of the United Nations,
> other obligations under international law or the provisions of the [Helsinki]
> Final Act, at violating the territorial integrity, political independence or the
> unity of a State. *No actions or situations in contravention of this principle will
> be recognized as legal by the participating States.* [Emphasis added.]

Accordingly, the reference in the *Helsinki Final Act* to a people
determining its external political status is interpreted to mean the
expression of a people's external political status through the government of the existing state, save in the exceptional circumstances
discussed below. As noted by Cassese, *supra*, at p. 287, given the
history and textual structure of this document, its reference to external self-determination simply means that "no territorial or other
change can be brought about by the central authorities of a State that
is contrary to the will of the whole people of that State".

[130] While the *International Covenant on Economic, Social and
Cultural Rights*, *supra*, and the *International Covenant on Civil and
Political Rights*, *supra*, do not specifically refer to the protection of
territorial integrity, they both define the ambit of the right to self-
determination in terms that are normally attainable within the
framework of an existing state. There is no necessary incompatibility between the maintenance of the territorial integrity of existing
states, including Canada, and the right of a "people" to achieve a
full measure of self-determination. A state whose government represents the whole of the people or peoples resident within its
territory, on a basis of equality and without discrimination, and
respects the principles of self-determination in its own internal
arrangements, is entitled to the protection under international law of
its territorial integrity.

(iii) Colonial and Oppressed Peoples

[131] Accordingly, the general state of international law with
respect to the right to self-determination is that the right operates
within the overriding protection granted to the territorial integrity of
"parent" states. However, as noted by Cassese, *supra*, at p. 334,

there are certain defined contexts within which the right to the self- [**440**
determination of peoples does allow that right to be exercised
"externally", which, in the context of this Reference, would potentially mean secession:

> ... the right to external self-determination, which entails the possibility of
> choosing (or restoring) independence, has only been bestowed upon two
> classes of peoples (those under colonial rule or foreign occupation), based
> upon the assumption that both classes make up entities that are inherently dis-
> tinct from the colonialist Power and the occupant Power and that their
> "territorial integrity", all but destroyed by the colonialist or occupying Power,
> should be fully restored;

[132] The right of colonial peoples to exercise their right to self-
determination by breaking away from the "imperial" power is now
undisputed, but is irrelevant to this Reference.

[133] The other clear case where a right to external self-
determination accrues is where a people is subject to alien subjugation, domination or exploitation outside a colonial context. This
recognition finds its roots in the *Declaration on Friendly Relations*,
supra:

> Every State has the duty to promote, through joint and separate action, the
> realization of the principle of equal rights and self-determination of peoples,
> in accordance with the provisions of the Charter, and to render assistance to
> the United Nations in carrying out the responsibilities entrusted to it by the
> Charter regarding the implementation of the principle, in order:
>
> (a) To promote friendly relations and co-operation among States; and
>
> (b) To bring a speedy end to colonialism, having due regard to the freely
>   expressed will of the peoples concerned;
>
> and bearing in mind that subjection of peoples to alien subjugation, domina-
> tion and exploitation constitutes a violation of the principle, as well as a denial
> of fundamental human rights, and is contrary to the Charter of the United
> Nations.

[134] A number of commentators have further asserted that the
right to self-determination may ground a right to unilateral secession in a third circumstance. Although this third circumstance has
been described in several ways, the underlying proposition is that,
when a people is blocked from the meaningful exercise of its right
to self-determination internally, it is entitled, as a last resort, to exercise it by secession. The *Vienna Declaration*, *supra*, requirement
that governments represent "the whole people belonging to the
territory without distinction of any kind" adds credence to the

[441] assertion that such a complete blockage may potentially give rise to a right of secession.

[135] Clearly, such a circumstance parallels the other two recognized situations in that the ability of a people to exercise its right to self-determination internally is somehow being totally frustrated. While it remains unclear whether this third proposition actually reflects an established international law standard, it is unnecessary for present purposes to make that determination. Even assuming that the third circumstance is sufficient to create a right to unilateral secession under international law, the current Quebec context cannot be said to approach such a threshold. As stated by the *amicus curiae*, Addendum to the factum of the *amicus curiae*, at paras. 15-16:

> [TRANSLATION] 15. The Quebec people is not the victim of attacks on its physical existence or integrity, or of a massive violation of its fundamental rights. The Quebec people is manifestly not, in the opinion of the *amicus curiae*, an oppressed people.
>
> 16. For close to 40 of the last 50 years, the Prime Minister of Canada has been a Quebecer. During this period, Quebecers have held from time to time all the most important positions in the federal Cabinet. During the 8 years prior to June 1997, the Prime Minister and the Leader of the Official Opposition in the House of Commons were both Quebecers. At present, the Prime Minister of Canada, the Right Honourable Chief Justice and two other members of the Court, the Chief of Staff of the Canadian Armed Forces and the Canadian ambassador to the United States, not to mention the Deputy Secretary-General of the United Nations, are all Quebecers. The international achievements of Quebecers in most fields of human endeavour are too numerous to list. Since the dynamism of the Quebec people has been directed toward the business sector, it has been clearly successful in Quebec, the rest of Canada and abroad.

[136] The population of Quebec cannot plausibly be said to be denied access to government. Quebecers occupy prominent positions within the government of Canada. Residents of the province freely make political choices and pursue economic, social and cultural development within Quebec, across Canada, and throughout the world. The population of Quebec is equitably represented in legislative, executive and judicial institutions. In short, to reflect the phraseology of the international documents that address the right to self-determination of peoples, Canada is a "sovereign and independent state conducting itself in compliance with the principle of equal rights and self-determination of peoples and thus possessed of a

government representing the whole people belonging to the territory [442 without distinction".

[137] The continuing failure to reach agreement on amendments to the Constitution, while a matter of concern, does not amount to a denial of self-determination. In the absence of amendments to the Canadian Constitution, we must look at the constitutional arrangements presently in effect, and we cannot conclude under current circumstances that those arrangements place Quebecers in a disadvantaged position within the scope of the international law rule.

[138] In summary, the international law right to self-determination only generates, at best, a right to external self-determination in situations of former colonies; where a people is oppressed, as for example under foreign military occupation; or where a definable group is denied meaningful access to government to pursue their political, economic, social and cultural development. In all three situations, the people in question are entitled to a right to external self-determination because they have been denied the ability to exert internally their right to self-determination. Such exceptional circumstances are manifestly inapplicable to Quebec under existing conditions. Accordingly, neither the population of the province of Quebec, even if characterized in terms of "people" or "peoples", nor its representative institutions, the National Assembly, the legislature or government of Quebec, possess a right, under international law, to secede unilaterally from Canada.

[139] We would not wish to leave this aspect of our answer to Question 2 without acknowledging the importance of the submissions made to us respecting the rights and concerns of aboriginal peoples in the event of a unilateral secession, as well as the appropriate means of defining the boundaries of a seceding Quebec with particular regard to the northern lands occupied largely by aboriginal peoples. However, the concern of aboriginal peoples is precipitated by the asserted right of Quebec to unilateral secession. In light of our finding that there is no such right applicable to the population of Quebec, either under the Constitution of Canada or at international law, but that on the contrary, a clear democratic expression of support for secession would lead under the Constitution to negotiations in which aboriginal interests would be taken into account, it becomes unnecessary to explore further the concerns of the aboriginal peoples in this Reference.

[443]   *(2) Recognition of a Factual/Political Reality: the "Effectivity"*
Principle

[140] As stated, an argument advanced by the *amicus curiae* on
this branch of the Reference was that, while international law may
not ground a positive right to unilateral secession in the context of
Quebec, international law equally does not prohibit secession and,
in fact, international recognition would be conferred on such a political reality if it emerged, for example, via effective control of the
territory of what is now the province of Quebec.

[141] It is true that international law may well, depending on the
circumstances, adapt to recognize a political and/or factual reality,
regardless of the legality of the steps leading to its creation.
However, as mentioned at the outset, effectivity, as such, does not
have any real applicability to Question 2, which asks whether a *right*
to unilateral secession exists.

[142] No one doubts that legal consequences may flow from
political facts, and that "sovereignty is a political fact for which no
purely legal authority can be constituted", H.W.R. Wade, "The Basis
of Legal Sovereignty", [1955] *Camb. L.J.* 172, at p. 196. Secession
of a province from Canada, if successful in the streets, might well
lead to the creation of a new state. Although recognition by other
states is not, at least as a matter of theory, necessary to achieve statehood, the viability of a would-be state in the international
community depends, as a practical matter, upon recognition by other
states. That process of recognition is guided by legal norms.
However, international recognition is not alone constitutive of statehood and, critically, does not relate back to the date of secession to
serve retroactively as a source of a "legal" right to secede in the first
place. Recognition occurs only after a territorial unit has been successful, as a political fact, in achieving secession.

[143] As indicated in responding to Question 1, one of the legal
norms which may be recognized by states in granting or withhold-
ing recognition of emergent states is the legitimacy of the process
by which the *de facto* secession is, or was, being pursued. The process of recognition, once considered to be an exercise of pure
sovereign discretion, has come to be associated with legal norms.
See, *e.g., European Community Declaration on the Guidelines on
the Recognition of New States in Eastern Europe and in the Soviet
Union*, 31 I.L.M. 1485 (1992), at p. 1487. While national interest

and perceived political advantage to the recognizing state obviously **[444]**
play an important role, foreign states may also take into account
their view as to the existence of a right to self-determination on the
part of the population of the putative state, and a counterpart domestic evaluation, namely, an examination of the legality of the
secession according to the law of the state from which the territorial
unit purports to have seceded. As we indicated in our answer to
Question 1, an emergent state that has disregarded legitimate obligations arising out of its previous situation can potentially expect to
be hindered by that disregard in achieving international recognition,
at least with respect to the timing of that recognition. On the other
hand, compliance by the seceding province with such legitimate
obligations would weigh in favour of international recognition. The
notion that what is not explicitly prohibited is implicitly permitted
has little relevance where (as here) international law refers the legality of secession to the domestic law of the seceding state and the law
of that state holds unilateral secession to be unconstitutional.

[144] As a court of law, we are ultimately concerned only with
legal claims. If the principle of "effectivity" is no more than that
"successful revolution begets its own legality" (S.A. de Smith,
"Constitutional Lawyers in Revolutionary Situations" (1968), 7
West. Ont. L. Rev. 93, at p. 96, it necessarily means that legality follows ahd does not precede the successful revolution. *Ex hypothesi*,
the successful revolution took place outside the constitutional
framework of the predecessor state, otherwise it would not be characterized as "a revolution". It may be that a unilateral secession by
Quebec would eventually be accorded legal status by Canada and
other states, and thus give rise to legal consequences; but this does
not support the more radical contention that subsequent recognition
of a state of affairs brought about by a unilateral declaration of
independence could be taken to mean that secession was achieved
under colour of a legal right.

[145] An argument was made to analogize the principle of effectivity with the second aspect of the rule of law identified by this
Court in the *Manitoba Language Rights Reference, supra*, at p. 753,
namely, avoidance of a legal vacuum. In that Reference, it will be
recalled, this Court declined to strike down all of Manitoba's legislation for its failure to comply with constitutional dictates, out of
concern that this would leave the province in a state of chaos. In so
doing, we recognized that the rule of law is a constitutional

[445] principle which permits the courts to address the practical consequences of their actions, particularly in constitutional cases. The similarity between that principle and the principle of effectivity, it was argued, is that both attempt to refashion the law to meet social reality. However, nothing of our concern in the *Manitoba Language Rights Reference* about the severe practical consequences of unconstitutionality affected our conclusion that, as a matter of law, all Manitoba legislation at issue in that case was unconstitutional. The Court's declaration of unconstitutionality was clear and unambiguous. The Court's concern with maintenance of the rule of law was directed in its relevant aspect to the appropriate remedy, which in that case was to suspend the declaration of invalidity to permit appropriate rectification to take place.

[146] The principle of effectivity operates very differently. It proclaims that an illegal act may eventually acquire legal status if, as a matter of empirical fact, it is recognized on the international plane. Our law has long recognized that through a combination of acquiescence and prescription, an illegal act may at some later point be accorded some form of legal status. In the law of property, for example, it is well known that a squatter on land may ultimately become the owner if the true owner sleeps on his or her right to repossess the land. In this way, a change in the factual circumstances may subsequently be reflected in a change in legal status. It is, however, quite another matter to suggest that a subsequent condonation of an initially illegal act retroactively creates a legal right to engage in the act in the first place. The broader contention is not supported by the international principle of effectivity or otherwise and must be rejected.

C. Question 3

> In the event of a conflict between domestic and international law on the right of the National Assembly, legislature or government of Quebec to effect the secession of Quebec from Canada unilaterally, which would take precedence in Canada?

[147] In view of our answers to Questions 1 and 2, there is no conflict between domestic and international law to be addressed in the context of this Reference.

IV. SUMMARY OF CONCLUSIONS

[148] As stated at the outset, this Reference has required us to consider momentous questions that go to the heart of our system of constitutional government. We have emphasized that the

Constitution is more than a written text. It embraces the entire [446] global system of rules and principles which govern the exercise of constitutional authority. A superficial reading of selected provisions of the written constitutional enactment, without more, may be misleading. It is necessary to make a more profound investigation of the underlying principles that animate the whole of our Constitution, including the principles of federalism, democracy, constitutionalism and the rule of law, and respect for minorities. Those principles must inform our overall appreciation of the constitutional rights and obligations that would come into play in the event a clear majority of Quebecers votes on a clear question in favour of secession.

[149] The Reference requires us to consider whether Quebec has a right to *unilateral* secession. Those who support the existence of such a right found their case primarily on the principle of democracy. Democracy, however, means more than simple majority rule. As reflected in our constitutional jurisprudence, democracy exists in the larger context of other constitutional values such as those already mentioned. In the 131 years since Confederation, the people of the provinces and territories have created close ties of interdependence (economically, socially, politically and culturally) based on shared values that include federalism, democracy, constitutionalism and the rule of law, and respect for minorities. A democratic decision of Quebecers in favour of secession would put those relationships at risk. The Constitution vouchsafes order and stability, and accordingly, secession of a province "under the Constitution" could not be achieved unilaterally, that is, without principled negotiation with other participants in Confederation within the existing constitutional framework.

[150] The Constitution is not a straitjacket. Even a brief review of our constitutional history demonstrates periods of momentous and dramatic change. Our democratic institutions necessarily accommodate a continuous process of discussion and evolution, which is reflected in the constitutional right of each participant in the federation to initiate constitutional change. This right implies a reciprocal duty on the other participants to engage in discussions to address any legitimate initiative to change the constitutional order. While it is true that some attempts at constitutional amendment in recent years have faltered, a clear majority vote in Quebec on a clear question in favour of secession would confer democratic legitimacy

[447] on the secession initiative which all of the other participants in Confederation would have to recognize.

[151] Quebec could not, despite a clear referendum result, purport to invoke a right of self-determination to dictate the terms of a proposed secession to the other parties to the federation. The democratic vote, by however strong a majority, would have no legal effect on its own and could not push aside the principles of federalism and the rule of law, the rights of individuals and minorities, or the operation of democracy in the other provinces or in Canada as a whole. Democratic rights under the Constitution cannot be divorced from constitutional obligations. Nor, however, can the reverse proposition be accepted. The continued existence and operation of the Canadian constitutional order could not be indifferent to a clear expression of a clear majority of Quebecers that they no longer wish to remain in Canada. The other provinces and the federal government would have no basis to deny the right of the government of Quebec to pursue secession, should a clear majority of the people of Quebec choose that goal, so long as in doing so, Quebec respects the rights of others. The negotiations that followed such a vote would address the potential act of secession as well as its possible terms should in fact secession proceed. There would be no conclusions predetermined by law on any issue. Negotiations would need to address the interests of the other provinces, the federal government, Quebec and indeed the rights of all Canadians both within and outside Quebec, and specifically the rights of minorities. No one suggests that it would be an easy set of negotiations.

[152] The negotiation process would require the reconciliation of various rights and obligations by negotiation between two legitimate majorities, namely, the majority of the population of Quebec, and that of Canada as a whole. A political majority at either level that does not act in accordance with the underlying constitutional principles we have mentioned puts at risk the legitimacy of its exercise of its rights, and the ultimate acceptance of the result by the international community.

[153] The task of the Court has been to clarify the legal framework within which political decisions are to be taken "under the Constitution", not to usurp the prerogatives of the political forces that operate within that framework. The obligations we have identified are binding obligations under the Constitution of Canada.

However, it will be for the political actors to determine what con- **[448]**
stitutes "a clear majority on a clear question" in the circumstances
under which a future referendum vote may be taken. Equally, in the
event of demonstrated majority support for Quebec secession, the
content and process of the negotiations will be for the political
actors to settle. The reconciliation of the various legitimate constitutional interests is necessarily committed to the political rather than
the judicial realm precisely because that reconciliation can only be
achieved through the give and take of political negotiations. To the
extent issues addressed in the course of negotiation are political, the
courts, appreciating their proper role in the constitutional scheme,
would have no supervisory role.

[154] We have also considered whether a positive legal entitlement to secession exists under international law in the factual
circumstances contemplated by Question 1, *i.e.*, a clear democratic
expression of support on a clear question for Quebec secession.
Some of those who supported an affirmative answer to this question
did so on the basis of the recognized right to self-determination that
belongs to all "peoples". Although much of the Quebec population
certainly shares many of the characteristics of a people, it is not necessary to decide the "people" issue because, whatever may be the
correct determination of this issue in the context of Quebec, a right
to secession only arises under the principle of self-determination of
peoples at international law where "a people" is governed as part of
a colonial empire; where "a people" is subject to alien subjugation,
domination or exploitation; and possibly where "a people" is denied
any meaningful exercise of its right to self-determination within the
state of which it forms a part. In other circumstances, peoples are
expected to achieve self-determination within the framework of
their existing state. A state whose government represents the whole
of the people or peoples resident within its territory, on a basis of
equality and without discrimination, and respects the principles of
self-determination in its internal arrangements, is entitled to maintain its territorial integrity under international law and to have that
territorial integrity recognized by other states. Quebec does not
meet the threshold of a colonial people or an oppressed people, nor
can it be suggested that Quebecers have been denied meaningful
access to government to pursue their political, economic, cultural
and social development. In the circumstances, the National

[449] Assembly, the legislature or the government of Quebec do not enjoy a right at international law to effect the secession of Quebec from Canada unilaterally.

[155] Although there is no right, under the Constitution or at international law, to unilateral secession, that is secession without negotiation on the basis just discussed, this does not rule out the possibility of an unconstitutional declaration of secession leading to a *de facto* secession. The ultimate success of such a secession would be dependent on recognition by the international community, which is likely to consider the legality and legitimacy of secession having regard to, amongst other facts, the conduct of Quebec and Canada, in determining whether to grant or withhold recognition. Such recognition, even if granted, would not, however, provide any retro-active justification for the act of secession, either under the Constitution of Canada or at international law.

[156] The reference questions are answered accordingly.

Answers to Questions 1 and 2: No;
not necessary to answer Question 3.

[Report: (1998) 161 DLR (4th) 385]

Diplomatic relations—Immunity—Former head of mission —Acts performed in the exercise of diplomatic functions— Whether immunity subsists after functions have terminated —Vienna Convention on Diplomatic Relations, 1961, Article 39(2) — Immunity from criminal jurisdiction — Whether commission of particularly serious crime may preclude reliance on diplomatic immunity—Whether State may take preventative measures against abuses of diplomatic immunity — Whether criminal prosecution constitutes preventative measure

Diplomatic relations — Immunity — Territorial scope — Whether immunity has *erga omnes* effect in third States or is only applicable in receiving State—Whether this question is regulated by treaty or customary international law — *Agrément* (consent) as basis of immunity—Vienna Convention on Diplomatic Relations, 1961, Article 4—Exception for diplomats in transit—Article 40 of Convention

State immunity—Jurisdiction—Whether war crimes, crimes against humanity or other crimes against international law may preclude State official from relying on State immunity — Significance of Article 7 of Charter of International Military Tribunal, 1945—Whether violation of *jus cogens* might preclude reliance on immunity — Whether any distinction between diplomatic and State immunity in this regard

State succession—Union of States—German reunification— Demise of German Democratic Republic with accesssion of its *Länder* to Federal Republic of Germany — Effect on treaties of German Democratic Republic with third States —Unification Treaty, 1990, Article 12—Effect of reunification on diplomatic relations of German Democratic Republic with third States—Whether accreditations expiring or taken over by Federal Republic—Continuity of the law— Criminal law — Prosecution of former head of foreign mission in German Democratic Republic for acts committed against Federal Republic—Whether permissible following absorption of German Democratic Republic into Federal Republic—Whether any rule of customary international law governing the position

Jurisdiction—Territorial—Criminal jurisdiction—Offences committed in West Berlin prior to German reunification in 1990—Whether committed within the territory of the Federal Republic of Germany—The law of the Federal Republic of Germany

FORMER SYRIAN AMBASSADOR TO THE GERMAN DEMOCRATIC REPUBLIC

(Case No 2 BvR 1516/96)

Federal Republic of Germany, Federal Constitutional Court (BVerfG) (Second Senate)

(Limbach, *President*; Kruis, Kirchhof, Winter, Sommer, Jentsch
and Hassemer, *Judges*)

10 *June* 1997

SUMMARY: *The facts*:—In 1983 a bomb attack at an arts centre in West
Berlin left one person dead and more than twenty people seriously injured.
The Syrian Ambassador to the German Democratic Republic (GDR) at the
time was implicated, in that he had allegedly failed to prevent the terrorist
group which carried out the attack from removing explosives from the Syrian
Embassy, where they had briefly been allowed to store them in accordance
with specific instructions from Syria to its Ambassador "to do everything
possible to assist the group". It was not known how the explosives had reached
West Berlin, although a Syrian Embassy official had refused a request from
the terrorists to transport them there in an Embassy bag, after consultation
with the Ambassador. The terrorists were, however, permitted to leave the
Embassy with the explosives and the attack occurred a few hours later.

Following German reunification and the demise of the GDR in 1990, an
arrest warrant was issued against the former Ambassador by a District Court
in Berlin in July 1994, charging him with being an accessory to murder and
the causing of an explosion. The former Ambassador challenged the warrant
but it was upheld by the Court of Appeal (*Kammergericht*) of Berlin on the basis
that immunity was not a bar to the proceedings even though, at the relevant
time, the accused had been accredited as the Ambassador of Syria in the
GDR.

The former Ambassador then lodged a constitutional complaint in respect
of the arrest warrant, arguing that it violated his rights under Articles 2(1)
(right to self-fulfilment), 2(2) (right to life and physical integrity), 20(3) (rule of
law), 101(1) (inadmissibility of courts with special jurisdiction) and 103(2)
(non-retroactivity of criminal law) of the Basic Law of the Federal Republic
(*Grundgesetz: GG*). He argued in particular that the Court of Appeal had been
wrong in holding that, at the relevant time, the complainant was only
exempted from the criminal jurisdiction of the GDR, but not from that of the
Federal Republic, since diplomatic immunity did not have *erga omnes* effect.

Held:—The constitutional complaint was rejected.

(1) The courts of the Federal Republic had criminal jurisdiction over the
offences at issue because the acts which the complainant was accused of
assisting had been committed within West Berlin and their effects were also
felt there. Accordingly, Federal criminal law was applicable even prior to
German reunification and had not been applied retroactively (pp. 604-5).

(2) The complainant had acted "in the exercise of his functions as a member
of the mission" within the meaning of the Vienna Convention on Diplomatic
Relations, 1961. In these circumstances, Article 39(2) of the Convention
provided that his diplomatic immunity continued to subsist even after his
functions came to an end. Where, as here, a diplomat acted as the head of a
mission, according to instructions received from his Government, his actions
were directly attributable to the sending State. It made no difference whether

598   FRG (FEDERAL CONSTITUTIONAL COURT)

or not the act in question violated the law of the receiving State, or whether it was lawful according to the law of the Federal Republic, or even whether it fulfilled diplomatic functions within the meaning of Article 3 of the Vienna Convention. If a criminal act could never be classified as official, there would be no substance to continuing immunity (pp. 605-7).

(3) Customary international law did not provide for any exception from diplomatic immunity for criminal prosecution, even for particularly serious violations of law. The rules of diplomatic law constituted a self-contained regime which exhaustively laid down the possible reactions to abuse of diplomatic privileges. While it was considered lawful for a State sometimes to take preventative measures to protect itself against gross abuses of diplomatic status, the case at issue concerned not prevention but a criminal prosecution for acts already committed (pp. 607-8).

(4) Article 7 of the Charter of the Nuremberg International Military Tribunal (and the similar provisions of the Statutes of the International Criminal Tribunals for Yugoslavia and Rwanda) provided that the official position of an accused, whether as a leader of a State or as a responsible government official, did not serve to free him from responsibility or mitigate punishment. On the basis of this rule, certain exemptions from immunity were discussed in case-law and doctrine in relation to war crimes, crimes against humanity and other crimes against international law, as well as violations of *jus cogens*. But this discussion applied to States and their organs only in the context of State immunity. Diplomatic immunity and State immunity were two different institutions of international law, each with their own rules, so that it could not be inferred that restrictions in one area also applied in the other. In any case, the complainant could not rely upon immunity as a State organ because the self-contained regime of diplomatic immunity, as a *lex specialis*, prevailed over the general immunity of State organs (pp. 608-9, 613-14).

(5) There was no general rule of customary international law whereby the continuing immunity codified in Article 39(2) of the Vienna Convention on Diplomatic Relations would be binding on third States other than the receiving State and therefore have *erga omnes* effect. This question was a matter for customary international law rather than treaty law since, according to the fifth recital of the Preamble to the Vienna Convention, the rules of customary international law continue to govern all questions not expressly regulated by the Convention. Diplomatic immunity applied only in the receiving State, and not in third States, precisely because the latter had not consented to the diplomat's activity. This principle was confirmed by the fact that Article 40 of the Vienna Convention exceptionally required third States to grant certain immunities to diplomats passing through their territory in transit to or from their receiving State. In other respects, diplomatic immunity was a self-contained regime which was not designed to cover relations between diplomats and third States (pp. 610-12).

(6) There was no rule of customary international law requiring that the obligation of the former GDR to recognize the continuing immunity of a diplomat under Article 39(2) of the Vienna Convention on Diplomatic Relations should be transferred to the Federal Republic by operation of the law of State succession. Indeed international law did not allow the Federal Republic and the GDR to decide unilaterally the fate of their treaties with

third parties. The wording of Article 12 of the Unification Treaty, 1990, confirmed this view by requiring only that the contracting parties should discuss the position of their treaties with a view to deciding upon their continued application or expiry. Furthermore, the Vienna Convention had already been in force in both parts of Germany prior to reunification so that the problem of succession did not arise in relation to it (pp. 614-16).

(7) The Federal Republic could not be forced to recognize the continuing immunity of the complainant by the previous actions of the GDR as a third State. What was decisive was that the Federal Republic itself had never accepted the complainant as a diplomat and had not taken over the accreditations given earlier by the GDR. With the reunification of Germany the GDR had disappeared as a State, its diplomatic relations had come to an end and all its accreditations of missions and diplomats had accordingly expired. Since prosecution of the complainant in the Federal Republic would have been entirely lawful under international law prior to 1990, reunification could not render such prosecution unlawful or give rise to an expectation of a bar to prosecution, based on either the law of diplomatic relations or State succession (pp. 616-17).

The following is the text of the judgment of the Court:[1]

[68]   OPERATIVE PART OF THE JUDGMENT

The constitutional complaint is rejected.

[69]   GROUNDS

A.

The constitutional complaint concerns an arrest warrant for complicity in murder and the causing of an explosion, which was issued against the former ambassador of a foreign State, who was accredited in the GDR [German Democratic Republic].

I.

1. From 1981 to 1989 the complainant was accredited in the GDR as the ambassador of a foreign State, of which he is a national. The Public Prosecutor's Office is investigating him in connection with a bombing attack perpetrated in West Berlin in 1983.

The investigation conducted by the Public Prosecutor's Office concluded that the bombing attack was planned and carried out by a

---

[1] The translation of the text of the judgment from German was prepared by Dr Michael Byers, Fellow of Jesus College, Oxford and Visiting Fellow, Max-Planck Institute for Public International and Comparative Law, Heidelberg. He wishes to thank Dr Claus Kress of the Federal Ministry of Justice, Bonn, for help in checking the translation.

terrorist group. The complainant's sending State had, in a telegram, instructed its embassy in East Berlin to provide every possible assistance to the group. In the middle of August 1983 a member of the terrorist group appeared in the embassy while the complainant was absent and requested permission from the then third secretary to deposit a bag in the embassy. In view of the telegram, which was known to him, the third secretary granted that permission.

Later, the member of the terrorist group returned to the embassy and asked the third secretary to transport the bag to West Berlin for him in an embassy car. At the same time, he revealed that there were explosives in the bag. The third secretary informed the complainant of the request. The complainant first ordered the third secretary to bring him the telegram, in order to read through the text carefully once again, and then decided that the third secretary could refuse to provide the transportation. After the third secretary had returned and informed the terrorist of this, the terrorist took the bag, left the embassy and conveyed the explosive in an unknown manner towards West Berlin.

A few hours later the attack **[70]** was carried out with those explosives. One person died and more than twenty people were seriously injured. A large amount of property damage was also caused.

2. On the basis of these suspicions the District Court issued an arrest warrant against the complainant for complicity in murder and the causing of an explosion (Sections 211, 311 paragraphs 1-3, 27, 52 of the Penal Code). The Provincial Court quashed the warrant for lack of sufficiently compelling evidence against the complainant.

3. The Court of Appeal (*Kammergericht*), on a decision of 10 April 1995, overruled the decision of the Provincial Court and restored the validity of the warrant. It did so on the basis that there was no immunity which barred the proceedings, although the complainant was at the relevant time ambassador in the GDR and the relevant offences had been committed in East Berlin. The relevant jurisdictional provision, Section 18(1) of the Constitution of the Courts Act (*Gerichtsverfassungsgesetz*) had not applied, according to Section 1 of the Introductory Act on the Constitution of the Courts Act (*Einführungsgesetz zum Gerichtsverfassungsgesetz*), in East Berlin prior to unification. Moreover, immunity after the termination of diplomatic status only applied in respect of acts performed in the exercise of official duties as a member of the mission. Providing assistance for a bomb attack did not form part of the functions performed by the complainant in his position as ambassador of his country in the former GDR.

The complainant was held to have contributed to the attack by omission. He had done nothing to prevent the explosives stored in the embassy building from being removed. His duty to act did not arise solely out of the complainant's domestic authority, together with his authority over objects deposited in the embassy. Rather he also provided material assistance with the attack (involvement) by permitting the storage of the explosives in the embassy building. The explosives, which had originally been seized by the GDR, had then been released by the Ministry for State Security. Nevertheless, the fact remained that keeping it in closely monitored East Berlin would otherwise have been difficult. After the complainant became aware of the presence of the explosives in the embassy building, he was under a duty to take steps to undo **[71]** the assistance thus afforded to the impending attack.

II.

1. After the First Chamber of the Second Senate [of the Federal Constitutional Court] decided, on 18 March 1996 (2 BvR 1504/95), not to hear a constitutional complaint directed against the warrant and the decision of the Court of Appeal, the complainant applied to the Court of Appeal to consider a previously unheard complaint under Section 33(a) of the Code of Criminal Procedure (*Sträfprozessordnung*) and quash the warrant. As a basis for this he argued, with the support of two expert opinions of Professors Dr Doehring and Dr Ress, that according to Article 39(2), second sentence, of the Vienna Convention on Diplomatic Relations of 18 April 1961 (*BGBl.* 1964 II, p. 959; hereinafter: VCDR), as well as universal customary international law, the immunity of an ambassador for official acts continued after the termination of his office.

The complainant argued that he had acted in the exercise of official duties. Criminal character alone could not preclude official acts. Otherwise every criminal act would be private, so that an exemption from penal jurisdiction for official acts would remain irrelevant. The complainant was asked to follow instructions and had done so. He was even ordered by his Government to help the terrorist group. He thus made an official decision. A personal interest in the furtherance of the matter was neither recognizable nor demonstrable. Moreover, he argued that State practice provides no evidence whatsoever of a separation of official from non-official acts, whether conducted in an open or concealed manner.

He claimed that the rule that so-called immunity *ratione materiae*, i.e. for official acts, continued after the termination of office, rested on the conception that official acts were attributable to the sending State. Although a special regime existed for diplomatic immunity, this case involved the immunity of the sending State. That immunity was to be respected by all the members of the international community. Such an **[72]** *erga omnes* effect of diplomatic immunity also made sense in terms of furthering relations between States, as well as in terms of the principle of State equality.

The complainant argued that the incorporation of the GDR into the Federal Republic of Germany altered nothing in regard to the already existing obligation of the Federal Republic to guarantee immunity for his official acts performed in the former GDR. Even if the obligation to guarantee immunity arose solely out of a legal relation between the sending State and the GDR, the Federal Republic as successor State was in any case still bound by such an obligation of the predecessor State, to uphold the fundamental norms of international legal relations. Moreover, diplomatic immunity also existed in the interests of third States like the sending State here. It applied even in the case of war or occupation and was part of universally applicable customary international law.

The complainant also argued that the dominant doctrine of unlimited immunity for official acts had not remained unchallenged, although it was also extremely doubtful whether those challenges were supported by legally significant practice. There were opinions in the literature that the immunity of war criminals and those who commit crimes against humanity could be forfeited, as could immunity for violations of norms of peremptory international law (*jus cogens*), in particular by the violation of minimum standards of human rights and also in connection with acts of international terrorism. However, the violation of the duty to retain the explosives in the embassy or give them back to the GDR did not represent an excess nor did it lie fully outside the outer limits of diplomatic relations. Nor, in his view, did it constitute a violation of *jus cogens*. Even if further legal violations of a particuarly serious kind were foreseeable, such as the intentional murder of a person or an attack, there was no parallel with the alleged situation, which was exceptional and involved new facts.

. . .

[73] 2. The Court of Appeal (*Kammergericht*), by a decision of 5 July 1996, upheld its decision of 10 April 1995.

It held that the complainant was at the relevant time only exempt from the criminal jurisdiction of the GDR. The immunity did not have effect *erga omnes*. Although the opposite view was put forward in international legal writings, this did not reflect any general rule of international law. This resulted in particular from Article 40 of the VCDR, according to which immunity in third States exists only under narrow conditions which were not fulfilled here.

The Federal Republic itself was also not bound by the rules on State succession to respect immunity, simply because the GDR had been required to recognize it at the time. A general rule of international law to this effect did not exist. Up until unification, criminal prosecution of the complainant by the Federal Republic would have been possible. There was no reasonable basis for the assumption that the ability to prosecute disappeared with the incorporation of the former GDR into the Federal Republic of Germany.

In addition, it seemed at least doubtful whether the act was committed in the exercise of the complainant's official duties. The decision of 10 April 1995 was not based on the conception that an official function alone could eliminate the criminal character of the manner of its performance. It was always possible that the official character would be negated if the manner of performance was, as here, generally to be regarded as no more than remotely connected to a diplomat's assigned tasks.

The complainant's duty to act had to be **[74]** affirmed . . . The established facts showed that the embassy building was misused for the storage of explosives by an embassy employee who was subject to the complainant's supervision and responsibility.

III.

The complainant in his constitutional complaint alleges violations of his rights under Articles 2(1), 2(2), 20(3), 101(1) and 103(2) of the Basic Law. He relies on expert opinions from Professors Dr Doehring and Dr Ress and argues that the Court of Appeal was mistaken with regard to the *erga omnes* effect of diplomatic immunity. He argues that diplomatic immunity *erga omnes* is a rule of customary international law, based on State practice. In support of this contention he relies, in accordance with Article 38(1)(d) of the Statute of the International Court of Justice of 26 June 1945 (*BGBl.* 1973 II, p. 505; hereinafter: ICJ Statute), on the teachings of prominent jurists of international law. In his view, the Court of Appeal wrongly failed to refer to these sources.

He argues that, as one would expect on the basis of the connection between diplomatic immunity *ratione materiae* and State immunity, the provisions of Articles 31 and 40 of the VCDR do not allow any interference with the extension of the effect of immunity to third States. A series of expressions of opinion in the literature, which seemingly speak against the *erga omnes* thesis, in reality concern only immunity *ratione personae*, while Article 39(2), second sentence, of the VCDR only regulates diplomatic immunity *ratione materiae* in respect of the receiving State. The position of diplomats in third States is not governed by this provision, but rather by the general rules of customary international law. Neither can it be objected, against the *erga omnes* thesis, that third States are left unprotected as against the acts of diplomats in another State. According to the complainant, this is not the position because, apart from the requirements set out in Article 40(1) of the VCDR, they are not obligated to allow a diplomat to enter the State concerned.

The complainant argues that diplomatic immunity *ratione materiae* and **[75]** State immunity are also, according to State practice and the literature of international law, separate legal institutions with different objects of protection and different spheres of application. Nevertheless, both legal institutions are comparable in so far as they serve to protect the sovereignty of the sending State. He argues that it would be paradoxical if State immunity could be circumscribed by the diplomat being subject to personal criminal jurisdiction, with the result that, in preliminary proceedings, a verdict over the conduct of the sending State could be rendered.

He also argues that the Court of Appeal failed to take account of the fact that the rules of State succession, at best, free the successor State from earlier treaty obligations, but not from following the norms of general international law.

Lastly, he argues that the Court of Appeal was required, by Article 100(2) of the Basic Law, to submit the important question of the scope of the continuing effect of diplomatic immunity to the Federal Constitutional Court for decision . . .

IV.

The Federal Constitutional Court gave the Berlin Senate, the Public Prosecutor at the Court of Appeal as well as the Federal Government, Federal Parliament and Federal Council the opportunity to make submissions to it.

On request, the Foreign Ministry transmitted a copy of a circular note of 24 August 1990, sent to the foreign missions accredited in Bonn, on the legal legation and protocol effects of the unification of the two German States. According to this note the diplomatic relations of the GDR disappeared with the accession, and the former accreditations lost their validity. Former diplomatic representations of foreign States in the GDR could occasionally continue, with the agreement of the Federal Republic of Germany, but only as offices of their Bonn embassy or as consular representations. In other cases the Foreign **[76]** Ministry was prepared to leave in effect the privileges and immunities provided for in the VCDR, for a period of up to three months after the accession of the GDR took effect. According to the Foreign Ministry, no protests were made against this procedure.

B.

The constitutional complaint is unfounded.

I.

The facts on which a sufficiently compelling case against the complainant were based constituted, for the Federal Republic of Germany, an internal act within the meaning of Sections 3 and 9 of the Penal Code, even at the time of their commission in 1983. According to these provisions, Federal German law is applicable to an act of complicity, *inter alia*, if the principal act was internal (on the meaning of "internal act" see Eser, in: Schönke/Schröder, *Strafgesetzbuch*, 25th edn, 1997, §9, especially margin note 12). An internal act was present here because the effect of the bomb attack occurred in West Berlin and the acts were also perpetrated there. The authorities of the Federal Republic of Germany had therefore been competent to bring the criminal prosecution according to Federal German law prior to unification.

This legal situation did not change as a result of reunification. The substantive criminal law of the Federal Republic has not been applied retroactively.

II.

. . .

[77] 1. . . .

[79] 2. . . . The complainant acted in the exercise of his official functions as a member of the mission and thereby fulfilled the requirements of Article 39(2), second sentence, of the VCDR for continuing immunity (a). There was no exception of unwritten [customary international] law applicable in that regard (b).

a) Article 39(2) of the VCDR provides:

When the functions of a person enjoying privileges and immunities have come to an end, such privileges and immunities shall normally cease at the moment when he leaves the country, or on expiry of a reasonable period in which to do so, but shall subsist until that time, even in case of armed conflict. However, with respect to acts performed by such a person in the exercise of his functions as a member of the mission, immunity shall continue to subsist.

aa) The question of whether the complainant was acting in the exercise of his official functions and therefore had immunity (Articles 29(2), 31(1), first sentence, VCDR) concerns the interpretation of Article 39(2), second sentence, of the VCDR, and thus international treaty law . . .

[80] bb) According to Article 39(2), second sentence, of the VCDR, diplomatic immunity for official acts continues to exist after the termination of the diplomat's position. What is to be understood as an official act follows from the purpose of this rule (see, on the interpretation of international treaties, Article 31(1) of the Vienna Convention on the Law of Treaties of 23 May 1969, *BGBl.* 1985 II, p. 926; hereinafter: VCLT): The official acts of diplomats are attributable to the sending State. Judicial proceedings against diplomats come, in their effects, close to proceedings against the sending State.

Continuing diplomatic immunity for official acts thus serves to protect the sending State itself (see in particular Denza, *Diplomatic Law*, 1976, p. 249; *Zoernsch* v. *Waldock*, English Court of Appeal, International Legal Materials (ILM) 1964, p. 425).[2] This view is reflected in the widely used terminology according to which immunity for official acts is described as *ratione materiae* or functional immunity and immunity for private acts as *ratione personae* or personal immunity (see, in particular, Dahm/ Delbrück/Wolfrum, *Völkerrecht*, vol. I/1, 2nd edn, 1989, pp. 277f.).

An official act in the sense of Article 39(2), second sentence, of the VCDR occurs, in particular, where the diplomat acts for his sending State as a delegated organ whose acts are attributable to the State (see Salmon, *Manuel de droit diplomatique*, 1994, pp. 458ff.). It is unimportant whether the act is in violation of the national law of the receiving State (see Salmon, *Manuel de droit diplomatique*, 1994, p. 466; the same is true even for consular immunity: 36 *BGHSt* 396 at 401; Dahm/Delbrück/ Wolfrum, Völkerrecht, vol. I/1, 2nd edn, 1989, p. 311; on the possibility of official acts of a criminal nature **[81]** see also Folz/Soppe, *Zur Frage der Völkerrechtmässigkeit von Haftbefehlen gegen Regierungsmitglieder anderer Staaten, Neue Zeitschrift für Strafrecht*, 1996, p. 576 at p. 578). These conclusions are derived directly from the meaning of diplomatic immunity, which only applies if the diplomat allegedly or actually violates the law of the receiving State. The guarantee of immunity has no purpose except in respect of such an illegal act.

cc) The complainant acted in the exercise of his official functions as a member of the mission, within the meaning of Article 39(2), second sentence, of the VCDR, because he is charged with an omission that lay within the sphere of his responsibility as ambassador, and which is to that extent attributable to the sending State.

The complainant was charged with having done nothing to prevent the return of the explosive. The Court of Appeal derived the relevant obligation of conduct out of the official responsibility of the complainant, as leader of the mission, for objects left in the embassy. After the explosive was left in the embassy and therefore in the complainant's sphere of control and responsibility, he was obligated, within the framework of his official duties, to decide how the explosive would then be dealt with. The complainant made such a decision, apparently on the basis of the telegraphed instruction from his sending State, so that private interests are not discernible (on the classification of activities on the basis of instructions see the Bingham Case in McNair, *International Law Opinions*, vol. I, 1956, p. 196 at p. 197; Denza, *Diplomatic Law*, 1976, pp. 249f.; Salmon, *Manuel de droit diplomatique*, 1994, pp. 458ff.). Instead, the complainant responded to the third secretary directly, in his position as the superior official, and, according to the view of the Court of Appeal, sought the best solution for the embassy.

[2 41 *ILR* 438.]

For the categorization as an official act, it is irrelevant whether the conduct is legal according to the legal order of the Federal Republic of Germany (see above B.II.2.a)bb)) and whether it fulfilled diplomatic functions in the sense of Article 3 of the VCDR (see also the position taken by the [Swiss] Federal Political Department on 12 May **[82]** 1961, *Schweizerisches Jahrbuch für internationales Recht* (*SJIR*) 21 (1964), p. 171; however, a different position was taken by the Federal Political Department on 31 January 1979, reproduced in *SJIR* 36 (1980), p. 210 at pp. 211f.). The commission of criminal acts does not simply concern the functions of the mission. If a criminal act was never considered as official, there would be no substance to continuing immunity.

b) In addition, there is no relevant customary international law exception from diplomatic immunity here (see Preamble to the VCDR, 5th paragraph) . . .

aa) Diplomatic immunity from criminal prosecution basically knows no exception for particularly serious violations of law. The diplomat can in such situations only be declared *persona non grata* (Article 9 VCDR). (See Denza, Diplomatic Agents and Missions, Privileges and Immunities, *Encyclopedia of Public International Law*, vol. I (1992), p. 1040 at p. 1043: Seidl-Hohenveldern, *Völkerrecht*, 9th edn, 1997, margin note 1028; Fisher, in: Ipsen, *Völkerrecht*, 3rd edn, 1990, pp. 446, 449; Shaw, *International Law*, 3rd edn, 1991, p. 473; Salmon, *Manuel de droit diplomatique*, 1994, p. 480; see also Dahm/Delbrück/Wolfrum, *Völkerrecht*, Vol. I/1, 2nd edn, 1989, p. 278; Brownlie, *Principles of Public International Law*, 4th edn, 1990, p. 357; Higgins, The Abuse of Diplomatic Privileges and Immunities: Recent United Kingdom Experience, AJIL 79 (1985), p. 641 at p. 649; Murty, *The International Law of Diplomacy*, 1989, pp. 347ff., 366ff., 416f.) The possibility nevertheless remains of proceeding against the sending State on the international law plane.

If the receiving State could also proceed against diplomats by recourse to means other than those foreseen by diplomatic law, the foundations of diplomatic relations which make the co-existence of States possible would be shaken. The inviolability of diplomats, as one of the oldest guarantees of customary international law, is a fundamental prerequisite for the maintenance of inter-State relations. In the course **[83]** of history States of all cultures have therefore recognized reciprocal obligations directed at this goal. The institutions of diplomacy, with their privileges and immunities, have emerged over the course of centuries as a universal instrument of effective cooperation within international society. They allow States, unrestricted by their different constitutional and social systems, to develop a mutual understanding and set aside their differences of opinion using friendly means (see [*United States*] *Diplomatic and Consular Staff Case* (Order 15 XII 79), International Court of Justice, Reports of Judgments, Advisory Opinions and Orders (ICJ Rep.) 1979, p. 6 at p. 19;[3] [*United States*] *Diplomatic and Consular Staff Case* (Judgment), ICJ Rep. 1980, p. 1 at pp. 42f.).[4]

The complexity of the modern international community demands, more than ever, that the rules which secure the ordered progress of relations between its members are durable and very carefully respected (see ICJ, *Diplomatic and Consular Staff Case* (Judgment), ICJ Rep. 1980, p. 1 at p. 43).[5] In addition, the special role of reciprocity in diplomatic law should be noted. Each receiving State is equally a sending State. Each restriction and each offence against diplomatic immunities and privileges can, legally or factually, react upon its own diplomats and their relatives abroad (see Higgins, The Abuse of Diplomatic Privileges and Immunities: Recent United Kingdom Experience, AJIL 79 (1985), p. 641 at pp. 641, 650).

The rules of diplomatic law therefore constitute a self-contained regime that exhaustively circumscribes the possible reactions to misuses of diplomatic privileges and immunities (see ICJ, *Diplomatic and Consular Staff Case* (Judgment), ICJ Rep. 1980, p. 1 at p. 40).[6]

bb) Only in respect of preventative measures is it examined, in both judicial decisions and the literature, whether the receiving State may protect itself against gross abuses of diplomatic status (see ICJ, *Diplomatic and Consular Staff Case* (Judgment), ICJ Rep. 1980, p. 1 at p. 40; Herdegen, The Abuse of Diplomatic Privileges **[84]** and Countermeasures not Covered by the Vienna Convention on Diplomatic Relations, *ŽaöRV* 46 (1986), p. 734 at pp. 747ff.; Mann, Inviolability and Other Problems of the Vienna Convention on Diplomatic Relations, in: *Festschrift Karl Doehring*, 1989, p. 553 at pp. 560ff.; Kokott, Missbrauch und Verwirkung von Souveränitätsrechten bei gravierenden Völkerrechtsverstössen, in: *Festschrift Rudolf Bernhardt*, 1995, p. 135 at pp. 136ff.; Brown, Diplomatic Immunity: State Practice under the Vienna Convention on Diplomatic Relations, ICLQ 37 (1988), p. 53 at pp. 86f.; Higgins, The Abuse of Diplomatic Privileges and Immunities: Recent United Kingdom Experience, AJIL 79 (1985), p. 641 at pp. 646ff.; Simma, Self-Contained Regimes, NYIL 16 (1985), p. 111 at pp. 120ff.; Jennings/Watts, *Oppenheim's International Law*, vol. I, 9th edn, 1992, p. 1080, fn. 30; see also already Grotius, *De iure belli ac pacis*, Part II, Ch. XVIII, §IV, 7). However, the case of the complainant does not concern prevention, but rather a warrant of arrest in criminal proceedings aimed at the punishment of a crime already committed.

cc) Article 7 of the Charter of the International Military Tribunal of Nuremberg (UNTS, vol. 82, p. 279)[7] and following it Article 7(2) of

[3 61 *ILR* 513 at 525.]   [5 *Ibid.* at 569.]
[4 61 *ILR* 530 at 568.]   [6 *Ibid.* at 566.]
[7 Article 7 provides: "The official position of defendants, whether as Heads of State or responsible officials in Government Departments, shall not be considered as freeing them from responsibility or mitigating punishment".]

the Statute of the International Criminal Tribunal for Yugoslavia (ILM 32 (1993), p. 1192), as well as Article 6(2) of the Statute for the International Criminal Tribunal for Rwanda (ILM 33 (1994), p. 1602) state that the official position of an accused, whether as a leader of a State or as a responsible official in a government department, does not serve to free him from responsibility or mitigate punishment. Exemptions from immunity for cases of war criminals, violations of international law and offences against *jus cogens* under international law have been discussed as developments of this rule (see Sunga, *Individual Responsibility in International Law for Serious Human Rights Violations*, 1992, *passim*; *Hugo Princz* v. *Federal Republic of Germany*, Court of Appeals for the District of Columbia, ILM 33 (1994), p. 1485 at pp. 1491ff.;[8] *Bruce Smith, Paul S. Hudson et al.* v. *Socialist People's Libyan Arab Jamahiriya*, Court of Appeals for the Second Circuit, ILM 36 (1997), p. 102 at pp. 104ff.;[9] Belsky/Merva/Roht-Arriaza, Implied Waiver under the FSIA: Proposed Exception to Immunity for Violations of Peremptory Norms of International Law, **[85]** California Law Review 77 (1989), pp. 365ff.; Reimann, A Human Rights Exception to Sovereign Immunity: Some Thoughts on *Princz* v. *Federal Republic of Germany*, Michigan Journal of International Law 16 (1995), p. 403 at 404ff.; Zimmermann, Sovereign Immunity and Violations of International *Jus Cogens*—Some Critical Remarks, Michigan Journal of International Law 16 (1995), p. 433; see also 28 USC Section 1605 (a)(7), ILM 36 (1997), p. 759). However, as the wording of Article 7 of the Charter of the International Military Tribunal of Nuremberg makes clear, these exceptions are relevant only to the applicable law of State immunity and the immunity of State organs that flows directly from it, in particular for members of the government, and not to diplomatic immunity.

dd) State immunity and diplomatic immunity represent two different institutions of international law, each with their own rules, so that no inference can be drawn from any restrictions in one sphere as to possible effects in the other (see, on the separation of diplomatic from State immunity, 16 *BVerfGE* 27 at 55).[10] According to Article 39(2)(2) of the VCDR this also applies to continuing immunity, although it is grounded in the protection of the sending State.

The drawing of conclusions from State immunity for diplomatic immunity *ratione materiae* is opposed by the personal element inherent in each case of diplomatic immunity. This personal element protects not the sending State but rather the diplomat personally as the acting organ. Whilst the State may not enjoy the protection of immunity for non-sovereign activity (see 16 *BVerfGE* 27 at 34ff.),[11] this does not mean that a person acting as a diplomatic organ thereby submits to

[8 103 *ILR* 594 at 609 ff.]   [10 45 *ILR* 57 at 76.]
[9 113 *ILR* 534 at 537ff.]   [11 *Ibid.* at 61.]

the jurisdiction of the receiving State (see Salmon, *Manuel de droit diplomatique*, 1994, p. 463; Denza, *Diplomatic Law*, 1976, p. 250). The separation between *acta jure imperii* and *acta jure gestionis*, which is characteristic of State immunity (see *BVerfGE, loc. cit.*), is rather just as unknown in the sphere of Article 39(2), second sentence, of the VCDR as it is in diplomatic immunity generally.

Diplomatic immunity for official acts is thus not simply a reflex of the immunity of the sending State. Instead, **[86]** it clarifies itself particularly in the special status of diplomats. Their presence on the territory of the receiving State and their authority to act there on behalf of the sending State is based on the consent of the receiving State in the form of the *agrément* (Article 4 VCDR). This consent legalizes the personal as well as functional diplomatic immunity. By contrast, State organs only achieve their status through an act of creation that is internal to the State (see Dinstein, Diplomatic Immunity from Jurisdiction *ratione materiae*, ICLQ 15 (1966), p. 76 at p. 88; on the absence of immunity for spies see 92 *BVerfGE* 277 at 321).[12]

3 . . .

a) There is no general rule of international law whereby the continuing immunity codified in Article 39(2), second sentence, of the VCDR extends beyond the provisions of this agreement, and therefore also against third States (on the *erga omnes* effect in international law, see *Barcelona Traction Case*, ICJ Rep. 1970, p. 1 at p. 32;[13] *East Timor Case* (Judgment), ILM 34 (1995), p. 1583 at p. 1589).[14]

aa) Universally applicable rules of customary international law and general principles of law both constitute general rules of international law [in the sense of Article 25 of the Basic Law] (see 23 *BVerfGE* 288 at 317; 94, 315 at 328). The development **[87]** of customary international law basically requires firstly a sufficient degree of State practice, that is to say a durable and uniform practice involving a widely based and representative participation (see 94 *BVerfGE* 315 at 332). Secondly, behind this practice there must also be *opinio juris sive necessitatis*, that is to say the conception as to what international law requires and allows or regards as necessary (see Verdross/Simma, *Universelles Völkerrecht*, 3rd edn, 1984, pp. 353 ff; Dahm/Delbrück/Wolfrum, *Völkerrecht*, vol. I/1, 2nd edn, 1989, pp. 59 ff.; see also Article 38(1)(b), ICJ Statute). Judicial decisions and the opinions of international law scholars are to be referred to as helpful material for the establishment of customary international law (Article 38(1)(d), ICJ Statute).

This question, whether according to Article 39(2), second sentence, of the VCDR continuing immunity applies *erga omnes*, concerns

---

[12 Judgment of the Federal Constitutional Court of 15 May 1995, to be published in a future volume of the *International Law Reports*.]

[13 46 *ILR* 1.]

[14 105 *ILR* 226 at 243.]

customary international law and not international treaty law. It does not concern the interpretation of provisions of the VCDR, but rather the question whether immunity can exist above and beyond the rules of the VCDR, outside the receiving State. According to the fifth paragraph of the Preamble to the VCDR, customary international law applies to those questions which are not regulated by the VCDR.

bb) Diplomatic immunity applies only in the receiving State. Third States have not consented to the activities of diplomats who have no duties to fulfil there. Since earliest times there has been agreement on this principle in the literature, as well as on the questions it raises (cf. Grotius, *De iure belli ac pacis*, Part II, Ch. XVIII, §V, 1; Bynkershoek, *De foro legatorum*, Ch. IX with further notes on the older literature; from the modern literature: Salmon, *Manuel de droit diplomatique*, 1994, p. 416; Zemanek, *Der durchreisende Gesandte, Österreichische Zeitschrift für öffentliches Recht (ÖZöR)* 4 (1952), p. 530 at p. 531; Sen, *A Diplomat's Handbook of International Law and Practice*, 3rd edn, 1988, p. 209; Gore-Booth/Pakenham, *Satow's Guide to Diplomatic Practice*, 5th edn, 1979, p. 154; Noël-Henry, Note on *V et Dicker* v. *D, Tribunal de première instance de Genève*, 29 March 1929, *Clunet* 54 (1929), p. 1184;[15] Cluzel, Note on *Sickles* v. *Sickles, Tribunal civile de la Seine*, 13 March 1909, *Clunet* 37 (1910), p. 533 at p. 534; see **[88]** also Dembinski, *The Modern Law of Diplomacy*, 1988, p. 185; Jennings/Watts, *Oppenheim's International Law*, Vol. I, 9th edn, 1992, p. 1116 is undecided). This principle is confirmed through the exceptions regulated by Article 40 of the VCDR. Such special rules would not be necessary if diplomatic immunity applied *erga omnes*.

Diplomatic law as a self-contained regime, with its integrated possibilities of protection and reaction, is in principle not designed to cover the relations between diplomats and third States. Although the receiving State must guarantee the immunity of diplomats, it does not stand unprotected as a result. It can rescind the *agrément* (Article 4 VCDR), declare a diplomat *persona non grata* (Article 9 VCDR) or even break off diplomatic relations (in this connection see Dinstein, Diplomatic Immunity from Jurisdiction *ratione materiae*, ICLQ 15 (1966), p. 76 at p. 88). This possibility of reaction is a necessary component of the self-contained regime within which diplomatic immunity is first guaranteed (see ICJ, *Diplomatic and Consular Staff Case* (Judgment), ICJ Rep. 1980, p. 1 at p. 40).[16] Also, under the immunity by which an envoy in transit is protected according to Article 40 of the VCDR, the relevant State has the possibility of denying the transit voyage (see Denza, *Diplomatic Law*, 1976, p. 259; Salmon, *Manuel de droit diplomatique*, 1994, p. 420). However, beyond this there do not exist possibilities of protection for third States, through which they could balance any duty to guarantee immunity.

[[15] 3 *Ann Dig* 325.]   [[16] 61 *ILR* 530 at 566.]

cc) The principle of the non-*erga omnes* effect of diplomatic immunity is confirmed by judicial State practice, which does not guarantee immunity for diplomats in third States (cf. *The New Chile Gold Mining Company* v. *Blanco*, Queen's Bench Division, 27 February 1888, British International Law Cases 6 (1967), p. 236 at p. 241; *Léon* v. *Diaz, Cour d'appel d'Amiens*, 29 March 1892, *Clunet* 19 (1892), p. 1137 at p. 1138; *Sickles* v. *Sickles, Tribunal civil de la Seine*, 13 March 1909, *Clunet* 37 (1910), p. 529 at p. 531; *Stoïesco* v. *Stoïesco, Tribunal civil de la Seine*, 9 November 1917, *Clunet* 45 (1918), p. 656; *V et Dicker* v. *D*,[17] *Tribunal de première instance de Genève*, 29 March 1929, *Clunet* 54 (1929), p. 1179 at pp. 1181, 1183). Further confirmation is found in Article 12(2) **[89]** of the Lateran Treaty of 11 February 1929 (English translation in British and Foreign State Papers, vol. 130, p. 791), in that for the territorial peculiarity of the Vatican it is expressly provided that diplomats accredited by the Holy See should also have international law privileges and immunities in Italy. If immunity already had effect *erga omnes* according to general international law, such an expressed agreement would not be necessary (on the exceptional position of Article 12 of the Lateran Treaty see Zemanek, *Der durchreisende Gesandte, ÖZöR* 4 (1952), p. 530 at p. 538; Salmon, *Manuel de droit diplomatique*, 1994, p. 419). Nor does this result conflict with the decision of the French Court of Appeal of Rouen, in which the recognition of an Austrian judgment against a United States ambassador accredited in Austria was denied on the basis of his immunity (*Salm* v. *Frazier, Cour d'appel de Rouen*, 12 July 1933, English translation in: AJIL 28 (1934), pp. 382f.).[18] It was not held that the ambassador was guaranteed immunity from the jurisdiction of the French courts. Rather, the Court took the view that recognition of the Austrian judgment would be a violation of the immunity of the accredited ambassador there and therefore refused to violate diplomatic immunity indirectly by recognizing a judgment which itself violated international law (see Grafton Wilson, *Salm* v. *Frazier:* Diplomatic Immunity, AJIL 28 (1934), pp. 339f.).

dd) Furthermore, the limited effect of immunity does not change at the · moment when the mission is terminated. Although personal immunity is extinguished from that moment forward, functional immunity for official acts continues according to the express provision of Article 39(2), second sentence, of the VCDR. Were this continuing immunity to apply *vis-à-vis* third States, the diplomat would be subject to the jurisdiction of the third State for his official acts during the period of his office, but suddenly immune with respect to the same official acts upon termination of the mission. Consequently, according to Article 39(2), second sentence, of the VCDR, immunities would no longer just continue to subsist, but would actually come into existence with worldwide effect. The proposition that a diplomat should enjoy a

[17] 3 *Ann Dig* 325.]   [18] 7 *Ann Dig* 379.]

wider immunity after the termination of his mission than before contradicts **[90]** the basic conception of the law of diplomatic immunity enshrined in Article 39(2) of the VCDR.

Consequently, contrary to the complainant's view, it does not follow from the fact that continuing immunity is functional and not personal that it also applies in third States. Continuing immunity does not express itself as a simple reflex of State immunity which has *erga omnes* effect (see above B.II.2.b)dd)). Otherwise immunity for official acts, which existed before the termination of the mission, albeit side by side with personal immunity (see Dinstein, Diplomatic Immunity from Jurisdiction *ratione materiae*, ICLQ 15 (1966), p. 76 at p. 79), would also have had *erga omnes* effect during the time of the diplomat's tenure of office.

ee) In addition, an *erga omnes* effect cannot be based on the argument that otherwise a third State could make acts of the sending State subject to judicial proceedings, thereby violating the latter State's immunity. State immunity does not forbid such proceedings. It applies only if the State as such is party to the judicial proceedings. If the diplomat alone is party as a natural person, only diplomatic immunity comes into question (see Ress, Final Report on Developments in the Field of State Immunity and Proposal for a Revised Draft Convention on State Immunity, *International Law Association, Report of the 66th Conference*, 1994, p. 453 at 478, 482).

Furthermore, judicial decisions concerning sovereign acts of other States, within the framework of preliminary questions, are not prohibited under international law and raise doubts only in the Anglo-American legal systems under the so-called Act of State Doctrine (see: 92 *BVerfGE* 277 at 322;[19] Verdross/Simma, *Universelles Völkerrecht*, 3rd edn, 1984, pp. 774ff.; Steinberger, State Immunity, *Encyclopaedia of Public International Law*, Part 10 (1987), p. 428 at p. 429; on the United States Act of State Doctrine see *Banco Nacional de Cuba* v. *Sabbatino*, 376 US, p. 398 at pp. 421ff.;[20] *W. S. Kirkpatrick & Co., Inc. et al.* v. *Environmental Tectonics Corp., International*, ILM 29 (1990), p. 184 at p. 187).[21]

[91] ff) Equally the complainant cannot rely on immunity as a State organ (see Verdross/Simma, *Universelles Völkerrecht*, 3rd edn, 1984, p. 773; Gloria, in: Ipsen, *Völkerrecht*, 3rd edn, 1990, p. 344; at some length, Folz/Soppe, *Zur Frage der Völkerrechtmässigkeit von Haftbefehlen gegen Regierungsmitglieder anderer Staaten, Neue Zeitschrift für Strafrecht*, 1996, p. 576). Such immunity does not depend on the recognition of a receiving State and can therefore have effect *erga omnes*. Nevertheless recourse, alongside the law of diplomatic immunity, to the general immunity of State organs is not possible for diplomats. The self-

[19 Judgment of the Federal Constitutional Court of 15 May 1995, to be published in a future volume of the *International Law Reports*.]
[20 35 *ILR* 2.]
[21 88 *ILR* 93.]

contained regime of diplomatic immunity, as a *lex specialis*, prevails over the general immunity of State organs (see also 92 *BVerfGE* 277 at 321).[22] Recourse to the immunity of State organs, when diplomatic immunity is not available, is denied both in the literature and in State practice. It would, moreover, render meaningless the existing restrictions on diplomatic immunity.

b) The obligation limited to the former GDR to recognize the continuing immunity of the complainant, according to Article 39(2), second sentence, of the VCDR, was not transferred to the Federal Republic of Germany by the international law of State succession.

aa) The question of State succession cannot be answered by Article 12 of the Unification Treaty (UT). This provision neither contains a set of binding legal consequences, nor is it relevant to the case at hand.

On the basis of the international law prohibition on treaties having effects on third parties, codified in Articles 34ff. of the VCLT, the Federal Republic and the GDR could not unilaterally decide, in a binding manner, the fate of their treaties concluded with third States (see Blumenwitz, *Staatennachfolge und die Einigung Deutschlands*, Part I, 1992, pp. 53f. and 103f.; Frowein, *Die Identität der Bundesrepublik Deutschland als Völkerrechtssubjekt, Handbuch des Staatsrechts*, vol. 8, 1995, §196 margin note 5; Drobnig, *Das Schicksal der Staatsverträge der DDR nach dem Einigungsvertrag, Deutsche Rechtszeitung*, 1991, p. 76 at p. 78; Wittkowski, *Die Staatensukzession in völkerrechtliche Verträge unter besonderer Berücksichtigung der Herstellung der staatlichen Einheit Deutschlands*, 1992, pp. 198, 285; **[92]** Mansel, *Staatsverträge und autonomes internationales Privat- und Verfahrensrecht nach der Wiedervereinigung, Juristische Rundschau*, 1990, p. 441 at p. 443; Dannemann, *Das staatsvertragliche Kollisionsrecht der GDR nach der Vereinigung, Deutsche Rechtszeitung*, 1991, p. 130 at p. 131; Silagi, *Staatsuntergang und Staatennachfolge*, 1996, p. 136; Magnus, *Deutsche Rechtseinheit im Zivilrecht, die Übergangsregelungen, Juristische Schulung*, 1992, p. 456 at p. 459; Enderlein/Graefrath, *Nochmals: Deutsche Einheit und internationales Kaufrecht, Betriebsberater*, 1991, Supplement 6, p. 8 at p. 11; also Herber, *Deutsche Einheit und internationales Kaufrecht, Betriebsberater*, 1990, Supplement 37, p. 1 at p. 3). The language of Article 12 of the Unification Treaty corresponds with this view, in that it only expresses a common conviction of the treaty parties and does not fix any particular legal consequences. Instead it signals the way for future diplomatic negotiations (see Drobnig, *Das Schicksal der Staatsverträge der GDR nach dem Einigungsvertrag, Deutsche Rechtszeitung*, 1991, p. 76 at pp. 78, 80; Papenfuss, *Die Behandlung der völkerrechtlichen Verträge der GDR im Zuge der Herstellung der Einheit Deutschlands*, 1997, pp. 77ff., on its coverage of the transition pp. 93ff.; Herber, *Deutsche Einheit und internationales Kaufrecht, Betriebsberater*, 1990, Supplement 37, p. 1 at p. 3; Enderlein/Graefrath, *Nochmals: Deutsche Einheit und internationales Kaufrecht, Betriebsberater*, 1991,

[[22] *Ibid.*]

Supplement 6, p. 8 at p. 11; Wittkowski, *Die Staatensukzession in völkerrechtliche Verträge unter besonderer Berücksichtigung der Herstellung der staatlichen Einheit Deutschlands*, 1992, pp. 292ff.; Silagi, *Staatsuntergang und Staatennachfolge*, 1992, pp. 139 and 155; see also the memorandum on the Unification Treaty, *Bundestags-Drucksache* 11/7760, p. 355 at p. 362). Article 12 of the Unification Treaty therefore indicates that international law requires neither the expiry of all treaties of the GDR (see the memorandum on the Unification Treaty, *Bundestags-Drucksache* 11/7760, p. 355 at p. 362) nor their general continued validity. It thus confirms the principle that, according to international law, neither is there a kind of universal succession of the successor State to all rights and obligations of the predecessor State, nor are such rights and obligations fully extinguished. Rather, individual rules have developed out of State practice for the different case situations (see O'Connell, *State Succession in Municipal Law and International Law*, vol. I, 1967, pp. 8ff., particularly p. 34; Blumenwitz, *Staatennachfolge und die Einigung Deutschlands*, Part I, 1992, p. 22; **[93]** Starke, *Introduction to International Law*, 10th edn, 1989, pp. 322ff.; Brownlie, *Principles of Public International Law*, 4th edn, 1990, p. 655; Shaw, *International Law*, 3rd edn, 1991, pp. 604ff.; Dahm/Delbrück/Wolfrum, *Völkerrecht*, vol. I/1, 2nd edn, 1989, p. 158; Fiedler, State Succession, *Encyclopaedia of Public International Law*, Part 10 (1987), p. 446 at p. 448; Epping, in Ipsen, *Völkerrecht*, 3rd edn, 1990, p. 315; Jennings/Watts, *Oppenheim's International Law*, vol. I, 9th edn, 1992, p. 209).

Furthermore, Article 12 of the Unification Treaty concerns State succession to the international law treaties of the GDR so far as they needed to be extinguished, reaffirmed or adapted. However, as the VCDR was already in force in both the Federal Republic and the GDR (*BGBl.* 1964 II, p. 959; *Gesetzblatt der DDR* 1973 II p. 29), it therefore also applied after unification in an unrestricted manner for the entire Federal Republic of Germany (on such situations see Oeter, German Unification and State Succession, *ZaöRV* 51 (1991), p. 349 at p. 368). The problem of State succession to international law treaties, as regulated by Article 12 of the Unification Treaty, therefore does not arise. Rather, what is involved here is the possible transfer of a particular obligation, to recognize the continuing immunity of the complainant. That obligation bound only the predecessor State, but emanated from a clause in a multilateral treaty binding that State both as predecessor and as successor State.

bb) There is no discernible State practice concerning such a general succession question, irrespective of the question whether examples of the kind of succession involved in the unification of Germany exist at all (see, on the one side, Blumenwitz, *Staatennachfolge und die Einigung Deutschlands*, Part I, 1992, pp. 28 and 46; and, on the other side, Dörr, *Die Inkorporation als Tatbestand der Staatensukzession*, 1995). Consequently, no support is found in general State practice for a rule of customary international law which would require the Federal Republic to recognize the complainant's continuing immunity. This is confirmed by Article 12 of the Unification Treaty, which itself applies to the international law treaties of the GDR, and not only to the individual obligations **[94]** contained therein. No general obligation exists under international law which would bind the successor State. Instead, there is an obligation to seek a negotiated solution in individual cases. The circular note from the Foreign Ministry of 24 August 1990 does not start from a different premise. It only concerns declarations on the absence of immunity according to Article 39(2), first sentence, of the VCDR for diplomats still accredited in the GDR at the time of the unification. It does not concern continuing immunity for the official acts of former diplomats.

cc) Accordingly, the criminal prosecution of the complainant by the Federal Republic of Germany, which was initially in conformity with international law, is not now, as a result of unification and through the operation of the law of State succession, in violation of international law. This view of the law is confirmed by balancing the shared interests concerned from the standpoint of the purpose of continuing immunity (on such balancing in relation to the law of State succession, see O'Connell, *State Succession in Municipal Law and International Law*, vol. II, 1967, p. 24; Starke, *Introduction to International Law*, 10th edn, 1989, p. 326; Papenfuss, *Die Behandlung der völkerrechtlichen Verträge der DDR im Zuge der Herstellung der Einheit Deutschlands*, 1997, p. 27; see also Dahm/Delbrück/Wolfrum, *Völkerrecht*, vol. I/1, 2nd edn, 1989, p. 160; Art. 12(1) of the Unification Treaty).

The sense of Article 39(2), second sentence, VCDR does not point in the direction of a transfer of obligation by way of State succession. That provision does not refer, so far as its scope of applicability is concerned, to the necessary protection of the sending State (which would favour an *erga omnes* effect) but rather to the absence of protection possibilities for third States in respect of the *agrément, persona non grata* procedures and the closing of the mission (see above B.II.3)a), bb) and dd)). However, the Federal Republic does not here find itself pushed into a different situation by a third State. It did not accept the complainant as a diplomat. What is crucial is that, with the disappearance of the GDR, it did not take over that State's earlier accreditation, in particular in the form of the *agrément*. With the unification of Germany the GDR as a State disappeared, and with it also disappeared its diplomatic relations with other States (on the termination of the mission through the disappearance of the sending or receiving State see Guggenheim, **[95]** *Lehrbuch des Völkerrechts*, vol. I, 1948, p. 456). Consequently the earlier accreditations expired. Diplomatic missions in the GDR did not, with unification, become missions of what at that time were third States in the Federal Republic of

Germany. As far as one can see, no foreign State has protested against this practice, which was notified in a circular note from the Foreign Ministry issued on 24 August 1990. Thus, if the Federal Republic of Germany had itself, by the time of unification, still not taken over the *agrément* of existing missions to the GDR, this above all precluded the retrospective transfer of the accreditation of all diplomats who, like the complainant, had once previously been accredited in the GDR.

The purpose of the law of diplomacy and of diplomatic immunity, to make possible effective cooperation and thereby peace within the community of nations, also requires that there should be no transmission of the obligations arising out of Article 39(2), second sentence, of the VCDR. The fact that it was permissible under international law for the Federal Republic, prior to unification, to institute judicial proceedings [of the type at issue], does not imply any prejudice to inter-State cooperation which might be of significance under international law. Nor would such proceedings, if brought by the Federal Republic, constitute such a prejudice merely as a result of the completion in the meantime of German unification.

In addition, the facts of the case are not relevant [from the standpoint of immunity] in so far as they concern the protection of expectations. An expectation of continuing freedom from prosecution is not protected by Article 39(2), second sentence, of the VCDR. Diplomatic immunity does not work directly to protect individual diplomats (see the fourth paragraph of the Preamble of the VCDR). Nor does Article 39(2), second sentence, of the VCDR protect an expectation, on the part of the sending State, that its sovereign acts will not become the object of judicial proceedings in litigation against its organs. Rather, the provision serves to protect the sending State, in the person of its envoys, before the courts of those States which have freely guaranteed the envoys entry. The sending State of the complainant could not, before unification, have had an expectation of a bar to prosecution in the Federal Republic of Germany, and cannot **[96]** subsequently acquire such an expectation, in consideration of the continuity of the Federal Republic of Germany (see in particular Blumenwitz, *Staatennachfolge und die Einigung Deutschlands*, Part I, 1992, p. 47; Enderlein/Graefrath, *Nochmals: Deutsche Einheit und internationales Kaufrecht, Betriebsberater*, 1991, Supplement No 6, p. 8 at p. 10; see also 92, 277 at 330, 348;[23] Art. 11 of the Unification Treaty).

III.

The decision at issue also does not violate Articles 2(1), 2(2)(2) taken in conjunction with 25 of the Basic Law. Therefore, the violation of a

[[23] Judgment of the Federal Constitutional Court of 15 May 1995, to be published in a future volume of the *International Law Reports*.]

basic right must be denied on the ground that the general rule of international law alleged by the complainant does not exist (see above B.II.3.).

IV.

. . .

[Report: 96 *BVerfGE*, p. 68 (in German)]

NOTE.—In the above judgment the Federal German Constitutional Court gave two important rulings concerning the existence of rules of customary international law: there was no rule of customary international law whereby the continuing immunity codified in Article 39(2) of the Vienna Convention on Diplomatic Relations, 1961 was binding on third States and therefore had *erga omnes* effect; there was no rule of customary international law requiring the Federal Republic of Germany to recognize that a diplomat formerly accredited to the German Democratic Republic was entitled to continuing immunity from criminal prosecution under Article 39(2) of the Convention by operation of the rules of State succession.

It has been argued by Professors Doehring and Ress that neither of these rulings corresponds with the current position under international law. Indeed these two professors put forward their views in expert opinions submitted to the Constitutional Court. They subsequently published their opinions, with a commentary, arguing that the Court had interpreted the legal effects of diplomatic immunity in an over-restrictive manner ("Diplomatische Immunität und Drittstaaten", *Archiv des Völkerrechts*, 37, 1999, p. 68 (in German)). There is also a critical note by Fassbender in English in 92 AJIL 74 (1998).

The above case may be contrasted with the treatment, prior to German reunification, of two members of the diplomatic staff of the Embassy of Iraq in East Berlin in August 1980. They were apprehended in West Berlin following a car chase after they had apparently delivered an explosive device to another Iraqi in an attempt to mount a terrorist attack on the Headquarters of the Association of Kurdish Students there. The two diplomats were in possession of special passes issued by the Foreign Ministry of the GDR granting them immunity on the territory of that State. That immunity was not recognized, however, by either the three Western Allied Powers responsible for Berlin or the local authorities in West Berlin.

The Iraqi Ambassador in East Berlin denied the allegations against the two diplomats and protested against a violation of diplomatic protocol. Nevertheless, the two diplomats were formally arrested and charged (by the prosecuting authorities in West Berlin) in September 1980 with attempted murder and possession of arms and explosives. After consultation, the Allied Powers decided the matter fell within those matters delegated to the Senate of West Berlin. The Senate, on the advice of the Government of the Federal Republic, decided merely to expel the two diplomats concerned (*RGDIP* 1981, *Chronique des faits internationaux*, p. 106 (in French)).

Territory — Conquest — Non-recognition — Annexation of Lithuania to Soviet Union—Soviet Union introducing new laws and Constitution in Lithuania—Subsequent national-ization of property, banks and large-scale industry

State succession—Continuity of States—Re-emergence of State—Lithuania—End of annexation by Soviet Union—Lithuania regaining independence—Supreme Council of Lithuania adopting Act of 11 March 1990 on the Restoration of the Independent State of Lithuania—Territory of Lithuania integral and indivisible—Act of 11 March 1990 on the Reinstatement of 12 May 1938 Constitution—Annulment of all laws introduced by Soviet Union — No re-establishment of laws in effect prior to 15 June 1940—Validity of Chapter 8 of 1938 Constitution "National Economy" remaining — Provisional Basic Law of the Republic of Lithuania—Restitution of right to private ownership—Whether private or State ownership of property — Whether property to be restored to former owners according to prescribed laws—Whether any public interest —Whether fair compensation appropriate

Human rights—Property rights—Right to private ownership of property — Right not to be arbitrarily deprived of property—Right enshrined in international legal instruments — Nationalization of property in Lithuania upon its annexation by Soviet Union in 1940 — Restoration of independence in Lithuania in 1990 — Right of private ownership reinstated — Whether property in Lithuania belonging to State or former landowners—Law of 18 June 1991 on the Procedure and Conditions of the Restoration of the Rights of Ownership to the Existing Real Property (the "Restoration Law")—Amended on 15 July 1993 ("law in dispute")—Whether provisions complying with Constitution of Lithuania—Whether parts of item 3 of law in dispute amending Parts 5 and 6 of the Restoration Law contradicting Constitution of Lithuania—Whether items 14, 15, 16, 17, 18 and 19 of law in dispute by which Article 12 of the Restoration Law has been appended by items 10, 11, 12, 13, 14 and 15 complying with Constitution of Lithuania—The law of the Republic of Lithuania

PROPERTY RESTITUTION CASE

(Case No 12/93)

Lithuania, Constitutional Court.	3 *May* 1994

(Algirdas Gailiūnas, Kęstutis Lapinskas, Zigmas Levickis, Pranas Vytautas Rasimavičius, Stasys Stačiokas, Teodora Staugaitienė, Stasys Šedbaras and Juozas Žilys JJ)

SUMMARY: *The facts:*—On 15 June 1940 the Soviet Union invaded, occupied and annexed the State of Lithuania. Lithuania's Constitution of 12 May 1938 was suspended and land, property, banks and large-scale industry were nationalized.[1] On 11 March 1990 the Supreme Council of Lithuania declared that the independent State of Lithuania was restored. The 12 May 1938 Constitution was reinstated upon the adoption of acts by the Supreme Council of the Republic of Lithuania. The laws which had been introduced under the Soviet Union were annulled.[2] However, laws existing prior to annexation were not re-established.[3] The Supreme Council also ratified the Provisional Basic Law of the Republic of Lithuania. On 15 November 1990 the Supreme Council made the statement that citizens were entitled to restoration of existing real property, according to the scope and procedure prescribed by laws and, if that was not possible, to receive due compensation.

A law "On the Procedure and Conditions of the Restoration of the Rights of Ownership to the Existing Real Property" was adopted on 18 June 1991 (the "Restoration Law") and amended on 15 July 1992 (the "law in dispute"). The petitioner, a group of members of the Lithuanian Parliament, asserted that certain provisions of the law in dispute did not comply with the Constitution of Lithuania in that they did not protect the property rights of the owner.[4] Persons described in Article 1 of the Restoration Law were still regarded as owners who had been deprived of the opportunity to use and manage their property. The party concerned, however, contended that all laws and resolutions adopted by the Supreme Council after 11 March 1990 had declared all land to be State property and denied the validity of the petitioner's request that the Court investigate compliance of the provisions with the Constitution.

Held:—(1) As the concept of "Property of the Republic of Lithuania" encompassed three forms of property, that is the private property of

[1] Declarations adopted by the Lithuanian Parliament on 22 and 23 July 1940 "On Proclaiming all the Land of Lithuania National Property" and "On Nationalization of Banks and Large-scale Industry".

[2] The 20 April 1978 Constitution of the Lithuanian SSR (Basic Law), the legislation of the USSR and the Union Republics and other USSR legislation in the Republic of Lithuania were all annulled.

[3] Item 4 of the Reinstatement of the Constitution of Lithuania.

[4] The petitioner maintained that the additions made to Article 12 of the Restoration Law by the law in dispute, by expanding the scope of land which was not to be returned to former owners, contradicted Article 46 of the Constitution which established that Lithuania's economy was to be based on the right to private ownership.

Lithuanian citizens, the property of groups of citizens and State property, according to Article 44 of the Provisional Basic Law of the Republic of Lithuania, it could not be said that the property described in Article 45 was the exclusive property of the State (p. 623).

(2) When the annexation of Lithuania by the Soviet Union was ended the main concern of the Supreme Council was the constitutional dissociation from the occupying State and its legal system and not the establishment of forms of property. This was revealed by the wording of Article 45 of the Provisional Basic Law which stated that all wealth should be national wealth and the exclusive property of Lithuania and not within the jurisdiction of any other State (p. 623).

(3) The restoration of the independence of Lithuania brought with it a return to an economic system based on the right to private ownership. The right to possess property was one of the most significant human rights. A person was not arbitrarily to be deprived of property. Thus, property could only be seized for the needs of society according to the procedure established by law. The principle of the protection of property and the right to property was enshrined in international legal instruments such as the Universal Declaration of Human Rights and the European Convention for the Protection of Human Rights and Fundamental Freedoms. As property nationalized by an occupation government was not taken on a lawful basis it was only factually and not legally managed by the State (pp. 623-5).

(4) Although the right to own property which had been contained in the 12 May 1938 Constitution was confirmed again in the legal system of Lithuania by new constitutional provisions, Article 44 of the Provisional Basic Law and Article 46 of the 1992 Constitution, there was no re-establishment of laws in effect prior to annexation. Chapter 8 of the Constitution "National Economy" remained but it was not possible to reconstruct the former system of property relations in its entirety (p. 625).

(5) Although the Supreme Council had demonstrated its belief that rights of ownership prior to annexation had been unlawfully nullified upon annexation, it also acknowledged that situations did exist whereby it was not possible for existing property to be returned in kind and where the provision of compensation was appropriate. Compensation had to be fair and it too ensured the restoration of property ownership rights (pp. 625-6).

(6) Parts 5 and 6 of Article 4 of the Restoration Law as amended by parts of item 3 of the law in dispute on the restoration of the right of ownership to land used for agricultural purposes did not contradict the Constitution. The right of the State to regulate conditions for such restoration was vital in order to preserve the productivity of the land and so protect public interest as well as the interests of former owners. A former landlord was not restricted to concluding a lease contract in order to restore rights of ownership and thus the principle of the inviolability of property was protected (pp. 627-30)

(7) The provision of item 14 of the law in dispute, appending item 10 to Article 12 of the Restoration Law concerning the buying out of land, contradicted Article 23 of the Constitution. A provision that land "may be" restored to former owners created legal ambiguity and left too much scope for subjective decision-making. Other provisions of item 14, however, did not contradict the Constitution. Given the change in circumstances surrounding

land tenure over the fifty years of annexation, it was appropriate that the State had the right to regulate conditions for the restoration of land. Land comprising orchards, nursery-gardens and such like could be bought out by the State on the ground of public interest as they comprised complete industrial-technological units and fulfilled a public need for specialized production (pp. 630-2).

(8) Item 15 of the law in dispute, appending item 11 to Article 12 of the Restoration Law, did not contradict the Constitution. This provision permitting the buying out of land containing certain irrigation systems for cattle-breeding complexes was necessary in that it protected a special technology which was needed in the public interest of ecological protection and protection of the natural environment (pp. 632-3).

(9) Item 16 of the law in dispute, appending item 12 to Article 12 of the Restoration Law, contradicted Article 23 of the Constitution as the provision allowed the buying out of forest districts and national parks for "the needs of forestry" as opposed to any objectively assessed public interest (p. 633).

(10) Item 17 of the law in dispute, appending item 13 to Article 12 of the Restoration Law, contradicted Article 23 of the Constitution. Although the buying out of land in a rural area was to be for the construction of residential houses, this was not in the public interest if the land was later to be privatized thus violating the rights of the former landowners (pp. 633-4).

(11) Item 18 of the law in dispute, appending item 14 to Article 12 of the Restoration Law, contradicted Article 23 of the Constitution. The buying out of internal waters based on whether they belonged to the water fund of the State or local government was not in the public interest. The provision imposed more conditions on the return of internal waters to former owners impairing their rights (pp. 634-5).

(12) Item 19 of the law in dispute, appending item 15 to Article 12 of the Restoration Law, did not contradict the Constitution as, in providing for the possibility of the State to buy out land establishing a farmer's holding, it avoided a potential conflict with the Law on Farmer's Holding (pp. 635-6).

The following is the text of the judgment of the Court:

[277] On 11 March 1990, the Supreme Council of the Republic of Lithuania adopted the Act on the Restoration of Independent State of Lithuania and declared thereby that the execution of sovereign powers of the Lithuanian State, heretofore constrained by alien forces in 1940, was restored, and Lithuania was once again an independent State. It was also declared that the Constitution of any other State had no jurisdiction within it.

The Supreme Council, by the 11 March 1990 Law "On the Reinstatement of the 12 May 1938 Constitution" annulled the 20 April 1978 Constitution of the Lithuanian SSR (Basic Law), also the fundamentals of legislation of the USSR and Union Republics, as well as other USSR legislation in the Republic of Lithuania. The Supreme Council by the same Law reinstated "the 12 May 1938 Constitution of Lithuania throughout the Republic of Lithuania, suspending those paragraphs and articles governing the status and powers of the President, the Seimas of the Republic, the Assembly, the State Council and the State Supervisory body". The validity of Chapter 8 of the 12 May 1938 Constitution entitled "National Economy", by norms of which property relations are regulated, was not terminated, and this meant the restitution of the institute of the right of private ownership.

The Supreme Council by 11 March 1990 Law "On the Provisional Basic Law of the Republic of Lithuania" terminated the validity of the 12 May 1938 Constitution of Lithuania and ratified the Provisional Basic Law of the Republic of Lithuania. In the first part of Article 44 of this Law it was established that: "The economy of Lithuania shall be based on the property of the Republic of Lithuania, which shall consist of the private property of its citizens, the property of groups of citizens, and state property." The provision is significant primarily because of the fact that the restitution of the institute of the right to private ownership was established again, i.e. its continuity with the constitutions of Lithuanian State was actually recognized. Secondly, three forms of property that existed and were recognized at that time in our State, were enumerated in said Law. Thirdly, all three legalized forms of property were joined under one concept: "Property of the Republic of Lithuania". Therefore, the arguments on the basis of which notions "property of the Republic of Lithuania" and "state property" are identified, are groundless, because it **[278]** is the relation of the whole to its part. Thus, the norm of the first part of Article 45 of the Provisional Basic Law that "the land, its mineral resources, inland and territorial waters, forests, flora and fauna, and other natural resources shall be the national wealth of Lithuania and the exclusive property of the Republic of Lithuania", did not mean that these objects of property were exclusive property of the State. It should be noted, that in the Provisional Basic Law only mineral resources of the land were declared to be the exclusive property of the Republic of Lithuania.

Taking the fact into consideration that between 15 June 1940 and 11 March 1990 Lithuania was occupied, annexed and incorporated into another State—the USSR—of primary importance to the Supreme Council on 11 March 1990 was not the precise establishment of the subjects, objects and forms of property, but the constitutional dissociation from the occupation State and its legal system, and detachment of the State of Lithuania and its citizens from the unlawful governing of the USSR. This was expressed by the wording of Article 45 of the Provisional Basic Law that all the wealth of Lithuania shall be its national wealth and the exclusive property of the Republic of Lithuania, therefore, jurisdiction of any other State shall not be applied to it. Principles of independence that had been set forth in the Act of the Restoration of Independent State of Lithuania, were once again constitutionally established by this norm. That meant return to an economic system based on the right to private ownership, from which Lithuania had been expelled by force against its will.

The right to possess property is one of the most significant human natural rights, and a person may not be arbitrarily deprived of it. It may only be seized for the needs of society according to the procedure established by law. Such principle of the protection of property and rights to property is also formulated in international legal instruments. For instance, in the second part of Article 17 of the Universal Declaration of Human Rights it is specified: "No one shall be arbitrarily deprived of his property." In the first part of Article 1 of the Protocol 1 pertaining to the European Convention for the Protection of Human Rights and Fundamental Freedoms it is maintained: "Every natural or legal person is entitled to the peaceful enjoyment of his possessions. No one shall be deprived of his possessions except in the public interest and subject to the conditions provided for by law and by the general principles of international law."

The independence of the Republic of Lithuania was destroyed by **[279]** force, in realization of unlawful secret agreements of 1939 between the USSR and Hitler's Germany. The unlawfulness of these agreements and their consequences was officially declared already in the February 1990 Resolution of the Supreme Council of the Lithuanian SSR "On 1939 Treaties between Germany and the USSR and elimination of their consequences to Lithuania". It was also stated in this resolution that elections to the People's Seimas, which took place on 14-15 July 1940, were carried out in violation to the Constitution of Lithuania, and it was declared that "the 21 July 1940 Declaration of the People's Seimas concerning Lithuania's entrance into the USSR is unlawful and null and void as it did not express the will of the Lithuanian People".

In the 11 March 1990 Law of the Republic of Lithuania "On the Reinstatement of the 12 May 1938 Constitution of Lithuania" it was stated, that the 12 May 1938 Constitution was suspended when on 15 June 1940 the Soviet Union committed aggression against the independent State of Lithuania and annexed it. Thus, the People's Seimas, which had been formed in violation to the Constitution of Lithuania, was used for the destruction of the economic system established in the Constitution, and for the unconstitutional enforcement of an economic system of an alien State on Lithuania. The Declaration of 22 July 1940 "On Proclaiming all the Land of Lithuania National Property", i.e. State-owned property, may serve as an example of such acts of the People's Seimas. The next day the People's Seimas adopted the "Declaration on Nationalization of Banks and Large-scale Industry", followed by nationalization of other property as well. Such overall nationalization and elimination of private property was carried out not only in rough violation of the 1938 Constitution of Lithuania, but also unlawfully denying human natural right to private ownership by force. Lawful State property could not and did not appear on the basis of such arbitrary acts of occupation government, as rights may not originate on unlawful basis. Therefore, property taken from people in such a way, may be considered as property which is only factually managed by the State.

The right of private ownership found its way back into the legal system of the State due to the constitutional provisions of Article 44 of the Provisional Basic Law and Article 46 of the 1992 Constitution. Thereby, the continuity of the provisions of the 12 May 1938 Constitution governing the property right has been confirmed. However, it is impossible to impartially reconstruct the complete former system of property relations which existed in Lithuania in 1940. In the Law "On **[280]** the Provisional Basic Law of the Republic of Lithuania" it was stated that even changes which took place during occupation period should not be ignored. In the preamble to this Law it is determined that the Supreme Council has taken into consideration the necessity of bringing the provisions of the 12 May 1938 Constitution of Lithuania "with today's changing political, economic and other social relations".

The Supreme Council by the 11 March 1990 Law "On the Reinstatement of the 12 May 1938 Constitution of Lithuania" did not terminate the validity of Chapter 8 of this Constitution entitled "National Economy", the norms of which regulate property relations, however, in item 4 of this Law established that "the reinstatement of the Constitution of Lithuania does not in itself re-establish other laws in effect in the Republic of Lithuania prior to 15 June 1940". While recognizing the restitution of property and continuity of property rights, the Supreme Council on 15 November 1990 confirmed the following statements: "The recognition of continuity of citizens' rights of ownership is unquestionable", (. . .) "To establish that citizens of Lithuania are entitled to the right to restore the existing real property in kind in the scope and procedure prescribed by laws, and when there is no such possibility, to receive due compensation".

The circumstance that there was a need to resolve the issue concerning continuity of the rights of ownership and to vote the recognition of the continuity of property rights of the citizens of the Republic of Lithuania shows that the Supreme Council considered the rights of ownership that had been possessed before nationalization (the right of a particular person to manage, use and dispose of property) as unlawfully nullified. The promulgation of the provision of continuity of property rights was a basis for the implementation of a limited restitution, i.e. for the protection of property rights that had been violated, in the conditions and procedure prescribed by laws.

While recognizing the continuity of property ownership rights, the Supreme Council by the statement of 15 November 1990 actually also ascertained that situations were possible when all the existing property could not be restored in kind. In such cases, it was provided for the possibility to receive compensation. The Constitutional Court indicates that the provision that, providing there is no possibility to restore property in kind, it must be adequately compensated for, does not contradict the principles of inviolability of property and protection of property ownership rights, because fair compensation also ensures restoration of property ownership rights.

[281] The realization of said rights is established in the Law of the Republic of Lithuania "On the Procedure and Conditions of the Restoration of the Rights of Ownership to the Existing Real Property". In Article 1 of this Law it was specified: "This Law shall legislate the procedures and conditions of the restoration of the right of ownership to the citizens of the Republic of Lithuania to the property which was nationalized under the laws of the USSR (Lithuanian SSR), or which was otherwise unlawfully made public, and which, on the day of enactment of this Law, is considered the property of the State, of the public, of co-operative organizations (enterprises), or of collective farms."

The Supreme Council by this Law has recognized that the rights of ownership to the property which was nationalized under the legal acts of the Lithuanian SSR, or which was otherwise unlawfully made public, must be restored. The legislator, while maintaining that the rights of ownership that had been unlawfully terminated, must be restored, also recognized that it had to be done in the procedure and conditions prescribed by laws. It is, on the one hand, overall forcible character of violation of the rights of ownership and, on the other hand, the decision to carry out only limited restitution which predestined the situation when the rights of former owners, that had been unlawfully terminated, could not be protected by means of norms of civil law that were in force at that time. For this purpose, a special law like the Law "On the Procedure and Conditions of the Restoration of the Rights of Ownership to the Existing Real Property", had to be enacted.

Under this Law, the rights of ownership shall be restored not to all former owners of property and not to all the property they had possessed. It contains special conditions, restrictions rather, which are applied to former owners of property who desire to restore their property in kind. Therefore, the statement, that by said Law an attempt is made only to regulate the procedure of the restoration of the rights of ownership, may not be considered as grounded.

The fundamentals of the restoration of the rights to private ownership and to land, which had been earlier violated, were formulated already in the legal acts of the Supreme Council of the Republic of

Lithuania. The establishment of additional conditions and restrictions, disregarding these acts, would not be in compliance with the principled provisions of the continuity and restoration of the rights of ownership, enacted by the legislator. After the enforcement of the Constitution of the Republic of Lithuania on 2 November 1992, laws that were amended or newly adopted laws had to be coordinated with it.

[282] Article 2 of the Law "On the Procedure and Conditions of the Restoration of the Rights of Ownership to the Existing Real Property" is titled: "Citizens Entitled to Restored Ownership Rights", and in this Article, a notion "former owner" is used to define such a person. He, i.e. "the owner of property", is not mentioned in the Law with regard to present time. While evaluating the status of a citizen, who tries to restore the unlawfully terminated rights of ownership, the fact when he acquires the right to manage, use and dispose of some specific property is of considerable importance.

Until his property is restituted or he is paid an appropriate compensation for it, the subjective rights of the former owner to a specific property are not restored yet. The law by itself shall not create subjective rights until it is applied to a specific subject pertaining to the restoration of a specific property. In such a situation the legal meaning of the decision of the institution authorized by the State to restore property in kind or compensate for it is, that only from this proper moment, the former owner acquires the rights of ownership to such property.

The legislator, having defined the procedure and conditions of the restoration of the rights of ownership, emphasized the priority of restoring the actual land property. However, in the event when, due to the factual present land-tenure relations and public interests, it is impossible to grant the actual property, the former owner is guaranteed the right to choose the manner of restoring the right of ownership in the procedure and conditions prescribed by laws.

The restoration of the rights of ownership and land reform are two inseparable processes. Their unity is expressed through their common object—land—therefore, the restoration of the rights of ownership to land is coordinated with land reform.

The aforementioned circumstances must be necessarily taken into consideration while evaluating the compliance of the legal norms of the Law in dispute with the Constitution.

1. On the compliance of the parts of item 3 of the Law "On Appending and Amending the Law 'On the Procedure and Conditions of the Restoration of the Rights of Ownership to the Existing Real Property'", adopted 15 July 1993, by which Parts 5 and 6 of Article 4 of the Law "On the Procedure and Conditions of the Restoration of the Rights of Ownership to the Existing Real Property" of 18 June

1991 have been amended, with the Constitution of the Republic of Lithuania.

In Parts 5 and 6 of Article 4 entitled "Conditions and Procedures **[283]** for the Restoration of the Right of Ownership to Land Situated in Rural Areas" of the Law "On the Procedure and Conditions of the Restoration of the Rights of Ownership to the Existing Real Property", adopted 18 June 1991, which has been amended by the Law in dispute, it is established: "The right of ownership to land used for agricultural purposes shall be restored to: persons establishing farmer's holding; members of agricultural companies and partnerships; persons planning to use the restored land for private economic purposes as well as other agricultural activities; persons, who intend to lease the restored land for other legal persons engaged in farming."

While restoring the right of ownership to the land used for agricultural purposes, it may be done only after identification of the use of this land. This may be either:

1) a person, regaining this land, provided that he is establishing a farmer's holding or is going to use this land for private economic purposes;

2) a tenant (a farmer, a person ready to engage in farming, or an agricultural company), consenting to lease the land (or portion thereof), which is unnecessary for the needs of the landowner's family, for at least 3-year-period. Preliminary consent to lease plots of land used for agricultural purposes, designed in the land-planning project, must be witnessed by a notary. The priority for renting the land goes to the present user of this land.

The specific purpose and status of land, in comparison to other objects of real property, predetermine special legal regulation of land relations. Thus, in the first part of Article 47 of the Constitution it is established that, land, internal waters, forests and parks may only belong to the citizens and the State of the Republic of Lithuania by the right of ownership. The only exception is set forth in the second part of Article 47 of the Constitution: "Plots of land may belong to a foreign state by the right of ownership for the establishment of its diplomatic and consular missions in accordance with the procedure and conditions established by law."

The second part of Article 54 of the Constitution contains the provision that the exhaustion of land shall be prohibited by law. This constitutional principle of land protection shows that land is interpreted as a public value having its social function—to serve the welfare of the **[284]** people. The society is not indifferent to the way the land is used, because it is in public interests to preserve the productivity of land. Therefore, the right of the State to regulate conditions of the restoration of the rights of ownership to land is vital in order to coordinate the interests of former owners with the public interests.

Parts 5 and 6 of Article 4 establish the conditions for the restoration of the rights of ownership, under which land used for agricultural purposes is returned in kind. The specific character of agricultural land is that it is used for agricultural production. Therefore, the legislator, while determining the conditions for the restoration of the land used for agricultural purposes, must neither impair the rights of former owners, nor ignore the public interest to use this land for agricultural purposes. Such public interest is based on the provision established in the third part of Article 46 of the Constitution that the State shall regulate economic activity so that it serves the general welfare of the people.

Parts 5 and 6 of Article 4 contain the provisions that land used for agricultural purposes may be restored to: 1) persons establishing a farmer's holding; 2) members of agricultural companies and partnerships; 3) persons who desire to use the land regained for personal economic needs and other agricultural activity. Said persons at present are already users of the land which is given back to them. It will further be used for its special purpose, therefore, their interests do not contradict public interests.

The provision of the fifth part of Article 4 that the land used for agricultural purposes may be restored "to persons who are going to lease the land which is restored to them for other natural and legal persons engaged in farming", to a portion of former landowners, i.e. to those who themselves are not going to use the land for agricultural purposes, prescribes an unusual condition.

The conclusion of lease contract is the owner's right based on his free will. The obligation to lease land, imposed on the owner, is not acceptable from the point of view of the traditions of civil law, as it restricts the freedom to dispose of land. Though, it must not be disregarded, that this is only a temporary measure used in the implementation of land reform. Land is restored to former owners ready to lease it, even if they would not use it for agricultural purposes. However, while applying unusual conditions for lease, which actually make the former owner lease the restored land for its real user, it is necessary to ensure the imposition of such imperative conditions on the **[285]** other party to the lease contract as well. Thus, in cases when the owner chooses the lease of the land (or a portion thereof) as a condition of the restoration of the land which he had in his ownership earlier, the factual user of this land must conclude a lease contract with a landowner. In the event that the factual land user refuses to conclude a lease contract, such land should be restored to the former owner as a person who has met the condition prescribed by law to lease land. Disputes among parties pertaining to the lease contract and conditions thereof are to be investigated in civil procedure. Another interpretation of the provisions of the Law concerning the land lease would mean the violation of the rights of the former landowner as well as the principle of equality among parties to the contract.

In the event that the former landowner does not desire to conclude said lease contract, he may choose another way of restoring the rights of ownership as an alternative. Such possibility to choose does not deny the principle of the inviolability of property, therefore, Parts 5 and 6 of Article 4 of the Law in dispute do not contradict the Constitution.

2. On the compliance of the items 14, 15, 16, 17, 18 and 19 of the Law "On Appending and Amending the Law 'On the Procedure and Conditions of the Restoration of the Rights of Ownership to the Existing Real Property'", adopted 15 July 1993, by which Article 12 of the Law "On the Procedure and Conditions of the Restoration of the Rights of Ownership to the Existing Real Property" of 18 June 1991 has been appended by items 10, 11, 12, 13, 14 and 15, with the Constitution of the Republic of Lithuania.

In Article 12 of the Law "On the Procedure and Conditions of the Restoration of the Rights of Ownership to the Existing Real Property" of 18 June 1991, which is entitled "The Buying out of Land" it is established: "Land required for State needs as well as other land shall be bought out from persons defined in Article 2 of this Law in the manner specified in Article 16 of this Law . . ."

This Article provides for the cases of buying out of land. The buying out of land regulated by said Article is not identical to the purchase according to the contract of sale which is regulated by the norms of civil law. The contract of sale, in accordance with general principles of making contracts, is based on the free will and equality of the parties. Under this contract, the owner himself assumes the obligation to transfer his property to the purchaser at a contract price, and nobody can make him conclude this contract. The notion "buying out", used in **[286]** Article 12, actually means the right of the institutions authorized by the State to adopt a decision not to restore the existing real property to the former owner provided that there are appropriate conditions established by the legislator himself. Buying out of the land is conditioned by the public interest in it but not by the will of the former owners and other persons specified in the Law. Buying out is not a voluntary transferral of one's property but its seizure compensating for its value. Said persons have only the right to choose the manner of compensation in the procedure prescribed by law. In case of disputes pertaining to the manner of compensation of property or its value, they may defend their interests in court.

While considering the issues of returning the land to former owners, facing the system of socio-economic relations, that was formed during the period of fifty years, is inevitable. Land-tenure has changed: land areas were planted with forests; new water bodies came into being; railways and motorways were built; the main network of oil and gas pipes was laid on; urban areas and land areas covered by industrial enterprises have expanded; large-scale specialized units of agricultural production have been built and are functioning at present. Due to such new circumstances, the right of the State to regulate the conditions of the restoration of the rights of ownership, so that the interests of former owners and public interests were coordinated to the utmost, should not be ignored. The activity of State and its institutions, trying to establish the procedure and conditions of the restoration of the unlawfully terminated rights of ownership, must be based on the constitutional provisions ensuring the protection of the rights of ownership and the general welfare of the people.

In item 10 of Article 12 it is established that land shall be bought out if "it is occupied by orchards, berry-fields, nursery-gardens, gardens with the installed irrigation systems of specialized agricultural enterprises". Such plots may be given back into ownership in kind, without changing the nature of land use, for the persons who shall lease it for agricultural enterprises using this land under the conditions specified in item 9 of said Article.

This norm provides for buying out of land containing orchards, berry-fields, nursery-gardens as well as gardens with installed irrigation systems, that belong to specialized agricultural enterprises. Farming lands of such agricultural enterprises are formed with reference to perspective farming using long-term investments. Apart from irrigation and reclamation systems, other special industrial objects, such as depositories, **[287]** refrigerators, equipment for production processing etc., are installed in these companies. Such orchards, berry-fields, nursery-gardens, gardens along with all the equipment comprise a complete industrial-technological unit. Therefore, special technologies, the same means of pest control can be used, and the cultivation of fruit and vegetables can be specialized.

Unconditional restoration of land would violate industrial-technological integrity of existing complexes, it even can lead to the ruining of all the operation of these units, so that their useful technological potential would be left unused. This would impair the public need for specialized production. The obligation to conclude a lease contract concerning the land to be returned is established meeting the interests of the former owner and society. With regard to the legislator's standpoint that the land must be used for agricultural purposes, the Constitutional Court expressed its opinion while resolving the issue whether Parts 5 and 6 of Article 4, which have been amended by the Law in dispute, are in conformity with the Constitution.

However, the provision of item 10, that plots of land "may be" returned is flawed as it creates legal ambiguity. Such a provision means that the right of the former owner to restore land in kind may be restricted even in cases when he agrees to lease land under conditions prescribed by the Law in dispute. The consent of the former owner to lease shows that he meets all the conditions established by the Law in dispute therefore, it must be evaluated as a juridical fact ensuring the restoration of the actual land property. However, in the presence of said provision ("may be"), this right of the former owner might be restricted by certain State institutions, officials or current land users. Such possibility of subjective decisions contradicts the provision that the restoration of the rights of ownership is predetermined only by the conditions established in the Law "On the Procedure and Conditions of the Restoration of the Rights of Ownership to the Existing Real Property". Therefore, the provision of item 10 of Article 12 that plots of land "may be" restored, contradicts Article 23 of the Constitution.

In item 11 of Article 12 it is established that land shall be bought out if it "contains irrigation systems for overhead irrigation of fodder areas by disposed waters of cattle-breeding complexes".

This norm expresses the legislator's desire to ensure the functioning of existing cattle-breeding complexes as special technologies. Such complexes were formed as integral production systems, the functioning of which cause ecological problems which must not be ignored. Disposed waters that appear in the production cycle of cattle-[288]breeding complexes, must be permanently discharged. For overhead irrigation of such waters plots of land of appropriate size are needed, on which system of two-way regulation of humidity regime—pumping stations, communications of underground pipelines and systems of overhead irrigation—would be installed. If such special technology of elimination of disposed waters were not used, natural environment would be threatened.

The objective situation is such that the industrial-technological process requires said plots of land with above-mentioned equipment. Therefore, such plots of land used for special purposes must necessarily be left near cattle-breeding complexes, because it is related to the public demand for the guarantee of ecological protection.

Due to systematic irrigation of land areas, an appropriate regime of the utilization of irrigated land, essential limitations on crop rotation must be applied. Upon restoration of such land to former owners, the interests of cattle-breeding complexes and individual landowners would inevitably clash. An attempt to combine those interests may face objective as well as subjective obstacles, and may cause disorder in the functioning of the existing ecologically safe production systems.

While solving the issues concerning the restoration of the rights of ownership and providing for the buying out of said plots of land, the legislator took into account not only economic but also ecological interests of society. Thereby, the legislator implemented the function of the State to concern itself with the protection of the natural environment, established in Article 54 of the Constitution. Therefore, there is no ground for recognizing that item 11 of Article 12 contradicts the Constitution.

In item 12 of Article 12 it is established, that land "of forest districts and national parks to be used for the needs of forestry shall be bought out according to the standards determined by the Ministry of Forestry".

Item 12 of Article 12 provides for the possibility not to return the land used for agricultural purposes in kind provided that this land, in compliance with the standards determined by the Ministry of Forestry, is assigned to forest districts and national parks. The restriction of the restoration of the right of ownership is related under this item to vague needs of forestry, without specifying any objective criteria for public interest. The statement that land not subject to restoration is necessary for the maintenance of horses needed for work in forests is not a convincing argument, because such utilization of land may not be regarded as public **[289]** interest. The right to draft standards for agricultural land to be used for the needs of forestry, vested in the Ministry of Forestry, is also groundless. In this case, governmental institution is entitled to the right to determine the size of plots of land to be bought out for its own needs. The establishment of new conditions to be applied in the restoration of the right of ownership is within the competence of the legislator. The Ministry of Forestry actually becomes an institution resolving issues concerning ownership, i.e. it restricts the rights of the former owners to restore land in kind. Whereas, land may be seized only upon a specific decision adopted in compliance with the provisions of the third part of Article 23 of the Constitution.

Limitations on the restoration of land, set forth in item 12, are not based on objectively expressed public interests, therefore, such restriction of the restoration of the rights of ownership of former owners contradicts Article 23 of the Constitution of the Republic of Lithuania.

In item 13 of Article 12 it is established that "land to be bought out in a rural area, shall be used for the construction of residential houses, common use of residents or other public needs in accordance with the settlement-development projects".

During the occupation period in Lithuania, upon denial of the private ownership to land and implementation of collectivization of agriculture as well as establishment of large-scale State farms, an appropriate structure of rural settlements was formed. That period saw the construction of many new rural settlements. Land, which before occupation used to be private property, was now used for the construction of these settlements. At present, the situation is such, when some land areas that used to be private property are now built over by residential houses, structures used for economic, cultural and other social purposes, therefore, this and other commonly used land in settlements may not be considered the existing real property and is not objectively possible to be returned for the former owners.

Due to the economic reform in general, and land reform taken apart, the perspectives of the development of rural settlements are subjected to changes as well. They change in the process of restoration of the rights of private ownership to land. Therefore, preliminary purchase of land for the future construction of residential houses in accordance with settlement-development projects, for common use of residents or for other public needs, may not be based on public interest.

Buying out of land in rural settlements according to the development projects provide for the possibility to privatize it later, i.e. **[290]** other persons will be allowed to acquire it. That would mean, however, the violation of the right of former owners to restore land.

In conformity with aforementioned arguments it is recognized that item 13 of Article 12 contradicts Article 23 of the Constitution.

In item 14 of Article 12 it is established that "rivers and lakes belonging to the water fund of the State and local governments shall be bought out if they are ascribed to water bodies not subject to privatization in accordance with the procedure established by the Government of the Republic of Lithuania".

The legislator, while adopting on 18 June 1991 the Law "On the Procedure and Conditions of the Restoration of the Rights of Ownership to the Existing Real Property", established the conditions which were applied to former owners while returning inland waters. In item 8 of the resolution of the Supreme Council of the Republic of Lithuania "On the Process of Enforcement and Application of the Law of the Republic of Lithuania 'On the Procedure and Conditions of the Restoration of the Rights of Ownership to the Existing Real Property'" it is determined that: "A person shall own any lake of the size determined by the Government of the Republic of Lithuania, water reservoir, canal, pond, and other surface water body, if it is surrounded on all sides by his property."

By way of implementing this resolution, the Government in paragraph 1, item 15 of resolution No 470 of 15 November 1991 established that the restored area of aforementioned waters along with land "must not exceed 5 hectares. In exceptional cases, the restored area may exceed 10 hectares, provided that the Deparment of the Environmental Protection of the Republic of Lithuania gives its consent thereto."

In conformity with earlier formulated provisions of the legislator, the process of the restoration of unlawfully terminated rights of ownership and returning of water bodies to their former owners has already been under way. New conditions that are determined in item 14 of Article 12 impose even more restrictions on the rights of former owners who have not restored their water bodies yet.

Only small in size water bodies have been returned. Therefore, the restrictions imposed on the restoration of such waters may not be justified by abstract public interest. In case that such interest is related to a specific water body, it may, regardless of its size, be seized only in accordance with the decision adopted under the provisions prescribed by the third part of Article 23 of the Constitution.

[291] In item 14 of Article 12, buying out of internal waters is based on their adherence to the State fund or the fund of local governments. This adherence of waters does not manifest public interest. On the contrary, due to this adherence, the possibility arises to ascribe any water bodies to this fund, in accordance with the provision that they are not subject to privatization. Such norm impairs the rights of former owners to restore water bodies in kind, therefore, item 14 of Article 12 contradicts Article 23 of the Constitution.

In item 15 of Article 12 it is established that "land taken into the state land fund for establishing a farmer's holding shall be bought out provided that at present it is leased by persons who are actually engaged in farming and have structures used for economic activity, but may not restore this land in kind".

It was the Law "On Farmer's Holding in the Lithuanian SSR", adopted on 4 July 1989, which at the end of Soviet period for the first time established the allocation of land for farmer's holdings. Those who desired to engage in farming were allotted land free of charge from the land fund designed for farmer's holdings. This fund appropriated land from the State reserve, State forest fund, State farms, collective farms as well as other enterprises and organizations (Article 7 of the Law "On Farmer's Holding in the Lithuanian SSR").

Said provisions were not nullified upon the adoption of the 11 March 1990 Law "On the Provisional Basic Law" in Article 3 of which it is established that: "Laws and other legal acts heretofore in force in Lithuania which do not conflict with the Provisional Basic Law of the Republic of Lithuania shall remain in effect in the Republic of Lithuania". With the presence of such norm, Land Code of the Republic of Lithuania, in accordance with the Law of 5 April 1990, was appended by Article 48-1 providing for the appropriation land into the land fund designed for farmer's holdings. Under this Law, plots of land were appropriated into the fund disregarding the right of ownership of former owners, although the institute of private property had already been returned into the legal system of the State. The allocation of land according to the Law on Farmer's Holding had not been terminated until the day of the enforcement of the Law on Land Reform of the Republic of Lithuania, i.e. until 1 September

1991 (Paragraph 1, item 1 of the Resolution of the Supreme Council "On the Procedure for the Enforcement of the Law on Land Reform of the Republic of Lithuania" of 25 July 1991).

The provisions of item 1, Article 8 of the Law on Land Reform **[292]** meant that the citizens, having received land under the Law on Farmer's Holding, had to buy out or lease from the State an additionally acquired plot. Such provisions show that the State took the obligation to protect the rights of citizens who had acquired land according to the Law on Farmer's Holding, and to pay an appropriate compensation for the former owners.

Thus, the State by laws provided the conditions for persons who acquired land into the ownership under the Law on Farmer's Holding, to settle on this land, engage in farming, as well as to have various structures there. Failing to provide the possibility for the State to buy out such land from the former owners, the contents of legal relations already regulated by laws would be changed. That would mean retroactive validity of Article 12 of the Law "On the Procedure and Conditions of the Restoration of the Rights of Ownership to the Existing Real Property" of 18 June 1991, because it would be applied to juridical facts and legal consequences which appeared on the basis of the Law on Farmer's Holding. Item 15 of Article 12 has eliminated the clash of laws, therefore it does not contradict the Constitution.

Conforming to Article 102 of the Constitution of the Republic of Lithuania as well as Articles 53, 54, 55 and 56 of the Law on the Constitutional Court of the Republic of Lithuania, the Constitutional Court has passed the following

ruling:

To recognize that concerning the Law of the Republic of Lithuania "On Appending and Amending the Law of the Republic of Lithuania 'On the Procedure and Conditions of the Restoration of the Rights of Ownership to the Existing Real Property'", adopted 15 July 1993:

1) those parts of item 3, by which Parts 5 and 6 of Article 4 of the Law "On the Procedure and Conditions of the Restoration of the Rights of Ownership to the Existing Real Property" of 18 June 1991 have been amended, do not contradict the Constitution of the Republic of Lithuania;

2) the provision "may be" of item 14, by which Article 12 of the Law "On the Procedure and Conditions of the Restoration of the Rights of Ownership to the Existing Real Property" of 18 June 1991 has been appended by item 10, contradicts Article 23 of the Constitution of the **[293]** Republic of Lithuania. Other provisions of this item do not contradict the Constitution of the Republic of Lithuania;

3) item 15, by which Article 12 of the Law "On the Procedure and Conditions of the Restoration of the Rights of Ownership to the Existing Real Property" of 18 June 1991 has been appended by item 11, does not contradict the Constitution of the Republic of Lithuania;

4) item 16, by which Article 12 of the Law "On the Procedure and Conditions of the Restoration of the Rights of Ownership to the Existing Real Property" of 18 June 1991 has been appended by item 12, contradicts Article 23 of the Constitution of the Republic of Lithuania;

5) item 17, by which Article 12 of the Law "On the Procedure and Conditions of the Restoration of the Rights of Ownership to the Existing Real Property" of 18 June 1991 has been appended by item 13, contradicts Article 23 of the Constitution of the Republic of Lithuania;

6) item 18, by which Article 12 of the Law "On the Procedure and Conditions of the Restoration of the Rights of Ownership to the Existing Real Property" of 18 June 1991 has been appended by item 14, contradicts Article 23 of the Constitution of the Republic of Lithuania;

7) item 19, by which Article 12 of the Law "On the Procedure and Conditions of the Restoration of the Rights of Ownership to the Existing Real Property" of 18 June 1991 has been appended by item 15, does not contradict the Constitution of the Republic of Lithuania.

This Constitutional Court ruling is final and not subject to appeal. The ruling is promulgated on behalf of the Republic of Lithuania.

[Report: East European Case Reporter of Constitutional Law, vol. 1 No 2, 1994, p. 270]

Relationship of international law and municipal law— Treaties—Human rights—European Convention for the Protection of Human Rights and Fundamental Freedoms, 1950 — Protocols Nos 1, 4 and 7 — Republic of Lithuania ratifying Convention and Protocols—International obligations of Republic of Lithuania—Requirement effectively to implement Convention—Constitution of Republic of Lithuania — Defining rights and freedoms to be guaranteed for individuals

within jurisdiction of the Republic of Lithuania—Article 7 of Constitution rendering any law or legal act contradicting Constitution invalid—Whether Articles 4, 5, 9 and 14 of Convention contradicting Articles 48, 20, 26 and 29 of the Constitution—Whether Article 2 of Protocol No 4, 1963 contradicting Article 32 of Constitution—The law of the Republic of Lithuania

HUMAN RIGHTS CONVENTION CASE

(Case No 22/94)

Lithuania, Constitutional Court.   5 *January* 1995

(Algirdas Gailiūnas, Kęstutis Lapinskas, Zigmas Levickis, Vladas Pavilonis, Pranas Vytautas Rasimavičius, Stasys Stačiokas, Teodora Staugaitienė, Stasys Šedbaras and Juozas Žilys JJ)

SUMMARY: *The facts*:—In May 1993 the Minister of Foreign Affairs of the Republic of Lithuania signed the European Convention for the Protection of Human Rights and Fundamental Freedoms, 1950 ("the Convention") and its Protocols Nos 1, 4 and 7. Article 1 of the Convention[1] obliged the Republic of Lithuania ("Lithuania") to ensure that its human rights legislation complied with the requirements of the Convention.

In February 1994 a working group convened by the President of the Republic under Decree No 233 concluded that certain articles of the Constitution of the Republic of Lithuania ("the Constitution") might not comply with the Convention. In that event Lithuania would have been unable to fulfil its international obligations as Article 7 of the Constitution deemed any law or other legal act which contradicted the Constitution to be invalid.

The petitioner, the President of Lithuania, inquired of the Court as to whether Articles 4,[2] 5,[3] 9[4] and 14[5] of the Convention and Article 2 of Protocol

---

[1] Article 1 of the Convention provides that:
The High Contracting Parties shall secure to everyone within their jurisdiction the rights and freedoms defined in Section 1 of this Convention.
[2] Article 4 of the Convention provides that:
    . . . (2) No one shall be required to perform forced or compulsory labour.
    (3) For the purpose of this article the term forced or compulsory labour shall not include (a) any work required to be done in the ordinary course of detention . . ."
Article 48 of the Constitution provides that:
    . . . labour which is performed by the convicts in places of confinement and which is regulated by law shall not be deemed as forced labour either . . .
[3] Article 5 of the Convention provides that:
    . . . (3) Everyone arrested or detained . . . shall be brought promptly before a judge . . .
Article 20 of the Constitution provides that:
    . . . a person detained in flagrante delicto must, within 48 hours, be brought to court.
[4] Article 9 of the Convention provides that:
    (1) Everyone has the right to freedom of thought, conscience and religion; this right includes freedom to change his religion or belief, and freedom, either alone or in community with others and in public or private, to manifest his religion or belief, in worship, teaching, practice and observance.

No 4[6] were consistent with Articles 48, 20, 26, 29 and 32 of the Constitution respectively.

Held:—Articles 4, 5, 9 and 14 of the Convention and Article 2 of Protocol No 4 were consistent with Articles 48, 20, 26, 29 and 32 of the Constitution respectively.

(1) By reason of the rule, prevalent in Europe, that international treaties be transformed into the municipal legal system of a State, every State ratifying the Convention was under a duty to implement its provisions effectively in order to fulfil its international obligations under the Convention. Such incorporation was established in the Constitution of Lithuania (p. 641).

(2) As a peculiar source of international law whose purpose was universal, the Convention was distinct from many other acts of international law. It acted as a constitutional guarantee for human rights and fundamental freedoms on an international level in the same way as the Constitution of Lithuania did on a national level. As such it was important to evaluate the relationship between the Convention and the Constitution (pp. 641-2).

(3) According to the legal system of Lithuania no law or legal act, including the Convention, could contradict its Constitution. In the event of a contradiction the Republic could not ensure the legal protection of Convention rights and freedoms in an effective remedy before a national authority provided for in Article 13 of the Convention. In order to avoid any legal obstacles, it was necessary for provisions of the Convention to become the constituent part of the domestic law of a State and thus to comply with the Constitution (p. 642).

(4) It was not possible, and nor did the Convention require, that domestic law norms comply literally with the contents and norms of the Convention.

(2) Freedom to manifest one's religion or beliefs shall be subject only to such limitations as are prescribed by law and are necessary in a democratic society in the interests of public safety, for the protection of public order, health or morals, or the protection of the rights and freedoms of others.
Article 26 of the Constitution provides that: ". . . a person's freedom to profess and propagate his or her faith" may be subject to limitations.
[5] Article 14 of the Convention provides that:
The enjoyment of the rights and freedoms set forth in this Convention shall be secured without discrimination on any ground such as sex, race, colour, language, religion, political or other opinion, national or social origin, association with a national minority, property, birth or other status.
Article 29 of the Constitution provides that:
All people shall be equal before the law, the court, and other State institutions and officers . . .
[6] Article 2 of Protocol No 4 provides that:
(1) Everyone lawfully within the territory of a State shall, within that territory, have the right to liberty of movement and freedom to choose his residence.
(2) Everyone shall be free to leave any country, including his own.
(3) No restrictions shall be placed on the exercise of these rights other than such as are in accordance with law and are necessary in a democratic society in the interests of national security or public safety for the maintenance of "ordre public", for the prevention of crime, for the protection of rights and freedoms of others.
(4) The rights set forth in paragraph 1 may also be subject, in particular areas, to restrictions imposed in accordance with law and justified by the public interest in a democratic society.
Article 32 of the Constitution provides that:
Citizens may move and choose their place of residence freely, and may leave Lithuania at their own will.

The Convention did not lay down specific means to be employed by a State to secure Convention rights (p. 642).

(5) The national authority of a State was empowered by the Constitution to determine the level of protection necessary to safeguard Convention rights by the laws of a State. National laws were not to be used as an excuse for the non-implementation and violation of Convention rights and freedoms as the State Party was under a duty to apply Convention norms in the domestic legal system. Exactly how the Convention was to be applied in municipal law depended upon the particular sphere of legal activity involved. Only domestic law could secure Convention rights in that it alone could provide the legal remedy within domestic as opposed to international jurisdiction (pp. 642-4).

(6) Although Article 138(3) of the Constitution provided that international agreements duly ratified were to be applied in the same way as domestic law, Article 7 of the Constitution provided that the Constitution prevailed in the event of any inconsistency with another law. As neither the Constitution nor the Convention contained a complete and final list of human rights and freedoms and as there was no action forbidden by the Constitution which was defined as a right or freedom by the Convention, it could not be said that Convention provisions contradicted the Constitution (pp. 644-6).

(7) It was necessary to examine concrete provisions in order to determine whether there were any Convention provisions which could not be applied in the legal system of Lithuania because they were not consistent with the Constitution. Article 4 of the Convention did not contradict Article 48 of the Constitution. As there was no provision in the Constitution for correctional labour as a criminal penalty, the Convention rule that there was a duty to work only for a person imprisoned or released from detention was not narrower in its scope (pp. 646-8).

(8) Article 5 of the Convention was in conformity with Article 20 of the Constitution. The requirement of the Convention to bring the detainee "promptly" before a judge did not differ in essence from the requirement of the Constitution to bring him "within forty-eight hours" to court. Even if the guarantee of the Convention was more extensive in that it encompassed "everyone" as opposed to the "person in flagrante delicto" in the Constitution, it was possible for the provisions to complement one another. The assessment of the lawfulness of the detention by a judge in the Convention, if evaluated nationally and not literally, did not contradict that of the validity of detention by the court in the Constitution (pp. 648-50).

(9) Article 9 of the Convention was in compliance with Article 26 of the Constitution. Although Article 9 of the Convention did not explicitly refer to a person's freedom to profess and propagate his beliefs as Article 26 of the Constitution did, it still secured freedom of religion albeit defined in different terms. Neither could it be said that the Constitution of Lithuania, with respect to freedom of faith or religion, restricted the right to profess religion or faith (pp. 650-1).

(10) Article 14 of the Convention did not contradict Article 29 of the Constitution. Although the Convention and the Constitution used different words with regard to discrimination, the norms were essentially the same (pp. 651-3).

(11) Article 2 of Protocol No 4 of the Convention was in compliance with Article 32 of the Constitution. Although Article 32 of the Constitution concerned "citizens" as opposed to the more general "everyone lawfully within the territory of a State" of the Protocol, the provisions encompassed each other. Article 2 of Protocol No 4 consisted of two interdependent parts, one implying freedom of movement and freedom to choose one's residence and the other referring only to persons lawfully within a State being entitled to such a right. According to domestic law, non-citizens lawfully within Lithuania had the same rights and freedoms as citizens unless the Constitution, other domestic laws or international agreements provided otherwise (pp. 653-4).

The following is the text of the judgment of the Court:

[82] The European Convention for the Protection of Human Rights and Fundamental Freedoms (hereinafter referred to as the Convention) was concluded in Rome on 4 November 1950 and entered into force on 3 September 1953. According to the first part of Article 66 of the Convention, it must be ratified. Protocol 4 of the Convention was concluded in Strasbourg on 16 September 1963 and came into force on 2 May 1968. On 14 May 1993, the Minister of Foreign Affairs of the Republic of Lithuania signed the Convention and its Protocols No 1, No 4 and No 7. These Protocols must also be ratified.

Section 1 of the Convention defines human rights and freedoms that, according to Articles 1 and 57 thereof, shall be secured by every State which has ratified the Convention to everyone within its jurisdiction. In Article 1 of the Convention it **[83]** is established that: "The High Contracting Parties shall secure to everyone within their jurisdiction the rights and freedoms defined in Section 1 of this Convention." Thus, every State which has ratified the Convention must effectively implement the provisions of the Convention (or its Protocols that have been signed by this State) in order to fully carry out all the obligations under it.

This general requirement is directly connected with the relation between the international law and domestic (national) laws of the States in general and with respect to separate problems, specifically— to the problem of human rights and freedoms. Nowadays, the system of so-called parallel adjustment of international and domestic law is perhaps the most widely spread in Europe; it is based on the rule that international treaties are transformed in the legal system of a State (i.e. are incorporated in it). Such way of realization of international agreements, the Convention among them, is established in the Constitution of the Republic of Lithuania.

The European Convention for the Protection of Human Rights and Fundamental Freedoms is a peculiar source of international law, the purpose of which is different from that of many other acts of international law. This purpose is universal, i.e. to strive for universal and effective recognition of the rights declared in the Universal Declaration of Human Rights and to achieve that they were observed while protecting and further implementing human rights and fundamental freedoms. With respect to its purpose, the Convention performs the same function as the constitutional guarantees for human rights, because the Constitution establishes the guarantees in a State and the Convention—on the international scale. That is why it is very significant to evaluate and establish the relation between the Convention and the Constitution.

Chapter 2 of the Constitution ("The Individual and the State"), also preamble, Chapters 3, 4 and 12 of the Constitution define the rights and freedoms to be guaranteed for individuals within the jurisdiction of the Republic of Lithuania.

[84] The legal system of the Republic of Lithuania is based on the fact that no law or other legal act as well as international agreements (in this case the Convention) may contradict the Constitution. In contrary case the Republic of Lithuania would not be able to ensure the legal protection of the rights and freedoms recognized by the Convention, which is prescribed in Article 13 of the Convention containing the basis for the implementation of the provisions of the Convention in the internal legal system of every State. This Article declares: "Everyone whose rights and freedoms as set forth in this Convention are violated shall have an effective remedy before a national authority notwithstanding that the violation has been committed by persons acting in an official capacity." Consequently, national authority, while implementing legal protection, must directly apply constitutional norms and realize the provisions of the Convention. The provisions must become the constituent part of the domestic law of a State and must meet no obstacles in their application in courts and other authorities providing legal protection.

It should also be emphasized that the requirement that the norms of the domestic law must literally comply with the contents of the norms of the Convention is not directly formulated in the Convention as the realization of this requirement would not be possible. Neither is it strictly specified in the Convention which ways should be employed for the realization of human rights established in the Convention. Every State itself establishes the ways it will use to ensure the application of the provisions of the Convention. At this point it is important to define the so-called limits of compliance, i.e. to determine a sufficiently effective protection of the rights specified in the Convention by the laws of a State. Such "limits of compliance" are provided by the national authority of a State on the basis of the powers prescribed to them by the Constitution. The European Court of Human Rights in its judgment of 6 February 1976 in the *Swedish Engine*

Drivers' Union Case[7] argued that neither Article 13 nor the Convention in general lays down for the Contracting State any given manner for **[85]** ensuring within their internal law the effective implementation of any of the provisions of the Convention.

However, the provisions of Sections 2, 3, 4 and 5 of the Convention concerning the international protection of human rights and freedoms established therein doubtlessly imply that the norms of the Convention must be really implemented and the violation of these rights and freedoms may not be explained by saying that national laws prescribe otherwise. Such validity of the Convention may be explained by the fact that a State Party to the Convention must secure the application of the norms of the Convention in the domestic legal system. Nevertheless, international agreements, the Convention among them, are differently applied in separate spheres of legal activity. Concrete ways and forms of their application are established by the laws of the Republic of Lithuania. In civil proceedings direct application of international agreements is established as a way of solving the competition between such agreements and the norms of laws of the Republic of Lithuania: in case that international agreements of the Republic of Lithuania set forth other rules than it is provided by the laws of the Republic of Lithuania, the rules of international agreements shall prevail (Civil Code, Article 606, and Code of Civil Procedure, Article 482). Said way of deciding the competition of norms shall not be applied in criminal proceedings. In such cases criminal laws and laws of criminal procedure of the Republic of Lithuania shall be directly applied, whereas international agreements shall be applicable only in special cases prescribed by the laws (Article 7(1) of the Criminal Code, and Articles 20, 21, 21(1), 21(2), 22, 22(1) and 22(2) of the Code of Criminal Procedure). If, in the process of application of a criminal law, doubts arose as to the guarantees for the realization of human rights established in the Convention, the issue of the constitutionality of the applied law should be settled in the procedure of constitutional review. On the other hand, human rights determined in the Convention cannot be realized without direct application of domestic law acts. Putting it otherwise, if only direct application **[86]** of the Convention is recognized, said rights cannot be secured because the Convention itself does not provide for any ways of realization of these rights in the States that have ratified the Convention, or legal responsibility of offenders, or appropriate procedures and special jurisdiction for judicial institutions of the States. The rule *ubi jus ibi remedium*, i.e. when the law provides the right it also provides the remedy, is obviously valid here. Such remedy in the legal system of a State is established by the laws of this State. The

Convention sets forth the remedy only for the cases when litigation concerning the protection of human rights established in it becomes the subject-matter of international jurisdiction.

In the third part of Article 138 it is determined: "International agreements which are ratified by the Seimas of the Republic of Lithuania shall be the constituent part of the legal system of the Republic of Lithuania." With respect to the Convention, this constitutional provision implies that upon its ratification and enforcement the Convention will become the constituent part of the legal system of the Republic of Lithuania and shall be applied in the same way as laws of the Republic of Lithuania. The provisions of the Convention in the system of legal sources of the Republic of Lithuania are equalled to the laws, because in Article 12 of the 21 May 1991 Law "On International Agreements of the Republic of Lithuania" (Official Gazette "Valstybės žinios" No 16-415, 1991; No 30-915, 1992) it is established that: "International agreements of the Republic of Lithuania shall have the power of law on the territory of the Republic of Lithuania."

Equal with laws application of the Convention in the domestic law of the Republic of Lithuania and the legal power of its provisions ipso facto does not ensure yet that the provisions of the Convention shall in all cases be effectively applied, because in the first part of Article 7 of the Constitution it is determined: "Any law or other statute which contradicts the Constitution shall be invalid." Although this constitutional provision by itself may not make the international agreement, the Convention in this case, **[87]** invalid, however it requires the compliance of the provisions of the international agreement with the constitutional provisions, because in contrary case it would be problematic to implement the Convention in the domestic law of the Republic of Lithuania.

While evaluating the contents of human rights established in the Constitution and in the Convention, it is necessary to take into consideration methodological basis for coordination of comparative constitutional law and international law. The provisions of the Convention might be recognized as contradicting the Constitution if:

(1) the Constitution established a complete and final list of rights and freedoms and the Convention set forth some other rights and freedoms;

(2) the Constitution prohibited some actions and the Convention defined them as one or another right or freedom;

(3) some provision of the Convention could not be applied in the legal system of the Republic of Lithuania because it was not consistent with some provision of the Constitution.

(1) Pursuant to the general analysis of the Constitution and the Convention it can be stated that neither the Constitution nor the Convention contain a complete and final list of human rights and

freedoms. This is also confirmed in Article 18 of the Constitution which establishes that "the rights and freedoms of individuals shall be inborn". No legal act may establish an exhaustive list of inborn rights and freedoms.

The interpretation of the compatibility (relation) of the norms of the Constitution and the Convention must be semantic, logical and not only literal. Literal interpretation of human rights alone is not acceptable for the nature of the protection of human rights. For example, in the second part of Article 5 of the International Covenant on Civil and Political Rights it is set forth that: "There shall be no restriction upon or derogation from any of the fundamental human rights recognized or existing in any State Party to the present Covenant pursuant to law, conventions, regulations or custom on the pretext that the present Covenant **[88]** does not recognize such rights or that it recognizes them to a lesser extent."

The literal interpretation of legal norms when applied as the only way of interpretation is not acceptable because while interpreting the contents of a legal norm not the particular wording of a certain rule is most significant, but the fact that the text should provide understanding beyond doubt that the instruction is given to certain subjects under certain conditions to act in appropriate way.

The formal literal interpretation of the provisions of the Convention is not recognized in the practice of the European Court of Human Rights as well. This Court on 27 June 1968 in the judgment in *Wemhoff Case*[8] and on 17 June 1970 in the judgment in *Delcourt Case*[9] repeated the same conclusion that, given that it is a law-making treaty, it is also necessary to seek the interpretation that is most appropriate in order to realize the aim and achieve the object of the treaty, not that which would restrict to the greatest possible degree the obligations undertaken by the parties.

The fact that the fundamental rights, freedoms and the guarantees in one or another verbal form are formulated in the Constitution does not allow yet to maintain that these wordings are in all cases absolute in the sense of their application. A law may provide a more extensive formulation of human rights, freedoms and their guarantees than their literal expression in concrete article or its part in the Constitution. Therefore, their broader application is possible only if it is provided by another legal act which has the power of law (in this case, by the Convention and its Protocols). In this case, the third part of Article 138 of the Constitution shall have determining significance, as it establishes the principle of incorporation of international agreements which are ratified by the Seimas, consequently also of their equal application with laws, in the legal system of the Republic of Lithuania.

[⁸ 41 *ILR* 281.]   [⁹ 47 *ILR* 169.]

Therefore, the provisions of the Convention, which define human rights and freedoms, may be applied along with the constitutional provisions provided they do not contradict the latter.

[89] (2) The Constitutional Court after a general analysis of the texts observes that no provision of the Constitution and no provision establishing human rights and freedoms in the Convention allows to maintain that the Constitution forbids some actions whereas the Convention defines them as one or another right or freedom.

While evaluating the interaction of the norms of the Constitution and the Convention and interpretation limits for mutual interaction, the provision of part 1, Article 6 of the Constitution, "the Constitution shall be an integral and directly applicable statute", should not be disregarded. The Constitutional Court emphasizes that the integrity of the Constitution first of all implies that constitutional provisions are related not only formally, i.e. according to the structure of their arrangement, but also according to their contents. This unanimity of norms implies that the preamble to the Constitution, its chapters and articles comprise the significant whole of the Constitution. The significance of the Constitution as integral and directly applicable act is exceptional only when evaluating constitutional provisions pertaining to human rights and freedoms. It is obvious that, while interpreting the contents of concrete constitutional provision, in many cases it is impossible to interpret it separately from other provisions of the Constitution. It is especially important to take this into account with regard to such Chapters of the Constitution as "the Individual and the State", "Society and the State", "National Economy and Labour" and others which contain guarantees for the implementation and means of legal protection of constitutional rights and freedoms.

(3) The Constitutional Court notes that it is possible to answer the question concerning compatibility of concrete provisions of the Convention with concrete articles of the Constitution only after analysing these concrete norms. Further in this conclusion it is presented the analysis of the norms of the Convention and the Constitution the compatibility of which has been questioned in the inquiry.

[90] 1. *On the compliance of Article 4 of the European Convention for the Protection of Human Rights and [Fundamental] Freedoms with the Constitution of the Republic of Lithuania*

In the inquiry of the President of the Republic it is indicated that the second part of Article 4 of the Convention declares that "no one shall be required to perform forced or compulsory labour", and the third part of this Article contains explanation what kind of work is not considered forced or compulsory. Item (a) of the third part provides that this is "any work required to be done in the ordinary course of detention imposed according to the provisions of Article 5 of this

Convention or during conditional release from such detention". Whereas, according to the provision of the fifth part of Article 48 of the Constitution, "labour which is performed by convicts in places of confinement and which is regulated by law shall not be deemed as forced labour either". Every criminal penalty provided in the Criminal Code may comprise the duty of a convict to work. This principle is realized by correctional labour penalty without imprisonment (Article 29 of Criminal Code). The rule formulated in the Convention provides the duty to work only for an individual who has been imprisoned or conditionally released from detention. In the inquiry it is stated that the rule prescribed by the Convention is of somewhat narrower scope, therefore the conclusion can be drawn that item (a) of part 3, Article 4 of the Convention contradicts part 5, Article 48 of the Constitution.

The Constitutional Court emphasizes that such interpretation of the interaction of norms of the Constitution and the Convention is inaccurate first of all because the Constitution does not provide for correctional labour as criminal penalty, in fact such labour is not even mentioned. The rule of the fifth part of Article 48 of the Constitution that labour which is performed by convicts and which is regulated by law shall not be deemed as forced labour either, does not imply, however, that laws must establish correctional labour penalty without imprisonment. It should also be noted that **[91]** the Criminal Code does not provide for the forced employment of a convict as penalty.

On the other hand, forced labour in item (a) of part 3, Article 4 of the Convention related to the application of Article 5 of the Convention, i.e. to lawful detention (or to conditional release from detention). Such standpoint has in essence been confirmed in the practice of the European Court of Human Rights and other courts of the States of Europe. For instance, *Van Droogenbroeck* case[10] the essence of which was forced work done by the recidivist executing a sentence including deprivation of liberty, because the work was required in order to save 12,000 Belgian francs. The European Court of Human Rights in its judgment of 24 June 1982 argued that in this case it was important to evaluate whether conditions of the plaintiff's detention complied with Article 5 of the Convention. The Court also pointed out that the work which Mr Van Droogenbroeck was asked to do did not go beyond what is "ordinary" in this context since it was calculated to assist him in reintegrating himself into society and had as its legal basis provisions which find an equivalent in certain other Member States of the Council of Europe.

The comparative analysis of Article 48 of the Constitution, Article 4 of the Convention and the practice of application of this Article allows to draw the conclusion that item (a), part 3, Article 4 of the European

[10 67 *ILR* 525.]

Convention for the Protection of Human Rights and Fundamental Freedoms does not contradict the Constitution of the Republic of Lithuania.

2. *On the compliance of Article 5 of the European Convention for the Protection of Human Rights and Fundamental Freedoms with the Constitution of the Republic of Lithuania*

In the inquiry of the President of the Republic it is specified that, first, the third part of Article 5 of the Convention prescribes that "everyone arrested or detained . . . shall be brought promptly before a judge". Meanwhile, in the third part of Article 20 it is established that "a person detained in flagrante delicto must, **[92]** within 48 hours, be brought to court". The comparison of these two rules allows to presume that the Convention provides for a more extensive guarantee as, under it, everyone detained in accordance with the criminal procedure shall be brought to court, whereas under the Constitution, only a person detained in flagrante delicto must be brought to court. In the inquiry it is emphasized that in this case it may be stated that this constitutional rule is a special norm, whereas part 2, Article 20 of the Constitution provides for a general norm which declares that "no person may be deprived of freedom except on the bases, and according to the procedures, which have been established in laws", however such conclusion may be presented only by the Constitutional Court.

Second, in the inquiry it is requested to establish whether the term "promptly" used in the Convention complies with the rule of 48 hours determined in the Constitution.

Finally, third, part 4 of Article 5 of the Convention contains the requirement that a judge should decide the lawfulness of detention, whereas under the Constitution the court must decide only the validity of the detention. The petitioner maintains that this difference is essential because a lawful detention is at the same time valid, whereas valid detention can be unlawful.

The Constitutional Court emphasizes that such doubts are not a significant basis for maintaining that the Convention contradicts the Constitution. In the introductory part of the argumentation of this conclusion it has already been stated that the fact that the Constitution does not establish any human rights, freedoms or their guarantees or provides somewhat different wording for them, does not imply, however, that such rights, freedoms or means of their realization may not be guaranteed in the legal system of the Republic of Lithuania. They may be, and usually are, stipulated in other legal acts and are realized while applying these acts. Taking separately, this also may be ensured by applying the Convention on the basis of part 3, Article 138 of the Constitution. It would not be possible **[93]** to apply the provisions of the Convention only in the case that they contradict according to their contents to the Constitution.

First of all, the Constitutional Court, having compared the concepts "shall be brought promptly before a judge" (Convention, Article 5, part 3) and "must, within 48 hours, be brought to court", emphasizes that they in essence do not contradict each other. In the practice of the application of the Convention the period of 48 hours conforms to the provision "promptly brought". In order to found this, there is no need to make an independent analysis of the application of the Convention, because it is universally recognized that the period of four days in cases of usual criminal offences and a five-day-period in exceptional cases are considered as conforming to the requirement of promptness. On the other hand, having compared the constitutions of other Member States of the Council of Europe, we can find analogous constitutional norms. For example, the same term of 48 hours is established in the Constitutions of Portugal and Italy (Articles 28 and 13, respectively), of 72 hours in the Constitution of Spain (Article 17). Thus, even the comparative analysis of the constitutions of Member States of the Council of Europe confirms the above-mentioned evaluation with respect to this issue.

Secondly, in the inquiry, while comparing part 3, Article 20 of the Constitution and part 3, Article 5 of the Convention, the conclusion is made that the Convention provides for a broader procedural guarantee, because under it everyone detained in accordance with the criminal procedure shall be brought to court, whereas under the Constitution only a person detained in flagrante delicto must be brought to court. The Constitutional Court observes that the main purpose of the provisions of part 3, Article 20 of the Constitution is to guarantee that such a person be brought to court. Even in the case that the conclusion made in the inquiry were true, it would be possible to coordinate both provisions. When applied together, they would only complement each other making only legal guarantee.

[94] Thirdly, although in the fourth part of Article 5 of the Convention it is required that a judge should decide the lawfulness of detention, whereas according to part 3, Article 20 of the Constitution the court must determine the validity of the detention, which, in the petitioner's opinion, is the essential difference, these provisions, however, when evaluated not literally but notionally, do not contradict each other. According to the Constitution as well as conforming to the Convention, the Constitutional Court must evaluate the lawfulness and the validity of detention. However, part 3, Article 20 of the Constitution may not be evaluated separately from the text of all this Article and other constitutional provisions concerning the guarantees of lawfulness. In the second part of said Article it is set

forth: "No person may be arbitrarily arrested or detained. No person may be deprived of freedom except on the basis, and according to the procedures, which have been established in laws." These provisions actually establish the principle of lawfulness of detention as a universal rule. The term "validity" used in Article 20 of the Constitution has a more extensive meaning than causative factual relation, i.e. it includes "lawfulness" as well.

Taking all this into consideration, the conclusion may be drawn that Article 5 of the European Convention for the Protection of Human Rights and Fundamental Freedoms is in conformity with the Constitution of the Republic of Lithuania.

3. *On the compliance of Article 9 of the European Convention for the Protection of Human Rights and Fundamental Freedoms with the Constitution of the Republic of Lithuania*

In the inquiry of the President of the Republic it is specified that the second part of Article 9 of the Convention provides for the possibility to restrict a person's "freedom to manifest one's religion or beliefs", whereas part 4, Article 26 of the Constitution declares that "a person's freedom to profess and propagate his or her religion or faith" may be subject to limitations. In the inquiry it is stated that, in the Convention as well as the Constitution, freedom to profess and propagate one's religion or beliefs is discerned into two independent **[95]** freedoms, therefore it may be maintained that the Convention does not prescribe any possibility to restrict a person's freedom to profess his or her religion or beliefs.

The Constitutional Court states that neither Article 9 nor any other article of the Convention contains two independent freedoms, i.e. a person's freedom to profess religion or beliefs and freedom to manifest religion or beliefs. The freedom to profess religion or beliefs is simply not mentioned in the Convention. In the first part of Article 9 of the Convention it is determined: "Everyone has the right to freedom of thought, conscience and religion; this right includes freedom to change his religion or belief and freedom, either alone or in community with others and in public or private, to manifest his religion or belief, in worship, teaching, practice and observance."

Thereby this text of the Convention differs not only from Article 26 of the Constitution but also from the texts of the first part of Article 18 of the International Covenant on Civil and Political Rights containing the word "to have". Consequently, international legal acts and the Constitution while securing to everyone freedom of religion, employ different terms to define this freedom.

Taking this into consideration, there is absolutely no basis for maintaining that Article 26 of the Constitution provides for the possibility to restrict a person's freedom to profess religion or beliefs.

On the contrary, the first part of Article 26 of the Constitution establishes a general principle: "Freedom of thought, conscience, and religion shall not be restricted", whereas the second part provides: "Every person shall have the right to freely choose any religion or faith and, either individually or with others, in public or in private, to manifest his or her religion or faith in worship, observance, practice or teaching."

The profession of religion or beliefs, when taken apart from manifestation and propagation, is a spiritual category implying the possession of religious and faith beliefs. It is not accidental that Lithuanian words "laisvė išpažinti" (freedom to profess) in the French and English texts of the first part of Article 18 of the Covenant on Civil and Political Rights correspond to "la liberté **[96]** d'avoir" and "freedom to have", respectively, the word-for-word translation of which would be "laisvė turėti" (religija ar tikėjima) "freedom to have" (religion or belief). In translations the word "to profess" was used instead of "to have" because the latter does not entirely reflect the spiritual nature of religion or faith and also the inner state of human soul. This state may not be restricted in any way if only by persecuting a person for his religion or faith, and even in such a case the persecution cannot deprive him of his religious beliefs or faith. In this case a general legal principle is valid: *lex non cogit ad impossiblia*—the law does not require impossible things.

The Constitutional Court states that the word "to profess" in the phrase "a person's freedom to profess and propagate his or her religion or faith may be subject only to those limitations prescribed by law" in part 4, Article 26 of the Constitution may be interpreted as corresponding in its sense to the words "one's religion" in the Convention. If part 4, Article 26 of the Constitution had provided separate limitations on the freedom to profess religion or faith, the phrase would be joined by the conjunction "or" instead of "and". The joining of the words "to profess" and "to propagate" by the conjunction "and" means nothing else but one's religion or beliefs. That is why this constitutional provision did not have any negative legal consequences in the legal system of the Republic of Lithuania with respect to freedom of faith or religion, there is no law restricting the right to profess religion or faith.

Taking all this into account the conclusion can be drawn that Article 9 of the European Convention for the Protection of Human Rights and Fundamental Freedoms is in compliance with the Constitution of the Republic of Lithuania.

4. On the compliance of Article 14 of the European Convention for the Protection of Human Rights and Fundamental Freedoms with the Constitution of the Republic of Lithuania

In the inquiry of the President of the Republic it is pointed out that the Convention prohibits only the so-called negative **[97]** discrimination, whereas the Constitution forbids "negative" as well as "positive" discrimination (granting of privileges). Furthermore, in the inquiry it is stated that the Convention establishes a longer list of the grounds for prohibiting discrimination: in the Constitution no mention is made of the colour of the skin, belonging to a national minority.

The Constitutional Court states that the so-called positive discrimination mentioned in the inquiry may not be considered as granting of privileges. The Constitution only establishes certain universally recognized special rights peculiar for a certain group of people, namely the rights of the members of national minorities, which are determined in Articles 37 and 45 of the Constitution. The Constitution also prescribes that the State shall take care of families bringing up children at home, and shall render them support, shall provide privileges for working mothers (Article 39), etc.

Such standpoint with regard to special human rights is peculiar also to the practice of the application of the Convention. The European Court of Human Rights in its judgment of 8 July 1986 in the case of *Lithgow and Others*[11] made the conclusion that the Contracting States enjoy a certain margin of appreciation in assessing whether and to what extent differences in otherwise similar situations justify a different treatment in law.

All this, along with the general non-discrimination rule, ensures the underlying principle of all people's equality. This is confirmed by the general rule established in the first part of Article 29 of the Constitution: "All people shall be equal before the law, the court, and other State institutions and officers."

The second part of this Article derives from the first one as it forbids violation of equality by determining that: "A person may not have his right restricted in any way, or be granted any privileges, on the basis of his or her sex, race, nationality, language, origin, social status, religion, convictions, or opinions." Here the phrase "a person may not have his rights restricted in any way, or be granted any privileges" is adequate to the phrase "the **[98]** enjoyment of the rights and freedom set forth in this Convention shall be secured without discrimination on any ground". The restriction of human rights on the basis of his or her sex, race, nationality, etc., is nothing else but discrimination which is prohibited by both the Convention and the Constitution.

The Constitutional Court argues that word-for-word comparison of the texts of the second part of Article 29 of the Constitution and Article 14 of the Convention allows to maintain that the Convention provides for more extensive non-discrimination guarantees, because it prohibits discrimination also on the basis of colour, association with a national minority, property, birth or other status. However, it is

[[11] 75 *ILR* 438.]

necessary to take into consideration the essential identity of the constitutional norms and the norms of the Convention concerning non-discrimination of people on any ground, and not the differences in verbal expression of separate non-discrimination indications. Besides, it should be noted that some different words used in the Constitution and in the Convention actually imply the same non-discrimination indication or embrace some of them. For example, it may be presumed that the word "faith" used in the Constitution embraces the word "religion" employed in the Convention. If it were evaluated otherwise, it might cause doubts where the Convention recognizes faith as a basis for non-discrimination. The notion "social status" used in the Constitution comprises the concepts "social origin" and "property" of the Convention. On the other hand, the fact that the phrase "social status" is not used in the Convention, and the phrase "social origin" is mentioned instead, does not imply the possibility to establish unequal rights for persons of separate social groups. The words "races", "nationalities", "national minorities" that are actually used to define the same non-discrimination basis, should be evaluated in the same way.

Consequently, complex and not formal word-for-word comparison of the provisions of the Constitution and the Convention allows to make a conclusion that Article 14 of the European Convention for the Protection of Human Rights and **[99]** Fundamental Freedoms does not contradict the Constitution of the Republic of Lithuania.

5. *On the compliance of Article 2 of Protocol No 4 of the European Convention for the Protection of Human Rights and Fundamental Freedoms with the Constitution of the Republic of Lithuania*

In the inquiry of the President of the Republic it is specified that part 1, Article 2 of Protocol No 4 prescribes that "everyone lawfully within the territory of a State shall, within that territory, have the right to liberty of movement and freedom to choose his residence". Meanwhile, in the first part of Article 32 of the Constitution it is declared that "citizens may move and choose their place of residence in Lithuania freely, and may leave Lithuania at their own will". The petitioner argues that systematic analysis of articles of the Constitution shows that the legislator uses concepts "person", "individual" and "citizen". The analysis of the texts in which these notions are used allows to maintain that they are not synonyms and have certain legal meaning. For instance, concepts "individual" and "person" used in Articles 22, 24, 25 and 26 of the Constitution which provide for universal human rights and freedoms (for a citizen of a State, a foreigner and a person without citizenship). Meanwhile, the concept "citizen" is employed only in those articles of the Constitution which establish specific rights concerning relation between a person and the Lithuanian State, i.e. concerning citizenship (e.g. Constitution, Article

32, parts 1, 2, 3; Article 33). Therefore, the petitioner has doubts whether Article 2 of Protocol No 4 of the Convention according to its scope is in conformity with the first part, Article 32 of the Constitution.

The Constitutional Court states that the norm of Article 2 of Protocol No 4 of the Convention that "everyone lawfully within the territory of a State shall, within that territory, have the right to liberty of movement and freedom to choose his residence" consists of two parts that are interdependent. One of them implies freedom of movement and freedom to choose one's residence, whereas another means that only persons that are lawfully within a State **[100]** shall be entitled to such right. Such persons may be citizens, foreigners and persons without citizenship. A citizen's being in his or her State is always lawful. In part 3, Article 32 of the Constitution it is set forth: "A person may not be prohibited from returning to Lithuania." Meanwhile, the conditions for the lawfulness of arrival, departure and being in a State of a foreigner or a person without citizenship are prescribed in the domestic law. Such conditions have been established in the Law of the Republic of Lithuania "On the Legal Status of Foreigners in the Republic of Lithuania" (Official Gazette "Valstybės žinios", No 27-729, 1991).

Foreigners and persons without citizenship that in accordance with said Law are lawfully within the Republic of Lithuania have the same rights and freedoms as citizens of the Republic of Lithuania unless the Constitution, this Law and other laws as well as international agreements prescribe otherwise. Thus, the provisions in question of Protocol No 4, when applied in the legal system of Lithuania along with the provisions of the Law "On the Legal Status of Foreigners in the Republic of Lithuania" and other laws of the Republic of Lithuania would include each other. There would be only one question to solve—whether in concrete case a foreigner or a person without citizenship is lawfully within territory of the Republic of Lithuania, so that he might fully exercise the right to movement and free choice of his place of residence.

The evaluation of all this results in the conclusion that Article 2 of Protocol No 4 of the European Convention for the Protection of Human Rights and Fundamental Freedoms is in compliance with the Constitution of the Republic of Lithuania.

Taking into consideration all the motives presented in the argument-ation of this conclusion and interpretation of some concepts of the Constitution and the Convention, and conforming to part 3, Article 105 of the Constitution; item 3, Article 73 and Article 83 of the Law on the Constitutional Court, the Constitutional Court has presented the following

[101]   *conclusion*:

Articles 4, 5, 9, 14 and Article 2 of Protocol No 4 of the European Convention for the Protection of Human Rights and Fundamental Freedoms are in compliance with the Constitution of the Republic of Lithuania.

This Constitutional Court conclusion is final and not subject to appeal.

[Report: Transcript]

Human rights—Procedure—United Nations Human Rights Committee—Nature of Committee—Whether a "judicial authority"—International Covenant on Civil and Political Rights, 1966—Whether State Party under an obligation to provide legal aid for petitioner to Human Rights Committee

Relationship of international law and municipal law — Treaties — International Covenant on Civil and Political Rights, 1966—Effect in the law of New Zealand—Whether New Zealand authorities required to grant legal aid for petition to United Nations Human Rights Committee—The law of New Zealand

WELLINGTON DISTRICT LEGAL SERVICES COMMITTEE *v.* TANGIORA[1]

New Zealand, Court of Appeal.   8 *July* 1997

(Richardson P, Gault, Thomas, Keith and Blanchard JJ)

SUMMARY: *The facts*:—The respondent, Pauline Tangiora, lodged a communication with the United Nations Human Rights Committee established under the International Covenant on Civil and Political Rights, 1966 ("the Covenant"). She claimed that the Treaty of Waitangi (Fisheries Claims) Settlement Act 1992 violated her rights under the Covenant. The Committee determined that the communication was admissible and the Government of

---

[1] The appellant was represented by Solicitor-General John McGrath QC, Peter Andrew and Natalie Baird and the solicitors were the Crown Law Office (Wellington). The respondent was represented by the Rt Hon Sir Geoffrey Palmer, Tony Shaw and Charl Hirschfeld and the solicitors were Wellington Maori Legal Services.

New Zealand filed a response. The respondent applied to the Wellington District Legal Services Committee, the appellant, for legal aid to pursue her petition before the Human Rights Committee. The appellant denied legal aid and the respondent sought a declaration that this refusal was unlawful. The High Court held that the Human Rights Committee was a "judicial authority" within the terms of the Legal Services Act and granted the respondent's declaration. The Wellington District Legal Services Committee appealed.

Held:—The appeal was allowed.

(1) The Human Rights Committee was not an "administrative tribunal or judicial authority" within the meaning of the Legal Services Act. In contrast to the International Court of Justice and tribunals such as the United Nations Administrative Tribunal, the Human Rights Committee was not a court. It did not take a decision but merely forwarded its "views" in respect of alleged violations. While those views were important to an assessment of the treaty obligations of States Parties to the Covenant, the express law relating to the Committee did not indicate that the views of the Committee were binding (pp. 660-2).

(2) There was no international obligation to provide legal aid in respect of proceedings before the Committee in light of which the Legal Services Act could have been given a broader interpretation (pp. 662-70).

Per Thomas J: The Human Rights Committee might, in fact, be a judicial authority but it was not necessary to express a concluded view on that question since the relevant provisions of the Legal Services Act were intended to apply only to domestic tribunals and judicial authorities (pp. 670-1).

The following is the text of the judgment of the Court:

The judgment of Richardson P, Gault, Keith and Blanchard JJ was **[131]** delivered by
KEITH J.

Summary	656
The International Bill of Rights	657
The Human Rights Committee	660
Relevant approaches to interpretation	662
The Legal Services Act 1991	665
Result	670

Summary
    The respondent, along with 18 others representing Maori iwi, lodged a communication with the Human Rights Committee set up under the International Covenant on Civil and Political Rights claiming that the Treaty of Waitangi (Fisheries Claims) Settlement Act 1992 violates her rights under the covenant. The committee has found the communication admissible and the New Zealand Government has filed a further lengthy response. The proceedings before this Court do not concern that substantive claim. Rather they concern the application for legal aid which the respondent made to the Wellington District Legal Services Committee in support of the substantive claim. The committee,

the appellant in this Court, ruled that legal aid could not be approved in respect of proceedings issued in Courts outside New Zealand. The respondent sought a declaration that that refusal was unlawful.

The only issue argued before Gallen J was whether the Human Rights Committee is a "judicial authority" within s 19(1)(e) of the Legal Services Act 1991, and accordingly falls within the list of bodies in respect of which legal aid can be granted. He held that it was and accordingly granted a declaration that the refusal was unlawful and invalid. His judgment is reported as *Tangiora v Wellington District Legal Services Committee* [1997] NZAR 118.

The Legal Services Committee appeals. For the reasons given in this judgment we allow the appeal. We hold that the Human Rights Committee is not "Any administrative tribunal or judicial authority" within the meaning of the Legal Services Act.

[132]   That result follows directly from the terms of the 1991 Act. We also conclude that in this case no questions about New Zealand's international obligations relating to legal aid are directly raised by the interpretation and application of the Legal Services Act. Before we address the terms of that Act and approaches to its interpretation we consider the International Bill of Rights and the Human Rights Committee. We do that as background to the issues relating to the claim for legal aid. To repeat, we are not concerned with the substantive claim relating to the Fisheries Settlement Act and the Sealords deal, now before the Human Rights Committee.

The International Bill of Rights
On 26 June 1945 "We the peoples of the United Nations" stated their determination in the Preamble to the Charter of the United Nations:

"to save succeeding generations from the scourge of war, which twice in our lifetime has brought untold sorrow to mankind, and
    to reaffirm faith in fundamental human rights, in the dignity and worth of the human person, in the equal rights of men and women and of nations large and small, and
    to establish conditions under which justice and respect for the obligations arising from treaties and other sources of international law can be maintained, and
    to promote social progress and better standards of life in larger freedom."

The prominent recognition in the second paragraph and to some extent in the fourth of the centrality of fundamental human rights in international relations was of huge significance. No longer could it be accepted, as it had been so disastrously only a few short years before, that the world community had no right to concern itself with violations of human rights committed by a state against its own people. The barriers of domestic jurisdiction and sovereignty were to be lowered, if not completely swept away.

The preambular provisions are reflected in arts 1(3), 13(1)(b), 55 and 56. The third of the purposes of the United Nations as set out in art 1(3) is:

"3. To achieve international co-operation in solving international problems of an economic, social, cultural, or humanitarian

character, and in promoting and encouraging respect for human
rights and for fundamental freedoms for all without distinction as
to race, sex, language, or religion."

Under art 56 all the members of the United Nations pledge themselves to
take joint and separate action in cooperation with the organisation for the
achievement of the purposes set out in art 55. That provision states in part that:

"With a view to the creation of conditions of stability and well-being
which are necessary for peaceful and friendly relations among nations
based on respect for the principle of equal rights and self-determination of
peoples, the United Nations shall promote:

. . .

   (c) universal respect for, and observance of, human rights and
      fundamental freedoms for all without distinction as to race, sex,
      language, or religion."

In the decades since 1945 members of the United Nations and related
bodies have striven to give content to those aspirations and broad undertakings
by: (1) stating substantive human rights obligations intended to be binding on **[133]**
states; and (2) developing effective means of implementing those obligations.
Notable among those steps are the components of what is often referred to as
the International Bill of Rights – the Universal Declaration of Human Rights
proclaimed by the United Nations General Assembly in 1948 as "a common
standard of achievement for all peoples and all nations", the International
Covenant on Economic, Social and Cultural Rights, the International Covenant
on Civil and Political Rights (ICCPR) and the (first) Optional Protocol, the last
three all being adopted in 1966, UNGA res 217A(III), 993 UNTS 3, 999 UNTS
171 and 302. New Zealand became bound by the covenants in 1979 and the
Optional Protocol in 1989. In the substantive claim before the Human Rights
Committee, the respondent alleges breaches of the ICCPR and invokes the
procedure available under the Optional Protocol.

The preamble to the ICCPR indicates its foundation and purposes:

"The States Parties to the present Covenant,

   Considering that, in accordance with the principles proclaimed in the
Charter of the United Nations, recognition of the inherent dignity and of
the equal and inalienable rights of all members of the human family is the
foundation of freedom, justice and peace in the world.

   Recognizing that these rights derive from the inherent dignity of the
human person,

   Recognizing that, in accordance with the Universal Declaration of
Human Rights, the ideal of free human beings enjoying civil and political
freedom and freedom from fear and want can only be achieved if
conditions are created whereby everyone may enjoy his civil and political
rights, as well as his economic, social and cultural rights,

   Considering the obligation of States under the Charter of the United
Nations to promote universal respect for, and observance of, human rights
and freedoms,

> *Realizing* that the individual, having duties to other individuals and to the community to which he belongs, is under a responsibility to strive for the promotion and observance of the rights recognized in the present Covenant,
> *Agree* upon the following articles: . . .."

Part III of the covenant sets out substantive rights including two relevant to the substantive claim before the committee: the right to be equal before the. Courts and tribunals (art 14) and rights in respect of minorities (art 27); art 1 (comprising the whole of Part I) about self-determination is also invoked. Part II is concerned with the national implementation of the obligations and Part IV with international processes. In Part II, art 2 requires each state party to the covenant to respect and to ensure to all individuals within its territory subject to its jurisdiction the rights recognised in the covenant without distinction of any kind. As well, the parties are obliged to adopt legislative or other measures necessary to give effect to the rights recognised in the covenant to the extent that their existing law is deficient. And finally, in art 2(3):

> "3. Each State Party to the present covenant undertakes:
>
> (a) To ensure that any person whose rights or freedoms as herein recognized are violated shall have an effective remedy, notwithstanding that the violation has been committed by persons acting in an official capacity;
>
> **[134]** (b) To ensure that any person claiming such a remedy shall have his right thereto determined by competent judicial, administrative or legislative authorities, or by any other competent authority provided for by the legal system of the State, and to develop the possibilities of judicial remedy;
>
> (c) To ensure that the competent authorities shall enforce such remedies when granted."

That provision was prominent in the judgments in this Court in *Baigent's Case* holding that a person whose rights under the New Zealand Bill of Rights Act 1990 had been breached might, in appropriate cases, be entitled to an award of compensation, *Simpson v Attorney-General [Baigent's Case]* [1994] 3 NZLR 667 at pp 676, 690 – 691, 699 and 718.

In principle and in practice it is those national means of implementation which must constitute the major means by which states give effect to their obligations under the covenant. In principle that is so given the substantive obligations of states set out in Part III emphasised by their implementation obligations in Part II. In practice that will also be so given the impossibility of a single central body, meeting on a part-time basis, handling the vast number of human rights disputes arising between individuals and governments around the world. The last resort character of the complaint remedies in the covenant and the Optional Protocol is emphasised as well by their express requirements that domestic remedies be exhausted before the committee considers a communication.

The Human Rights Committee

The Human Rights Committee which consists of 18 members elected to four-year terms under Part IV of the covenant by the states parties to it has three functions. The first is to consider the reports submitted to it on a periodic basis by states parties to the covenant on the measures they have adopted to give effect to the rights recognised in the covenant and on the progress made in the enjoyment of those rights (art 40). Secondly, a procedure is available between states which accept it enabling one state to make a communication to the effect that another state is not fulfilling its obligations under the covenant (arts 41 – 42). The third procedure, the one in issue in the present case, is also available only against states which have separately accepted it, by becoming party to the Optional Protocol. Under art 1 of the Protocol the committee is competent to receive and consider communications from individuals who claim to be victims of a violation by such a state party of any of the rights set out in the covenant.

The question the Court has to decide is whether, when the Human Rights Committee is carrying out that final function, it is "Any administrative tribunal or judicial authority" within the meaning of s 19(1)(e) of the Legal Services Act 1991. If it is, a person who has made a communication to the committee may be entitled to legal aid in accordance with the other provisions of that Act.

Before turning to the New Zealand legislation and the approach to its interpretation that should be adopted, we note some aspects of the character, procedures and powers of the committee, when it is dealing with individual communications under the Optional Protocol.

In the first place, the committee is not called a Court (by contrast to the International Court of Justice) or a tribunal (by contrast to the United Nations Administrative Tribunal), or even a commission (by contrast to the Fact-Finding Commissions provided for in the Hague Conventions on the **[135]** Peaceful Settlement of International Disputes, 1901 UKTS 9). The history of the drafting of the covenant shows that the choice of a lesser title was a deliberate one. The negative implication of the title for judicial status is not affected by the fact that members serve in their personal capacities, make solemn declarations of office and enjoy certain privileges and immunities; that is also true of members of a number of international bodies which could not be characterised as judicial.

Second, the process set out in the Protocol is exiguous. It is not that expected of a judicial body or tribunal. Under art 3, the committee is first required to consider as inadmissible anonymous communications, communications which are an abuse of the right of submission, or communications which are incompatible with the covenant. Subject to those constraints the communication need not take any particular form. The committee need not follow any express procedure in undertaking that consideration. If those hurdles have been overcome the committee brings the communication to the attention of the state party in question which within six months is obliged to submit written explanations or statements "clarifying the matter and the remedy, if any, that may have been taken by that State", art 4. The committee is then to consider communications received under the Protocol in the light of all the information made available to it by the individual and the state party. If the matter is not being considered by some other international process and if the individual has exhausted available domestic remedies, the committee examines the communications in closed meetings and "shall forward its views to the State Party concerned and to the individual", art 5. It is to include in its annual report to the General Assembly on its activities a summary of its activities under the Protocol, art 6.

While these provisions have been considerably developed by the Rules of Procedure and the practices of the committee the procedures are not obviously those of a Court or tribunal-like body. They are even limited compared with the procedures the committee applies when dealing with complaints brought by one state against another. For instance, in that situation the committee must make available its good offices to the states parties concerned with a view to a friendly solution of the matter on the basis of respect for human rights and fundamental freedoms as recognised in the covenant. The states parties have an express right to be represented when the matter is being considered in the committee and to make oral and written submissions. If that process is unsuccessful the committee has the power, with the consent of the states parties, to appoint an ad hoc conciliation commission which is required to fully consider the matter. It, too, has the power to call upon the states parties to supply any other relevant information.

More significant than that internal contrast are the differences between the provisions regulating the committee and those governing other bodies set up to resolve disputes of an international character. We take just one example arising from a multilateral treaty negotiated at about the same time as the covenant – the International Convention on the Settlement of Investment Disputes between states and nationals of other states which was concluded in 1965, 1175 UNTS 438. It sets up, principally by way of the rules which have been adopted in accordance with it, an arbitral procedure following the standard processes of international commercial arbitration and giving both parties full opportunities to present evidence and argument to the arbitrators.

[136]   The contrast can be carried forward into the third area, that is the powers of the Human Rights Committee. All it can do under the Optional Protocol is to forward its "views" to the state party in question and the individual concerned. They are views on the issue whether the state has breached its obligations. That aspect of the function might suggest a judicial role. But against that characterisation is the wording of the Protocol: it is not the language of binding obligation, as the legislative history once again emphasises. It is true there have been important subsequent developments designed to enhance the force of the "views" adopted by the committee. Nothing that we say should be seen as questioning at all the importance of those developments and others designed to strengthen the committee's procedures. Nor do we question in any way the duty of the states parties to the covenant to consider in good faith what steps they must take to give effect to their obligations under the covenant in accordance with the general principles of international law, as proclaimed, for example, in art 26 of the Vienna Convention on the law of treaties:

"Every treaty in force is binding upon the parties to it and must be performed by them in good faith" (1155 UNTS 331, 339).

No doubt the views stated and the comments made by the committee should where appropriate have an important relevance to the states parties' assessment of those obligations, as this Court has indicated, eg *R v Goodwin (No 2)* [1993] 2 NZLR 390 at p 393.

The fact remains however that when international obligations to comply with findings made following dispute settlement procedures are being created, plain language to that effect is available and is ordinarily used. Again, to take the example of the ICSID Convention, the parties to the arbitration process set up under it must accept the binding force of the award. Article 53(1) provides:

"The award shall be binding on the parties and shall not be subject to any appeal or to any other remedy except those provided for in this Convention. Each party shall abide and comply with the terms of the award except to the extent that enforcement shall have been stayed pursuant to the relevant provisions of this Convention."

Even the qualifications in that provision help emphasise the different position of the committee. Neither element – that the award is binding and that that binding character is subject to limits – is to be found in the express law relating to the committee.

The above brief review of the character, procedures and powers of the committee raises real doubts whether the committee could be characterised in any general sense as an administrative tribunal or judicial authority; see eg *Tertiary Institutes Allied Staff Association Inc v Tahana* [1998] 1 NZLR 41 at pp 45 – 51. A comparison with the same three features of the European Court of Human Rights set up under the European Convention on Human Rights of 1950 – the only existing human rights model when the covenant was being drafted – increases those doubts. Any general characterisation would not however be decisive since the characterisation does have to be made in the particular context of the Legal Services Act. The issue is one of the interpretation of the relevant provision of that Act. We take up that matter in the next two parts of this judgment.

Relevant approaches to interpretation   **[137]**

In his judgment Gallen J recorded that in this case the appropriate approach towards statutory interpretation was "very much in contention". He continued at p 123:

"Speaking in general terms, it is the view for the plaintiff that the Act should be interpreted in the light of the appropriate response of the New Zealand Government and New Zealand governmental agencies towards international obligations. The defendant takes the view that the Act should be interpreted according to those rules of interpretation which have evolved within the common law and which have been set out with more or less precision in a large number of judicial decisions.

In determining the matter, I think that both approaches need to be taken into account. There is ample authority from the Court of Appeal and I accept that international obligations are to be taken seriously and that the acceptance of such obligations, particularly in relation to human rights, is a matter of significance – as such it ought to reflect in statutory interpretation.

Older attitudes based on the primacy of domestic law and the general irrelevance for the purposes of domestic law of international law must, I think, be considered as having lost a good deal of their authority in the contemporary climate of a world where international obligations are taken seriously and in some cases become the focus of international action. At the same time, the rules of interpretation which have been worked out and applied, are necessary to ensure some degree of certainty in the application of domestic law and the ordering of the affairs of persons subject to it. In the light of those observations, I proceed to consider the specific submissions made."

We begin with two brief statements taken from a recent judgment of this Court about the role of treaty provisions in the interpretation of legislation. The first states:

". . . the presumption of statutory interpretation that so far as its wording allows legislation should be read in a way which is consistent with New Zealand's international obligations, eg *Rajan v Minister of Immigration* [1996] 3 NZLR 543 at p 551. That presumption may apply whether or not the legislation was enacted with the purpose of implementing the relevant text" (*New Zealand Air Line Pilots' Association Inc v Attorney-General* [1997] 3 NZLR 269 at p 289).

The Court secondly pointed out that the statutory language in issue in that case could be read in the context of the relevant international text. There was, the Court said, no legislative provision which stood in the way of that contextual use of the international provisions. That use of the international provisions to assist the reading of the national text does not expressly depend on the existence of relevant international obligations. We return to that second, somewhat wider approach later. For the moment we consider whether there are relevant international obligations by reference to which s 19 of the Legal Services Act might fall to be interpreted.

The international obligations suggested in this case were: (1) an obligation to provide civil legal aid, including aid facilitating access to the Human Rights Committee; and (2) an obligation to ensure "an equality of arms" between the **[138]** parties; according to the respondent that equality, on the facts of this case, required the grant of legal aid.

The first possibility received only limited attention in argument before us and rightly so. The only express obligation relating to legal aid in the covenant relates to criminal proceedings at the trial level, art 14(3)(d). Civil proceedings are not the subject of any such explicit obligation at any level of national Courts, let alone at the international level. The information about state practice available to us also does not begin to support the existence of an obligation to provide legal aid in respect of a communication to the Human Rights Committee. While there is some provision for financial assistance within the European human rights system, that assistance is provided by the European Commission of Human Rights itself, Gomien, Harris and Zwaak, *Law and Practice of the European Convention on Human Rights and the European Social Charter* (1996) p 52. The Ministry of Foreign Affairs and Trade sought information from 17 countries which are parties to the Optional Protocol and which together provided a broad geographic sample. Of those countries only the Netherlands definitely provides legal aid for communications to the committee although Finland is contemplating making such a provision. In other jurisdictions, including some Australian states, the position is not clear as the situation has not yet arisen. Among the countries which do not provide such financial assistance are Austria, Canada, Denmark, France, Germany, Italy and Norway. The French reply is perhaps of some wider relevance since legal aid is available in that country before "juridiction" – a word that is understood by the French authorities as applying the legal aid scheme only to cases being heard by French Courts. Those replies are consistent with the statement in the 1996 book just cited that domestic legal aid systems in most Council of Europe countries do not cover the costs of pursuing international legal actions.

The covenant does not expressly refer to "equality of arms". Rather art 14(1) of the covenant requires that:

"1. All persons shall be equal before the courts and tribunals."

and art 26 that:

"All persons are equal before the law and are entitled without any discrimination to the equal protection of the law."

The argument might also be related to the obligation under art 2 of the covenant quoted earlier. Those provisions are however concerned with Courts, tribunals, rights and remedies made available by a state party through its own legal system or enforced through that system. Moreover, in none of the cases to which we were referred is there any suggestion that the principle creates an obligation to fund access to the committee. The situation in this case is sharply different from that where the state creates a difficult financial hurdle for those seeking justice, as Laws J emphasised in *R v Lord Chancellor, ex parte Witham* [1997] 2 All ER 779 at p 788 c – e.

We accordingly conclude that there is no relevant international obligation by reference to which the Legal Services Act is to be interpreted in this case. That is not however the end of the matter so far as the international texts are concerned since the respondent urged here, as in the High Court, that the Act should be interpreted in the light of "the appropriate response of the New Zealand Government and New Zealand governmental agencies towards international obligations". In so far as that proposition requires an approach to the interpretation of legislation which seeks consistency with international obligations we see no difficulty with it and we have already dealt with it. The **[139]** argument before us was however put in a broader way, calling in aid a passage from the report of the Legislation Advisory Committee, "Legislative Change:

Guidelines on Process and Content" (rev ed, 1991) para 44, a report which the *Cabinet Office Manual* (August 1996) para 5.26 endorses. The respondent invoked the emphasised sentence which should however be read in context:

> "44 In a very wide and increasing range of areas, New Zealand is committed by its treaty obligations or by customary international law to make particular provision in its domestic laws. Appendix E [to the report] is a list of primary legislation which appears to raise treaty issues. It includes about one quarter of all public Acts. Any proposal to amend that legislation should prompt the question whether there is a treaty which must be taken into consideration. Again, appropriate and timely consultation, especially with the Ministry of External Relations and Trade is essential. *Even where there is no direct obligation, there might be an international standard, especially in the human rights area, which is relevant to the preparation of new legislation and to the replacement and amendment of the old.* It may also be relevant to the interpretation of legislation." (Emphasis added.)

We read the emphasised sentence as saying no more than that in some circumstances the legislature might go further than New Zealand's international obligations require and draw on international standards which do not have obligatory force. That is an option available to those responsible for the preparation and enactment of legislation.

But as the passage also indicates that non-obligatory material may also be relevant to the interpretative process as it was for instance in *Van Gorkom v Attorney General* [1977] 1 NZLR 535 at pp 542 – 543, affirmed [1978] 2 NZLR 387. The international text might provide part of the context in which legislation might be read, as occurred in the *ALPA* case mentioned earlier. International law might for instance help indicate the content of "judicial authority" or "administrative tribunal" – but not as a matter of international obligation and only as one part of the context and possibly an inconsequential one at that. We do not see the interpretative role of the Courts as extending to determining "the appropriate response" of New Zealand towards its international obligations – at least if that process runs beyond the approaches mentioned in this part of the judgment.

The Legal Services Act 1991

Against that background of international human rights law and appropriate approaches to the interpretation of legislation which might be related to that law, we turn to the provisions of the Legal Services Act.

According to its title it is an "Act to make legal assistance and legal services more readily available to persons of insufficient means". The Legal Aid Act 1969 similarly was an Act to make legal aid "more readily available". Prominent in the reasons given by the Ministers of Justice in 1969 and 1989 for a state-funded system was the basic responsibility of the state to ensure that its citizens have access to the legal system. Both cited art 7 of the Universal Declaration of Human Rights which like art 26 of the ICCPR quoted earlier provides that "all . . . are entitled without any discrimination to equal protection of the law".

Such broad propositions do not of course dictate the detail of the support **[140**
to be provided – to whom it is to be given as having insufficient means, in
respect of what legal services, in which Courts and tribunals, and in what
amounts (and with what contributions or repayments)? Decisions are to be
made about those matters, in the first place by Ministers in proposing
legislation, by Parliament in enacting it, and by those responsible for its
administration. The answers might very well vary from time to time, as appears
from a comparison of the law before 1969 (when only criminal legal aid was
provided for), between 1969 and 1991 and since 1991. That is not to say that
there may not be some rights in respect of legal aid, as there are for criminal
trials, see the New Zealand Bill of Rights Act 1990, s 24(f) and the Criminal
Justice Act 1985, s 10, and also art 14(3)(d) of the ICCPR.

One critical area of decision for the legislature concerns the Courts and
other bodies in respect of which legal aid may be granted. So far as civil
proceedings are concerned, Parliament provided this answer in s 19(1):

. . .

(a) Civil proceedings in any District Court or Family Court:

(b) Civil proceedings in the High Court or the Court of Appeal:

(c) Appeals to the Judicial Committee of the Privy Council in civil
proceedings in any case where –

(i) The applicant has succeeded in the Court of Appeal and is
the respondent in the appeal to the Privy Council, if the grant of
aid is approved by the Minister; or

(ii) The Attorney-General certifies that a question of law of
exceptional public importance is involved and that the grant of aid
is desirable in the public interest:

(d) Proceedings commenced by way of application in a Youth Court
under Part VII of the Children, Young Persons, and Their Families
Act 1989 or in respect of any review of any determination of, or
any order made in, a Youth Court in any such proceedings:

(e) Proceedings in –

(i) The Maori Land Court; or

(ii) The Maori Appellate Court; or

(iii) The Employment Court; or

(iv) The Employment Tribunal; or

(v) *Any administrative tribunal or judicial authority* (not
being a tribunal or an authority in respect of any decision of which
an appeal lies to any of the bodies referred to in any of
paragraphs (g) to (j) of this subsection) –

in any case where the District Subcommittee considering the
application is of the opinion –

(vi) That the case is one that requires legal representation
having regard to the nature of the proceedings and to the
applicant's personal interest; and

(vii) That the applicant would suffer substantial hardship if
aid were not granted:

(f) Proceedings in the Waitangi Tribunal:

(g) Proceedings in the Compensation Court or before the Accident Compensation Appeal Authority:

(h) Proceedings before the Social Security Appeal Authority:

(i) Proceedings before the Tenancy Tribunal:

141] (j) Proceedings before any body (by whatever name called) established by the Government of New Zealand to determine appeals against decisions made by immigration officers (within the meaning of the Immigration Act 1987) and relating to the status of persons as refugees:

(k) All applications, submissions, and appeals under the Resource Management Act 1991 or to the Environment Court under any other Act:

(l) All applications, submissions, and appeals to any Council or body in any case where an appeal in relation to its decision lies to the Planning Tribunal. (Emphasis added.)

The emphasised words in para (e)(v) are the ones immediately in issue.

The separate inclusion of paras (f) and (j) helps make a point touched on earlier, that bodies without powers of decision may not easily be characterised as "Any administrative tribunal or judicial authority". Doubts raised in 1987 on that score about the Waitangi Tribunal by the Legal Aid Appeal Authority were met by Parliament in the following year expressly adding the tribunal to the list in the 1969 Act; *Decision No LAA 11/87* (1987) 6 NZAR 443 and Treaty of Waitangi (State Enterprises) Act 1988, s 15.

Subsection (4) excludes certain proceedings from the list (relator actions, election petitions and proceedings for dissolution of marriage; see also subs (3)) and subs (5) requires separate applications in respect of appeals or reviews to which paras (b), (d), (e), (k) or (l) apply. Those provisions can be seen as indicating the care with which the list is constructed. That care is also to be seen in an amendment to s 19 made later in 1991 essentially excluding from the coverage of the Act proceedings before the newly established immigration tribunals (subs (4A)). That exclusion is to be contrasted with the addition to the Bill, made in the course of its passage, of the refugee body referred to in para (j). The procedural obligations to be found in and arising from the 1951 Convention relating to the Status of Refugees may have helped to distinguish that body from the new statutory bodies and to justify eligibility for legal aid. The refugee body is the only named body included in the list which is not established by or under statute or which does not have authority conferred on it by statute.

The list of bodies in s 19(1) can usefully be put into four groups. The first and second are particularly identified. The third and the fourth require a further judgment to ensure eligibility:

(1) paras (a), (b) and (d) cover the Courts of general and related jurisdiction without the additional standards to be found in paras (c) and (e);

(2) paras (f) – (l) list particular specified tribunals again without additional standards (for the Waitangi Tribunal see also ss 72 – 76);

(3) para (c) provides for appeals to the Privy Council but only if the Minister of Justice or Attorney-General agree; that executive or non-judicial requirement also appears in the provisions for criminal legal aid: cf s 4(b) with s 4(a); and

(4) para (e) – that in issue in this case – requires further judgments about the proceedings, the personal interest and substantial hardship.

The extra element in respect of appeals to the Privy Council is particularly significant: legal aid is available in respect of those appeals only if the Minister of Justice or Attorney-General agrees, while all other legal aid decisions are **[142** made by the legal services bodies or the Courts originally or on appeal. Access to that final stage in the New Zealand Court system is to be tightly controlled. By contrast, on the respondent's argument, there would be no such executive constraint on legal aid supporting access to a *next* stage of complaint, beyond the Judicial Committee: it is relevant to recall that domestic remedies must be exhausted before the committee can be approached. (In fact a challenge to the Sealord agreement relating to the proposed legislation which is in issue in the Human Rights Committee did come to this Court, *Te Runanga o Wharekauri Rekohu Inc v Attorney-General* [1993] 2 NZLR 301.)

The requirement for the further judgments in the case of the fourth group is also significant. It is understandable given the large number and wide range of administrative tribunals to be found in New Zealand. A report of the Legislation Advisory Committee on "Administrative Tribunals" presented to the Minister of Justice in late 1988 and published in 1989 referred to more than 100 tribunals and discussed more than 50 of them under nine headings, including disputes between individuals, environmental and planning matters, economic matters, censorship, welfare and benefits, taxation, and licensing.

One plain implication to be drawn from this list is of considerable caution once it extends beyond those in groups (1) and (2) – the major original and appellate judicial and tribunal jurisdictions. As well the final appeal in the regular Court system is subject to unique executive control.

Another implication arising from the list is that it is firmly limited to bodies established within the New Zealand legal system and then only to the bodies listed or indicated. By contrast to the action that it took in relation to the refugee appeal body, a body established by a Minister, Parliament did not expressly respond to the suggestion of a scholarly commentator that it extend legal aid to the committee, Elkind [1990] NZLJ 96, 100.

The care in the construction of the list and the careful limits placed on it are to be seen as well in the exclusion from the Act as enacted of legal proceedings originally included in the 1989 Bill. The Minister in 1991 explained those exclusions in this way:

"The demands for legal aid have risen dramatically in recent years – in particular, for civil legal aid. The Government is determined to be fiscally responsible. Competing demands for the taxpayers' dollars must be, and under this Government will be, carefully weighed in the balance. The Government considers that it is not responsible behaviour to borrow the amount spent today on legal aid and to burden future generations with that cost. Therefore it has been necessary to delete from the Bill all new categories for which legal aid was to become available. Those categories include legal aid for appearances before royal commissions, for the dissolution of marriage, for groups making claims in the Maori Land Court, and for groups in the environmental sector. Legal aid for all those proceedings for which it is available under the present Acts will continue, including – but at present in a different form – hearings before the Waitangi Tribunal" (515 *New Zealand Parliamentary Debates* at p 2009).

He later made the point that the fund available for legal aid is not a bottomless pit and spoke of the conflict between the demand-driven nature of legal aid and the need to ration resources.

[143]   Prudent financial management is emphasised in the statement of the principal functions of the Legal Services Board established to administer the schemes provided for in the Act. Like the board under the 1969 Act it is:

> (c) To ensure that the operation of the criminal legal aid scheme and the civil legal aid scheme is as inexpensive, expeditious, and efficient as is consistent with the spirit of this Act: (s 95(c); Legal Aid Act 1969, s 5(1)(c); see also the emphasis in the annual report provision on financial reporting, s 111).

Against that account of the provisions of the Act we return to the question whether the expression "Any administrative tribunal or judicial authority" includes the Human Rights Committee. The answer is plainly No. The 1991 Act, including s 19, is concerned only with Courts, tribunals and related bodies which are established under New Zealand law, by or with the authority of Parliament, and which Parliament in a careful way lists or indicates. (As already noted, the refugee appeal body is an exception to that proposition in so far as it requires parliamentary establishment or authority. That body is established under the common law rather than by or with the authority of statute but it was of course expressly added.) The ruling in the most relevant decision to which we were referred, *Arbitrators' Institute of New Zealand Inc v Legal Services Board* [1995] 2 NZLR 202, is consistent with that proposition.

The Act does not extend to Courts or tribunals established beyond New Zealand except to the limited extent provided for in respect of the Privy Council. In particular the Human Rights Committee does not come within the scope of the Act.

The respondent understandably emphasised various statements which this Court has made about the status of the Human Rights Committee and the significance of its views, one of which is mentioned earlier in this judgment. In [2] particular in *Tavita v Minister of Immigration* [1994] 2 NZLR 257 at p 260, this Court said:

> "That committee is in substance a judicial body of high standing."

When making that statement the Court was not of course concerned with the particular issue of statutory interpretation involved in this case. Nor was it when the other statements were made. Rather they concern the authority that should be accorded to the views of the committee (*R v Goodwin (No 2)* at p 393), the views that it has expressed on matters before the Court (*Baigent's Case* at p 699), and the significance of New Zealand's acceptance of the Optional Protocol for the remedies available under the Bill of Rights (*Baigent's Case* at p 691). This Court has recently cautioned against using in one context the characterisation of a body or function as judicial made for a quite different purpose, *Tertiary Institutes Allied Staff Association Inc v Tahana*, above. Accordingly we do not see these statements as affecting the meaning of s 19. Nor, to return to an earlier part of the judgment, do we see that meaning as affected by any possible argument based on the general characterisation of the committee: as indicated, there must be great doubt whether it can be characterised in some general sense as an administrative tribunal or a judicial authority. In any event, the analysis of the terms of s 19(1)(e)(v) in context and by reference to the purpose of the Legal Services Act leads us to the conclusion stated earlier – s 19 is limited to Courts, tribunals and related bodies which are established under New Zealand law, by or with the authority of Parliament, and which Parliament in a careful way lists or indicates. The Human Rights **[144]** Committee is not such a body.

Result

Accordingly, the appeal succeeds. The statement of claim is dismissed. The order for costs made in favour of the respondent in the High Court is quashed. Counsel may submit memoranda on costs in both Courts if they wish.

THOMAS J. I have had the advantage of reading Keith J's draft judgment, and I agree that the appeal should be allowed. I wish, however, to restrict the basis of my concurrence to the question of the interpretation of s 19(1)(e) of the Legal Services Act 1991.

After an admirable and comprehensive review of the International Bill of Rights and the Human Rights Committee, Keith J reaches the conclusion that his review of the character, procedures and powers of the committee raises real doubts whether the committee could be characterised in any general sense as a judicial authority. I do not wish, or consider it necessary, to reach a concluded view on this issue. Although the committee may lack many of the characteristics of a judicial authority, particularly the power to issue decisions which are binding and enforceable, I incline to think that, when the committee determines a substantive claim by reaching a "view" whether or not the state party is in breach of its obligations under the International Covenant on Civil and Political Rights, it has made a definitive and final ruling on that claim. The fact the state party may choose not to comply with the committee's directions in any particular case does not detract from the fact that to all intents and purposes the committee's "view" that there is a breach is determinative of the issue. In reaching what is effectively a definitive ruling, I apprehend that the committee is exercising a judicial or quasi-judicial function which may be sufficient to clothe it with the mantle of a "judicial authority". But because I believe the meaning of s 19(1)(e) of the Legal Services Act is plain, I do not need to press my opinion to a firm conclusion.

For the reasons given by Keith J, I take the view that s 19(1)(e) is intended to apply to domestic tribunals and judicial authorities only. I cannot accept that any other interpretation would accord with Parliament's intent.

Appeal allowed.

[Report: [1998] 1 NZLR 129]

INDEX

For references to particular articles of treaties, see the Table of Treaties, p. xxxiii.

A

Aboriginal rights. *See* Canada, aboriginal rights; Canada, aboriginal title; Canada, Indian peoples in; Finland, Sami rights

Act of State—
    declaration of diplomat as *persona non grata* 443-5
    judicial review 445
    sovereign activity—
      —international law, under 613

Alien—
    equality of treatment 653-4
    non-national, whether synonymous 338-41
    rights—
      —rights and freedoms of citizen 653-4

Ambassador. *See also* Diplomatic agent
    State immunity, jurisdiction—
      —entitlement 613-14

Applicable law—
    Head of State—
      —authority to act on behalf of State in international relations 103
    secession of part of a State—
      —international law 546, 579
      —municipal law 133-46, 580, 590
    State, creation—
      —international law 117-20
      —municipal law 121-3

Arbitrary act—
    interference under law—
      —conformity with provisions, aims and objectives of International Covenant on Civil and Political Rights (1966), need for 342-3
    test—
      —proportionality 348-9
      —reasonableness 342-3

Australia—
    broadcasting—
      —Australian Content Standard. *See also* New Zealand, Closer Economic Relations Trade Agreement (1983) *below*
      ——compatibility with treaty obligations 386-415
      ——transmission quota as 391
      —programme content 393-5
    law of—
      —Broadcasting Services Act 1992—
      ——Section 4(1) 400
      ——Section 122(1)(a) 387
      ——Section 122(1)(b) 389-91, 405-7
      ——Sections 122(1)(b) and 160(d), conflict 389-414
      ——Section 128(1) 401
      ——Section 158 386, 400

Australia *(cont.)*
——Section 159 386
——Section 160 386-7, 389-91, 400-1
——validity of act in breach of 412-14
legislation—
—implementation by broadcasting authority in conformity with treaty obligations 407
—validity—
——conflict with international obligations 410-12
legislation, interpretation—
—aids—
——context 393-5, 405, 406
——legislative history 392-3
—guidelines—
——conformity with treaty 407-10
——every word to be given meaning 405
——intention of legislature 398-9
——object and purpose 404-5
——ordinary grammatical meaning 406-7
——Statute as a whole 404-5
—phrases—
——"Australian content" 389-95, 402
—presumptions—
——conformity, international law 395
New Zealand, Closer Economic Relations Trade Agreement (1983)—
—MFN clause—
——Australian Content Standard (broadcasting), compatibility with 386-415
——text 387

B

Belgium—
act of State—
—declaration of diplomat as *persona non grata* 443-5
—judicial review 445
American Battle Monuments Commission—
—legal personality 440
diplomatic relations—
—declaration of diplomat as *persona non grata*—
——act of State 443-5
employment contract—
—applicable law 425
international organizations—
—legal personality 426
international organizations, privileges and immunities—
—immunity, execution—
——*exequatur* as preliminary step 429
——nature of assets as test 428-9
——waiver, need for 428, 429
—immunity, jurisdiction—
——employment contract 425
—waiver 425
jurisdiction—
—nexus—

——payment of compensation 417
——registered office 416
law of—
—Judicial Code—
——Article 635 417
service of process—
—date of 420
—means—
——diplomatic channels 420
——registered post 420, 440-1
State immunity, jurisdiction—
—classification of act—
——establishment of Office for Management of Public Debt (recovery of compensation in respect of expropriation of private property) 417-18
——private person test 421, 433
—customary international law—
——European Convention on State Immunity (1972) 422
—employment contract—
——dismissal 419, 421-3, 435
——European Convention on State Immunity (1972), relevance 422
——language teacher 434
——nationality of employee, relevance 422
—entitlement to raise—
——Court *ex proprio motu* 431
—expropriation 417
—preliminary issue 417
treaties—
—applicability—
——non-party, to 434
—publication, need for 426, 439-40
Bosnia-Herzegovina—
armed conflict—
—international, whether 174-5
boundaries—
—administrative dividing lines 74-80
— conversion into international boundaries 76-80
—Arbitration Commission of the Conference on Yugoslavia 76-7, 116-17
—Dayton Agreements (1995) 79
—demarcation lines 75
federal unit of SFRY, whether 130-2
Framework Agreement for the Federation (1994) 77-9
Genocide Convention (1948)—
—applicability 23-7, 67-8
——date of 25
—succession mechanism 23-7, 183-203
Head of State—
—authority to act on behalf of State in international relations 34-5, 102-15
—existence of state of war or emergency, relevance 108-13
international protectorate, as 94-6
proclamation of sovereignty—
—legality 115-16, 132-57
recognition 96-102
—FRY reservation 200-3
—political basis 98-102

Bosnia-Herzegovina *(cont.)*
  secession, right of 130-57
  Statehood—
    —Dayton Agreements (1995)—
      ——dependence on effective implementation of 89-94
    —effective government 80-93
    —population—
      ——absence of consensus between separate groups 73-4
    —Republika Srpska and Herceg-Bosna, relevance 80-8
    —territory 71-3, 74-80
  treaties—
    —State succession 23-5, 46-8, 115-17, 183-203
Boundaries—
  uti possidetis—
    —Yugoslavia 77
Broadcasting—
  content standard—
    —MFN clause, compatibility with 386-415
    —transmission quota as 391
  programme content 393-5

                                       C
Canada—
  aboriginal rights. *See also* aboriginal title *below*
    —abandonment—
      ——burden of proof 462
    —alienation—
      ——restrictions on 463, 476, 498-500
    —basis—
      ——occupation or use of specific land 456-7, 463, 467
      ——operation of law rather than Crown grant 463
      ——practices, customs and traditions pre-dating contact with Europeans 469-70,
        473-4
    —common law recognition 467, 469, 481
    —constitutionalization. *See* aboriginal title, Constitution Act 1982 *below*
    —consultation with minority representatives, relevance 516, 534
    —critical date—
      ——contact with Europeans 469-70, 473-4, 481
      ——England's assertion of sovereignty 460, 463
    —development, possibility of 469-70
    —extinction—
      ——act inconsistent with continuing right, implied by 460-1, 466-7, 470
      ——clear and plain intention, need for 460, 464-5, 469, 475, 522-3
      ——Crown's power of unilateral 457, 460, 464
      ——fiduciary obligation of Crown. *See below*
      ——laws of general application, by 465-6
      ——possibility of 463, 511
      ——provincial power over. *See below*
    —fiduciary obligation of Crown—
      ——to ensure aboriginal activities not unduly impaired 461, 512-17, 529
      ——to enter into and conduct negotiations in good faith 524
    —land rights 476
    —nature—

——*ad hoc* 466
——communal pursuit of subsistence activities 456-7, 463, 472-3
——jurisdictional 459, 464, 468, 472, 473-6
——personal 457
——proprietary 457-8, 463, 467
——usufructuary 457
——negotiations relating to 464, 466, 469, 473, 535
——Crown's obligation of good faith 524
—oil or gas benefits 496-7
—priority over competing and inconsistent activities 457
—provincial power over 465-7, 470, 518-23
——"core of Indianness" 520-1
——general legislation affecting 521-2
——legislation relating specifically to Indians 521
——rights not relating to land 521
——rights relating to land 521
—reconciliation of prior aboriginal occupation and Crown sovereignty 481, 504, 514-15
—regulation—
——legitimate and justifiable Crown interests, need for 457, 533-4
——possibility of 463
—requirements—
——continuity 481-2, 494-7
——integrality to claimants' culture 467-8, 470, 497-500
——long-standing practice 456, 463-4, 468, 472
——occupation pre-dating England's assertion of sovereignty 459-60, 463-4, 468
——occupation of specific territory 459-60, 463-4, 468
——occupation to the exclusion of other organized societies 459-60, 468, 474
——organized society 459-60
—self-government 470-1, 474-7, 517
——as alternative to jurisdiction 478-9
—territorial limits 476
——evidence of 488-90
—title to land, distinguished 520
—trapping—
——whether aboriginal right 472
aboriginal title. *See also* aboriginal rights *above*; Indian peoples in *below*
—aboriginal rights, distinguished 511
—affirmation by Constitution Act 1982 452, 470
—alienation, restrictions on 492, 528-9
—basis—
——activities 491-2, 503-4
——occupation 472, 493, 528
——possession 472
——relationship between common law and pre-existing aboriginal law 493
——*Royal Proclamation, 1763* 493, 532-3
——use 472
—at common law 492-500
—Constitution Act 1982 500-3. *See also* Constitution Act 1982, Section 35(1) *below*
—critical date—
——assertion of sovereignty 481-2, 504-8, 531-2
—evidence of 452
——occupancy 498

Canada *(cont.)*
 ——occupation prior to assertion of sovereignty 504-8
 ——oral histories 453, 471, 481-90
 —extinction. *See* power of province to extinguish *below*
 —interference with—
 ——compensation 516-17, 535
 ——requirements 514-16
 —joint 509-11
 —nature—
 ——aboriginal rights 469
 ——communal 493
 ——ownership and jurisdiction 472, 478, 527-8
 ——right in land 452, 491-2, 502-3
 ——right to exclusive use and occupation for variety of purposes not necessarily integral to aboriginal cultures 494-7, 529
 ——*sui generis* 453, 469, 481, 492-500, 528
 ——uncertainty 478-9
 —power of province to extinguish 453, 470-1, 535
 —requirements—
 ——continuity 508-9, 528, 530, 531-2
 ——defined territory 530-1
 ——exclusive occupation 509-11, 524, 531, 532
 ——practices relating to traditional way of life 530, 532
 —reserve lands, relevance of legislation relating to 529-30
applicable law—
 —secession of part of State—
 ——international law 546
 ——municipal law 590
British Columbia—
 —aboriginal rights in 452-535
confederation—
 —history 550-5
Constitution—
 —constitutional/parliamentary supremacy, distinguished 564-5
 —cultural and linguistic minorities, pursuit of collective goals 559-60
 —entrenchment, reasons for—
 ——protection of division of powers 565
 ——protection of human rights 565
 ——protection of minority groups 565, 566
 —referendum. *See below*
 —sovereignty of people, expression of 569
 —unwritten principles—
 ——aid to interpretation 556-7, 558
 ——democracy 560-3
 ——effect 557
 ——federalism 557-60
 ——protection of minorities 566-8
 —written nature 555-7
Constitution Act 1867—
 —Section 91(24) 465, 518-19, 520-2
 —Section 101 540-2
Constitution Act 1982—
 —Section 35(1) 452-3, 466, 468, 469, 491-517
 ——self-government, right to 517

——Section 52(1) 564
Constitution, interpretation—
——aids—
————unwritten underlying principles 556-7
——guidelines—
————text as a whole 556
democracy—
——majority rule 561-3, 592
————competing majorities 562-3, 566
——referendum, role 565
——rule of law, need for 562-3, 572. *See also* rule of law *below*
——sovereign will of the people, supremacy 560, 562
evidence of—
——territorial limits of aboriginal rights 488-90
——title—
————occupancy 498
————oral histories 453
Indian peoples in—
——Gitksan and Wet'suwet'en people—
————demography 454, 473
————history 454-5
————oral histories 485-8
————social organization 455-6
————territorial boundaries 461-2, 473
——jurisdiction over—
————interjurisdictional immunity 520-1
————jurisdiction over land, distinguished 520
——rights 452-535. *See also* aboriginal rights *above*
——title. *See* aboriginal title *above*
international law—
——municipal courts, application by 545-6
————binding effect on other States or international courts 545
judicial restraint 574-5
jurisdiction—
——Indian peoples—
————jurisdiction over land, distinguished 520
justiciability—
——advisory jurisdiction—
————hypothetical question 546
————legal nature of question 546-7
——imprecise or ambiguous question 548-9
——judicial restraint, need for 574-5
——legal problem, limited to 575-6
——secession 574-7, 593-4
law of—
——Constitution Acts. *See* Constitution Act 1867 and Constitution Act 1982 *above*
——Indian Act 1985—
————Section 88 466, 522-3
——Indian Oil and Gas Act 496-7
——Supreme Court Act 1985—
————constitutional validity of Section 53 541-9
legislation, interpretation—
——phrases—
————"Indians" 520-1

Canada *(cont.)*
——"lands reserved for the Indians" 518-20
legislative powers—
——distribution between province and federal government 557-9
political question doctrine—
——clarification of legal framework for democratic decisions 547
Quebec—
——"people", whether 594
——right of self-expression 587-8
——secession, right of 539-95. *See also* secession, right of province *below*
referendum—
——democratic, whether 565, 572
——legal effect 570, 593
——legitimacy, conferring 571
——negotiation, obligation following 570-4, 593
——secession, relevance to 570-1, 592-3
remedies—
——need for 576
——political process as 576
rule of law—
——definition 563-6
——constitutionalism distinguished 564-5
——remedy for breach 590-1
secession, right of province—
——amendment to Constitution, need for 568-9, 574
——applicable law—
——international law 546, 579
——municipal law 590
——complementary rights of federal government and other provinces 571-3
——*de facto* 578, 589, 595
——international law, under 579-91
——legitimacy—
——recognition 576, 593
——refusal to negotiate, effect 576-7
——referendum 570-1, 592-3
——unilateral 568-95
Supreme Court—
——advisory function 543-4
——international law, right to apply 545-6
——jurisdiction—
——advisory function. *See above*
——application of federal laws, whether limited to 541
——important questions of fact or law concerning any matter 544
——interpretation of Constitution Acts 544
——original jurisdiction 541-2
——questions concerning the powers of the legislature or government of a Canadian province 544
——primacy over provincial court of appeal 542
Civil war—
Bosnia-Herzegovina. *See* Bosnia-Herzegovina, armed conflict
Genocide Convention (1948), applicability 28
Compensation—
for—
——interference with minority rights 516-17, 535

Constitution (State)—
constitutional/parliamentary supremacy, distinguished 564-5
entrenchment, reasons for—
——protection of division of powers 565
——protection of human rights 565
——protection of minority groups 565, 566
interpretation—
——aids—
————unwritten underlying principles 556-7, 558
——guidelines—
————text as a whole 556
property rights, protection of 624-36
treaties. *See* Treaties, constitutional compatibility
unwritten principles—
——aid to interpretation 556-7
——democracy 560-3
——effect 557
——federalism 557-60
——protection of minorities 566-8
written 555-7
Counterclaim—
admissibility—
——Court's discretion 242-3, 245, 250-3
——criminal cases 248-50
——ICJ—
————*Bosnia and Herzegovina* v. *Yugoslavia* 206-53
————oral hearings, need for 227, 236
——State immunity cases 241-2
————ILC Draft Articles on Jurisdictional Immunities of States and their Property
     (1991) 241-2
autonomy 216-17, 222-3
basis—
——consistency of decision-making 217-18
——procedural economy 217-18, 235-6
defence on merits, distinguished 217
—— *United States Diplomatic and Consular Staff in Tehran* 217
definition 246-50
equality of parties 220, 226
joinder—
——automatic, whether 224-6
legal nature 223
requirements—
——"direct connection with the subject-matter of the claim of the other party" 218,
     224-31, 245
————*Case concerning the Diversion of Water from the Meuse* 229
————Court's discretion to determine 218, 224-7
————facts of the same nature 218
————factual connection 218, 228
————legal connection 218, 228-31
————part of the same factual complex 218, 230
——reasonable time-scale for decision 220
——reciprocity of obligations, relevance 218-19
——"within the jurisdiction of the Court" 245
————as recognized by the parties 218

Counterclaim *(cont.)*
  third party—
    —effect on admissibility 243, 253
    —protection—
    ——transmission of Order 220
Courts, municipal—
  advisory functions 543-4
  appeal court's right to exercise original jurisdiction 541-2
Customary international law—
  diplomatic privileges and immunities—
    —matters not covered by the Vienna Convention on Diplomatic Relations
      (1961) 611
    —State succession—
    ——incorporation of receiving State into forum State, effect 615-16, 618
    —third State, in 610-12
  evidence of—
    —State practice: *qv*
    —treaty. *See* treaties and other international instruments reflecting *below*
  jus cogens: *qv*
  requirements—
    —constant and uniform practice 186, 610
    —general acceptance 186, 610
    —*jus cogens*: *qv*
    —*opinio juris* 610
    —State practice: *qv*
  State practice: *qv*
  treaties and other international instruments reflecting—
    —European Convention on State Immunity (and Protocol) (1972) 422, 431, 432-4
    —Vienna Convention on Diplomatic Relations (1961)—
    ——preservation of customary international law 611
    —Vienna Convention on the Law of Treaties (1969) 196
    —Vienna Convention on the Succession of States in respect of Treaties (1978)
      186-92

D

Democracy—
  majority rule 561-3, 592
    —competing majorities 562-3, 566
  referendum, role 565
  rule of law, need for 562-3
  supremacy of sovereign will of the people 560, 562
Deportation—
  family life, respect for 341
    —unlawful or arbitrary interference 337, 348-9
  grounds—
    —criminal record 342-3
  inhuman or degrading treatment, whether 330
Diplomatic agent—
  agrément, need for 616-17
    —State succession, and 616-17
  criminal offence—
    —remedy—
    ——declaration as *persona non grata* 607

functions—
—bomb attack, assistance 600, 603
Diplomatic privileges and immunities. *See also* International organizations, privileges
  and immunities; State immunity, jurisdiction
abuse—
  —measures to prevent 608
  ——break of diplomatic relations 611
  ——refusal of permission to transit 611
  ——withdrawal of *agrément* 611
  —remedies—
  ——expulsion 618
agrément, dependence on 610, 616-17
basis—
  —foreign relations considerations 607
  —protection of own diplomats abroad 607
  —protection of sending State 609, 616, 617
criminal jurisdiction—
  —serious violation of law 607
customary international law—
  —State succession—
  ——incorporation of receiving State into forum State, effect 615-16, 618
entitlement—
  —termination of diplomatic status—
  ——continuation after, functional basis for 600, 605-6
  ——protection of State as basis 609
functional 603, 605-7. *See also* Diplomatic agent, functions
  —act attributable to State 606
  —act illegal under sending State law 606
  —criminal act 606, 607
  —failure to prevent bomb attack 606
  —personal immunity, distinguished 606, 609-10, 612-13
  —termination of status, after 600, 605-6, 612-13
immunity, jurisdiction—
  —functional. *See* Diplomatic agent, functions
purpose. *See* basis *above*
State immunity, and 605-6. *See also* Ambassador, State immunity, jurisdiction
  —distinction 608-10, 613-14
  —primacy 613-14
State succession—
  —incorporation of receiving State into forum State, effect 602, 614, 615-17
  ——customary international law 615-16, 618
  ——State practice 615-16
third State, in 602
  —customary international law 610-12
  —effects doctrine 604-5
  —general principle of international law 602
  —Lateran Treaty (1929) as evidence against 612
  —recognition of judgment delivered by courts of receiving State 612
  —State practice 612
  —termination of mission, relevance 612-13
  —third State as successor State, relevance 602
Vienna Convention on Diplomatic Relations (1961)—
  —customary international law—
  ——residual matters 611

Diplomatic relations—
  declaration of diplomat as *persona non grata*—
    —act of State 443-5
Discrimination—
  compensation by successor government for expropriation of property under
    communist regime 268-76
Dispute settlement. *See also* International Court of Justice (ICJ)
  Genocide Convention (1948) 39-41, 204-5
  methods—
    —failure to make treaty provision 662

                                      E
Employment contract—
  applicable law 425
European Convention on Human Rights (1950)—
  constitutional compatibility 642-55
  implementation—
    —obligation 641-2
    —procedure—
      ——national discretion 642-3
  municipal law, and—
    —direct effect 644
  phrases—
    —"religion"—
      ——"faith" 653
    —"social origin"—
      ——"social status" 653
  remedy for breach—
    —international proceedings, limited to 643-4
Evidence of—
  territorial limits of aboriginal rights 488-90
  title—
    —occupancy 498
    —oral histories 453
Expropriation, compensation—
  discrimination—
    —compensation by successor government for property confiscated under
      communist regime 265-76
Expulsion of national—
  International Covenant on Civil and Political Rights (1966) 344-5

                                      F
Fair trial—
  non-disclosure of prosecution evidence—
    —international tribunal's right to question conduct of defence lawyer 298-9
  proceedings—
    —international tribunal's right to question 297
  right to—
    —effective representation 353-5
    —*non bis in idem* 365
Federal State—
  Canadian Confederation, history 550-5

constituent State—
—requirements—
——Bosnia-Herzegovina 130-2
—secession—
——*de facto* 578, 589, 595
cultural and linguistic minorities, pursuit of collective goals 559-60
jurisdiction—
—primacy of federal appeal court 542
legislative powers—
—distribution 468, 557-9
representation—
—federal organs 154-7
Finland—
Sami rights—
—enjoyment of own culture—
——measures affecting 316-18
——reindeer husbandry, effect of logging and road construction 316-18
France—
freedom of expression—
—anti-semitic remarks, prohibition 372-3
international organizations, privileges and immunities—
—immunity, jurisdiction—
——execution, distinguished 428
law of—
—Freedom of the Press Law (1881)—
——Gayssot Act (1990) amending, legality 358-83
legislation—
—implementation by courts in conformity with treaty obligations 378-80

G

General principles of—
international law. *See* International law, general principles
Genocide—
definition—
—single act as 240
Genocide Convention (1948). *See* Genocide Convention (1948)
obligation not to commit—
—*erga omnes* 175
obligation to implement rule prohibiting 175-6
Genocide Convention (1948)—
accession—
—Dayton Agreements (1995) as basis 200-3
—notification of succession 200-3
—relevance 194-5
applicability—
—critical date 30
—nature of conflict, relevance 28, 174-5
breach—
—individual 45
—State responsibility for act of genocide 29, 40-1, 44-5, 177-9, 180-2
—State responsibility for act of ruler or public officials 29
—territorial jurisdiction, relevance 28-9, 176-82
dispute settlement provisions 22-35, 38-43, 44, 179-82, 193-4

Genocide Convention *(cont.)*
—retroactive, whether 204-5
humanitarian treaty, whether 184-5
jurisdiction—
—competent tribunal of State in which act committed 44
—ICJ 42-3, 44-5
—International Criminal Court (ICC) 42-3
—international penal institution 43, 44
—organ of UN 43
notification of succession, effect 194-201
object and purpose—
—protection of rights of individuals and groups of persons 39, 41-2
obligations—
—*erga omnes* nature 39, 218-19
—*jus cogens* nature 193-4
——dispute settlement provisions 193-4
—non-derogable 62-3
—reciprocal, whether 218-19
—to prevent and punish crime of genocide—
——preambular nature of obligation 39, 63
——remedy for breach 39-40
——territorial scope 28-9, 174, 176-82
parties to—
—Bosnia-Herzegovina 23-5, 46-7
——reservation in respect of, relevance 200-2
——succession mechanism 23-7, 183-203
—Federal Republic of Yugoslavia (FRY) 23, 165-74
—members of UN 24
—recognition, relevance 25-7
rights—
—vested 63
State responsibility. *See* breach, State responsibility for act of genocide *above*
State succession 23-5, 45-8, 52-66, 71, 183-203. *See also* Treaties, State succession, human rights conventions
—gap, avoidance of 45-8, 64-5, 67-8
Germany, Democratic Republic (GDR)—
diplomatic relations—
—effect of unification 616-17
Germany, Federal Republic (FRG)—
act of State—
—sovereign activity—
——international law, under 613
ambassador—
—State immunity, jurisdiction—
——entitlement 613-14
Basic Law *(GG)*—
—Article 2(1) 603
—Article 2(2) (right to life) 603
—Article 20(3) 603
—Article 101(1) 603
—Article 103(1) 603
customary international law—
—diplomatic privileges and immunities—
——incorporation of receiving State into forum State, effect 615-16, 618

——matters not covered by the Vienna Convention on Diplomatic Relations (1961) 611
——third State, in 610-12
—requirements—
——constant and uniform practice 610
——general acceptance 610
——*opinio juris* 610
diplomatic agent—
—*agrément*, need for 616-17
——State succession, and 616-17
—criminal offence—
——remedy, declaration as *persona non grata* 607
—functions—
——bomb attack, assistance 600, 603
diplomatic privileges and immunities—
—abuse—
——measures to prevent 608, 611
—*agrément*, dependence on 610, 616-17
—basis—
——foreign relations considerations 607
——protection of own diplomats abroad 607
——protection of sending State 609, 616, 617
—criminal jurisdiction—
——serious violation of law 607
—customary international law—
——State succession—
—incorporation of receiving State into forum State, effect 615-16, 618
—entitlement—
——termination of diplomatic status, continuation after 600, 605-6, 609
—functional 603, 605-7
——act attributable to State 606
——act illegal under sending State law 606
——criminal act 606, 607
——failure to prevent bomb attack 606
——personal immunity, distinguished 606, 609-10, 612-13
—— termination of status, after 600, 605-6, 612-13
—incorporation of receiving State into forum State, effect—
——customary international law 615-16, 618
——State practice 615-16
—State immunity, and 605-6
——distinction 608-10, 613-14
——primacy 613-14
—State succession—
——incorporation of receiving State into forum State, effect 602, 614, 615-17
—third State, in 602
——customary international law 610-12
——effects doctrine 604-5
——general principle of international law 602
——Lateran Treaty (1929) as evidence against 612
——recognition of judgment delivered by courts of receiving State 612
——State practice 612
——termination of mission, relevance 612-13
——third State as successor State, relevance 602

Germany, Federal Republic *(cont.)*
  German Democratic Republic (GDR), and—
    —diplomatic relations—
      ——effect of unification 616-17
    —treaties, succession to—
      ——Unification Treaty 614-15
  international law—
    —general principles—
      ——customary international law as 610
      ——general principles of law as 610
    —sources—
      ——arbitral and judicial decisions 610
      ——writings of publicists 610
  jurisdiction—
    —effects doctrine 604-5
    —sovereign act of third State 613
  law of—
    —GDR, application in 600
    —Penal Code—
      ——Section 3 604-5
      ——Section 9 604-5
  State agency—
    —"agent or instrumentality of foreign State"—
      ——ambassador 613-14
  State practice—
    —diplomatic privileges and immunities—
      ——third State, in 612
  treaties—
    —State succession—
      ——*ad hoc* 615
      ——agreement of all parties, need for 614
      ——treaties concluded by the German Democratic Republic (GDR) 614

H

Head of State—
  authority to act on behalf of State in international relations 34-5, 102-15
    —applicable law—
      ——international law 103
    —domestic law, relevance 103
  recognition—
    —evidence of 35, 104-5
Human rights—
  legal rights, whether limited to 644-5
  municipal law—
    —incorporation into 645
Hungary—
  expropriation, compensation—
    —property confiscated under communist regime—
      ——discriminatory, whether 265-76
  law of—
    —Act XXV (1991) (compensation for confiscation of property) 269-76
      ——discriminatory, whether 274-6
    —Act LXXVIII (1993) (privatization of residential property)—
      ——discriminatory, whether 274-6

property—
　　—privatization of State-owned residential property—
　　　—priority to tenants, fairness 276

I

Inhuman or degrading treatment—
failure of State to investigate prison conditions 298
Interim measures—
UNHRC 256, 306
International Court of Justice (ICJ)—
　ad hoc judge—
　　—appointment—
　　　—*Application of Genocide Convention* 11
　　—purpose 236
　admissibility—
　　—international dispute, need for 34
　consent to jurisdiction—
　　—evidence of—
　　　—Head of State's letter in another forum 31-2
　　—Head of State's authority, relevance 34-5
　　—implied—
　　　—conduct in proceedings 33
　　—request for provisional measures 33-4
　　—"unequivocal indication . . . of a voluntary and undisputed acceptance" 33-4
　counterclaim: *qv*
　judgments—
　　—interpretation—
　　　—official publication of Court 439-40
　jurisdiction—
　　—basis—
　　　—Genocide Convention (1948), Article IX 22-35, 38-43, 44, 179-82
　　　—Treaty of Saint-Germain-en-Laye (1919) 32-3
　　—genocide cases 42-3
　　—objection to—
　　　—abuse of rights under Statute or Rules of Court 35
　　　—value to Court 35
　　—preliminary objections, purpose 166
　　—*ratione temporis*—
　　　—critical date 30
　　—restrictive interpretation 42-3
　legal dispute—
　　—disagreement relating to performance of treaty obligations 27-30
　　　—breach of treaty, distinguished 42
　　　—infringement of rights of State, need for 38-42
　　—international dispute between States 70-1
　procedure—
　　—formalism, need to avoid 25-7
　　—oral hearings, need for 227, 236, 237-8
　　—Rules of Court. *See below*
　Rules of Court—
　　—31 206, 212
　　—35(4) 237
　　—36(2) 237

International Court of Justice (ICJ) *(cont.)*
—43 (notification to States party to Genocide Convention) 11
—44 206
—45 206
—49(2) 216
—53(2) (public availability of pleadings) 12
—56(2) 237
—67 237
—79 237
—79(1) (preliminary objections) 12, 35, 210
—79(7) 166, 237
—80 206, 216-19, 223-9, 237-8, 244-5
—80(1) 212, 216, 218, 224-6, 234, 245
—80(2) 216, 218, 234
—80(3) 212, 214, 226-8, 234, 235-6, 238
seisin—
—unilateral—
——*forum prorogatum* 45, 48-50
International Covenant on Civil and Political Rights (1966)—
arbitrary act—
—conformity with provisions, aims and objectives of Covenant, need for 342-3
—test—
——proportionality 348-9
——reasonableness 342-3
death penalty—
—accordance with law, need for 354
deportation—
—decision in accordance with law 330, 337
—inhuman or degrading treatment, whether 330
—respect for family life 337, 341
entry to one's own country—
—deportation or expulsion, relevance 335, 340
equality of arms 664-5
expulsion—
—national 344-5
fair trial—
—*non bis in idem* 365
—non-disclosure of prosecution evidence 298-9
—right to—
——effective representation 353-5
freedom of expression—
—anti-semitic remarks 372-3
—restrictions on 372-3
implementation—
—national measures as primary means 659
inhuman or degrading treatment—
—death row 297-8
——three-year delay in hearing appeal 297-8
—deportation 330
—failure of State to investigate prison conditions 298
minority rights—
—consultation with minority representatives, relevance 317
—enjoyment of own culture 316-18
——cumulative effect of measure affecting 318

obligations under—
——entry into force as critical date—
————continuing violation 268-9, 285
——provision of effective and enforceable remedy for violation 299, 355
phrases—
——"his own country" 330-1, 335-6, 337-49
————"country of nationality", distinguished 335, 346
————failure to acquire nationality, relevance 336-7, 343-4, 347-8
————stateless person 335
——"victim"—
————"actually affected" 261-2, 372
property rights 268
——discrimination in respect of compensation by successor government for expropriation under communist regime 265-76
remedies—
——avoidance of future violations 355
——commutation of death penalty 354
——compensation 299
restrictions on rights—
——courts' interpretation of law in compliance with treaty obligations, relevance 378-80
——requirements—
————compliance of law with provisions of Covenant 372
————conformity with aims and objectives of Covenant 372, 374, 380-1
————legitimate purpose 372
————necessity 373, 374-7, 378-9, 380-3
————proportionality 376-7, 380-1
————provision by law 372, 380-1
International law—
basis—
——consent 192
——customary international law 192
general principles—
——customary international law as 610
——general principles of law as 610
——*Lotus* principle ("what is not prohibited is allowed") 590
——self-determination 581
——territorial integrity 483, 580, 582, 584-5
municipal courts, application by 545-6
——binding effect on other States or international courts 545
municipal law, and—
——municipal law as part of international law 121-3
peremptory norms. *See Jus cogens*
sources—
——arbitral and judicial decisions 610
————municipal courts 545
——customary international law: *qv*
——general practice accepted as law. *See* State practice
——State practice: *qv*
——writings of publicists 610
International Law Commission (ILC)—
Draft Articles on Jurisdictional Immunities of States and Their Property (1991)—
——counterclaims 241-2
Draft Code of Offences against the Peace and Security of Mankind (1976)—

International Law Commission (ILC) *(cont.)*
—State responsibility 178-9
International organizations—
legal personality 426
International organizations, privileges and immunities—
immunity, execution—
—*exequatur* as preliminary step 429
—nature of assets as test 428-9
—waiver, need for 428, 429
immunity, jurisdiction—
—employment contract 425
—execution, distinguished 428
waiver 425

J

Judicial restraint 574-5
Jurisdiction—
effects doctrine 604-5
Indian peoples in Canada—
—interjurisdictional immunity 520-1
—jurisdiction over land, distinguished 520
nexus—
—payment—
——of compensation 417
—registered office 416
sovereign act of third State 613
Jus cogens—
basis—
—multilateral treaties 192
derogation 164-5
effectiveness principle, effect on 119-20
Justiciability—
advisory jurisdiction—
—hypothetical question 546
—legal nature of question 546-7
imprecise or ambiguous question 548-9
legal problem, limited to 575-6

L

Legal personality—
American Battle Monuments Commission 440
Legislation—
implementation by broadcasting authority in conformity with treaty obligations 407
implementation by courts in conformity with treaty obligations 378-80
validity—
—conflict with international obligations 410-12
Legislation, interpretation—
aids—
—context 393-5, 405, 406
—legislative history 392-3
—treaty—
——unincorporated 663

guidelines—
—conformity with treaty 407-10
—every word to be given meaning 405
—intention of legislature 398-9
—object and purpose 404-5
—ordinary grammatical meaning 406-7
—Statute as a whole 404-5
presumptions—
—conformity—
——international law 395
——international obligations 662-3
Life, right to—
nuclear tests 255-62
Lithuania—
alien—
—equality of treatment 653-4
—rights—
——rights and freedoms of citizen 653-4
Constitution 1938—
—Art. 2 642
—Art. 3 642
—Art. 4 642
—Art. 6 646
—Art. 7 644
—Art. 12 642
—Art. 20(2) 648-9
—Art. 20(3) 649-50
—Art. 23 633, 635
—Art. 26(4),650-1
—Art. 29 652-3
—Art. 32 653-4
—Art. 46 629
—Art. 47 628
—Art. 48(5) 647-8
—Art. 54 628, 633
—Art. 102 636
—Art. 138 644, 645
—restoration 622-3
European Convention on Human Rights (1950)—
—constitutional compatibility 642-55
——Article 4 (forced or compulsory labour) 646-8
——Article 5 (prompt hearing) 648-50
——Article 9 (freedom of religion) 650-1
——Article 14 (discrimination) 651-3
——Protocol 4, Article 2 (freedom of movement) 653-4
—implementation—
——obligation 641-2
——procedure, national discretion 642-3
—municipal law, and—
——direct effect 644
human rights—
—legal rights, whether limited to 644-5
independence, declaration of 622
law of—

Lithuania *(cont.)*
—Civil Code—
——Art. 606 643
—Civil Procedure Code—
——Art. 482 643
—Law on International Agreements of the Republic of Lithuania 1991—
——Art. 12 644
—Law on Land Reform 1990 635-6
—Law on the Legal Status of Foreigners in the Republic of Lithuania 1991 654
—Law on the Procedure and Conditions of the Restoration of the Rights of Ownership to Existing Real Property 1990 626-7
——Law Appending and Amending 1993 627-8
—Law on the Provisional Basic Law of the Republic of Lithuania 1990 623-4
—Law on the Reinstatement of the 12 May 1938 Constitution 1990 622-3
——effect on other laws in force prior to 15 June 1940 625
—property rights 623-37
property—
—public good 628-9, 634, 635
property rights—
—continuity 624-6
—restoration 626-37
——compensation for non-restoration 626-7
——limitations on 629-36
treaties—
—implementation—
——means, choice 642
——obligation 641
—municipal law, and—
——part of, whether 644
—primacy—
——civil matters 643
——criminal matters 643-4
Lotus principle ("what is not prohibited is allowed"). *See under* International law, general principles

M

Minority rights—
constitutional principle 566-8
enjoyment of own culture 316-18
—measures affecting—
——consultation with minority representatives, relevance 317, 516, 534
——cumulative effect 318
——threshold 316-18
—reindeer husbandry—
——logging and road construction 316-18

N

New Zealand—
International Covenant on Civil and Political Rights (1966)—
—implementation—
——national measures as primary means 659
law of—

—Legal Services Act 1991 665-71
legislation, interpretation—
—aids—
——treaty 663
—presumptions—
——conformity, international obligations 662-3
UNHRC—
—"administrative tribunal or judicial authority", whether 657, 660-5
—legal aid—
——obligation to provide 664-71
Nuclear tests—
threat of catastrophic accident, whether 262
threat to life, whether 255-62

P
Permanent Court of International Justice (PCIJ)—
Rules of Court (1922)—
—39 247
—40 223, 247
Political question doctrine—
clarification of legal framework for democratic decisions 547
Property—
privatization of State-owned residential property—
—priority to tenants, fairness 276
public good 628-9, 634, 635
rights—
—arbitrary deprivation 624
—continuity 624-6
—human right 624
—International Covenant on Civil and Political Rights (1966) 268, 274-6
—restoration—
——compensation for non-restoration 626-7
——limitations on 629-36
Proportionality—
arbitrary act, test 348-9

Q
Quebec. *See under* Canada

R
Recognition, State—
constitutive theory 589
implied—
—treaty 200
legality of State, effect on 165, 201-2
political act, whether 96-102, 589-91
requirements—
—Restatement of Foreign Relations Law (Second) (1965) 97-8
retroactive effect—
—legitimization of secession 589-90, 595

Referendum—
  democratic, whether 565
  legality 135-46
  procedure 135-46
Remedies—
  commutation of death penalty 354
  need for 576, 643
  political process as 576
Revolution—
  definition—
    —illegitimate change of legal order 590
Rule of law—
  definition 563-6
    —constitutionalism distinguished 564-5

S

Sami. *See* Finland, Sami rights
Secession. *See also* Self-determination
  applicable law—
    —municipal law 133-46, 580, 590
  of dependent territories and part of existing State distinguished 188-91
  "effectivity" principle 589-91. *See also* State, creation, effectiveness principle
  referendum 570-1, 592-3
  right of constituent part of a federal State—
    —amendment to Constitution, need for 135-7, 568-9, 574
    —Bosnia-Herzegovina 130-57
    —*de facto* 578, 589, 595
    —unilateral right 579
  self-determination, distinguished 584
  State succession, distinguished 116-17
  territorial integrity 150-3, 162-4, 580, 582, 584-5
Self-determination. *See also* Secession
  general principle of international law 581
  Helsinki Final Act (1975) 163-4, 582, 585
  International Covenant on Civil and Political Rights (1966) 581, 585
  International Covenant on Economic, Social and Cultural Rights (1966) 581, 585
  multi-ethnic State, in 121, 133-4
  "people" 147, 583
    —municipal law, under 147
    —Quebec 594
    —Yugoslavia 123-30, 143
  peremptory norm of international law 146-7, 202
  right—
    —colonial people 585-6, 594-5
    —oppressed people 586, 594-5
    —"people" 580-8, 594-5
    —people denied right of self-expression 586-8, 594-5
    —within existing State 582-5
  secession, distinguished 584
  UN Charter 581
  UNGA Resolution 2158 (XXV) (Declaration on Principles of International Law concerning Friendly Relations and Cooperation among States in accordance with the Charter of the UN) 581-2

Service of process—
    date of 420
    means—
        —diplomatic channels 420
        —registered post 420, 440-1
Sources of international law. *See* International law, sources
Sovereignty—
    rights—
        —territorial integrity 152
State—
    creation—
        —applicable law—
            ——international law 117-20
            ——municipal law 121-3
        —effectiveness principle 118-20
        —legality—
            ——recognition, effect 165
    territorial integrity, importance 580, 582, 584-5
    "territory", distinguished—
        —loss of territory, relevance 172-3
State agency—
    "agent or instrumentality of foreign State"—
        —ambassador 613-14
State immunity, jurisdiction. *See also* Diplomatic privileges and immunities; International
    organizations, privileges and immunities
    classification of act—
        —establishment of Office for Management of Public Debt (recovery of
            compensation in respect of expropriation of private property) 417-18
        —private person test 421, 433
    customary international law—
        —European Convention on State Immunity (1972) 422, 432-4
    employment contract—
        —dismissal 419, 421-3
            ——refusal of work permit as ground for 435
        —European Convention on State Immunity (1972), relevance—
            ——non-party 422
        —language teacher 434
        —nationality of employee—
            ——relevance 422
    entitlement to raise—
        —Court *ex proprio motu* 431
    expropriation 417
    preliminary issue 417
    restrictive—
        —customary international law 434
State practice. *See also* Customary international law
    diplomatic privileges and immunities—
        —third State, in 612
    treaties—
        —State succession 186-92
State responsibility—
    criminal acts—
        —ILC Draft Code of Offences against the Peace and Security of Mankind (1976)
            178-9

State responsibility *(cont.)*
  genocide 29
  Genocide Convention (1948) 29, 40-2, 44-5, 177-9, 180-2
State succession—
  diplomatic privileges and immunities, effect on. *See* Diplomatic privileges and
    immunities, State succession
  treaties. *See* Treaties, State succession
Statehood. *See also* Recognition, State
  Bosnia-Herzegovina 71-102
  definition. *See* requirements *below*
  federal State—
    —States within 77
  requirements—
    —capacity to enter into relations with other States 72
    —defined territory 71-2, 74-80
    —effective government 72, 79-94
    —independence 79
    —population 72-4
    —recognition 71
    —Restatement of the Foreign Relations Law of the United States (Second) (1965)
      97-8
    —sovereignty 73

                                      T
Territorial integrity—
  general principle of international law 483, 580, 582, 584-5
  secession 150-3, 162-4, 580, 582
  self-determination, and 162, 583
  UN Charter 161-2
Treaties—
  accession—
    —notification of succession 194-201
  applicability—
    —non-party, to—
      ——evidence of customary international law, as 434
  constitutional compatibility—
    —need for 642
  customary international law—
    —Vienna Convention on the Succession of States in respect of Treaties (1978)
      185-92
  depositary—
    —powers 183-4
  humanitarian—
    —Genocide Convention (1948), whether 184-5
  implementation—
    —means—
      ——choice 642
    —obligation 641
  multilateral—
    —*jus cogens*, creation of 193
  municipal law, and—
    —part of, whether 644
  parties—

—States, whether limited to 100
primacy—
—civil matters 643
—criminal matters 643-4
publication, need for 426
reservations—
—recognition of State, prevention of implied 200-1
State succession—
—*ad hoc* 615
—agreement of all parties, need for 614
—automatic 185-91
——Vienna Convention on the Succession of States in respect of Treaties (1978) 185-92
—Bosnia-Herzegovina. *See* Bosnia-Herzegovina, treaties
—clean slate principle 54-6
——human rights conventions 56-66
—customary international law—
——Vienna Convention on the Succession of States in respect of Treaties (1978) 185-92
—*de facto* succession 158
—*de jure* 158-61
—Genocide Convention (1948) 23-5, 46-8, 52-66, 183-203
—human rights conventions 52-3, 184-5
——confirmatory nature 58
——customary international law as basis 59
——*erga omnes* nature 56-7
——gap, avoidance 60-1, 64-6, 67-8
——general principles of human rights and humanitarian law, and 58-9
——principle of continuity 61-2
——*res inter alios acta* 62
——stability, protection of 60-1
——State sovereignty, relevance 57-8
—legality of creation of successor State, relevance 115-16, 157-74
——Vienna Convention on the Succession of States in respect of Treaties (1978) 158-61
—multilateral treaties 190-1
—*res inter alios* principle 62
—State practice 186-92
—statement of intention to remain bound 23
—succession of dependent territory and secession of part of State, distinguished 189-90
—treaties concluded by the German Democratic Republic (GDR) 614
—Treaty of Saint-Germain-en-Laye (1919) 32-3
suspension—
—human rights treaties during civil war 62
Vienna Convention on the Law of Treaties (1969)—
—customary international law 196
Vienna Convention on the Succession of States in respect of Treaties (1978)—
—customary international law 185-92
—entry into force 186, 191
Treaty interpretation—
guidelines—
—human rights, protection 344

U

United Nations Human Rights Committee (UNHRC)—
"administrative tribunal or judicial authority", whether 657, 660-5
admissibility—
——continuing effects 268-9, 285
——exhaustion of local remedies. *See below*
——State's acceptance, relevance 306
——State's failure to challenge 297
——sufficiency of evidence 352-3
exhaustion of local remedies—
——dismissal of identical case in national courts 365
——dismissal of petition for leave to appeal 297
——effective remedy, need for 364-5
——failure to complain about trial before Special Criminal Court 285-6
——failure to seek judicial review 286
——previous "act of government" finding by national courts 260
interim measures 256, 306
——compensation as effective remedy, relevance 331
——irreparable damage, need for 331
judicial body, whether 657, 660-5
jurisdiction—
——evaluation of facts and evidence—
————national courts, for 297
——right to question conduct of trial 297
——right to question defence lawyer's conduct 298-9
————consultation with accused 354
legal aid—
——obligation to provide 664-71
Rules of Procedure—
——85 (composition of Committee) 356 n. 1
——86 (interim measures) 256, 325, 331
——87 (admissibility) 261, 285, 330
——91 (information and observations on admissibility) 325
United Nations Secretary-General—
responsibilities—
——parties to multilateral treaties, determination of 169-74, 183-4

W

War—
armed conflict—
——Bosnia-Herzegovina. *See* Bosnia-Herzegovina, armed conflict
Words and phrases—
"Australian content" 389-95, 402
"Indians" 520-1
"lands reserved for the Indians" 518-20
non bis in idem 365
"people" 583
——Quebec 594
"religion"—
——"faith" 653
"social origin"—
——"social status" 653
ubi jus ibi remedium 643

Y

Yugoslavia—
  Constitution—
    —community of peoples 128-30
    —history 123-9
Yugoslavia, Federal Republic of (FRY)—
  succession to Socialist Federal Republic of Yugoslavia (SFRY)—
    —treaties—
      ——Genocide Convention (1948) 169
      ——statement of intention to be bound by 23, 166-9
      ——UN Secretary-General, role 169-74
Yugoslavia, Socialist Federal Republic (SFRY)—
  Constitution—
    —secession—
      ——need for amendment 135-7
    "process of dissolution" 116-17
  referendum—
    —legality 135-46
    —procedure 135-46
  representation—
    —federal organs 154-7
  secession—
    —amendment to Constitution, need for 135-7
    —State succession, distinguished 116-17

Z

Zaire—
  "Zairianization"—
    —sovereign act 417

CONSOLIDATED TABLE OF CASES
VOLUMES 101-115

ARRANGED ALPHABETICALLY

(Cases which are reported only in a note are distinguished from cases which are reported in full by the insertion of the word "note" in parentheses after the page number of the report.)

44123 Ontario Ltd *v.* Crispus Kiyonga and Others **103**, 259

A Limited *v.* B Bank and Bank of X **111**, 590

AAP Ltd *v.* Republic of Sri Lanka. *See* Asian Agricultural Products Ltd *v.* Republic of Sri Lanka

Abbott *v.* Republic of South Africa (Decision No 107/92) **113**, 411

Abdelghafar and Another *v.* United Arab Emirates. *See* United Arab Emirates *v.* Abdelghafar and Another

Abebe-Jira and Others *v.* Negewo **107**, 447

Adams *v.* Jamaica (Communication No 607/1994) **115**, 286

Agyepong **111**, 531

Ahmad *v.* Wigen and Others. *See* In the Matter of the Extradition of Atta; Ahmad *v.* Wigen and Others

Ahmed *v.* Government of the Kingdom of Saudi Arabia. *See* Government of the Kingdom of Saudi Arabia *v.* Ahmed

Al-Adsani *v.* Government of Kuwait and Others **103**, 420, **107**, 536

Alicog *v.* Kingdom of Saudi Arabia and Others **113**, 509

Antarctica Legal Status Case (Case No VI R 185/87) **108**, 654

Antares Aircraft LP *v.* Federal Republic of Nigeria and Nigerian Airports Authority **107**, 225

Antonio Lorenzo. See R *v.* Pesquera Concar SA (Owners of the *Antonio Lorenzo*)

Argentina/Chile, Dispute Concerning the Course of the Frontier between BP 62 and Mount Fitzroy. *See* Dispute Concerning the Course of the Frontier between BP 62 and Mount Fitzroy (Argentina/Chile) ("Laguna del Desierto")

Arizona (State of) *v.* Willoughby **114**, 586

Arriba Ltd *v.* Petroleos Mexicanos **103**, 490

Asian Agricultural Products Ltd *v.* Republic of Sri Lanka **106**, 416

Askir *v.* Boutros-Ghali and Others **113**, 516

Association Greenpeace France **106**, 231

Atta, the Extradition of. *See* In the Matter of the Extradition of Atta; Ahmad *v.* Wigen and Others

Attorney-General (Commonwealth) *v.* Tse Chu-Fai and Another **114**, 383

Australian Federation of Islamic Councils Inc. *v.* Westpac Banking Corporation **104**, 405

Australian Paper Manufacturers Ltd *v.* CIL Inc. **107**, 89 (note)

Autocephalous Greek-Orthodox Church of Cyprus and the Republic of Cyprus *v.* Goldberg and Feldman Fine Arts, Inc. **108**, 488

Autronic AG Case **101**, 134

Avagliano *v.* Sumitomo Shoji America Inc. *See* Sumitomo Shoji America, Inc. *v.* Avagliano; Avagliano *v.* Sumitomo Shoji America, Inc.

Avions Marcel Dassault Bréguet Aviation (SA) *v.* Association Européenne Droit contre Raison d'Etat **106**, 216

Aziz *v.* Caruzzi **101**, 358

Banai *v.* Canadian High Commission and Others **107**, 600

Bank of Credit and Commerce International (Overseas) Ltd (In Liquidation) *v.* Price Waterhouse (A Firm) and Others **111**, 604

Barrandon *v.* United States of America **113**, 464

Beahan *v.* State **103**, 203

Beaumartin *v.* France **107**, 50

Beldjoudi *v.* France **111**, 159

Bereciartua-Echarri **111**, 509

Biljabu and Others *v.* State of Western Australia **112**, 662

Billaud and Bessoles *v.* Secretary-General (Joined Cases Nos 24/25) **110**, 602

Biocare (SA) *v.* Gécamines (Zaire) and Republic of Zaire **115**, 415

Blaškić. *See* Prosecutor *v.* Blaškić (Application to Vary Conditions of Detention) (Case IT-95-14-T) *and* Prosecutor *v.* Blaškić (Objection to the Issue of *Subpoenae Duces Tecum*) (Cases IT-95-14-PT and IT-95-14-AR 108 *bis*)

Boimah *v.* United Nations General Assembly **113**, 499

Bordes and Temeharo *v.* France (Communication No 645/1995) **115**, 254

Bosnia and Herzegovina *v.* Yugoslavia. *See* Case Concerning Application of the Convention on the Prevention and Punishment of the Crime of Genocide (Bosnia and Herzegovina *v.* Yugoslavia) (Preliminary Objections) (Order on Counter-claims)

Brannigan *v.* Davison ("Winebox Case") **108**, 622. *See also* KPMG Peat Marwick and Others *v.* Davison; Controller and Auditor-General *v.* Davison; Brannigan and Others *v.* Davison ("Winebox Case") *and* European Pacific Group Ltd and Others *v.* KPMG Peat Marwick and Others ("Winebox Case")

Brasserie du Pêcheur SA *v.* Federal Republic of Germany (Case C-46/93) **111**, 1

British Consulate-General in Naples *v.* Toglia (Case No 2329) **101**, 379

British Council of Turkish Cypriot Associations and Another, *ex parte. See* R *v.* Secretary of State for Foreign and Commonwealth Affairs, *ex parte* British Council of Turkish Cypriot Associations and Another

British Telecommunications plc, *ex parte. See* R *v.* HM Treasury, *ex parte* British Telecommunications plc (Case 392/93)

Butler *v.* Attorney-General and Refugees Status Appeals Authority **114**, 568

Bwalya *v.* Zambia (Communication No 314/1988) **114**, 320

Caglar *v.* Billingham (Inspector of Taxes) and Related Appeals **108**, 510

Camacq Corporation, *ex parte. See* R *v.* Inland Revenue Commissioners, *ex parte* Camacq Corporation and Another

Cameroon *v.* Nigeria. *See* Case Concerning the Land and Maritime Boundary Between Cameroon and Nigeria (Cameroon *v.* Nigeria) (Request for the Indication of Provisional Measures)

Can and Others *v.* United States of America **107**, 255

Canada *v.* Cargnello (Decision No 4017/1998) **114**, 559

Canadian Overseas Ores Ltd *v.* Compania de Acero del Pacifico **101**, 470

Carbonar *v.* Magurno (Decision No 9675/1993) **114**, 534

Cargill International SA *v.* M/T Pavel Dybenko **103**, 572

Case Concerning Application of the Convention on the Prevention and Punishment of the Crime of Genocide (Bosnia and Herzegovina *v.* Yugoslavia) (Order on Counter-claims) **115**, 1, 206

Case Concerning Application of the Convention on the Prevention and Punishment of the Crime of Genocide (Bosnia and Herzegovina *v.* Yugoslavia) (Preliminary Objections) **115**, 1, 10

Case Concerning East Timor (Portugal *v.* Australia) **105**, 226

Case Concerning the Land and Maritime Boundary Between Cameroon and Nigeria (Cameroon *v.* Nigeria) (Request for the Indication of Provisional Measures) **106**, 144

Case Concerning Maritime Delimitation and Territorial Questions between Qatar and Bahrain (Qatar *v.* Bahrain) (Jurisdiction and Admissibility—First and Second Decisions) (Order) **102**, 1

Category "A" Claims against Iraq (Reports and Recommendations made by the Panel of Commissioners Concerning Claims for Departure from Iraq or Kuwait) (First, Second, Third, Fourth, Fifth and Sixth Instalments) **109**, 1

Category "B" Claims against Iraq (Reports and Recommendations made by the Panel of Commissioners Concerning Claims for Serious

Personal Injury or Death) (First, Second (Parts One and Two) and Third Instalments) **109**, 118

Category "C" Claims against Iraq (Reports and Recommendations made by the Panel of Commissioners Concerning Individual Claims up to US $100, 000) (First, Second, Third and Fourth Instalments) **109**, 205

Centre for Industrial Development v. Naidu **115**, 424

CERN Official Taxation Case **102**, 174

Chahal v. United Kingdom **108**, 385. See also R v. Secretary of State for the Home Department, ex parte Chahal

Chahal, ex parte. See R v. Secretary of State for the Home Department, ex parte Chahal

Chambre Syndicale des Transports Aeriens **111**, 500

Champel Bellevue SA v. State of Geneva **102**, 180

Chemical Weapons Deployment (Danger to Life) Case (Case Nos 2 BvR 624, 1080, 2029/83) **106**, 389

Cheng **111**, 530

Chile/Argentina, Dispute Concerning the Course of the Frontier between BP 62 and Mount Fitzroy. See Dispute Concerning the Course of the Frontier between BP 62 and Mount Fitzroy (Argentina/Chile) ("Laguna del Desierto")

Chiou Yaou Fa v. Morris **101**, 164

Chorherr v. Austria **107**, 5

Church v. Ferraino and Others (Case No 283) **101**, 370

Cicippio and Others v. Islamic Republic of Iran **107**, 296

Ciric v. Canada; Minister of Employment and Immigration **104**, 267

Coco v. State of Argentina **113**, 491

Coin Security Group (Pty) Ltd v. Smit NO and Others **103**, 1

Collée v. Gécamines Commerciale **115**, 435 (note)

Collins and Others v. Weinberger and Others **101**, 580

Commercial Bank of Kuwait v. Rafidain Bank and Central Bank of Iraq **107**, 261

Commission of the European Communities v. Council of the European Union (Case C-25/94) **113**, 339

Commission of the European Communities v. Grand Duchy of Luxembourg (Case C-473/93) **113**, 279

Compania Naviera Panlieve SA v. Public Prosecutor **101**, 409

Competence of the European Community to Conclude International Agreements Concerning Services and the Protection of Intellectual Property (Opinion 1/94). See Re the Competence of the European Community to Conclude International Agreements Concerning Services and the Protection of Intellectual Property (Opinion 1/94)

Condor and Filvem v. Minister of Justice (Case No 329) **101**, 394

Consarc Corporation and Others v. Iraqi Ministry and Others **106**, 408

Consul-General of Belgium in Naples v. Esposito (Case No 666) **101**, 376

Controller and Auditor-General v. Davison. See KPMG Peat Marwick and Others v. Davison; Controller and Auditor-General v. Davison; Brannigan and Others v. Davison ("Winebox Case") and European Pacific Group Ltd and Others v. KPMG Peat Marwick and Others ("Winebox Case")

Coreck Maritime GmbH v. Sevrybokholodflot **107**, 658

Corporal Punishment by Organs of the State, ex parte Attorney-General of Namibia. See Ex parte Attorney-General of Namibia, In re Corporal Punishment by Organs of the State

Cox v. Canada (Communication No 539/1993) **114**, 347

Cruise Missiles (Danger to Life) Case (Case Nos 2 BvR 1160, 1565 and 1714/83) **106**, 353

Cruise Missiles Deployment (German Approval) Case (Case No 2 BvE 13/83) **106**, 364

Cruz Varas and Others v. Sweden **108**, 283

Dalfino v. Governing Council of European Schools and European School of Brussels I **108**, 638

Dame X v. Conseil d'Etat du Canton de Genève **102**, 195

Dankha **111**, 503

Davoudian **111**, 505 (note)

De Luca v. United Nations Organization and Others **113**, 503
De Queiroz v. State of Portugal **115**, 430
Delgamuukw and Others v. The Queen in Right of British Columbia and Others; First Nations Summit and Others, Interveners **115**, 446
DeMauro Construction Corporation v. United States **101**, 554
Dillenkofer and Others v. Federal Republic of Germany (Cases C-178/94 et al.) **111**, 130 (note)
Dioulo **113**, 489
Dispute Concerning the Course of the Frontier between BP 62 and Mount Fitzroy (Argentina/Chile) ("Laguna del Desierto") **113**, 1
Doe I and Doe II v. Karadžić. See Kadić v. Karadžić; Doe I and Doe II v. Karadžić
Dokmanović. See Prosecutor v. Mrkšić, Radić, Šljivančanin and Dokmanović (Decision on the Motion for Release by the Accused Slavko Dokmanović) (Case IT-95-13a-PT)
Dow v. Attorney-General **103**, 128
Drexel Burnham Lambert Group Inc. v. Committee of Receivers for Galadari et al.; Refco Inc. v. Galadari et al. **103**, 532
Du Pree and Others v. United States **101**, 465
Duvalier v. State of Haiti **113**, 448
Duvalier and Madame Duvalier **111**, 528

EAL (Delaware) Corporation, Electra Aviation Inc. et al. v. European Organization for the Safety of Air Navigation ("Eurocontrol") and English Civil Aviation Authority **107**, 318
East Timor (Portugal v. Australia). See Case Concerning East Timor (Portugal v. Australia)
Eckert International Inc. v. Government of the Sovereign Democratic Republic of Fiji **107**, 347
Economic Community of West African States and Another v. Bank of Credit and Commerce International **113**, 472
Egypt (Arab Republic of) v. Gamal-Eldin **104**, 673
Erdemović. See Prosecutor v. Erdemović

(Sentencing Appeal) (Case IT-96-22-A); Prosecutor v. Erdemović (Sentencing Judgment) (Case IT-96-22-T)
Eritrea/Yemen Arbitration. See Government of the State of Eritrea and Government of the Republic of Yemen (Phase One: Territorial Sovereignty and Scope of the Dispute)
Estonia (Republic of) **113**, 477
European Molecular Biology Laboratory Arbitration **105**, 1
European Pacific Group Ltd and Others v. KPMG Peat Marwick and Others ("Winebox Case") **104**, 501. See also KPMG Peat Marwick and Others v. Davison; Controller and Auditor-General v. Davison; Brannigan and Others v. Davison ("Winebox Case") and Brannigan v. Davison ("Winebox Case")
European School v. Hermans-Jacobs and Heuvelmans-Van Iersel (Case No 12/94) **108**, 642
European School Employee Bonus Case (Case No 2 C 2.90) **108**, 664
Ex parte Attorney-General of Namibia, In re Corporal Punishment by Organs of the State **103**, 81
Export Group and Others v. Reef Industries Inc. and Mexican Coffee Institute **107**, 393

Factortame Ltd, ex parte. See R v. Secretary of State for Transport, ex parte Factortame Ltd and Others (No 4) (Case C-48/93)
Faurisson v. France (Communication No 550/1993) **115**, 355
FdCS v. Minister for Foreign Affairs **101**, 438
Fickling v. Commonwealth of Australia **103**, 447
Food and Agriculture Organization v. Colagrossi (Case No 5942) **101**, 385
Food and Agriculture Organization v. INPDAI **101**, 361
Footwear Distributors and Retailers of America v. United States **107**, 269
Forafrique Burkinabe SA v. Commission of the European Communities (Case C-182/91) **113**, 382
Foremost-McKesson Inc. and Another v. Islamic Republic of Iran and Others **101**, 536

Former Syrian Ambassador to the German Democratic Republic (Case No 2 BvR 1516/96) **115**, 595

Forth Tugs Ltd v. Wilmington Trust Co. **106**, 641

France (Republic of) v. Heeralall and Attorney-General. *See* Heeralall v. Commissioner of Prisons; Republic of France v. Heeralall and Attorney-General

François v. State of Canada **115**, 418

Franklin Mint Corporation and Others v. Trans World Airlines, Inc. *See* Trans World Airlines, Inc. v. Franklin Mint Corporation and Others

French Consulate Disabled Employee Case (Case No AZ 1K 4/88) **114**, 507

French Republic v. Commission of the European Communities (Case C-327/91) **101**, 30

Fusco v. O'Dea **103**, 318

Gabay v. Mostazafan Foundation of Iran and Mostazafan Foundation of New York **107**, 242

Garcia-Ramirez **111**, 524 (note)

Gates and Others v. Victor Fine Foods and Others **107**, 371

General Comment No 24 on Issues relating to Reservations made upon Ratification or Accession to the Covenant or the Optional Protocols thereto, or in relation to Declarations under Article 41 of the Covenant **107**, 64

Genocide, Application of the Convention on the Prevention and Punishment of the Crime of. *See* Case Concerning Application of the Convention on the Prevention and Punishment of the Crime of Genocide (Bosnia and Herzegovina v. Yugoslavia) (Preliminary Objections) (Order on Counterclaims)

Germany–Poland Border Treaty Constitutionality Case (Case No 2 BvR 1613/91) **108**, 656

Gerritsen v. de la Madrid Hurtado and Others **101**, 476

Gestra v. Italy (Application No 21072/92) **111**, 147

Giaffreda v. French Republic (Case No 12315/1992) **114**, 558 (note)

Gil v. Canada (*Re* Gil and Minister of Employment and Immigration) **107**, 146

GISTI **111**, 499

GISTI and MRAP **106**, 198

Goldman v. Thai Airways International Ltd **101**, 316

Government of the Kingdom of Saudi Arabia v. Ahmed **104**, 629

Government of Kuwait and Others v. Al-Adsani. *See* Al-Adsani v. Government of Kuwait and Others

Government of the Republic of Namibia and Another v. Cultura 2000 and Another **103**, 104

Government of the State of Eritrea and Government of the Republic of Yemen (Phase One: Territorial Sovereignty and Scope of the Dispute) **114**, 1

Governor of Pitcairn and Associated Islands v. Sutton **104**, 508

Grant v. South-West Trains Ltd (Case C-249/96) **112**, 344

Groppera Radio AG and Others Case **101**, 96

Groupement d'Entreprises Fougerolle v. CERN **102**, 209

Guatemala (Republic of) v. SINCAFC **113**, 450 (note)

Gueye et al. v. France (Communication No 196/1985) **114**, 312

Gül v. Switzerland **111**, 271

Haiti (Republic of) and Others v. Duvalier and Others **107**, 490

Haji v. Nungu and Another **103**, 243

Heathrow Airport User Charges. *See* United States of America–United Kingdom Arbitration Concerning Heathrow Airport User Charges

Hedley Lomas (Ireland) Ltd, *ex parte*. *See* R v. Ministry of Agriculture, Fisheries and Food, *ex parte* Hedley Lomas (Ireland) Ltd (Case C-5/94)

Heeralall v. Commissioner of Prisons; Republic of France v. Heeralall and Attorney-General **107**, 168

Heinz v. Contracting Parties to the European Patent Convention (Application No 21090/92) **111**, 142

Hilao and Others v. Estate of Marcos. *See Re* Estate of Ferdinand Marcos Human Rights Litigation; Hilao and Others v. Estate of Marcos

Hintermann v. Western European Union **113**, 487

Hipperson and Others v. Director of Public Prosecutions **111**, 584

Hirsch v. State of Israel and State of Germany **113**, 543

Holland v. Ireland (Communication No 593/1994) **115**, 277

Holy See v. Starbright Sales Enterprises Inc. **102**, 163

Horta and Others v. Commonwealth of Australia **104**, 450

Hudson v. Socialist People's Libyan Arab Jamahiriya and Others. *See* Smith v. Socialist People's Libyan Arab Jamahiriya and Others; Hudson v. Socialist People's Libyan Arab Jamahiriya *and* Smith v. Socialist People's Libyan Arab Jamahiriya Human Rights Convention Case (Case No 22/94) **115**, 637

Iberia Lineas Aereas de España, *ex parte*. *See* R v. Secretary of State for Transport, *ex parte* Iberia Lineas Aereas de España

In the Matter of the Extradition of Atta; Ahmad v. Wigen and Others **104**, 52

In the Matter of the Extradition of Suarez-Mason **104**, 12

In the Matter of Tadić (Application for a Formal Request for Deferral) (Case IT-94-1-I) **101**, 1

In the Matter of: Tariffs Applied by Canada to Certain US-Origin Agricultural Products (CDA-95-2008-01) **110**, 542

Ingram v. Commonwealth of Australia and Peacock (Minister for Foreign Affairs) **107**, 76

International Catholic Migration Commission v. Calleja (Director of Bureau of Labor Relations) and Trade Unions of the Philippines and Allied Services (Case No 85750) **102**, 149

International Institute of Refrigeration v. Elkaim **113**, 438

International Military Operations (German Participation) Case (Case Nos 2 BvE 3/92, 5/93, 7/93 and 8/93) **106**, 319

Iraq v. Dumez **106**, 284

Iraqi Airways Company and the Republic of Iraq v. Kuwait Airways

Corporation. *See* Kuwait Airways Corporation v. Iraqi Airways Company and the Republic of Iraq

Islamic Republic of Iran Shipping Lines and Another v. Public Prosecutor and Another **101**, 453

Janini v. Kuwait University **107**, 367

Jayetilleke v. High Commission of the Bahamas **107**, 622

Jersild v. Denmark **107**, 23

JK v. Public Prosecutor **101**, 447

Joseph v. Office of the Consulate-General of Nigeria and Others **101**, 485

Jungquist v. Sheikh Sultan Bin Khalifa al Nahyan **113**, 522

Kaba-Camara v. Fonds National de Solidarité **106**, 316

Kadić v. Karadžić; Doe I and Doe II v. Karadžić **104**, 135

Kaiser Bauxite Company v. Government of Jamaica **114**, 142

Kalenga v. Zambia (Communication No 326/1988) **114**, 326

Kamrudin Pirbhai, Chimanbhai Shivabhai Amin and Vrajlal Jamnadas Vasant, *ex parte*. *See* R v. Secretary of State for Foreign and Commonwealth Affairs, *ex parte* Kamrudin Pirbhai, Chimanbhai Shivabhai Amin and Vrajlal Jamnadas Vasant

Kanthal Australia Pty Ltd v. Minister for Industry, Technology and Commerce **107**, 90

Kapisanan (Organized Labor Association in Line Industries and Agriculture) v. Secretary for Labor and Employment and International Rice Research Institute (Case No 89331) **102**, 149

Karadžić. *See* Prosecutor v. Karadžić and Mladić (Rule 61) (Cases IT-95-5-R61 and IT-95-18-R61) *and* Prosecutor v. Karadžić, Mladić and Stanišić (Request for Deferral) (Case IT-95-5-D)

Khan v. Canada (Communication No 15/1994) **108**, 268

Kiraly v. Richards **107**, 101

Kline and Others v. Kaneko and Others **101**, 497

Klöckner Industrie-Anlagen GmbH and Others v. Republic of Cameroon **114**, 152

Kolompar v. Belgium **111**, 195

Koné **111**, 543

Koskotas v. Roche and Others **104**, 110
KPMG Peat Marwick and Others v. Davison; Controller and Auditor-General v. Davison; Brannigan and Others v. Davison ("Winebox Case") **104**, 526. See also Brannigan v. Davison ("Winebox Case") and European Pacific Group Ltd and Others v. KPMG Peat Marwick and Others ("Winebox Case")
Kramer Italo Ltd v. Government of the Kingdom of Belgium; Embassy of Belgium, Nigeria **103**, 299
Kremzow v. Republic of Austria (Case C-299/95) **113**, 263
Kryla v. Kappy **106**, 226
Kuwait Airways Corporation v. Iraqi Airways Company and the Republic of Iraq **103**, 340
Kuwait News Agency v. Parrott **113**, 457

Labyad v. Ilari **101**, 361 (note)
Lafontant v. Aristide **103**, 581
Laguna del Desierto. See Dispute Concerning the Course of the Frontier between BP 62 and Mount Fitzroy (Argentina/Chile) ("Laguna del Desierto")
Länsman (J.) et al. v. Finland (Communication No 671/1995) **115**, 300
Largueche v. Tancredi Fenu (Case No 9321) **101**, 377
Larkins v. National Labor Relations Commission and Others (Case No 92432) **102**, 148 (note)
Lasidi SA and Others v. Financiera Avenida SA and Others **101**, 505
Launder, ex parte. See R v. Secretary of State for the Home Department, ex parte Launder
Legality of the Threat or Use of Nuclear Weapons (Request by the United Nations General Assembly for an Advisory Opinion) **110**, 163
Legality of the Use by a State of Nuclear Weapons in Armed Conflict (Request by the World Health Organization for an Advisory Opinion) **110**, 1
Libyan Arab Jamahiriya v. Trobbiani (Decision No 145/1990) **114**, 520
Liu v. Republic of China **101**, 519
Loizidou v. Turkey (Merits) **108**, 443
Loizidou v. Turkey (Preliminary Objections) **103**, 622

London Branch of the Nigerian Universities Commission v. Bastians **107**, 613
Lonrho Exports Ltd v. Export Credits Guarantee Department **108**, 596
López Ostra v. Spain **111**, 210
Lujambio Galdeano **111**, 505

Mabo and Another v. State of Queensland and Another (No 1) **112**, 412
Mabo and Others v. State of Queensland (No 2) **112**, 457
MacArthur Area Citizens Association v. Republic of Peru **107**, 196
McElhinney v. Williams and Her Majesty's Secretary of State for Northern Ireland **103**, 311, **104**, 691
Makenete v. Lekhanya and Others **103**, 27
Manauta v. Embassy of Russian Federation **113**, 429
Mangope v. Van der Walt and Another NNO **103**, 6
Marcos and Marcos v. Federal Department of Police **102**, 198
Maritime Delimitation and Territorial Questions between Qatar and Bahrain (Qatar v. Bahrain). See Case Concerning Maritime Delimitation and Territorial Questions between Qatar and Bahrain (Qatar v. Bahrain) (Jurisdiction and Admissibility—First and Second Decisions) (Order)
Markt Intern Verlag GmbH and Klaus Beermann Case **101**, 69
Martić. See Prosecutor v. Martić (Rule 61) (Case IT-95-11-R61)
Melchers and Co. v. Federal Republic of Germany (Application No 13258/87) **111**, 131
Melia v. United States **104**, 1
Menten v. Federal Republic of Germany **101**, 443
Minister for Foreign Affairs and Trade and Others v. Magno and Another **101**, 202
Minister for Immigration and Ethnic Affairs v. Teoh **104**, 460
Ministre du Budget v. N'guyen Van Gio **106**, 225 (note)
Ministry of Defence of the Government of the United Kingdom v. Joel Ndegwa **103**, 235
Ministry for Economic and Financial Affairs of the Islamic Republic of Iran

v. Société Framatome and Others **113**, 452

Mladić. *See* Prosecutor *v.* Karadžić, Mladić and Stanišić (Request for Deferral) (Case IT-95-5-D) *and* Prosecutor *v.* Karadžić and Mladić (Rule 61) (Cases IT-95-5-R61 and IT-95-18-R61)

Mobutu and Republic of Zaire *v* Société Logrine **113**, 481

Moran *v.* Kingdom of Saudi Arabia **107**, 303

Morocco (Kingdom of) *v.* DR **115**, 421

Mouracade *v.* Arab Republic of Yemen **113**, 462

Mrkšić. *See* Prosecutor *v.* Mrkšić, Radić, Šljivančanin and Dokmanović (Decision on the Motion for Release by the Accused Slavko Dokmanović) (Case IT-95-13a-PT); Prosecutor *v.* Mrkšić, Radić and Šljivančanin (Rule 61) (Case IT-95-13-R61)

Muiden Chemie BV *v.* State Secretary for Economic Affairs **101**, 449

Mukoro *v.* European Bank for Reconstruction and Development and Another **107**, 604

Muller *v.* United States of America (Case No 10 Sa 1506/97) **114**, 512

Mushikiwabo and Others *v.* Barayagwiza **107**, 457

Mutombo *v.* Switzerland (Communication No 13/1993) **108**, 256

MvdV *v.* Minister for Foreign Affairs **101**, 406

N, C, F and AG *v.* Italy (Application No 24236/94) **111**, 153

N and Others *v.* European School, Munich (Case No 7 CS 89.90) **108**, 649

Nacci *v.* Bari Institute of the International Centre for Advanced Mediterranean Agronomic Studies (Decision No 5565/1994) **114**, 539

Najohn *v.* United States **104**, 7

Narrainen *v.* Norway (Communication No 3/1991) **112**, 317

Nasri *v.* France **111**, 252

National Iranian Gas Corporation *v.* Pipeline Services and Another **113**, 446

National Oil Co. of Zimbabwe (Private) Ltd and Others *v.* Sturge **107**, 505

National Sanitation Services *v.* Embassy of Cuba **113**, 434

NATO AWACS Bosnia Case (Interim Measures) (Case No 2 BvQ 11/93) **106**, 352 (note)

Netherlands *v.* Bergings en transport-beddrijf Van den Akker and Another **101**, 436

Netherlands *v.* Dissotis Shipping Corporation **101**, 436

New Zealand *v.* France. *See* Request for an Examination of the Situation in Accordance with Paragraph 63 of the Court's Judgment of 20 December 1974 in the *Nuclear Tests (New Zealand* v. *France) Case* (Order)

N'guyen Duy Thong **106**, 229

Nikolić. *See* Prosecutor *v.* Nikolić (Rule 61) (Case IT-94-2-R61)

Norwegian Embassy *v.* Quattri (Decision No 12771/1991) **114**, 525

Oen Yin Choy *v.* Robinson **104**, 43

Office for Cereals of Tunisia *v.* Société Bec Frères **113**, 485

Opel Austria GmbH *v.* Council of the European Union (Case T-115/94) **113**, 295

Opinion 1/94. *See Re* the Competence of the European Community to Conclude International Agreements Concerning Services and the Protection of Intellectual Property (Opinion 1/94)

Opinion 2/94. *See Re* Accession of the European Community to the Convention for the Protection of Human Rights and Fundamental Freedoms (Opinion 2/94)

Ortiz *v.* Gramajo. *See* Xuncax and Others *v.* Gramajo; Ortiz *v.* Gramajo

Panattoni *v.* Federal Republic of Germany (Case No 6172) **101**, 385 (note)

Paprocki *v.* German State (Bonn) and Another **104**, 684

Pareroultja and Others *v.* Tickner and Others **112**, 638

Paul and Others *v.* Avril **103**, 553

Perrini *v.* Académie de France (Decision No 5126/1994) **114**, 536

Philipp Brothers *v.* Sierra Leone and Commission of the European Communities **107**, 517

PMJ *v.* Public Prosecutor **101**, 430

Portugal *v.* Australia (Case Concerning East Timor). *See* Case Concerning East Timor (Portugal *v.* Australia)

Prefect of Essonne *v.* Ariste **111**, 546

Prefect of Hérault *v.* Dakoury **111**, 525

Prefect of La Gironde *v.* Mahmedi **106**, 204

Price *v.* Jamaica (Communication No 572/1994) **115**, 350

Princz *v.* Federal Republic of Germany **103**, 594

Project Blue Sky Inc. and Others *v.* Australian Broadcasting Authority **115**, 384

Propend Finance Pty Limited and Others *v.* Sing and Others **111**, 611

Property Restitution Case (Case No 12/93) **115**, 619

Prosecutor *v.* Blaškić (Application ˙to Vary Conditions of Detention) (Case IT-95-14-T) **108**, 68

Prosecutor *v.* Blaškić (Objection to the Issue of *Subpoenae Duces Tecum*) (Cases IT-95-14-PT and IT-95-14-AR 108 *bis*) **110**, 607

Prosecutor *v.* Erdemović (Sentencing Appeal) (Case IT-96-22-A) **111**, 298

Prosecutor *v.* Erdemović (Sentencing Judgment) (Case IT-96-22-T) **108**, 180

Prosecutor *v.* Karadžić and Mladić (Rule 61) (Cases IT-95-5-R61 and IT-95-18-R61) **108**, 85

Prosecutor *v.* Karadžić, Mladić and Stanišić (Request for Deferral) (Case IT-95-5-D) **108**, 1

Prosecutor *v.* Martić (Rule 61) (Case IT-95-11-R61) **108**, 39

Prosecutor *v.* Mrkšić, Radić and Šljivančanin (Rule 61) (Case IT-95-13-R61) **108**, 53

Prosecutor *v.* Mrkšić, Radić, Šljivančanin and Dokmanović (Decision on the Motion for Release by the Accused Slavko Dokmanović) (Case IT-95-13a-PT) **111**, 458

Prosecutor *v.* Nikolić (Rule 61) (Case IT-94-2-R61) **108**, 21

Prosecutor *v.* Rajić (Review of Indictment) (Case IT-95-12-I) **108**, 10

Prosecutor *v.* Rajić (Rule 61) (Case IT-95-12-R61) **108**, 141

Prosecutor *v.* Tadić (Judgment) (Case IT-94-1-T) **112**, 1

Prosecutor *v.* Tadić (Jurisdiction) (Cases IT-94-1-T and IT-94-1-AR72) **105**, 419

Prosecutor *v.* Tadić (Protective Measures for Victims and Witnesses) (Case IT-94-1-T) **105**, 599

Prosecutor *v.* Tadić (Sentencing Judgment) (Case IT-94-1-T) **112**, 286

Qatar *v.* Bahrain. *See* Case Concerning Maritime Delimitation and Territorial Questions between Qatar and Bahrain (Qatar *v.* Bahrain) (Jurisdiction and Admissibility—First and Second Decisions) (Order)

Quebec, Certain Questions relating to the Secession from Canada. *See* Re Reference by the Governor in Council Concerning Certain Questions relating to the Secession of Quebec from Canada

Quinn *v.* France **111**, 232

R *v.* Abbrederis **107**, 80

R *v.* Donyadideh and Others **101**, 259

R *v.* Finta (No 3) **104**, 284

R *v.* HM Treasury, *ex parte* British Telecommunications plc (Case C-392/93) **111**, 130 (note)

R *v.* Inland Revenue Commissioners, *ex parte* Camacq Corporation and Another **103**, 327

R *v.* MacDonald **101**, 281

R *v.* Ministry of Agriculture, Fisheries and Food, *ex parte* Hedley Lomas (Ireland) Ltd (Case C-5/94) **111**, 130 (note)

R *v.* Ministry of Defence, *ex parte* Smith and Others **112**, 367

R *v.* Pesquera Concar SA (Owners of the *Antonio Lorenzo*) **108**, 632

R *v.* Salvador, Wannamaker, Campbell and Nunes **101**, 269

R *v.* Secretary of State for Foreign and Commonwealth Affairs, *ex parte* British Council of Turkish Cypriot Associations and Another **112**, 735

R *v.* Secretary of State for Foreign and Commonwealth Affairs, *ex parte* Kamrudin Pirbhai, Chimanbhai Shivabhai Amin and Vrajlal Jamnadas Vasant **107**, 461

R *v.* Secretary of State for the Home Department, *ex parte* Chahal **108**, 363. *See also* Chahal *v.* United Kingdom

R *v.* Secretary of State for the Home Department, *ex parte* Launder **114**, 402

R *v.* Secretary of State for Transport, *ex parte* Factortame Ltd and Others (No 4) (Case C-48/93) **111**, 1

R *v.* Secretary of State for Transport, *ex parte* Iberia Lineas Aereas de España **107**, 481

R *v.* Vincent **104**, 204

Radić. *See* Prosecutor *v.* Mrkšić, Radić and Šljivančanin (Rule 61) (Case IT-95-13-R61) *and* Prosecutor *v.* Mrkšić, Radić, Šljivančanin and Dokmanović (Decision on the Motion for Release by the Accused Slavko Dokmanović) (Case IT-95-13a-PT)

Rafidain Bank and Iraqi Ministry for Industry *v.* Consarc Corporation **106**, 274

Rajić. *See* Prosecutor *v.* Rajić (Review of Indictment) (Case IT-95-12-I) *and* Prosecutor *v.* Rajić (Rule 61) (Case IT-95-12-R61)

Rastello and Permanent Delegation of Commission of European Community to International Organizations in Geneva *v.* Caisse Cantonale Genevoise de Compensation and Another **102**, 183

Rattigan and Others *v.* Chief Immigration Officer, Zimbabwe and Others **103**, 224

Re Accession of the European Community to the Convention for the Protection of Human Rights and Fundamental Freedoms (Opinion 2/94) **108**, 225

Re Almirante and Cecovini (Case No 300/84) **101**, 362

Re Attorney-General of Canada and Ward; United Nations High Commissioner for Refugees *et al.* **104**, 222

Re the Competence of the European Community to Conclude International Agreements Concerning Services and the Protection of Intellectual Property (Opinion 1/94) **105**, 75

Re Election for the Fifth Constituency of Val d'Oise **111**, 496

Re Estate of Ferdinand E. Marcos Human Rights Litigation; Trajano *v.* Marcos and Another **103**, 521

Re Estate of Ferdinand Marcos Human Rights Litigation; Hilao and Others *v.* Estate of Marcos **104**, 119

Re Gil and Minister of Employment and Immigration. *See* Gil *v.* Canada (*Re* Gil and Minister of Employment and Immigration)

Re Hashim and Others **107**, 405

Re Hawkins **106**, 310

Re Lane (Case No 2266) **106**, 305

Re Mitchell and The Queen **101**, 293

Re P (No 1) **114**, 478

Re P (No 2) **114**, 485

Re Pan American World Airways Inc. and Others' Application **101**, 352

Re Paramount Airways Ltd (In Administration) **101**, 337

Re Protocol No 6 to the European Convention on Human Rights **111**, 495

Re Rafidain Bank **101**, 332

Re Reference by the Governor in Council Concerning Certain Questions relating to the Secession of Quebec from Canada **115**, 536

Re Regina and Palacios **101**, 306

Re Rudolph and Minister of Employment and Immigration **104**, 195

Re Schmidt **111**, 548

Re Wood and Hansard **103**, 234 (note)

Refco Inc. *v.* Galadari *et al. See* Drexel Burnham Lambert Group Inc. *v.* Committee of Receivers for Galadari *et al.*; Refco Inc. *v.* Galadari *et al.*

Reid *v.* Republic of Nauru **101**, 193

Rekhou **106**, 222

Request for an Examination of the Situation in Accordance with Paragraph 63 of the Court's Judgment of 20 December 1974 in the *Nuclear Tests (New Zealand* v. *France) Case* (Order) **106**, 1

Reservations, General Comment No 24 on Issues relating to. *See* General Comment No 24 on Issues relating to Reservations made upon Ratification or Accession to the Covenant or the Optional Protocols thereto, or in relation to Declarations under Article 41 of the Covenant

Residence Miremont SA and Another *v.* Administrative Tribunal of Geneva and Another **102**, 189

Robert *v.* Procureur de la République **113**, 450

Rocklea Spinning Mills Pty Ltd *v.* Anti-Dumping Authority and Another **107**, 104

Romero v. Ministry of Defence and United Nations **113**, 436

Roumeliotis v. European School **108**, 642 (note)

Rush-Presbyterian-St Luke's Medical Center and Others v. Hellenic Republic and Others **101**, 509

S v. December **107**, 186

S and S Machinery Co. v. Masinexport-import **107**, 239

Saiga, M/V (No 1) (Saint Vincent and the Grenadines v. Guinea) **110**, 736

Saignie v. Embassy of Japan **113**, 492

Sanders and Moreau v. Veridiano, Rossi and Wyers (Case No L-46930) **102**, 148 (note)

Sara et al. v. Finland (Communication No 431/1990) **114**, 331

SAT Fluggesellschaft mbH v. European Organization for the Safety of Air Navigation ("Eurocontrol") (Case C-364/92) **101**, 9

Scaniainventor v. Commissioner of Patents **107**, 82

Schmidt v. Home Secretary of the Government of the United Kingdom, the Commissioner of the Metropolitan Police and Jones **103**, 322

Schoenmakers v. Director of Public Prosecutions **101**, 174

SCK and FNK v. Commission of the European Communities **113**, 277 (note)

Seetransport Wiking Trader Schiffarhts-gesellschaft MBH and Co., Kommanditgesellschaft v. Navimpex Centrala Navala **103**, 559

Senghor v. International Bank for West Africa and Republic of Senegal **113**, 460

Shugaba Abdulrahaman Darman v. Federal Minister of Internal Affairs and Others **103**, 268

Siderman de Blake and Others v. Republic of Argentina and Others **103**, 454

Sierra Leone and Commission of the European Communities v. Philipp Brothers. See Philipp Brothers v. Sierra Leone and Commission of the European Communities

Sierra Leone Telecommunications Co. Ltd v. Barclays Bank plc **114**, 466

Sing and Others v. Propend Finance Pty Limited and Others. See Propend Finance Pty Limited and Others v. Sing and Others

SL and Others v. Federal Republic of Germany (Case No III ZR 59/92) **108**, 668

Slebos Research BV v. Minister for Economic Affairs **101**, 427

Šljivančanin. See Prosecutor v. Mrkšić, Radić and Šljivančanin (Rule 61) (Case IT-95-13-R61) and Prosecutor v. Mrkšić, Radić, Šljivančanin and Dokmanović (Decision on the Motion for Release by the Accused Slavko Dokmanović) (Case IT-95-13a-PT)

Smith v. Socialist People's Libyan Arab Jamahiriya **113**, 534

Smith v. Socialist People's Libyan Arab Jamahiriya and Others; Hudson v. Socialist People's Libyan Arab Jamahiriya **107**, 382. See also Smith v. Socialist People's Libyan Arab Jamahiriya

Smith, ex parte. See R v. Ministry of Defence, ex parte Smith and Others

Société Ouest Africaine des Bétons Industriels (SOABI) and Others v. State of Senegal **113**, 440

Société Robatel SLPI **106**, 192

Somers v. Hungary (Communication No 566/1993) **115**, 263

Southern Pacific Properties (Middle East) Ltd v. Arab Republic of Egypt (Award) **106**, 501

Southern Pacific Properties (Middle East) Ltd v. Arab Republic of Egypt (Jurisdiction) **106**, 501

Spaans v. Netherlands (Application No 12516/86) **107**, 1

SPP (Middle East) Ltd v. Arab Republic of Egypt. See Southern Pacific Properties (Middle East) Ltd v. Arab Republic of Egypt

Stanišić. See Prosecutor v. Karadžić, Mladić and Stanišić (Request for Deferral) (Case IT-95-5-D)

Stena Rederi AB v. Comision de Contratos del Comite Ejecutivo General del Sindicato Revolucionario de Trabajadores Petroleros de la Republica Mexicana SC **103**, 433

Stewart v. Canada (Communication No 538/1993) **115**, 318

Stichting Greenpeace Nederland and Another *v.* Vulcanus II Shipping Company and Another **101**, 432

Stichting Verbiedt de Kruisraketten (SVK) and Others **106**, 400

Straub *v.* A. P. Green Inc. and Atlas Turner Inc. **107**, 359

Stupni Do Case. *See* Prosecutor *v.* Rajić (Review of Indictment) (Case IT-95-12-I) *and* Prosecutor *v.* Rajić (Rule 61) (Case IT-95-12-R61)

Suarez-Mason, the Extradition of. *See* In the Matter of the Extradition of Suarez-Mason

Sumitomo Shoji America, Inc. *v.* Avagliano; Avagliano *v.* Sumitomo Shoji America, Inc. **101**, 570

Swiss Confederation **106**, 256

Swiss Federal Prosecutor *v.* Kruszyk and Others **102**, 176

Syndicat des Copropriétaires du 14/16 Boulevard Flandrin **113**, 470

T *v.* Belgium **115**, 442

T *v.* Immigration Officer; T *v.* Secretary of State for the Home Department **107**, 552

T *v.* Secretary of State for the Home Department **104**, 656. *See also* T *v.* Immigration Officer; T *v.* Secretary of State for the Home Department

Tabion *v.* Mufti **107**, 452

Tadić. *See* In the Matter of Tadić (Application for a Formal Request for Deferral) (Case IT-94-1-I) *and* Prosecutor *v.* Tadić (Jurisdiction) (Cases IT-94-1-T and IT-94-1-AR72) *and* Prosecutor *v.* Tadić (Protective Measures for Victims and Witnesses) (Case IT-94-1-T) *and* Prosecutor *v.* Tadić (Judgment) (Case IT-94-1-T) *and* Prosecutor *v.* Tadić (Sentencing Judgment) (Case IT-94-1-T)

Tariffs Applied by Canada to Certain US-Origin Agricultural Products (CDA-95-2008-01). *See* In the Matter of: Tariffs Applied by Canada to Certain US-Origin Agricultural Products (CDA-95-2008-01)

Tavita *v.* Minister of Immigration **101**, 455

Toonen *v.* Australia (Communication No 488/1992) **112**, 328

Trajano *v.* Marcos and Another. *See Re*

Estate of Ferdinand E. Marcos Human Rights Litigation; Trajano *v.* Marcos and Another

Trans World Airlines, Inc. *v.* Franklin Mint Corporation and Others; Franklin Mint Corporation and Others *v.* Trans World Airlines, Inc. **101**, 587

Transaero Inc. *v.* La Fuerza Aerea Boliviana **107**, 308

Travel Associates Inc. *v.* Kingdom of Swaziland **107**, 219

Trinh *v.* Citibank NA **107**, 203

Turkish National Extradition Case (Case No 4 ARs 22/86) **106**, 298

United Arab Emirates *v.* Abdelghafar and Another **104**, 646, **107**, 626

United Kingdom and Governor of Hong Kong **106**, 233

United Nations General Assembly, Request for an Advisory Opinion. *See* Legality of the Threat or Use of Nuclear Weapons (Request by the United Nations General Assembly for an Advisory Opinion)

United Nations Somalia Peace-Keeping Force (Interim Measures) (Case No 2 BvQ 17/93) **106**, 352 (note)

United States of America *v.* Lo Gatto (Decision No 4483/1995) **114**, 555

United States of America *v.* Lui Kin-Hong, a.k.a. Jerry Lui **114**, 606

United States of America *v.* Matta-Ballesteros **107**, 429

United States of America *v.* Moats **103**, 480

United States of America *v.* Perières **113**, 494

United States of America, Lamachia and Others *v.* Rodrigo and Genove (Case No 79470) **102**, 132

United States of America and Others *v.* Ceballos and Bautista (Case No 80018) **102**, 132

United States of America and Others *v.* Guinto, Valencia and Others (Case No 76607) **102**, 132

United States of America and Others *v.* Ruiz de Guzman and Co. (Case No L-35645) **102**, 122

United States of America–United Kingdom Arbitration Concerning Heathrow Airport User Charges **102**, 215

United States Lines Inc. *v.* World Health Organization **107**, 182
Universal Consolidated Companies Inc. *v.* Bank of China **107**, 353

Vaessen *v.* American Battle Monuments Commission **115**, 435
Victrawl Pty Ltd *v.* Telstra Corporation Ltd and Others **107**, 122
Vilvarajah and Others *v.* United Kingdom **108**, 321
Vukovar Hospital Case. *See* Prosecutor *v.* Mrkšić, Radić and Šljivančanin (Rule 61) (Case IT-95-13-R61)

Walker *v.* State of New South Wales **112**, 658
Walker *et al. v.* Bank of New York Inc. **104**, 277
Walter Fuller Aircraft Sales Inc. *v.* Republic of the Philippines **103**, 503
Watershed Nigeria Ltd *v.* Brew-Graves **107**, 178
Weinberger, Secretary of Defense and Others *v.* Rossi and Others **101**, 562
Well Blowout Control Claim (the "WBC Claim") (Report and Recommendations made by the Panel of Commissioners Appointed to Review the Well Blowout Control Claim) **109**, 479
Wellington District Legal Services Committee *v.* Tangiora **115**, 655
Western Australia (State of) *v.* Commonwealth of Australia **112**, 662
Westland Helicopters Ltd *v.* Arab Organization for Industrialization **108**, 564
Westminster City Council *v.* Government of the Islamic Republic of Iran **108**, 557
Wickes *v.* Olympic Airways **101**, 615
Wik Peoples (The) *v.* State of Queensland and Others **112**, 638 (note)
Williams and Her Majesty's Secretary of State for Northern Ireland *v.*

McElhinney. *See* McElhinney *v.* Williams and Her Majesty's Secretary of State for Northern Ireland
Wilton Feyenoord BV *v.* Minister for Economic Affairs **101**, 418
"Winebox Case". *See* KPMG Peat Marwick and Others *v.* Davison; Controller and Auditor-General *v.* Davison; Brannigan and Others *v.* Davison ("Winebox Case") *and* Brannigan *v.* Davison ("Winebox Case") *and* European Pacific Group Ltd and Others *v.* KPMG Peat Marwick and Others ("Winebox Case")
World Health Organization, Request for an Advisory Opinion. *See* Legality of the Use by a State of Nuclear Weapons in Armed Conflict (Request by the World Health Organization for an Advisory Opinion)
Wororra Peoples and Another *v.* State of Western Australia **112**, 662

X *v.* Argentina (Case No 2 AZR 513/95) **114**, 502
X *v.* Secretary-General (Case No 22) **110**, 599
Xuncax and Others *v.* Gramajo; Ortiz *v.* Gramajo **104**, 165

Yemen/Eritrea Arbitration. *See* Government of the State of Eritrea and Government of the Republic of Yemen (Phase One: Territorial Sovereignty and Scope of the Dispute)
Yendall *v.* Commonwealth of Australia **107**, 590
Young *v.* Registrar, Court of Appeal and Another (No 3) **104**, 418

Z *v.* Geneva Supervisory Authority for the Enforcement of Debts and Bankruptcy **102**, 205
Zaire *v.* D'Hoop and Another **106**, 294
Zambian Embassy *v.* Sendanayake (Decision No 5941/1992) **114**, 532

CONSOLIDATED TABLE OF CASES VOLUMES 101-115

ARRANGED ACCORDING TO COURTS
AND TRIBUNALS (INTERNATIONAL CASES)
AND COUNTRIES (MUNICIPAL CASES)

(Cases which are reported only in a note are distinguished from cases which are reported in full by the insertion of the word "note" in parentheses after the page number of the report.)

I. DECISIONS OF INTERNATIONAL TRIBUNALS

Arbitral Tribunals (Various)

1990
European Molecular Biology Laboratory (EMBL)–Federal Republic of Germany (European Molecular Biology Arbitration) **105**, 1

1992
United States–United Kingdom, Court of Arbitration established under the Air Services Agreement of 23 July 1977 (Arbitration Concerning Heathrow Airport User Charges) (Award on the First Question) **102**, 215, 224

1993
United States–United Kingdom, Court of Arbitration established under the Air Services Agreement of 23 July 1977 (Arbitration Concerning Heathrow Airport User Charges) (Supplementary Decision) **102**, 215, 564

1994
Argentina–Chile, Dispute Concerning the Course of the Frontier between BP 62 and Mount Fitzroy ("Laguna del Desierto") **113**, 1, 17

1995
Argentina–Chile, Dispute Concerning the Course of the Frontier between BP 62 and Mount Fitzroy ("Laguna del Desierto") **113**, 1, 194

1996
Canada–United States, Arbitral Panel Established Pursuant to Article 2008 of the North American Free Trade Agreement (In the Matter of: Tariffs Applied by Canada to Certain US-Origin Agricultural Products) (CDA-95-2008-01) **110**, 542

1998
Arbitration Tribunal established by Agreement of 3 October 1996 (Government of the State of Eritrea and Government of the Republic of Yemen (Phase One: Territorial Sovereignty and Scope of the Dispute)) **114**, 1

International Centre for the Settlement of Investment Disputes, Arbitration Tribunals. *See below*

Court of First Instance of the European Communities

1997
Opel Austria GmbH *v.* Council of the European Union (Case T-115/94) **113**, 295
SCK and FNK *v.* Commission of the European Communities **113**, 277 (note)

Court of Justice of the European Communities

1993
Forafrique Burkinabe SA *v.* Commission of the European Communities (Case C-182/91) **113**, 382

1994
French Republic *v.* Commission of the

European Communities (Case C-327/
91) **101**, 30
Opinion 1/94 (*Re* the Competence of the
European Community to Conclude
International Agreements Concerning
Services and the Protection of
Intellectual Property) **105**, 75
SAT Fluggesellschaft mbH *v.* European
Organization for the Safety of Air
Navigation ("Eurocontrol") (Case C-
364/92) **101**, 9

1996
Brasserie du Pêcheur SA *v.* Federal
Republic of Germany (Case C-46/93)
111, 1
Commission of the European Comm-
unities *v.* Council of the European
Union (Case C-25/94) **113**, 339
Commission of the European Comm-
unities *v.* Grand Duchy of Luxembourg
(Case C-473/93) **113**, 279
Dillenkofer and Others *v.* Federal
Republic of Germany (Cases C-178/
94 *et al.*) **111**, 130 (note)
Opinion 2/94 (*Re* Accession of the
European Community to the
Convention for the Protection of
Human Rights and Fundamental
Freedoms) **108**, 225
Regina *v.* HM Treasury, *ex parte* British
Telecommunications plc (Case C-
392/93) **111**, 130 (note)
Regina *v.* Ministry of Agriculture,
Fisheries and Food, *ex parte* Hedley
Lomas (Ireland) Ltd (Case C-5/94)
111, 130 (note)
Regina *v.* Secretary of State for
Transport, *ex parte* Factortame Ltd and
Others (No 4) (Case C-48/93) **111**, 1

1997
Kremzow *v.* Republic of Austria (Case
C-299/95) **113**, 263

1998
Grant *v.* South-West Trains Ltd (Case C-
249/96) **112**, 344

European Commission of Human Rights

1988
Spaans *v.* Netherlands (Application No
12516/86) **106**, 1

1990
Melchers and Co. *v.* Federal Republic of
Germany (Application No 13258/87)
111, 131

1994
Heinz *v.* Contracting Parties to the Euro-
pean Patent Convention (Application
No 21090/92) **111**, 142

1995
Gestra *v.* Italy (Application No 21072/
92) **111**, 147
N, C, F and AG *v.* Italy (Application No
24236/94) **111**, 153

European Court of Human Rights

1989
Markt Intern Verlag GmbH and Klaus
Beermann Case **101**, 69

1990
Autronic AG Case **101**, 134
Groppera Radio AG and Others Case
101, 96

1991
Cruz Varas and Others *v.* Sweden **108**,
283
Vilvarajah and Others *v.* United
Kingdom **108**, 321

1992
Beldjoudi *v.* France **111**, 159
Kolompar *v.* Belgium **111**, 195

1993
Chorherr *v.* Austria **107**, 5

1994
Beaumartin *v.* France **107**, 50
Jersild *v.* Denmark **107**, 23
López Ostra *v.* Spain **111**, 210

1995
Loizidou *v.* Turkey (Preliminary
Objections) **103**, 622
Nasri *v.* France **111**, 252
Quinn *v.* France **111**, 232

1996
Chahal *v.* United Kingdom **108**, 385
Gül *v.* Switzerland **111**, 271
Loizidou *v.* Turkey (Merits) **108**, 443

International Centre for the Settlement of Investment Disputes, Arbitration Tribunals

1975
Kaiser Bauxite Company *v.* Government of Jamaica **114**, 142

1983
Klöckner Industrie-Anlagen GmbH and Others *v.* Republic of Cameroon (Merits) **114**, 152, 157

1985
Klöckner Industrie-Anlagen GmbH and Others *v.* Republic of Cameroon (Annulment) **114**, 152, 243
Southern Pacific Properties (Middle East) Ltd *v.* Arab Republic of Egypt (Jurisdiction) **106**, 501, 512

1988
Southern Pacific Properties (Middle East) Ltd *v.* Arab Republic of Egypt (Jurisdiction) **106**, 501, 531

1990
Asian Agricultural Products Ltd *v.* Republic of Sri Lanka **106**, 416

1992
Southern Pacific Properties (Middle East) Ltd *v.* Arab Republic of Egypt (Award) **106**, 501, 589

International Court of Justice

1994
Case Concerning Maritime Delimitation and Territorial Questions between Qatar and Bahrain (Qatar *v.* Bahrain) (Jurisdiction and Admissibility) (First Decision) **102**, 1, 9

1995
Case Concerning East Timor (Portugal *v.* Australia) **105**, 226
Case Concerning Maritime Delimitation and Territorial Questions between Qatar and Bahrain (Qatar *v.* Bahrain) (Jurisdiction and Admissibility) (Second Decision) **102**, 1, 47
Case Concerning Maritime Delimitation and Territorial Questions between Qatar and Bahrain (Qatar *v.* Bahrain) (Order) **102**, 1, 119

Request for an Examination of the Situation in Accordance with Paragraph 63 of the Court's Judgment of 20 December 1974 in the *Nuclear Tests (New Zealand* v. *France) Case* (Order) **106**, 1

1996
Case Concerning Application of the Convention on the Prevention and Punishment of the Crime of Genocide (Bosnia and Herzegovina *v.* Yugoslavia) (Preliminary Objections) **115**, 1, 10
Case Concerning the Land and Maritime Boundary Between Cameroon and Nigeria (Cameroon *v.* Nigeria) (Request for the Indication of Provisional Measures) **106**, 144
Legality of the Threat or Use of Nuclear Weapons (Request by the United Nations General Assembly for an Advisory Opinion) **110**, 163
Legality of the Use by a State of Nuclear Weapons in Armed Conflict (Request by the World Health Organization for an Advisory Opinion) **110**, 1

1997
Case Concerning Application of the Convention on the Prevention and Punishment of the Crime of Genocide (Bosnia and Herzegovina *v.* Yugoslavia) (Order on Counter-claims) **115**, 1, 206

International Criminal Tribunal for the Former Yugoslavia

1994
In the Matter of Tadić (Application for a Formal Request for Deferral) (Case IT-94-1-I) **101**, 1

1995
Prosecutor *v.* Karadžić, Mladić and Stanišić (Request for Deferral) (Case IT-95-5-D) **108**, 1
Prosecutor *v.* Nikolić (Rule 61) (Case IT-94-2-R61) **108**, 21
Prosecutor *v.* Rajić (Review of Indictment) (Case IT-95-12-I) **108**, 10
Prosecutor *v.* Tadić (Jurisdiction) (Appeals Chamber) (Case IT-94-1-AR72) **105**, 419, 453

Prosecutor v. Tadić (Jurisdiction) (Trial Chamber) (Case IT-94-1-T) **105**, 419, 427

Prosecutor v. Tadić (Protective Measures for Victims and Witnesses) (Case IT-94-1-T) **105**, 599

1996

Prosecutor v. Blaškić (Application to Vary Conditions of Detention) (Case IT-95-14-T) **108**, 68

Prosecutor v. Erdemović (Sentencing Judgment) (Case-IT-96-22-T) **108**, 180

Prosecutor v. Karadžić and Mladić (Rule 61) (Cases IT-95-5-R61 and IT-95-18-R61) **108**, 85

Prosecutor v. Martić (Rule 61) (Case IT-95-11-R61) **108**, 39

Prosecutor v. Mrkšić, Radić and Šljivančanin (Rule 61) (Case IT-95-13-R61) **108**, 53

Prosecutor v. Rajić (Rule 61) (Case IT-95-12-R61) **108**, 141

1997

Prosecutor v. Blaškić (Application to Vary Conditions of Detention) (Case IT-95-14-T) **108**, 68

Prosecutor v. Blaškić (Objection to the Issue of *Subpoenae Duces Tecum*) (Case IT-95-14-AR 108 *bis*) (Appeals Chamber) **110**, 606, 677, 681, 688

Prosecutor v. Blaškić (Objection to the Issue of *Subpoenae Duces Tecum*) (Case IT-95-14-PT) (Trial Chamber II) **110**, 606, 616

Prosecutor v. Erdemović (Sentencing Appeal) (Case IT-96-22-A) **111**, 298

Prosecutor v. Mrkšić, Radić, Šljivančanin and Dokmanović) (Decision on the Motion for Release by the Accused Slavko Dokmanović) (Case IT-95-13a-PT) **111**, 458

Prosecutor v. Tadić (Judgment) (Case IT-94-1-T) **112**, 1

Prosecutor v. Tadić (Sentencing Judgment) (Case IT-94-1-T) **112**, 286

International Tribunal for the Law of the Sea

1997

M/V Saiga (No 1) (Saint Vincent and the Grenadines v. Guinea) **110**, 736

OECD Administrative Tribunal

1997

Billaud and Bessoles v. Secretary-General (Joined Cases Nos 24/25) **110**, 602

X v. Secretary-General (Case No 22) **110**, 599

United Nations Committee against Torture

1994

Khan v. Canada (Communication No 15/1994) **108**, 268

Mutombo v. Switzerland (Communication No 13/1993) **108**, 256

United Nations Committee on the Elimination of Racial Discrimination

1994

Narrainen v. Norway (Communication No 3/1991) **112**, 317

United Nations Compensation Commission

1994

Category "A" Claims against Iraq (Report and Recommendations made by the Panel of Commissioners Concerning the First Instalment of Claims for Departure from Iraq or Kuwait) **109**, 1, 14

Category "B" Claims against Iraq (Reports and Recommendations made by the Panel of Commissioners Concerning the First and Second (Part One) Instalments of Claims for Serious Personal Injury or Death) **109**, 118, 126, 162

Category "C" Claims against Iraq (Report and Recommendations made by the Panel of Commissioners Concerning the First Instalment of Individual Claims up to US $100, 000) **109**, 205, 214

1995

Category "A" Claims against Iraq (Reports and Recommendations made by the Panel of Commissioners Concerning the Second, Third, Fourth and Fifth Instalments of

Claims for Departure from Iraq or Kuwait) **109**, 1, 46, 56, 64, 94
Category "B" Claims against Iraq (Reports and Recommendations made by the Panel of Commissioners Concerning the Second (Part Two) and Third Instalments of Claims for Serious Personal Injury or Death) **109**, 118, 183, 194

1996
Category "A" Claims against Iraq (Report and Recommendations made by the Panel of Commissioners Concerning the Sixth Instalment of Claims for Departure from Iraq or Kuwait) **109**, 1, 99
Category "C" Claims against Iraq (Reports and Recommendations made by the Panel of Commissioners Concerning the Second, Third and Fourth Instalments of Individual Claims up to US $100, 000) **109**, 205, 448, 466, 470
Well Blowout Control Claim (the "WBC Claim") (Report and Recommendations made by the Panel of Commissioners Appointed to Review the Well Blowout Control Claim) **109**, 479, 485

United Nations Human Rights Committee

1989
Gueye *et al. v.* France (Communication No 196/1985) **114**, 312

1993
Bwalya *v.* Zambia (Communication No 314/1988) **114**, 320
Kalenga *v.* Zambia (Communication No 326/1988) **114**, 326

1994
Cox *v.* Canada (Communication No 539/1993) **114**, 347
General Comment No 24 on Issues relating to Reservations made upon Ratification or Accession to the Covenant or the Optional Protocols thereto, or in relation to Declarations under Article 41 of the Covenant **107**, 64
Sara *et al. v.* Finland (Communication No 431/1990) **114**, 331
Toonen *v.* Australia (Communication No 488/1992) **112**, 328

1996
Adams *v.* Jamaica (Communication No 607/1994) **115**, 286
Bordes and Temeharo *v.* France (Communication No 645/1995) **115**, 254
Faurisson *v.* France (Communication No 550/1993) **115**, 355
Holland *v.* Ireland (Communication No 593/1994) **115**, 277
Länsman *et al. v.* Finland (Communication No 671/1995) **115**, 300
Price *v.* Jamaica (Communication No 572/1994) **115**, 350
Somers *v.* Hungary (Communication No 566/1993) **115**, 263
Stewart *v.* Canada (Communication No 538/1993) **115**, 318

II. DECISIONS OF MUNICIPAL COURTS

Argentina

1992
National Sanitation Services *v.* Embassy of Cuba **113**, 434

1994
Manauta *v.* Embassy of Russian Federation **113**, 429

1995
Romero *v.* Ministry of Defence and United Nations **113**, 436

Australia

1980
Ingram *v.* Commonwealth of Australia and Peacock (Minister for Foreign Affairs) **106**, 76

1981
Australian Paper Manufacturers Ltd *v.* CIL Inc. **107**, 89 (note)
R *v.* Abbrederis **107**, 80
Scaniainventor *v.* Commissioner of Patents **107**, 82

1987
Chiou Yaou Fa *v.* Morris **101**, 164
Kanthal Australia Pty Ltd *v.* Minister for Industry, Technology and Commerce **107**, 90

1988
Australian Federation of Islamic Councils Inc. *v.* Westpac Banking Corporation **104**, 405
Mabo and Another *v.* State of Queensland and Another (No 1) **112**, 412

1991
Schoenmakers *v.* Director of Public Prosecutions **101**, 174

1992
Mabo and Others *v.* State of Queensland (No 2) **112**, 457
Minister for Foreign Affairs and Trade and Others *v.* Magno and Another **101**, 202
Reid *v.* Republic of Nauru **101**, 193

1993
Kiraly *v.* Richards **107**, 101
Pareroultja and Others *v.* Tickner and Others **112**, 638
R *v.* Donyadideh **101**, 259
Young *v.* Registrar, Court of Appeal and Another (No 3) **104**, 418

1994
Horta and Others *v.* Commonwealth of Australia **104**, 450
Walker *v.* State of New South Wales **112**, 658

1995
Biljabu and Others *v.* State of Western Australia **112**, 662
Minister for Immigration and Ethnic Affairs *v.* Teoh **104**, 460
Rocklea Spinning Mills Pty Ltd *v.* Anti-Dumping Authority and Another **107**, 104

State of Western Australia *v.* Commonwealth of Australia **112**, 662
Victrawl Pty Ltd *v.* Telstra Corporation Ltd and Others **107**, 122
Wororra Peoples and Another *v.* State of Western Australia **112**, 662

1996
The Wik Peoples *v.* State of Queensland and Others **112**, 638 (note)

1998
Attorney-General (Commonwealth) *v.* Tse Chu-Fai and Another **114**, 383
Project Blue Sky Inc. and Others *v.* Australian Broadcasting Authority **115**, 384

Belgium

1982
Dalfino *v.* Governing Council of European Schools and European School of Brussels I **108**, 638

1989
François *v.* State of Canada **115**, 418
Kingdom of Morocco *v.* DR **115**, 421
SA Biocare *v.* Gécamines (Zaire) and Republic of Zaire **115**, 415

1990
Collée *v.* Gécamines Commerciale **115**, 435 (note)

1991
Centre for Industrial Development *v.* Naidu **115**, 424
Roumeliotis *v.* European School **108**, 642 (note)

1992
De Queiroz *v.* State of Portugal **115**, 430

1993
Rafidain Bank and Iraqi Ministry for Industry *v.* Consarc Corporation **106**, 274

1994
European School *v.* Hermans-Jacobs and Heuvelmans-Van Iersel (Case No 12/94) **108**, 642

1995
Iraq *v.* Dumez **106**, 284
Zaire *v.* D'Hoop and Another **106**, 294

1997
Vaessen *v.* American Battle Monuments
Commission **115**, 435

1998
T *v.* Belgium **115**, 442

Botswana

1992
Dow *v.* Attorney-General **103**, 128

Canada

1981
R *v.* Salvador, Wannamaker, Campbell
and Nunes **101**, 269

1982
R *v.* MacDonald **101**, 281

1983
Re Mitchell and The Queen **101**, 293

1984
Re Regina and Palacios **101**, 306

1992
Re Rudolph and Minister of Employment and Immigration **104**, 195

1993
Ciric *v.* Canada; Minister of Employ-
ment and Immigration **104**, 267
R *v.* Vincent **104**, 204
Re Attorney-General of Canada and
Ward; United Nations High Com-
missioner for Refugees *et al.* **104**, 222

1994
Gil *v.* Canada (*Re* Gil and Minister of
Employment and Immigration) **107**,
146
R *v.* Finta (No 3) **104**, 284
Walker *et al. v.* Bank of New York Inc.
104, 277

1997
Delgamuukw and Others *v.* The Queen
in Right of British Columbia and
Others; First Nations Summit and
Others, Interveners **115**, 446

1998
Re Reference by the Governor in
Council Concerning Certain Questions
relating to the Secession of Quebec
from Canada **115**, 536

Cook Islands

1995
European Pacific Group Ltd and Others
v. KPMG Peat Marwick and Others
("Winebox Case") **104**, 501

Falkland Islands

1996
R *v.* Pesquera Concar SA (Owners of the
Antonio Lorenzo) **108**, 632

France

1981
Rekhou **106**, 222

1983
Dankha **111**, 503

1984
Garcia-Ramirez **111**, 524 (note)
Kryla *v.* Kappy **106**, 226
Lujambio Galdeano **111**, 505

1985
Re Protocol No 6 to the European
Convention on Human Rights **111**,
495

1987
Ministre du Budget *v.* N'guyen Van Gio
106, 225 (note)

1988
Bereciartua-Echarri **111**, 509
International Institute of Refrigeration *v.*
Elkaim **113**, 438

Re Election for the Fifth Constituency of Val d'Oise **111**, 496
Société Robatel SLPI **106**, 192

1989
Société Ouest Africaine des Bétons Industriels (SOABI) and Others *v.* State of Senegal **113**, 440, 441

1990
Duvalier *v.* State of Haiti **113**, 448
GISTI **111**, 499
Kuwait News Agency *v.* Parrott **113**, 457
Ministry for Economic and Financial Affairs of the Islamic Republic of Iran *v.* Société Framatome and Others **113**, 452
National Iranian Gas Corporation *v.* Pipeline Services and Another **113**, 446
Republic of Guatemala *v.* SINCAFC **113**, 450 (note)
Robert *v.* Procureur de la République **113**, 450
SA Avions Marcel Dassault Bréguet Aviation *v.* Association Européenne Droit contre Raison d'Etat **106**, 216, 217
Senghor *v.* International Bank for West Africa and Republic of Senegal **113**, 460

1991
Mouracade *v.* Arab Republic of Yemen **113**, 462
Prefect of Hérault *v.* Dakoury **111**, 525
Société Ouest Africaine des Bétons Industriels (SOABI) and Others *v.* State of Senegal **113**, 440, 444

1992
Barrandon *v.* United States of America **113**, 464, 465
Davoudian **111**, 505 (note)
Duvalier and Madame Duvalier **111**, 528
GISTI and MRAP **106**, 198
Prefect of La Gironde *v.* Mahmedi **106**, 204
SA Avions Marcel Dassault Bréguet Aviation *v.* Association Européenne Droit contre Raison d'Etat **106**, 216, 221
Syndicat des Copropriétaires du 14/16 Boulevard Flandrin **113**, 470

1993
Cheng **111**, 530
Economic Community of West African States and Another *v.* Bank of Credit and Commerce International **113**, 472
Republic of Estonia **113**, 477
United Kingdom and Governor of Hong Kong **106**, 233

1994
Agyepong **111**, 531
Chambre Syndicale des Transports Aeriens **111**, 500
Mobutu and Republic of Zaire *v* Société Logrine **113**, 481
N'guyen Duy Thong **106**, 229
Swiss Confederation **106**, 256

1995
Association Greenpeace France **106**, 231
Barrandon *v.* United States of America **113**, 464, 466
Dioulo **113**, 489
Hintermann *v.* Western European Union **113**, 487
Office for Cereals of Tunisia *v.* Société Bec Frères **113**, 485

1996
Coco *v.* State of Argentina **113**, 491
Koné **111**, 543
Prefect of Essonne *v.* Ariste **111**, 546

1997
Saignie *v.* Embassy of Japan **113**, 492
United States of America *v.* Perières **113**, 494

Germany, Federal Republic of

1983
Cruise Missiles (Danger to Life) Case (Case Nos 2 BvR 1160, 1565 and 1714/83) **106**, 353

1984
Cruise Missiles Deployment (German Approval) Case (Case No 2 BvE 13/83) **106**, 364

1987
Chemical Weapons Deployment (Danger to Life) Case (Case Nos 2 BvR 624, 1080, 2029/83) **106**, 389

Turkish National Extradition Case (Case No 4 ARs 22/86) **106**, 298

1988
French Consulate Disabled Employee Case (Case No AZ 1K 4/88) **114**, 507

1989
N and Others *v.* European School, Munich (Case No 7 CS 89.90) **108**, 649

1991
Antarctica Legal Status Case (Case No VIR 185/87) **108**, 654

1992
European School Employee Bonus Case (Case No 2 C 2.90) **108**, 664
Germany–Poland Border Treaty Constitutionality Case (Case No 2 BvR 1613/91) **108**, 656

1993
NATO AWACS Bosnia Case (Interim Measures) (Case No 2 BvQ 11/93) **106**, 352 (note)
SL and Others *v.* Federal Republic of Germany (Case No III ZR 59/92) **108**, 668
United Nations Somalia Peace-Keeping Force (Interim Measures) (Case No 2 BvQ 17/93) **106**, 352 (note)

1994
International Military Operations (German Participation) Case (Case Nos 2 BvE 3/92, 5/93, 7/93 and 8/93) **106**, 319

1996
X *v.* Argentina (Case No 2 AZR 513/95) **114**, 502

1997
Former Syrian Ambassador to the German Democratic Republic (Case No 2 BvR 1516/96) **115**, 595

1998
Muller *v.* United States of America (Case No 10 Sa 1506/97) **114**, 512

Ireland

1994
Fusco *v.* O'Dea **103**, 318
McElhinney *v.* Williams and Her Majesty's Secretary of State for Northern Ireland **103**, 311
Schmidt *v.* Home Secretary of the Government of the United Kingdom, the Commissioner of the Metropolitan Police and Jones **103**, 322

1995
McElhinney *v.* Williams and Her Majesty's Secretary of State for Northern Ireland **104**, 691

Italy

1983
Aziz *v.* Caruzzi **101**, 358
Labyad *v.* Ilari **101**, 361 (note)

1984
Food and Agriculture Organization *v.* INPDAI **101**, 361
Re Almirante and Cecovini (Case No 300/84) **101**, 362

1986
Church *v.* Ferraino and Others (Case No 283) **101**, 370
Consul-General of Belgium in Naples *v.* Esposito (Case No 666) **101**, 376
Re Lane (Case No 2266) **106**, 305

1987
Largueche *v.* Tancredi Fenu (Case No 9321) **101**, 377
Panattoni *v.* Federal Republic of Germany (Case No 6172) **101**, 385 (note)

1989
British Consulate-General in Naples *v.* Toglia (Case No 2329) **101**, 379

1990
Libyan Arab Jamahiriya *v.* Trobbiani (Decision No 145/1990) **114**, 520

1991
Norwegian Embassy *v.* Quattri (Decision No 12771/1991) **114**, 525

1992
Condor and Filvem *v.* Minister of Justice (Case No 329) **101**, 394
Food and Agriculture Organization *v.* Colagrossi (Case No 5942) **101**, 385
Giaffreda *v.* French Republic (Case No 12315/1992) **114**, 558 (note)
Re Hawkins **106**, 310
Zambian Embassy *v.* Sendanayake (Decision No 5941/1992) **114**, 532

1993
Carbonar *v.* Magurno (Decision No 9675/1993) **114**, 534

1994
Nacci *v.* Bari Institute of the International Centre for Advanced Mediterranean Agronomic Studies (Decision No 5565/1994) **114**, 539
Perrini *v.* Académie de France (Decision No 5126/1994) **114**, 536

1995
United States of America *v.* Lo Gatto (Decision No 4483/1995) **114**, 555

1998
Canada *v.* Cargnello (Decision No 4017/1998) **114**, 559

Kenya

1983
Ministry of Defence of the Government of the United Kingdom *v.* Joel Ndegwa **103**, 235

Lesotho

1992
Makenete *v.* Lekhanya and Others **103**, 27

Lithuania

1994
Property Restitution Case (Case No 12/93) **115**, 619

1995
Human Rights Convention Case (Case No 22/94) **115**, 637

Luxembourg

1994
Kaba-Camara *v.* Fonds National de Solidarité **106**, 316

Mauritius

1992
Heeralall *v.* Commissioner of Prisons **107**, 168, 170

1993
Republic of France *v.* Heeralall and Attorney-General **107**, 168, 175

Namibia

1991
Ex parte Attorney-General of Namibia, *In re* Corporal Punishment by Organs of the State **103**, 81

1993
Government of the Republic of Namibia and Another *v.* Cultura 2000 and Another **103**, 104

The Netherlands

1983
MvdV *v.* Minister for Foreign Affairs **101**, 406

1984
Compania Naviera Panlieve SA *v.* Public Prosecutor **101**, 409
Wilton Feyenoord BV *v.* Minister for Economic Affairs **101**, 418

1985 .
PMJ *v.* Public Prosecutor **101**, 430
Slebos Research BV *v.* Minister for Economic Affairs **101**, 427

1986
Compania Naviera Panlieve SA *v.* Public Prosecutor **101**, 409
FdCS *v.* Minister for Foreign Affairs **101**, 438
Netherlands *v.* Bergings en transport-beddrijf Van den Akker and Another **101**, 436

Netherlands *v.* Dissotis Shipping Corporation **101**, 436

1987
JK *v.* Public Prosecutor **101**, 447
Menten *v.* Federal Republic of Germany **101**, 443

1988
Islamic Republic of Iran Shipping Lines and Another *v.* Public Prosecutor and Another **101**, 453
Muiden Chemie BV *v.* State Secretary for Economic Affairs **101**, 449

1989
Stichting Greenpeace Nederland and Another *v.* Vulcanus II Shipping Company and Another **101**, 432
Stichting Verbiedt de Kruisraketten (SVK) and Others **106**, 400

New Zealand

1993
Tavita *v.* Minister of Immigration **101**, 455 .

1994
Governor of Pitcairn and Associated Islands *v.* Sutton **104**, 508

1996
Brannigan *v.* Davison ("Winebox Case") **108**, 622
KPMG Peat Marwick and Others *v.* Davison; Controller and Auditor-General *v.* Davison; Brannigan and Others *v.* Davison ("Winebox Case") **104**, 526

1997
Butler *v.* Attorney-General and Refugees Status Appeals Authority **114**, 568
Wellington District Legal Services Committee *v.* Tangiora **115**, 655

Nigeria

1980
Shugaba Abdulrahaman Darman *v.* The Federal Minister of Internal Affairs and Others **103**, 268

1988
Kramer Italo Ltd *v.* Government of the Kingdom of Belgium; Embassy of Belgium, Nigeria **103**, 299

1990
Watershed Nigeria Ltd *v.* Brew-Graves **106**, 178

Philippines

1983
United States Lines Inc. *v.* World Health Organization **107**, 182

1985
United States of America and Others *v.* Ruiz de Guzman and Co. (Case No L-35645) **102**, 122

1988
Sanders and Moreau *v.* Veridiano, Rossi and Wyers (Case No L-46930) **102**, 148 (note)

1990
International Catholic Migration Commission *v.* Calleja (Director of Bureau of Labor Relations) and Trade Unions of the Philippines and Allied Services (Case No 85750) **102**, 149
Kapisanan (Organized Labor Association in Line Industries and Agriculture) *v.* Secretary for Labor and Employment and International Rice Research Institute (Case No 89331) **102**, 149
United States of America, Lamachia and Others *v.* Rodrigo and Genove (Case No 79470) **102**, 132
United States of America and Others *v.* Ceballos and Bautista (Case No 80018) **102**, 132
United States of America and Others *v.* Guinto, Valencia and Others (Case No 76607) **102**, 132

1994
The Holy See *v.* Starbright Sales Enterprises Inc. **102**, 163

1995
Larkins *v.* National Labor Relations Commission and Others (Case No 92432) **102**, 148 (note)

South Africa

1990
Coin Security Group (Pty) Ltd *v.* Smit
NO and Others **103**, 1

1994
Mangope *v.* Van der Walt and Another
NNO **103**, 6
S *v.* December **107**, 186

Spain

1992
Abbott *v.* Republic of South Africa
(Decision No 107/92) **113**, 411

Switzerland

1982
CERN Official Taxation Case **102**, 174

1983
Swiss Federal Prosecutor *v.* Kruszyk and
Others **102**, 176, 177

1984
Champel Bellevue SA *v.* State of Geneva
102, 180
Rastello and Permanent Delegation of
Commission of European Community
to International Organizations in
Geneva *v.* Caisse Cantonale Genevoise
de Compensation and Another **102**,
183
Swiss Federal Prosecutor *v.* Kruszyk and
Others **102**, 176, 179

1985
Residence Miremont SA and Another *v.*
Administrative Tribunal of Geneva
and Another **102**, 189

1987
Dame X *v.* Conseil d'Etat du Canton de
Genève **102**, 195

1989
Marcos and Marcos *v.* Federal Department of Police **102**, 198

1990
Z *v.* Geneva Supervisory Authority for

the Enforcement of Debts and
Bankruptcy **102**, 205

1992
Groupement d'Entreprises Fougerolle *v.*
CERN **102**, 209

Tanzania

1986
Haji *v.* Nungu and Another **103**, 243

Uganda

1992
44123 Ontario Ltd *v.* Crispus Kiyonga
and Others **103**, 259

United Kingdom, England

1983
Goldman *v.* Thai Airways International
Ltd **101**, 316

1984
R *v.* Secretary of State for Foreign and
Commonwealth Affairs, *ex parte*
Kamrudin Pirbhai, Chimanbhai
Shivabhai Amin and Vrajlal Jamnadas
Vasant **107**, 461, 464
Yendall *v.* Commonwealth of Australia
107, 590

1985
R *v.* Secretary of State for Foreign and
Commonwealth Affairs, *ex parte*
Kamrudin Pirbhai, Chimanbhai
Shivabhai Amin and Vrajlal Jamnadas
Vasant **107**, 461, 475
R *v.* Secretary of State for Transport, *ex
parte* Iberia Lineas Aereas de España
107, 481

1986
Westminster City Council *v.* Government of the Islamic Republic of Iran
108, 557

1988
Republic of Haiti and Others *v.* Duvalier
and Others **106**, 490

1989

R v. Inland Revenue Commissioners, ex parte Camacq Corporation and Another **103**, 327

1990

Banai v. Canadian High Commission and Others **107**, 600

National Oil Company of Zimbabwe (Private) Ltd and Others v. Sturge **107**, 505

1991

Re Rafidain Bank **101**, 332

1992

In re Pan American World Airways Inc. and Others' Application **101**, 352

In re Paramount Airways Ltd (In Administration) **101**, 337

Kuwait Airways Corporation v. Iraqi Airways Company and the Republic of Iraq **103**, 340, 344

1993

Government of the Kingdom of Saudi Arabia v. Ahmed **104**, 629, 631

In re Schmidt **111**, 548

Kuwait Airways Corporation v. Iraqi Airways Company and the Republic of Iraq **103**, 340, 367

Philipp Brothers v. Sierra Leone and Commission of the European Communities **107**, 516, 519

R v. Secretary of State for the Home Department, ex parte Chahal **108**, 363

1994

Jayetilleke v. High Commission of the Bahamas **107**, 622

London Branch of the Nigerian Universities Commission v. Bastians **107**, 613

Mukoro v. European Bank for Reconstruction and Development and Another **107**, 604

Philipp Brothers v. Sierra Leone and Commission of the European Communities **107**, 516, 524

T v. Secretary of State for the Home Department **104**, 656

United Arab Emirates v. Abdelghafar and Another **104**, 647

Westland Helicopters Ltd v. Arab Organization for Industrialization (AOI) **108**, 564

1995

Al-Adsani v. Government of Kuwait and Others **103**, 420

Arab Republic of Egypt v. Gamal-Eldin **104**, 673

Government of the Kingdom of Saudi Arabia v. Ahmed **104**, 629, 640

Kuwait Airways Corporation v. Iraqi Airways Company and the Republic of Iraq **103**, 340, 391

Paprocki v. German State (Bonn) and Another **104**, 684

Regina v. Ministry of Defence, ex parte Smith and Others **112**, 367

United Arab Emirates v. Abdelghafar and Another **107**, 626, 628, 632

1996

A Limited v. B Bank and Bank of X **111**, 590

Al-Adsani v. Government of Kuwait and Others **107**, 536

Bank of Credit and Commerce International (Overseas) Ltd (In Liquidation) v. Price Waterhouse (A Firm) and Others **111**, 604

Caglar v. Billingham (Inspector of Taxes) and Related Appeals **108**, 510

Hipperson and Others v. Director of Public Prosecutions **111**, 584

Lonrho Exports Ltd v. Export Credits Guarantee Department **108**, 596

Propend Finance Pty Limited and Others v. Sing and Others **111**, 611

Regina v. Secretary of State for the Home Department, ex parte Launder **114**, 402, 407

T v. Immigration Officer; T v. Secretary of State for the Home Department **107**, 552

1997

Re P (No 1) **114**, 478

Regina v. Secretary of State for the Home Department, ex parte Launder **114**, 402, 436

1998

Re P (No 2) **114**, 485

Regina v. Secretary of State for Foreign and Commonwealth Affairs, ex parte British Council of Turkish Cypriot Associations and Another **112**, 735

Sierra Leone Telecommunications Co. Ltd v. Barclays Bank plc **114**, 466

United Kingdom, Scotland

1985
Forth Tugs Ltd *v.* Wilmington Trust Co. **107**, 641

1993
Coreck Maritime GmbH *v.* Sevrybok-holodflot **107**, 658

United States of America

1977
Du Pree and Others *v.* United States **101**, 465

1978
DeMauro Construction Corporation *v.* United States **101**, 554

1981
Melia *v.* United States **104**, 1

1982
Sumitomo Shoji America, Inc. *v.* Avagliano; Avagliano *v.* Sumitomo Shoji America, Inc. **101**, 570
Weinberger, Secretary of Defense and Others *v.* Rossi and Others **101**, 562

1983
Collins and Others *v.* Weinberger and Others **101**, 580

1984
Canadian Overseas Ores Ltd *v.* Compania de Acero del Pacifico **101**, 470
Trans World Airlines, Inc. *v.* Franklin Mint Corporation and Others; Franklin Mint Corporation and Others *v.* Trans World Airlines, Inc. **101**, 587
Wickes *v.* Olympic Airways **101**, 615

1986
Najohn *v.* United States **104**, 7

1987
Boimah *v.* United Nations General Assembly **113**, 499
Gerritsen *v.* de la Madrid Hurtado and Others **101**, 476
Joseph *v.* Office of the Consulate-General of Nigeria and Others **101**, 485

MacArthur Area Citizens Association *v.* Republic of Peru **106**, 196

1988
In the Matter of the Extradition of Suarez-Mason **104**, 12
Kline and Others *v.* Kaneko and Others **101**, 497
Oen Yin Choy *v.* Robinson **104**, 43
Trinh *v.* Citibank NA **107**, 203

1989
Ahmad *v.* Wigen and Others **104**, 52, 79
In the Matter of the Extradition of Atta **104**, 52, 60
Lasidi SA and Others *v.* Financiera Avenida SA and Others **101**, 505
Liu *v.* Republic of China **101**, 519
Rush-Presbyterian-St Luke's Medical Center and Others *v.* Hellenic Republic and Others **101**, 509

1990
Ahmad *v.* Wigen and Others **104**, 52, 105
Autocephalous Greek Orthodox Church of Cyprus and the Republic of Cyprus *v.* Goldberg and Feldman Fine Arts, Inc. **108**, 488
Foremost-McKesson Inc. and Another *v.* Islamic Republic of Iran and Others **101**, 536
Travel Associates Inc. *v.* Kingdom of Swaziland **107**, 219

1991
Antares Aircraft LP *v.* Federal Republic of Nigeria and Nigerian Airports Authority **107**, 225, 227
Fickling *v.* Commonwealth of Australia **103**, 447
Koskotas *v.* Roche and Others **104**, 110
Stena Rederi AB *v.* Comision de Contratos del Comite Ejecutivo General del Sindicato Revolucionario de Trabajadores Petroleros de la Republica Mexicana SC **103**, 433

1992
Arriba Ltd *v.* Petroleos Mexicanos **103**, 490
In re Estate of Ferdinand E. Marcos Human Rights Litigation; Trajano *v.* Marcos and Another **103**, 521
Princz *v.* Federal Republic of Germany **103**, 594, 598

S and S Machinery Co. *v.* Masinexport-import **107**, 239

Siderman de Blake and Others *v.* Republic of Argentina and Others **103**, 454

United States of America *v.* Moats **103**, 480

Walter Fuller Aircraft Sales Inc. *v.* Republic of the Philippines **103**, 503

1993

Antares Aircraft LP *v.* Federal Republic of Nigeria and Nigerian Airports Authority **107**, 225, 234

Cargill International SA *v.* M/T Pavel Dybenko **103**, 572

Drexel Burnham Lambert Group Inc. *v.* Committee of Receivers for Galadari *et al.*; Refco Inc. *v.* Galadari *et al.* **103**, 532

Gabay *v.* Mostazafan Foundation of Iran and Mostazafan Foundation of New York **107**, 242

Paul and Others *v.* Avril **103**, 553

Seetransport Wiking Trader Schiffarhtsgesellschaft MBH and Co., Kommanditgesellschaft *v.* Navimpex Centrala Navala **103**, 559

1994

Alicog *v.* Kingdom of Saudi Arabia and Others **113**, 509

Can and Others *v.* United States of America **107**, 255

Cicippio and Others *v.* Islamic Republic of Iran **107**, 296

Commercial Bank of Kuwait *v.* Rafidain Bank and Central Bank of Iraq **107**, 261

Consarc Corporation and Others *v.* Iraqi Ministry and Others **106**, 408

De Luca *v.* United Nations Organization and Others **113**, 503

EAL (Delaware) Corp., Electra Aviation Inc. *et al. v.* European Organization for the Safety of Air Navigation ("Eurocontrol") and English Civil Aviation Authority **107**, 318

Eckert International Inc. *v.* Government of the Sovereign Democratic Republic of Fiji **107**, 347

Footwear Distributors and Retailers of America *v.* United States **107**, 269

In re Estate of Ferdinand Marcos Human Rights Litigation; Hilao and Others *v.* Estate of Marcos **104**, 119

Kadić *v.* Karadžić; Doe I and Doe II *v.* Karadžić **104**, 135, 140

Lafontant *v.* Aristide **103**, 581

Moran *v.* Kingdom of Saudi Arabia **107**, 303

Princz *v.* Federal Republic of Germany **103**, 594, 604

Straub *v.* A. P. Green Inc. and Atlas Turner Inc. **107**, 359

Transaero Inc. *v.* La Fuerza Aerea Boliviana **107**, 308

Universal Consolidated Companies Inc. *v.* Bank of China **107**, 353

1995

Export Group and Others *v.* Reef Industries Inc. and Mexican Coffee Institute **107**, 393

Gates and Others *v.* Victor Fine Foods and Others **107**, 371

In re Hashim and Others **107**, 405

Janini *v.* Kuwait University **107**, 367

Kadić *v.* Karadžić; Doe I and Doe II *v.* Karadžić **104**, 135, 149

Smith *v.* Socialist People's Libyan Arab Jamahiriya and Others; Hudson *v.* Socialist People's Libyan Arab Jamahiriya **107**, 382

State of Arizona *v.* Willoughby **114**, 586

United States of America *v.* Matta-Ballesteros **107**, 429

Xuncax and Others *v.* Gramajo; Ortiz *v.* Gramajo **104**, 165

1996

Abebe-Jira and Others *v.* Negewo **107**, 447

Askir *v.* Boutros-Ghali and Others **113**, 516

Jungquist *v.* Sheikh Sultan Bin Khalifa al Nahyan **113**, 522

Mushikiwabo and Others *v.* Barayagwiza **107**, 457

Smith *v.* Socialist People's Libyan Arab Jamahiriya **113**, 534

Tabion *v.* Mufti **107**, 452

1997

Hirsch *v.* State of Israel and State of Germany **113**, 543

Smith *v.* Socialist People's Libyan Arab Jamahiriya **113**, 534

United States of America *v.* Lui Kin-Hong, a.k.a. Jerry Lui **114**, 606

Zimbabwe

1991
Beahan *v.* State **103**, 203

1994
In re Wood and Hansard **103**, 234 (note)
Rattigan and Others *v.* Chief Immigration Officer, Zimbabwe and Others **103**, 224